# 2005/2006

## Twelfth Edition

# The Complete Learning Disabilities Directory

Associations • Products • Resources • Magazines
Books • Services • Conferences • Web Sites

A SEDGWICK PRESS Book

Grey House Publishing

| | |
|---|---|
| PUBLISHER: | Leslie Mackenzie |
| EDITORIAL DIRECTOR: | Laura Mars-Proietti |
| PRODUCTION MANAGERS: | Gabby Templet, Neil O'Connor |
| PRODUCTION ASSISTANT: | Bobbie-Jo Scutt |
| MARKETING DIRECTOR: | Jessica Moody |

A Sedgwick Press Book
Grey House Publishing, Inc.
185 Millerton Road
Millerton, NY  12546
518.789.8700
FAX 518.789.0545
www.greyhouse.com
e-mail: books @greyhouse.com

First edition published 1993
Twelfth edition published 2005
Printed in the USA
The complete learning disabilities directory. -- 1994-

   v. ; 27.5 cm.
   Annual
   Continues: Complete directory for people with learning disabilities
   Includes index.

1. Learning disabled--Education--United States--Directories. 2. Learning disabilities--United States--Bibliography. 3. Education, Special--United States--Bibliography. 4. Education, Special--United States--Directory. 5. Learning Disorders--rehabilitation--United States--Bibliography. 6. Learning Disorders--rehabilitation--United States--Directory. 7. Rehabilitation Centers--United States--Bibliography. 8. Rehabilitation Centers--United States—Directory.

LC4704.6 .C66
371.9025
ISBN  1-59237-092-6      softcover

# Preface

The National Center for Learning Disabilities is pleased to recognize this latest edition of *The Complete Learning Disabilities Directory*. With opportunities to access information both via print and online, it continues to be a valuable resource to parents, professionals and individuals with LD.

So much in the field of learning disabilities has changed since the first edition of this guide was published over a decade ago. Public awareness of the needs of students with LD has increased dramatically, and efforts to provide special education students with access to the general education curriculum has had a dramatic impact upon schools and their models of instruction and support. Our understanding of the science underlying different sub-types of learning disabilities has grown, and with new knowledge about effective instructional practices, opportunities for students with learning disabilities have never been better.

And that's where *The Complete Learning Disabilities Directory* can make a difference. By listing organizations and material resources in over 100 categories, it offers thousands of easy-to-access entries for individuals who are searching for information about LD that will help them make informed decisions about school, work, and leisure activities. It serves as a catalog of organizations, products, and Web sites that covers the landscape in terms of variety and need, and provides multiple points of entry to help find the best set of resources for individuals with LD of all ages.

Some keys to success for individuals with learning disabilities? A solid understanding of one's learning disability, a readiness to self-advocate for specific types of help and appropriate accommodations, a willingness to be creative and flexible in searching for and negotiating access to services and supports, an organized and thoughtful system for anticipating problems and seeking solutions (including building and cultivating a community of support), and the optimism and courage to persist and overcome the inevitable challenges that arise for individuals with LD throughout their lives. This Directory can be helpful in addressing all of these needs.

For more than 25 years, NCLD too has been addressing these challenges by promoting public awareness and understanding of learning disabilities, conducting educational programs, and offering services that advance research-based knowledge, and providing national leadership in shaping public policy. We are pleased to be listed in this Directory and encourage readers to also visit our Web site at www.LD.org for access to our LDInfoZone, featured newsletters, policy updates, and lots more, including a free, online early literacy screening tool (www.GetReadytoRead.org).

Thank you Grey House Publishing for once again, providing the public with this guide.

*Dr. Sheldon H. Horowitz*
Director of Professional Services
National Center for Learning Disabilities

# Table of Contents

## Exchange Programs

## Government Agencies

## Literacy & Learning Skills

## Media: Books

## Media: Pamphlets

## Media: Magazines & Newsletters

## Media: Publishers

## Media: Audio & Video

**Glossary**

# Introduction

Welcome to the twelfth edition of *The Complete Learning Disabilities Directory* (*LDD*). Published since 1992, *LDD* continues to be a comprehensive and sought after resource for professionals, families and individuals in the learning disabilities community. This edition marks the second recognized by the **National Center for Learning Disabilities** as a valuable resource for the LD community. We thank **NCLD** for this recognition and for the preceding Preface.

In addition to the 6,275 listings, *The Complete Learning Disabilities Directory* includes several Fact Sheets developed by the **National Center for Learning Disabilities**: LD at a Glance; Being an Advocate for Your Pre-School Child; Being an Advocate for Your School-Aged Child; Self-Advocacy for Teens and Adults; LD and the Arts.

Again this year, our update process was rigorous. Nearly 80% of entries have been updated. You'll find the best in Summer Programs, Publishers of LD material, and Classroom Resources. Other strong chapters include ADD, Literacy, Learning Centers, Media, and Transitional Skills.

The Table of Contents is your guide to this database in print form. *The Complete Learning Disabilities Directory's* 6,275 listings are arranged into 21 major chapters and 100 sub chapters making it easy to pinpoint the exact type of desired reference, including Associations, National/State Programs, Publications, Audio/Video, Web Sites, Products, Conferences, Schools, Learning/Testing Centers, and Summer Programs. Listings provide thousands of valuable contact points, including 5,898 fax numbers, 5,546 web sites, and 9,264 key executives, descriptions, founding year, designed-for age, and size of LD population.

*The Complete Learning Disabilities Directory* provides comprehensive and far-reaching coverage not only for individuals with LD, but for parents, teachers, professionals and friends. Users will find answers to legal and advocacy questions, as well as specially designed computer software.

This valuable resource includes three indexes: Entry Name Index; Geographic Index; and Subject Index and a Glossary that includes hundreds of definitions and abbreviations for specific disabilities, treatment plans, and legal phrases, such as Auditory Sequencing, FBA (functional behavior assessment) and LRE (least restrictive environment). The Glossary will eliminate guesswork and increase your knowledge base as you search for listings or network in the LD community.

*The Complete Learning Disabilities Directory*, 2005/06, makes it possible, in this age of information overload, to have one resource with important LD information readily available at every school and library across the country, not just at state or district level special education resource centers. Now, every special education teacher, student, or parent can have at their fingertips a wealth of information on the critical resources that are available to help individuals achieve in school and in their community.

This data is also available as **The Complete Learning Disabilities Directory – Online Database**. Using the **Online Database**, researchers have access to all of the important data in a quick-to-find, easy-to-navigate format.

# User Guide

Descriptive listings in *The Complete Learning Disabilities Directory (LDD)* are organized into 21 chapters and 84 subchapters. You will find the following types of listings throughout the book:

- National Agencies & Associations
- State Agencies & Associations
- Camps & Summer Programs
- Exchange Programs
- Classroom & Computer Resources
- Print & Electronic Media
- Schools & Learning Centers
- Testing & Training Resources
- Conferences & Workshops

Below is a sample listing illustrating the kind of information that is or might be included in an entry. Each numbered item of information is described in the paragraphs on the following page.

---

1 ▶ 1234

2 ▶ **Association for Children and Youth with Disabilities**

3 ▶ **1704 L Street NW**

**Washington, DC  20036**

4 ▶ **075-785-0000**

5 ▶ **FAX: 075-785-0001**

6 ▶ **800-075-0002**

7 ▶ **TDY: 075-785-0002**

8 ▶ **info@AGC.com**

9 ▶ **www.AGC.com**

10 ▶ Peter Rancho, Director
Nancy Williams, Information Specialist
Tanya Fitzgerald, Marketing Director
William Alexander, Editor

11 ▶ Advocacy organization that ensures children and youth with learning disabilities receive the best possible education. Services include speaking with an informed specialist, free publications, database searches, and referrals to other organizations.

12 ▶ *$6.99*

13 ▶ *204 pages*

14 ▶ *Paperback*

# User Key

1 → **Record Number**: Entries are listed alphabetically within each category and numbered sequentially. The entry numbers, rather than page numbers, are used in the indexes to refer to listings.

2 → **Organization Name**: Formal name of organization. Where organization names are completely capitalized, the listing will appear at the beginning of the alphabetized section. In the case of publications, the title of the publication will appear first, followed by the publisher.

3 → **Address**: Location or permanent address of the organization.

4 → **Phone Number**: The listed phone number is usually for the main office of the organization, but may also be for sales, marketing, or public relations as provided by the organization.

5 → **Fax Number**: This is listed when provided by the organization.

6 → **Toll-Free Number**: This is listed when provided by the organization.

7 → **TDY**: This is listed when provided by the organization. It refers to Telephone Device for the Deaf.

8 → **E-Mail**: This is listed when provided by the organization and is generally the main office e-mail.

9 → **Web Site**: This is listed when provided by the organization and is also referred to as an URL address. These web sites are accessed through the Internet by typing http:// before the URL address.

10 → **Key Personnel**: Name and title of key executives within the organization.

11 → **Organization Description**: This paragraph contains a brief description of the organization and their services.

### The following apply if the listing is a publication:

12 → **Price:** The cost of each issue or subscription, often with frequency information. If the listing is a school or program, you will see information on age group served and enrollment size.

13 → **Number of Pages**: Total number of pages for publication.

14 → **Paperback:** The available format of the publication: paperback; hardcover; spiral bound.

# National Center *for* Learning Disabilities
## *The power to hope, to learn, and to succeed*

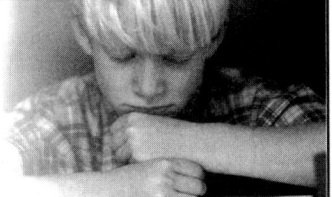

## LD at a Glance

Learning disabilities are real. A person can be of average or above-average intelligence, not have any major sensory problems (like blindness or hearing impairment), and yet struggle to keep up with people of the same age in learning and regular functioning.

### What is a learning disability?

A learning disability (LD) is a neurological disorder that affects the brain's ability to receive, process, store and respond to information. The term learning disability is used to describe the seeming unexplained difficulty a person of at least average intelligence has in acquiring basic academic skills. These skills are essential for success at school and work, and for coping with life in general.
LD is not a single disorder. It is a term that refers to a group of disorders.

### How can one tell if a person has a learning disability?

Learning disabilities can affect a person's ability in the areas of:
- Listening
- Speaking
- Reading
- Writing
- Mathematics

Other features of a learning disability are:
- A distinct gap between the level of achievement that is expected and what is actually being achieved
- Difficulties that can become apparent in different ways with different people
- Difficulties that manifest themselves differently throughout development
- Difficulties with socio-emotional skills and behavior.

A learning disability is not a disease, so there is no cure, but there are ways to overcome the challenges it poses through identification and accommodation.

***Identification:*** If there is reason to think a person might have LD, it is important to collect observations by parents, teachers, doctors and others regularly in contact with that person. If there does seem to be a pattern of trouble that is more than just an isolated case of difficulty, the next step is to seek help from school or consult a learning specialist for an evaluation.

***Accommodation and Modification:*** Depending on the type of learning disability and its severity, as well as the person's age, different kinds of assistance can be provided. Under the Individuals with Disabilities Education Act (IDEA) of 1997 and Americans with Disabilities Act (ADA) of 1990 people of all ages with LD are protected against discrimination and have a right to different forms of assistance in the classroom and workplace.

### What causes learning disabilities?

Experts aren't exactly sure what causes learning disabilities. LD may be due to:
- Heredity - often learning disabilities run in the family, so it's not uncommon to find that people with LD have parents or other relatives with similar difficulties.
- Problems during pregnancy and birth - LD may be caused by illness or injury during or before birth. It may also be caused by drug and alcohol use during pregnancy, low birth weight, lack of oxygen and premature or prolonged labor.
- Incidents after birth - Head injuries, nutritional deprivation and exposure to toxic substances (i.e. lead) can contribute to LD.

Learning disabilities are NOT caused by economic disadvantage, environmental factors or cultural differences. In fact, there is frequently no apparent cause for LD.

Each type of strategy should be considered when planning instruction and support. A person with dysgraphia will benefit from help from both specialists and those who are closest to the person. Finding the most beneficial type of support is a process of trying different ideas and openly exchanging thoughts on what works best.

## Are learning disabilities common?

Currently, almost 2.9 million school-aged children in the US are classified as having specific learning disabilities (SLD) and receive some kind of special education support. They are approximately 5% of all school-aged children in public schools. These numbers do not include children in private and religious schools or home-schooled children.

Studies show that learning disabilities do not fall evenly across racial and ethnic groups. For instance, in 2001, 1% of white children and 2.6% of non-hispanic black children were receiving LD-related special education services*. The same studies suggest that this has to do with economic status and not ethnic background. LD is not caused by economic disadvantage, but the increased risk of exposure to harmful toxins (lead, tobacco, alcohol, etc.) at early stages of development are prevalent in low-income communities.

## What can one do about learning disabilities?

Learning disabilities are lifelong, and although they won't go away, they don't have to stop a person from achieving goals. Help is available if they are identified. Learning disabilities affect every person differently, and the disorder can range from mild to severe. Sometimes people have more than one learning disability. In addition, approximately one third of people with LD also have attention deficit hyperactivity disorder (AD/HD), which makes it difficult for them to concentrate, stay focused or manage their attention to specific tasks.

## LD and children

Early identification is vital in helping a child to succeed academically, as well as socially. If you think your child is displaying signs of a learning disability, share them with classroom teachers and others who come in contact with your child. Observe the way your child develops the language, motor coordination and social skills and behaviors important for success in school. And rememberearly is better-even preschoolers can show signs of risk for LD.

Don't panic. Not all children who are slow to develop skills have LD. If your child does have a learning disability, early intervention with specialized teaching strategies can help to overcome difficulties. As a parent, it is important to learn as much as you can and to help your child understand that he or she is not alone: other children struggle too, and adults are there to help.

## LD and adulthood

It is never too late to get help for a learning disability. Finding out about a learning disability can be a great relief to adults who could not explain the reason for their struggles in the past. Testing specialists are available for people of all ages, and assistance is available for every stage of life. Taking the initiative to seek out support and services than can provide help is the first step to overcoming a learning disability.

Many adults (some of whom are unaware of their LD) have developed ways to cope with their difficulties and are able to lead successful, functioning lives. LD shouldn't hinder a person from attaining goals. Regardless of the situation, understanding the specific challenges and learning strategies to deal with LD directly at every stage can alleviate a lot of frustration and make successful living much easier.

* Executive Summary, National Research Council, 2001

# National Center *for* Learning Disabilities
### *The power to hope, to learn, and to succeed*

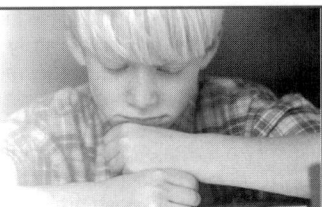

## Being an Advocate for Your Pre-school Child

Being an advocate means knowing how to ensure that your child gets the help he or she needs to be successful. For children who experience learning difficulties, it's never too early to start looking for ways to help them succeed in learning. Even before formal schooling starts, there are things you can do to make sure your child gets help early, so that learning can be a fun and productive experience. Below are the first steps you should take if you suspect your child has difficulty learning:

- Observe your child and start a log of the behavior you think suggests learning delays or difficulties.
- Talk to your child about what you are observing. Try to learn more about the problems he or she appears to be having through play so that you can share specific examples with people who might be able to help. Be sure to enthusiastically praise your child's successes and good effort often.
- Meet with your child's pediatrician, bringing along your list of observations. Be open and honest about your concerns and don't be afraid to ask questions like "Why is my child having trouble?" or "Is this something that will go away by itself?" or "Is this within the normal range of development?" Ask if developmental screenings are available; or if another medical professional (i.e., a neurologist) or an early childhood specialist (i.e., speech/language pathologist, psychologist, special educator) should evaluate your child. If you are concerned about your child's progress, don't wait to pursue further evaluation.
- Ask the pediatrician or your local school district whom you should contact to arrange an evaluation for your child. An evaluation will provide you with the information you need to make important decisions, and will determine whether your child could be eligible for early intervention or preschool services. Evaluation findings are strictly confidential. It is up to you to decide with whom the information is shared.
- Early intervention services are services for infants and toddlers up to age two that are designed to identify and address a problem or delay as early as possible. Preschool services are specially designed programs offered by public schools and are available for eligible children with disabilities beginning at age three. Until age five, these services are voluntary-you can wait to decide whether you want to enroll your child in a program that provides special help.
- Once you request an evaluation, it is your right to have it completed within a set period of time, usually within 30 school days of your signing a written consent for your child to be evaluated. Don't be shy about calling or visiting the evaluation site to keep the process moving.
- Bring all information about your child that you think is relevant to meetings and evaluations. When speaking to doctors, therapists or school administrators be prepared to tell them your observations about your child's strengths and weaknesses, likes and dislikes, as well as what goals you are progressing towards with your child. Your input is vital in helping provide a full picture of your child to people who probably don't know him or her well.
- Keep a log of the names, organizations and phone numbers of all people you speak to and the information they give you. Also ask for a copy of all reports and correspondence about your child.

Public Law (P.L.) 105-17 of the federal Individual with Disabilities Education Act guarantees certain rights to young children (ages zero to five) with special needs. Among those are:

- Children ages zero through two with disabilities have the right to early intervention services. If a state chooses, it can also serve infants and toddlers at risk for developing disabilities.
- Children ages three to five with disabilities have the right to special education.
- Each child has the right to special services that are based on an evaluation and assessment of the child's particular needs at no cost to the child's family.
- Children with disabilities have the right to receive teaching and instruction designed to meet their specific needs. In the case of infants and toddlers these needs are documented in an Individualized Family Services Plan (IFSP) and focus on the development of the child; for children age three and older, service and support plans are stated in an Individualized Education Plan (IEP). These plans outline:

    - The developmental levels of the child (in the case of children ages zero to two)
    - The outcomes expected to be achieved for the child
    - The services that will be provided
    - When and where they will be provided
    - When the plan will be updated next.

- An IFSP recognizes the family as a child's greatest developmental resource, so that each plan is structured around the strengths of the family to support the special needs of the child. A group of specialists, who can include doctors, therapists, child development specialists, social workers and others, is also part of the team and can help the family support the child. Services provided may include speech therapy, social work and others. IFSPs are reviewed at least every six months.
- An IEP is a similar plan that moves away from the family and focuses on a child's education. The IEP team also includes teachers and school administrators who come in contact with child. IEPs are reviewed at least every year.
- Parents or guardians have the right to be included in making any decisions about their child's educational needs and services. This includes appealing or consenting to any decisions made through the evaluation and assessment process.

Every child is entitled to a free and appropriate public education, and part of your role as a parent and caregiver is to make sure that the rights of your child are protected. Becoming familiar with the laws and services that exist to assist your child is the first step towards learning success.

National Center for Learning Disabilities
www.ld.org

# National Center **for** Learning Disabilities

*The power to hope, to learn, and to succeed*

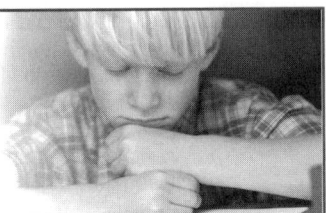

## Being an Advocate for your School-Aged Child

Your child has the right to a free and appropriate public school education. Getting involved in his or her education is among the most important things you can do as your child's advocate. As you'll see below, you have a right to be a part of every decision regarding your child's education, including the process of finding out if your child needs special services. You know your child best, and your input should be considered at every opportunity.

In order to make sure that your child with learning disabilities gets the help he or she needs throughout his or her school career, you should familiarize yourself with the rights you have as your child's advocate. These rights are federally mandated by the Individuals with Disabilities Education Act (IDEA).

### Your child's rights in determining eligibility for special education and related services:

- You have the right to request that your child be evaluated to determine if he or she is eligible for special education and related services. This evaluation is more than just a single test. The school must gather information from you, your child's teacher and others who would be helpful. An assessment of your child must then be conducted in all the areas that may be affected by the suspected disability
- If the public school agrees that your child may have a learning disability and may need special help, the school must evaluate your child at no cost to you.
- Teachers or other professionals can recommend that your child be evaluated, but the school must get your explicit written consent before any part of the evaluation is started.
- If the public school system refuses to give your child an evaluation, they must explain in writing the reasons for refusal, and must also provide information about how you can challenge their decision.
- All tests and interviews must be conducted in your child's native language. The evaluation process cannot discriminate against your child because he or she is not a native English speaker, has a disability or is from a different racial or cultural background.
- Your child cannot be determined eligible for special education services only because of limited English proficiency or because of lack of instruction in reading or math.
- You have the right to be a part of the evaluation team that decides what information is needed to determine whether your child is eligible.
- You have the right to a copy of all evaluation reports and paperwork related to your child.

### Your child's rights once determined eligible for special education and related services:

- A meeting to design an Individualized Education Plan (IEP) must be held within 30 days of your child being found eligible for special education services. An IEP should set reasonable learning goals for your child and state the services that the school district will provide.
- You and your child have the right to participate in the development of the IEP, along with a team that will include: your child's teachers, a representative from the school administration who is qualified to recommend and supervise special programs and services as well as representatives from other agencies that may be involved in your child's transition services (if your child is age 16 or older). You can also request an advisor to help you better understand your rights and responsibilities as a parent, and request that this person be present.
- Your child has a right to the least restrictive environment possible. Unless members of the IEP team can justify removal from the general education classroom, your child should receive instruction and support with classmates that do not have disabilities. Also be sure that special education services or supports are available to help your child participate in extracurricular activities such as clubs and sports.
- During an IEP meeting, the IEP team will develop goals for any related services, such as occupational therapy, which could help your child. Be sure the team specifies how often and for how long these services will be provided as well as in what setting the services will be provided. This team will also identify behavioral strategies to support your child's learning in school and at home.
- Be sure to discuss what kind of assistive technology devices-such as speech recognition software, electronic organizers or books on tape-could help your child. Assistive technology services include evaluating your child for specific devices, providing the device and training your child to use the device.

381 Park Avenue South • Suite 1401 • New York, NY 10016-8806 • 212-545-7510 • 212-545-9665 fax • www.ld.org • www.getreadytoread.org

- You have the right to challenge the school's decisions concerning your child. If you disagree with a decision that 's been made, discuss it with the school and see if an agreement can be reached. If all efforts don't work, IDEA provides other means of protection for parents and children under the law. These other ways of settling your dispute allow parents and school personnel to resolve disagreements. Options include mediation with an impartial third person, a due process hearing or a formal hearing in a court of law.
- An IEP meeting must be held once a year and comprehensive re-evaluation must be done every three years. However, you may request an IEP meeting at any time.

## Other tips for advocating for your child:

- Collect as much information as possible. Be sure to keep copies of all reports and paperwork. Also, keep a log of all the people you speak to, their phone numbers and other pertinent information, as well as the time and date of your call and the details of the conversation. After making a call, you can send a follow-up letter reminding the person of the important points, such as any information they promised to provide you or information you think should be in that person's files. Also learn as much as possible about IDEA and other laws that could help your child.
- Talk to your child about school. Find out what he/she likes and dislikes and what kind of frustrations he/ she is experiencing. Understanding what your child is going through is an essential part of being an advocate.
- Don't be afraid to ask questions or say no. It's important to work together with the school to plan your child's education, so make sure you know to what you are agreeing. Don't be afraid to ask for clarification, request further testing, or challenge the school's decision regarding services.
- Stay level-headed. Being involved in a process where lots of people are talking about your child can be very emotional. Remember that the people involved are there to help, even if you disagree with them. You will be most helpful to your child, if you hear everyone out and express yourself calmly and specifically.
- Get support from others. Talking to other parents with children who have similar difficulties may give you ideas and tips you can benefit from. It's also good to team up with other parents to bring your concerns to the school system or agencies.

# National Center for Learning Disabilities
*The power to hope, to learn, and to succeed*

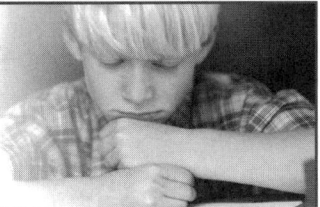

## Self-Advocacy for Teens and Adults

Having learning disabilities often means having special needs. As an adult it's up to you to make sure your rights are being respected and that the accommodations you need are available to you. Whether at school or at work, being an advocate for yourself means understanding your rights, understanding how you work best and working with others to ensure that your special needs are met.

LD.org has a section called **Living with LD** that has details about dealing with the different aspects of learning disabilities (LD) that you may face as a teenager and as an adult. Here, we'll focus on how to be your own best spokesperson at school and at work.

### Being your own advocate in high school

- Attend all your IEP (Individualized Education Plan) meetings. You have a right to be there and should take an active part in the meetings. It's a great opportunity to talk to teachers, administrators and others that are involved with your education (including your parents or guardians) about how you learn and what kinds of services and supports you need to do well in school. Make sure the specific accommodations you need are outlined in your IEP.
- Set goals for yourself and think realistically about reaching them. Part of your IEP process calls for establishing a transition plan as early as possible, outlining your path to graduation, what you want to do after high school and the accommodations you might need after you leave. If you hope to go to college, what subjects do you want to study? What college are you interested in? Will that college permit you to substitute requirements or have them waived? To get into that school, what grades will you need to get and which classes should you take? Don't feel like once you decide on something that it's set in stone - adjusting your goals is an important part of realizing what you want and what it will take to achieve success.
- Be aware of what you're good at, what you struggle with, what activities you have a passion for and what your ideal job or project would be - being able to share this kind of information with others is a valuable part of representing yourself.
- Learn as much as you can about your LD. The more you know about your specific learning disability, the easier it will be for you to figure out how you learn best and the accommodations you will need to be successful.
- Meet with your teachers and counselors outside of the IEP meeting to talk about your classes, about the accommodations you may have (extra time on tests or a note-taking buddy, for example) and other helpful strategies, as well as what you're interested in pursuing next.
- Request that your school update your LD documentation before you leave high school.

### Being your own advocate in college

Once you graduate from high school, responsibility for attending to your special needs moves away from the educational system and onto your shoulders. It's up to you to make your college career successful. Here are some tips:

- Make sure you arrive on campus able to provide current documentation of your disability.
- Know your rights. You have a right to participate in educational programs without discrimination and to receive reasonable accommodations in courses and exams.
- Meet with your advisors to talk about what you want to learn; discuss what challenges you may encounter and how you can accommodate for them.
- If you need specific support and services, you must disclose your learning disability to your instructors and others who can help you.

- Find out right away if there are any curriculum requirements and how you can best select classes to complement your strengths. For instance, if you have dyscalculia, is there a class that fulfills the math requirement that doesn't involve a lot of computation?
- Request accommodations early. Don't wait until the end of the semester to ask for extra time on finals, or tell your professor you would like to substitute an oral presentation on the day before a research paper is due. It is your responsibility to manage your time and to do what you can to succeed.

## Being your own advocate at work

- Focus on the skills you have to choose a job that suits your strengths.
- Under the law, you cannot be discriminated against in the workplace because of your learning disability. This means you cannot get fired, demoted or denied opportunities that others are given because you have a learning disability. However, you must be able to fulfill the expectations your job demands. You have a right to reasonable accommodations, as long as they don't put an unreasonable financial burden on your employer.
- Have proper documentation of your LD and your need for accommodations. This can be a letter or report from someone who evaluated you. It should outline the methods used to identify your LD, an explanation of your LD and how it affects your performance, as well as a recommendation for accommodations.
- Talk to your employer about your learning disability. Information shared must be kept confidential and can be shared with others only with your explicit permission. Be honest and share as much information as is appropriate for your employer to have so that you can work out strategies to help you succeed on the job.

# National Center *for* Learning Disabilities
### *The power to hope, to learn, and to succeed*

## LD and the Arts

The arts are more than a fun, superficial way to keep kids occupied. Art activities can help children with learning disabilities begin to overcome the challenges they face in learning in many different ways. Of course, having a learning disability does not necessarily mean that a person has an exceptional artistic talent. However, music, art, crafts and dance can give students with learning disabilities a chance to express themselves through different media and gain confidence along the way.

### Unlocking confidence

A feeling of self-worth - the knowledge that you can do something - is a critical part of the learning process. Children with learning disabilities often come to think they are incapable of learning because of their ongoing difficulties in school. A paintbrush, a costume, a drum or paper, scissors and glue can be new tools for self-expression that boost confidence while providing opportunities for learning and practice

### Learning through art

The arts can open the world of learning to students who have trouble with traditional teaching methods. The arts are intellectual disciplines - requiring complex thinking and problem solving - that offer students the opportunity to construct their own understanding of the world.
- Drawing and painting reinforce motor skills and can also be a way of learning shapes, contrasts, boundaries, spatial relationships, size and other math concepts.
- Music teaches children about rhythm, sound and pitch. Beats can help children learn rhymes and other features of reading such as phonological awareness. Using repetitive songs to learn academic facts (like the alphabet song or multiplication tables) can make the learning experience easier and more fun.
- Dance provides children with a social way to learn about sequencing, rhythm and following directions. While developing coordination and motor control, students can also learn counting and directionality, which can enhance reading and writing concepts - such as understanding the difference between similar looking letters (like p/b/d/q) and telling left from right.
- Performing plays is an opportunity for children to immerse themselves in a theme and learn about it in a profound and personal way. Acting out historical or literary figures and events gives students a sense of ownership about what they've learned, allowing them to acquire a deeper appreciation of the subject matter.
- Crafts offer children the opportunity to express themselves in two- and three-dimensional ways. Students can develop vital problem-solving skills without having to rely on areas of expression that may be more challenging.

### Arts as a means of assessment

Timed tests and take-home reports are traditional means of academic assessment that can be especially difficult for individuals with learning disabilities. Creative projects offer these students the freedom to show what they know without the constraints of printed text. Offering students art projects or multi-media presentations as a way to demonstrate an understanding of material they've learned can be an excellent alternative.

Because a person has difficulty learning through hearing alone or seeing alone, that does not mean they cannot learn. The arts offer individuals with learning disabilities dynamic ways of learning, and just as importantly, a way to fully discover their own self-worth.

## Legal

**1  ADA Clearinghouse and Resource Center**
National Center for State Courts
300 Newport Avenue
Williamsburg, VA 23185
800-616-6165
FAX 757-564-2002
http://www.ncsc.online.org

Disseminates information on ADA compliance to state and local court systems. Will develop a diagnostic checklist and strategies for compliance specifically relevant to the state and local courts.

**2  ADA Information Line**
US Department of Justice
US Department of Justice Civil Righ
Washington, DC 20530
202-514-0301
800-514-0301
FAX 202-307-1198
TDY:202-514-0301
http://www.ada.gov
*Alexander Acosta, Assistant Attorney General*
*Alberto Gonzales, Attorney General*

Answers questions about Title II (public services) and Title III (public accommodations) of the Americans with Disabilities Act (ADA). Provides materials and technical assistance on the provisions of the ADA.

**3  ADA Technical Assistance Programs**
US Department of Justice
950 Pennsylvania Avenue NW
Washington, DC 20530
202-514-2000
http://www.usdoj.gov

Federally funded regional resource centers that provide information and referral, technical assistance, public awareness, and training on all aspects of the Americans with Disabilities Act (ADA).

**4  American Bar Association Center on Children and the Law: Information Line**
Market Bar Association
740 15th Street NW
Washington, DC 20005
202-662-1000
800-285-2221
FAX 202-662-1032
TDY:202-662-1012
http://www.abanet.org
e-mail: service@abanet.org
*Michael Stratton, Administrative Assistant*
*John Parry, Director*

Provides information on legal issues and referrals to local Bar Associations.

**5  Community Alliance for Special Education**
1600 Howard Street
San Francisco, CA 94103
415-431-2285
FAX 415-431-2289
*Laura Gonzalez, Intake Worker*
*Cristina Martinez, Coordinator*

Provides special education advocacy, representation at individual education program (IEP) meetings and due process proceedings, free technical assistance consultations and training throughout the San Francisco Bay area.

**6  Disability Rights Education & Defense Fund (DREDF)**
2212 6th Street
Berkeley, CA 94710
510-644-2555
800-348-423
FAX 510-841-8645
TDY:800-466-4232
http://www.dredf.org
e-mail: dredf@dredf.org
*Susan Henderson, Administration Director*
*Mary Breslin, Co-Founder*

A nonprofit organization dedicated to advancing the civil rights of individuals with disabilities through legislation, litigation, informal and formal advocacy, and education and training of lawyers, advocates and clients with respect to disability issues. DREDF operates a Department of Justice funded national ADA information hotline for Titles II and III of the ADA. DREDF also provides training, advocacy, technical assistance and referrals for parents of disabled children.

**7  ED Law Center**
PO Box 81-7327
Hollywood, FL 33081 1327
954-966-4489
FAX 954-966-8561
http://www.edlaw.net

Provides information on special education law and offers listing of attorneys.

**8  Equal Employment Opportunity Commission**
1801 L Street NW
Washington, DC 20507
202-663-4900
800-669-4000
FAX 202-663-4639
TDY:800-669-6820
http://www.eeoc.gov
*Cari Dominguez, Chairman*
*Noami Churchill, Vice Chairman*

Federal agency that provides assistance with discrimination complaints about employment.

**9  Home School Legal Defense Association**
PO Box 3000
Purcellville, VA 20134
540-338-5600
FAX 540-338-2733
http://www.hslda.org
*Betty Statnick, Special Needs Coordinator*
*Mike Smith, President*

A membership organization that offers legal assistance for homeschooling issues.

**10  Legal Services for Children**
Legal Services for Children
1254 Market Street
San Francisco, CA 94102
415-863-3762
FAX 415-863-7708
http://www.lsc-sf.org
*Shannan Wilber, Executive Director*
*Helen Jiang, Office Assistant*

# Associations & Organizations /National Programs

Founded in 1975. Nonprofit law firm for children and youth. Legal Services for Children provides free legal and social services to children and youth under 18 years old in the San Francisco Bay area.

**11  National Association for Community Mediation**

**National Association for Community Mediation**
**1527 New Hampshire Avenue NW**
**Washington, DC  20036 1206        202-667-9700**
**FAX 202-667-8629**
**http://www.nafcm.org**
**e-mail: nafcm@nafcm.org**
*Joanne Hartman, Executive Director*
*Linda Baron, Director*

Supports the maintenance and growth of community-based mediation programs and processes; acts as a resource for mediation information; locates a center to help individuals and groups resolve disputes.

**12  National Association of Protection and Advocacy Systems (NAPAS)**

**900 2nd Street NE**
**Washington, DC  20002        202-408-9514**
**FAX 202-408-9520**
**TDY:202-408-9521**
**http://www.protectionandadvocacy.com**
**e-mail: info@napas.org**
*Curtis Decker, Executive Director*
*Nachama Wilker, Deputy Director*

NAPAS, the voluntary national membership association of protection and advocacy systems and client assistance programs, assumes leadership in promoting and strengthening the role and performance of its members in providing quality-based advocacy services. NAPAS has a vision of a society where people with disabilities exercise self-determination and choice and have equal opportunity and full participation.

**13  National Center for Youth Law**

**405 14th Street**
**Oakland, CA  94612 2701        510-835-8098**
**FAX 510-835-8099**
**http://www.youthlaw.org**
**e-mail: info@youthlaw.org**
*John O'Toole, Director*

Uses the law to protect children from harms caused by poverty, and to improve the lives of children living in poverty. Works to protect abused and neglected children through work with advocates, foster parents and others striving to reform state child welfare systems. Expands access to health care for children and youth through the state and federal levels to see that children get the health insurance and health care services to which they are entitled.

**14  National Council of Juvenile and Family Court Judges (NCJFCJ)**

**1041 N Virginia Street, 3rd Floor**
**Reno, NV  89507        775-784-6012**
**FAX 775-784-6628**
**http://www.ncjfcj.org**
**e-mail: admin@ncjfcj.unr.edu**
*David Gamble, Director*
*David Humke, Associate Project Attorney*

Founded in 1937 by a group of judges dedicated to improving the effectiveness of the nation's juvenile courts, the National Council of Juvenile and Family Court Judges (NCJFCJ) strives to increase awareness and sensitivity to children's issues. The National Council focuses on providing meaningful assistance to the judges, court administrators and related professionals in whose care the concerns of children and their families have been entrusted.

**15  Public Interest Law Center of Philadelphia**

**125 S 9th Street**
**Philadelphia, PA  19107        215-627-7100**
**FAX 215-627-3183**
**TDY:215-627-7300**
**e-mail: pubint@aol.com**
*Stephen Gold, attorney*
*Michael Churchhill, Executive Director*

A public interest law firm with a disabilities project specializing in class action by individuals and organizations.

## National Programs

**16  ABLE DATA**

**USDE National Institution on Disability and Rehabi**
**8630 Fenton Street**
**Silver Spring, MD  20910        301-608-8998**
**800-227-0216**
**FAX 301-608-8958**
**TDY:301-608-8912**
**http://www.abledata.com**
**e-mail: abledata@macroint.com**
*Katherine Belknap, Project Director*
*Janice Benton, Information Services*

Sponsored by the National Institute on Disability and Rehabilitation Research (NIDRR) of the US Department of Education; provides information on more than 27,000 assistive technology products, including detailed descriptions of each product, price and company information.

**17  ADA Information Hotline**

**Great Lakes Disability & Business Technical Center**
**374 Congress Street**
**Boston, MA  02210        617-695-1225**
**800-949-4232**
**FAX 617-482-8099**
**TDY:617-695-1225**
**http://www.adaptenv.org**
**e-mail: info@adaptiveEsvironments.org**
*Valerie Fletcher, Director*
*Gabriela Sims, Assistant Director*

Provides technical assistance, information services and outreach regarding the Americans with Disabilities Act.

**18  AVKO Dyslexia Research Foundation**

3084 W Willard Road
Clio, MI  48420 7801                 810-686-9283
                                     866-285-6612
                              FAX 810-686-1101
                              http://www.avko.org
                     e-mail: donmccabe@aol.org
*Don McCabe, Research Director*
*Ann McCabe, Office Manager*

AVKO is a nonprofit, tax exempt membership organization founded in 1974. The AVKO Dyslexia Research Foundation has been founded to help determine what dyslexia is, why traditional methods of teaching and writing fail and help most dyslexics learn to read and write.

**19  Academy for Educational Developmentities Center**

Academy for Educational Development
1825 ConneCourticut Avenue NW
Washington, DC  20009 5721         202-884-8000
                                     800-953-2553
                              FAX 202-884-8400
                              http://www.aed.org
                     e-mail: admindc@aed.org
*Denise Borders, Senior Vice President/Director*
*Edward Russell, Chairman*

A nonprofit organization established by the National Institute for Literacy, which provides information regarding learning disabilities and trends impacting the provision of literacy services.

**20  Alliance for Technology Access**

1304 Southpoint Boulevard
Petaluma, CA  94954                707-778-3011
                                     800-914-3017
                              FAX 707-765-2080
                              TDY:707-778-3015
                              http://www.ataccess.org
                     e-mail: atainfo@ataccess.org
*Mary Lester, Executive Director*
*Libbie Butler, Program Coordinator*

A national organization dedicated to providing access to technology for people with disabilities through its coalition of 39 community-based resource centers in 28 states and in the Virgin Islands. Each center provides information, awareness, and training for professionals and provides guided problem solving and technical assistance for individuals with disabilities and family members.

**21  American Academy of Pediatrics National Headquarters**

141 NW Point Boulevard
Elk Grove Village, IL  60007       847-434-4000
                                     800-433-9016
                              FAX 847-434-8000
                              http://www.aap.org
                     e-mail: ealden@aap.org
*Maureen DeRosa, Director Marketing/Publications*
*Errol Alden, Executive Director*

An organization of 55,000 pediatricians that publishes professional and patient education materials. Brochures include Learning Disabilities and Children, Guidelines for Parents, Understanding the ADHD Child and Learning Disabilities and Young Adults.

**22  American Art Therapy Association**

1202 Allanson Road
Mundelein, IL  60060 3808          847-949-6064
                                     888-290-0878
                              FAX 847-566-4580
                              http://www.arttherapy.org
                     e-mail: info@arttherapy.org
*Ed Stygar, Executive Director*
*Betty Perri, Administrative Assistant*

An organization of professionals dedicated to the belief that the creative process involved in the making of art is healing and life enhancing. Its mission is to serve its members and the general public by providing standards of professional competence, and developing and promoting knowledge in, and of, the field of art therapy.

**23  American Association for Adult and Continuing Education**

4380 Forbes Boulevard
Lanham, MD  20706                  301-918-1900
                              FAX 301-918-1846
                              http://www.aca.org
                     e-mail: aaace10@aol.com
*Stephen Steurer PhD, Executive Director*
*Jeff Washington, Executive Administrator*

Mission is to provide leadership for the field of adult and continuing education: by expanding opportunities for adult growth and development; unifying adult educators; fostering the development and dissemination of theory, research, information and best practices; promoting identity and standards for the profession; and advocating relevant public policy and social change initiatives.

**24  American Association for the Advancement of Science (AAAS)**

1200 New York Avenue NW
Washington, DC  20005              202-326-6400
                              FAX 202-789-0455
                              http://www.aaas.org
                     e-mail: webmaster@aaas.org
*Jill Perla, Senior Manager Operations*
*Melissa Risenthan, Program Associate*

According to AAAS's constitution, its mission is to: further the work of scientists; facilitate cooperation among them; foster scientific freedom and responsibility; improve the effectiveness of science in the promotion of human welfare; advance education in science and increase the public's understanding and appreciation of the promise of scientific methods in human progress.

**25  American Association of Collegiate Registrars and Admissions Officers**

One Dupont Circle NW
Washington, DC  20036              202-293-9161
                              FAX 202-872-8857
                              http://www.aacrao.org
                     e-mail: info@aacrao.org
*Dan Gardner, Information Specialist*
*Jerry Sullivan, Executive Director*

The mission is to provide professional development, guidelines and voluntary standards to be used by higher education officials regarding the best practices in records management, admissions, enrollment management, administrative information technology and student services.

**26    American Association of Health Plans**

American Health Insurance Plan
601 Pennsylvania Avenue NW
Washington, DC  20004                202-778-3200
                                    FAX 202-331-7487
                                    http://www.ahip.org
                                    e-mail: webmaster@ahip.org
*Karen Ignani, President*
*Scott Styles, Vice President*

National trade association representing more than
1,000 health maintenance organizations, preferred
provider organizations, point-of-service plans, and
other similar health plans that care for more than 140
million Americans.

**27    American Camping Association**

American Camping Association
5000 State Road 67 N
Martinsville, IN  46151              765-342-8456
                                    800-428-2267
                                    FAX 765-342-2065
                                    TDY:765-342-8456
                                    http://www.acacamps.org
                                    e-mail: acacamps@acacamps.org
*Peg Smith, Executive Director*
*Marge Scanlin, Executive Officer of Research*

Provides support, education and information on best
practices and accreditation programs for camp programs throughout the US. Offers an online bookstore
with outdoor education, youth development, adventure resources and a web site with an interactive,
searchable database of camps.

**28    American Coaching Association**

PO Box 353
Lafayette Hill, PA  19444            610-825-4505
                                    FAX 610-825-4505
                                    http://www.americoach.com
Links people who want coaching with people who do
coaching; coaches help individuals to set goals, accept
limitations and acknowledge strengths, develop social skills and create strategies that enable them to be
more effective in managing their day-to-day lives.

**29    American College Testing Program**

ACT Universal Testing
PO Box 168
Iowa City, IA  52243 0168            319-337-1000
                                    FAX 319-339-3021
                                    TDY:319-337-1701
                                    http://www.act.org
                                    e-mail: sandy.schlote@act.org
*Sandy Schlote, Testing Coordinator*
*Ed Colby, Public Relations*

Helps individuals and organizations make informed
decisions about education and work. We provide information for life's transitions.

**30    American Council of the Blind (ACB)**

1155 15th Street NW
Washington, DC  20005                202-467-5081
                                    800-424-8666
                                    FAX 202-467-5085
                                    http://www.acb.org
                                    e-mail: info@acb.org
*Melanie Bronson, Acting Executive Director*
*Tatricia Moreira, Executive Assistant*

A national membership organization established to
promote the independence, dignity and well-being of
blind and visually-impaired people. Members are
blind, visually-impaired or fully sighted people from
all walks of life. People who are blind and visually-impaired comprise the vast majority of members
and are responsible for governing, administering and
setting organizational policy. Formed in 1961, ACB is
one of the largest US organizations of blind people.

**31    American Counseling Association**

5999 Stevenson Avenue
Alexandria, VA  22304                703-823-9800
                                    800-347-6647
                                    FAX 800-473-2329
                                    TDY:703-823-6862
                                    http://www.counseling.org
                                    e-mail: aca@counseling.org
*Sam Gladding, President*
*Kathy Rollins, Member Representative*

The mission is to enhance the quality of life in society
by promoting the development of professional counselors, advancing the counseling profession, and using the profession and practice of counseling to
promote respect for human dignity and diversity.

**32    American Dance Therapy Association (ADTA)**

2000 Century Plaza, Suite 108
Columbia, MD  21044                  410-997-4040
                                    FAX 410-997-4048
                                    http://www.adta.org
                                    e-mail: info@adta.org
*Tina Erfer, Eastern Region*
*Stacey Hurst, Central Region*
*Nancy Goldov, Western Region*

ADTA stimulates communication among
dance/movement therapists and members of allied
professions through publication of the ADTA Newsletter, the American Journal of Dance Therapy, mono-
graphs, bibliographies and conference proceedings.

**33    American Occupational Therapy Association**

4720 Montgomery Lane
Bethesda, MD  20824                  301-652-2682
                                    800-7292-682
                                    FAX 301-652-7711
                                    TDY:800-377-8555
                                    http://www.aota.org
                                    e-mail: praota@aota.org
*Jodi Greenblatt, Public Relations Department*
*Mary , Administrative Assistant*

Advances the quality, availability, use, and support of
occupational therapy through standard setting, advocacy, education, and research on behalf of its members and the public.

**34    American Printing House for the Blind**

1839 Frankfort Avenue
Louisville, KY  40206                502-895-2405
                                    800-223-1839
                                    FAX 502-899-2274
                                    http://www.aph.org
                                    e-mail: info@aph.org
*Tuck Tinsley III, President*
*Kathy Smiddy, Executive Secretary*
*Tony Grantz, Business Development Manager*

To promote the independence of blind and visually-impaired persons by providing special media,
tools, and materials needed for education and life.

**35  American Psychological Association**

American Psychological Association
750 1st Street NE
Washington, DC  20002                202-336-5500
                                     800-374-2721
                              FAX 202-336-5500
                              TDY:202-336-6123
                              http://www.apa.org
                              e-mail: psycinfo@apa.org
*Diane Halpern, PhD, President of the Board*
*Norman Anderson, Director*

Works to advance psychology as a science, a profession, and a means of promoting human welfare.

**36  American Public Human Services Association (APHSA)**

810 1st Street NE
Washington, DC  20002                202-682-0100
                                     888-628-2792
                              FAX 202-289-6555
                              http://www.aphsa.org
                              e-mail: jfriedman@aphsa.org
*Jerry Friedman, Executive Director*
*Elaine Ryan, Director Government Affairs*

The association's mission is to develop, promote, and implement public human service policies that improve the health and well-being of families, children, and adults. APHSA is also an umbrella for several component groups.

**37  American Red Cross**

2025 E Street NW
Washington, DC 20006                 202-303-4498
                              http://www.redcross.org
                              e-mail: info@usa.redcross.org
*Marsha Evans, President/CEO*

A humanitarian organization led by volunteers, guided by its Congressional Charter and the fundamental principles of the International Red Cross Movement, will provide relief to victims of disasters and help people prevent, prepare for, and respond to emergencies.

**38  American Rehabilitation Counseling Association (ARCA)**

5999 Stevenson Avenue
Alexandria, VA  22304                703-823-9800
                                     800-347-6647
                              FAX 703-461-9260
                              TDY:937-775-3153
                              http://www.counseling.org
                              e-mail: stephen.fortson@right.edu
*John Laforge MD, President*
*Stephen , Department Chairman*

In its pursuit of its mission, ARCA exercises leadership in developing the profession and science of rehabilitation counseling and advocates for the maintenance of standards in rehabilitation counseling, practice and education.

**39  American Speech-Language-Hearing Association**

American Speech-Language-Hearing Association on
10801 Rockville Pike
Rockville, MD  20852                 301-897-5700
                                     800-638-8255
                              FAX 301-571-0457
                              TDY:301-897-5700
                              http://www.asha.org
                              e-mail: actioncenter@asha.org
*Eileen Pietrarton, Executive Director*
*Dolores Battle, President of the Board*

A certifying body of 98,000 professionals providing speech, language and hearing services to the public. It is an accrediting agency for college and university graduate school programs in speech-language pathology and audiology.

**40  Appalaciha Educational Laboratory**

Appalachia Educational Laboratory
1031 Quarrier Street
Charleston, WV  25301 1348          304-347-0400
                                     800-624-9120
                              FAX 304-347-0487
                              TDY:304-347-0448
                              http://www.ael.org
*Caroline Reymolts, Senior Executive Assistant*
*Terry Eidell, Chief Executive Officer*

Economic, cultural, social or other factors related to educational programs and practices for rural residents.

**41  Assistive Technology Industry Association**

401 N Michigan Avenue
Chicago, IL  60611 4267             617-524-0035
                                     877-687-2842
                              FAX 312-673-6659
                              http://www.atia.org
                              e-mail: nfo@atia.org
*Caroline Vanhowe, Director*
*David Dikter, Executive Director*

A nonprofit membership organization of organizations manufacturing or selling technology-based devices for people with disabilities, or providing services associated with or required by people with disabilities.

**42  Association of Educational Therapists**

1804 W Burbank Boulevard
Burbank, CA  91506
                                     800-286-4267
                              http://www.aetonline.org
                              e-mail: aetla@aol.com

A national professional organization dedicated to establishing ethical professional standards, defining the roles and responsibilities of the educational therapist, providing opportunities for professional growth, and to studying techniques and technologies, philosophies and research related to the practice of educational therapy.

**43  Association on Higher Education and Disability**

Waltham, MA  02454                   781-788-0003
                              FAX 781-788-0033
                              http://www.AHEAD.org
                              e-mail: AHEAD@ahead.org
*Stephan Smith, Executive Director*
*Tri To, Operations Manager*

An international, muiticultural organization of professionals committed to full participation in higher education for persons with disabilities. The Association is a vital resource, promoting excellence through education, communication and training.

**44    Association on Higher Education and Disability (AHEAD)**

**University of Massachusetts-Boston**
**Waltham, MA  02454          781-788-0003**
**                               FAX 781-788-0033**
**                        http://www.ahead.org**
**        e-mail: ahead@postbox.acs.ohio-state.edu**
*Stephan Smith, Executive Director*
*Tri Do, Operations Manager*

An organization of professionals committed to full participation in higher education for persons with disabilities; provides information resources and training on issues related to disabilities.

**45    Attention Deficit Disorder Association**

**PO Box 543**
**Pottstown, PA  19464          484-945-2101**
**                               FAX 610-970-7520**
**                        http://www.add.org**
**                  e-mail: mail@add.org**
*Hildegard Rutter, Assistant*
*David Giwerc, VP*

A national nonprofit organization that provides information, resources and networking to adults with AD/HD.

**46    Autism Research Institute**

**4182 Adams Avenue**
**San Diego, CA  92116          619-281-7165**
**                               FAX 619-563-6840**
**        http://www.autismresearchinstitute.com**
*Bernard Rimland, Director*
*Matt Cobler, Assistant to the Director*

A nonprofit organization established in 1967 devoted to conducting research and to disseminating the results of research on the causes of autism and on methods of preventing, diagnosing and treating autism and other severe behavioral disorders of childhood.

**47    Autism Society of America**

**7910 Woodmont Avenue**
**Bethesda, MD  20814 3067          301-657-0881**
**                                   800-328-8476**
**                            FAX 301-657-0869**
**              http://www.autism-society.org**
**          e-mail: info@autism-society.org**
The mission is to promote lifelong access and opportunities for persons within the autism spectrum and their families, and to help them to be fully included, participating members of their communities through advocacy, public awareness, education and research related to autism.

**48    Autism Treatment Center of America**

**2080 S Undermountain Road**
**Sheffield, MA  01257          413-229-2100**
**                               800-714-2779**
**                        FAX 413-229-3202**
**              http://www.son-rise.org**
**      e-mail: correspondence@option.org**
*Barry Kaufman, Co-Founder*
*Tania Hills, Marketing Assistant*

Provides innovative training programs for parents and professionals caring for children challenged by Autism, Autism Spectrum Disorders, Pervasive Developmental Disorder (PDD) and other developmental difficulties. The Son-Rise Program teaches a specific yet comprehensive system of treatment and education designed to help families and caregivers enable their children to dramatically improve in all areas of learning.

**49    Birth Defect Research for Children (BDRC)**

**930 Woodcock Road**
**Orlando, FL  32803          407-895-0802**
**                             FAX 407-895-0824**
**                  http://www.birthdefects.org**
**              e-mail: abcd@birthdefects.org**
*Betty Mekdeci, Executive Director*

Nonprofit organization that provides parents and expectant parents with information about birth defects and support services for their children. BDRC has a parent matching program that links families who have children with similar birth defects.

**50    Boy Scouts of America**

**Scouting for the Handicapped Services**
**1325 W Walnut Hill Lane**
**Irving, TX  75015          972-580-2000**
**                            FAX 972-580-2502**
**                  http://www.scouting.org**
*Joe Glascock, Chief Scout Executive*
*Roy Williams, Assistant Executive*

Provides an educational program for boys and young adults to build character, to train in the responsibilities of participating citizenship, and to develop personal fitness.

**51    Brain Injury Association**

**8201 Greensboro Drive**
**McLean, VA  22101          703-761-0750**
**                            800-444-6443**
**                       FAX 703-236-6001**
**                 http://www.biausa.org**
*Ian Elliot, President*

Mission is to create a better future through brain injury prevention, research, education and advocacy.

**52    Career College Association (CCA)**

**10 G Street NE**
**Washington, DC  20002          202-336-6700**
**                                FAX 202-336-6828**
**                         http://www.career.org**
**                   e-mail: cca@career.org**
*Nick Glakas, President*
*Ruth Lestwich, Vice President*

Represents more than 1,000 private for profit post secondary schools, institutes, colleges and universities.

**53 Center for Applied Special Technology (CAST)**
39 Cross Street
Peabody, MA 01960      978-531-8555
FAX 978-531-0192
http://www.cast.org
e-mail: cast@cast.org

An educational, not-for-profit organization that uses technology to expand opportunities for all people, including those with disabilities; develops learning models, approaches and tools that are usable by a wide range of learners.

**54 Clearinghouse on Disability Information**
Office of Special Education and Rehabilitative Svc
US Department of Education
Washington, DC 20202 2524    202-205-8241
http://www.ed.gov/offices/osers/index.html

**55 Closing the Gap**
Computer Technology in Special Education & Rehab.
520 Main Street
Henderson, MN 56044      507-248-3294
FAX 507-248-3810
http://www.closingthegap.com
e-mail: info@closingthegap.com
*Sarah Anderson, Administrative Assistant*

Provides information on the use of computer-related technology by and for persons with disabilities.

**56 Commission on Accreditation of Rehabilitation Facilities (CARF)**
Commission on Accreditation of Rehabilitation Fac
4891 E Grant Road
Tucson, AZ 85712      520-325-1044
888-281-6531
FAX 520-318-1129
TDY:888-281-6531
http://www.carf.org
e-mail: feedback@carf.org
*Brian PhD, President/CEO*
*Linda Pitney, Human Resources Coordinator*

Promotes the quality, value and optimal outcomes of services through a consultative accreditation process that centers on enhancing the lives of the persons served.

**57 Communication Aids: Manufacturers Association**
205 W Randolph
Chicago, IL 60606      312-229-5444
800-441-2262
FAX 312-229-5445
TDY:800-441-2262
http://www.aacproducts.org
e-mail: cama@northshore.net
*James Neils, President*

A nonprofit organization of the world's leading manufacturers of augmentative and alternative communication software and hardware.

**58 Computer Learning Foundation**
Po Box 60007
Palo Alto, CA 94306-0007     408-720-8898
FAX 408-720-8777
http://www.computerlearning.org
e-mail: clf@computerlearning.org
*Sally Alden, Executive Director*

An international nonprofit educational foundation, dedicated to improving the quality of education and preparation of youth for the workplace through the use of technology. To accomplish its mission, the foundation provides numerous projects and materials to help parents and educators use technology effectively with children.

**59 Council for Exceptional Children**
Council for Exceptional Children
1110 N Glebe Road
Arlington, VA 05704      703-620-3660
888-232-7733
FAX 703-264-9494
TDY:866-915-5000
http://www.cec.sted.org
e-mail: cathym@cec.sped.org
*Dr Albritten, M.D., Executive Director*
*Betty Bryant, Program Manager*

TED promotes the preparation and continuing professional development of effective professionals in special education and related service fields. Members receive Teacher Education and Special Education quarterly and the TED Lines newsletter three times a year.

**60 Council for Exceptional Children (CEC)**
Council for Exceptional Children
1110 N Glebe Road
Arlington, VA 05704      703-620-3660
800-224-6830
FAX 703-264-9494
TDY:866-915-5000
http://www.cec.sped.org
e-mail: cec@cec.sped.org
*Drew Albritten, M.D., Executive Director*
*Betty Bryant, Program Manager*

CEC is a non-profit association. Accomplishes its mission which is carried out in support of special education professionals and others working on behalf of individuals with exceptionalities, by advocating for appropriate governmental policies, by setting professional standards and by providing continuing professional development.

**61 Council for Learning Disabilities**
PO Box 4014
Leesburg, VA 20177      571-258-1010
FAX 571-258-1011
http://www.cldinternational.org
*Joyce Rademacher, President*
*Mary Provost, Vice President*

An international organization that promotes effective teaching and research. CLD is composed of professionals who represent diverse disciplines and who are committed to enhancing the education and life span development of individuals with learning disabilities.

**62 Council on Rehabilitation Education**
1835 Rohlwing Road
Rolling Meadows, IL 60008    847-394-1785
FAX 847-394-2108
http://www.core-rehab.org
e-mail: dclink@wans.net
*Donald Linkowski, Executive Director*
*Sue Denys, Executive Admin Assistant*

Seeks to provide effective delivery of rehabilitation services to individuals with disabilities by stimulating and fostering continuing review and improvement of master's degree level rehabilitation counselor education programs.

**63    Distance Education and Training Council (DETC)**

1601 18th Street NW
Washington, DC  20009          202-234-5100
                               FAX 202-332-1386
                               http://www.detc.org
                               e-mail: detc@detc.org
*Michael Lambert, Executive Director*
*Jennifer Tobia, Information Specialist*

Nonprofit educational association located in Washington, DC. DETC serves as a clearinghouse of information about the distance study/correspondence field and sponsors a nationally recognized accrediting agency called the Accrediting Commission of the Distance Education and Training Council.

**64    Division for Culturally and Linguistically Diverse Learners**
Council for Exceptional Children
1110 N Glebe Road
Arlington, VA  05704           703-620-3660
                               888-232-7733
                               FAX 703-620-2521
                               TDY:866-915-5000
                               http://www.cec.sped.org
                               e-mail: cathym@cec.sped.org
*Drew Albritten M.D., Executive Director*
*Betty Bryant, Program Manager*
*Gwendolyn Webb-Johnson, Division President*

Dedicated to advancing and improving educational opportunities for culturally and linguistically diverse learners with disabilites and/or who are gifted, their families and the professionals who serve them.

**65    Division for Early Childhood**
Council for Exceptional Children
1110 N Glebe Road
Arlington, VA  05704           703-620-3660
                               888-232-7733
                               FAX 703-264-9494
                               TDY:866-915-5000
                               http://www.cec.sped.org
                               e-mail: cathym@cec.sped.org
*Drew Albritten, MD, Executive Director*
*Betty Bryant, Program Manager*

Organization designed for individuals who work with, or on behalf of children with special needs, birth through eight, and their families. Members include early childhood intervention professionals as well as parents of children who have disabilities, are gifted, or are at risk of future developmental problems. Members receive two quarterly publications as well as discounts on other DEC publications and the annual conference.

**66    Division for Learning Disabilities**
Council for Exceptional Children
1110 N Glebe Road
Arlington, VA  05704           703-620-3660
                               800-224-6830
                               FAX 703-264-9494
                               TDY:866-915-5000
                               http://www.cec.sped.org
                               e-mail: cathym@cec.sped.org
*Drew Albritten, MD, Executive Director*
*Betty Bryant, Program Manager*

Promotes improved services, research and legislation for individuals with learning disabilities. Members include teachers, teacher educators, administrators, policy makers, researchers, parents and related service providers. Members receive a quarterly journal and three newsletters per year.

**67    Division for Research**
Council for Exceptional Children
1110 N Glebe Road
Arlington, VA  05704           703-620-3660
                               888-232-7733
                               FAX 703-264-9494
                               TDY:866-915-5000
                               http://www.cec.sped.org
                               e-mail: cathym@cec.sped.org
*Drew Albritten, MD, Executive Director*
*Betty Bryant, Program Manager*

Devoted to the advancement of research related to the education of individuals with disabilities and/or who are gifted. Members include university, public and private school teachers, researchers, administrators, psychologists, speech/language clinicians, parents of children with special learning needs and other related professionals and service personnel. Members receive quarterly journal and newsletter three times a year.

**68    Division on Career Development**
Council for Exceptional Children
1110 N Glebe Road
Arlington, VA  05704           703-620-3660
                               888-232-7733
                               FAX 703-264-9494
                               TDY:866-915-5000
                               http://www.cec.sped.org
                               e-mail: cathym@cec.sped.org
*Drew Albritten, MD, Executive Director*
*Betty Bryant, Program Manager*

Focuses on the career development of individuals with disabilities and/or who are gifted and their transition from school to adult life. Members include professionals and others interested in career development and transition for individuals with any exception at any age. Members receive a journal twice yearly and newsletter three times per year.

**69  Division on Visual Impairments**

Council for Exceptional Children
1110 N Glebe Road
Arlington, VA  05704                     703-620-3660
                                         888-232-7733
                                     FAX 703-264-9494
                                     TDY:866-915-5000
                               http://www.cec.sped.org
                             e-mail: cathym@cec.sped.org
*Drew Albritten, MD, Executive Director*
*Betty Bryant, Program Manager*

Advances the education of children and youth who
have visual impairments that impede their educational
progress. Members include teachers, teacher educators, other practitioners and administrators. Members
receive quarterly newsletter.

**70  Dyslexia Research Institute**

5746 Centerville Road
Tallahassee, FL  32309               850-893-2216
                                 FAX 850-893-2440
                          http://www. dylexia-add.org
                        e-mail: dri@dyslexia-add.org
*Patrica Hardman PhD, Director*
*Robyn Rennick MS, Assistant Director*

Addresses academic, social and self-concept issues
for dyslexic and ADD children and adults. College
prep courses, study skills, advocacy, diagnostic testing, seminars, teacher training, day school, tutoring
and an adult literacy and life skills programs are available using an accredited MSLE approach.

**71  Easter Seals**

230 W Monroe Street
Chicago, IL  60606                   312-726-6200
                                     800-221-6827
                                 FAX 312-726-1494
                                 TDY:312-726-4258
                         http://www.easter-seals.com
                        e-mail: info@easter-seals.com
*James Williams, Chairman*
*James Williams Jr, President/CEO*

Easter Seals' mission is to create solutions that change
lives for children and adults with disabilities, their
families, and their communities. We work to identify
the needs of people with disabilities and to provide appropriate developmental and rehabilitation services.
Our Easter Seals operate 450 sites that provide services to children and adults with disabilities and their
families. All sites provide different services. Call to
inquire about Easter Seals in your community.

**72  Educational Advisory Group**

2222 E Lake Avenue E
Seattle, WA  98102                   206-323-1838
                                 FAX 206-267-1325
                        http://www.apianeducation.com
                       e-mail: info@apianeducation.com
*Yvonne Jones, Associate*
*Paul Auchterlonie, Director*

Specializes in matching children with the learning environments that are best for them and works with families to help them identify concerns and establish
priorities about their child's education.

**73  Educational Equity Concepts**

100 5th Avenue
New York, NY  10011                  212-243-1110
                                 FAX 212-627-0407
                             http://www.edequity.org
                         e-mail: information@edequity.org
*Ellen Rubin, Executive Director*
*Anna Orellana, Project Assistant*

A national nonprofit organization that promotes bias
free learning through innovative programs and materials. Founded in 1982, our mission is to decrease discrimination based on gender, race/ethnicity,
disability, and level of family income.

**74  Educational Testing Service: SAT Services for
Students with Disabilities**

College Board SAT Program
PO Box 6200
Princeton, NJ  08541                 609-771-7137
                                 FAX 609-771-7944
                         http://www.collegeboard.org
                     e-mail: ssd@info.collegeboard.org
*Margie Griffin, Department Head of Disability*
*Michael Hart, Administrative Assistant*

Offers testing accommodations to attempt to minimize the effect of disabilities on test performance.
The SAT Program tests eligible students with documented visual, physical, hearing, or learning disabilities who require testing accommodations for SAT.

**75  Families and Advocates Partnership for
Education FAPE**

PACER Center
8161 Normandale Blvd.
Minneapolis, MN  55437               952-838-9000
                                 FAX 952-838-0199
                              http://www.fape.org
*Paula Goldberg, Director*

The FAPE project is a strong partnership that aims to
improve the educational outcomes for children with
disabilities. FAPE links families, advocates, and
self-advocates to communicate the new focus of the
Individuals with Disabilities Education Act (IDEA).
The project represents the needs of six million children with disabilities.

**76  Federation for Children with Special Needs**

1135 Tremont Street
Boston, MA  02120                    617-236-7210
                                     800-331-0688
                                 FAX 617-572-2094
                                 TDY:617-236-7210
                              http://www.fcsn.org
                          e-mail: fcsninfo@fcsn.org
*Richard Robison, Executive Director*
*Sarah Miranda, Assistant Director*

The mission of the Federation is to provide information, support and assistance to parents of children with
disabilities, their professional partners and their communities. Major services are information and referral
and parent and professional training.

**77    General Educational Development Testing Service**

American Council on Education
1 Dupont Circle NW
Washington, DC  20036          202-939-9490
                               800-626-9433
                           FAX 202-833-4760
                         http://www.acenet.edu
                       e-mail: ged@ace.nche.edu
*Joan Auchtner, Executive Director*
*Lyn Schaeser, Director*

**78    HEATH Resource Center**

George Washington University
2121 K St. NW
Washington, DC  20036          202-973-0903
                               800-544-3284
                           FAX 202-973-0908
                        http://www.heath.gwu.edu
                     e-mail: askheath@heath.gwu.edu
*Lynda West, Publications Manager*
*Joel Gomez, Co-Principal Investigator*
*Pamela Ekpone, Director*

Higher Education and Adult Training for People with
Handicaps (HEATH) is a national clearinghouse that
provides free information on postsecondary education
and related issues for individuals with learning disabilities

**79    Independent Living Research Utilization Program**

Institute of Rehabilitation and Research
2323 S Shepherd Drive
Houston, TX  77019             713-520-0232
                           FAX 713-520-5785
                           TDY:713-520-0232
                           http://www.ilru.org
                         e-mail: ilru@ilru.org
*Linda CoVan, Director*

National center for information, training, research,
and technical assistance in independent living. Its
goal is to expand the body of knowledge in independent living and to improve utilization of results of research programs and demonstration projects in this
field. It is a program of The Institute for Rehabilitation
and Research, a nationally recognized medical rehabilitation facility for persons with disabilities.

**80    Institute for Educational Leadership**

4455 Court Avenue NW
Washington, DC  20008          202-822-8405
                           FAX 202-872-4050
                           http://www.iel.org
                         e-mail: iel@iel.org
*Elizabeth Hale, President*
*Louise Clarke, Chief Administrator*
*Bert Berkley, Chairman of the Board*

Mission is to improve education and the lives of children and their families through positive and visionary
change. Everyday, we face that challenge by bringing
together diverse constituencies and empowering leaders with knowledge and applicable ideas.

**81    Institutes for the Achievement of Human Potential**

8801 Stenton Avenue
Wyndmoore, PA  19038           215-233-2050
                               800-736-4663
                           FAX 215-233-9312
                          http://www.iahp.org/
                       e-mail: institutes@iahp.org
*Glenn Doman, Founder*
*Janet Doman, Executive Director*

Nonprofit educational organization that serves children by introducing parents to the field of child brain
development. Parents learn how to enhance significantly the development of their children physically,
intellectually and socially in a joyous and sensible
way. The goal of the institute is to raise significantly
the intellectual, physical, and social abilities of all
children. Accepts brain injured children, however severely hurt, and helps them advance.

**82    International Dyslexia Association: National
Headquarters**

8600 Lasalle Road, Chester Building
Baltimore, MD  21286           410-296-0232
                               800-223-3123
                           FAX 410-321-5069
                         http://www.interdys.org
                     e-mail: MBIDA4@hotmail.com
*Cathy Rosemond, President*

Nonprofit, scientific and educational organization
dedicated to the study and treatment of dyslexia. Focus is educating parents, teachers and professionals in
the field of dyslexia in effective teaching methodologies. Programs and services include: information and
referral; public awareness; medical and educational
research; governmental affairs; conferences and publications.

**83    International Reading Association**

800 Barksdale Road
Newark, DE  19714              302-731-1600
                               800-628-8508
                           FAX 302-731-1057
                         http://www.reading.org
                      e-mail: pubinfo@reading.org
*Beth Cady, Public Information Associate*

A professional association with more then 80,000
members in nearly 100 counties dedicated to promoting higher achievement levels in literacy, reading and
communication worldwide.

**84    Landmark Outreach Program**

Landmark School
429 Hale Street
Prides Crossing, MA  01965     978-236-3010
                           FAX 978-927-7268
                       http://www.landmarkschool.org
                   e-mail: jbloom@landmarkschool.org
*Robert Broudo, Head Master*
*Kathryn Frye, Administrative Assistant*

Provides consultation and training to public and private schools, professional organizations, parent groups, and businesses on topics related to individuals with learning disabilities. Services are individually designed to meet the client's specific needs and can range from a two-hour workshop to a year-long training project. Options include consulting services, training workshops, summer training program, seminars and parent workshops.

**85    Learning Disabilities Association of America (LDA)**

Learning Disabilities Association of America
4156 Library Road
Pittsburgh, PA  15234 1349          412-341-1515
                                    888-300-6710
                                FAX 412-344-0224
                        http://www.ldaamerica.org
                        e-mail: info@ldaamerica.org
*Jane Browning, Executive Director*
*Marianne Toombs, President*
*Suzanne Fornaro, VP*

Formed on behalf of children with learning disabilities in 1964, LDA is the only national organization devoted to defining and finding solutions for the broad spectrum of learning disabilities. LDA has 50 state affiliates with more than 350 local chapters. Membership totals over 50,000, including parents, professionals from many sectors and concerned citizens. Makes available publications, rental films, a newsletter and journal. Holds an annual international conference.

**86    Learning Resource Network**

1130 Hostetler
Manhattan, KS  66502          785-539-5376
                              800-678-5376
                          FAX 785-539-7766
                          http://www.lern.org
                          e-mail: rebel@lern.org
*William Draves, Director*

This network for educators provides resources to adult education and adult basic education service providers.

**87    MATRIX: A Parent Network and Resource Center**

555 Northgate Drive
San Rafael, CA  94903          415-884-3535
                               800-578-2592
                           FAX 415-884-3555
                           TDY:415-884-3554
                    http://www.matrixparents.org
                    e-mail: info@matrixparents.org
*Nora Thompson, Executive Director*
*Sudy Jensen, Information Research Manager*

A place where parents can turn to when they discover that their child has a special need or disability and a place for parents to find emotional support and information from parents who have been there.

**88    Menninger Clinic: Center for Learning Disabilities**

2801 Gessner
Houston, TX  77280 9045          713-275-5000
                                 800-351-9058
                             FAX 713-275-5107
                    http://www.meninger.clinic.com
                        e-mail: info@menninger.edu
*Ian Aitken, President/CEO*
*Rozanna Davis, Vice President*

The mission of Menninger is to be a national resource providing psychiatric care and treatment of the highest standard, searching for new knowledge and better understanding of mental illness and human behavior, teaching what we know and what we learn, and applying this knowledge in useful ways to promote individual growth and better mental health.

**89    Nat'l Association for the Education ofAfrican American Children with Learning Disabilities**

PO Box 09521
Columbus, OH  43209          614-237-6021
                         FAX 614-238-0929

The NAEAACLD has the latest information on educating African American Children with learning disabilities and links to many other resources.

**90    Nat'l Association for the Education of African American Children with Learning Disabilities**

PO Box 09521
Columbus, OH  43209          614-237-6021
                         FAX 614-238-0929

The NAEAACLD has the latest information on educating African American Children with learning disabilities and links to many other resources.

**91    National Admission, Review, Dismissal: Individualized Education Plan Advocates**

PO Box 16111
Sugar Land, TX  77496          281-265-1506
                           FAX 253-295-9954
                           http://www.narda.org
                e-mail: louisadvo@mylinuxisp.com
*Louis Geigerman, President*

National ARD Advocates is dedicated to obtaining the appropriate educational services for children with special needs.

**92    National Adult Education Professional Development Consortium**

444 N Capitol Street NW
Washington, DC  20001          202-624-5250
                           FAX 202-624-1497
                           http://www.naepdc.org
                           e-mail: dc1@naepdc.org
*Patricia Bennett,MD, Executive Director*

The Consortium, incorporated in 1990 by state adult education directors, provides professional development, policy analysis, and dissemination of information important to state staff in adult education.

**93** **National Association for Adults with Special Learning Needs**

PO Box 716
Bryn Mawr, PA 19010          610-525-8336
                            800-869-8336
                        FAX 610-446-6129
                    http://www.ldonline.org
            e-mail: 75250.1273@compuserv.com

A nonprofit organization designed to organize, establish, and promote an effective national and international coalition of professionals, advocates, and consumers of lifelong learning for the purpose of educating adults with special learning needs.

**94** **National Association for Gifted Children**

1707 L Street NW
Washington, DC 20036          202-785-4268
                        FAX 202-785-4248
                        http://www.nagc.org
                    e-mail: nacg@nagc.org
*Richard Olenchak, President*

An organization of parents, educators, other professionals and community leaders who unite to address the unique needs of children and youth with demonstrated gifts and talents as well as those children who may be able to develop their talent potential with appropriate educational experiences. We support and develop policies and practices that encourage and respond to the diverse expressions of gifts and talents in children and youth from all cultures.

**95** **National Association for the Education of Young Children (NAEYC)**

1509 16th Street NW
Washington, DC 20036 1426          202-232-8777
                                800-424-2460
                            FAX 202-328-1846
                            http://www.naeyc.org
                        e-mail: naeyc@naeyc.org
*Jane Crompton, President*
*James Wagner, Relationship Associate*

NAEYC exists for the purpose of leading and consolidating the efforts of individuals and groups working to achieve health development and constructive education for all young children. Primary attention is devoted to assuring the provision of high quality early childhood programs for young children.

**96** **National Association of Developmental Disabilities Councils (NADDC)**

1234 Massachusetts Avenue NW
Washington, DC 20005          202-347-1234
                        FAX 202-347-4023
                        http://www.naddc.org
                    e-mail: info@naddc.org
*Karen Flippo, Executive Director*
*Pat Seybold, President*

A national organization for Developmental Disabilities Councils that advocate and work for change on behalf of people with developmental and other disabilities, and their families. NADDC promotes national policy to enhance the quality of life for all people with developmental disabilities.

**97** **National Association of Private Special Education Centers**

1522 K Street NW
Washington, DC 20005          202-408-3338
                        FAX 202-408-3340
                        http://www.napsec.com
                    e-mail: napsec@aol.com
*Sherry Kolbe, Executive Director/CEO*
*Alison Figi, Communications Coordinator*
*Dr. Mike Rice, President*

A nonprofit association whose mission is to ensure access for individuals to private special education as a vital component of the continuum of appropriate placement and services in American education. The association consists solely of private special education schools that serve both privately and publicly placed children with disabilities.

**98** **National Business and Disability Council**

201 IU Willets Road
Albertson, NY 11507          516-465-1515
                        FAX 516-465-3730
                        http://www.nbdc.com
            e-mail: mcgowan@business-disability.com.
*Lynn Broder, Membership Specialist*
*Mike McGowan, Information Service Assistant*

A leading resource for employers seeking to integrate people with disabilities into the workplace and companies seeking to reach them in the consumer marketplace. As a non-profit we are providing educational, vocational, rehabilitation and research opportunities for persons with disabilities through the Henry Viscardi School, the Edwin W Martin, Jr. Career and Employment Institute, the Research and Training Institute and the Mary Jean and Frank P Smeal Learning Center.

**99** **National Camp Association**

610 5th Avenue
New York, NY 10185          212-645-0653
                        800-966-2267
                    FAX 845-354-5501
                http://www.summercamp.org
            e-mail: info@summercamp.org
*Jeffrey Solomon, Executive Director*

Dedicated to helping parents find the right sleep-away camp for their children.

**100** **National Center for ESL Literacy Education (NCLE)**

4646 40th Street NW
Washington, DC 20016 1859          202-362-0700
                                866-845-3378
                            FAX 202-363-7204
                        http://www.cal.org/ncle
                        e-mail: ncle@cal.org
*Joy Peyton, Vice President*
*Miriam Burt, Associate Director*

A national organization focusing on literacy education for adults and out-of-school youth learning English as a second language. NCLE publishes many documents on its website.

**101**    **National Center for Family Literacy**

325 W Main Street
Louisville, KY 40202 4237      502-584-1133
     877-FAMLIT-1
     FAX 502-584-0172
     http://www.famlit.org
     e-mail: ncfl@famlit.org
*Sharon Darling, President*
*Patricia West, Administrator Assistant*

Provides leadership for family literacy development nationwide; promote policies at the national and state level to support family literacy; designs, develops and demonstrates new family literacy practices that address the needs of families in a changing social, economic and political landscape; deliver high quality, dynamic, research-based training, staff development and technical assistance; conducts research to expand the knowledge base of family literacy.

**102**    **National Center for Learning Disabilities (NCLD)**

**National Center for Learning Disabilities**
381 Park Avenue S
New York, NY 10016      212-545-7510
     888-575-7373
     FAX 212-545-9665
     http://www.ld.org
     e-mail: help@ncld.org
*James Wendorf, Executive Director*
*Marcia Pauyo, Executive Assistant*

The National Center for Learning Disabilities' (NCLD) mission is to increase opportunities for all individuals with learning disabilities to achieve their potential. NCLD accomplishes its mission by increasing public awareness and understanding of learning disabilities, conducting educational programs and services that promote research-based knowledge, and providing national leadership in shaping public policy. We provide solutions that help people with LD participate fully in society.

**103**    **National Center of Higher Education for Learning Problems (HELP)**

**Myers Hall**
520 18th Street
Huntington, WV 20004      304-696-6313
     FAX 304-696-3231
     TDY:202-272-2074
     e-mail: mquigley@ncd.gov
*Barbara Guyer, Director HELP Program*
*Debbie , Coordinator Diagnostics*

The HELP program offers a full battery of comprehensive psychoeducational tests to determine if an individual has learning and/or attention deficits. The team of professionals can identify specific problems for all ages, such as school age children, college students, medical students, and professionals.

**104**    **National Clearinghouse for Professions in Special Education**

**Council for Exceptional Children**
1110 N Glebe Road
Arlington, VA 22201      703-620-3660
     888-232-7733
     http://www.cec.sped.org
     e-mail: ncpse@cec.sped.org
*Lynn Boyer, Director*
*Rebecca Presgrares, Administrative Specialist*

Committed to enhancing the nation's capacity to recruit, prepare, and retain well qualified diverse educators and related services professionals for children with disabilities.

**105**    **National Council on Disability**

1331 F Street NW
Washington, DC 20006      202-272-2004
     FAX 202-272-2022
     http://www.ncd.gov
     e-mail: mquigley@ncd.gov
*Lex Frieden, Chairman*
*Ethel Briggs, Executive Director*

An independent federal agency comprised of 15 members appointed by the President and confirmed by the Senate.

**106**    **National Council on Independent Living Programs**

1916 Wilson Boulevard
Arlington, VA 22201      703-525-3406
     800-224-6830
     FAX 703-525-3409
     TDY:703-525-4153
     http://www.ncil.org
     e-mail: ncil@ncil.org
*John Lancaster, Executive Director*
*Denise Law, Administrative Assistant*

A membership organization that advances the independent living philosophy and advocates for the human rights of, and services for, people with disabilities to further their full integration and participation in society.

**107**    **National Council on Rehabilitation Education**

**Emporia State University**
1200 Commercial Street
Emporia, KS 66801      620-341-1200
     FAX 620-341-5073
     http://www.rehabeducators.org
*Kay Schallenkamp, President*
*Vilia Tarvydes PhD CRC, Board President*

An organization which has as its purpose promoting the improvement of rehabilitation services available to people with disabilities through quality education and rehabilitation research.

**108**    **National Data Bank for Disabled Students Services**

**University of Maryland**
Shoemaker Building
College Park, MD 20742      301-314-7682
     FAX 301-405-0813
     http://www.counseling.umd.edu/dss
*Robert Giannell, Coordinator*

Provides colleges the means for accessing statistics related to services, staff, budget and other components of disabled student services programs across the country.

**109    National Dissemination Center for Children with Disabilities**

**NICHCY**
**PO Box 1492**
**Washington, DC  20013-149**
                        202-884-8200
                        800-695-0285
                FAX 202-884-8441
                TDY:800-695-0285
                http://www.nichcy.org
                e-mail: nichcy@aed.org
*Susan Ripley, Executive Director*

An information and referral clearinghouse that provides free information on disabilities and disability related issues. Services include speaking with an information specialist, receiving free publications, database searches and referrals to other organizations. Also provides a state resource sheet which identifies resources in each state including state agencies, disability organizations and parent groups.

**110    National Early Childhood Technical Assistance Center**

**Univ of N Carolina at Chapel Hill**
**Chapel Hill, NC  27599 8040**
                        919-962-2001
                FAX 919-966-7463
                TDY:919-843-3269
                http://www.nectas.unc.edu
                e-mail: nectas@unc.edu
*Pascal Trohanis, Director*
*Judi Shaver, Coordinator*

Assists states and other designated governing jurisdictions as they develop multidisciplinary, coordinated and comprehensive services for young children with special needs and their families

**111    National Education Association (NEA)**

**1201 16th Street NW**
**Washington, DC  20036 3290**
                        202-833-4000
                FAX 202-822-7974
                http://www.nea.org
*Rug Weaver, President*

NEA is a volunteer-based organization supported by a network of staff at the local, state and national level. At the local level, NEA affiliates are active in a wide variety of activities, everything from conducting professional workshops on discipline and other issues that affect faculty and school support staff to bargaining contracts for school district employees. At the state level, NEA affiliate activities are equally wide-ranging.

**112    National Federation of the Blind**

**1800 Johnson Street**
**Baltimore, MD  21230**
                        410-659-9314
                FAX 410-685-5653
                http://www.nfb.org
                e-mail: nfb@nfb.org
*Betsy Zaborowski, MD, Executive Director*
*Mrs , Director Community Relations*

The purpose of the National Federation of the Blind is two-fold: to help blind persons achieve self-confidence and self-respect and to act as a vehicle for collective self expression for the blind. Provides public education about blindness, information and referral services, scholarships, literature and publications about blindness, aids and appliances and other adaptive equipment for the blind, advocacy services and protection of civil rights and job opportunities for the blind.

**113    National Institute of Art and Disabilities**

**551 23rd Street**
**Richmond, CA  94804**
                        510-620-0290
                FAX 510-620-0326
                http://www.niadart.org
                e-mail: admin@niadart.org
*Pat Coleman, Executive Director*
*Elias Katz, President*

Mission is to provide an art program for people with developmental disabilities which promotes creative expression, independence, dignity and community integration.

**114    National Jewish Council for Disabilities Summer Program**

**YACHAD East Coast Adventure**
**11 Broadway**
**New York, NY  10004**
                        212-613-8369
                FAX 212-613-0796
                http://www.njcd.org
                e-mail: yadbyad@ou.org
*Nechama Braun, Administrator*

**115    National Lekotek Center**

**3204 W Armitage Avenue**
**Chicago, IL  60647**
                        773-276-5164
                        800-366-7529
                FAX 773-276-8644
                http://www.lekotek.org
                e-mail: lekotek@lekotek.org
*Diana Nielander, Executive Director*

The mission of the National Lekotek Center is driven by the philosophy that children learn best when play is a family-centered activity that includes all children, regardless of their abilities or disabilities, in family and community activities. We offer play-centered services to children with disabilities and supportive services to their families. We also offer computer play, parent support and national resources for families and professionals.

**116    National Organization for Rare Disorders (NORD)**

**Nord Literature**
**55 Kenosia Avenue**
**Danbury, CT  01968**
                        203-744-0100
                        800-999-6673
                FAX 203-798-2291
                TDY:203-797-9590
                http://www.rarediseases.org
                e-mail: orphan@rarediseases.org
*James Broatch, Chairman*
*Maria Hardin, Vice President*

NORD is an international clearing house on rare disorders. It provides information in understandable language, supplies information on support groups, networking with patients and families; hosts an annual conference for patients and the medical community. Offers medication assistance programs, funding for research, cost options for travel to medical facilities, and a Medical Equipment Exchange.

**117  National Organization on Disability (NOD)**
**910 16th Street NW**
**Washington, DC  20006**          202-293-5960
                              FAX 202-293-7999
                              TDY:202-293-5968
                              http://www.nod.org
                              e-mail: ability@nod.org
*Alan Reich, Founder*
*Michael Deland, Chairman*

Promotes the full and equal participation of America's 54 million men, women and children with disabilities in all aspects of life. Funded entirely by private sector contributions, NOD is the only national disability network organization concerned with all disabilities, all age groups and all disability issues.

**118  National Rehabilitation Association**
**633 S Washington Street**
**Alexandria, VA  22314**          703-836-0850
                              888-258-4295
                              FAX 703-836-0848
                              TDY:703-836-0849
                        http://www.nationalrehab.org
                        e-mail: info@nationalrehab.org
*Annemarie Hohman, Executive Director*
*Jon D'Angelo, Director*

A member organization whose mission is providing opportunities through knowledge and diversity for professionals in the field of rehabilitation of people with disabilities.

**119  National Rehabilitation Information Center**
**4200 Forbes Boulevard**
**Lanham, MD  20706**          301-459-5900
                          800-346-2742
                          FAX 301-459-4263
                          TDY:301-459-5984
                        http://www.naric.com
                  e-mail: naricinfo@heitechservices.com
*Mark Odum, Director*
*Jessica Chaiken, Media Manager*

A library and information center on all aspects of disability and rehabilitation.

**120  PACER Center**
**8661 Normandale Boulevard**
**Minneapolis, MN  55437**          952-838-9000
                              800-537-2237
                              FAX 952-838-0199
                              http://www.pacer.org
                              e-mail: pacer@pacer.org
*Paula Goldberg, Executive Director*

The mission of PACER Center is to expand opportunities and enhance the quality of life of children and young adults with disabilities and their families, based on the concept of parents helping parents.

**121  Parent Educational Advocacy Training Center (PEATC)**
**6320 Augusta Drive**
**Springfield, VA  22150**          703-923-0010
                              800-869-6782
                              FAX 703-923-0030
                              TDY:703-923-0010
                              http://www.peatc.org
                              e-mail: partners@peatc.org
*Cherie Takemoto, Executive Director*
*Gail Ryder, Administrative Coordinator*

Assists the families of children with disabilities through education, information and training. PEATC builds parent-professional partnerships to promote success in school and community life through information and assistance to families in understanding and negotiating the education and service systems for their children with disabilities.

**122  Parents Helping Parents: Family Resource for Children with Special Needs**
**3041 Olcott Street**
**Santa Clara, CA  95054**          408-727-5775
                              866-747-4040
                              FAX 408-727-0182
                              TDY:408-748-8399
                              http://www.php.com
                              e-mail: general@php.com
*Alexandra Cramer, Administrative Assistant*

Helping children with special needs receive the resources, love, hope, respect, health care, education and other services they need to achieve their full potential by providing them with strong families and dedicated professionals to serve them.

**123  Pioneers Division**
**Council for Exceptional Children**
**1110 N Glebe Road**
**Arlington, VA  05704**          703-620-3660
                              888-232-7733
                              FAX 703-264-9494
                              TDY:866-915-5000
                              http://www.cec.sped.org
                              e-mail: cathym@cec.sped.org
*Drew Albritten MD, Executive Director*
*Betty Bryant, Program Manager*

Promotes activities and programs to increase awareness of the educational needs of children with disabilities and/or who are gifted, and the services available to them. Supports CEC's programs and activities. Membership is only open to CEC life members, retired life members and members of twenty years' standing. Members receive newsletter three times yearly.

**124  Promote Real Independence for Disabled & Elderly Foundation**
**391 Long Hill Road**
**Groton, CT  06340**          860-445-7320
                          800-332-9122
                          FAX 860-445-1448
                    http://www.sewtiqueonline.com
                    e-mail: dresspride@aol.com
*Evelyn Kennedy, Executive Director*

Rehabilitation assistance utilizing fashion and grooming along with home management and independence in dressing. Speakers and resources are available for outreach services.

**125  RFB&D Learning Through Listening**
Anne T MacDonald Center
20 Roszel Road
Princeton, NJ  08540                 609-452-0606
                                     800-221-4792
                              FAX 609-987-8116
                            http://www.rfbd.org
                      e-mail: custserv@rfbd.org
*John Kelly, President/CEO*
*Pat Sullivan, Contact*

The nation's educational library for people with print disabilities. We provide educational materials in recorded and computerized formats from kindergarten through postgraduate level.

**126  Reach for Learning**
1221 Marin Avenue
Albany, CA  94706                    510-524-6455
                              FAX 510-524-5154
*Corinne Gustafson, Director*

Educational center providing diagnosis, instruction, consultation for children, youth, adults with learning disabilities or under achievement.

**127  Rehabilitation Engineering and Assistive Technology Society of North America (RESNA)**
1700 N Moore Street
Arlington, VA  22209 1903            703-524-6686
                              FAX 703-524-6630
                              TDY:703-524-6639
                            http://www.resna.org
                      e-mail: resna@resna.org
*Larry Lencak, Director*

Dedicated to improving the potential of people with disabilities to achieve their goals through the use of technology; maintains listing of State Assistive Technology Programs. Services include an annual conference and publications.

**128  Rehabilitation International**
25 E 21st Street
New York, NY  10010                  212-420-1500
                              FAX 212-505-0871
                http://www.rehab-international.org
          e-mail: rehabintl@rehab-international.org
*Lex Frieden, President*
*Blanca Ceno, Administrative Assistant*

A federation of national and international organizations and agencies working for the prevention of disability, the rehabilitation of people with disabilities and the equalization of opportunities within society on behalf of persons with disabilities and their families throughout the world.

**129  Rural Clearinghouse for Lifelong Education & Development**
Kansas State University
101 College Court Building
Manhattan, KS  66506                 913-532-5560
                              FAX 913-532-5637
                  e-mail: abyers@ksuksu.edu
*Jacqueline Spears, Director*

A national effort to improve rural access to continuing education.

**130  Sertoma International/Sertoma Foundation**
1912 E Meyer Boulevard
Kansas City, MO  64132               816-333-8300
                              FAX 816-333-4320
                            http://www.sertoma.org
                   e-mail: infosertoma@sertoma.org
*Steven Murphy, Executive Director*
*Ronda Aldridge, Administrative Assistant*

Activities focus on helping people with speech and hearing problems, but also have programs in the areas of youth, national heritage, drug awareness and community services.

**131  Son-Rise Program**
Autism Treatment Center of America
2080 S Undermountain Road
Sheffield, MA  01257                 413-229-2100
                                     800-714-2779
                              FAX 413-229-8931
                            http://www.son-rise.org
                   e-mail: information@son-rise.org
*Sean Fitzgerald, Marketing Associate*
*Barry Kauffman, Co-Founder*
*Bryn Hogan, Director*

Since 1983, the Autism Treatment Center of America has provided innovative training programs for parents and professionals caring for children challenged by autism, autism spectrum disorders, pervasive developmental disorder (PDD) and other developmental difficulties. The Son-Rise Program teaches a specific yet comprehensive system of treatment and education designed to help families and caregivers enable their children to dramatically improve in all areas of learning.

**132  Stuttering Foundation of America**
3100 Walnut Grove Road
Memphis, TN  38111 0749              901-452-7343
                                     800-992-9392
                              FAX 901-452-3931
                      http://www.stutteringhelp.org
                   e-mail: stutter@stutteringhelp.org
*Jane Fraser, President*
*Joan Warner, Information Resource*

Provides information to parents of children, adults, and teens who may have a stuttering problem.

**133  Team of Advocates for Special Kids**
100 W Cerritos Avenue
Anaheim, CA  92805                   714-533-8275
                              FAX 714-533-2533
                            http://www.taskca.org
                   e-mail: tasca@yahoo.com
*Marta Anchondo, Executive Director*
*Brenda Smith, Assistant Director*

A parent training and information center serving families of children with disabilities. Provides support, legal rights information, phone advocacy, workshops and referral services. Conducts assistive technology assessments for ages 12 months through adulthood and workshops on adapted toys, adaptive hardware and specialized software. Newsletter with legal updates, technology and disability information.

**134 Technology and Media Division**
**Council for Exceptional Children**
**1110 N Glebe Road**
**Arlington, VA  05704**          703-620-3660
                                  888-232-7733
                             FAX 703-264-9494
                             TDY:866-915-5000
                        http://www.cec.sped.org
                    e-mail: cathym@cec.sped.org
*Drew Albritten, M.D., Executive Director*
*Betty Bryant, Program Manager*

Promotes the availability and effective use of technology and media for individuals with disabilities and/or who are gifted. Members include special education teachers, speech and language therapists, rehabilitation therapists, counselors, researchers, teacher educators and others. Members receive two quarterly newsletters.

**135 Thinking and Learning Connection**
**239 Whitclem Court**
**Palo Alto, CA  94306**           650-493-3497
                             FAX 650-494-3499

*Lynne Stietzel, Co-Director*
*Eric Stietzel, Co-Director*

A group of independent associates committed to teaching students to learn new paths of knowledge and understanding. Our primary focus is working with dyslexic and dyscalculia. Individualized educational programs utilize extensive multisensory approaches to teach reading, spelling, handwriting, composition, comprehension, and mathematics. The students are actively involved in learning processes that integrate visual, auditory, and tactile techniques.

**136 Very Special Arts (VSA)**
**VSA Arts**
**1300 ConneCourticut Avenue NW**
**Washington, DC  20036**          202-737-0645
                                   800-933-8721
                             FAX 202-737-0725
                         http://www.vsarts.org
                      e-mail: info@vsarts.org
*Soula Antoniou, President*
*Veda Herman, Chief Executive Officer*

Founded in 1974 by Jean Kennedy Smith as an affiliate of the John F. Kennedy Center for the Performing Arts, and led by president Doris Dixon, VSA is an international organization that creates learning opportunities through the arts for people with disabilities. The organization offers arts-based programs in creative writing, dance, drama, music and the visual arts implemented primarily through our vast network in 39 states and 70 international affiliates.

**137 Washington PAVE: Specialized Training of Military Parents**
**Wapave**
**6316 S 12th Street**
**Tacoma, WA  98465**              253-565-2266
                                   800-572-7368
                             FAX 253-566-8052
                             TDY:253-565-2266
                  http://www.washingtonpave.org
          e-mail: wapave9@washingtonpave.com
*Joanne Butts, Executive Director*
*Elama Rounds, Financial Officer*

STOMP, a parent directed project exists to empower military parents, individuals with disabilities, and service providers with knowledge, skills and resources so that they might access services to create a collaborative environment for a family and professional partnerships without regard to geographic location.

**138 World Institute on Disability (WID)**
**510 16th Street**
**Oakland, CA  94612**             510-763-4100
                             FAX 510-763-4109
                        http://www.wid.org
                   e-mail: webpoobah@wid.org
A nonprofit public policy center dedicated to promoting independence and full societal inclusion of people with disabilities. Since its founding in 1983 by Ed Roberts, WID has earned a reputation for high quality research and public education on a wide range of issues. Newsletter is published on a regular basis.

**139 Young Adult Institute (YAI): National Institute for People with Disabilities**
**460 W 34th Street**
**New York, NY  10001 2382**       212-273-6100
                             FAX 212-629-4113
                             TDY:212-290-2787
                        http://www.yai.org
                     e-mail: staff@yai.org
*Joel Levy DSW, CEO*
*Philip Levy PhD, President/COO*
*Abbe Wittenberg, Professional Information*
Award-winning network of not-for-profit health and human service agencies for people with developmental and learning disabilities. YAI has received national acclaim for its television series, On Our Own, and its Emmy nominated training videos and manuals. YAI conferences on MR/DD have been co-sponsored by prestigious organizations such as the United Nations and the President's Committee on Mental Retardation.

---

## Alabama

---

**140 Division of Rehabilitation Services and Childrens Rehabilitation Services**
**3800 E Highway 34**
**Pierre, SD  57501**              605-773-3195
                                   800-265-968
                             FAX 605-773-5483
                             TDY:605-773-5990
                  http://www.state.sd.us/dhs/drs
*Grady Kickul, Executive Director*

Our mission is to assist individuals with disabilities to obtain employment, economic self-sufficiency, personal idependence and full inclusion in society.

**141 Learning Disabilities Association of Alabama**
**PO Box 11588**
**Montgomery, AL  36111**          334-277-9151
                             FAX 334-284-9357
                        http://www.ldaal.org
                   e-mail: alabama@ldaal.org
*Mattie Ray, President*
*Linda Graham, Vice President*

Educational, support and advocacy group for individuals with learning disabilities and Attention Deficit Disorder.

**142 UAB Sparks Center for Developmental and Learning Disorders**

University of Alabama at Birmingham
1720 7th Avenue S
Birmingham, AL 35233          205-934-5471
800-UAB-CIRC
FAX 205-975-2380
http://www.uap.com
e-mail: sparksinfo@civmail.circ.uab.edu
*Dr Friedlander, Executive Director*
*Alvin Vogtle, Social Worker*

The Sparks Clinics provide an extensive range of interdisciplinary offerings including comprehensive diagnosis, evaluation and treatment of the needs of children and adults with mental retardation and developmental disabilities. Each of the clinics consults with clients in a context that considers the unique needs of individuals and their family members. Additionally, the Sparks Clinics complex is a major site for clinical research.

## Alaska

**143 Center for Human Development (CHD) University Affiliated Program**

University of Alaska
2210 ARCA Drive
Anchorage, AK 99508          907-272-8270
800-243-2199
FAX 907-274-4802
TDY:907-264-6206
http://www.alaskachd.org
e-mail: info@alaskachd.orgdu
*Karen Ward PhD, Director*
*Beverly Tallman, Associate Director*

Provides training, research, and support for people with developmental disabilities. The CHD is an interdisciplinary unit within the University of Alaska Anchorage, under the College of Health, Education, and Social Welfare. Faculty and staff represent a variety of disiplines. The center has a variety of projects which provide paid work experience for student assistants.

**144 Learning Disabilities Association of Alaska (LDAALaska)**

PO Box 243172
Anchorage, AK 99524 3172          907-563-LDAA
http://www.ldaalaska.org
e-mail: info@ldaalaska.org
*Colleen Deal, Contact*

A nonprofit organization whose members are individuals with learning disabilities, their families, and the professionals who work with them.

## Arizona

**145 Arizona Center for Disability Law**

Arizona Center for Disability Law
100 N Stone Avenue
Tucson, AZ 85701          520-327-9547
800-922-1447
FAX 502-884-0992
TDY:520-327-9547
http://www.acdl.com
e-mail: center@acdl.com
*Leslie Cohen, Executive Director*
*Anabel Reyes, Support Staff*

Advocates for the legal rights of persons with disabilities to be free from abuse, neglect and discrimination.

**146 Institute for Human Development: Northern Arizona University**

PO Box 5630
Flagstaff, AZ 86011          928-523-4791
FAX 928-523-9127
http://www.nau.edu.ihd
e-mail: richard.carroll@nau.edu
*Richard Carroll PhD, Director*

Training, research and support for people with development disabilities.

**147 Parent Information Network**

Arizona Department of Education
1535 W Jefferson Street
Phoenix, AZ 85007          602-542-4361
800-352-4558
FAX 602-542-5440
http://www.ade.az.gov
e-mail: rkeniso@ade.az.gov
*Rita Kenison, Parent Network/Coordinator*
*Joanne Philips, Director*

Provides free training and information to parents on federal and state laws and regulations for special education, parental rights and responsibilities, parent involvement, advocacy, behavior, standards and disability related resources. Provides a clearinghouse of information targeted to parents of children with disabilities. Also assists schools in promoting positive parent/professional/ regional partnerships.

## Arkansas

**148 Center for Applied Studies in Education Learning (CASE)**

University of Arkansas at Little Rock
1120 Marshall Street
Little Rock, AR 72202          501-569-3422
FAX 501-569-8503
http://www.ualr.edu/coedept/CASE
e-mail: rhbradley@ualr.edu
*R Bradley, Professor*

Improves the quality of education and human services in Arkansas and globally through a number of inter-related activities: conducting research on the effectiveness of programs and practices in education and human services; providing technical assistance in statistics, research design, measurement methodologies, data management, and program evaluation to students, faculty, and external groups and agencies; providing formal and informal consultation, technical assistance and instruction.

**149 Disability Rights Center**

1100 N University Avenue
Little Rock, AR 72207        501-296-1775
                            800-482-1174
                       FAX 501-296-1779
                       TDY:501-296-1775
        http://www.arkdisabilityrights.org
    e-mail: panda@arkdisabilityrights.org
*Nan Ellen East, Executive Director*
*Eddie Miller, CAP Director*

Protection and advocacy system for Arkansas.

**150 Learning Disabilities Association of Arkansas (LDAA)**

7509 Cantrell Road
Little Rock, AR 72207        501-666-8777
                        FAX 501-666-4070
              http://www.ldaarkansas.org
              e-mail: ldaa@sbcglobal.net
*Dana Jackson, Executive Administrator*

A nonprofit, volunteer organization of parents and professionals. It is devoted to defining and finding solutions to the broad spectrum of learning problems. LDAA is a state affiliate to ACLD

## California

**151 Bay Area Adult Dyslexic Support Group**

239 Whitelem
Palo Alto, CA 94306         650-493-3497
                       FAX 650-494-3499
*Lynne Stietzel, Contact*

A support group for any adults with learning differences interested in sharing or listening.

**152 Berkeley Planning Associates**

4440 Grand Avenue
Oakland, CA 94610          510-465-7884
                       FAX 510-465-7885
                       TDY:510-465-4493
                 http://www.bpacal.com
                 e-mail: info@bpacal.com
*Frances Laskey, Human Resources Director*

Conducts social policy research and program evaluations in various topic areas, including disability policy. Although the research typically does not focus on specific disabilities, the reports or other deliverables deriving from the projects may include specific information relating to particular disabilities, and are available for purchase.

**153 California Association of Special Education & Services**

CASES Executive Office
1722 J Street
Sacramento, CA 95814        916-447-7061
                       FAX 916-447-1320
                  http://www.capses.com
                  e-mail: info@capses.com
*Janeth Serrano, Executive Director*
*Rita Celaya, Executive Assistant*

The purposes are to serve as a liaison between the public and private sectors and to lend support for a continuum of programs and objectives which improve the delivery of services provided to the exceptional individual.

**154 Client Assistance Program (CAP)California Division of Persons with Disabilities**

PO Box 944222
Sacramento, CA 94244        916-263-7367
                            800-952-5544
                       FAX 916-263-7464
   http://www.dor.ca.gov/public/contacts
             e-mail: capinfo@dor.ca.gov
*Sheila Mentkowski, Chief Officer*
*Catherine Campisi, Director*

The CAP is mandated by the Federal Rehabilitation Act. CAP provides free services to consumers and applicants of projects, programs, and facilities funded under the Rehabilitation Act. CAP services involve the analysis of issues a consumer/applicant may have and provision of advocacy services regarding Rehabilitation Act funded services.

**155 Dyslexia Awareness and Resource Center**

928 Carpinteria Street
Santa Barbara, CA 93103     805-963-7339
                       FAX 805-963-6581
            http://www.dyslexiacenter.com
            e-mail: info@dyslexiacenter.com
*Leslie Esposito CFRE, Executive Director*
*Joan Esposito, Founder/Director Programs*

The mission of the Center is to inform, educate and raise awareness of parents, students, adult dyslexics, professionals, educators, law enforcement agencies, employers and mental and health professionals about dyslexia, attention disorders and other learning disabilities and the characteristics that often accompany them. The Center accomplishes its mission by providing comprehensive information, workshops, and advocacy information and programs free of charge.

**156 International Dyslexia Association: Los Angeles Branch**

4383 Tujunga Avenue
Studio City, CA 91604       818-506-8866
                       FAX 818-506-1111
                http://www.interdys.org
              e-mail: dyslexiala@aol.com
*Wynne Good, Contact*

The Los Angeles County Branch of The International Dyslexia Association believes that all individuals have the right to realize their potential, that individual learning abilities can be strengthened, and that language and reading skills can be achieved.

**157** **International Dyslexia Association: Northern California Branch**

PO Box 78008
San Francisco, CA 94107 8808      650-328-7667
                                  800-ABC-D123
                                  FAX 415-753-0701
http://www.dyslexia-ncbida.org
*Francis Dickson, President*

Founded to increase public awareness of dyslexia in Northern California and Northern Nevada.

**158** **International Dyslexia Association: San Diego Branch**

2515 Camino Del Rio Drive
San Diego, CA 92138 7448      619-295-3722
                              FAX 760-723-7168
http://www.dyslexiasd.org
            e-mail: pph@tfb.com
*Jose Cruz, President*

An international 501(c)(3) nonprofit, scientific and educational organization dedicated to the study and treatment of dyslexia. All branches hold at least one public meeting, workshop or conference per year.

**159** **Learning Disabilities Association of California**

PO Box 601067
Sacramento, CA 95860      916-725-7881
                          866-532-6322
                          FAX 916-725-8786
http://www.volunteerinfo.org
            e-mail: lda@June.com

Support and advocacy for children and adults with learning disabilities.

**160** **Lutheran Braille Workers: Sight Saving Division**

LBW Inc.
Yucaipa, CA 92399      909-795-8977
                       FAX 909-795-8970
http://www.lbwinc.org
            e-mail: lbw@lbwinc.org
*Loyd Coppenger, Executive Director*

Provides the message of Salvation to the blind and visually impaired throughout the world.

**161** **Recording for the Blind & Dyslexic: Los Angeles**

Recording for the Blind & Dyslexic: Los Angeles
5022 Hollywood Boulevard
Los Angeles, CA 90027      323-664-5525
                           800-499-5525
                           FAX 323-664-1881
http://www.rfbdla.org
            e-mail: los_angeles@rfbdla.org
*Carol Smith, Executive Director*
*Stacey Eubank, Outreach Director*

A national, nonprofit organization providing recorded textbooks, library services and other educational materials to students who cannot read standard print because of a visual, physical or learning disability. $50.00 registration fee and a $25.00 annual renewal fee. No fee for students whose schools are members.

**162** **Recording for the Blind & Dyslexic: Northern California Unit**

488 W Charleston Road
Palo Alto, CA 94306      650-493-3717
                         800-221-4792
                         FAX 650-493-5513
http://www.rfbd.org
*John Stevenson, Executive Director*
*Valley Brown, Outreach Director*

A national network of thirty three studios with headquarters in Princeton, NJ. The sole purpose is to provide educational materials in recorded and computerized formats at every academic level. The materials are for all people unable to read standard print because of a visual, perceptual (dyslexia), or other physical disability.

**163** **Recording for the Blind & Dyslexic: Santa Barbara Chapter**

3970 La Colina Road
Santa Barbara, CA 93110      805-687-6393
                             FAX 805-682-8197
http://www.rfbd.org
            e-mail: timowens@rfbd.org
*Tim Owens, Director*

The Santa Barbara Unit was founded in 1976. Over 300 volunteers produce textbooks on tape for students at local schools and around the country.

**164** **Recording for the Blind and Dyslexic: Inland Empire-Orange County Unit**

1844 W 11th Street
Upland, CA 91786      909-949-4316
                      FAX 909-981-8457
                      http://www.rfbd.org
            e-mail: mdavis@rfbd.org
*Sherry Weekes, Production Director*
*Mike Davis, Executive Director*
*Maggie Tupman, Educational Outreach Director*

Volunteers record texts on audio cassettes and computer disks for the visually, physically and perceptually disabled.

# Colorado

**165** **International Dyslexia Association: RockyMountain Branch**

PO Box 3598
Boulder, CO 80307      303-721-9425
            e-mail: ida_rmb@yahoo.com
*Shelia Phillips, President*

An international 501(c)(3) nonprofit, scientific and educational organization dedicated to the study and treatment of dyslexia. All branches hold at least one public meeting, workshop or conference per year.

**166** **Learning Disabilities Association of Colorado**

4596 E Iliff Avenue
Denver, CO 80222      303-894-0992
                      FAX 303-830-1645
                      http://www.ldanatl.org
            e-mail: info@ldacolorado.com
*Tim Carroll, Public Relations*

A non-profit volunteer organization dedicated to advocacy and education of learning disabled children and adults.

**167  Rocky Mountain Disability and Business Technical Assistance Center**

Meeting the Challenge Incorporated
3630 Sinton Road
Colorado Springs, CO  80907          719-444-0268
                                                    800-949-4232
                                      FAX 719-444-0269
                                      TDY:719-444-0268
                              http://www.adainformation.org
                              e-mail: rmdbtac@mtc-inc.com
*Patrick Going, Project Director*
*Cristi Harris, Assistant Director*

Provides information, training and technical assistance to employers, people with disabilities and other entities with responsibilities and rights under the ADA of 1990.

# Connecticut

**168  Connecticut Association for Children and Adults with LD**

CACLD
25 Van Zant Street
East Norwalk, CT  06855          203-838-5010
                                      FAX 203-866-6108
                              http://www.CACLD.org
                              e-mail: CACLD@opt.online.net
*Beryl Kaufman, Executive Director*
*Ida Kubaryth, Office Manager*

Helping children and adults with learning disabilities and attention disorders.

**169  Connecticut Association of Private Special Education Facilities (CAPSEF)**

330 Main Street
Hartford, CT  06106          860-525-1318
                                      FAX 860-541-6484
                              http://www.capsef.org
                              e-mail: info@capsef.org
*Alan Deckman, Executive Director*
*Allyson Deckman, Assistant Executive Director*

Provides a basis for unity and action to serve the common interests among all private education facilities, including cost reporting, the state approval process and the private special education community.

**170  Connecticut Capitol Region Educational Council**

Administrator Capitol Education Council
111 Charter Oak Avenue
Hartford, CT  06106          860-247-2732
                                      877-850-2832
                                      FAX 860-246-3304
                              http://www.crec.org
                              e-mail: pfernandez@rss.crec.org
*Paula Fernandez, Executive Director/Case Worker*
*Tom Parvenski, Director*

CREC is a nonprofit, regional educational service center serving 35 greater Hartford public school districts. It was founded in 1966 by local school districts working together to solve common problems. Today, CREC administers more than 100 programs and services spanning the entire educational spectrum with the same goal in mind. We work with local boards of education of the capitol region to improve the quality of public education for all learners.

**171  Learning Disabilities Association of Connecticut**

999 Asylum Avenue
Hartford, CT  06105          860-560-1711
                                      FAX 860-560-1750
                              http://www.ldact/org
                              e-mail: ldact@idact.org
*William Bossi, President*
*Fran Ficocelli, Office Manager*

Helps families and individuals in Connecticut who are affected by learning disabilities. Assists both children and adults in securing appropriate education and employment opportunities.

**172  Parent-to-Parent Network of Connecticut**

Family Center Dept. of CT Children's Med. Center
282 Washington
Hartford, CT  06106          860-545-9021
                                      FAX 860-545-9201
                              http://www.ccmckids.org
                              e-mail: mcole@ccmckids.org
*Laura Glomb, Network Director*

A group of trained parent volunteers who help other parents who are seeking professional information and emotional support. Parent volunteers attend a series of training workshops designed to prepare them to provide support and information to other parents.

**173  Recording for the Blind & Dyslexic: Connecticut Chapter**

209 Orange Street
New Haven, CT  06510          203-624-4334
                                      FAX 203-865-0203
                              http://www.rfbd.org
                              e-mail: connecticut@rfbd.org
*Anne Fortunato, Studio Director*

Provides textbooks on tape and computer disks to individuals who cannot read standard print because of a visual, perceptual or physical disability. Books span the entire educational spectrum from kindergarten through post graduate work and professional support. Master Tape Library contains almost 80,000 books on tape including a wide variety of science and technology books.

**174  Special Education Resource Center of Connecticut**

25 Industrial Park Road
Middletown, CT  06457          860-632-1485
                                      800-842-8678
                                      FAX 860-632-8870
                              http://www.ctserc.org
                              e-mail: info@ctserc.org
*Marianne Koerner, Director*
*Susan Bussolari, Coordinator*

Serves as a centralized resource for professionals, families, and community members on early intervention, special education and pupil services for individuals with special needs.

## District of Columbia

**175** **Georgetown University Medical Center Child Development Center**

3307 M Street NW
Washington, DC 20007     202-687-8635
     FAX 202-687-8899
http://www.gucdc.georgtown.edu
e-mail: info@georgetown.edu
*Phyllis Magrab, Director*
*Vernicy Thompson, Assistant*

Seeks to improve the quality of life for all children and youth, especially those with special needs and their families. Founded on an interdisciplinary approach to service, training programs, research, community outreach, and public policy.

**176** **Learning Disabilities Association: District of Columbia**

PO Box 6350
Washington, DC 20015     202-624-8581
     FAX 202-667-9140

A nonprofit organization whose members are individuals with learning disabilities, their families, and the professionals who work with them.

**177** **Recording for the Blind & Dyslexic of Metropolitan Washington**

National Organization
5225 Wisconsin Avenue NW
Washington, DC 20015     202-244-8990
     FAX 202-244-1346
http://www.rfbd.org
e-mail: washingtondc@rfbd.org
*Betsy O'Connell, Executive Director*
*Anelie Dergunder, Advisory Committee*
*Elizabeth Ratigan, Chairman*

Provides unlimited numbers of recorded textbooks to students with documented learning disability. Serves students in the District of Columbia, Montgomery and Prince Georges counties Maryland, and Northern Virginia.

**178** **University Legal Services: Client Assistance Program**

University Legal Services
2001 Street NE
Washington, DC 20002     202-547-0198
     877-211-4638
     FAX 202-547-2662
     TDY:202-547-2657
http://www.dcpanda.org
e-mail: info@napas.org
*Joe Cooney, Executive Director*
*William Finland, Administrative Assistant*

Provides legal assistance to students and consumers.

## Florida

**179** **Florida Advocacy Center for Persons with Disabilities**

2671 W Executive Center Circle
Tallahassee, FL 32301     850-488-9071
     800-342-0823
     FAX 850-488-8640
     TDY:800-346-4127
http://www.advocacycenter.org
e-mail: advocacyn@aol.com
*Elizabeth Hollifield, Board Member*
*Douglas Jones, President*

The Advocacy Center for Persons with Disabilities is a nonprofit organization providing protection and advocacy services in the State of Florida. Our mission is to advance the dignity, equality, self-determination and expressed choices of individuals with disabilities.

**180** **Florida Bureau of Instructional Support & Community Services**

325 W Gaines Street
Tallahassee, FL 32399     850-488-1570
     FAX 850-921-8246
http://www.fldoe.org
e-mail: michele.polland@fldoe.org
*Michele Polland, Interim Bureau Chief*

The bureau has a broad range of responsibilities in the outgoing examination of state and federal laws, rules and regulations affecting public education and coordinating among other agencies, the delivery of services to public school students in Florida.

**181** **Florida Protection & Advocacy Agency for Persons with Disabilities**

2671 Executive Center Circle W
Tallahassee, FL 32301     850-488-9071
     800-342-0823
     FAX 850-488-8640
     TDY:800-346-4127
*Grisom Hubrk, Advocacy Center Manager*
*Hubert Grissom, Interim Executive Director*

Offers help for people with disabilities.

**182** **International Dyslexia Association: Florida Branch**

10770 SW 84 Street
Miami, FL 33173     305-252-3474
     FAX 305-274-0337
http://www.interdys.org
*Carole Reprensek, President*

An international 501(c)(3) nonprofit, scientific and educational organization dedicated to the study and treatment of dyslexia. All branches hold at least one public meeting, workshop or conference per year.

**183    Learning Disabilities Association of Florida**
331 E Henry Street
Punta Gorda, FL  33950                    941-637-8957
                                 http://www.lda-fl.org
                           e-mail: ldaf00@sunline.net
*Gail Kurz, Executive Board Member*

**184    Learning Disabilities Association of Florida**
331 E Henry Street
Punta Gorda, FL  33950                    941-637-8957
                                   FAX 941-637-0617
                                 http://www.lda-fl.org
                           e-mail: ldaf00@sunline.net
*Cheryl Kron, Executive Secretary*

The Learning Disabilities Association of Florida is a nonprofit volunteer organization of parents, professionals and LD adults.

**185    Mailman Center for Child Development:
         University of Miami Department of Pediatrics**
University of Miami School of Medicine
PO Box 01820
Miami, FL  33101                          305-243-5790
                                   FAX 305-326-7594
                      http://www.pediatrics.med.miami.edu
                           e-mail: reuben@miami.edu
*Ruben Garcia, Director*

The mission is to enhance the lives of individuals with developmental disabilities and their families by supporting personal and family relationships and facilitating independence, productivity, integration and inclusion.

## Georgia

**186    International Dyslexia Association: Georgia
         Branch**
1951 Greystone Road NW
Atlanta, GA  30318                        404-256-1232
                                          800-223-3123
                                   FAX 404-351-7652
                                 http://www.idaga.org
         e-mail: info@midaga.org  rdavis@schenk.org
*Rosalie Davis, President*

An international nonprofit, scientific and educational organization dedicated to the study and treatment of dyslexia. All branches hold at least one public meeting, workshop or conference per year.

**187    Recording for the Blind & Dyslexic: Georgia
         Chapter**
Recording For The Blind & Dyslexic
120 Florida Avenue
Princeton, NJ  30605                      706-549-1313
                                   FAX 706-227-6161
                                 http://www.rfbd.org
*Lenore Martin, Executive Director*
*Fred Smith, Production Director*

Offers recordings of educational books on audio cassette and computer disk.

## Hawaii

**188    Aloha Special Technology Access Center**
710 Green Street
Honolulu, HI  96813                       808-523-5547
                                   FAX 808-536-3765
                              http://www.aloha.astachi.com
                           e-mail: astachi@yahoo.com
*Eric Arveson, Program Coordinator*

A private, nonprofit group of volunteers, parents of disabled children, adults with disabilities and professionals in the field of health and education. The aim of the center is to increase the awareness and use of computers by disabled people through a program of educational activities and events. This technology empowers people through communication, access to information and markets, and entry to new job opportunities.

**189    Assistive Technology Resource Centers of Hawaii**
414 Kuwili Street
Honolulu, HI  96817                       808-532-7110
                                          800-645-3007
                                   FAX 808-532-7120
                                   TDY:808-532-7110
                                 http://www.atrc.org
                             e-mail: atrc@atrc.org
*Barbara Fischlowitz-Leong, Executive Director*
*May Choy, Administrative Assistant*

A non-profit organization that is dedicated to linking individuals with technology so all people can participate in every aspect of community life. Empowers individuals to maintain dignity and control in their lives by promoting technology through advocacy, training. information, and education

**190    International Dyslexia Association: Hawaii
         Branch**
International Dyslexia Association
PO Box 61610
Honolulu, HI  96839                       808-538-7007
                                   FAX 808-566-6837
                              http://www.dyslexia-hawaii.org
                           e-mail: info@HIBIDA.org
*Sally Lambert, Co-President*
*Sue Voit, Co-President*

An international 501(c)(3) nonprofit, scientific and educational organization dedicated to the study and treatment of dyslexia. All branches hold at least one public meeting, workshop or conference per year.

**191    Learning Disabilities Association of Hawaii
         (LDAH)**
200 N Vineyard Boulevard
Honolulu, HI  96817                       808-536-9684
                                          800-533-9684
                                   FAX 808-5376780
                                 http://www.ldahawaii.org
                           e-mail: ldah@ldaHawaii.org
*Jennifer Schember-Lang, Executive Director*
*Jasmine Williams, Supervisor*

A nonprofit agency founded in 1968 by parents of children with learning disabilities. LDAH serves families of children with learning disabilities and other special needs that interfere with learning by providing educational advocacy training and support in order to remove barriers and promote awareness and full educational opportunity.

# Idaho

**192  Comprehensive Advocacy of Idaho**
4477 Emerald Street
Boise, ID  83706          208-336-5353
                          866-262-3462
                    FAX 208-336-5396
                    TDY:208-336-5353
http://www.users.moscow.com/co-ad
e-mail: coadinc@cableone.net
*Linda Flesner, Administrative Assistant*

Private, nonprofit legal services organization designated by the Governor as the Protection and Advocacy System for the state of Idaho. Operates federally funded grant programs to protect the legal rights of persons with disabilities.

**193  Idaho High Researchers Employment & Trainig**
High Researchers-ARC
140 E 2nd Street
Mountain Home, ID  83647      208-587-5804
                              800-559-5804
                        TDY:208-343-2950
*Lisa Cahill, Contact*

# Illinois

**194  Child Care Association of Illinois**
300 E Monroe
Springfield, IL  62701      217-528-4409
                      FAX 217-528-6498
http://www.cca-il.org
*Margaret Berglind, President/Executive Director*
*Barb Olzani, Administrative Assistant*

A voluntary, nonprofit organization dedicated to improving the delivery of social services to the abused, neglected, and troubled children, youth and families of Illinois.

**195  Illinois Catholic Guild for the Blind**
180 N Michigan Avenue
Chicago, IL  60601          312-236-8569
                      FAX 312-236-8128
http://www.guildfortheblind.org
e-mail: info@guildfortheblind.org
*Kathy Firak, Operations Manager*

Support and information for families and individuals with visual disabilities.

**196  Illinois Protection & Advocacy Agency:Equip for Equality**
20 N. Michigan Ave
Chicago, IL  60602          312-341-0022
                          800-537-2632
                    FAX 312-341-0295
                    TDY:312-341-0022
http://www.equipforequality.org
e-mail: hn6177@handsnet.org
*Peter Grosz, Relations Manager*

Equip for Equality is a not-for-profit Federally-funded organization that advocates for disability rights in the state of Illinois.

**197  International Dyslexia Association: Illinois/Missouri Branch**
751 Roosevelt Road, Building 7
Glen Ellyn, IL  60137          630-469-6900
                        FAX 630-469-6810
http://www.interdys.org
e-mail: ilbranch_ida@ameritech.net
*Carolyn Swallow PhD, Executive Director*
*Gail Oliphant, Assistant*

Formed to increase public awareness of dyslexia in Illinois and Eastern Missouri. We have been serving individuals with dyslexia, their families, and professionals for 25 years. One of our primary objectives is to increase early intervention efforts.

**198  Jewish Children's Bureau of Chicago**
216 W Jackson Boulevard
Chicago, IL  60606          312-444-2090
                      FAX 312-855-3754
http://www.jcbchicago.org
e-mail: robertbloom@jcbchicago.org
*Robert Bloom MD, Executive Director*

Provides Jewish children and their families a range of services which preserve, strengthen and protect the emotional well-being of children.

**199  Learning Disabilities Association of Illinois**
10101 S Roberts Road
Palos Hills, IL  60465          708-430-7532
                        FAX 708-430-7592
http://www.ldanatl.org/illinois
e-mail: ldaofil@ameritech.net
*Sharon Schussler, Administrative Assistant*

A nonprofit organization dedicated to the advancement of the education and general welfare of children and youth of normal or potentially normal intelligence who have learning disabilities of a perceptual, conceptual or coordinative nature or related problems.

**200  Recording for the Blind & Dyslexic: Chicago Loop Studio & Administrative Offices**
18 S Michigan Avenue
Chicago, IL  60603          312-236-8715
                      FAX 312-236-8719
http://www.rfbd.org
e-mail: jburbank@rfbd.org
*David Smith, Studio Director*
*Jessica Burbank, Office Administrator*

Offers information on recordings of books on audio cassette and computer disk.

**201**  **Recording for the Blind & Dyslexic: Lois C Klein Studio**
9612C W 143rd Street
Orland Park, IL  60462          312-349-9356
http://www.rfbd.org
e-mail: selhenicky@rfbd.org
*Sandy Elhenicky, Studio Director*

Offers information on recordings of books on audio cassette and computer disk.

**202**  **Recording for the Blind & Dyslexic: Naperville Chapter**
1266 E Chicago Avenue
Naperville, IL  60540          630-420-0722
FAX 630-420-8975
http://www.rfbd.org
e-mail: nleone@rfbd.org
*Nina Leone, Production Director*

One of 21 units of a national nonprofit organization that provides educational materials in recorded and computerized formats for people who cannot effectively read standard print due to a visual, perceptual or other physical disability.

## Indiana

**203**  **Bridgepointe Goodwill & Easter Seals**
1329 Applegate Lane
Clarksville, IN  47129          812-283-7908
800-660-3355
FAX 812-283-6248
TDY:812-283-7908
e-mail: cmarshall@bridgepointe.org
*Karen Marshall, Director*
*Gary Turlle, Assistant Director*

Helps children and adults with disabilities expand their independence.

**204**  **Indiania Vocation Rehabilitation Services Goodwill Industries**
1452 Vaxter Avenue
Clarksville, IN  47131          812-288-8261
877-228-1967
FAX 812-282-7048
*Delbert Hatyden, Interim Area Supervisor*

Purpose is to assist the community by providing services which allow individuals to maximize their potential and to participate in work, family and the community. To do this we will provide rehabilitation, education and training.

**205**  **International Dyslexia Association: Indiana Branch**
1100 W 42nd Street
Indianapolis, IN  46208          317-926-1450
870-984-9824
FAX 317-927-9285
http://www.inbsida.com
e-mail: inbofida@hotmail.com
*Yvonne Gill, President*

An international nonprofit, scientific and educational organization dedicated to the study and treatment of dyslexia. All branches hold at least one public meeting, workshop or conference per year.

**206**  **Learning Disabilities Association of Indiana (LDA-IN)**
Kathy-Communications
PO Box 20584
Indianapolis, IN  46220          574-272-3058
800-284-2519
FAX 574-272-3058
http://www.lda-in.org
e-mail: ldain@ldain.org
*Sharon Harris, Director*

LDA-IN is the state chapter of the Learning Disabilities Association of America. LDA-IN is an all volunteer group that provides information and support. Membership brings national and state newsletters and reduced conference fees. Dues ($25.00 per year) permit LDA to fund projects and provide free and inexpensive literature to anyone who requests information. Fall state conference is held in Indianapolis.

**207**  **Southwestern Indiana Easter Seal**
Rehabilitation Center
3701 Bellemeade Avenue
Evansville, IN  47714          812-479-1411
FAX 812-437-2634
http://www.easterslealswindiana.com
e-mail: info@evansvillerehab.com
*Ray Rasior, President*
*Kelly Reeds, Parents Coordinator*

Helps children and adults with disabilities expand their independence.

## Iowa

**208**  **International Dyslexia Association: Iowa Branch**
2215 Westdale Drive SW
Cedar Rapids, IA  52404          319-551-2851
FAX 319-365-1038
http://www.interdys.org
e-mail: sue_ida_ia@yahoo.com
*Pat McGuire, President*

An international nonprofit, scientific and educational organization dedicated to the study and treatment of dyslexia. All branches hold at least one public meeting, workshop or conference per year.

**209**  **Iowa Center for Disabilities and Development**
100 Hawkins Drive
Iowa City, IA  52242          319-353-6135
877-686-0031
FAX 319-356-8284
TDY:877-686-0032
http://www.uihealthcare.com/cdd
e-mail: disability-resources@uiowa.edu
*Dennis Harper PHD, Director*
*Elayne Sexsmith, Assistant Director*

Center for people with disabilities or special needs.

**210  Iowa Program for Assistive Technology**
Center for Disabilities and Development
100 Hawkins Drive
Iowa City, IA  52242 1011          319-356-0550
                                   800-779-2001
                              FAX 319-384-5139
                              TDY:877-686-0032
                        http://www.uiowa.edu/infotech/
                        e-mail: jane-gay@uiowa.edu
*Jane Gay, Director*
*Amy Mikelson, Outreach Coordinator*
*Alicia Audry, Secretary*

Provides free information and referral about available
assistive technology, used equipment referral service,
and bimonthly newsletter. Makes referral for free legal advocacy relating to access to AT devices and services.

**211  Learning Disabilities Association of Iowa**
321 E-6 Good Morning Iowa
Cedar Falls, IA  50309          515-280-8558
                               800-450-8667
                          FAX 515-243-1902
                        http://www.askresource.org
                        e-mail: hloyd@askresource.org
*Jule Reynolds, President*
*Harvey Lold, Culture Art Specialist*

A nonprofit organization whose members are individuals with learning disabilities, their families, and the
professionals who work with them.

## Kansas

**212  International Dyslexia Society: Kansas Western
Missouri Branch**
2812 SW Osborn Road
Topeka, KS  66614          816-838-7323
                     http://www.hcity.com/kwmida
                     e-mail: ks_wmo_ida@hotmail.com
*C Anderson, President*

Focuses efforts on Kansas and Western Missouri. By
hosting events and establishing a presence, the leaders
have begun to work with parents, schools and teachers
to help children with dyslexia. Maintains a list of individuals who have specialized training and who are
available for remediation of reading, writing and
spelling problems. Provides information for parents
and teachers, an annual spring conference, quarterly
newsletter dealing with local issues, and teacher training.

**213  Kansas Advocacy & Protective Services**
3745 SW Wanamaker Road
Topeka, KS  66610          785-273-9661
                          877-776-1541
                     FAX 785-273-9414
                     TDY:785-273-9661
                http://www.drckansas.org
                e-mail: info@ksadv.org
*Tim Voth, Intake Coordinator*
*Kathleen Wilson, Advocate*

Works in partnership with persons with disabilities to
protect, advocate for, and advance their human, legal
and service rights.

**214  Learning Disabilities Association of Kansas**
PO Box 4424
Topeka, KS  66604          785-273-4505
                      FAX 785-228-9527
                      http://www.ldakansas.org
                      e-mail: marciasu@aol.com
*Andrea Blair, Manhattan President*

Information and referral service to parents of the
learning disabled child and to adults with learning disabilities.

## Kentucky

**215  Learning Disabilities Association of Kentucky**
LDA of America Learning Disabilities Association
2210 Goldsmith Lane
Louisville, KY  40218          502-473-1256
                               877-587-1256
                          FAX 502-473-4695
                          http://www.ldaofky.org
                          e-mail: ldaofky@yahoo.com
*Catherine Senn, Executive Director*
*Tim Wood, Executive Director*

Embraces the challenge to educate the general public
on the characteristics of learning disabilities such as
attention deficit disorder, dyslexia and more.

**216  Recording for the Blind & Dyslexic: Kentucky
Chapter**
Recording for the Blind & Dyslexic Kentucky
Chapte
240 Haldeman Avenue
Louisville, KY  40206          502-895-9068
                          FAX 502-897-1145
                          http://www.rfbd.org
                          e-mail: mbrown@rfbd.org
*Martha Brown, Executive Director*
*Maureen Gaynor, Assistant Director*

Offers information on recordings of books on audio
cassette and computer disk.

## Maine

**217  Learning Disabilities Association of Maine (LDA)**
Learning Disabilities Association of Maine (LDA)
97 Rocky Shore Land
Oakland, ME  04963          207-465-7700
                          FAX 207-465-4844
                          http://www.ldame.org
                          e-mail: ldame@ldame.org
*Cathy Lashin-Otisfield, President*
*Brenda Bennett, Executive Director*

LDA of Maine is a statewide, nonprofit, volunteer organization including individuals with learning disabilities, their families, and professionals. The
organization is dedicated to enhancing the quality of
life for all individuals with learning disabilities and
their families, to alleviating the restricting effects of
learning disabilities, and to supporting endeavors to
determine the causes of learning disabilities.

**218    Maine Parent Federation**

PO Box 2067
**Augusta, ME  04338**                              207-623-2144
                                                    800-870-7746
                                              FAX 207-623-2148
                                              TDY:207-623-2144
                                         http://www.mpf.org
                              e-mail: parentconnnect@mpf.org
*Janice LaChance, Executive Director*
*Ellen McGuire, Coordinator*

Parent Training and Information Program views parents as full partners in the educational process and a significant source of support and assistance to each other. Funded by the Division of Personnel Preparation, Office of Special Education Programs, these programs provide training and information to parents to enable them to participate more effectively with professionals in meeting the educational needs of disabled children.

## Maryland

**219    International Dyslexia Association: Maryland Branch**

PO Box 792
**Brooklandville, MD  21022**          410-825-2881
                          e-mail: MBIDA4@hotmail.com
*Cathy Rommel, President*

**220    Learning Disabilities Association of Maryland**

PO Box 792
**Brooklandville, MD  21022**          410-825-2881
                          e-mail: MBIDA4@hotmail.com
*Cathy Rommel, President*

Nonprofit, volunteer association dedicated to enhancing the quality of life for all individuals with learning disabilities and their families.

**221    Maryland Association of University Centers on Disabilities**

**1010 Wayne Avenue**
**Silver Spring, MD  20910**                301-588-8252
                                      FAX 301-588-2842
                                   http://www.aucd.org
                              e-mail: gjesien@aucd.org
*George Jesien PhD, Executive Director*
*David Johnson, PhD, Board President*

Helps member agencies to enhance quality of life for people with developmental disabilities through disciplinary training and technical assistance with information and research.

## Massachusetts

**222    Adaptive Environments**

**Adaptive Environments**
**374 Congress Street**
**Boston, MA  02210**                       617-695-1225
                                            800-949-4232
                                      FAX 617-482-8099
                                      TDY:617-695-1225
                    http://www.adaptiveenvironments.org
                    e-mail: info@adaptiveenvironments.org
*Valerie Fletcher, Executive Director*
*Andy Washburn, Information Specialist*

Adaptive Environments promotes design that works for everyone across the spectrum of ability and age and enhances human experience.

**223    Learning Disabilities Association of Massachusetts (LDAM)**

**PO Box 142**
**Weston, MA  02493**                       781-891-5009
                                      FAX 781-647-5141
                       http://www.easter-sealsutah.org
                    e-mail: gbrenda@easter-sealsutah.org
*Mike Fitzgerald, Chief Executive Officer*
*Mike Medoro, Assistant Chief Executive*

Works to enhance the lives of individuals with learning disabilities, with emphasis on the underserved. To identify and support unrecognized strengths/capabilities of persons with learning disabilities. Strive to increase awareness and understanding of LD through multilingual media productions/publications that serve populations across cultures. Educational enrichment programs are designed to serve individuals with learning disabilities, their families and the professionals in their lives.

**224    Massachusetts Association of 766 Approved Private Schools (MAAPS)**

**591 N Avenue**
**Wakefield, MA  01880**                    781-245-1220
                                      FAX 781-245-5294
                          http://www.spedschools.com
                       e-mail: maaps@spedschools.com
*James Major, Executive Director*
*Rita Greenberg, Business Manager*

Nonprofit association of Chapter 766 approved private schools dedicated to providing educational programs and services to students with special needs throughout Massachusetts. Concerned that children with special needs have appropriate, quality education and that they and their families know the rights, policies, procedures and options that make the education process a productive reality for special needs children.

**225    Massachusetts Shriver Center: University Affiliated Program**

**200 Trapelo Road**
**Waltham, MA  02254**                      781-642-0223
                                      FAX 781-642-2238

*William McIlvane, Director*
*Charles Hamad, Associate Director*
*Laura Massei, Administrator*

The Center promotes the understanding of neurological, cognitive and behavioral development associated with disabilities, emphasizing mental retardation. We conduct basic and applied research to determine the biological and environmental factors that influence typical and atypical development and provide training and service programs that directly benefit people with developmental disabilities and their families.

**226  Recording for the Blind & Dyslexic: Boston**

**Recruiting for the Blind & Dyslexic**
**58 Charles Street**
**Princeton, NJ  02141**            617-577-1111
                                    FAX 617-577-1113
                                    http://www.rfbd.org
                                    e-mail: ajones@rfod.org
*Christina Raimo, Executive Director*
*Kelly Hill, Outreach Coordinator*
*Amy Deangelis, Director Educational Outreach*

A nonprofit volunteer organization and educational library serving people who cannot effectively read standard print because of visual impairment, dyslexia or other physical disability. We strive to create opportunities for individual success by providing accessible educational material. Comprehensive source of recorded textbooks and other educational printed matter. One-time registration fee of $50.00 plus a $25.00 annual fee. School memberships are available.

**227  Recording for the Blind & Dyslexic: Berkshire/Lenox/Williamstown**

**55 Pittsfield/Lenox Rd, Lenox 01240**
**Williamstown, MA  01267**          413-637-0889
                                     800-221-4792
                                     http://www.rfbd.org
                                     e-mail: cosorio@rfbd.org
*Alan Alibozek, Studio Director*
*Cristina Osorio, Studio Director*

The Berkshire United Way operates recording studios in both Lenox and Williamstown. The studios offer information on recordings of books on audio cassette and computer disk, and provides outreach to: four western counties of Massachusetts; Albany, Columbia, Rensselaer, Saratoga, Schenectady and Washington counties in New York; Bennington County in Vermont; Litchfield County in Connecticut.

# Michigan

**228  International Dyslexia Association: Michigan Branch**

**International Dyslexia Association**
**4050 Waverly Place**
**Ann Arbor, MI  48105**            734-663-9884
                                    http://www.idamib.org
                                    e-mail: postmaster@idamib.org
*Sally Burden, President*

An international 501(c)(3) nonprofit, scientific and educational organization dedicated to the study and treatment of dyslexia. All branches hold at least one public meeting, workshop or conference per year.

**229  Learning Disabilities Association of Michigan (LDA)**

**200 Museum Drive**
**Lansing, MI  48933**              517-485-8160
                                    888-597-7809
                                    FAX 517-485-8462
                                    http://www.ldaofmichigan.org
                                    e-mail: info@ldaofmichigan.org or
                                            ldami@aol.com
*Ed Schlitt, President*
*Flo Curtis, Head of the Office*

A nonprofit, volunteer association that is dedicated to enhancing the quality of life for all individuals with learning disabilities and their families through advocacy, education, training, services and support of research. Our goal is to see LD understood and addressed and the individuals with learning disabilities will thrive and participate fully in society.

*1,200 Members*

**230  Michigan Citizens Alliance to Uphold Special Education (CAUSE)**

**6412 Centurion Drive**
**Lansing, MI  48917**              517-886-9167
                                    800-221-9105
                                    FAX 517-886-9366
                                    TDY:888-814-4013
                                    http://www.causeonline.org
                                    e-mail: info@causeonline.org
*Patricia Keller, Executive Director*
*Francis Spring, Assistant Director*

Provides a collaborative forum where consumers and providers can actively support an individualized, Free and Appropriate Education (FAPE) that enables all students to maximize their options in the world community. Our priority is the protection of the rights of students with disabilities. We are a Parent Training Information Center providing free information, referrals, support, advocacy and workshops for parents/professionals working with children who have special needs.

**231  Recording for the Blind & Dyslexic Learning Through Listening: Michigan Unit**

**5600 Rochester Road**
**Troy, MI  48085**                 248-879-0101
                                    FAX 248-879-9927
                                    http://www.rfbd.org
                                    e-mail: creeb@rfbd.org
*Carla Reeb, Executive Director*
*Zan Shore, Studio Director*

Recording for the Blind & Dyslexic is the nation's educational library serving people who cannot effectively read standard print because of visual impairment, dyslexia or other physical disability. We provide textbooks, educational and professional materials in an audio format. The Michigan Unit's outreach volunteers offer students and their parents training sessions at the studio by appointment.

## Minnesota

**232  International Dyslexia Association: Upper Midwest Branch**
**5021 Vernon Avenue**
**Minneapolis, MN  55436**          651-450-7589
                    e-mail: umbida@hotmail.com
*Trish Vickman, President*

An international 501(c)(3) nonprofit, scientific and educational organization dedicated to the study and treatment of dyslexia. All branches hold at least one public meeting, workshop or conference per year in Minnesota, North Dakota and South Dakota.

**233  Minnesota Access Services**
**Minneapolis Public Schools Community Education**
**3131 19th Avenue S**
**Minneapolis, MI  55407**          612-668-4326
                       FAX 612-627-3101
                http://www.mplscommunityed.com
*Jack Tamble, Department Head*

Provides outreach and integration services for adults with disabilities.

**234  Minnesota Disability Law Center**
**430 1st Avenue N**
**Minneapolis, MN  55401**          612-332-1441
                          800-292-4150
                       FAX 612-334-5755
                       TDY:612-332-4668
                       http://www.mndlc.org
                e-mail: mndlc@midmnlegal.org
*Luther Granquist, Attorney*
*Pamela Hoopes, Director*

Mission is to protect, promote and expand the rights of people with disabilities and mental illness.

## Mississippi

**235  International Dyslexia Association: Mississippi**
**PO Box 2485**
**Laurel, MS  39442**          601-428-0857
                    FAX 601-362-9180
*Judy Robinson, President*

An international 501(c)(3) nonprofit, scientific and educational organization dedicated to the study and treatment of dyslexia. All branches hold at least one public meeting, workshop or conference per year.

## Montana

**236  Montana Advocacy Program (MAP): Helena**
**Montana Advocacy Program (MAP) Inc.: Helena**
**400 N Park, 2nd Floor**
**Helena, MT  59624**          406-449-2344
                          800-245-4743
                       FAX 406-449-2418
                     http://www.mtadv.org
              e-mail: advocate@mtadv.org or
                       bernie@mtadv.org
*Bernadette Franks-Ongoy, Executive Director*
*Liesl Beck, Advocacy Specialist*
*Karin Billings, Advocacy Specialist*

A nonprofit corporation administering eight protection and advocacy programs and one private program that advocate the rights of Montanans with disabilities. MAP staff include professional advocates and attorneys. Mission is to protect and advocate the human, legal and civil rights of Montanans with mental and physical disabilities while advancing dignity, equality and self-determination.

**237  Montana Advocacy Program (MAP): Missoula Office**
**1280 S 3rd West, Suite 4**
**Missoula, MT  59801**          406-541-4357
                          800-245-4743
                       FAX 406-541-4360
                     http://www.mtadu.org
                e-mail: bernie@mtadv.org
*Bernadette Franks-Ongoy, Executive Director*
*Liesl Beck, Advocacy Specialist*
*Karin Billings, Advocacy Specialist*

A nonprofit corporation administering eight protection and advocacy programs and one private program that advocate the rights of Montanans with disabilities. MAP staff include professional advocates and attorneys. Mission is to protect and advocate the human, legal and civil rights of Montanans with mental and physical disabilities while advancing dignity, equality and self-determination.

**238  Montana Parents, Let's Unite for Kids (PLUK)**
**516 N 32nd Street**
**Billings, MT  59101**          406-255-0540
                          800-222-7585
                       FAX 406-255-0523
                     http://www.pluk.org/
                e-mail: plukinfo@pluk.org
*Dennis Moore, Executive Director*

PLUK is a private, nonprofit organization formed by parents of children with disabilities and chronic illnesses. Its purpose is to provide information, support, training and assistance to aid parents with their children at home, in school and as adults. We keep current on best practices in education, medicine, law, human services, rehabilitation, and technology to insure families with disabilites have access to high quality services.

## Nebraska

**239   International Dyslexia Association of Nebraska**

2830 Kipling Circle
Lincoln, NE  68516                       402-434-6434
                                  FAX 410-321-5069
                            http://www.interdys.org
                            e-mail: gcarlson@lps.org
*Gwelda Carlson, President*

An international 501(c)(3) nonprofit, scientific and
educational organization dedicated to the study and
treatment of dyslexia. All branches hold at least one
public meeting, workshop or conference per year.

**240   Learning Disabilities Association of Nebraska**

1941 S 42nd Street
Omaha, NE  68105 2942                    402-348-1567
                                  FAX 402-934-1479
                            http://www;ldonline.com
                            e-mail: LDAofNE@aol.com
*Sharon Bloechle, Administration Director*

Support groups for parents and teachers, information
for school and community regarding ADHD and LD
children/adults, book and video library, educational
seminars and conferences, parent panel for discussion, summer camp (ages 8-15) and verified
LD/ADHD students. Monthly newsletter.

## Nevada

**241   Nevada Economic Opportunity Board:
Community Action Partnership**

PO Box 270880
Las Vegas, NV  89127 4880                702-647-1510
                                  FAX 702-647-6639
                            http://www.eobcc.org-www.cap.org
*Mary Twitty, Acting Interim Director*
*Connie Coleman, Office Manager*

Located in one of the fastest growing and most diverse
communities in the United States, the Economic Opportunity Board of Clark County is a highly innovative Community Action Agency. Our mission is to
eliminate poverty by providing programs, resources,
services, and advocacy for self-sufficiency and economic empowerment.

## New Hampshire

**242   Easter Seals New Hampshire**

555 Auburn Street
Manchester, NH  03103                    603-623-8863
                                         800-870-8728
                                  FAX 603-625-1148
                            http://www.eastersealsnh.org
*Larry Gammon, President/Chief Executive Office*
*Betty Burke, Assistant Executive Officer*

Easter Seals New Hampshire is one of the most comprehensive affiliates in the nation, assisting more than
18,000 children and adults with disabilities through a
network of more than a dozen service sites around the
state and in Vermont. Each center provides top-qual-
ity, family-focused and innovative services tailored to
meet the specific needs of the particular community it
serves.

**243   Learning Disabilities Association of New
Hampshire**

35 Marty Drive
Merrimack, NH  03054                     603-424-6667
                            e-mail: hhlda@aol.com
*Jan Carlton, Adult Issues*

Resources for people with learning disabilities.

**244   New Hampshire Disabilities Rights Center (DRC)**

18 Low Avenue
Concord, NH  03301                       603-228-0432
                                         800-834-1721
                                  TDY:603-228-0432
                            http://www.drcnh.org
                            e-mail: advocacy@drcnh.org
*Richard Cohen, Esq, Executive Director*
*Ronald Lospennato, Legal Director*

New Hampshire's protective and advocacy system for
individuals with a disability, a development disability, and mental illness. Information about your rights;
referral to someone who can help you; legal advice
about your situation; legal representation. Fully accessible office. DRC is independent from state service
providers and dedicated to equal enjoyment of civil
and legal rights for people with disability. We are authorized by federal statute to pursue legal and administrative remedies.

**245   New Hampshire Easter Seals Early Intervention
Program**

25 Nashua Road
Londonderry, NH  03053                   603-432-1945
                                  FAX 603-749-0981
                            http://www.eastersealsnh.org
                            e-mail: formerg@eastersealsnh.org
*Gloria Fulmer, Contact*

Helps people with learning disabilities cope.

**246   New Hampshire-ATEC Services**

67 Communications Drive
Laconia, NH  03246                       603-528-3060
                                         800-932-5837
                                  FAX 603-524-0702
                            http://www.nhassistivetechnology.org
                            e-mail: lorraineh@atechservices.org
*Lorraine Halton, MA, Clinical Director*
*Therese Wilkhomm, Executive Director*
*Donna Furlong, BS, Administrative Assistant*

ATECH's mission is to enable comunity participation
and achievement of personal goals through the provision of education, information, and assistive technology services for persons with disability. Technical
Division: Leo Benoit, Concord 603-226-2900;
Sales/Marketing: Paul Luff, Concord 800-427-3338

**247** **Parent to Parent of New Hampshire**
Upper Valley Support Group
12 Flynn Street
Lebanon, NH 03766     603-448-6393
800-698-LINK
http://www.parenttoparentnh.org
e-mail: p2p@nhsupport.net
*Philip Eller, Administrative Coordinator*

If you are a parent of a child with special challenges and you would like to speak to a parent whose child has similar needs - someone who will understand, Parent to Parent is a network of families willing to share experiences. Should you call a Supporting Parent will contact you by phone or visit within 24 hours. All information will be kept confidential and there is no cost for the service.

## New Jersey

**248** **American Self-Help Clearinghouse of New Jersey**
Saint Clare's Health Services
100 E Hanover Avenue
Cedar Knolls, NJ 07927 2020     973-326-6789
800-367-6274
FAX 973-326-9467
http://www.njgroups.org
e-mail: ashc@cybernex.net
*Ed Madara, President*
*Howard Lerner, Office Assistant*

Puts callers in touch with any of several hundred national and international self-help groups covering a wide range of illnesses, disabilities, addictions, bereavement and stressful life situations.

**249** **Family Support Center of New Jersey**
Lions Head Office Park
Brick, NJ 08723     723-262-8020
800-372-6510
FAX 732-262-4373
TDY:800-852-7899
http://www.familysupportnj.com
e-mail: fsnj@familysupport.com
*Veronica Trathen, Director*
*Natalie Trump, Resources Coordinator*

A clearinghouse offering up-to-date information on all types of disabilities as well as national, state and local support programs and services. We offer free services including telephone helpline, resource data base, private respite care networks, lending library, OPTIONS manual, cash subsidy program, speakers bureau, assistive technology.

**250** **International Dyslexia Association of New Jersey**
PO Box 32
Long Valley, NJ 07853     908-879-1179
FAX 908-876-3621
http://www.interdys.org
e-mail: NJIDA@msn.com
*Georgette Dickman, President*
*Mary , Branch Office Administrator*

An international nonprofit, scientific and educational organization dedicated to the study of dyslexia. We offer tutoring and testing referrals, as well as support teacher education and hold outreach programs. Teacher Scholarships are offered to our Annual Fall Conferences, Wilson Reading Overviews and Project Read programs. Newsletter published bi-annually.

**251** **New Jersey Family Resource Associates**
35 Haddon Avenue
Shrewsbury, NJ 07702     732-747-5310
FAX 732-747-1896
http://www.familyresourceassociates.org
e-mail: frabook@aol.com
*Nancy Phalanucorn, Executive Director*

Private, nonprofit agency servicing children with disabilities and their families. Sibling support services are provided via newsletters and sibling groups. Also recreational technology resources and family support programs. State funded infant program services for children aged birth to 3.

**252** **New Jersey Protection and Advocacy (NJP&A)**
210 S Broad Street
Trenton, NJ 08608     609-292-9742
800-922-7233
FAX 609-777-0187
TDY:800-852-7899
http://www.njpanda.org
e-mail: advoc@njpanda.org
*Sarah Mitchell, Executive Director*
*Joseph Young, Deputy Director*

NJP&A is a private nonprofit consumer driven organization established to advocate for and protect the civil, human, and legal rights of citizens of New Jersey with disabilities.

## New Mexico

**253** **International Dyslexia Association of New Mexico**
PO Box 25891
Albuquerque, NM 87125     505-255-8234
FAX 505-262-8547
http://www.interdys.org
e-mail: swlda@southwestlda.com
*Linda Curry, President*

Committed to the training of teachers and other professionals in appropriate instructional methods for individuals with dyslexia. Provides a 24-hour hotline with information and assistance for dyslexia related problems. There are eight regional offices: Gallup 772-2844, Farmington 326-1525, Taos 776-8279, Las Cruces, 525-8076, Hobbs 393-6269, Silver City 535-2399, El Paso 915-921-6835, Santa Fe 995 0801. Offers support with tutor/diagnostic referrals, conferences/events and college scholarships.

**254    Learning Disabilities Association of New Mexico: Las Cruces**

PO Box 20001/3SPE
Las Cruces, NM 88003          505-646-5971
                             FAX 505-867-3398
http://www.education.nmsu.edu/projects/NMLDA
e-mail: epoel@nmsu.edu
*Elisa Wolf Poel MD, President*
*Pam Gough, Vice-President*

A nonprofit organization of volunteers including individuals with learning disabilities. Dedicated to identifying causes and promoting prevention of learning disabilities and enhancing the quality of life for individuals with LD by encouraging effective identification and intervention, fostering research, protecting rights under the law. LDA seeks to accomplish this through awareness, advocacy, empowerment, education, service and collaboarative efforts.

**255    Learning Disabilities Association of New Mexico: Albuquerque**

6301 Menaul Boulevard NE
Albuquerque, NM 87110          505-851-2545
http://www.vivanewmexico.com/nm/nmldal
*Patricia Useem, President*

---

# New York

**256    Advocates for Children of New York**

151 W 30th Street
New York, NY 10001          212-947-9779
                           FAX 212-947-9790
http://www.advocatesforchildren.org
e-mail: info@advocatesforchildren.org
Works on behalf of children from infancy to the age of 21 who are at greatest risk for school-based discrimination and academic failure.

**257    Attention Deficit Disorder of Westchester County**

10 W Hyatt Avenue
Mount Kisco, NY 10549          914-241-0682
                              FAX 914-241-0684
Helps and guides people on how to cope with ADD.

**258    Developmental Disability Center of New York**

St. Lukes-Roosevelt Hospital
New York, NY 10019          212-523-6230
                           FAX 212-523-6241
*Steven Wolf MD, Director*
*Barbara Fedun, Administrative Assistant*

Working in neurology. Offers pre-school program.

**259    International Dyslexia Association of Suffolk County**

728 Route 25A
Northport, NY 11768          631-423-7834
                            FAX 631-261-7834
http://www.interdys.org/3-suff.stm
e-mail: ckent@optonline.net
*Carol Kent, President*

Our objectives are to increase awareness of dyslexia in the community; provide support for parents and teachers; promote teacher training. We offer a telephone message system for information requests; sponsor an annual conference and four topic workshops as well as a summer Orton-Gillingham course. We have a network of local school officials, parents, attorneys and other professionals to help parents navigate the channels of the school system.

**260    International Dyslexia Association: Buffalo Branch**

c/o Gow School
South Wales, NY 14139          716-687-2030
http://www.interdys.org - www.gow.org
e-mail: bufida@gow.org
*Kathy Rose, President*
*Joan Weaver, Office Assistant*

Strives to be a resource for information and services that address the full scope of dyslexia in a way that builds cooperation, partnership and understanding among professional communities and dyslexic individuals so that everyone is valued and has the opportunity to be productive and fulfilled in life. Newsletter and teacher training scholarships.

**261    International Dyslexia Association: New York**

71 W 23rd Street
New York, NY 10010          212-691-1930
                           FAX 212-633-1620
http://www.nybida.org
e-mail: info@nybida.org
*Eileen Marzola, President*
*Linda Selvin, Executive Director*

This is a nonprofit organization whose mission is to provide continuing education in appropriate diagnostic remedial approaches and to support the rights of people with dyslexia in order that they may lead fulfilling lives. To this end, the NYB-IDA disseminates information, publishes a quarterly newsletter, and provides information and referral services, teacher training, conferences, adult support groups, and workshops for parents. Annual teen conference.

**262    International Dyslexia Association: Troy, New York Branch**

Capital District Regional Group
1046 Madison Avenue
Troy, NY 12180          518-272-4064
e-mail: ldteams@taconic.net
An international, nonprofit, scientific and educational organization dedicated to the study of dyslexia.

**263    Learning Disabilites Association of Central New York**

722 West Manlius Street
East Syracuse, NY 13057          315-432-0665
                                FAX 315-431-0606
http://www.ldacny.org
e-mail: LDACNY@LDACYN.org
*Agnes Gavin, Executive Director*

We provide many services at no cost to clients including educational consultations about LD/ADD to assist parents; adult services including consultations with a coordinator for education, employment, housing and finances; adult recreation with an emphasis on social skills and outings; referral services including tutors, psychologists, counselors, evaluations. We have a library, an A/V resource center and employment services.

**264    Learning Disabilites Association: New York Capital Region**

**Learning Disabilities Association: New York Capit**
**2995 Curry Road Extension**
**Schenectady, NY  12303         518-356-6410**
                                **FAX 518-356-3603**
                                **TDY:518-356-6410**
                        **http://www.wildwood.edu**
                   **e-mail: LDACNY@LDACYN.org**
*Mary Allen, Executive Director*
*Marie Gunner, Director Family Support Services*

Sponsors Wildwood Programs for children and adults with LD, autism and other neurological disabilities. Programs include: Wildwood School—Preschool through Young Adult; Camp Wildwood; Wildwood Recreational Services, such as Saturday recreation, Thursday evening teen community center, and nights and weekend adult recreation; Wildwood Family Services and Service Coordination; Wildwood Residential Services; Employment/Vocational Services; and Captain's Choice small business employment opportunity.

**265    Learning Disabilities Association of Kenmore/Fredonia, New York**

**2555 Elmwood Avenue**
**Kenmore, NY  14217         716-874-7200**
                            **FAX 716-874-7205**
                   **http:// www.ldaoswny.org**
            **e-mail: information@ldaoswny.org**
*Mike Helman, Executive Director*
*Brenda Frazier, Executive Assistant*

To create conditions under which persons with learning disabilities, neurological impairments, and developmental disabilities are given opportunities to make choices and develop and achieve independence. The association also addresses each individual's health, future, participation in the community, and personal relationships. LDA Southern Fredonia Tier branch can be reached at 716-679-1601.

**266    Learning Disabilities Association of NewYork City**

**27 W 20th Street**
**New York, NY  10011         212-645-6730**
                            **FAX 212-924-8896**
                   **http://www.ldanyc.com**
               **e-mail: ldanyc@verizon.net**
*Stephen Baldwin, Executive Director*

The Learning Disabilities Association of New York City is a non profit, citywide organization affiliated with the Learning Disabilities Association of New York State and the Learning Disabilities Association of America. The Association is dedicated to facilitating access to needed services for individuals with learning disabilities and to providing support for those individuals and their families. All services are provided at no cost to consumers.

**267    Learning Disabilities of the Genesee Valley**
**339 East Avenue**
**Rochester, NY  14604         585-263-3323**
                        **http://www.ldagvi.org**
                   **e-mail: info@ldagvi.org**
*James Buchholz, President*
*Timothy McNamara, VP*
*Margaret Mecredy, Secretary*

Providing ongoing parent/student support services including after school and saturday programs, summer recreation, GED/Adult Education, library, movies, sports events, concerts, miniature golf, bowling and employment services. We offer comprehensive Service Coordination to develop, implement and maintain an Individualized Service Plan (ISP) that covers the spectrum of a person's life and functions as a daily guide.

**268    National Center for Learning Disabilities (NCLD)**

**National Center for Learning Disabilities**
**381 Park Avenue S**
**New York, NY  10016 1401         212-545-7510**
                                **888-575-7373**
                            **FAX 212-545-9665**
                   **http://www.tetreadytoread.org**
                       **e-mail: help@ncld.org**
*Sheldon Horowitz EdD, Director Professional Services*
*Marcia Pauyo, Executive Assistant*

Provides national leadership in support of children and adults with learning disabilities by offering information and an online resource locator, developing and supporting innovative educational programs, such as Get Ready to Read! (including an early literacy screening tool), providing leadership in guiding policy in Washington, and promoting awareness of learning disabilities. Also offers guidance regarding No Child Left Behind Act.

**269    New York Easter Seal Society**
**11 West 42nd Street**
**New York, NY  10036         212-398-0648**
                            **800-727-8785**
                        **FAX 518-456-5094**
                   **http://www.ny.easter-seals.org**
*James Berry, Director*

Although it was created to help polio victims, the New York Easter Seal society now helps children and adults disabled from any cause to live independently if living in New York State.

**270    Resources for Children with Special Needs in New York**

**116 E 16th Street**
**New York, NY  10003         212-677-4650**
                            **FAX 212-254-4070**
                   **http://www.resourcesnyc.org**
               **e-mail: info@resourcesnyc.org**
*Karen Schlesinger, Executive Director*
*Helene Crane, Associate Director*

An independent, nonprofit organization that provides information and referral, case management and support, individual and systemic advocacy, parent and professional training and library services to New York City parents and caregivers of children with disabilities and special needs and to professionals who work with them. Our publications include: Camps 2004; After School and more; The Comprehensive Directory; and Schools for Children with Autism Spectrum Disorders.

**271    Strong Center for Developmental Disabilities**
**Golisano Children's Hospital at Strong**
**601 Elmwood Avenue**
**Rochester, NY  14642**                585-275-0355
                                       FAX 585-275-3366
   **http://www.urmc.rochester.edu/gchas/div/scdd**
            **e-mail: scdd@cc.urmc.rochester.edu**
*Philip Davidson PhD, Chief*
*Cathy Imhos, Office Manager*

Strong is a University Center of Excellence for Developmental Disabilaity, Education, Research, Service and a federally designated interdisciplinary division of the Department of Pediatrics involving faculty, students, departments, schools of the University of Rochester and area institutions of higher learning. Interdisciplinary diagnoses and treatment are provided to children and adults with developmental disabilities and their families from the western New York region.

**272    Westchester Institute for Human Development**
**Westchester Medical Center**
**Cedarwood Hall**
**Valhalla, NY  10595 1689**              914-493-8202
                                       FAX 914-493-1973
              **http://www.nymc.edu/wyhd**
                 **e-mail: WIHD@nymc.edu**
*Ansley Bacon, Director*
*David O'Hara, Associate Director*

Enhances the quality of life of individuals with or at risk for disabilities, and their families. We believe that all people have the right to live independently, enjoy self-determination, contribute to society, and participate fully in the mainstream of daily life. Our work is based on a vision of a society that includes individuals with disabilities as full participants, valued citizens and friends.

## North Carolina

**273    All Kinds of Minds of North Carolina**
**54 W 1450 Valley Road**
**Chapel Hill, NC  27517**               919-933-8082
                                       FAX 919-843-9955
           **http://www.allkindsofminds.org**
          **e-mail: revans@allkindsofminds.org**
*Robert Evans, President*
*Mel Levine, Co-Chair*
*Charles R Schwab, Co-Chair*

Helps students measurably improve their success in school and in life by providing programs that integrate educational, scientific expertise. Our goal is to make the Institute's programs and services broadly accessible to parents, teachers, clinicians and students who struggle with differences in learning, and to change the educational environment supporting these children.

**274    Learning Disabilities Association of North Carolina (LDANC)**
**PO Box 68084**
**Raleigh, NC  27613 8084**              919-493-5362
                                       FAX 919-489-0788
                     **http://www.Idanc.org**
              **e-mail: idanc@mindspring.com**
*Pat Lillie, Director*

For 29 years, LDANC has been committed to improving the lives of, and serving as a voice for, all persons in the state with learning disabilities and or attention disorders. Branches: Asheville: 828-250-5317; Charlotte: 704-542-0470; Dare County: vgrist@mindspring.com; Guilford County: 336-855-5900; Orange County: bmblack@email.unc.edu; Eastern Carolina: 252-321-1111; Wake County: 919-616-8766; Winston-Salem: 336-722-6810.

## North Dakota

**275    Learning Disabilities Association of North Dakota**
**7840 Arcata Drive**
**Dismarck, ND  58503**                 701-222-1490
                                       FAX 701-222-1490
*Henry Heidt, President*

A nonprofit organization whose members are individuals with learning disabilities, their families, and the professionals who work with them.

## Ohio

**276    Easter Seals: Youngstown, Ohio**
**299 Edwards Street**
**Youngstown, OH  44502**                330-743-1168
                                       FAX 330-743-1616
                                       TDY:330-743-1168
              **http://www.mtc.easter-seals.org**
*Karen Sklenar CHE, President/CEO*
*Bill Addington, Contact*

Occupational, physical and speech therapy available.

**277    Learning Disabilities Association of Central Ohio**
**PO Box 835**
**Worthington, OH  43085**
                                       FAX 614-436-7450
*Elliot Resnick, President*

## Oklahoma

**278 Center for Learning & Leadership (UAP)**
College of Medicine
PO Box 26901
Oklahoma City, OK  73190

405-271-4500
800-627-6827
FAX 405-271-1459
TDY:405-271-1464
http://www.ouhsc.edu
e-mail: firstname-lastname@ouhsc.edu
*Valerie Williams, Director*

The UAP is a federally designated organization dedicated to promoting the independence, productivity and inclusion of people with disabilities in the life of the community. The core value of the UAP is to build an accepting, respectful and accessible environment for all.

**279 Learning Disabilities Association of Oklahoma**
PO Box 2315
Stillwater, OK  74076

800-532-6365
FAX 405-377-4745
http://www.ldao.com
e-mail: lado@fullnet.net
*Susan Parker, President*

## Oregon

**280 Eugene Easter Seal Service Center**
Stewart Aquatic Center
3575 Donald Street
Eugene, OR  97405

541-344-2247
800-224-5289
FAX 541-687-0803
*Diane Madrigale, Director*

Helps individuals with disabilities and special needs, and their families, live better lives.

**281 International Dyslexia Association: Oregon Branch (ORBIDA)**
PO Box 3677
Portland, OR  97208

503-228-4455
800-530-2234
FAX 503-228-3152
http://www.orbida.org
e-mail: orbida@aracnet.com
*Gary Wright, President*

An international 501(c)(3) nonprofit, scientific and educational organization dedicated to the study and treatment of dyslexia. All branches hold at least one public meeting, workshop or conference per year.

**282 International Dyslexia Society: Oregon Branch**
PO Box 3677
Portland, OR  97208

503-228-4455
FAX 503-228-3152
*Elizabeth Barton, President*

An international nonprofit, scientific and educational organization dedicated to the study of dyslexia.

**283 Learning Disabilities Association of Oregon: Beaverton**
PO Box 1221
Beaverton, OR  97008

503-641-3768
FAX 503-641-3769
http://www.ldanetl.org/
e-mail: Oregon@LDAwebpage1.html
*Donna Newton, President*

A nonprofit organization whose members are individuals with learning disabilities, their families, and the professionals who work with them.

**284 Oregon Disabilities Commission**
1257 Ferry Street SE
Salem, OR  97301

503-378-3142
800-358-3117
FAX 503-378-3599
http://www.odc.state.or.us/
*Daniel Knight, Executive Director*
*Wendy Leedle, Executive Assistant*

State ADA coordinator and building code advisor offers resources and advice to the governor and state legislative on disability issues.

**285 University of Oregon for Excellence in Developmental Disabilities**
Center on Human Development College of Education

5252 University of Education
Eugene, OR  97403

541-346-3591
FAX 541-346-2594
http://www.uoregon.edu/~uocedd/
*Jane Squires, Associate Director*
*Hill Walker, Chief Executive Officer*

To improve quality of life for persons with developmental disabilities and their families within community settings.

## Pennsylvania

**286 Adult Basic Educational Development Programs in Pennsylvania**
Philadelphia Library for the Blind
919 Walnut Street
Philadelphia, PA  19107

215-683-3213
FAX 215-683-3211
e-mail: sltdlind@library.thila.gov
*Vicky Collins, Director*

Adult basic education, GED classes and GED testing for the disabled.

**287 Easter Seal Society of Western Pennsylvania: Fayette Division**
2525 Railroad Street
Pittsburgh, PA  15222

724-437-4047
FAX 724-437-5485
*Alice Young, Division Director*

Speech, language, learning disabilities and hearing evaluations and therapy for all ages. PA licensed preschool on the premises. Open five days per week; 12 months. Call for an appointment or information on the programs provided.

**288 Huntingdon County PRIDE**
307 10th Street
Huntingdon, PA 16652 814-643-5724
FAX 814-643-6085
e-mail: pride@huntingdon.net
*Sandra Bair, Executive Director*

Speech evaluation and therapy, occupational therapy, advocacy, equipment, self-determination, specific assistance, home modification consulting, summer recreation, therapeutic horseback riding and swimming, social/recreation, information and referral.

**289 Learning Disabilities Association of Pennsylvania (LDA)**
Toomey Building
Uwchland, PA 19480 610-458-8193
http://www.ldanet.org/Pennsylvania/Index.html
*Anna McHugh, President*

LDA of Pennsylvania is a nonprofit organization of dedicated individuals whose mission is to promote quality education and to support the general welfare of children and adults with learning disabilities.

**290 Pennsylvania Center for Disability Law and Policy**

Pennsylvania Center for Disability Law and Policy
1617 JFK Boulevard
Philadelphia, PA 19103 215-557-7112
800-742-8877
FAX 215-557-7602
http://www.equalemployment.org/
e-mail: info@equalemployment.org
*Stephen Esquire, Director*
*Jamie Esquire, Managing Attorney*

CDLP provides advocacy and legal representation to persons with disabilities in employment, disability rights and education areas.

**291 Philadelphia Dyslexia Association**
International Dyslexia Association
PO Box 251
Bryn Mawr, PA 19010 610-527-1548
FAX 610-527-5011
http://www.gpbida.org
e-mail: dyslexia@gpbida.org
*John Kruidenier, President*
*Marianne Cook, Office Manager*

A nonprofit, scientific and educational organization dedicated to the study of dyslexia.

## South Carolina

**292 International Dyslexia Association: South Carolina Branch**
213 Hominy Hills Drive
Six Mile, SC 29682 803-772-8065
FAX 803-772-8065
*Felicia Robbins, President*

An international 501(c)(3) nonprofit, scientific and educational organization dedicated to the study and treatment of dyslexia. All branches hold at least one public meeting, workshop or conference per year.

**293 Literacy Volunteers of America: Laurence County**

221 W Laurens Street
Laurens, SC 29360 864-984-0466
FAX 864-984-2920
e-mail: lclc@backroads.net
*JoAn Boehm, Director*

Laurence County Literacy Council promotes literacy for people of all ages in Laurence County.

**294 South Carolina Center for Disability Resourses: Department of Pediatrics**
University of South Carolina School of Medicine
8301 Farrow Road
Columbia, SC 29203 803-935-5231
FAX 803-935-5059
http://www.cdd.sc.edu
*Richard Ferrante, Director*
*Leah Perry, Administrative Assistant*

Committed to promoting the independence, productivity, and inclusion of persons with a wide range of disabilities.

## South Dakota

**295 Learning Disabilities Association of South Dakota**
National Organization of Learning Disabilities Ass
PO Box 9760
Rapid City, SD 57709 605-388-9291
888-388-5553
http://www.geocities.com/athens/ithaca/8835
e-mail: dthom@rapidnet.com
*Dee Thompson, Executive Director*

The Association conducts workshops and conferences, assists local communities, collaborates with other organizations with similar missions and concerns, and provides 1-on-1 assistance to individuals and families. Most visible among its efforts is the Association's statewide annual conference.

**296 South Dakota Center for Disabilities**
UST School of Medicine
1400 W 22nd Street
Sioux Falls, SD 57105 605-357-1439
800-658-3080
FAX 605-357-1438
TDY:800-658-3080
http://www.usd.edu/cd
*Judy Struck, Executive Director*
*Paula Koller, Assistant Executive*

Center focuses on academic training, community education and technical assistance, information dissemination, research and evaluation, and services and support.

## Tennessee

**297  International Dyslexia Society: Tennessee West/Middle Tennessee Branch**

6525 Brownlee Drive
Nashville, TN  37205        615-896-5987
                            877-836-6432
                        FAX 615-353-6412
                        TDY:615-896-5987
                http://www.tn-interdys.org
*Susan Smartt, President*

An international nonprofit, scientific and educational organization dedicated to the study of dyslexia.

**298  Recording for the Blind & Dyslexic: Tennessee Chapter**

205 Badger Road
Oak Ridge, TN  37830        865-482-3496
                        FAX 865-483-9934
                    http://www.rfbd.org
                e-mail: kperry@rfbd.org
*Brian Jenkins, Executive Director*
*Karen Perry, Outreach Director*

Part of the national, nonprofit organization which records educational and career-related materials for print impaired students and professionals. The special focus is educational books. Blind and other print impaired students at every level, from elementary through graduate school, depend on RFBD tapes for the texts they need.

## Texas

**299  Easter Seals of Central Texas**

Easter Seals National
919 W 28 1/2 Street
Austin, TX  78705           512-478-2581
                        FAX 512-476-1638
        http://www.essentialtx.easterseals.com
        e-mail: dclowers@eastersealstx.com
*Kevin Coleman, President/CEO*
*Miriam Nisenbaum, Outpatient Rehabilitation*

Easter Seals - Central Texas creates solutions and changes lives of children and adults with disabilities.

**300  Easter Seals of Greater Dallas**

4443 N Josey Lane
Carrollton, TX  75010       972-394-8900
                            800-580-4718
                        FAX 972-394-6266
                http://www.easterseals.com
                e-mail: info@easterseals.com
*Elizabeth Hart, Director*
*Sam Gibson, Vice President*

To help children and adults with disabilities and special needs achieve their highest level of independence and self-esteem, regardless of ability to pay.

**301  Learning Disabilities Association of Texas**

Learning Disabilities Association of Texas
1011 W 31st Street
Austin, TX  78705           512-458-8234
                            800-604-7500
                        FAX 512-458-3826
                    http://www.ldat.org
                e-mail: contact@ldat.org
*Ann Robinson, State Coordinator*

Support, information and referral services for persons with learning disabilities, their families and the professionals who serve them.

**302  Learning Disabilities Association: El Paso Council**

8929 Viscount Boulevard
El Paso, TX  79925          915-591-8080
                        FAX 915-591-8150
                e-mail: eplda@elpn.com
*Lina Monroy, Director*

Support, information and referral services for persons with learning disabilities, their families and the professionals who serve them.

**303  North Texas Rehabilitation Center**

1005 Midwestern Parkway
Wichita Falls, TX  76302    940-322-0771
                            800-861-1322
                        FAX 940-766-4943
                    http://www.ntrehab.org
*Kathy Mickus, Child Achievement Supervisor*
*Susan Griffin, Cashier/Operator*

A rehabilitation center for people with disabilities. Physical therapy, occupational therapy, speech language therapy, and academic services available.

## Vermont

**304  Learning Disabilities Association of Vermont**

PO Box 1041
Manchester Center, VT  05255    802-362-3127
                            FAX 802-362-3128
                e-mail: chthurston@juno.com
*Christina Thurston, President*

A nonprofit organization whose members are individuals with learning disabilities, their families, and the professionals who work with them.

**305  Vermont Protection and Advocacy**

National Association of Protection & Advocacy Syst
141 Main Street
Montpelier, VT  05602       802-229-1355
                            800-834-7890
                        FAX 802-229-1359
                    http://www.vtpa.org
                e-mail: info@vtpa.org
*Christopher Holliday, Supervising Attorney*
*Marshe Bancroft, Intake Paralegal*

Mission is to defend and advance the rights of people who have been labeled mentally ill.

## Virginia

**306  Learning Disabilities Association of Virginia**
N4001 North 9th Street
Arlington, VA  22203                703-243-2614
                                   FAX 703-243-0894
                           http://www.ldavirginia.org
                        e-mail: info@ldavirginia.org/na
*Anna Johnson, President*
*Justine Maloney, Volunteer*

A nonprofit organization whose members are individuals with learning disabilities, their families, and the professionals who work with them.

## Washington

**307  Learning Disabilities Association of Washington**
7819 159th Place NE
Redmond, WA  98052                 425-882-0820
                                   800-536-2343
                                   FAX 425-861-4642
                              http://www.ldawa.org
                        e-mail: dsiegel@ldawa.org
*Phil Mortenson, President*

Promotes and provides services and support to improve the quality of life for individuals and families affected by learning and attentional disabilities.

**308  Washington Parent Training Project: PAVE**
6316 S 12th Street
Tacoma, WA  98465                  253-565-2266
                                   800-572-7368
                                   FAX 253-566-8052
                                   TDY:253-569-2266
                        http://www.washingtonpave.org
                   e-mail: wapave9@washingtonpave.com
*Joanne Butts, Executive Director*
*Elma Rounds, Chief Financial Officer*

PAVE helps parents understand their child's school program and to become their child's best advocate. The parent resource coordinators on staff, all of whom are parents of children with disabilities, help other parents learn about the rights of children with special learning needs.

**309  Washington Protection & Advocacy Agency**
1401 E Jefferson
Seattle, WA  98122                 206-324-1521
                                   800-562-2702
                                   FAX 425-776-0601
                              e-mail: wpas@wpas.org
*Mark Stroh, Executive Director*
*Abby Ceja, Administrative Assistant*

## Wisconsin

**310  Easter Seals of Southeast Wisconsin**
3090 N 53rd Street
Milwaukee, WI  53210               414-449-4444
                                   FAX 414-449-4447
                   e-mail: agency@wi-se.easter-seals.org
*Dob Glowacki, Executive Director*
*Sheolia Underwoods, Office Manager*

Two child development centers in southeast Wisconsin offer an integrated environment for children ages 6 weeks-12 years. Birth-Three Early Intervention Services provide speech, physical, and occupational therapies. After School Recreation Program provides recreational activities for ages 12-21 with a range of disabilities. The Adult Recreation program offers classes and recreation opportunities to adults with disabilities. Call for additiional programs.

**311  International Dyslexia Association: Wisconsin Branch**
7415 North Avenue
Madison, WI  53562                 608-238-4343
                                   FAX 608-238-6093
                           e-mail: bbliss@chorus.net
*Irene Meinholz, Chief Executive Officer*

Clearinghouse for information on dyslexia. Offers information on testing and tutoring throughout the state. Has lists of Wisconsin residents who have been trained to tutor using the Orton-Gillingham method. Also trains teachers and parents to use this method. There is a Dane County Dyslexia Support Group meeting 3rd Tuesday of every month.

## National Programs

**312   Attention Deficit Disorder Association**

Attention Deficit Disorder Association
PO Box 543
Pottstown, PA  19464                  484-945-2101
                                      FAX 610-970-7520
                                      http://www.add.org
                                      e-mail: mail@add.org
*David Giwerc, President*
*Linda Anderson, Vice President*
*David Giwerc, VP*

A national nonprofit organization that provides information, resources and networking to adults with AD/HD.

**313   Attention Deficit Disorder Warehouse**

300 NW 70th Avenue
Plantation, FL  33317                 954-792-8100
                                      800-233-9273
                                      FAX 954-792-8545
                                      http://www.addwarehouse.com
                                      e-mail: sales@addwarehouse.com
*Jared Pincuh, Phone Sales*

Comprehensive collection of ADHD-related books, videos, training programs, games, professional texts and assessment products. Because of its tremendous depth, and the quality of the products we carry, our catalog is a recommended source of help in practically every book written on ADHD, and is provided to patients by hundreds of health professionals across the country.

**314   Attention Deficit Information Network**

58 Prince Street
Needham, MA  02492                    781-455-9895
                                      http://www.addinfonetwork.com
                                      e-mail: adin@gis.net

A nonprofit volunteer organization that offers support and information to families of children and adults with ADD, and to professionals.

**315   Children and Adults with Attention Deficit Hyperactivity Disorder (CHADD)**

8181 Professional Place
Landover, MD  20785                   301-306-7070
                                      800-233-4050
                                      FAX 301-306-7090
                                      http://www.chadd.org
                                      e-mail: national@chadd.org
*Mary Durheim, President*
*Marsha Bokman, Chief Administrative Officer*

CHADD is a national nonprofit organization providing education, advocacy and support for individuals with AD/HD.

**316   Dyslexia Research Institute**

5746 Centerville Road
Tallahassee, FL  32309                850-893-2216
                                      FAX 850-893-2440
                                      http://www.dyslexia-add.org
                                      e-mail: dri@dyslexia-add.org
*Patrica Hardman PhD, Director*
*Robyn Rennick MS, Assistant Director*

Addresses academic, social and self-concept issues for dyslexic and ADD children and adults. College prep courses, study skills, advocacy, diagnostic testing, seminars, teacher training, day school, tutoring and an adult literacy and life skills program is available using an accredited MSLE approach.

**317   Learning Disabilities Association of America**

Learning Disabilities Association of America
4156 Library Road
Pittsburgh, PA  15234 1349            412-341-1515
                                      888-300-6710
                                      FAX 412-344-0224
                                      http://www.ldaamerica.org
                                      e-mail: info@ldaamerica.org
*Jane Browning, Executive Director*
*Marianne Toombs, President*
*Suzanne Fornaro, VP*

An information and referral center for parents and professionals dealing with Attention Deficit Disorders, and other learning disabilities. Free materials and referral service to nearest chapter.

**318   School Based Assessment of Attention Deficit Disorders**

Nat'l Clearinghouse of Rehab. Training Materials
206 West 6th Street.
Stillwater, OK  74078 4080            405-744-2000
                                      800-223-5219
                                      FAX 405-744-2001
                                      TDY:405-744-2002
                                      http://www.nchrtm.okstate.edu
                                      e-mail: ahlerti@okstate.edu
*Charles Seasley, Director*
*Carolyn Cail, Assistant Director*

To promote the exchange of information and enhance the outcome of the public rehabilitation program by collecting, archiving and disseminating the rehabilitation training materials developed by Rehabilitation Services Administration Grantees.

## Publications

**319   ADD Challenge: A Practical Guide for Teachers**

Research Press
PO Box 9177
Champaign, IL  61826                  217-352-3273
                                      800-519-2707
                                      FAX 217-352-1221
                                      http://www.researchpress.com
                                      e-mail: rp@researchpress.com
*Russ Pence, President*
*Susan Allen, Office Manager*

Provides educators with practical information about the needs and treatment of children and adolescents with ADD. The book addresses the defining characteristics of ADD, common treatment approaches, myths about ADD, matching intervention to student, use of behavior-rating scales and checklists evaluating interventions, regular verses, special class placement, helps students regulate their own behavior and more. Case examples are used throughout. *$17.95*

*196 pages*
*ISBN 0-878223-45-2*

**320 ADD and Adults: Strategies for Success**

CHADD
8181 Professional Place
Landover, MD 20785
301-306-7070
800-233-4050
FAX 301-306-7090
http://www.chadd.org
e-mail: national@chadd.org
*Mary Durheim, President*
*Marsha Bokman, Chief Administrative Officer*

A series of articles written by many of the nation's leading experts. Includes important topics/issues such as: Diagnosing ADD in Adults; Coaching, Anger Management Training, Succeeding in the Workplace with ADD; Adults with ADD and the Military; Using Strategies and Services for Success in College; Interpersonal and Social Problems in Adults with ADD, and much more. *$19.00*

*118 pages*

**321 ADD and Creativity: Tapping Your Inner Muse**

Taylor Publishing
1550 W Mockingbird Lane
Dallas, TX 75235
214-637-2800
800-677-2800
FAX 214-819-8580
http://www.taylorpublishing.com
e-mail: brosser@taylorpublishing.com
*Lynn Weiss, PhD, Author*
*Boyd Rosser, Director*
*Stacy Young, Office Manager*

Raises and answers questions about the dynamic between the two components and shows how they can be a wonderful gift but also a painful liability if not properly handled. Real-life stories and inspirational affirmations throughout.

*Paperback*
*ISBN 0-878339-60-4*

**322 ADD and Romance: Finding Fulfillment in Love, Sex and Relationships**

Taylor Publishing
1550 W Mockingbird Lane
Dallas, TX 75235
214-637-2800
800-677-2800
FAX 214-819-8580
http://www.taylorpublishing.com
e-mail: brosser@taylorpublishing.com
*Jonathan Scott Halverstadt, Author*
*Boyd Rosser, Director*
*Charles Kass, Assistant Director*

A look at how attention deficit disorder can damage romantic relationships when partners do not take time, or do not know how to address this problem. This book provides the tools needed to build and sustain a more satisfying relationship.

*240 pages  Paperback*
*ISBN 0-878332-09-0*

**323 ADD and Success**

Taylor Publishing
1550 W Mockingbird Lane
Dallas, TX 75235
214-637-2800
800-677-2800
FAX 214-819-8580
http://www.taylorpublishing.com
e-mail: brosser@taylorpublishing.com
*Lynn Weiss, PhD, Author*
*Boyd Rosser, Director*
*Charles Kass, Assistant Director*

Presents the stories of 13 individuals and their experiences and challenges of living with adult attention disorder and achieving success.

*224 pages  Paperback*
*ISBN 0-878339-94-9*

**324 ADD in Adults**

Taylor Publishing
1550 W Mockingbird Lane
Dallas, TX 75235
214-637-2800
800-677-2800
FAX 214-819-8580
http://www.taylorpublishing.com
e-mail: brosser@taylorpublishing.com
*Lynn Weiss, PhD, Author*
*Boyd Rosser, Director*
*Charles Kass, Assistant Director*

Updated version of this best-selling book on the topic of ADD helps others to understand and live with the issues related to ADD.

*Paperback*
*ISBN 0-878339-79-5*

**325 ADD: Helping Your Child**

Warner Books
1271 Avenue of the Americas
New York, NY 10020
800-759-0190
http://www.twbookmark.com
*Warren Umansky, Author*
*Barbara Smalley, Author*

This guide to an organic condition that affects between three and ten percent of grade-school children is designed to help parents obtain accurate diagnosis, improve their child's self-esteem, develop classroom strategies, and become informed about medicine. *$10.99*

*244 pages  Paperback*
*ISBN 0-446670-13-8*

**326 ADHD**

Learning Disabilities Association of America
4156 Library Road
Pittsburgh, PA 15234 1349
412-341-1515
FAX 412-344-0224
http://www.ldaamerica.org
e-mail: info@ldaamerica.org
*Larry B Silver, MD, Author*
*Marianne Toombs, President*

A booklet for parents offering information on Attention Deficit-Hyperactivity Disorders and learning disabilities. *$3.95*

**327 ADHD Challenge Newsletter**
PO Box 2277
West Newbury, MA 01960
800-233-2322
FAX 800-233-2322
*Jean Harrison, Executive Director*

National newsletter on ADD/ADHD that presents interviews with nationally-known scientists, as well as physicians, psychologists, social workers, educators, and other practitioners in the field of ADHD. *$35.00*

*12 pages Bimonthly*

**328 ADHD Report**
**Guilford Publications**
**72 Spring Street**
**New York, NY 10012**
212-431-9800
800-365-7006
FAX 212-966-6708
http://www.guilford.com
e-mail: info@guilford.com
*Michael Gordon, Editor*
*Shelby Keiser, Editor*

Presents the most up-to-date information on the evaluation, diagnosis and management of ADHD in children, adolescents and adults. This important newsletter is an invaluable resource for all professionals interested in ADHD. *$77.00*

*Bimonthly*
*ISSN 1065-8025*

**329 Attention Deficit Disorder in Adults Workbook**
**Taylor Publishing**
**1550 W Mockingbird Lane**
**Dallas, TX 75235**
214-637-2800
800-677-2800
FAX 214-819-8580
http://www.taylorpublishing.com
e-mail: brosser@taylorpublishing.com
*Lynn Weiss, Author*
*Boyd Rosser, Director*
*Charles Kass, Assistant Director*

Dr. Lynn Weiss's best-selling Attention Deficit Disorder In Adults has sold over 125,000 copies since its publication in 1991. This updated volume still contains all the original information — how to tell if you have ADD, ways to master distraction, ADD's impact on the family, and more—plus the newest treatments available. *$17.99*

*192 pages Paperback*
*ISBN 0-878338-50-0*

**330 Attention Deficit Disorder: A Concise Source of Information for Parents**
**Temeron Books**
**PO Box 896**
**Bellingham, WA 98227**
360-738-4016
FAX 360-738-4016
http://www.temerondetselig.com
e-mail: temeron@telusplanet.net
*H Moghadam, MD and Joel Fagan, MD, Author*

The authors travel from a brief historical review of ADD, through a description of symptoms and consequences, to a discussion of treatment. *$15.95*

*128 pages Paperback*
*ISBN 1-550590-82-0*

**331 Attention Deficit Disorder: A Different Perception**

**Underwood-Miller**
**708 Westover Drive**
**Lancaster, PA 17601**
717-285-2255
FAX 717-285-2255
*Thomas Hartmann, Author*

Attention Deficit Disorder is a disease that stigmatizes millions of Americans and causes many of them to fail—first in school, then later in adult life. It has been estimated that 90% of the prison population has ADD. This book takes a unique look at the disorder, suggesting that it is not really a disease, but rather an evolutionary adaptation to life in a hunting society. *$9.95*

*180 pages Paperback*
*ISBN 0-887331-56-4*

**332 Attention Deficit Disorders: Assessment & Teaching**
**Brooks/Cole Publishing Company**
**511 Forest Lodge Road**
**Pacific Grove, CA 93950**
831-373-0728
FAX 831-375-6414
*Janet W Lerner, et al., Author*
*Janet Lerner, Contact*

*Paperback $18.95*
*ISBN 0-534250-44-0*

**333 Attention Deficit Hyperactivity Disorder: Handbook for Diagnosis & Treatment**
**Western Psychological Services**
**12031 Wilshire Boulevard**
**Los Angeles, CA 90025**
310-478-2061
800-648-8857
FAX 310-478-7838
http://www.wpspublish.com
e-mail: custsve@wpspublish.com
*Russell A Barkley, PhD, Author*
*Greg Gillmar, Director*
*Russell Barkley, PhD*

This second edition helps clinicians diagnose and treat Attention Deficit Hyperactivity Disorder. Written by an internationally recognized authority in the field, it covers the history of ADHD, its primary symptoms, associated conditions, developmental course and outcome, and family context. A workbook companion manual is also available.

*700 pages Hardcover*

**334 Attention Deficit-Hyperactivity Disorder: Is It a Learning Disability?**

Georgetown University, School of Medicine
37th and O Street NW
Washington, DC 20007          202-687-0100
                              FAX 202-662-9444
                              TDY:202-444-3353
http://www.georgetownuniversityhospital.org
e-mail:
joy.darss@georgetownuniversityhospital.org
*Larry Silver, Author*
*Joy Darss MD, Chairman*

Offers information on learning disabilities and related disorders.

**335 Attention-Deficit Hyperactivity Disorder**

72 Spring Street
New York, NY 10012          212-431-9800
                            800-365-7006
                            FAX 212-966-6708
                            http://www.guilford.com
                            e-mail: info@guilford.com
*Russell A Barkley, Author*
*Michael Gordon, Editor*
*Shelby Keiser, Editor*

Provides a comprehensive analysis of ADHD. *$55.00*

*747 pages*

**336 CHADD Educators Manual**

CHADD
8181 Professional Place
Landover, MD 20785          301-306-7070
                            800-233-4050
                            FAX 301-306-7090
                            http://www.chadd.org
                            e-mail: national@chadd.org
*Mary Fowler, Author*
*Mary Durheim, President*
*Marsha Bokman, Chief Administrative Officer*

An in-depth look at Attention Deficit Disorders from an educational perspective. *$10.00*

**337 Children with ADD: A Shared Responsibility**

Council for Exceptional Children
1110 N Glebe Road
Arlington, VA 22201 5704          703-620-3660
                                  888-232-7733
                                  FAX 703-264-9494
                                  TDY:866-915-5000
                                  http://www.cec.sped.org/
                                  e-mail: service@cec.sped.org
*Drew Albritten MD, Executive Director*
*Betty Bryant, Program Manager*

This book represents a consensus of what professionals and parents believe ADD is all about and how children with ADD may best be served. Reviews the evaluation process under IDEA and 504 and presents effective classroom strategies.

*35 pages*
*ISBN 0-865862-33-8*

**338 Cognitive-Behavioral Therapy with ADHD Children: Child, Family & School**

Western Psychological Services
12031 Wilshire Boulevard
Los Angeles, CA 90025          310-478-2061
                               800-648-8857
                               FAX 310-478-7838
                               http://www.wpspublish.com
                               e-mail: custsve@wpspublish.com
*Lauren Braswell, Michael L Bloomquist, Author*

Presents a model for treating Attention-Deficit Hyperactivity Disorder and associated disruptive behavior disorders that is uniquely sensitive to environmental and developmental factors. It applies cognitive-behavioral techniques in settings where problems actually occur — at home and at school — thus encouraging a truly effective therapeutic partnership that involves not only the child, but also the school and family. *$52.00*

*391 pages*

**339 Coping: Attention Deficit Disorder: A Guide for Parents and Teachers**

Temeron Books
PO Box 896
Bellingham, WA 98227
                              FAX 360-738-4016
                     http://www.temerondetselig.com
                   e-mail: temeron@telusplanet.net
*Mary Ellen Beugin, Author*

The author investigates medical and behavioral interventions that can be tried with ADD children and gives suggestions on coping with these children at home and at school. *$15.95*

*173 pages Paperback*
*ISBN 1-550590-13-8*

**340 Driven to Distraction: Attention Deficit Disorder from Childhood Through Adulthood**

2107 Wilson Blvd
Arlington, VA 22201-3042          703-524-7600
                                  800-950-6264
                                  FAX 703-524-9094
                                  TDY:703-516-7227
                                  http://www.nami.org
*Edward Hallowell, Author*
*John Ratey, Author*

Through vivid stories of the experience of their patients, Drs. Hallowell and Ratey show the varied forms ADD takes — from the hyperactive search for high stimulation to the floating inattention of daydreaming — and the transforming impact of precise diagnosis and treatment.

*ISBN 0-684801-28-0*

**341 Dyslexia Research and Resource Guide**

Books on Special Children
PO Box 305
Congers, NY 10920          413-256-8164
                           FAX 413-256-8896
                           http://www.boscbooks.com
                           e-mail: contact@boscbook.com
*CS Spafford, Author*
*Marcia Young, President*

A definitive book on dyslexia, which is defined as a reading disorder whereby an individual fails to attain reading skills. Book has resources, teaching ideas and strategies for people with LD. Other forms of LD discussed, such as memory disorders, math disabilities, ADHD, aphasia, etc. *$47.00*

*340 pages  hardcover*
*ISBN 0-205159-07-9*

**342    Fact Sheet-Attention Deficit Hyperactivity Disorder**

**Learning Disabilities Association of America**
**4156 Library Road**
**Pittsburgh, PA  15234**                          **412-341-1515**
                                                   **FAX 412-344-0224**
                          **http://www.ldaamerica.org**
                          **e-mail: info@ldaamerica.org**
*Jane Browning, Executive Director*
*Marianne Toombs, President*
*Connie Parr, VP*

A pamphlet offering factual information on ADHD. *$10.00*

**343    Focus Magazine**

**Attention Deficit Disorder Association**
**PO Box 543**
**Pottstown, PA  19464**                          **484-945-2101**
                                                  **FAX 610-970-7520**
                          **http://www.add.org**
                          **e-mail: mail@add.org**
*David Giwerc, President*
*Linda Anderson, Vice President*
*David Giwerc, VP*

The National Attention Deficit Disorder Association is an organization focused on the needs of adults and young adults with ADD/ADHD, and their children and families. We seek to serve individuals with ADD, as well as those who love, live with, teach, counsel and treat them.

**344    Focus Your Energy: Succeeding in Business with ADD**

**Pocket Books**
**1230 Avenue of The Americas**
**New York, NY  10024**                           **212-698-7000**
                                                  **FAX 212-698-7007**
                          **http://www.simonsays.com**
                  **e-mail: jackromano@simonandschuster.com**
*Thom Hartmann, Author*
*Jack Romano, President*
*David England, Vice President*

Focus Your Energy will help you to understand and overcome the symptoms of ADD that may be holding you back, and take advantage of the traits that mark you for success. *$10.00*

*Paperback*
*ISBN 0-671516-89-2*

**345    Getting a Grip on ADD: A Kid's Guide to Understanding & Coping with ADD**

**Educational Media Corporation**
**6021 Wish Avenue**
**Encino, CA  91316**                             **818-708-0962**
                                                  **FAX 818-345-2980**
                          **http://www.educationalmedia.com**
*Kim Frank, Author*
*Susan Smith, Author*

Help your elementary and middle school students cope more effectively with Attention Deficit Disorders. *$9.95*

*64 pages  Paperback*
*ISBN 0-932796-60-3*

**346    Helping Your Child with Attention-Deficit Hyperactivity Disorder**

**Learning Disabilities Association of America**
**4156 Library Road**
**Pittsburgh, PA  15234**                          **412-341-1515**
                                                   **FAX 412-344-0224**
                          **http://www.ldaamerica.org**
                          **e-mail: info@ldaamerica.org**
*Jane Browning, Executive Director*
*Marianne Toombs, President*
*Connie Parr, VP*

A parents's guide to identifying, understanding and helping your child with ADD. *$12.95*

**347    Helping Your Hyperactive-Attention Deficit Child**

**Prima Publishing**
**3000 Lava Ridge Court**
**Roseville, CA  95661**                          **916-787-7000**
                                                  **800-632-8676**
                                                  **FAX 916-787-7001**
                          **http://www.primagame.com**
                          **e-mail: scoodwin@primagame.com**
*John F Taylor, Author*
*Debra Kempker, President*
*Julie Asbury, Office Manager*

For parents on how to help your child with ADD. *$19.95*

*ISBN 1-559584-23-8*

**348    How to Own and Operate an Attention Deficit Disorder**

**Learning Disabilities Association of America**
**4156 Library Road**
**Pittsburgh, PA  15234**                          **412-341-1515**
                                                   **FAX 412-344-0224**
                          **http://www.ldaamerica.org**
                          **e-mail: info@ldaamerica.org**
*Jane Browning, Executive Director*
*Marianne Toombs, President*
*Connie Parr, VP*

Clear, informative and sensitive introduction to ADHD. Packed with practical things to do at home and school, the author offers her insight as a professional and mother of a son with ADHD. *$10.45*

*43 pages*

**349    How to Teach ADD-ADHD Children**

**Council for Exceptional Children**
**1110 N Glebe Road**
**Arlington, VA  22201 5704**                     **703-620-3660**
                                                  **888-232-7733**
                                                  **FAX 703-264-9494**
                                                  **TDY:866-915-5000**
                          **http://www.cec.sped.org**
                          **e-mail: service@cec.sped.org**
*Drew Albritten, M.D., Executive Director*
*Betty Bryant, Program Manager*

Practical techniques, strategies, and interventions for helping children with attention problems and hyperactivity. *$27.95*

*245 pages*
*ISBN 0-876264-13-6*

**350  Hyperactive Child Book**

**St. Martin's Press**
**175 5th Avenue**
**New York, NY  10010**                212-674-5151
                                        800-321-9299
                                        FAX 212-420-9314
                        http://www.stmartins.com
                e-mail: george.witte@stmartins.com
*Patricia Kennedy, Author*
*George Witte, President*
*Lydia Fusetti, Author*

Treating, educating and living with an ADHD child. *$12.95*

*ISBN 0-312112-86-6*

**351  Hyperactive Child, Adolescent and Adult**

**Oxford University Press**
**198 Madison Avenue**
**New York, NY  10016**                212-726-6000
                                        800-451-7556
                                        FAX 212-726-6440
                        http://www.aup-usa.org
                e-mail: laura.brown@oup.com
*Paul H Wender MD, Author*
*Laura Brown, President*
*Terry Dickerson, Office Manager*

How does one know if a youngster is hyperactive? How do you know if you are hyperactive yourself? The answers may lie in this easy-to-read and comprehensive volume written by one of the leading researchers in the field. *$9.95*

*172 pages*

**352  Hyperactivity, Attention Deficits and School Failure: Better Ways**

**Learning Disabilities Association of America**
**4156 Library Road**
**Pittsburgh, PA  15234**              412-341-1515
                                        FAX 412-344-0224
                        http://www.ldaamerica.org
                e-mail: info@ldaamerica.org
*Jane Browning, Executive Director*
*Marianne Toombs, President*

*$6.00*

**353  International Reading Association Newspaper: Reading Today**

**International Reading Association**
**800 Barksdale Road**
**Newark, DE  19714**                  302-731-1600
                                        800-628-8508
                                        FAX 302-731-1057
                        http://www.reading.org
                e-mail: pubinfo@reading.org
*Janet Butler, Public Information Associate*

The International Reading Association is a professional membership organization dedicated to promoting high levels of literacy for all by improving the quality of reading instruction, disseminating research and information about reading, and encouraging the lifetime reading habit. Our members include classroom teachers, reading specialists, consultants, administrators, supervisors, university faculty, researchers, psychologists, librarians, media specialistss and parents.

**354  LD Child and the ADHD Child**

**John F Blair, Publisher**
**1406 Plaza Drive**
**Winston-Salem, NC  27103**           336-768-1374
                                        800-222-9796
                                        FAX 336-768-9194
                        http://www.blairpub.com
                e-mail: blairpub@blairpub.com
*Suzanne H Stevens, Author*
*Ed Southern, Sales Director*
*Carolyn Sakowski, President*

The author recommends other options that can be explored to treat LD and ADHD children without drugs. *$12.95*

*261 pages  Paperback*
*ISBN 0-895871-42-4*

**355  LDA Alabama Newsletter**

**Learning Disabilities Association Alabama**
**PO Box 11588**
**Montgomery, AL  36111**              334-277-9151
                                        FAX 334-284-9357
                        http://www.ldaal.org
                e-mail: alabama@ldaal.org
*Debbie Gibson, President*

Educational, support, and advocacy group for individuals with learning disabilities and ADD.

**356  LDA Georgia Newsletter**

**Learning Disabilities Association Georgia**
**130 W Wieuca Road**
**Atlanta, GA  30342**                 404-303-7774
                                        FAX 404-303-7161
                        http://www.ldag.org
                e-mail: services@ldag.org
*Christopher Lee, Executive Director*
*Franches Rolster, President*

Information and helpful articles on learning disabilities. Mailed free four times a year to members. *$40.00*

*Quarterly*

**357  LDA Illinois Newsletter**

**Learning Disabilities Association Illinois**
**10101 S Roberts Road**
**Palos Hills, IL  60465**             708-430-7532
                                        FAX 708-430-7592
                        http://www.idanatl.org/illinois
                e-mail: ldaosil@ameritech.net
*Sharon Schussler, Administrative Assistant*

A nonprofit organization dedicated to the advancement of the education and general welfare of children and youth of normal or potentially normal intelligence who have perceptual, conceptual, coordinative or related learning disabilities.

**358 Maybe You Know My Kid: A Parent's Guide to Identifying ADHD**

Birch Lane Press
120 Enterprise Avenue S
Secaucus, NJ 07094
201-866-0186
800-447-2665
FAX 201-866-1886
http://www.secaucus.birchlanepress.com
e-mail: mmpsec@carroll.com

*Mary Fowler, Author*
*Tal Goldgraber, President*

A guide for parents of children diagnosed with ADD discusses the recent changes in the education of these children and offers practical guidelines for improving educational performance. *$13.25*

*222 pages*

**359 Natural Therapies for Attention Deficit Hyperactivity Disorder**

Comprehensive Psychiatric Resources
831 Beacon Street
Newton Centre, MA 02459
617-332-1336
FAX 617-332-9936
http://www.natualadd.com
e-mail: cprinc2@aol.com

A full day workshop professionally recorded on six audiotapes featuring Dr. James M. Greenblatt, M.D., neuropsychiatrist. Dr. Greenblatt explores updated research on nutrition and ADD, food additives, food allergies, fatty acids and more, provides practical treatment strategies and helps you make informed choices between effective and worthless therapies.

**360 Parent's Guide to Attention Deficit Disorders**

Dell Publishing
1540 Broadway
New York, NY 10036
212-354-6500
FAX 212-782-9523
http://www.randomhouse.com

*Lisa J Bain, Author*
*R Moss, Author*
*H Dunlap, Author*

In this first book in a new series with the renowned Children's Hospital of Philadelphia, doctors at the hospital discuss the conditions known as ADD and offer means of diagnosing them, up-to-date medical and behavioral therapies, and a listing of organizations specializing in their treatment.

**361 Parenting Attention Deficit Disordered Teens**

Connecticut Association for Children and Adults wi
25 Van Zant Street
East Norwalk, CT 06855
203-838-5010
FAX 203-866-6108
http://www.CACLD.org
e-mail: cacld@optonline.net

*Patricia C Land, Author*
*Beryl Kaufman, Executive Director*
*Carol Maloney, Executive Assistant*

Small pamphlet with amazingly detailed outline of the various problems of adolescents with ADHD. *$3.25*

*14 pages $2.50 shipping*

**362 Parents' Hyperactivity Handbook: Helping the Fidgety Child**

Plenum Publishers
233 Spring Street
New York, NY 10013
212-620-8000
FAX 212-463-0742
http://www.springer.com
e-mail: derk.haank@springer.coom

*DM Paltin, Author*
*Derk Haank, President*
*Myrtle Bannis, Office Manager*

*305 pages $27.50*
*ISBN 0-306444-65-8*

**363 Putting on the Brakes**

American Psychological Association
750 1st Street NE
Washington, DC 20002
202-336-5500
800-374-2721
FAX 202-336-5502
TDY:202-336-6123
http://www.apa.org
e-mail: apeditor@apa.org

*Patricia Quinn, Author*
*Judith Stern, Author*

This is one of the most popular books written on attention deficit-hyperactivity disorder and a most useful resource for kids with ADHD. The authors describe the symptoms and theories of ADHD in warm, kid-friendly terms and discuss family support, medication, and tips on getting organized.

**364 Rethinking Attention Deficit Disorders**

Brookline Books
300 Bedford St
Machester, OH 03101
617-734-6772
FAX 603-922-3348
http://www.brooklinebooks.com
e-mail: brooklinebks@delphi.com

*Milt Budoff, President*

Groundbreaking analysis of ADHD. *$27.95*

*ISBN 1-571290-37-0*

**365 Shelley, the Hyperactive Turtle**

Woodbine House
6510 Bells Mill Road
Bethesda, MD 20817
301-897-3570
800-843-7323
FAX 301-897-5838
http://www.woodbinehouse.com
e-mail: info@woodbinehouse.com

*Susan Stokes, Editorial in Chief*
*Irvin Shapell, Publisher*

Shelley the turtle has a very hard time sitting still, even for short periods of time. During a visit to the doctor, Shelley learns that he is hyperactive, and that he can take medicine every day to control his wiggly feeling. *$ 12.95*

*20 pages Hardcover*
*ISBN 0-933149-31-X*

**366 Special Parent, Special Child: Parents of Children with Disabilities**

**Books on Special Children**
4 Harkness Road
Pelham, MA  01002                845-638-1236
FAX 845-638-0847
http://www.boscbooks.com
e-mail: irene@boscbooks.com
*T Sullivan, Author*
*Marcia Young, Owner*

Parents share the depths of their feelings, despair and disappointments. Author asks his mother about his blindness, then speaks with parents of six children with disabilities: blind; deaf; Cerebral Palsy; leukemia; ADD; and Down Sydrome. Discusses initial reaction upon learning their child had a disability, family repercussions, advocacy and other special insights. *$24.95*

*239 pages  hardcover*
*ISBN 0-874777-82-8*

**367 Teach and Reach Students with Attention Deficit Disorders**

**Multi-Growth Resources**
12345 Jones Road
Houston, TX  77070                713-890-5334
e-mail: multigrowthresources@compuserve.com
*Nancy Eisenberg, Author*
*Pamela Esser, Author*

Handbook and resource guide for parents and educators of students with ADHD. *$23.95*

*200 pages*
*ISBN 0-963084-71-2*

**368 Understanding and Teaching Children With Autism**

**Books on Special Children**
22 Webster Court
Amherst, MA  01002                845-638-1236
FAX 845-638-0847
http://www.boscbooks.com
e-mail: irene@boscbooks.com
*R Jordan, Author*
*Marcia Young, President*

The triad of impairment: social, language and communication and thought behavior aspects of development discussed. Difficulties in interacting, transfer of learning and bizarre behaviors are part of syndrome. Many LD are associated with autism. *$57.00*

*175 pages  hardcover*
*ISBN 0-471958-88-3*

**369 Why Can't Johnny Concentrate: Coping With Attention Deficit Problems**

**Bantam Doubleday Dell**
1540 Broadway
New York, NY  10036                212-782-9000
800-323-9872
FAX 212-302-7985
http://www.randomhouse.com
*R Moss, Author*
*H Dunlap, Author*

How to cope with ADD problems.

**370 Why Can't My Child Behave?**

**Pear Tree Press**
PO Box 30146
Alexandria, VA  22310                800-321-3287
FAX 703-768-3619
http://www.childbehave.com
*Jane Hersey, Author*

This book shows how foods and food additives can trigger learning and behavior problems in sensitive people. It provides practical guidance on using a simple diet to uncover the causes of ADD and ADHD. *$22.00*

*400 pages*
*ISSN 0965-1105*

**371 You Mean I'm Not Lazy, Stupid or Crazy?**

**Scribner**
1230 Avenue of Americas
New York, NY  10020                212-698-7000
800-622-6611
FAX 212-698-7007
*Peggy Ramundo, Author*
*Kate Kelly, Author*

This new book is the first written by ADD adults for other ADD adults. A comprehensive guide, it provides accurate information, practical how-to's, and moral support. Among other issues, readers will get information on: unique differences in ADD adults; the impact on their lives; up-to-date research findings; treatment options available for adults; and much more. *$24.95*

*444 pages*
*ISBN 1-882522-00-1*

## Web Sites

**372 www.add.org**
**Attention Deficit Disorder Association**

The National Attention Deficit Disorder Association is an organization focused on the needs of adults and young adults with ADD/ADHD, and their children and families. We seek to serve individuals with ADD, as well as those who love, live with, teach, counsel and treat them.

**373 www.addhelpline.org**
**ADD Helpline for Help with ADD**

A site dedicated to providing information and support to all parents, regardless of their choice of treatment, belief or approach toward ADD/ADHD.

**374 www.additudemag.com**
**Attitude Magazine**

ADDitude: The Happy Healthy Lifestyle Magazine for People with ADD offers articles, information and support.

**375**  www.addvance.com
**ADDvance Online Newsletter**

A resource for girls and women with ADD. Site has books, tapes, support groups, chat and links.

**376**  www.addwarehouse.com
**ADD Warehouse**

The world's largest collection of ADHD-related books, videos, training programs, games, professional texts and assessment products.

**377**  www.adhdnews.com/ssi.htm

Guidance in applying for Social Security disability benefits on behalf of a child who has ADHD.

**378**  www.cec.sped.org
**Council for Exceptional Children**

Dedicated to improving educational outcomes for individuals with exceptionalities, students with disabilities, and/or the gifted.

**379**  www.chadd.org
**National Resource Center on AD/HD**

CHADD works to improve the lives of people affected by AD/HD.

**380**  www.childdevelopmentinfo.com
**Child Development Institute**

*Robert Myers MD, President*

Online information on child development, child psychology, parenting, learning, health and safety as well as childhood disorders such as attention deficit disorder, dyslexia and autism. Provides comprehensive resources and practical suggestions for parents.

**381**  www.dyslexia.com
**Davis Dyslexia Association**

Links to internet resources for learning. Includes dyslexia, Autism and Asperger's Syndrome, ADD/ADHD and other learning disabilities.

**382**  www.my.webmd.com
**Web MD Health**

Medical website with information which includes learning disabilities, ADD/ADHD, etc.

**383**  www.ncgiadd.org
**National Center for Gender Issues and AD/HD**

Offers knowledge and understanding of girls and women with ADHD to improve their lives.

**384**  www.nichcy.org
**Nat'l Dissemination Center for Children Disabiliti**

Provides information on disabilties in children and youth and programs and services.

**385**  www.oneaddplace.com
**One A D D Place**

A virtual neighborhood of information and resources relating to ADD, ADHD and learning disorders.

**386**  www.therapistfinder.net

Locate psychologists, psychiatrists, social workers, family counselors, and more specializing in all disorders.

## Publications

**387  Directory of Summer Camps for Children with Learning Disabilities**

**Learning Disabilities Association of America**
**4156 Library Road**
**Pittsburgh, PA  15234**          412-341-1515
                                   FAX 412-344-0224
                                   http://www.ldaamerica.org
                                   e-mail: info@ldaamerica.org
*Jane Browning, Executive Director*
*Marianne Toombs, President*

Offers a full range of listings for the learning disabled.
*$4.00*

**388  Guide to ACA Accredited Camps**

**American Camping Association**
**5000 State Road 67 N**
**Martinsville, IN  46151**          765-342-8456
                                     800-428-2267
                                     FAX 765-349-6357
                                     TDY:765-342-8456
                                     http://www.acacamps.org
                                     e-mail: bookstore@acacamps.org
*Melody Snider, Bookstore Director*
*Harriet Gamble, Director of Communications*

A national listing of accredited camping programs.
Listed by activity, special clientele, camp name, and
specific disabilities. *$14.95*

*285 pages  Annually*
*ISBN 0-876031-66-1*

**389  Guide to Summer Camps and Summer Schools**

**Porter Sargent Publishers**
**11 Beacon Street**
**Boston, MA  02108**          617-523-1670
                               800-342-7470
                               FAX 603-669-7945
                               http://www.portersargent.com
                               e-mail: orders@portersargent.com
*Dan McKeever, Senior Editor*
*John Yonce, General Manager*
*Leslie Weston, Production Manager*

Covers a broad spectrum of recreational and educational summer opportunities in the US and abroad.
Current facts from 1300 camps and schools, as well as
programs for those with special needs and disabilities.
*$27.00*

*640 pages  Biannual/Paper*
*ISBN 0-875581-45-5*

**390  Learning Disabilities: Guide for Directors of Specialized Camps**

**Learning Disabilities Association of America**
**4156 Library Road**
**Pittsburgh, PA  15234**          412-341-1515
                                   FAX 412-344-0224
                                   http://www.ldaamerica.org
                                   e-mail: info@ldaamerica.org
*Jane Browning, Executive Director*
*Marianne Toombs, President*

*$6.50*

**391  Learning Disabled: Camp Directors Guide on Integration**

**Learning Disabilities Association of America**
**4156 Library Road**
**Pittsburgh, PA  15234**          412-341-1515
                                   FAX 412-344-0224
                                   http://www.ldaamerica.org
                                   e-mail: info@ldaamerica.org
*Jane Browning, Executive Director*
*Marianne Toombs, President*

*$6.50*

## Alabama

**392  Camp ASCCA**

**Easter Seals of Alabama**
**PO Box 21**
**Jacksons Gap, AL  36861**          256-825-9226
                                     800-843-2267
                                     FAX 256-825-8332
                                     http://www.alabama.easter-seals.org
                                     e-mail: info@campascca.org
*Matt Rickman, Camp Director*
*John Stevenson, Administrator*

Helps children and adults with disabilities achieve
equality, dignity and maximum independence. This is
to be accomplished through a safe and quality program of camping, recreation and education in a
year-round barrier-free environment. Founded 1976.

**393  Easter Seals Gulf Coast**

**2448 Gordon Smith Drive**
**Mobile, AL  36617**          251-471-1581
                               800-411-0068
                               FAX 251-476-4303
                               e-mail: esmob@zebra.net
*Frank Harkins, CEO*
*Loretta Yound, Office Manager*

Camperships camping and recreation services offered.

## Arizona

**394  Easter Seals Arizona**

**Easter Seals Arizona**
**2075 S Cootonwood Drive**
**Tempe, AZ  85004 1996**          602-252-6061
                                   800-626-6061
                                   FAX 602-252-6065
                                   e-mail: brian@azseals.org
*Michael Sitzterald, Chief Executive Officer*

The following are camping and recreation services offered: Adventure, camp respite for children,
camperships, canoeing, day camping for children,
recreational services for children and water skiing.

**395  Easter Seals Tucson**

**7634 North La Cholla Boulevard**
**Tucson, AZ  85711**          520-745-5222
                               FAX 520-745-9030
*Bernard Kennady, Office Manager*

The following are camping and recreation services offered: Camp respite for children.

## Arkansas

**396   Easter Seals Adult Services Center**
**Easter Seals Adult Services Center**
**11801 Fairview Road**
**Little Rock, AR  72212**                501-221-8400
                                          877-533-3600
                              FAX 501-221-8842
                   e-mail: mail@easter-seals.org
*Sharon Moone-Jochums, President/CEO*
*Johnny Baldwin, Vice President*

Day camping for children. Founded 1976.

## California

**397   Easter Seals Bay Area: San Jose**
**Easter Seals Bay Area**
**730 Empey Way**
**San Jose, CA  95128**                   408-295-0228
                              FAX 408-275-9858
                        http://www.esba.org
                   e-mail: polson@esba.org
*Peter Olson, Director Health & Wellness*
*Cheryl Bergevin, Office Manager*

Recreational services for adults.

**398   Easter Seals Bay Area: Tri-Valley Campus**
**7425 Larkdale Avenue**
**Dublin, CA  94568**                     925-828-8857
                              FAX 925-828-5245
            http://www.easter-sealsbayarea.com
                   e-mail: kcarnahan@esba.org
*Bryant Potts, Service Supervisor*
*Ron Halog, Program Manager*

Recreational services for adults.

**399   Easter Seals Central California**
**9010 Soquel Drive**
**Aptos, CA  95003 4002**                 831-684-2166
                              FAX 831-685-6055
            http://www.centralcal.easterseals.com
              e-mail: centralcal@easterseals.com
*Donna Alvarez, Vice President Finance & Service*
*Bruce Hinman, President*

The following are camping and recreational services offered: Recreational services for adults, residential camping programs and therapeutic horseback riding.

**400   Easter Seals Central California: Camp Harmon**
**9010 Soquel Drive**
**Aptos, CA  95006**                      831-684-2380
                              FAX 831-684-1018
            http://www.centralcal.easterseals.com
                   e-mail: jennifer@es-cc.org
*Jennifer Johnson, Camping Services Coordinator*
*Bruce Hinman, President*

The following are camping and recreational services offered: Easter Seals own and operated camps and residential camping programs.

**401   Easter Seals Eureka**
**3289 Edgewood Road**
**Eureka, CA  95501**                     707-445-8841
                                          800-675-7325
                              FAX 707-445-3106
            e-mail: hgale@noca-ea-easterseals.com
*Helen Gale, Program Manager*
*Kathy Cook, Office Manager*

The following are camping and recreational services offered: Camperships, computer program, day camping for children, recreational services for adults and recreational services for children.

**402   Easter Seals Monterey**
**9010 Soquel Drive**
**Aptos, CA  93942**                      831-684-2166
                              FAX 831-684-1018
                   e-mail: dalvarez@es-cc.org
*Donna Alvarez, Vice President Finance & Service*
*Bruce Hinman, President*

Recreational services for adults.

**403   Easter Seals Northern California**
**20 Pimentel Court**
**Novato, CA  94949**                     415-382-7450
                              FAX 415-382-6052
            http://www.noca.easter-seals.com
              e-mail: jreinhardt@ca-no.easter-seals.org
*Jackie Reinhardt, President/CEO*
*Janet Clarke, Administrative Assistant*

The following are camping and recreational services offered: Before/After school program (Ages 6 through 18), camp respite for adults, camperships, recreational services for adults and recreational services for children.

**404   Easter Seals Northern California: RohnertPark**
**5440 State Farm Drive**
**Rohnert Park, CA  94928**               707-584-1443
                                          800-234-7325
                              FAX 707-584-3438
                              TDY:707-584-1889
            http://www.noc.easterseals.com
              e-mail: skreuzer@ca-no.easter-seals.org
*Susanne Kreuzer, Vice President Program Services*
*Jackie Rainheadt, Senior President*

The folllowing are camping and recreational services offered: Camp respite for adults, camperships, day camping for children, recreational services for children and residential camping programs.

**405   Easter Seals Superior California**
**3205 Hurley Way**
**Sacramento, CA  95864 3898**            916-485-6711
                                          888-877-3257
                              FAX 916-485-6711
            http://www.easterseals-superiorca.org
              e-mail: info@easterseals-superiorca.org
*Gary Kasai, President/CEO*
*Joanna Budd, Manager*

Camping and recreational services offered are: Swim programs.

**406  Easter Seals Superior California: Stockton**
102 W Bianchi Road
Stockton, CA  95207 7132          209-473-0441
                                 FAX 209-473-4128
        http://www.easterseals-superiorca.org
        e-mail: info@easterseals-superiorca.org
*Gary Kasai, President/CEO*
*Joanna Budd, Manager*

Camping and recreational services offered are: Swim programs.

**407  Easter Seals Tri-Counties California**
**National Organization of Easter Seals**
10730 Henderson Road
Ventura, CA  93004 1898          805-647-1141
                                 FAX 805-647-1148
        http://www.ca_tr.easterseals.com
        e-mail: eastertc@pacbell.net
*Jamie Polis, Assistant Aquatic Director*

Camping and recreational services offered are: Camperships and swim programs.

**408  Los Angeles School of Gymnastics Day Camp**
8450 Higuera Street
Culver City, CA  90232          310-204-1980
                                888-849-6627
                                FAX 310-204-6864
        http://www.lagymnastics.com
        e-mail: info@lagymnastics.com
*Alla Svirsky, Executive Director*
*Tanya Barber, General Manager*

Runs summer and winter camps for boys and girls. Founded 1975.

## Colorado

**409  Easter Seals Camp Rocky Mountain Village**
PO Box 115
Empire, CO  80438          303-569-2333
                           FAX 303-569-3857
        e-mail: campinfo@cess.org
*Roman Krafczyk, Camp Director*

Camping and recreational services are: Adventure, camp respite for adults, camp respite for children, camperships, conference rental, family retreats, recreational services for adults, recreational services for children, residential camping programs, swim programs and therapeutic horseback riding.

**410  Easter Seals Colorado**
5755 W Alameda Avenue
Lakewood, CO  80226 3500          303-233-1666
                                  FAX 303-233-1028
*Lynn Robinson, CEO*

Camping and recreational services offered are: Swim programs.

**411  Easter Seals Southern Colorado**
225 S Academy Boulevard
Colorado Springs, CO  80910 2768  719-574-9002
                                  FAX 719-574-1330
        http://www.co-so.easterseals.com
        e-mail: contactus@easter-sealssc.org
*Paula Waldera-Hundt, Project Director*
*Christine Bucher, Executive Director*

Camping and recreational services offered: Camp respite for adults, camp respite for children and camperships.

**412  Learning Camp**
PO Box 1146
Vail, CO  81658          970-524-2706
                         FAX 970-524-4178
        http://www.learningcamp.com
        e-mail: info@learningcamp.com
*Ann Cathcart, Founder/Director*
*Tom Macht, Director*

Summer camp that focuses on helping children with learning disabilities, such as dyslexia, ADD, ADHD and other learning challenges.

## Connecticut

**413  CREC Summer School**
**Administrator Capitol Education Council**
111 Charter Oak Avenue
Hartford, CT  06106          860-298-9079
                             877-850-2832
                             FAX 860-246-3304
        http://www.crec.org
        e-mail: pfernandez@rss.crec.org
*Paula Fernandez, Executive Director/Case Worker*

Offers an educationally oriented program with recreational opportunities, strong behavior management and highly structured groupings.

**414  Camp Hemlocks Easter Seals**
**Smith Street**
Hebron, CT  06248          617-226-2640
                           800-244-2756
                           FAX 508-751-6444
        http://www.eastersealsma.org
        e-mail: rozf@eastersealsma.org

Offers an environment that allows campers with disabilities optimal independence.

**415  Camp Horizons**
PO Box 323
South Windham, CT  06266          860-456-1032
                                  FAX 860-456-4721
        http://www.camphorizons.org
        e-mail: staffpage@camphorizons.org
*Chris McNaboe, Executive Director*
*Janice Chamberlain, Associate Director*
*Lauren Perrotti, Director*

To provide high quality residential, recreational, support and work programs for people who are developmentally disabled or who have other challenging social and emotional needs.

**416  Camp Lark**

**Litchfield County Association for Retarded Citizen**
**84 Main Street**
**Torrington, CT  06790**          860-482-9364
                                  FAX 860-489-2492
*Katherine Marchand-Beyer, Director Community*
*Services*

Program offers arts and crafts, swimming, field sports, archery, outdoor education, music, drama and adventure courses. Once a week overnights are offered and the program runs in conjunction with the Torrington YMCA camp, Northwest YMCA, Camp Torymca. Additional staff supports are available when needed.

**417  Camp Tepee**

**204 Stanley Road**
**Monroe, CT  06468**             203-261-2566
                                  FAX 203-261-3146
*Dawn Dalryntle, Executive Director*
*Sally Schoonmaker, Office Manager*

Each summer, over 1,700 campers experience exciting thrills and make memories that last a lifetime. We are a fully modernized facility located on 47 beautiful acres nestled in the Stephney section of Monroe, CT. We pride ourselves on providing a safe and nurturing environment in which children of all ages conquer new challenges, make new friends, and share in the unique and wonderful experience that is day camp.

**418  Cyber Launch Pad**

**Learning Incentive**
**139 N Main Street**
**West Hartford, CT  06107**      860-236-5807
                                  FAX 860-233-9945
         http://www.tli.com/learningincentive.com
               e-mail: tli@learningincentive.com
*Aileen Stan-Spence MD, Director*
*Mary Austin, Office Manager*

Half days camp where children and their parents learn to use Cyberslate which is learning keyboarding, word processing, programming and remedial sessions in reading, writing and arithmetic for learning disabled children.

**419  Eagle Hill Southport School**

**214 Main Street**
**Southport, CT  06490**          203-254-2044
                                  FAX 203-255-4052
              http://www.eaglehillsouthport.org
              e-mail: info@eaglehillsouthport.org
*Lea Sylvertro, Administrative Assistant*
*Dede Warner, Administrative Assistant*

The summer program at Eagle Hill is designed to help students 6 to 13 years old maintain their academic progress.

**420  Eagle Hill Summer Program**

**45 Glenville Road**
**Greenwich, CT  06831**          203-622-9240
                                  FAX 203-622-0914
              http://www.eaglehillschool.org
              e-mail: info@eaglehillschool.org
*Mark Griffin, Director*
*Abby Hanrahan, Teacher Camp*

Designed for children experiencing academic difficulty. Open to boys and girls ages 5-11.

**421  East Hartford Special Education Camp**

**East Hartford Park and Recreation Department**
**50 Chapman Place**
**East Hartford, CT  06108**      860-528-1458
                                  FAX 860-282-8239
              http://www.ci.east-hartford.ct.us
*Roger Moss, Director*
*Jim Uhrij, Assistant Director*

For East Hartford residents only. A day camp offering swimming, sports, arts and crafts, projects, music and field trips.

**422  Easter Seals Camp Hemlocks**

**85 Jones Street**
**Hebron, CT  06248**             860-228-9496
                                  800-832-4409
                                  FAX 860-228-2091
              e-mail: johnq@eastersealsofct.org
*Mark Kline, Director Camping & Recreation*

Camping and recreational services offered are: Camp respite for adults, camp respite for children, camperships, computer program, conference rental, family retreats, recreational services for adults, recreational services for children, residential camping programs and swim programs.

**423  Haddam-Killingworth Recreation Department**

**95 Little City Road**
**Higganum, CT  06441**           860-345-8334
                                  FAX 860-345-8252
              http://www.hkrec.com
              e-mail: hkrec@snet.net
*Frank Sparks, Director*
*Robyne Brennan, Assistant Director*

Programs offered include arts and crafts, games, sports workshops, field trips, movies, special events and a carnival.

**424  Kiwanis Easter Seal Day Camp**

**Easter Seal Rehabilitation Center**
**Munson Road**
**Wolcott, CT  06716**            203-879-2343
*Alice Hubbell, Director*
*Ronnie Genova, Manager*

Programs offered include swimming, athletics, camping, hiking, outdoor education, music activities, arts and crafts and special day activities.

**425 Marvelwood Summer**
Marvelwood School
PO Box 3001
Kent, CT 06757          860-927-0047
                        800-440-9107
                   FAX 860-927-0021
http://www.themarvelwoodschool.net
e-mail: marvelwood.school@snet.net
*Todd Holt, Director Admissions*
*Katherine Almquist, Director Summer Admissions*

A coeducational boarding and day school enrolling 150 students in grades 9-12. Provides an environment in which young people of varying abilities and learning needs can prepare for success in college and in life. In a nurturing, structured community, students who have not thrived academically in traditional settings are guided and motivated to reach and exceed their personal potential.

**426 Middletown Summer Day Programs**
Middletown Parks and Recreation Department
319 Butternut Street
Middletown, CT 06457     860-343-6620
                    FAX 860-344-3319
*Wesley Downing, Director*

These camps offer a variety of recreational and social activities. Each camp will be integrated with at least 12% population of children with disabilities. Campers must be Middletown residents.

**427 Milford Recreation Department Camp Happiness**
70 W River Street
Milford, CT 06460        203-783-3280
                    FAX 203-783-3284
http://www.ci.milford.ct.us/parkrec.html
e-mail: cschneider@ci.milford.ct.us
*Marelene Sanchez, Director Summer Camp*
*Paul Tiscitelli, Recreation Supervisor*

A camp specifically designed for learning disabled children from the Milford area.

**428 Norwalk Public Schools: Special Education Summer Programs**
125 E Avenue
Norwalk, CT 06851        203-854-4133
                    FAX 203-854-4125
http://www.norwalkpublicschool.net
e-mail: corda@norwalkpublicschool.net
*Salvador Corda, Superintendent*
*Barbara Sacks, Assistant*

Offers pre-school/elementary students developmental and remedial academics.

**429 Shriver Summer Developmental Program**
Nathan Hale School
5 Taylor Road
Enfield, CT 06082        860-763-8899
                    FAX 860-763-8897
http://www.ensieldschool.org
e-mail: leann.beaulieu@ensieldschool.org
*Leann Beaulieu, Principal*
*Kathi Steinert, Assistant Principal*

Academic/recreational program including instructional swimming for the learning disabled.

**430 Timber Trails Camps**
Connecticut Valley Girl Scout Council
340 Washington Street
Hartford, CT 06106       860-522-0163
                    FAX 860-548-0325
http://www.girlscouts-ct.org
e-mail: info@girlscouts-ct.org
*Theresa Miller, Camps Director*
*Janet Kissin, Acting Director*

All girls age 6 to 17 who can function in a group in a mainstream environment are welcome, including those with chronic illnesses, learning disabilities, and physcial or emotional needs.

**431 Wilderness Challenge**
Wheeler Clinic
91 NW Drive
Plainville, CT 06062     860-747-6801
                        800-793-3588
                    FAX 860-793-3520
http://www.wheelerclinic.org
e-mail: alarouche@wheelerclinic.org
*David Berkowitz MD, Executive Director*
*Mary Hess, Director for Research*

A three-week program offering therapeutic outdoor education programs which include a variety of non-competitive group games and activities.

**432 YMCA: Valley-Shore**
201 Spencer Plains Road
Westbrook, CT 06498      860-399-9622
                    FAX 860-399-8349
http://www.vsymca.org
e-mail: ymca@valley.shoresnet.net
*Bryan McFarland, Camp Director*
*Joan Camire, Office Manager*

Day camps which include music, arts and crafts, swimming, hiking, sports, games, nature study, archery and overnight camp outs.

# Delaware

**433 Cedars Academy**
PO Box 103
Bridgeville, DE 19933    302-337-3200
                    FAX 302-337-8496
http://www.cedarsacademy.com
*Mary Pauer, Headmaster*
*Robin Abel, Executive Director*

A seven week program which encourages positive feelings of self worth and increased interpersonal skills. Activities include camping, sailing and art.

## District of Columbia

**434   Summer Camps for Children who are Deaf or Hard of Hearing**

National Deaf Education Network and Clearinghouse

Gallaudet University
Washington, DC  20002            202-651-5000
                                FAX 202-651-5704
                        http://www.pr.gallaudet.edu
                e-mail: public.relations@gallaudet.edu
*I King Jordan, President*
*Paul Kelly, Vice President*

To serve as a comprehensive, multipurpose facility of higher education for deaf and hard of hearing.

## Florida

**435   3D Learner Program**

State Land of Learning Disability Association
3121 NW 108th Drive
Coral Springs, FL  33065          954-341-2578
                                FAX 954-796-3883
                          http://www.3dlearner.com
                      e-mail: succes@3dlearner.com
*Mark Halpert, Co-Director*
*Mira Halpert, Co-Director*

3D Learner Program, a one-week program for struggling students who learn best when they see and experience information. We have had students from all over the US. We address attention, self-esteem and reading with a natural and effective method. Our students make immediate gains and often see significant gains with 3 months.

**436   ΛLERT-US**

Coalition for Independent Living
6800 Forest Hill Boulevard
West Palm Beach, FL  33413        561-966-4288
                                  800-683-7337
                                FAX 561-641-6619
                            http://www.cilo.org
*Shelly Gottsagen, Executive Director*
*Linda Kirtley, Administrative Assistant*

To promote the independence for peole with disabilties.

**437   Easter Seals Florida: Central Florida**

31600 Camp Challenge Road
Sorrento, FL  32776 9729
                                  800-377-3257
                        http://www.fl.easterseals.com
                   e-mail: mguinta@fl.easter-seals.org
*Melissa Guinta, Director Camping & Recreation*

Camping and recreational services offered are: Camp respite for adults, camperships, conference rental and residential camping programs.

**438   Easter Seals Volusia and Flagler Counties**

Easter Seals Volusia and Flagler Counties of Chica
1219 Dunn Avenue
Daytona Beach, FL  32120          386-255-4568
                                  877-255-4568
                                FAX 386-258-7677
                 e-mail: info@fl-vf.easter-seals.org
*Lynn Sinnott, President*
*Catherine Colwell, Vice President*

Camping and recreational services are: Day camping for children.

**439   Eckerd Family Youth Alternatives**

100 N Starcrest Drive
Clearwater, FL  33765             727-461-2990
                                FAX 727-442-5911
                              http://www.eckerd.org
*Karen Waddell, CEO*
*Timmy Doyel, Administrative Assistant*

Designed to combine the wilderness living experience with the reality treatment perspective, the psychology perspective and behavior modification techniques. Founded 1968

**440   YMCA: Lakeland**

3620 Cleveland Heights Boulevard
Lakeland, FL  33803               863-644-3528
                                FAX 863-644-2517
                            http://www.ymcawcs.org
*Alice Colins, CEO*
*Sharon Andrews, Administrative Assistant*

Camp runs June through July, and is coed, ages 12-16.

## Georgia

**441   Easter Seals Southern Georgia**

1906 Palmyra Road
Albany, GA  31701 1598            229-439-7061
                                  800-365-4583
                                FAX 229-435-6278
                e-mail: benglish@swga-easterseals.org
*Beth English, Executive Director*
*Cana Cooper, Assistant of Human Resource*

Camping and recreational services offered are: Camp respite for adults, camp respite for children, day camping for children and therapeutic horseback riding.

**442   Squirrel Hollow**

Bedford School Organization
5665 Milam Road
Fairburn, GA  30213               770-774-8001
                                FAX 770-774-8005
                   http://www.thebedfordschool.org
               e-mail: bbox@thebedfordschool.org
*Betsy Box, Director*
*Bonnie Sides, Secretary*

The five week camp meets on campus of Atlanta Christian College and includes a camping trip in the north Georgia mountains.

## Hawaii

**443  Easter Seals Hawaii: Oahu Service Center**
710 Green Street
Honolulu, HI  96813                   808-536-1015
                                      888-241-7450
                               FAX 808-536-3765
          http://www.eastersealshawaii.org
          e-mail: nicole@eastersealshawaii.org
*Nicole Deligans, Assistant Coordinator*
*Lin Joseth, Director*

Camping and recreational services offered are: Residential camping programs.

## Illinois

**444  Camp Algonquin**
1889 Cary Road
Algonquin, IL  60102                  847-658-8212
                               FAX 847-658-8431
          http://www.campalgonquin.org
          e-mail: info@campalgonquin.org
*Jim Roth, Executive Director*
*Graham Little, Education Director*

To inspire, educate and strengthen individuals, families and groups toward growth, achievement, positive community and environmental stewardship through education, experiential and recreational opportunities.

**445  Camp Little Giant: Touch of Nature Environmental Center**
Southern Illinois University
1208 Touch of Nature Road
Carbondale, IL  62901 6888            618-453-1121
                               FAX 618-453-1188
          http://www.pso.siu.edu/tonec
          e-mail: tonec@tonec.siu.edu
*Randy Osborn, Program Coordinator*
*Chilang Lanlessna, Registrar*

A residential camp program designed to meet the recreational needs of adults and children with disabilities.

**446  Easter Seals Camping and Recreation List**
National Easter Seals Society
230 W Monroe Street
Chicago, IL  60606                    312-726-6200
                                      800-221-6827
                               FAX 312-726-1494
          http://www.easter-seals.com
          e-mail: info@easter-seals.com
*Jim Williams, CEO*
*Rosemary Garza, Interim Specialist*

Various programs with the united purpose of giving disabled children a fun and safe camping or recreational experience. Call for information on activities in your state.

**447  Easter Seals Central Illinois**
2715 N 27th Street
Decatur, IL  62526                    217-429-1052
                               FAX 217-423-7605
          http://www.easterseals-ci.org
          e-mail: info@easterseals-ci.org
*Janet Kelsheimer, President*
*Margie Malone, Office Manager*

The following are Camping and Recreational services offered: Recreational services for adults and recreational services for children.

**448  Easter Seals Jayne Shover Center**
National Easter Seals Society
799 S McLean Boulevard
Elgin, IL  60123                      847-742-3264
                               FAX 847-742-9436
          http://www.il-js.easterseals.com
          e-mail: admin@il-js.easterseals.com
*Susan Dilley, Chief Executive Officer*

The following are Camping and Recreational services offered: Recreational services for adult and recreational services for children.

**449  Easter Seals Joliet**
National Easter Seals Society
212 Barney Drive
Joliet, IL  60435 2830                815-773-9362
                               FAX 815-773-9365
          http://www.joliet.easterseals.com
          e-mail: dcondotti@il-wg.easter-seals.org
*Debra Condotti, President*
*Carol Baces, Human Resource Director*

The following are camping and recreational services offered: Camperships.

**450  Easter Seals Missouri**
602 E 3rd Street
Alton, IL  62002                      618-462-7325
                               FAX 618-462-8170
          http://www.mo.easter-seals.org
          e-mail: mail@mo.easter-seals.org
*Craig Byrd, CEO*
*Susan Gunning, Development Therapist*

The following are camping and recreational services offered: Camperships.

**451  Easter Seals UCP: Peoria**
Easter Seals of Peoria Bloomington
20 Timber Pointe Lane
Hudson, IL  61748                     309-365-8021
                               FAX 309-365-8934
          e-mail: kpodeszwa@easterseals.com
*Kurt Podeszwa, Director Camping/Outdoor Program*
*Jerrilyn Zavata, Registrar*

The following are Camping and Recreational services offered: Recreational services for adults and recreational services for children.

**452  Western Du Page Special Recreation Association**
116 N Schmale Road
Carol Stream, IL  60188       630-681-0962
                             FAX 630-681-1262
                             TDY:630-681-0962
                             http://www.wdsra.com
                             e-mail: info@wdsra.com
*Jane Hodgkinson, Executive Director*
*Nancy Miner, Superintendent Recreation*

Offers year-round recreational services and programs to special residents of its nine member communities.

## Indiana

**453  Camp Brosend: Brosend Ministries**
7599 Brosend Road
Newburgh, IN  47630 2881       812-853-3466
                               FAX 812-853-5585
                    http://www.campbrosend.org
*Kevin Heil, Director*

Campers enjoy a wide variety of program activities while building confidence.

**454  Easter Seals ARC of Northeast Indiana**
2542 Thompson Avenue
Fort Wayne, IN  46807       260-456-4534
                            800-234-7811
                            FAX 260-745-5200
                e-mail: shinkle@easarc.org
*Steve Hinkle, CEO*

The following are camping and recreational services offered: Recreational services for adults and camp respite for adults.

**455  Easter Seals Wayne & Union Counties**
Easter Seals Central Indiana
5632 US Highway 40 E
Centerville, IN  47330 0086       765-855-2482
                                  FAX 765-855-2482
            http://www.eastersealswu.tripod.com
                    e-mail: easterseals@juno.com
*Patricia Powers, Program Director*
*Pat Bowers, Executive Director*

The following are camping and recreational services offered: Camperships and recreational services for children.

**456  Englishton Park Academic Remediation & Training**
PO Box 228
Lexington, IN  47138       812-889-2046
                http://www.englishtonpark.org
                e-mail: tbarnet@venus.net
*Thomas Barnett, Co-Director*
*Lisa Barnett, Co-Director*

To improve academic skills, change attitudes toward learning, modify behavior interferring with learning in the classroom. Founded 1968

## Iowa

**457  Easter Seals Camp Sunnyside**
Easter Seals
401 NE 66th Avenue
Des Moines, IA  50313       515-274-1529
                            FAX 515-274-6434
            e-mail: info@eastersealsia.org
*Claire Lecroy, Director*
*Sherri Nielsen, Administrator*

The following are Camping and Recreational services offered: Adventure, camp respite for children, day camping for children, easter seals own and operated camps and residential camping programs.

## Kentucky

**458  Bethel Mennonite Camp**
2773 Bethel Church Road
Clayhole, KY  41317       606-666-4911
                          FAX 606-666-4216
              http://www.bethelcamp.org
              e-mail: grow@bethelcamp.org
*Roger Voth, Director*

A camp with an emphasis on bible study. Founded 1957

**459  Camp Kysoc**
Kentucky EasterSeal Society
1902 Easterday Road
Carrollton, KY  40504 1499       502-732-5333
                                 FAX 502-732-0783
                  e-mail: fun@kysoc.org
*Jim Edert, Executive Director*
*Tammy Richmond, Assistant Director*

Traditional outdoor camp program.

**460  Easter Seals Camp KYSOC**
Kentucky EasterSeal Society
1902 Easterday Road
Carrolton, KY  40504 1499       502-732-5333
                                FAX 502-732-0783
                  e-mail: fun@kysoc.org
*Jim Edert, Director*
*Tammy Richmond, Assistant Director*

The following are camping and recreational services offered: Camp respite for adults, camp respite for children, camperships, canoeing, day camping for children and family retreats.

**461  Easter Seals Kentucky**
2050 Versailles Road
Lexington, KY  40504 1499       859-254-5701
                                800-888-5377
                                FAX 859-367-7155
                http://www.cardinalhill.org
                e-mail: kgg@cardinalhill.org
*Kerry Gillihan, President/CEO*

The following are camping and recreational services offered: Daycamping for children.

**462  Easter Seals of Northern Kentucky**

31 Spiral Drive
Florence, KY  41042                859-491-1171
                             FAX 859-491-8132
                       http://www.cardinalhill.org
             e-mail: clw@cardinalhill-northernky.org
*Cynthia Lawhorn-Williams, Executive Director*

The following are camping and recreational services
offered: Daycamping for children.

## Louisiana

**463  Easter Seals Louisiana**

National Organization
305 Baronne Street
New Orleans, LA  70112 1617        504-523-7325
                                   800-695-7325
                             FAX 504-523-3465
                       e-mail: essla@aol.com
*Mark Stafford, Corporate Program Director*
*Daniel Underwoods, President*

The following are camping and recreational services
offered: Camperships.

**464  Med-Camps of Louisiana**

102 Thomas Road
West Monroe, LA  71291             318-329-8405
                             FAX 318-329-8407
                       http://www.medcamps.com
                 e-mail: caledseney@medcamps.com
*Caled Seney, Director*
*Gabriel Davison, Vice President*

Regardless of special needs this camp offers participants a sense of well being, belonging, accomplishment and self worth.

## Maine

**465  Camp Waban**

Waban's Projects
5 Dunaway Drive
Sanford, ME  04073                 207-324-7955
                             FAX 207-324-6050
                       http://www.waban.org
                 e-mail: waban@gwi.net
*Jan Fraser, Executive Director*

This program provides campers from a wide
geograhic area a chance to enjoy the outdoors in a
theraputic recreational setting.

## Maryland

**466  Camp Fairlee Manor**

Easter-Seals Delaware
22242 Bay Shore Road
Chestertown, MD  21620             410-778-0566
                             FAX 410-778-0567
                       http://www.de.easterseals.com
                 e-mail: fairlee@esdel.org
*Dan Tabacheck, Camping Director*
*Dessie Rochester, Administrative Assistant*

Dedicated to providing social, recreational and educational activities for participants while helping them
achieve greater independence.

**467  Jemicy Community Outreach**

Jemicy Community Outreach
11 Celadon Road
Owings Mills, MD  21117            410-356-7656
                             FAX 410-653-1972
                       http://www.jemicyschool.org
                 e-mail: dlasalle@jemicyschool.org
*Dave Lasalle, Director*
*Ben Shisrin, Headmaster*

Two special camps for dyslexic children that blends
fun camp activities which includes swimming and nature experiences.

**468  Kamp A-Kom-plish**

9035 Ironsides Road
Nanjemoy, MD  20662                301-870-3226
                             FAX 301-870-2620
                       http://www.kampakomplish.org
                 e-mail: kampakomplish@melwood.com
*Heidi Aldous, Director*

A sleep-away camp for for children and teens aged 8 to
16 years old. Located on 108 acres there are air-condi-
tioned cabins, fishing, boating and trails for hiking.
Founded 1968

## Massachusetts

**469  Camp Half Moon for Boys & Girls**

PO Box 188
Great Barrington, MA  01230        413-528-0940
                             FAX 413-528-0941
                       http://www.camphalfmoon.com
                 e-mail: info@camphalfmoon.com
*Ed Mann, Director/Owner*
*Til Mann, Director/Owner*
*Gretchen Mann, Director/Owner*

The philosophy is based on six principles: structure,
social values, sound learning skills, spirit, guidance
and individuality. Half Moon provides a safe orderly
environment that stresses skill improvement rather
than high competition.

**470    Camp Joy**
**Boston Centers for Youth & Families**
**1483 Tremont Street**
**Roxbury, MA  02120**                    617-635-4920
                                          FAX 617-635-5074
        **e-mail: michaeltriant@ci.boston.ma.us**
*Michael Triant, Program Manager*
*Kevin Stanton, Dir. After/Out School Services*

A therapeutic recreational program for special needs children and adults. Currently serving over 700 participants with a professionally qualified staff of 290 at 15 sites throughout the city. Serves the physically and cognitively challenged, multi-handicapped, behaviorally involved, legally blind/visually impaired, deaf/hearing impaired, learning disabled, and pre-school special needs children.

**471    Camp Lapham**
**731 S Road**
**Ashby, MA  01431**                      781-834-2700
                                          FAX 781-834-2701
   **http://www.crossroads4kids.org/lapham.html**
        **e-mail: office@crossroads4kids.org**
*Ian Moorhouse, Director*

Designed to meet the needs of children who thrive in a small, structured environment. The program emphasis includes anger and behavior management, along with strong self-image building all in a fun, noncompetitive camp atmosphere. With a maximum of 50 children enrolled per session and a low camper to counselor ratio of 1 to 4, the campers experience success in a more family-like atmosphere which enables each child to focus on personal goals and nonviolent methods of interaction.

**472    Camp Polywog**
**Malden YMCA**
**83 Pleasant Street**
**Malden, MA  02148**                     781-324-7680
                                          FAX 781-324-7856
                                          TDY:781-324-7680
*Susan Hogan, Program Director*
*Beth Caneron, Associate Executive Director*

Offers a gym, swimming, city tours and more. Structured recreation that teaches.

**473    Camp Ramah**
**35 Highland Circle**
**Needham, MA  02494**                    781-449-7090
                                          FAX 781-449-6331
            **http://www.campramahne.org**
        **e-mail: billym@campramahne.org**
*Sally Rosensield, Director*
*Erica Silverman, Assistant Manager*

Young people have fun while developing skills, strong friendships and a Jewish conciousness that lasts a lifetime through a variety of experiences such as sports, nature, music, study, Shabbat and Judaica.

**474    Camp Six Acres**
**475 Winthrop Street**
**Medford, MA  02155**                    781-391-2220
                                          FAX 781-393-4864
*Roz Abukasis, Program Director*
*Mary Hoarty, Manager*

Two week camp for mild to moderately mentally impaired children. Transportation is provided free of charge.

**475    Carroll School Summer Camp Summer Camp**
**25 Baker Bridge Road**
**Lincoln, MA  01773**                    781-259-8342
                                          FAX 781-259-8361
            **http://www.carrollschool.org**
        **e-mail: info@carrollschool.org**
*Philp Burling, Head School*

Summer at Carroll is designed to offer academic intervention and remediation to children diagnosed with primary language learning difficulties, such as dyslexia. Small group teaching, individualized instruction and attention to the needs of goals of the students are what Carroll prides themselves on.

**476    Crossroads for Kids**
**119 Myrtle Street**
**Duxbury, MA  02332**                    781-834-2700
                                          888-543-7284
                                          FAX 781-834-2701
            **http://www.crossroads4kids.org**
        **e-mail: office@crossroads4kids.org**
*Jeffery Rumph, Executive Director*

The daily programs provide a good balance between active and quiet, sport, cultural, group and individual activities. We place campers into smaller, age appropriate groups so they receive the extra support, care and encouragement they need to feel at home here at camp.

**477    Easter Seals Massachusetts**
**484 Main Street**
**Worcester, MA  01608 1817**             508-751-6345
                                          800-244-2756
                                          FAX 508-831-9768
            **http://www.eastersealsma.org**
        **e-mail: maryd@eastersealsma.org**
*Mary D'Antonino, Disability Resource Manager*

The following are camping and recreational services offered: Camp respite for adults, camp respite for children, canoeing, computer camp, computer program, day camping for children, residential camping programs, sailing, swim programs, therapeutic horseback riding and water skiing.

**478 Kolburne School Summer ProgramSummer Program**

Kolburne School
343 NM Southfield Road
New Marlborough, MA 01230        413-229-8787
                                FAX 413-229-4165
                        http://www.kolburne.net
                        e-mail: info@kolburne.net
*Jeane Weinstein, Executive Director*
*Christopher Ezzo, Chief Administrator*

A family operated residential treatment center located in the Berkshire Hills of Massachusetts. Through integrated treatment services, effective behavioral management, recreational programming, and positive staff relationships, our students develop the emotional stability, interpersonal skills and academic/vocational background necessary to return home with success.

**479 Landmark Summer Adventure Ropes Program**

Landmark School
429 Hale Street
Prides Crossing, MA 01965        978-236-3010
                                FAX 978-927-7268
                        http://www.landmarkschool.org
                        e-mail: jbloom@landmarkschool.org
*Robert Broudo, Headmaster*
*Carolyn Orsini, Director of Admission*

The adventure ropes program offers students 10 years and older an opportunity to spend part of their summer experience in an outdoor adventure-based program. Students spend half the day on the ropes understanding group dynamics and developing self esteem. They spend the next half of the day in a one-to-one language tutorial, a math class, and a language arts class.

**480 Landmark Summer Marine Science Program**

Landmark School
429 Hale Street
Prides Crossing, MA 01965        978-236-3010
                                FAX 978-927-7268
                        http://www.landmarkschool.org
                        e-mail: jbl@landmarkschool.org
*Robert Broudo, Headmaster Admission*
*Carolyn Orsini, Director of Admission*

A program offered to students who are interested in the natural and physical world. Students spend half the day exploring local coastal ecosystems, working on research teams and collecting data. The other half of the day is spent in academic or preparatory classes in which students develop their language skills through a one on one tutorial and language arts and math classes.

**481 Landmark Summer Seamanship Program**

Landmark School
429 Hale Street
Prides Crossing, MA 01965        978-236-3010
                                FAX 978-927-7268
                        http://www.landmarkschool.org
                        e-mail: jbloom@landmarkschool.org
*Robert Broudo, Headmaster*
*Carolyn Orsini, Director of Admission*

Students attend academic classes for half of the school day and learn seamanship and sailing skills during the other half.

**482 Patriots' Trail Girl Scout Council SummerCamp**

985 Berkeley Street
Boston, MA 02116                 617-350-8335
                                FAX 617-482-9045
                                TDY:800-882-1662
                http://www.ptgirlscouts.org/camp.htm
                e-mail: SummerCamp@ptgirlscouts.org
*Mimi Moran, President*
*Shannon O'brien, Chief Executive Officer*

Canoeing, swimming, windsurfing, life-saving, sailing, biking and trips.

**483 Ramah in New England**

Camp Ramah
39 Bennett Street
Palmer, MA 01069                 413-283-9771
                                FAX 781-449-6331
                        http://www.campramahne.org
                        e-mail: billym@campramahne.org
*Billy Mencow, Director*
*Joel Stavsky, Business Manager*

Offers a special program to meet the social and religious needs of developmentally challenged Jewish adolescents. The program provides the youth with a full experience in boating, swimming, sports, and the arts.

**484 Valleyhead**

79 Reservoir Road
Lenox, MA 01240                  413-637-3635
                                FAX 413-637-3501
                        http://www.valleyhead.org
                        e-mail: cmacbeth@valleyhead.org
*Christine Macbeth ACSW LICSW, Executive Director*

A residential school for girls nestled in the scenic Berkshire Hills of Lenox, Massachusetts. We provide a home and education for girls ages 12-22 with emotional needs. Most of our girls come from abusive and traumatic backgrounds.

# Michigan

**485 Adventure Learning Center at Eagle Village**

5044 175th Avenue
Hersey, MI 49639                 231-832-1424
                                 800-748-0061
                                FAX 231-832-1468
                        http://www.eaglevillage.org
                        e-mail: alc@eaglevillage.org
*Jeremy Shafer, Summer Camp Director*
*Mark Anderson, Program Manager*

Offers a variety of fun camp experiences for any child, including those with emotional and/or behavioral impairments. Challenging activities make the camps rewarding experiences.

**486    Easter Seals Genesee County**
1420 W Third Avenue
Flint, MI  48504 4897            810-238-0475
                                 FAX 810-238-9270
        e-mail: kwright@essmichigan.org
*Kindra Wright, Executive Director*
*Rosemary Parnow, Office Manager*

The following are camping and recreational services offered: Recreational services for adults, recreational services for children, residential camping programs and therapeutic horseback riding.

**487    Easter Seals Michigan**
4065 Saladin Drive SE
Grand Rapids, MI  49546 6299     616-942-2081
                                 800-75-SEALS
                                 FAX 616-942-5932
                                 TDY:248-338-1188
        http://www.essmichigan.org
*John Kersten, President*
*John Collison, Chairman*

The following are camping and recreational services offered: Camperships.

**488    Easter Seals Michigan: Saginaw**
Easter Seals Michigan
1401 North Michigan
Saginaw, MI  48602 1516          989-797-0880
                                 800-757-3257
                                 FAX 989-797-0888
        http://www.esfmichigan.org
        e-mail: esofmi@aol.comesfmichigan.org
*Julie Dorcey, Regional Director*
*Sue Combs, Administrative Assistant*

The following are camping and recreational services offered: Camperships.

**489    Fowler Center Summer Camp**
2315 Harmon Lake Road
Mayville, MI  48744              989-673-2050
                                 FAX 989-673-6355
        http://www.thefowlercenter.org
        e-mail: info@thefowlercenter.org
*John Fowler, Chairman/Founder*
*Tom Hussnann, Executive Director*

The Fowler Center is an outdoor recreation and education facility that provides programs with paraticular emphasis on people with developmental and physical disabilities.

---
# Minnesota
---

**490    Camp Buckskin**
PO Box 389
Ely, MN  55731                   218-365-2121
        http://www.campbuckskin.com
        e-mail: buckskin@spacestar.net
*Tom Bauer, Director*

Buckskin operates a therapeutic summer program for youth with ADD/ADHD and related difficulties. We have two 32-day sessions which utilize a combination of traditional camp activities and academics (reading, writing, environmental education) to allow multiple successes which develop self-confidence and improves self-esteem. High staff to camper ratio provides individualized instruction. The program is supportive, yet provides adequate structure to improve social skills and peer relations.

**491    Camp Chi Rho**
9 Rustic Lodge W
Minneapolis, MN  55409           612-827-7123
                                 FAX 612-825-8824
        http://www.chirhocenter.org
        e-mail: sjchirho@aol.com
*Sandra Rader, Camp Director*
*James Greenlee, Executive Director*

A year round ecumenical retreat and conference center available for rental.

**492    Camp Confidence**
1620 Mary Fawcett Memorial Drive
East Gull Lake, MN  56401        218-828-2344
                                 FAX 218-828-2618
        http://www.campconfidence.com
        e-mail: info@campconfidence.com
*Jeff Olsen, Executive Director*
*Shelli Fairone, Office Manager*

A year-round center for persons with developmental disabilities specializing in recreation and outdoor education. Aimed at promoting self confidence and self esteem and the necessary skills to become full, contributing members of society.

**493    Camp Friendship**
Friendship Ventures
10509 108th Street NW
Annandale, MN  55302             952-852-0101
                                 800-450-8376
                                 FAX 952-852-0123
        http://www.friendshipventures.org
        e-mail: fv@friendshipventures.org
*Georgann Rumsey, President*

A summer resident camp that is open to anyone five or older who has developmental and/or physical disabilities.

**494    Winnebago**
19708 Camp Winnebago Road
Caledonia, MN  55921             507-724-2351
                                 FAX 507-724-3786
        http://www.campwinnebago.org
*Theresa Burroughs, Director*
*Cathy Greeley, Director*

## Nebraska

**495** **Camp Easter Seals**
National Easter Seals Society
7171 Mercy Road
Omaha, NE 68106                   402-345-2200
                              FAX 402-345-2500
http://www.ne.easter-seals.com
e-mail: mtufte@ne.easter-seals.com
*Mike Tufte, Camp Director*
*Joanne Schulte, Product Support*

Residential camp for people with disabilities. Encourages independence, social development and self confidence.

**496** **Camp Kitaki YMCAYMCA**
6000 Cornhusker Highway
Lincoln, NE 68507                 402-434-9225
                              FAX 402-434-9226
http://www.ymcalincoln.org
e-mail: campkitaki@ymcalincoln.org
*Chris Klingenberg, Camp Director*
*Barb Bettin, President*

A Christian camp for children with ADD and other disabilities. Archery, climbing, horseback riding, fishing and aquatic activities are some of the activities.

**497** **Easter Seals Nebraska**
National Easter Seals Society
7171 Mercy Road
Omaha, NE 68106                   402-345-2200
                                  800-650-9880
                              FAX 402-345-2500
e-mail: mtufte@ne.easter-seals.com
*Mike Tufte, Camp Recreation & Respite*
*Joanne Schulte, Product Support*

The following are camping and recreational services offered: Camp respite for adults, camp respite for children, camperships, recreational services for children and residential camping programs.

## New Hampshire

**498** **Camp Calumet Lutheran**
Ossipee Lake Road
Ossipee, NH 03890                 603-539-3223
                              FAX 603-539-3385
http://www.calumet.org/contact.htm
e-mail: boomchickaboom@calumet.org
*Donald Johnson, Executive Director*

Families and adults, young and not so young come to this beautiful site for fellowship, relaxation and a Christian community atmosphere.

**499** **Camp Runels**
270 Gage Hill Road
Pelham, NH 03076                  603-635-1662
                              FAX 603-635-2366
*Karen Martin, Program Director*

General camping, aquatics, arts, drama, hiking, sailing and more.

**500** **Easter Seals Camp Carpenter**
555 Auburn Street
Manchester, NH 03103              603-623-8863
                                  800-870-8728
                              FAX 603-625-1148
http://www.eastersealsnh.org
*Larry Gammon, President/Chief Executive Office*
*Betty Burke, Assistant Executive Officer*

Promote and assure maximum independence and quality of life for people with disabilities and their families.

**501** **Easter Seals New Hempshire**
555 Auborn Strreet
Manchester, NH 03103              603-621-3601
                                  800-870-8728
                              FAX 603-625-1148
http://www.eastersealsnh.org
e-mail: Eastersealsnh@eastersealsnh.org
*Heather Rich, Camp Director*

The following are camping and recreational services offered: Camp respite for adults, camperships, day camping for children, recreational services for children and residential camping programs.

## New Jersey

**502** **Alpine Scout Camp**
Boy Scout of America
Route 9W
Alpine, NJ 07620                  201-768-1910
                              FAX 201-784-1663
*Tony Cardiello, Director*
*Nelita Barreto, Director*

Offers short term camping for scouts.

**503** **Camp Merry Heart Easter SealsEaster Seals**
Easter Seals of New Jersey
21 O'Brien Road
Hackettstown, NJ 07840            908-852-3896
                              FAX 908-852-9263
http://www.eastersealsmj.org
e-mail: campmerryheart@mendhamrotary.org
*Alex Humanick, Director Camping*
*Mary Simpson, Office Manager*

A coed camp for people with disabilities.

**504** **Camp Tikvah**
Jewish Community Center on the Palisades
411 E Clinton Avenue
Tenafly, NJ 07670                 201-569-7900
                              FAX 201-569-7448
http://www.jcconthepalisades.org
*Shmuel Abramson, Coordinator*

Camp Tikvah is designed to meet the special needs of children and adolescents who have been classified with mild neurological and/or perceptual impairment.

**505**  **Easter Seals Camp Merry Heart**
21 O'Brien Road
Hackettstown, NJ 07840          908-852-3896
                              FAX 908-852-9263
                          http://www.eastersealnj
                e-mail: ahumanick@nj.easter-seals.org
*Alex Humanick, Director*
*Mary Simpson, Office Manager*

The following are camping and recreational services offered: Camp respite for adults, camperships, canoeing, day camping for children, recreational services for adults and residential camping programs.

**506**  **Elks Camp Moore**
New Jersey Elks Association
PO Box 375
Pompton Lakes, NJ 07083          973-835-1542
                              FAX 973-835-4125
                              TDY:609-271-0138
                    e-mail: elkscampmoore@aol.com
*Todd Garmer, Director*
*Laurid Miller, Assistant Director*

Serving children with asthma, behavior disorders and learning disabilities. Activities include hiking, water sports and arts and crafts.

**507**  **Harbor Hills Day Camp**
75 Doby Road
Mt Freedom, NJ 07970          973-895-3200
                              FAX 973-895-7239
                              http://www.hhdc.com
                          e-mail: info@hhdc.com
*Robyn Tanny, Executive Director*

A seven-week, co-ed day camp for children ages 5-15 with special needs. Provides a nurturing and supportive summer. The camp is oriented towards youngsters with learning disabilities and/or attention deficit disorders. It may also be appropriate for children with other types of learning challenges.

**508**  **Round Lake Camp**
21 Plymouth Street
Fairfield, NJ 07004          973-575-3333
                              FAX 973-575-4188
                    http://www.roundlakecamp.org/
                          e-mail: rlc@njycamps.org
*Eugene Bell, Contact*

A camp for children who have been identified with ADD, and/or mild social disorders.

## New Mexico

**509**  **Easter Seals New Mexico**
2819 Richmond Drive NE
Albuquerque, NM 87107 1918          505-888-3811
                                    800-279-5261
                              FAX 505-888-0490
                          e-mail: esnm1@aol.com
*Marlis Hadley, President/CEO*

The following are camping and recreational services offered: Residential camping programs.

## New York

**510**  **Camp Agape Pioneer Retreat Center Pioneer Retreat Center**
9324 Lake Shore Road
Angola, NY 14006          716-549-1420
                              FAX 716-549-6018
                          http://www.pioneercamp.org
                          e-mail: pioneercamp@wzrd.com
*Linda Gage, Executive Director*
*Christi Julis, Program Director*

Offers a variety of activities for growing in faith and in service towards one another. Children, teens, adults and seniors are welcome all summer.

**511**  **Camp Dunnabeck at kildonan SchoolKildonan School**
425 Morse Hill Road
Amenia, NY 12501          845-373-8111
                              FAX 845-373-9793
                          http://www.kildonan.org
*Bonnie Wilson, Director of Admissions*

Specializes in helping intelligent children with specific reading, writing and spelling disabilities. Provides Orton-Gillingham tutoring with camp activities, including swimming, sailing, waterskiing, horseback riding, ceramics, tennis and woodworking.

**512**  **Camp HASC**
5902 14th Ave
Brooklyn, NY 11219
                              http://www.hasc.net
                          e-mail: chayam.hasc@verizon.net
*Chaya Miller, Director*

Provides over 300 mentally and physcially handicapped children and adults with the opportunity to enjoy a seven week sleep away camp experience.

**513**  **Camp Huntington**
56 Bruceville Road
High Falls, NY 12440          845-687-7840
                              FAX 845-687-7211
                          http://www.kidscamps.com
                          e-mail: camphtgtn@aol.com
For boys and girls with learning disabilities and developmental disabilities, ADD and PDD.

**514  Camp Kehilla**

**Sid Jacobson Jewish Community Center**
**300 Forest Drive**
**East Hills, NY  11548**          516-484-1545
                              FAX 516-484-7354
                        e-mail: afields@jcca.org
*Ashley Fields, Director*

A summer day camp for high functioning children and teens with minimal learning disabilities, speech and language delays and ADHD.


**515  Camp Northwood**

**132 State Route 365**
**Remsen, NY  13438**          315-831-3621
                              FAX 315-831-5867
                        http://www.nwood.com
                    e-mail: campinfo@nwood.com
*Gordon Felt, Director/Owner*
*Donna Felt, Director/Owner*

Oriented toward a population of socially immature, isolated, nonaggresive children ranging in age from 8-18 that experience difficulties in social and academic settings due to a variety of types of learning challenges.


**516  Camp Pa-Qua-Tuck**

**PO Box 677**
**Center Moriches, NY  11934**     631-878-1070
                              FAX 631-878-2596
            http://www.camppaquatuck.org/contact.html
                e-mail: camppaquatuck@webtv.net
*Garrett Nagle PhD, Executive Director*

Handicapped children experience the joys of boating, fishing, campfires and more. In a supportive, enriching environment they are encouraged to reach beyond the limits of their handicaps and join with their fellow campers in activities designed to enhance their lives.


**517  Camp Sunshine-Camp Elan**

**Mosholu-Montefiore Community Center**
**3450 Dekalb Avenue**
**Bronx, NY  10467**          718-882-4000
                              FAX 718-882-6369
                        http://www.mmcc.org
                    e-mail: daycamp@mmcc.org
*Mike Halpern, Director*
*Donald Blustone, Assistant Director*

Serves children who are intellectually limited, emotionally impaired and/or demonstrate special learning disabilities.


**518  Coda's Day Camp**

**Community Opportunity Development Agency**
**564 Thomas S Boyland Street**
**Brooklyn, NY  11212**          718-345-4779
*Emil DeLoache MD, Director*


**519  Cross Island YMCA Day Camp**

**23810 Hillside Avenue**
**Bellerose, NY  11426**          718-479-0505
                              FAX 718-465-1665
                http://www.ymcanyc.org/crossislands
                    e-mail: mwright@mcanyc.org
*Michele Wright, Director*

Day camp offers opportunity to improve self esteem through age appropriate, structured activities and trips.


**520  Easter Seals Albany**

**Easter Seals New Hampshire**
**292 Washington Avenue Extension**
**Albany, NY  12203**          518-456-4880
                              800-727-8785
                        FAX 518-456-5094
                e-mail: info@ny.easter-seals.org
*Larry Gammon, President*
*Althea Whitmore, Administrative Assistant*

The following are camping and recreational services offered: Camp respite for children, camperships, day camping for children and recreational services for children.


**521  Easter Seals East Rochester**

**International Easter Seals**
**349 W Commercial Street**
**East Rochester, NY  14445 2402**     585-264-9550
                              FAX 585-264-9547
                        http://www.easterseals.org
                e-mail: info@ny.easter-seals.org
*Larry Gammon, President*
*Michael Donneloy, Vice President*

The following are camping and recreational services offered: Recreational services for children.


**522  GAP Summer Program**

**Syosset/Woodbury Community Park**
**977 Hicksville Road**
**Massapequa, NY  11758**          516-797-7900
                              FAX 516-797-7919
                    http://www.oysterbaytown.com
*Mary Ryan, Director*
*Mary Hurst, Assistant Director*

A program for children with mental and learning disabilities.


**523  Gow Summer Programs**

**Emery Road**
**South Wales, NY  14139**          716-655-2900
                              FAX 716-652-3457
                        http://www.gow.org
                    e-mail: summer@gow.org
*Brett Marcoux, Director*
*Lorri Beefing, Secretary to the Director*

For boys and girls who have experienced past academic difficulties and have learning differences but possess the potential for success.

**524   Harlem Branch YWCA Summer Day Camp**
YWCA
154 W 127th Street
New York, NY  10027          212-283-8543
                              FAX 212-491-3178
*Charles Taylor, Director*
*Elaine Edmonds, Executive Officer*

Camp size 50 per session, coed.

**525   Jimmy Vejar Day Camp**
United Cerebral Palsy of Westchester
PO Box 555118
Rye Brook, NY  10573          914-937-3800
                        FAX 914-937-0967
               http://www.ucpw.orgwww.oucp
               e-mail: elatainer@ucpw.org
*Evan Latanier, Director*

Camp for people with disabilities.

**526   Kamp Kiwanis**
NY District Kiwanis Foundation
9020 Kiwanis Road
Taberg, NY  13471          315-336-4568
                        FAX 315-336-3845
               http://www.kiwanis-ny.org/kamp
               e-mail: kampkiwanis@mybizz.net
*Rebecca Lopez, Director*
*Luke Coemence, Assistant Director*

Serves youths with many forms of disabilities to include ADD, autism, and learning disabilities.

**527   MAC Mainstreaming at Camp**
Frost Valley YMCA
460 W 34th Street
New York, NY  10001          212-273-6658
                        FAX 212-273-6161
                        http://www.yai.org
*Joel Levy DSW, CEO*

MAC is designed to serve children with developmental disabilities and to promote inclusion into the broader camp community.

**528   Maplebrook School**
5142 Route 22
Amenia, NY  12501          845-373-9511
                        FAX 845-373-7029
               http://www.maplebrookschool.org
               e-mail: mbsechs@aol.com
*Jennifer Scully, Director Admissions*
*Jenni Hill, Assistant Director*

Academic instruction is given in the morning hours of each weekday and afternoon hours are filled with culturally enriching classes in drama, dance and art.

**529   New Country Day Camp**
Educational Alliance
197 E Broadway
New York, NY  10002          212-780-2300
                        FAX 212-979-1225
                        http://www.edalliance.org
*Robin Bernstein, Executive Director*

Clients must be toilet trained. A special program for teens and young adults emphasizes independent living skills and prevocational training.

**530   Parkside School**
48 W 74th Street
New York, NY  10023          212-721-8888
                        FAX 212-721-1547
*A. Miller, Director*

A New York State chartered, not-for-profit school established in 1986 for children with language-based learning problems in the New York City area. An educational setting that promotes active participation in learning.

**531   Queens REACH Camp Smile**
80-30 Parkland Q Gardens
Queen, NY  11415          718-699-4213
                        FAX 718-699-4243
                        TDY:718-699-4213
               http://www.nyc.gov/parks
               e-mail: alwilliams@nyc.gov/parks
*Adrian Benepe, Commissioner*
*Al Williams, Director*

**532   Samuel Field/Bay Terrace YM & YWHA Special Services**
58-20 Little Neck Parkway
Little Neck, NY  11362          718-225-6750
                        FAX 718-423-8276
               http://www.samuelfieldy.org
               e-mail: samfieldy@aol.com
*Steven Goodman, Vice President*
*William Frumkin, President*

Committed to providing the residents of northeast Queens and western Nassau with an outstanding array of high quality and diverse services, innovative programming and a wide variety of community events and celebrations.

**533   School Vacation Camps: Youth with Development Disabilities**
YWCA of White Plains-Central Westchester
515 N Street
White Plains, NY  10605          914-949-6227
                        FAX 914-949-8903
               http://www.ywca.whiteplains.org
*Amy Kohn, Director*
*Leressa Crockett, Chief Operating Officer*

Camp for people with developmental disabilities.

**534  Shield Summer Play Program**

Shield Institute
14461 Roosevelt Avenue
Flushing, NY  11354          718-886-1534
                            FAX 718-961-7669
                            http://www.shield.org
                            e-mail: webmaster@shield.org
*Helen Berman, Director*

**535  Summit Travel Program**

Summit Travel
18 E. 41st St
New York, NY  10017          212-689-3880
                            FAX 212-689-4347
                            http://www.summitcamp.com
*Gil Skyer MD, Director*

Represents the logical extension of the camping program for young adults who have outgrown the traditional camping experience, but still require opportunities for structured and supervised social experiences as well as recreational opportunities of a more adult nature. This program offers 1,2,3 and 6 week programs of domestic and/or foreign travel.

**536  Trailblazers Camp JCC of N Westchester JCC of Northern Westchester**

600 Bear Ridge Road
Pleasantville, NY  10570          914-741-0333
                                FAX 914-741-6150
                    http://www.rosenthaly.org
*Tom Naviglis, Camp Director*
*Carolyn Hagano, Contact*

Located on 19 acres of scenic woodland. Offers a swim program, softball, arts and crafts, music, drama and Jewish culture for children with special needs.

**537  YAI/Rockland County Association for the Learning Disabled (YAI/RCALD)**

2 Crosfield Avenue
West Nyack, NY  10994          845-358-5700
                            FAX 845-358-6119
                    e-mail: taustin@yai.org
*Joel Levy, Chief Executive Officer*

YAI/RCALD conducts a wide variety of programs, supervised by experienced and professional staff, designed to build life skills, promote self-esteem, provide information exchange and offer other support services for individuals with learning and other developmental disabilities. The programs include, vocational evaluation and placements, recreational, residential, camping, service coordination and support groups.

## North Carolina

**538  Camp Timberwolf**

PO Box 457
Hendersonville, NC  28793          828-697-9379
                    http://www.camptimberwolf.com
                    e-mail: timberwolf@camptimberwolf.com
*Tony Coburn, Director*

An camping program specifically designed for boys and girls with ADD, ADHD, LD, OCD and similar behavioral challanges.

**539  SOAR Camp**

2319 Rosemount Road
Balsam, NC  28707          828-456-3435
                        FAX 828-456-3449
                        http://www.soarnc.org
*Jonathan Jones, Executive Director*
*John Wilson, Director*

Features success-oriented, high-adventure programs for learning disabled and ADD preteens, teens and adults. Emphasis is placed on developing self-confidence, social skills, problem-solving techniques, a willingness to attempt new challenges and the motivation that comes through successful goal orientation.

**540  Talisman Summer Camp**

601 Camp Elliot Road
Hendersonville, NC  28711          828-669-8639
                                888-972-7736
                            FAX 828-669-2521

Includes three programs for children with learning disabilities, high functioning Autism and Asperger's Snydrome.

**541  Wilderness Experience**

Ashe County 4-H
134 Government Circle
Jefferson, NC  28640          336-219-2650
                            FAX 336-229-2682
                    e-mail: george_santucci@ncsu.edu
*Julie Landry, Director*
*Vickie Moore, Assistant Director*

## Ohio

**542  Camp Cheerful: Achievement Center for Children**

Achievement Center for Children
15000 Cheerful Lane
Strongsville, OH  44136          440-238-6200
                            FAX 440-238-1858
                e-mail: tim.fox@achievementctrs.org
*Tim Fox, Director*
*Barb Fields, Office Manager*

A residential camp for children who are high functioninig autistic, and Asbergers Syndrome

**543  Camp Happiness at Corde Campus**

Catholic Charities Disability Services
7911 Detroit Avenue
Cleveland, OH  44102          216-334-2963
                            FAX 216-334-2905
*Molly Worthington, Camp Director*

To provide educational, social and recreational services to children and adults with developmental disabilities during the summer months.

**544 Camp Happiness at St. Augustine**
**Catholic Charities Disability Services**
**7911 Detroit Avenue**
**Cleveland, OH 44102**     **216-334-2963**
                          **FAX 216-334-2905**
*Molly Worthington, Camp Director*

To provide educational, social and recreational services to children and adults with developmental disabilities during the summer months.

**545 Camp Happiness at St. Joseph Center**
**Catholic Charities Disability Services**
**7911 Detroit Avenue**
**Cleveland, OH 44102**     **216-334-2963**
                          **FAX 216-334-2905**
*Molly Worthington, Camp Director*

To provide educational, social and recreational services to children and adults with developmental disabilities during the summer months.

**546 Camp Nuhop**
**404 Hillcrest Drive**
**Ashland, OH 44805**     **419-289-2227**
                         **FAX 419-289-2227**
             **http://www.campnuhop.org**
      **e-mail: campnuhop@zoominternet.net**
*Jerry Dunlap, Director*
*Trevor Dunlap, Assistant Director*
*Fred Boll, Director*

A residential camp for all children with learning disabilities, attention deficit disorders and behavior disorders.

**547 Camp Success at Marburn AcademyMarburn Academy**
**1860 Walden Drive**
**Columbus, OH 43229**     **614-433-0822**
                          **FAX 614-433-0812**
           **http://www.marburnacademy.org**
      **e-mail: bdavidson@marburnacademy.org**
*Barbara Davidson, Director*
*Linda Welch, Office Administrator Secretary*

A four program academic day camp for children with LD and dyslexia.

**548 Camp-I-Can**
**Children's Home of Cincinnati, The**
**5050 Madison Road**
**Cincinnati, OH 45227**     **513-272-2800**
                            **800-639-4965**
                          **FAX 513-272-2807**
        **http://www.thechildrenshomecinti.org**
     **e-mail: wyoung@thechildrenshomecinti.org**
*Stephen Black, President*
*Wesley Young, Vice President*

A summer day camp that enhances creativity and promotes positive social skills.

**549 Easter Seals Broadview Heights**
**Easter Seals North East Ohio**
**1929 A E Royalton Road**
**Broadview Heights, OH 44147**     **440-838-0990**
                                   **888-325-8532**
                                 **FAX 440-838-8440**
          **e-mail: spowers@eastersealsneo.org**
*Susan Powers, Director Rehabilitation Services*
*Sheila Dunn, President*

The following are camping and recreational services offered: Camperships and day camping for children.

**550 Easter Seals Central and Southeast Ohio**
**565 Children's Drive W**
**Columbus, OH 43205 0166**     **614-228-5523**
                               **FAX 614-228-8249**
        **http://www.eastersealscentralohio.org**
       **e-mail: tshiverd@easterseals-cseohio.org**
*Karen Zucherman, Director*
*Marty Fisher, Administrative Assistant*

The following are camping and recreational services offered: Aquatics.

**551 Easter Seals Cincinnati**
**231 Clark Road**
**Cincinnati, OH 45215**     **513-821-9890**
                            **800-288-1123**
                          **FAX 513-821-9895**
    **http://www.twatsoon.oh-sw.easterseals.com**
      **e-mail: twatson@oh-sw.easter-seals.com**
*Tammy Watson, CEO*

The following are camping and recreational services offered: Adventure.

**552 Easter Seals Lorain**
**Easter Seals Lorain**
**1909 N Ridge Road**
**Lorain, OH 44055 3344**     **440-277-7337**
                             **888-723-5602**
                           **FAX 440-277-7339**
         **e-mail: eastersealsnwohio.org**
*Kevin Walter, Director*
*Stephanie Engle, Billing Specialist*

The following are camping and recreational services offered: Camperships and day camping for children.

**553 Easter Seals Marietta**
**Easter Seals**
**609 Putnam Street**
**Marietta, OH 45750 0031**     **740-374-8876**
                               **800-860-5523**
                             **FAX 740-374-4501**
*Melanie Alloway, Office Manager*
*Randy Burchett, Facility Manager*

The following are camping and recreational services offered: Camp respite for children and therapeutic horseback riding.

**554  Easter Seals Northeast Ohio**
3085 W Market Street
Akron, OH  44333 3363         330-836-9741
                             FAX 330-836-4967
              e-mail: susan@eastersealsneo.org
*Susan Powers, Director Rehabilitation Services*
*Jenny Mason, Programmer Assistant*

The following are camping and recreational services
offered: Swim programs.

**555  Easter Seals Youngstown**
299 Edwards Street
Youngstown, OH  44502         330-743-1168
                             FAX 330-743-1616
         e-mail: jwalston@mtc.easter-seals.com
*Janet Walston, Manager Pediatric Services*
*Vickie Villano, Director*

The following are camping and recreational services
offered: Recreationsl/Day care for Ages 6-12.

**556  Pilgrim Hills Camp**
33833 Township Road 20
Brinkhaven, OH  43006         740-599-6314
                              800-282-0740
                             FAX 740-599-9790
          e-mail: campregistrar@ocucc.org
*Cynthia Speller, Camp Director*

Many camp programs for all children including learning disabled.

**557  Recreation Unlimited Farm and Fun**
7700 Piper Road
Ashley, OH  43003             740-548-7006
                             FAX 740-747-2640
          http://www.recreationunlimited.org
          e-mail: info@recreationunlimited.org
*Paul Huplin, Director*
*Michelle Higgins, Administrative Assistant*

Is a not-for-profit organization providing programs in
sports, recreation and education for individuals with
physical and developmental disabilities on an accessible 165-acre campus in a safe, fun and challenging environment.

## Oklahoma

**558  Camp Arrowhead YMCA YMCA**
500 N Broadway
Oklahoma City, OK  73102      405-733-9622
                             FAX 405-733-9626
*Tammy Newton, Camp Director*
*Mike Roark, President*

A camp that puts Christian principles into practice
through programs that build healthy spirit, mind and
body.

**559  Camp Fire USA**
National Camp Fire USA
706 S Boston
Tulsa, OK  74119              918-592-2267
                              888-553-2267
                             FAX 918-592-3473
           http://www.tulsaccampfire.org
           e-mail: vproctor@Tulsacampfire.org
*Denny Winters, Camp Director*
*Vicky Proctor, Company Director*

A coed overnight non-competitive camp building self
esteem.

**560  Easter Seals Oklahoma**
701 NE 13th Street
Oklahoma City, OK  73104      405-239-2525
                             FAX 405-239-2278
              e-mail: esok1@coxinet.net
*Patricia Filer, President*
*Linda Maisch, Administrative Assistant*

The following are camping and recreational services
offered: Camperships.

## Oregon

**561  Easter Seals Central Pennsylvania**
501 Valley View Boulevard
Altoona, PA  16603            814-944-5014
                             FAX 814-944-6500
       e-mail: jhanlin@eastersealscentralpa.org
*Jeanne Hanlin, CEO*

The following are camping and recreational services
offered: Day camping for children, recreational services for children and therapeutic horseback riding.

**562  Easter Seals Medford**
33 N Central Avenue
Medford, OR  97501            541-842-2199
                             FAX 541-842-4048
          e-mail: medford@or.easter-seals.org
*Diane Mathews, Program Coordinator*

The following are camping and recreational services
offered: Day camping for children, recreational services for adults and recreational services for children.

**563  Easter Seals Oregon**
Easter Seals National
5757 SW Macadam Avenue
Portland, OR  97239           503-228-5108
                              800-556-6020
                             FAX 503-228-1352
           http://www.oreasterseals.com
           e-mail: info@or.easter-seals.com
*David Chedeallier, Director*
*Debbie Seymour, Office Manager*

The following are camping and recreational services
offered: Residential camping programs.

**564**  **Mobility International USA**
PO Box 10767
Eugene, OR  97401  541-343-1284
FAX 541-343-6812
http://www.miusa.org
e-mail: info@miusa.org
*Susan Sygall, Director*
*Joan Anderson, Administrative Assistant*

A nonprofit organization founded in 1981 to empower people with disabilities around the world through international exchange promoting cross-cultural understanding and providing leadership and disability rights training to people with disabilities. We also provide consultation, publications, resources and technical assistance promoting the full participation of people with disabilities in international exchange opportunities and at all levels of the international development process.

**565**  **Upward Bound Camp for Special Needs**
PO Box C
Stayton, OR  97383  503-897-2447
FAX 503-897-4116
http://www.upwardboundcamp.org
e-mail: ubc@open.org
*Jerry Pierce, Co Director*
*Heidi Gott, Assistant Director*

Christian-based camp for people with developmental disabilities age 12 and up. Activities include fishing, hiking, swimming, arts and crafts, archery, Bible study, nature explorations, campfires, games, basketball, volleyball, horseshoes and badminton. Founded 1978

# Pennsylvania

**566**  **Camp Hebron**
957 Camp Hebron Road
Halifax, PA  17032  717-896-3441
800-864-7747
FAX 717-896-3391
http://www.camphebron.org
e-mail: hebron@camphebron.org
*Lanny Millette, Executive Director*
*Mike Ford, Program Director*

A place where people connect with God, nature and each other. This is accomplished through the creation of a Christ-centered sanctuary where people find renewal and growth through recreation, teaching and fellowship in God's creation.

**567**  **Camp Joy**
3325 Swamp Creek Road
Schwenksville, PA  19473  610-754-6878
FAX 610-754-7880
http://www.campjoy.com
e-mail: campjoy@fast.net
*Angus Murray, Director*

Sleeover and day camp for kids and adults with developmental disabilities: mental retardation, autism, brain injury and neurological disorders.

**568**  **Easter Seals Bethlehem**
2200 Industrial Drive
Bethlehem, PA  18017 2198  610-866-8092
FAX 610-866-3450
http://www.easterseals-easternpa.org
e-mail:
barbara.carlson@easterseals-easternpa.org
*Barbara Carlson, Vice President Program*
*Frank Malone, Office Manager*

The following are camping and recreational services offered: Recreational services for children and day camp for children.

**569**  **Easter Seals Downingtown**
797 E Lancaster Avenue
Downingtown, PA  19335  610-873-3990
FAX 610-873-3992
http://www.easterseals-sepa.org
e-mail: dkeiths@easterseals-sepa.org
*Donna Keiths, Division Director*
*April Williams, Secretary*

The following are camping and recreational services offered: Day camping for children, recreational services for children.

**570**  **Easter Seals Eastern Pennsylvania**
1040 Liggett Avenue
Reading, PA  19611  610-775-1431
FAX 610-796-1954
*Naggie Goss, Director*
*Anna Mountz, Office Manager*

The following are camping and recreational services offered: Camperships, day camping for children and recreational services for children.

**571**  **Easter Seals Franklin**
Easter Seals
200 12th Street
Franklin, PA  16323 0231  814-437-3071
FAX 814-433-2226
http://www.westernpa.easter-seals.com
e-mail: dgriffith@pa-ws.easter-seals.org
*Donna Griffith, Division Director*
*Lyn Cross, Division Secretary*

The following are camping and recreational services offered: Day camping for children, recreational services for children.

**572**  **Easter Seals Kulpsville**
1161 Forty Foot Road
Kulpsville, PA  19443  215-368-7000
FAX 216-368-1199
e-mail: bstrasser@easterseals-sepa.org
*Carl Webster, Executive Director*

The following are camping and recreational services offered: Day camping for children, recreational services for children.

**573  Easter Seals Levittown**

2400 Trenton Road
Levittown, PA  19056          215-945-7200
                             FAX 215-945-4073
          e-mail: lremick@easterseals-sepa.org
*Adrienne Young, Division Director*
*Pat Van, Administrative Assistant*

The following are camping and recreational services offered: Day camping for children, recreational services for children.

**574  Easter Seals Media**

468 N Middletown Road
Media, PA  19063          610-565-2353
                         FAX 610-565-5256
          http://www.easterseals.com
          e-mail: jwright@easterseals-sepa.org
*Donna Keiths, Division Director*

The following are camping and recreational services offered: Day camping for children, recreational services for children.

**575  Easter Seals South Central Pennsylvania**

2201 S Queen Street
York, PA  17402 4695          717-741-3891
                             FAX 717-741-5359
*Matt Ernst, Director Therapeutic Recreation*

The following are camping and recreational services offered: Adventure, day camping for children, recreational services for adults, recreational services for children, sports camp, swim programs, therapeutic horseback riding, water skiing and snow skiing.

**576  Easter Seals of Southeastern Pennsylvania**

3975 Conshohocken Avenue
Philadelphia, PA  19131 5484          215-879-1001
                                     FAX 215-879-8424
          e-mail: jpodgajny@easterseals-sepa.org
*John Podgajny, Division Director*
*Sandy Miller, Administrative Assistant*

The following are camping and recreational services offered: Day camping for children, recreational services for adults and recreational services for children.

**577  Summit Camp Program**

Summit Camp Program New York Office
18 E 41st Street
New York, NY  10017          212-689-3880
                             800-323-9908
          http://www.summitcamp.com
          e-mail: summitcamp@aol.com
*Mayer Stiskin, Director*
*Ninette Stiskin, Director*

Summit camp in Honsdales Pennsylvania serves boys and girls diagnosed with Attention Deficit Disorders, Asperger Snydrome and learning disabilities.

**578  Wesley Woods**

Western Pennsylvania Constant of the United Method
RR 1
Grand Valley, PA  16420          814-436-7802
                                 800-295-0420
                            FAX 814-436-7669
          http://www.wesleywoods.com
          e-mail: info@wesleywoods.com
*Herb West, Director*
*Jeff Mazza, Business Manager*

The mission is to meet spiritual needs of children, youth, and adults in a Christian camp and retreat setting.

## South Carolina

**579  Easter Seals Greenville**

Easter Seals South Carolina
1122 Rutherford Road
Greenville, SC  29609          864-232-4185
                               FAX 864-232-8161
          e-mail: eastersgvl@aol.com
*Barbara Jardno, Director*
*Patti Reins, Assistant Director*

The following are camping and recreational services offered: Residential camping program.

**580  Easter Seals Pierre**

1351 N Harrison Avenue
Pierre, SD  57501 2373          605-224-5879
                               FAX 605-224-1033
          http://www.sd.easterseals.com
          e-mail: administrator@sd.easter-seals.com
*Ann Bush, CEO*

The following are camping and recreational services offered: Day camping for children.

## Tennessee

**581  Camp Discovery Tennessee Jaycees Tennessee Jaycees Foundation**

400 Camp Discovery Lane
Gainesboro, TN  38562          615-293-4497
                               FAX 423-265-7879
          http://www.camp-discovery.org
          e-mail: hickman_sped@yahoo.com
*Dawn Hickman, Director*
*John Garner, President/Jaycees Foundation*

Provides summer camp for people with special needs.

**582  Easter Seals Camp**

Easter Seal Camp
6300 Benders Ferry Road
Mt. Juliet, TN  37122          615-444-2829
                               FAX 615-444-8576
          http://www.eastersealscn.com
          e-mail: escamp@bellsouth.net
*Jodi Franke, Director Camping*
*Tenny Williams, Office Manager*

The following are camping and recreational services offered: Camp respite for adults, camp respite for children, camperships and residential camping programs.

**583    River's Way Outdoor Adventure Center**
889 Stoney Hollow Road
Bluff City, TN  37618             423-538-0405
                                   FAX 423-538-8183
                        http://www.riversway.org
                        e-mail: tom@riversway.org
*Tom Hanlon, Executive Director*
*Jamie Scott, Director*

Providing opportunities for youth of all abilities to work, learn and have fun together in educational and outdoor adventure settings. Founded 1993

## Texas

**584    ADD/ADHD Summer Camp**
River Oaks Academy
10600 Richmond Avenue
Houston, TX  77042                713-783-7200
                                   FAX 713-783-7286
                        http://www.riveracademy.com
                        e-mail: roainfo@riveroaks.org
*Sandra Phares MD, Director*
*Burton Chapman, Registrar*

A specialized summer camp for children and adolescents with ADHD or conduct disorder.

**585    Easter Seals Central Texas**
919 W 28 1/2 Street
Austin, TX  78705 3595            512-478-2581
                                   FAX 512-476-1638
                        e-mail: dclowers@eastersealstx.com
*Kevin Coleman, President/CEO*
*Miriam Nisenbaum, Outpatient Rehabilitation Direct*

The following are camping and recreational services offered: Day camping for children.

**586    El Paso LDA Vacation Adventure**
8929 Viscount Boulevard
El Paso, TX  79925                915-591-8080
                                   FAX 915-591-8150
                        e-mail: eplda@elpn.com
*Barbara Monroy, Director*
*Lina Monroy, Executive Director*

Summer developmental learning program for children currently placed in Special Education or section 504 programs.

**587    Girl Scout Camp La Jita**
Girls Scout of America
10443 Gulfdale Street
San Antonio, TX  78216            210-349-2404
                                   FAX 210-349-2666
                        http://www.sagirlscouts.org
                        e-mail: jlarose@sagirlscout.org
*Kathy Grantham, Executive Director*
*Jean Larose, Administrative Assistant*

Mainstream camp open to children with disabilities.

**588    Rocking L Guest Ranch**
240 Van Zandt County Road #3837
Wills Point, TX  75169            903-560-0246
                                   FAX 972-495-1131
                        http://www.rockinglguestranch.com
                        e-mail: bradlarsen@rockinglranch.com
*Brad Larsen, Owner*
*Alicia Larsen, Owner*

Campers benefit mentally, physically and socially from the camp experience. Additional activities include canoeing, fishing, volleyball, basketball and swimming.

**589    Star Ranch: Summer Program**
149 Camp Scenic Loop
Ingram, TX  78025                 830-367-4868
                                   FAX 830-367-2814
                        http://www.starranch.org
                        e-mail: pbrouse@starranch.org
*Cody Schrank, Program Coordinator*
*Paul Brouse, Program Director*
*Rand Southard, Executive Director*

A camp that teaches Christian values and is geared specifically to deal with children that have severe learning disabilities.

## Utah

**590    Camp Easter Seals East**
8003 Franklin Farm Drive
Richmond, VA  22514               804-746-1007
                                   866-874-4153
                                   FAX 804-746-9214
                        http://www.va.easterseals.com
                        e-mail: info@va.easter-seals.org
*Ginger Ellis, Director Program Administration*
*Whitney Nida, Grant Writer*

The following are camping and recreational services offered: Family retreats.

**591    Camp Easter Seals West**
Route 2
New Castle, VA  24127 9566        540-864-5750
                                   FAX 540-864-6797
                        http://www.va.easterseals.org
                        e-mail: dduerk@va.easter-seals.org
*Deborah Duerk, Director*

The following are camping and recreational services offered: Adventure, camperships, canoeing, conference rental, family retreats, residential camping programs, climbing wall, creative arts, finishing marksmanship, nature study, occupational therapy, swimming, sports camp, speech therapy and therapeutic horseback riding.

**592   Easter Seals Utah**

638 E Wilmington Avenue
Salt Lake City, UT  84106 1491        801-486-3778
                                     800-388-1991
                                FAX 801-486-3123
                     http://www.eastersealsutah.org
                  e-mail: poyd@eastersealsutah.org
*Richard Starley, President*
*Patti Poyd, Office Manager*

The following are camping and recreational services offered: Camp respite for children and day camping for children.

**593   Reid Ranch**

3310 S 2700 E
Salt Lake City, UT  84109          801-486-5083
                                   800-468-3274
                              FAX 801-485-0561
                       http://www.reidranch.com
                    e-mail: greid@reidranch.com
*Gardner Reid, Owner*

Provides students, ages 8-18, with an opportunity to receive small group and tutorial instruction in reading and language skills development. The program operates three weeks during the summer.

## Vermont

**594   Easter Seals Vermont**

641 Comstock Road
Berlin, VT  05602                  802-223-4744
                                   888-372-2636
                              FAX 802-229-0848
                       e-mail: mjohnso@eseals.org
*Mark Johnson, Vice President*

The following are camping and recreational services offered: Camp respite for children, camperships.

**595   Silver Towers Camp**

1116 US Route 5
East Dummerston, VT  05346
                                   800-385-8524
                       http://www.silvertowers.com
                       e-mail: enc550@sover.net
*Earl Cavanagh*

A one-week residential camp for exceptional people six years old and up to enjoy varied opportunities for personal enrichment and development of social skills, including swimming, arts and crafts, sing alongs, music, dancing and bowling

## Virginia

**596   Fairfax County Community and Recreation**

12011 Government Center Pkwy.
Fairfax, VA  22035                 703-324-5532
                                FAX 703-222-9788
                                TDY:703-222-9693
                     http://www.fairfaxcounty.gov\rec
*Patricia Sranckewitz, Agency Director*
*Sara Mumsord, Branch Manager*

Therapeutic recreation services summer activities for children with disabilities to include LD and ADHA.

**597   Sensational Explorers Day Camp**

PO Box 10693
Burke, VA  22009                   703-764-3495
*Nancy Malina, Director*

A camp for high functioning children with sensory integration needs. The camp is run by sensory integration clinicians.

**598   Summer Adventure Program**

Trinity College
125 Michigan Avenue NE
Washington, DC  20017              202-244-8089
                                FAX 202-244-8065
                       e-mail: lciotassoc@aol.com
*Lynne Israel, Director*

A six week day camp to enhance sensory motor development. Activities include tactile activity, gross and fine motor skills, swimming instruction, music, language and visualization skills.

## Washington

**599   Camp Easter Seals West**

17809 S Vaughn Road
Vaughn, WA  98394                  253-884-2722
                                FAX 253-884-0200
                           http://www.seals.org
                    e-mail: eastersealare@seals.org
*Mary McIntyre, Office Manager*
*Mike Mooney, Summer Camp Director*
*Lori Hall, Respite Coordinator*

The camp offers six day sessions geared to the age, level of ability and needs of the camper. Includes a wide range of activities including horseback riding, dancing and waterfront activities.

**600   Camp Killoqua/Camp Fire USA Camp Fire USA**

Snohomish County Council
4312 Rucker Avenue
Everett, WA  98203                 425-258-5437
                                FAX 452-252-2267
                http://www.campfireusasnohomish.org
                e-mail: info@campfireusasnohomish.org
*David Sursace, Director*
*Carol Johnson, Assistant Director*

Provides a unique outdoor experience for youth and adults offering a full range of options and opportunities.

**601 Camp Sweyolakan**
524 N Mullan Road
Spokane, WA 99206
509-747-6191
800-386-2324
FAX 509-747-4913
http://www.campfireinc.org
e-mail: campfireinc@campfireinc.org
*Peggy Clark, Camp Director*
*Judy Lippman, Special Programs*

Both resident and day camp on 300 wooded acres is open to all boys, girls, adults, those with special needs and families.

**602 Easter Seals Spokane**
Easter Seals
W 606 Sharp
Spokane, WA 99201 2424
509-326-8292
FAX 509-326-2261
e-mail: gperkins@wa.easter-seals.org
*Ginette Perkins, Program Manager*
*Stefanie Butlar, Assistant Director*

The following are camping and recreational services offered: Recreational services for children and residential camping programs.

**603 Easter Seals Washington**
17809 S Vaughn Road KPN
Vaughn, WA 98394 0313
253-884-2722
FAX 253-884-0200
http://www.seals.org
e-mail: camp@seals.org
*Mary McIntyre, Office Manager*
*Mike Mooney, Summer Camp Director*

The following are camping and recreational services offered: Camp respite for adults, camp respite for children, camperships, computer program, conference rental, family retreats, residential camping programs and swim programs.

## West Virginia

**604 Easter Seals West Virginia**
Easter Seals West Virginia
1305 National Road
Wheeling, WV 26003 5780
304-242-1390
800-677-1390
FAX 304-243-5880
e-mail: ateaster@stargate.net
*Lorie Untch, President/CEO*
*Kim Davis, Community Relations Assistant*

The following are camping and recreational services offered: Day camping for children, sports camp and therapeutic horseback riding.

**605 Mountain Milestones**
Stepping Stones
15 Cottage Street
Morgantown, WV 26501
304-296-0150
800-982-8799
FAX 304-296-0194
http://www.steppingstonecenter.net
e-mail: abilitywv@hotmail.com
*Susan Fox, Director*
*Jack Porter, President*
*Adam Bullian, Recreation Coordinator*

People with disabilities of all ages can take part in a variety of recreation programs that include adventures, team sports, special events and camps.

## Wisconsin

**606 Bike Farm Summer Camp**
Bleffingway Family Service
2780 230th Street
Cushing, WI 54006
715-648-5773
FAX 715-648-6800
http://www.bikefarm.org
e-mail: sclark@bikefarm.org
*Stephen Clark, Director*
*Carl Gaede, Supervisor*

Residential and day camp that provides an opportunity through activities to create, support and grow.

**607 Easter Seals Camp Wawbeek**
101 Nob Hill Road
Madison, WI 53713
608-277-8288
800-422-2324
FAX 608-277-8333
TDY:608-277-8031
http://www.eastersealswisconsin.com
e-mail: wawbeek@wi-easterseals.org
*Valerie Croissant, Director*
*Nance Roepke, Executive Vice President*

The following are camping and recreational services offered: Adventure, camperships, canoeing, conference rental, day camping for children, family retreats, residential camping programs and swim programs.

**608 Easter Seals Madison**
101 Nob Hill Road
Madison, WI 53713 3969
608-277-8288
800-422-2324
FAX 608-277-8333
TDY:608-277-8031
http://www.eastersealswisconsin.com
e-mail: tpaprock@wi-easterseals.org
*Valerie Croissant, Director*
*Nance Roepke, Executive Vice President*

The following are camping and recreational services offered: Vacation get-away program.

**609 Easter Seals Menomonee Falls**
N79W14845 Homestead Drive
Norwalkee, WI 53051
262-253-5550
FAX 262-253-6503
*Julie Hagenstein, CDC Director*

The following are camping and recreational services offered: Before/After school program for Ages 6 through 18, recreational services for adults and recreational services for children.

**610   Easter Seals Southeastern Wisconsin**

3090 N 53rd Street
Milwaukee, WI 53210 1699          414-449-4444
                                  FAX 414-449-4447
          e-mail: agency@easterseals-sewi.org
*Dob Glowacki, CEO*
*Sheolia Underwoods, Office Manager*

The following are camping and recreational services offered: Before/After school program for Ages 6 through 18.

**611   Timbertop Nature Adventure Camp**

Stevens Point Area YMCA
1000 Division Street
Stevens Point, WI 54481          715-342-2980
                                 FAX 715-342-2987
          http://www.spymca.org
          e-mail: pmatthai@spymca.org
*Audrey Shmeeckle, Operations Director; Executive*
*Jackie Clussman, Special Needs Director*

For youth identified by their school districts as needing extra help for a learning disability. Combines traditional camp activities focused on dealing with learning disabilities in a structured daily setting. Special attention is paid to peer relations, building self-confidence and learning new skills.

**612   Wisconsin Elk/Easter Seals Respite Camp**

101 Nob Hill Road
Madison, WI 53713          608-277-8288
                           800-422-2342
                      FAX 608-277-8333
                      TDY:608-277-8031
     http://www.eastersealswisconsin.com
          e-mail: respite1@wi-easterseals.org
*Valerie Croissant, Director*
*Nance Roepke, Executive Vice President*

The following are camping and recreational services offered: Camp respite for adults, camp respite for children, canoeing, family retreats, residential camping programs and swim programs.

## Language Arts

**613** **100% Concepts: Intermediate**

LinguiSystems
3100 4th Avenue
East Moline, IL  61244                309-775-2300
                                        800-776-4332
                                   FAX 309-755-2377
                                   TDY:800-933-8331
                      http://www.linguisystems.com
                  e-mail: service@linguisystems.com
*LinguiSystems Staff, Author*
*Linda Bowers, Owner*
*Rosemary Huisingh, Owner*

Concepts learning doesn't stop in the early grades. Your older students with language disorders need to understand the terms they hear in the classroom. These terrific activities will help. Teach higher level concepts, including location and direction, quality or condition, comparison, time and occurrence, and relationship. *$37.95*

*174 pages  Ages 10-14*

**614** **100% Concepts: Primary**

LinguiSystems
3100 4th Avenue
East Moline, IL  61244                309-775-2300
                                        800-776-4332
                                   FAX 309-755-2377
                                   TDY:800-933-8331
                      http://www.linguisystems.com
                  e-mail: service@linguisystems.com
*LinguiSystems Staff, Author*
*Linda Bowers, Owner*
*Rosemary Huisingh, Owner*

Concepts are the building blocks of language. This approach gives students practice with familiar concepts in different formats for strong language comprehension skills. You'll teach tons of concepts, including following directions, grouping, association, math, and time. *$37.95*

*157 pages  Ages 5-9*

**615** **100% Grammar**

LinguiSystems
3100 4th Avenue
East Moline, IL  61244                309-775-2300
                                        800-776-4332
                                   FAX 309-755-2377
                                   TDY:800-933-8331
                      http://www.linguisystems.com
                  e-mail: service@linguisystems.com
*Mike LoGiudice, Carolyn LoGiudice, Author*
*Linda Bowers, Owner*
*Rosemary Huisingh, Owner*

Make the link between grammar and communication skills with this incredible resource. You'll get relevant, fun activities to develop clear, accurate, excellent communication skills. Covers all the essential grammar areas including nouns, pronouns, complements, verbals, clauses, and fine points. *$37.95*

*174 pages  Ages 9-14*

**616** **100% Grammar LITE**

LinguiSystems
3100 4th Avenue
East Moline, IL  61244                309-775-2300
                                        800-776-4332
                                   FAX 309-755-2377
                                   TDY:800-933-8331
                      http://www.linguisystems.com
                  e-mail: service@linguisystems.com
*Mike LoGiudice, Carolyn LoGiudice, Author*
*Linda Bowers, Owner*
*Rosemary Huisingh, Owner*

Teach one grammar concept at a time. Compared to 100% Grammar, this resource is lighter in the amount of content per page and contextual demands of the practice items. The fun art and light approach will appeal to your hardest-to-teach students. The book is divided into two sections covering parts of speech and sentence structures. *$37.95*

*178 pages  Ages 9-14*

**617** **100% Vocabulary: Intermediate**

LinguiSystems
3100 4th Avenue
East Moline, IL  61244                309-775-2300
                                        800-776-4332
                                   FAX 309-755-2377
                                   TDY:800-933-8331
                      http://www.linguisystems.com
                  e-mail: service@linguisystems.com
*Vicki Rothstein, Rhoda Zacker, Author*
*Linda Bowers, Owner*
*Rosemary Huisingh, Owner*

Teach vocabulary through an organized, systematic approach that works. These challenging semantic exercises teach word flexibility and verbal reasoning skills. You'll teach strategies for understanding word relationships with activities for classification, absurdities, comparisons, exclusion and more. *$37.95*

*188 pages  Ages 9-14*

**618** **100% Vocabulary: Primary**

LinguiSystems
3100 4th Avenue
East Moline, IL  61244                309-775-2300
                                        800-776-4332
                                   FAX 309-755-2377
                                   TDY:800-933-8331
                      http://www.linguisystems.com
                  e-mail: service@linguisystems.com
*Vicki Rothstein, Rhoda Zacker, Author*
*Linda Bowers, Owner*
*Rosemary Huisingh, Owner*

Help younger students begin to understand complex word relationships with these outstanding exercises. Students work through a hierarchy of task complexity based on how we think about words. Students will recognize answers with yes/no or true/false, choose answers from alternatives, and infer answers when information isn't directly stated. *$37.95*

*187 pages  Ages 6-9*

**619   125 Vocabulary Builders**

LinguiSystems
3100 4th Avenue
East Moline, IL  61244                    309-775-2300
                                          800-776-4332
                                    FAX 309-755-2377
                                    TDY:800-933-8331
                        http://www.linguisystems.com
                    e-mail: service@linguisystems.com
*LinguiSystems Staff, Author*
*Linda Bowers, Owner*
*Rosemary Huisingh, Owner*

This resource goes beyond teaching words by teaching students how to recognize, learn, and integrate new words into their daily vocabulary. Gives students strategies for connecting new vocabulary words to each other, to curriculum and to their prior experience. Your students will learn and remember sets of words because they're used in meaningful ways. *$35.95*

*158 pages  Ages 10-15*

**620   Ablenet**

2808 North Fairview Avenue
Roseville, MN  55414                      612-379-0956
                                          800-322-0956
                                    FAX 651-294-2259
                          http://www.ablenetinc.com
              e-mail: customerservice@ablenetinc.com
*Cheryl Volkman, Chief Developmental Officer*
*Rick Osterhaus, Chief Executive Officer*

Simple assistive technology for teaching children with disabilities including communication aids, switches, environmental control, mounting systems, literacy and teacher resources, kits and more.

**621   American Heritage Children's Dictionary**

Sunburst Technology
400 Columbus Avenue
Valhalla, NY  10595 1349                  914-747-3310
                                          800-321-7511
                                    FAX 914-747-4109
                          http://www.sunburst.com
                    e-mail: support@sunburst.com
*Katie Birmingham, Office Manager*

This multimedia dictionary uses sound, color illustrations and animations to demonstrate the spelling, definition and pronunciation of 13,000 words. Three additional word games enhance the students' language usage and vocabulary levels. Available formats in MAC CD-ROM, Win CD-ROM. *$99.95*

**622   Analogies 1, 2 & 3**

Educators Publishing Service
31 Smith Place
Cambridge, MA  02139 9031                 617-547-6706
                                          800-435-7728
                                    FAX 888-440-2665
                          http://www.epsbooks.com
                    e-mail: eps@epsbooks.com
*Arthur Liebman, Author*
*Steve Kote, President*
*Jennifer Avery, Contact*

Studying analogies helps students to sharpen reasoning ability, develop critical thinking, understand relationships between words and ideas, learn new vocabulary, and prepare for the SAT's and for standardized tests.

**623   Artic Shuffle**

LinguiSystems
3100 4th Avenue
East Moline, IL  61244                    309-775-2300
                                          800-776-4332
                                    FAX 309-755-2377
                                    TDY:800-933-8331
                        http://www.linguisystems.com
                    e-mail: service@linguisystems.com
*Tobie Nan Kaufman, Author*
*Linda Bowers, Owner*
*Rosemary Huisingh, Owner*

Your students can play Go Fish, Crazy Eights, or Concentration while they practice their target sounds. Use them for vocabulary drills or naming practice. *$89.95*

*Ages 5-Adult*

**624   Artic-Pic**

Speech Bin
1965 25th Avenue
Vero Beach, FL  32960                     772-770-0007
                                          800-477-3324
                                    FAX 772-770-0006
                          http://www.speechbin.com
                    e-mail: info@speechbin.com
*Shane Peters, Product Coordinator*
*Jen Binney, Owner*

You're just going to love this topsy-turvy upside-down book! Artic-Pic is a clever book that gives you delightful interactive practice materials for those troublesome r and s sounds. You get twenty story poems for each phoneme, each with Artic-Pic answer choices featuring the target sound in varying co-articulatory contexts. Item number 1513. *$19.95*

**625   ArticBURST Articulation Practice for S, R, Ch, and Sh**

LinguiSystems
3100 4th Avenue
East Moline, IL  61244                    309-775-2300
                                          800-776-4332
                                    FAX 309-755-2377
                                    TDY:800-933-8331
                        http://www.linguisystems.com
                    e-mail: service@linguisystems.com
*LinguiSystems Staff, Author*
*Linda Bowers, Owner*
*Rosemary Huisingh, Owner*

Here's a fun quick thinking game for your older students and clients who continue to need articulation therapy. You'll get a set of cards for each of the toughest sounds. Players have to think of a word with their target sound in these four areas: rhyming, compounds, antonyms, and synonyms. *$37.95*

*Ages 10-Adult*

**626  Articulation 3-Vowels: Software**

**Speech Bin**
**1965 25th Avenue**
**Vero Beach, FL  32960**                  570-770-0007
                                          800-477-3324
                                    FAX 888-329-2246
                              http://www.speechbin.com
                              e-mail: info@speechbin.com
*Jen Binney, Owner*

This terrific articulation software is a speech-language pathologist's dream come true! It gives you 572 full-color photo stimuli featuring those troublesome r-controlled vowels and r clusters in 76 categories. *$99.00*

**627  AtoZap!**

**Sunburst Technology**
**400 Columbus Avenue**
**Valhalla, NY  10595 1349**                914-747-3310
                                          800-321-7511
                                    FAX 914-747-4109
                                http://www.sunburst.com
                              e-mail: support@sunburst.com
*Katie Birmingham, Office Manager*

A whimsical world of magical talking alphabet blocks and energetic playful characters this program provides young children with exciting opportunities to explore new concepts through open-ended activities and games. Mac/Win CD-ROM

**628  Autism & PPD: Concept Development**

**LinguiSystems**
**3100 4th Avenue**
**East Moline, IL  61244**                 309-775-2300
                                          800-776-4332
                                    FAX 309-755-2377
                                    TDY:800-933-8331
                              http://www.linguisystems.com
                            e-mail: service@linguisystems.com
*Pam Britton Reese, Nena Challenner, Author*
*Linda Bowers, Owner*
*Rosemary Huisingh, Owner*

This great program teaches a variety of concepts grouped by themes. The simple, realistic artwork provides the visual clues so many students need. As students work through each concept-building program, they'll also develop important language skills such as naming, attributes, categorizing, and giving descriptions. *$155.70*

*Ages 3-8*

**629  Autism & PPD: Pictured Stories and Language Activities**

**LinguiSystems**
**3100 4th Avenue**
**East Moline, IL  61244**                 309-775-2300
                                          800-776-4332
                                    FAX 309-755-2377
                                    TDY:800-933-8331
                              http://www.linguisystems.com
                            e-mail: service@linguisystems.com
*Patricia Snair Koski, Author*
*Linda Bowers, Owner*
*Rosemary Huisingh, Owner*

These sequential picture stories focus on simple, easy-to-follow elements. The repetition, structure, and routine make this a great program for students with autism, PPD, or delayed language development. It's a field tested program that works. *$149.75*

*Ages 3-8*

**630  Basic Signing Vocabulary Cards**

**Harris Communications**
**15155 Technology Drive**
**Eden Prairie, MN  55344 2277**           952-906-1180
                                          800-825-6758
                                    FAX 952-906-1099
                                    TDY:800-825-9187
                              http://www.harriscomm.com
                              e-mail: mail@harriscomm.com

Designed to build signed English vocabulary at a beginners level. Two sets. *$6.95*

*100 cards/set*

**631  Basic Words for Children: Software**

**Speech Bin**
**1965 25th Avenue**
**Vero Beach, FL  32960**                  772-770-0007
                                          800-477-3324
                                    FAX 772-770-0006
                              http://www.speechbin.com
                              e-mail: info@speechbin.com
*Shane Peters, Product Coordinator*
*Jen Binney, Owner*

This exciting software uses beautiful full color photos and action videos to teach 100 basic words essential for the young child's vocabulary. Item number L197: English, Item number L174: Spanish. *$99.00*

**632  Blonigen Fluency Program**

**Speech Bin**
**1965 25th Avenue**
**Vero Beach, FL  32960**                  570-770-0007
                                    FAX 561-770-0006
                              http://www.speechbin.com
                              e-mail: info@speechbin.com
*Julie Blonigen, Author*
*Jen Binney, Owner*

The Blonigen Fluency Program is a systematic approach to teaching the stuttering modification technique of prolongation to treat stuttering in 7-17 year olds. It features easy-to-follow step-by-step directions and exercises to identify and alter disfluency patterns and gain control over the moment of stuttering. *$24.95*

*Ages 7-17*

**633  Bubbleland Word Discovery**

**Sunburst Technology**
**400 Columbus Avenue**
**Valhalla, NY  10595 1349**               914-747-3310
                                          800-321-7511
                                    FAX 914-747-4109
                                http://www.sunburst.com
                              e-mail: support@sunburst.com
*Katie Birmingham, Office Manager*

Build and sharpen language arts skills with this multimedia dictionary. Students explore ten familiar locations that include a pet shop, zoo, toy store, hospital, playground, beach and airport where they engage in 40 activities that build word recognition, pronunciation and spelling skills.

**634    Carolina Picture Vocabulary Test**

Pro-Ed
8700 Shoal Creek Boulevard
Austin, TX  78757 6897          512-451-3246
                                800-897-3202
                          FAX 800-397-7633
                    http://www.proedinc.com
*Thomas Layton and David Holmes, Author*
*Roy Fitzgerald, Department Head*

A norm-referenced, validated, receptive sign vocabulary test for deaf and hearing-impaired children. *$133.00*

**635    Central Auditory Processing Kit**

LinguiSystems
3100 4th Avenue
East Moline, IL  61244          309-775-2300
                                800-776-4332
                          FAX 309-755-2377
                          TDY:800-933-8331
                 http://www.linguisystems.com
         e-mail: service@linguisystems.com
*Mary Ann Mokhemar, Author*
*Linda Bowers, Owner*
*Rosemary Huisingh, Owner*

This unique, comprehensive program addresses auditory processing skills with a direct focus on academics including decoding, following directions, and more. Three books cover a wide range of skills including auditory memory, discrimination, closure, synthesis, figure ground, cohesion, and compensatory strategies. *$89.95*

*180 pages  Ages 6-13*

**636    Complete Oral-Motor Program for Articulation: Book Only**

LinguiSystems
3100 4th Avenue
East Moline, IL  61244          309-775-2300
                                800-776-4332
                          FAX 309-755-2377
                          TDY:800-933-8331
                 http://www.linguisystems.com
         e-mail: service@linguisystems.com
*Harriet Pehde, Ann Geller, Bonnie Lechner, Author*
*Linda Bowers, Owner*
*Rosemary Huisingh, Owner*

Manual guides you through oral-motor lessons with clear instructions for exercise. Students will increase oral-motor awareness, strength and tone. There's even a specific sound remediation program for S, Z, Sh, Ch, J, and R. *$ 39.95*

*159 pages  Ages 3-12*

**637    Complete Oral-Motor Program for Articulation**

LinguiSystems
3100 4th Avenue
East Moline, IL  61244          309-775-2300
                                800-776-4332
                          FAX 309-755-2377
                          TDY:800-933-8331
                 http://www.linguisystems.com
         e-mail: service@linguisystems.com
*Harriet Pehde, Ann Geller, Bonnie Lechner, Author*
*Linda Bowers, Owner*
*Rosemary Huisingh, Owner*

These authors have pooled their years of experience to create this big, best selling kit. You'll get everything you need to help students increase awareness, strength and tone of oral musculature, associate oral-motor function to speech sound musculature, associate oral-motor function to speech sound production, and improve overall articulation skills. *$119.95*

*159 pages  Ages 3-12*

**638    Complete Oral-Motor Program for Articulation: Refill Kit**

LinguiSystems
3100 4th Avenue
East Moline, IL  61244          309-775-2300
                                800-776-4332
                          FAX 309-755-2377
                          TDY:800-933-8331
                 http://www.linguisystems.com
         e-mail: service@linguisystems.com
*Harriet Pehde, Ann Geller, Bonnie Lechner, Author*
*Linda Bowers, Owner*
*Rosemary Huisingh, Owner*

Refill kit for Complete Oral-Motor Program for Articulation. *$54.95*

*Ages 3-12*

**639    Create-A-Story**

Speech Bin
1965 25th Avenue
Vero Beach, FL  32960           772-770-0007
                                800-477-3324
                          FAX 772-770-0006
                 http://www.speechbin.com
           e-mail: info@speechbin.com
*Shane Peters, Product Coordinator*
*Jen Binney, Owner*

Here's a powerful language learning game that simplifies the creative process of storytelling and writing for 5-99-year-olds. It fosters their imaginations, organizes their thoughts, and boosts their confidence as they build a narrative. The game can be played by 1-6 players as groups or individuals. Item number C151. *$44.95*

**640    Curious George Pre-K ABCs**

Sunburst Technology
400 Columbus Avenue
Valhalla, NY  10595 1349        914-747-3310
                                800-321-7511
                          FAX 914-747-4109
                    http://www.sunburst.com
          e-mail: support@sunburst.com
*Katie Birmingham, Office Manager*

Children go on a lively adventure with Curious George visiting six multi level activities that provide an animated introduction to letters and their sounds. Students discover letter names and shapes, initial letter sounds, letter pronunciations, the order of the alphabet and new vocabulary words during the fun exursions with Curious George. Mac/Win CD-ROM

**641  Curriculum Vocabulary Game**

LinguiSystems
3100 4th Avenue
East Moline, IL  61244          309-775-2300
                               800-776-4332
                          FAX 309-755-2377
                          TDY:800-933-8331
              http://www.linguisystems.com
          e-mail: service@linguisystems.com
*Paul Johnson, Stephen Johnson, Author*
*Linda Bowers, Owner*
*Rosemary Huisingh, Owner*

The organized lessons teach the classroom vocabulary your students need to know. Each lesson is curricular, flexible, and comprehensive. You'll tap all the learning styles in your case-load. Activities work through a hierarchy from introducing the concepts, to hands-on activities, to writing and take home practice. *$44.95*

*Ages 9-13*

**642  Daily Starters: Quote of the Day**

LinguiSystems
3100 4th Avenue
East Moline, IL  61244          309-775-2300
                               800-776-4332
                          FAX 309-755-2377
                          TDY:800-933-8331
              http://www.linguisystems.com
          e-mail: service@linguisystems.com
*Dave Wisniewski, Author*
*Linda Bowers, Owner*
*Rosemary Huisingh, Owner*

Get your students off to a focused start in therapy or in the classroom. These quick activities help older students integrate several language arts skills at once including writing, thinking, grammar, punctuation, vocabulary, and more. *$21.95*

*142 pages  Ages 12-18*

**643  Dyslexia: An Introduction to the Orton-Gillingham Approach**

Educators Publishing Service
31 Smith Place
Cambridge, MA  02139 9031          617-547-6706
                                   800-225-5750
                              FAX 888-440-2665
                  http://www.epsbooks.com
                  e-mail: eps@epsbooks.com
*Steve Kote, President*
*Gunnar Voltz, Vice President*

This ten-lesson, online course provides an introduction to the Orton-Gillingham approach to teaching students with dyslexia. Topics include: the nature of the individual with dyslexia; principles of the Orton-Gillingham approach; multisensory instruction and the brain; and the phonology, structure, and history of the English language.

**644  ESPA Success in Language Arts Literacy**

Harcourt Achieve
6277 Sea Harbor Drive
Orlando, FL  32887                 252-480-3200
                                   800-844-1464
                              FAX 800-269-5232
                  http://www.steckvaughn.com
              e-mail: info@steckvaughn.com
*Steck-Vaughn Staff, Author*
*Tim McEwen, President/CEO*
*Jeff Johnson, Dir Marketing Communications*
*Chris Lehmann, Team Coordinator*

Prepares students for one of their most important early assessments. Especially in the early years, children learn at their own pace. Make sure your students aren't exposed to an early disappointment by providing a thorough preparation for the ESPA.

**645  Early Communication Skills**

Therapro
225 Arlington Street
Framingham, MA  01702 8723          508-872-9494
                                    800-257-5376
                               FAX 508-875-2062
                  http://www.theraproducts.com
              e-mail: info@theraproducts.com
*Libby Kumin PhD, Author*
*Karen Conrad, President*
*Paul Rock, Owner*

Provides professional expertise in understandable terms. Parents and professionals learn how their skills are evaulated by professionals, and what activities they can practice with a child immediately to encouarge a childs's communication skill development. *$19.95*

*368 pages  Ages Birth-K*

**646  Early Listening Skills**

Therapro
225 Arlington Street
Framingham, MA  01702 8723          508-872-9494
                                    800-257-5376
                               FAX 508-875-2062
                  http://www.theraproducts.com
              e-mail: info@theraproducts.com
*Diana Williams, Author*
*Karen Conrad, President*
*Paul Rock, Owner*

Two hundred activities designed to be photocopied for classroom or home. Includes materials on auditory detection, discrimination, recognition, sequencing and memory. Describes listening projects and topics for the curriculum. Activity sheets for parents are included. A practical, comprehensive and effective manual for professionals working with preschool children or the older child with special needs. *$55.00*

**647  Earobics Step 2: Home Version**

Speech Bin
1965 25th Avenue
Vero Beach, FL  39260               772-770-0007
                                    800-477-3324
                               FAX 772-770-0006
                  http://www.speechbin.com
              e-mail: info@speechbin.com
*Shane Peters, Product Coordinator*
*Jen Binney, Owner*

Step 2 teaches critical language comprehension skills and trains the critical auditory skills children need for success in learning. It offers hundreds of levels of play, appealing graphics, and entertaining music to train the critical auditory skills young children need for success in learning. Item number C483. *$59.00*

**648    Earobics Step 2: Specialist/Clinician Version**

Speech Bin
1965 25th Avenue
Vero Beach, FL  32960                772-770-0007
                                     800-477-3324
                          FAX 772-770-0006
                 http://www.speechbin.com
                 e-mail: info@speechbin.com
*Shane Peters, Product Coordinator*
*Jen Binney, Owner*

Earobics features: tasks and level counter with real time display; adaptive training technology for individualized programs; and reporting to track and evaluate each individual's progress. Step 2 teaches critical language comprehension skills and trains the critical auditory skills children need for success in learning. Item number C484. *$299.00*

**649    Easy Does It for Fluency: Intermediate**

LinguiSystems
3100 4th Avenue
East Moline, IL  61244                309-775-2300
                                      800-776-4332
                         FAX 309-755-2377
                         TDY:800-933-8331
                 http://www.linguisystems.com
                 e-mail: service@linguisystems.com
*Barbara Roseman, Karin Johnson, Author*
*Linda Bowers, Owner*
*Rosemary Huisingh, Owner*

This program addresses the motor, linguistic, and psychosocial components of stuttering as students work toward fluent speech. This updated and revised version of an old favorite will help your students become fluent. *$49.95*

*165 pages  Ages 6-11*

**650    Easy Does It for Fluency: Preschool/Primary**

LinguiSystems
3100 4th Avenue
East Moline, IL  61244                309-775-2300
                                      800-776-4332
                         FAX 309-755-2377
                         TDY:800-933-8331
                 http://www.linguisystems.com
                 e-mail: service@linguisystems.com
*Barbara Roseman, Karin Johnson, Author*
*Linda Bowers, Owner*
*Rosemary Huisingh, Owner*

This systematic program of fluency shaping uses slow, easy speech for the youngest stutterers. The therapy manual contains step-by-step activities with goals and objectives. There are also sample lesson plans for individualizing therapy, strategies and materials to involve care givers. *$49.95*

*117 pages  Ages 2-6*

**651    Elementary Spelling Ace ES-90**

Franklin Electronic Publishers
1 Franklin Plaza
Burlington, NJ  08016                609-386-2500
                                     800-525-9673
                         FAX 609-239-5948
                 http://www.franklin.com
                 e-mail: info@frankling.com
*John Applegate, Director*
*Bettie Albertson, Executive Assistant*

Designed for elementary children, provides them with spelling correction for over 80,000 words. Accompanied by Webster's Elementary Dictionary. *$34.95*

**652    Every Child a Reader**

Sunburst Technology
400 Columbus Avenue
Valhalla, NY  10595 1349             914-747-3310
                                     800-321-7511
                         FAX 914-747-4109
                 http://www.sunburst.com
                 e-mail: support@sunburst.com
*Katie Birmingham, Office Manager*

Traditional reading strategies in a rich literary context. Designed to promote independent reading and develop oral and written language expression.

**653    Explode the Code: Wall Chart**

Educators Publishing Service
31 Smith Place
Cambridge, MA  02139 9031            617-547-6706
                                     800-225-5750
                         FAX 888-440-2665
                 http://www.epsbooks.com
                 e-mail: eps@epsbooks.com
*Nancy M Hall, Rena Price, Author*
*Steve Kote, President*
*Gunnar Voltz, Vice President*

Learning sounds is exciting with the new Explode The Code alphabet chart! Each letter is represented by a colorful character from the series and is stored inside a felt pocket embroidered with the letter's name.

**654    Expressive Language Kit**

LinguiSystems
3100 4th Avenue
East Moline, IL  61244                309-775-2300
                                      800-776-4332
                         FAX 309-755-2377
                         TDY:800-933-8331
                 http://www.linguisystems.com
                 e-mail: service@linguisystems.com
*Linda Bowers, Rosemary Huisingh, Carolyn LoGiudice, Author*
*Linda Bowers, Owner*
*Rosemary Huisingh, Owner*

It's our biggest language therapy kit ever. The focus is on strengthening expressive language skills so your students will become effective communicators. A combination of colorful photographs, picture cards, and activity sheets work together to create an outstanding expressive language program. A comprehension therapy manual is included to help you direct this incredibly wide variety of language activities. *$149.95*

*250 pages  Ages 5-11*

**655  Famous African Americans**

**Harcourt Achieve**
**6277 Sea Harbor Drive**
**Orlando, FL  32887**                    **252-480-3200**
                                           **800-844-1464**
                                           **FAX 800-269-5232**
                             **http://www.steckvaughn.com**
                             **e-mail: info@steckvaughn.com**
*Booth, Author*
*Tim McEwen, President/CEO*
*Jeff Johnson, Dir Marketing Communications*
*Chris Lehmann, Team Coordinator*

Introduce students to dozens of African-American achievers while improving language and thinking skills. High interest, three-page lessons highlight a defining moment in each individual's life and provide activities to build and apply skills in a curriculum context. Subjects are drawn from such diverse fields as science, government, education, sports, fine arts, and the military.

**656  Figurative Language**

**Harcourt Achieve**
**6277 Sea Harbor Drive**
**Orlando, FL  32887**                    **252-480-3200**
                                           **800-531-5015**
                                           **FAX 800-699-9459**
                             **http://www.steckvaughn.com**
                             **e-mail: info@steckvaughn.com**
*Steck-Vaughn Staff, Author*
*Tim McEwen, President/CEO*
*Jeff Johnson, Dir Marketing Communications*
*Chris Lehmann, Team Coordinator*

A delightful series that promotes critical thinking and vocabulary development through the use of literal and figurative language.

**657  First Phonics**

**Sunburst Technology**
**400 Columbus Avenue**
**Valhalla, NY  10595 1349**              **914-747-3310**
                                           **800-321-7511**
                                           **FAX 914-747-4109**
                             **http://www.sunburst.com**
                             **e-mail: support@sunburst.com**
*Katie Birmingham, Office Manager*

Targets the phonics skills that all children need to develop, sounding out the first letter of a word. This program offers four different engaging activities that you can customize to match each child's specific need.

**658  Fluharty Preschool Speech & Language Screening Test 2**

**Speech Bin**
**1965 25th Avenue**
**Vero Beach, FL  32960**                 **772-770-0007**
                                           **800-477-3324**
                                           **FAX 888-329-2246**
                             **http://www.speechbin.com**
                             **e-mail: info@speechbin.com**
*Nancy Buono Fluharty, Author*
*Shane Peters, Product Coordinator*
*Jen Binney, Owner*

Carefully normed on 705 children, the Fluharty yields standard scores, percentiles, and age equivalents. The form features space for speech-language pathologist to note phonological processess, voice quality, and fluency; a Teacher Questionnaire is also provided. Item number P882. *$153.00*

**659  Focus on Listening**

**Harcourt Achieve**
**6277 Sea Harbor Drive**
**Orlando, FL  32887**                    **252-480-3200**
                                           **800-531-5015**
                                           **FAX 800-699-9459**
                             **http://www.steckvaughn.com**
                             **e-mail: info@steckvaughn.com**
*Cimchowski, Author*
*Tim McEwen, President/CEO*
*Jeff Johnson, Dir Marketing Communications*
*Chris Lehmann, Team Coordinator*

A one-of-a-kind solution for students who need to improve their listening skills, students who are tested for their listening ability, or students who need practice with comprehending oral instructions. This program uses audio cassettes and teacher read material to practice listening comprehension of narrative, informational, persuasive, and workplace language.

**660  Follow Me! 2**

**LinguiSystems**
**3100 4th Avenue**
**East Moline, IL  61244**                **309-775-2300**
                                           **800-776-4332**
                                           **FAX 309-775-2377**
                                           **TDY:800-933-8331**
                             **http://www.linguisystems.com**
                             **e-mail: service@linguisystems.com**
*Grace Frank, Author*
*Linda Bowers, Owner*
*Rosemary Huisingh, Owner*

These activities are relevant to classroom listening demands. The directions relate specifically to an accompanying worksheet. It's a pick-up-and-use-now resource to teach the vocabulary of language arts, math, social studies and more. *$34.95*

*201 pages  Ages 7-11*

**661  Fun with Language: Book 1**

**Therapro**
**225 Arlington Street**
**Framingham, MA  01702 8723**            **508-872-9494**
                                           **800-257-5376**
                                           **FAX 508-875-2062**
                             **http://www.theraproducts.com**
                             **e-mail: info@theraproducts.com**
*Kathleen Yardley, Author*
*Karen Conrad, President*

A wonderful reproducible workbook of thinking and language skill exercises for children ages 4-8. Perfect when you need something on a moment's notice. Over 100 beautifully illustrated exercises in the following categories: Spatial Relationships; Opposites; Categorizing; Following Directions; Temporal Concepts; Syntax & Morphology; Same and Different; Plurals; Memory; Reasoning; Storytelling; and Describing. Targets both receptive and expressive language as well as problem- solving skills. *$55.00*

**662** **GEPA Success in Language Arts Literacy and Mathematics**

Harcourt Achieve
6277 Sea Harbor Drive
Orlando, FL 32887          252-480-3200
                          800-844-1464
                          FAX 800-269-5232
                    http://www.steckvaughn.com
                    e-mail: info@steckvaughn.com
*Steck-Vaughn Staff, Author*
*Tim McEwen, President/CEO*
*Jeff Johnson, Dir Marketing Communications*
*Chris Lehmann, Team Coordinator*

With these workbooks, you can ensure that your students are becoming more proficient users of language and math as well as more skilled test takers. Your students will gain valuable practice answering the types of questions found on the GEPA, such as open-ended and enhanced multiple choice items.

**663** **Get the Story! City News: Country News CD-ROM**

Harcourt Achieve
6277 Sea Harbor Drive
Orlando, FL 32887          252-480-3200
                          800-844-1464
                          FAX 800-269-5232
                    http://www.steckvaughn.com
                    e-mail: info@steckvaughn.com
*Tim McEwen, President/CEO*
*Jeff Johnson, Dir Marketing Communications*
*Chris Lehmann, Team Coordinator*

Develop investigation and communication skills in the context of publishing a newspaper. Students take on the roles of editors, reporters, and photographers to get the scoop on events in a big city, in a small town, and on a farm. Tasks include gathering information through interviews and clips files.

**664** **Goldman-Fristoe Test of Articulation: 2nd Edition**

Speech Bin
1965 25th Avenue
Vero Beach, FL 32960          772-770-0007
                             800-477-3324
                        FAX 772-770-0006
                    http://www.speechbin.com
                    e-mail: info@speechbin.com
*Shane Peters, Product Coordinator*
*Jen Binney, Owner*

The Goldman-Fristoe has been revised! This 2000 edition of your perennial articulation testing favorite systematically measures a child's production of 39 consonant sounds and blends. Its age range is expanded to 2-21 years, and age-based standard scores have separate gender norms. Item number A195. *$209.99*

**665** **HELP 1**

LinguiSystems
3100 4th Avenue
East Moline, IL 61244          309-775-2300
                              800-776-4332
                         FAX 309-775-2375
                         TDY:800-933-8331
                    http://www.linguisystems.com
                    e-mail: service@linguisystems.com
*Andrea Lazzari, Patricia Peters, Author*
*Linda Bowers, Owner*
*Rosemary Huisingh, Owner*

Get the books clinicians have relied on for years as their number one therapy resource. Written by two speech-language pathologists who know language remediation, this series has set the industry standard for practical, pick-up-and-use-now language therapy activities. HELP 1 includes activities for auditory discrimination, question comprehension, auditory association, and auditory memory. *$39.95*

*163 pages  Ages 6-Adult*

**666** **HELP 2**

LinguiSystems
3100 4th Avenue
East Moline, IL 61244          309-775-2300
                              800-776-4332
                         FAX 309-755-2377
                         TDY:800-933-8331
                    http://www.linguisystems.com
                    e-mail: service@linguisystems.com
*Andrea Lazzari, Patricia Peters, Author*
*Linda Bowers, Owner*
*Rosemary Huisingh, Owner*

Get the books clinicians have relied on for years as their number one therapy resource. Written by two speech-language pathologists who know language remediation, this series has set the industry standard for practical, pick-up-and-use-now language therapy activities. HELP 2 includes activities for word-finding, categorization, answering different question forms and grammar practice. *$39.95*

*175 pages  Ages 6-Adult*

**667** **HELP 3**

LinguiSystems
3100 4th Avenue
East Moline, IL 61244          309-775-2300
                              800-776-4332
                         FAX 309-755-2377
                         TDY:800-933-8331
                    http://www.linguisystems.com
                    e-mail: service@linguisystems.com
*Andrea Lazzari, Patricia Peters, Author*
*Linda Bowers, Owner*
*Rosemary Huisingh, Owner*

Get the books clinicians have relied on for years as their number one therapy resource. Written by two speech-language pathologists who know language remediation, this series has set the industry standard for practical, pick-up-and-use-now language therapy activities. HELP 3 includes activities for basic concepts, paraphrasing, thinking and problem-solving, and social language skills. *$39.95*

*194 pages  Ages 6-Adult*

**668    HELP 4**

LinguiSystems
3100 4th Avenue
East Moline, IL  61244                    309-775-2300
                                          800-776-4332
                                  FAX 309-755-2377
                                  TDY:800-933-8331
                      http://www.linguisystems.com
                  e-mail: service@linguisystems.com
*Andrea Lazzari, Patricia Peters, Author*
*Linda Bowers, Owner*
*Rosemary Huisingh, Owner*

Get the books clinicians have relied on for years as their number one therapy resource. Written by two speech-language pathologists who know language remediation, this series has set the industry standard for practical, pick-up-and-use-now language therapy activities. HELP 4 includes activities for defining and describing activities, written language exercises, linguistic concepts, and the language of humor and riddles. *$39.95*

*190 pages  Ages 6-Adult*

**669    HELP 5**

LinguiSystems
3100 4th Avenue
East Moline, IL  61244                    309-775-2300
                                          800-776-4332
                                  FAX 309-755-2377
                                  TDY:800-933-8331
                      http://www.linguisystems.com
                  e-mail: service@linguisystems.com
*Andrea Lazzari, Patricia Peters, Author*
*Linda Bowers, Owner*
*Rosemary Huisingh, Owner*

Get the books clinicians have relied on for years as their number one therapy resource. Written by two speech-language pathologists who know language remediation, this series has set the industry standard for practical, pick-up-and-use-now lanuage therapy activities. HELP 5 includes activities for processing information and messages; comparing and contrasting words; understanding math language and concepts; and communicating needs, feelings, and opinions. *$39.95*

*190 pages  Ages 6-Adult*

**670    HELP for Articulation**

LinguiSystems
3100 4th Avenue
East Moline, IL  61244                    309-775-2300
                                          800-776-4332
                                  FAX 309-755-2377
                                  TDY:800-933-8331
                      http://www.linguisystems.com
                  e-mail: service@linguisystems.com
*Andrea Lazzari, Author*
*Linda Bowers, Owner*
*Rosemary Huisingh, Owner*

This pick-up-and-use resource gives you a great variety of target sounds and activities. The hierarchy of tasks ensures mastery along the way and keeps your articulation therapy organized. Best of all, it's designed to span ages 6 through adult so you'll have articulation practice for your entire caseload. *$39.95*

*195 pages  Ages 6-Adult*

**671    HELP for Auditory Processing**

LinguiSystems
3100 4th Avenue
East Moline, IL  61244                    309-775-2300
                                          800-776-4332
                                  FAX 309-755-2377
                                  TDY:800-933-8331
                      http://www.linguisystems.com
                  e-mail: service@linguisystems.com
*Andrea Lazzari, Patricia Peters, Author*
*Linda Bowers, Owner*
*Rosemary Huisingh, Owner*

Functional communication improves when auditory processing skills are strong. Work on skills necessary to receive, interpret, and internalize language. Work through a hierarchy of auditory processing strategies with exercises for processing information in word classes, following a variety of directions, listening for sounds in words, and more. *$39.95*

*190 pages  Ages 6-Adult*

**672    HELP for Grammar**

LinguiSystems
3100 4th Avenue
East Moline, IL  61244                    309-775-2300
                                          800-776-4332
                                  FAX 309-755-2377
                                  TDY:800-933-8331
                      http://www.linguisystems.com
                  e-mail: service@linguisystems.com
*Andrea Lazzari, Author*
*Linda Bowers, Owner*
*Rosemary Huisingh, Owner*

Get in-depth grammar practice arranged in developmental order so skill builds upon skill. Get grammar training and practice with oral and written language exercises including identifying and matching grammar types, categorizing grammar types, applying grammar skills in context, and more. *$39.95*

*191 pages  Ages 8-Adult*

**673    HELP for Vocabulary**

LinguiSystems
3100 4th Avenue
East Moline, IL  61244                    309-775-2300
                                          800-776-4332
                                  FAX 309-755-2377
                                  TDY:800-933-8331
                      http://www.linguisystems.com
                  e-mail: service@linguisystems.com
*Andrea Lazzari, Author*
*Linda Bowers, Owner*
*Rosemary Huisingh, Owner*

Your students will expand word knowledge and learn to apply vocabulary skills in context with these great exercises. The hierarchy of tasks lets you see where breakdowns occur. Each page is a complete lesson with an IEP goal and ready-to-use exercise. *$39.95*

*180 pages  Ages 8-Adult*

**674    HELP for Word Finding**

LinguiSystems
3100 4th Avenue
East Moline, IL  61244          309-775-2300
                                800-776-4332
                          FAX 309-755-2377
                          TDY:800-933-8331
                http://www.linguisystems.com
              e-mail: service@linguisystems.com
*Andera Lazzari, Patricia Peters, Author*
*Linda Bowers, Owner*
*Rosemary Huisingh, Owner*

Expand the speed, quality, and variety of word recall
strategies within practical, everyday context. Stimulus items progress in difficulty within each task to
cover a broad age range as well as range of ability. Clients practice word-finding strategies with exercises
for automatic associations, words grouped in themes,
and more. *$39.95*

*179 pages  Ages 6-Adult*

**675    HSPA Success in Language Art Literacy**

Harcourt Achieve
6277 Sea Harbor Drive
Orlando, FL  32887            252-480-3200
                              800-844-1464
                        FAX 800-269-5232
                http://www.steckvaughn.com
              e-mail: info@steckvaughn.com
*Steck-Vaughn Staff, Author*
*Tim McEwen, President/CEO*
*Jeff Johnson, Dir Marketing Communications*
*Chris Lehmann, Team Coordinator*

These workbooks ensure your students are
enchancing their language arts skills, while learning
and practicing the skills they need for improved test
performance.

**676    HearFones**

Speech Bin
1965 25th Avenue
Vero Beach, FL  32960         772-770-0007
                              800-477-3324
                        FAX 772-770-0006
                http://www.speechbin.com
              e-mail: info@speechbin.com
*Shane Peters, Product Coordinator*
*Jen Binney, Owner*

This unique nonelectronic self-contained headset is
made of composite and plastic materials, and it's easy
to clean. It lets users hear themselves more directly
and clearly so they can analyze their own speech
sound production and voice quality. Item number
N261. *$29.00*

**677    I Can Say R**

Speech Bin
1965 25th Avenue
Vero Beach, FL  32960         772-770-0007
                              800-477-3324
                        FAX 772-770-0006
                http://www.speechbin.com
              e-mail: info@speechbin.com
*Shane Peters, Product Coordinator*
*Jen Binney, Owner*

Helping children overcome problems saying R sounds
is one of the most perplexing dilemmas speech and
language pathologists face in their caseloads. Here's a
terrific book packed with innovative practice materials to make that task easier. Item number 1477. *$26.95*

**678    Idiom's Delight**

Academic Therapy Publications
20 Commercial Boulevard
Novato, CA  94949             415-883-3314
                              800-422-7249
                        FAX 888-287-9975
                http://www.academictherapy.com
              e-mail: sales@academictherapy.com
*John Arena, Author*
*Jim Arena, Vice President*
*Anna Arena, President*

Offers 75 idioms and accompanying reproducible activities. Delightful illustrations portraying humorous
literal interpretations of idioms are sprinkled throughout the book to enhance enjoyment. *$14.00*

*64 pages*
*ISBN 0-878798-89-7*

**679    Island Reading Journey**

Sunburst Technology
400 Columbus Avenue
Valhalla, NY  10595 1349      914-747-3310
                              800-321-7511
                        FAX 914-747-4109
                http://www.sunburst.com
              e-mail: support@sunburst.com
*Katie Birmingham, Office Manager*

Enhance your reading program with meaningful summary and extension activities for 100 intermediate
level books. Students read for meaning while they engage in activities that test for comprehension, build
writing skills with reader response and essay questions, develop usage skills with cloze activities and
improve vocabulary/word attack skills.

**680    Just for Kids: Apraxia**

LinguiSystems
3100 4th Avenue
East Moline, IL  61244        309-775-2300
                              800-776-4332
                        FAX 309-755-2377
                        TDY:800-933-8331
                http://www.linguisystems.com
              e-mail: service@linguisystems.com
*Martha Drake, Author*
*Linda Bowers, Owner*
*Rosemary Huisingh, Owner*

Work through a sequence of skills to help your young
students achieve intelligibility. Sessions are organized using the alphabet as a theme. Each phase gives
you all the materials you need including goals, for
moving to the nest phase, family letter for take-home
practice, supplemental word lists, oral-mouth posture
pictures, and ABC flash cards. *$39.95*

*157 pages  Ages 4-8*

**681    Just for Kids: Articulation Stories**

LinguiSystems
3100 4th Avenue
East Moline, IL  61244                     309-775-2300
                                           800-776-4332
                                      FAX 309-755-2377
                                      TDY:800-933-8331
                           http://www.linguisystems.com
                    e-mail: service@linguisystems.com
*Jennifer Preschern, Author*
*Linda Bowers, Owner*
*Rosemary Huisingh, Owner*

Work through target sounds at the word, carrier sentence, sentence, and conversation levels. For each target sound, you'll get a wonderful organized lesson with child-centered vocabulary, appealing pictures, fun stories and interactive activities. *$39.95*

*175 pages  Ages 4-9*

**682    Just for Kids: Grammar**

LinguiSystems
3100 4th Avenue
East Moline, IL  61244                     309-775-2300
                                           800-776-4332
                                      FAX 309-755-2377
                                      TDY:800-933-8331
                           http://www.linguisystems.com
                    e-mail: service@linguisystems.com
*Janet Lanza, Lynn Flahive, Author*
*Linda Bowers, Owner*
*Rosemary Huisingh, Owner*

This kid friendly approach to grammar teaches the parts of speech your students need to know. The practice centers around natural, meaningful activities. Each chapter includes a pre-and post-test, picture cards, sequence story, rebus story, and family letter. *$39.95*

*186 pages  Ages 4-9*

**683    Just for Kids: Phonological Processing**

LinguiSystems
3100 4th Avenue
East Moline, IL  61244                     309-775-2300
                                           800-776-4332
                                      FAX 309-755-2377
                                      TDY:800-933-8331
                           http://www.linguisystems.com
                    e-mail: service@linguisystems.com
*Lynn Flahive, Janet Lanza, Author*
*Linda Bowers, Owner*
*Rosemary Huisingh, Owner*

Teach phonological processing skills through fun, themed activities. You'll love each comprehensive, pick-up-and-use-now lesson! This terrific program gives you 22 theme-related lessons that target common phonological processes. *$39.95*

*188 pages  Ages 4-9*

**684    Just for Me! Game**

LinguiSystems
3100 4th Avenue
East Moline, IL  61244                     309-775-2300
                                           800-776-4332
                                      FAX 309-755-2377
                                      TDY:800-933-8331
                           http://www.linguisystems.com
                    e-mail: service@linguisystems.com
*Margaret Warner, Author*
*Linda Bowers, Owner*
*Rosemary Huisingh, Owner*

Follow-up on the early language skills from all five Just for Me! books with this fun new game. It's a hands-on approach as youngsters mix up specially designed puzzle pieces to make funny faces. Each piece gives you five questions. That's 360 questions in all! Each puzzle piece covers an early language skill and corresponds to one part of the face. *$37.95*

*Ages 4-7*

**685    Just for Me! Grammar**

LinguiSystems
3100 4th Avenue
East Moline, IL  61244                     309-775-2300
                                           800-776-4332
                                      FAX 309-755-2377
                                      TDY:800-933-8331
                           http://www.linguisystems.com
                    e-mail: service@linguisystems.com
*Margaret Warner, Author*
*Linda Bowers, Owner*
*Rosemary Huisingh, Owner*

Teach oral grammar to your youngest students. Through a variety of engaging activities, your students will become familiar with basic parts of speech, correct word order, and simple grammar concepts. These activities provide a solid foundation for later formal grammar training in the classroom. *$24.95*

*150 pages  Ages 3-6*

**686    Just for Me! Vocabulary**

LinguiSystems
3100 4th Avenue
East Moline, IL  61244                     309-775-2300
                                           800-776-4332
                                      FAX 309-755-2377
                                      TDY:800-933-8331
                           http://www.linguisystems.com
                    e-mail: service@linguisystems.com
*Margaret Warner, Author*
*Linda Bowers, Owner*
*Rosemary Huisingh, Owner*

Your youngest students will love these fun cut-and-create activities for vocabulary. Each unit starts with poem introducing the key vocabulary words for the unit. *$24.95*

*148 pages  Ages 3-6*

**687    Kaufman Speech Praxis Test**

Speech Bin
1965 25th Avenue
Vero Beach, FL  32960                772-770-0007
                                     800-477-3324
                                     FAX 772-770-0006
                              http://www.speechbin.com
                              e-mail: info@speechbin.com
*Shane Peters, Product Coordinator*
*Jen Binney, Owner*

This standardized test utlilizes a hierarchy of simple to complex motor-speech movements, from oral movement and simple phonemic/syllable to complex phonemic/syllable level. The complete kit contains manual, guide, and 25 test booklets. Item number W325. *$150.00*

**688    Keys to Excellence in Integrated Language Arts**

Harcourt Achieve
6277 Sea Harbor Drive
Orlando, FL  32887                252-480-3200
                                 800-844-1464
                                 FAX 800-269-5232
                        http://www.steckvaughn.com
                        e-mail: info@steckvaughn.com
*Steck-Vaughn Staff, Author*
*Tim McEwen, President/CEO*
*Jeff Johnson, Dir Marketing Communications*
*Chris Lehmann, Team Coordinator*

Extensive instruction and assessment for improved test scores. Instruction and preparation for integrated language arts assessments. Boosts skills and scores.

**689    LILAC**

Speech Bin
1965 25th Avenue
Vero Beach, FL  32960                772-770-0007
                                     800-477-3324
                                     FAX 772-770-0006
                              http://www.speechbin.com
                              e-mail: info@speechbin.com
*Shane Peters, Product Coordinator*
*Jen Binney, Owner*

LILAC uses direct and naturalistic teaching in a creative approach that links spoken language learning to reading and writing. Activities to develop semantic, syntactic, expressive, and receptive language skills are presented sequentially from three-to five-year-old developmental levels. Item number 1428. *$27.95*

**690    Language Activity Resource Kit: LARK**

Speech Bin
1965 25th Avenue
Vero Beach, FL  32960                772-770-0007
                                     800-477-3324
                                     FAX 772-770-0006
                              http://www.speechbin.com
                              e-mail: info@speechbin.com
*Shane Peters, Product Coordinator*
*Jen Binney, Owner*

It's portable, stimulating, and easy-to-use with your adults who have aphasia and related disorders; you'll find many uses for it in your practice. The LARK includes a manual and 30 common objects familiar to adults represented in a variety of ways. Item number Q894. *$135.00*

**691    Language Arts Handbook**

Harcourt Achieve
6277 Sea Harbor Drive
Orlando, FL  32887                252-480-3200
                                 800-844-1464
                                 FAX 800-269-5232
                        http://www.steckvaughn.com
                        e-mail: info@steckvaughn.com
*Steck-Vaughn Staff, Author*
*Tim McEwen, President/CEO*
*Jeff Johnson, Dir Marketing Communications*
*Chris Lehmann, Team Coordinator*

This comprehensive, all in one handbook of reproducibles provides activities on every aspect of language arts skills. Each book's grade appropriate content and organization are easy to follow and thorough in scope.

**692    Language Exercises**

Harcourt Achieve
6277 Sea Harbor Drive
Orlando, FL  32887                252-480-3200
                                 800-844-1464
                                 FAX 800-269-5232
                        http://www.steckvaughn.com
                        e-mail: info@steckvaughn.com
*Jones, Author*
*Tim McEwen, President/CEO*
*Jeff Johnson, Dir Marketing Communications*
*Chris Lehmann, Team Coordinator*

Provides focused practice in six complex areas of language. Each book consists of six units addressing key skill areas such as vocabulary, sentences, grammar usage, capitalization and punctuation, composition, readiness and study skills.

**693    Language Handbooks**

Harcourt Achieve
6277 Sea Harbor Drive
Orlando, FL  32887                252-480-3200
                                 800-844-1464
                                 FAX 800-269-5232
                        http://www.steckvaughn.com
                        e-mail: info@steckvaughn.com
*Steck-Vaughn Staff, Author*
*Tim McEwen, President/CEO*
*Jeff Johnson, Dir Marketing Communications*
*Chris Lehmann, Team Coordinator*

Language reference, modeling, and practice combined. These comprehensive reference and practice resources cover grammar usage, mechanics, and writing at appropriate levels for grades 1-6.

**694    Language Practice**

Harcourt Achieve
6277 Sea Harbor Drive
Orlando, FL  32887                252-480-3200
                                 800-844-1464
                                 FAX 800-269-5232
                        http://www.steckvaughn.com
                        e-mail: info@steckvaughn.com
*Moeller, Author*
*Tim McEwen, President/CEO*
*Jeff Johnson, Dir Marketing Communications*
*Chris Lehmann, Team Coordinator*

Focuses students attention on the six most complex areas of language or only on the ones that need work. Now teachers can fine tune language skills with consistent, grade appropriate instruction with exercises covering vocabulary, sentences, grammar usage, capitalization and punctuation, composition, readiness and study skills.

**695  Language Processing Kit**

**LinguiSystems**
**3100 4th Avenue**
**East Moline, IL  61244**          309-775-2300
800-776-4332
FAX 309-755-2377
TDY:800-933-8331
http://www.linguisystems.com
e-mail: service@linguisystems.com
*Gail Richard, Mary Anne Hanner, Author*
*Linda Bowers, Owner*
*Rosemary Huisingh, Owner*

You'll get a variety of activities in developmental progression for improving processing skills. It's your comprehensive follow-up to the Language Processing Test-Revised. You'll also get an outline of compensatory cueing and prompting strategies with helpful tips on how to teach them. *$124.95*

*143 pages  Ages 5-11*

**696  Language Rehabilitation**

**Pro-Ed**
**8700 Shoal Creek Boulevard**
**Austin, TX  78757 6897**          512-451-3246
800-897-3202
FAX 800-397-7633
http://www.proedinc.com
*James Martinoff, Rosemary Martinoff, Author*
*Donald Hammill MD, President*

Offers practical exercises for developing language in older children or rebuilding language in aphasic adults. *$99.00*

**697  LanguageBURST: A Language and Vocabulary Game**

**LinguiSystems**
**3100 4th Avenue**
**East Moline, IL  61244**          309-775-2300
800-776-4332
FAX 309-755-2377
TDY:800-933-8331
http://www.linguisystems.com
e-mail: service@linguisystems.com
*Lauri Whiskeyman, Author*
*Linda Bowers, Owner*
*Rosemary Huisingh, Owner*

Expand your student's language and vocabulary skills with this quick- thinking game. Many of the items are based on the curriculum for grades 3-8 so your therapy is classroom-relevant. Students think quickly as they practice skills in four key language areas: fill-in-the-blank; categories; comparing and contrasting; and attributes. *$37.95*

*Ages 9-15*

**698  Learning 100 Language Clues Vocabulary and Spelling**

**Harcourt Achieve**
**6277 Sea Harbor Drive**
**Orlando, FL  32887**          252-480-3200
800-844-1464
FAX 800-269-5232
http://www.steckvaughn.com
e-mail: info@steckvaughn.com
*Steck-Vaughn Staff, Author*
*Tim McEwen, President/CEO*
*Jeff Johnson, Dir Marketing Communications*
*Chris Lehmann, Team Coordinator*

Help your learners build vocabulary and spelling skills through a variety of exercises, including word attack, usage, dictionary, context clues, spelling, and cloze exercises. Use this print-based program alone or in conjunction with Language Clues Software to build vocabulary by providing instruction, practice, and reinforcement through the application of 19 essential skills.

**699  Learning 100 Thinking Strategies Series**

**Harcourt Achieve**
**6277 Sea Harbor Drive**
**Orlando, FL  32887**          252-480-3200
800-844-1464
FAX 800-699-9459
http://www.steckvaughn.com
e-mail: info@steckvaughn.com
*Steck-Vaughn Staff, Author*
*Tim McEwen, President/CEO*
*Jeff Johnson, Dir Marketing Communications*
*Chris Lehmann, Team Coordinator*

Make your students better listeners and readers. Criterion referenced tests help you evaluate comprehension skills. Audio cassettes and written instructions help learners develop essential thinking processes and communication skills.

**700  Letter Sounds**

**Sunburst Technology**
**400 Columbus Avenue**
**Valhalla, NY  10595 1349**          914-747-3310
800-321-7511
FAX 914-747-4109
http://www.sunburst.com
e-mail: service@sunburst.com
*Katie Birmingham, Office Manager*

Students develop phonemic awareness skills as they make the connection between consonant letters and their sounds.

**701 Linamood Program (LIPS Clinical Version):Phoneme Sequencing Program**

LinguiSystems
3100 4th Avenue
East Moline, IL  61244          309-775-2300
                               800-776-4332
                            FAX 309-755-2377
                           TDY:800-933-8331
                      http://www.linguisystems.com
                   e-mail: service@linguisystems.com
*Patricia Lindamood, Phyllis Lindamood, Author*
*Linda Bowers, Owner*
*Rosemary Huisingh, Owner*

Help your students develop phoneme awareness for competence in reading, spelling, and speech. This multisensory program meets the needs of the many children and adults who don't develop phonemic awareness through traditional methods. *$247.00*

*Birth-Adult*

**702 Listening Kit**

LinguiSystems
3100 4th Avenue
East Moline, IL  61244          309-775-2300
                               800-776-4332
                            FAX 309-755-2377
                           TDY:800-933-8331
                      http://www.linguisystems.com
                   e-mail: service@linguisystems.com
*Susan Simms, Mark Barrett, Rosemay Huisingh, Author*
*Linda Bowers, Owner*
*Rosemary Huisingh, Owner*

This listening curriculum combines thinking, reasoning, and language skills for improved listening and attending. It's an unbeatable combination. The Listening Book organizes listening skills into the areas of paying attention, listening with an open mind and reasoning. *$119.95*

*185 pages  Ages 5-11*

**703 Listening and Speaking for Job and Personal Use**

AGS Publishing
4201 Woodland Road
Circle Pines, MN  55014 1796    651-287-7220
                               800-328-2560
                            FAX 800-471-8457
                       http://www.agsnet.com
                    e-mail: agsmail@agsnet.com
*L Ann Masters, Author*
*Karen Dahlen, Associate Director*
*Matt Keller, Marketing Manger*

With an interest level of High School through Adult, and a reading level of Grade 5-6, this series has modules in Listening Skills and Speaking Skills. Self-paced texts have applications-oriented exercises.

**704 Listening for Articulation All Year 'Round**

LinguiSystems
3100 4th Avenue
East Moline, IL  61244          309-775-2300
                               800-776-4332
                            FAX 309-755-2377
                           TDY:800-933-8331
                      http://www.linguisystems.com
                   e-mail: service@linguisystems.com
*Brenda Brumbaugh, Nan Thompson-Trenta, Author*
*Linda Bowers, Owner*
*Rosemary Huisingh, Owner*

Get your young students on their way to intelligible speech with this book devoted to early-developing sounds. Pictures and activities can be used for phonology or articulation therapy. The program includes practice with minimal pairs, tips for establishing production, a variety of stimulus pictures, and activity sheets organized by phoneme. *$39.95*

*208 pages  Ages 5-10*

**705 Listening for Language All Year 'Round**

LinguiSystems
3100 4th Avenue
East Moline, IL  61244          309-775-2300
                               800-776-4332
                            FAX 309-755-2377
                           TDY:800-933-8331
                      http://www.linguisystems.com
                   e-mail: service@linguisystems.com
*Brenda Brumbaugh, Nan Thompson-Trenta, Author*
*Linda Bowers, Owner*
*Rosemary Huisingh, Owner*

Reinforce word relationships while you teach these important language concepts: synonyms, antonyms, classification, comparisons, multiple meanings, and idioms. Special notebook activities give structured writing practice. *$39.95*

*196 pages  Ages 7-11*

**706 Listening for Vocabulary All Year 'Round**

LinguiSystems
3100 4th Avenue
East Moline, IL  61244          309-775-2300
                               800-776-4332
                            FAX 309-755-2377
                           TDY:800-933-8331
                      http://www.linguisystems.com
                   e-mail: service@linguisystems.com
*Brenda Brumbaugh, Nan Thompson-Trenta, Author*
*Linda Bowers, Owner*
*Rosemary Huisingh, Owner*

Save time and energy with these ready-to-use listening and vocabulary lessons that match the themes of your school year. This book includes language stories, hands-on listening activities, home lessons, and terrific artworks! *$ 39.95*

*196 pages  Ages 5-8*

**707 Look! Listen! & Learn Language!: Software**
**Speech Bin**
**1965 25th Avenue**
**Vero Beach, FL 32960**
772-770-0007
800-477-3324
FAX 772-770-0006
http://www.speechbin.com
e-mail: info@speechbin.com
*Shane Peters, Product Coordinator*
*Jen Binney, Owner*

Interactive activities for children with autism, PDD, Down syndrome, language delay, or apraxia include: hello; Match Same to Same; Quack; Let's talk About It; visual scanning/attention and match ups! Item number L177. *$99.00*

**708 M-SS-NG L-NKS**
**Sunburst Technology**
**400 Columbus Avenue**
**Valhalla, NY 10595 1349**
914-747-3310
800-321-7511
FAX 914-747-4109
http://www.sunburst.com
e-mail: service@sunburst.com
*Katie Birmingham, Office Manager*

This award-winning program is an engrossing language puzzle. A passage appears with letters or words missing. Students complete it based on their knowledge of word structure, spelling, grammar, meaning in context, and literary style.

**709 MCLA: Measure of Cognitive-Linguistic Abilities**
**Speech Bin**
**1965 25th Avenue**
**Vero Beach, FL 32960**
772-770-0007
800-477-3324
FAX 772-770-0006
http://www.speechbin.com
e-mail: info@speechbin.com
*Shane Peters, Product Coordinator*
*Jen Binney, Owner*

The MCLA includes the Family Questionnaire, Information Processing Checklist, Communication Functioning Interview and these valuable subtests: functional reading, paragraph comprehension, story recall and oral mechanism screening. The MCLA is normed for individuals 16 to 55+ years. Item number 1450. *$89.00*

**710 Many Voices of Paws**
**Speech Bin**
**1965 25th Avenue**
**Vero Beach, FL 32960**
772-770-0007
800-477-3324
FAX 772-770-0006
http://www.speechbin.com
e-mail: info@speechbin.com
*Julie Reville, Author*
*Jan Binney, Editor-in-Chief*
*Shane Peters, Product Coordinator*

The Many Voices of Paws shows young stuttering children how to modify their speaking rates and vocal behaviors in a way that's easy for them to understand. Beautifully illustrated, the story about Paws, the cat, combines pretending, talking, and playful interaction and helps children accept their disfluencies in a positive way. Item number 1568. *$19.95*

*64 pages*
*ISBN 0-937857-11-4*

**711 Max's Attic: Long & Short Vowels**
**Sunburst Technology**
**400 Columbus Avenue**
**Valhalla, NY 10595 1349**
914-747-3310
800-321-7511
FAX 914-747-4109
http://www.sunburst.com
e-mail: service@sunburst.com
*Katie Birmingham, Office Manager*

Filled to the rafters with phonics fun, this animated program builds your students' vowel recognition skills.

**712 Maxwell's Manor: A Social Language Game**
**LinguiSystems**
**3100 4th Avenue**
**East Moline, IL 61244**
309-775-2300
800-776-4332
FAX 309-755-2377
TDY:800-933-8331
http://www.linguisystems.com
e-mail: service@linguisystems.com
*Carolyn LoGiudice, Nancy McConnell, Author*
*Linda Bowers, Owner*
*Rosemary Huisingh, Owner*

This fun game will teach your students the social skills they need to get along with others, be more accepted by their peers, and be successful in the classroom. Maxwell, the loveable dog, leads the way as your students practice positive social language skills. *$44.95*

*Ages 4-9*

**713 Middle School Language Arts**
**Harcourt Achieve**
**6277 Sea Harbor Drive**
**Orlando, FL 32887**
252-480-3200
800-844-1464
FAX 800-269-5232
http://www.steckvaughn.com
e-mail: info@steckvaughn.com
*Steck-Vaughn Staff, Author*
*Tim McEwen, President/CEO*
*Jeff Johnson, Dir Marketing Communications*
*Chris Lehmann, Team Coordinator*

This skill-specific series reinforces and enhances the middle school language arts curriculum. It provides teachers and parents with a tool to focus on the skills that students need to review and reinforce. The lessons provide step-by-step instructions and follow-up activities to enable students to work independently.

**714  Mike Mulligan & His Steam Shovel**

Sunburst Technology
400 Columbus Avenue
Valhalla, NY  10595 1349          914-747-3310
                                 800-321-7511
                            FAX 914-747-4109
                      http://www.sunburst.com
                 e-mail: service@sunburst.com
*Katie Birmingham, Office Manager*

This CD-ROM version of the Caldecott classic lets students experience interactive book reading and participate in four skills-based extension activities that promote memory, matching, sequencing, listening, pattern recognition and map reading skills.

**715  Mouth Madness**

Speech Bin
1965 25th Avenue
Vero Beach, FL  32960            772-770-0007
                                 800-477-3324
                            FAX 772-770-0006
                     http://www.speechbin.com
                  e-mail: info@speechbin.com
*Shane Peters, Product Coordinator*
*Jen Binney, Owner*

This unique manual uses oral imitation, motor planning, and breath control activities to improve the articulation and feeding skills of preschool and primary children. Games, manipulative tasks, silly sentences, rhymes, and funny faces target higher organizational levels of motor planning. Item number C758. *$51.95*

**716  My First Phonics Book**

Speech Bin
1965 25th Avenue
Vero Beach, FL  32960            772-770-0007
                                 800-477-3324
                            FAX 772-770-0006
                     http://www.speechbin.com
                  e-mail: info@speechbin.com
*Shane Peters, Product Coordinator*
*Jen Binney, Owner*

Shows that words are made of sounds, then helps to recognize the letter symbols for the sounds. It's organized in easy-to-locate alphabetical order of sounds, with one page for each of the 42 sounds of English. Item number H585. *$16.95*

**717  Myrtle's Beach: A Phonological Awareness and Articulation Game**

LinguiSystems
3100 4th Avenue
East Moline, IL  61244           309-775-2300
                                 800-776-4332
                            FAX 309-755-2377
                          TDY:800-933-8331
                    http://www.linguisystems.com
               e-mail: service@linguisystems.com
*LinguiSystems Staff, Author*
*Linda Bowers, Owner*
*Rosemary Huisingh, Owner*

Myrtle's Beach is a fun place to practice phonological awareness, articulation, and language skills. The flexible format allows you to meet the varied needs of all the students in your speech and language groups. *$44.95*

*Ages 4-9*

**718  No-Glamour Grammar**

LinguiSystems
3100 4th Avenue
East Moline, IL  61244           309-775-2300
                                 800-776-4332
                            FAX 309-755-2377
                          TDY:800-933-8331
                    http://www.linguisystems.com
               e-mail: service@linguisystems.com
*Suzanna Mayer Watt, Author*
*Linda Bowers, Owner*
*Rosemary Huisingh, Owner*

This best-selling grammar book teaches all the basic grammar skills your students need. The no-frills approach is great for students with language or learning disorders. You'll teach one skill at a time with tons of practice pages. The units progress in difficulty as students master each grammar skill. *$41.95*

*415 pages  Ages 8-12*

**719  No-Glamour Grammar 2**

LinguiSystems
3100 4th Avenue
East Moline, IL  61244           309-775-2300
                                 800-776-4332
                            FAX 309-755-2377
                          TDY:800-933-8331
                    http://www.linguisystems.com
               e-mail: service@linguisystems.com
*Diane Hyde, Author*
*Linda Bowers, Owner*
*Rosemary Huisingh, Owner*

Get more grammar skill practice with a variety of activity sheets. From nouns to verbs, adjectives to adverbs, your students will apply their knowledge to these challenging, fun activity pages. *$41.95*

*320 pages  Ages 8-12*

**720  No-Glamour Vocabulary**

LinguiSystems
3100 4th Avenue
East Moline, IL  61244           309-775-2300
                                 800-776-4332
                            FAX 309-755-2377
                          TDY:800-933-8331
                    http://www.linguisystems.com
               e-mail: service@linguisystems.com
*Diane Hyde, Author*
*Linda Bowers, Owner*
*Rosemary Huisingh, Owner*

With one vocabulary skill to a page, students can focus on the semantic areas that give them the most trouble. These vocabulary worksheets target absurdities, multiple meanings, associations, definitions, synonyms, antonyms, and more. *$41.95*

*278 pages  Ages 7-12*

**721  Oral-Motor Activities for School-Aged Children**
**LinguiSystems**
**3100 4th Avenue**
**East Moline, IL  61244**              **309-775-2300**
                                        **800-776-4332**
                                    **FAX 309-755-2377**
                                    **TDY:800-933-8331**
                       **http://www.linguisystems.com**
                  **e-mail: service@linguisystems.com**
*Elizabeth Mackie, Author*
*Linda Bowers, Owner*
*Rosemary Huisingh, Owner*

Multisensory, oral-motor approach to treating articulation disorders. Great for older students with developmental delays or any student who needs to improve oral-motor function for better speech production. *$39.95*

*171 pages  Ages 7-12*

**722  Oral-Motor Activities for Young Children**
**LinguiSystems**
**3100 4th Avenue**
**East Moline, IL  61244**              **309-775-2300**
                                        **800-776-4332**
                                    **FAX 309-755-2377**
                                    **TDY:800-933-8331**
                       **http://www.linguisystems.com**
                  **e-mail: service@linguisystems.com**
*Elizabeth Mackie, Author*
*Linda Bowers, Owner*
*Rosemary Huisingh, Owner*

Whether your are new to oral-motor skills training or an experienced oral-motor skills clinician, these activities get results. *$39.95*

*119 pages  Ages 3-8*

**723  PLAID**
**Speech Bin**
**1965 25th Avenue**
**Vero Beach, FL  32960**              **772-770-0007**
                                       **800-477-3324**
                                   **FAX 772-770-0006**
                        **http://www.speechbin.com**
                      **e-mail: info@speechbin.com**
*Shane Peters, Product Coordinator*
*Jen Binney, Owner*

PLAID is a top-notch clinical tool that gives you practical practice materials featuring twenty different phonemes — just what you need for your apraxic and aphasic adults — all in one resource. Item number 1424. *$29.95*

**724  Pair-It Books: Early Emergent Stage 1**
**Harcourt Achieve**
**6277 Sea Harbor Drive**
**Orlando, FL  32887**                 **252-480-3200**
                                       **800-844-1464**
                                   **FAX 800-269-5232**
                      **http://www.steckvaughn.com**
                    **e-mail: info@steckvaughn.com**
*Steck-Vaughn Staff, Author*
*Tim McEwen, President/CEO*
*Jeff Johnson, Dir Marketing Communications*
*Chris Lehmann, Team Coordinator*

Includes 30 eight-page books with simple concepts, predictable and repetitive text patterns, and a strong matching of art or photos to support the text.

**725  Pair-It Books: Early Emergent Stage 1 in Spanish**
**Harcourt Achieve**
**6277 Sea Harbor Drive**
**Orlando, FL  32887**                 **252-480-3200**
                                       **800-844-1464**
                                   **FAX 800-269-5232**
                      **http://www.steckvaughn.com**
                    **e-mail: info@steckvaughn.com**
*Steck-Vaughn Staff, Author*
*Tim McEwen, President/CEO*
*Jeff Johnson, Dir Marketing Communications*
*Chris Lehmann, Team Coordinator*

Includes 30 eight-page books with simple concepts, predictable and repetitive text patterns, and a strong matching of art or photos to support the text. Six big books encourage shared reading and strategy instruction. Students can read these texts with ease and view themselves as successful readers.

**726  Pair-It Books: Early Emergent Stage 2**
**Harcourt Achieve**
**6277 Sea Harbor Drive**
**Orlando, FL  32887**                 **252-480-3200**
                                       **800-844-1464**
                                   **FAX 800-269-5232**
                      **http://www.steckvaughn.com**
                    **e-mail: info@steckvaughn.com**
*Steck-Vaughn Staff, Author*
*Tim McEwen, President/CEO*
*Jeff Johnson, Dir Marketing Communications*
*Chris Lehmann, Team Coordinator*

A series of 20 books, each containing 16 pages, that gradually become more difficult and reflect more complex text structures such as dialogue, content vocabulary and question and answer formats. All stories are available on audio cassette, and four are available in big book format.

**727  Pair-It Books: Early Emergent Stage 2 in Spanish**
**Harcourt Achieve**
**6277 Sea Harbor Drive**
**Orlando, FL  32887**                 **252-480-3200**
                                       **800-844-1464**
                                   **FAX 800-269-5232**
                      **http://www.steckvaughn.com**
                    **e-mail: info@steckvaughn.com**
*Steck-Vaughn Staff, Author*
*Tim McEwen, President/CEO*
*Jeff Johnson, Dir Marketing Communications*
*Chris Lehmann, Team Coordinator*

A series of 20 books, each containing 16 pages, that encourage native Spanish speakers with early reading success in their first language. Simple concepts, predictable language, and well chosen art support students efforts.

**728  Pair-It Books: Early Fluency Stage 3**
**Harcourt Achieve**
**6277 Sea Harbor Drive**
**Orlando, FL  32887**                 **252-480-3200**
                                       **800-844-1464**
                                   **FAX 800-269-5232**
                      **http://www.steckvaughn.com**
                    **e-mail: info@steckvaughn.com**
*Steck-Vaughn Staff, Author*
*Tim McEwen, President/CEO*
*Jeff Johnson, Dir Marketing Communications*
*Chris Lehmann, Team Coordinator*

A series of 30 books, each containing either 16 or 24 pages, and six big books that introduce tables, folktales, tall tales and plays that invite readers to respond in writing.

**729  Pair-It Books: Early Skills**
Harcourt Achieve
6277 Sea Harbor Drive
Orlando, FL  21887              252-480-3200
                               800-844-1464
                          FAX 800-269-5232
                   http://www.steckvaughn.com
                   e-mail: info@steckvaughn.com
*Steck-Vaughn Staff, Author*
*Tim McEwen, President/CEO*
*Jeff Johnson, Dir Marketing Communications*
*Chris Lehmann, Team Coordinator*

Give students an early start on academic achievement
with grade appropriate, cross-curricular excercises.
Easy-to-understand lessons with helpful graphics are
ideal for independent or small group learning.

**730  Pair-It Books: Fluency Stage 4**
Harcourt Achieve
6277 Sea Harbor Drive
Orlando, FL  32887             252-480-3200
                               800-844-1464
                          FAX 800-269-5232
                   http://www.steckvaughn.com
                   e-mail: info@steckvaughn.com
*Steck-Vaughn Staff, Author*
*Tim McEwen, President/CEO*
*Jeff Johnson, Dir Marketing Communications*
*Chris Lehmann, Team Coordinator*

A series of 20 books, each containing 24 or 32 pages,
and four big books. Readers encounter diaries, journals, biographies, and mysteries and explore written
responses in a variety of formats. Students emerge as
confident readers and writers of both narrative and informational texts.

**731  Pair-It Books: Proficiency Stage 5**
Harcourt Achieve
6277 Sea Harbor Drive
Orlando, FL  32887             252-480-3200
                               800-844-1464
                          FAX 800-269-5232
                   http://www.steckvaughn.com
                   e-mail: info@steckvaughn.com
*Steck-Vaughn Staff, Author*
*Tim McEwen, President/CEO*
*Jeff Johnson, Dir Marketing Communications*
*Chris Lehmann, Team Coordinator*

A series of 30 books, each containing 32 or 40 pages,
that take readers from fluency to proficiency, presenting a wide variety of genres and text structures. Offers
helpful strategies and activities for improving phonics
skills, vocabulary, and reading and language skills, as
well as take-home letters in Spanish and English.

**732  Pair-It Books: Transition Stage 2-3**
Harcourt Achieve
6277 Sea Harbor Drive
Orlando, FL  32887             252-480-3200
                               800-844-1464
                          FAX 800-269-5232
                   http://www.steckvaughn.com
                   e-mail: info@steckvaughn.com
*Tim McEwen, President/CEO*
*Jeff Johnson, Dir Marketing Communications*
*Chris Lehmann, Team Coordinator*

A series of 20 books, each containing 16 pages, that
provide readers with a gradual transition into early
fluency. All stories are available on audio cassette,
and four are avaiable in big book format.

**733  Patterns Across the Curriculum**
Harcourt Achieve
6277 Sea Harbor Drive
Orlando, FL  32887             252-480-3200
                               800-844-1464
                          FAX 800-269-5232
                   http://www.steckvaughn.com
                   e-mail: info@steckvaughn.com
*Steck-Vaughn Staff, Author*
*Tim McEwen, President/CEO*
*Jeff Johnson, Dir Marketing Communications*
*Chris Lehmann, Team Coordinator*

Develop students awareness and understanding of
patterns in the real world. Exercises allow students to
identify, complete, extend, and create patterns. Developed across math, language, social studies, and
science. This flexible organization allows teachers to
utilize content specific activities in coordination with
other classroom assignments, providing additional
richness in learning.

**734  Patty's Cake: A Describing Game**
LinguiSystems
3100 4th Avenue
East Moline, IL  61244         309-775-2300
                               800-776-4332
                          FAX 309-755-2377
                          TDY:800-933-8331
                   http://www.linguisystems.com
                   e-mail: service@linguisystems.com
*Julie Cole, Author*
*Linda Bowers, Owner*
*Rosemary Huisingh, Owner*

Teach describing skills with Patty's Cake. Two levels
of play in this fun game give you flexibility to meet individual students learning needs. Players describe
age-appropriate picture vocabulary cards by naming
attributes such as category, function, shape, color, or
location. Your students will improve their skills in listening, memory, word retrieval, categorizing, naming
attributes, formulating sentences, and giving descriptions. *$44.95*

*Ages 4-9*

**735  PhonicsMart CD-ROM**
Harcourt Achieve
6277 Sea Harbor Drive
Orlando, FL  32887             252-480-3200
                               800-844-1464
                          FAX 800-269-5232
                   http://www.steckvaughn.com
                   e-mail: info@steckvaughn.com
*Steck-Vaughn Staff, Author*
*Tim McEwen, President/CEO*
*Jeff Johnson, Dir Marketing Communications*
*Chris Lehmann, Team Coordinator*

Five interactive games offer practice and reinforcement in 19 phonics skills at a variety of learning levels! Over 700 key words are vocalized, and each is
accompanied by sound effects, colorful illustrations,
animation, or video clips!

**736** **Phonological Awareness Kit**

LinguiSystems
3100 4th Avenue
East Moline, IL  61244          309-775-2300
                               800-776-4332
                        FAX 309-755-2377
                        TDY:800-933-8331
               http://www.linguisystems.com
            e-mail: service@linguisystems.com
*Carolyn Robertson, Wanda Salter, Author*
*Linda Bowers, Owner*
*Rosemary Huisingh, Owner*

Help your students learn to use phonological information to process oral and written language with this fan-
tastic kit. Written by an SLP and special educator, this
best-seller links sound awareness, oral language, and
early reading and writing skills. The kit uses a
multisensory approach to ensure success for all learning styles. *$69.95*

*115 pages  Ages 5-8*

**737** **Phonological Awareness Kit: Intermediate**

LinguiSystems
3100 4th Avenue
East Moline, IL  61244          309-775-2300
                               800-776-4332
                        FAX 309-755-2377
                        TDY:800-933-8331
               http://www.linguisystems.com
            e-mail: service@linguisystems.com
*Carolyn Robertson, Wanda Salter, Author*
*Linda Bowers, Owner*
*Rosemary Huisingh, Owner*

Now there's hope for your older students who have
struggled with reading through their early school
years. Give them strategies to crack the reading code
with this comprehensive program. Great for students
with deficits in auditory processing, decoding, and
written language. *$69.95*

*116 pages  Ages 9-14*

**738** **Phonological Awareness Test: Computerized
Scoring**

LinguiSystems
3100 4th Avenue
East Moline, IL  61244          309-755-2377
                               800-776-4332
                        FAX 800-577-4555
                        TDY:800-933-8331
               http://www.linguisystems.com
            e-mail: service@linguisystems.com
*Carolyn Robertson, Wanda Salter, Author*
*Linda Bowers, Owner*
*Rosemary Huisingh, Owner*

Designed to save time, this optional CD-ROM software allows you to accurately, conveniently, and
quickly score The Phonological Awareness Test. Just
plug in the raw scores and the program does everything else. You'll be able to print out all the scores you
need to include in a student's assessment report.
*$69.95*

*Ages 5-9*

**739** **Phonology: Software**

Speech Bin
1965 25th Avenue
Vero Beach, FL  32960          772-770-0007
                               800-477-3324
                        FAX 772-770-0006
               http://www.speechbin.com
            e-mail: info@speechbin.com
*Shane Peters, Product Coordinator*
*Jen Binney, Owner*

This unique software gives you six entertaining
games to treat children's phonological disorders. The
program uses target patterns in a pattern cycling approach to phonological processes. Item number L183.
*$99.00*

**740** **Plunk's Pond: A Riddles Game for Language**

LinguiSystems
3100 4th Avenue
East Moline, IL  61244          309-775-2300
                               800-776-4332
                        FAX 309-755-2377
                        TDY:800-933-8331
               http://www.linguisystems.com
            e-mail: service@linguisystems.com
*LinguiSystems Staff, Author*
*Linda Bowers, Owner*
*Rosemary Huisingh, Owner*

Encourage divergent thinking, sharpen listening
skills, and improve vocabulary with this fun riddle
game. With a picture on one side and three clues on the
other, these cards are great for all kinds of therapy
games. Target attributes such as function, color, category, and more. *$44.95*

*Ages 4-9*

**741** **Poetry in Three Dimensions: Reading, Writing
and Critical Thinking Skills through Poetry**

Educators Publishing Service
31 Smith Place
Cambridge, MA  02139 9031          617-547-6706
                                   800-225-5750
                            FAX 888-440-2665
                   http://www.epsbooks.com
                e-mail: eps@epsbooks.com
*Carol Clark, Alison Draper, Author*
*Steve Kote, President*
*Jennifer Avery, Contact*

Help your students improve their reading comprehension and writing through the study of poetry in this
collection of multicultural poems. With poems and
questions on facing pages, students are encouraged to
annotate the text of the poem and to go back to the text
to respond to the questions.

**742** **Polar Express**

Sunburst Technology
400 Columbus Avenue
Valhalla, NY  10595 1349          914-747-3310
                                  800-321-7511
                           FAX 914-747-4109
                  http://www.sunburst.com
               e-mail: service@sunburst.com
*Katie Birmingham, Office Manager*

Share the magic and enchantment of the holiday season with this CD-ROM version of Chris Van Allsburg's Caldecott-winning picture book.

**743    Preschool Motor Speech Evaluation & Intervention**

**Speech Bin**
**1965 25th Avenue**
**Vero Beach, FL  32960**            772-770-0007
                                      800-477-3324
                              FAX 800-329-2246
                         http://www.speechbin.com
                          e-mail: info@speechbin.com
*Shane Peters, Product Coordinator*
*Jen Binney, Owner*

This comprehensive criterion-based assessment tool differentiates motor-based speech disorders from those of phonology and determines if speech difficulties of children 18 months to six years old are characteristic of: oral nonverbal apraxia; dysarthria; developmental verbal dyspraxia; hypersensitivity; differences in tone and hyposensitivity. Item number J322. *$59.00*

**744    Progress with Puppets: Speech and Language Activities for Children**

**Therapro**
**225 Arlington Street**
**Framingham, MA  01702 8723**        508-872-9494
                                      800-257-5376
                              FAX 508-875-2062
                        http://www.theraproducts.com
                        e-mail: info@theraproducts.com
*Joanne Hanson MS CCC-SLP, Author*
*Karen Conrad, President*

A much needed book of activities to use during therapy with puppets. Great ideas for working on chewing and feeding, language stimulation, articulation training, fluency and more. Suggestions offered for use with the Puppets that Swallow. *$29.95*

**745    Promoting Communication in Infants & Children**

**Speech Bin**
**1965 25th Avenue**
**Vero Beach, FL  32960**            772-770-0007
                                      800-477-3324
                              FAX 772-770-0006
                         http://www.speechbin.com
                          e-mail: info@speechbin.com
*Shane Peters, Product Coordinator*
*Jen Binney, Owner*

Gives you down-to-earth information, activities, and step-by-step suggestions for stimulating children's speech and language skills. Topics are conveniently organized, concisely presented, and written in easy-to-understand language. Item number 1512. *$14.95*

**746    Python Path Phonics Word Families**

**Sunburst Technology**
**400 Columbus Avenue**
**Valhalla, NY  10595 1349**          914-747-3310
                                      800-321-7511
                              FAX 914-747-4109
                         http://www.sunburst.com
                        e-mail: service@sunburst.com
*Katie Birmingham, Office Manager*

Your students improve their word-building skills by playing three fun strategy games that involve linking one-or two-letter consonant beginnings to basic word endings.

**747    RULES**

**Speech Bin**
**1965 25th Avenue**
**Vero Beach, FL  32960**            772-770-0007
                                      800-477-3324
                              FAX 772-770-0006
                         http://www.speechbin.com
                          e-mail: info@speechbin.com
*Shane Peters, Product Coordinator*
*Jen Binney, Owner*

Faced with young children whose speech is unintelligible? RULES is the perfect program for these preschool and elementary children. It remediates the processes: cluster reduction;, final consonant deletion, stopping; and prevocalic voicing. Item number 1557. *$43.95*

**748    Receptive One-Word Picture Vocabulary Test (ROWPVT-2000)**

**Speech Bin**
**1965 25th Avenue**
**Vero Beach, FL  32960**            772-770-0007
                                      800-477-3324
                              FAX 772-770-0006
                         http://www.speechbin.com
                          e-mail: info@speechbin.com
*Shane Peters, Product Coordinator*
*Jen Binney, Owner*

This administered, untimed measure assesses the vocabulary comprehension of 0-2 through 11-18 years. New full-color test pictures are easy to recognize; many new test items have been added. It is ideal for children unable or reluctant to speak because only a gestural response is required. Item number A305. *$140.00*

**749    Remediation of Articulation Disorders (RAD)**

**Speech Bin**
**1965 25th Avenue**
**Vero Beach, FL  32960**            772-770-0007
                                      800-477-3324
                              FAX 772-770-0006
                         http://www.speechbin.com
                          e-mail: info@speechbin.com
*Shane Peters, Product Coordinator*
*Jen Binney, Owner*

RAD treats articulation and speech intelligibility as important parameters of language. It gives you thematic pictures and worksheets to facilitate the development of critical sounds. Each picture also has a problem-solving element that provides rich opportunities for discussion and narratives. Item number 1420. *$19.95*

**750** **Retell Stories**

**Speech Bin**
**1965 25th Avenue**
**Vero Beach, FL 32960**      **772-770-0007**
**800-477-3324**
**FAX 772-770-0006**
**http://www.speechbin.com**
**e-mail: info@speechbin.com**
*Shane Peters, Product Coordinator*
*Jen Binney, Owner*

You'll use them for pre-/post-testing, treatment sessions, and home practice. This approach emphasizes systematic training of error phonemes in a semantically potent core vocabulary of the child's own words. It enables children to use whole words intelligibly as powerful tools for real-life communication. Item number 1441. *$17.95*

**751** **Ridgewood Grammar**

**Educators Publishing Service**
**31 Smith Place**
**Cambridge, MA 02139 9031**      **617-547-6706**
**800-225-5750**
**FAX 888-440-2665**
**http://www.epsbooks.com**
**e-mail: eps@epsbooks.com**
*Terri Wiss, Nancy Bison, Author*
*Steve Kote, President*
*Jennifer Avery, Contact*

Grammar is an important part of any student's education. This new series, from the school district that developed the popular Ridgewood Analogies books, teaches 3rd, 4th, and 5th graders about the parts of speech and their use in sentences.

**752** **Rocky's Mountain: A Word-finding Game**

**LinguiSystems**
**3100 4th Avenue**
**East Moline, IL 61244**      **309-775-2300**
**800-776-4332**
**FAX 309-755-2377**
**TDY:800-933-8331**
**http://www.linguisystems.com**
**e-mail: service@linguisystems.com**
*Gina Williamson, Susan Shields, Author*
*Linda Bowers, Owner*
*Rosemary Huisingh, Owner*

Tackle stubborn word-finding problems with this fun game! Game cards are organized by four word-finding strategies so you can pick the strategy that best meets your students' needs. Teach these strategies for word-finding: visual imagery; word association; sound/letter cueing; and categories. *$44.95*

*Ages 4-9*

**753** **Room 14**

**LinguiSystems**
**3100 4th Avenue**
**East Moline, IL 61244**      **309-775-2300**
**800-776-4332**
**FAX 309-755-2377**
**TDY:800-933-8331**
**http://www.linguisystems.com**
**e-mail: service@linguisystems.com**
*Carolyn Wilson, Author*
*Linda Bowers, Owner*
*Rosemary Huisingh, Owner*

Build social skills by offering a variety of teaching approaches to meet the language and learning needs of your students. Through stories, comprehension activities, and organized lessons, students learn to: make and keep friends. fit in at school, handle feelings, and be responsible for their actions. *$59.95*

*198 pages Ages 6-10*

**754** **SLP's IDEA Companion**

**LinguiSystems**
**3100 4th Avenue**
**East Moline, IL 61244**      **309-775-2300**
**800-776-4332**
**FAX 309-755-2375**
**TDY:800-933-8331**
**http://www.linguisystems.com**
**e-mail: service@linguisystems.com**
*Shaila Lucas, Author*
*Linda Bowers, Owner*
*Rosemary Huisingh, Owner*

Set goals and objectives that match the guidelines outlined in the Individuals with Disabilities Education Act. You'll be able to link your therapy goals to the classroom curriculum, determine appropriate benchmarks for students, and determine levels of performance using the baseline measures provided in the book. *$39.95*

*162 pages Ages 5-18*

**755** **SPARC Artic Junior**

**LinguiSystems**
**3100 4th Avenue**
**East Moline, IL 61244**      **309-775-2300**
**800-776-4332**
**FAX 309-755-2377**
**TDY:800-933-8331**
**http://www.linguisystems.com**
**e-mail: service@linguisystems.com**
*Beverly Plass, Author*
*Linda Bowers, Owner*
*Rosemary Huisingh, Owner*

Reach intelligibility goals faster with these take-home exercises. The practice words have been carefully selected to control the phonetic context. It's a programmed, research-based approach that will get results. Activities are divided by primary and secondary phonological processes. *$39.95*

*211 pages Ages 3-7*

**756 SPARC Artic Scenes**

LinguiSystems
3100 4th Avenue
East Moline, IL 61244        309-775-2300
                            800-776-4332
                         FAX 309-755-2377
                         TDY:800-933-8331
                    http://www.linguisystems.com
                 e-mail: service@linguisystems.com
*Susan Rose Simms, Author*
*Linda Bowers, Owner*
*Rosemary Huisingh, Owner*

Each picture scene is loaded with target sounds to get
the most speech practice in your limited therapy time.
You'll take care of your entire caseload with these articulation and language activities. Activities include
vocabulary lists, story starts, thinking questions, categorizing and multiple meanings. *$39.95*

*207 pages  Ages 4-10*

**757 SPARC for Grammar**

LinguiSystems
3100 4th Avenue
East Moline, IL 61244        309-775-2300
                            800-776-4332
                         FAX 309-755-2377
                         TDY:800-933-8331
                    http://www.linguisystems.com
                 e-mail: service@linguisystems.com
*Susan Thomsen, Kathy Donnelly, Author*
*Linda Bowers, Owner*
*Rosemary Huisingh, Owner*

Teach grammar in meaningful contexts! The lessons
provide a wealth of opportunities for your students to
hear, repeat, answer questions and tell stories using
targeted language structures. *$39.95*

*165 pages  Ages 4-10*

**758 SPARC for Phonology**

LinguiSystems
3100 4th Avenue
East Moline, IL 61244        309-775-2300
                            800-776-4332
                         FAX 309-755-2377
                         TDY:800-933-8331
                    http://www.linguisystems.com
                 e-mail: service@linguisystems.com
*Susan Thomsen, Kathy Donnelly, Author*
*Linda Bowers, Owner*
*Rosemary Huisingh, Owner*

This excellent resource includes 80 pages of 16 pictures each... that's 1280 pictures in all! Each picture
page has corresponding 20-word auditory bombard-
ment list. These great lessons cover syllable reduction, consonant deletion, cluster reduction, gliding,
vowelization, fronting, backing, stopping, stridency
deletion, affrication, deaffrication, voicing and
devoicing. *$39.95*

*165 pages  Ages 4-10*

**759 SPARC for Vocabulary**

LinguiSystems
3100 4th Avenue
East Moline, IL 61244        309-775-2300
                            800-776-4332
                         FAX 309-755-2377
                         TDY:800-933-8331
                    http://www.linguisystems.com
                 e-mail: service@linguisystems.com
*Susan Thomsen, Kathy Donnelly, Author*
*Linda Bowers, Owner*
*Rosemary Huisingh, Owner*

Teach vocabulary skills through themes! Rapid-nam-
ing skills will improve as vocabulary knowledge increases. This invaluable picture resource gets your
students learning and thinking about new words.
*$39.95*

*165 pages  Ages 4-10*

**760 Scissors, Glue, and Artic, Too!**

LinguiSystems
3100 4th Avenue
East Moline, IL 61244        309-775-2300
                            800-776-4332
                         FAX 309-755-2377
                         TDY:800-933-8331
                    http://www.linguisystems.com
                 e-mail: service@linguisystems.com
*Susan Rose Simms, Author*
*Linda Bowers, Owner*
*Rosemary Huisingh, Owner*

Hands-on projects that beg to be talked about are perfect for young students in articulation therapy. This
wonderfully illustrated manual is filled with puzzles,
books, animals, and more that come to life in the hands
of students. *$39.95*

*189 pages  Ages 4-9*

**761 Scissors, Glue, and Grammar, Too!**

LinguiSystems
3100 4th Avenue
East Moline, IL 61244        309-775-2300
                            800-776-4332
                         FAX 309-755-2377
                         TDY:800-933-8331
                    http://www.linguisystems.com
                 e-mail: service@linguisystems.com
*Susan Boegler, Debbie Abruzzini, Author*
*Linda Bowers, Owner*
*Rosemary Huisingh, Owner*

Even your youngest students can learn correct grammar and syntax skills. This interactive approach is the
perfect resource. These cut-and-paste activities are so
much fun, your students won't realize they're learning regular and irregular verbs, comparatives and superlatives, wh- questions, and more! *$39.95*

*174 pages  Ages 4-9*

**762    Scissors, Glue, and Phonological Processes, Too!**
**LinguiSystems**
**3100 4th Avenue**
**East Moline, IL  61244**            309-775-2300
                                      800-776-4332
                                FAX 309-755-2377
                                TDY:800-933-8331
                          http://www.linguisystems.com
                          e-mail: service@linguisystems.com
*Gayle H Daly, Author*
*Linda Bowers, Owner*
*Rosemary Huisingh, Owner*

Eliminate error patterns with minimal pair contrasts at the word and phrase level. Watch your young students cut and paste their way to better speech with these engaging, interactive activities. *$39.95*

*174 pages  Ages 4-9*

**763    Scissors, Glue, and Vocabulary, Too!**
**LinguiSystems**
**3100 4th Avenue**
**East Moline, IL  61244**            309-775-2300
                                      800-776-4332
                                FAX 309-755-2377
                                TDY:800-933-8331
                          http://www.linguisystems.com
                          e-mail: service@linguisystems.com
*Barb Truman, Patti Halfman, Lauri Whiskeyman,*
*Author*
*Linda Bowers, Owner*
*Rosemary Huisingh, Owner*

These cut-and-paste activities keep young students motivated. The rich vocabulary content gets them using new words in new ways. You'll not only teach vocabulary skills but listening and following directions too. Each lesson gives you a list of key vocabulary, scripted directions, a family letter, and several enrichment activites. *$39.95*

*187 pages  Ages 4-9*

**764    Sequential Spelling 1-7 with Student Response Book**
**AVKO Dyslexia Research Foundation**
**3084 W Willard Road**
**Clio, MI  48420 7801**              810-686-9283
                                      866-285-6612
                                FAX 810-686-1101
                                http://www.avko.org
                          e-mail: donmccabe@aol.org
*Don McCabe, Author*
*Don McCabe, Research Director*
*Ann McCabe, Office Manager*

Sequential Spelling uses immediate student self-correction. It builds from easier words of a word family such as all and then builds on them to teach; all, tall, stall, install, call, fall, ball, and their inflected forms such as: stalls, stalled, stalling, installing, installment. *$79.95*

*72 pages*
*ISBN 1-664003-00-0*

**765    Sign Language Classroom Resource**
**Harris Communications**
**15155 Technology Drive**
**Eden Prairie, MN  55344 2277**      952-906-1180
                                      800-825-6758
                                FAX 952-906-1099
                                TDY:800-825-9187
                          http://www.harriscomm.com
                          e-mail: info@harriscomm.com
*Traci Jacobson, Author*
*Robert Harris, Owner*
*Patty Johnson, Vice President*

Learn basic signs quickly and easily. Contains pictures of 100 essential signs. Each picture is presented on an 8.5x11 page and may be copied for bulletin boards or classroom walls. Also includes smaller versions of the pictures to distribute to individual students and family members. *$32.00*

*143 pages  Paperback*

**766    Silly Sentences**
**Speech Bin**
**1965 25th Avenue**
**Vero Beach, FL  32960**             772-770-0007
                                      800-477-3324
                                FAX 772-770-0006
                          http://www.speechbin.com
                          e-mail: info@speechbin.com
*Shane Peters, Product Coordinator*
*Jen Binney, Owner*

Children love to have fun. Silly Sentences lets them have fun while they play these engaging card games to learn: subject verb agreement, speech sound articulation; S+ V+ O sentences, questioning and answering; humor and absurdities and present progressive verbs. Item number P506. *$41.00*

**767    Soaring Scores CTB: TerraNova Reading and Language Arts**
**Harcourt Achieve**
**6277 Sea Harbor Drive**
**Orlando, FL  32887**                252-480-3200
                                      800-844-1464
                                FAX 800-269-5232
                          http://www.steckvaughn.com
                          e-mail: info@steckvaughn.com
*Steck-Vaughn Staff, Author*
*Tim McEwen, President/CEO*
*Jeff Johnson, Dir Marketing Communications*
*Chris Lehmann, Team Coordinator*

Through a combination of targeted instructional practice and test-taking tips, these workbooks help students build better skills and improve CTB-TerraNova test scores. Initial lessons address reading comprehension and language arts. The authentic practice test mirrors the CTB's format and content.

**768    Soaring Scores in Integrated Language Arts**

Harcourt Achieve
6277 Sea Harbor Drive
Orlando, FL  32887                    252-480-3200
                                      800-844-1464
                          FAX 800-269-5232
                  http://www.steckvaughn.com
                  e-mail: info@steckvaughn.com
*Steck-Vaughn Staff, Author*
*Tim McEwen, President/CEO*
*Jeff Johnson, Dir Marketing Communications*
*Chris Lehmann, Team Coordinator*

Help your students develop the right skills and strategies for success on integrated arts assessments. Soaring Scores presents three sets of two lengthy, thematically linked literature selections. Students develop higher-order thinking skills as they respond to open-ended questions about the selections.

**769    Soaring Scores on the CMT in Language Arts& on the CAPT in Reading and Writing Across Disciplines**

Harcourt Achieve
6277 Sea Harbor Drive
Orlando, FL  32887                    252-480-3200
                                      800-844-1464
                          FAX 800-269-5232
                  http://www.steckvaughn.com
                  e-mail: info@steckvaughn.com
*Steck-Vaughn Staff, Author*
*Tim McEwen, President/CEO*
*Jeff Johnson, Dir Marketing Communications*
*Chris Lehmann, Team Coordinator*

Make every minute count when you are preparing for the CMT or CAPT. Fine tune your language arts test preparation with the program developed specifically for the Connecticut's assessments. Questions are correlated to Connecticut's content standards for reading and responding, producing text, applying English language conventions, and exploring and responding to texts.

**770    Soaring Scores on the NYS English Language Arts Assessment**

Harcourt Achieve
6277 Sea Harbor Drive
Orlando, FL  32887                    252-480-3200
                                      800-844-1464
                          FAX 800-269-5232
                  http://www.steckvaughn.com
                  e-mail: info@steckvaughn.com
*Steck-Vaughn Staff, Author*
*Tim McEwen, President/CEO*
*Jeff Johnson, Dir Marketing Communications*
*Chris Lehmann, Team Coordinator*

With these workbooks, students receive instructional practice for approaching the assessment's reading, listening and writing questions.

**771    Soaring on the MCAS in English Language Arts**

Harcourt Achieve
6277 Sea Harbor Drive
Orlando, FL  32887                    252-480-3200
                                      800-844-1464
                          FAX 800-269-5232
                  http://www.steckvaughn.com
                  e-mail: info@steckvaughn.com
*Steck-Vaughn Staff, Author*
*Tim McEwen, President/CEO*
*Jeff Johnson, Dir Marketing Communications*
*Chris Lehmann, Team Coordinator*

Instructional practice in the first section builds skills for the MCAS language, literacy, and composition questions. A practice test models the MCAS precisely in design and length.

**772    Sound Connections**

Speech Bin
1965 25th Avenue
Vero Beach, FL  32960                 772-770-0007
                                      800-477-3324
                          FAX 772-770-0006
                  http://www.speechbin.com
                  e-mail: info@speechbin.com
*Shane Peters, Product Coordinator*
*Jen Binney, Owner*

This program teaches the critical connections between the sounds kids hear and speaking, reading, and writing. Dozens of activities and worksheets, 19 phoneme-based stories, and 100s of pictures. Item number 1487. *$41.95*

**773    Sounds Abound**

LinguiSystems
3100 4th Avenue
East Moline, IL  61244                309-775-2300
                                      800-776-4332
                          FAX 309-755-2377
                          TDY:800-933-8331
                  http://www.linguisystems.com
                  e-mail: service@linguisystems.com
*Hugh Catts, Tina Olsen, Author*
*Linda Bowers, Owner*
*Rosemary Huisingh, Owner*

Delayed speech and language skills DO impact reading skills. Give your young students an edge with Sounds Abound. They'll connect letters with sounds as they meet their speech and language goals. This best-selling manual is loaded with activities for speech sound awareness, rhyming skills, beginning and ending sounds, segmenting and blending sounds, and putting sounds together with letters. *$37.95*

*190 pages  Ages 4-9*

**774    Sounds Abound Game**

LinguiSystems
3100 4th Avenue
East Moline, IL  61244                309-775-2300
                                      800-776-4332
                          FAX 309-755-2377
                          TDY:800-933-8331
                  http://www.linguisystems.com
                  e-mail: service@linguisystems.com
*Hugh Catts, Tina Olsen, Author*
*Linda Bowers, Owner*
*Rosemary Huisingh, Owner*

Teach critical features about sounds in words for better language skills. Your students will love this fun game because it's easy to play. This game targets the sounds students use the most: f; s; p; t; and m. These essential sounds are critical for early literacy success. *$39.95*

*Ages 4-9*

**775    Sounds Abound Multisensory Phonological Awareness**

**LinguiSystems**
**3100 4th Avenue**
**East Moline, IL  61244**          309-775-2300
                                                      800-776-4332
                                   FAX 309-755-2377
                                   TDY:800-933-8331
                            http://www.linguisystems.com
                   e-mail: service@linguisystems.com
*Jill Teachworth, Author*
*Linda Bowers, Owner*
*Rosemary Huisingh, Owner*

The multisensory approach in this phonological program reinforces knowledge and retention of sound-symbol correspondence. Students will learn through their best modality as they look, listen, feel, play, and even sing the sounds. *$37.95*

*201 pages  Ages 4-7*

**776    Source for Apraxia Therapy**

**LinguiSystems**
**3100 4th Avenue**
**East Moline, IL  61244**          309-775-2300
                                                      800-776-4332
                                   FAX 309-755-2377
                                   TDY:800-933-8331
                            http://www.linguisystems.com
                   e-mail: service@linguisystems.com
*Kathryn J Tomlin, Author*
*Linda Bowers, Owner*
*Rosemary Huisingh, Owner*

This resource combines a visual-auditory-kinesthetic approach to help your clients improve intelligibility. Three sections target phoneme production, articulation, fluency, and phrasing, and paralinguistic drills. You'll know just where to start therapy for clients with mild, moderate, or severe apraxia. *$41.95*

*195 pages  Adults*

**777    Source for Bilingual Students with Language Disorders**

**LinguiSystems**
**3100 4th Avenue**
**East Moline, IL  61244**          309-775-2300
                                                      800-776-4332
                                   FAX 309-755-2377
                                   TDY:800-933-8331
                            http://www.linguisystems.com
                   e-mail: service@linguisystems.com
*Celeste Roseberry-McKibbin, Author*
*Linda Bowers, Owner*
*Rosemary Huisingh, Owner*

Focus on teaching vocabulary and phonolgical awareness skills, the most important skills your bilingual students need for overall English proficiency and literacy. This resource gives you activities and materials based on a hierarchy of second language acquisition, *$41.95*

*250 pages  Ages 5-18*

**778    Source for Processing Disorders**

**LinguiSystems**
**3100 4th Avenue**
**East Moline, IL  61244**          309-775-2300
                                                      800-776-4332
                                   FAX 309-755-2377
                                   TDY:800-933-8331
                            http://www.linguisystems.com
                   e-mail: service@linguisystems.com
*Gail J Richard, Author*
*Linda Bowers, Owner*
*Rosemary Huisingh, Owner*

This great resource helps you differentiate between language processing disorders and auditory processing disorders. Chapters cover: the neurology of processing and learning; the central auditory processing model; the language processing model; and a lot more! *$41.95*

*181 pages  Ages 5-Adult*

**779    Source for Stuttering and Cluttering**

**LinguiSystems**
**3100 4th Avenue**
**East Moline, IL  61244**          309-775-2300
                                                      800-776-4332
                                   FAX 309-755-2377
                                   TDY:800-933-8331
                            http://www.linguisystems.com
                   e-mail: service@linguisystems.com
*David A Daly, Author*
*Linda Bowers, Owner*
*Rosemary Huisingh, Owner*

Author David Daly, a former stutterer and respected speech pathologist, puts his clinical expertise and personal passion into this comprehensive program. Your clients will become fluent, confident speakers with this excellent, field-tested resource. *$44.95*

*210 pages  Ages 13-Adult*

**780    Source for Syndromes**

**LinguiSystems**
**3100 4th Avenue**
**East Moline, IL  61244**          309-775-2300
                                                      800-776-4332
                                   FAX 309-755-2377
                                   TDY:800-933-8331
                            http://www.linguisystems.com
                   e-mail: service@linguisystems.com
*Gail J Richard, Debra Reichert Hoge, Author*
*Linda Bowers, Owner*
*Rosemary Huisingh, Owner*

Do you often wish someone would just tell you what to do with a specific youngster on your caseload? The Source for Syndromes can do just that. Learn about the speech-language characteristics for each sydrome with a focus on communication issues. This resource covers pertinent information for such sydromes such as Angelman, Asperger's, Autism, Rett's Tourette's, Williams, and more. *$41.95*

*147 pages  Ages Birth-18*

**781  Spectral Speech Analysis: Software**

**Speech Bin**
**1965 25th Avenue**
**Vero Beach, FL  32960**          772-770-0007
                                  800-477-3324
                          FAX 772-770-0006
                 http://www.speechbin.com
              e-mail: info@speechbin.com
*Shane Peters, Product Coordinator*
*Jen Binney, Owner*

This exciting new software uses visual feedback as an effective speech treatment tool. Speech-language pathologists can record speech and corresponding visual displays for clients who then try to match either auditory or visual targets. These built-in visual patterns can be displayed as either sophisticated spectrograms or real-time waveforms. Item number P227 — windows only. *$159.95*

**782  Speech & Language & Voice & More**

**Speech Bin**
**1965 25th Avenue**
**Vero Beach, FL  32960**          772-770-0007
                                  800-477-3324
                          FAX 772-770-0006
                 http://www.speechbin.com
              e-mail: info@speechbin.com
*Shane Peters, Product Coordinator*
*Jen Binney, Owner*

Contains eighty-eight practically perfect reproducible games and activities ideal for your K-5 clients. It gives you: manipulable activities to keep active leaners learning; tasks to match a multitude of interests and abilities; and vocal hygiene worksheets targeted to reduce vocal abuse. Item number 1496. *$19.95*

**783  Speech Sports**

**Speech Bin**
**1965 25th Avenue**
**Vero Beach, FL  32960**          772-770-0007
                                  800-477-3324
                          FAX 772-770-0006
                 http://www.speechbin.com
              e-mail: info@speechbin.com
*Shane Peters, Product Coordinator*
*Jen Binney, Owner*

Speech Sports makes every child in your caseload a shining sports star. Reproducible gameboards and language activities feature 19 different sports from boating to skating, bowling to running, basketball to soccer. Item number 1590. *$24.95*

**784  Speech Viewer III**

**Speech Bin**
**1965 25th Avenue**
**Vero Beach, FL  32960**          772-770-0007
                                  800-477-3324
                          FAX 772-770-0006
                 http://www.speechbin.com
              e-mail: info@speechbin.com
*Shane Peters, Product Coordinator*
*Jen Binney, Owner*

SpeechViewer III creates entertaining interactive displays that let them do just that! It has all the Visual Voice Tools and so much more! Begin with simple sound awareness and advance to complex speech tasks, increasing phoneme awareness and improving speech sound production. Users enjoy constant and objective real time visual feedback from graphical speech displayed. Item number E280 — windows only. *$899.00*

**785  Speech-Language Delights**

**Speech Bin**
**1965 25th Avenue**
**Vero Beach, FL  32960**          772-770-0007
                                  800-477-3324
                          FAX 772-770-0006
                 http://www.speechbin.com
              e-mail: info@speechbin.com
*Shane Peters, Product Coordinator*
*Jen Binney, Owner*

Cook up lots of fun with Speech-Language Delights! Delectably delicious speech and language activities and games provide rich opportunities and hands-on activities with food-related themes to enrich K-8 kids. Item number 1541. *$ 29.95*

**786  SpeechCrafts**

**Speech Bin**
**1965 25th Avenue**
**Vero Beach, FL  32960**          772-770-0007
                                  800-477-3324
                          FAX 772-770-0006
                 http://www.speechbin.com
              e-mail: info@speechbin.com
*Shane Peters, Product Coordinator*
*Jen Binney, Owner*

Children love to create decorative and useful objects. They also love the surprise of using common and ordinary objects in unexpected ways. Best of all, children learn best when engaged in tangible, concrete, hands-on projects that are designed to enhance learning. Activities develop skills in: sequencing; language; basic concepts; vocabulary; articulation and following directions. Item number 1490. *$23.95*

**787  Spelling: A Thematic Content-Area Approach Reproducibles**

**Harcourt Achieve**
**6277 Sea Harbor Drive**
**Orlando, FL  32887**             252-480-3200
                                  800-844-1464
                          FAX 800-269-5232
                 http://www.steckvaughn.com
              e-mail: info@steckvaughn.com
*Kelley, Author*
*Tim McEwen, President/CEO*
*Jeff Johnson, Dir Marketing Communications*
*Chris Lehmann, Team Coordinator*

Help students master the words they will use most frequently in the classroom. Organized lessons incorporate word analysis of letter patterns, correlations to appropriate literature, writing exercises, and application and extension activities.

**788  Stepping Up to Fluency**
Speech Bin
1965 25th Avenue
Vero Beach, FL  32960          772-770-0007
                               800-477-3324
                          FAX 772-770-0006
                    http://www.speechbin.com
                   e-mail: info@speechbin.com
*Shane Peters, Product Coordinator*
*Jen Binney, Owner*

Stepping Up to Fluency gives you a systematic program to help your clients from five years old to adults understand their disfluencies and gain control of their speech in 25-35 sessions. It presents high-interest strategies and materials in two levels, K-3 and grade 4 to adult. Item number 1360. *$34.95*

**789  Stories and More: Time and Place**
Riverdeep
500 Redwood Boulevard
Novato, CA  94947              415-763-4700
                               800-362-2890
                          FAX 415-763-4385
                     http://www.edmark.com
                  e-mail: info@riverdeep.net
*Barry O'Callaghan, Chairman/CEO*
*Simon Calver, COO*
*John Rim, VP CFO*

Combines three well-loved stories - The House on Maple Street, Roxaboxen, and Galimoto with engaging activities that strengthen students' reading comprehension.

**790  Straight Speech**
Speech Bin
1965 25th Avenue
Vero Beach, FL  32960          772-770-0007
                               800-477-3324
                          FAX 772-770-0006
                    http://www.speechbin.com
                   e-mail: info@speechbin.com
*Jane Folk, Author*
*Jan Binney, Editor-in-Chief*
*Shane Peters, Product Coordinator*

Lateral lisps can be one of the most preplexing articulation problems you encounter. Straight Speech gives you an effective, easy-to-implement program for lateral lisps. Developed by an experienced speech-language specialist, Straight Speech is a practical, step-by-step program tailored to meet this long-standing need. Item number 1525. *$22.95*

*80 pages*
*ISBN 0-937857-32-7*

**791  Stuttering: Helping the Disfluent Preschool Child**
Speech Bin
1965 25th Avenue
Vero Beach, FL  32960          772-770-0007
                               800-477-3324
                          FAX 772-770-0006
                    http://www.speechbin.com
                   e-mail: info@speechbin.com
*Shane Peters, Product Coordinator*
*Jen Binney, Owner*

Written in the warm encouraging style for which this author is known, Stuttering: Helping the Disfluent Preschool Child is the perfect tool for parents and teachers of young stuttering children. It uses a Speech Thermometer to show them ways to turn talking into an area of strength. Item number 1489. *$13.95*

**792  Sunken Treasure Adventure: Beginning Blends**
Sunburst Technology
400 Columbus Avenue
Valhalla, NY  10595 1349       914-747-3310
                               800-321-7511
                          FAX 914-747-4109
                     http://www.sunburst.com
                 e-mail: service@sunburst.com
*Katie Birmingham, Office Manager*

Focus on beginning blends sounds and concepts with three high-spirited games that invite students to use two letter consonant blends as they build words.

**793  TARGET**
Speech Bin
1965 25th Avenue
Vero Beach, FL  32960          772-770-0007
                               800-477-3324
                          FAX 772-770-0006
                    http://www.speechbin.com
                   e-mail: info@speechbin.com
*Shane Peters, Product Coordinator*
*Jen Binney, Owner*

TARGET is the kind of resource aphasia clinicians beg for — a practical resource that answers not only the what and how questions of treatment but also the why. It describes dozens of treatment methods and gives you practical exercises and activities to implement each technique. Item number 1434. *$49.95*

**794  TOLD-P3: Test of Language Development Primary**
Speech Bin
1965 25th Avenue
Vero Beach, FL  32960          772-770-0007
                               800-477-3324
                          FAX 772-770-0006
                    http://www.speechbin.com
                   e-mail: info@speechbin.com
*Shane Peters, Product Coordinator*
*Jen Binney, Owner*

This revised test of 4-8 year olds' language gives unbiased test items that reflect the most modern language theories, Two new subtests — Phonemic Analysis and Relational Vocabulary, full-color contemporary photos young children like and norms include minority and disability groups. Item number P501. *$246.00*

**795   TOPS Kit-Adolescent: Tasks of Problem Solving**

LinguiSystems
3100 4th Avenue
East Moline, IL  61244                   309-775-2300
                                          800-776-4332
                                     FAX 309-755-2377
                                  TDY:800-933-8331
                          http://www.linguisystems.com
                    e-mail: service@linguisystems.com
*Linda Bowers, Rosemary Huisingh, Mark Barrett,*
*Author*
*Linda Bowers, Owner*
*Rosemary Huisingh, Owner*

Teach your teens how to use their language skills to think, think, think. We combine literacy, thinking, writing, humor, and language arts practice to cover these thinking skills: using content to make references; analyzing information; taking another's point of view; and more. It's a literacy- based approach that gets dramatic results! *$59.95*

*192 pages  Ages 12-18*

**796   TOPS Kit-Elementary: Tasks of Problem Solving**

LinguiSystems
3100 4th Avenue
East Moline, IL  61244                   309-775-2300
                                          800-776-4332
                                     FAX 309-755-2377
                                  TDY:800-933-8331
                          http://www.linguisystems.com
                    e-mail: service@linguisystems.com
*Linda Bowers, Rosemary Huisingh, Mark Barrett,*
*Author*
*Linda Bowers, Owner*
*Rosemary Huisingh, Owner*

Reveal thinking and language skills your students didn't know they had with this remarkable kit. TOPS Kit-Elementary combines thinking and expressive language skills to develop better communications. *$119.95*

*209 pages  Ages 6-12*

**797   Take Home: Oral-Motor Exercises**

LinguiSystems
3100 4th Avenue
East Moline, IL  61244                   309-775-2300
                                          800-776-4332
                                     FAX 309-755-2377
                                  TDY:800-933-8331
                          http://www.linguisystems.com
                    e-mail: service@linguisystems.com
*Lisa Loncar-Belding, Author*
*Linda Bowers, Owner*
*Rosemary Huisingh, Owner*

Stop writing your own take-home letters and exercises for carryover! These homework pages work on the earliest developing vowel and consonant sounds. Created for use with deaf and hearing-impaired students, this resource is great for all of your oral-motor and articulation cases. *$31.95*

*129 pages  Ages 2-6*

**798   Take Home: Phonological Awareness**

LinguiSystems
3100 4th Avenue
East Moline, IL  61244                   309-775-2300
                                          800-776-4332
                                     FAX 309-755-2377
                                  TDY:800-933-8331
                          http://www.linguisystems.com
                    e-mail: service@linguisystems.com
*Carolyn Robertson, Wanda Salter, Author*
*Linda Bowers, Owner*
*Rosemary Huisingh, Owner*

These activities are easy for parents and caregivers to follow. Activities are organized at the word, syllable, phoneme, and grapheme level. You'll target these skills: rhyming; blending; isolation; segmentation; deletion; substitution; and phoneme-grapheme correspondence. *$31.95*

*144 pages  Ages 5-8*

**799   Take Home: Preschool Language Development**

LinguiSystems
3100 4th Avenue
East Moline, IL  61244                   309-775-2300
                                          800-776-4332
                                     FAX 309-755-2377
                                  TDY:800-933-8331
                          http://www.linguisystems.com
                    e-mail: service@linguisystems.com
*Martha Drake, Author*
*Linda Bowers, Owner*
*Rosemary Huisingh, Owner*

Home follow-up is essential for your little ones with speech and language delays. Get everything you need for a comprehensive take-home program with this time saver! Each take-home lesson is easy to follow. *$31.95*

*191 pages  Ages 1-5*

**800   Talk About Fun**

Speech Bin
1965 25th Avenue
Vero Beach, FL  32960                     772-770-0007
                                          800-477-3324
                                     FAX 772-770-0006
                           http://www.speechbin.com
                        e-mail: info@speechbin.com
*Shane Peters, Product Coordinator*
*Jen Binney, Owner*

Talk About Fun takes advantage of children's natural love of play and making things to achieve your speech-language goals. Target phonemes featured include p-b-m, t-d-n, f, k-g, s, sh-ch-j, i, and consonant blends. Carryover projects, sequence stories, and letters to parents are an added bonus. Item number 1485. *$29.95*

**801   Talkable Tales**

Speech Bin
1965 25th Avenue
Vero Beach, FL  32960                     772-770-0007
                                          800-477-3324
                                     FAX 772-770-0006
                           http://www.speechbin.com
                        e-mail: info@speechbin.com
*Shane Peters, Product Coordinator*
*Jen Binney, Owner*

Talkable Tales gives you a wealth of stories to build speech and language skills. Comprehension and challenge questions accompany each story. Stories are a uniform length so you may use them with groups working on multiple sounds. Each has ten key words containing the target sound. Item number 1540. $25.95

**802    Talking Time**
**Speech Bin**
**1965 25th Avenue**
**Vero Beach, FL  32960**          **772-770-0007**
                                    **800-477-3324**
                             **FAX 772-770-0006**
                      **http://www.speechbin.com**
                      **e-mail: info@speechbin.com**
*Jeanette Stickel, Author*
*Jan Binney, Editor-in-Chief*
*Shane Peters, Product Coordinator*

Talking times gives you sequenced activities to foster language and cognitive programs by parents, family members, and caregivers. Talking Time also includes guidelines for language development and directions and rationale for use. Item number 1589. *$17.95*

*64 pages*
*ISBN 0-937857-24-6*

**803    Teaching Phonics: Staff Development Book**
**Harcourt Achieve**
**6277 Sea Harbor Drive**
**Orlando, FL  32887**          **252-480-3200**
                                **800-844-1464**
                         **FAX 800-269-5232**
                  **http://www.steckvaughn.com**
                  **e-mail: info@steckvaughn.com**
*Steck-Vaughn Staff, Author*
*Tim McEwen, President/CEO*
*Jeff Johnson, Dir Marketing Communications*
*Chris Lehmann, Team Coordinator*

Fine-tune your instructional approach with fresh insights from phonics experts. This resource offers informative articles and timely tips for teaching phonics in the integrated language arts classroom.

**804    Test for Auditory Comprehension of Language: TACL-3**
**Speech Bin**
**1965 25th Avenue**
**Vero Beach, FL  32960**          **772-770-0007**
                                    **800-477-3324**
                             **FAX 888-329-2246**
                      **http://www.speechbin.com**
                      **e-mail: info@speechbin.com**
*Elizabeth Carrow-Woolfolk, Author*
*Shane Peters, Product Coordinator*
*Jen Binney, Owner*

The newly revised TACL-3 evaluates the 0-3 to 9-11 year-old's understanding of spoken language in three subtests: Vocabulary, Grammatical Morphemes and Elaborated Phrases and Sentences. Each test item is a word or sentence read aloud by the examiner; the child responds by pointing to one of three pictures. Item number P792. $261.00

**805    Test of Early Language Development 3rd Edition: TELD-3**
**Speech Bin**
**1965 25th Avenue**
**Vero Beach, FL  32960**          **772-770-0007**
                                    **800-477-3324**
                             **FAX 772-770-0006**
                      **http://www.speechbin.com**
                      **e-mail: info@speechbin.com**
*Shane Peters, Product Coordinator*
*Jen Binney, Owner*

TELD-3 for children 0-2 through 7-11 quickly and easily measures receptive and expressive language and yields an overall Spoken Language Score. Stimulus pictures are colorful and contemporary. Standardized on 2,217 children, this test has little or no bias. Item number P576. $272.00

**806    Test of Language Development: Intermediate (TOLD-I:3)**
**Speech Bin**
**1965 25th Avenue**
**Vero Beach, FL  32960**          **772-770-0007**
                                    **800-477-3324**
                             **FAX 772-770-0006**
                      **http://www.speechbin.com**
                      **e-mail: info@speechbin.com**
*Shane Peters, Product Coordinator*
*Jen Binney, Owner*

This well-normed test is one popular measure of language development; it's an ideal choice for speech-language pathologists' use in schools. The complete kit includes an examiner's manual, picture stimulus book, and 25 test forms. Item number P574. *$179.00*

**807    That's LIFE! Life Skills**
**LinguiSystems**
**3100 4th Avenue**
**East Moline, IL  61244**          **309-775-2300**
                                     **800-776-4332**
                              **FAX 309-755-2377**
                             **TDY:800-933-8331**
                   **http://www.linguisystems.com**
                   **e-mail: service@linguisystems.com**
*Patricia Smith, Author*
*Linda Bowers, Owner*
*Rosemary Huisingh, Owner*

Students get hands-on language experience in everyday events. Units are organized by consumer affairs, government, health concerns, money matters, going places, and homemaking. Tasks include identifying vocabulary, making inferences, predicting, and more. $37.95

*192 pages  Ages 12-18*

**808    Therapy Guide for Language & Speech Disorders: Volume 1**
**Speech Bin**
**1965 25th Avenue**
**Vero Beach, FL  32960**          **772-770-0007**
                                    **800-477-3324**
                             **FAX 772-770-0006**
                      **http://www.speechbin.com**
                      **e-mail: info@speechbin.com**
*Shane Peters, Product Coordinator*
*Jen Binney, Owner*

This structured language rehabilitation program contains 429 color-coded pages containing exercises for listening, reading comprehension, speech and language, gestures, writing, and number skills. A word communication notebook and worksheets suitable for carryover are included. Item number V368. *$47.95*

**809  Therapy Guide for Language and Speech Disorders: Volume 2**

**Speech Bin**
**1965 25th Avenue**
**Vero Beach, FL  32960**          772-770-0007
                                    800-477-3324
                        FAX 772-770-0006
              http://www.speechbin.com
              e-mail: info@speechbin.com
*Shane Peters, Product Coordinator*
*Jen Binney, Owner*

Volume 2 answers your need for materials at a higher level. This large print workbook covers oral language comprehension, word retrieval, sentence formulation, general knowledge, thought organization, definitions, number skills, and daily needs. Item number V370. *$38.95*

**810  Thought Organization Workbook**

**Therapro**
**225 Arlington Street**
**Framingham, MA  01702 8723**      508-872-9494
                                    800-257-5376
                        FAX 508-875-2062
              http://www.theraproducts.com
              e-mail: info@theraproducts.com
*Therapro Staff, Author*
*Karen Conrad, President*

Completing letter and word puzzles, composing sentences and organizing shapes, numbers, events and language. *$10.50*

**811  Tic-Tac-Artic and Match**

**LinguiSystems**
**3100 4th Avenue**
**East Moline, IL  61244**          309-775-2300
                                    800-776-4332
                        FAX 309-755-2377
                        TDY:800-933-8331
              http://www.linguisystems.com
              e-mail: service@linguisystems.com
*Carol A Vaccariello, Author*
*Linda Bowers, Owner*
*Rosemary Huisingh, Owner*

Tic-Tac-Artic and Match gives you five games on every page and tons of practice per session. Each page has 16 pictures for one target phoneme. To play Tic-Tac-Artic, use the special game template to create four different tic-tac-toe style games. *$34.95*

*157 pages  Ages 4-12*

**812  Visual Voice Tools**

**Speech Bin**
**1965 25th Avenue**
**Vero Beach, FL  32960**          772-770-0007
                                    800-477-3324
                        FAX 772-770-0006
              http://www.speechbin.com
              e-mail: info@speechbin.com
*Shane Peters, Product Coordinator*
*Jen Binney, Owner*

Seven visual voice tools help your clients develop vocal control through engaging visual and auditory feedback. The tools include: Sound Presence; Loudness Range; Voice Presence; Voice Timing; Voice Onset; Pitch Range and Pitch Control. Item number E278. *$199.95*

**813  Vocabulary Connections**

**Harcourt Achieve**
**6277 Sea Harbor Drive**
**Orlando, FL  32887**              252-480-3200
                                    800-844-1464
                        FAX 800-269-5232
              http://www.steckvaughn.com
              e-mail: info@steckvaughn.com
*Steck-Vaughn Staff, Author*
*Tim McEwen, President/CEO*
*Jeff Johnson, Dir Marketing Communications*
*Chris Lehmann, Team Coordinator*

Keep students engaged in building vocabulary through crossword puzzles and cloze passages, and by using words in context and making analogies. Lessons build around thematically organized literature and nonfiction selections provide meaningful context for essential vocabulary words.

**814  Vocabulary Play by Play**

**LinguiSystems**
**3100 4th Avenue**
**East Moline, IL  61244**          309-775-2300
                                    800-776-4332
                        FAX 309-755-2377
                        TDY:800-933-8331
              http://www.linguisystems.com
              e-mail: service@linguisystems.com
*Caolyn LoGiudice, Mike LoGiudice, Author*
*Linda Bowers, Owner*
*Rosemary Huisingh, Owner*

Students with language-learning disabilities need ten times more encounters with new vocabulary words than their nondisabled peers. Vocabulary Play by Play gives students the built-in encounters with vocabulary they need for school success. *$44.95*

*Ages 9-15*

**815  Vowel Patterns**

**Sunburst Technology**
**400 Columbus Avenue**
**Valhalla, NY  10595 1349**        914-747-3310
                                    800-321-7511
                        FAX 914-747-4109
              http://www.sunburst.com
              e-mail: service@sunburst.com
*Katie Birmingham, Office Manager*

Some vowels are neither long nor short. In this investigation, students explore and learn to use abstract vowels.

**816   Vowel Scramble**

**LinguiSystems**
**3100 4th Avenue**
**East Moline, IL  61244**          **309-775-2300**
                                     **800-776-4332**
                              **FAX 309-755-2377**
                              **TDY:800-933-8331**
                     **http://www.linguisystems.com**
                **e-mail: service@linguisystems.com**
*Carolyn LoGiudice, Author*
*Linda Bowers, Owner*
*Rosemary Huisingh, Owner*

Your student will love this fun new way to practice
spelling and phonological awareness skills. Players
earn points by using letter tiles to complete words on
the game board. *$44.95*

*Ages 7-12*

**817   Warmups and Workouts**

**Speech Bin**
**1965 25th Avenue**
**Vero Beach, FL  32960**          **772-770-0007**
                                   **800-477-3324**
                            **FAX 772-770-0006**
                     **http://www.speechbin.com**
                **e-mail: info@speechbin.com**
*Shane Peters, Product Coordinator*
*Jen Binney, Owner*

Easy-to-follow step-by-step instructions demonstrate
how to help children achieve reliable production of r
sounds, practice them in words of increasing complexity, and improve their phonic skills simultaneously.
Item number 1486. *$26.95*

**818   Weekly Language Practice**

**Harcourt Achieve**
**6277 Sea Harbor Drive**
**Orlando, FL  32887**          **252-480-3200**
                                **800-844-1464**
                         **FAX 800-269-5232**
                  **http://www.steckvaughn.com**
             **e-mail: info@steckvaughn.com**
*Keely Hoffman, Ken Bowser, Author*
*Tim McEwen, President/CEO*
*Jeff Johnson, Dir Marketing Communications*
*Chris Lehmann, Team Coordinator*

Each activity page features five activity strips, one for
each day of the week, and is backed up by a convenient
answer key for the teacher that includes explanations
and extensions.

**819   Winning in Speech**

**Speech Bin**
**1965 25th Avenue**
**Vero Beach, FL  32960**          **772-770-0007**
                                   **800-477-3324**
                            **FAX 772-770-0006**
                     **http://www.speechbin.com**
                **e-mail: info@speechbin.com**
*Michelle Waugh, Author*
*Shane Peters, Product Coordinator*
*Jen Binney, Owner*

This delightful workbook gives your 7-14 year olds a
wealth of information about stuttering and how to
handle it. Winning in Speech shows them how they
can modify their stuttering behaviors through everyday experiences. Item number 1594. *$22.95*

*40 pages*
*ISBN 0-937857-29-7*

**820   Wizard of Rs**

**Speech Bin**
**1965 25th Avenue**
**Vero Beach, FL  32960**          **772-770-0007**
                                   **800-477-3324**
                            **FAX 772-770-0006**
                     **http://www.speechbin.com**
                **e-mail: info@speechbin.com**
*Shane Peters, Product Coordinator*
*Jen Binney, Owner*

This wizard makes those troublesome r problems
diappear like magic! It gives you a practical approach
with a wide range of scripted activities and helpful criterion-referenced testing, oral-motor exercises, remedial techniques and review of musculature. Item
number P756. *$22.00*

**821   Workbook for Aphasia**

**Speech Bin**
**1965 25th Avenue**
**Vero Beach, FL  32960**          **772-770-0007**
                                   **800-477-3324**
                            **FAX 772-770-0006**
                     **http://www.speechbin.com**
                **e-mail: info@speechbin.com**
*Shane Peters, Product Coordinator*
*Jen Binney, Owner*

This book gives you materials for adults who have recovered a significant degree of speaking, reading,
writing, and comprehension skills. It includes 106
excercises divided into eight target areas. Item number W331. *$48.95*

**822   Workbook for Language Skills**

**Speech Bin**
**1965 25th Avenue**
**Vero Beach, FL  32960**          **772-770-0007**
                            **FAX 772-770-0006**
                     **http://www.speechbin.com**
                **e-mail: info@speechbin.com**
*Shane Peters, Product Coordinator*
*Jen Binney, Owner*

This workbook features 68 real-world exercises designed for use with mildly to severely cognitive and
language-impaired individuals. The workbook is divided in seven target areas: Sentence Completion;
General Knowledge; Word Recall; Figurative Language; Sentence Comprehension; Sentence Construction and Spelling. Item number W333. *$48.95*

**823 Workbook for Verbal Expression**

Speech Bin
1965 25th Avenue
Vero Beach, FL 32960      772-770-0007
800-477-3324
FAX 772-770-0006
http://www.speechbin.com
e-mail: info@speechbin.com
*Shane Peters, Product Coordinator*
*Jen Binney, Owner*

Is a book of 100s of excerises from simple naming, automatic speech sequences, and repetition exercises to complex tasks in sentence formulation and abstract verbal reasoning. Item number 1435. *$43.95*

**824 Writing Trek Grades 4-6**

Sunburst Technology
400 Columbus Avenue
Valhalla, NY 10595 1349      914-747-3310
800-321-7511
FAX 914-747-4109
http://www.sunburst.com
e-mail: service@sunburst.com
*Katie Birmingham, Office Manager*

Enhance your students' experience in your English language arts classroom with twelve authentic writing projects that build students' competence while encouraging creativity.

**825 Writing Trek Grades 6-8**

Sunburst Technology
400 Columbus Avenue
Valhalla, NY 10595 1349      914-747-3310
800-321-7511
FAX 914-747-4109
http://www.sunburst.com
e-mail: service@sunburst.com
*Katie Birmingham, Office Manager*

Twelve authentic language arts projects, activities, and assignments develop your students' writing confidence and ability.

**826 Writing Trek Grades 8-10**

Sunburst Technology
400 Columbus Avenue
Valhalla, NY 10595 1349      914-747-3310
800-321-7511
FAX 914-747-4109
http://www.sunburst.com
e-mail: service@sunburst.com
*Katie Birmingham, Office Manager*

Help your students develop a concept of genre as they become familiar with the writing elements and characteristics of a variety of writing forms.

**827 Your Child's Speech and Language**

Speech Bin
1965 25th Avenue
Vero Beach, FL 32960      772-770-0007
800-477-3324
FAX 772-770-0006
http://www.speechbin.com
e-mail: info@speechbin.com
*Shane Peters, Product Coordinator*
*Jen Binney, Owner*

This delightfully illustrated 52- page book provides helpful information about speech and language development from infancy through five years. It shows how to determine if speech is developing normally and ways to stimulate its growth. It's ideal for parent training and baby showers too! Item number P652. *$17.00*

# Life Skills

**828 Ablenet**

2808 North Fairview Avenue
Roseville, MN 55414      612-379-0956
800-322-0956
FAX 651-294-2259
http://www.ablenetinc.com
e-mail: customerservice@ablenetinc.com
*Cheryl Volkman, Chief Developmental Officer*
*Rick Osterhaus, Chief Executive Officer*

Simple assistive technology for teaching children with disabilities including communication aids, switches, environmental control, literacy and teacher resources, kits and more.

**829 Activities for the Elementary Classroom**

Curriculum Associates
PO Box 2001
North Billerica, MA 01862 9914      978-667-8000
800-225-0248
FAX 800-366-1158
http://www.curriculumassociates.com
e-mail: ca@infocurriculumassociates.com
*Ernest Kern, Editor*
*Frank Ferguson, President*

Challenge your students to make a hole in a 3" x 5" index card large enough to poke their heads through. Or offer to pour them a glass of air. You'll have their attenion — the first step toward learning — when you use the high-interest, hands-on activities in these exciting teacher resource books.

**830 Activities of Daily Living: A Manual of Group Activities and Written Exercises**

Therapro
225 Arlington Street
Framingham, MA 01702 8723      508-872-9494
800-257-5376
FAX 508-875-2062
http://www.theraproducts.com
e-mail: info@theraproducts.com
*Karen McCarthy COTA/L, Author*
*Karen Conrad, President*

Designed to provide group leaders easy access to structured plans for Activities of Daily Living (ADL) Groups. Organized into five modules: Personal Hygiene; Laundry Skills; Money Management; Leisure Skills and Nutrition. Each includes introduction, assessment guidelines, worksheets to copy, suggested board work, and wrap-up discussions. Appropriate for adult or adolescent programs, school systems and programs for the learning disabled. *$25.00*

*136 pages*

**831    Aids and Appliances for Indepentent Living**

**Maxi**
**PO Box 3209**
**Farmingdale, NY  11735**              631-752-0521
                                        800-522-6294
                                   FAX 631-752-0689
                                   TDY:631-752-0738
                           http://www.maxiaids.com
*Elliot Zaretsky, President*
*Barbara Collins, Contact*

Thousands of products to make life easier. Eating, dressing, communications, bed, bath, kitchen, writing aids and more.

**832    Artic-Action**

**Speech Bin**
**1965 25th Avenue**
**Vero Beach, FL  32960**              772-770-0007
                                       800-477-3324
                                  FAX 772-770-0006
                          http://www.speechbin.com
                        e-mail: info@speechbin.com
*Denise Grigas, Author*
*Jan Binney, Editor-in-Chief*
*Shane Peters, Product Coordinator*

Take the doldrums out of speech drills with this terrific collection of ideas! Clever tasks facilitate learning through hands-on experiences and provide a rich language learning environment for K-5 children. Activities encourage cooperative learning, turn taking, conversational discourse and social interaction. Item number 1524. *$18.95*

*144 pages*
*ISBN 0-937857-37-8*

**833    Barnaby's Burrow: An Auditory Processing Game**

**LinguiSystems**
**3100 4th Avenue**
**East Moline, IL  61244**              309-775-2300
                                        800-776-4332
                                   FAX 309-755-2375
                                   TDY:800-933-8331
                         http://www.linguisystems.com
                     e-mail: service@linguisystems.com
*Barb Truman, Author*
*Linda Bowers, Owner*
*Rosemary Huisingh, Owner*

Your students will practice good auditory processing skills as they help Barnaby the rabbit get to his burrow. This delightful game gives you tons of auditory processing tasks at increasing levels of difficulty. 300 game cards provide you stimulus items for phonological awareness, following directions, absurdities, and identifying main ideas and details. *$44.95*

*Ages 4-9*

**834    Boredom Rx**

**Speech Bin**
**1965 25th Avenue**
**Vero Beach, FL  32960**              772-770-0007
                                       800-477-3324
                                  FAX 772-770-0006
                          http://www.speechbin.com
                        e-mail: info@speechbin.com
*Kristel Aderholdt, Author*
*Jan Binney, Editor-in-Chief*
*Shane Peters, Product Coordinator*

Fun-filled tasks help school-age kids improve their practical skills in listening, pragmatics, remembering, and following directions. Item number 1583. *$29.95*

**835    Brainopoly: A Thinking Game**

**LinguiSystems**
**3100 4th Avenue**
**East Moline, IL  61244**              309-775-2300
                                        800-776-4332
                                   FAX 309-755-2377
                                   TDY:800-933-8331
                         http://www.linguisystems.com
                     e-mail: service@linguisystems.com
*LinguiSystems Staff, Author*
*Linda Bowers, Owner*
*Rosemary Huisingh, Owner*

Target all the critical thinking, problem-solving, and decision-making skills your older students need to meet the demands of the classroom curriculum. Each game section has 50 questions divided into two levels of difficulty. That's 450 total questions! Students will practice using predicting, inferring, deduction skills, and more! *$44.95*

*Ages 10-15*

**836    Categorically Speaking**

**Speech Bin**
**1965 25th Avenue**
**Vero Beach, FL  32960**              772-770-0007
                                       800-477-3324
                                  FAX 772-770-0006
                          http://www.speechbin.com
                        e-mail: info@speechbin.com
*Shane Peters, Product Coordinator*
*Jen Binney, Owner*

This game for two to four players or two teams gives 6-10 year-olds experience in asking questions, evaluating information they receive, and using it to solve problems. To play, they must use specified question formats to get clues about pictures, recognize similarities and differences, identify salient features of objects, and encode and decode messages. Item number Q849. *$51.00*

**837    Changes Around Us CD-ROM**

**Harcourt Achieve**
**6277 Sea Harbor Drive**
**Orlando, FL  32887**                 252-480-3200
                                       800-844-1464
                                  FAX 800-269-5232
                          http://www.steckvaughn.com
                        e-mail: info@steckvaughn.com
*Steck-Vaughn Staff, Author*
*Tim McEwen, President/CEO*
*Jeff Johnson, Dir Marketing Communications*
*Chris Lehmann, Team Coordinator*

Nature is the natural choice for observing change. By observing and researching dramatic visual sequences such as the stages of development of a butterfly, children develop a broad understanding of the concept of change. As they search this multimedia database for images and information about plant and animal life cycles and seasonal change, students strengthen their abilities in research, analysis, problem-solving, critical thinking and communication.

**838 Classroom Visual Activities**

Therapro
225 Arlington Street
Framingham, MA  01702 8723          508-872-9494
                                    800-257-5376
                               FAX 508-875-2062
                        http://www.theraproducts.com
                        e-mail: info@theraproducts.com
*Regina G Richards MA, Author*
*Karen Conrad, President*

This work presents a wealth of activities for the development of visual skills in the areas of pursuit, scanning, aligning, and locating movements; eye hand coordination, and fixation activity. Each activity lists objectives and criteria for success and gives detailed instuctions. *$15.00*

*80 pages*

**839 Cognitive Strategy Instruction for Middle & High Schools**

Brookline Books
300 Bedford St
Manchester, NH  03101          617-734-6772
                          FAX 603-922-3348
                   http://www.brooklinebooks.com
                   e-mail: info@brooklinebooks.com
*Eileen Wood, Vera Woloshyn, Teena Willoughby, Author*

Presents cognitive strategies empirically validated for middle and high school students, with an emphasis for teachers on how to teach and support the strategies. *$26.95*

*286 pages*
*ISBN 1-571290-07-9*

**840 Complete Guide to Running, Walking and Fitness for Kids**

Therapro
225 Arlington Street
Framingham, MA  01702 8723          508-872-9494
                                    800-257-5376
                               FAX 508-875-2062
                        http://www.theraproducts.com
                        e-mail: info@theraproducts.com
*Tim Erson MS PT, Author*
*Karen Conrad, President*

This should be every child's first book of fitness. Many tips on how to get started, such as stretching, dressing wisely, where to run, racing, aerobics and more. Includes a logbook and journal for 1 year, with weekly goals, encouraging messages, training notes, and so on. *$18.95*

*263 pages*

**841 Coping for Kids Who Stutter**

Speech Bin
1965 25th Avenue
Vero Beach, FL  32960          772-770-0007
                               800-477-3324
                          FAX 772-770-0006
                      http://www.speechbin.com
                      e-mail: info@speechbin.com
*Shane Peters, Product Coordinator*
*Jen Binney, Owner*

Coping for Kids Who Stutter educates people of all ages about the confusing and frustrating communication disorder of stuttering. This matter-of-fact book presents a muiltitude of facts about stuttering and gives lots of good advice about what to do about it in a nonthreatening, convincing manner. Item number 1543. *$18.95*

**842 Definition Play by Play**

LinguiSystems
3100 4th Avenue
East Moline, IL  61244          309-775-2300
                                800-776-4332
                           FAX 309-755-2377
                           TDY:800-933-8331
                    http://www.linguisystems.com
                    e-mail: service@linguisystems.com
*Sharon Spencer, Author*
*Linda Bowers, Owner*
*Rosemary Huisingh, Owner*

Teach your students to give accurate, cohesive definitions by identifying and organizing critical attributes of words. As players move along the board, they describe an object card by these attributes: function; what goes with it; size/shape; color; parts; what it's made of; and location. *$44.95*

*Ages 8-14*

**843 Effective Listening**

Speech Bin
1965 25th Avenue
Vero Beach, FL  32960          772-770-0007
                               800-477-3324
                          FAX 772-770-0006
                      http://www.speechbin.com
                      e-mail: info@speechbin.com
*Shane Peters, Product Coordinator*
*Jen Binney, Owner*

Effective Listening gives you creative lessons in a stimulating format that takes the drudgery out of listening drills. Its LISTEN techniques provide structured strategies to improve auditory processing skills. Item number 1355. *$25.95*

**844 Fine Motor Activities Guide and Easel Activities Guide**

Therapro
225 Arlington Street
Framingham, MA  01702 8723          508-872-9494
                                    800-257-5376
                               FAX 508-875-2062
                        http://www.theraproducts.com
                        e-mail: info@theraproducts.com
*Jane Berry OTR/L, Author*
*Karen Conrad, President*

These guides have always been included in the above kits and can now be purchased separately. Useful for activity plans or teacher-educator-parent consultations. Perfect hand-outs as part of your inservice packet (no need to write out ideas, photocopy materials, etc). Package of 10 booklets.

## 845 Fine Motor Fun

**Therapro**
**225 Arlington Street**
**Framingham, MA 01702 8723** **508-872-9494**
**800-257-5376**
**FAX 508-875-2062**
**http://www.theraproducts.com**
**e-mail: info@theraproducts.com**
*Maryanne Bruni BS OT, Author*
*Karen Conrad, President*

Fine motor skills are the hand skills that allow us to do things like hold a pencil, cut with scissors, eat with a fork, and use a computer. This practical guide shows parents and professionals how to help children with Down Syndrome from infancy to 12 years improve fine motor functioning. *$16.95*

*191 pages Ages Birth-12*

## 846 Finger Frolics: Fingerplays

**Therapro**
**225 Arlington Street**
**Framingham, MA 01702 8723** **508-872-9494**
**800-257-5376**
**FAX 508-875-2062**
**http://www.theraproducts.com**
**e-mail: info@theraproducts.com**
*Liz Cromwell, Dixie Hibner, Author*
*Karen Conrad, President*

Invaluable for occupational therapists, speech/language pathologists and teachers. Over 350 light and humorous fingerplays help children with rhyming and performing actions which develop fine motor and language skills. *$10.95*

## 847 Follow Me!

**LinguiSystems**
**3100 4th Avenue**
**East Moline, IL 61244** **309-775-2300**
**800-776-4332**
**FAX 309-755-2377**
**TDY:800-933-8331**
**http://www.linguisystems.com**
**e-mail: service@linguisystems.com**
*Grace W Frank, Author*
*Linda Bowers, Owner*
*Rosemary Huisingh, Owner*

Lessons are organized by grade level so you can control the lesson complexity as your students listen and follow oral directions. Get 91 listen-and-do lessons, each with a reproducible student worksheet to teach concepts such as location, association, exclusion, sequencing, and more. *$34.95*

*187 pages Ages 5-9*

## 848 Follow Me! 2

**LinguiSystems**
**3100 4th Avenue**
**East Moline, IL 61244** **309-775-2300**
**800-776-4332**
**FAX 309-755-2377**
**TDY:800-933-8331**
**http://www.linguisystems.com**
**e-mail: service@linguisystems.com**
*Grace Frank, Author*
*Linda Bowers, Owner*
*Rosemary Huisingh, Owner*

These activities are relevant to classroom listening demands. The directions relate specifically on an accompanying worksheet. It's a pick-up-and-use-now resource to teach the vocabulary of language arts, math, social studies and more. *$34.95*

*201 pages Ages 7-11*

## 849 HELP Elementary

**LinguiSystems**
**3100 4th Avenue**
**East Moline, IL 61244** **309-775-2300**
**800-776-4332**
**FAX 309-755-2377**
**TDY:800-933-8331**
**http://www.linguisystems.com**
**e-mail: service@linguisystems.com**
*Andrea Lazzari, Patricia Peters, Author*
*Linda Bowers, Owner*
*Rosemary Huisingh, Owner*

The look and content of these activities appeal specifically to your elementary-aged students. The no-frills, ready-to-use approach fits your precious time. These worksheets are perfect for oral or written practice. Help students improve question comprehension, association, specific word-finding, grammar, and more. *$39.95*

*207 pages Ages 6-12*

## 850 HELP for Memory

**LinguiSystems**
**3100 4th Avenue**
**East Moline, IL 61244** **309-775-2300**
**800-776-4332**
**FAX 309-755-2377**
**TDY:800-933-8331**
**http://www.linguisystems.com**
**e-mail: service@linguisystems.com**
*Andrea Lazzari, Author*
*Linda Bowers, Owner*
*Rosemary Huisingh, Owner*

Help clients and students acquire memory strategies they'll use in daily life. These exercises incorporate attention, discrimination, categorization, and association to cover the broad range of memory skills. These functional memory tasks are arranged in a hierarchy to build skill upon skill. Help clients organize and retrieve information through exercises for coding and grouping items for recall, applying memory techniques to daily life skills, and more. *$39.95*

*178 pages Ages 8-Adult*

**851 HELP for Middle School**

**LinguiSystems**
**3100 4th Avenue**
**East Moline, IL 61244** 309-775-2300
800-776-4332
FAX 309-755-2377
TDY:800-933-8331
http://www.linguisystems.com
e-mail: service@linguisystems.com
*Andrea Lazzari, Author*
*Linda Bowers, Owner*
*Rosemary Huisingh, Owner*

Get ready-to-use activities relevant to middle school students. Your students will tune in and make progress! Middle school clinicians are singing the praises of this great resource. You'll get IEP goals and great language activities for vocabulary, grammer, question comprehension, following directions, test taking, and expression. *$39.95*

*183 pages Ages 10-15*

**852 Hands-On Activities for Exceptional Students**

**Peytral Publications**
**PO Box 1162**
**Minnetonka, MN 55345** 952-949-8707
877-739-8725
FAX 952-906-9777
http://www.peytral.com
e-mail: help@peytral.com
*Beverly Thorne, Author*
*Peggy Hammeken, Owner/Publisher*

This execptional new release is developed for educators of students who have cognitive delays who will eventually work in a sheltered employment environment. If you need new ideas at your fingertips, this practical book is for you. *$19.95*

*112 pages Special Ed*
*ISBN 1-890455-31-8*

**853 Health**

**Harcourt Achieve**
**6277 Sea Harbor Drive**
**Orlando, FL 32887** 252-480-3200
800-844-1464
FAX 800-269-5232
http://www.steckvaughn.com
e-mail: info@steckvaughn.com
*Steck-Vaughn Staff, Author*
*Tim McEwen, President/CEO*
*Jeff Johnson, Dir Marketing Communications*
*Chris Lehmann, Team Coordinator*

Lessons and projects focus on nutrition, outdoor safety, smart choices, and exercise. Designed to make children more health conscious. Activity formats include fill in the blank, word puzzles, multiple choice, crosswords, and more.

**854 Hidden Senses: Your Balance Sense & Your Muscle Sense**

**Therapro**
**225 Arlington Street**
**Framingham, MA 01702 8723** 508-872-9494
800-257-5376
FAX 508-875-2062
http://www.theraproducts.com
e-mail: info@theraproducts.com
*Jane Koomar PhD, Barbara Friedman MA, Author*
*Karen Conrad, President*

These movement books are back in print! Help children discover the crucial, yet seldom mentioned body awareness senses that help them in movement, coordination, strength and perception. The authors, both practicing OTs, explain simply and clearly how the body senses work. Colorful and vibrant images bring the explanations to life.

**855 It's All in Your Head: A Guide to Understanding Your Brain and Boosting Your Brain Power**

**Therapro**
**225 Arlington Street**
**Framingham, MA 01702 8723** 508-872-9494
800-257-5376
FAX 508-875-2062
http://www.theraproducts.com
e-mail: info@theraproducts.com
*Susan L Barrett, Author*
*Karen Conrad, President*

By popular demand from therapists, we are carrying this popular book for children. An owners manual on the brain, written especially for kids, this upbeat, engaging book is great for ages 9-14. *$9.95*

*151 pages*

**856 Just for Me! Concepts**

**LinguiSystems**
**3100 4th Avenue**
**East Moline, IL 61244** 309-775-2300
800-776-4332
FAX 309-755-2377
TDY:800-933-8331
http://www.linguisystems.com
e-mail: service@linguisystems.com
*Margaret Warner, Author*
*Linda Bowers, Owner*
*Rosemary Huisingh, Owner*

These fun color, cut, fold and play pages will keep youngsters busy learning basic concepts. Teach basic concepts in four areas: spatial, attributes, quantity, and temporal. *$24.95*

*150 pages Ages 3-6*

**857 Key Concepts in Personal Development**

**Marshsilm Enterprises**
**8025 Ward Parkway Plaza**
**Kansas City, MO 64114** 816-523-1059
800-821-3303
FAX 866-333-7421
http://www.marshmedia.com
e-mail: info@marshmedia.com
*Joan Marsh, President*
*Sarah Lynch, Shipping Manager*

Our videos, books, and teaching guides bring character education to the classroom. These kits are invaluable aids in teaching everyday values like honesty, anger control, trustworthiness, perseverance, understanding and respect. They help you prepare youngsters to meet challenges and greet opportunities with skill and optimism.

**858    LD Teacher's IEP Companion Software**

**LinguiSystems**
**3100 4th Avenue**
**East Moline, IL  61244**        **309-775-2300**
                                **800-776-4332**
                        **FAX 309-755-2377**
                        **TDY:800-933-8331**
                **http://www.linguisystems.com**
                **e-mail: service@linguisystems.com**
*Molly Lyle, Author*
*Linda Bowers, Owner*
*Rosemary Huisingh, Owner*

Create customized, professional reports with these terrific academic goals and objectives. You'll have individual objectives from nine skill areas at the click of your mouse! Save time with the software version of the best-selling book! For both PC and Macintosh. *$69.95*

*Ages 5-18*

**859    Life Management Skills I**

**Therapro**
**225 Arlington Street**
**Framingham, MA  01702 8723**        **508-872-9494**
                                **800-257-5376**
                        **FAX 508-875-2062**
                **http://www.theraproducts.com**
                **e-mail: info@theraproducts.com**
*Therapro Staff, Author*
*Karen Conrad, President*

Topics include: assertion; discharge planning; emotion identification; exercise; goal setting; leisure; motivation; nutrition; problem solving; risk taking; self awareness; self esteem; sleep; stress management; support systems; time management; and values clarification. *$39.95*

**860    Life Management Skills II**

**Therapro**
**225 Arlington Street**
**Framingham, MA  01702 8723**        **508-872-9494**
                                **800-257-5376**
                        **FAX 508-875-2062**
                **http://www.theraproducts.com**
                **e-mail: info@theraproducts.com**
*Therapro Staff, Author*
*Karen Conrad, President*

Topics include: activities of daily living; anger management; assertion; verbal and nonverbal communication; coping skills; grief/loss; humor; life balance; money management; parenting; reminiscence; safety issues; self esteem; image; steps to recovery; stress management; support systems and time management. *$41.95*

**861    Life Management Skills III**

**Therapro**
**225 Arlington Street**
**Framingham, MA  01702 8723**        **508-872-9494**
                                **800-257-5376**
                        **FAX 508-875-2062**
                **http://www.theraproducts.com**
                **e-mail: info@theraproducts.com**
*Therapro Staff, Author*
*Karen Conrad, President*

Using the same format as books I and II, this new book has 50 handouts including 5 forms on both men's and women's issues. Includes 9 pages of generic forms that everyone can use. Topics include: aging; body image; communication; conflict resolution; coping skills; creative expression; healthy living; job readiness; nurturance; relapse prevention; relationships and many more. *$41.95*

**862    Life Management Skills IV**

**Therapro**
**225 Arlington Street**
**Framingham, MA  01702 8723**        **508-872-9494**
                                **800-257-5376**
                        **FAX 508-875-2062**
                **http://www.theraproducts.com**
                **e-mail: info@theraproducts.com**
*Therapro Staff, Author*
*Karen Conrad, President*

Topics include: activities of daily living; combating stigma; communication; coping with serious mental illness; home management; humor; job readiness; journalizing; leisure; parenting; relationships; responsibility; self esteem; sexual health; social skills; stress mangagement; suicide issues and values. *$41.95*

**863    Life-Centered Career Education: Daily Living Skills**

**Council for Exceptional Children**
**1110 N Glebe Road**
**Arlington, VA  22201 5704**        **703-620-3660**
                                **888-232-7733**
                        **FAX 703-264-9494**
                        **TDY:866-915-5000**
                **http://www.cec.sped.org**
                **e-mail: service@cec.sped.org**
*Donn Brolin, Author*
*Drew Albritten MD, Executive Director*
*Betty Bryant, LCCE Program Manager*

LCCE teaches you to prepare students to function independently and productively as family members, citizens, and workers, and to enjoy fulfilling personal lives. LCCE is a motivating and effectiev classroom, home, and community-based curriculum.

**864    Listening for Basic Concepts All Year' Round**

**LinguiSystems**
**3100 4th Avenue**
**East Moline, IL  61244**        **309-775-2300**
                                **800-776-4332**
                        **FAX 309-755-2377**
                        **TDY:800-933-8331**
                **http://www.linguisystems.com**
                **e-mail: service@linguisystems.com**
*Brenda Brumbaugh, Nan Thompson-Trenta, Author*
*Linda Bowers, Owner*
*Rosemary Huisingh, Owner*

Mastering concepts is guaranteed with this book because you teach them in fun, themed contexts. Teach 86 space, quanity, and attribute concepts. Concept tests give you built-in accountablility. *$39.95*

*186 pages  Ages 5-8*

**865    Living Skills**

**Speech Bin**
**1965 25th Avenue**
**Vero Beach, FL  32960**                      772-770-0007
                                               800-477-3324
                                               FAX 772-770-0006
                                   http://www.speechbin.com
                                   e-mail: info@speechbin.com
*Shane Peters, Product Coordinator*
*Jen Binney, Owner*

Living Skills meets the challenges and special needs of children and adolescents with traumatic brain injury. A wealth of activities help restore cognitive, perceptual, and functional skills. Item number 1350. *$39.95*

**866    MORE: Integrating the Mouth with Sensory & Postural Functions**

**Therapro**
**225 Arlington Street**
**Framingham, MA  01702 8723**          508-872-9494
                                        800-257-5376
                                        FAX 508-875-2062
                                http://www.theraproducts.com
                                e-mail: info@theraproducts.com
*Particia Oetter OTR/L, Eileen Richter OTR, Author*
*Karen Conrad, President*

MORE is an acronym for Motor components, Oral organization, Respiratory demands and Eye contact and control; elements of toys and items that can be used to facilitate integration of the mouth with sensory and postural development, as well as self-regulation and attention. A theoretical framework for the treatment of both sensorimotor and speech/language problems is presented, methods for evaluating therapeutic potential of motor toys, and activities designed to improve functions. *$46.00*

**867    Memory Workbook**

**Therapro**
**225 Arlington Street**
**Framingham, MA  01702 8723**          508-872-9494
                                        800-257-5376
                                        FAX 508-875-2062
                                http://www.theraproducts.com
                                e-mail: info@theraproducts.com
*Therapro Staff, Author*
*Karen Conrad, President*

Recalling daily activities, seasons, months of the year, shapes, words and pictures. *$10.50*

**868    One-Handed in a Two-Handed World**

**Therapro**
**225 Arlington Street**
**Framingham, MA  01702 8723**          508-872-9494
                                        800-257-5376
                                        FAX 508-875-2062
                                http://www.theraproducts.com
                                e-mail: info@theraproducts.com
*Tommye K Mayer, Author*
*Karen Conrad, President*

A personal guide to managing single handed. Written by a woman who has lived one-handed for many years, this book shares a methodology and mindset necessary for managing. It details a wide array of topics including personal care, daily chores, office work, traveling, sports, relationships and many more. A must for patients and therapists. *$19.95*

*250 pages*

**869    Peabody Developmental Motor Scales-2**

**Speech Bin**
**1965 25th Avenue**
**Vero Beach, FL  32960**                      772-770-0007
                                               800-477-3324
                                               FAX 888-329-2246
                                   http://www.speechbin.com
                                   e-mail: info@speechbin.com
*Rhonda Folio, Rebecca Fewell, Author*
*Shane Peters, Product Coordinator*
*Jen Binney, Owner*

PDMS-2 gives you in-depth standardized assessment of motor skills in children birth to six years. Subtests include: fine motor object manipulation; grasping; gross motor; locomotion; reflexes; visual-motor integration and stationary. Item number P624. *$413.00*

*Ages Birth-6*

**870    People at Work**

**AGS Publishing**
**4201 Woodland Road**
**Circle Pines, MN  55014 1796**          651-287-7220
                                          800-328-2560
                                          FAX 800-471-8457
                                   http://www.agsnet.com
                                   e-mail: agsmail@agsnet.com
*Karen Dahlen, Associate Director*
*Matt Keller, Marketing Manager*

With an interest level of High School through Adult, ABE and ESL and a reading level of Grades 3-4, this program is a simple, thorough teaching plan for every day of the school year. The program's 180 sessions are divided into eighteen study units that each survey an entire occupational cluster of eight jobs while focusing on one or two writing skills. *$26.95*

**871    Putting the Pieces Together: Volume 4**

**Speech Bin**
**1965 25th Avenue**
**Vero Beach, FL  32960**                      772-770-0007
                                               800-477-3324
                                               FAX 772-770-0006
                                   http://www.speechbin.com
                                   e-mail: info@speechbin.com
*Shane Peters, Product Coordinator*
*Jen Binney, Owner*

This helpful volume gives you enjoyable materials and effective strategies for conceptualization, problem-solving, inductive and deductive reasoning, organization, judgement sequencing, attention/concentration, visual field neglect, and cognitve system reintegration. Item number V360. *$47.95*

**872  Reading and Writing Workbook**

Therapro
225 Arlington Street
Framingham, MA  01702 8723       508-872-9494
                                 800-257-5376
                            FAX 508-875-2062
                   http://www.theraproducts.com
                   e-mail: info@theraproducts.com
*Therapro Staff, Author*
*Karen Conrad, President*

Writing checks and balancing a checkbook, copying words and sentences, and writing messages and notes. Helps with recognition and understanding of calendars, phone books and much more. *$10.50*

**873  Real World Situations**

Harcourt Achieve
6277 Sea Harbor Drive
Orlando, FL  32887            252-480-3200
                              800-844-1464
                         FAX 800-269-5232
                   http://www.steckvaughn.com
                   e-mail: info@steckvaughn.com
*Steck-Vaughn Staff, Author*
*Tim McEwen, President/CEO*
*Jeff Johnson, Dir Marketing Communications*
*Chris Lehmann, Team Coordinator*

Practice the practical problem-solving skills students need every day.

**874  Responding to Oral Directions**

Speech Bin
1965 25th Avenue
Vero Beach, FL  32960         772-770-0007
                              800-477-3324
                         FAX 772-770-0006
                   http://www.speechbin.com
                   e-mail: info@speechbin.com
*Shane Peters, Product Coordinator*
*Jen Binney, Owner*

Help children of all ages who function at first through sixth-grade levels learn to identify unclear directions and ask for clarification. Nine units teach them how to handle: recognizing directions, carryover and generalization; unreasonable, distorted, vague, unfamiliar, lenngthy, unknown, and mixed directions. Item number 975. *$49.00*

**875  SEALS II Self-Esteem and Life Skills II**

Therapro
225 Arlington Street
Framingham, MA  01702 8723       508-872-9494
                                 800-257-5376
                            FAX 508-875-2062
                   http://www.theraproducts.com
                   e-mail: info@theraproducts.com
*Therapro Staff, Author*
*Karen Conrad, President*

Adapted from Life Management Skills III and IV, this book is for youth, ages 12-18 with age-appropriate language, graphics, and illustrations. Includes 80 activity-based handouts related to body image, communication, conflict resolution, coping skills, creative expression, humor, job readiness, leisure skills, nurturance and more. *$43.95*

**876  Scissors, Glue, and Concepts, Too!**

LinguiSystems
3100 4th Avenue
East Moline, IL  61244        309-775-2300
                              800-776-4332
                         FAX 309-755-2377
                         TDY:800-933-8331
                   http://www.linguisystems.com
                   e-mail: service@linguisystems.com
*Susan Boegler, Debbie Abruzzini, Author*
*Linda Bowers, Owner*
*Rosemary Huisingh, Owner*

Your young students will learn to follow directions and understand basic concepts in context. Concepts for each activity are grouped as they naturally occur in our language. Teach over 50 concepts including right/left, above/below, empty/full, and more. *$39.95*

*199 pages  Ages 5-8*

**877  Sensory Motor Issues in Autism**

Speech Bin
1965 25th Avenue
Vero Beach, FL  32960         772-770-0007
                              800-477-3324
                         FAX 772-770-0006
                   http://www.speechbin.com
                   e-mail: info@speechbin.com
*Shane Peters, Product Coordinator*
*Jen Binney, Owner*

This resource for professionals and parents explains sensory processing disorders and their relationship to autism. It shows how to improve a child's responses to sensation, teach motor skills using daily living activities, and provide an effective learning environment. Item number C971. *$20.95*

**878  So What Can I Do?**

Therapro
225 Arlington Street
Framingham, MA  01702 8723       508-872-9494
                                 800-257-5376
                            FAX 508-875-2062
                   http://www.theraproducts.com
                   e-mail: info@theraproducts.com
*Gail Kushnir, Author*
*Karen Conrad, President*

A book to help children develop their own solutions to everyday problems. Cartoon illustrations feature common situations for children to analyze. The adult asks the child, so what can you do? The child is then encouraged to think of creative solutions, developing their emotional intelligence and improving coping skills. 58 problems to solve. *$10.95*

**879  Special Needs Program**

Dallas Metro Care
3330 S Lancaster Road
Dallas, TX  75216             214-371-0474
                         FAX 214-371-3933
*Cecilia Castillo, Director*
*John Gorman, Supervisor*

The special needs curriculum teaches students with disabilities the life skills they need to achieve self-sufficiency. The program focuses on and enhances coping skills.

**880** **Stepwise Cookbooks**

**Therapro**
225 Arlington Street
Framingham, MA 01702 8723   508-872-9494
                            800-257-5376
                         FAX 508-875-2062
                 http://www.theraproducts.com
                 e-mail: info@theraproducts.com
*Beth Jackson OTR, Author*
*Karen Conrad, President*

A chance for children and adults at all developmental levels to participate in fun-filled hands-on cooking activities while developing independence. These cookbooks were developed by an OT working with children and teenagers with cognitive and physical challenges. Only one direction is presented on a page to reduce confusion. Recipes are represented by large Boardmaker symbols from Mayer Johnson. Large, easy-to-read text with dividing lines for visual clarity.

**881** **Strategies for Problem-Solving**

**Harcourt Achieve**
6277 Sea Harbor Drive
Orlando, FL 32887          252-480-3200
                          800-844-1464
                       FAX 800-269-5232
                 http://www.steckvaughn.com
                 e-mail: info@steckvaughn.com
*Yellin, Author*
*Tim McEwen, President/CEO*
*Jeff Johnson, Dir Marketing Communications*
*Chris Lehmann, Team Coordinator*

Show students more than one way to approach a problem, and you hand them the key to effective problem solving. These reproducible activities build math reasoning and critical thinking skills, reinforce core concepts, and reduce math anxiety too. *$8.49*

**882** **Survey of Teenage Readiness and Neurodevelopmental Status**

**Educators Publishing Service**
31 Smith Place
Cambridge, MA 02139 9031   617-547-6706
                          800-225-5750
                       FAX 888-440-2665
                 http://www.epsbooks.com
                 e-mail: eps@epsbooks.com
*Melvin D Levine MD FAAP, Author*
*Steve Kote, President*

Developed by Dr. Mel Livine and Dr. Stephen Hooper, The Survey of Teenage Readiness and Neurodevelopmental Status capitalizes on adolescents' evolving metacognitive abilities by directly asking them for their perceptions of how they are functioning in school and how they process information across a variety of neurocognitive and psychosocial domains.

**883** **Swallow Right**

**Speech Bin**
1965 25th Avenue
Vero Beach, FL 32960       772-770-0007
                          800-477-3324
                       FAX 772-770-0006
                 http://www.speechbin.com
                 e-mail: info@speechbin.com
*Shane Peters, Product Coordinator*
*Jen Binney, Owner*

This 12-session program evaluates and treats oral myofunctional disorders. 40 reproducible sequential exercises train individuals from five years to adult how to swallow correctly. Easy-to-use evaluation and tracking forms, checklist, and carryover strategies make this book a real time-saver! Item number Q858. *$44.00*

**884** **TARGET**

**Speech Bin**
1965 25th Avenue
Vero Beach, FL 32960       772-770-0007
                          800-477-3324
                       FAX 772-770-0006
                 http://www.speechbin.com
                 e-mail: info@speechbin.com
*Shane Peters, Product Coordinator*
*Jen Binney, Owner*

TARGET is the kind of resource aphasia clinicians beg for — a practical resource that answers not only the what and how questions of treatment but also the why. It describes dozens of treatment methods and gives you practical exercises and activities to implement each technique. Item number 1434. *$49.95*

**885** **TOPS Kit- Adolescent: Tasks of Problem Solving**

**LinguiSystems**
3100 4th Avenue
East Moline, IL 61244      309-775-2300
                          800-776-4332
                       FAX 309-755-2377
                      TDY:800-933-8331
                 http://www.linguisystems.com
                 e-mail: service@linguisystems.com
*Linda Bowers, Rosemary Huisingh, Mark Barrett, Author*
*Linda Bowers, Owner*
*Rosemary Huisingh, Owner*

Teach your teens how to use their language skills to think, think, think. We combine literacy, thinking, writing, humor, and language arts practice to cover these thinking skills: using content to make references; analyzing information; taking another's point of view; and more. It's a literacy-based approach that gets dramatic results! *$59.95*

*192 pages  Ages 12-18*

**886** **TOPS Kit-Elementary: Tasks of Problem Solving**

**LinguiSystems**
3100 4th Avenue
East Moline, IL 61244      309-775-2300
                          800-776-4332
                       FAX 800-577-4555
                      TDY:800-933-8331
                 http://www.linguisystems.com
                 e-mail: service@linguisystems.com
*Linda Bowers, Owner*
*Rosemary Huisingh, Owner*

Reveal thinking and language skills your students didn't know they had with this remarkable kit. TOPS Kit-Elementary combines thinking and expressive language skills to develop better communications.

*Ages 6-12*

**887   Target Spelling**

Harcourt Achieve
6277 Sea Harbor Drive
Orlando, FL  32887                    252-480-3200
                                     800-844-1464
                              FAX 800-269-5232
                    http://www.steckvaughn.com
                    e-mail: info@steckvaughn.com
*Scarborough, Author*
*Tim McEwen, President/CEO*
*Jeff Johnson, Dir Marketing Communications*
*Chris Lehmann, Team Coordinator*

You can differentiate instructions to address a variety of learning styles and profiles and meet the needs of special education students.

**888   Teaching Dressing Skills: Buttons, Bows and More**

Therapro
225 Arlington Street
Framingham, MA  01702 8723           508-872-9494
                                     800-257-5376
                              FAX 508-875-2062
                    http://www.theraproducts.com
                    e-mail: info@theraproducts.com
*Marcy Coppelman Goldsmith OTR/L BCP, Author*
*Karen Conrad, President*

Consists of 5 fold-out pamphlets for teaching children and adults of varying abilities the basic dressing skills: shoe tying, buttoning, zippering, dressing and undressing. Each task is broken down with every step clearly illustrated and specific verbal directions given to avoid confusion and to eliminate excess verbiage that can distract the learner. The author, an experienced OT, has included the needed prerequisites for each task, many great teaching tips and more. *$12.95*

*5 Pamphlets*

**889   That's Life Picture Stories**

AGS Publishing
4201 Woodland Road
Circle Pines, MN  55014 1796         651-287-7220
                                     800-328-2560
                              FAX 800-471-8457
                    http://www.agsnet.com
                    e-mail: agsmail@agsnet.com
*Tana Reiff, Vince Clews, Author*
*Karen Dahlen, Associate Director*
*Matt Keller, Marketing Manager*

With an interest level of high school through adult, ABE and ESL and a reading level of Grades 3-4, these eight picture stories describe how four families face daily challenges and solve practical problems. Features comic-book-style art and speech balloons. Families represent varied ethnic backgrounds. DramaTape cassettes featuring professional actors, music and sound effects available. *$105.99*

**890   That's Life! Social Language**

LinguiSystems
3100 4th Avenue
East Moline, IL  61244               309-775-2300
                                     800-776-4332
                              FAX 309-755-2377
                              TDY:800-933-8331
                    http://www.linguisystems.com
                    e-mail: service@linguisystems.com
*Carolyn LoGiudice, Nancy McConnell, Author*
*Linda Bowers, Owner*
*Rosemary Huisingh, Owner*

Teach your students to be effective and appropriate communicators in a wide variety of situations. Through direct instruction, role-playing activities, and discussion, your students will learn the how and why of social language interaction. *$37.95*

*176 pages  Ages 12-18*

**891   That's Life: A Game of Life Skills**

LinguiSystems
3100 4th Avenue
East Moline, IL  61244               309-775-2300
                                     800-776-4332
                              FAX 309-755-2344
                              TDY:800-933-8331
                    http://www.linguisystems.com
                    e-mail: service@linguisystems.com
*Patricia Smith, Author*
*Linda Bowers, Owner*
*Rosemary Huisingh, Owner*

Help your older students refine their language skills to negotiate the real-world with this fun game. Get 100 thinking and language questions for each of these life areas: consumer affairs; government; health concerns; money matters; going places; and homemaking. *$44.95*

*Ages 12-18*

**892   ThemeWeavers: Animals Activity Kit**

Riverdeep
500 Redwood Boulevard
Novato, CA  94947                    415-763-4700
                                     800-362-2890
                              FAX 415-763-4385
                    http://www.edmark.com
                    e-mail: info@riverdeep.net
*Barry O'Callaghan, Chairman/CEO*
*Simon Calver, COO*
*John Rim, VP CFO*

ThemeWeavers: Animals is the essential companion for theme-based teaching. Dozens of animal-themed, interactive activities immediately engage your students to practice fundamental skills in math, language arts, science, social studies and more. Easy-to-use tools allow you to modify these activities or create your own to meet specific classroom needs.

**893   ThemeWeavers: Nature Activity Kit**

Riverdeep
500 Redwood Boulevard
Novato, CA  94947                    415-763-4700
                                     800-362-2890
                              FAX 415-763-4385
                    http://www.edmark.com
                    e-mail: info@riverdeep.net
*Barry O'Callaghan, Chairman/CEO*
*Simon Calver, COO*
*John Rim, VP CFO*

ThemeWeavers: Nature Activity Kit is an all-in-one solution for theme-based teaching. In just a few minutes, you can select from dozens of ready-to-use activities centering on the seasons and weather and be ready for the next day's lesson! Interactive and engaging activities cover multiple subject areas such as language arts, math, science, social studies and art.

**894    Thinkin' Science ZAP**

**Riverdeep**
**500 Redmond Boulevard**
**Novato, CA  94947**          415-763-4700
                              800-362-2890
                          FAX 415-763-4385
                      http://www.edmark.com
                   e-mail: info@riverdeep.net
*Barry O'Callaghan, Chairman/CEO*
*Simon Calver, COO*
*John Rim, CFO*

It is a dark and stormy night as you step backstage to be guest director at the Wonder Dome, the world-famous auditorium of light, sound, and electricity. But great zotz! The Theater has been zapped by lightning, and the Laser Control System is on the fritz! Can you learn all about light, sound and electricity to rescue the show? *$69.95*

**895    Time: Concepts & Problem-Solving**

**Harcourt Achieve**
**6277 Sea Harbor Drive**
**Orlando, FL  32887**          252-480-3200
                               800-844-1464
                           FAX 800-269-5232
                    http://www.steckvaughn.com
                  e-mail: info@steckvaughn.com
*Steck-Vaughn Staff, Author*
*Tim McEwen, President/CEO*
*Jeff Johnson, Dir Marketing Communications*
*Chris Lehmann, Team Coordinator*

Develop concepts of telling time, identifying intervals, calculating elapsed time, and solving problems that deal with time changes, lapses, and changes over the AM/PM cusp.

**896    Tips for Teaching Infants & Toddlers**

**Speech Bin**
**1965 25th Avenue**
**Vero Beach, FL  32960**          772-770-0007
                                  800-477-3324
                              FAX 772-770-0006
                       http://www.speechbin.com
                     e-mail: info@speechbin.com
*Shane Peters, Product Coordinator*
*Jen Binney, Owner*

This multisensory approach to Early Intervention is a whole year's worth of weekly thematic lessons which let children see, hear, feel, manipulate, smell, and taste. Item number 1235. *$45.95*

**897    Travel the World with Timmy Deluxe**

**Riverdeep**
**500n Redmond Boulevard**
**Novato, CA  94947**          415-763-4700
                              800-362-2890
                          FAX 415-763-4385
                      http://www.edmark.com
                   e-mail: info@riverdeep.net
*Barry O'Callaghan, Chairman/CEO*
*Simon Calver, COO*
*John Rim, CFO*

France and Russia are the newest destinations for Edmark's favorite world traveler, Timmy! In this delightful and improved program, students will enjoy expanding their understanding of the world around them. With wonderful stories, songs, games, and printable crafts, early learners discover how their international neighbors live, dress, sing, eat and play.

**898    Visual Perception and Attention Workbook**

**Therapro**
**225 Arlington Street**
**Framingham, MA  01702 8723**          508-872-9494
                                       800-257-5376
                                   FAX 508-875-2062
                         http://www.theraproducts.com
                       e-mail: info@theraproducts.com
*Therapro Staff, Author*
*Karen Conrad, President*

Simple mazes, visual discrimination and visual form constancy task, telling time and much more! *$10.50*

**899    Workbook for Cognitive Skills**

**Speech Bin**
**1965 25th Avenue**
**Vero Beach, FL  32960**          772-770-0007
                                  800-477-3324
                              FAX 772-770-0006
                       http://www.speechbin.com
                     e-mail: info@speechbin.com
*Shane Peters, Product Coordinator*
*Jen Binney, Owner*

This workbook of perceptual and problem-solving exercises provides challenging material that's easy to read. Designed for adults and adolescents who have cognitive disorders. Item number W336. *$48.95*

**900    Workbook for Memory Skills**

**Speech Bin**
**1965 25th Avenue**
**Vero Beach, FL  32960**          772-770-0007
                              FAX 772-770-0006
                       http://www.speechbin.com
                     e-mail: info@speechbin.com
*Jan Binney, Editor in Chief*
*Shane Peters, Product Coordinator*

Helpful in treating individuals with deficits in attention and memory skills secondary to: traumatic brain injury; cognitive disorganization; early stage dementia; brain damage; learning disability; and progressive disease. Item number 1488. *$44.95*

**901   Workbook for Reasoning Skills**

**Speech Bin**
**1965 25th Avenue**
**Vero Beach, FL  32960**          772-770-0007
                                  800-477-3324
                              FAX 772-770-0006
                       http://www.speechbin.com
                       e-mail: info@speechbin.com
*Shane Peters, Product Coordinator*
*Jen Binney, Owner*

This workbook is designed for adults and children who need practice in reasoning, thinking, and organizing. Includes 67 exercises created for individuals with closed head injuries and mild to moderate cognitive deficits. Item number W332. *$48.95*

**902   Workbook for Word Retrieval**

**Speech Bin**
**1965 25th Avenue**
**Vero Beach, FL  32960**          772-770-0007
                                  800-477-3324
                              FAX 772-770-0006
                       http://www.speechbin.com
                       e-mail: info@speechbin.com
*Beth M Kennedy, Author*
*Jan Binney, Editor-in-Chief*
*Shane Peters, Product Coordinator*

Helpful materials treat individuals with deficits in attention and memory skills secondary to: Traumatic brain injury, Congnitive disorganization, Early stage dementia, Brain damage, Learning disability and Progressive disease. Item number 1523. *$42.95*

*248 pages*

**903   Working With Words-Volume 3**

**Speech Bin**
**1965 25th Avenue**
**Vero Beach, FL  32960**          772-770-0007
                                  800-477-3324
                              FAX 772-770-0006
                       http://www.speechbin.com
                       e-mail: info@speechbin.com
*Shane Peters, Product Coordinator*
*Jen Binney, Owner*

Stimulate the reasoning skills of your brain-injured patients with this large print workbook of puzzles and word games. Activities include word builders, word hunters, word puzzlers, and word games challenging exercises for older children and adults. Item number V371. *$38.95*

**904   Working for Myself**

**AGS Publishing**
**4201 Woodland Road**
**Circle Pines, MN  55014 1796**          651-287-7220
                                          800-328-2560
                                      FAX 800-471-8457
                               http://www.agsnet.com
                               e-mail: agsmail@agsnet.com
*Tana Reiff, Author*
*Karen Dahlen, Associate Director*
*Matt Keller, Marketing Manager*

With an interest level of High School through Adult, ABE and ESL and a reading level of Grades 3-4, this series of ten easy-to-read books tells the stories of ordinary people who successfully build small businesses. Students will learn that energy, problem-solving skills and thorough preparation can make the difference between success and failure.

## Math

**905   Algebra Stars**

**Sunburst Technology**
**400 Columbus Avenue**
**Valhalla, NY  10595 1349**          914-747-3310
                                      800-321-7511
                                  FAX 914-747-4109
                           http://www.sunburst.com
                           e-mail: service@sunburst.com
*Katie Birmingham, Office Manager*

Students build their understanding of algebra by constructing, categorizing, and solving equations and classifying polynomial expressions using algebra tiles.

**906   American Guidance Service Learning Disabilities Resources**

**Instruction & Assessment AGS Special Needs Catalog**
**PO Box 716**
**Bryn Mawr, PA  19010**          610-525-8336
                                  800-869-8336
                              FAX 610-525-8337
                       http://www.ldonline.org
*Dr. Richard Cooper, Author*

A collection of alternative techniques which Dr. Cooper has found useful in teaching arithmetic to individuals with learning problems. *$9.95*

**907   Attack Math**

**Educators Publishing Service**
**31 Smith Plaza**
**Cambridge, MA  02139 9031**          617-547-6706
                                       800-225-5750
                                   FAX 888-440-2665
                            http://www.epsbooks.com
                            e-mail: eps@epsbooks.com
*Carol Greenes, George Immerzeel, Linda Shulman, Author*
*Steve Kote, President*
*Gunnar Voltz, Vice President*

This series, for grades 1-6, teaches the four arithmetic operations: addition, subtraction, multiplication and division. Each operation is covered in three books, with book one teaching the basic facts and books two and three teaching multi-digit computation with whole numbers. A checkpoint and testpoint monitor progress at the middle and end of each book.

**908 Awesome Animated Monster Maker Math**

Sunburst Technology
400 Columbus Avenue
Valhalla, NY 10595 1349          914-747-3310
                                 800-321-7511
                            FAX 914-747-4109
                      http://www.sunburst.com
                  e-mail: service@sunburst.com
*Katie Birmingham, Office Manager*

With an emphasis on building core math skills, this humorous program incorporates the monstrous and the ridiculous into a structured learning environment. Students choose from six skill levels tailored to the 3rd to 8th grade.

**909 Awesome Animated Monster Maker Math & Monster Workshop**

Sunburst Technology
400 Columbus Avenue
Valhalla, NY 10595 1349          914-747-3310
                                 800-321-7511
                            FAX 914-747-4109
                      http://www.sunburst.com
                  e-mail: service@sunburst.com
*Katie Birmingham, Office Manager*

Students develop money and strategic thinking skills with this irresistable game that has them tinker about making monsters.

**910 Awesome Animated Monster Maker Number Drop**

Sunburst Technology
400 Columbus Avenue
Valhalla, NY 10595 1349          914-747-3310
                                 800-321-7511
                            FAX 914-747-4109
                      http://www.sunburst.com
                  e-mail: service@sunburst.com
*Katie Birmingham, Office Manager*

Your students will think on their mathematical feet estimating and solving thousands of number problems in an arcade-style game designed to improve their performance in numeration, money, fractions, and decimals.

**911 Basic Essentials of Mathematics**

Harcourt Achieve
6277 Sea Harbor Drive
Orlando, FL 32887               252-480-3200
                                 800-844-1464
                            FAX 800-269-5232
                   http://www.steckvaughn.com
                 e-mail: info@steckvaughn.com
*Shea, Author*
*Tim McEwen, President/CEO*
*Jeff Johnson, Dir Marketing Communications*
*Chris Lehmann, Team Coordinator*

Ideal for basic math skill instruction, test practice, or any situation requiring a thorough, confidence-building review. It provides a complete lesson - instruction, examples, and computation exercises.

**912 Basic Math for Job and Personal Use**

AGS Publishing
4201 Woodland Road
Circle Pines, MN 55014 1796     651-287-7220
                                 800-328-2560
                            FAX 800-471-8457
                         http://www.agsnet.com
                   e-mail: agsmail@agsnet.com
*Merle Wood, Jeanette Powell, Author*
*Karen Dahlen, Associate Director*
*Matt Keller, Marketing Manager*

With an interest level of high school through adult, and a reading level of Grade 3-4, this series has modules in addition, subtraction, multiplication and division.

**913 Building Mathematical Thinking**

Educators Publishing Service
31 Smith Place
Cambridge, MA 02139 9031        617-547-6706
                                 800-225-5750
                            FAX 888-440-2665
                      http://www.epsbooks.com
                  e-mail: eps@epsbooks.com
*Marsha Stanton, Author*
*Steve Kote, President*
*Gunnar Voltz, Vice President*

In this new math program, the units covered are presented as a series of Skinny Concepts that serve as manageable building blocks that eventually become entire topics. The Students Journal provides exercises for each Skinny Concept, encourages students to seek their own conclusions for problem solving, and provides space for the students ideas.

**914 Building Perspective**

Sunburst Technology
400 Columbus Avenue
Valhalla, NY 10595 1349          914-747-3310
                                 800-321-7511
                            FAX 914-747-4109
                      http://www.sunburst.com
                  e-mail: support@sunburst.com
*Katie Birmingham, Office Manager*

Develop spatial perception and reasoning skills with this award-winning program that will sharpen your students' problem-solving abilities.

**915 Building Perspective Deluxe**

Sunburst Technology
400 Columbus Avenue
Valhalla, NY 10595 1349          914-747-3310
                                 800-321-7511
                            FAX 914-747-4109
                      http://www.sunburst.com
                  e-mail: support@sunburst.com
*Katie Birmingham, Office Manager*

New visual thinking challenges await your students as they engage in three spacial reasoning activities that develop their 3D thinking, deductive reasoning and problem solving skills

**916 Calculator Math for Job and Personal Use**

4201 Woodland Road
Circle Pines, MN 55014 1796      651-287-7220
                                 800-328-2560
                            FAX 800-471-8457
                         http://www.agsnet.com
                      e-mail: agsmail@agsnet.com

With an interest level of high school through adult, and a reading level of Grade 3-4, this series has modules in basic math with a calculator and fractions, decimals, and percentages using a calculator.

**917 Combining Shapes**

Sunburst Technology
400 Columbus Avenue
Valhalla, NY 10595 1349      914-747-3310
                             800-321-7511
                        FAX 914-747-4109
                     http://www.sunburst.com
                  e-mail: support@sunburst.com
*Katie Birmingham, Office Manager*

Students discover the properties of simple geometric figures through concrete experience combining shapes. Measurements, estimating and operation skills are part of this fun program.

**918 Combining and Breaking Apart Numbers**

Sunburst Technology
400 Columbus Avenue
Valhalla, NY 10595 1349      914-747-3310
                             800-321-7511
                        FAX 914-747-4109
                     http://www.sunburst.com
                  e-mail: support@sunburst.com
*Katie Birmingham, Office Manager*

Students develop their number sense as they engage in "real life" dilemmas, which demonstrates the basic concepts of operations.

**919 Comparing with Ratios**

Sunburst Technology
400 Columbus Avenue
Valhalla, NY 10595 1349      914-747-3310
                             800-321-7511
                        FAX 914-747-4109
                     http://www.sunburst.com
                  e-mail: support@sunburst.com
*Katie Birmingham, Office Manager*

Students learn that ratio is a way to compare amounts by using multiplication and division. Through five engaging activities, students recognize and describe ratios, develop proportional thinking skills, estimate ratios, determine equivalent ratios, and use ratios to analyze data.

**920 Concert Tour Entrepreneur**

Sunburst Technology
400 Columbus Avenue
Valhalla, NY 10595 1349      914-747-3310
                             800-321-7511
                        FAX 914-747-4109
                     http://www.sunburst.com
                  e-mail: support@sunburst.com
*Katie Birmingham, Office Manager*

Your students improve math, planning and problem solving skills as they manage a band in this music management business simulation.

**921 Creating Patterns from Shapes**

Sunburst Technology
400 Columbus Avenue
Valhalla, NY 10595 1349      914-747-3310
                             800-321-7511
                        FAX 914-747-4109
                     http://www.sunburst.com
                  e-mail: support@sunburst.com
*Katie Birmingham, Office Manager*

Students discover patterns by exploring the properties of radiating and tiling patterns through Native American basket weaving and Japanese fish print themes.

**922 Data Explorer**

Sunburst Technology
400 Columbus Avenue
Valhalla, NY 10595 1349      914-747-3310
                             800-321-7511
                        FAX 914-747-4109
                     http://www.sunburst.com
                  e-mail: support@sunburst.com
*Katie Birmingham, Office Manager*

This easy-to-use CD-ROM provides the flexibility needed for eleven different graph types including tools for long-term data analysis projects.

**923 Decimals and Percentages for Job and Personal Use**

AGS Publishing
4201 Woodland Road
Circle Pines, MN 55014 1796      651-287-7220
                                 800-328-2560
                            FAX 800-471-8457
                         http://www.agsnet.com
                      e-mail: agsmail@agsnet.com
*Merle Wood, Jeanette Powell, Author*
*Karen Dahlen, Associate Director*
*Matt Keller, Marketing Manager*

With an interest level of high school through adult, and a reading level of Grade 3-4, this series has modules in decimals, fractions and percentages.

**924    Decimals: Concepts & Problem-Solving**

Harcourt Achieve
6277 Sea Harbor Drive
Orlando, FL  32887                          252-480-3200
                                            800-844-1464
                                       FAX 800-269-5232
                          http://www.steckvaughn.com
                          e-mail: info@steckvaughn.com
*Steck-Vaughn Staff, Author*
*Tim McEwen, President/CEO*
*Jeff Johnson, Dir Marketing Communications*
*Chris Lehmann, Team Coordinator*

This easy to implement, flexible companion to the classroom mathematics curriculum emcompasses decimal concepts such as values and names, equivalent decimals, mixed decimals, patterns, comparing, ordering, estimating and more. *$ 8.49*

**925    ESPA Math Practice Tests D**

Harcourt Achieve
6277 Sea Harbor Drive
Orlando, FL  32887                          252-480-3200
                                            800-844-1464
                                       FAX 800-269-5232
                          http://www.steckvaughn.com
                          e-mail: info@steckvaughn.com
*Steck-Vaughn Staff, Author*
*Tim McEwen, President/CEO*
*Jeff Johnson, Dir Marketing Communications*
*Chris Lehmann, Team Coordinator*

If you are concerned about your students' performance on the math portion of the ESPA, these workbooks can give them the boost they need. Each follows the New Jersey State standards in mathematics, giving students additional practice with the same kinds of questions they will face on the test day. Workbooks include three practice tests, with 50 multiple choice and open-ended questions each.

**926    ESPA Success in Mathematics**

Harcourt Achieve
6277 Sea Harbor Drive
Orlando, FL  32887                          252-480-3200
                                            800-844-1464
                                       FAX 800-269-5232
                          http://www.steckvaughn.com
                          e-mail: info@steckvaughn.com
*Steck-Vaughn Staff, Author*
*Tim McEwen, President/CEO*
*Jeff Johnson, Dir Marketing Communications*
*Chris Lehmann, Team Coordinator*

Ensure a positive experience on the ESPA with the preparatory program that follows the New Jersey State standards in mathematics, including instruction and practice in all five content clusters. Modeled instruction provides strategies to help students get the right answer on both multiple choice and open-ended questions.

**927    Elementary Math Bundle**

Sunburst Technology
400 Columbus Avenue
Valhalla, NY  10595 1349                    914-747-3310
                                            800-321-7511
                                       FAX 914-747-4109
                             http://www.sunburst.com
                          e-mail: support@sunburst.com
*Katie Birmingham, Office Manager*

Number sense and operations are the focus of the Elementary Math Bundle. Students engage in activities that reinforce basic addition and subtraction skills. This product comes with Splish Splash Math, Ten Tricky Tiles and Numbers Undercover.

**928    Equation Tile Teaser**

Sunburst Technology
400 Columbus Avenue
Valhalla, NY  10595 1349                    914-747-3310
                                            800-321-7511
                                       FAX 914-747-4109
                             http://www.sunburst.com
                          e-mail: support@sunburst.com
*Katie Birmingham, Office Manager*

Students develop logic thinking and pre-algebra skills solving sets of numbers equations in three challenging problem-solving activities.

**929    Equivalent Fractions**

Sunburst Technology
400 Columbus Avenue
Valhalla, NY  10595 1349                    914-747-3310
                                            800-321-7511
                                       FAX 914-747-4109
                             http://www.sunburst.com
                          e-mail: support@sunburst.com
*Katie Birmingham, Office Manager*

This exciting investigation develops students' conceptual understanding that every fraction can be named in many different but equivalent ways.

**930    Estimation**

Harcourt Achieve
6277 Sea Harbor Drive
Orlando, FL  32887                          252-480-3200
                                            800-844-1464
                                       FAX 800-269-5232
                          http://www.steckvaughn.com
                          e-mail: info@steckvaughn.com
*Steck-Vaughn Staff, Author*
*Tim McEwen, President/CEO*
*Jeff Johnson, Dir Marketing Communications*
*Chris Lehmann, Team Coordiantor*

Students learn to make sensible estimates, educated guesses, and logical choices, then use tools to check their estimates for accuracy. Practice includes estimation in measurement of length, weight, capacity, temperature, time and money.

**931    Factory Deluxe**

Sunburst Technology
400 Columbus Avenue
Valhalla, NY  10595 1349                    914-747-3310
                                            800-321-7511
                                       FAX 914-747-4109
                             http://www.sunburst.com
                          e-mail: support@sunburst.com
*Katie Birmingham, Office Manager*

Five activities explore shapes, rotation, angles, geometric attributes, area formulas, and computation. Includes journal, record keeping, and on-screen help. This program helps sharpen geometry, visual thinking and problem solving skills.

**932    Focus on Math**

**Harcourt Achieve**
**6277 Sea Harbor Drive**
**Orlando, FL  32887**                    **252-480-3200**
**800-844-1464**
**FAX 800-269-5232**
**http://www.steckvaughn.com**
**e-mail: info@steckvaughn.com**
*Steck-Vaugh Staff, Author*
*Tim McEwen, President/CEO*
*Jeff Johnson, Dir Marketing Communications*
*Chris Lehmann, Team Coordinator*

Consists of four sections and in each you will learn more about addition and subtraction, multiplication and division, fractions, decimals, measurements, geometry and problem solving.

**933    Follow Me! 2**

**LinguiSystems**
**3100 4th Avenue**
**East Moline, IL  61244**                    **309-775-2300**
**800-776-4332**
**FAX 309-755-2377**
**TDY:800-933-8331**
**http://www.linguisystems.com**
**e-mail: service@linguisystems.com**
*Grace Frank, Author*
*Linda Bowers, Owner*
*Rosemary Huisingh, Owner*

These activities are relevant to classroom listening demands. The directions relate specifically on an accompanying worksheet. It's a pick-up-and-use-now resource to teach the vocabulary of language arts, math, social studies, and more. *$34.95*

*201 pages  Ages 7-11*

**934    Fraction Attraction**

**Sunburst Technology**
**400 Columbus Avenue**
**Valhalla, NY  10595 1349**                    **914-747-3310**
**800-321-7511**
**FAX 914-747-4109**
**http://www.sunburst.com**
**e-mail: support@sunburst.com**
*Katie Birmingham, Office Manager*

Build the fraction skills of ordering, equivalence, relative sizes and multiple representations with four, multi-level, carnival style games.

**935    Fraction Operations**

**Sunburst Technology**
**400 Columbus Avenue**
**Valhalla, NY  10595 1349**                    **914-747-3310**
**800-321-7511**
**FAX 914-747-4109**
**http://www.sunburst.com**
**e-mail: support@sunburst.com**
*Katie Birmingham, Office Manager*

Students build on their concepts of fraction meaning and equivalence as they learn how to perform operations with fractions.

**936    Fractions: Concepts & Problem-Solving**

**Harcourt Achieve**
**6277 Sea Harbor Drive**
**Orlando, FL  32887**                    **252-480-3200**
**800-844-1464**
**FAX 800-269-5232**
**http://www.steckvaughn.com**
**e-mail: info@steckvaughn.com**
*Steck-Vaughn Staff, Author*
*Tim McEwen, President/CEO*
*Jeff Johnson, Dir Marketing Communications*
*Chris Lehmann, Team Coordinator*

This companion to the classroom mathematics curriculum emcompasses many of the standards established at each grade level. Each activity page targets a specific skill to help bolster students who need additional work in a particular area of fractions.

**937    Funny Monster for Tea**

**Sunburst Technology**
**400 Columbus Avenue**
**Valhalla, NY  10595 1349**                    **914-747-3310**
**800-321-7511**
**FAX 914-747-4109**
**http://www.sunburst.com**
**e-mail: support@sunburst.com**
*Katie Birmingham, Office Manager*

This interactive, read-along rhyme features six activities for young students to learn about time, practice spelling, investigate math and explore poetry, music and art.

**938    GEPA Success in Language Arts Literacy and Mathematics**

**Harcourt Achieve**
**6277 Sea Harbor Drive**
**Orlando, FL  32887**                    **252-480-3200**
**800-844-1464**
**FAX 800-269-5232**
**http://www.steckvaughn.com**
**e-mail: info@steckvaughn.com**
*Steck-Vaugh Staff, Author*
*Tim McEwen, President/CEO*
*Jeff Johnson, Dir Marketing Communications*
*Chris Lehmann, Team Coordinator*

Build skills as you improve scores on the GEPA. Better test scores don't always mean better skills. With these workbooks, you can ensure that your students are becoming more proficient users of language and math as well as more skilled test-takers. Your students will gain valuable practice answering the types of questions found on the GEPA, such as open-ended and enhanced multiple-choice items.

**939 Geometry for Primary Grades**

Harcourt Achieve
6277 Sea Harbor Drive
Orlando, FL 32887           252-480-3200
                           800-844-1464
                        FAX 800-269-5232
                    http://www.steckvaughn.com
                    e-mail: info@steckvaughn.com
*Steck-Vaughn Staff, Author*
*Tim McEwen, President/CEO*
*Jeff Johnson, Dir Marketing Communications*
*Chris Lehmann, Team Coordinator*

Self-explanatory lessons ideal for independent work
or as homework. Transitions from concrete to pictorial to abstract.

**940 Get Up and Go!**

Sunburst Technology
400 Columbus Avenue
Valhalla, NY 10595 1349      914-747-3310
                            800-321-7511
                         FAX 914-747-4109
                     http://www.sunburst.com
                    e-mail: support@sunburst.com
*Katie Birmingham, Office Manager*

Students interpret and construct timelines through
three descriptive activities in the animated program.
Students are introduced to timelines as they participate in an interactive story.

**941 Grade Level Math**

Harcourt Achieve
6277 Sea Harbor Drive
Orlando, FL 32887           252-480-3200
                           800-844-1464
                        FAX 800-269-5232
                    http://www.steckvaughn.com
                    e-mail: info@steckvaughn.com
*Steck-Vaughn Staff, Author*
*Tim McEwen, President/CEO*
*Jeff Johnson, Dir Marketing Communications*
*Chris Lehmann, Team Coordinator*

Easy to understand practice exercises help students
build conceptual knowledge and computation skills
together. Each book addresses essential grade appropriate math areas.

**942 Graphers**

Sunburst Technology
400 Columbus Avenue
Valhalla, NY 10595 1349      914-747-3310
                            800-321-7511
                         FAX 914-747-4109
                     http://www.sunburst.com
                    e-mail: support@sunburst.com
*Katie Birmingham, Office Manager*

Students develop data analysis skills with this easy to
use graphing tool. With over 30 pictorial data sets and
16 lessons, students learn to construct and interpret
six different graph types.

**943 Green Globs & Graphing Equations**

Sunburst Technology
400 Columbus Avenue
Valhalla, NY 10595 1349      914-747-3310
                            800-321-7511
                         FAX 914-747-4109
                     http://www.sunburst.com
                    e-mail: support@sunburst.com
*Katie Birmingham, Office Manager*

As students explore parabolas, hyperbolas, and other
graphs, they discover how altering an equation
changes a graph's shape or position.

**944 Grouping and Place Value**

Sunburst Technology
400 Columbus Avenue
Valhalla, NY 10595 1349      914-747-3310
                            800-321-7511
                         FAX 914-747-4109
                     http://www.sunburst.com
                    e-mail: support@sunburst.com
*Katie Birmingham, Office Manager*

Students develop their understanding of our number
system, learning to think about numbers in groups of
ones, tens, and hundreds, and discovering the meaning of place value.

**945 Hidden Treasures of Al-Jabr**

Sunburst Technology
400 Columbus Avenue
Valhalla, NY 10595 1349      914-747-3310
                            800-321-7511
                         FAX 914-747-4109
                     http://www.sunburst.com
                    e-mail: support@sunburst.com
*Katie Birmingham, Office Manager*

Beginning algebra students undertake three challenges that develop skills in the areas of solving linear
equations, substituting variables, grouping like variables, using systems of equations and translating algebra word problems into equations.

**946 High School Math Bundle**

Sunburst Technology
400 Columbus Avenue
Valhalla, NY 10595 1349      914-747-3310
                            800-321-7511
                         FAX 914-747-4109
                     http://www.sunburst.com
                    e-mail: support@sunburst.com
*Katie Birmingham, Office Manager*

Each program in this bundle focuses on a specific area
to ensure that your students master the math skills
they need. This bundle allows students to master basics of Algebra, explore equations and graphs, practice learning with algebra graphs, use trigonometric
functions, apply math concepts to practical situations
and improve problem solving and data analysis skills.

**947  Higher Scores on Math Standardized Tests**

Harcourt Achieve
6277 Sea Harbor Drive
Orlando, FL  32887                    252-480-3200
                                       800-844-1464
                                  FAX 800-269-5232
                      http://www.steckvaughn.com
                      e-mail: info@steckvaughn.com
*Steck-Vaughn Staff, Author*
*Tim McEwen, President/CEO*
*Jeff Johnson, Dir Marketing Communications*
*Chris Lehmann, Team Coordinator*

These grade level math test preparation series provide focused practice in areas where students have shown a weakness in previous standardized tests. Improves test scores by zeroing in on the skills requiring remediation.

**948  Hot Dog Stand: The Works**

Sunburst Technology
400 Columbus Avenue
Valhalla, NY  10595 1349               914-747-3310
                                       800-321-7511
                                  FAX 914-747-4109
                          http://www.sunburst.com
                      e-mail: support@sunburst.com
*Katie Birmingham, Office Manager*

Students practice math, problem-solving, and communication skills in a multimedia business simulation that challenges students with unexpected events.

**949  How the West Was 1+3x4**

Sunburst Technology
400 Columbus Avenue
Valhalla, NY  10595 1349               914-747-3310
                                       800-321-7511
                                  FAX 914-747-4109
                          http://www.sunburst.com
                      e-mail: support@sunburst.com
*Katie Birmingham, Office Manager*

Students use order of operations to construct equations and race along number line trails.

**950  Ice Cream Truck**

Sunburst Technology
400 Columbus Avenue
Valhalla, NY  10595 1349               914-747-3310
                                       800-321-7511
                                  FAX 914-747-4109
                          http://www.sunburst.com
                      e-mail: support@sunburst.com
*Katie Birmingham, Office Manager*

Elementary students learn important problem solving, strategic planning and math operation skills, as they become owners of a busy ice cream truck.

**951  Intermediate Geometry**

Harcourt Achieve
6277 Sea Harbor Drive
Orlando, FL  32887                    252-480-3200
                                       800-844-1464
                                  FAX 800-269-5232
                      http://www.steckvaughn.com
                      e-mail: info@steckvaughn.com
*Steck-Vaughn Staff, Author*
*Tim McEwen, President/CEO*
*Jeff Johnson, Dir Marketing Communications*
*Chris Lehmann, Team Coordinator*

Prepares intermediate and middle school students for a successful experience in high school geometry. Intermediate geometry provides a study of the concepts, computation, problem-solving, and enrichment of topics identified by NCTM standards. This three-book series links the informal explorations of geometry in primary grades to more formalized processes taught in high school.

**952  Introduction to Patterns**

Sunburst Technology
400 Columbus Avenue
Valhalla, NY  10595 1349               914-747-3310
                                       800-321-7511
                                  FAX 914-747-4109
                          http://www.sunburst.com
                      e-mail: support@sunburst.com
*Katie Birmingham, Office Manager*

Students discover patterns found in art and nature, exploring linear and geometric designs, predicting outcomes and creating patterns of their own.

**953  It's Elementary!**

Educators Publishing Service
31 Smith Place
Cambridge, MA  02139 9031             617-547-6706
                                       800-225-5750
                                  FAX 888-440-2665
                          http://www.epsbooks.com
                      e-mail: eps@epsbooks.com
*M J Owen, Author*
*Steve Kote, President*
*Gunnar Voltz, Vice President*

These new books helps make math word problems less intimidating for students in grades 2 through 5 by teaching them how to identify key words, draw pictures, and disregard unnecessary information. Captivating illustrations provide visual reinforcement of addition, subtraction, multiplication and division problems.

**954  Maps & Navigation**

Sunburst Technology
400 Columbus Avenue
Valhalla, NY  10595 1349               914-747-3310
                                       800-321-7511
                                  FAX 914-747-4109
                          http://www.sunburst.com
                      e-mail: support@sunburst.com
*Katie Birmingham, Office Manager*

This exciting nautical simulation provides students with opportunities use their math and science skills.

**955**   **Mastering Math**

**Harcourt Achieve**
**6277 Sea Harbor Drive**
**Orlando, FL  32887**          **252-480-3200**
                                        **800-844-1464**
                              **FAX 800-269-5232**
                    **http://www.steckvaughn.com**
                    **e-mail: info@steckvaughn.com**
*Steck-Vaughn Staff, Author*
*Tim McEwen, President/CEO*
*Jeff Johnson, Dir Marketing Communications*
*Chris Lehmann, Team Coordinator*

Now low level readers can succeed at math with this easy to read presentation. Makes basic math concepts accessible to all students.

**956**   **Math Assessment System**

**Harcourt Achieve**
**6277 Sea Harbor Drive**
**Orlando, FL  32887**          **252-480-3200**
                                        **800-844-1464**
                              **FAX 800-269-5232**
                    **http://www.steckvaughn.com**
                    **e-mail: info@steckvaughn.com**
*Steck-Vaughn Staff, Author*
*Tim McEwen, President/CEO*
*Jeff Johnson, Dir Marketing Communications*
*Chris Lehmann, Team Coordinator*

This easy-to-administer program generates individual scores, class scores, and an item analysis two times per year, providing a benchmark and two clear indicators of student progress.

**957**   **Math Detectives**

**Harcourt Achieve**
**6277 Sea Harbor Drive**
**Orlando, FL  32887**          **252-480-3200**
                                        **800-844-1464**
                              **FAX 800-269-5232**
                    **http://www.steckvaughn.com**
                    **e-mail: info@steckvaughn.com**
*Steck-Vaughn Staff, Author*
*Tim McEwen, President/CEO*
*Jeff Johnson, Dir Marketing Communications*
*Chris Lehmann, Team Coordinator*

Put student sleuths on the trail of mathematical problem solving and critical thinking with short mysteries even limited readers can manage. Use these motivating, grade-level mysteries as individual assignments, math center materials, group projects, or whole-class activities.

**958**   **Math Enrichment**

**Harcourt Achieve**
**6277 Sea Harbor Drive**
**Orlando, FL  32887**          **252-480-3200**
                                        **800-844-1464**
                              **FAX 800-269-5232**
                    **http://www.steckvaughn.com**
                    **e-mail: info@steckvaughn.com**
*Steck-Vaughn Staff, Author*
*Tim McEwen, President/CEO*
*Jeff Johnson, Dir Marketing Communications*
*Chris Lehmann, Team Coordinator*

Features alternate ways to help children become mathematical thinkers and master the basic rules and concepts. It has relevance to the reader, promoting and expanding critical thinking skills through puzzles, mazes, games, charts, tables, symbols and codes, and more.

**959**   **Math Scramble**

**LinguiSystems**
**3100 4th Avenue**
**East Moline, IL  61244**          **309-775-2300**
                                            **800-776-4332**
                              **FAX 309-755-2377**
                              **TDY:800-933-8331**
                    **http://www.linguisystems.com**
                    **e-mail: service@linguisystems.com**
*Paul F Johnson, Author*
*Linda Bowers, Owner*
*Rosemary Huisingh, Owner*

It's great for students with learning disabilities who need a different approach to learning and memorizing basic math facts. Students can play with your guidance or as independent practice. *$44.95*

*Ages 5-12*

**960**   **Mathematics Skills Books**

**Harcourt Achieve**
**6277 Sea Harbor Drive**
**Orlando, FL  32887**          **252-480-3200**
                                        **800-844-1464**
                              **FAX 800-269-5232**
                    **http://www.steckvaughn.com**
                    **e-mail: info@steckvaughn.com**
*Steck-Vaughn Staff, Author*
*Tim McEwen, President/CEO*
*Jeff Johnson, Dir Marketing Communications*
*Chris Lehmann, Team Coordinator*

Affordable, focused reviews of fundamental math principles. Six 48 page books. Complete series of focused books offers practice in all basic mathematics skill areas with a consistent approach.

**961**   **Maximize Math Success for the Special Populations You Serve**

**Saxon Publishers**
**Harcourt 6277 C. Harvard Drive Seah**
**Norman, FL  32887**          **405-329-7071**
                                        **800-284-7019**
                              **FAX 866-378-2249**
                    **http://www.saxonpublishers.com**
                    **e-mail: info@saxonpublishers.com**
*Tim Mcquine, President/CEO*

An adaptation that helps special populations with math where other teaching methods have failed.

**962**   **Maya Math**

**Sunburst Technology**
**400 Columbus Avenue**
**Valhalla, NY  10595 1349**          **914-747-3310**
                                              **800-321-7511**
                              **FAX 914-747-4109**
                    **http://www.sunburst.com**
                    **e-mail: support@sunburst.com**
*Katie Birmingham, Office Manager*

Students discover the importance of place value and the number zero as they learn a different number and calendar system.

**963 Measurement: Practical Applications**

Harcourt Achieve
6277 Sea Harbor Drive
Orlando, FL 32887
252-480-3200
800-844-1464
FAX 800-269-5232
http://www.steckvaughn.com
e-mail: info@steckvaughn.com

*Steck-Vaughn Staff, Author*
*Tim McEwen, President/CEO*
*Jeff Johnson, Dir Marketing Communications*
*Chris Lehmann, Team Coordinator*

Concentrated practice on the measurement skills we use on a daily basis. This practical presentation of both customary and metric units helps the student to understand the importance of measurement skills in everyday life. Hands on activities and real life situations create logical applications so measurements make sense.

**964 Memory Fun!**

Sunburst Technology
400 Columbus Avenue
Valhalla, NY 10595 1349
914-747-3310
800-321-7511
FAX 914-747-4109
http://www.sunburst.com
e-mail: support@sunburst.com

*Katie Birmingham, Office Manager*

Welcome to Tiny's attic where students build memory, matching, counting and money sense through a variety of fun matching activities.

**965 Middle School Geometry: Basic Concepts**

Harcourt Achieve
6277 Sea Harbor Drive
Orlando, FL 32887
252-480-3200
800-844-1464
FAX 800-269-5232
http://www.steckvaughn.com
e-mail: info@steckvaughn.com

*Steck-Vaughn Staff, Author*
*Tim McEwen, President/CEO*
*Jeff Johnson, Dir Marketing Communications*
*Chris Lehmann, Team Coordinator*

Provides students with enough comprehensive, skill specific practice in the key areas of geometry to ensure mastery. Ideal for junior high or high school students in need of remediation.

**966 Middle School Math**

Harcourt Achieve
6277 Sea Harbor Drive
Orlando, FL 32887
252-480-3200
800-844-1464
FAX 800-269-5232
http://www.steckvaughn.com
e-mail: info@steckvaughn.com

*Steck-Vaughn Staff, Author*
*Tim McEwen, President/CEO*
*Jeff Johnson, Dir Marketing Communications*
*Chris Lehmann, Team Coordinator*

This skill-specific series reinforces and enhances the middle school math curriculum. It provides teachers and parents with a tool to focus on the skills that students need to review and reinforce. The lessons provide step-by-step instructions, sample problems, and practices that enable students to work independently.

**967 Middle School Math Bundle**

Sunburst Technology
400 Columbus Avenue
Valhalla, NY 10595 1349
914-747-3310
800-321-7511
FAX 914-747-4109
http://www.sunburst.com
e-mail: support@sunburst.com

*Katie Birmingham, Office Manager*

This bundle helps improve student's logical thinking, number sense and operation skills. This product comes with Math Arena, Building Perspective Deluxe, Equation Tile Teasers and Easy Sheet.

**968 MindTwister Math**

Riverdeep
500 Redmond Boulevard
Novato, CA 94947
415-763-4700
800-362-2890
FAX 415-763-4385
http://www.edmark.com
e-mail: info@riverdeep.net

*Barry O'Callaghan, Chairman/CEO*
*Simon Calver, COO*
*John Rim, CFO*

MindTwister Math provides a challenging review of third grade math and problem-solving skills in a fast-paced, multi-player game show format. Thousands of action-packed challenges encourage students to practice essential math facts including addition, subtraction, mutiplication and division and develop more advanced mathematical problem-solving skills such as visualization, deduction, sequencing, estimating and pattern recognition.

**969 Mirror Symmetry**

Sunburst Technology
400 Columbus Avenue
Valhalla, NY 10595 1349
914-747-3310
800-321-7511
FAX 914-747-4109
http://www.sunburst.com
e-mail: support@sunburst.com

*Katie Birmingham, Office Manager*

Students advance their understanding of geometric properties and spatial relationships by exploring lines of symmetry within a single geometric shape.

**970  Multiplication & Division**

Harcourt Achieve
6277 Sea Harbor Drive
Orlando, FL  32887                         252-480-3200
                                           800-844-1464
                                      FAX 800-269-5232
                              http://www.steckvaughn.com
                              e-mail: info@steckvaughn.com
*Steck-Vaughn Staff, Author*
*Tim McEwen, President/CEO*
*Jeff Johnson, Dir Marketing Communications*
*Chris Lehmann, Team Coordinator*

Skill specific activities focus on the concepts and inverse relationships of multiplication and division. Explains in simplified terms how the process of multiplication undoes the process of division, and vice versa.

**971  My Mathematical Life**

Sunburst Technology
400 Columbus Avenue
Valhalla, NY  10595 1349                   914-747-3310
                                           800-321-7511
                                      FAX 914-747-4109
                                http://www.sunburst.com
                              e-mail: support@sunburst.com
*Katie Birmingham, Office Manager*

Students discover the math involved in everyday living as they take a character from high school graduation to retirement, advising on important health, education, career, and financial decisions.

**972  Number Meanings and Counting**

Sunburst Technology
400 Columbus Avenue
Valhalla, NY  10595 1349                   914-747-3310
                                           800-321-7511
                                      FAX 914-747-4109
                                http://www.sunburst.com
                              e-mail: support@sunburst.com
*Katie Birmingham, Office Manager*

Students develop their understanding of number meaning and uses with experiences practicing estimating, using number meanings, and making more-and-less comparisons.

**973  Number Sense & Problem Solving CD-ROM**

Sunburst Technology
400 Columbus Avenue
Valhalla, NY  10595 1349                   914-747-3310
                                           800-321-7511
                                      FAX 914-747-4109
                                http://www.sunburst.com
                              e-mail: support@sunburst.com
*Katie Birmingham, Office Manager*

Build number and operation skills with these three programs: How the West Was One + Three x Four, Divide and Conquer and Puzzle Tanks.

**974  Numbers Undercover**

Sunburst Technology
400 Columbus Avenue
Valhalla, NY  10595 1349                   914-747-3310
                                           800-321-7511
                                      FAX 914-747-4109
                                http://www.sunburst.com
                              e-mail: support@sunburst.com
*Katie Birmingham, Office Manager*

As children try to solve the case of missing numbers, they practice telling time, measuring and estimating, counting, and working with money.

**975  Patterns Across the Curriculum**

Harcourt Achieve
6277 Sea Harbor Drive
Orlando, FL  32887                         252-480-3200
                                           800-844-1464
                                      FAX 800-269-5232
                              http://www.steckvaughn.com
                              e-mail: info@steckvaughn.com
*Steck-Vaughn Staff, Author*
*Tim McEwen, President/CEO*
*Jeff Johnson, Dir Marketing Communications*
*Chris Lehmann, Team Coordinator*

Develop students awareness and understanding of patterns in the real world. Exercises allow students to identify, complete, extend, and create patterns. Developed across four curriculum areas: math, language, social studies, and science. Flexible organization allows teachers to utilize content specific activities in coordination with other classroom assignments, providing additional richness in learning.

**976  Penny Pot**

Sunburst Technology
400 Columbus Avenue
Valhalla, NY  10595 1349                   914-747-3310
                                           800-321-7511
                                      FAX 914-747-4109
                                http://www.sunburst.com
                              e-mail: support@sunburst.com
*Katie Birmingham, Office Manager*

Students learn about money as they count combinations of coins in this engaging program.

**977  Problemas y mas**

Harcourt Achieve
6277 Sea Harbor Drive
Orlando, FL  32887                         252-480-3200
                                           800-531-5015
                                      FAX 800-699-9459
                              http://www.steckvaughn.com
                              e-mail: joan.phifer@harcourt.com
*Tim McEwen, President/CEO*
*Joan Phifer, Manager*
*Chris Lehmann, Team Coordinator*

This ESL math practice and strategy tool is in three levels the same as Problems Plus, but expressly for your Spanish fluent ESL learners.

**978 Problems Plus Levels B-H**

**Harcourt Achieve**
**6277 Sea Harbor Drive**
**Orlando, FL 32887**            252-480-3200
                                800-531-5015
                             FAX 800-699-9459
                       http://www.steckvaughn.com
                       e-mail: info@steckvaughn.com
*Steck-Vaughn Staff, Author*
*Tim McEwen, President/CEO*
*Jeff Johnson, Dir Marketing Communications*
*Chris Lehmann, Team Coordinator*

A one-of-a-kind guide to solving open-ended math problems. Doesn't just give answers to test questions. With its innovative problem-solving plan, this series teaches math thinking and problem attack strategies, plus offers practice in higher order thinking skills students need to solve open-ended math problems successfully.

**979 Puzzle Tanks**

**Sunburst Technology**
**400 Columbus Avenue**
**Valhalla, NY 10595 1349**      914-747-3310
                                800-321-7511
                             FAX 914-747-4109
                        http://www.sunburst.com
                       e-mail: support@sunburst.com
*Katie Birmingham, Office Manager*

A problem-solving program that uses logic puzzles involving liquid measurements.

**980 Representing Fractions**

**Sunburst Technology**
**400 Columbus Avenue**
**Valhalla, NY 10595 1349**      914-747-3310
                                800-321-7511
                             FAX 914-747-4109
                        http://www.sunburst.com
                       e-mail: support@sunburst.com
*A Birmingham, Office Manager*
*Mark Sotir, President*

In this investigation students work with one interpretation of a fraction and the relationship between parts and wholes by working with symbolic and visual representations.

**981 Sequencing Fun!**

**Sunburst Technology**
**400 Columbus Avenue**
**Valhalla, NY 10595 1349**      914-747-3310
                                800-321-7511
                             FAX 914-747-4109
                        http://www.sunburst.com
                       e-mail: support@sunburst.com
*A Birmingham, Office Manager*
*Mark Sotir, President*

Text, pictures, animation, and video clips provide a fun-filled program that encourages critical thinking skills.

**982 Shape Up!**

**Sunburst Technology**
**400 Columbus Avenue**
**Valhalla, NY 10595 1349**      914-747-3310
                                800-321-7511
                             FAX 914-747-4109
                        http://www.sunburst.com
                       e-mail: support@sunburst.com
*A Birmingham, Office Manager*
*Mark Sotir, President*

Students actively create and manipulate shapes to discover important ideas about mathematics in an electronic playground of two and three dimensional shapes.

**983 Shapes Within Shapes**

**Sunburst Technology**
**400 Columbus Avenue**
**Valhalla, NY 10595 1349**      914-747-3310
                                800-321-7511
                             FAX 914-747-4109
                        http://www.sunburst.com
                       e-mail: service@sunburst.com
*A Birmingham, Office Manager*
*Mark Sotir, President*

Students identify shapes within shapes, then rearrange them to develop spatial sense and deepen their understanding of the properties of shapes.

**984 Soaring Scores AIMS Mathematics**

**Harcourt Achieve**
**6277 Sea Harbor Drive**
**Orlando, FL 32887**            252-480-3200
                                800-531-5015
                             FAX 800-699-9459
                       http://www.steckvaughn.com
                       e-mail: info@steckvaughn.com
*Steck-Vaughn Staff, Author*
*Tim McEwen, President/CEO*
*Jeff Johnson, Dir Marketing Communications*
*Chris Lehmann, Team Coordinator*

Emphasize problem-solving and conceptual understanding to succeed with Arizona mathematics standards such as number sense, data analysis and probability, patterns, algebra and functions, measurement and discrete mathematics, and mathematics structure.

**985 Soaring Scores in Math Assessment**

**Harcourt Achieve**
**6277 Sea Harbor Drive**
**Orlando, FL 32887**            252-480-3200
                                800-531-5015
                             FAX 800-699-9459
                       http://www.steckvaughn.com
                       e-mail: info@steckvaughn.com
*Steck-Vaughn Staff, Author*
*Tim McEwen, President/CEO*
*Jeff Johnson, Dir Marketing Communications*
*Chris Lehmann, Team Coordinator*

Classroom Resources /Math

Students get 48 pages of modeled instruction and practice tests covering exactly the types of questions they'll face on assessments, which include open-ended, multiple choice, and free response problems with fill in grids. A review test helps assess, diagnose, and prescribe additional work quickly.

**986  Soaring Scores on the CMT in Mathematics & Soaring Scores on the CAPT in Mathematics**

**Harcourt Achieve**
**6277 Sea Harbor Drive**
**Orlando, FL  32887**              252-480-3200
                                    800-531-5015
                                 FAX 800-699-9459
                      http://www.steckvaughn.com
                       e-mail: info@steckvaughn.com
*Steck-Vaughn Staff, Author*
*Tim McEwen, President/CEO*
*Jeff Johnson, Dir Marketing Communications*
*Chris Lehmann, Team Coordinator*

Build the skills, strategies, and confidence your students need to do their best on the mathematics portion of the CMT and CAPT with this focused test preparation program. The instructional portion offers hints and strategies for each type of question students will face. Content standards and strands accompany each modeled problem.

**987  Soaring Scores on the CSAP Mathematics Assessment**

**Harcourt Achieve**
**6277 Sea Harbor Drive**
**Orlando, FL  32887**              252-480-3200
                                    800-531-5015
                                 FAX 800-699-9459
                      http://www.steckvaughn.com
                       e-mail: info@steckvaughn.com
*Steck-Vaughn Staff, Author*
*Tim McEwen, President/CEO*
*Jeff Johnson, Dir Marketing Communications*
*Chris Lehmann, Team Coordinator*

Make the most of your CSAP test preparation. The best way to prepare your students for Colorado's unique achievement assessment is to use the program designed specifically for that purpose.

**988  Soaring Scores on the ISAT Mathematics**

**Harcourt Achieve**
**6277 Sea Harbor Drive**
**Orlando, FL  32887**              252-480-3200
                                    800-531-5015
                                 FAX 800-699-9459
                      http://www.steckvaughn.com
                       e-mail: info@steckvaughn.com
*Steck-Vaughn Staff, Author*
*Tim McEwen, President/CEO*
*Jeff Johnson, Dir Marketing Communications*
*Chris Lehmann, Team Coordinator*

Developed to ensure peak performance on Illinois new math assessment. This test preparation product offers grade specific materials and authentic practice designed to help students approach the ISAT in mathematics strategically and confidently.

**989  Soaring Scores on the MEAP Math Test**

**Harcourt Achieve**
**6277 Sea Harbor Drive**
**Orlando, FL  32887**              252-480-3200
                                    800-531-5015
                                 FAX 800-699-9459
                      http://www.steckvaughn.com
                       e-mail: info@steckvaughn.com
*Steck-Vaughn Staff, Author*
*Tim McEwen, President/CEO*
*Jeff Johnson, Dir Marketing Communications*
*Chri Lehmann, Team Coordinator*

Focus your MEAP math preparation where it will do the most good. This targeted test preparation program delivers the instruction, strategies, and practice your students need to be accomplished test takers.

**990  Spatial Relationships**

**Sunburst Technology**
**400 Columbus Avenue**
**Valhalla, NY  10595 1349**        914-747-3310
                                    800-321-7511
                                 FAX 914-747-4109
                        http://www.sunburst.com
                      e-mail: support@sunburst.com
*Mark Sotir, President*
*Mary , Administrative Assistant*

Students explore location by identifying the positions of objects and creating paths between places. Children develop spatial abilities and language needed to communicate about our world.

**991  Spatial Sense CD-ROM**

**Sunburst Technology**
**400 Columbus Avenue**
**Valhalla, NY  10595 1349**        914-747-3310
                                    800-321-7511
                                 FAX 914-747-4109
                        http://www.sunburst.com
                      e-mail: support@sunburst.com
*Mark Sotir, President*

Your students will strenghten their spatial perception, spatial reasoning and problem-solving skills with three great programs now on one CD-ROM.

**992  Splish Splash Math**

**Sunburst Technology**
**400 Columbus Avenue**
**Valhalla, NY  10595 1349**        914-747-3310
                                    800-321-7511
                                 FAX 914-747-4109
                        http://www.sunburst.com
                      e-mail: support@sunburst.com
*Mark Sotir, President*

Students learn and practice basic operation skills as they engage in this high interest program that keeps them motivated. Great visual rewards and three levels of difficulty keep students challanged.

**993  Statistics & Probability**

**Harcourt Achieve**
**6277 Sea Harbor Drive**
**Orlando, FL 32887**                     **252-480-3200**
                                          **800-531-5015**
                                      **FAX 800-699-9459**
                      **http://www.steckvaughn.com**
                      **e-mail: info@steckvaughn.com**
*Steck-Vaughn Staff, Author*
*Tim McEwen, President/CEO*
*Jeff Johnson, Dir Marketing Communications*
*Chris Lehmann, Team Coordinator*

A working knowledge of statistics and probability increases problem solving skills, and provides students with the skills to be able to more effectively gather, describe, organize, and interpret information in their world.

**994  Strategic Math Series**

**Edge Enterprises**
**708 W 9th Street**
**Lawrence, KS 66044 2846**             **785-749-1473**
                                        **877-767-1487**
                                   **FAX 785-749-0207**
                   **e-mail: info@edgenterprise.inc.com**
*Cecil D Mercer and Susan Peterson Miller, Author*
*Jacqueline Schafer, Managing Editor*
*Carolyn Mitchell, Accounting Department*

The Strategic Math Series are a group of seven manuals designed for any aged student who needs to learn basic math facts and operations. Each manual is built upon the concrete-representational-abstract method of instruction. Within this approach, understanding of mathematics is developed through the use of concrete objects, representational drawings and an easy-to-learn strategy that turns all students into active problem-solvers. Available as a series or individually.

**995  Strategies for Problem-Solving**

**Harcourt Achieve**
**6277 Sea Harbor Drive**
**Orlando, FL 32887**                     **252-480-3200**
                                          **800-531-5015**
                                      **FAX 800-699-9459**
                      **http://www.steckvaughn.com**
                      **e-mail: info@steckvaughn.com**
*Steck-Vaughn Staff, Author*
*Tim McEwen, President/CEO*
*Jeff Johnson, Dir Marketing Communications*
*Chris Lehmann, Team Coordinator*

Show students more than one way to approach a problem, and you hand them the key to effective problem solving. These reproducible activities build math reasoning and critical thinking skills, reinforce core concepts, and reduce math anxiety, too.

**996  Strategies for Success in Mathematics**

**Harcourt Achieve**
**6277 Sea Harbor Drive**
**Orlando, FL 32887**                     **252-480-3200**
                                          **800-531-5015**
                                      **FAX 800-699-9459**
                      **http://www.steckvaughn.com**
                      **e-mail: info@steckvaughn.com**
*Steck-Vaughn Staff, Author*
*Tim McEwen, President/CEO*
*Jeff Johnson, Dir Marketing Communications*
*Chris Lehmann, Team Coordinator*

Teach your students specific problem-solving skills and test taking strategies for success with math and math assessments. Practice thoroughly covers five math clusters: numerical operations, patterns and functions, algebraic concepts, measurement and geometry, and data analysis.

**997  Sunbuddy Math Playhouse**

**Sunburst Technology**
**400 Columbus Avenue**
**Valhalla, NY 10595 1349**               **914-747-3310**
                                          **800-321-7511**
                                      **FAX 914-747-4109**
                      **http://www.sunburst.com**
                      **e-mail: support@sunburst.com**
*Mark Sotir, President*

An entertaining play, hidden math-related animations, and four multi-level interactive activities encourage children to explore math and reading.

**998  Take Off With...**

**Harcourt Achieve**
**6277 Sea Harbor Drive**
**Orlando, FL 32887**                     **252-480-3200**
                                          **800-531-5015**
                                      **FAX 800-699-9459**
                      **http://www.steckvaughn.com**
                      **e-mail: info@steckvaughn.com**
*Steck-Vaughn Staff, Author*
*Tim McEwen, President/CEO*
*Jeff Johnson, Dir Marketing Communications*
*Chris Lehmann, Team Coordinator*

Youngsters build number sense with concepts such as counting, sequencing and dividing, sorting, sets, and graphing, memory games, board games, and guessing games.

**999  Teddy Bear Press**

**Teddy Bear Press**
**3639 Midway Drive**
**San Diego, CA 92110**                   **619-223-7311**
                                      **FAX 858-674-0423**
                   **http://www.teddybearpress.net**
                   **e-mail: fparker@teddybearpress.net**
*Fran Parker, Author*
*Fran Parker, President*

Introduces number concepts 1-10 using the pre-primer words found in the I Can Read series.
*$20.00*

**1000  Ten Tricky Tiles**

**Sunburst Technology**
**400 Columbus Avenue**
**Valhalla, NY 10595 1349**               **914-747-3310**
                                          **800-321-7511**
                                      **FAX 914-747-4109**
                      **http://www.sunburst.com**
                      **e-mail: support@sunburst.com**
*Mark Sotir, President*

Students develop their arithmetic and logic skills with three levels of activities that involve solving sets of numbers sentences.

**1001 Weekly Math Practice**

Harcourt Achieve
6277 Sea Harbor Drive
Orlando, FL 32887
252-480-3200
800-531-5015
FAX 800-699-9459
http://www.steckvaughn.com
e-mail: info@steckvaughn.com
*Steck-Vaughn Staff, Author*
*Tim McEwen, President/CEO*
*Jeff Johnson, Dir Marketing Communications*
*Chris Lehmann, Team Coordinator*

Keep students sharp throughout the year with 36 weeks of brief, daily activities in math. Each activity page features five activity strips, one for each day of the week, and is backed up by a convenient answer key for the teacher that includes explanations and extensions.

**1002 Zap! Around Town**

Sunburst Technology
400 Columbus Avenue
Valhalla, NY 10595 1349
914-747-3310
800-321-7511
FAX 914-747-4109
http://www.sunburst.com
e-mail: support@sunburst.com
*Mark Sotir, President*

Students develop mapping and direction skills in this easy-to-use, animated program featuring Shelby, your friendly Sunbuddy guide.

## Preschool

**1003 2's Experience Fingerplays**

Therapro
225 Arlington Street
Framingham, MA 01702 8723
508-872-9494
800-257-5376
FAX 508-875-2062
http://www.theraproducts.com
e-mail: info@theraproducts.com
*Liz Wilmes, Dick Wilmes, Author*
*Karen Conrad, President*

A wonderful collection of fingerplays, songs and rhymes for the very young child. Fingerplays are short, easy to learn, and full of simple movement. Chant or sing the fingerplays and then enjoy the accompanying games and activities. *$12.95*

*159 pages*

**1004 28 Instant Song Games**

Therapro
225 Arlington Street
Framingham, MA 01702 8723
508-872-9494
800-257-5376
FAX 508-875-2062
http://www.theraproducts.com
e-mail: info@theraproducts.com
*MaBoAubLo, Barbara Sher, Author*
*Karen Conrad, President*

Gets kids up and moving in no time! Includes numerous games of body awareness, movement play, self expression, imagination and language play. Booklet and 75 minute audio tape. *$21.00*

*Audio Tape*

**1005 Artic Shuffle**

LinguiSystems Incorporated.
3100 4th Avenue
East Moline, IL 61244
309-775-2300
800-776-4332
FAX 309-755-2377
TDY:800-933-8331
http://www.linguisystems.com
e-mail: service@linguisystems.com
*Tobie Nan Kaufman, Author*
*Linda Bowers, Owner*
*Rosemary Huisingh, Owner*

Why are these card decks best-sellers? Because they're real playing cards! Your students can play Go Fish, Crazy Eights, or Concentration while they practice their target sounds. Use them for vocabulary drills or naming practice. *$89.95*

*Ages 5-Adult*

**1006 Curious George Preschool Learning Games**

Sunburst Technology
400 Columbus Avenue
Valhalla, NY 10595
914-747-3310
800-321-7511
FAX 914-747-4109
http://www.sunburst.com
e-mail: support@sunburst.com
*Mark Sotir, President*

Join Curious George in Fun Town and play five arcade-style games that promote the visual and auditory discrimination skills all students need before they begin to read. Mac/Win CD-ROM

**1007 Devereux Early Childhood Assessment (DECA)**

Kaplan Early Learning Company
PO Box 609
Lewisville, NC 27023
336-766-7374
800-334-2014
FAX 800-452-7526
http://www.kaplanco.com
e-mail: info@kaplanco.com
*Hal Kaplan, President/CEO*
*Paul LeBuffe, Assistant Director*

Strength-based standardized, norm-referenced behavior rating scale designed to promote resilience and measure protective factors in children ages 2-5. Through the program, early childhood professionals and families learn specific strategies to support young children's social and emotional development and to enhance the ovall quality of early childhood programs.

**1008 Devereux Early Childhood Assessment: Clinical Version (DECA-C)**

Kaplan Early Learning Company
PO Box 609
Lewisville, NC 27023          336-766-7374
                              800-334-2014
                              FAX 800-452-7526
                              http://www.kaplanco.com
                              e-mail: info@kaplanco.com
*Paul LeBuffe, Author*
*Hal Kaplan, President/CEO*
*Paul LeBuffe, Assistant Director*
*Pat Conte, Publishing Director*

DECA-C is designed to support early intervention efforts to reduce or eliminate significant emotional and behavioral concerns in preschool children. This can be used for guide interventions, identify children needing special services, assess outcomes and help programs meet Head Start, IDEA, and similar requirements. Kit includes: 1 Manual, 30 Record Forms, and 1 Norms Reference Card. *$125.95*

**1009 Early Movement Skills**

Therapro
225 Arlington Street
Framingham, MA 01702 8723     508-872-9494
                              800-257-5376
                              FAX 508-875-2062
                              http://www.theraproducts.com
                              e-mail: info@theraproducts.com
*Naomi Benari, Author*
*Karen Conrad, President*

Easy to follow, reproducible gross motor activities are graded from very simple (even for the passive child) to more demanding (folk dancing). Each of the 150 pages offers an activity with its objective, a clear instruction of the activity, rationale, and alternative movements and games. Many activities involve music and rythm. A great source for early intervention and early childhood programs. *$58.00*

**1010 Early Screening Inventory: Revised**

Harcourt
6277 Sea Harbor Dr
Orlando, FL 32887             407-345-2000
                             http://www.harcourt.com
*Gail Ribalta, Vice President Marketing*

A developmental screening instrument for 3-to-6-year olds. Provides a norm-referenced overview of visual-motor/adaptive, language and cognition, and gross motor development. Meets IDEA and Head Start requirements for early identification and parental involvement. Test in English or Spanish in 15-20 minutes. Training video and materials available.

**1011 Early Sensory Skills**

Therapro
225 Arlington Street
Framingham, MA 01702 8723     508-872-9494
                              800-257-5376
                              FAX 508-875-2062
                              http://www.theraproducts.com
                              e-mail: info@theraproducts.com
*Jackie Cooke, Author*
*Karen Conrad, President*

A wonderful book filled with practical and fun activities for stimulating vision, touch, taste and smell. Invaluable for anyone working with children 6 months to 5 years, this manual outlines basic principals followed by six sections containing activities, games and topics to excite the senses. Introductions are easy to follow, and materials for the sensory work are readily accessible in the everyday environment. *$52.50*

**1012 Early Visual Skills**

Therapro
225 Arlington Street
Framingham, MA 01702 8723     508-872-9494
                              800-257-5376
                              FAX 508-875-2062
                              http://www.theraproducts.com
                              e-mail: info@theraproducts.com
*Diana Williams, Author*
*Karen Conrad, President*

A beautifully designed, easy to follow reproducible book for working with young children on visual perceptual skills. Most of the activities are nonverbal and can be used with children who have limited language. Each section has both easy and challenging activities for school and for parents working with children at home. Activities include sorting, color and shape matching, a looking walk, games to develop visual memory and concentration and many more. *$52.50*

*208 pages*

**1013 Family Literacy Package**

Harcourt Achieve
6277 Sea Harbor Drive
Orlando, FL 32887            252-480-3200
                             800-531-5015
                             FAX 800-699-9459
                             http://www.steckvaughn.com
                             e-mail: info@steckvaughn.com
*Steck-Vaughn Staff, Author*
*Tim McEwen, President/CEO*
*Jeff Johnson, Dir Marketing Communications*
*Chris Lehmann, Team Coordinator*

Parent Package: includes materials that provide valuable academic and life coping resources for parents. Manual and companion video tapes prepare staff members for effective implementation. Child Package: includes materials that develop reading readiness and encourage positive parent-child interaction. Manual and companion video tapes prepare staff members to direct preschool learning and to facilitate supportive new relationships.

**1014 Fluharty Preschool Speech & Language Screening Test-2**

Speech Bin
1965 25th Avenue
Vero Beach, FL 32960          772-770-0007
                              800-477-3324
                              FAX 772-770-0006
                              http://www.speechbin.com
                              e-mail: info@speechbin.com
*Shane Peters, Product Coordinator*
*Jen Binney, Owner*

Carefully normed on 705 children, the Fluharty yields standard scores, percentiles, and age equivalents. The form features space for speech-language pathologist to note phonological processes, voice quality, and fluency; a Teacher Questionnaire is also provided. Item number P882 *$153.00*

**1015  For Parents and Professionals: Preschool**

LinguiSystems
3100 4th Avenue
East Moline, IL  61244          309-775-2300
                                800-776-4332
                          FAX 309-755-2377
                          TDY:800-933-8331
                http://www.linguisystems.com
           e-mail: service@linguisystems.com
*Marilyn A Ianni, Karin A Mullin, Author*
*Linda Bowers, Owner*
*Rosemary Huisingh, Owner*

Get tips and activities to facilitate developing communication skills in young children. You'll target social development, fine and gross motor development, cognitive growth, and receptive and expressive language skills. Each activity gives you three levels of increasing complexity for children functioning at different developmental levels. *$37.95*

*181 pages  Ages 2-5*

**1016  Funology Fables**

Speech Bin
1965 25th Avenue
Vero Beach, FL  32960          772-770-0007
                               800-477-3324
                          FAX 772-770-0006
                   http://www.speechbin.com
                 e-mail: info@speechbin.com
*Shane Peters, Product Coordinator*
*Jen Binney, Owner*

Funology Fables targets specific phonemes and critical early concepts, such as matching, sequencing, opposites, comparisons, quantity, size, and space. Reproducible Talking Tales and activities include 32 six-part sequence stories. Item number 1484. *$45.00*

**1017  Goal Oriented Gross & Fine Motor Lesson Plans for Early Childhood Classes**

Therapro
225 Arlington Street
Framingham, MA  01702 8723     508-872-9494
                               800-257-5376
                          FAX 508-875-2062
                http://www.theraproducts.com
              e-mail: info@theraproducts.com
*Donna Weiss MA OTR, Author*
*Karen Conrad, President*

Practical and convinient format covers 224 activities grouped into 12 monthly units, making it easy to incorporate gross and fine motor activities into a daily class schedule. Provides challenges for groups whose abilities span early childhood, from 2.5 to 5.5 years of age. *$32.00*

*77 pages*

**1018  HELP for Preschoolers at Home**

Therapro
225 Arlington Street
Framingham, MA  01702 8723     508-872-9494
                               800-257-5376
                          FAX 508-875-2062
                http://www.theraproducts.com
              e-mail: info@theraproducts.com
*Therapro Staff, Author*
*Karen Conrad, President*

Three hundred pages of practical, home-based activities that can be easily administered by the parents or the child's home-care provider. Upon completion of their assessments, teachers and therapists provide parents with these handouts to help them work on skills at home in conjunction with the program. *$72.50*

*Ages 3-6*

**1019  IEP Companion Software**

LinguiSystems
3100 4th Avenue
East Moline, IL  61244          309-775-2300
                                800-776-4332
                          FAX 309-755-2377
                          TDY:800-933-8331
                http://www.linguisystems.com
           e-mail: service@linguisystems.com
*Carolyn Wilson, Janet Lanza, Jeannie Evans, Author*
*Linda Bowers, Owner*
*Rosemary Huisingh, Owner*

Get IEP goals from the best-selling book with the click of your mouse. Writing complete reports is easy! You'll get to choose from hundreds of individual and classroom goals and objectives for all the important speech and language areas. Just click on the specific goals you want to create your individualized report. *$69.95*

*Birth-Adult*

**1020  Just for Me! Grammar**

LinguiSystems
3100 4th Avenue
East Moline, IL  61244          309-775-2300
                                800-776-4332
                          FAX 309-755-2377
                          TDY:800-933-8331
                http://www.linguisystems.com
           e-mail: service@linguisystems.com
*Margaret Warner, Author*
*Linda Bowers, Owner*
*Rosemary Huisingh, Owner*

Teach oral grammar to your youngest students! Through a variety of engaging activities, your students will become familiar with basic parts of speech, correct word order, and simple grammar concepts. These activities provide a solid foundation for later formal grammar training in the classroom. *$24.95*

*150 pages  Ages 3-6*

**1021  LAP-D Kindergarten Screen Kit**

Kaplan Early Learning Company
PO Box 609
Lewisville, NC  27023          336-766-7374
                               800-334-2014
                          FAX 800-452-7526
                     http://www.kaplanco.com
                  e-mail: info@kaplanco.com
*Hal Kaplan, President/CEO*
*Pat Conte, Publishing Director*

Concise, standardized screening deice normed on 5 year old children. Tasks are in four domains: fine, motor, gross motor, cognititve, and language. The Kindergarten Kit includes the technical manual, examiners, manual, and materials to assist in determining pure outcomes. *$124.95*

**1022  LILAC**

**Speech Bin**
**1965 25th Avenue**
**Vero Beach, FL  32960**               570-770-0007
                                        FAX 561-770-0006
                            **http://www.speechbin.com**
                            **e-mail: info@speechbin.com**
*Shane Peters, Product Coordinator*
*Jen Binney, Owner*

LILAC uses direct and naturalistic teaching in a creative approach that links spoken language learning to reading and writing. Activities to develop semantic, syntactic, expressive, and receptive language skills are presented sequentially from three-to-five-year old developmental levels. *$21.95*

**1023  Learning Accomplishment Profile Diagnostic Normed Screens for Age 3-5**

**Kaplan Early Learning Company**
**PO Box 609**
**Lewisville, NC  27023**               336-766-7374
                                        800-334-2014
                                        FAX 800-452-7526
                            **http://www.kaplanco.com**
                            **e-mail: info@kaplanco.com**
*Hal Kaplan, President/CEO*
*Pat Conte, Publishing Director*

For 3-5 years. Create reliable developmental snapshots in fine motor, gross motor, cognitive, language, personal/social, and self-help skill domains. *$349.95*

**1024  Learning Accomplishment Profile (LAP-R) KIT**

**Kaplan Early Learning Company**
**PO Box 609**
**Lewisville, NC  27023**               336-766-7374
                                        800-334-2014
                                        FAX 800-452-7526
                            **http://www.kaplanco.com**
                            **e-mail: info@kaplanco.com**
*Hal Kaplan, President/CEO*
*Pat Conte, Publishing Director*

A criterion-referenced assessment instrument measuring development in six domains: gross motor, fine motor, cognitive, language, self-help and social/emotional. Kit includes all materials necessary for assessing 20 children. *$ 299.95*

**1025  Learning Accomplishment Profile Diagnostic Normed Assessment (LAP-D)**

**Kaplan Early Learning Company**
**PO Box 609**
**Lewisville, NC  27023**               336-766-7374
                                        800-334-2014
                                        FAX 800-452-7526
                            **http://www.kaplanco.com**
                            **e-mail: info@kaplanco.com**
*Hal Kaplan, President/CEO*
*Pat Conte, Publishing Director*

A comprehensive developemtal assessment tool for children between the ages of 30 and 72 months. LAP-D consists of a hierarchy of developmental skills arranged in four developmental domains: fine motor, gross motor, cognitive and language. *$624.95*

**1026  Linamood Program (LIPS Clinical Version)-Phoneme Sequencing Program for Reading, Spelling,Speech**

**LinguiSystems**
**3100 4th Avenue**
**East Moline, IL  61244**              309-775-2300
                                        800-776-4332
                                        FAX 309-755-2377
                                        TDY:800-933-8331
                            **http://www.linguisystems.com**
                            **e-mail: service@linguisystems.com**
*Patricia Linamood, Phyllis Linamood, Author*
*Linda Bowers, Owner*
*Rosemary Huisingh, Owner*

Help your students develop phoneme awareness for competence in reading, spelling, and speech. This multisensory program meets the needs of the many children and adults who don't develop phonemic awareness through traditional methods. *$247.00*

   *Birth-Adult*

**1027  Make Every Step Count: Birth to 1 Year**

**Therapro**
**225 Arlington Street**
**Framingham, MA  01702 8723**          508-872-9494
                                        800-257-5376
                                        FAX 508-875-2062
                            **http://www.theraproducts.com**
                            **e-mail: info@theraproducts.com**
*Stephanie Parks MA, Author*
*Karen Conrad, President*

A great book with many ideas for parents to use at home to foster child development. *$16.50*

   *94 pages*

**1028  Make It Today for Pre-K Play**

**Therapro**
**225 Arlington Street**
**Framingham, MA  01702 8723**          508-872-9494
                                        800-257-5376
                                        FAX 508-875-2062
                            **http://www.theraproducts.com**
                            **e-mail: info@theraproducts.com**
*Joyce Hamman, Author*
*Karen Conrad, President*

Many ideas for making and using toys for motor development. Includes a nice checklist for balance, directional terms, body awareness, and gross and fine motor skills. For each piece of equipment, specific directions are given on how to make it; teaching tips, many ideas for using in curriculum integration. *$7.95*

**1029  Mouth Madness**

**Speech Bin**
**1965 25th Avenue**
**Vero Beach, FL  32960**               772-770-0007
                                        800-477-3324
                                        FAX 772-770-0006
                            **http://www.speechbin.com**
                            **e-mail: info@speechbin.com**
*Shane Peters, Product Coordinator*
*Jen Binney, Owner*

This unique manual uses oral imitation, motor planning, and breath control activities to improve the articulation and feeding skills of preschool and primary children. Games, manipulative tasks, silly sentences, rhymes, and funny faces target higher organizational levels of motor planning. Item number C758. *$51.95*

**1030 Partners for Learning (PFL)**

**Kaplan Early Learning Company**
**PO Box 609**
**Lewisville, NC 27023**          336-766-7374
                                  800-334-2014
                        FAX 800-452-7526
                    http://www.kaplanco.com
                    e-mail: info@kaplanco.com
*Hal Kaplan, President/CEO*
*Pat Conte, Publishing Director*

This resource uses cards, books, posters, and support materials to supply teaching ideas and to support child development. PARTNERS for Learning encourages cognitive, social, motor, and language development. The kit provides materials for curriculum planning and self-assessment. *$199.95*

**1031 Preschool**

**Harcourt Achieve**
**6277 Sea Harbor Drive**
**Orlando, FL 32887**          252-480-3200
                               800-531-5015
                     FAX 800-699-9459
                http://www.steckvaughn.com
                e-mail: info@steckvaughn.com
*Davis, Author*
*Tim McEwen, President/CEO*
*Jeff Johnson, Dir Marketing Communications*
*Chris Lehmann, Team Coordinator*

This series provides age appropriate activities to foster childrens' desire to read and create a print rich classroom to enhance their emergent literacy. Multiple lesson plans save teachers time by providing suggested lessons that cover the purpose, materials, direct teaching, and application of new skills. This is a great resource for center ideas that provide opportunities for children to think creatively, explore new ideas, and use problem-solving skills.

**1032 Preschool Motor Speech Evaluation &**
**Intervention**

**Speech Bin**
**1965 25th Avenue**
**Vero Beach, FL 32960**          772-770-0007
                                  800-477-3324
                        FAX 772-770-0006
                    http://www.speechbin.com
                    e-mail: info@speechbin.com
*Shane Peters, Product Coordinator*
*Jen Binney, Owner*

This comprehensive criterion-based assessment tool differentiates motor-based speech disorders from those of phonology and determines if speech difficulties of children 18 months to six years old are characteristic of: oral nonverbal apraxia; dysarthria; developmental verbal dyspraxia; hypersensitivity; differences in tone and hyposensitivity. Item number J322. *$59.00*

**1033 Promoting Communication in Infants & Children**
**Speech Bin**
**1965 25th Avenue**
**Vero Beach, FL 32960**          772-770-0007
                                  800-477-3324
                        FAX 772-770-0006
                    http://www.speechbin.com
                    e-mail: info@speechbin.com
*Shane Peters, Product Coordinator*
*Jen Binney, Owner*

Promoting Communication in Infants and Young Children gives you down-to-earth information, activities, and step-by-step suggestions for stimulating children's speech and language skills. Topics are conveniently organized, concisely presented, and written in easy-to-understand language. Item number 1512. *$14.95*

**1034 RULES**

**Speech Bin**
**1965 25th Avenue**
**Vero Beach, FL 32960**          772-770-0007
                                  800-477-3324
                        FAX 772-770-0006
                    http://www.speechbin.com
                    e-mail: info@speechbin.com
*Shane Peters, Product Coordinator*
*Jen Binney, Owner*

Faced with young children whose speech is unintelligible? RULES is the perfect program for these preschool and elementary children. It remediates the processes: cluster reduction; final consonant deletion; stopping and prevocalic voicing. Item number 1557. *$43.95*

**1035 Receptive One-Word Picture Vocabulary Test**
**(ROWPVT-2000)**

**Speech Bin**
**1965 25th Avenue**
**Vero Beach, FL 32960**          772-770-0007
                                  800-477-3324
                        FAX 772-770-0006
                    http://www.speechbin.com
                    e-mail: info@speechbin.com
*Shane Peters, Product Coordinator*
*Jen Binney, Owner*

This administered, untimed measure assessess the vocabulary comprehension of 0-2 through 11-18 years. New full-color test pictures are easy to recognize; many new test items have been added. It is ideal for children unable or reluctant to speak because only a gestural response is required. Item number A305. *$140.00*

**1036 Right from the Start: Behavioral Intervention for**
**Young Children with Autism: A Guide**

**Therapro**
**225 Arlington Street**
**Framingham, MA 01702 8723**          508-872-9494
                                       800-257-5376
                             FAX 508-875-2062
                        http://www.theraproducts.com
                        e-mail: info@theraproducts.com
*Mary Jane Weiss PhD, Sandra Harris PhD, Author*
*Karen Conrad, President*

This informative and user-friendly guide helps parents and service providers explore programs that use early intensive behavioral intervention for young children with autism and related disorders. Within these programs, many children improve in intellectual, social and adaptive functioning, enabling them to move on to regular elementary and preschools. Benefits all children, but primarily useful for children age five and younger. *$14.95*

*138 pages*

**1037  SPARC Artic Junior**

**LinguiSystems**
**3100 4th Avenue**
**East Moline, IL  61244**          **309-775-2300**
**800-776-4332**
**FAX 309-755-2377**
**TDY:800-933-8331**
**http://www.linguisystems.com**
**e-mail: service@linguisystems.com**
*Beverly Plass, Author*
*Linda Bowers, Owner*
*Rosemary Huisingh, Owner*

Reach intelligibility goals faster with these take-home exercises. The practice words have been carefully selected to control the phonetic context. It's a programmed, research-based approach that will get results. Activities are divided by primary and secondary phonological processes. *$39.95*

*211 pages  Ages 3-7*

**1038  Sensory Motor Activities for Early Development**

**Therapro**
**225 Arlington Street**
**Framingham, MA  01702 8723**          **508-872-9494**
**800-257-5376**
**FAX 508-875-2062**
**http://www.theraproducts.com**
**e-mail: info@theraproducts.com**
*Chia Swee Hong, Helen Gabriel, Cathy St John, Author*
*Karen Conrad, President*

A complete package of tried and tested gross and fine motor activities. Many activities to stimulate sensory and body awareness, encourage basic movement, promote hand skills, and enhance spatial/early perceptual skills. Master handouts throughout to give to parents for home practice activities for working in small groups. *$44.50*

**1039  Silly Sentences**

**Speech Bin**
**1965 25th Avenue**
**Vero Beach, FL  32960**          **772-770-0007**
**800-477-3324**
**FAX 772-770-0006**
**http://www.speechbin.com**
**e-mail: info@speechbin.com**
*Shane Peters, Product Coordinator*
*Jen Binney, Owner*

Children love to have fun. Silly Sentences lets them have fun while they play these engaging card games to learn: subject verb agreement; speech sound articulation; S+ V+ O sentences; questioning and answering; humor and absurdities; and present progressive verbs. Item number P506. *$41.00*

**1040  Sound Connections**

**Speech Bin**
**1965 25th Avenue**
**Vero Beach, FL  32960**          **772-770-0007**
**800-477-3324**
**FAX 772-770-0006**
**http://www.speechbin.com**
**e-mail: info@speechbin.com**
*Shane Peters, Product Coordinator*
*Jen Binney, Owner*

This program teaches the critical connections between the sounds kids hear and speaking, reading, and writing. Dozens of activities and worksheets, 19 phoneme-based stories, and 100s of pictures. Item number 1487. *$41.95*

**1041  Source for Early Literacy Development**

**LinguiSystems**
**3100 4th Avenue**
**East Moline, IL  61244**          **309-775-2300**
**800-776-4332**
**FAX 309-755-2377**
**TDY:800-933-8331**
**http://www.linguisystems.com**
**e-mail: service@linguisystems.com**
*Linda K Crowe, Sara S Reichmuth, Author*
*Linda Bowers, Owner*
*Rosemary Huisingh, Owner*

This great resource gives you the latest information on children's emergent reading and writing from birth through age eight. You'll also get helpful strategies to facilitate literacy development for future academic success! *$ 41.95*

*151 pages  Birth-8*

**1042  Stuttering: Helping the Disfluent Preschool Child**

**Speech Bin**
**1965 25th Avenue**
**Vero Beach, FL  32960**          **772-770-0007**
**800-477-3324**
**FAX 772-770-0006**
**http://www.speechbin.com**
**e-mail: info@speechbin.com**
*Shane Peters, Product Coordinator*
*Jen Binney, Owner*

Written in the warm encouraging style for which this author is known, Stuttering: Helping the Disfluent Preschool Child is the perfect tool for parents and teachers of young stuttering children. It uses a Speech Thermometer to show them ways to turn talking into an area of strength. Item number 1489. *$13.95*

**1043  Take Home: Preschool Language Development**

**LinguiSystems**
**3100 4th Avenue**
**East Moline, IL  61244**          **309-775-2300**
**800-776-4332**
**FAX 309-755-2377**
**TDY:800-933-8331**
**http://www.linguisystems.com**
**e-mail: service@linguisystems.com**
*Martha Drake, Author*
*Linda Bowers, Owner*
*Rosemary Huisingh, Owner*

Home follow-up is essential for your little ones with speech and language delays. Get everything you need for a comprehensive take-home program with this time saver! Each take-home lesson is easy to follow. *$31.95*

*191 pages  Ages 1-5*

**1044    Test for Auditory Comprehension of Language: TACL-3**

**Speech Bin**
**1965 25th Avenue**
**Vero Beach, FL  32960**                    772-770-0007
                                                      800-477-3324
                                        FAX 772-770-0006
                           http://www.speechbin.com
                           e-mail: info@speechbin.com
*Shane Peters, Product Coordinator*
*Jen Binney, Owner*

The newly revised TACL-3 evaluates the 0-3 to 9-11-year old's understanding of spoken language in three subtests: Vocabulary, Grammatical Morphemes and Elaborated Phrases and Sentences. Each test item is a word or sentence read aloud by the examiner; the child responds by pointing to one of three pictures. Item number P792. *$261.00*

**1045    Tips for Teaching Infants & Toddlers**

**Speech Bin**
**1965 25th Avenue**
**Vero Beach, FL  32960**                    772-770-0007
                                                      800-477-3324
                                        FAX 772-770-0006
                           http://www.speechbin.com
                           e-mail: info@speechbin.com
*Shane Peters, Product Coordinator*
*Jen Binney, Owner*

This multisensory approach to Early Intervention is a whole year's worth of weekly thematic lessons which let children see, hear, feel, manipulate, smell, and taste. Item number 1235. *$45.95*

**1046    What Am I? Game**

**Harcourt Achieve**
**6277 Sea Harbor Drive**
**Orlando, FL  32887**                       252-480-3200
                                                      800-531-5015
                                        FAX 800-699-9459
                           http://www.steckvaughn.com
                           e-mail: info@steckvaughn.com
*Steck-Vaughn Staff, Author*
*Tim McEwen, President/CEO*
*Jeff Johnson, Dir Marketing Communications*
*Chris Lehmann, Team Coordinator*

Turn animal identity into a guessing game. Children guess the identities of amazing animals from a series of clues and up close views. A world map pinpoints each animal's habitat, and a quick quiz reinforces fun facts.

**1047    When Pre-Schoolers are Not on Target: Guide for Parents & Early Childhood Educators**

**Learning Disabilities Association of America**
**LDA Literary Depository**
**Pittsburgh, PA  15234**                    412-341-1515
                                        FAX 412-344-0224
                           http://www.ldaamerica.org
                           e-mail: ldanatl@usaor.net
*Jane Browning, Executive Director*
*Mary , Office Manager*

New booklet provides information on early identification of learning disabilities and appropriate intervention strategies to professionals who work with preschool children. Available in Spanish. Discounts for multiples. *$4.00*

**1048    Your Child's Speech and Language**

**Speech Bin**
**1965 25th Avenue**
**Vero Beach, FL  32960**                    772-770-0007
                                                      800-477-3324
                                        FAX 772-770-0006
                           http://www.speechbin.com
                           e-mail: info@speechbin.com
*Shane Peters, Product Coordinator*
*Jen Binney, Owner*

This delightfully illustrated 52- page book provides helpful information about speech and language development from infancy through five years. It shows how to determine if speech is developing normally and ways to stimulate its growth. It's ideal for parent training and baby showers too! Item number P652. *$17.00*

---

# Reading

**1049    100% Reading: 2-Book Intermediate Set**

**LinguiSystems**
**3100 4th Avenue**
**East Moline, IL  61244**                   309-775-2300
                                                      800-776-4332
                                        FAX 309-755-2377
                                   TDY:800-933-8331
                           http://www.linguisystems.com
                           e-mail: service@linguisystems.com
*LinguiSystems Staff, Author*
*Linda Bowers, Owner*
*Rosemary Huisingh, Owner*

Our reading series uses a developmental approach based on the latest research in phonological awareness and early reading skills. Intermediate books are for ages 8-10. Great as a reading curriculum or to supplement your current reading program. *$69.90*

*200 pages  Ages 8-10*

**1050    100% Reading: 3-Book Primary Set**

**LinguiSystems**
**3100 4th Avenue**
**East Moline, IL  61244**                   309-775-2300
                                                      800-776-4332
                                        FAX 309-755-2377
                                   TDY:800-933-8331
                           http://www.linguisystems.com
                           e-mail: service@linguisystems.com
*LinguiSystems Staff, Author*
*Linda Bowers, Owner*
*Rosemary Huisingh, Owner*

Our reading series uses a developmental approach based on the latest research in phonological awareness and early reading skills. Primary books are for ages 5-7. Great as a reading curriculum or to supplement your current reading program. *$104.85*

*200 pages  Ages 5-7*

**1051  100% Reading: Decoding and Word Recognition: 5-book set**

LinguiSystems
3100 4th Avenue
East Moline, IL  61244          309-775-2300
                                800-776-4332
                         FAX 309-755-2377
                         TDY:800-933-8331
                  http://www.linguisystems.com
                e-mail: service@linguisystems.com

*LinguiSystems Staff, Author*
*Linda Bowers, Owner*
*Rosemary Huisingh, Owner*

Our reading series uses a developmental approach based on the latest research in phonological awareness and early reading skills. Primary books are for ages 5-7. Intermediate books are for ages 8-10. Great as a reading curriculum or to supplement your current reading program. *$174.75*

*200 pages  Ages 5-10*

**1052  100% Reading: Intermediate Book 1**

LinguiSystems
3100 4th Avenue
East Moline, IL  61244          309-775-2300
                                800-776-4332
                         FAX 309-755-2377
                         TDY:800-933-8331
                  http://www.linguisystems.com
                e-mail: service@linguisystems.com

*LinguiSystems Staff, Author*
*Linda Bowers, Owner*
*Rosemary Huisingh, Owner*

Our reading series uses a developmental approach based on the latest research in phonological awareness and early reading skills. Great as a reading curriculum or to supplement your current reading program. Intermediate Book 1 covers: schwa, vowel sounds, consonant sounds, hard and soft c and g sound, and silent letters. *$34.95*

*211 pages  Ages 8-10*

**1053  100% Reading: Intermediate Book 2**

LinguiSystems
3100 4th Avenue
East Moline, IL  61244          309-775-2300
                                800-776-4332
                         FAX 309-755-2377
                         TDY:800-933-8331
                  http://www.linguisystems.com
                e-mail: service@linguisystems.com

*LinguiSystems Staff, Author*
*Linda Bowers, Owner*
*Rosemary Huisingh, Owner*

Our reading series uses a developmental approach based on the latest research in phonological awareness and early reading skills. Great as a reading curriculum or to supplement your current reading program. Intermediate Book 2 covers: syllables, root words and affixes, plurals and possessive, contractions, homonyms, and word endings. *$34.95*

*221 pages  Ages 8-10*

**1054  100% Reading: Primary Book 1**

LinguiSystems
3100 4th Avenue
East Moline, IL  61244          309-775-2300
                                800-776-4332
                         FAX 309-755-2377
                         TDY:800-933-8331
                  http://www.linguisystems.com
                e-mail: service@linguisystems.com

*LinguiSystems Staff, Author*
*Linda Bowers, Owner*
*Rosemary Huisingh, Owner*

Our reading series uses a developmental approach based on the latest research in phonological awareness and early reading skills. Primary books are ages 5-7. Great as a reading curriculum or to supplement your current reading program. Primary Book 1 covers: sight words, short vowels, long vowels, and sorry vowels oo, ow, oi, aw, er. *$34.95*

*194 pages  Ages 5-7*

**1055  100% Reading: Primary Book 2**

LinguiSystems
3100 4th Avenue
East Moline, IL  61244          309-775-2300
                                800-776-4332
                         FAX 309-755-2377
                         TDY:800-933-8331
                  http://www.linguisystems.com
                e-mail: service@linguisystems.com

*LinguiSystems Staff, Author*
*Linda Bowers, Owner*
*Rosemary Huisingh, Owner*

Our reading series uses a developmental approach based on the latest research in phonological awareness and early reading skills. Primary books are ages 5-7. Great as a reading curriculum or to supplement your current reading program. Primary Book 2 covers: sight words, beginning consonants, and ending constants. *$34.95*

*200 pages  Ages 5-7*

**1056  100% Reading: Primary Book 3**

LinguiSystems
3100 4th Avenue
East Moline, IL  61244          309-775-2300
                                800-776-4332
                         FAX 309-755-2377
                         TDY:800-933-8331
                  http://www.linguisystems.com
                e-mail: service@linguisystems.com

*LinguiSystems Staff, Author*
*Linda Bowers, Owner*
*Rosemary Huisingh, Owner*

Our reading series uses a developmental approach based on the latest research in phonological awareness and early reading skills. Primary books are ages 5-7. Great as a reading curriculum or to supplement your current reading program. Primary Book 3 covers: intial blends, final blends, consonant digraphs, vowel digraphs, vowel dipthongs, sounds of y. *$34.95*

*233 pages  Ages 5-7*

**1057  125 Ways to Be a Better Reader**

**LinguiSystems**
**3100 4th Avenue**
**East Moline, IL  61244**                    309-775-2300
                                              800-776-4332
                                              FAX 309-755-2377
                                              TDY:800-933-8331
                              http://www.linguisystems.com
                        e-mail: service@linguisystems.com
*Elizabeth M Wadlington, Paula S Currie, Author*
*Linda Bowers, Owner*
*Rosemary Huisingh, Owner*

Get 125 strategies to improve decoding and
conprehension skills. You'll improve reading abilities and attitudes in seven major areas including: getting ready to read, decoding, comprehension, content
area reading, reading for test, reading reference materials, and the reading-writing connection. *$35.95*

*180 pages  Ages 10-16*

**1058  Ablenet**

**2808 North Fairview Avenue**
**Roseville, MN  55113**                      612-379-0956
                                              800-322-0956
                                              FAX 612-379-9143
                              http://www.ablenetinc.com
                    e-mail: customerservice@ablenetinc.com
*Cheryl Volkman, Chief Developmental Officer*
*Sheree Christianson, Sales Administrator*

Simple assistive technology for teaching children
with disabilities including communication aids,
switches, environmental control, mounting systems,
literacy and teacher resources, kits and more.

**1059  Animals of the Rain Forest: Steadwell**

**Harcourt Achieve**
**6277 Sea Harbor Drive**
**Orlando, FL  32887**                        252-480-3200
                                              800-531-5015
                                              FAX 800-699-9459
                              http://www.steckvaughn.com
                          e-mail: info@steckvaughn.com
*Steck-Vaughn Staff, Author*
*Tim McEwen, President/CEO*
*Jeff Johnson, Dir Marketing Communications*
*Chris Lehmann, Team Coordinator*

When reading is a struggle, academic success is even
harder to achieve. Now you can put social studies and
science curriculum content within reach of every student with this series. Designed specifically for limited
readers.

**1060  Ants in His Pants: Absurdities and Realities of
Special Education**

**Peytral Publications**
**PO Box 1162**
**Minnetonka, MN  55345**                     952-949-8707
                                              877-739-8725
                                              FAX 952-906-9777
                              http://www.peytral.com
                          e-mail: help@peytral.com
*Michael F Giangreco, Author*
*Kevin Ruelle, Illustrator*
*Peggy Hammeken, Owner/Publisher*

With wit, humor and profound one liners, Michael
Giagreco will transform your thinking as you take a
lighter look at the sometimes comical and occasionally harsh truths in the ever changing field of special
education. *$19.95*

*128 pages*
*ISBN 1-890455-42-3*

**1061  AppleSeeds**

**Cobblestone Publishing - Division of Cane Pub. Co.**
**30 Grove Street**
**Peterborough, NH  03458**                   603-924-7209
                                              800-821-0115
                                              FAX 603-924-7380
                              http://www.cricketmag.com
                    e-mail: custsvc@cobblestone.mv.com
*John Olbrych, Publisher*
*Susan Buckley, Editor*
*Lou Waryncia, Editorial Director*

A delightful way to develop the love of nonfiction
reading. Each full color issue comes jam-packed with
fascinating articles, photographs, illustrations, time
lines, maps, activities and contests. *$29.95*

*36 pages  9 times a year*

**1062  Basic Level Workbook for Aphasia**

**Speech Bin**
**1965 25th Avenue**
**Vero Beach, FL  32960**                     772-770-0007
                                              800-477-3324
                                              FAX 772-770-0006
                              http://www.speechbin.com
                          e-mail: info@speechbin.com
*Shane Peters, Product Coordinator*
*Jen Binney, Owner*

If you work with adolescents and adults with mild to
moderate language deficits or limited, impaired, or
emerging reading skills, this workbook is what you've
been waiting for! The mMaterial is relevant to their
lives, interests, experiences, and vocabulary. Item
number W324. *$48.95*

**1063  Beyond the Code**

**Educators Publishing Service**
**31 Smith Place**
**Cambridge, MA  02139 9031**                 617-547-6706
                                              800-225-5750
                                              FAX 888-440-2665
                              http://www.epsbooks.com
                          e-mail: eps@epsbooks.com
*Nancy M Hall, Author*
*Steven Corte, President*

Beyond the Code gives beginning readers experience
reading original stories as well as thinking about what
they have read. This companion series follows the
same phonetic progression as the frist 4 books of the
popular Explode the Code program.

**1064  Book Reports Plus**

**Harcourt Achieve**
**6277 Sea Harbor Drive**
**Orlando, FL  32887**        252-480-3200
                             800-531-5015
                        FAX 800-699-9459
                 http://www.steckvaughn.com
                 e-mail: info@steckvaughn.com

*Steck-Vaughn Staff, Author*
*Tim McEwen, President/CEO*
*Jeff Johnson, Dir Marketing Communications*
*Chris Lehmann, Team Coordinator*

Readers of all levels and abilities will be able to participate in activities that allow them to respond to literature in nontraditional ways. Six units include written and oral reports, dramatizations, and other expressive media. Multiple graphic organizers reinforce the habits of planning and preparing for reading, writing, and presenting.

*96 pages*

**1065  Bridges to Reading Comprehension**

**Harcourt Achieve**
**6277 Sea Harbor Drive**
**Orlando, FL  32887**        252-480-3200
                             800-531-5015
                        FAX 800-699-9459
                 http://www.steckvaughn.com
                 e-mail: info@steckvaughn.com

*Steck-Vaughn Staff, Author*
*Tim McEwen, President/CEO*
*Jeff Johnson, Dir Marketing Communications*
*Chris Lehmann, Team Coordinator*

Lets your readers build skills in the context of high quality fiction and nonfiction selections.

**1066  Careers**

**Harcourt Achieve**
**6277 Sea Harbor Drive**
**Orlando, FL  32887**        252-480-3200
                             800-531-5015
                        FAX 800-699-9459
                 http://www.steckvaughn.com
                 e-mail: info@steckvaughn.com

*Heyworth, Author*
*Tim McEwen, President/CEO*
*Jeff Johnson, Dir Marketing Communications*
*Chris Lehmann, Team Coordinator*

Develop reading skills while expanding students frames of reference in employment. A highly accessible preview of vocational, technical, and professional career opportunities on both today's and tomorrow's job market. Eight thematic units per title present overviews of careers in health, science, community service, agriculture and forestry circuitry, communications, entertainment and the creative industries.

**1067  Claims to Fame**

**Educators Publishing Service**
**31 Smith Place**
**Cambridge, MA  02139 9031**        617-547-6706
                                     800-225-5750
                                FAX 888-440-2665
                         http://www.epsbooks.com
                         e-mail: eps@epsbooks.com

*Carol Einstein, Author*
*Steven Corte, President*

The three exercises after each reading are tailored to the content of each story. In Thinking About What You Have Read, students check and extend their understanding of the story. Working with Words asks students to think about and experiment with vaious word meanings.

**1068  Clues to Meaning**

**Educators Publishing Service**
**31 Smith Place**
**Cambridge, MA  02139 9031**        617-547-6706
                                     800-225-5750
                                FAX 888-440-2665
                         http://www.epsbooks.com
                         e-mail: eps@epsbooks.com

*Ann L Staman, Author*
*Steven Korte, President*
*Gunnar Voltz, Vice President*

A versatile series which teaches beginning readers to use the sounds of letters as one strategy among many in learning to read.

**1069  Connect-A-Card**

**Speech Bin**
**1965 25th Avenue**
**Vero Beach, FL  32960**        772-770-0007
                                 800-477-3324
                            FAX 772-770-0006
                     http://www.speechbin.com
                     e-mail: info@speechbin.com

*Shane Peters, Product Coordinator*
*Jen Binney, Owner*

How to teach your 6-12 year olds how to build tons of sentences, each using two illustrated phrase cards plus a common conjunction. Word cards feature four coordinating and, but, or, yet and eleven subordinating after, although, because, before, if, since, so that, unless, until, when, while conjunctions; clear black and white picture cards foster creative sentence construction. Item number Q974. *$35.00*

**1070  Cosmic Reading Journey**

**Sunburst Technology**
**400 Columbus Avenue**
**Valhalla, NY  10595 1349**        914-747-3310
                                    800-321-7511
                               FAX 914-747-4109
                        http://www.sunburst.com
                        e-mail: support@sunburst.com

*Mark Sotir, President*

This reading comprehension program provides meaningful summary and writing activities for the 100 books that early readers and their teachers love most.

**1071  Creepy Cave Initial Consonants**

Sunburst Technology
400 Columbus Avenue
Valhalla, NY  10595 1349          914-747-3310
                                 800-321-7511
                             FAX 914-747-4109
                     http://www.sunburst.com
                 e-mail: support@sunburst.com
*Mark Sotir, President*

Help your students develop letter recognition and
phonemic awareness skills matching words with the
same initial consonant letter in a Creepy Cave.

**1072  Curious Creatures Program:**
**Owls-Spiders-Wolves-Snakes-Bats**

Curriculum Associates
PO Box 2001
North Billerica, MA  01862 9914     978-667-8000
                                    800-225-0248
                                FAX 800-366-1158
               http://www.curriculumassociates.com
          e-mail: ca@infocurriculumassociates.com
*Louis Jame Taris, James Robert Taris, Author*
*Frank Ferguson, President*
*Fred Ferguson, Vice President Corporate Develop*

Users of this award-winning multimedia program say
awesome! They learn little known facts about animals
that make most of us cringe. Designed to encourage reluctant readers in grades 4 and above, the program is
also appropriate for on-level students in grades 2-3.
Students learn the language of life science as they
strengthen their reading and comprehension skills.

**1073  Decoding Games**

LinguiSystems
3100 4th Avenue
East Moline, IL  61244             309-775-2300
                                   800-776-4332
                               FAX 309-755-2377
                              TDY:800-933-8331
                   http://www.linguisystems.com
              e-mail: service@linguisystems.com
*Tina Sanford, Author*
*Linda Bowers, Owner*
*Rosemary Huisingh, Owner*

Get three fun games in one handy case. These colorful
games target tricky decoding skills your students need
for strong reading skills. *$39.95*

*Ages 6-10*

**1074  Dyslexia Training Program**

Educators Publishing Service
31 Smith Place
Cambridge, MA  02139 9031          617-547-6706
                                   800-225-5750
                               FAX 888-440-2665
                    http://www.epsbooks.com
                e-mail: eps@epsbooks.com
*Texas Scottish Rite Hospital For Children, Author*
*Steven Korte, President*
*Gunnar Voltz, Vice President*

Introduces reading and writing skills to dyslexic children through a two-year, cumulative series of daily
one-hour videotaped lessons and accompanying student's books and teacher's guides.

**1075  Earobics Step 1 Home Version**

Speech Bin
1965 25th Avenue
Vero Beach, FL  32960              772-770-0007
                                  800-477-3324
                              FAX 772-770-0006
                   http://www.speechbin.com
               e-mail: info@speechbin.com
*Shane Peters, Product Coordinator*
*Jen Binney, Owner*

Step 1 offers hundreds of levels of play, appealing
graphics, and entertaining music to train the critical
auditory skills young children need for success in
learning. Item number C481. *$59.00*

**1076  Earobics Step 1 Specialist/Clinician Version**

Speech Bin
1965 25th Avenue
Vero Beach, FL  32960              772-770-0007
                                  800-477-3324
                              FAX 772-770-0006
                   http://www.speechbin.com
               e-mail: info@speechbin.com
*Shane Peters, Product Coordinator*
*Jen Binney, Owner*

Earobics is a dazzling software that teaches phonological awareness and auditory processing. It systematically — anf enjoyably — trains these critical skills for
development ages four to seven years. Item number
C482. *$299.00*

**1077  Earobics for Adolescents & Adults Home Version**

Speech Bin
1965 25th Avenue
Vero Beach, FL  32960              772-770-0007
                                  800-477-3324
                              FAX 772-770-0006
                   http://www.speechbin.com
               e-mail: info@speechbin.com
*Shane Peters, Product Coordinator*
*Jen Binney, Owner*

Two users may use the Home Version which offers
hundreds of levels of play, age-appropriate graphics,
and entertaining music. This level is also available in
a professional version for specialists and clinicians.
Item number C485. *$59.00*

**1078  Earobics for Adolescents & Adults**
**Specialist/Clinician Version**

Speech Bin
1965 25th Avenue
Vero Beach, FL  32960              772-770-0007
                                  800-477-3324
                              FAX 772-770-0006
                   http://www.speechbin.com
               e-mail: info@speechbin.com
*Shane Peters, Product Coordinator*
*Jen , Owner*

The Clinician/Specialist Version has twelve name slots per workstation and goal writing and charting capability to save professional time. This level is also available in a Home Version limited to two users. Both versions offer hundreds of levels of play, appealing graphics, and entertaining music. Item number C486. *$299.00*

## 1079 Emergent Reader

**Sunburst Technology**
**400 Columbus Avenue**
**Valhalla, NY 10595 1349**       **914-747-3310**
**800-321-7511**
**FAX 914-747-4109**
**http://www.sunburst.com**
**e-mail: support@sunburst.com**
*Mark Sotir, President*

This story-reading program supports the efforts of beginning readers by developing their sight word vocabularies.

## 1080 Every Child a Reader

**Sunburst Technology**
**400 Columbus Avenue**
**Valhalla, NY 10595 1349**       **914-747-3310**
**800-321-7511**
**FAX 914-747-4109**
**http://www.sunburst.com**
**e-mail: support@sunburst.com**
*Mark Sotir, President*

Traditional reading strategies in a rich literary context. Designed to promote independent reading and develop oral and written language expression.

## 1081 Explode the Code

**Educators Publishing Service**
**31 Smith Place**
**Cambridge, MA 02139 9031**       **617-547-6706**
**800-225-5750**
**FAX 888-440-2665**
**http://www.epsbooks.com**
**e-mail: eps@epsbooks.com**
*Nancy M Hall, Rena Price, Author*
*Steven Corte, President*

Explode the Code provides a sequential, systematic approach to phonics in which students blend sounds to build vocabulary and read words, phrases, sentences, and stories.

## 1082 Expressway to Reading

**Harcourt Achieve**
**6277 Sea Harbor Drive**
**Orlando, FL 32887**       **252-480-3200**
**800-531-5015**
**FAX 800-699-9459**
**http://www.steckvaughn.com**
**e-mail: info@steckvaughn.com**
*Davis, Author*
*Tim McEwen, President/CEO*
*Jeff Johnson, Dir Marketing Communications*
*Chris Lehmann, Team Coordinator*

Now parents can make everyday activities fun exercises in reading. These skill building and practice activities turn ordinary errands into opportunities for progress.

## 1083 Funology Fables

**Speech Bin**
**1965 25th Avenue**
**Vero Beach, FL 32960**       **772-770-0007**
**800-477-3324**
**FAX 772-770-0006**
**http://www.speechbin.com**
**e-mail: info@speechbin.com**
*Shane Peters, Product Coordinator*
*Jen Binney, Owner*

Funology Fables targets specific phonemes and critical early concepts, such as matching, sequencing, opposites, comparisons, quantity, size, and space. Reproducible Talking Tales and activities include 32 six-part sequence stories. Item number 1484. *$45.00*

## 1084 Great Series

**Harcourt Achieve**
**6277 Sea Harbor Drive**
**Orlando, FL 32887**       **252-480-3200**
**800-531-5015**
**FAX 800-699-9459**
**http://www.steckvaughn.com**
**e-mail: info@steckvaughn.com**
*Billings, Author*
*Tim McEwen, President/CEO*
*Jeff Johnson, Dir Marketing Communications*
*Chris Lehmann, Team Coordinator*

Human drama makes beginning reading worth the effort. Eight exciting titles build confidence as they build skills. Short, easy-to-read selections enable limited readers to succeed with material that matters.

## 1085 Handprints

**Educators Publishing Service**
**31 Smith Place**
**Cambridge, MA 02139 9031**       **617-547-6706**
**800-225-5750**
**FAX 888-440-2665**
**http://www.epsbooks.com**
**e-mail: eps@epsbooks.com**
*Ann L Staman, Author*
*Steven Corte, President*

Handprints is a set of 50 storybooks and 4 workbooks for beginning readers in kindergarten and first grade. The storybooks increase in difficulty very gradually and encourage the new readers to use meaning, language, and print cues as they read.

**1086 High Interest Nonfiction**

Harcourt Achieve
6277 Sea Harbor Drive
Orlando, FL 32887                252-480-3200
                                800-531-5015
                        FAX 800-699-9459
                http://www.steckvaughn.com
                e-mail: info@steckvaughn.com
*Steck-Vaughn Staff, Author*
*Tim McEwen, President/CEO*
*Jeff Johnson, Dir Marketing Communications*
*Chris Lehmann, Team Coordinator*

Whether you want to promote the joy of reading or the thrill of reading riveting nonfiction, this series does the job. Amazing stories of adventure, mystery, escape, disaster, rescue, challenge, firsts, and heroes capture and hold student interest.

**1087 High Interest Nonfiction for Primary Grades**

Harcourt Achieve
6277 Sea Harbor Drive
Orlando, FL 32887                252-480-3200
                                800-531-5015
                        FAX 800-699-9459
                http://www.steckvaughn.com
                e-mail: info@steckvaughn.com
*Steck-Vaughn Staff, Author*
*Tim McEwen, President/CEO*
*Jeff Johnson, Dir Marketing Communications*
*Chris Lehmann, Team Coordinator*

Introduce students to a new type of reading in which the reader gains information! As students read nonfiction, they continue to develop and build comprehension skills and reading strategies. Fun and exciting stories are organized into four units that support the curriculum, such as people, animals, Earth and space , and more.

**1088 High Noon Books**

Academic Therapy Publications
20 Commercial Boulevard
Novato, CA 94949                415-883-3314
                                800-422-7249
                        FAX 888-287-9975
                http://www.academictherapy.com
                e-mail: sales@academictherapy.com
*Anna Arena, President*
*Jim Arena, Vice President*

Serving the field of learning disabilities for 35 years. High-interest books for reluctant readers, phonic remedial reading lessons, streamlined Shakespeare, etc.

**1089 I Can Read**

Teddy Bear Press
3639 Midway Drive
San Diego, CA 92110                619-223-7311
                        FAX 619-255-2158
                http://www.teddybearpress.net
                e-mail: fparker@teddybearpress.net
*Fran Parker, Author*
*Fran Parker, President*

A series of 7 reading books and 7 workbooks, a set of 52 flashcards and teacher manual which uses a sight word approach to teach beginning readers. These teacher created books and workbooks present an easy to use beginning reading program which provides repetition, visual motor, visual discrimination and word comprehension activities. It was created to teach young, learning disabled children and has been successfully employed to teach beginning readers of varying ages and abilities. *$80.00*

**1090 I Can See the ABC's**

Teddy Bear Press
3639 Midway Drive
San Diego, CA 92110                619-223-7311
                        FAX 619-255-2158
                http://www.teddybearpress.net
                e-mail: fparker@teddybearpress.net
*Fran Parker, Author*
*Fran Parker, President*

A big 11x17 which contains the pre-primer words found in the I Can Read program while introducing the alphabet. *$20.00*

**1091 Inclusion: Strategies for Working with Young Children**

Peytral Publications
PO Box 1162
Minnetonka, MN 55345                952-949-8707
                                877-739-8725
                        FAX 952-906-9777
                http://www.peytral.com
                e-mail: help@peytral.com
*Lorraine O Moore PhD, Author*
*Peggy Hammeken, Owner/Publisher*

This exceptional resource is a gold mine of developmentally based ideas to help children between the ages of 3-7 or older students who may be developmentally delayed. This is a very practical and easy-to-use publication which is appropriate for early childhood teachers, K-2 general and special education teachers. *$21.95*

*185 pages  Educators*
*ISBN 1-890455-33-4*

**1092 Island Reading Journey**

Sunburst Technology
400 Columbus Avenue
Valhalla, NY 10595 1349                914-747-3310
                                800-321-7511
                        FAX 914-747-4109
                http://www.sunburst.com
                e-mail: support@sunburst.com
*Mark Sotir, President*

Enhance your reading program with meaningful summary and extension activities for 100 intermediate level books. Students read for meaning while they engage in activities that test for comprehension, build writing skills with reader response and essay questions, develop usage skills with cloze activities and improve vocabulary/word attack skills.

**1093 It's a...Safari: Software**

**Speech Bin**
**1965 25th Avenue**
**Vero Beach, FL 32960**          772-770-0007
                                  800-477-3324
                            FAX 772-770-0006
                       http://www.speechbin.com
                       e-mail: info@speechbin.com
*Shane Peters, Product Coordinator*
*Jen Binney, Owner*

It's a Safari improves these critical skills: auditory processing; reading; spelling and comprehension. This unique Locu Tour language software presents a total of 100 short stories which describe the animals and people of Africa. Item number L190. *$29.00*

**1094 Just for Me! Phonological Awareness**

**LinguiSystems**
**3100 4th Avenue**
**East Moline, IL 61244**           309-775-2300
                                    800-776-4332
                              FAX 309-755-2377
                              TDY:800-933-8331
                       http://www.linguisystems.com
                       e-mail: service@linguisystems.com
*Margaret Warner, Author*
*Linda Bowers, Owner*
*Rosemary Huisingh, Owner*

Youngsters will love this cut, color, and create approach to sound awareness. You'll love how they begin to learn strong reading and literacy skills. The hands-on activities help students learn rhyming, syllables, compound words, beginning and ending sounds, short and long vowels, and beginning blends. *$24.95*

*154 pages  Ages 3-6*

**1095 Kids Media Magic 2.0**

**Sunburst Technology**
**400 Columbus Avenue**
**Valhalla, NY 10595**              914-747-3310
                                   800-321-7511
                             FAX 914-747-4109
                       http://www.sunburst.com
                       e-mail: service@sunburst.com
*Mark Sotir, President*

The first multimedia word processor designed for young children. Help your child become a fluent reader and writer. The Rebus Bar automatically scrolls over 45 vocabulary words as students type.

**1096 LD Teacher's IEP Companion**

**LinguiSystems**
**3100 4th Avenue**
**East Moline, IL 61244**           309-775-2300
                                    800-776-4332
                              FAX 309-755-2377
                              TDY:800-933-8331
                       http://www.linguisystems.com
                       e-mail: service@linguisystems.com
*Molly Lyle, Author*
*Linda Bowers, Owner*
*Rosemary Huisingh, Owner*

These IEP goals are organized developmentally by skill area with individual objectives and classroom activity suggestions. Goals and objectives cover these academic areas: math; reading; writing; literacy concepts; attention skills; study skills; classroom behavior; social interaction; and transition skills. *$39.95*

*169 pages  Ages 5-18*

**1097 Learning 100 Computerized Reading Skills**

**Harcourt Achieve**
**6277 Sea Harbor Drive**
**Orlando, FL 32887**               252-480-3200
                                    800-531-5015
                              FAX 800-699-9459
                       http://www.steckvaughn.com
                       e-mail: info@steckvaughn.com
*Steck-Vaughn Staff, Author*
*Tim McEwen, President/CEO*
*Jeff Johnson, Dir Marketing Communications*
*Chris Lehmann, Team Coordinator*

Now you can determine each individual's precise reading level and mastery of individual comprehension skills automatically with this extraordinary accurate, easy-to-use program. Computer-administered cloze and criterion referenced tests yield the results you need as well as personalized prescriptions.

**1098 Learning 100 Computerized Reading Skills: Inventory**

**Harcourt Achieve**
**6277 Sea Harbor Drive**
**Orlando, FL 32887**               252-480-3200
                                    800-531-5015
                              FAX 800-699-9459
                       http://www.steckvaughn.com
                       e-mail: info@steckvaughn.com
*Steck-Vaughn Staff, Author*
*Tim McEwen, President/CEO*
*Jeff Johnson, Dir Marketing Communications*
*Chris Lehmann, Team Coordinator*

Planning and placement without the guesswork. Now you can determine each individual's precise reading level and mastery of individual comprehension skills automatically with this extraordinary accurate, easy-to-use program.

**1099 Learning 100 Go Books**

**Harcourt Achieve**
**6277 Sea Harbor Drive**
**Orlando, FL 32887**               252-480-3200
                                    800-531-5015
                              FAX 800-699-9459
                       http://www.steckvaughn.com
                       e-mail: info@steckvaughn.com
*Steck-Vaughn Staff, Author*
*Tim McEwen, President/CEO*
*Jeff Johnson, Dir Marketing Communications*
*Chris Lehmann, Team Coordinator*

Go Books offer readers at all levels the opportunity to experience reading success with real-life content in an enjoyable environment. Softcover anthologies offer variety. Each book contains stories dealing with real-life situations in both fiction and nonfiction presentations.

**1100    Learning 100 Language Clues Software**

**Harcourt Achieve**
**6277 Sea Harbor Drive**
**Orlando, FL  32887**                 252-480-3200
                                       800-531-5015
                                   FAX 800-699-9459
                         http://www.steckvaughn.com
                         e-mail: info@steckvaughn.com
*Steck-Vaughn Staff, Author*
*Tim McEwen, President/CEO*
*Jeff Johnson, Dir Marketing Communications*
*Chris Lehmann, Team Coordinator*

When learners have control over their instruction, they are motivated to succeed. This program lets users customize instruction to their individual needs. They can control the speed of presentation, the number of times a word is used, and the length of time each word appears.

**1101    Learning 100 System**

**Harcourt Achieve**
**6277 Sea Harbor Drive**
**Orlando, FL  32887**                 252-480-3200
                                       800-531-5015
                                   FAX 800-699-9459
                         http://www.steckvaughn.com
                         e-mail: info@steckvaughn.com
*Steck-Vaughn Staff, Author*
*Tim McEwen, President/CEO*
*Jeff Johnson, Dir Marketing Communications*
*Chris Lehmann, Team Coordinator*

Deliver research-based reading strategies in the context of real-life stories. If your readers need extra motivation, this program is a must. Compelling, relevant stories coupled with audio instruction build vocabulary, comprehension, and confidence. Built on findings from 40 years of reading research, Learning 100 Reading Strategies is a proven performer for low-level readers.

**1102    Learning 100 Write and Read**

**Harcourt Achieve**
**6277 Sea Harbor Drive**
**Orlando, FL  32887**                 252-480-3200
                                       800-531-5015
                                   FAX 800-699-9459
                         http://www.steckvaughn.com
                         e-mail: info@steckvaughn.com
*Steck-Vaughn Staff, Author*
*Tim McEwen, President/CEO*
*Jeff Johnson, Dir Marketing Communications*
*Chris Lehmann, Team Coordinator*

Helps learners succeed with reading and writing opportunities they encounter every day. Learners improve grammar, mechanics, usage, style, and paragraphing skills through a proven program based on more than 40 years of research.

**1103    Let's Go Read 1: An Island Adventure**

**Riverdeep**
**500 Redmond Boulevard**
**Novato, CA  94947**                  415-763-4700
                                       800-362-2890
                                   FAX 415-763-4385
                            http://www.edmark.com
                            e-mail: info@riverdeep.net
*Barry O'Callaghan, Chairman/CEO*
*Simon Calver, COO*
*John Rim, CFO*

Take off with Robby the Raccoon, Emily the Squirrel and the Reading Rover on an exciting adventure to an island inhabited by the alphabet. Motivated by the delight of mastering new challenges, your child will play through more than 35 fun activties that install and reinforce the essential skills for successful reading.

**1104    Let's Go Read 2: An Ocean Adventure**

**Riverdeep**
**500 Redmond Boulevard**
**Novato, CA  94947**                  415-763-4700
                                       800-362-2890
                                   FAX 415-763-4385
                            http://www.edmark.com
                            e-mail: info@riverdeep.net
*Barry O'Callaghan, Chairman/CEO*
*Simon Calver, COO*
*John Rim, CFO*

Building upon your child's mastery of letters, Let's Go Read: 2 explores how letters combine to form words, and how words combine to express meaning. Dozens of captivating, skill-building activities teach your child the skills to sound out, recognize, build and comprehend hundreds of new words. It's an endlessly fun voyage toward reading fluency!

**1105    Let's Read**

**Educators Publishing Service**
**31 Smith Place**
**Cambridge, MA  02139 9031**          617-547-6706
                                       800-225-5750
                                   FAX 888-440-2665
                            http://www.epsbooks.com
                            e-mail: eps@epsbooks.com
*Leonard Bloomfield, Clarence and Robert*
*Barnhart, Author*
*Steven Corte, President*

Using a linguistic approach to teaching reading skills, this series emphasizes relationship of spelling to sound, presenting the concepts together, and providing nine reading books and accompanying workbooks for practice. Provides classroom directions and suggestions for supplementary exercises.

**1106    Lighthouse Low Vision Products**

**Lighthouse International**
**111 East 59th Street**
**New York, NY  10022 1202**           212-821-9740
                                       800-829-0500
                                   FAX 212-821-9707
                            http://www.lighthouse.org
                            e-mail: info@lighthouse.com
*Wendy Maurice, Managing Director*
*Barbara Silverstone, President/CEO*

Helping people who are blind or partially sighted to lead independent and productive lives.

**1107  Linamood Program (LIPS Clinical
Version):Phoneme Sequencing Program for
Reading, Spelling,Speech**

**LinguiSystems**
**3100 4th Avenue**
**East Moline, IL  61244**            309-775-2300
                                      800-776-4332
                                  FAX 309-755-2377
                                  TDY:800-933-8331
                        http://www.linguisystems.com
                        e-mail: service@linguisystems.com
*Patricia Linamood, Phyllis Linamood, Author*
*Linda Bowers, Owner*
*Rosemary Huisingh, Owner*

Help your students develop phoneme awareness for
competence in reading, spelling, and speech. This
multisensory program meets the needs of the many
children and adults who don't develop phonemic
awareness through traditional methods. *$247.00*

*Birth-Adult*

**1108  Mastering Reading Series**

**AGS Publishing**
**4201 Woodland Road**
**Circle Pines, MN  55014 1796**      651-287-7220
                                      800-328-2560
                                  FAX 800-471-8457
                        http://www.agsnet.com
                        e-mail: agsmail@agsnet.com
*Kevin Brueggeman, President*
*Matt Keller, Marketing Manager*

With an interest level of High School through Adult,
and a reading level of Grade 3-7, this series will help
your students build reading and life skills while learning about specific occupations. Each series features
four books of increasing complexity in reading level,
allowing learners to work at their own pace to master
essential reading skills. The five series titles are: Office Work; Health Care; Commercial Trucking; Food
Service and Manufacturing.

**1109  Megawords**

**Educators Publishing Service**
**31 Smith Place**
**Cambridge, MA  02139 9031**         617-547-6706
                                      800-225-5750
                                  FAX 888-440-2665
                        http://www.epsbooks.com
                        e-mail: eps@epsbooks.com
*Kristin Johnson, Polly Baird, Author*
*Steven Corte, President*

A series with a systematic, multisensory approach to
learning the longer words encountered from fourth
grade on. Students first work with syllables, then combine the syllables into words, use them in context, and
work to increase their reading and spelling proficiency. Teacher's Guide and Answer Key available.

**1110  Mike Mulligan & His Steam Shovel**

**Sunburst Technology**
**400 Columbus Avenue**
**Valhalla, NY  10595 1349**          914-747-3310
                                      800-321-7511
                                  FAX 914-747-4109
                        http://www.sunburst.com
                        e-mail: service@sunburst.com
*Mark Sotir, President*

This CD-ROM version of the Caldecott classic lets
students experience interactive book reading and participate in four skills-based extension activities that
promote memory, matching, sequencing, listening,
pattern recognition and map reading skills.

**1111  More Primary Phonics**

**Educators Publishing Service**
**31 Smith Place**
**Cambridge, MA  02139 9031**         617-547-6706
                                      800-225-5750
                                  FAX 888-440-2665
                        http://www.epsbooks.com
                        e-mail: eps@epsbooks.com
*Barbara Makar, Author*
*Steven Corte, President*

Reinforces and expands skills developed in Primary
Phonics. Workbooks and storybooks contain the same
phonetic elements, sight words and phonetic sequences as workbooks 1 and 2.

**1112  Mythopoly**

**LinguiSystems**
**3100 4th Avenue**
**East Moline, IL  61244**            309-775-2300
                                      800-776-4332
                                  FAX 309-755-2377
                                  TDY:800-933-8331
                        http://www.linguisystems.com
                        e-mail: service@linguisystems.com
*Mike LoGiudice, Carolyn LoGiudice, Author*
*Linda Bowers, Owner*
*Rosemary Huisingh, Owner*

Boost your student's reading and listening comprehension skills with this wonderful game. Engaging
stories from classical mythology help students understand references to mythological concepts in literature and everyday life. The reading level of the 25
stories ranges from grades 3.5 to 5.2. *$44.95*

*Ages 10-18*

**1113  New Way: Learning with Literature**

**Harcourt Achieve**
**6277 Sea Harbor Drive**
**Orlando, FL  32887**                252-480-3200
                                      800-531-5015
                                  FAX 800-699-9459
                        http://www.steckvaughn.com
                        e-mail: info@steckvaughn.com
*Steck-Vaughn Staff, Author*
*Tim McEwen, President/CEO*
*Jeff Johnson, Dir Marketing Communications*
*Chris Lehmann, Team Coordinator*

# Classroom Resources /Reading

Do you need additional literature your primary readers can read independently? Steck-Vaughn offers a large collection of developmentally appropriate titles at attractive prices.

**1114 Next Stop**

**Educators Publishing Service**
**31 Smith Place**
**Cambridge, MA 02139 9031**     **617-547-6706**
**800-225-5750**
**FAX 888-440-2665**
**http://www.epsbooks.com**
**e-mail: eps@epsbooks.com**
*Tanya Auger, Author*
*Steven Corte, President*

Increase reading and language skills while exploring different literacy genres. This series is intended for students who are ready to move beyond phonetically controlled readers to the nest stop-real chapter books that will help prepare them for the more challenging literature they will encounter in later grades.

**1115 PATHS**

**Speech Bin**
**1965 25th Avenue**
**Vero Beach, FL 32960**     **772-770-0007**
**800-477-3324**
**FAX 772-770-0006**
**http://www.speechbin.com**
**e-mail: info@speechbin.com**
*Shane Peters, Product Coordinator*
*Jen Binney, Owner*

PATHS gives you a step-by-step comprehensive program for students who have experienced difficulty in academic learning. It targets skills critical for academic achievements: phonological awareness; phonemic relationships; phonemic processing; and listening and memory. Item number 1491. *$21.95*

**1116 Patterns of English Spelling**

**AVKO Dyslexia Research Foundation**
**3084 W Willard Road**
**Clio, MI 48420 7801**     **810-686-9283**
**866-285-6612**
**FAX 810-686-1101**
**http:// www.spelling.org**
**e-mail: avkoemail@aol.com**
*Don McCabe, Author*
*Don McCabe, Research Director*

Use the index to locate the page upon which you can find all the words that share the same patterns. If you look up the word cat, you will find all the pages where all the at words are located. If you look up the word precious you will find all the words ending in cious. There are ten volumes which can be purchased all together or separately. *$119.95*

*Whole set*

**1117 Phonemic Awareness: The Sounds of Reading**

**Peytral Publication**
**PO Box 1162**
**Minnetonka, MN 55345**     **952-949-8707**
**877-739-8725**
**FAX 952-906-9777**
**http://www.peytral.com**
**e-mail: help@peytral.com**
*Victoria Groves Scott, Author*
*Victoria Scott, Author*
*Peggy Peytral, Publisher*

In this dynamic new video, Dr. Scott demonstrates the principal components of phonemic awareness: identification; comparison; segmentation; blending and rhyming. This video will help you to better understand phonemic awareness training and will show you how to apply these components not only to the reading curriculum but to all subjects through the school day. Filmed in actual classroom settings. *$59.95*

*25 minute video*
*ISBN 1-890455-29-6*

**1118 Phonological Awareness Kit**

**LinguiSystems**
**3100 4th Avenue**
**East Moline, IL 61244**     **309-775-2300**
**800-776-4332**
**FAX 309-755-2377**
**TDY:800-933-8331**
**http://www.linguisystems.com**
**e-mail: service@linguisystems.com**
*Carolyn Robertson, Wanda Salter, Author*
*Linda Bowers, Owner*
*Rosemary Huisingh, Owner*

Help your students learn to use phonological information to process oral and written language with this fantastic kit. Written by an SLP and special educator, this best-seller links sound awareness, oral language, and early reading and writing skills. The kit uses a multisensory approach to ensure success for all learning styles. *$69.95*

*115 pages Ages 5-8*

**1119 Poetry in Three Dimensions: Reading, Writing and Critical Thinking Skills through Poetry**

**Educators Publishing Service**
**31 Smith Place**
**Cambridge, MA 02139 9031**     **617-547-6706**
**800-225-5750**
**FAX 888-440-2665**
**http://www.epsbooks.com**
**e-mail: eps@epsbooks.com**
*Carol Clark, Alison Draper, Author*
*Steven Corte, President*

Help your students improve their reading comprehension and writing through the study of poetry in this collection of multicultural poems. With poems and questions on facing pages, students are encouraged to annotate the text of the poem and to go back to the text to respond to the questions.

144

**1120  Polar Express**

**Sunburst Technology**
**400 Columbus Avenue**
**Valhalla, NY  10595 1349**          **914-747-3310**
                                       **800-321-7511**
                                  **FAX 914-747-4109**
                       **http://www.sunburst.com**
           **e-mail: service@sunburst.com**
*Mark Sotir, President*

Share the magic and enchantment of the holiday season with this CD-ROM version of Chris Van Allsburg's Caldecott-winning picture book.

**1121  Prehistoric Creaures Then & Now: Steadwell**

**Harcourt Achieve**
**6277 Sea Harbor Drive**
**Orlando, FL  32887**                 **252-480-3200**
                                       **800-531-5015**
                                  **FAX 800-699-9459**
                   **http://www.steckvaughn.com**
           **e-mail: info@steckvaughn.com**
*Steck-Vaughn Staff, Author*
*Tim McEwen, President/CEO*
*Jeff Johnson, Dir Marketing Communications*
*Chris Lehmann, Team Coordinator*

When reading is a struggle, academic success is even harder to achieve. Now you can put social studies and science curriculum content within reach of every students with Steadwell Books — the series designed specifically for limited readers. Attention-getting photos and informative illustrations, maps, and time lines communicate the social studies and science concepts found in the text.

**1122  Primary Phonics**

**Educators Publishing Service**
**31 Smith Place**
**Cambridge, MA  02139 9031**          **617-547-6706**
                                       **800-225-5750**
                                  **FAX 888-440-2665**
                       **http://www.epsbooks.com**
           **e-mail: eps@epsbooks.com**
*Barbara Makar, Author*
*Steven Corte, President*

This revised program of storybooks and coordinated workbooks teaches reading for grades K-2. There is a set of ten storybooks to go with each of the first five workbooks. A Primary Phonics Picture Dictionary contains 2,500 commonly used words, including most of the words in the series. This series' individualized nature permits students to progress at their own speed. Teacher's manual available.

**1123  Racing Through Time on a Flying Machine**

**Harcourt Achieve**
**6277 Sea Harbor Drive**
**Orlando, FL  32887**                 **252-480-3200**
                                       **800-531-5015**
                                  **FAX 800-699-9459**
                   **http://www.steckvaughn.com**
           **e-mail: info@steckvaughn.com**
*Elizabeth Werley-Prieto, Mike Lester, Author*
*Tim McEwen, President/CEO*
*Jeff Johnson, Dir Marketing Communications*
*Chris Lehmann, Team Coordinator*

Traveling through time to visit Thomas Edison and Leonardo da Vinci inspires young Keene to become an inventor himself.

**1124  Read On! Plus**

**Sunburst Technology**
**400 Columbus Avenue**
**Valhalla, NY  10595 1349**          **914-747-3310**
                                       **800-321-7511**
                                  **FAX 914-747-4109**
                       **http://www.sunburst.com**
           **e-mail: support@sunburst.com**
*Mark Sotir, President*

Promote skills and strategies that improve reading comprehension, and build appreciation for literature and the written word.

**1125  Read-A-Bit**

**LinguiSystems**
**3100 4th Avenue**
**East Moline, IL  61244**             **309-775-2300**
                                       **800-776-4332**
                                  **FAX 309-755-2377**
                             **TDY:800-933-8331**
                   **http://www.linguisystems.com**
           **e-mail: service@linguisystems.com**
*Dagmar Kafka, Author*
*Linda Bowers, Owner*
*Rosemary Huisingh, Owner*

Get 15 games in one box! Six decks of cards with different levels of reading difficulty work with and without the colorful game board to give you plenty of flexibility. You'll work through a hierarchy of reading skills from primer to grade 3. Students practice consonants, vowels, controlled R sounds, sight words, and more. *$41.95*

*Ages 5-9*

**1126  Reader's Quest I**

**Sunburst Technology**
**400 Columbus Avenue**
**Valhalla, NY  10595 1349**          **914-747-3310**
                                       **800-321-7511**
                                  **FAX 914-747-4109**
                       **http://www.sunburst.com**
           **e-mail: support@sunburst.com**
*Mark Sotir, President*

These reading workshops provide students with direct reading instruction, interactive practice activities, and practical strategies to ensure reading success.

**1127  Reader's Quest II**

**Sunburst Technology**
**400 Columbus Avenue**
**Valhalla, NY  10595 1349**          **914-747-3310**
                                       **800-321-7511**
                                  **FAX 914-747-4109**
                       **http://www.sunburst.com**
           **e-mail: support@sunburst.com**
*Mark Sotir, President*

# Classroom Resources /Reading

These reading workshops provide students with direct reading instruction, interactive practice activities, and practical strategies to ensure reading success.

**1128  Reading Comprehension Bundle**

Sunburst Technology
400 Columbus Avenue
Valhalla, NY  10595 1349          914-747-3310
                                 800-321-7511
                            FAX 914-747-4109
                         http://www.sunburst.com
                    e-mail: support@sunburst.com
*Mark Sotir, President*

This collection for the intermediate-level classroom develops the skills students need to read for meaning and understanding.

**1129  Reading Comprehension Game Intermediate**

LinguiSystems
3100 4th Avenue
East Moline, IL  61244           309-775-2300
                                 800-776-4332
                            FAX 309-755-2377
                            TDY:800-933-8331
                      http://www.linguisystems.com
                  e-mail: service@linguisystems.com
*Linda Bowers, Rosemary Huisingh, Carolyn
LoGiudice, Author
Linda Bowers, Owner
Rosemary Huisingh, Owner*

This game gives you fun, repetitive practice in three essential reading comprehension skills. The first is Reading for Details including cloze, referents, sequencing, describing, and more! The second is Reading for Understanding including main idea, paraphrasing, context clues, defining, and more. The thrid area is Going Beyond including making references, predicting, and making associations. *$44.95*

*Ages 12-18*

**1130  Reading Comprehension Materials (Volume 5)**

Speech Bin
1965 25th Avenue
Vero Beach, FL  32960            772-770-0007
                                 800-477-3324
                            FAX 772-770-0006
                       http://www.speechbin.com
                    e-mail: info@speechbin.com
*Shane Peters, Product Coordinator
Jen Binney, Owner*

Three hundred and fifty-one pages of practical large-print materials give older children and adults practice thinking about words, following directions, and telling what/who stories, stories in part, short stories, and more. Stories are either high-interest factual stories or relate to everyday experiences. Tasks are versatile and a variety of difficulties for maximum use. Item number V372. *$49.95*

**1131  Reading Comprehension Series**

Harcourt Achieve
6277 Sea Harbor Drive
Orlando, FL  32887               252-480-3200
                                 800-531-5015
                            FAX 800-699-9459
                      http://www.steckvaughn.com
                   e-mail: info@steckvaughn.com
*Resnick, Author
Tim McEwen, President/CEO
Jeff Johnson, Dir Marketing Communications
Chris Lehmann, Team Coordinator*

Develop basic reading skills! Short stories sustain interest! Brief, captivating selections feature children and animals in contemporary situations. Exercises build comprehension skills! Exercises cover all aspects of reading comprehension, including main idea, sequencing, facts, and inferences.

**1132  Reading Comprehension in Varied Subject Matter**

Educators Publishing Service
31 Smith Plaza
Cambridge, MA  02139 9031        617-547-6706
                                 800-225-5750
                            FAX 888-440-2665
                         http://www.epsbooks.com
                     e-mail: eps@epsbooks.com
*Jane Ervin, Author
Steven Corte, President*

Ten workbooks that present a wide range of people and situations with new reading selections, new vocabulary, and a new writing exercise. Each book contains 31 selections in the subject areas of social studies, science, literature, mathematics, philosophy, logic, language, and the arts.

**1133  Reading Pen**

Wizcom Technologies
257 Great Road
Acton, MA  01720                 978-635-5357
                                 888-777-0552
                            FAX 978-929-9228
                       http://www.wizcomtech.com
                  e-mail: usasales@wizcomtech.com
*Ranz Itchiyake, President
Chris Anderton, Business Development Officer*

Portable assitive reading device that reads words aloud and can be used anywhere. Scans a word from printed text, displays the word in large characters, reads the word aloud from built-in speaker or ear phones and defines the word with the press of a button. Displays syllables, keeps a history of scanned words, adjustable for left or right-handed use. Includes a tutorial video and audio cassette. Not recommended for persons with low vision or impaired fine motor control. *$279.00*

**1134  Reading Power Modules Books**

Harcourt Achieve
6277 Sea Harbor Drive
Orlando, FL  32887                252-480-3200
                                  800-531-5015
                              FAX 800-699-9459
                      http://www.steckvaughn.com
                      e-mail: info@steckvaughn.com
*Tim McEwen, President/CEO*
*Joan Phifer, Manager*
*Chris Lehmann, Team Coordinator*

Supplementary reading based on 4 decades of reading research. Companion books give students and teachers a choice of formats. High interest stories reinforce reading comprehension skills while building vocabulary, spelling skills, reading fluency, and speed.

**1135  Reading Power Modules Software**

Harcourt Achieve
6277 Sea Harbor Drive
Orlando, FL  32887                252-480-3200
                                  800-531-5015
                              FAX 800-699-9459
                      http://www.steckvaughn.com
                      e-mail: info@steckvaughn.com
*Steck-Vaughn Staff, Author*
*Tim McEwen, President/CEO*
*Jeff Johnson, Dir Marketing Communications*
*Chris Lehmann, Team Coordinator*

This program provides practice and reinforcement of reading comprehension skills while building spelling and reading skills and vocabulary. Exercises include requiring learners to type the new vocabulary word after it flashes on the screen, fill-in-the-blank exercises, timed reading exercises, comprehension checks, vocabulary review in multiple-choice format, and vocabulary games.

**1136  Reading Readiness**

Harcourt Achieve
6277 Sea Harbor Drive
Orlando, FL  32887                252-480-3200
                                  800-531-5015
                              FAX 800-699-9459
                      http://www.steckvaughn.com
                      e-mail: info@steckvaughn.com
*Steck Vaughn Staff, Author*
*Tim McEwen, President/CEO*
*Jeff Johnson, Dir Marketing Communications*
*Chris Lehmann, Team Coordinator*

Build a firm foundation for reading success with thematic workbooks that introduce readiness skills through literature. Fun-filled nursery rhymes, riddles, and tongue twisters focus on the key words and sound/letter patterns that precede decoding skills.

**1137  Reading Skills Bundle**

Sunburst Technology
400 Columbus Avenue
Valhalla, NY  10595 1349          914-747-3310
                                  800-321-7511
                              FAX 914-747-4109
                        http://www.sunburst.com
                      e-mail: support@sunburst.com
*Mark Sotir, President*

Teach beginning reading with teacher-developed programs that sequentially present phonics, phonemic awareness, word recognition, and reading comprehension concepts.

**1138  Reading Who? Reading You!**

Sunburst Technology
400 Columbus Avenue
Valhalla, NY  10595 1349          914-747-3310
                                  800-321-7511
                              FAX 914-747-4109
                        http://www.sunburst.com
                      e-mail: support@sunburst.com
*Mark Sotir, President*

Teach beginning reading skills effectively with phonics instruction built into engaging games and puzzles that have children asking for more.

**1139  Reading and Writing Workbook**

Therapro
225 Arlington Street
Framingham, MA  01702 8723        508-872-9494
                                  800-257-5376
                              FAX 508-875-2062
                     http://www.theraproducts.com
                     e-mail: info@theraproducts.com
*Therapro Staff, Author*
*Karen Conrad, President*

Writing checks and balancing a checkbook, copying words and sentences, and writing messages and notes. Helps with recognition and understanding of calendars, phone books and much more. *$10.50*

**1140  Reading for Content**

Educators Publishing Service
31 Smith Place
Cambridge, MA  02139 9031         617-547-6706
                                  800-225-5750
                              FAX 888-440-2665
                          http://www.epsbooks.com
                       e-mail: eps@epsbooks.com
*Carol Einstein, Author*
*Steven Corte, President*

Reading for Content is a series of 4 books designed to help students improve their reading comprehension skills. Each book contains 43 pasages followed by 4 questions. Two questions ask for a recall of main ideas, and two ask the student to draw conclusions from what they have just read.

**1141  Reading for Job and Personal Use**

AGS Publishing
4201 Woodland Road
Circle Pines, MN  55014 1796      651-287-7220
                                  800-328-2560
                              FAX 800-471-8457
                            http://www.agsnet.com
                       e-mail: agsmail@agsnet.com
*Joyce Hing-McGowan, Author*
*Kevin Brueggeman, President*
*Matt Keller, Marketing Manager*

# Classroom Resources /Reading

The practical, real-life exercises in these texts teach students how to read and comprehend catalogs, training manuals, letters and memos, signs, reports, charts, and more. *$14.95*

**1142  Ready to Read**

**Educators Publishing Service**
**31 Smith Place**
**Cambridge, MA  02139 9031**        617-547-6706
                                    800-225-5750
                               FAX 888-440-2665
                         http://www.epsbooks.com
                        e-mail: eps@epsbooks.com
*Phyllis Bertin, Eileen Perlman, Author*
*Steven Corte, President*

Ready to Read contains activities for teaching sound/symbol association, blending, word recognition, reading, spelling and handwriting, including individual words, phrases, sentences, and connected text.

**1143  Reasoning & Reading Series**

**Educators Publishing Service**
**31 Smith Place**
**Cambridge, MA  02139 9031**        617-547-6706
                                    800-225-5750
                               FAX 888-440-2665
                         http://www.epsbooks.com
                        e-mail: eps@epsbooks.com
*Joanne Carlisle, Author*
*Steven Corte, President*

These workbooks develop basic language and thinking skills that build the foundation for reading comprehension. Exercises reinforce reading as a critical reasoning activity. Many exercises encourage students to come up with their own response in instances where there is no single correct answer. In other cases, exercises lend themselves to students working collaboratively to see how many different answers satisfy a question.

**1144  Right into Reading: A Phonics-Based Reading and Comprehension Program**

**Educators Publishing Service**
**31 Smith Place**
**Cambridge, MA  02139 9031**        617-547-6706
                                    800-225-5750
                               FAX 888-440-2665
                         http://www.epsbooks.com
                        e-mail: eps@epsbooks.com
*Jane Ervin, Author*
*Steven Corte, President*

Right into Reading introduces phonics skills in a carefully ordered sequence of bite-size lessons so that students can progress easily and successfully from one reading level to the next. The stories and selections are unusually diverse and interactive.

**1145  Roots, Prefixes & Suffixes**

**Sunburst Technology**
**400 Columbus Avenue**
**Valhalla, NY  10595 1349**        914-747-3310
                                    800-321-7511
                               FAX 914-747-4109
                         http://www.sunburst.com
                       e-mail: support@sunburst.com
*Mark Sotir, President*

Students learn to decode difficult and more complex words as they engage in six activities where they construct and dissect words with roots, prefixes and suffixes.

**1146  See Me Add**

**Teddy Bear Press**
**3639 Midway Drive**
**San Diego, CA  92110**            619-223-7311
                               FAX 619-255-2158
                    http://www.teddybearpress.net
                   e-mail: fparker@teddybearpress.net
*Fran Parker, Author*
*Fran Parker, President*

Introduces the concept of addition using simple story problems and the basic sight word vocabulary found in the I Can Read and Reading Is Fun programs. *$20.00*

**1147  See Me Subtract**

**Teddy Bear Press**
**3639 Midway Drive**
**San Diego, CA  92110**            619-223-7311
                               FAX 619-255-2158
                    http://www.teddybearpress.net
                   e-mail: fparker@teddybearpress.net
*Fran Parker, Author*
*Fran Parker, President*

Introduces the concept of subtraction using simple story problems. *$20.00*

**1148  Short Classics**

**Harcourt Achieve**
**6277 Sea Harbor Drive**
**Orlando, FL  32887**              252-480-3200
                                    800-531-5015
                               FAX 800-699-9459
                       http://www.steckvaughn.com
                     e-mail: info@steckvaughn.com
*Steck-Vaughn Staff, Author*
*Tim McEwen, President/CEO*
*Jeff Johnson, Dir Marketing Communications*
*Chris Lehmann, Team Cooridnator*

These shortened easy-to-read presentations use carefully controlled vocabulary while maintaining the style of the original authors. Your students can broaden their horizons and build self-esteem as they succeed with literary classics.

**1149  Soaring Scores CTB: TerraNova Reading and Language Arts**

Harcourt Achieve
6277 Sea Harbor Drive
Orlando, FL  32887                    252-480-3200
                                      800-531-5015
                                   FAX 800-699-9459
                            http://www.steckvaughn.com
                            e-mail: info@steckvaughn.com

*Steck-Vaughn Staff, Author*
*Tim McEwen, President/CEO*
*Jeff Johnson, Dir Marketing Communications*
*Chris Lehmann, Team Coordinator*

Through a combination of targeted instructional practice and testing-taking tips, these workbooks help students build better skills and improve CTB-TerraNova tests scores. Initial lessons address reading comprehension and language arts. The authentic practice test mirrors the CTB's format and content.


**1150  Soaring Scores on the ISAT Reading and Writing**

Harcourt Achieve
6277 Sea Harbor Drive
Orlando, FL  32887                    252-480-3200
                                      800-531-5015
                                   FAX 800-699-9459
                            http://www.steckvaughn.com
                            e-mail: info@steckvaughn.com

*Steck-Vaughn Staff, Author*
*Tim McEwen, President/CEO*
*Jeff Johnson, Dir Marketing Communications*
*Chris Lehmann, Team Cooridnator*

Highly targeted instruction and practice tests help students approach the ISAT strategically and confidently. Writing prompts ask students to write a persuasive, expository, or narrative essay. Modeled questions practice both multiple-choice and open-ended queries.


**1151  Sounds Abound Program**

LinguiSystems
3100 4th Avenue
East Moline, IL  61244                309-775-2300
                                      800-776-4332
                                   FAX 309-755-2377
                                   TDY:800-933-8331
                            http://www.linguisystems.com
                            e-mail: service@linguisystems.com

*Orna Lenchner PhD, Blanche Podhajski PhD, Author*
*Linda Bowers, Owner*
*Rosemary Huisingh, Owner*

This program boosts emergent reading and beginning literacy through a hierarchy of skills. Activities target rhyming, syllables, sound recognition, sound production, sound blending, phoneme-grapheme correspondence, and more phonological skills. *$109.95*

*112 pages  Ages 4-8*


**1152  Source for Aphasia Therapy**

LinguiSystems
3100 4th Avenue
East Moline, IL  61244                309-775-2300
                                      800-776-4332
                                   FAX 309-755-2377
                                   TDY:800-933-8331
                            http://www.linguisystems.com
                            e-mail: service@linguisystems.com

*Lisa A Arnold, Author*
*Linda Bowers, Owner*
*Rosemary Huisingh, Owner*

Therapy exercises are organized into three groups: receptive language, reading comprehension, and expressive language. Each section is organized in a hierarchy to meet each client's individual needs. You'll cover imitating gestures, following commands, understanding symbols and signs, naming and describing objects, and much more! *$41.95*

*183 pages  Adults*


**1153  Source for Dyslexia and Dysgraphia**

LinguiSystems
3100 4th Avenue
East Moline, IL  61244                309-775-2300
                                      800-776-4332
                                   FAX 309-755-2377
                                   TDY:800-933-8331
                            http://www.linguisystems.com
                            e-mail: service@linguisystems.com

*Regina G Richards, Author*
*Linda Bowers, Owner*
*Rosemary Huisingh, Owner*

From diagnosis to developmental strategies to how-to techniques, this is the definitivie SOURCE on students who have difficulty with the reading and writing process. *$41.95*

*308 pages  Ages 6-18*


**1154  Source for Early Literacy Development**

LinguiSystems
3100 4th Avenue
East Moline, IL  61244                309-775-2300
                                      800-776-4332
                                   FAX 309-755-2377
                                   TDY:800-933-8331
                            http://www.linguisystems.com
                            e-mail: service@linguisystems.com

*Linda K Crowe, Sara S Reichmuth, Author*
*Linda Bowers, Owner*
*Rosemary Huisingh, Owner*

This great resource gives you the latest information on children's emergent reading and writing from birth through age eight. You'll also get helpful strategies to facilitate literacy development for future academic success! *$ 41.95*

*151 pages  Birth-8*

**1155 Specialized Program Individualizing Reading Excellence (SPIRE)**

Educators Publishing Service
31 Smith Place
Cambridge, MA  02139 9031

800-225-5750
FAX 207-985-3878
http://www.espbooks.com
e-mail: spire@espbooks.com

*Sheila Clark-Edmonds, President*

SPIRE is a comprehensive multisensory reading and language arts program for students with learning differences.

**1156 Starting Comprehension**

Educators Publishing Service
31 Smith Place
Cambridge, MA  02139 9031

617-547-6706
800-225-5750
FAX 888-440-2665
http://www.epsbooks.com
e-mail: eps@epsbooks.com

*Ann L Staman, Author*
*Steven Corte, President*

A reading series of 12 workbooks that develops essential comprehension skills at the earliest reading level. It is divided into two different strands, one for students who have a strong visual sense, the other for those who learn sounds easily. Vocabulary introduced within context of exercises, using most of the words in the books. Student relates the details of the passage to the main idea.

**1157 Stories and More: Animal Friends**

Riverdeep
500 Redmond Boulevard
Novato, CA  94947

415-763-4700
800-362-2890
FAX 415-763-4385
http://www.elmark.com
e-mail: info@riverdeep.net

*Barry O'Callaghan, Chairman/CEO*
*Simon Calver, COO*
*John Rim, CFO*

Stories and More: Animal Friends features three well-known stories — The Gunnywolf, The Trek, and Owl and the Moon — with engaging activities that strengthen students reading comprehension. A scaffolding of pre-reading, reading, and post-reading activities for each story helps kindergarten and 1st grade students practice prediction and sequencing skills; appreciate the importance of character and setting; and respond to literature through writing, drawing, and speaking. *$ 69.95*

**1158 Stories and More: Time and Place**

Riverdeep
500 Redwod Boulevard
Novato, CA  97947

415-763-4700
800-362-2890
FAX 415-763-4385
http://www.edmark.com
e-mail: info@riverdeep.net

*Barry O'Callaghan, Chairman/CEO*
*Simon Calver, COO*
*John Rim, CFO*

Stories and More: Time and Place combines three well-loved stories — The House on Maple Street, Roxaboxen, and Galimoto — with — engaging activities that strengthen students' reading comprehension. In these books, the setting plays a primary role. Second and third grade students learn the importance of time, culture, and place in our lives.

**1159 Success Stories 1, 2**

Educators Publishing Service
31 Smith Plaza
Cambridge, MA  02139 9031

617-547-6706
800-225-5750
FAX 888-440-2665
http://www.epsbooks.com
e-mail: eps@epsbooks.com

*Elizabeth H Butcher, Nancy A Simonetti, Author*
*Steven Corte, President*

These workbooks contain high-interest phonetically structured stories. Each book contains 60 stories, each story focusing on an individual grapheme or syllable pattern.

**1160 Take Me Home Pair-It Books**

Harcourt Achieve
6277 Sea Harbor Drive
Orlando, FL  32887

252-480-3200
800-531-5015
FAX 800-699-9459
http://www.steckvaughn.com
e-mail: info@steckvaughn.com

*Park, Author*
*Tim McEwen, President/CEO*
*Jeff Johnson, Dir Marketing Communications*
*Chris Lehmann, Team Coordinator*

Make reading time a family favorite. Our most popular Pair-It Book titles in convenient take-home packages make it easy to get parents involved in reinforcing reading.

**1161 Taking Your Camera To...Steadwell**

Harcourt Achieve
6277 Sea Harbor Drive
Orlando, FL  32887

252-480-3200
800-531-5015
FAX 800-699-9459
http://www.steckvaughn.com
e-mail: info@steckvaughn.com

*Park, Author*
*Tim McEwen, President/CEO*
*Jeff Johnson, Dir Marketing Communications*
*Chris Lehmann, Team Coordinator*

Give limited readers unlimited access to major countries! Each title devotes a spread to the land, the people, major cities, lifestyles, places to visit, government and religion, earning a living, sports and school, food and holidays, quick facts, statistics and maps, and the future.

**1162  That's LIFE! Reading Comprehension**

**LinguiSystems**
**3100 4th Avenue**
**East Moline, IL  61244**          309-775-2300
                                     800-776-4332
                                 FAX 309-755-2377
                                 TDY:800-933-8331
                    http://www.linguisystems.com
                  e-mail: service@linguisystems.com
*LinguiSystems Staff, Author*
*Linda Bowers, Owner*
*Rosemary Huisingh, Owner*

Get two programs in one. Each high-interest reading passage is written at an upper and lower reading level to meet your students' needs. These lessons are great for individuals or classroom istruction. Each story is followed by thought-provoking comprehension questions, including multiple choice, fill-in-the-blank, true/false, and critical thinking questions. *$37.95*

*191 pages  Ages 11-18*

**1163  Tic-Tac-Read and Match: Fun Phonics Games**

**LinguiSystems**
**3100 4th Avenue**
**East Moline, IL  61244**          309-775-2300
                                     800-776-4332
                                 FAX 309-755-2377
                                 TDY:800-933-8331
                    http://www.linguisystems.com
                  e-mail: service@linguisystems.com
*Carol A Vaccariello, Author*
*Linda Bowers, Owner*
*Rosemary Huisingh, Owner*

Two-books set offers fun activities to reinforce reading. Use the whole page to play Read and Match. Use the nine shaded areas to play Tic-Tac-Read. Students move progressively through a hierarchy of phonics skills as they read the words aloud while playing. *$38.90*

*160 pages  Ages 7-14*

**1164  Transition Stage 2-3**

**Harcourt Achieve**
**6277 Sea Harbor Drive**
**Orlando, FL  32887**              252-480-3200
                                     800-531-5015
                                 FAX 800-699-9459
                     http://www.steckvaughn.com
                    e-mail: info@steckvaughn.com
*Steck-Vaughn Staff, Author*
*Tim McEwen, President/CEO*
*Jeff Johnson, Dir Marketing Communications*
*Chris Lehmann, Team Coordinator*

A series of 20 books, each containing 16 pages, that provide readers with a gradual transition into early fluency. All stories are available on audio cassette, and four are available in big book format.

**1165  Understanding Me**

**Churchill Center and School for Learning Disabili**
**1035 Price School Lane**
**Saint Louis, MO  63124**          314-997-4343
                                 FAX 314-997-2760
                    http://www.churchillschool.org
                 e-mail: churchill@churchillschool.org
*Sandra Gilligan, Director*
*Jenny , Outreach Coordinator*

A student workbook of activities that have been developed to reinforce the language and vocabulary found in 'Keeping Ahead in School' by Dr. Melvin Levine. The workbook is comprised of blackline masters which can be reproduced. *$ 20.00*

**1166  Vocabulary**

**Harcourt Achieve**
**6277 Sea Harbor Drive**
**Orlando, FL  32887**              252-480-3200
                                     800-531-5015
                                 FAX 800-699-9459
                     http://www.steckvaughn.com
                    e-mail: info@steckvaughn.com
*Steck-Vaughn Staff, Author*
*Tim McEwen, President/CEO*
*Jeff Johnson, Dir Marketing Communications*
*Chris Lehmann, Team Coordinator*

Improve reading comprehension where it matters most by introducing new words in the context of content area articles. Twenty-five highly visual lessons include a high-interest story with vocabulary words highlighted, a full-page graphic application activity, and reinforcement and extension activities presented as computer pull-down menus.

**1167  Vowels: Short & Long**

**Sunburst Technology**
**400 Columbus Avenue**
**Valhalla, NY  10595 1349**        914-747-3310
                                     800-321-7511
                                 FAX 914-747-4109
                         http://www.sunburst.com
                    e-mail: support@sunburst.com
*Mark Sotir, President*

Introduce students to vowels and the role they play in the structure of words. By engaging in word building activities, students learn to identify short and long vowels and regular spelling patterns.

**1168  Warmups and Workouts**

**Speech Bin**
**1965 25th Avenue**
**Vero Beach, FL  32960**           772-770-0007
                                     800-477-3324
                                 FAX 772-770-0006
                        http://www.speechbin.com
                    e-mail: info@speechbin.com
*Shane Peters, Product Coordinator*
*Jen Binney, Owner*

Easy-to-follow step-by-step instructions demonstrate how to help children achieve reliable production of r sounds, practice them in words of increasing complexity, and improve their phonic skills simultaneously. Item number 1486. *$26.95*

**1169 Wilson Language Training**

**Wilson Reading System**
**175 W Main Street**
**Millbury, MA 01527 1956**          508-865-5699
                                    800-899-8454
                              FAX 508-865-9644
                    http://www.wilsonlanguage.com
                    e-mail: info@wilsonlanguage.com
*Judith Nicholas, Administrator Training*
*Barbara Wilson, President*

Our mission is to instruct teachers, or other professionals in a related field, how to succeed with students who have not learned to read, write and spell despite great effort. Established in order to provide training in the Wilson Reading System, the Wilson staff provides Two-Day Overview Workshops as well as certified Level I and II training.

**1170 Word Parts**

**Sunburst Technology**
**400 Columbus Avenue**
**Valhalla, NY 10595 1349**          914-747-3310
                                    800-321-7511
                              FAX 914-747-4109
                      http://www.sunburst.com
                    e-mail: support@sunburst.com
*Mark Sotir, President*

Students build skills with compound and polysyllabic words by learning to chunk big words into manageable parts.

**1171 Word Scramble 2**

**LinguiSystems**
**3100 4th Avenue**
**East Moline, IL 61244**          309-775-2300
                                  800-776-4332
                            FAX 309-755-2377
                          TDY:800-933-8331
                   http://www.linguisystems.com
                   e-mail: service@linguisystems.com
*Paul F Johnson, Author*
*Linda Bowers, Owner*
*Rosemary Huisingh, Owner*

Customers loved the best-selling Word Scramble game and kept asking for more. Take your students to a new level of decoding practice with Word Scramble 2. This game is perfect for your students who've mastered CVC words and are ready for more challenging decoding practice. *$44.95*

*Ages 7-14*

**1172 Wordly Wise 3000 ABC 1-9**

**Educators Publishing Service**
**31 Smith Place**
**Cambridge, MA 02139 9031**          617-547-6706
                                    800-225-5750
                              FAX 888-440-2665
                      http://www.epsbooks.com
                      e-mail: eps@epsbooks.com
*Kenneth Hodkinson, Sandra Adams, Author*
*Steven Corte, President*

Three thousand new and carefully selected words taken from literature, textbooks and SAT-prep books, are the basis of this new series that teaches vocabulary through reading, writing, and a variety of exercises for grades 4-12.

**1173 Wordly Wise ABC 1-9**

**Educators Publishing Service**
**31 Smith Place**
**Cambridge, MA 02139 9031**          617-547-6706
                                    800-225-5750
                              FAX 888-440-2665
                      http://www.epsbooks.com
                      e-mail: eps@epsbooks.com
*Kenneth Hodkinson, Author*
*Steven Corte, President*

Vocabulary workbook series employs crossword puzzles, riddles, word games and a sense of humor to make the learning of new words an interesting experience.

**1174 Workbook for Aphasia**

**Speech Bin**
**1965 25th Avenue**
**Vero Beach, FL 32960**          772-770-0007
                                800-477-3324
                          FAX 772-770-0006
                    http://www.speechbin.com
                    e-mail: info@speechbin.com
*Shane Peters, Product Coordinator*
*Jen Binney, Owner*

This book gives you materials for adults who have recovered a significant degree of speaking, reading, writing, and comprehension skills. It includes 106 excercises divide into eight target areas. Item number W331. *$48.95*

---

# Science

---

**1175 Ablenet**

**Ablenet**
**2808 North Fairview Avenue**
**Roseville, MN 55113**          612-379-0956
                                800-322-0956
                          FAX 651-294-2259
                    http://www.ablenetinc.com
                e-mail: customerservice@ablenetinc.com
*Cheryl Volkman, Chief Developmental Officer*
*Ken Sobtzak, Technical Support*

Simple assistive technology for teaching children with disabilities including communication aids, environmental control, mounting systems, literacy and teacher resources, kits and more.

**1176  Animals and Their Homes CD-ROM**

Harcourt Achieve
6277 Sea Harbor Drive
Orlando, FL  32887          252-480-3200
                          800-531-5015
                     FAX 800-699-9459
              http://www.steckvaughn.com
              e-mail: info@steckvaughn.com

*Steck-Vaughn Staff, Author*
*Tim McEwen, President/CEO*
*Jeff Johnson, Dir Marketing Communications*
*Chris Lehmann, Team Coordinator*

This interactive simulation encourages students to explore animals habitats and environmental needs and create appropriate environments for a variety of animals. Students use the Animal Book to create a customized habitat display and write or record their own observations and ideas.

**1177  Animals in Their World CD-ROM**

Harcourt Achieve
6277 Sea Harbor Drive
Orlando, FL  32887          252-480-3200
                          800-531-5015
                     FAX 800-699-9459
              http://www.steckvaughn.com
              e-mail: info@steckvaughn.com

*Steck-Vaughn Staff, Author*
*Tim McEwen, President/CEO*
*Jeff Johnson, Dir Marketing Communications*
*Chris Lehmann, Team Coordinator*

This multimedia database motivates children to explore, compare, and contrast habitats, behaviors, and physicl characteristics of 58 animals in nine categories, such as carnivore or herbivore, hatched or born, and with or without backbone.

**1178  Curious Creatures Program:**
**Owls-Spiders-Wolves-Snakes-Bats**

Curriculum Associates
PO Box 2001
North Billerica, MA  01862 9914     978-667-8000
                                   800-225-0248
                              FAX 800-366-1158
           http://www.curriculumassociates.com
           e-mail: ca@infocurriculumassociates.com

*Louis James Taris, James Robert Taris, Author*
*Frank Ferguson, President*
*Fred Ferguson, Vice President Corporate Develop*

Users of this award-winning multimedia program say awesome! They learn little known facts about animals that make most of us cringe. Designed to encourage reluctant readers in grades 4 and above, the program is also appropriate for on-level students in grades 2-3. Students learn the language of life science as they strengthen their reading and comprehension skills.

**1179  Deep in the Rain Forest**

Harcourt Achieve
6277 Sea Harbor Drive
Orlando, FL  32887          252-480-3200
                          800-531-5015
                     FAX 800-699-9459
              http://www.steckvaughn.com
              e-mail: info@steckvaughn.com

*Pirotta, Author*
*Tim McEwen, President/CEO*
*Jeff Johnson, Dir Marketing Communications*
*Chris Lehmann, Team Coordinator*

Now even young readers can investigate the wonder and importance of the rain forest. Hands-on activities, large photos, and meaningful tests in each of these titles relate rain forest facts to a child's world and introduce conservation and environmental protection issues.

**1180  Dive to the Ocean Deep: Voyages of Exploration and Discovery**

Harcourt Achieve
6277 Sea Harbor Drive
Orlando, FL  32819          252-480-3200
                          800-531-5015
                     FAX 800-699-9459
              http://www.steckvaughn.com
              e-mail: info@steckvaughn.com

*Steck-Vaughn Staff, Author*
*Tim McEwen, President/CEO*
*Jeff Johnson, Dir Marketing Communications*
*Chris Lehmann, Team Coordinator*

These exciting titles draw readers in with true tales of discovery using a documentary approach. Renowned scientists show real world science at work in the depths of the ocean. *$27.11*

*64 pages*

**1181  Harcourt Brace: The Science Book of....**

Harcourt Achieve
6277 Sea Harbor Drive
Orlando, FL  32887          252-480-3200
                          800-531-5015
                     FAX 800-699-9459
              http://www.steckvaughn.com
              e-mail: info@steckvaughn.com

*Ardley, Author*
*Tim McEwen, President/CEO*
*Jeff Johnson, Dir Marketing Communications*
*Chris Lehmann, Team Coordinator*

Encourage independent scientific inquiry. Set up a classroom library of 16 hardcover titles that offer dozens of exploration opportunities with basic science principles. Ordinary classroom or household materials are all you need. Full-color photos of preparations and experiments are ideal for independent work. Practical examples relate each experiment to real world.

**1182  Learn About Life Science: Animals**

Sunburst Technology
400 Columbus Avenue
Valhalla, NY  10595 1349          914-747-3310
                                 800-321-7511
                            FAX 914-747-4109
                  http://www.sunburst.com
                  e-mail: service@sunburst.com

*Mark Sotir, President*

Learn about animal classification, adaptation to climate, domestication and special relationships between humans and animals.

**1183** **Learn About Life Science: Plants**

**Sunburst Technology**
**400 Columbus Avenue**
**Valhalla, NY 10595 1349**          **914-747-3310**
                                     **800-321-7511**
                                **FAX 914-747-4109**
                     **http://www.sunburst.com**
               **e-mail: service@sunburst.com**
*Mark Sotir, President*

Students explore the world of plants. From small seeds to tall trees students learn what plants are and what they need to grow.

**1184** **Learn About Physical Science: Simple Machines**

**Sunburst Technology**
**400 Columbus Avenue**
**Valhalla, NY 10595 1349**          **914-747-3310**
                                     **800-321-7511**
                                **FAX 914-747-4109**
                     **http://www.sunburst.com**
               **e-mail: service@sunburst.com**
*Mark Sotir, President*

Students delve into the mechanical world learning about the ways simple machines make our work easier.

**1185** **Life Cycles**

**Harcourt Achieve**
**6277 Sea Harbor Drive**
**Orlando, FL 32887**          **252-480-3200**
                               **800-531-5015**
                          **FAX 800-699-9459**
               **http://www.steckvaughn.com**
           **e-mail: info@steckvaughn.com**
*Hogan, Author*
*Tim McEwen, President/CEO*
*Jeff Johnson, Dir Marketing Communications*
*Chris Lehmann, Team Coordinator*

Dramatic photos tell the story of animal growth and development. This softcover series enriches any classroom science curriculum. Animal development is a complex subject but this series makes it understandable for young readers with simple text and informative images that follow each animal from birth to maturity.

**1186** **Maps & Navigation**

**Sunburst Technology**
**400 Columbus Avenue**
**Valhalla, NY 10595 1349**          **914-747-3310**
                                     **800-321-7511**
                                **FAX 914-747-4109**
                     **http://www.sunburst.com**
               **e-mail: support@sunburst.com**
*Mark Sotir, President*

This exciting nautical simulation provides students with opportunities to use their math and science skills.

**1187** **Our Universe: Steadwell**

**Harcourt Achieve**
**6277 Sea Harbor Drive**
**Orlando, FL 32887**          **252-480-3200**
                               **800-531-5015**
                          **FAX 800-699-9459**
               **http://www.steckvaughn.com**
           **e-mail: info@steckvaughn.com**
*Vogt, Author*
*Tim McEwen, President/CEO*
*Jeff Johnson, Dir Marketing Communications*
*Chris Lehmann, Team Coordinator*

Unravel the mysteries of space! A complex universe becomes amazingly clear in these easy-to-read titles.

**1188** **Patterns Across the Curriculum**

**Harcourt Achieve**
**6277 Sea Harbor Drive**
**Orlando, FL 32887**          **252-480-3200**
                               **800-531-5015**
                          **FAX 800-699-9459**
               **http://www.steckvaughn.com**
           **e-mail: info@steckvaughn.com**
*Steck-Vaughn Staff, Author*
*Tim McEwen, President/CEO*
*Jeff Johnson, Dir Marketing Communications*
*Chris Lehmann, Team Coordinator*

Develop students awareness and understanding of patterns in the real world! Exercises allow students to identify, complete, extend, and create patterns. Developed across four curriculum areas: Math, Language, Social Studies, and Science. Flexible organization allows teachers to utilize content-specific activities in coordination with other classroom assignments, providing additional richness in learning.

**1189** **Prehistoric Creaures Then & Now: Steadwell**

**Harcourt Achieve**
**6277 Sea Harbor Drive**
**Orlando, FL 32887**          **252-480-3200**
                               **800-531-5015**
                          **FAX 800-699-9459**
               **http://www.steckvaughn.com**
           **e-mail: info@steckvaughn.com**
*Steck-Vaughn Staff, Author*
*Tim McEwen, President/CEO*
*Jeff Johnson, Dir Marketing Communications*
*Chris Lehmann, Team Coordinator*

Now limited readers can dig into the details of dinosaurs! Each information-packed title includes a special spread with a project, a profile of a dinosaur expert, or a description of a recent dinosaur discovery.

**1190  Space Academy GX-1**

**Riverdeep**
**500 Redmond Boulevard**
**Novato, CA  94947**                    **415-763-4700**
                                        **800-362-2890**
                                   **FAX 415-763-4385**
                              **http://www.elmark.com**
                          **e-mail: info@riverdeep.net**
*Barry O'Callaghan, Chairman/CEO*
*Simon Calver, COO*
*John Rim, CFO*

Explore the solar system with Space Academy GX-1!
Fully aligned with national science standards and
state curricula, Space Academy GX-1, students investigate the astronomical basis for seasons, phases of the
moon, gravity, orbits, and more. As students succeed,
Grow Slides adjust to offer more advanced topics and
problems.

**1191  Steck-Vaughn Science Centers**

**Harcourt Achieve**
**6277 Sea Harbor Drive**
**Orlando, FL  32887**                   **252-480-3200**
                                        **800-531-5015**
                                   **FAX 800-699-9459**
                       **http://www.harcourtachieve.com**
                   **e-mail: info@harcourtachieve.com**
*Steck-Vaughn Staff, Author*
*Tim McEwen, President/CEO*
*Jeff Johnson, Dir Marketing Communications*
*Chris Lehmann, Team Coordinator*

Organized by theme, these books will supplement the
study of weather, prehistoric life, plants, animals of
the ocean, animals of the rain forest, earth and space,
and energy.

**1192  Talking Walls**

**Riverdeep**
**500 Redmond Boulevard**
**Novato, CA  94947**                    **415-763-4700**
                                        **800-362-2890**
                                   **FAX 415-763-4385**
                              **http://www.elmark.com**
                          **e-mail: info@riverdeep.net**
*Barry O'Callaghan, Chairman/CEO*
*Simon Calver, COO*
*John Rim, CFO*

The Talking Walls Software Series is a wonderful
springboard for a student's journey of exploration and
discovery. This comprehensive collection of researched resources and materials enables students to
focus on learning while conducting a guided search
for information.

**1193  Talking Walls: The Stories Continue**

**Riverdeep**
**500 Redmond Boulevard**
**Novato, CA  94947**                    **415-763-4700**
                                        **800-362-2890**
                                   **FAX 415-763-4385**
                              **http://www.elmark.com**
                          **e-mail: info@riverdeep.net**
*Barry O'Callaghan, Chairman/CEO*
*Simon Calver, COO*
*John Rim, CFO*

Using the Talking Walls Software Series, students
discover the stories behind some of the world's most
fascinating walls. The award-winning books, interactive software, carefully chosen Web sites, and suggested classroom activities build upon each other,
providing a rich learning experience that includes
text, video, and hands-on projects.

**1194  ThemeWeavers: Nature Activity Kit**

**Riverdeep**
**500 Redmond Boulevard**
**Novato, CA  94947**                    **415-763-4700**
                                        **800-362-2890**
                                   **FAX 415-763-4385**
                              **http://www.elmark.com**
                          **e-mail: info@riverdeep.net**
*Barry O'Callaghan, Chairman/CEO*
*Simon Calver, COO*
*John Rim, CFO*

ThemeWeavers: Nature Activity Kit is an all-in-one
solution for theme-based teaching. In just a few minutes, you can select from dozens of ready-to-use activities centering on the seasons and weather and be
ready for the next day's lesson! Interactive and engaging activities cover multiple subject areas such as language arts, math, science, social studies and art.

**1195  Thinkin' Science**

**Sunburst Technology**
**400 Columbus Avenue**
**Valhalla, NY  10595 1349**             **914-747-3310**
                                        **800-321-7511**
                                   **FAX 914-747-4109**
                             **http://www.sunburst.com**
                        **e-mail: service@sunburst.com**
*Mark Sotir, President*

Five environments introduce students to the scientific
methods and concepts needed to understand basic
earth, life and physical sciences. Students learn to
think like scientists as they solve problems using hypothesis, experimentation, observation and deduction.

**1196  Thinkin' Science ZAP!**

**Sunburst Technology**
**400 Columbus Avenue**
**Valhalla, NY  10595 1349**             **914-747-3310**
                                        **800-321-7511**
                                   **FAX 914-747-4109**
                             **http://www.sunburst.com**
                        **e-mail: service@sunburst.com**
*Mark Sotir, President*

Working with laser beams, electrical circuits, and
"visible" sound waves, students practice valuable
thinking skills, observation, prediction, dedutive reasoning, conceptual modeling, theory building and hypothesis testing while experimenting within
scientifically accurate learning environment.

**1197 True Tales**

**Harcourt Achieve**
**6277 Sea Harbor Drive**
**Orlando, FL 32887**       252-480-3200
                           800-531-5015
                        FAX 800-699-9459
                   http://www.steckvaughn.com
                   e-mail: info@steckvaughn.com
*Billings, Author*
*Tim McEwen, President/CEO*
*Jeff Johnson, Dir Marketing Communications*
*Chris Lehmann, Team Coordinator*

If you have been looking for reading comprehension materials for limited readers, your search is over. True Tales presents powerful real-lfe events with direct connections to geography and science at reading level 3. Gripping accounts of personal triumph and tragedy put geography and science in a very real context. Accompanying activities develop reading and language arts, science, and geography skills students need to boost test scores.

**1198 Turnstone Explorer Kits**

**Harcourt Achieve**
**6277 Sea Harbor Drive**
**Orlando, FL 32887**       252-480-3200
                           800-531-5015
                        FAX 800-699-9459
                   http://www.steckvaughn.com
                   e-mail: info@steckvaughn.com
*Steck-Vaughn Staff, Author*
*Tim McEwen, President/CEO*
*Jeff Johnson, Dir Marketing Communications*
*Chris Lehmann, Team Coordinator*

Encourage inquiry with an insider's look at science exploration! Energize discovery-based learning through nonfiction literature, hands-on exploration, and challenging application projects. Put budding scientists in touch with real thing. Action-packed kits bring the experience of scientific exploration to life.

**1199 Untamed World**

**Harcourt Achieve**
**6277 Sea Harbor Drive**
**Orlando, FL 32887**       252-480-3200
                           800-531-5015
                        FAX 800-699-9459
                   http://www.steckvaughn.com
                   e-mail: info@steckvaughn.com
*Karen Dudley, Marie Levine, Patricia Schroeder,*
*Author*
*Tim McEwen, President/CEO*
*Jeff Johnson, Dir Marketing Communications*
*Chris Lehmann, Team Coordinator*

A vivid view of wild animals through science and literature! Awe-inspiring creatures of the land and sea are as fascinating in fact as in folklore. These titles offer both views, combining a thorough nonfiction resource with riveting reading. Topics include life span, classification, the food chain, social organization, communication, and seasonal activities.

**1200 Virtual Labs: Electricity**

**Riverdeep**
**500 Redmond Boulevard**
**Novato, CA 94947**        415-763-4700
                           800-362-2890
                        FAX 415-763-4385
                    http://www.elmark.com
                    e-mail: info@riverdeep.net
*Barry O'Callaghan, Chairman/CEO*
*Simon Calver, COO*
*John Rim, CFO*

Five environments introduce students to the scientific methods and conepts needed to understand basic Earth, life, and physical sciences. Students will learn to think like scientists as they solve problems using hypothesis, experimentation, observation, and deduction. *$69.95*

**1201 Virtual Labs: Light**

**Riverdeep**
**500 Redmond Boulevard**
**Novato, CA 94947**        415-763-4700
                           800-362-2890
                        FAX 415-763-4385
                    http://www.elmark.com
                    e-mail: info@riverdeep.com
*Barry O'Callaghan, Chairman/CEO*
*Simon Calver, COO*
*John Rim, CFO*

Designed to integrate directly into the physcial science curricula, Virtual Labs: Light combines easy-to-use experiments and highly accurate simulations with over 40 reproducible lab worksheets. Carefully sequenced levels of virtual experiments — basic, extension, and challenge — provide a safe means for students to perform hands-on activities with lasers and an assortment of optical tools.

## Social Skills

**1202 2's Experience Fingerplays**

**Therapro**
**225 Arlington Street**
**Framingham, MA 01702 8723**   508-872-9494
                               800-257-5376
                            FAX 508-875-2062
                    http://www.theraproducts.com
                    e-mail: info@theraproducts.com
*Liz Wilmes, Dick Wilmes, Author*
*Karen Conrad, President*

A wonderful collection of fingerplays, songs and rhymes for the very young child. Fingerplays are short, easy to learn, and full of simple movement. Chant or sing the fingerplays and then enjoy the accompanying games and activities. *$12.95*

*159 pages*

**1203 28 Instant Song Games**

**Therapro**
**225 Arlington Street**
**Framingham, MA  01702 8723**          **508-872-9494**
                                                              **800-257-5376**
                                              **FAX 508-875-2062**
                            **http://www.theraproducts.com**
                               **e-mail: info@theraproducts.com**
*MaBoAubLo, Barbara Sher, Author*
*Karen Conrad, President*

Gets kids up and moving in no time! Includes numerous games of body awareness, movement play, self expression, imagination and language play. Booklet and 75 minute audio tape. *$21.00*

*Audio Tape*

**1204 Ablenet**

**Ablenet**
**2808 North Fairview Avenue**
**Roseville, MN  55113**          **612-379-0956**
                                            **800-322-0956**
                              **FAX 651-294-2259**
                **http://www.ablenetinc.com**
    **e-mail: customerservice@ablenetinc.com**
*Cheryl Volkman, Chief Developmental Officer*
*Ken Sobtzak, Technical Support*

Simple assistive technology for teaching children with disabilities including communication aids, switches, environmental control, mounting systems, literacy and teacher resources, kits and more.

**1205 Active Learning Series**

**Therapro**
**225 Arlington Street**
**Framingham, MA  01702 8723**          **508-872-9494**
                                                              **800-257-5376**
                                              **FAX 508-875-2062**
                            **http://www.theraproducts.com**
                               **e-mail: info@theraproducts.com**
*Therapro Staff, Author*
*Karen Conrad, President*

A favorite of parents and caregivers. Over 300 innovative and easy-to-do activities in each book. The activities are easy to read and can be done with one child in a group. Helps caregivers to choose the right activities for each child. Ideas on setting up environments, and an easy system for writing plans, helps caregivers set the stage for a good activity program. Each book contains a complete planning guide. Activities for listening, talking, physical development and more.

**1206 Activities Unlimited**

**Therapro**
**225 Arlington Street**
**Framingham, MA  01702 8723**          **508-872-9494**
                                                              **800-257-5376**
                                              **FAX 508-875-2062**
                            **http://www.theraproducts.com**
                               **e-mail: info@theraproducts.com**
*A Cleveland, B Caton, L Adler, Author*
*Karen Conrad, President*

Helps young children develop fine and gross motor skills, increase their language, become self-reliant and play cooperatively. An innovative resource that immediately attracts and engages children. Short of time? Need a good idea? Count on Activites Unlimited. *$19.95*

**1207 Activities for a Diverse Classroom: Connecting Students**

**PEAK Parent Center**
**611 N Weber**
**Colorado Springs, CO  80903**          **719-531-9400**
                                                              **800-284-0251**
                                              **FAX 719-531-9452**
                                              **TDY:719-531-5403**
                            **http://www.peakparent.org**
                               **e-mail: info@peakparent.org**
*Leah Katz, Caren Sax, Douglas Fisher, Author*
*Barbara Buswell, Executive Director*
*Amy Schaub, Administration/Communications*

Offers elementary school teachers 18 fun and enriching do it tomorrow activities designed to build acceptance, belonging, and friendships among all students throughout the academic year. Each activity includes extension ideas for linking students' learning to the general education curriculum. *$10.00*

*80 pages*
*ISBN 1-884720-20-X*

**1208 Activity Schedules for Children with Autism: Teaching Independent Behavior**

**Therapro**
**225 Arlington Street**
**Framingham, MA  01702 8723**          **508-872-9494**
                                                              **800-257-5376**
                                              **FAX 508-875-2062**
                            **http://www.theraproducts.com**
                               **e-mail: info@theraproducts.com**
*Lynn McClannahan PhD, Patricia Krantz PhD, Author*
*Karen Conrad, President*

An activity schedule is a set of pictures or words that cue a child to follow a sequence of activities. When mastered, the children are more self-directed and purposeful at home, school and leisure activites. In this book, parents and professionals can find detailed instructions and examples, assess a child's readiness to use activity schedules, and understand graduated guidance and progress monitoring. Great for promoting independence in children with autism. *$14.95*

*117 pages*

**1209 Alert Program With Songs for Self-Regulation**

**Therapro**
**225 Arlington Street**
**Framingham, MA  01702 8723**          **508-872-9494**
                                                              **800-257-5376**
                                              **FAX 508-875-2062**
                            **http://www.theraproducts.com**
                               **e-mail: info@theraproducts.com**
*Mary Sue Williams OTR, Sherry Shellenberger OTR, Author*
*Karen Conrad, President*

This program compares the body to an engine, running either high, low, or just right. Side A is an overview, Side B has 15 songs for self-regulation. Extremely successful in helping kids recognize and change their own engine speeds.

*Audio Tape*

**1210  An Introduction to How Does Your Engine Run?**

Therapro
225 Arlington Street
Framingham, MA 01702 8723          508-872-9494
                                   800-257-5376
                               FAX 508-875-2062
                    http://www.theraproducts.com
                    e-mail: info@theraproducts.com
*Mary Sue Williams OTR, Sherry Shellenberger
OTR, Author
Karen Conrad, President*

Introduces the entire Alert Program, which explains
how we regulate our arousal states. Describes the use
of sensorimotor strategies to manage levels of alertness. This program is fun for students and the adults
working with them, and translates easily into real life.
*$40.00*

**1211  Andy and His Yellow Frisbee**

Therapro
225 Arlington Street
Framingham, MA 01702 8723          508-872-9494
                                   800-257-5376
                               FAX 508-875-2062
                    http://www.theraproducts.com
                    e-mail: info@theraproducts.com
*Mary Thompson, Author
Karen Conrad, President*

A heartwarming story about Andy, a boy with autism.
Like many children with autism, Andy has a fascina-
tion with objects in motion. His talent for spinning his
Frisbee and a new classmate's curiosity set this story
in motion. Rosie, the watchful and protective sister,
supplies backround on Andy and autism, as well as a
sibling's perspective. *$14.95*

*19 pages*

**1212  Artic-Riddles**

Speech Bin
1965 25th Avenue
Vero Beach, FL 32960               772-770-0007
                                   800-477-3324
                               FAX 772-770-0006
                       http://www.speechbin.com
                       e-mail: info@speechbin.com
*Shane Peters, Product Coordinator
Jen Binney, Owner*

Tired of the same old games? Artic-Riddles is a collection of speech materials with a tantalizing new twist!
Each deck of twenty cards has an eye-catching picture
on the front and five riddle clues on the back. Games
provide speech sound practice; at the same time, they
develop and reinforce skills in listening, turn taking,
recalling, reasoning, vocabulary, naming, inferring,
answering questions, and drawing conclusions. Item
number 1401. *$54.95*

**1213  Autism & PDD: Primary Social Skills Lessons**

LinguiSystems
3100 4th Avenue
East Moline, IL 61244              309-775-2300
                                   800-776-4332
                               FAX 309-755-2377
                               TDY:800-933-8331
                    http://www.linguisystems.com
                    e-mail: service@linguisystems.com
*Pam Britton Reese, Nena C Challenner, Author
Linda Bowers, Owner
Rosemary Huisingh, Owner*

These structured lessons teach social skills through
rebus stories. The pictures help students read the lesson with you. Here are just some of the social skill areas you'll address: using a quiet voice, self-care
skills, school behavior, hurting self or others, table social skills, getting a check-up. *$109.75*

*60 pages  Ages 3-8*

**1214  Autism & PPD: Adolescent Social Skills Lessons**

LinguiSystems
3100 4th Avenue
East Moline, IL 61244              309-775-2300
                                   800-776-4332
                               FAX 309-755-2377
                               TDY:800-933-8331
                    http://www.linguisystems.com
                    e-mail: service@linguisystems.com
*Pam Britton Reese, Nena C Challenner, Author
Linda Bowers, Owner
Rosemary Huisingh, Owner*

These lessons target the social skills your students
with autism need to succeed in school and in life.
From school schedule changes to staying healthy to
job skills, you'll cover all the important skills your
students need. Each book includes instructional and
behavioral lessons. *$109.75*

*65 pages  Ages 12-18*

**1215  Autism & PPD: Adolescent Social Skills
Lessons-Health & Hygiene**

LinguiSystems
3100 4th Avenue
East Moline, IL 61244              309-775-2300
                                   800-776-4332
                               FAX 309-755-2377
                               TDY:800-933-8331
                    http://www.linguisystems.com
                    e-mail: service@linguisystems.com
*Pam Britton Reese, Nena C Challenner, Author
Linda Bowers, Owner
Rosemary Huisingh, Owner*

Use these rebus story lessons to teach your students
important social skills related to health and hygiene.
The instructional lessons teach what to say or do in social situations that are sometimes overwhelming to
the student with autism and PPD. The behavioral lessons target specific social problems that need to be
stopped. *$21.95*

*63 pages  Ages 12-18*

**1216 Breakthroughs Manual: How to Reach Students with Autism**

**Therapro**
**225 Arlington Street**
**Framingham, MA 01702 8723**      **508-872-9494**
                                   **800-257-5376**
                              **FAX 508-875-2062**
                    **http://www.theraproducts.com**
                    **e-mail: info@theraproducts.com**
*Karen Sewell, Author*
*Karen Conrad, President*

This manual features practical suggestions for everyday use with preschool through high school students. Covers communication, behavior, academics, self-help, life and social skills. Includes reproducible lesson plans and up to date listing of classroom materials and catalog supply companies. *$59.00*

*243 pages*

**1217 Broccoli-Flavored Bubble Gum**

**Harcourt Achieve**
**6277 Sea Harbor Drive**
**Orlando, FL 32887**            **252-480-3200**
                                   **800-531-5015**
                              **FAX 800-699-9459**
                    **http://www.steckvaughn.com**
                    **e-mail: info@steckvaughn.com**
*Justin McGivern, Patrick Girouard, Author*
*Tim McEwen, President/CEO*
*Jeff Johnson, Dir Marketing Communications*
*Chris Lehmann, Team Coordinator*

A young boy gains fame and fortune encouraging kids to eat their vegetables.

*32 pages*

**1218 Busy Kids Movement**

**Therapro**
**225 Arlington Street**
**Framingham, MA 01702 8723**      **508-872-9494**
                                   **800-257-5376**
                              **FAX 508-875-2062**
                    **http://www.theraproducts.com**
                    **e-mail: info@theraproducts.com**
*Therapro Staff, Author*
*Karen Conrad, President*

Full of ideas for developing youngsters' gross motor skills. Games, dramatics, action songs, music and rythm activities. *$9.95*

*64 pages*

**1219 Calm Down and Play**

**Childswork**
**45 Executive Dr**
**Plainview, NY 11803 9020**
                                   **800-962-1141**
                              **FAX 877-434-6553**
                    **http://www.childswork.com**
*Sally Germain, Editorial*

Filled with fun and effective activities to help children: calm down and control their impulses; focus, concentrate, and organize their thoughts; identify and verbalize feelings; channel and release excess energy appropriately; and build self-esteem and confidence. *$17.95*

*Ages 5-12*

**1220 Case of the Crooked Candles**

**Harcourt Achieve**
**6277 Sea Harbor Drive**
**Orlando, FL 32887**            **252-480-3200**
                                   **800-531-5015**
                              **FAX 800-699-9459**
                    **http://www.steckvaughn.com**
                    **e-mail: info@steckvaughn.com**
*Jonathan Conn, Author*
*Tim McEwen, President/CEO*
*Jeff Johnson, Dir Marketing Communications*
*Chris Lehmann, Team Coordinator*

A pair of felonious fruit bats is no match for Detective Dog and his alert animal assistants.

*32 pages*

**1221 Cooperative Thinking Strategies**

**Edge Enterprises**
**708 W 9th Street**
**Lawrence, KS 66044 2846**       **785-749-1473**
                              **FAX 785-749-0207**
                    **e-mail: edge@midusa.net**
*D Sue Vernon, Donald Deshler, Jean Schumaker, Author*
*Jacqueline Schafer, Managing Editor*

Cooperative Thinking Strategies are a group of strategies students can use to think, learn and work together productively. The strategies are designed to improve the students' ability to interact and work with others as they restructure and manipulate information in group tasks. Instruction in these strategies has been designed to be delivered in general education classes in which a diversity of students are enrolled, including students with disabilities. Available as a series or individually.

**1222 Courageous Pacers Classroom Chart**

**Therapro**
**225 Arlington Street**
**Framingham, MA 01702 8723**      **508-872-9494**
                                   **800-257-5376**
                              **FAX 508-875-2062**
                    **http://www.theraproducts.com**
                    **e-mail: info@theraproducts.com**
*Therapro Staff, Author*
*Karen Conrad, President*

Highly recommended to accompany the Courageous Pacers Program. Assists in keeping record of 12 students' progress in walking and lifting. A great visual tool to view progress.

**1223 Courageous Pacers Program**

**Therapro**
**225 Arlington Street**
**Framingham, MA 01702 8723**      **508-872-9494**
                                   **800-257-5376**
                              **FAX 508-875-2062**
                    **http://www.theraproducts.com**
                    **e-mail: info@theraproducts.com**
*Tim Erson MS PT, Author*
*Karen Conrad, President*

This fun and easy program was developed to help students become more active. Research shows that students who are more active, do better in school. The goal of the program is simple: get students to walk 100 miles and lift 10,000 pounds in a year.

*92 pages*

**1224   Dance Land**

**Therapo**
**225 Arlington Street**
**Framingham, MA  01702 8723        508-872-9494**
**                                                            800-257-5376**
**                                                  FAX 508-875-2062**
**                                  http://www.theraproducts.com**
**                                  e-mail: info@theraproducts.com**
*Fitz-Taylor, McDonald, Hicman, Lande, Wiz, Author*
*Karen Conrad, President*

Safe fun for kids of all abilities. Engages listeners in rythmic expression, which is fundamental to physical, cognitive and emotional development. Dance activities designed by physical and occupational therapists. 33 page book included. Many sensory motor activites included. 50 minute audio tape. *$21.00*

*Audio Tape*

**1225   Eden Family of Services**

**Eden Services**
**One Eden Way**
**Princeton, NJ  08540               609-987-0099**
**                                                  FAX 609-987-0243**
**                                  http://www.edenservices.org**
**                                  e-mail: info@edenservices.org**
*David Holmes EdD, Executive Director/President*
*Joani Truch, Administration/Communications*

Provides year round educational services, early intervention, parent training, respite care, outreach services, community based residential services and employment opportunities for individuals with autism.

**1226   Emotions Activity Manuals**

**Therapo**
**225 Arlington Street**
**Framingham, MA  01702 8723        508-872-9494**
**                                                            800-257-5376**
**                                                  FAX 508-875-2062**
**                                  http://www.theraproducts.com**
**                                  e-mail: info@theraproducts.com**
*Therapo Staff, Author*
*Karen Conrad, President*

Great new manuals to use with the EMOTIONS products (poster, cards and flashcards). 63 different tried and true activities from therapists, educators and counselors form the US and Canada. Simply produced, includes an EMOTIONS page.

**1227   Expression Connection**

**Speech Bin**
**1965 25th Avenue**
**Vero Beach, FL  32960               772-770-0007**
**                                                            800-477-3324**
**                                                  FAX 772-770-0006**
**                                  http://www.speechbin.com**
**                                  e-mail: info@speechbin.com**
*Shane Peters, Product Coordinator*
*Jen Binney, Owner*

This criterion-referenced assessment protocol and structured instructional program moves elementary school children from simple narratives to complex stories and establishes the critical concepts that underline coherent oral expression. Item number 1586. *$43.95*

**1228   Expressive Language Kit**

**LinguiSystems**
**3100 4th Avenue**
**East Moline, IL  61244               309-775-2300**
**                                                            800-776-4332**
**                                                  FAX 309-755-2377**
**                                                  TDY:800-933-8331**
**                                  http://www.linguisystems.com**
**                                  e-mail: service@linguisystems.com**
*Linda Bowers, Rosemary Huisingh, Carolyn LoGiudice, Author*
*Linda Bowers, Owner*
*Rosemary Huisingh, Owner*

It's our biggest language therapy kit ever. The focus is on strengthening expressive language skills so your students will become effective communicators. A combination of colorful photographs, picture cards, and activity sheets work together to create an outstanding expressive language program. A comprehension therapy manual is included to help you direct this incredibly wide variety of language activities. *$149.95*

*250 pages  Ages 5-11*

**1229   Face to Face: Resolving Conflict Without Giving in or Giving Up**

**National Association for Community Mediation**
**1527 New Hampshire Avenue, NW**
**Washington, DC  20036 1206        202-667-9700**
**                                                  FAX 202-466-8629**
**                                  http://www.nafcm.org\nafcm**
**                                  e-mail: nafcm@nafcm.org**
*Jan Bellard,Hilda Gutierrez Baldoquin,Andrew Sachs, Author*
*Linda Baron, Executive Director*
*Joanne Galindo, Associate Director*

Modular curriculum for training program for AmeriCorps members. Addresses conflict at the personal level, interpersonal level, and group collaboration. Includes workbook. *$69.95*

*266 pages*

**1230   Forms for Helping the ADHD Child**

**Childswork**
**45 Executive Dr**
**Plainview, NY  11803 9020**
**                                                  800-962-1141**
**                                                  FAX 877-434-6553**
**                                  http://www.childswork.com**
*Sally Germain, Editorial*

Forms, charts, and checklists for treating children with Attention Deficit Hyperactivity Disorder cover a wide range of approaches. Includes effective aids in assessing, treating, and monitoring the progress of the ADHD child. *$ 31.95*

*100 pages*

**1231  Friendzee: A Social Skills Game**
LinguiSystems
3100 4th Avenue
East Moline, IL  61244                309-775-2300
                                       800-776-4332
                                  FAX 309-755-2377
                                   TDY:800-933-8331
                          http://www.linguisystems.com
                        e-mail: service@linguisystems.com
*Diane A Figula, Author*
*Linda Bowers, Owner*
*Rosemary Huisingh, Owner*

This game uses a communication-based approach to teaching social skills. Skills are taught through the themes of home, school, and community. Stimulus items teach these social skills: body language; tone of voice; polite forms; giving information; listening; asking questions; and problem solving. *$39.95*

*Ages 7-11*

**1232  Funsical Fitness With Silly-cise CD: Motor Development Activities**
Therapro
225 Arlington Street
Framingham, MA  01702 8723          508-872-9494
                                     800-257-5376
                                FAX 508-875-2062
                         http://www.theraproducts.com
                         e-mail: info@theraproducts.com
*Karen Conrad, President*

This unique blending of developmentally appropriate gross motor, sensory integration, and aerobic activities is guaranteed to build children's strength, balance endurance, coordination, and self confidence. Leads children through four 15-minute classes of Wacky Walking, Grinnastics, Brain Gym, Warm Ups, Adventurobics, and Chill Out activities. *$15.00*

*Ages 3-9*

**1233  Games We Should Play in School**
Therapro
225 Arlington Street
Framingham, MA  01702 8723          508-872-9494
                                     800-257-5376
                                FAX 508-875-2062
                         http://www.theraproducts.com
                         e-mail: info@theraproducts.com
*Frank Aycox, Author*
*Karen Conrad, President*

Includes over 75 interactive, fun, social games; describes how to effectively lead Social Play sessions in the classroom. Students become more cooperative, less antagonistic and more capable of increased attentiveness. Contains the secrets to enriching the entire school environment. *$16.50*

*154 pages*

**1234  Goal Oriented Gross & Fine Motor Lesson Plans for Early Childhood Classes**
Therapro
225 Arlington Street
Framingham, MA  01702 8723          508-872-9494
                                     800-257-5376
                                FAX 508-875-2062
                         http://www.theraproducts.com
                         e-mail: info@theraproducts.com
*Donna Weiss MA OTR, Author*
*Karen Conrad, President*

Practical and convinient format covers 224 activities grouped into 12 monthly units, making it easy to incorporate gross and fine motor activities into a daily class schedule. Provides challenges for groups whose abilities span early childhood, from 2.5 to 5.5 years of age. *$32.00*

*77 pages*

**1235  Hidden Child: Linwood Method for Reaching the Autistic Child**
Therapro
225 Arlington Street
Framingham, MA  01702 8723          508-872-9494
                                     800-257-5376
                                FAX 508-875-2062
                         http://www.theraproducts.com
                         e-mail: info@theraproducts.com
*Jeanne Simmons, Sabine Oiski PhD, Author*
*Karen Conrad, President*

This book provides an explanation of autism, then a step-by-step analysis of the Linwood method of establishing relationships, patterning good behavior, overcoming compulsions, developing skills, and fostering social and emotional development. This guidebook for teachers and therapists also has a message for parents.

**1236  High Interest Sports**
Harcourt Achieve
6277 Sea Harbor Drive
Orlando, FL  32887                   252-480-3200
                                     800-531-5015
                                FAX 800-699-9459
                         http://www.steckvaughn.com
                         e-mail: info@steckvaughn.com
*Fetty, Author*
*Tim McEwen, President/CEO*
*Jeff Johnson, Dir Marketing Communications*
*Chris Lehmann, Team Coordinator*

Exercise is an important part of a healthy lifestyle. By providing a variety of activities, games, and sports, we give students as opportunity to choose the exercise that fits their personal needs. These books provide the basic framework of a variety of sports and schoolyard games, making it an excellent resource for the classroom teacher.

**1237 Inclusive Early Childhood Classroom: Easy Ways to Adapt Learning Centers for All Children**

**Therapro**
**225 Arlington Street**
**Framingham, MA 01702 8723**     **508-872-9494**
**800-257-5376**
**FAX 508-875-2062**
**http://www.theraproducts.com**
**e-mail: info@theraproducts.com**
*Patti Gould, Joyce Sullivan, Author*
*Karen Conrad, President*

A great inclusion resource! This long awaited book by two experienced occupational therapists offers many concrete suggestions that are easy to implement. Gives teachers tools to make classrooms more effective environments for ALL students. *$24.95*

*203 pages*

**1238 Jarvis Clutch: Social Spy**

**Educators Publishing Service**
**31 Smith Place**
**Cambridge, MA 02139 9031**     **617-547-6706**
**800-225-5750**
**FAX 888-440-2665**
**http://www.epsbooks.com**
**e-mail: eps@epsbooks.com**
*Melvin D Levine MD FAAP, Author*
*Steven Corte, President*

In Jarvis Clutch social spy, Dr. Mel Levine teams up with eight grader Jarvis Clutch for an insider's look at life on the middle school social scene. Jarvis's wry and insightful observations of student interactions at Eastern Middle School bring to light the myriad social challenges that adolescents face every day, including peer pressure, the need to seem cool, the perils of dating., Include the commentary in Jarivs' Spy Notes!

**1239 Kids with Special Needs: Information & Activities to Promote Awareness & Understanding**

**Therapro**
**225 Arlington Street**
**Framingham, MA 01702 8723**     **508-872-9494**
**800-257-5376**
**FAX 508-875-2062**
**http://www.theraproducts.com**
**e-mail: info@theraproducts.com**
*Dee Konczal, Veronica Getskow, Author*
*Karen Conrad, President*

Children with disabilities have a need to be accepted and understood by other children. This book provides simulation activities to better understand what it's like to have a disability. Background information about communicative developmental, physical and learning disabilities is also offered. Includes a comprehensive resource list. *$16.95*

*200 pages*

**1240 Learning in Motion**

**Therapro**
**225 Arlington Street**
**Framingham, MA 01702 8723**     **508-872-9494**
**800-257-5376**
**FAX 508-875-2062**
**http://www.theraproducts.com**
**e-mail: info@theraproducts.com**
*Angermeir, Krzyzanowski, Keller-Moir, Author*
*Karen Conrad, President*

Written by 3 OTs, this book is for the busy therapist or teacher of preschoolers to second graders. Provides group activities using gross, fine andsensory motor skills in theme based curricula. Every lesson plan contains goals, objectives, materials and adaptations to facilitate inclusion and multilevel instructions. Includes 130 lesson plans with corresponding parent letters that explain the lesson and provide home follow-up activities. *$50.00*

*379 pages*

**1241 Look At It This Way**

**Therapro**
**225 Arlington Street**
**Framingham, MA 01702 8723**     **508-872-9494**
**800-257-5376**
**FAX 508-875-2062**
**http://www.theraproducts.com**
**e-mail: info@theraproducts.com**
*Roma Lee, Author*
*Karen Conrad, President*

Although the play and toy activities in this book are designed for children with visual impairment, they can be used with other children as well. Chapters include Learning to Look, Learning to Listen, Learning to Feel, and Using the Sense of Smell. *$32.00*

*129 pages*

**1242 Maxwell's Manor: A Social Language Game**

**LinguiSystems**
**3100 4th Avenue**
**East Moline, IL 61244**     **309-775-2300**
**800-776-4332**
**FAX 309-755-2377**
**TDY:800-933-8331**
**http://www.linguisystems.com**
**e-mail: service@linguisystems.com**
*Carolyn LoGiudice, Nancy McConnell, Author*
*Linda Bowers, Owner*
*Rosemary Huisingh, Owner*

This fun game will teach your students the social skills they need to get along with others, be more accepted by their peers, and be successful in the classroom. Maxwell, the loveable dog, leads the way as your students practice positive social language skills. *$44.95*

*Ages 4-9*

**1243 Moving Right Along**

**Therapro**
**225 Arlington Street**
**Framingham, MA 01702 8723**        **508-872-9494**
                                    **800-257-5376**
                                **FAX 508-875-2062**
                        **http://www.theraproducts.com**
                        **e-mail: info@theraproducts.com**
*Barbara Sher MA OTR, Author*
*Karen Conrad, President*

A collection of 264 easy, spur of the moment, movement games for young children to increase coordination, balance, rythm and enhance their sense of mastery. Great resource for parents, teachers, PT's and OT's. *$14.50*

**1244 Moving and Learning Across the Curriculum: 315 Games to Make Learning Fun**

**Therapro**
**225 Arlington Street**
**Framingham, MA 01702 8723**        **508-872-9494**
                                    **800-257-5376**
                                **FAX 508-875-2062**
                        **http://www.theraproducts.com**
                        **e-mail: info@theraproducts.com**
*Rae Pica, Author*
*Karen Conrad, President*

Gives children the chance to be physically involved in the experience of learning concepts. A great way to include gross motor skills across 6 major content areas: art; language arts; mathematics; music; science and social studies. *$4.00*

**1245 New Language of Toys: Teaching Communication Skills to Children with Special Needs**

**Therapro**
**225 Arlington Street**
**Framingham, MA 01702 8723**        **508-872-9494**
                                    **800-257-5376**
                                **FAX 508-875-2062**
                        **http://www.theraproducts.com**
                        **e-mail: info@theraproducts.com**
*Sue Schwarz PhD, Joan Heller Miller EdM, Author*
*Karen Conrad, President*

Play time becomes a fun and educational experience with this revised hands-on approach for developing communication skills using everyday toys. Includes a fresh assortment of toys, books and new chapters on computer technology, language learning, videotapes and television. *$16.95*

*289 pages  Ages Birth-6*

**1246 Patterns Across the Curriculum**

**Harcourt Achieve**
**6277 Sea Harbor Drive**
**Orlando, FL 32887**                **252-480-3200**
                                    **800-531-5015**
                                **FAX 800-699-9459**
                        **http://www.steckvaughn.com**
                        **e-mail: info@steckvaughn.com**
*Steck-Vaughn Staff, Author*
*Tim McEwen, President/CEO*
*Jeff Johnson, Dir Marketing Communications*
*Chris Lehmann, Team Coordinator*

Develop students' awareness and understanding of patterns in the real world! Exercises allow students to identify, complete, extend, and create patterns. Developed across four curriculum areas: Math; Language; Social Studies; and Science. Flexible organization allows teachers to utilize content-specific activities in coordination with other classroom assignments, providing additional richness in learning.

**1247 Peer Pals**

**AGS Publishing**
**4201 Woodland Road**
**Circle Pines, MN 55014 1796**        **651-287-7220**
                                    **800-328-2560**
                                **FAX 800-471-8457**
                        **http://www.agsnet.com**
                        **e-mail: agsmail@agsnet.com**
*Robert P Bowman, John N Chanaca, Author*
*Kevin Brueggeman, President*
*Matt Keller, Marketing Manager*

A peer helping program designed to improve study skills, self-esteem, and decision making. The program uses a big sister/big brother approach, as grade 3-6 students are paired with grade K-2 students. *$33.99*

*ISBN 0-886711-62-2*

**1248 Play Helps: Toys and Activities for Children with Special Needs**

**Therapro**
**225 Arlington Street**
**Framingham, MA 01702 8723**        **508-872-9494**
                                    **800-257-5376**
                                **FAX 508-875-2062**
                        **http://www.theraproducts.com**
                        **e-mail: info@theraproducts.com**
*Roma Lear, Author*
*Karen Conrad, President*

This unique book features many homemade ideas for all ages, including the very young child. All the toys can be adapted to meet individual needs. The text is divided into sections on each of the five senses: sight, hearing, touch, taste and smell. Anyone working with children will find this book indispensable. *$42.00*

*200 pages  3rd Edition*

**1249 Reaching Out, Joining In: Teaching Social Skills to Young Children with Autism**

**Therapro**
**225 Arlington Street**
**Framingham, MA 01702 8723**        **508-872-9494**
                                    **800-257-5376**
                                **FAX 508-875-2062**
                        **http://www.theraproducts.com**
                        **e-mail: info@theraproducts.com**
*Mary Jane Weiss PhD BCBA, Sandra Harris PhD, Author*
*Karen Conrad, President*

Describes how to help young children diagnosed within the autism spectrum with one of their most challenging areas of development, social behavior. Focuses on four broad topics: play skills; the language of social skills; undestanding another person's perspective; and using these skills in an inclusive classroom. The authors present concrete strategies to teach basic play skills, how to play with others, to recognize social cues and engage in social conversation. Practical and accessible. *$16.95*

*215 pages*

**1250 Right from the Start: Behavioral Intervention for Young Children with Autism: A Guide**

**Therapro**
**225 Arlington Street**
**Framingham, MA 01702 8723**          **508-872-9494**
**800-257-5376**
**FAX 508-875-2062**
**http://www.theraproducts.com**
**e-mail: info@theraproducts.com**
*Mary Jane Weiss PhD BCBA, Sandra Harris PhD, Author*
*Karen Conrad, President*

This informative and user-friendly guide helps parents and service providers explore programs that use early intensive behavioral intervention for young children with autism and related disorders. Within these programs, many children improve in intellectual, social and adaptive functioning, enabling them to move on to regular elementary and preschools. Benefits all children, but primarily useful for children age five and younger. *$14.95*

*138 pages*

**1251 Room 14**

**LinguiSystems**
**3100 4th Avenue**
**East Moline, IL 61244**          **309-775-2300**
**800-776-4332**
**FAX 309-755-2377**
**TDY:800-933-8331**
**http://www.linguisystems.com**
**e-mail: service@linguisystems.com**
*Carolyn Wilson, Author*
*Linda Bowers, Owner*
*Rosemary Huisingh, Owner*

Build social skills by offering a variety of teaching approaches to meet the language and learning needs of your students. Through stories, comprehension activities, and organized lessons, students learn to: make and keep friends: fit in at school; handle feelings; and be responsible for their actions. *$59.95*

*198 pages  Ages 6-10*

**1252 S'Cool Moves for Learning: A Program Designed to Enhance Learning Through Body-Mind**

**Therapro**
**225 Arlington Street**
**Framingham, MA 01702 8723**          **508-872-9494**
**800-257-5376**
**FAX 508-875-2062**
**http://www.theraproducts.com**
**e-mail: info@theraproducts.com**
*Debra Heiberger MA, Margot Heiniger-White MA, Author*
*Karen Conrad, President*

The movement activities described in this book are organized in a way that is easy to integrate into the class routine throughout the day. The Minute Moves for the Classroom included in several chapters is a handy reference of movement activities which help make the transition from one activity to another fun and smooth. *$35.00*

**1253 Self-Perception: Organizing Functional Information Workbook**

**Therapro**
**225 Arlington Street**
**Framingham, MA 01702 8723**          **508-872-9494**
**800-257-5376**
**FAX 508-875-2062**
**http://www.theraproducts.com**
**e-mail: info@theraproducts.com**
*Therapro Staff, Author*
*Karen Conrad, President*

Recognizing human and animal body parts, discriminating between right and left, and exploring attitudes, emotions, humor and personal problem-solving. *$10.50*

**1254 Simple Steps: Developmental Activities for Infants, Toddlers & Two Year-Olds**

**Therapro**
**225 Arlington Street**
**Framingham, MA 01702 8723**          **508-872-9494**
**800-257-5376**
**FAX 508-875-2062**
**http://www.theraproducts.com**
**e-mail: info@theraproducts.com**
*Karen Miller, Author*
*Karen Conrad, President*

Three hundred activities linked to the latest research in brain development. Outlines a typical developmental sequence in 10 domains: social/emotional, fine motor; gross motor; language; cognition; sensory; nature; music and movement; creativity and dramatic play. Chapters on curriculum development and learning environment also included. *$24.95*

*293 pages*

**1255 Solutions Kit for ADHD**

**Childswork**
**45 Executive Dr**
**Plainview, NY 11803 9020**
**800-962-1141**
**FAX 877-434-6553**
**http://www.childswork.com**
*Sally Germain, Editorial*

This comprehensive kit is packed with hands-on materials for a multi-modal approach to working with ADHD kids aged 5 through 12. *$105.00*

*Ages 5-12*

**1256 Song Games for Sensory Integration**

**Therapro**
**225 Arlington Street**
**Framingham, MA 01702 8723**          **508-872-9494**
**800-257-5376**
**FAX 508-875-2062**
**http://www.theraproducts.com**
**e-mail: info@theraproducts.com**
*Aubrey Carton, Lois Hickman, Author*
*Karen Conrad, President*

For young children with sensory processing challenges, 15 play-along routines help remediate everything from bilateral skills to vestibular dysfunction. Narrative is helpful for parents. Includes a 51 page book filled with ideas for extending therapeutic value of these activites. 87 minute audio tape. *$21.00*

*Audio Tape*

**1257 Source for Syndromes**

**LinguiSystems**
**3100 4th Avenue**
**East Moline, IL 61244**          **309-775-2300**
**800-776-4332**
**FAX 309-755-2377**
**TDY:800-933-8331**
**http://www.linguisystems.com**
**e-mail: service@linguisystems.com**
*Gail J Richard, Debra Reichert Hoge, Author*
*Linda Bowers, Owner*
*Rosemary Huisingh, Owner*

Do you often wish someone would just tell you what to do with a specific youngster on your caseload? The Source for Syndromes can do just that. Learn about the speech-language characteristics for each sydrome with a focus on communication issues. This resource covers pertinent information for such sydromes such as Angelman, Asperger's, Autism, Rett's Tourette's, Williams, and more. *$41.95*

*117 pages Ages Birth-18*

**1258 Start to Finish: Developmentally Sequenced Fine Motor Activities for Preschool Children**

**Therapro**
**225 Arlington Street**
**Framingham, MA 01702 8723**          **508-872-9494**
**800-257-5376**
**FAX 508-875-2062**
**http://www.theraproducts.com**
**e-mail: info@theraproducts.com**
*Nory Marsh, Author*
*Karen Conrad, President*

Seventy stimulating activities target 4 areas of fine motor development normally acquired between 3 and 5: hand manipulation, pencil grasp, scissors skill and grasp, and visual motor skills. Each 30 minute activity has skills, projected goal, supplies needed, instructions and modifications provided and needs limited preparation time. *$57.50*

**1259 Stop, Relax and Think**

**Childswork**
**45 Executive Dr**
**Plainview, NY 11803 9020**
**800-962-1141**
**FAX 877-434-6553**
**http://www.childswork.com**
*Sally Germain, Editorial*

In this board game, active impulsive children learn motor control, relaxation skills, how to express their feelings, and how to problem-solve. Can be used both as a diagnostic and a treatment tool, and behaviors learned in the game can be generalized into the home or classroom. *$52.00*

*Ages 6-12*

**1260 Stop, Relax and Think Ball**

**Childswork**
**45 Executive Dr**
**Plainview, NY 11803 9020**
**800-962-1141**
**FAX 877-434-6553**
**http://www.childswork.com**
*Sally Germain, Editorial*

This ball teaches children to control their impulsivity by helping them understand and control their actions. *$22.00*

**1261 Stop, Relax and Think Card Game**

**Childswork**
**45 Executive Dr**
**Plainview, NY 11803 9020**
**800-962-1141**
**FAX 877-434-6553**
**http://www.childswork.com**
*Sally Germain, Editorial*

Players are dealt Stop, Relax and Think cards and also Stressed Out, Confused, and Discouraged cards. As they acquire more cards, they must choose different self-control skills, and they learn the value of patience and cooperating with others to achieve a goal. *$21.95*

*Ages 6-12*

**1262 Stop, Relax and Think Scriptbook**

**Childswork**
**45 Executive Dr**
**Plainview, NY 11803 9020**
**800-962-1141**
**FAX 877-434-6553**
**http://www.childswork.com**
*Sally Germain, Editorial*

In this uniquely designed book, children can practice what to say and how to act in eight different scenarios common to children with behavioral problems. The counselor and the child sit across from each other and read the scripts. *$24.95*

*Ages 8-12*

**1263 Stop, Relax and Think Workbook**

**Childswork**
**45 Executive Dr**
**Plainview, NY 11803 9020**
**800-257-5376**
**FAX 877-434-6553**
**http://www.childswork.com**
*Sally Germain, Editorial*

This new workbook contains more than 60 paper and pencil activities that teach children such important skills as: thinking about consequences, staying focused and completing a task, engaging in quiet activities without disturbing others, and more. *$19.95*

*Ages 6-12*

**1264 Successful Movement Challenges**

Therapro
225 Arlington Street
Framingham, MA 01702          508-872-9494
                             800-257-5376
                        FAX 508-875-2062
            http://www.theraproducts.com
            e-mail: info@theraproducts.com
*Jack Capon, Author*
*Karen Conrad, President*

Extensive and exciting movement activities for children in preschool, elementary and special education. Includes movement exploration challenges using parachutes, balls, hoops, ropes, bean bags, rythm sticks, scarves and much more. This popular publication also includes body conditioning, mat activities and playground apparatus activities. Everyone enjoys the creative and carefully designed movement experiences. *$14.25*

*127 pages*

**1265 Surface Counseling**

Edge Enterprises
708 W 9th Street
Lawrence, KS 66044 2846          785-749-1473
                            FAX 785-749-0207
        e-mail: nfo@edgenterprise.inc.com
*Joe N Crank, Donald D Deshler, Jean B
Schumaker, Author*
*Jacqueline Schafer, Managing Editor*
*Carolyn Mitchell, Accounting Department*

Details a set of relationship-building skills necessary for establishing a trusting, cooperative relationship between adults and youths and a problem-solving strategy that youths can learn to use by themselves. Includes study guide questions, model dialogues and role-play activities. Useful for any adult who has daily contact with children and adolescents.

*60 pages Paperback*

**1266 Survival Guide for Kids with LD**

Therapro
225 Arlington Street
Framingham, MA 01702 8723          508-872-9494
                                  800-257-5376
                             FAX 508-875-2062
                http://www.theraproducts.com
                e-mail: info@theraproducts.com
*Gary Fisher PhD, Rhonda Cummings EdD, Author*
*Karen Conrad, President*

Popular book that is highly reccommended. Contains vital information, practical advice, step-by-step strategies, and encouragement for children labeled Learning Disabled. *$9.95*

**1267 Taking Part**

AGS Publishing
4201 Woodland Road
Circle Pines, MN 55014 1796          651-287-7220
                                    800-328-2560
                               FAX 800-471-8457
                     http://www.agsnet.com
                e-mail: agsmail@agsnet.com
*Gwendolyn Cartledge, James Kleefield, Author*
*Kevin Brueggeman, President*
*Matt Keller, Marketing Manager*

A social skills program for students in preschool to grade 3 that teaches skills identified by research to be essential to social development: expressing oneself; playing with peers; responding to aggression; cooperating with peers; communicating nonverbally and making conversation. The program focuses on cooperative or group play skills and conflict resolution. Materials include a manual, puppets, stickers and posters. *$90.99*

*ISBN 0-886714-21-4*

**1268 That's Life! Social Language**

LinguiSystems
3100 4th Avenue
East Moline, IL 61244          309-775-2300
                              800-776-4332
                         FAX 309-755-2377
                       TDY:800-933-8331
            http://www.linguisystems.com
            e-mail: service@linguisystems.com
*Linda Bowers, Owner*
*Rosemary Huisingh, Owner*

Teach your students to be effective and appropriate communicators in a wide variety of situations. Through direct instruction, role-playing activities, and discussion, your students will learn the how and why of social language interaction.

*Ages 12-18*

**1269 Tools for Students Video**

Therapro
225 Arlington Street
Framingham, MA 01702 8723          508-872-9494
                                  800-257-5376
                             FAX 508-875-2062
                http://www.theraproducts.com
                e-mail: info@theraproducts.com
*Therapro Staff, Author*
*Karen Conrad, President*

This 30 minute video is a fun and participatory how-to video which provides solutions to the problems indentified in the Tools for Teachers Video. It can be used by teachers in the classroom and by parents at home. There are 25 sensory tools for movement, proprioception, mouth and hand fidgets, calming and recess. Pencil-holding and hand games to develop hand manipulation skills are also demonstrated. *$25.95*

*Video*

**1270 Tools for Teachers Video**

Therapro
225 Arlington Street
Framingham, MA 01702 8723          508-872-9494
                                  800-257-5376
                             FAX 508-875-2062
                http://www.theraproducts.com
                e-mail: info@theraproducts.com
*Therapro Staff, Author*
*Karen Conrad, President*

This video, designed by an OT to provide a logical approach to sensory integration and hand skill strategies for anyone to use, is ideal for in-services. Within 20 minutes, you'll learn how to help students calm down, focus, and increase their self-awareness. This is a great tool for teachers and therapists (shows how to inplement sensory diet into classroom), administrators and parents. *$25.95*

*Video*

**1271 Understanding Argumentative Communication: How Many Ways Can You Ask for a Cookie?**

**Therapro**
**225 Arlington Street**
**Framingham, MA  01702 8723**      **508-872-9494**
**800-257-5376**
**FAX 508-875-2062**
**http://www.theraproducts.com**
**e-mail: info@theraproducts.com**
*Christine Derse MEd, Janice Lopes MSEd, Author*
*Karen Conrad, President*

Ten uncomplicated lesson plans for classroom use. Teach a complete overview of all that Argumentative Communication encompasses or give students a brief awareness lesson about just one type of communication. Lessons can be used either consecutively or singly. Includes defining communication, gestures, sign language, object boards, picture boards, headsticks, eye pointing, scanning with picture boards, picture boards in sentence format and computers for argumentative communication. *$17.95*

*142 pages*

**1272 Updown Chair**

**Rehab and Educational Aids for Living**
**187 N Main Street**
**Dolgeville, NY  13329**
**800-696-7041**
**FAX 315-429-3071**
**http://www.realdesign.inc**
**e-mail: rdesign@twcny.rr.com**
*Kris Wohnsen, Co-Owner*

The updown chair is designed for children from 43"-63" in height. It combines optimal positioning and sitting comfort with ease of adjustment. Changing the seat height can be done quickly and safely with our exclusive foot lever activation which uses a pneumatic cylinder assist. Children can be elevated to just the right position for floor or table top activities.

*5-15 years*

**1273 What's Up? A That's LIFE! Game of Social Language**

**LinguiSystems**
**3100 4th Avenue**
**East Moline, IL  61244**      **309-775-2300**
**800-776-4332**
**FAX 309-755-2377**
**TDY:800-933-8331**
**http://www.linguisystems.com**
**e-mail: service@linguisystems.com**
*Carolyn LoGiudice, Nancy McConnell, Author*
*Linda Bowers, Owner*
*Rosemary Huisingh, Owner*

Here's a game with strategy, fast action, and competition. Your older students will love it! Teach appropriate social communication with this game. Peer evaluation is built-in so students can track progress. *$44.95*

*Ages 12-16*

**1274 Who Cares?**

**Therapro**
**225 Arlington Street**
**Framingham, MA  01702 8723**      **508-872-9494**
**800-257-5376**
**FAX 508-875-2062**
**http://www.theraproducts.com**
**e-mail: info@theraproducts.com**
*Therapro Staff, Author*
*Karen Conrad, President*

This series of small handbooks for children teaches them about diversity. *$7.99*

*32 pages  Hardcover*

**1275 Wikki Stix Hands On-Learning Activity Book**

**Therapro**
**225 Arlington Street**
**Framingham, MA  01702 8723**      **508-872-9494**
**800-257-5376**
**FAX 508-875-2062**
**http://www.theraproducts.com**
**e-mail: info@theraproducts.com**
*Therapro Staff, Author*
*Karen Conrad, President*

Loaded with great ideas for using Wikki Stix. For all ages and curriculums. *$3.50*

**1276 Workbook for Verbal Expression**

**Speech Bin**
**1965 25th Avenue**
**Vero Beach, FL  32960**      **772-770-0007**
**800-477-3324**
**FAX 772-770-0006**
**http://www.speechbin.com**
**e-mail: info@speechbin.com**
*Shane Peters, Product Coordinator*
*Jen Binney, Owner*

A book of 100s of excercises from simple naming, automatic speech sequences, and repetition exercises to complex tasks in sentence formulation and abstract verbal reasoning. Item number 1435. *$43.95*

## Social Studies

**1277 A Knock at the Door**

**Harcourt Achieve**
**6277 Sea Harbor Drive**
**Orlando, FL  32887**      **252-480-3200**
**800-531-5015**
**FAX 800-699-9459**
**http://www.steckvaughn.com**
**e-mail: info@steckvaughn.com**
*Eric Sonderling, Wendy Wassink Ackison, Author*
*Tim McEwen, President/CEO*
*Jeff Johnson, Dir Marketing Communications*
*Chris Lehmann, Team Coordinator*

The frightened stranger's identity remains a secret until the day a Nazi soldier knocks on the door.

# Classroom Resources /Social Studies

**1278  A World So Different**

Harcourt Achieve
6277 Sea Harbor Drive
Orlando, FL  32887                   252-480-3200
                                     800-531-5015
                                  FAX 800-699-9459
                          http://www.steckvaughn.com
                          e-mail: info@steckvaughn.com
*Steck-Vaughn Staff, Author*
*Tim McEwen, President/CEO*
*Jeff Johnson, Dir Marketing Communications*
*Chris Lehmann, Team Coordinator*

As generations of family members recall how dramatically technology has changed everyday life, Sarah wonders what changes are in store for her generation.

**1279  American Government Today: Steadwell**

Harcourt Achieve
6277 Sea Harbor Drive
Orlando, FL  32887                   252-480-3200
                                     800-531-5015
                                  FAX 800-699-9459
                          http://www.steckvaughn.com
                          e-mail: info@steckvaughn.com
*Sanders, Author*
*Tim McEwen, President/CEO*
*Jeff Johnson, Dir Marketing Communications*
*Chris Lehmann, Team Coordinator*

Give limited readers unlimited access to social studies and citizenship topics! Whether applying for citizenship or studying for GED Test, learners need to know about our nation's capital and the democracy it hosts. In this series, even limited readers can get a clear picture of a complex system.

**1280  Calliope**

Cobblestone Publishing
30 Grove Street
Peterborough, NH  03458              603-924-7209
                                     800-821-0115
                                  FAX 603-924-7380
                          http://www.cricketmag.com
                          e-mail: custsvc@cobblestone.mv.com
*Rosalie Baker, Editor*
*Malcom Jensen, Publisher*
*Charles Baker, Editor*

Winner of the coveted 1998 Educational Press Association's Golden Lamp Award. Calliope brings to the classroom a fresh and exciting look at world history, one theme at a time. *$29.95*

*52 pages  9 times anually*

**1281  Discoveries: Explore the Desert Ecosystem**

Sunburst Technology
400 Columbus Avenue
Valhalla, NY  10595 1349             914-747-3310
                                     800-321-7511
                                  FAX 914-747-4109
                          http://www.sunburst.com
                          e-mail: service@sunburst.com
*Mark Sotir, President*

This program invites students to explore the plants, animals, culture and georgraphy of the Sonoran Desert by day and by night.

**1282  Discoveries: Explore the Everglades Ecosystem**

Sunburst Technology
400 Columbus Avenue
Valhalla, NY  10595 1349             914-747-3310
                                     800-321-7511
                                  FAX 914-747-4109
                          http://www.sunburst.com
                          e-mail: service@sunburst.com
*Mark Sotir, President*

This multi curricular research program takes students to the Everglades where they anchor their exploration photo realistic panaramas of the habitiat.

**1283  Discoveries: Explore the Forest Ecosystem**

Sunburst Technology
400 Columbus Avenue
Valhalla, NY  10595 1349             914-747-3310
                                     800-321-7511
                                  FAX 914-747-4109
                          http://www.sunburst.com
                          e-mail: service@sunburst.com
*Mark Sotir, President*

This theme based CD-ROM enables students of all abilities to actively research a multitude of different forest ecosystems in the Appalachian National Park.

**1284  Easybook Deluxe Writing Workshop: Colonial Times**

Sunburst Technology
400 Columbus Avenue
Valhalla, NY  10595 1349             914-747-3310
                                     800-321-7511
                                  FAX 914-747-4109
                          http://www.sunburst.com
                          e-mail: service@sunburst.com
*Mark Sotir, President*

Writing workshops combine theme-based activities with the award-winning EasyBook Deluxe.

**1285  Easybook Deluxe Writing Workshop: Immigration**

Sunburst Technology
400 Columbus Avenue
Valhalla, NY  10595 1349             914-747-3310
                                     800-321-7511
                                  FAX 914-747-4109
                          http://www.sunburst.com
                          e-mail: support@sunburst.com
*Mark Sotir, President*

Writing workshops combine theme-based activities with the award-winning EasyBook Deluxe.

**1286  Easybook Deluxe Writing Workshop: Rainforest & Astronomy**

**Sunburst Technology**
**400 Columbus Avenue**
**Valhalla, NY  10595 1349**          **914-747-3310**
                                     **800-321-7511**
                              **FAX 914-747-4109**
                              **http://www.sunburst.com**
                       **e-mail: support@sunburst.com**
*Mark Sotir, President*

Writing workshops combine theme-based activities with the award-winning EasyBook Deluxe.

**1287  Explorers & Exploration: Steadwell**

**Harcourt Achieve**
**6277 Sea Harbor Drive**
**Orlando, FL  32887**              **252-480-3200**
                                    **800-531-5015**
                              **FAX 800-699-9459**
                              **http://www.steckvaughn.com**
                       **e-mail: info@steckvaughn.com**
*Steck-Vaughn Staff, Author*
*Tim McEwen, President/CEO*
*Jeff Johnson, Dir Marketing Communications*
*Chris Lehmann, Team Coordinator*

Long ago adventures are still a thrill in these vividly illustrated titles. Maps, diagrams, and contemporary prints lend an authenic air. A time line and list of events in the appropriate century put history in perspective.

**1288  First Biographies**

**Harcourt Achieve**
**6277 Sea Harbor Drive**
**Orlando, FL  32887**              **252-480-3200**
                                    **800-531-5015**
                              **FAX 800-699-9459**
                              **http://www.steckvaughn.com**
                       **e-mail: info@steckvaughn.com**
*Steck-Vaughn Staff, Author*
*Tim McEwen, President/CEO*
*Jeff Johnson, Dir Marketing Communications*
*Chris Lehmann, Team Coordinator*

True stories of true legends! Legendary figures triumph over tough challenges in these brief biographies. Beginning readers learn about favorite heroes and heroines in books they can read for themselves.

**1289  Footsteps**

**Cobblestone Publishing**
**30 Grove Street**
**Peterborough, NH  03458**         **603-924-7209**
                                    **800-821-0115**
                              **FAX 603-924-7380**
                              **http://www.cricketmag.com**
                       **e-mail: custsvc@cobblestone.mv.com**
*John Olbrych, Publisher*
*Charles Baker III, Editor*

Celebrate the heritage of African-Americans and explore their contributions to the development of our culture from the Colonial period through today. Interviews from descendents of figures from the past, maps, illustrations, and photographs complement the nonfiction articles. *$23.95*

*52 pages  5 times a year*

**1290  Imagination Express Destination Time Trip USA**

**Sunburst Technology**
**400 Columbus Avenue**
**Valhalla, NY  10595 1349**          **914-747-3310**
                                     **800-321-7511**
                              **FAX 914-747-4109**
                              **http://www.sunburst.com**
                       **e-mail: service@sunburst.com**
*Mark Sotir, President*

Student's travel through time to explore the history and development of a fictional New England town. An online scrapbook lets them learn about architecture, fashion, entertainment and events of the six major periods in U.S. history.

**1291  Make-a-Map 3D**

**Sunburst Technology**
**400 Columbus Avenue**
**Valhalla, NY  10595 1349**          **914-747-3310**
                                     **800-321-7511**
                              **FAX 914-747-4109**
                              **http://www.sunburst.com**
                       **e-mail: support@sunburst.com**
*Mark Sotir, President*

Students learn basic mapping, geography and navigation skills. Students design maps of their immediate surroundings by dragging and dropping roads and buildings and adding landmarks, land forms and traffic signs.

**1292  Maps & Navigation**

**Sunburst Technology**
**400 Columbus Avenue**
**Valhalla, NY  10595 1349**          **914-747-3310**
                                     **800-321-7511**
                              **FAX 914-747-4109**
                              **http://www.sunburst.com**
                       **e-mail: support@sunburst.com**
*Mark Sotir, President*

This exciting nautical simulation provides students with opportunities to use their math and science skills.

**1293  Patterns Across the Curriculum**

**Harcourt Achieve**
**6277 Sea Harbor Drive**
**Orlando, FL  32887**              **252-480-3200**
                                    **800-531-5015**
                              **FAX 800-699-9459**
                              **http://www.steckvaughn.com**
                       **e-mail: info@steckvaughn.com**
*Steck-Vaughn Staff, Author*
*Tim McEwen, President/CEO*
*Jeff Johnson, Dir Marketing Communications*
*Chris Lehmann, Team Coordinator*

Develop students' awareness and understanding of patterns in the real world. Exercises allow students to identify, complete, extend, and create patterns. Developed across math, language, social studies, and science. This flexible organization allows teachers to utilize content specific activities in coordination with other classroom assignments, providing additional richness in learning.

**1294    Prehistoric Creaures Then & Now: Steadwell**

Harcourt Achieve
6277 Sea Harbor Drive
Orlando, FL  32887                    252-480-3200
                                     800-531-5015
                               FAX 800-699-9459
                        http://www.steckvaughn.com
                     e-mail: info@steckvaughn.com
*Steck-Vaughn Staff, Author*
*Tim McEwen, President/CEO*
*Jeff Johnson, Dir Marketing Communications*
*Chris Lehmann, Team Coordinator*

Now limited readers can dig into the details of dinosaurs! Each information-packed title includes a special spread with a project, a profile of a dinosaur expert, or a description of a recent dinosaur discovery.

**1295    Story of the USA**

Educators Publishing Service
31 Smith Place
Cambridge, MA  02139 9031            617-547-6706
                                     800-225-5750
                               FAX 888-440-2665
                         http://www.epsbooks.com
                        e-mail: eps@epsbooks.com
*Franklin Escher Jr, Author*
*Steven Corte, President*

A series of four workbooks for grades 4-8 which presents basic topics in American History: Book 1, Explorers and Settlers - Book 2, A Young Nation Solves Its Problems - Book 3, America Becomes A Giant - and Book 4, Modern America. A list of vocabulary words introduces each chapter and study questions test students' knowledge.

**1296    Talking Walls Bundle**

Sunburst Technology
400 Columbus Avenue
Valhalla, NY  10595 1349             914-747-3310
                                     800-321-7511
                               FAX 914-747-4109
                         http://www.sunburst.com
                      e-mail: service@sunburst.com
*Mark Sotir, President*

Broaden students' perspective of cultures around the world with this two program CD-ROM bundle. From the Great Wall of China to the Berlin Wall to the Vietnam Memorial, students explore 28 "walls" that represent examples of the greatest human achievements to the most intimate expressions of individuality.

**1297    Test Practice Success: American History**

Harcourt Achieve
6277 Sea Harbor Drive
Orlando, FL  32887                    252-480-3200
                                     800-531-5015
                               FAX 800-699-9459
                        http://www.steckvaughn.com
                     e-mail: info@steckvaughn.com
*Steck-Vaughn Staff, Author*
*Tim McEwen, President/CEO*
*Jeff Johnson, Dir Marketing Communications*
*Chris Lehmann, Team Coordinator*

When you are trying to meet history standards, standardized test preparation is hard to schedule. Now you can do both at the same time. Steck-Vaughn/Berrent Test Practice Success: American History refreshes basic skills, familiarizes students with test formats and directions, and teaches test-taking strategies, while drawing on the material students are studying in class.

**1298    True Tales**

Harcourt Achieve
6277 Sea Harbor Drive
Orlando, FL  32877                    252-480-3200
                                     800-531-5015
                               FAX 800-699-9459
                        http://www.steckvaughn.com
                     e-mail: info@steckvaughn.com
*Billings, Author*
*Tim McEwen, President/CEO*
*Jeff Johnson, Dir Marketing Communications*
*Chris Lehmann, Team Coordinator*

If you have been looking for reading comprehension materials for limiteed readers, your search is over. True Tales presents powerful real-lfe events with direct connections to geography and science at reading level 3. Gripping accounts of personal triumph and tragedy put geography and science in a very real context. Accompanying activities develop reading and language arts, science, and geography skills students need to boost test scores.

## Study Skills

**1299    125 Ways to Be a Better Student**

LinguiSystems
3100 4th Avenue
East Moline, IL  61244               309-775-2300
                                     800-776-4332
                               FAX 309-755-2377
                               TDY:800-933-8331
                        http://www.linguisystems.com
                   e-mail: service@linguisystems.com
*Paula Currie, Mary deBrueys, Jill Exnicios, Author*
*Linda Bowers, Owner*
*Rosemary Huisingh, Owner*

Eliminate poor study habits! Help your students develop positive attitudes toward school with these study strategies. Students will get organized and take responsibility for their classroom attitude with these terrific lessons. Lessons are complete with key vocabulary, informative handouts, and practice activities.
*$35.95*

*136 pages  Ages 10-18*

**1300    125 Ways to Be a Better Test-Taker**

**LinguiSystems**
**3100 4th Avenue**
**East Moline, IL  61244**                    **309-775-2300**
**800-776-4332**
**FAX 309-755-2377**
**TDY:800-933-8331**
**http://www.linguisystems.com**
**e-mail: service@linguisystems.com**
*Andrea M Lazzari, Judy W Wood, Author*
*Linda Bowers, Owner*
*Rosemary Huisingh, Owner*

Help your students with test-taking strategies they can use right away. Through activities and practice tests, students learn test-taking strategies including: looking for key words in true/false questions;, answering the multiple-choice questions you know first;, drawing lines through answers you've used in matching questions, re-reading passages for comprehension tasks;, and adding details to a main idea in an essay test. *$35.95*

*150 pages  Ages 12-18*

**1301    Crash Course for Study Skills**

**LinguiSystems**
**3100 4th Avenue**
**East Moline, IL  61244**                    **309-775-2300**
**800-776-4332**
**FAX 309-755-2377**
**TDY:800-933-8331**
**http://www.linguisystems.com**
**e-mail: service@linguisystems.com**
*Marty Soper, Author*
*Linda Bowers, Owner*
*Rosemary Huisingh, Owner*

These helpful study strategies teach your students to take responsibility for their own learning. It's a practical, motivating approach that works! Students will learn to set goals, manage time, take notes, improve study habits, and understand their personal learning styles. *$35.95*

*172 pages  Ages 12-18*

**1302    Experiences with Writing Styles**

**Harcourt Achieve**
**6277 Sea Harbor Drive**
**Orlando, FL  32887**                    **252-480-3200**
**800-531-5015**
**FAX 800-699-9459**
**http://www.steckvaughn.com**
**e-mail: info@steckvaughn.com**
*Steck-Vaughn Staff, Author*
*Tim McEwen, President/CEO*
*Jeff Johnson, Dir Marketing Communications*
*Chris Lehmann, Team Coordinator*

Give your students experience applying the writing process in nine relevant situations, from personal narratives to persuasive paragraphs to research reports. Units provide a clear definition of each genre and plenty of practice with prewriting, writing, revising, proofreading, and publishing.

**1303    INSPECT: A Strategy for Finding and Correcting Spelling Errors**

**Edge Enterprises**
**708 W 9th Street**
**Lawrence, KS  66044 2846**                    **785-749-1473**
**FAX 785-749-0207**
**e-mail: nfo@edgenterprise.inc.com**
*David B McNaughton and Charles A Hughes, Author*
*Jacqueline Schafer, Managing Editor*
*Carolyn Mitchell, Accounting Department*

A strategy for detecting and correcting spelling errors in work generated with a word processing-based spellchecker. Can also be adapted for use with hand-held spellcheckers. The manual comes with IBM and Macintosh computer disks containing practice passages appropriate for upper elementary-aged students, junior-high students and high-school students. The passages can be used with such word processing programs as MS Word, Claris Works and MS Works.

*36 pages  Paperback*

**1304    Keyboarding Skills**

**Educators Publishing Service**
**31 Smith Place**
**Cambridge, MA  02139 9031**                    **617-547-6706**
**800-225-5750**
**FAX 888-440-2665**
**http://www.epsbooks.com**
**e-mail: eps@epsbooks.com**
*Diana Hanbury King, Author*
*Steven Corte, President*

This innovative touch typing method enables students of all ages to learn to type quickly and easily. After learning the alphabet, students can practice words, phrases, numbers, symbols and punctuation.

**1305    LD Teacher's IEP Companion**

**LinguiSystems**
**3100 4th Avenue**
**East Moline, IL  61244**                    **309-775-2300**
**800-776-4332**
**FAX 309-755-2377**
**TDY:800-933-8331**
**http://www.linguisystems.com**
**e-mail: service@linguisystems.com**
*Molly Lyle, Author*
*Linda Bowers, Owner*
*Rosemary Huisingh, Owner*

These IEP goals are organized developmentally by skill area with individual objectives and classroom activity suggestions. Goals and objectives cover these academic areas: math, reading, writing, literacy concepts, attention skills, study skills, classroom behavior, social interaction, and transition skills. *$39.95*

*169 pages  Ages 5-18*

**1306  Learning Strategies Curriculum**

Edge Enterprises
708 W 9th Street
Lawrence, KS  66044 2846          785-749-1473
                                 FAX 785-749-0207
            e-mail: nfo@edgenterprise.inc.com
*Jacqueline Schafer, Managing Editor*
*Carolyn Mitchell, Accounting Department*

A learning strategy is an individual's approach to a
learning task. It includes how a person thinks and acts
when planning, executing and evaluating performance on the task and its outcomes. In short, learning
strategy instruction focuses on how to learn and how
to effectively use what has been learned. Manuals
range from sentence writing to test taking. All require
training. For information, contact the Kansas Center
for Research on Learning, 3061 Dole Center, Lawrence 66045 (785-864-4780)

**1307  Peer Pals**

AGS Publishing
4201 Woodland Road
Circle Pines, MN  55014 1796      651-287-7720
                                  800-328-2560
                             FAX 800-471-8457
                        http://www.agsnet.com
                 e-mail: agsmail@agsnet.com
*Robert P Bowman,John N Chanaca, Author*
*Kevin Brueggeman, President*
*Matt Keller, Marketing Manager*

A peer helping program designed to improve study
skills, self-esteem, and decision-making. The program uses a big sister/big brother approach, as grade
3-6 students are paired with grade K-2 students.
*$33.99*

*ISBN 0-886711-62-2*

**1308  SLANT: A Starter Strategy for Class
Participation**

Edge Enterprises
708 W 9th Street
Lawrence, KS  66044 2846          785-749-1473
                                 FAX 785-749-0207
            e-mail: nfo@edgenterprise.inc.com
*Edwin S Ellis, Author*
*Jacqueline Schafer, Managing Editor*
*Carolyn Mitchell, Accounting Department*

An easy-to-learn strategy that students of all ages can
use to combine nonverbal, cognitive and verbal behaviors to increase their class participation. Specifically, students learn how to use appropriate
posture, track the speaker, activate their thinking and
contribute information. Once exposed to this strategy,
students not only increase their amount of class participation, but understand how their use of positive participation behaviors can influence the reactions of
others.

*8 pages  Pamphlet*

**1309  School Power: Strategies for Succeeding in School**

Therapro
225 Arlington Street
Framingham, MA  01702 8723        508-872-9494
                                  800-257-5376
                             FAX 508-875-2062
                 http://www.theraproducts.com
              e-mail: info@theraproducts.com
*Jeanne Schumm PhD, Marguite Radencich PhD,
Author*
*Karen Conrad, President*

A great book for students, parents and teachers. Helps
students get organized, take notes, study smarter,
write better, handle homework and more. Includes 17
reproducible handout masters. *$16.95*

*136 pages*

**1310  Study Skills and Learning Strategies for
Transition**

HEATH Resource Center
2121 K Street NW
Washington, DC  20036             202-973-0904
                                  800-544-3284
                             FAX 202-973-0908
                     http://www.heath.gwu.gov
                  e-mail: askheath@gwu.edu
*Dan Gardner, Publications Manager*
*Pamela Ekpone, Director*

The curriculum guide provides students with learning
disabilities the skills and strategies they will need to
increase their level of success within the high school
curriculum. *$15.00*

**1311  Super Study Wheel: Homework Helper**

Therapro
225 Arlington Street
Framingham, MA  01702 8723        508-872-9494
                                  800-257-5376
                             FAX 508-875-2062
                 http://www.theraproducts.com
              e-mail: info@theraproducts.com
*Therapro Staff, Author*
*Karen Conrad, President*

The fun and simple way to find study tips. Developed
by learning specialists and an occupational therapist,
the Super Study Wheel is an idea-packed resource
(with 101 tips) to improve study skills in 13 areas. As a
visual, motor and kinesthetic tool, it is very helpful to
students with unique learning styles. *$6.95*

## Toys & Games, Catalogs

**1312  Ablenet**

Ablenet
2808 North Fairview Avenue
Roseville, MN  55113              612-379-0956
                                  800-322-0956
                             FAX 651-294-2259
                      http://www.ablenetinc.com
          e-mail: customerservice@ablenetinc.com
*Cheryl Volkman, Chief Developmental Officer*
*Ken Sobtzak, Technical Support*

Simple assistive technology for teaching children with disabilities including communication aids, switches, mounting systems, environmental control, literacy and teacher resources, kits and more.

**1313 Enabling Devices/Toys for Special Children**

**Enabling Devices**
**385 Warburton Avenue**
**Hastings On Hudson, NY  10706**      **914-478-0960**
                                      **800-832-8697**
                                **FAX 914-478-7030**
                        **http://www.enablingdevices.com**
                        **e-mail: info@enablingdevices.com**
*Steven Kanor PhD, President/CEO*
*Karen O'Connor, VP Operations*

A designer, manufacturer and distributor of unique and affordable assitive and adaptive technologies for the physically and mentally challenged, ED/TFSC's products are sought by parents, teachers, and professionals alike.

**1314 Maxi Aids**

**42 Executive Blouevard**
**Farmingdale, NY  11735**            **631-752-0521**
                                      **800-522-6294**
                                **FAX 631-752-0689**
                                **TDY:516-752-0738**
                        **http://www.maxiaids.com**
                        **e-mail: sales@maxiaids.com**

Aids and appliances for independent living with products designed especially for the visually impaired, blind, hard of hearing, deaf, deaf-blind, arthritic and the physically challenged. New educational games and toys section.

**1315 PCI Educational Publishing**

**PO Box 34270**
**San Antonio, TX  78265**
                                      **800-594-4263**
                        **http://www.pcieducation.com**
                        **e-mail: info@pcieducation.com**
*Jeff McLane, President/CEO*
*Janie Haugen-McLane, Senior VP/Founder*
*Richard Resnik, VP Sales/Marketing*

Offers 14 programs in a gameboard format to improve life and social skills including Cooking Class, Community Skills, Looking Good, Eating Skills, Workplace Skills, Behavior Skills, Time Skills, Money Skills, Safety Skills, Household Skills, Social Skills, Health Skills, Survival Skills and Recreation Skills. Also offers a Life Skills catalog with over 140 additional products.

**1316 School Specialtities**

**Guidance Channel**
**135 Dupont Street**
**Plainview, NY  11803 0760**         **516-349-5520**
                                      **800-962-9020**
                                **FAX 800-262-1886**
                        **http://www.childswork.com**
                        **e-mail: info@childswork.com**
*Carmine Russo, President*

The most complete source for toys, books and games to help children with their mental health needs, including hundreds of items that deal with ADD, behavior problems, learning disabilities, physical disabilities, sleep disorders, stress and more.

**1317 Therapro**

**225 Arlington Street**
**Framingham, MA  01702 8723**        **508-872-9494**
                                      **800-257-5376**
                                **FAX 508-875-2062**
                        **http://www.theraproducts.com**
                        **e-mail: info@theraproducts.com**
*Karen Conrad, President*

Therapro offers for families and professionals a 100+ page catalog with the following: handwriting and fine motor products; perceptual, cognitive and language activities; publications and assessments.

*116 pages*

---

## Toys & Games, Products

**1318 Animal Match-Ups**

**Therapro**
**225 Arlington Street**
**Framingham, MA  01702 8723**        **508-872-9494**
                                      **800-257-5376**
                                **FAX 508-875-2062**
                        **http://www.theraproducts.com**
                        **e-mail: info@theraproducts.com**
*Therapro Staff, Author*
*Karen Conrad, President*

A wonderful visual memory game designed to appeal to young children. Learn to recognize 28 animals by collecting matching pairs from remembered positions. Develops attention and memory. *$8.95*

*Ages 3+*

**1319 Artic Shuffle**

**LinguiSystems**
**3100 4th Avenue**
**East Moline, IL  61244**            **309-775-2300**
                                      **800-776-4332**
                                **FAX 309-755-2377**
                                **TDY:800-933-8331**
                        **http://www.linguisystems.com**
                        **e-mail: service@linguisystems.com**
*Tobie Nan Kaufman, Author*
*Linda Bowers, Owner*
*Rosemary Huisingh, Owner*

Why are these card decks best-sellers? Because they're real playing cards! Your students can play Go Fish, Crazy Eights, or Concentration while they practice their target sounds. Use them for vocabulary drills or naming practice. *$89.95*

*Ages 5-Adult*

**1320 ArticBURST Articulation Practice for S, R, Ch, and Sh**

**LinguiSystems**
**3100 4th Avenue**
**East Moline, IL  61244**            **309-775-2300**
                                      **800-776-4332**
                                **FAX 309-755-2377**
                                **TDY:800-933-8331**
                        **http://www.linguisystems.com**
                        **e-mail: service@linguisystems.com**
*LinguiSystems Staff, Author*
*Linda Bowers, Owner*
*Rosemary Huisingh, Owner*

Here's a fun quick-thinking game for your older students and clients who continue to need articulation therapy. You'll get a set of cards for each of the toughest sounds. Players have to think of a word with their target sound in these four areas: rhyming, compounds, antonyms, and synonyms. *$37.95*

*Ages 10-Adult*

**1321    BUSY BOX Activity Centers**

**Enabling Devices**
**385 Warburton Avenue**
**Hastings On Hudson, NY 10706        914-478-0960**
**800-832-8697**
**FAX 914-478-7030**
**http://www.enablingdevices.com**
**e-mail: info@enablingdevices.com**
*Steven Kanor PhD, President/CEO*
*Karen O'Connor, VP Operations*

With their bright colors and exciting variety of textures and shapes that are designed to invite exploration that results in rewards including buzzers, music box melodies, radio, vibrations, puffs of air, flashing lights, and even a model that talks. Encourages hand-eye coordination, fine motor skills, gross arm movement. A full line of activity centers are available to meet the needs of the learning disabled, hearing impaired, visually impaired and multisensory impaired.

**1322    Barnaby's Burrow: An Auditory Processing Game**

**LinguiSystems**
**3100 4th Avenue**
**East Moline, IL 61244        309-775-2300**
**800-776-4332**
**FAX 309-755-2377**
**TDY:800-933-8331**
**http://www.linguisystems.com**
**e-mail: service@linguisystems.com**
*Barb Truman, Author*
*Linda Bowers, Owner*
*Rosemary Huisingh, Owner*

Your students will practice good auditory processing skills as they help Barnaby the rabbit get to his burrow. This delightful game gives you tons of auditory processing tasks at increasing levels of difficulty. 300 game cards provide stimulus items for: phonological awareness; following directions; absurdities; and identifying main idea and details. *$44.95*

*Ages 4-9*

**1323    Beads and Baubles**

**Therapro**
**225 Arlington Street**
**Framingham, MA 01702 8723        508-872-9494**
**800-257-5376**
**FAX 508-875-2062**
**http://www.theraproducts.com**
**e-mail: info@theraproducts.com**
*Therapro Staff, Author*
*Karen Conrad, President*

A basic stringing activity great for developing fine motor skills. Over 100 pieces in various shapes, colors, and sizes to string on a lace. Three laces included. *$7.50*

**1324    Beads and Pattern Cards: Complete Set**

**Therapro**
**225 Arlington Street**
**Framingham, MA 01702 8723        508-872-9494**
**800-257-5376**
**FAX 508-875-2062**
**http://www.theraproducts.com**
**e-mail: info@theraproducts.com**
*Therapro Staff, Author*
*Karen Conrad, President*

Colorful wooden sphers, cubes, cylinders and laces provide pre-reading/early math practice and help develop shape/color sorting and recognition skills. *$26.50*

**1325    Big-Little Pegboard Set**

**Therapro**
**225 Arlington Street**
**Framingham, MA 01702 8723        508-872-9494**
**800-257-5376**
**FAX 508-875-2062**
**http://www.theraproducts.com**
**e-mail: info@theraproducts.com**
*Therapro Staff, Author*
*Karen Conrad, President*

Kids love to play with this set of 25 safe, brightly colored hardwood pegs and a durable foam rubber board. *$16.99*

**1326    Blend It! End It!**

**LinguiSystems**
**3100 4th Avenue**
**East Moline, IL 61244        309-775-2300**
**800-776-4332**
**FAX 309-755-2377**
**TDY:800-933-8331**
**http://www.linguisystems.com**
**e-mail: service@linguisystems.com**
*Heather Koepke, Author*
*Linda Bowers, Owner*
*Rosemary Huisingh, Owner*

Get this fun, quick-thinking game to work on phonics and spelling skills. Players write as many words as they can that include a specific initial blend or word ending. You get 36 initial word blends including: bl-, cr-. sk-, th-, tw-. *$42.95*

*Ages 7-14*

**1327    Brainopoly: A Thinking Game**

**LinguiSystems**
**3100 4th Avenue**
**East Moline, IL 61244        309-775-2300**
**800-776-4332**
**FAX 309-755-2377**
**TDY:800-933-8331**
**http://www.linguisystems.com**
**e-mail: service@linguisystems.com**
*LinguiSystems Staff, Author*
*Linda Bowers, Owner*
*Rosemary Huisingh, Owner*

Target all the critical thinking, problem-solving, and decision-making skills your older students need to meet the demands of the classroom curriculum. Each game section has 50 questions divided into two levels of difficulty. That's 450 total questions! Students will practice using predicting, inferring, deduction skills, and more! *$44.95*

*Ages 10-15*

**1328  Categorically Speaking**

**Speech Bin**
**1965 25th Avenue**
**Vero Beach, FL  32960**          772-770-0007
                                  800-477-3324
                            FAX 772-770-0006
               http://www.speechbin.com
               e-mail: info@speechbin.com
*Shane Peters, Product Coordinator*
*Jen Binney, Owner*

This game for two to four players or two teams gives 6-10 years-olds experience in asking questions, evaluating information they receive, and using it to solve problems. To play, they must use specified question formats to get clues about pictures, recognize similarities and differences, identify salient features of objects, and encode and decode messages. Item number Q849. *$49.00*

**1329  Children's Cabinet**

**1090 S Rock Boulevard**
**Reno, NV  89502**              775-856-6200
                                800-753-5500
                          FAX 775-856-6208
            http://www.childrenscabinet.org
            e-mail: mail@childrenscabinet.org
*Mary Brown, Executive Director*
*Rose Sparks, Assistant Executive*

The Children's Cabinet is our community's stand to ensure every child and family has the services and resources to meet fundamental development, care, and learning needs.

**1330  Clip Art Collections: The Environment & Space**

**Sunburst Technology**
**Elgin, IL  60123**                Not availabl
                                  800-321-7511
                            FAX 888-800-3028

*Mark Sotir, CEO*
*Morton Cohen, VP/CFO*
*Daniel Figurski, VP Sales*

This thematic clip art collection is a perfect creativity tool for the classroom.

**1331  Clip Art Collections: The US & The World**

**Sunburst Technology**
**101 Castleton Street**
**Pleasantville, NY  10570**        914-747-3310
                            FAX 914-747-4109

*Mark Sotir, President*

This thematic clip art collection is a perfect tool for the classroom.

**1332  Colored Wooden Counting Cubes**

**Therapro**
**225 Arlington Street**
**Framingham, MA  01702 8723**       508-872-9494
                                   800-257-5376
                             FAX 508-875-2062
                http://www.theraproducts.com
                e-mail: info@theraproducts.com
*Therapro Staff, Author*
*Karen Conrad, President*

100 cubes in 6 colors are perfect for counting, patterning, and building activities. Activity Guide included. *$19.95*

**1333  Come Play with Me**

**Therapro**
**225 Arlington Street**
**Framingham, MA  01702 8723**       508-872-9494
                                   800-257-5376
                             FAX 508-875-2062
                http://www.theraproducts.com
                e-mail: info@theraproducts.com
*Therapro Staff, Author*
*Karen Conrad, President*

This three-dimensional game is so much fun while working on language, matching and visual observation skills. Toys are everywhere! Balls in the livingroom, trains in the kitchen, bears in the bedroom. Look, I found the blocks! Can you be the first to collect all of the toys you need for your toybox? *$19.95*

*Ages 3-6*

**1334  Communication Aids**

**Enabling Devices**
**385 Warburton Avenue**
**Hastings On Hudson, NY  10706**    914-478-0960
                                   800-832-8697
                             FAX 914-478-7030
                http://www.enabling devices. com
                e-mail: info@enablingdevices.com
*Steven Kanor PhD, President/CEO*
*Karen O'Connor, VP Operations*

Designed to encourage independence by allowing the user to speak your pre-recorded messages.

**1335  Create-A-Story**

**Speech Bin**
**1965 25th Avenue**
**Vero Beach, FL  32960**          772-770-0007
                                  800-477-3324
                            FAX 772-770-0006
               http://www.speechbin.com
               e-mail: info@speechbin.com
*Shane Peters, Product Coordinator*
*Jen Binney, Owner*

Here's a powerful language learning game that simplifies the creative process of story-telling and writing for 5-99 years-olds. It fosters their imaginations, organizes their thoughts, and boosts their confidence as they build a narrative. The game can be played by 1-6 players as groups or individuals. Item number C151. *$44.95*

**1336 Decoding Games**
**LinguiSystems**
**3100 4th Avenue**
**East Moline, IL 61244**          309-775-2300
                                    800-776-4332
                              FAX 309-755-2377
                              TDY:800-933-8331
                  http://www.linguisystems.com
                  e-mail: service@linguisystems.com
*Tina Sanford, Author*
*Linda Bowers, Owner*
*Rosemary Huisingh, Owner*

Get three fun games in one handy case. These colorful games target tricky decoding skills your students need for strong reading skills. $39.95

*Ages 6-10*

**1337 Definition Play by Play**
**LinguiSystems**
**3100 4th Avenue**
**East Moline, IL 61244**          309-775-2300
                                    800-776-4332
                              FAX 309-755-2377
                              TDY:800-933-8331
                  http://www.linguisystems.com
                  e-mail: service@linguisystems.com
*Sharon Spencer, Author*
*Linda Bowers, Owner*
*Rosemary Huisingh, Owner*

Teach your students to give accurate, cohesive definitions by identifying and organizing critical attributes of words. As players move along the board, they describe an object card by these attributes: function; what goes with it; size/shape; color; parts; what it's made of; and location. $44.95

*Ages 8-14*

**1338 Disc-O-Bocce**
**Therapro**
**225 Arlington Street**
**Framingham, MA 01702 8723**     508-872-9494
                                    800-257-5376
                              FAX 508-875-2062
                  http://www.theraproducts.com
                  e-mail: info@theraproducts.com
*Therapro Staff, Author*
*Karen Conrad, President*

Requested by therapists working with adults, this item is also great for children. Hundreds of uses include tossing the discs onto the ground and stepping on them to follow their path, tossing and trying to hit the same color disc on the floor, or using the discs to toss in a game of tic-tac-toe on the floor. Includes 12 colorful bocce discs in a storage box with handle. $17.95

**1339 Earobics Step 1 Home Version**
**Speech Bin**
**1965 25th Avenue**
**Vero Beach, FL 32960**          772-770-0007
                                    800-477-3324
                              FAX 772-770-0006
                  http://www.speechbin.com
                  e-mail: info@speechbin.com
*Shane Peters, Product Coordinator*
*Jen Binney, Owner*

Step 1 offers hundreds of levels of play, appealing graphics, and entertaining music to train the critical auditory skills young children need for success in learning. Item number C481. $59.00

**1340 Earobics Step 2 Home Version**
**Speech Bin**
**1965 25th Avenue**
**Vero Beach, FL 39260**          772-770-0007
                                    800-477-3324
                              FAX 772-770-0006
                  http://www.speechbin.com
                  e-mail: info@speechbin.com
*Shane Peters, Product Coordinator*
*Jen Binney, Owner*

Step 2 teaches critical language comprehension skills and trains the critical auditory skills children need for success in learning. It offers hundreds of levels of play, appealing graphics, and entertaining music to train the critical auditory skills young children need for success in learning. Item number C483. $59.00

**1341 Earobics Step 2 Specialist-Clinician Version**
**Speech Bin**
**1965 25th Avenue**
**Vero Beach, FL 32960**          772-770-0007
                                    800-477-3324
                              FAX 772-770-0006
                  http://www.speechbin.com
                  e-mail: info@speechbin.com
*Shane Peters, Product Coordinator*
*Jen Binney, Owner*

Earobics features: Tasks and Level Counter with real time display, adaptive training technology for individualized programs and reporting to track and evaluate each individual's progress. Step 2 teaches critical language comprehension skills and trains the critical auditory skills children need for success in learning. Item number C484. $299.00

**1342 Eye-Hand Coordination Boosters**
**Therapro**
**225 Arlington Street**
**Framingham, MA 01702 8723**     508-872-9494
                                    800-257-5376
                              FAX 508-875-2062
                  http://www.theraproducts.com
                  e-mail: info@theraproducts.com
*Therapro Staff, Author*
*Karen Conrad, President*

A book of 92 masters that can be used over and over again with work sheets that are appropriate for all ages. These are perceptual motor activities that involve copying and tracing in the areas of visual tracking, discrimination and spatial relationships. $14.00

*92 pages*

**1343 Familiar Things**
**Therapro**
**225 Arlington Street**
**Framingham, MA 01702 8723**     508-872-9494
                                    800-257-5376
                              FAX 508-875-2062
                  http://www.theraproducts.com
                  e-mail: info@theraproducts.com
*Therapro Staff, Author*
*Karen Conrad, President*

Identify and match shapes of common objects with these large square, rubber pieces. *$19.99*

**1344 Fishing!**

Therapro
225 Arlington Street
Framingham, MA 01702 8723          508-872-9494
                                   800-257-5376
                              FAX 508-875-2062
                       http://www.theraproducts.com
                       e-mail: info@theraproducts.com
*Therapro Staff, Author*
*Karen Conrad, President*

Encourages eye-hand coordination. Rubber hook safely catches velcro on chipboard fish. *$6.95*

**1345 Flagship Carpets**

Blue Ridge Industries
1546 Progress Road
Ellijay, GA 30540 0507          706-695-4055
                                800-848-4055
                           FAX 706-276-1980
                      http://www.flagshipcarpets.com
                      e-mail: info@flagshipcarpets.com
*Vicki Winkler, Director Sales*

Offers a variety of carpet games like hopscotch, the alphabet, geography maps, custom logo mats and more.

**1346 Geoboard Colored Plastic**

Therapro
225 Arlington Street
Framingham, MA 01702 8723          508-872-9494
                                   800-257-5376
                              FAX 508-875-2062
                       http://www.theraproducts.com
                       e-mail: info@theraproducts.com
*Therapro Staff, Author*
*Karen Conrad, President*

Teach eye/hand coordination skills while strengthening pincher grasp with rubber bands. *$3.25*

**1347 Geometrical Design Coloring Book**

Therapro
225 Arlington Street
Framingham, MA 01702 8723          508-872-9494
                                   800-257-5376
                              FAX 508-875-2062
                       http://www.theraproducts.com
                       e-mail: info@theraproducts.com
*Spyros Horemis, Author*
*Karen Conrad, President*

Color these 46 original designs of pure patterns and abstract shapes for a striking and beautiful result, regardless of skill level. Most designs are made of a combination of small and large areas. *$3.95*

*48 pages*

**1348 Geosafari**

Lakeshore Learning Materials
2695 E Dominguez Street
Carson, CA 90895          310-537-8600
                          800-421-5354
                     FAX 800-537-5403
              http://www.lakeshorelearning.com
              e-mail: orders@lakeshorelearning.com
*Michael Kaplan, President*
*Ralph Muro, Sales Department*

A fast-paced electronic game teaching geography in an exciting new way. *$99.50*

*Item #ED8700*

**1349 Get in Shape to Write**

Therapro
225 Arlington Street
Framingham, MA 01702 8723          508-872-9494
                                   800-257-5376
                              FAX 508-875-2062
                       http://www.theraproducts.com
                       e-mail: info@theraproducts.com
*Phillip Bongiorno MA OTR, Author*
*Karen Conrad, President*

Practice the visula perceptual motor skills needed for writing with these colorful, fun, and engaging activities. The 23 reusable activities will keep a student's interest while they learn to process auditory, visual, and motoor movement patterns. In addition, learn concepts of matching and sorting colors, shapes and familiar objects. *$12.95*

*Ages 3+*

**1350 Gram's Cracker: A Grammar Game**

LinguiSystems
3100 4th Avenue
East Moline, IL 61244          309-775-2300
                               800-776-4332
                          FAX 309-755-2377
                          TDY:800-933-8331
                   http://www.linguisystems.com
                   e-mail: service@linguisystems.com
*Julie Cole, Author*
*Linda Bowers, Owner*
*Rosemary Huisingh, Owner*

Gram the mouse is in the house! Students will love helping Gram get to his mouse hole as they practice these grammar skills: pronouns; plurals; possessives; past tense verbs; comparatives and superlatives; copulas; present progressives; has and have; and negatives. *$44.95*

*Ages 4-9*

**1351 Grammar Scramble: A Grammar and Sentence-Building Game**

LinguiSystems
3100 4th Avenue
East Moline, IL 61244          309-775-2300
                               800-776-4332
                          FAX 309-755-2377
                          TDY:800-933-8331
                   http://www.linguisystems.com
                   e-mail: service@linguisystems.com
*Rick Bowers, Linda Bowers, Author*
*Linda Bowers, Owner*
*Rosemary Huisingh, Owner*

Students will improve their grammar and thinking skills as they form intersecting sentences in crossword style. Students receive word tiles divide into these parts of speech: nouns; verbs; pronouns; adjectives; adverbs; articles; interrogatives; prepositions; and conjunctions. *$44.95*

*Ages 8-Adult*

**1352    Gramopoly: A Parts of Speech Game**

**LinguiSystems**
**3100 4th Avenue**
**East Moline, IL  61244**            **309-775-2300**
                                      **800-776-4332**
                                **FAX 309-755-2377**
                                **TDY:800-933-8331**
                **http://www.linguisystems.com**
        **e-mail: service@linguisystems.com**
*Raelene Hudson, Author*
*Linda Bowers, Owner*
*Rosemary Huisingh, Owner*

This best-selling game turns on the grammar lights for your older students. Assign each player a sentence from three levels of difficulty. Players must purchase parts of speech to complete their sentence. *$44.95*

*Ages 10-15*

**1353    Half and Half Design and Color Book**

**Therapro**
**225 Arlington Street**
**Framingham, MA  01702 8723**        **508-872-9494**
                                      **800-257-5376**
                                **FAX 508-875-2062**
                **http://www.theraproducts.com**
            **e-mail: info@theraproducts.com**
*Therapro Staff, Author*
*Karen Conrad, President*

Geometric designs appropriate for all ages. The client draws over dotted lines to finish the other half of the printed design. *$15.00*

*72 pages*

**1354    Hands, Feet and Arrows**

**Therapro**
**225 Arlington Street**
**Framingham, MA  01702 8723**        **508-872-9494**
                                      **800-257-5376**
                                **FAX 508-875-2062**
                **http://www.theraproducts.com**
            **e-mail: info@theraproducts.com**
*Therapro Staff, Author*
*Karen Conrad, President*

This kit has many possibilities for working on gross motor, sensory integration and academic skills. Its variety and ability to easily change to new tasks challenges all levels of abilities. Includes: 12 round sturdy plastic pieces (3 red, 3 yellow, 3 blue and 3 green) and stickers to go on the plastic pieces (3 right & 3 left feet, 3 right & 3 left hands, and 3 arrows). Guaranteed to provide many hours of fun. *$52.95*

**1355    Hooray I Can Read!**

**Therapro**
**225 Arlington Street**
**Framingham, MA  01702 8723**        **508-872-9494**
                                      **800-257-5376**
                                **FAX 508-875-2062**
                **http://www.theraproducts.com**
            **e-mail: info@theraproducts.com**
*Ravensburger, Author*
*Karen Conrad, President*

Have fun learning letters, sounds and more with 200 age appropriate questions and answers. Turn the dial until a question appears in the window, choose an answer and flip up the question mark to check it. 1-2 Players. *$18.95*

*Ages 6-8*

**1356    Huffy Woofers**

**Therapro**
**225 Arlington Street**
**Framingham, MA  01702 8723**        **508-872-9494**
                                      **800-257-5376**
                                **FAX 508-875-2062**
                **http://www.theraproducts.com**
            **e-mail: info@theraproducts.com**
*Therapro Staff, Author*
*Karen Conrad, President*

Safe giant ring toss game. Great for either indoor or outdoor activity. Includes a foam base and 6 rings, 3 red and 3 blue. *$18.95*

**1357    Idiom Game**

**LinguiSystems**
**3100 4th Avenue**
**East Moline, IL  61244**            **309-775-2300**
                                      **800-776-4332**
                                **FAX 309-755-2377**
                                **TDY:800-933-8331**
                **http://www.linguisystems.com**
        **e-mail: service@linguisystems.com**
*Dave Wisniewski, Author*
*Linda Bowers, Owner*
*Rosemary Huisingh, Owner*

Idioms give our language richness but confuse our students! Give your students practice with 800 of the most commonly used idiomatic expressions in our language. Each card provides multiple-choice questions at a lower and upper level. *$44.95*

*Ages 10-16*

**1358    Just for Me! Game**

**LinguiSystems**
**3100 4th Avenue**
**East Moline, IL  61244**            **309-775-2300**
                                      **800-776-4332**
                                **FAX 309-755-2377**
                                **TDY:800-933-8331**
                **http://www.linguisystems.com**
        **e-mail: service@linguisystems.com**
*Margaret Warner, Author*
*Linda Bowers, Owner*
*Rosemary Huisingh, Owner*

Follow-up on the early language skills from all five Just for Me! books with this fun new game. It's a hands-on approach as youngsters mix up specially-designed puzzle pieces to make funny faces. Each piece gives you five questions. That's 360 questions in all! Each puzzle piece covers an early language skill and corresponds to one part of the face. *$37.95*

*Ages 4-7*

**1359 LanguageBURST: A Language and Vocabulary Game**

**LinguiSystems**
**3100 4th Avenue**
**East Moline, IL  61244**          **309-775-2300**
                                    **800-776-4332**
                              **FAX 309-755-2377**
                              **TDY:800-933-8331**
              **http://www.linguisystems.com**
              **e-mail: service@linguisystems.com**
*Lauri Whiskeyman, Author*
*Linda Bowers, Owner*
*Rosemary Huisingh, Owner*

Expand your students' language and vocabulary skills with this quick- thinking game. Many of the items are based on the curriculum for grades 3-8 so your therapy is classroom-relevent. Students think quickly as they practice skills in four key language areas: fill-in-the-blank; categories; comparing and contrasting; and attributes. *$37.95*

*Ages 9-15*

**1360 Link N' Learn Activity Book**

**Therapo**
**225 Arlington Street**
**Framingham, MA  01702**          **508-872-9494**
                                   **800-257-5376**
                             **FAX 508-875-2062**
              **http://www.theraproducts.com**
              **e-mail: info@theraproducts.com**
*Therapro Staff, Author*
*Karen Conrad, President*

A nice accompaniment to the color rings. There are great cognitive activities included. *$8.95*

*80 pages*

**1361 Link N' Learn Activity Cards**

**Therapo**
**225 Arlington Street**
**Framingham, MA  01702 8723**          **508-872-9494**
                                        **800-257-5376**
                                  **FAX 508-875-2062**
              **http://www.theraproducts.com**
              **e-mail: info@theraproducts.com**
*Therapro Staff, Author*
*Karen Conrad, President*

Learn patterning, sequencing and color discrimination and logic skills with this set of 20 cards that show life-sized links. An instructor's guide is included. *$6.95*

**1362 Link N' Learn Color Rings**

**Therapo**
**225 Arlington Street**
**Framingham, MA  01702 8723**          **508-872-9494**
                                        **800-257-5376**
                                  **FAX 508-875-2062**
              **http://www.theraproducts.com**
              **e-mail: info@theraproducts.com**
*Therapro Staff, Author*
*Karen Conrad, President*

These easy to hook and separate colorful 1-1/2" plastic rings can be used in color sorting, counting, sequencing, and other perceptual/cognitive activities. *$6.95*

**1363 Magicatch Set**

**Therapo**
**225 Arlington Street**
**Framingham, MA  01702 8723**          **508-872-9494**
                                        **800-257-5376**
                                  **FAX 508-875-2062**
              **http://www.theraproducts.com**
              **e-mail: info@theraproducts.com**
*Therapro Staff, Author*
*Karen Conrad, President*

This Velcro catch game offers a much higher degree of success and feeling of security than traditional ball tossing games. 7 1/2 inch neon catching paddles and 2 1/2 inch ball, in a mesh bag. No latex. *$7.50*

**1364 Magnetic Fun**

**Therapo**
**225 Arlington Street**
**Framingham, MA  01702 8723**          **508-872-9494**
                                        **800-257-5376**
                                  **FAX 508-875-2062**
              **http://www.theraproducts.com**
              **e-mail: info@theraproducts.com**
*Therapro Staff, Author*
*Karen Conrad, President*

One swipe of the magic wand can pick up small objects without the need for a refined pincher grasp. *$13.95*

**1365 Maxwell's Manor: A Social Language Game**

**LinguiSystems**
**3100 4th Avenue**
**East Moline, IL  61244**          **309-775-2300**
                                    **800-776-4332**
                              **FAX 309-755-2377**
                              **TDY:800-933-8331**
              **http://www.linguisystems.com**
              **e-mail: service@linguisystems.com**
*Carolyn LoGiudice, Nancy McConnell, Author*
*Linda Bowers, Owner*
*Rosemary Huisingh, Owner*

This fun game will teach your students the social skills they need to get along with others, be more accepted by their peers, and be successful in the classroom. Maxwell, the loveable dog, leads the way as your students practice positive social language skills. *$44.95*

*Ages 4-9*

**1366  Maze Book**

**Therapro**
**225 Arlington Street**
**Framingham, MA  01702 8723**     508-872-9494
                                   800-257-5376
                              FAX 508-875-2062
                    http://www.theraproducts.com
                    e-mail: info@theraproducts.com
*Therapro Staff, Author*
*Karen Conrad, President*

Significantly more challenging than the ABC Mazes; rich in perceptual activities. *$10.00*

*32 pages*

**1367  Myrtle's Beach: A Phonological Awareness and Articulation Game**

**LinguiSystems**
**3100 4th Avenue**
**East Moline, IL  61244**     309-775-2300
                               800-776-4332
                          FAX 309-755-2377
                          TDY:800-933-8331
                 http://www.linguisystems.com
                 e-mail: service@linguisystems.com
*LinguiSystems Staff, Author*
*Linda Bowers, Owner*
*Rosemary Huisingh, Owner*

Myrtle's Beach is a fun place to practice phonologial awareness, articulation, and language skills. The flexible format allows you to meet the varied needs of all the students in your speech and language groups. *$44.95*

*Ages 4-9*

**1368  Opposites Game**

**Therapro**
**225 Arlington Street**
**Framingham, MA  01702 8723**     508-872-9494
                                   800-257-5376
                              FAX 508-875-2062
                    http://www.theraproducts.com
                    e-mail: info@theraproducts.com
*Therapro Staff, Author*
*Karen Conrad, President*

Children can explore the concept of opposites by matching and then joining these tiles. Self correcting feature allows for both independent and supervised play. Helps build observation and recognition skills. *$8.50*

**1369  PLAID**

**Speech Bin**
**1965 25th Avenue**
**Vero Beach, FL  32960**     772-770-0007
                              800-477-3324
                         FAX 772-770-0006
                http://www.speechbin.com
                e-mail: info@speechbin.com
*Shane Peters, Product Coordinator*
*Jen Binney, Owner*

PLAID is a top-notch clinical tool that gives you practical practice materials featuring twenty different phonemes — just what you need for your apraxic and aphasic adults — all in one resource. Item number 1424. *$29.95*

**1370  Parquetry Blocks & Pattern Cards**

**Therapro**
**225 Arlington Street**
**Framingham, MA  01702 8723**     508-872-9494
                                   800-257-5376
                              FAX 508-875-2062
                    http://www.theraproducts.com
                    e-mail: info@theraproducts.com
*Therapro Staff, Author*
*Karen Conrad, President*

Encourages visual perceptual skills and challenges a person's sense of design and color with squares, triangles, and rhombuses in six colors.

**1371  Patty's Cake: A Describing Game**

**LinguiSystems**
**3100 4th Avenue**
**East Moline, IL  61244**     309-775-2300
                               800-776-4332
                          FAX 309-755-2377
                          TDY:800-933-8331
                 http://www.linguisystems.com
                 e-mail: service@linguisystems.com
*Julie Cole, Author*
*Linda Bowers, Owner*
*Rosemary Huisingh, Owner*

Teach describing skills with Patty's Cake. Two levels of play in this fun game give you flexibility to meet individual students' learning needs. Players describe age-appropriate picture vocabulary cards by naming attributes such as category, function, shape, color, or location. Your students will improve their skills in: listening; memory; word retrieval; categorizing; naming attributes; formulating sentences; and giving descriptions. *$44.95*

*Ages 4-9*

**1372  Peabody Articulation**

**Speech Bin**
**1965 25th Avenue**
**Vero Beach, FL  32960**     772-770-0007
                              800-477-3324
                         FAX 772-770-0006
                http://www.speechbin.com
                e-mail: info@speechbin.com
*Shane Peters, Product Coordinator*
*Jen Binney, Owner*

You'll use these colorful stimulus cards in dozens of games and activities. Ten PAD decks — 480 cards — feature 18 frequently misarticulated consonants and blends. Each deck includes 40 picture cards, word list, two response cards, and five blank cards. Item number A180. *$140.99*

**1373  Pegboard Set**

**Therapro**
**225 Arlington Street**
**Framingham, MA  01702 8723**     508-872-9494
                                   800-257-5376
                              FAX 508-875-2062
                    http://www.theraproducts.com
                    e-mail: info@theraproducts.com
*Therapro Staff, Author*
*Karen Conrad, President*

Pegboard has 100 holes and measures 5-3/4 inch square. The pegs come in six bright colors. The 20 double-sided pattern cards or 40 different patterns present 5 levels of difficulty. *$14.99*

**1374    Phonology: Software**

**Speech Bin**
**1965 25th Avenue**
**Vero Beach, FL  32960**              772-770-0007
                                       800-477-3324
                                  FAX 772-770-0006
                          **http://www.speechbin.com**
                          **e-mail: info@speechbin.com**
*Shane Peters, Product Coordinator*
*Jen Binney, Owner*

This unique software gives you six entertaining games to treat children's phonological disorders. The program uses target patterns in a pattern cycling approach to phonological processes. Item number L183. *$99.00*

**1375    Plastic Cones**

**Therapro**
**225 Arlington Street**
**Framingham, MA  01702 8723**         508-872-9494
                                       800-257-5376
                                  FAX 508-875-2062
                        **http://www.theraproducts.com**
                        **e-mail: info@theraproducts.com**
*Therapro Staff, Author*
*Karen Conrad, President*

The 12-inch versions of the construction project cones are bright orange and made of lightweigth vinyl. Hole in top. *$5.95*

**1376    Plunk's Pond: A Riddles Game for Language**

**LinguiSystems**
**3100 4th Avenue**
**East Moline, IL  61244**             309-775-2300
                                       800-776-4332
                                  FAX 309-755-2377
                                  TDY:800-933-8331
                        **http://www.linguisystems.com**
                        **e-mail: service@linguisystems.com**
*LinguiSystems Staff, Author*
*Linda Bowers, Owner*
*Rosemary Huisingh, Owner*

Encourage divergent thinking, sharpen listening skills, and improve vocabulary with this fun riddle game. With a picture on one side and three clues on the other, these cards are great for all kinds of therapy games. Target attributes such as function, color, category, and more! *$44.95*

*Ages 4-9*

**1377    Primer Pak**

**Therapro**
**225 Arlington Street**
**Framingham, MA  01702 8723**         508-872-9494
                                       800-257-5376
                                  FAX 508-875-2062
                        **http://www.theraproducts.com**
                        **e-mail: info@theraproducts.com**
*Therapro Staff, Author*
*Karen Conrad, President*

A challenging sampler of manipulatives. Four Fit-A-Space disk puzzles with basic shapes, an 8x8 Alphabet Puzzle, three Lacing Shapes for primary lacing, and 24 Locktagons to form structures. *$14.99*

**1378    Punctuation Play-by-Play**

**LinguiSystems**
**3100 4th Avenue**
**East Moline, IL  61244**             309-775-2300
                                       800-776-4332
                                  FAX 309-755-2377
                                  TDY:800-933-8331
                        **http://www.linguisystems.com**
                        **e-mail: service@linguisystems.com**
*Carolyn LoGiudice, Mike LoGiudice, Author*
*Linda Bowers, Owner*
*Rosemary Huisingh, Owner*

Punctuation Play-by-Play engages students in a lively game as they practice essential punctuation skills including: capitalization; end marks; apostrophes; commas; quotation marks; colons; semicolons. Question cards are divided into two levels of difficulty. *$44.95*

*Ages 10-18*

**1379    Read-A-Bit**

**LinguiSystems**
**3100 4th Avenue**
**East Moline, IL  61244**             309-775-2300
                                       800-776-4332
                                  FAX 309-755-2377
                                  TDY:800-933-8331
                        **http://www.linguisystems.com**
                        **e-mail: service@linguisystems.com**
*Dagmar Kafka, Author*
*Linda Bowers, Owner*
*Rosemary Huisingh, Owner*

Get 15 games in one box! Six decks of cards with different levels of reading difficulty work with and without the colorful game board to give you plenty of flexibility. You'll work through a hierarchy of reading skills from primer to grade 3. Students practice consonants, vowels, controlled R sounds, sight words, and more. *$41.95*

*Ages 5-9*

**1380    Reading Comprehension Game Intermediate**

**LinguiSystems**
**3100 4th Avenue**
**East Moline, IL  61244**             309-775-2300
                                       800-776-4332
                                  FAX 309-755-2377
                                  TDY:800-933-8331
                        **http://www.linguisystems.com**
                        **e-mail: service@linguisystems.com**
*Linda Bowers, Rosemary Huisingh, Carolyn*
*LoGiudice, Author*
*Linda Bowers, Owner*
*Rosemary Huisingh, Owner*

This game gives you fun, repetitive practice in three essential reading comprehension skills. The first is Reading for Details including cloze, referents, sequencing, describing, and more! The second is Reading for Understanding including main idea, paraphrasing, context clues, defining, and more. The third area is Going Beyond including making references, predicting, and making associations. *$44.95*

*Ages 12-18*

**1381  Rhyming Sounds Game**

Therapro
225 Arlington Street
Framingham, MA  01702 8723          508-872-9494
                                    800-257-5376
                                    FAX 508-875-2062
                        http://www.theraproducts.com
                        e-mail: info@theraproducts.com
*Therapro Staff, Author*
*Karen Conrad, President*

Introduces 32 different rhyming sounds as players match the ending sound of the picture tile to the corresponding object on the category boards. Includes sorting/storage tray, 56 picture tiles, and 4 category cards with self-checking feature. No reading required. *$9.95*

**1382  Rocky's Mountain: A Word-finding Game**

LinguiSystems
3100 4th Avenue
East Moline, IL  61244              309-775-2300
                                    800-776-4332
                                    FAX 309-755-2377
                                    TDY:800-933-8331
                        http://www.linguisystems.com
                        e-mail: service@linguisystems.com
*Gina Williamson, Susan Shields, Author*
*Linda Bowers, Owner*
*Rosemary Huisingh, Owner*

Tackle stubborn word-finding problems with this fun game! Game cards are organized by four word-finding strategies so you can pick the strategy that best meets your students' needs. Teach these strategies for word-finding: visual imagery; word association; sound/letter cueing; and categories. *$44.95*

*Ages 4-9*

**1383  SPARC for Grammar**

LinguiSystems
3100 4th Avenue
East Moline, IL  61244              309-775-2300
                                    800-776-4332
                                    FAX 309-755-2377
                                    TDY:800-933-8331
                        http://www.linguisystems.com
                        e-mail: service@linguisystems.com
*Susan Thomsen, Kathy Donnelly, Author*
*Linda Bowers, Owner*
*Rosemary Huisingh, Owner*

Teach grammar in meaningful contexts! The lessons provide a wealth of opportunities for your students to hear, repeat, answer questions and tell stories using targeted language structures. *$39.95*

*165 pages  Ages 4-10*

**1384  Self-Control Games & Workbook**

Western Psychological Services
12031 Wilshire Boulevard
Los Angeles, CA  90025              310-478-2061
                                    800-648-8857
                                    FAX 310-478-7838
                        http://www.wpspublish.com
                        e-mail: custsve@wpspublish.com
*Berthold Berg, PhD, Author*
*Greg Gilmore, Executive Vice President*

This game is designed to teach self-control in academic and social situations. Addresses a total of 24 impulsive, inattentive and hyperactive behaviors. The companion workbook reinforces the use of positive self-statements, and problem-solving techniques, instead of expressing anger. *$62.50*

**1385  Sequenced Inventory of Communication Development Revised(SICD)**

Speech Bin
1965 25th Avenue
Vero Beach, FL  32960               772-770-0007
                                    800-477-3324
                                    FAX 888-329-2246
                        http://www.speechbin.com
                        e-mail: info@speechbin.com
*Dona Hedrick, Elizabeth Prather, Annette Tobin, Author*
*Shane Peters, Product Coordinator*
*Jen Binney, Owner*

SICD uses appealing toys to assess communication skills of children at all levels of ability including those with impaired hearing or vision. SICD looks at child and environment, measuring receptive and expressive language. Item number W710. *$395.00*

**1386  Shape and Color Sorter**

Therapro
225 Arlington Street
Framingham, MA  01702 8723          508-872-9494
                                    800-257-5376
                                    FAX 508-875-2062
                        http://www.theraproducts.com
                        e-mail: info@theraproducts.com
*Therapro Staff, Author*
*Karen Conrad, President*

This simple and safe task of perception includes 25 crepe foam rubber pieces to sort by shape or color. Comes in five bright colors, each color representing a shape. Shapes fit nicely onto five large pegs. *$14.99*

**1387  Shapes**

Therapro
225 Arlington Street
Framingham, MA  01702 8723          508-872-9494
                                    800-257-5376
                                    FAX 508-875-2062
                        http://www.theraproducts.com
                        e-mail: info@theraproducts.com
*Therapro Staff, Author*
*Karen Conrad, President*

This 8 1/2 x 11 inch high quality coloring book will help children learn to recognize shapes while improving their fine motor and perceptual skills. *$1.50*

*30 pages*

**1388  Silly Sentences**

Speech Bin
1965 25th Avenue
Vero Beach, FL  32960               772-770-0007
                                    800-477-3324
                                    FAX 772-770-0006
                        http://www.speechbin.com
                        e-mail: info@speechbin.com
*Shane Peters, Product Coordinator*
*Jen Binney, Owner*

Children love to have fun. Silly Sentences lets them have fun while they play these engaging card games to learn: subject + verb agreement; speech sound articulation; S+ V+ O sentences; questioning and answering; humor and absurdities and present progressive verbs. Item number P506. *$41.00*

**1389    Snail's Pace Race Game**

**Therapro**
**225 Arlington Street**
**Framingham, MA  01702 8723**      **508-872-9494**
                                    **800-257-5376**
                          **FAX 508-875-2062**
              **http://www.theraproducts.com**
                  **e-mail: info@theraproducts.com**
*Therapro Staff, Author*
*Karen Conrad, President*

This classic, easy color game is back and is fun for all to play. Roll the colored dice to see which wooden snail will move closer to the finish line. Promotes color recognition, understanding of taking turns, and sharing. *$ 19.95*

**1390    Sounds Abound Game**

**LinguiSystems**
**3100 4th Avenue**
**East Moline, IL  61244**      **309-775-2300**
                                **800-776-4332**
                      **FAX 309-755-2377**
                      **TDY:800-933-8331**
              **http://www.linguisystems.com**
                  **e-mail: service@linguisystems.com**
*Orna Lenchner PhD, Blanche Podhajski PhD, Author*
*Linda Bowers, Owner*
*Rosemary Huisingh, Owner*

Teach critical features about sounds in words for better language skills. Your students will love this fun game because it's easy to play. This game targets the sounds students use the most — f, s, p, t, and m. These essential sounds are critical for early literacy success. *$109.95*

*112 pages  Ages 4-8*

**1391    Speech & Language & Voice & More...**

**Speech Bin**
**1965 25th Avenue**
**Vero Beach, FL  32960**      **772-770-0007**
                                **800-477-3324**
                      **FAX 772-770-0006**
              **http://www.speechbin.com**
                  **e-mail: info@speechbin.com**
*Shane Peters, Product Coordinator*
*Jen Binney, Owner*

Contains 88 practically perfect reproducible games and activities ideal for your K-5 clients. It gives you: manipulable activities to keep active leaners learning; tasks to match a multitude of interests and abilities and vocal hygiene worksheets targeted to reduce vocal abuse. Item number 1496. *$19.95*

**1392    Speech Sports**

**Speech Bin**
**1965 25th Avenue**
**Vero Beach, FL  32960**      **772-770-0007**
                                **800-477-3324**
                      **FAX 772-770-0006**
              **http://www.speechbin.com**
                  **e-mail: info@speechbin.com**
*Shane Peters, Product Coordinator*
*Jen Binney, Owner*

Speech Sports makes every child in your caseload a shining sports star. Reproducible gamesboards and language activities feature 19 different sports from boating to skating, bowling to running, basketball to soccer. Item number 1590. *$24.95*

**1393    Speech-Language Delights**

**Speech Bin**
**1965 25th Avenue**
**Vero Beach, FL  32960**      **772-770-0007**
                                **800-477-3324**
                      **FAX 772-770-0006**
              **http://www.speechbin.com**
                  **e-mail: info@speechbin.com**
*Shane Peters, Product Coordinator*
*Jen Binney, Owner*

Cook up lots of fun with Speech-Language Delights! Delectably delicious speech and language activities and games provide rich opportunities and hands-on activities with food-related themes to enrich K-8 kids. Item number 1541. *$ 29.95*

**1394    Spider Ball**

**Therapro**
**225 Arlington Street**
**Framingham, MA  01702 8723**      **508-872-9494**
                                    **800-257-5376**
                          **FAX 508-875-2062**
              **http://www.theraproducts.com**
                  **e-mail: info@theraproducts.com**
*Therapro Staff, Author*
*Karen Conrad, President*

Easy to catch, won't roll away! This foam rubber ball has rubber legs that make it incredibly easy to catch. Invented by a PE teacher to help children improve their ball playing skills. The Spiderball's legs act as brakes bringing it to a stop when rolled and minimizing the time needed to chase a missed ball. 2 1/4 inch diameter. *$4.50*

**1395    Squidgie Flying Disc**

**Therapro**
**225 Arlington Street**
**Framingham, MA  01702 8723**      **508-872-9494**
                                    **800-257-5376**
                          **FAX 508-875-2062**
              **http://www.theraproducts.com**
                  **e-mail: info@theraproducts.com**
*Therapro Staff, Author*
*Karen Conrad, President*

This is a great flexible flying disc that is amazingly easy to throw and travels over long distances. It is soft and easy to catch. It will even float in the pool! *$4.95*

**1396 String-A-Long Lacing Activity**

Therapro
225 Arlington Street
Framingham, MA 01702 8723     508-872-9494
800-257-5376
FAX 508-875-2062
http://www.theraproducts.com
e-mail: info@theraproducts.com

*Therapro Staff, Author*
*Karen Conrad, President*

A lacing activity that develops hand eye coordination and concentration as children create 2 colorful bead buddies. Each buddy has 4 laces attached to its painted heal now build the body with 23 beads! *$18.00*

*Ages 4+*

**1397 That's Life: A Game of Life Skills**

LinguiSystems
3100 4th Avenue
East Moline, IL 61244     309-775-2300
800-776-4332
FAX 309-755-2377
TDY:800-933-8331
http://www.linguisystems.com
e-mail: service@linguisystems.com

*Patricia Smith, Author*
*Linda Bowers, Owner*
*Rosemary Huisingh, Owner*

Help your older students refine their language skills to negotiate the real world with this fun game. Get 100 thinking and language questions for each of these life area: consumer affairs, government, health concerns, money matters, going places, and homemaking. *$44.95*

*Ages 12-18*

**1398 Things in My House: Picture Matching Game**

Therapro
225 Arlington Street
Framingham, MA 01702 8723     508-872-9494
800-257-5376
FAX 508-875-2062
http://www.theraproducts.com
e-mail: info@theraproducts.com

*Therapro Staff, Author*
*Karen Conrad, President*

Strengthen visual discrimination, sorting, and organizing skills. Young children enjoy finding correct matches in this fun first game. The colorful graphics depicting familiar household objects and activities encourage verbalization and imaginative play. *$10.95*

**1399 Tic-Tac-Artic and Match**

LinguiSystems
3100 4th Avenue
East Moline, IL 61244     309-775-2300
800-776-4332
FAX 309-755-2377
TDY:800-933-8331
http://www.linguisystems.com
e-mail: service@linguisystems.com

*Carol A Vaccariello, Author*
*Linda Bowers, Owner*
*Rosemary Huisingh, Owner*

Tic-Tac-Artic and Match gives you five games on every page and tons of practice per session. Each page has 16 pictures for one target phoneme. To play Tic-Tac-Artic, use the special game template to create four different tic-tac-toe style games. *$34.95*

*Ages 4-12*

**1400 Toddler Tote**

Therapro
225 Arlington Street
Framingham, MA 01702 8723     508-872-9494
800-257-5376
FAX 508-875-2062
http://www.theraproducts.com
e-mail: info@theraproducts.com

*Therapro Staff, Author*
*Karen Conrad, President*

Offers one Junior Fit-A-Space panel that has large geometric shapes; 4 Shape Squares providing basic shapes in a more challenging size; 2 Peg Play Vehicles and Pegs introducing early peg board skills; 3 Familiar Things and 2 piece puzzles and a handy take-along bag. *$14.99*

**1401 Tools of the Trade Game**

Therapro
225 Arlington Street
Framingham, MA 01702 8723     508-872-9494
800-257-5376
FAX 508-875-2062
http://www.theraproducts.com
e-mail: info@theraproducts.com

*Therapro Staff, Author*
*Karen Conrad, President*

Introduces 32 different occupations and the tools they use. Tool picture tiles are sorted into compartments which correspond to the category card, showing people dressed for their jobs. Includes sorting tray, 56 tool tiles and 4 category cards with self-checking feature. No reading required. *$9.95*

**1402 Vowel Scramble**

LinguiSystems
3100 4th Avenue
East Moline, IL 61244     309-775-2300
800-776-4332
FAX 309-755-2377
TDY:800-933-8331
http://www.linguisystems.com
e-mail: service@linguisystems.com

*Carolyn LoGiudice, Author*
*Linda Bowers, Owner*
*Rosemary Huisingh, Owner*

Your student will love this fun new way to practice spelling and phonological awareness skills. Players earn points by using letter tiles to complete words on the game board. *$44.95*

*Ages 7-12*

**1403  Whistle Set**
Therapro
225 Arlington Street
Framingham, MA  01702 8723        508-872-9494
                                          800-257-5376
                                     FAX 508-875-2062
                        http://www.theraproducts.com
                       e-mail: info@theraproducts.com
*Therapro Staff, Author*
*Karen Conrad, President*

The whistles in this collection are colorful and sturdy.
Most feature moving parts as well as noise-makers to
stimulate both ocular and oral motor skills. Includes
nine whistles. Respiratory demand ranges from easy
to difficult. *$17.50*

**1404  Wikki Stix-Neon & Primary**
Therapro
225 Arlington Street
Framingham, MA  01702 8723        508-872-9494
                                          800-257-5376
                                     FAX 508-875-2062
                        http://www.theraproducts.com
                       e-mail: info@theraproducts.com
*Therapro Staff, Author*
*Karen Conrad, President*

Colorful, nontoxic waxed strings which are easily
molded to create various forms, shapes and letters.
Combine motor planning skill with fine motor skill by
following simple shapes with Wikki Stix and then coloring in the shape. *$4.95*

*Each*

**1405  Wonder Ball**
Therapro
225 Arlington Street
Framingham, MA  01702 8723        508-872-9494
                                          800-257-5376
                                     FAX 508-875-2062
                        http://www.theraproducts.com
                       e-mail: info@theraproducts.com
*Therapro Staff, Author*
*Karen Conrad, President*

This 3 inch ball made of many small suction cups feels
good in the palm of the hand and, when thrown against
a smooth surface, will firmly stick. Pulling it from the
surface requires strength, resulting in proprioceptive
stimulation. *$1.95*

**1406  Wooden Pegboard**
Therapro
225 Arlington Street
Framingham, MA  01702 8723        508-872-9494
                                          800-257-5376
                                     FAX 508-875-2062
                        http://www.theraproducts.com
                       e-mail: info@theraproducts.com
*Therapro Staff, Author*
*Karen Conrad, President*

This 10 inch square, laquer-finished wooden board
has 100 drilled holes. *$10.95*

**1407  Wooden Pegs**
Therapro
225 Arlington Street
Framingham, MA  01702 8723        508-872-9494
                                          800-257-5376
                                     FAX 508-875-2062
                        http://www.theraproducts.com
                       e-mail: info@theraproducts.com
*Therapro Staff, Author*
*Karen Conrad, President*

Smooth 2 inch pegs in 6 colors for use in design and
pattern making with the wooden pegboard above. Set
of 100 pegs. *$4.95*

**1408  WriteOPOLY**
LinguiSystems
3100 4th Avenue
East Moline, IL  61244                309-775-2300
                                          800-776-4332
                                     FAX 309-755-2377
                                     TDY:800-933-8331
                        http://www.linguisystems.com
                     e-mail: service@linguisystems.com
*Paul F Johnson, Author*
*Linda Bowers, Owner*
*Rosemary Huisingh, Owner*

End writer's block for even your most reluctant writers with this fun game. Improve written language
skills with WriteOPOLY. Students travel around a
colorful game board buying properties and filling out
Writing Plan sheets. *$ 44.95*

*Ages 9-14*

# Writing

**1409  100% Grammar**
LinguiSystems
3100 4th Avenue
East Moline, IL  61244                309-775-2300
                                          800-776-4332
                                     FAX 309-755-2377
                                     TDY:800-933-8331
                        http://www.linguisystems.com
                     e-mail: service@linguisystems.com
*Mike LoGiudice, Carolyn LoGiudice, Author*
*Linda Bowers, Owner*
*Rosemary Huisingh, Owner*

Make the link between grammar and communication
skills with this incredible resource. You'll get relevant, fun activities to develop clear, accurate, excellent communication skills. 100% Grammar
thoroughly covers all the essential grammar areas including: nouns; pronouns; complements; verbals;
clauses; and fine points. *$37.95*

*174 pages  Ages 9-14*

**1410  100% Grammar LITE**

LinguiSystems
3100 4th Avenue
East Moline, IL  61244                    309-775-2300
                                          800-776-4332
                                   FAX 309-755-2377
                                   TDY:800-933-8331
                         http://www.linguisystems.com
                    e-mail: service@linguisystems.com
*Mike LoGiudice, Carolyn LoGiudice, Author*
*Linda Bowers, Owner*
*Rosemary Huisingh, Owner*

Teach one grammar concept at a time. Compared to 100% Grammar, this resource is lighter in the amount of content per page and contextual demands of the practice items. The fun art and light approach will appeal to your hardest-to-teach students. The book is divided into two sections covering parts of speech and sentence structures. *$37.95*

*178 pages  Ages 4-19*

**1411  100% Punctuation**

LinguiSystems
3100 4th Avenue
East Moline, IL  61244                    309-775-2300
                                          800-776-4332
                                   FAX 309-755-2377
                                   TDY:800-933-8331
                         http://www.linguisystems.com
                    e-mail: service@linguisystems.com
*Mike LoGiudice, Carolyn LoGiudice, Author*
*Linda Bowers, Owner*
*Rosemary Huisingh, Owner*

Good written language requires the appropriate touches. On-target punctuation is essential for clear writing. This resource puts fun, zip, and humor into teaching this necessary skill. Each unit gives you a teacher guide, a skill overview, light-hearted activity sheets, and a handy quiz for accountability. *$37.95*

*179 pages  Ages 9-14*

**1412  100% Punctuation LITE**

LinguiSystems
3100 4th Avenue
East Moline, IL  61244                    309-775-2300
                                          800-776-4332
                                   FAX 309-755-2377
                                   TDY:800-933-8331
                         http://www.linguisystems.com
                    e-mail: service@linguisystems.com
*LinguiSystems Staff, Author*
*Linda Bowers, Owner*
*Rosemary Huisingh, Owner*

Good punctuation is essential for clear written communication. This light approach makes it fun to teach and fun to learn. Get practice pages for: capitals; end marks; apostrophes; commas; quotation marks; letters; abbreviations; colons; and semicolons. *$37.95*

*183 pages  Ages 9-14*

**1413  100% Spelling**

LinguiSystems
3100 4th Avenue
East Moline, IL  61244                    309-775-2300
                                          800-776-4332
                                   FAX 309-755-2377
                                   TDY:800-933-8331
                         http://www.linguisystems.com
                    e-mail: service@linguisystems.com
*LinguiSystems Staff, Author*
*Linda Bowers, Owner*
*Rosemary Huisingh, Owner*

Demystify spelling by helping students tackle one pattern at a time. Your students will discover and retain spelling rules by searching for spelling patterns. Each set of three lessons targets a specific spelling pattern. These activity sheets are great for independent work, group work, and take-home practice. *$37.95*

*187 pages  Ages 8-14*

**1414  100% Story Writing**

LinguiSystems
3100 4th Avenue
East Moline, IL  61244                    309-775-2300
                                          800-776-4332
                                   FAX 309-755-2377
                                   TDY:800-933-8331
                         http://www.linguisystems.com
                    e-mail: service@linguisystems.com
*Dave Wisniewski, Katarina Hempstead, Author*
*Linda Bowers, Owner*
*Rosemary Huisingh, Owner*

Your students experience success with writing because you give them strategies to sequence, plan, and write a great story! You'll get 50 well-developed topics for your students to choose from. Work on organizing thoughts before writing, sequencing story events, writing paragraphs, and using storyboards to visualize a story. *$37.95*

*149 pages  Ages 9-14*

**1415  100% Writing 4-book Set**

LinguiSystems
3100 4th Avenue
East Moline, IL  61244                    309-775-2300
                                          800-776-4332
                                   FAX 309-755-2377
                                   TDY:800-933-8331
                         http://www.linguisystems.com
                    e-mail: service@linguisystems.com
*Dave Wisniewski, Author*
*Linda Bowers, Owner*
*Rosemary Huisingh, Owner*

Awaken the slumbering interest in writing that your students unknowingly possess. This set of books shows students how to organize thoughts into cohesive, interesting writing. Even students who hate to write will produce solidly-crafted products. *$131.80*

*150 pages  Ages 12-15*

**1416   100% Writing: Comparison and Contrast**

LinguiSystems
3100 4th Avenue
East Moline, IL  61244          309-775-2300
                                800-776-4332
                         FAX 309-755-2377
                         TDY:800-933-8331
                http://www.linguisystems.com
                e-mail: service@linguisystems.com
*Dave Wisniewski, Author*
*Linda Bowers, Owner*
*Rosemary Huisingh, Owner*

Help your students to learn to write comparison and
contrast with this helpful resource. Chapters walk students through introductory, body, and concluding
paragraphs. Along the way they'll practice helpful
strategies of identifying workable comparisons and
meaningful contrasts. *$37.95*

*183 pages  Ages 12-15*

**1417   100% Writing: Exposition**

LinguiSystems
3100 4th Avenue
East Moline, IL  61244          309-775-2300
                                800-776-4332
                         FAX 309-755-2377
                         TDY:800-933-8331
                http://www.linguisystems.com
                e-mail: service@linguisystems.com
*Dave Wisniewski, Author*
*Linda Bowers, Owner*
*Rosemary Huisingh, Owner*

Get helpful handouts, instructions, and practice sheets
to help students learn all about expository writing.
Chapters cover introductory paragraph, building body
paragraphs, concluding paragraph, using quotations
in definition, and much more! *$37.95*

*143 pages  Ages 12-15*

**1418   100% Writing: Narration**

LinguiSystems
3100 4th Avenue
East Moline, IL  61244          309-775-2300
                                800-776-4332
                         FAX 309-755-2377
                         TDY:800-933-8331
                http://www.linguisystems.com
                e-mail: service@linguisystems.com
*Dave Wisniewski, Author*
*Linda Bowers, Owner*
*Rosemary Huisingh, Owner*

Your students will learn all they need to know about
narrative writing with this incredible resource. Chapters cover introducing narration, consistency of tense,
use of dialogue sequencing an incident, using specific
vocabulary, variety in sentence structure, character
and setting development, and much more! *$37.95*

*187 pages  Ages 12-15*

**1419   100% Writing: Persuasion**

LinguiSystems
3100 4th Avenue
East Moline, IL  61244          309-775-2300
                                800-776-4332
                         FAX 309-755-2377
                         TDY:800-933-8331
                http://www.linguisystems.com
                e-mail: service@linguisystems.com
*Dave Wisniewski, Author*
*Linda Bowers, Owner*
*Rosemary Huisingh, Owner*

Teach all the basics of writing persuasion. Students
will learn how to write a simple five-paragraph persuasion, understand fact vs. opinion, circling in persuasion, appealing to logic and emotion, and much
more. *$37.95*

*143 pages  Ages 12-15*

**1420   125 Ways to Be a Better Writer**

LinguiSystems
3100 4th Avenue
East Moline, IL  61244          309-775-2300
                                800-776-4332
                         FAX 309-755-2377
                         TDY:800-933-8331
                http://www.linguisystems.com
                e-mail: service@linguisystems.com
*Paul F Johnson, Author*
*Linda Bowers, Owner*
*Rosemary Huisingh, Owner*

Your students will be eager to write in these fun, relevant contexts. Train functional, confident writers
with 125 strategies for better writing skills.
Easy-to-grasp strategies and practice pages help your
students learn the writing process, express their
thoughts clearly, write better sentences and paragraphs, and more. *$35.95*

*166 pages  Ages 12-18*

**1421   125 Writing Projects**

LinguiSystems
3100 4th Avenue
East Moline, IL  61244          309-775-2300
                                800-776-4332
                         FAX 309-755-2377
                         TDY:800-933-8331
                http://www.linguisystems.com
                e-mail: service@linguisystems.com
*Paul F Johnson, Author*
*Linda Bowers, Owner*
*Rosemary Huisingh, Owner*

Help your students discover themselves as successful
writers. This handy resource gives you activities arranged in a hierarchy to meet the needs of all the levels
you teach. *$35.95*

*171 pages  Ages 10-17*

**1422 Author's Toolkit**

Sunburst Technology
400 Columbus Avenue
Valhalla, NY 10595 1349          914-747-3310
                                 800-321-7511
                           FAX 914-747-4109
                      http://www.sunburst.com
           e-mail: support@sunburst.com
*Mark Sotir, President*

Students can use this comprehensive tool to organize ideas, make outlines, rough drafts, edit and print all their written work.

**1423 Blend It! End It!**

LinguiSystems
3100 4th Avenue
East Moline, IL 61244          309-775-2300
                               800-776-4332
                         FAX 309-755-2377
                         TDY:800-933-8331
                http://www.linguisystems.com
        e-mail: service@linguisystems.com
*Heather Koepke, Author*
*Linda Bowers, Owner*
*Rosemary Huisingh, Owner*

Get this fun quick-thinking game to work on phonics and spelling skills. Players write as many words as they can including a specific initial blend or word ending. You get 36 initial word blends including: bl-, cr-, spl-. sk-, th-, tw-. *$42.95*

*Ages 7-14*

**1424 Callirobics: Advanced Exercises**

Therapro
225 Arlington Street
Framingham, MA 01702 8723          508-872-9494
                                   800-257-5376
                             FAX 508-875-2062
                  http://www.theraproducts.com
         e-mail: info@theraproducts.com
*Therapro Staff, Author*
*Karen Conrad, President*

Allows those who have finished earlier Callirobics programs to continue improving their handwriting in a fun and creative way. Callirobics Advanced lets one create shapes to popular music from around the world. *$27.95*

*Book and CD*

**1425 Callirobics: Exercises for Adults**

Therapro
225 Arlington Street
Framingham, MA 01702 8723          508-872-9494
                                   800-257-5376
                             FAX 508-875-2062
                  http://www.theraproducts.com
         e-mail: info@theraproducts.com
*Therapro Staff, Author*
*Karen Conrad, President*

Callirobics-for-Adults is a program designed to help adults regain handwriting skills to music. The music assists as an auditory cue in initiating writing movements, and will help develop a sense of rhythm in writing. The program consists of two sections: exercises of simple graphical shapes that help adults gain fluency in the writing movement, and exercises of various combinations of cursive letters. *$30.95*

**1426 Callirobics: Handwriting Exercises to Music**

Therapro
225 Arlington Street
Framingham, MA 01702 8723          508-872-9494
                                   800-257-5376
                             FAX 508-875-2062
                  http://www.theraproducts.com
         e-mail: info@theraproducts.com
*Therapro Staff, Author*
*Karen Conrad, President*

Ten structured sessions, each with 2 exercises and 2 pieces of music. Includes stickers and a certificate book. *$27.95*

*Book and CD*

**1427 Callirobics: Prewriting Skills with Music**

Therapro
225 Arlington Street
Framingham, MA 01702 8723          508-872-9494
                                   800-257-5376
                             FAX 508-875-2062
                  http://www.theraproducts.com
         e-mail: info@theraproducts.com
*Therapro Staff, Author*
*Karen Conrad, President*

These 11 handwriting exercises are a series of simple and enjoyable graphical patterns to be traced by the child while listening to popular melodies. *$27.95*

*Book and CD*

**1428 Caps, Commas and Other Things**

Academic Therapy Publications
20 Commercial Boulevard
Novato, CA 94949          415-883-3314
                          800-422-7249
                    FAX 888-287-9975
          http://www.academictherapy.com
      e-mail: sales@academictherapy.com
*Sheryl Pastorek, Author*
*Betty Kratoville, Editor*
*Anna Arena, President*

A writing program for regular, remedial and EST students in grades 3 through 12 and adults in basic education classes remedial ESL. Six levels on capitalization and punctuation, four levels on written expression. Specific lesson plans with reproducible worksheets. *$20.00*

*264 pages*
*ISBN 0-878793-25-9*

**1429  Create-A-Story**

**Speech Bin**
**1965 25th Avenue**
**Vero Beach, FL  32960**            772-770-0007
                                     800-477-3324
                              FAX 772-770-0006
                     http://www.speechbin.com
                     e-mail: info@speechbin.com
*Shane Peters, Product Coordinator*
*Jen Binney, Owner*

Here's a powerful language learning game that simplifies the creative process of storytelling and writing for 5-99 year olds. It fosters their imaginations, organizes their thoughts, and boosts their confidence as they build a narrative. The game can be played by 1-6 players as groups or individuals. Item number C151. *$44.95*

**1430  D'Nealian Handwriting from A to Z**

**Therapro**
**225 Arlington Street**
**Framingham, MA  01702 8723**            508-872-9494
                                          800-257-5376
                                    FAX 508-875-2062
                        http://www.theraproducts.com
                        e-mail: info@theraproducts.com
*Donald Thurber, Author*
*Karen Conrad, President*

Up to date books for D'Nealian manuscript and cursive handwriting. In the manuscript children master each lowercase and uppercase letter in natural progressive stages first by tracing with their fingers, then by writing the letters, and finally by writing words that begin with the letter. *$9.95*

**1431  Daily Starters: Quote of the Day**

**LinguiSystems**
**3100 4th Avenue**
**East Moline, IL  61244**            309-775-2300
                                      800-776-4332
                               FAX 309-755-2377
                               TDY:800-933-8331
                       http://www.linguisystems.com
                       e-mail: service@linguisystems.com
*Dave Wisniewski, Author*
*Linda Bowers, Owner*
*Rosemary Huisingh, Owner*

Get your students off to a focused start in therapy or in the classroom. These quick activities help older students integrate several language arts skills at once including writing, thinking, grammar, punctuation, vocabulary, and more. *$21.95*

*142 pages  Ages 12-18*

**1432  Do-A-Dot Activity Books**

**Therapro**
**225 Arlington Street**
**Framingham, MA  01702 8723**            508-872-9494
                                          800-257-5376
                                    FAX 508-875-2062
                        http://www.theraproducts.com
                        e-mail: info@theraproducts.com
*Therapro Staff, Author*
*Karen Conrad, President*

Do-A-Dot Activity Books are great for pre-writing skill books, printed on heavy paper stock, with each page perforated for easy removal. They promote eye-hand coordination and visual recognition. *$4.95*

**1433  Draw-Write-Now, A Drawing and Handwriting Course for Kids**

**Therapro**
**225 Arlington Street**
**Framingham, MA  01702 8723**            508-872-9494
                                          800-257-5376
                                    FAX 508-875-2062
                        http://www.theraproducts.com
                        e-mail: info@theraproducts.com
*Therapro Staff, Author*
*Karen Conrad, President*

A great way to incorporate visual motor skills and handwriting with curriculum studies. Based on a teacher's idea that handwriting utilizes many of the same skills as drawing, these books feature easy to follow drawing lessons that are broken down into a series of steps. Students can use the practice text provided to write about their drawings. The books cover a variety of themes and subjects. *$10.95*

**1434  Dysgraphia: Why Johnny Can't Write: 3rd Edition**

**Therapro**
**225 Arlington Street**
**Framingham, MA  01702 8723**            508-872-9494
                                          800-257-5376
                                    FAX 508-875-2062
                        http://www.theraproducts.com
                        e-mail: info@theraproducts.com
*D Cavey, Author*
*Karen Conrad, President*

Dysgraphia is a serious writing difficulty. This book provides guidelines for recognizing dysgraphic children and explains their special writing needs. Offers valuable tips, ideas and methods to promote success and self regard. *$15.95*

*61 pages*

**1435  Easybook Deluxe**

**Sunburst Technology**
**400 Columbus Avenue**
**Valhalla, NY  10595 1349**            914-747-3310
                                        800-321-7511
                                 FAX 914-747-4109
                         http://www.sunburst.com
                         e-mail: service@sunburst.com
*Mark Sotir, President*

Designed to support the needs of a wide range of writers, this book publishing tool provides students with a creative environment to write, design and illustrate stories and reports, and to print their work in book formats.

**1436  Easybook Deluxe Writing Workshop: Colonial Times**

Sunburst Technology
400 Columbus Avenue
Valhalla, NY  10595 1349          914-747-3310
                                 800-321-7511
                          FAX 914-747-4109
                      http://www.sunburst.com
                 e-mail: service@sunburst.com
*Mark Sotir, President*

Writing workshops combine theme-based activities with the award-winning EasyBook Deluxe.

**1437  Easybook Deluxe Writing Workshop: Immigration**

Sunburst Technology
400 Columbus Avenue
Valhalla, NY  10595 1349          914-747-3310
                                 800-321-7511
                          FAX 914-747-4109
                      http://www.sunburst.com
                 e-mail: support@sunburst.com
*Mark Sotir, President*

Writing workshops combine theme-based activities with the award-winning EasyBook Deluxe.

**1438  Easybook Deluxe Writing Workshop: Rainforest & Astronomy**

Sunburst Technology
400 Columbus Avenue
Valhalla, NY  10595 1349          914-747-3310
                                 800-321-7511
                          FAX 914-747-4109
                      http://www.sunburst.com
                 e-mail: support@sunburst.com
*Mark Sotir, President*

Writing workshops combine theme-based activities with the award-winning EasyBook Deluxe.

**1439  Easybook Deluxe Writing Workshop: Whales & Oceans**

Sunburst Technology
400 Columbus Avenue
Valhalla, NY  10595 1349          914-747-3310
                                 800-321-7511
                          FAX 914-747-4109
                      http://www.sunburst.com
                 e-mail: support@sunburst.com
*Mark Sotir, President*

Writing workshops combine theme-based activities with the award-winning EasyBook Deluxe.

**1440  Experiences with Writing Styles**

Harcourt Achieve
6277 Sea Harbor Drive
Orlando, FL  32887               252-480-3200
                                 800-531-5015
                          FAX 800-699-9459
                      http://www.steckvaughn.com
                 e-mail: info@steckvaughn.com
*Steck-Vaughn Staff, Author*
*Tim McEwen, President/CEO*
*Jeff Johnson, Dir Marketing Communications*
*Chris Lehmann, Team Coordinator*

Give your students experience applying the writing process in nine relevant situations, from personal narratives to persuasive paragraphs to research reports. Units provide a clear definition of each genre and plenty of practice with prewriting, writing, revising, proofreading, and publishing.

**1441  Fonts 4 Teachers**

Therapro
225 Arlington Street
Framingham, MA  01702 8723       508-872-9494
                                 800-257-5376
                          FAX 508-875-2062
                      http://www.theraproducts.com
                 e-mail: info@theraproducts.com
*Therapro Staff, Author*
*Karen Conrad, President*

A software collection of 31 True Type fonts for teachers, parents and students. Fonts include Tracing, lined and unlined Traditional Manuscript and Cursive (similar to Zaner Blouser and D'Nealian), math, clip art, decorative, time, American Sign Language symbols and more. The included manual is very informative, with great examples of lesson plans and educational goals. *$39.95*

*Windows/Mac*

**1442  From Scribbling to Writing**

Therapro
225 Arlington Street
Framingham, MA  01702 8723       508-872-9494
                                 800-257-5376
                          FAX 508-875-2062
                      http://www.theraproducts.com
                 e-mail: info@theraproducts.com
*Suzanne Naville, Pia Marbacher, Author*
*Karen Conrad, President*

Ideas, exercises and practice pages for all children preparing to write. Contains line drawing exercises, forms to complete, and forms for encouraging good flow of movement during writing. *$29.95*

*99 pages*

**1443  Fun with Handwriting**

Therapro
225 Arlington Street
Framingham, MA  01702 8723       508-872-9494
                                 800-257-5376
                          FAX 508-875-2062
                      http://www.theraproducts.com
                 e-mail: info@theraproducts.com
*Therapro Staff, Author*
*Karen Conrad, President*

One hundred and one ways to improve handwriting. Includes key to writing legibly, chalkboard activities, evaluation tips, and real world handwriting projects. *$16.00*

*160 pages  Spiral-bound*

**1444  Getting It Write**

**Therapro**
**225 Arlington Street**
**Framingham, MA  01702 8723**          **508-872-9494**
                                        **800-257-5376**
                                **FAX 508-875-2062**
                **http://www.theraproducts.com**
                **e-mail: info@theraproducts.com**
*LouAnne Audette OTR, Anne Karson OTR, Author*
*Karen Conrad, President*

A 6-week course for individuals or groups of 4-10 children, 6-12 years. Weekly, 1/2 hour classes begin with a short orientation followed by 25 minutes of games and sensory motor activities, from prewriting to writing practice, from basic strokes to letter formation. Reproducible manuscript and cursive worksheets are included along with homework assignments. *$58.95*

*215 pages*

**1445  Getting Ready to Write: Preschool-K**

**Therapro**
**225 Arlington Street**
**Framingham, MA  01702 8723**          **508-872-9494**
                                        **800-257-5376**
                                **FAX 508-875-2062**
                **http://www.theraproducts.com**
                **e-mail: info@theraproducts.com**
*Therapro Staff, Author*
*Karen Conrad, President*

A wonderful little book for any handwriting program. Includes many basic skills needed for beginning writing such as matching like objects, finding differences, writing basic strokes, left to right sequence, etc. *$6.50*

*97 pages*

**1446  Getty-Dubay Italic Handwriting Series: The Natural Way to Write**

**Therapro**
**225 Arlington Street**
**Framingham, MA  01702 8723**          **508-872-9494**
                                        **800-257-5376**
                                **FAX 508-875-2062**
                **http://www.theraproducts.com**
                **e-mail: info@theraproducts.com**
*Barbara Getty, Inga Dubay, Author*
*Karen Conrad, President*

This method produces fast and legible handwriting by consistently using an elliptical shape and letter slope (5 degrees) which conforms to natural hand movements and requires very few pencil lifts. A great handwriting program for all children and for adults. Also, use this method with student's handwriting problems. You will see an immediate difference. Has long term effects, when the practice stops, the good handwriting continues!

*Video available*

**1447  Grammar Scramble: A Grammar and Sentence-Building Game**

**LinguiSystems**
**3100 4th Avenue**
**East Moline, IL  61244**              **309-775-2300**
                                        **800-776-4332**
                                **FAX 309-755-2377**
                                **TDY:800-933-8331**
                **http://www.linguisystems.com**
                **e-mail: service@linguisystems.com**
*Rick Bowers, Linda Bowers, Author*
*Linda Bowers, Owner*
*Rosemary Huisingh, Owner*

Students will improve their grammar and thinking skills as they form intersecting sentences in crossword style. Students receive word tiles divided into these parts of speech: nouns; verbs; pronouns; adjectives; adverbs; articles; interrogatives; prepostions; and conjunctions. *$44.95*

*Ages 8-Adult*

**1448  Grammar and Writing for Job and Personal Use**

**AGS Publishing**
**4201 Woodland Road**
**Circle Pines, MN  55014 1796**        **651-287-7220**
                                        **800-328-2560**
                                **FAX 800-471-8457**
                        **http://www.agsnet.com**
                **e-mail: agsmail@agsnet.com**
*Joyce Hing-McGowan, Author*
*Kevin Brueggeman, President*
*Matt Keller, Marketing Manager*

With an interest level of high school through adult, and a reading level of Grade 5-6, this series has modules in Improving Basic Grammar and Writing Skills and Writing for Employment. Self-paced texts are filled with exercises that teach students the basic rules of English grammar and how to apply them to actual writing situations.

**1449  Gramopoly: A Parts of Speech Game**

**LinguiSystems**
**3100 4th Avenue**
**East Moline, IL  61244**              **309-775-2300**
                                        **800-776-4332**
                                **FAX 309-755-2377**
                                **TDY:800-933-8331**
                **http://www.linguisystems.com**
                **e-mail: service@linguisystems.com**
*Raelene Hudson, Author*
*Linda Bowers, Owner*
*Rosemary Huisingh, Owner*

This best-selling game turns on the grammar lights for your older students. Assign each player a sentence from three levels of difficulty. Players must purchase parts of speech to complete their sentence. *$44.95*

*Ages 10-15*

**1450**  **HELP for Grammar**
LinguiSystems
3100 4th Avenue
East Moline, IL  61244          309-775-2300
                                       800-776-4332
                                 FAX 309-755-2377
                                 TDY:800-933-8331
                          http://www.linguisystems.com
                          e-mail: service@linguisystems.com
*Andrea Larazzi, Author*
*Linda Bowers, Owner*
*Rosemary Huisingh, Owner*

Get in-depth grammar practice arranged in developmental order so skill builds upon skill. Get grammar training and practice with oral and written language exercises including identifying and matching grammar types, categorizing grammar types, applying grammar skills in context, and more. *$39.95*

*191 pages  Ages 8-Adult*

**1451**  **Handwriting Readiness for Preschoolers**
Therapro
225 Arlington Street
Framingham, MA  01702 8723      508-872-9494
                                       800-257-5376
                                 FAX 508-875-2062
                          http://www.theraproducts.com
                          e-mail: info@theraproducts.com
*Donald Thurber, Author*
*Karen Conrad, President*

As teacher recites directions, children trace lower case manuscript letters with finger (Book 1) or crayon (Book 2), developing letter recognition skills and writing readiness. *$9.95*

*32 pages*

**1452**  **Handwriting Without Tears**
8801 MacArthur Boulevard
Cabin John, MD  20818           301-263-2700
                                       888-983-8409
                                 FAX 301-263-2707
                          http://www.hwtears.com
                          e-mail: Jan@hwtears.com
*Jan Olsen, Occupational Therapist*

An easy and fun method for children of all abilities to learn printing and cursive.

**1453**  **Handwriting without Tears Workbooks**
Therapro
225 Arlington Street
Framingham, MA  01702 8723      508-872-9494
                                       800-257-5376
                                 FAX 508-875-2062
                          http://www.theraproducts.com
                          e-mail: info@theraproducts.com
*Therapro Staff, Author*
*Karen Conrad, President*

These workbooks are excellent for both classroom and individual instruction. Minimal preparation time is needed to use the clear and easy-to-follow lesson guides. *$5.95*

**1454**  **Handwriting: Cursive ABC Book**
Therapro
225 Arlington Street
Framingham, MA  01702 8723      508-872-9494
                                       800-257-5376
                                 FAX 508-875-2062
                          http://www.theraproducts.com
                          e-mail: info@theraproducts.com
*Therapro Staff, Author*
*Karen Conrad, President*

The perfect at-home reinforcement with fully illustrated excerpts from children's literature, model letters, practice space and tear-out alphabet cards. *$9.95*

*56 pages*

**1455**  **Handwriting: Manuscript ABC Book**
Therapro
225 Arlington Street
Framingham, MA  01702 8723      508-872-9494
                                       800-257-5376
                                 FAX 508-875-2062
                          http://www.theraproducts.com
                          e-mail: info@theraproducts.com
*Therapro Staff, Author*
*Karen Conrad, President*

Illustrated rhymes, practice letters and words, coloring and tear out alphabet cards teach letter formation. *$9.95*

*56 pages*

**1456**  **Home/School Activities Manuscript Practice**
Therapro
225 Arlington Street
Framingham, MA  01702 8723      508-872-9494
                                       800-257-5376
                                 FAX 508-875-2062
                          http://www.theraproducts.com
                          e-mail: info@theraproducts.com
*Therapro Staff, Author*
*Karen Conrad, President*

Directions for forming lower and upper case letters, and numbers, with space for practice. Activities use letters in words and sentences. *$9.95*

*64 pages*

**1457**  **Introduction to Journal Writing**
Harcourt Achieve
6277 Sea Harbor Drive
Orlando, FL  32887              252-480-3200
                                       800-531-5015
                                 FAX 800-699-9459
                          http://www.steckvaughn.com
                          e-mail: info@steckvaughn.com
*Steck-Vaughn Staff, Author*
*Tim McEwen, President/CEO*
*Jeff Johnson, Director Marketing Communication*
*Chris Lehmann, Team Coordinator*

The more students write as young children, the higher quality their writing will be, now and as they go on through life. Journal Writing is not about spelling and grammar. It's a highly personal outpouring of thoughts and experiences.

**1458 Just for Kids: Grammar**

LinguiSystems
3100 4th Avenue
East Moline, IL  61244          309-775-2300
                               800-776-4332
                          FAX 309-755-2377
                          TDY:800-933-8331
              http://www.linguisystems.com
              e-mail: service@linguisystems.com
*Janet Lanza, Lynn Flahive, Author*
*Linda Bowers, Owner*
*Rosemary Huisingh, Owner*

This kid-friendly approach to grammar teaches the parts of speech your students need to know. The practice centers around natural, meaningful activities. Each chapter includes: a pre-and post-test, picture cards, sequence story, rebus story, and family letter. *$39.95*

*186 pages  Ages 4-9*

**1459 LD Teacher's IEP Companion**

LinguiSystems
3100 4th Avenue
East Moline, IL  61244          309-775-2300
                               800-776-4332
                          FAX 309-755-2377
                          TDY:800-933-8331
              http://www.linguisystems.com
              e-mail: service@linguisystems.com
*Molly Lyle, Author*
*Linda Bowers, Owner*
*Rosemary Huisingh, Owner*

These IEP goals are organized developmentally by skill area with individual objectives and classroom activity suggestions. Goals and objectives cover these academic areas: math; reading; writing; literacy concepts; attention skills; study skills; classroom behavior; social interaction; and transition skills. *$39.95*

*169 pages  Ages 5-18*

**1460 Learning 100 Writing Strategies**

Harcourt Achieve
6277 Sea Harbor Drive
Orlando, FL  32887             252-480-3200
                               800-531-5015
                          FAX 800-699-9459
                http://www.steckvaughn.com
                e-mail: info@steckvaughn.com
*Steck-Vaughn Staff, Author*
*Tim McEwen, President/CEO*
*Jeff Johnson, Director Marketing Communication*
*Chris Lehmann, Team Coordinator*

Use the writing process as a tool to build reading comprehension, writing proficiency, and learner confidence. Help learners make a successful connection between reading and writing. Writing Strategies gives learners thorough instruction in the writing process and challenges them to apply their new skills in an everyday writing task that provides ongoing success and encouragement.

**1461 Learning Grammar Through Writing**

Educators Publishing Service
31 Smith Place
Cambridge, MA  02139 9031      617-547-6706
                               800-225-5750
                          FAX 888-440-2665
                     http://www.epsbooks.com
                     e-mail: eps@epsbooks.com
*Sandra M Bell, James I Wheeler, Author*
*Steven Corte, President*

Learning Grammar through Writing contains grammar and composition rules explained and reference-numbered. Basic grammatical rules, common stylistic and grammatical writing errors, and commonly confused words and expressions are a few of the topics.

**1462 Let's Write Right: Teacher's Edition**

AVKO'S Dyslexia Research Foundation
3084 W Willard Road
Clio, MI  48420 7801           810-686-9283
                               866-285-6612
                          FAX 810-686-1101
                     http://www.spelling.org
                     e-mail: avkoemail@aol.com
*Don McCabe, Author*
*Don McCabe, Research Director*

This is a teacher's lesson plan book which uses an approach designed specifically for dyslexics to teach reading and spelling skills through the side door of penmanship exercises with an empasis on legibility. Student books are handy but are not required. *$19.95*

**1463 Let's-Do-It-Write: Writing Readiness Workbook**

Therapro
225 Arlington Street
Framingham, MA  01702 8723     508-872-9494
                               800-257-5376
                          FAX 508-875-2062
                http://www.theraproducts.com
                e-mail: info@theraproducts.com
*Gail Kushnir, Author*
*Karen Conrad, President*

A great variety of prewriting activities and exercises focusing on development of eye-hand coordination and motor, sensory and cognitive skills. Also, helps improve sitting posture, cutting skills, pencil grasp, spatial orientation and problem-solving. Written by an occupational therapist who is a special educator. *$19.95*

*112 pages*

**1464 Linamood Program (LIPS Clinical Version):Phoneme Sequencing Program for Reading, Spelling,Speech**

LinguiSystems
3100 4th Avenue
East Moline, IL  61244          309-775-2300
                               800-776-4332
                          FAX 309-755-2377
                          TDY:800-933-8331
              http://www.linguisystems.com
              e-mail: service@linguisystems.com
*Patricia Linamood, Phyllis Linamood, Author*
*Linda Bowers, Owner*
*Rosemary Huisingh, Owner*

Help your students develop phoneme awareness for competence in reading, spelling, and speech. This multisensory program meets the needs of the many children and adults who don't develop phonemic awareness through traditional methods. *$247.00*

*Birth-Adult*

**1465  MAXI**

**Aids and Appliances for Independent Living**
**PO Box 3209**
**Farmingdale, NY  11735**          516-752-0521
                                   800-522-6294
                              FAX 516-752-0689
                              TDY:516-752-0738
                         http://www.maxiaids.com
                      e-mail: sales@maxiaids.com
*Elliot Zaretsky, President*

Thousands of products to make life easier. Eating, dressing, communications, bed, bath, kitchen, writing aids and more.

**1466  Manual for Learning to Use Manuscript and Cursive Handwriting**

**Educators Publishing Service**
**31 Smith Place**
**Cambridge, MA  02139 9031**          617-547-6706
                                       800-225-5750
                                  FAX 888-440-2665
                             http://www.epsbooks.com
                          e-mail: eps@epsbooks.com
*Beth Slingerland, Author*
*Steven Corte, President*

This multisensory handwriting program is divided into two parts, manuscript and cursive, which can be used either consecutively or independently.

**1467  Media Weaver 3.5**

**Sunburst Technology**
**400 Columbus Avenue**
**Valhalla, NY  10595 1349**          914-747-3310
                                      800-321-7511
                                 FAX 914-747-4109
                            http://www.sunburst.com
                         e-mail: support@sunburst.com
*Mark Sotir, President*

Publishing becomes a multimedia event with this dynamic word processor that contains hundreds of media elements and effective process writing resources.

**1468  Middle School Writing: Expository Writing**

**Harcourt Achieve**
**6277 Sea Harbor Drive**
**Orlando, FL  32887**          252-480-3200
                                800-531-5015
                           FAX 800-699-9459
                      http://www.steckvaughn.com
                   e-mail: info@steckvaughn.com
*Steck-Vaughn Staff, Author*
*Tim McEwen, President/CEO*
*Jeff Johnson, Director Marketing Communication*
*Chris Lehmann, Team Coordinator*

An effective comprehensive review and reinforcement of the writing and research skills students will need. Effectively used in both school and home setting. Ideal for junior high or high school students in need of remediation.

**1469  My Handwriting Word Book**

**Therapro**
**225 Arlington Street**
**Framingham, MA  01702 8723**          508-872-9494
                                        800-257-5376
                                   FAX 508-875-2062
                           http://www.theraproducts.com
                       e-mail: info@theraproducts.com
*Therapro Staff, Author*
*Karen Conrad, President*

Children practice writing everyday words — two letter words, words for days, months, numbers, family names and more. *$9.95*

*64 pages*

**1470  PAF Handwriting Programs for Print, Cursive (Right or Left-Handed)**

**Educators Publishing Service**
**31 Smith Place**
**Cambridge, MA  02139 9031**          617-547-6706
                                       800-225-5750
                                  FAX 888-440-2665
                             http://www.epsbooks.com
                          e-mail: eps@epsbooks.com
*Phyllis Bertin, Eileen Perlman, Author*
*Steven Corte, President*

These workbooks can be used in conjunction with the PAF curriculum or independently as a classroom penmanship program. They were specifically designed to accommodate all students including those with fine-motor, visual-motor and graphomotor weaknesses. The workbooks contain both large models for introducing motor patterns and smaller models to facilitate the transition to primary and loose-leaf papers. A detailed instruction booklet accompanies each workbook.

**1471  PATHS**

**Speech Bin**
**1965 25th Avenue**
**Vero Beach, FL  32960**          772-770-0007
                                   800-477-3324
                              FAX 772-770-0006
                         http://www.speechbin.com
                      e-mail: info@speechbin.com
*Shane Peters, Product Coordinator*
*Jen Binney, Owner*

PATHS gives you a step-by-step comprehensive program for students who have experienced difficulty in academic learning. It targets skills critical for academic achievements: phonological awareness, phonemic relationships, phonemic processing and listening and memory. Item number 1491. *$21.95*

**1472 Phonological Awareness Kit**

LinguiSystems
3100 4th Avenue
East Moline, IL 61244    309-775-2300
800-776-4332
FAX 309-755-2377
TDY:800-933-8331
http://www.linguisystems.com
e-mail: service@linguisystems.com
*Carolyn Robertson, Wanda Salter, Author*
*Linda Bowers, Owner*
*Rosemary Huisingh, Owner*

Help your students learn to use phonological informa-tion to process oral and written language with this fan-tastic kit. Written by an SLP and special educator, this best-seller links sound awareness, oral language, and early reading and writing skills. The kit uses a multisensory approach to ensure success for all learn-ing styles. *$69.95*

*115 pages  Ages 5-8*

**1473 Phonological Awareness Kit: Intermediate**

LinguiSystems
3100 4th Avenue
East Moline, IL 61244    309-775-2300
800-776-4332
FAX 309-755-2377
TDY:800-933-8331
http://www.linguisystems.com
e-mail: service@linguisystems.com
*Carolyn Robertson, Wanda Salter, Author*
*Linda Bowers, Owner*
*Rosemary Huisingh, Owner*

Now there's hope for your older students who have struggled with reading through their early school years. Give them strategies to crack the reading code with this comprehensive program. Great for students with deficits in auditory processing, decoding, and written language. *$69.95*

*116 pages  Ages 9-14*

**1474 Prewriting Curriculum Enrichment Series**

Therapro
225 Arlington Street
Framingham, MA  01702 8723    508-872-9494
800-257-5376
FAX 508-875-2062
http://www.theraproducts.com
e-mail: info@theraproducts.com
*Peggy Hundley Spitz OTR, Author*
*Karen Conrad, President*

This series offers a wide variety of thematically re-lated developmental activities: Trace & Draw; Crafts and Costumes; Cooking; Stories to Color & Read; and Games. Enough activities for several years. Many reproducable worksheets are included. Ideal for pre-school programs. Helps all levels of development with hand skills, eye-hand coordination, perception and sensory motor awareness. *$22.50*

*180 pages*

**1475 Punctuation Play-by-Play**

LinguiSystems
3100 4th Avenue
East Moline, IL 61244    309-775-2300
800-776-4332
FAX 309-755-2377
TDY:800-933-8331
http://www.linguisystems.com
e-mail: service@linguisystems.com
*Carolyn LoGiudice, Mike LoGiudice, Author*
*Linda Bowers, Owner*
*Rosemary Huisingh, Owner*

Punctuation Play-by-Play engages students in a lively game as they practice essential punctuation skills in-cluding: capitalization; end marks; apostrophes; com-mas; quotation marks; colons; semicolons. Question cards are divides into two levels of difficulty. *$44.95*

*Ages 10-18*

**1476 Punctuation, Capitalization, and Handwriting for Job and Personal Use**

AGS Publishing
4201 Woodland Road
Circle Pines, MN  55014 1796    651-287-7220
800-328-2560
FAX 800-471-8457
http://www.agsnet.com
e-mail: agsmail@agsnet.com
*Renae B Humberg, Author*
*Kevin Brueggeman, President*
*Matt Keller, Marketing Manager*

With an interest level of high school through adult, and a reading level of Grade 5-6, this series has mod-ules in Punctuation, Capitalization and Handwriting. *$299.00*

**1477 Reading and Writing Workbook**

Therapro
225 Arlington Street
Framingham, MA  01702 8723    508-872-9494
800-257-5376
FAX 508-875-2062
http://www.theraproducts.com
e-mail: info@theraproducts.com
*Therapro Staff, Author*
*Karen Conrad, President*

Writing checks and balancing a checkbook, copying words and sentences, and writing messages and notes. Helps with recognition and understanding of calen-dars, phone books and much more. *$10.50*

**1478 Report Writing**

Harcourt Achieve
6277 Sea Harbor Drive
Orlando, FL 32887    252-480-3200
800-531-5015
FAX 800-699-9459
http://www.steckvaughn.com
e-mail: info@steckvaughn.com
*Steck-Vaughn Staff, Author*
*Tim McEwen, President/CEO*
*Jeff Johnson, Director Marketing Communication*
*Chriss Lehmann, Team Coordinator*

Here is the complete, step-by-step guide to learning the tools, skills, and time management techniques necessary for researching, organizing, outlining, and writing reports.

**1479 SLP's IDEA Companion**

LinguiSystems
3100 4th Avenue
East Moline, IL 61244      309-775-2300
800-776-4332
FAX 309-755-2377
TDY:800-933-8331
http://www.linguisystems.com
e-mail: service@linguisystems.com
*Shaila Lucas, Author*
*Linda Bowers, Owner*
*Rosemary Huisingh, Owner*

Get goals and objectives that match the guidelines outlined in the individuals with Disabilities Education Act. You'll be able to link your therapy goals to the classroom curriculum, determine appropriate benchmarks for students, and determine levels of performance using the baseline measures provided in the book. *$39.95*

*162 pages Ages 5-18*

**1480 Soaring Scores on the ISAT Reading and Writing**

Harcourt Achieve
6277 Sea Harbor Drive
Orlando, FL 32887      252-480-3200
800-531-5015
FAX 800-699-9459
http://www.steckvaughn.com
e-mail: info@steckvaughn.com
*Steck-Vaughn Staff, Author*
*Tim McEwen, President/CEO*
*Jeff Johnson, Director Marketing Communication*
*Chris Lehmann, Team Coordinator*

Highly targeted instruction and practice tests help students approach the ISAT strategically and confidently. Writing prompts ask students to write a persuasive, expository, or narrative essay. Modeled questions practice both multiple-choice and open-ended queries.

**1481 Spelling Charts: Intermediate**

LinguiSystems
3100 4th Avenue
East Moline, IL 61244      309-775-2300
800-776-4332
FAX 800-577-4555
TDY:800-933-8331
http://www.linguisystems.com
e-mail: service@linguisystems.com
*Linda Bowers, Owner*
*Rosemary Huisingh, Owner*

Good spelling doesn't stop in the primary grades. Help your older students understand word families with this great resource. It's a valuable tool for spelling, writing, and vocabulary skills. You get 45 full-color cards to use as charts, overheads, or take-home practice.

**1482 Spelling Charts: Primary**

LinguiSystems
3100 4th Avenue
East Moline, IL 61244      309-775-2300
800-776-4332
FAX 800-577-4555
TDY:800-933-8331
http://www.linguisystems.com
e-mail: service@linguisystems.com
*Linda Bowers, Owner*
*Rosemary Huisingh, Owner*

Tap into phonological awareness skills with these full-color charts. Use them as classroom charts, overheads, or take-home practice. They're great for large group, small group, or individual teaching. Each chart features words grouped by rhyming families or similar word endings.

**1483 Spelling for Job and Personal Use**

AGS Publishing
4201 Woodland Road
Circle Pines, MN 55014 1796      651-287-7220
800-328-2560
FAX 800-471-8457
http://www.agsnet.com
e-mail: agsmail@agsnet.com
*Merle Wood, Author*
*Kevin Brueggeman, President*
*Matt Keller, Marketing Manager*

With an interest level of high school through adult, and a reading level of Grade 5-6, this series has modules in Using the Dictionary, Guides to Spelling and Spelling the 100 Most Used Words.

**1484 StartWrite**

Therapro
225 Arlington Street
Framingham, MA 01702 8723      508-872-9494
800-257-5376
FAX 508-875-2062
http://www.theraproducts.com
e-mail: info@theraproducts.com
*Therapro Staff, Author*
*Karen Conrad, President*

With this easy-to-use software package, you can make papers and handwriting worksheets to meet individual student's needs. Type letters, words, or numbers and they appear in a dot format on the triple line guide. Change letter size, add shading, turn on or off guide lines and arrow strokes and place provided clipart. Fonts include Manuscript and Cursive, Modern Manuscript and Cursive and Italic Manuscript and Cursive. Useful manual included. *$39.95*

*Windows/Mac*

**1485 Strategies for Success in Writing**

Harcourt Achieve
6277 Sea Harbor Drive
Orlando, FL 32887      252-480-3200
800-531-5015
FAX 800-699-9459
http://www.steckvaughn.com
e-mail: info@steckvaughn.com
*Steck-Vaughn Staff, Author*
*Tim McEwen, President/CEO*
*Jeff Johnson, Director Marketing Communication*
*Chriss Lehmann, Team Coordinator*

Help your students gain success and master all the steps in writing through essay-writing strategies and exercises in proofreading, editing, and revising written work. This program also helps students approach tests strategically.

## 1486 Sunbuddy Writer

**Sunburst Technology**
**400 Columbus Avenue**
**Valhalla, NY  10595 1349**　　　　914-747-3310
　　　　　　　　　　　　　　　　800-321-7511
　　　　　　　　　　　　　　FAX 914-747-4109
　　　　　　　　　　　http://www.sunburst.com
　　　　　　　　　e-mail: support@sunburst.com
*Mark Sotir, President*

An easy-to-use picture and word processor designed especially for young writers.

## 1487 TOPS Kit: Adolescent-Tasks of Problem Solving

**LinguiSystems**
**3100 4th Avenue**
**East Moline, IL  61244**　　　　　309-775-2300
　　　　　　　　　　　　　　　　800-776-4332
　　　　　　　　　　　　　　FAX 309-755-2377
　　　　　　　　　　　　　TDY:800-933-8331
　　　　　　　　　http://www.linguisystems.com
　　　　　　　e-mail: service@linguisystems.com
*Linda Bowers, Rosemary Huisingh, Mark Barrett, Author*
*Linda Bowers, Owner*
*Rosemary Huisingh, Owner*

Teach your teens how to use their language skills to think, think, think. We combine literacy, thinking, writing, humor, and language arts practice to cover these thinking skills: using content to make references; analyzing information; taking another's point of view; and more. It's a literacy- based approach that gets dramatic results! *$59.95*

*192 pages  Ages 12-18*

## 1488 Tool Chest: For Teachers, Parents and Students

**Therapro**
**225 Arlington Street**
**Framingham, MA  01702 8723**　　　508-872-9494
　　　　　　　　　　　　　　　　800-257-5376
　　　　　　　　　　　　　　FAX 508-875-2062
　　　　　　　　　　http://www.theraproducts.com
　　　　　　　　e-mail: info@theraproducts.com
*Henry OT Services, Author*
*Karen Conrad, President*

Ideas for self-regulation and handwriting skills. 26+ activities, each on its own page, with rationale, supplies needed, instructions and related projects. Provides a fast way to prepare for OT activities. Supports the videotapes Tools for Teachers and Tools for Students. *$19.95*

## 1489 Type-It

**Educators Publishing Service**
**31 Smith Place**
**Cambridge, MA  02139 9031**　　　617-547-6706
　　　　　　　　　　　　　　　　800-225-5750
　　　　　　　　　　　　　　FAX 888-440-2666
　　　　　　　　　　　　http://www.epsbooks.com
　　　　　　　　　　e-mail: eps@epsbooks.com
*Joan Duffy, Author*
*Steven Corte, President*

A linguistically oriented beginning 'touch-system' typing manual. A progress chart allows students to pace their progress in short, easily attainable units, often enabling them to proceed with little or no supervision.

## 1490 Vowel Scramble

**LinguiSystems**
**3100 4th Avenue**
**East Moline, IL  61244**　　　　　309-775-2300
　　　　　　　　　　　　　　　　800-776-4332
　　　　　　　　　　　　　　FAX 309-755-2377
　　　　　　　　　　　　　TDY:800-933-8331
　　　　　　　　　http://www.linguisystems.com
　　　　　　　e-mail: service@linguisystems.com
*Carolyn LoGiudice, Author*
*Linda Bowers, Owner*
*Rosemary Huisingh, Owner*

Your student will love this fun new way to practice spelling and phonological awareness skills. Players earn points by using letter tiles to complete words on the game board. *$44.95*

*Ages 7-12*

## 1491 Workbook for Aphasia

**Speech Bin**
**1965 25th Avenue**
**Vero Beach, FL  32960**　　　　　772-770-0007
　　　　　　　　　　　　　　　　800-477-3324
　　　　　　　　　　　　　　FAX 772-770-0006
　　　　　　　　　　　http://www.speechbin.com
　　　　　　　　　e-mail: info@speechbin.com
*Shane Peters, Product Coordinator*
*Jen Binney, Owner*

This book gives you materials for adults who have recovered a significant degree of speaking, reading, writing, and comprehension skills. It includes 106 exercises divided into eight target areas. Item number W331. *$48.95*

## 1492 Write On! Plus: Beginning Writing Skills

**Sunburst Technology**
**400 Columbus Avenue**
**Valhalla, NY  10595 1349**　　　　914-747-3310
　　　　　　　　　　　　　　　　800-321-7511
　　　　　　　　　　　　　　FAX 914-747-4109
　　　　　　　　　　　http://www.sunburst.com
　　　　　　　　　e-mail: support@sunburst.com
*Mark Sotir, President*

This classic process writing series teaches a wide range of core writing and literature skills through hundreds of motivating and challenging activities.

**1493  Write On! Plus: Elementary Writing Skills**

Sunburst Technology
400 Columbus Avenue
Valhalla, NY  10595 1349          914-747-3310
                                 800-321-7511
                            FAX 914-747-4109
                     http://www.sunburst.com
                  e-mail: support@sunburst.com
*Mark Sotir, President*

This classic process writing series teaches a wide range of core writing and literature skills through hundreds of motivating and challenging activities.

**1494  Write On! Plus: Essential Writing**

Sunburst Technology
400 Columbus Avenue
Valhalla, NY  10595 1349          914-747-3310
                                 800-321-7511
                            FAX 914-747-4109
                     http://www.sunburst.com
                  e-mail: support@sunburst.com
*Mark Sotir, President*

This classic process writing series teaches a wide range of core writing and literature skills through hundreds of motivating and challenging activities.

**1495  Write On! Plus: Growing as a Writer**

Sunburst Technology
400 Columbus Avenue
Valhalla, NY  10595 1349          914-747-3310
                                 800-321-7511
                            FAX 914-747-4109
                     http://www.sunburst.com
                  e-mail: support@sunburst.com
*Mark Sotir, President*

This classic process writing series teaches a wide range of core writing and literature skills through hundreds of motivating and challenging activities.

**1496  Write On! Plus: High School Writing Skills**

Sunburst Technology
400 Columbus Avenue
Valhalla, NY  10595 1349          914-747-3310
                                 800-321-7511
                            FAX 914-747-4109
                     http://www.sunburst.com
                  e-mail: support@sunburst.com
*Mark Sotir, President*

This classic process writing series teaches a wide range of core writing and literature skills through hundreds of motivating and challenging activities.

**1497  Write On! Plus: Literature Studies**

Sunburst Technology
400 Columbus Avenue
Valhalla, NY  10595 1349          914-747-3310
                                 800-321-7511
                            FAX 914-747-4109
                     http://www.sunburst.com
                  e-mail: support@sunburst.com
*Mark Sotir, President*

This classic process writing series teaches a wide range of core writing and literature skills through hundreds of motivating and challenging activities.

**1498  Write On! Plus: Middle School Writing Skills**

Sunburst Technology
400 Columbus Avenue
Valhalla, NY  10595 1349          914-747-3310
                                 800-321-7511
                            FAX 914-747-4109
                     http://www.sunburst.com
                  e-mail: support@sunburst.com
*Mark Sotir, President*

This classic process writing series teaches a wide range of core writing and literature skills through hundreds of motivating and challenging activities.

**1499  Write On! Plus: Responding to Great Literature**

Sunburst Technology
400 Columbus Avenue
Valhalla, NY  10595 1349          914-747-3310
                                 800-321-7511
                            FAX 914-747-4109
                     http://www.sunburst.com
                  e-mail: support@sunburst.com
*Katie Birmingham, Office Manager*

This classic process writing series teaches a wide range of core writing and literature skills through hundreds of motivating and challenging activities.

**1500  Write On! Plus: Spanish/ English Literacy Series**

Sunburst Technology
400 Columbus Avenue
Valhalla, NY  10595 1349          914-747-3310
                                 800-321-7511
                            FAX 914-747-4109
                     http://www.sunburst.com
                  e-mail: support@sunburst.com
*Mark Sotir, President*

This classic process writing series teaches a wide range of core writing and literature skills through hundreds of motivating and challenging activities.

**1501  Write On! Plus: Steps to Better Writing**
**Sunburst Technology**
**400 Columbus Avenue**
**Valhalla, NY  10595 1349**          **914-747-3310**
**800-321-7511**
**FAX 914-747-4109**
**http://www.sunburst.com**
**e-mail: support@sunburst.com**
*Mark Sotir, President*

This classic process writing series teaches a wide range of core writing and literature skills through hundreds of motivating and challenging activities.

**1502  Write On! Plus: Writing with Picture Books**
**Sunburst Technology**
**400 Columbus Avenue**
**Valhalla, NY  10595 1349**          **914-747-3310**
**800-321-7511**
**FAX 914-747-4109**
**http://www.sunburst.com**
**e-mail: support@sunburst.com**
*Mark Sotir, President*

This classic process writing series teaches a wide range of core writing and literature skills through hundreds of motivating and challenging activities.

**1503  Write from the Start**
**Therapro**
**225 Arlington Street**
**Framingham, MA  01702 8723**          **508-872-9494**
**800-257-5376**
**FAX 508-875-2062**
**http://www.theraproducts.com**
**e-mail: info@theraproducts.com**
*Ion Teodorescu, Lois M Addy, Author*
*Karen Conrad, President*

This program addresses the handwriting process in two ways. First, it assists in developing the intrinsic muscles of the hand to gain the control required to form letter shapes and to create appropriate spaces between words. Secondly, it helps to develop perceptual skills that are required to orient letters and organize the page. Each book has sections to be copied. Two books consisting of eye hand, spatial organization, graphic and perceptual challenges.

*128 pages*

**1504  WriteOPOLY**
**LinguiSystems**
**3100 4th Avenue**
**East Moline, IL  61244**          **309-775-2300**
**800-776-4332**
**FAX 309-755-2377**
**TDY:800-933-8331**
**http://www.linguisystems.com**
**e-mail: service@linguisystems.com**
*Paul F Johnson, Author*
*Linda Bowers, Owner*
*Rosemary Huisingh, Owner*

End writer's block for even your most reluctant writers with this fun game. Improve written language skills with WriteOPOLY. Students travel around a colorful game board buying properties and filling out Writing Plan sheets. *$ 44.95*

*Ages 9-14*

**1505  Writer's Resources Library 2.0**
**Sunburst Technology**
**400 Columbus Avenue**
**Valhalla, NY  10595 1349**          **914-747-3310**
**800-321-7511**
**FAX 914-747-4109**
**http://www.sunburst.com**
**e-mail: service@sunburst.com**
*A Birmingham, Owner*
*Mark Sotir, President*

Students quickly access seven reference resources with this indispensable writing tool.

**1506  Writestart**
**Therapro**
**225 Arlington Street**
**Framingham, MA  01702 8723**          **508-872-9494**
**800-257-5376**
**FAX 508-875-2062**
**http://www.theraproducts.com**
**e-mail: info@theraproducts.com**
*Therapro Staff, Author*
*Karen Conrad, President*

A great prewriting kit with 30 beautifully illustrated 8x8 reusable cards. The activities progress from simple pre-writing activities such as mazes and tracking, up to formation of upper and lower case letters, all hosted by a green dinosaur. Includes a special pencil and triangular grip. *$16.95*

**1507  Writing Trek Grades 4-6**
**Sunburst Technology**
**400 Columbus Avenue**
**Valhalla, NY  10595 1349**          **914-747-3310**
**800-321-7511**
**FAX 914-747-4109**
**http://www.sunburst.com**
**e-mail: service@sunburst.com**
*A Birmingham, Owner*
*Mark Sotir, President*

Enhance your students' experience in your English language arts classroom with twelve authentic writing projects that build students' competence while encouraging creativity.

**1508  Writing Trek Grades 6-8**
**Sunburst Technology**
**400 Columbus Avenue**
**Valhalla, NY  10595 1349**          **914-747-3310**
**800-321-7511**
**FAX 914-747-4109**
**http://www.sunburst.com**
**e-mail: service@sunburst.com**
*A Birmingham, Owner*
*Mark Sotir, President*

Twelve authentic language arts projects, activities, and assignments develop your students' writing confidence and ability.

**1509   Writing Trek Grades 8-10**

Sunburst Technology
400 Columbus Avenue
Valhalla, NY  10595 1349          914-747-3310
                                 800-321-7511
                            FAX 914-747-4109
                          http://www.sunburst.com
                     e-mail: service@sunburst.com
*A Birmingham, Owner*
*Mark Sotir, President*

Help your students develop a concept of genre as they
become familiar with the writing elements and characteristics of a variety of writing forms.

## Learning Disabilities

**1510  Access Expo and Conference**

Fairfield Factor
30 Main Street
Danbury, CT  06810          203-798-8850
FAX 203-798-8779
http://www.fairfieldfactor.com
e-mail: mail@fairfieldfactor.com

Offers information on the latest technology, assistive devices and more for the disabled.

**1511  Active Parenting Workshops**

Active Parenting Publishers
1955 Vaughn Road NW
Kennesaw, GA  30144 7808          770-429-0565
800-825-0060
FAX 770-429-0334
http://www.activeparenting.com
e-mail: cservice@activeparenting.com
*Michael Popkin PhD, President*
*Susan Hopkins, Marketing*

Conducts nationwide parenting workshops recognized by the National Board of Certified Counselors. Offers parenting education curriculum for parents of ADD/ADHD children.

**1512  American Council on Rural Special Education Conference**

Utah State University
2865 Old Main Hill
Logan, UT  84322 2865          801-626-6268
FAX 801-626-7427
http://www.extension.usu.edu/acres
e-mail: jmayhew@weber.edu
*Jack Mayhew MD, Program Chair*
*Carolyn Mitchell, Accounting Department*

Conference of special educators, teachers and professors working with exceptional needs students. Keynote speakers, silent auction.

*March*

**1513  American Counseling Association Convention**

ACA Membership Division
5999 Stevenson Avenue
Alexandria, VA  22304          703-823-0252
800-347-6647
FAX 703-823-0252
http://www.counseling.org
e-mail: webmaster@counseling.org
*Mark Pope MD, President*
*Debra Bass, Marketing*
*Robin Hayes, Convention/Meetings*

Keynote speakers and workshops as well as exhibits are offered.

*April*

**1514  American Speech-Language-Hearing Association Annual Convention**

American Speech Language-Hearing Association
10801 Rockville Pike
Bethesda, MD  20852          301-897-5700
800-638-8255
FAX 301-571-0457
TDY:301-897-5700
http://www.asha.org
e-mail: epietrarton@asha.com
*Eileen Pietrarton, Executive Director*
*Cheyrl Russel, Convention/Meetings*

Topics addressed include hearing impairments, special education and speech communication. 10,000 attendees.

*November*

**1515  Annual Postsecondary Learning Disability Training Institute Workshop**

University of Connecticut
362 Fairfield Road
Storrs, CT  06269          860-486-3321
FAX 860-486-5799
http://www.cped.uconn.edu
e-mail: carrol.waite@uconn.edu
*Stan Shaw, Institute Coordinator*
*Carrol Waite, Program Assistant*

Focus of the Institute's workshop is to assist concerned professionals to meet the unique needs of college students with learning disabilities and other hidden disabilities.

*June*

**1516  Assessing Learning Problems Workshop**

Learning Disabilities Resources
PO Box 716
Bryn Mawr, PA  19010          610-525-8336
800-869-8336
FAX 610-525-8337
http://www.ldonline.org

This workshop includes behavioral manifestations of information processing problems and how to relate these to learning processes.

**1517  Association Book Exhibit: Brain Research**

Association Book Exhibit
8727A Cooper Road
Alexandria, VA  22309          703-619-5030
FAX 703-619-5035
http://www.bookexhibit.com
e-mail: info@bookexhibit.com
*Mark Trocchi, Owner*

Attendence is 800-1,000. Every serious publisher of Neuroscience material represented.

**1518  CACLD Spring & Fall Conferences**

Connecticut Assoc. for Children & Adults with LD
25 Van Zant Street
East Norwalk, CT  06855          203-838-5010
FAX 203-866-6108
http://www.CACLD.org
e-mail: cacld@optonline.net
*Marie Armstrong, Conference Coordinator*
*Beryl Kaufman, Executive Director*

Offers speakers, workshops, presentations and more for professionals and parents dealing with learning disability and attention disorder in their daily life. Also offers a stand on college for students with LD and ADD, exhibitors and a giant bookstore.

**1519    CEC Federation Conference: Arkansas**

**Council for Exceptional Children**
**105 N 6th Street**
**Heber Springs, AR  72543          501-362-2404**
**FAX 501-329-7409**
**e-mail: dido@ozarkisp.net**

Annual conference held at Hot Springs Convention Centerin Hot Springs, AR.

*November*

**1520    CEC Federation Conference: Kansas**

**Council for Exceptional Children**
**1011 Price Boulevard**
**Atchison, KS  66002          785-462-2940**
**http://www.kscec.org**
**e-mail: jstewart719@yahoo.com**
*Janette Stewart, President*

Exhibits and workshop sessions for educators building a brighter tomorrow.

*October*

**1521    CEC Federation Conference: Pennsylvania**

**Council of Exceptional Children**
**West Chester University**
**West Chester, PA  19383          610-436-1060**
**FAX 610-436-3102**
**http://www.pfcec.org**
**e-mail: vmcginley@wcupa.edu**
*Vicki McGinley MD, Convention Chair*

Annual conference for parents and educators involved with the Pennsylvania Council of Exceptional Children.

*November*

**1522    CEC Federation Conference: Virginia**

**Council for Exceptional Children**
**1110 N Glede Road**
**Arlington, VA  22201          703-264-9454**
**FAX 703-264-1637**
**http://www.cec.sped.org**
**e-mail: victore@cec.sped.org**
*Victor Erickson, Exhibits Manager*
*Liz Martinez, Publications Director*

Find a wealth of information targeted just for educators. Choose from more than 600 workshops, lectures, demonstrations, mini workshops, panels and poster sessions.

*April*

**1523    Center on Disabilities Conference**

**California State University**
**401 Golden Shore**
**Long Beach, CA  90802          562-951-4000**
**FAX 562-951-4986**
**http://www.csun.edu**
**e-mail: ctrdis@csun.edu**
*Charles Reed MD, Chancellor*
*Tom Roberts, Director of Contract Services*

Focuses on issues pertaining to the disabled learner and gifted education. 2,000 attendees.

**1524    Closing the Gap Conference**

**PO Box 68**
**Henderson, MN  56044          507-248-3294**
**FAX 507-248-3810**
**http://www.closingthegap.com**
**e-mail: info@closingthegap.com**
*Jan Latzke, Registration*

Annual international conference with over 100 exhibitors concerned with the use of computer technology in special education and rehabilitation.

*October*

**1525    College Students with Learning Disabilities Workshop**

**Learning Disabilities Resources**
**PO Box 716**
**Bryn Mawr, PA  19010          610-525-8336**
**800-869-8336**
**FAX 610-525-8337**
**http://www.ldonline.org**

This workshop is designed to provide both information and motivation to both students and college personnel.

**1526    Communication Aid Manufacturers Association (CAMA) Workshops**

**205 W Randolf Street**
**Evanston, IL  60204**
**800-441-2262**
**FAX 847-869-5689**
**TDY:800-441-2262**
**http://www.aacproducts.org**
**e-mail: cama@northshore.net**
*James Neils, Association Administrator*
*Chris Murin, Workshop Coordinator*

CAMA sponsors workshops throughout the US and Canada that demonstrates a variety of communication products from leading manufacturers. The Association strives to keep up with the latest in augmentative and alternative communication (ACC) technology, and promotes understanding of software and hardware, appropriate for clients with learning disabilities. Members teach functional use in a variety of speaking situations.

**1527    ConnSENSE Conference**

**University of Connecticut**
**233 Glenbrook Road**
**Storrs, CT  06269 4174          860-486-2020**
**FAX 860-486-4412**
**TDY:860-486-2077**
**http://www.csd.uconn.edu**
**e-mail: jennifer.lucia@uconn.edu**
*Donna Korbel, Director*
*Jennifer Lucia, Associate Director*
*Christine Morello, Associate Director*

Annual conference on technology for people with special needs.

**1528  Council for Exceptional Children: Teacher Education Division Conference**

Peabody College/Vanderbilt University
2201 W End Avenue
Nashville, TN  37235          615-322-7311
                             FAX 615-343-5555
*Patricia Cegelka, Contact*

Topics addressed include personnel, productivity and teacher education.

**1529  Council for Learning Disabilities International Conference**

Council for Learning Disabilities
PO Box 4014
Leesburg, VA  20177          571-258-1010
                             FAX 571-258-1011
             http://www.cldinternational.org
                  e-mail: info@mcs-amc.com
*Andrea Falzarano, Executive Director*

Focuses on all aspects pertaining to learning disabled individuals from a teaching and research perspective. Over 1000 attendees.

*October*

**1530  Council of Administrators of Special Education Conference**

Fort Valley State University
1005 State University Drive
Fort Valley, GA  31030          478-825-7667
                                800-585-1753
                             FAX 478-825-7811
                http://www.casecec.org
             e-mail: purcell@belsouth.net
*Steve Milliken, President*
*Luann Purcell, Executive Director*

Our mission is to provide leadership and support to members by shaping policies and practices that impact the quality of education.

*January*

**1531  Counseling Individuals with Learning Disabilities Workshop**

Learning Disabilities Resources
PO Box 716
Bryn Mawr, PA  19010          610-525-8336
                              800-869-8336
                           FAX 610-525-8337
                http://www.ldonline.org

In this workshop, Dr. Cooper discusses reasons why some individuals with learning disabilities often do respond well to traditional therapies.

**1532  Creative Mind Workshop: Making Magic with Children and Art**

P Buckley Moss Foundation for Children's Education
601 Shenandoah Village Drive
Waynesboro, VA  22980          540-932-1728
                            FAX 540-941-8865
             http://www.mossfoundation.org
          e-mail: foundation@mossfoundation.org
*Randy Myers, President*
*Dell Philpott, Program coordinator*

Instructional and collaborative strategies for including the visual and performing arts in the education of students with special needs.

**1533  Eden Family of Services**

Eden Services
One Eden Way
Princeton, NJ  08540          609-987-0099
                           FAX 609-987-0243
                http://www.edenservices.org
               e-mail: info@edenservices.org
*David Holmes EdD, Executive Director/President*
*Anne Holmes, Director Outreach Support*
*Joani Truch, Administration/Communications*

Provides year-round educational services, early intervention, parent training and workshops, respite care, outreach services, community based residential services and employment opportunities for individuals with autism.

**1534  Educating Children: Summer Training Institute at Muskingum College**

Ecsti Administrative Services
163 Stormont Stet
New Concord, OH  43762          740-826-8038
                             FAX 740-826-6038
             http://www.ecsti@muskingum.edu
            e-mail: rschmitz@muskingum.edu
*Rolf Schmitz, Medical Doctor*

For public or private school, child care center or family day care teachers, parents, administrators, Head Start, undergraduate/graduate students and other education-related professionals.

**1535  Educational Computer Conference**

Annual International Conference
19 Calvert Court
Piedmont, CA  94611          510-594-1249
                             888-594-1249
                          FAX 510-594-1838
                http://www.trld.com
             e-mail: registration@trld.com
*Diane Frost, CEO*

Focusing on actual classroom and administrative applications for technology, reading and learning difficulties. Hands on workshops are featured.

*January*

**1536  Hearsay Workshops**

1325 Ramblewood Trail
S Euclid, OH  44121          216-382-0383
                          FAX 216-382-0385
                http://www.hearsayinfo.com
             e-mail: mlandis@hearsayinfo.com
*Marilyn Landis, President*

Hearsay offers a variety of training programs and workshops for those working with the hearing impaired population. Workshops and seminars are individualized to meet the special needs of each program. Follow up and online coaching available.

**1537  Inclusion of Learning Disabled Students in Regular Classrooms Workshop**

Learning Disabilities Resources
PO Box 716
Bryn Mawr, PA  19010        610-525-8336
                            800-869-8336
                        FAX 610-525-8337
                    http://www.ldonline.org

This workshop provides teachers with practical suggestions and techniques for including students with learning problems.

**1538  Innovative Instructional Techniques Workshop**

Learning Disabilities Resources
PO Box 716
Bryn Mawr, PA  19010        610-525-8336
                            800-869-8336
                        FAX 610-525-8337
                    http://www.ldonline.org

In this workshop, Dr. Cooper provides an overview of the various techniques he has developed for helping students with learning problems in reading, writing, spelling and math.

**1539  Interest-Driven Learning Workshop**

383 DeSoto Drive
New Smyna Beach, FL  32169      386-427-4473
                                800-245-5733
                            FAX 386-427-4473
                        http://www.drpeet.com
                    e-mail: drpeet@drpeet.com

*Bill Peet MD, CEO*

Provides affordable low and high-tech tools that will help people of all ages and abilities learn to read, write and communicate with support from assistive technology as needed.

**1540  International Adolescent Conference: Programs for Adolescents**

Behavioral Institute for Children and Adolescents
3585 Lexington Avenue N
Arden Hills, MN  55126        651-484-5510
                          FAX 651-483-3879
              http://www.behavioralinstitute.org

*Sheldon Braaten, Executive Director*
*Melissa Knoll, Managing Director*

Information on programs for the developmental needs of children and adolescents with behavioral disorders. Transdisciplinary knowledge and skill, training related, to serve children and youth who have emotional/behavioral disorders.

**1541  International Dyslexia Association Conference: Maryland**

International Dyslexia Association
8600 Lasalle Road, Chester Building
Baltimore, MD  21286        410-296-0232
                            800-ABC-D123
                        FAX 410-321-5069
                    http://www.interdys.org
                e-mail: info@interdys.org

*J Viall, Executive Director*
*Judith Dudek, Director Marketing*
*Cindy Ciresi, Director Conference*

Each year IDA sponsors an international conference. Sessions meet the needs and interests of a wide range of consumers.

*November*

**1542  International Dyslexia Association Conference: Illinois**

Illinois Branch of the International Dyslexia Asso
751 Roosevelt Road, Building 7
Glen Ellyn, IL  60137        630-469-6900
                         FAX 630-469-6810
            e-mail: ilbranch_ida@ameritech.net
*Lisa Hannum, President*
*Gail Oliphant, Office Manager*

This conference will have approximately 500 attendees and 20 exhibitors.

*November*

**1543  LDR Workshop: What Are Learning Disabilities, Problems and Differences?**

Learning Disabilities Resources
PO Box 716
Bryn Mawr, PA  19010        610-525-8336
                            800-869-8336
                        FAX 610-525-8337
                    http://www.ldonline.org

In this workshop, Dr. Cooper draws on personal experiences with a learning disability and on his clinical work with thousands of individuals with a wide variety of learning problems to provide the participants with an understanding of the positive and negative aspects of being, living and learning differently.

**1544  Landmark Outreach Program Workshops**

Landmark School
429 Hale Street
Prides Crossing, MA  01965      978-236-3010
                            FAX 978-927-7268
                http://www.landmark outreach.org
                e-mail: outreach@landmarkschool.org
*Dan Ahearn, Program Director*
*Trish Newhall, Associate Director*

Provides consultation and training to public and private schools, professional organizations, parent groups, and businesses on topics related to individuals with learning disabilities. Services are individually designed to meet the client's specific needs and can range from a two-hour workshop to a year-long training project. Options include: consulting services; training workshops; summer training program; seminars; and parent workshops.

**1545  Learning Disabilities Association Conference: International**

4156 Library Road
Pittsburgh, PA  15234 1349      412-341-1515
                            FAX 412-344-0224
                    http://www.ldaamerica.org
                e-mail: info@ldaamerica.org
*Jane Browning, Executive Director*
*Reed Powell, Membership Coordinator*

Topics addressed at the conference include advocacy, adult literacy and learning disabled education.

*March*

**1546 Learning Disabilities Association of Texas Conference**

1011 W 31st Street
Austin, TX 78705                        512-458-8234
                                        800-604-7500
                                    FAX 512-458-3826
                                 http://www.ldat.org
                            e-mail: contact@ldat.org
*Ann Robinson, State Coordinator*

Promotes the educational and general welfare of individuals with learning disabilities.

**1547 Learning Disabilities and the World of Work Workshop**

Learning Disabilities Resources
PO Box 716
Bryn Mawr, PA 19010                     610-525-8336
                                        800-869-8336
                                    FAX 610-525-8337
                              http://www.ldonline.org

This workshop is designed for employers, parents or professionals working with individuals with learning disabilities.

**1548 Learning Problems and Adult Basic Education Workshop**

Learning Disabilities Resources
Bryn Mawr, PA 19010                     610-525-8336
                                        800-869-8336
                                    FAX 610-525-8337
                              http://www.ldonline.org

This workshop for adult educators discusses the manifestations of learning problems in adults.

**1549 Life After High School for the Student with LD/ADD Conference**

Connecticut Assoc. for Children & Adults with LD
25 Van Zant Street
East Norwalk, CT 06855                  203-838-5010
                                    FAX 203-866-6108
                               http://www.CACLD.org
                         e-mail: cacld@optonline.net
*Beryl Kaufman, Executive Director*
*Carol Maloney, Conference Coordinator*

Conference held for parents, students and professionals. Features workshops, panels, exhibitors and a bookstore.

*Spring*

**1550 Life Lines in the Classroom: LR Consulting & Workshops**

925 S Mason Road
Katy, TX 77450 3874                     281-395-4978
                                    FAX 281-392-8379
                           http://www.lrconsulting.com
*Marlene Johnson, Curriculum and Instruction*
*Mary Fitzgerald, Special Education*

Offers a variety of staff development training options regarding inclusive and special educational issues.

**1551 Lindamood-Bell Research & Training Conferences**

Lindamood-Bell Learning Processes
416 Higuera Street
San Luis Obispo, CA 93401               805-541-3836
                                        800-233-1819
                                    FAX 805-541-8756
                                 http://www.lblp.com
                              e-mail: rbell@lblp.com
*Rodney Bell, Training Coordinator*

Offers workshops nationwide for educators using Lindamood-Bell teaching methods. Twenty or more workshops annually. Inservices also available.

**1552 Melvin-Smith Learning Center Annual Conference**

EDU-Theraputics
775 Kimball Avenue
Seaside, CA 93955                       831-620-1908
                                        800-505-3276
                                    FAX 831-620-1907
                       http://www.edu-theraputics.com
                            e-mail: edu-t@erc1.com
*Joan Smith, Director*

National conference entitled Strategies for Success in Overcoming Learning Handicaps. Special Sessions: 1) Strategic Planning for Learning Centers; 2) Administration and Interpretation of Receptive Expressive Observation of Memory Skills. Workshops: 1) Reading for Nonreaders; 2) Setting Structure for Homework Success; 3) Developing Attention Focus Skills and many more. Call for conference program. Exhibitors welcome.

**1553 National Center for Family Literacy Conference**

325 W Main Street
Louisville, KY 40202 1859               502-584-1133
                                       877-FAMLIT-1
                                    FAX 502-584-0172
                                http://www.famlit.org
                             e-mail: ncfl@famlit.org
*Sharon Darling, President*
*Patricia West, Administrative Assistant*

National Center for Family Literacy will be holding a conference with approximately 40-50 exhibitors and 2,000-2,400 attendees.

*March*

**1554 National Head Start Association Academy Workshop**

1651 Prince Street
Alexandria, VA 22314                    703-739-0875
                                    FAX 703-739-0878
                                  http://www.nhsa.org
                           e-mail: rlewisriar@nhsa.org
*Diane Whitehead, Program Development*
*Ruby Lewis-Riar, Conferences*
*Cheyrl Thompson, Conferences*

Both Adminstrator and Mid-Manager credentials are offered in a six day, institute style setting, workshop. Family Services and Health credentials are offered through a self study format.

*September*

**1555  National Head Start Association Parent Conference**

1651 Prince Street
Alexandria, VA  22314          703-739-0875
                              FAX 703-739-0878
                       http://www.nhsa.org
                 e-mail: rlewisriar@nhsa.org
*Diane Whitehead, Program Development*
*Ruby Lewis-Riar, Conferences*
*Cheyrl Thompson, Conferences*

Newest information on enhancing parent involvement, child development, and sharpening parenting skills. More than 100 workshops.

**1556  New England Joint Conference on Specific Learning Disabilities**

58 Prince Street
Needham, MA  02492          781-455-9895
                           FAX 781-449-1332
                 http://www.addinfonetwork.org
                        e-mail: adin@gis.net
*Linda Downer, Conference Coordinator*

Dynamic, informative conference with the goal being to improve services for language/learning-disabled individuals by encouraging dialogue among the many disciplines, organizations and professions involved in the field of learning disabilities.

**1557  North American Montessori Teachers' Association Conference**

13693 Butternut Road
Buton, OH  44021          440-834-4011
                         FAX 440-834-4016
                http://www.montessori-namta.org
            e-mail: staff@montessori-namta.org
*Katherine Wilson, Conference Coordinator*
*Kristin Sasaki, Office Manager*

Montessori method of teaching is discussed as well as topics pertaining to all levels of special education. This and other conferences are held in different locations and months throughout the year. Please contact us for more information.

*Quarterly*

**1558  Pacific Rim Conference on Disabilities**

University of Hawaii Center on Disability Studies
1776 University Avenue
Honolulu, HI  96822          808-956-9810
                            FAX 808-956-7878
                  http://www.pacrim.hawaii.edu
                     e-mail: cds@hawaii.com
*Martha Guinan, Organizer*
*Valerie Shearer, Organizer*

Participants from the US and other Pacific Rim nations study such topics as lifelong inclusion in education and community, new technology, family support, employment and adult services.

*March*

**1559  Pennsylvania Training and Technical Assistance Network Workshops**

Department of Education Pennsylvania
6340 Flank Drive
Harrisburg, PA  17112          717-541-4960
                               800-360-7282
                           FAX 717-541-4968
                           TDY:800-654-5984
                    http://www.pattan.k12.pa.us
           e-mail: fwarkomski@pattan k12pa.us
*Fran Warkomski, Executive Director*
*Carol Maloney*

Works collaboratively with intermediate units in the areas of professional development, technical assistance and information dissemination to support school districts throughout the Commonwealth. Training and resources are available regarding assistive technology services, short term loans, demonstrations, and production of large print and Braille for student use.

**1560  Social Skills Workshop**

Learning Disabilities Resources
PO Box 716
Bryn Mawr, PA  19010          610-525-8336
                              800-869-8336
                          FAX 610-525-8337
                      http://www.ldonline.org

This workshop is relevant for individuals with learning disabilities, parents or professionals.

**1561  Son-Rise Program Start-Up Workshops**

Autism Treatment Center of America
2080 S Undermountain Road
Sheffield, MA  01257          413-229-2100
                              800-714-2779
                          FAX 413-229-8931
                    http://www.son-rise.org
              e-mail: information@son-rise.org
*Sean Fitzgerald, Assistant Director*
*Camila Titone, Front Office Asst.*

Since 1983, the Autism Treatment Center of America has provided innovative training programs for parents and professionals caring for children challenged by autism, autism spectrum disorders, pervasive developmental disorder (PDD) and other developmental difficulties. The Son-Rise Program teaches a specific yet comprehensive system of treatment and education designed to help families and caregivers enable their children to dramatically improve in all areas of learning.

**1562  Symposium Series on Assistive Technology**

Center on Disabilities/California State University
1811 Nordhoff Street
Northridge, CA  91330          818-677-2578
                           FAX 818-677-4929
                           TDY:818-677-2579
                      http://www.csun.com
                 e-mail: ctrdis@csun.edu
*Joanne Moreno, Coordinator*
*Sonya Hernandez, Coordinator*

Series of workshops that will address specific areas of assistive technology through in depth one and two day training workshops.

**1563 TASH Annual Conference**
29 W Susquehanna Avenue
Baltimore, MD 21204    410-828-8274
FAX 410-828-6706
http://www.tash.org
e-mail: info@tash.org
*Nancy Weiss, Executive Director*
*Kelly Nelson, Conference Coordinator*

Progressive international conference that focuses on strategies for achieving full inclusion for people with disabilities. This invigorating conference, which brings together the best hearts and minds in the disability movement, features over 450 breakout sessions, exhibits, roundtable discussions, poster sessions and much more.

*December*

**1564 Teaching Math Workshop**
Learning Disabilities Resources
PO Box 716
Bryn Mawr, PA 19010    610-525-8336
800-869-8336
FAX 610-525-8337
http://www.ldonline.org
A workshop for teachers on how to teach math to individuals with learning problems.

**1565 Teaching Reading Workshop**
Learning Disabilities Resources
PO Box 716
Bryn Mawr, PA 19010    610-525-8336
800-869-8336
FAX 610-525-8337
http://www.ldonline.org
This workshop explains how to teach individuals with reading problems, dyslexia, ADD, and specific learning disabilities.

**1566 Teaching Spelling Workshop**
Learning Disabilities Resources
PO Box 716
Bryn Mawr, PA 19010    610-525-8336
800-869-8336
FAX 610-525-8337
http://www.ldonline.org
Spelling is a problem which directly affects an individual's ability to write.

**1567 Technology and Persons with Disabilities Conference**
California State University, Northridge
18111 Nordhoff Street
Northridge, CA 91330 8340    818-677-2578
FAX 818-677-4929
http://www.csun.edu/cod
e-mail: ctrdis@csun.edu
*Joanne Moreno, Exhibits Coordinator*
*Sonya Hernandez, Speakers Coordinator*

Comprehensive, international conference where technologies across all ages, disabilities, levels of education and training, employment and independent living are addressed.

*March*

**1568 Tic Tac Toe: Math Training Workshop**
Learning Disabilities Resources
PO Box 716
Bryn Mawr, PA 19010    610-525-8336
800-869-8336
FAX 610-525-8337
http://www.ldonline.org
This two hour workshop provides teachers with instruction in Tic Tac Toe Math and how to teach it.

**1569 US International Council on Disabilities Conference**
1630 ConneCourticut Avenue NW
Washington, DC 20009    202-429-2706
FAX 202-429-9574
http://www.usid.org
e-mail: usid.org@verizon.net
*Ilene Zeitzer, Interim Executive Director*

Annual conference offers information for professionals in the areas of rehabilitation research, assistive technology and more.

*September*

**1570 Wilson Language Training**
Wilson Reading System
175 W Main Street
Millbury, MA 01527 1956    508-865-5699
800-599-8454
FAX 508-865-9644
http://www.wilsonlanguage.com
e-mail: info@wilsonlanguage.com
*Judith Nicholas, Administrator Training*

Our workshops instruct teachers, or other professionals in a related field, how to succeed with students who have not learned to read, write and spell despite great effort. Established in order to provide training in the Wilson Reading System, the Wilson staff provides Two-Day Overview Workshops as well as certified Level I and II training.

**1571 Wilson Reading System**
Wilson Language Training
175 W Main Street
Millbury, MA 01527    508-865-5699
800-899-8454
FAX 508-865-9644
http://www.wilsonlanguage.com
*Judith Nicholas, Administrator Training*
*Duane Armstrong*

Wilson Reading System workshops are research-based programs designed for individuals who have difficulty with written language in the areas of decoding and spelling. Wilson Language Training was established in order to provide training in the Wilson Reading System. The Wilson staff provides two-day Overview Workshops as well as certified Level I and Level II training. A noncertified Level I training is now offered on line.

**1572  Young Adult Institute Conference on Developmental Disabilities**

460 W 34th Street
New York, NY  10001 2382          212-273-6100
                                  FAX 212-629-4113
                                  TDY:212-290-2787
                                  http://www.yai.org
                                  e-mail: ahorowitz@yai.org

*Ben Nivin, Conference Director*
*Andrea lafayette, Conference Manager*
*Aimee Horowitz, Project Director*

Annual conference of developmental disabilities. In-depth sessions on the keys to success in developmental and learning disabilities.

   *May*

## Assistive Devices

**1573 ABLEDATA**

**USDE National Institution on Disability and Rehabi**
**8630 Fenton Street**
**Silver Spring, MD 20910**          301-608-8998
                                     800-227-0216
                                FAX 301-608-8958
                                TDY:301-608-8912
                          http://www.abledata.com
                       e-mail: abledata@oremacro.com
*Katherine Belknap, Project Director*
*Janice Benton, Information Services*
*David Johnson, Publications Director*

Database contains descriptions of more than 30,000 commercially available, one-of-a-kind, and do-it-yourself products for rehabilitation and independent living. A wealth of information on assistive technology.

**1574 ARTIC Technologies**

**1000 John R Road**
**Troy, MI 48083**                   248-588-7370
                                FAX 248-588-1424
                          http://www.artictech.com
                          e-mail: info@artictech.com

Manufacturers of speed boards for the blind and visually impaired. Accessibility appliances for low vision and blindness.

**1575 Ablenet**

**Ablenet**
**2808 North Fairview Avenue**
**Roseville, MN 55113**              612-379-0956
                                     800-322-0956
                                FAX 651-294-2259
                          http://www.ablenetinc.com
                  e-mail: customerservice@ablenetinc.com
*Cheryl Volkman, Chief Developmental Officer*
*Ken Sobtzak, Technical Support*

Simple assistive technology for teaching children with disabilities including communication aids, switches, environmental control, mounting systems, literacy and teacher resources, kits and more.

**1576 Adaptive Device Locator System (ADLS)**

**Academic Software**
**3504 Tates Creek Road**
**Lexington, KY 40517**              859-552-1020
                                FAX 859-273-1943
                            http://www.acsw.com
                        e-mail: asistaff@acsw.com
*Warren Lacefield, President*
*Penny Ellis, COO*

System describes thousands of devices, cross references over 600 vendors and illustrates devices graphically. The ADLS databases include a full spectrum of living aids, products ranging from specialized eating utensils to dressing aids, electronic switches, computer hardware and software, adapted physical education devices and much more. Now accessible on the internet through Adaptworld.com and Acsw.com *$195.00*

**1577 Arcade Adventure**

**Dunamis**
**Lawrenceville, GA 30044**          770-279-1144
                                     800-828-2443
                                FAX 770-279-0809
                          http://www.dunamisinc.com
                        e-mail: info@dunamisinc.com
*Ben Satterfield, President*
*Matt Satterfield, College/LD Sales*

Game-style program helps more advanced switch users build hand-eye coordination and problem solving skills. *$50.00*

**1578 Braille' n Speak Classic**

**American Printing House for the Blind**
**1839 Frankfort Avenue**
**Louisville, KY 40206**             502-895-2405
                                     800-223-1839
                                FAX 502-899-2274
                             http://www.aph.org
                          e-mail: info@aph.org
*Fred Gissoni, Customer Support*
*Allan Lovell, Customer Relations Manager*

This computerized, talking device has many features useful to student and adult braille users (word processors, print-to-braille translator, talking clocks/calculators and much more). *$929.95*

**1579 CCT Telephone Interface**

**Consultants for Communication Technology**
**508 Bellevue Terrace**
**Pittsburgh, PA 15202**             412-761-6062
                                FAX 412-761-7336
                          http://www.concommtech.com
                       e-mail: kathy@concommtech.com
*Kathleen PhD, Speech Pathologist*
*Sharon Money, Office Manager*

Device allows output from your communication software to be transmitted directly through the telephone. Requires CCT software. *$300.00*

**1580 Communication Aids: Manufacturers Association**

**205 W Randolph**
**Chicago, IL 60606**                312-229-5444
                                     800-441-2262
                                FAX 312-229-5445
                                TDY:800-441-2262
                          http://www.aacproducts.org
                       e-mail: cama@northshore.net
*James Neils, President*

A nonprofit organization of the world's leading manufacturers of augmentative and alternative communication software and hardware.

**1581 Connect Outloud**

**Freedon Scientific**
**11800 31st Court N**
**St.Petersburg, FL 33716 1805**     727-803-8000
                                     800-444-4443
                                FAX 727-803-8001
                       http://www.freedomscientific.com
                    e-mail: info@freedomscientific.com
*Lee Hamilton, CEO*

Designed to allow beginners through experienced blind or low vision computer users to access the Internet through speech and Braille output. Based on our JAWS for Windows technology, and offers additional access to Windows XP. *$ 249.00*

**1582  Consultants for Communication Technology**

Consultants for Communication Technology
508 Bellevue Terrace
Pittsburgh, PA  15202                        412-761-6062
                                        FAX 412-761-7336
                        http://www.concommtech.com
                        e-mail: cct@concommtech.com
*Kathleen PhD, Speech Pathologist*
*Sharon Money, Office Manager*

Manufactures and distributes a line of augmentative communication products for persons with speech impairments. In addition we have software products for environmental control, word processing and phone management. All products can be used with only one muscle movement or from the full keyboard.

**1583  Controlpad 24**

Genovation
17741 Mitchell N
Irvine, CA  92614                        949-833-3355
                                        800-822-4333
                                        FAX 949-833-0322
                        http://www.genovation.com
                        e-mail: sales@genovation.com
*Edward Lopez, Project Manager*
*Chris Fructus, Director Marketing*

Fully programmable 24 key pad. Its principal purpose is to provide single keystroke macros.

**1584  Creature Games Series**

Dunamis
3545 Cruse Road
Lawrenceville, GA  30044                770-279-1144
                                        800-828-2443
                                        FAX 770-279-0809
                        http://www.dunamisinc.com
                        e-mail: info@dunamisinc.com
*Ben Satterfield, President*
*Matt Satterfield, College/LD Sales*

Everybody loves computer games, but these games are unique. They can be enjoyed by children with severe/profound disabilities, including those functioning as low as 4 months of age. *$80.00*

**1585  Dunamis**

Dunamis
3545 Cruse Road
Lawrenceville, GA  30044                770-279-1144
                                        800-828-2443
                                        FAX 770-279-0809
                        http://www.dunamisinc.com
                        e-mail: info@dunamisinc.com
*Ben Satterfield, President*
*Matt Satterfield, College/LD Sales*

Since 1984 we have been committed to helping you find the technology you need to accomplish your goals and realize your dreams. We offer assistive technology that is the most appropriate available, at the highest quality and the most competitive price possible.

**1586  Dyna Vox SystemsDyna Vox Systems**

2100 Wharton Street
Pittsburgh, PA  15203                    412-381-4883
                                        800-344-1778
                                FAX 412-381-5241
                        http://www.dynavoxtech.com
                        e-mail: sale@dynavoxtech.com
*Joanne Kaufmann, President*

Dynamic display, touch screen augmentative communication devices that allow the user to create messages by choosing preprogrammed items, or create novel messages. Each device comes with DynaSyms, a comprehensive, language-based system with more than 2600 symbols. Word and symbol prediction helps individuals construct long messages quickly by offering a continuous stream of logical words and/or symbols. A built-in environmental control unit (ECU) allows users to access TVs, VCRs, and computers. *$4500.00*

**1587  EZ Keys/Key Wiz**

Words+
1220 W Avenue J
Lancaster, CA  93534                     661-723-6523
                                        800-869-8521
                                FAX 661-723-2114
                        http://www.world-plus.com
                        e-mail: info@world-plus.com
*Jeff Dahlen, President*
*Sandy Arnold, Accounting Manager*

Assistance program that provides keyboard control, dual word prediction, abbreviation-expansion and speech output while running standard software. *$695.00*

**1588  Franklin Language Master**

Freedon Scientific
11800 31st Court N
St. Petersburg, FL  33716 1805          727-803-8000
                                        800-444-4443
                                FAX 727-803-8001
                        http://www.freedomscientific.com
                        e-mail: info@freedomscientific.com
*Lee Hamilton, CEO*

Versatile hand-held dictionary full speech controls to read screens or speak individual words at the speed you choose. At less than 6 inches square, this lightweight tool is designed for maximum efficiency. Large-type display, high contrast screen and black on white QWERTY keyboard. For blind users, orientation features include active screen announcing and raised dots on location keys. *$450.00*

**1589  Genie Color TV**

TeleSensory
520 Almanor Avenue
Sunnyvale, CA  94043                     408-616-8700
                                        800-227-8418
                                FAX 408-616-8753
                        http://www.telesensory.com
                        e-mail: info@telesensory.com
*Ken Stokes, President*
*Jennifer Street, Marketing Director*

Brings clarity and comfort to reading and writing. Since many people with low vision find that specific color combinations enhance legibility, VersiColor offers 24 customized foreground and background color combinations to choose from in addition to a full color mode. Genie can also connect to a computer for use with Telesensory's Vista screen magnification system. *$2995.00*

**1590  Genovation**

**17741 Mitchell N**
**Irvine, CA  92614**                    **949-833-3355**
                                         **800-822-4333**
                               **FAX 949-822-4333**
                        **http://www.genovation.com**
                      **e-mail: sales@genovation.com**
*Edward Lopez, Project Manager*
*Chris Fructus, Director Marketing*

Produces a wide variety of computer input devices for data-entry, and custom applications. Produces the Function Keypad 682 for people with limited dexterity. It is programmable, allowing the user to store macros (selected patterns of key strokes) into memory, and relegendable keys allow easy labeling of user-programmed functions. Additional options such as larger keys (1x2), allow reconfiguration to meet the user's needs. Call toll-free for pricing and availability.

**1591  Home Row Indicators**

**Hooleon Corporation**
**417 Building A, S 6th Street/304 We**
**Melrose, NM  86326**                    **928-634-7515**
                                         **800-937-1337**
                               **FAX 928-634-4620**
                          **http://www.hooleon.com**
                        **e-mail: sales@hooleon.com**
*Joan Crozier, President*

Plastic adhesive labels with a raised bump in the center allowing the user to designate home row keys, or any other key, for quick recognition.

**1592  Hub**

**Alliance for Technology Access**
**1304 Southpoint Boulevard**
**Petaluma, CA  94954**                    **707-778-3011**
                               **FAX 707-765-2080**
                               **TDY:707-778-3015**
                         **http://www.ataccess.org**
                      **e-mail: atainfo@ataccess.org**
*Mary Lester, Executive Director*
*Kelly , Administrator and Development As*

Interactive information service provides quick and efficient access to information on assistive technology tools and services to consumers, families and service providers.

**1593  IBM Independence Series**

**IBM**
**11400 Burnet Road**
**Austin, TX  78758**
                                         **800-IBM-4YOU**
                               **FAX 512-838-9367**
                         **http://www.IBM.com/able**
*Dennis O'Brien, Product Manager*

A group of products designed to help individuals with disabilities to achieve greater personal and professional independence through the use of technology. Products include Keyguard, AccessDOS, THINKable/2, Screen Reader/2, Screen Magnifier/2, SpeechViewer II, THINKable/DOS and Screen Reader/DOS.

**1594  IntelliKeys**

**IntelliTools**
**1720 Corporate Circle**
**Petaluma, CA  94954**                    **707-773-2000**
                                         **800-899-6687**
                               **FAX 707-773-2001**
                        **http://www.intellitools.com**
                      **e-mail: info@intellitools.com**
*Beth Davis, Director*

Alternative, touch-sensitive keyboard. Plugs into any MAC, APPLE, or IBM compatible computer, no interface needed. *$395.00*

**1595  JAWS for Windows**

**Freedon Scientific**
**11800 31st Court N**
**St.Petersburg, FL  33716 1805**          **727-803-8000**
                                         **800-444-4443**
                               **FAX 727-803-8001**
                     **http://www.freedomscientific.com**
                   **e-mail: info@freedomscientific.com**
*Lee Hamilton, CEO*

Works with your PC to provide access to today's software applications and the internet. With its internal software speech synthesizer and the computer's sound card, information from the screen is read aloud, providing technology to access a wide variety of information, education and job related applications.

**1596  Large Print Keyboard**

**Hooleon Corporation**
**417 Building 3565, S 6th Street/304**
**Melrose, NM  86326**                    **928-634-7515**
                                         **800-937-1337**
                               **FAX 928-634-4620**
                          **http://www.hooleon.com**
                        **e-mail: sales@hooleon.com**
*Joan Crozier, President*

Keyboard with 104 keys features large print on all the keys.

**1597  Large Print Lower Case Labels**

**Hooleon Corporation**
**417 Building A, S 6th Street/304 W**
**Melrose, NM  86326**                    **928-634-7515**
                                         **800-937-1337**
                               **FAX 928-634-4620**
                          **http://www.hooleon.com**
                        **e-mail: sales@hooleon.com**
*Joan Crozier, President*

For children learning the keyboard.

**1598  Lekotek of Georgia Shareware**

Lekotek of Georgia
1955 Cliff Valley Way NE
Atlanta, GA  30329          404-633-3430
                           FAX 404-633-1242
                    http://www.lekotekga.org
            e-mail: lekotekga@mindspring.com
*Helena Prokesh, Executive Director*
*Peggy McWilliams, Tech Specialist*

Software created by our staff using Intellipics, Intellipics Studio or Hyperstudio. Players are included to run this shareware. Color overlays for intellemusic are included. Input methods are mouse, switch, touch window, head mouse and intellikeys if applicable. Subjects are colors and emotions, early childhood music in English and Spanish, shapes and sounds, pictures and letters.

**1599  Micro IntroVoice**

Voice Connection
10522 Covington Circle
Villa Park, CA  92861        714-997-8777
                           FAX 714-628-1321
                    http://www.voicecnx.com
                   e-mail: voicecnx@aol.com
*Shirley Dworak, Vice President Marketing*

A complete voice input/output system which provides voice recognition of 1,000 words with accuracy of 98 percent and unlimited text-to-speech and recorded speech for voice prompting and varification. Micro IntroVoice works with DOS and Windows applications for entering commands or data. *$1095.00*

**1600  Open Book**

Freedon Scientific
11800 31st Court N
St.Petersburg, FL  33716 1805    727-803-8000
                                 800-444-4443
                             FAX 727-803-8001
                  http://www.freedomscientific.com
                  e-mail: info@freedomscientific.com
*Lee Hamilton, CEO*

Allows you to convert printed documents or graphic based text into an electronic text format using accurate optical character recognition and quality speech. The many powerful low vision tools allow you to customize how the document appears on your screen, while other features provide portability. *$995.00*

**1601  OutSPOKEN**

Alva Access Group
436 14th Street
Oakland, CA  94612           510-451-2582
                             888-318-2582
                         FAX 510-451-0878
                     http://www.aagi.com
                   e-mail: info@aagi.com
*Larry Lake, Owner*

Gives blind and learning disabled persons access to mainstream Macintosh software via speech output. *$395.00*

**1602  Personal Communicating Device**

ABOVO
96 Rhinebeck Avenue
Springfield, MA  01129       413-594-5279
                           FAX 413-594-5809

A portable, handheld electronic device designed for single finger communication by people who wish to communicate through typing.

**1603  Phonic Ear Auditory Trainers**

Phonic Ear
3880 Cypress Drive
Petaluma, CA  94954          707-769-1110
                             800-227-0735
                         FAX 707-769-9624
                         TDY: 707-769-126
                  http://www.phonicear.com
            e-mail: marketing@phonicear.com
*Paul Hickey, Vice President Sales*
*J Merline, Director Marketing*
*Cindy Pedersen, Customer Service Manager*

A line of learning disabled communication equipment.

**1604  QuicKeys**

CE Software
PO Box 65580
West Des Moines, IA  50265     515-221-1801
                               800-523-7638
                           FAX 515-221-1806
                    http://www.cesoft.com
                  e-mail: sales@cesoft.com
*John Kirk, Controller*
*Joe Gray, Human Resources Director*

Assigns Macintosh functions to one keystroke.

**1605  Reading Pen**

Wizcom Technologies
257 Great Road
Acton, MA  01720             978-635-5357
                             888-777-0552
                         FAX 978-929-9228
                  http://www.wizcomtech.com
             e-mail: sales@wizcomtech.com
*Raz Itzhaki, President*
*Peter Lovitz, Office Manager*

Portable assistive reading device that reads words aloud and can be used anywhere. Scans a word from printed text, displays the word in large characters, reads the word aloud from built-in speaker or ear phones and defines the word with the press of a button. Displays syllables, keeps a history of scanned words, adjustable for left or right-handed use. Includes a tutorial video and audio cassette. Not recommended for persons with low vision or impaired fine motor control.

**1606  Scan It-Switch It**

UCLA Intervention Program for Handicapped Children
1000 Veteran Avenue
Los Angeles, CA  90095       310-825-4821
                         FAX 310-206-7744
                  http://www.bol.ucla.edu
            e-mail: scislo@madnet.uclu.edu
*Sharon Cislo, Administrative Assistant*
*Kit Kehr, Executive Director*

Helps teach horizontal and vertical scanning using a single switch or TouchWindow. Instruction progresses through five levels of difficulty from capturing a single object with a moving box to using scanning to select matching items. *$45.00*

**1607  Self-Adhesive Braille Keytop Labels**

**Hooleon Corporation**
**411 S 6th Street, Building B**
**Melrose, AZ  86326**  520-634-7515
800-937-1337
FAX 520-634-4620
http://www.hooleon.com
e-mail: sales@hooleon.com
*Joan Crozier, President*

Transparent with raised braille allows both sighted and nonsighted users to use same keyboard.

**1608  Switch Accessible Trackball**

**Lekotek of Georgia**
**1955 Cliff Valley Way NE**
**Atlanta, GA  30329**  404-633-3430
FAX 404-633-1242
http://www.lekotekga.org
e-mail: email@lekotekga.com
*Helena Prokesh, Executive Director*
*Peggy McWilliams, Tech Specialist*

Universal to Mac or Windows, this device aids computer navigation where traditional devices are not used. Trackball guards available. *$125.00*

**1609  Switch It Software Bundle**

**Dunamis**
**3423 Fowler Boulevard**
**Lawrenceville, GA  30044**  770-279-1144
800-828-2443
FAX 770-279-0809
http://www.dunamisinc.com
e-mail: info@dunamisinc.com
*Ben Satterfield, President*
*Matt Satterfield, College/LD Sales*

Collection of 4 software programs that follow a developmental learning sequence.

**1610  Talking Typer**

**American Printing House for the Blind**
**1839 Frankfort Avenue**
**Louisville, KY  40206**  502-895-2405
800-223-1839
FAX 502-899-2274
http://www.aph.org
e-mail: info@aph.org
*Fred Gissoni, Technical Support*
*Allan Lovell, Customer Relations Manager*

Designed to reinforce keyboarding skills for visually impaired Apple VI users and their teachers.

**1611  Talking Utilities for DOS 3.3**

**American Printing House for the Blind**
**1839 Frankfort Avenue**
**Louisville, KY  40206**  502-895-2405
800-223-1839
FAX 502-899-2274
http://www.aph.org
e-mail: info@aph.org
*Fred Gissoni, Customer Support*
*Allan Lovell, Customer Relations Manager*

A talking version of System Master with features added for speech synthesis users. *$15.00*

**1612  Talking Utilities for ProDOS**

**American Printing House for the Blind**
**1839 Frankfort Avenue**
**Louisville, KY  40206**  502-895-2405
800-223-1839
FAX 502-899-2274
http://www.aph.org
e-mail: info@aph.org
*Fred Gissoni, Customer Support*
*Allan Lovell, Customer Relations Manager*

A speech-accessible version of Apple's ProDOS User's Disk. *$10.00*

**1613  Text 2000**

**American Printing House for the Blind**
**1839 Frankfort Avenue**
**Louisville, KY  40206**  502-895-2405
800-223-1839
FAX 502-899-2274
http://www.aph.org
e-mail: info@aph.org
*Fred Gissoni, Customer Support*
*Allan Lovell, Customer Relations Manager*

Allows students to read textbooks in a number of ways, including synthetic speech, large type sized to the screen and refreshable braille. *$112.00*

**1614  Ufonic Voice System**

**Compass Learning**
**7878 N 16th Street**
**Phoenix, AZ  85020**  602-678-7272
800-551-1121
FAX 602-230-7034
http://www.compasslearning.com
e-mail: mholt@compasslearning.com
*Rajeev Turi, President*
*Mark Holt, Office Manager*

Consists of the interface card, amplifier/speaker with dual headphones and volume control, and provides human sounding speech in instructional software developed for this use. *$245.00*

**1615  Unicorn Expanded Keyboard**

**IntelliTools**
**1720 Corporate Circle**
**Petaluma, CA  94954**  707-773-2000
800-899-6687
FAX 707-773-2001
http://www.intellitools.com
e-mail: info@intellitools.com
*Beth Davis, Director*

Alternative keyboard with large, user-defined keys, requires interface. Smaller version is also available. *$315.00*

**1616  Unicorn Smart Keyboard**

**IntelliTools**
**55 Leveroni Court**
**Novato, CA  94949**          707-773-2000
                              800-899-6687
                              FAX 415-382-5950

Works with any standard keyboard and offers seven overlays and a cable for one type of computer.

**1617  Universal Numeric Keypad**

**Genovation**
**17741 Mitchell N**
**Irvine, CA  92614**          949-833-3355
                              800-822-4333
                              FAX 949-833-4333
                    http://www.genovation.com
                    e-mail: sales@genovation.com
*Chris Fructus, Director Marketing*
*Edward Lopez, Product Manager*

A 21 key numeric keypad that works with any laptop or portable computer.

**1618  Up and Running**

**IntelliTools**
**1720 Corporate Circle**
**Petaluma, CA  94954**          707-773-2000
                              800-899-6687
                              FAX 707-773-2001
                    http://www.intellitools.com
                    e-mail: info@intellitools.com
*Beth Davis, Director*

A custom overlay kit for the Unicorn Keyboard that provides instant access to a wide range of software including over 60 popular educational programs. *$69.95*

**1619  VISTA**

**TeleSensory**
**520 Almanor Avenue**
**Sunnyvale, CA  94086**          408-616-8700
                              800-227-8418
                              FAX 408-616-8720
                    http://www.telesensory.com
                    e-mail: info@telesensory.com
*Ken Stokes, President*
*Jennifer Street, Marketing*

Image enlarging system that magnifies the print and graphics on the screen from three to 16 times. *$2495.00*

**1620  Visagraph II Eye-Movement Recording System**

**Taylor Associated Communications**
**200 E 2nd Street**
**Huntington Station, NY  11746**     631-549-3000
                              800-732-3587
                              FAX 631-549-3156
                    http:// www.readingplus.com
                    e-mail: info@readingplus.com
*Stanford Taylor, President*

Measures reading performance efficiency, visual and functional proficiency, perceptual development, and information processing competence.

**1621  VoiceNote**

**Pulse Date Human Ware**
**175 Mason Circle**
**Concord, CA  94520**          925-680-7100
                              800-722-3393
                              FAX 925-681-4630
                    http://www.pulsedata.com
                    e-mail: usa@pulsedata.com
*Phil Rance, Chief Executive Officer*

Speech synthesizer without a braille display. Most of the great features that are on BrailleNote are here, but on a smaller and lighter unit. Choose from either a braille key or a QWERTY input, depending on your preference.

**1622  Window-Eyes**

**GW Micro**
**725 Airport N Office Park**
**Fort Wayne, IN  46825**          260-489-3671
                              FAX 260-489-2608
                    http://www.gwmicro.com
                    e-mail: support@gwmicro.com
*Dan Weirich, President*
*Mike Lawler, Technical Support*

Screen reader that is adaptable to your specific needs and preferances. Works automatically so you can focus on your application program, not so much on operating the screen reader.

## Books & Periodicals

**1623  AppleWorks Education**

**AACE**
**PO Box 3728**
**Norfolk, VA  23514**          757-623-7588
                              FAX 703-997-8760
                    http://www.aace.org
                    e-mail: info@aace.org
*Gary Marks, Publisher*
*Tracy Jacobs, Office Manager*

Covers educational uses of AppleWorks software. *$25.00*

**1624  AppleWorks Manuals: Special Editions**

**American Printing House for the Blind**
**1839 Frankfort Avenue**
**Louisville, KY  40206**          502-895-2405
                              800-223-1839
                              FAX 502-899-2274
                    http://www.aph.org
                    e-mail: info@aph.org
*Fred Gissoni, Customer Support*
*Allan Lovell, Customer Relations Manager*

Designed for visually impaired users. Includes AppleWorks tutorials on cassette and AppleWorks Reference Manual on computer diskette. *$23.90*

**1625  Art Express and the Literacy Curriculum**

**Center for Best Practices in Early Childhood
Western Illnois University
Macomb, IL  61455                 309-298-1634
                                  FAX 309-298-2305
                    http://www.mprojects.wiu.edu
                    e-mail: PL-Hutinger@wiu.edu**
*Patricia EdD, Director
Joyce Johanson, Coordinator*

Make your classroom come alive with art, music, movement, and dramatic play. Innovative, yet practical guide for helping teachers implement a comprehensive expressive arts curriculum in their classrooms include tips for arranging the environment. *$20.00*

*16-20 pages*

**1626  Bibliography of Journal Articles on
Microcomputers & Special Education**

**Special Education Resource Center
25 Industrial Park Road
Middletown, CT  06457              860-632-1485
                                  FAX 860-632-8870**
*Stephen Kramer, Compiler*

This pamphlet offers information on a wide variety of professional journals in the fields of microcomputers and special education.

**1627  Closing the Gap Newsletter**

**PO Box 68
Henderson, MN  56044              507-248-3294
                                  FAX 507-248-3810
                    http://www.closingthegap.com
                    e-mail: info@closingthegap.com**
*Jan Latzke, Communications*

Bimonthly newsletter on the use of computer technology in special education and rehabilitation. CTG also sponsors an annual international conference. *$34.00*

*40 pages
ISSN 0886-1935*

**1628  Computer Access-Computer Learning**

**Special Needs Project
324 State Street
Santa Barbara, CA  93101          805-962-8087
                                  800-333-6867
                                  FAX 805-962-5087
                    http://www.specialneeds.com
                    e-mail: books@specialneeds.com**
*Ginny LaVine, Author
Hod Gray, Director
Laraine Gray, Conference Coordinator*

A resource manual in adaptive technology. *$22.50*

*226 pages*

**1629  Computers in Head Start Classrooms**

**Learning Disabilities Association of America
4156 Library Road
Pittsburgh, PA  15234             412-341-1515
                                  FAX 412-344-0224
                    http://www.ldaamerica.com
                    e-mail: ldanatl@usaor.net**
*Jane Browning, Executive Director
Mary , Office Manager*

*$7.00*

**1630  MACcessories: Guide to Peripherals**

**Western Illinois University: Macomb Projects
27 Horrabin Hall
Macomb, IL  61455                 309-298-1634
                                  FAX 309-298-2305
                    http://www.mprojects.wiu.edu
                    e-mail: PL-Hutinger@wiu.edu**
*Patricia EdD, Director
Joyce Johanson, Coordinator*

Designed to help the Macintosh user understand peripheral devices. Includes descriptions of each device, advantages and disadvantages of each, procedures for installation, troubleshooting tips, suggested software and company resources. *$15.00*

*41 pages*

**1631  Opening Windows: A Talking and Tactile
Tutorial for Microsoft Windows**

**American Printing House for the Blind
1839 Frankfort Avenue
Louisville, KY  40206             502-895-2405
                                  800-223-1839
                                  FAX 502-895-1509
                    http://www.aph.org
                    e-mail: info@aph.org**
*Fred Gissoni, Customer Support
Allan Lovell, Customer Relations Manager*

Includes raised line graphics, cassette and computer diskette designed to acquaint visually impaired computer users with Windows 3.1 operating environment. *$50.00*

**1632  Switch to Turn Kids On**

**Western Illinois University: Macomb Projects
27 Horrabin Hall
Macomb, IL  61455                 309-298-1634
                                  FAX 309-298-2305
                    http://www.mprojects.wiu.edu
                    e-mail: PL-Hutinger@wiu.edu**
*Patricia EdD, Director
Joyce Johanson, Coordinator*

Guide to homemade switches gives information on conducting a switch workshop and constructing a battery interrupter as well as various kinds of switches (tread switches, ribbon switches, mercury switches, pillow switches). Contains illustrations and step-by-step instructions. *$12.00*

*47 pages*

## Centers & Organizations

**1633   Activating Children Through Technology (ACCT)**

Western Illinois University: Macomb Projects
27 Horrabin Hall
Macomb, IL  61455                       309-298-1634
                                   FAX 309-298-2305
                        http://www.mprojects.wiu.edu
                        e-mail: PL-Hutinger@wiu.edu
*Patricia EdD, Director*
*Joyce Johanson, Coordinator*

ACTT integrates assistive technology into early
childhood services for children with disabilities from
birth to 8 years old. It helps them gain control over
their environment, develop autonomy, communicate,
develop problem-solving skills and participate in an
inclusive environment. ACTT provides training to
families and educators and has written materials and
software available. *$16.00*

**1634   Adaptive Technology Laboratory**

Center for Adaptive Technology Department
501 Crescent Street
New Haven, CT  06515                    203-392-6790
                                   FAX 203-392-5796
                           http://www.southernct.edu
                        e-mail: cat@southernct.edu
*Bo Zamfir, Adaptive Technology Coordinator*
*Hessan Abbas, University Assistant*

Helps individuals with visual, orthopedic and learning disabilities to gain computer access through the
use of the latest technology.

**1635   Artificial Language Laboratory**

Michigan State University
405 Computer Center
East Lansing, MI  48824 1042            517-353-5399
                                   FAX 517-353-4766
                        http://www.ms.edu/~artlang/
                        e-mail: artlang@ msu.edu
*John Eulenberg PhD, Director*
*Stephen Blosser, Rehab Engineer*

Multidisciplinary teaching and research center involved in basic and applied research concerning the
computer processing of formal linguistic structures.

**1636   Assistive Technology Information Network**

IA University Assistive Technology
University Hospital School
Iowa City, IA  52242 1011               319-355-4463
                                        800-331-3027
                                   FAX 319-356-8284
                             http://www.uiowa.edu
                        e-mail: jane-gay@uiowa.edu
*Jane Gray, Director*
*Mary Quigley, Director*

Computer accesssed solutions for physically challenged students.

**1637   Association for Educational Communications and
Technology**

Association for Educational Communications and
Tec
1800 N Stonelake Drive
Bloomington, IN  47408                  812-335-7675
                                   FAX 812-335-7678
                             http://www.aect.org
                        e-mail: rxaver@aect.org
*Phillip Harris MD, Executive Director*
*Richard Xaver, Electronic Services*

Provides leadership in educational communications
and technology by linking professionals holding a
common interest in the use of educational technology
and its application to the learning process.

**1638   Birmingham Alliance for Technology Access
Center**

Birmingham Independent Living Center
206 13th Street S
Birmingham, AL  35233 1317              205-251-2223
                                   FAX 205-251-0605
                        e-mail: minorris@bellsouth.net
*Mike Norris, Information Specialist*
*Dan Kessler, Director*

Information dissemination, network, referral service,
support services, and training. Disabilities served are
cognitive, hearing, learning, physical, speech and vision.

**1639   Bluegrass Technology Center**

961 Beasley Street
Lexington, KY  40509                    859-294-4343
                                        800-209-7769
                                   FAX 859-294-0704
                                   TDY:800-209-7767
                        http://www.bluegrass-tech.org
                        e-mail: office@bluegrass-tech.org
*Jean Isaacs, Director Technology*
*Debbie Sharon, Director Education*
*Penny Ellis, Assistive Technology Consultant*

Provides support to all persons with disabilities in
their efforts to access technology and to increase
awareness and understanding of how that technology
can enhance their abilities to participate more fully in
their community, assisting individuals directly or in-
directly by working with their caregivers, therapists,
vocational counselors, case managers, educators, employers, and community members.

**1640   CAST**

40 Harvard Mills Square
Wakefield, MA  01880 3233               781-245-2212
                                        888-858-9994
                                   FAX 781-245-5212
                                   TDY:781-245-9320
                             http://www.cast.org
                        e-mail: djordon@cast.org
*David Rose MD, Co-Executive Director*
*David Gordon, Communications*

Nonprofit organization whose mission is to expand
educational opportunities for all children through innovative uses of computer technology. Provides direct services to individuals, offers consultation and
training, conducts research and develops software and
implementation models for education.

**1641** **CITE Technology Access Center**

215 E New Hampshire Street
Orlando, FL 32804      407-898-2483
FAX 407-895-5255
http://www.centralfloridalighthouse.org
e-mail: jgideons@cite-fl.com
*Lee Nasehi, Executive Director*
*Karen Morehouse, Children's Services*

Community based technology resource center seeks to redefine human potential by making technology a regular part of the lives of people with disabilities. Dedicated to increasing the use of technology by children and adults with disabilities, their families, educators and employers. CITE exists to solve the problem of where people can find out about the power of technology and get the expertise and assistance they need to make computers work for them.

**1642** **CMECSU Technology Project for Learners with Low Incidence Disabilities**

3335 W St. Germain Street
Saint Cloud, MN 56301      763-255-4913
*Dixie Anderson*

A regional educational organization that works within a nine county region. Maintains a demonstration center with about 500 public domain software programs. Offers specialized equipment for loan to students.

**1643** **Carolina Computer Access Center**

401 E 9th Street
Charlotte, NC 28202      704-342-3004
FAX 704-342-1513
http://www.bellsouth.net
e-mail: ccacnc@bellsouth.net
*Linda Schilling, Director*
*Allison Schilling, Communications Specialist*

Demonstrations, assessments, workshops, and information on assistive technologies.

**1644** **Center for Accessible Technology**

Center for Accessible Technology
2547 8th Street
Berkeley, CA 94710      510-841-3224
FAX 510-841-7956
http://www.cforat.org
e-mail: info@cforat.org
*Dimitri Belser, Executive Director*
*Eric Smith, Program Director*

Provides access to the tools of expression for people with disabilities. Offers information and traning on assistive computer technology and adapted art programs, allowing people with disabilities to participate fully in work, school, and community activities.

**1645** **Center for Enabling Technology**

College of New Jersey
Forcina 102
Ewing, NJ 08628      609-771-3016
FAX 609-637-5172
http://www.tcnj.edu
e-mail: educat@tcnj.edu
*Terry O'Connor, Dean*
*Christine Schindler, Director*

Ongoing projects that match assistive devices to the children who need them. Training and educational workshops.

**1646** **Comprehensive Services for the Disabled**

Comprehensive Services for the Disabled
Belmar Boulevard & Woodfield Avenue
Wall, NJ 07719      732-681-5632
800-784-2919
FAX 732-681-5632
*Donald DeSanto, Executive Director*
*Anthony Aquilino, Director*
*Jennifer DeSanto, Administrative Assistant*

Helps special students realize their potential and bring college admission a step closer. Program designed to meet the needs and maximize the unique talents of each individual. The staff consists of highly qualified teachers who see beyond labels and reach the person inside. By pacing scholastics to each student's ability, the college increases understanding and makes learning a positive experience. Instruction is tailored to each individual.

**1647** **Computer Access Center**

Computer Access Center
6234 W 87th Street
Los Angeles, CA 90045      310-338-5977
FAX 310-338-9318
http://www.cac.org
e-mail: cac@cac.org
*Mary Glicksman, Director*

Computer resource center serving primarily as a place where people with all types of disabilities can preview equipment. Workshops, seminars, after school clubs for children and individual consultations are provided.

**1648** **Computer Accommodation Lab**

Woodrow Wilson Rehab Center
Box 1500
Fishersville, VA 22939 1500      540-332-7000
800-345-9972
FAX 540-332-7132
http://www.wwrc.net
e-mail: colemawl@wwrc.state.va.us
*Twana Afton, Resource Specialist*
*Richard Luck, Director*

Provides assessments for adolescents and adults in appropriate access to computers, including alternative input strategies, mouse applications, and software solutions.

**1649** **Computer Learning Foundation**

47 Northgate Boulevard
Sacramento, CA 95834      916-595-4766
FAX 916-565-0220
http://www.computerlearning.org
e-mail: clf@computerlearning.org
*Sally Alden, Executive Director*

An international nonprofit educational foundation, dedicated to improving the quality of education and preparation of youth for the workplace through the use of technology. To accomplish its mission, the foundation provides numerous projects and materials to help parents and educators use technology effectively with children.

**1650 Dialog Information Services**
Dialog Information Services
11000 Regency Parkway
Cary, NC 27511         919-462-8600
         800-334-2564
        FAX 919-468-9890
        http://www.dialog.com
        e-mail: customer@dialog.com
*Roy Martin, President*

Offers access to over 390 data bases containing information on various aspects of disabling conditions and services to disabled individuals.

**1651 Disabled Children's Computer Group**
Center for Accessible Technology
2547 8th Street
Berkeley, CA 94710       510-841-3224
        FAX 510-841-7956
        http://www.cforat.org
        e-mail: info@cforat.org
*Eric Smith, Program Director*
*Dimitri Belser, Executive Director*

Resource center for parents, professionals, developers and individuals with disabilities, filled with computers, software, adapted toys and adaptive technology.

**1652 Eastern Tennessee Technology Access Center**
4918 N Broadway
Knoxville, TN 37918      865-219-0130
        FAX 865-219-0137
        http://www.korrnet.org/ettac
        e-mail: etstactn@aol.com
*Louis Symington, Director*

Assistive technology resource and information center for individuals with disabilities, their families and professionals who work with them. Workshops, consultations, tutoring, information and product reviews available.

**1653 Exceptional Child Education Resource (ECER)**
Council for Exceptional Children
1110 N Glebe Road
Arlington, VA 22201      703-620-3660
        888-232-7733
       FAX 703-264-9494
        http://www.cec.sped.org/
        e-mail: victore@cec.sped.org
*Victor Erickson, Exhibits Manager*
*Liz Martinez, Publications Director*

This database contains citations and abstracts of print and nonprint materials dealing with exceptional children, those who have disabilities and those who are gifted. Resources in all areas of special education and related services (including services provided by audiologists, speech therapists, occupational therapists, physical therapists, and educational psychologists) are covered in ECER.

**1654 High Tech Center for the Disabled of the California Community Colleges**
Foothill-DeAnza Community College District
21050 McClellan Road
Cupertino, CA 95014      408-996-4636
        800-411-8954
       FAX 408-996-6042
        http://www.htctu.fhda.edu
        e-mail: cbrown@htctu.net
*Carl Brown, Director*

Provides training for faculty and staff of the California community colleges in access technologies.

**1655 Learning Independence Through Computers**
LINC
1001 Eastern Avenue
Baltimore, MD 21202      410-659-5462
       FAX 410-659-5472
        http://www.linc.org
        e-mail: lincmd@aol.com
*Mary Salkever, Executive Director*
*Susan Pompa, Director Program Management*

Resource center that offers specially adapted computer technology to children and adults with a variety of disabilities. State-of-the-art systems allow consumers to achieve their potential for productivity and independence at home, school, work and in the community. Also offers a quarterly newsletter called Connections.

**1656 National Technology Center**
American Foundation for the Blind
11 Penn Plaza
New York, NY 10001      212-502-7600
        800-232-5463
       FAX 212-502-7777
        http://www.afb.org
        e-mail: afbinfo@afb.net
*Carl Augusto, President*

Demonstrates and evaluates equipment and publishes evaluations in the Journal of Visual Impairment & Blindness.

**1657 New Breakthroughs**
89911 Greenwood Drive
Eugene, OR 97402      541-741-5070
       FAX 541-896-0123
*Carol Berger, Contact*

Facilitated communication and information in all areas of assistive, alternative communication. Technological education materials, workshops and training in new special education advancements are available.

**1658 Northern Illinois Center for Adaptive Technology**
3615 Louisiana Road
Rockford, IL 61108 6195    815-229-2163
       FAX 815-229-2135
        http://www.nicat.ataccess.org
        e-mail: davegrass@earthlink.net
*Dave Grass, Director*

Nonprofit computer and adaptive devices resource center operated by parents, consumers, volunteers and professionals dedicated to providing information, seminars and individual needs technology. It is the goal of the center to help people with disabilities reach their full potential by providing them with information on the latest technology and by matching adaptive devices to their disabilities allowing them to more effectively interface with their environment.

**1659 Project TECH**

**Massachusetts Easter Seal Society**
**484 Main Street**
**Worcester, MA 01608 1817**      617-226-2640
800-922-8290
FAX 508-831-9768
http://www.eastersealsma.org
e-mail: maryd@eastersealsma.org
*Kirk Joslin, President*
*Mary D'Antonio, Information Specialist*

Assistive technology services, suited to an individual's needs. Transition from school to work, employment planning, occupational skills and more are coached here.

**1660 RESNA Technical Assistance Project**

**Rehabilitation Engineering & Asst Technology: NA**
**1700 N Moore Street**
**Arlington, VA 22209**      703-524-6686
FAX 703-524-6630
TDY:703-524-6639
http://www.resna.org
e-mail: membership@resna.org
*Larry Pencak, Executive Director*
*Shannon Marullo, Professional Services*
*Nell Bailey, Director Projects*

Provides technical assistance to states in the development and implementation of consumer responsive statewide programs of technology-related assistance under the Technology Related Assistance for Individuals with Disabilities Act of 1988.

**1661 Special Education Preview Center**

**Ruth Eason School**
**648 Old Mill Road**
**Millersville, MD 21108**      410-222-3815
FAX 410-222-3817

*Paulette Tanaue, Principal*
*Linda Abe, Secretary*

**1662 Tech-Able**

**Tech-Able**
**1114 Brett Drive SW**
**Conyers, GA 30094**      770-922-6768
FAX 770-992-6769
http://www.techable.org
e-mail: techable@techable.org
*Carolyn McGonagill, Director*
*Pat Hanus, Executive Assistant*
*Joe Tedesco, Assistive Tech. Practitioner*

Assistive technology demonstration and information center. Provides demonstrations of computer hardware and software specially designed to assist people with disabilities. Serves a wide range of disabilities and virtually all age groups. Also custom fabrication of key guards and switches.

**1663 Technology Access Center**

**2222 Metrocenter Boulevard**
**Nashville, TN 37228**      615-248-6733
800-368-4651
FAX 615-259-2536
TDY:615-248-6733
http://www.tac.ataccess.org
e-mail: techaccess@mindstate.com
*Bob Kibler, Director*
*Lynn Magner, Service Coordinator*

Serves the community as a resource center and carries out specific projects related to assistive technology.

**1664 Technology Access Foundation**

**Technology Access Foundation**
**3803 S Edmunds Street**
**Seattle, WA 98112**      206-725-9095
FAX 206-725-9097
http://www.techaccess.org
e-mail: taf@techaccess.org
*Trish Millines-Dziko, Executive Director*
*Sherry Williams, Program Manager*

Provides information, consultation and technical assistance on assistive technology for people with disabilities, including computer hardware and software technology, and adaptive and assistive equipment.

**1665 Technology Assistance for Special Consumers**

**United Cerebral Palsy**
**915 Monroe Street**
**Huntsville, AL 35804**      256-532-5996
FAX 256-532-2355
http://www.tasc.ataccess.org
e-mail: tasc@hiwaay.net
*Lisa Snyder, Resource Center Specialist*
*Sandra Schmidt, Office Manager*

Offers a computer resource center which has both computers and software for use at the center or for short-term.

**1666 Technology Utilization Program**

**National Aeronautics and Space Administration**
**300 E Street**
**Washington, DC 20002**      202-358-0000
FAX 202-358-4338
http://www.hq.nasa.gov
*Sean O'Keith, President*

Adapts aerospace technology to the development of equipment for the disabled, sick and elderly persons.

**1667 Technology for Language and Learning**

**PO Box 327**
**East Rockaway, NY 11518**      516-625-4550
FAX 516-621-3321
*Joan Tanenhaus, Executive Director*

An organization dedicated to advancing the use of computers and technology for children and adults with special language and learning needs. Public domain computer software for special education.

**1668 Tidewater Center for Technology Access**

Special Education Annex
960 Windsor Oaks Boulevard
Virginia Beach, VA 23462      757-474-8650
FAX 757-474-8648

Offers resources and information, equipment loans, hands-on exploration of assistive technologies, equipment and software awareness, consultations and inter-agency collaborations.

**1669 West Tennessee Special Technology
AccessResource Center**

119 Old Humbode Road
Jackson, TN 38305      731-668-3888
800-464-5619
FAX 731-668-1666
http://www.starcenter.tn.org
e-mail: jduke@starcenter.tn.org
*Judy Duke, Manager Information & Outreach*
*Joan Page, Administrative Assistant*

Technology center for people with disabilities. Some of the services are: music therapy, art therapy, augmentative communication evaluation and training, vocational evaluation, job placement, vision department, environmental controls.

# Games

**1670 A Day at Play**

**Don Johnston**
26799 W Commerce Drive
Volo, IL 60073      847-740-0749
800-999-4660
FAX 847-740-7326
http://www.donjohnston.com
e-mail: info@donjohnston.com
*Angie Leboida, Marketing/Channel Development*
*Ruth Ziolkowski, President*

A Day at Play and Out and About, programs in the UKanDu Little Books Series, are early literacy programs that consist of several create-your-own four-page animated stories that help build language experience for early readers. Students fill in the blanks to complete a sentence on each page and then watch the page come alive with animation and sound. After completing the story, students can print it out to make a book which can be read over and over again.

**1671 Academic Drill Builders: Wiz Works**

**SRA Order Services**
220 E Danieldale Road
DeSoto, TX 75115
800-843-8855
http://www.sraonline.com
*Jerry Chaffin, Author*

A program using an arcade game format for the creation, editing, pacing and monitoring of 36 drill and practice games. Grades K-8. *$49.00*

**1672 Alpine Tram Ride**

**Merit Software**
132 W 21 Street
New York, NY 10011      212-675-8567
800-753-6488
FAX 212-675-8607
http://www.meritsoftware.com
e-mail: sales@meritsoftware.com
*Ben Weintrap, President*

Teaches cognitive redevelopment skills. *$12.95*

**1673 Blocks in Motion**

**Don Johnston**
26799 W Commerce Drive
Volo, IL 60073      847-740-0749
800-999-4660
FAX 847-740-7326
http://www.donjohnston.com
e-mail: info@donjohnston.com
*Christine Filler, Marketing/Channel Development*
*Ruth Ziolkowski, President*

An art and motion program that makes drawing, creating and animating fun and educational for all users. Based on the Piagetian theory for motor-sensory development, this program promotes the concept that the process is as educational and as much fun as the end result. Good fine motor skills are not required for students to be successful and practice critical thinking. *$99.00*

**1674 CONCENTRATE! On Words and Concepts**

**Laureate Learning Systems**
110 E Spring Street
Winooski, VT 05404      802-655-4755
800-562-6801
FAX 802-655-4757
http://www.laureatelearning.com
e-mail: info@laureatelearning.com
*Mary Wilson, President*
*Bernard Fox, VP*

A series of educational games that reinforces the lessons of the Words and Concepts Series while developing short term memory skills. *$105.00*

**1675 Camp Frog Hollow**

**Don Johnston**
26799 W Commerce Drive
Volo, IL 60073      847-740-0749
800-999-4660
FAX 847-740-7326
http://www.donjohnston.com
e-mail: info@donjohnston.com
*Christine Filler, Marketing/Channel Development*
*Ruth Ziolkowski, President*

Camp Frog Hollow chronicles the further adventures of K.C. and Clyde as they head off to summer camp. This entertaining approach to reading, literacy and learning can be beneficial for individual reading lessons or large group activities. The journaling feature provides students the opportunity to record their thoughts and feelings while the tracking feature provides a record of progress for the teacher/parent.

**1676 Create with Garfield**

SRA Order Services
220 E Danieldale Road
DeSoto, TX 75115

800-843-8855
http://www.sraonline.com

For students to create cartoons, posters and labels by choosing a variety of backgrounds, props and Garfield characters.

**1677 Create with Garfield: Deluxe Edition**

SRA Order Services
220 E Danieldale Road
DeSoto, TX 75115

800-843-8855
http://www.sraonline.com

*Ahead Designes, Author*

A program to be used by children to create and print cartoons, posters or labels featuring Garfield and his friends.

**1678 Dino-Games**

Academic Software
331 W 2nd Street
Lexington, KY 40507

859-552-1020
FAX 859-231-0725
http://www.acsw.com
e-mail: asistaff@acsw.com

*Penny Ellis, COO*

Single switch software programs designed for early switch practice. CD-ROM for Mac or PC. Visit web site for demonstrations. *$39.00*

**1679 Dinosaur Days**

Queue
1 Controls Drive
Shelton, CT 06432

203-335-0906
800-232-2224
FAX 203-336-2481
http://www.queueinc.com
e-mail: jck@queueine.com

*Monica Kantrowitz, President*

Students can create their own unique dinosaurs choosing from hundreds of prehistoric parts. *$49.95*

**1680 Early Games for Young Children**

Software to Go-Gallaudet University
800 Florida Avenue NE
Washington, DC 20002

202-651-5705
FAX 202-651-5109
http://www.clerccenter.gallaudet.edu
e-mail: afbinfo@afb.net

*Ken Kurlychek, Project Coordinator*

**1681 Eden Institute Curriculum Adaptive Physical Education**

One Eden Way
Princeton, NJ 08540

609-987-0099
FAX 609-987-0243
http://www.edenservices.org
e-mail: info@edenservices.org

*David Holmes, Executive Director and President*
*Anne Holmes, Director Outreach Support*

This volume contains teaching programs in the area of sensory integration and adaptive physical education for students with autism. *$50.00*

**1682 Eency-Weency Spider Game**

UCLA Intervention Program for Handicapped Children
1000 Veteran Avenue
Los Angeles, CA 90095

310-825-4821
FAX 310-206-7744
http://www.bol.ucla.edu
e-mail: scislo@madnet.uclu.edu

*Sharon Cislo, Administrative Assistant*
*Kit Kehr, Executive Director*

Board game with spiders moving up the drain spout to win. The scanner randomly selects the sun (move up one space) or rain (move down one space). Scan speed can be modified to allow children with various abilities to compete more equally. *$35.00*

**1683 Every Day Is a Holiday: Summer/Fall**

UCLA Intervention Program for Handicapped Children
1000 Veteran Avenue
Los Angeles, CA 90095

310-825-4821
FAX 310-206-7744
http://www.bol.ucla.edu
e-mail: scislo@madnet.uclu.edu

*Sharon Cislo, Administrative Assistant*
*Kit Kehr, Executive Director*

Explore the major holidays of the year. Summer/Fall includes July 4th, Birthday, Halloween and Thanksgiving. *$45.00*

**1684 Every Day Is a Holiday: Winter/Spring**

UCLA Intervention Program for Handicapped Children
1000 Veteran Avenue
Los Angeles, CA 90095

310-825-4821
FAX 310-206-7744
http://www.bol.ucla.edu
e-mail: scislo@madnet.uclu.edu

*Sharon Cislo, Administrative Assistant*
*Kit Kehr, Executive Director*

Explore the major holidays of the year. Winter/Spring includes Hanukkah, Christmas, Valentine's Day and Easter. *$45.00*

**1685  Fast Food Game**

UCLA Intervention Program for Handicapped
Children
1000 Veteran Avenue
Los Angeles, CA  90095          310-825-4821
                              FAX 310-206-7744
                              http://www.bol.ucla.edu
                              e-mail: scislo@madnet.uclu.edu
*Sharon Cislo, Administrative Assistant*
*Kit Kehr, Executive Director*

Board game activity where players advance by selecting Fast Food items. The children press their switches
to spin a spinner which randomly points to a fast food
item or sick face. Press the switch to move to the next
square with the selected item on it. If you get a sick
face you lose your turn. *$35.00*

**1686  Garfield Trivia Game**

SRA Order Services
220 E Danieldale Road
DeSoto, TX  75115
                              800-843-8855
                              http://www.sraonline.com
*Jerry Chaffin, Author*

Designed for the student's creative side. Students can
apply their knowledge to 300 intriguing questions
about Garfield and his friends.

**1687  Incredible Adventures of Quentin**

Queue
1 Controls Drive
Shelton, CT  06432          203-335-0906
                              800-232-2224
                              FAX 203-336-2481
                              http://www.queueinc.com
                              e-mail: jck@queueine.com
*Monica Kantrowitz, President*

Students can interact with the story on a screen, with
wonderful visual and sound effects, animation and
music, for a multisensory learning experience.
*$225.00*

**1688  KC & Clyde in Fly Ball**

Don Johnston
26799 W Commerce Drive
Volo, IL  60073          847-740-0749
                              800-999-4660
                              FAX 847-740-7326
                              http://www.donjohnston.com
                              e-mail: info@donjohnston.com
*Christine Filler, Marketing/Channel Development*
*Ruth Ziolkowski, President*

In the UKanDu Series of interactive software which is
designed to promote learning, independence, and accommodate special needs. Word interaction and context are stressed as students progress through the story
and make decisions on how the storyline will advance.
Active interaction at the word level is encouraged by
UKanDu the wordbird, the tour guide to language in
this story. *$95.00*

**1689  Listen with Your Ears**

UCLA Intervention Program for Handicapped
Children
1000 Veteran Avenue
Los Angeles, CA  90095          310-825-4821
                              FAX 310-206-7744
                              http://www.bol.ucla.edu
                              e-mail: scislo@madnet.uclu.edu
*Sharon Cislo, Administrative Assistant*
*Kit Kehr, Executive Director*

Auditory discrimination game in which the user identifies an object or action by the sound it makes.
Twenty-four choices include: snoring, laughing, cat,
doorbell, fire truck, dog, cow, and many more. *$45.00*

**1690  Maze-O**

Software to Go by Gallaudet University
800 Florida Avenue NE
Washington, DC  20002          202-651-5705
                              FAX 202-651-5109
                              http://www.clerccenter.gallaudet.edu
                              e-mail: afbinfo@afb.net
*Ken Kurlychek, Project Coordinator*
*Karen Kauutz, Administrative Assistant*

**1691  Mind Over Matter**

Learning Well
111 Kane Street
Baltimore, MD  21224          516-326-2101
                              800-645-6564
                              FAX 800-413-7442
*Michael Heins, Author*

A game program that challenges students to solve 185
visual word puzzles or create their own puzzles, using
symbols and graphics.

**1692  Monkey Business**

Merit Software
132 W 21st Street
New York, NY  10011          212-675-8567
                              800-753-6488
                              FAX 212-675-8607
                              http://www.meritsoftware.com
                              e-mail: sales@meritsoftware.com
*Ben Weintrap, President*

Choose one of the three levels of difficulty and play
until a minimum score is reached. *$10.95*

**1693  Monsters & Make-Believe**

Queue
1 Controls Drive
Shelton, CT  06432          203-335-0906
                              800-232-2224
                              FAX 203-336-2481
                              http://www.queueinc.com
                              e-mail: jck@queueine.com
*Monica Kantrowitz, President*
*Peter Uhrynowski, Controller*

Children of all ages will love making monsters from over 100 body parts. Use the text processor to write about characters and add speech bubbles and type to the dialogue. *$49.95*

**1694    Monty Plays Scrabble**

**Software to Go-Gallaudet University**
**800 Florida Avenue NE**
**Washington, DC  20002**               **202-651-5705**
                             **FAX 202-651-5109**
**http://www.clerccenter.gallaudet.edu**
**e-mail: afbinfo@afb.net**
*Ken Kurlychek, Project Coordinator*
*Karen Kauutz, Administrative Assistant*

**1695    Multi-Scan**

**Academic Software**
**3504 Tates Creek Road**
**Lexington, KY  40517**               **859-552-1020**
                             **FAX 859-273-1943**
**http://www.acsw.com**
**e-mail: asistaff@acsw.com**
*Warren Lacefield, President*
*Penny Ellis, COO*

Single switch activity center containing educational games such as numerical dot to dot, concentration, mazes, and matching, for PCs and Macintosh CD-ROM. Handbook for adaptive switches available. *$149.00*

**1696    Note Speller**

**Electronic Courseware Systems**
**1713 S State Street**
**Champaign, IL  61820**               **217-359-7099**
                             **800-832-4965**
                             **FAX 217-359-6578**
**http://www.ecsmedia.com**
**e-mail: Sales@ecsmedia.com**
*Jodie Varner, Director Marketing/Sales*

A drill-and-practice game designed to teach notes presented on the alto, treble, or bass staff. Note Speller has four levels of difficulty. This is one of eighty music education titles published by Electronic Courseware Systems *$39.95*

**1697    On a Green Bus**

**Don Johnston**
**26799 W Commerce Drive**
**Volo, IL  60073**               **847-740-0749**
                             **800-999-4660**
                             **FAX 847-740-7326**
**http://www.donjohnston.com**
**e-mail: info@donjohnston.com**
*Christine Filler, Marketing/Channel Development*
*Ruth Ziolkowski, President*

An early literacy program in the UKandDu Little Books Series consisting of several create-your-own four-page animated stories that help build language experience for early readers. Students fill in the blanks, completing sentences on each page. After completing the story, students can print it out to make a book which can be read over and over again.

**1698    Path Tactics**

**Software to Go-Gallaudet University**
**800 Florida Avenue NE**
**Washington, DC  20002**               **202-651-5705**
                             **FAX 202-651-5109**
**http://www.clerccenter.gallaudet.edu**
**e-mail: afbinfo@afb.net**
*Ken Kurlychek, Project Coordinator*
*Karen Kauutz, Administrative Assistant*

**1699    Pitch Explorer**

**Electronic Courseware Systems**
**1210 Lancaster Drive**
**Champaign, IL  61821**               **217-359-7099**
                             **800-832-4965**
                             **FAX 217-359-6578**
**http://www.ecsmedia.com**
**e-mail: sales@ecsmedia.com**
*Jodie Varner, Director Education/Marketing*

Enables a computer to detect pitches produced by voice or instruments. Comes with microphone and is geared towards elementary and junior high students. Available for Mac or IBM. *$295.00*

**1700    Seek and Find**

**UCLA Intervention Program for Handicapped Children**
**1000 Veteran Avenue**
**Los Angeles, CA  90095**               **310-825-4821**
                             **FAX 310-206-7744**
**http://www.bol.ucla.edu**
**e-mail: scislo@madnet.uclu.edu**
*Sharon Cislo, Administrative Assistant*
*Kit Kehr, Executive Director*

Game promoting matching, figure/ground, and auditory discrimination utilizing four scenes: park; campground; city; play room. *$55.00*

**1701    Ships Ahoy**

**Software to Go-Gallaudet University**
**800 Florida Avenue NE**
**Washington, DC  20002**               **202-651-5705**
                             **FAX 202-651-5109**
**http://www.clerccenter.gallaudet.edu**
**e-mail: afbinfo@afb.net**
*Ken Kurlychek, Project Coordinator*
*Karen Kauutz, Administrative Assistant*

**1702    Son of Seek and Find**

**UCLA Intervention Program for Handicapped Children**
**1000 Veteran Avenue**
**Los Angeles, CA  90095**               **310-825-4821**
                             **FAX 310-206-7744**
**http://www.bol.ucla.edu**
**e-mail: scislo@madnet.uclu.edu**
*Sharon Cislo, Administrative Assistant*
*Kit Kehr, Executive Director*

Game promoting matching, figure/ground, and auditory discrimination utilizing three scenes: farm; classroom; house. *$55.00*

**1703 Switch It-See It**

**UCLA Intervention Program for Handicapped Children**
**1000 Veteran Avenue**
**Los Angeles, CA 90095** 310-825-4821
FAX 310-206-7744
http://www.bol.ucla.edu
e-mail: scislo@madnet.uclu.edu
*Sharon Cislo, Administrative Assistant*
*Kit Kehr, Executive Director*

Colorful animated graphics and sound effects encourage visual tracking from left to right, up and down, and on the diagonal. Graphics include: bear; fish; mouse; rocket; and others. *$35.00*

*Mac*

**1704 Teddy Barrels of Fun**

**SRA Order Services**
**220 E Danieldale Road**
**DeSoto, TX 75115**
800-843-8855
http://www.sraonline.com
A graphic design program that includes over 200 pieces of art for creating pictures, posters and labels, and word processing capabilities to develop writing skills and creative thinking. *$42.00*

**1705 Tennis Anyone?**

**Software to Go-Gallaudet University**
**800 Florida Avenue NE**
**Washington, DC 20002** 202-651-5705
FAX 202-651-5109
http://www.clerccenter.gallaudet.edu
e-mail: afbinfo@afb.net
*Ken Kurlychek, Project Coordinator*
*Karen Kauutz, Administrative Assistant*

**1706 Tune It II: Music Pitch Matcher**

**Electronic Courseware Systems**
**1713 S State Street**
**Champaign, IL 61820** 217-359-7099
800-832-4965
FAX 217-359-6578
http://www.ecsmedia.com
e-mail: sales@ecsmedia.com
*Jodie Varner, Director Education/Marketing*

A fun program designed to help students practice in matching pitches. Two pitches are played with the second one sounding out of tune with the first. The student adjusts the second pitch until it matches the first. Records are kept for students' scores. Tune It II is one of 80 programs in music education published by Electronic Courseware Systems.

**1707 Worm Squirm**

**UCLA Intervention Program for Handicapped Children**
**1000 Veteran Avenue**
**Los Angeles, CA 90095** 310-825-4821
FAX 310-206-7744
http://www.bol.ucla.edu
e-mail: scislo@madnet.uclu.edu
*Sharon Cislo, Administrative Assistant*
*Kit Kehr, Executive Director*

Maze game designed to teach directionality. A worm is directed through the maze by pushing the appropriate arrows on the overlay. *$35.00*

**1708 Zoo Time**

**UCLA Intervention Program for Handicapped Children**
**1000 Veteran Avenue**
**Los Angeles, CA 90095** 310-825-4821
FAX 310-206-7744
http://www.bol.ucla.edu
e-mail: scislo@madnet.uclu.edu
*Sharon Cislo, Administrative Assistant*
*Kit Kehr, Executive Director*

Five familiar zoo animals: kangaroo, elephant, monkey, giraffe and bird are depicted on an overlay. Level I, the child selects any animal. Level II, the child selects an animal by name. Level III, the child selects an animal by its actions. *$35.00*

## Language Arts

**1709 Alphabet Circus**

**SRA Order Services**
**220 E Danieldale Road**
**DeSoto, TX 75115**
800-843-8855
http://www.sraonline.com
Software to teach letter recognition. *$35.00*

**1710 Alphabetizing**

**Aquarius Instructional**
**PO Box 128**
**Indian Rocks Beach, FL 34655** 727-595-7890
800-338-2644
FAX 727-595-2685
http://www.philliproy.com
e-mail: info@philliproy.com
*Ashley Sutton, Office Manager*
*Ruth Bragman, President*

Teaches language arts skills to early childhood students. *$45.00*

**1711 American Sign Language Dictionary on CD-ROM**

**Harris Communications**
**15155 Technology Drive**
**Eden Prairie, MN 55344**     **952-906-1180**
**800-825-6758**
**FAX 952-906-1099**
**TDY:952-906-1180**
**http://www.harriscomm.com**
**e-mail: info@harriscomm.com**
*Martin Sternberg, Author*
*Robert Harris, President*
*Patty Johnson, Vice President*

Combines text, video, and animation to create a leading interactive reference tool that makes learning ASL easy and fun. Contains 2400 signs, searching capabilities in 5 languages, new learning games, and expanded sections in fingerspelling. *$79.95*

*448 pages  CD-ROM*

**1712 American Sign Language Dictionary: Software**

**Speech Bin**
**1965 25th Avenue**
**Vero Beach, FL 32960**     **772-770-0007**
**800-477-3324**
**FAX 772-770-0006**
**http://www.speechbin.com**
**e-mail: info@speechbin.com**
*Shane Peters, Product Coordinator*
*Jen Binney, Owner*

The CD includes captivating video clips that show 2,500+ words, phrases, and idioms in sign language. The videos may be played at normal speed, slow motion, and stop action. Animations explain origins of selected signs; drills and games are provided to reinforce learning. Item number M545 for Windows $24.95 Item number M540 for MAC. *$29.95*

**1713 AtoZap!**

**Sunburst Technology**
**400 Columbus Avenue**
**Valhalla, NY 10595**     **914-747-3310**
**800-321-7511**
**FAX 914-747-4109**
**http://www.sunburst.com**
**e-mail: service@sunburst.com**
*A Birmingham, Owner*
*Mark Sotir, President*

When users select an A, little airplanes that fly madly about appear. Users select T and students have their own telephone to talk to any one of nine animated friends. This program for prereaders has an activity for every letter.

**1714 Auditory Skills**

**Psychological Software Services**
**6555 Carrollton Avenue**
**Indianapolis, IN 46220**     **317-257-9672**
**FAX 317-257-9674**
**http://www.neuroscience.cnter.com**
**e-mail: nsc@netdirect.net**
*Odie Bracy MD, President*
*Nancy Bracy, Assistant Director*

Four computer programs designed to aid in the remediation of auditory discrimination problems. *$50.00*

**1715 Basic Language Units: Grammar**

**Continental Press**
**520 E Bainbridge Street**
**Elizabethtown, PA 17022**     **717-367-1836**
**800-233-0759**
**FAX 888-834-1303**
**http://www.continentalpress.com**
*Robyn Fitzpatrick*

Sentence disks include sentence types, subjects and predicates and phrases and clauses (Apple).

**1716 Basic Skills Products**

**EDCON Publishing Group**
**30 Montauk Boulevard**
**Oakdale, NY 11769**     **631-567-7227**
**888-553-3266**
**FAX 631-567-8745**
**TDY:631-567-7227**
**http://www.edconpublishing.com**
**e-mail: info@edconpublishing.com**
*Dale Solimene, President*
*Roberto Fuentes, Office Manager*

Deals with basic math and language arts. Free catalog available.

**1717 Blackout! A Capitalization Game**

**Software to Go-Gallaudet University**
**800 Florida Avenue NE**
**Washington, DC 20002**     **202-651-5705**
**FAX 202-651-5109**
**http://www.clerccenter.gallaudet.edu**
**e-mail: afbinfo@afb.net**
*Ken Kurlychek, Project Coordinator*
*Karen Kauutz, Administrative Assistant*

**1718 Boppie's Great Word Chase**

**SRA Order Services**
**220 E Danieldale Road**
**DeSoto, TX 75115**     **800-843-8855**
**http://www.sraonline.com**
*Stephen Schlapp, Author*

A program that helps refine spelling and word recognition skills.

**1719 Bubblegum Machine**

**Kid Smart, LLC.**
**8252 S Harvard Avenue**
**Tulsa, OK 74137**     **918-494-7878**
**800-285-3475**
**FAX 918-494-7884**
**e-mail: sales@heartsoft.com**

A vocabulary enrichment program that challenges students to rhyme, build words out of provided vocabulary or a user-created one. *$39.95*

**1720 Capitalization Plus**

**Software to Go-Gallaudet University**
**800 Florida Avenue NE**
**Washington, DC 20002**          **202-651-5705**
                                **FAX 202-651-5109**
        **http://www.clerccenter.gallaudet.edu**
                **e-mail: afbinfo@afb.net**
*Ken Kurlychek, Project Coordinator*
*Karen Kauutz, Administrative Assistant*

**1721 Circletime Tales Deluxe**

**Don Johnston**
**26799 W Commerce Drive**
**Volo, IL 60073**                **847-740-0749**
                                **800-999-4660**
                        **FAX 847-740-7326**
        **http://www.donjohnston.com**
                **e-mail: info@donjohnston.com**
*Christine Filler, Marketing/Channel Development*
*Ruth Ziolkowski, President*

An interactive CD-ROM that introduces and reinforces pre-literacy concepts using nursery rhymes and songs familiar to many children. This English/Spanish program emphasizes listening to and learning basic concepts such as opposites, directionality, colors and counting.

**1722 Cognitive Rehabilitation**

**Technology for Language and Learning**
**PO Box 327**
**East Rockaway, NY 11518**          **516-625-4550**
                                **FAX 516-621-3321**

A series of public domain programs that strengthen cognitive skills, memory, language and visual motor skills. *$20.00*

**1723 Construct-A-Word I & II**

**SRA Order Services**
**220 E Danieldale Road**
**DeSoto, TX 75115**

                                **800-843-8855**
        **http://www.sraonline.com**
Students blend beginnings and endings to create words. *$99.00*

**1724 Crypto Cube**

**Software to Go-Gallaudet University**
**800 Florida Avenue NE**
**Washington, DC 20002**          **202-651-5705**
                                **FAX 202-651-5109**
        **http://www.clerccenter.gallaudet.edu**
                **e-mail: afbinfo@afb.net**
*Ken Kurlychek, Project Coordinator*
*Karen Kauutz, Administrative Assistant*

**1725 Curious George Pre-K ABCs**

**Sunburst Technology**
**400 Columbus Avenue**
**Valhalla, NY 10595**            **914-747-3310**
                                **800-321-7511**
                        **FAX 914-747-4109**
        **http://www.sunburst.com**
                **e-mail: support@sunburst.com**
*A Birmingham, Owner*
*Mark Sotir, President*

Children go on a lively adventure with Curious George visiting six multi level activities that provide an animated introduction to letters and their sounds. Students discover letter names and shapes, initial letter sounds, letter pronunciations, the order of the alphabet and new vocabulary words during the fun exursions with Curious George. Mac/Win CD-ROM

**1726 Double-Up**

**Research Design Associates**
**5 Main Street**
**Freeville, NY 13068**            **607-844-4601**
                                **FAX 607-844-3310**
                **e-mail: adra@twcny.rr.com**
Takes one or two sentences and puts words in alphabetical order. *$139.95*

**1727 Dr. Peet's Talk Writer for Windows & Mac**

**Interest Driven Learning**
**383 DeSoto Drive**
**New Smryna Beach, FL 32169**      **386-427-4473**
                                **800-245-5733**
                        **FAX 386-426-0100**
                **http://www.drpeet.com**
                **e-mail: drpeet@drpeet.com**
*Bill Peet MD, CEO*

For developmental ages 3-8. Price ranges from $39.95 to $59.95.

**1728 Easy as ABC**

**Software to Go-Gallaudet University**
**800 Florida Avenue NE**
**Washington, DC 20002**          **202-651-5705**
                                **FAX 202-651-5109**
        **http://www.clerccenter.gallaudet.edu**
                **e-mail: afbinfo@afb.net**
*Ken Kurlychek, Project Coordinator*
*Karen Kauutz, Administrative Assistant*

**1729 Eden Institute Curriculum: Classroom**

**One Eden Way**
**Princeton, NJ 08540**            **609-987-0099**
                                **FAX 609-987-0243**
                **http://www.edenservices.org**
                **e-mail: info@edenservices.org**
*David Holmes, Executive Director/President*
*Anne Holmes, Director Outreach Support*

This volume is geared toward students with autism who have mastered some basic academic skills and are able to learn in a small group setting. Teaching programs include academics, domestic and social skills. *$100.00*

**1730  Elephant Ears: English with Speech**

Ballard & Tighe
480 Atlas Street
Brea, CA 92821          714-990-4332
                       800-321-4332
                       FAX 714-255-9828
                       http://www.ballard-tighe.com
                       e-mail: info@ballard-tighe.com
*Bob Batson, Vice President for Finance*

Features instruction and assessment of prepositions in a 3-part diskette. *$49.00*

**1731  Emerging Literacy**

Technology for Language and Learning
PO Box 327
East Rockaway, NY 11518          516-625-4550
                                 FAX 516-621-3321

A five-volume set of stories. *$25.00*

**1732  English 4-Pack**

Dataflo Computer Services
531 US Route 4
Lebanon, NH 03766          603-448-2223

These programs provide various spelling problems through word scrambling, letter substitution and spelling bee simulation. *$39.95*

**1733  English Info**

Phillip Roy
13064 Indian Rocks Road
Largo, FL 33774          727-593-2700
                         800-255-9085
                         FAX 727-595-2685
                         http://www.philliproy.com
                         e-mail: info@philliproy.com
*Ruth Bragman, President*
*Phil Padol, Director*

Offers informational disks on teaching nouns, pronouns, adjectives and more. *$350.00*

**1734  Essential Learning Systems**

Creative Education Institute
5000 Lakewood Drive
Waco, TX 76710          254-751-1188
                        800-234-7319
                        FAX 254-751-1199
                        http://www.cei-waco.com
                        e-mail: info@cei-waco.com
*Terry Irwin, President*
*Ric Klein, Marketing Director*

Enables special education, learning disabled and dyslexic students to develop the skills they need to learn. Using computer exercises to appropriately stimulate the brain's language areas, the lagging learning skills can be developed and patterns of correct language taught.

**1735  First Phonics**

Sunburst Technology
400 Columbus Avenue
Valhalla, NY 10595          914-747-3310
                            800-321-7511
                            FAX 914-747-4109
                            http://www.sunburst.com
                            e-mail: support@sunburst.com
*A Birmingham, Owner*
*Mark Sotir, President*

Targets the phonics skills that all children need to develop, sounding out the first letter of a word. This program offers four different engaging activities that you can customize to match each child's specific need.

**1736  Grammar Examiner**

Software to Go-Gallaudet University
800 Florida Avenue NE
Washington, DC 20002          202-651-5705
                              FAX 202-651-5109
                              http://www.clerccenter.gallaudet.edu
                              e-mail: afbinfo@afb.net
*Ken Kurlychek, Project Coordinator*
*Karen Kauutz, Administrative Assistant*

**1737  Grammar Toy Shop**

Software to Go-Gallaudet University
800 Florida Avenue NE
Washington, DC 20002          202-651-5705
                              FAX 202-651-5109
                              http://www.clerccenter.gallaudet.edu
                              e-mail: afbinfo@afb.net
*Ken Kurlychek, Project Coordinator*
*Karen Kauutz, Administrative Assistant*

**1738  Gremlin Hunt**

Merit Software
132 W 21 Street
New York, NY 10011          212-675-8567
                            800-753-6488
                            FAX 212-675-8607
                            http://www.meritsoftware.com
                            e-mail: sales@meritsoftware.com
*Ben Weintrap, President*

Gremlins test visual discrimination and memory skills at three levels. *$9.95*

**1739  High Frequency Vocabulary**

Technology for Language and Learning
PO Box 327
East Rockaway, NY 11518          516-625-4550
                                 FAX 516-621-3321

Each volume of the series has 10 stories that teach specific vocabulary. *$35.00*

**1740  Hint and Hunt I & II**

SRA Order Services
220 E Danieldale Road
DeSoto, TX  75115

800-843-8855
http://www.sraonline.com

With these programs, students can actually see and hear how changing vowels can make a new word. *$99.00*

**1741  Homonyms**

Software to Go-Gallaudet University
800 Florida Avenue NE
Washington, DC  20002

202-651-5705
FAX 202-651-5109
http://www.clerccenter.gallaudet.edu
e-mail: afbinfo@afb.net

*Ken Kurlychek, Project Coordinator*
*Karen Kauutz, Administrative Assistant*

**1742  HyperStudio Stacks**

Technology for Language and Learning
PO Box 327
East Rockaway, NY  11518

516-625-4550
FAX 516-621-3321

Offers various volumes in language arts, social studies and reading. *$10.00*

**1743  Hyperlingua**

Research Design Associates
5 Main Street
Freeville, NY  13068

607-844-4601
FAX 607-844-3310
e-mail: adra@twcny.rr.com

Allows teachers to create on-screen printing language drills. *$69.95*

**1744  IDEA Cat I, II and III**

Ballard & Tighe
480 Atlas Street
Brea, CA  92821

714-990-4332
800-321-4332
FAX 714-255-9828
http://www.ballard-tighe.com
e-mail: info@ballard-tighe.com

*Bob Batson, Vice President for Finance and O*

Computer-assisted teaching of English language lessons reinforces skills of Level I, II, and III of the IDEA Oral Program. *$142.00*

**1745  Individualized Keyboarding: Improving Reading/Spelling Skills via Keyboard**

AVKO Educational Research Foundation
3084 W Willard Road
Clio, MI  48420

810-686-9283
866-285-6612
FAX 810-686-1101
http://www.spelling.org
e-mail: avkoemail@aol.com

*Don McCabe, Author*

Students learn spelling patterns and acquire important word recognition skills as they slowly and methodically learn proper fingering and keystrokes on a typewriter or computer keyboard. *$12.95*

*ISBN 1-564004-01-5*

**1746  Katie's Farm**

Lawrence Productions
1800 S 35th Street
Galesburg, MI  49053

269-665-7075
800-421-4157
FAX 269-665-7060
http://www.lpi.com
e-mail: sales@lpi.com

*Edwin Wright, President*
*Karen Morehouse, Operations Manager*

Designed to encourage exploration and language development. *$29.95*

**1747  Key Words**

Humanities Software
PO Box 950
Hood River, OR  97031

541-386-6737
800-245-6737
FAX 541-386-1410
e-mail: tldye@humanitiessoftware.com

*Sherry Mayer, Marketing Director*
*Charlotte Arnold, Marketing Director*

Learning to keyboard goes hand-in-hand with language play, learning word families, and phonics rules. Six original passages at each of sixteen levels provide reading pleasure and finger dances that pop. You'll tell your students to stop. Key Words is available in versions for all your needs — elementary, high school, emergent literacy and remedial education. One computer, lab pack and school community site and network license. *$49.00*

**1748  Keys to Success: Computer Keyboard Skills for Blind Children**

Life Science Associates
1 Fennimore Road
Bayport, NY  11705

631-472-2111
FAX 631-472-8146
e-mail: lifesciassoc@pipeline.com

*Joe Frank, Manager*

A talking program that provides keyboard tutorial, keyboard practice, timed keyboard practice and a timed game for two players.

**1749  Kid Pix**

Riverdeep
222 3rd Avenue SE
Cedar Rapids, IA  52401

888-242-6747
800-362-2890
FAX 800-567-2714
http://www.riverdeep.net

*Joseph Durett, President*

A painting program that combines special effect art tools, sounds and magic screen transformations. *$59.95*

**1750** **Kids Media Magic 2.0**

Sunburst Technology
400 Columbus Avenue
Valhalla, NY 10595

914-747-3310
800-321-7511
FAX 914-747-4109
http://www.sunburst.com
e-mail: service@sunburst.com

*A Birmingham, Owner*
*Mark Sotir, President*

The first multimedia word processor designed for young children. Help your child become a fluent reader and writer. The Rebus Bar automatically scrolls over 45 vocabulary words as students type.

**1751** **Language Carnival I**

SRA Order Services
220 E Danieldale Road
DeSoto, TX 75115

800-843-8855
http://www.sraonline.com

*David Ertmer, Author*

A diskette of four games using humor to help students develop language and thinking skills.

**1752** **Language Carnival II**

SRA Order Services
220 E Danieldale Road
DeSoto, TX 75115

800-843-8855
http://www.sraonline.com

*David Ertmer, Author*

A diskette of four games using humor to help students develop language and thinking skills.

**1753** **Language Master: MWD-640**

Franklin Learning Resources
1 Franklin Plaza
Burlington, NJ 08016

609-386-8997
800-525-9673
FAX 609-387-1787

A language master without speech defining over 83,000 words, spelling correction capability, pick/edit feature, vocabulary enrichment activities and advanced word list. *$79.95*

**1754** **Learn to Match**

Technology for Language and Learning
PO Box 327
East Rockaway, NY 11518

516-625-4550
FAX 516-621-3321

Ten volume set of picture-matching disks. *$50.00*

**1755** **Letter Sounds**

Sunburst Technology
400 Columbus Avenue
Valhalla, NY 10595 1349

914-747-3310
800-321-7511
FAX 914-747-4109
http://www.sunburst.com
e-mail: service@sunburst.com

*A Birmingham, Owner*
*Mark Sotir, President*

Students develop phonemic awareness skills as they make the connection between consonant letters and their sounds.

**1756** **Letters and First Words**

C&C Software
5713 Kentford Circle
Wichita, KS 67220

316-683-6056
800-752-2086

*Carol Clark, President*

Helps children learn to identify letters and recognize their associated sounds. *$30.00*

**1757** **Level III - Phonics Based Reading: Grades 1, 2 & 3**

Lexia Learning Systems
2 Lewis Street
Lincoln, MA 01773

781-259-8752
800-435-3942
FAX 781-259-1349
http://www.lexialearning.com
e-mail: info@lexialearning.com

*John Bower, President*

Five activity areas with 64 branching units and practice with 535 one-syllable words and 90 two-syllable words, sentences and stories. *$250.00*

**1758** **Look! Listen! & Learn Language!: Software**

Speech Bin
1965 25th Avenue
Vero Beach, FL 32960

772-770-0007
800-477-3324
FAX 772-770-0006
http://www.speechbin.com
e-mail: info@speechbin.com

*Shane Peters, Product Coordinator*
*Jen Binney, Owner*

Interactive activities for children with autism, PDD, Down syndrome, language delay, or apraxia include: hello; Match Same to Same; Quack; Let's talk About It; visual scanning/attention and match ups! Item number L177. *$99.00*

**1759** **M-SS-NG L-NKS**

Sunburst Technology
400 Columbus Avenue
Valhalla, NY 10595

914-747-3310
800-321-7511
FAX 914-747-4109
http://www.sunburst.com
e-mail: service@sunburst.com

*A Birmingham, Owner*
*Mark Sotir, President*

This award-winning program is an engrossing language puzzle. A passage appears with letters or words missing. Students complete it based on their knowledge of word structure, spelling, grammar, meaning in context, and literary style.

**1760    Make It Go**

KidTECH
4181 Pinewood Lake Drive
Bakersfield, CA  93309          661-396-8676
                               FAX 661-396-8760

A collection of seven original cause and effect programs. *$20.00*

**1761    Make-A-Flash**

Teacher Support Software
3542 NW 97th Boulevard
Gainesville, FL  32606          352-332-6404
                               800-228-2871
                               FAX 352-332-6779
                    http://www.tssoftware.com
                    e-mail: rsmith2447@aol.com
*Ruth Smith, Educational Software Consultant*

A flash card program displaying and printing large, easy-to-read letters or numbers. *$69.95*

**1762    Mark Up**

Research Design Associates
5 Main Street
Freeville, NY  13068           607-844-4601
                               FAX 607-844-3310
                    e-mail: adra@twcny.rr.com

A sentence reconstruction program which presents learners with four options for the study of grammar. *$49.95*

**1763    Max's Attic: Long & Short Vowels**

Sunburst Technology
400 Columbus Avenue
Valhalla, NY  10595 1349        914-747-3310
                               800-321-7511
                               FAX 914-747-4109
                    http://www.sunburst.com
                    e-mail: service@sunburst.com
*A Birmingham, Owner*

Filled to the rafters with phonics fun, this animated program builds your students' vowel recognition skills.

**1764    McGee**

Lawrence Productions
1800 S 35th Street
Galesburg, MI  49053           269-665-7075
                               800-421-4157
                               FAX 269-665-7060
                               http://www.lpi.com
                               e-mail: sales@lpi.com
*Edwin Wright, President*

An independent exploration with no words. Available in IBM, Mac and IIGS formats. *$34.95*

**1765    Memory I**

Psychological Software Services
6555 Carrollton Avenue
Indianapolis, IN  46220         317-257-9672
                               FAX 317-257-9674
                    http://www.neuroscience.cnter.com
                    e-mail: nsc@netdirect.net
*Odie Bracy MD, President*
*Nancy Bracy, Assistant Director*

Consists of four computer programs designed to provide verbal and nonverbal memory exercises. *$110.00*

**1766    Memory II**

Psychological Software Services
6555 Carrollton Avenue
Indianapolis, IN  46220         317-257-9672
                               FAX 317-257-9674
                    http://www.neuroscience.cnter.com
                    e-mail: nsc@netdirect.net
*Odie Bracy MD, President*
*Nancy Bracy, Assistant Director*

These programs allow for work with encoding, categorizing and organizing skills. *$150.00*

**1767    Microcomputer Language Assessment and Development System**

Laureate Learning Systems
110 E Spring Street
Winooski, VT  05404            802-655-4755
                               800-562-6801
                               FAX 802-655-4757
                    http://www.laureatelearning.com
                    e-mail: info@laureatelearning.com
*Mary Wilson, President*

A series of seven diskettes designed to teach over 45 fundamental syntactic rules. Students are presented two or three pictures, depending on the grammatical construction being trained with optional speech and/or text and asked to select the picture which represents the correct construction. *$775.00*

**1768    Mike Mulligan & His Steam Shovel**

Sunburst Technology
400 Columbus Avenue
Valhalla, NY  10595 1349        914-747-3310
                               800-321-7511
                               FAX 914-747-4109
                    http://www.sunburst.com
                    e-mail: service@sunburst.com
*A Birmingham, Owner*

This CD-ROM version of the Caldecott classic lets students experience interactive book reading and participate in four skills-based extension activities that promote memory, matching, sequencing, listening, pattern recognition and map reading skills.

**1769    My Action Book**

KidTECH
4181 Pinewood Lake Drive
Bakersfield, CA  93309          661-396-8676
                               FAX 661-396-8760

Designed to teach familiar action vocabulary through live voice, song and animation. *$30.00*

**1770 Old MacDonald II**

UCLA Intervention Program for Handicapped
Children
1000 Veteran Avenue
Los Angeles, CA 90095          310-825-4821
                              FAX 310-206-7744
                         http://www.bol.ucla.edu
                    e-mail: scislo@madnet.uclu.edu
*Sharon Cislo, Administrative Assistant*
*Kit Kehr, Executive Director*

An early preposition program involving in, on top, behind, in front of, next to and between depicted in a
farm scene. *$35.00*

**1771 Optimum Resource**

18 Hunter Road
Hilton Head Island, SC 29926      843-689-8000
                                  888-784-2592
                             FAX 843-689-8008
                         http://www.stickybear.com
                    e-mail: stickyb@stickybear.com
*Christopher Gintz, COO*
*Richard Hefter, Chief Executive Officer*

An educational software publishing company for
grades K-12. Our software titles are available in Consumer, School, Labpack or Site License versions.
Please call for further details. Prices range from
$59.95 for Consumer to $699.95 for Site Licenses.

**1772 Padded Food**

UCLA Intervention Program for Handicapped
Children
1000 Veteran Avenue
Los Angeles, CA 90095          310-825-4821
                              FAX 310-206-7744
                         http://www.bol.ucla.edu
                    e-mail: scislo@madnet.uclu.edu
*Sharon Cislo, Administrative Assistant*
*Kit Kehr, Executive Director*

Program overlay depicts familiar foods and can be
used as a matching or categorizing program. *$35.00*

   *Mac*

**1773 Phonology: Software**

Speech Bin
1965 25th Avenue
Vero Beach, FL 32960          772-770-0007
                              800-477-3324
                         FAX 772-770-0006
                    http://www.speechbin.com
               e-mail: info@speechbin.com
*Shane Peters, Product Coordinator*
*Jen Binney, Owner*

This unique software gives you six entertaining games
to treat children's phonological disorders. The program uses target patterns in a pattern cycling approach
to phonological processess. Item number L183.
*$99.00*

**1774 Prefixes**

American Printing House for the Blind
1839 Frankfort Avenue
Louisville, KY 40206          502-895-2405
                              800-223-1839
                         FAX 502-899-2274
                         http://www.aph.org
                    e-mail: info@aph.org
*Fred Gissoni, Customer Support*
*Allan Lovell, Customer Relations Manager*

An interactive software program that teaches about
five common prefixes — un, re, dis, pre, and in — for
Apple II computers. *$34.95*

**1775 Python Path Phonics Word Families**

Sunburst Technology
400 Columbus Avenue
Valhalla, NY 10595 1349       914-747-3310
                              800-321-7511
                         FAX 914-747-4109
                    http://www.sunburst.com
               e-mail: service@sunburst.com
*A Birmingham, Owner*
*Mark Sotir, President*

Your child improves their word-building skills by
playing three fun strategy games that involve linking
one-or two-letter consonant beginnings to basic word
endings.

**1776 Read, Write and Type Learning System**

Talking Fingers
1 St. Vincents Street
San Rafael, CA 94903          415-472-3104
                              800-674-9126
                         FAX 415-472-7812
                    http://www.readwritetype.com
               e-mail: info@talkingfingers.com
*Janine Herron, Director*

This 40-lesson adventure is a powerful tool for 6-8
year-olds just learning to read, for children of other
cultures learning to read and write in English, and for
students of any age who are struggling to become successful readers and writers.

**1777 Reading Riddles with the Boars**

Queue
1 Controls Drive
Shelton, CT 06432             203-335-0906
                              800-232-2224
                         FAX 203-336-2481
                    http://www.queueinc.com
               e-mail: jck@queueine.com
*Monica Kantrowitz, President*
*Peter Uhrynowski, Controller*

Children are naturally curious about pictures. This
program uses pictures to teach over 1,000 vocabulary
words. *$39.95*

**1778  Reading Rodeo**

**Heartsoft**
**3101 N Hemlock Circle**
**Broken Arrow, OK  74012**          918-494-7878
                                     800-285-4018
                              FAX 800-285-3475
                     e-mail: sales@heartsoft.com

Utilizes over 100 artist drawn pictures to show students how to distinguish between words beginning with different initial consonant sounds. *$39.95*

**1779  Rhubarb**

**Research Design Associates**
**5 Main Street**
**Freeville, NY  13068**          607-844-4601
                           FAX 607-844-3310
                  e-mail: adra@twcny.rr.com

Allows teachers to quickly and easily enter reading passages tailored to needs of their classes. *$69.95*

**1780  Same or Different**

**Merit Software**
**132 W 21 Street**
**New York, NY  10011**          212-675-8567
                                 800-753-6488
                          FAX 212-675-8607
                http://www.meritsoftware.com
                e-mail: sales@meritsoftware.com
*Ben Weintrap, President*

Requires students to make important visual discriminations which involve shape, color and whole/part relationships. *$9.95*

**1781  Sensible Speller: Talking APH Edition**

**American Printing House for the Blind**
**1839 Frankfort Avenue**
**Louisville, KY  40206**          502-895-2405
                                   800-223-1839
                            FAX 502-899-2274
                         http://www.aph.org
                         e-mail: info@aph.org
*Fred Gissoni, Customer Support*
*Allan Lovell, Customer Relations Manager*

A speech output version of the spelling checker program from Sensible Software, for Apple IIs using the ProDOS Operating System. *$65.00*

**1782  Sequencing Fun!**

**Sunburst Technology**
**400 Columbus Avenue**
**Valhalla, NY  10595 1349**          914-747-3310
                                      800-321-7511
                               FAX 914-747-4109
                           http://www.sunburst.com
                           e-mail: service@sunburst
*A Birmingham, Owner*
*Mark Sotir, President*

Text, pictures, animation and video clips provide a fun filled program that encourages critical thinking skills.

**1783  Show Time**

**Software to Go - Gallaudet University**
**800 Florida Avenue NE**
**Washington, DC  20002**          202-651-5705
                            FAX 202-651-5109
             http://www.clerccenter.gallaudet.edu
                         e-mail: afbinfo@afb.net
*Ken Kurlychek, Project Coordinator*
*Karen Kauutz, Administrative Assistant*

**1784  Sight Words**

**UCLA Intervention Program for Handicapped Children**
**1000 Veteran Avenue**
**Los Angeles, CA  90095**          310-825-4821
                             FAX 310-206-7744
                          http://www.bol.ucla.edu
                  e-mail: scislo@madnet.uclu.edu
*Sharon Cislo, Administrative Assistant*
*Kit Kehr, Executive Director*

Early sight vocabulary program with six categories to choose from: school; outside; home; toys; food; clothing. Teacher options include: scan speed selection; switch or spacebar selection. *$35.00*

Mac

**1785  Soft Tools**

**Psychological Software Services**
**6555 Carrollton Avenue**
**Indianapolis, IN  46220**          317-257-9672
                             FAX 317-257-9674
                http://www.neuroscience.cnter.com
                       e-mail: nsc@netdirect.net
*Odie Bracy MD, President*
*Nancy Bracy, Assistant Director*

Menu-driven disk versions of the computer programs published in the Cognitive Rehabilitation Journal. *$50.00*

**1786  Solving Word Problems**

**Phillip Roy**
**PO Box 130**
**Indian Rocks Beach, FL  33785**          727-593-2700
                                           800-255-9085
                                    FAX 727-595-2685
                            http://www.philliproy.com
                         e-mail: info@philliproy.com
*Ashley Sutton, Office Manager*
*Ruth Bragman, President*

Offers 3 disks on how to solve word problems. *$115.00*

**1787  Sound Match**

**Enable/Schneier Communication Unit**
**1603 Court Street**
**Syracuse, NY  13208**          315-455-7591
                          FAX 315-455-1230
                      http://www.enablecny.org
               e-mail: enablecny@enablecny.org
*Sarah Bollinger, Executive Director*
*Prudence York, Assistant Executive*

Presents a variety of sounds/noises requiring gross levels of auditory discrimination and matching. *$25.00*

**1788  Speaking Speller**

**American Printing House for the Blind**
**1839 Frankfort Avenue**
**Louisville, KY  40206**                502-895-2405
                                          800-223-1839
                                     FAX 502-899-2274
                                    http://www.aph.org
                                   e-mail: info@aph.org
*Fred Gissoni, Customer Support*
*Allan Lovell, Customer Relations Manager*

A spelling program with speech output for students and teachers. For Apple II computers using either ProDOS or DOS 3.3. *$28.95*

**1789  Spell a Word**

**RJ Cooper & Associates**
**27601 Forbes Road #39**
**Laguna Niguel, CA  92677**             949-582-2572
                                          800-752-6673
                                     FAX 949-582-3169
                                http://www.rjcooper.com
                               e-mail: info@rjcooper.com
*RJ Cooper, Owner/Developer*

A large print, talking, spelling program. It uses an errorless learning method. It has both a drill and test mode, which a supervisor can set. Letters, words or phrases are entered by a supervisor and recorded by supervisor, peer, or sibling. Available for Apple II, Mac, Windows. *$99.00*

**1790  Spellagraph**

**Software to Go-Gallaudet University**
**800 Florida Avenue NE**
**Washington, DC  20002**                202-651-5705
                                     FAX 202-651-5109
                         http://www.clerccenter.gallaudet.edu
                               e-mail: afbinfo@afb.net
*Ken Kurlychek, Project Coordinator*
*Karen Kauutz, Administrative Assistant*

**1791  Spelling Ace**

**Franklin Learning Resources**
**1 Franklin Plaza**
**Burlington, NJ  08016**                609-386-8997
                                          800-525-9673
                                     FAX 609-387-1787

The basic spelling corrector with 80,000 words. Sound-Alikes feature identifies commonly confused words. *$25.00*

**1792  Spelling Mastery**

**SRA Order Services**
**220 E Danieldale Road**
**DeSoto, TX  75115**
                                          800-843-8855
                               http://www.sraonline.com

Six animated games offer practice for spelling in grades 1 to 3. *$49.00*

**1793  Stanley Sticker Stories**

**Riverdeep**
**222 3rd Avenue SE**
**Cedar Rapids, IA  52401**              888-242-6747
                                          800-362-2890
                                     FAX 800-567-2714
                                http://www.riverdeep.net

Kids love Mille, Bailey, Sammy and Trudy, the characters from Edmark's award-winning Early Learning Series. Now they can feature these and other Edmark characters in their very own animated storybooks building spelling and writing skills and expanding creativity along the way. The fun-filled program from the educational software experts at Edmark gives kids the power to build stories that come to life right on screen. *$59.95*

**1794  Stickybear Software**

**Optimum Resource**
**18 Hunter Road**
**Hilton Head Island, SC  29926**        843-689-8000
                                          888-784-2592
                                     FAX 843-689-8008
                              http://www.stickybear.com
                          e-mail: stickyb@stickybear.com
*Christopher Gintz, COO*
*Richard Hefter, Chief Executive Officer*

An educational software publishing company for grades K-12. Our software titles are available in Consumer, School, Labpack or Site License versions. Please call for further details. Prices range from $59.95 for Consumer to $699.95 for Site Licenses.

**1795  Sunken Treasure Adventure: Beginning Blends**

**Sunburst Technology**
**400 Columbus Avenue**
**Valhalla, NY  10595 1349**             914-747-3310
                                          800-321-7511
                                     FAX 914-747-4109
                                http://www.sunburst.com
                            e-mail: service@sunburst.com
*A Birmingham, Owner*
*Mark Sotir, President*

Focus on beginning blends sounds and concepts with three high-spirited games that invite students to use two letter consonant blends as they build words.

**1796  Syllasearch I, II, III, IV**

**SRA Order Services**
**220 E Danieldale Road**
**DeSoto, TX  75115**
                                          800-843-8855
                               http://www.sraonline.com

Students learn how to read multi-syllable words accurately and automatically with this new game that uses actual human speech for instruction and correction. *$99.00*

**1797  Talking Nouns**

Laureate Learning Systems
110 E Spring Street
Winooski, VT  05404          802-655-4755
                             800-562-6801
                     FAX 802-655-4757
            http://www.laureatelearning.com
            e-mail: info@laureatelearning.com
*Mary Wilson, President*
*Bernard Fox, Vice President*

An interactive communication product that helps
build expressive language and augmentative communication skills. *$130.00*

**1798  Talking Nouns II**

Laureate Learning Systems
110 E Spring Street
Winooski, VT  05404          802-655-4755
                             800-562-6801
                     FAX 802-655-4757
            http://www.laureatelearning.com
            e-mail: info@laureatelearning.com
*Mary Wilson, President*
*Bernard Fox, Vice President*

Designed to build expressive language and
augmentative communication skills. *$130.00*

**1799  Talking Verbs**

Laureate Learning Systems
110 E Spring Street
Winooski, VT  05404          802-655-4755
                             800-562-6801
                     FAX 802-655-4757
            http://www.laureatelearning.com
            e-mail: info@laureatelearning.com
*Mary Wilson, President*
*Bernard Fox, Vice President*

Builds expressive language and augmentative communication skills. *$130.00*

**1800  Texas School for the Deaf Sign Language**

Harris Communications
15155 Technology Drive
Eden Prairie, MN  55344          952-906-1180
                                 800-825-6758
                         FAX 952-906-1099
                         TDY:952-906-1198
                http://www.harriscomm.com
                e-mail: info@harriscomm.com
*Texas School for the Deaf, Author*
*Robert Harris, Owner*
*Patty Johnson, President*

Colorful picture book of four popular fables with fun
animation on CD-ROM. Has the option to have the
story voiced, with computer highlighting words as
they are spoken. *$79.95*

   *CD-ROM*

**1801  Twenty Categories**

Laureate Learning Systems
110 E Spring Street
Winooski, VT  05404          802-655-4755
                             800-562-6801
                     FAX 802-655-4757
            http://www.laureatelearning.com
            e-mail: info@laureatelearning.com
*Mary S Wilson, Author*
*Mary Wilson, President*
*Bernard Fox, Vice President*

Designed to use with children and adults, these two
diskettes provide instruction in both abstracting the
correct category for a noun and placing a noun in the
appropriate category. *$100.00*

**1802  Type to Learn 3**

Sunburst Technology
400 Columbus Avenue
Valhalla, NY  10595 1349          914-747-3310
                                  800-321-7511
                          FAX 914-747-4109
                     http://www.sunburst.com
                     e-mail: service@sunburst
*A Birmingham, Owner*
*Mark Sotir, President*

With the 25 lessons in this animated update of Type to
Learn, students embark on time travel missions to
learn keyboarding skills.

**1803  Type to Learn Jr.**

Sunburst Technology
400 Columbus Avenue
Valhalla, NY  10595 1349          914-747-3310
                                  800-321-7511
                          FAX 914-747-4109
                     http://www.sunburst.com
                     e-mail: service@sunburst
*A Birmingham, Owner*
*Mark Sotir, President*

One of the first steps to literacy is learning how to use
the keyboard. Age appropriate instruction and three
practice activities help students use the computer with
greater ease.

**1804  Type to Learn Jr. New Keys for Kids**

Sunburst Technology
400 Columbus Avenue
Valhalla, NY  10595 1349          914-747-3310
                                  800-321-7511
                          FAX 914-747-4109
                     http://www.sunburst.com
                     e-mail: service@sunburst
*A Birmingham, Owner*
*Mark Sotir, President*

With new keys to learn, your early keyboarders focus
on using the letter and number keys, the shift key,
home row and are introduced to selected internet symbols.

**1805  Vowel Patterns**

Sunburst Technology
400 Columbus Avenue
Valhalla, NY  10595 1349                 914-747-3310
                                         800-321-7511
                                    FAX 914-747-4109
                              http://www.sunburst.com
                         e-mail: service@sunburst.com
*A Birmingham, Owner*
*Mark Sotir, President*

Some vowels are neither long nor short. In this investigation, students explore and learn to use abstract vowels.

**1806  Word Invasion: Academic Skill Builders in Language Arts**

SRA Order Services
220 E Danieldale Road
DeSoto, TX  75115
                                         800-843-8855
                              http://www.sraonline.com
*Jerry Chaffin, Author*

A program using an arcade game format to provide practice in identifying words representing six parts of speech: nouns; pronouns; verbs; adjectives; adverbs and prepositions. *$49.00*

**1807  Word Master: Academic Skill Builders in Language Arts**

SRA Order Services
220 E Danieldale Road
DeSoto, TX  75115
                                         800-843-8855
                              http://www.sraonline.com
*Jerry Chaffin, Author*

A program using arcade game format to provide practice in identifying parts of antonyms, synonyms or homonyms at three difficulty levels. *$49.00*

**1808  Word Wise I and II: Better Comprehension Through Vocabulary**

SRA Order Services
220 E Danieldale Road
DeSoto, TX  75115
                                         800-843-8855
                              http://www.sraonline.com
*Isabel Beck, Author*

A series of two software programs for developing and improving reading comprehension by building vocabulary knowledge.

## Life Skills

**1809  Big/Little I**

UCLA Intervention Program for Handicapped Children
1000 Veteran Avenue
Los Angeles, CA  90095                   310-825-4821
                                    FAX 310-206-7744
                                http://www.bol.ucla.edu
                         e-mail: scislo@madnet.uclu.edu
*Sharon Cislo, Administrative Assistant*
*Kit Kehr, Executive Director*

Program for one to four players in which a little bear scans big and little objects commonly seen by young children. *$35.00*

    *Mac*

**1810  Big/Little II**

UCLA Intervention Program for Handicapped Children
1000 Veteran Avenue
Los Angeles, CA  90095                   310-825-4821
                                    FAX 310-206-7744
                                http://www.bol.ucla.edu
                         e-mail: scislo@madnet.uclu.edu
*Sharon Cislo, Administrative Assistant*
*Kit Kehr, Executive Director*

Children construct a big or little bear by choosing the appropriate size body parts and articles of clothing.

**1811  Boars Tell Time**

Queue
1 Controls Drive
Shelton, CT  06432                       203-335-0906
                                         800-232-2224
                                    FAX 203-336-2481
                               http://www.queueinc.com
                           e-mail: jck@queueine.com
*Monica Kantrowitz, President*
*Peter Uhrynowski, Controller*

The Boars help youngsters to learn both analog and digital time. *$39.95*

**1812  Bozons' Quest**

Laureate Learning Systems
110 E Spring Street
Winooski, VT  05404                      802-655-4755
                                         800-562-6801
                                    FAX 802-655-4757
                          http://www.laureatelearning.com
                     e-mail: info@laureatelearning.com
*Mary Wilson, President*
*Bernard Fox, Vice President*

A computer game designed to teach cognitive skills and strategies and left/right discrimination skills. *$32.50*

**1813 Braille 'n Speak Scholar**

American Printing House for the Blind
1839 Frankfort Avenue
Louisville, KY 40206     502-895-2405
     800-223-1839
FAX 502-899-2274
http://www.aph.org
e-mail: info@aph.org
*Roseann Broome, Marketing*
*Allan Lovell, Customer Relations Manager*

This portable, computerized, talking device has many features useful to student and adult braille users (word processors, print-to-braille translator, talking clocks/calculators and much more). *$929.95*

**1814 Buddy's Body**

UCLA Intervention Program for Handicapped
Children
1000 Veteran Avenue
Los Angeles, CA 90095     310-825-4821
FAX 310-206-7744
http://www.bol.ucla.edu
e-mail: scislo@madnet.uclu.edu
*Sharon Cislo, Administrative Assistant*
*Kit Kehr, Executive Director*

Body parts program containing two levels with animation. Level I contains facial features. Level II contains larger body parts. In each level, children are asked to identify body parts by pressing the part on the overlay. Each level has its own overlay. *$35.00*

**1815 Calendar Fun with Lollipop Dragon**

SVE & Churchill Media
6465 N Avendale Avenue
Chicago, IL 60631     773-775-9550
     800-829-1900
FAX 773-775-5091
http://www.SVEmedia.com
e-mail: custserve@SVEmedia.com
*Mark Bentoing, President*

Young students learn the calendar basics. *$84.00*

**1816 Coin Changer**

Kid Smart, LLC.
8252 S Harvard Avenue
Tulsa, OK 74137     918-494-7878
     800-285-3475
FAX 800-285-4018
e-mail: sales@hearsoft.com

Uses large coin graphics which help teach money skills. *$39.95*

**1817 Comparison Kitchen**

SRA Order Services
220 E Danieldale Road
DeSoto, TX 75115
     800-843-8855
http://www.sraonline.com
Strengthens students' visual perception of sizes and amounts as well as their visual discrimination of objects by color, shape and size. *$35.00*

**1818 Contemporary Living**

Aquarius Instructional
PO Box 128
Indian Rocks Beach, FL 33785     727-595-7890
     800-338-2644
FAX 727-595-2685
http://www.philliproy.com
e-mail: info@philliproy.com
*Ashley Sutton, Office Manager*
*Ruth Bragman, President*

Through the use of high-interest, low-reading levels, these programs promote self-concept. *$115.00*

**1819 Critical Thinking for Contemporary Lifestyles**

Phillip Roy
PO Box 130
Indian Rocks Beach, FL 33785     727-593-2700
     800-255-9085
FAX 727-595-2685
http://www.philliproy.com
e-mail: info@philliproy.com
*Ashley Sutton, Office Manager*
*Ruth Bragman, President*

This program of 14 titles offers to help improve employment, independent living, and community life skills. *$825.00*

**1820 Eden Institute Curriculum: Volume I**

Eden Services
One Logan Drive
Princeton, NJ 08540     609-987-0099
FAX 609-987-0243
http://www.members.aol.com/edensvcs
e-mail: info@edenservices.org
*David Holmes, Executive Director/President*
*Anne Holmes, Director Outreach Support*

Learning readiness, preacademic, academic, prevocational, self-care, domestic, social and play skills programs for young students with autism. *$200.00*

**1821 Electric Crayon**

Merit Software
132 W 21 Street
New York, NY 10011     212-675-8567
     800-753-6488
FAX 212-675-8607
http://www.meritsoftware.com
e-mail: sales@meritsoftware.com
*Ben Weintrap, President*

A tool to help preschool and primary aged children learn about and enjoy the computer. *$14.95*

**1822 Family Fun**

UCLA Intervention Program for Handicapped
Children
1000 Veteran Avenue
Los Angeles, CA 90095     310-825-4821
FAX 310-206-7744
http://www.bol.ucla.edu
e-mail: scislo@madnet.uclu.edu
*Sharon Cislo, Administrative Assistant*
*Kit Kehr, Executive Director*

Family members and household items (TV, table, tub, crib, etc.) are represented graphically on an overlay. The program can be utilized as a matching activity or for representational play. *$35.00*

**1823  Feelings**

**UCLA Intervention Program for Handicapped Children**
**1000 Veteran Avenue**
**Los Angeles, CA  90095**                   310-825-4821
                                         FAX 310-206-7744
                                **http://www.bol.ucla.edu**
                        **e-mail: scislo@madnet.uclu.edu**
*Sharon Cislo, Administrative Assistant*
*Kit Kehr, Executive Director*

Five feelings: happy, sad, scared, love and tired, are depicted on an overlay. Level I describes each emotion. Level II, the child associates an emotion with an action. Level III, the child chooses a picture to describe his or her feelings. *$35.00*

**1824  First Categories**

**Laureate Learning Systems**
**110 E Spring Street**
**Winooski, VT  05404**                      802-655-4755
                                             800-562-6801
                                       FAX 802-655-4757
                      **http://www.laureatelearning.com**
                      **e-mail: info@laureatelearning.com**
*Mary Wilson, President*
*Bernard Fox, Vice President*

A program that trains categorization skills with a natural sounding voice and pictures of 60 nouns in six categories. *$100.00*

**1825  First R**

**Milliken Publishing**
**11643 Lilburn Park Road**
**Saint Louis, MO  63146**                   314-991-4220
                                             800-325-4136
                                       FAX 314-991-4807
                         **http://www.millikenpub.com**
                    **e-mail: webmaster@millikenpub.com**
*Thomas Moore, Chairman*
*Lourie Avery, Accountant*

A phonetically-based word recognition program with emphasis on comprehension. *$325.00*

**1826  First Verbs**

**Laureate Learning Systems**
**110 E Spring Street**
**Winooski, VT  05404**                      802-655-4755
                                             800-562-6801
                                       FAX 802-655-4757
                      **http://www.laureatelearning.com**
                      **e-mail: info@laureatelearning.com**
*Mary Wilson, President*
*Bernard Fox, Vice President*

A program that trains and tests 40 early developing verbs using animated pictures and a natural sounding female voice. *$225.00*

**1827  First Words**

**Laureate Learning Systems**
**110 E Spring Street**
**Winooski, VT  05404**                      802-655-4755
                                             800-562-6801
                                       FAX 802-655-4757
                      **http://www.laureatelearning.com**
                      **e-mail: info@laureatelearning.com**
*Mary Wilson, President*
*Bernard Fox, Vice President*

A talking program that trains and tests 50 early developing nouns presented within 10 categories. *$225.00*

**1828  First Words II**

**Laureate Learning Systems**
**110 E Spring Street**
**Winooski, VT  05404**                      802-655-4755
                                             800-562-6801
                                       FAX 802-655-4757
                      **http://www.laureatelearning.com**
                      **e-mail: info@laureatelearning.com**
*Mary Wilson, President*
*Bernard Fox, Vice President*

Continues the training of First Words with training and testing of an additional 50 early developing nouns presented within the same 10 categories as used in First Words. *$225.00*

**1829  Fish Scales**

**SRA Order Services**
**220 E Danieldale Road**
**DeSoto, TX  75115**
                                             800-843-8855
                               **http://www.sraonline.com**
Graphics, animation and sound will capture players' attention as they learn how things are measured for height, length and distance. *$35.00*

**1830  Following Directions: Left and Right**

**Laureate Learning Systems**
**110 E Spring Street**
**Winooski, VT  05404**                      802-655-4755
                                             800-562-6801
                                       FAX 802-655-4757
                      **http://www.laureatelearning.com**
                      **e-mail: info@laureatelearning.com**
*Mary Wilson, President*
*Bernard Fox, Vice President*

Provides practice in following directions and exercises short-term memory while reinforcing left/right discrimination concepts. *$165.00*

**1831  Following Directions: One and Two Level Commands**

**Laureate Learning Systems**
**110 E Spring Street**
**Winooski, VT  05404**                      802-655-4755
                                             800-562-6801
                                       FAX 802-655-4757
                      **http://www.laureatelearning.com**
                      **e-mail: info@laureatelearning.com**
*Eleanor Semel, Author*
*Mary Wilson, President*
*Bernard Fox, Vice President*

Designed for a broad range of students experiencing difficulty in processing, remembering and following oral commands, a program of exercises on short and long-term memory highlighting specific spatial, directional and ordinary vocabulary.

**1832 Food Facts**

**American Printing House for the Blind**
**1839 Frankfort Avenue**
**Louisville, KY 40206**          502-895-2405
                              800-223-1839
                         FAX 502-899-2274
                         http://www.aph.org
                         e-mail: info@aph.org
*Fred Gissoni, Customer Support*
*Allan Lovell, Customer Relations Manager*

An interactive software program for Apple II computer that teaches about nutrition of common foods. *$39.70*

**1833 Getting Clean with Herkimer I**

**UCLA Intervention Program for Handicapped**
**Children**
**1000 Veteran Avenue**
**Los Angeles, CA 90095**        310-825-4821
                         FAX 310-206-7744
                    http://www.bol.ucla.edu
                e-mail: scislo@madnet.uclu.edu
*Sharon Cislo, Administrative Assistant*
*Kit Kehr, Executive Director*

Help Herkimer, the visitor from outer space, find the things he can use to get clean and look good in the bath, at the sink, or in the shower. Grooming items such as brush, comb, soap, towel, washcloth, toothbrush, tooth paste, sponge and bubble bath are illustrated. *$75.00*

**1834 Getting Clean with Herkimer II**

**UCLA Intervention Program for Handicapped**
**Children**
**1000 Veteran Avenue**
**Los Angeles, CA 90095**        310-825-4821
                         FAX 310-206-7744
                    http://www.bol.ucla.edu
                e-mail: scislo@madnet.uclu.edu
*Sharon Cislo, Administrative Assistant*
*Kit Kehr, Executive Director*

Find the things that Herkimer cannot use to get clean or look good. *$45.00*

**1835 Getting Clean with Herkimer III**

**UCLA Intervention Program for Handicapped**
**Children**
**1000 Veteran Avenue**
**Los Angeles, CA 90095**        310-825-4821
                         FAX 310-206-7744
                    http://www.bol.ucla.edu
                e-mail: scislo@madnet.uclu.edu
*Sharon Cislo, Administrative Assistant*
*Kit Kehr, Executive Director*

Emphasis is on grooming items, with cooking and health care items also shown. Teaches children to categorize objects according to their functions. *$45.00*

**1836 Information Station**

**SVE & Churchill Media**
**6465 N Avendale Ave**
**Chicago, IL 60631**            773-775-9550
                              800-829-1900
                         FAX 773-775-5091
                    http://www.SVEmedia.com
                e-mail: custserve@SVEmedia.com
*Mark Bentoing, President*

Students who boot up this software will find themselves floating miles above the earth orbiting the planet in an information station satellite. *$144.00*

**1837 Job Readiness Software**

**Lawrence Productions**
**1800 S 35th Street**
**Galesburg, MI 49053**          269-665-7075
                              800-421-4157
                         FAX 269-665-7060
                         http://www.lpi.com
                    e-mail: sales@lpi.com
*Edwin Wright, President*
*Karen Morehouse, Operations Manager*

Four programs: Job Attitudes: Assessment and Improvement; Filling Out Job Applications; Successful Job Interviewing; and Resumes Made Easy. *$99.00*

   *CD*

**1838 Knowledgeworks**

**Milliken Publishing**
**11643 Lilburn Park Road**
**Saint Louis, MO 63146**        314-991-4220
                              800-325-4136
                         FAX 314-991-4807
                    http://www.millikenpub.com
                e-mail: webmaster@millikenpub.com
*Victoria Scott, Manager-Sales*
*Lourie Avery, Accountant*

Math and reading software for on track and remediation.

   *Price varies*

**1839 Let's Go Shopping I**

**UCLA Intervention Program for Handicapped**
**Children**
**1000 Veteran Avenue**
**Los Angeles, CA 90095**        310-825-4821
                         FAX 310-206-7744
                    http://www.bol.ucla.edu
                e-mail: scislo@madnet.uclu.edu
*Sharon Cislo, Administrative Assistant*
*Kit Kehr, Executive Director*

Classification game in which children select the appropriate items that belong in the corresponding store (toy or grocery). *$35.00*

**1840** Let's Go Shopping II: Clothes & Pets

**UCLA Intervention Program for Handicapped Children**
1000 Veteran Avenue
Los Angeles, CA 90095          310-825-4821
                              FAX 310-206-7744
                    http://www.bol.ucla.edu
                  e-mail: scislo@madnet.uclu.edu
*Sharon Cislo, Administrative Assistant*
*Kit Kehr, Executive Director*

Classification game in which children select the appropriate items that belong in the corresponding store (clothes or pet).

**1841** Lion's Workshop

**Merit Software**
132 W 21 Street
New York, NY 10011          212-675-8567
                            800-753-6488
                        FAX 212-675-8607
                http://www.meritsoftware.com
              e-mail: sales@meritsoftware.com
*Ben Weintrap, President*

Presents various objects with parts missing or with like objects to be matched. *$9.95*

**1842** Marsh Media

**Marshware**
PO Box 8082
Shawnee Mission, KS 66208          816-523-1059
                                   800-821-3303
                               FAX 816-333-7421
                     http://www.marshmedia.com
                  e-mail: order@marshmedia.com
*Joan Marsh, President*
*Sarah Lynch, Shipping Manager*

Marsh Media publishes closed captioned health and guidance videos for the classroom and school library. Catalog available.

**1843** Math Spending and Saving

**World Class Learning**
111 Kane Street
Baltimore, MD 21224          410-633-0730
                         FAX 410-633-2758
                    http://www.wclm.com
*Paul Edwards, Author*
*Bruce Brown, President*

Designed for secondary students and adults, this program focuses on personal financial management, comparison shopping and calculation of essential banking transactions.

**1844** Money Skills

**MarbleSoft**
12301 Central Avenue NE
Blaine, MN 55434          763-755-1402
                      FAX 763-862-2920
                 http://www.marblesoft.com
               e-mail: sales@marblesoft.com
*Valerie Reit, Sales*

Money Skills 2.0 includes five activities that teach counting money and making change: Coins and Bills; Counting Money; Making Change; how much change? and the Marblesoft Store. Teaches American, Canadian and European money using clear, realistic pictures of the money. Single and dual-switch scanning options on all difficulty levels. Runs on Macintosh and Windows computers. *$60.00*

**1845** My House: Language Activities of Daily Living

**Laureate Learning Systems**
110 E Spring Street
Winooski, VT 05404          802-655-4755
                        FAX 802-655-4757
                http://www.laureatelearning.com
              e-mail: info@laureatelearning.com
*Mary Wilson, President*
*Bernard Fox, Vice President*

A language-simulation program designed for communicatively low-functioning clients. *$1200.00*

**1846** NOMAD Talking Touch Pad

**American Printing House for the Blind**
1839 Frankfort Avenue
Louisville, KY 40206          502-895-2405
                              800-223-1839
                          FAX 502-899-2274
                      http://www.aph.org
                    e-mail: info@aph.org
*Fred Gissoni, Customer Support*
*Allan Lovell, Customer Relations Manager*

Connects to a computer to make tactile pictures talk. Uses include teaching about tactile graphics, training in orientation and mobility, and a talking directory for buildings and campuses. *$750.00*

**1847** Occupations

**UCLA Intervention Program for Handicapped Children**
1000 Veteran Avenue
Los Angeles, CA 90095          310-825-4821
                              FAX 310-206-7744
                    http://www.bol.ucla.edu
                  e-mail: scislo@madnet.uclu.edu
*Sharon Cislo, Administrative Assistant*
*Kit Kehr, Executive Director*

Companion game to Community Vehicles. Game identifying 6 community helpers: Fireman, teacher, police officer, gas station attendant, dentist, and doctor. Level I, the child selects any community helper. Level II, the child chooses the community helper associated with the scene. *$36.00*

**1848** Optimum Resource

18 Hunter Road
Hilton Head Island, SC 29926          843-689-8000
                                      888-784-2592
                                  FAX 843-689-8008
                        http://www.stickybear.com
                      e-mail: stickyb@stickybear.com
*Christopher Gintz, COO*
*Robert Stangroom, Product Manager*

An educational software publishing company for grades K-12. Our software titles are available in Consumer, School, Labpack or Site License versions. Please call for further details. Prices range from $59.95 for Consumer to $699.95 for Site Licenses.

**1849  PAVE: Perceptual Accuracy**

**Software to Go-Gallaudet University**
**800 Florida Avenue NE**
**Washington, DC  20002**          **202-651-5705**
                                   **FAX 202-651-5109**
        **http://www.clerccenter.gallaudet.edu**
                    **e-mail: afbinfo@afb.net**
*Ken Kurlychek, Project Coordinator*
*Karen Kauutz, Administrative Assistant*

**1850  Padded Vehicles**

**UCLA Intervention Program for Handicapped**
**Children**
**1000 Veteran Avenue**
**Los Angeles, CA  90095**          **310-825-4821**
                                    **FAX 310-206-7744**
                **http://www.bol.ucla.edu**
            **e-mail: scislo@madnet.uclu.edu**
*Sharon Cislo, Administrative Assistant*
*Kit Kehr, Executive Director*

Children Identify 10 Vehicles — airplane, helicopter, motorcycle, police car, truck, ambulance, garbage truck, school bus, fire engine and tractor, which are illustrated on the overlay. Level I, the child selects any vehicle, Level II, the child selects the vehicle by name. *$36.00*

**1851  Paper Dolls I: Dress Me First**

**UCLA Intervention Program for Handicapped**
**Children**
**1000 Veteran Avenue**
**Los Angeles, CA  90095**          **310-825-4821**
                                    **FAX 310-206-7744**
                **http://www.bol.ucla.edu**
            **e-mail: scislo@madnet.uclu.edu**
*Sharon Cislo, Administrative Assistant*
*Kit Kehr, Executive Director*

Five articles of clothing (shoes, socks, jacket, pants, and T-shirt for boy, overall and dress for girl) are depicted on an overlay to dress the paper doll. *$36.00*

**1852  Paper Dolls II: Dress Me Too**

**UCLA Intervention Program for Handicapped**
**Children**
**1000 Veteran Avenue**
**Los Angeles, CA  90095**          **310-825-4821**
                                    **FAX 310-206-7744**
                **http://www.bol.ucla.edu**
            **e-mail: scislo@madnet.uclu.edu**
*Sharon Cislo, Administrative Assistant*
*Kit Kehr, Executive Director*

Twelve articles of clothing are depicted on an overlay to dress the paper doll (boy or girl). Options include dressing for: school day; sunny day; rainy day; or silly day. *$36.00*

**1853  Pic Talk**

**UCLA Intervention Program for Handicapped**
**Children**
**1000 Veteran Avenue**
**Los Angeles, CA  90095**          **310-825-4821**
                                    **FAX 310-206-7744**
                **http://www.bol.ucla.edu**
            **e-mail: scislo@madnet.uclu.edu**
*Sharon Cislo, Administrative Assistant*
*Kit Kehr, Executive Director*

Developed as a pre-primer for an alternative communication device for nonreaders who are severely physically disabled. Program includes 6 categories—places, things, action, foods, and feelings — with 54 picture vocabulary. *$ 35.00*

**1854  Pick a Meal**

**UCLA Intervention Program for Handicapped**
**Children**
**1000 Veteran Avenue**
**Los Angeles, CA  90095**          **310-825-4821**
                                    **FAX 310-206-7744**
                **http://www.bol.ucla.edu**
            **e-mail: scislo@madnet.uclu.edu**
*Sharon Cislo, Administrative Assistant*
*Kit Kehr, Executive Director*

This game is designed to promote good nutrition for children and/or individuals who are low functioning. Level I teaches the 4 basic food groups. Level II helps the individual learn how to select balanced meals for each meal of the day. There is no printout data collection, but scan speed selection is available. *$35.00*

**1855  Print Shop**

**Riverdeep**
**222 3rd Avenue SE**
**Cedar Rapids, IA  52401**          **888-242-6747**
                                     **800-362-2890**
                                **FAX 800-567-2714**
                **http://www.riverdeep.net**
*David Valsam, Author*
*Jospeh Durett, President*

A program allowing the user to automatically design and print greeting cards, letterhead stationery, banners, signs and other graphic designs on regular computer paper.

**1856  Print Shop Companion**

**Riverdeep**
**222 3rd Avenue SE**
**Cedar Rapids, IA  52401**          **888-242-6747**
                                     **800-362-2890**
                                **FAX 800-567-2714**
                **http://www.riverdeep.net**
*Roland Gustafsson, Author*
*Joseph Durett, President*

A program designed to expand the capabilities of The Print Shop with 12 new printing fonts, 50 new borders, additional graphic design options, custom calendar production and more.

**1857  Print Shop Graphics Library**

Riverdeep
222 3rd Avenue SE
Cedar Rapids, IA  52401          888-242-6747
                                 800-362-2890
                            FAX 800-567-2714
                    http://www.riverdeep.net
*David Balsam, Author*
*Joseph Durett, President*

Designed to be used with The Print Shop, this program with 120 additional graphic designs focuses on holidays, zodiac signs, animals, sports, school children and creative patterns.

**1858  Print Shop Graphics Library: Disk 2**

Riverdeep
222 3rd Avenue SE
Cedar Rapids, IA  52401          888-242-6747
                                 800-362-2890
                            FAX 800-567-2714
                    http://www.riverdeep.net
*David Balsam, Author*
*Joseph Durett, President*

Designed to supplement The Print Shop, this diskette with 120 additional graphics and a graphic editor focuses on graphics used on the job, as hobbies, places, travel, health, animals, sports and music.

**1859  Puzzle Works Readiness**

Continental Press
520 E Bainbridge Street
Elizabethtown, PA  17022          717-367-1836
                                  800-233-0759
                             FAX 888-834-1303

This series of five disks uses colorful graphics and reward techniques that are especially suited to the interests and needs of special learners. *$25.95*

**1860  Quiz Castle**

Software to Go-Gallaudet University
800 Florida Avenue NE
Washington, DC  20002          202-651-5705
                          FAX 202-651-5109
            http://www.clerccenter.gallaudet.edu
                     e-mail: afbinfo@afb.net
*Ken Kurlychek, Project Coordinator*
*Karen Kauutz, Administrative Assistant*

**1861  Remembering Numbers and Letters**

Relevant Publications
PO Box 128
N Largo, FL  33770-1815          727-595-7890
                                 800-338-2644
                            FAX 727-595-2685
            http://www.relevantpublication.com
          e-mail: info@relevantpublication.com
*Phil Padol, President*
*Phil Padol, Director*

Students work at their own pace and select their own numbers and letters with which to work. *$29.95*

**1862  Resumes Made Easy**

Lawrence Productions
1800 S 35th Street
Galesburg, MI  49053          269-665-7075
                              800-421-4157
                         FAX 269-665-7060
                    http://www.lpi.com
                e-mail: sales@lpi.com
*George Spengler, Author*
*Edwin Wright, President*
*Karen Morehouse, Operations Manager*

An interactive program covering what a resume is, how a resume is prepared and what is to be included in a resume. *$29.95*

**1863  Seasons**

UCLA Intervention Program for Handicapped Children
1000 Veteran Avenue
Los Angeles, CA  90095          310-825-4821
                           FAX 310-206-7744
                    http://www.bol.ucla.edu
            e-mail: scislo@madnet.uclu.edu
*Sharon Cislo, Administrative Assistant*
*Kit Kehr, Executive Director*

Game is designed to help teach children and/or low functioning individuals to identify attributes of the four seasons. Students select a season from the menu, then objects from each season scan the bottom of the screen. The child selects items matching the season using the mouse, switch, space bar, or TouchWindows. When a season is completed, there is an option to type a brief statement about the scene. *$45.00*

**1864  Secondary Print Pack**

Failure Free
140 W Cabarrus Avenue
Concord, NC  28025          314-569-0211
                            800-221-1274
                       FAX 314-569-2834
            e-mail: ffsales@concord.nc.com

Thousands of independent activities teaching over 750 words. *$1929.00*

**1865  Stickybear Software**

Optimum Resource
18 Hunter Road
Hilton Head Island, SC  29926          843-689-8000
                                       888-784-2592
                                  FAX 843-689-8008
                       http://www.stickybear.com
                e-mail: stickyb@stickybear.com
*Christopher Gintz, COO*
*Richard Hefter, Chief Executive Officer*

An educational software publishing company for grades K-12. Our software titles are available in Consumer, School, Labpack or Site License versions. Please call for further details. Prices range from $59.95 for Consumer to $699.95 for Site Licenses.

**1866   Switch It-Change It**

**UCLA Intervention Program for Handicapped Children**
**1000 Veteran Avenue**
**Los Angeles, CA  90095**          **310-825-4821**
                                   **FAX 310-206-7744**
                      **http://www.bol.ucla.edu**
                      **e-mail: scislo@madnet.uclu.edu**
*Sharon Cislo, Administrative Assistant*
*Kit Kehr, Executive Director*

Switch-activated cause and effect program presents colorful, common objects. Designed to be paired with three-dimensional objects for matching, identification and selection. Geared toward the young and/or low functioning. *$35.00*

   *Mac*

**1867   Tea Party**

**UCLA Intervention Program for Handicapped Children**
**1000 Veteran Avenue**
**Los Angeles, CA  90095**          **310-825-4821**
                                   **FAX 310-206-7744**
                      **http://www.bol.ucla.edu**
                      **e-mail: scislo@madnet.uclu.edu**
*Sharon Cislo, Administrative Assistant*
*Kit Kehr, Executive Director*

Follow-up classification game to Let's Go Shopping. Children shop at four different stores to select items for a tea party. *$36.00*

**1868   Teenage Switch Progressions**

**RJ Cooper & Associates**
**27601 Forbes Road #39**
**Laguna Nigel, CA  92677**          **949-582-2572**
                                    **800-752-6673**
                                **FAX 949-582-3169**
                      **http://www.rjcooper.com**
                      **e-mail: info@rjcooper.com**
*RJ Cooper, Owner/Developer*

Five activities for teenage persons working on switch training, attention training, life skills simulation and following directions. *$75.00*

**1869   TeleSensory**

**Telesensory**
**520 Almanor Avenue**
**Sunnyvale, CA  94043**          **408-616-8700**
                                 **800-227-8418**
                             **FAX 408-616-8720**
                      **http://www.telesensory.com**
                      **e-mail: info@telesensory.com**
*Ken Stokes, President*
*Jennifer Street, Marketing*

Helps visually impaired people become more independent with the most comprehensive products available anywhere for reading, writing, taking notes and using computers.

**1870   This Is the Way We Wash Our Face**

**UCLA Intervention Program for Handicapped Children**
**1000 Veteran Avenue**
**Los Angeles, CA  90095**          **310-825-4821**
                                   **FAX 310-206-7744**
                      **http://www.bol.ucla.edu**
                      **e-mail: scislo@madnet.uclu.edu**
*Sharon Cislo, Administrative Assistant*
*Kit Kehr, Executive Director*

Familiar Nursery song with singing and animation depicted in picture form on an overlay. Five verses are: washing your face; brushing your teeth; combing your hair; getting dressed; and eating. *$36.00*

**1871   Tools for Life**

**Oakwood Solutions**
**2926 Hidden Hollow Road**
**Oshkosh, WI  54904**          **920-231-4667**
                               **800-933-1933**
                           **FAX 920-231-4809**
                      **http://www.conovercompany.com**
                      **e-mail: conover@execpc.com**
*Terry Schmidtz, President*
*Becky Schmidtz, Member*

Tools for life software assists in the transition from school to the community and workplace. Functional literary, functional life skills, functional social skills, functional work skills. *$2535.00*

# Math

**1872   2+2**

**RJ Cooper & Associates**
**27601 Forbes Road #39**
**Laguna Nigel, CA  92677**          **949-582-2572**
                                    **800-752-6673**
                                **FAX 949-582-3169**
                      **http://www.rjcooper.com**
                      **e-mail: info@rjcooper.com**
*RJ Cooper, Owner/Developer*

This large print, talking, early academic program is for drilling math facts, including addition, subtraction, multiplication and division. It uses an errorless learning method. *$89.00*

**1873   Access to Math**

**Don Johnston**
**26799 W Commerce Drive**
**Volo, IL  60073**          **847-740-0749**
                            **800-999-4660**
                        **FAX 847-740-7326**
                      **http://www.donjohnston.com**
                      **e-mail: info@donjohnston.com**
*Christine Filler, Marketing/Channel Development*
*Ruth Ziolkowski, President*

The Macintosh talking math worksheet program that's two products in one. For teachers, it makes customized worksheets in a snap. For students who struggle, it provides individualized on-screen lessons.

**1874    Algebra Stars**

**Sunburst Technology**
**400 Columbus Avenue**
**Valhalla, NY  10595 1349**              **914-747-3310**
                                         **800-321-7511**
                                    **FAX 914-747-4109**
                          **http://www.sunburst.com**
                  **e-mail: service@sunburst.com**
*A Birmingham, Owner*
*Mark Sotir, President*

Students build their understanding of algebra by constructing, categorizing, and solving equations and classifying polynomial expressions using algebra tiles.

**1875    Alien Addition: Academic Skill Builders in Math**

**SRA Order Services**
**220 E Danieldale Road**
**DeSoto, TX  75115**
                                         **800-843-8855**
                          **http://www.sraonline.com**
*Jerry Chaffin, Author*

A program using an arcade game format to provide practice in addition of numbers 0 through 9. *$49.00*

**1876    Awesome Animated Monster Maker Math**

**Sunburst Technology**
**400 Columbus Avenue**
**Valhalla, NY  10595 1349**              **914-747-3310**
                                         **800-321-7511**
                                    **FAX 914-747-4109**
                          **http://www.sunburst.com**
                  **e-mail: service@sunburst.com**
*A Birmingham, Owner*
*Mark Sotir, President*

With an emphasis on building core math skills, this humorous program incorporates the monstrous and the ridiculous into a structured learning environment. Students choose from six skill levels tailored to the 3rd to 8th grade.

**1877    Awesome Animated Monster Maker Math & Monster Workshop**

**Sunburst Technology**
**400 Columbus Avenue**
**Valhalla, NY  10595 1349**              **914-747-3310**
                                         **800-321-7511**
                                    **FAX 914-747-4109**
                          **http://www.sunburst.com**
                  **e-mail: service@sunburst.com**
*A Birmingham, Owner*
*Mark Sotir, President*

Students develop money and strategic thinking skills with this irresistable game that has them tinker about making monsters.

**1878    Awesome Animated Monster Maker Number Drop**

**Sunburst Technology**
**400 Columbus Avenue**
**Valhalla, NY  10595 1349**              **914-747-3310**
                                         **800-321-7511**
                                    **FAX 914-747-4109**
                          **http://www.sunburst.com**
                  **e-mail: service@sunburst.com**
*A Birmingham, Owner*
*Mark Sotir, President*

Your students will think on their mathematical feet estimating and solving thousands of number problems in an arcade-style game designed to improve their performance in numeration, money, fractions, and decimals.

**1879    Basic Math Competency Skill Building**

**Educational Activities Software**
**PO Box 754**
**Baldwin, NY  11520**                    **516-867-7878**
                                         **800-645-2796**
                                    **FAX 516-379-7429**
                     **e-mail: learn@edact.com**
*Michael Conlon, Author*
*Alan Stern, Sales Director*
*Melissa Slevin, Assistant*

An interactive, tutorial and practice program to teach competency with arithmetic operations, decimals, fractions, graphs, measurement and geometric concepts. *$369.00*

**1880    Basic Skills Products**

**EDCON Publishing Group**
**30 Montauk Boulevard**
**Oakdale, NY  11769**                    **631-567-7227**
                                         **888-553-3266**
                                    **FAX 631-567-8745**
                                    **TDY:631-567-7227**
                     **http://www.edconpublishing.com**
                  **e-mail: info@edconpublishing.com**
*Dale Solimene, President*
*Roberto Fuentes, Office Manager*

Deals with basic math and language arts. Free catalog available.

**1881    Big: Calc**

**Don Johnston**
**26799 W Commerce Drive**
**Volo, IL  60073**                       **847-740-0749**
                                         **800-999-4660**
                                    **FAX 847-740-7326**
                          **http://www.donjohnston.com**
                  **e-mail: info@donjohnston.com**
*Christine Filler, Marketing/Channel Development*
*Ruth Ziolkowski, President*

A Macintosh calculator program for people with special needs but also beneficial for users who need the auditory reinforcement of a talking calculator. Features include big numbers, high-quality speech and versatile layouts. Encourages math motivation.

**1882 Boars 1, 2, 3! Counting with the Boars**

Queue
1 Controls Drive
Shelton, CT 06432
203-335-0906
800-232-2224
FAX 203-336-2481
http://www.queueinc.com
e-mail: jck@queueine.com

*Monica Kantrowitz, President*
*Peter Uhrynowski, Controller*

The Boars teach young learners basic keyboard skills while they identify numbers from 1-10 and count familiar objects in a variety of colorful scenes. *$39.95*

**1883 Boars Store**

Queue
1 Controls Drive
Shelton, CT 06432
203-335-0906
800-232-2224
FAX 203-336-2481
http://www.queueinc.com
e-mail: jck@queueine.com

*Monica Kantrowitz, President*
*Peter Uhrynowski, Controller*

Shopping at the Boars Store offers students an exciting way to learn to count money and make change. *$39.95*

**1884 Building Perspective**

Sunburst Technology
400 Columbus Avenue
Valhalla, NY 10595 1349
914-747-3310
800-321-7511
FAX 914-747-4109
http://www.sunburst.com
e-mail: support@sunburst.com

*A Birmingham, Owner*
*Mark Sotir, President*

Develop spatial perception and reasoning skills with this award-winning program that will sharpen your students' problem-solving abilities.

**1885 Building Perspective Deluxe**

Sunburst Technology
400 Columbus Avenue
Valhalla, NY 10595 1349
914-747-3310
800-321-7511
FAX 914-747-4109
http://www.sunburst.com
e-mail: support@sunburst.com

*A Birmingham, Owner*
*Mark Sotir, President*

New visual thinking challenges await your students as they engage in three spacial reasoning activities that develop their 3D thinking, deductive reasoning and problem solving skills

**1886 Combining Shapes**

Sunburst Technology
400 Columbus Avenue
Valhalla, NY 10595 1349
914-747-3310
800-321-7511
FAX 914-747-4109
http://www.sunburst.com
e-mail: support@sunburst.com

*A Birmingham, Owner*
*Mark Sotir, President*

Students discover the properties of simple geometric figures through concrete experience combining shapes. Measurements, estimating and operation skills are part of this fun program.

**1887 Combining and Breaking Apart Numbers**

Sunburst Technology
400 Columbus Avenue
Valhalla, NY 10595 1349
914-747-3310
800-321-7511
FAX 914-747-4109
http://www.sunburst.com
e-mail: support@sunburst.com

*A Birmingham, Owner*
*Mark Sotir, President*

Students explore part-whole relationships and develop number sense by combining and breaking apart numbers in a variety of problem-solving situations.

**1888 Comparing with Ratios**

Sunburst Technology
400 Columbus Avenue
Valhalla, NY 10595 1349
914-747-3310
800-321-7511
FAX 914-747-4109
http://www.sunburst.com
e-mail: support@sunburst.com

*A Birmingham, Owner*
*Mark Sotir, President*

Students learn that ratio is a way to compare amounts by using multiplication and division. Through five engaging activities, students recognize and describe ratios, develop proportional thinking skills, estimate ratios, determine equivalent ratios, and use ratios to analyze data.

**1889 Conceptual Skills**

Psychological Software Services
6555 Carrollton Avenue
Indianapolis, IN 46220
317-257-9672
FAX 317-257-9674
http://www.neuroscience.cnter.com
e-mail: nsc@netdirect.net

*Odie Bracy MD, President*
*Nancy Bracy, Assistant Director*

Twelve programs designed to enhance skills involved in relationships, comparisons and number concepts. *$50.00*

**1890  Concert Tour Entrepreneur**

Sunburst Technology
400 Columbus Avenue
Valhalla, NY  10595 1349          914-747-3310
                                 800-321-7511
                            FAX 914-747-4109
                       http://www.sunburst.com
                    e-mail: support@sunburst.com
*A Birmingham, Owner*
*Mark Sotir, President*

Your students improve math, planning and problem solving skills as they manage a band in this music management business simulation.

**1891  Counters**

Software to Go-Gallaudet University
800 Florida Avenue NE
Washington, DC  20002            202-651-5705
                            FAX 202-651-5109
              http://www.clerccenter.gallaudet.edu
                     e-mail: afbinfo@afb.net
*Ken Kurlychek, Project Coordinator*
*Karen Kauutz, Administrative Assistant*

**1892  Counting Critters**

Software to Go-Gallaudet University
800 Florida Avenue NE
Washington, DC  20002            202-651-5705
                            FAX 202-651-5109
              http://www.clerccenter.gallaudet.edu
                     e-mail: afbinfo@afb.net
*Ken Kurlychek, Project Coordinator*
*Karen Kauutz, Administrative Assistant*

**1893  DLM Math Fluency Program: Addition Facts**

SRA Order Services
220 E Danieldale Road
DeSoto, TX  75115
                                 800-843-8855
                       http://www.sraonline.com
*Ted Hasselbring, Author*

A program using drill and practice, arcade games, student record keeping, worksheet production and testing to develop the ability to recall basic addition math facts. *$32.00*

**1894  DLM Math Fluency Program: Division Facts**

SRA Order Services
220 E Danieldale Road
DeSoto, TX  75115
                                 800-843-8855
                       http://www.sraonline.com
*Ted Hasselbring, Author*

A series of 10-minute sessions in this diskette program easily retrieves answers to basic division facts up to 144 divided by 12.

**1895  DLM Math Fluency Program: Multiplication Facts**

SRA Order Services
220 E Danieldale Road
DeSoto, TX  75115
                                 800-843-8855
                       http://www.sraonline.com
*Ted Hasselbring, Author*

A series of 10-minute sessions easily retrieves answers to basic multiplication facts up to 12x12. *$32.00*

**1896  DLM Math Fluency Program: Subtraction Facts**

SRA Order Services
220 E Danieldale Road
DeSoto, TX  75115
                                 800-843-8855
                       http://www.sraonline.com
*Ted Hasselbring, Author*
*Terry Avon, Head Supervisor*

A series of sessions that easily retrieve answers to basic subtraction facts up to 24x12. *$32.00*

**1897  Data Explorer**

Sunburst Technology
101 Castleton Street
Poleasantville, NY  10570        914-747-3310
                                 800-321-7511
                            FAX 914-747-4109
                       http://www.sunburst.com
                    e-mail: support@nysunburst.com
*A Birmingham, Owner*
*Mark Sotir, President*

This easy-to-use CD-ROM provides the flexibility needed for eleven different graph types including tools for long-term data analysis projects.

**1898  Dragon Mix: Academic Skill Builders in Math**

SRA Order Services
220 E Danieldale Road
DeSoto, TX  75115
                                 800-843-8855
                       http://www.sraonline.com
*Jerry Chaffin, Author*

A program providing practice in multiplication of numbers 0 through 9 and division of problems with answers 0 through 9. *$49.00*

**1899  Eighth Through Tenth-Grade MathCompetencies**

Phillip Roy
PO Box 130
Indian Rocks Beach, FL  33785    727-593-2700
                                 800-255-9085
                            FAX 727-595-2685
                       http://www.philliproy.com
                    e-mail: info@philliproy.com
*Ashley Sutton, Office Manager*
*Ruth Bragman, President*

# Computer Resources /Math

Offers 59 disks on reading numerals and comparing, solving word problems with fractions, word problems, measurement, averages, geometry, graphs and more. *$1775.00*

**1900 Elementary Math Bundle**

Sunburst Technology
400 Columbus Avenue
Valhalla, NY 10595 1349          914-747-3310
                                800-321-7511
                            FAX 914-747-4109
                        http://www.sunburst.com
                    e-mail: support@sunburst.com
*A Birmingham, Owner*
*Mark Sotir, President*

Number sense and operations are the focus of the Elementary Math Bundle. Students engage in activities that reinforce basic addition and subtraction skills. This product comes with Splish Splash Math, Ten Tricky Tiles and Numbers Undercover.

**1901 Elements of Mathematics**

Electronic Courseware Systems
1713 S State Street
Champaign, IL 61820          217-359-7099
                             800-832-4965
                          FAX 217-359-6578
                       http://www.ecsmedia.com
                     e-mail: sales@ecsmedia.com
*Jodie Varner, Director Education/Marketing*

This program includes two lessons and a test in the addition of simple and complex fractions. Test results are stored for both student and instructor accessibility. Includes such graphics as pie slices. Elements of Mathematics is one of several programs published by Electronic Courseware Systems.

**1902 Equation Tile Teaser**

Sunburst Technology
400 Columbus Avenue
Valhalla, NY 10595 1349          914-747-3310
                                800-321-7511
                            FAX 914-747-4109
                        http://www.sunburst.com
                    e-mail: support@sunburst.com
*A Birmingham, Owner*
*Mark Sotir, President*

Students develop logic thinking and pre-algebra skills solving sets of numbers equations in three challenging problem-solving activities.

**1903 Equations**

Software to Go-Gallaudet University
800 Florida Avenue NE
Washington, DC 20002          202-651-5705
                           FAX 202-651-5109
                    http://www.clerccenter.gallaudet.edu
                       e-mail: afbinfo@afb.net
*Ken Kurlychek, Project Coordinator*
*Karen Kauutz, Administrative Assistant*

**1904 Equivalent Fractions**

Sunburst Technology
400 Columbus Avenue
Valhalla, NY 10595 1349          914-747-3310
                                800-321-7511
                            FAX 914-747-4109
                        http://www.sunburst.com
                    e-mail: support@sunburst.com
*A Birmingham, Owner*
*Mark Sotir, President*

This exciting investigation develops students' conceptual understanding that every fraction can be named in many different but equivalent ways.

**1905 Excelling in Mathematics**

Phillip Roy
PO Box 130
Indian Rocks Beach, FL 33785          727-593-2700
                                      800-255-9085
                                   FAX 727-595-2685
                            http://www.philliproy.com
                         e-mail: info@philliproy.com
*Ashley Sutton, Office Manager*
*Ruth Bragman, President*

A series of tutorial math programs designed to provide instruction for above average math students to prepare them for college math. *$795.00*

**1906 Factory Deluxe**

Sunburst Technology
400 Columbus Avenue
Valhalla, NY 10595 1349          914-747-3310
                                800-321-7511
                            FAX 914-747-4109
                        http://www.sunburst.com
                    e-mail: support@sunburst.com
*A Birmingham, Owner*
*Mark Sotir, President*

Five activities explore shapes, rotation, angles, geometric attributes, area formulas, and computation. Includes journal, record keeping, and on-screen help. This program helps sharpen geometry, visual thinking and problem solving skills.

**1907 Fast-Track Fractions**

SRA Order Services
220 E Danieldale Road
DeSoto, TX 75115
                                      800-843-8855
                            http://www.sraonline.com

Students solve problems that compare, add, subtract, multiply and divide fractions. *$46.00*

**1908 Fifth Through Seventh Grade Math Competencies**

Aquarius Instructional
PO Box 128
Indian Rocks Beach, FL 33785          727-595-7890
                                      800-338-2644
                                   FAX 727-595-2685
                            http://www.philliproy.com
                         e-mail: info@philliproy.com
*Ashley Sutton, Office Manager*
*Ruth Bragman, President*

Offers 32 disks on reading money values, ordering numbers, multiplying whole numbers, dividing whole numbers, adding and subtracting decimals and more. *$995.00*

**1909  Fraction Attraction**
Sunburst Technology
400 Columbus Avenue
Valhalla, NY  10595 1349          914-747-3310
800-321-7511
FAX 914-747-4109
http://www.sunburst.com
e-mail: support@sunburst.com
*A Birmingham, Owner*
*Mark Sotir, President*

Build the fraction skills of ordering, equivalence, relative sizes and multiple representations with four, multi-level, carnival style games.

**1910  Fraction Fairy Tales with the Boars**
Queue
1 Controls Drive
Shelton, CT  06432          203-335-0906
800-232-2224
FAX 203-336-2481
http://www.queueinc.com
e-mail: jck@queueine.com
*Monica Kantrowitz, President*
*Peter Uhrynowski, Controller*

The Boars teach students about fractions in their favorite fairy tale surroundings. *$39.95*

**1911  Fraction Fuel-Up**
SRA Order Services
220 E Danieldale Road
DeSoto, TX  75115
800-843-8855
http://www.sraonline.com
Players practice reducing, renaming, finding equivalent fractions and adding/subtracting fractions. *$46.00*

**1912  Fraction Operations**
Sunburst Technology
400 Columbus Avenue
Valhalla, NY  10595 1349          914-747-3310
800-321-7511
FAX 914-747-4109
http://www.sunburst.com
e-mail: support@sunburst.com
*A Birmingham, Owner*
*Mark Sotir, President*

Students build on their concepts of fraction meaning and equivalence as they learn how to perform operations with fractions.

**1913  Get Up and Go!**
Sunburst Technology
400 Columbus Avenue
Valhalla, NY  10595 1349          914-747-3310
800-321-7511
FAX 914-747-4109
http://www.sunburst.com
e-mail: support@sunburst.com
*A Birmingham, Owner*
*Mark Sotir, President*

Students interpret and construct timelines through three descriptive activities in the animated program. Students are introduced to timelines as they participate in an interactive story.

**1914  Handling Money**
Aquarius Instructional
PO Box 128
Indian Rocks Beach, FL  33785          727-595-7890
800-338-2644
FAX 727-595-2685
http://www.philliproy.com
e-mail: info@philliproy.com
*Ashley Sutton, Office Manager*
*Ruth Bragman, President*

This program teaches students how to count money and make change in paper and coin. *$75.00*

**1915  Hey, Taxi!**
Queue
1 Controls Drive
Shelton, CT  06432          203-333-7268
800-232-2224
FAX 203-336-2481
http://www.queueinc.com
e-mail: jck@queueine.com
*Monica Kantrowitz, President*
*Peter Uhrynowski, Controller*

Children maneuver their cab through the city streets to pick up passengers that solve basic math facts problems to collect their fares. *$39.95*

**1916  Learning About Numbers**
C&C Software
5713 Kentford Circle
Wichita, KS  67220          316-683-6056
800-752-2086
*Carol Clark, President*

Three segments use computer graphics to provide students with an experience in working with numbers. *$25.00*

**1917  Math Machine**
Software to Go-Gallaudet University
800 Florida Avenue NE
Washington, DC  20002          202-651-5705
FAX 202-651-5109
http://www.clerccenter.gallaudet.edu
e-mail: afbinfo@afb.net
*Ken Kurlychek, Project Coordinator*
*Karen Kauutz, Administrative Assistant*

**1918  Math Masters: Addition and Subtraction**

SRA Order Services
220 E Danieldale Road
DeSoto, TX  75115

800-843-8855
http://www.sraonline.com

*Jerry Chaffin, Author*

Designed to supplement math curriculum, this program covers addition and subtraction for all numbers from 0 through 25.

**1919  Math Masters: Multiplication and Division**

SRA Order Services
220 E Danieldale Road
DeSoto, TX  75115

800-843-8855
http://www.sraonline.com

*Jerry Chaffin, Author*

Designed to supplement math curriculum, this program covers multiplication and division for all numbers from 0 through 25.

**1920  Math Shop**

Software to Go-Gallaudet University
800 Florida Avenue NE
Washington, DC  20002

202-651-5705
FAX 202-651-5109
http://www.clerccenter.gallaudet.edu
e-mail: afbinfo@afb.net

*Ken Kurlychek, Project Coordinator*
*Karen Kauutz, Administrative Assistant*

**1921  Math Skill Games**

Software to Go-Gallaudet University
800 Florida Avenue NE
Washington, DC  20002

202-651-5705
FAX 202-651-5109
http://www.clerccenter.gallaudet.edu
e-mail: afbinfo@afb.net

*Ken Kurlychek, Project Coordinator*
*Karen Kauutz, Administrative Assistant*

**1922  Math Spending and Saving**

World Class Learning
111 Kane Street
Baltimore, MD  21224

410-633-0730
FAX 410-633-2758
http://www.wclm.com

*Paul Edwards, Author*
*Bruce Brown, President*

Designed for secondary students and adults, this program focuses on personal financial management, comparison shopping and calculation of essential banking transactions.

**1923  Math for All Ages: A Sequential MathProgram**

Phillip Roy
PO Box 130
Indian Rocks Beach, FL  33785

727-593-2700
800-255-9085
FAX 727-595-2685
http://www.philliproy.com
e-mail: info@philliproy.com

*Ashley Sutton, Office Manager*
*Ruth Bragman, President*

Offers 16 disks on adding, subtracting, multiplication and division.

**1924  Math for Everyday Living**

Educational Activities
PO Box 392
Baldwin, NY  11520

516-223-4666
800-645-3739
FAX 516-379-7429
e-mail: learn@edact.com

*Ann Edson, Author*
*Carol Stern, President*
*Rose Falco, Sales/Marketing*

Designed for secondary students, a tutorial and practice program with simulated activities for applying math skills in making change, working with sales slips, unit pricing, computing gas mileage and sales tax. *$129.00*

**1925  Mighty Math Astro Algebra**

Riverdeep
222 3rd Avenue SE
Cedar Rapids, IA  52401

888-242-6747
800-362-2890
FAX 800-567-2714
http://www.riverdeep.net

In Astro Algebra, you're the captain of the Algebra Centauri spaceship! Traveling through the galaxy, you meet fascinating alien species and use algebra to help them out of predicaments. Four expert crew members Skler, Max, Mialee and Tyric are standing by to help you understand, strategize, calculate and check your work. *$59.95*

**1926  Mighty Math Calculating Crew**

Riverdeep
222 3rd Avenue SE
Cedar Rapids, IA  52401

888-242-6747
800-362-2890
FAX 800-567-2714
http://www.riverdeep.net

Calculating Crew teaches your 3rd, 4th, 5th, or 6th grader the concepts, facts and thinking skills necessary to build math confidence and develop a strong, lasting understanding of math! Wanda Wavelet, Captain Nick Knack and Dr. Gee guide your child through thousands of skill-building problems! *$59.95*

**1927 Mighty Math Cosmic Geometry**
**Riverdeep**
**222 3rd Avenue SE**
**Cedar Rapids, IA 52401**          **888-242-6747**
                                    **800-362-2890**
                          **FAX 800-567-2714**
                          **http://www.riverdeep.net**

Cosmic Gemetry teaches you the concepts and problem-solving skills you need to master geometry and build math confidence! Polyhedral characters such as Dodeca, Hexa and Lcosa are your guides on this fun-filled exploration of Planet Geometry. *$59.95*

**1928 Mighty Math Countdown**
**Riverdeep**
**222 3rd Avenue SE**
**Cedar Rapids, IA 52401**          **888-242-6747**
                                    **800-362-2890**
                          **FAX 800-567-2714**
                          **http://www.riverdeep.net**

Kids love to visit Carnival Countdown, where addition, subtraction, early multiplication, division and logic are always center ring! This breakthrough math progam offers your child three years of math learning and ensures math success by teaching kindergarten through 2nd grade math concepts and problem-solving. With Carnival Countdown, learning math is as much fun as a trip to the circus! *$59.95*

**1929 Mighty Math Number Heroes**
**Riverdeep**
**222 3rd Ave SE**
**Cedar Rapids, IA 52401**          **888-242-6747**
                                    **800-362-2890**
                          **FAX 800-567-2714**
                          **http://riverdeep.net**

Number Heroes teaches kids the basics and problem-solving skills they need to succeed in math. With the help of Fraction Man, Star Brilliant and other math superheroes, kids understand dozens of math concepts and solve thousands of problems while learning multiplication and division, fractions, 2D geometry and probability. Help your children master 3rd through 6th-grade math with the Number Heroes! *$59.95*

**1930 Mighty Math Zoo Zillions**
**Riverdeep**
**222 3rd Ave SE**
**Cedar Rapids, IA 52401**          **888-242-6747**
                                    **800-362-2890**
                          **FAX 800-567-2714**
                          **http://www.riverdeep.net**

Mighty Math Zoo Zillions teaches your kindergartener, 1st grader or 2nd grader the concepts, facts and thinking skills necessary to build math confidence and develop a strong, lasting understanding of math! Armadillo Annie, the Otter Twins and other animal friends guide your child on this exciting mathematical adventure! *$59.95*

**1931 Millie's Math House**
**Riverdeep**
**222 3rd Ave SE**
**Cedar Rapids, IA 52401**          **888-242-6747**
                                    **800-362-2890**
                          **FAX 800-567-2714**
                          **http://www.riverdeep.net**
*Tina Martin, Education Marketing*

Now featuring addition, subtraction and counting to 30, the award-winning Millie's Math House has been enhanced to offer even more learning! In seven activities, children explore numbers, shapes, sizes, patterns, addition and subtraction as they build mouse houses, create wacky bugs, count animated critters, make jellybean cookies and answer math challenges posed by Dorothy the Duck! *$59.95*

**1932 Number Farm**
**Software to Go-Gallaudet University**
**800 Florida Avenue NE**
**Washington, DC 20002**          **202-651-5705**
                          **FAX 202-651-5109**
                **http://www.clerccenter.gallaudet.edu**
                **e-mail: afbinfo@afb.net**
*Ken Kurlychek, Project Coordinator*
*Karen Kauutz, Administrative Assistant*

**1933 Number Please**
**Merit Software**
**132 W 21 Street**
**New York, NY 10011**          **212-675-8567**
                                **800-753-6488**
                          **FAX 212-675-8607**
                **http://www.meritsoftware.com**
                **e-mail: sales@meritsoftware.com**
*Ben Weintrap, President*

Students are challenged to remember combinations of 4, 7 and 10 digit numbers. *$9.95*

**1934 Number Sense & Problem Solving CD-ROM**
**Sunburst Technology**
**400 Columbus Avenue**
**Valhalla, NY 10595 1349**          **914-747-3310**
                                     **800-321-7511**
                          **FAX 914-747-4109**
                **http://www.sunburst.com**
                **e-mail: support@sunburst.com**
*A Birmingham, Owner*
*Mark Sotir, President*

Build number and operation skills with these three programs: How the West Was One + Three x Four, Divide and Conquer and Puzzle Tank.

**1935 Number Stumper**
**Software to Go-Gallaudet University**
**800 Florida Avenue NE**
**Washington, DC 20002**          **202-651-5705**
                          **FAX 202-651-5109**
                **http://www.clerccenter.gallaudet.edu**
                **e-mail: afbinfo@afb.net**
*Ken Kurlychek, Project Coordinator*
*Karen Kauutz, Administrative Assistant*

**1936 Optimum Resource**

18 Hunter Road
Hilton Head Island, SC 29926      843-689-8000
888-784-2592
FAX 843-689-8008
http://www.stickybear.com
e-mail: stickyb@stickybear.com
*Christopher Gintz, COO*
*Robert Stangroom, Product Manager*

An educational software publishing company for grades K-12. Our software titles are available in Consumer, School, Labpack or Site License versions. Please call for further details. Prices range from $59.95 for Consumer to $699.95 for Site Licenses.

**1937 Race Car 'rithmetic**

**Software to Go-Gallaudet University**
**800 Florida Avenue NE**
**Washington, DC 20002**      202-651-5705
FAX 202-651-5109
http://www.clerccenter.gallaudet.edu
e-mail: afbinfo@afb.net
*Ken Kurlychek, Project Coordinator*
*Karen Kauutz, Administrative Assistant*

**1938 Read and Solve Math Problems #1**

**Educational Activities**
**PO Box 392**
**Baldwin, NY 11520**      516-223-4666
800-645-3739
FAX 516-379-7429
e-mail: learn@edact.com
*Ann Edson, Author*
*Carol Stern, President*
*Rose Falco, Sales/Marketing*

A tutorial and practice program for students which focuses on recognition of key words in solving arithmetic word problems, writing equations and solving word problems. *$109.00*

**1939 Read and Solve Math Problems #2**

**Educational Activities**
**PO Box 392**
**Baldwin, NY 11520**      516-223-4666
800-645-3739
FAX 516-379-7429
e-mail: learn@edact.com
*Ann Edson, Author*
*Carol Stern, President*
*Rose Falco, Sales/Marketing*

A tutorial and practice program for students which focuses on recognition of key words in solving two-step arithmetic problems, writing equations and solving two-step word problems. *$109.00*

**1940 Read and Solve Math Problems #3 Fractions, Two-Step Problems**

**Educational Activities**
**PO Box 392**
**Baldwin, NY 11520**      516-223-4666
800-645-3739
FAX 516-379-7429
e-mail: learn@edact.com
*Ann Edson, Author*
*Carol Stern, President*
*Rose Falco, Sales/Marketing*

Designed for students, this tutorial and practice program provides initial instruction and experience in critical thinking and problem-solving using fractions and mixed numbers. *$109.00*

**1941 Shape Up!**

**Sunburst Technology**
**400 Columbus Avenue**
**Valhalla, NY 10595 1349**      914-747-3310
800-321-7511
FAX 914-747-4109
http://www.sunburst.com
e-mail: support@sunburst.com
*A Birmingham, Owner*
*Mark Sotir, President*

Students actively create and manipulate shapes to discover important ideas about mathematics in an electronic playground of two and three dimensional shapes.

**1942 Spatial Sense CD-ROM**

**Sunburst Technology**
**400 Columbus Avenue**
**Valhalla, NY 10595 1349**      914-747-3310
800-321-7511
FAX 914-747-4109
http://www.sunburst.com
e-mail: support@sunburst.com
*A Birmingham, Owner*
*Mark Sotir, President*

Your students will strenghten their spatial perception, spatial reasoning and problem-solving skills with three great programs now on one CD-ROM.

**1943 Splish Splash Math**

**Sunburst Technology**
**400 Columbus Avenue**
**Valhalla, NY 10595 1349**      914-747-3310
800-321-7511
FAX 914-747-4109
http://www.sunburst.com
e-mail: support@sunburst.com
*A Birmingham, Owner*
*Mark Sotir, President*

Students learn and practice basic operation skills as they engage in this high interest program that keeps them motivated. Great visual rewards and three levels of difficulty keep students challanged.

**1944 Third and Fourth Grade Math Competencies**

**Phillip Roy**
**PO Box 130**
**Indian Rocks Beach, FL 33785**      727-593-2700
800-255-9085
FAX 727-595-2685
http://www.philliproy.com
e-mail: info@philliproy.com
*Ashley Sutton, Office Manager*
*Ruth Bragman, President*

Offers various programs of 40 disks on geometry, money, measurement, adding whole numbers, subtracting whole numbers and more. *$1175.00*

**1945 This Old Man**

**UCLA Intervention Program for Handicapped Children**
**1000 Veteran Avenue**
**Los Angeles, CA 90095**      310-825-4821
FAX 310-206-7744
http://www.bol.ucla.edu
e-mail: scislo@madnet.uclu.edu
*Sharon Cislo, Administrative Assistant*
*Kit Kehr, Executive Director*

Uses the song This Old Man in singing and signing to teach numbers and counting 1-10. *$35.00*

**1946 Zap! Around Town**

**Sunburst Technology**
**400 Columbus Avenue**
**Valhalla, NY 10595 1349**      914-747-3310
800-321-7511
FAX 914-747-4109
http://www.sunburst.com
e-mail: support@sunburst.com
*A Birmingham, Owner*
*Mark Sotir, President*

Students develop mapping and direction skills in this easy-to-use, animated program featuring Shelby, your friendly Sunbuddy guide.

# Preschool

**1947 Creature Series**

**Laureate Learning Systems**
**110 E Spring Street**
**Winooski, VT 05404**      802-655-4755
800-562-6801
FAX 802-655-4757
http://www.laureatelearning.com
e-mail: info@laureatelearning.com
*Mary Wilson, President*
*Bernard Fox, Vice President*

Programs designed to improve visual and auditory attention and teach cause and effect, turn taking, and switch use. *$95.00*

**1948 Curious George Visits the Library**

**Software to Go-Gallaudet University**
**800 Florida Avenue NE**
**Washington, DC 20002**      202-651-5705
FAX 202-651-5109
http://www.clerccenter.gallaudet.edu
e-mail: afbinfo@afb.net
*Ken Kurlychek, Project Coordinator*
*Karen Kauutz, Administrative Assistant*

**1949 Dinosaur Game**

**UCLA Intervention Program for Handicapped Children**
**1000 Veteran Avenue**
**Los Angeles, CA 90095**      310-825-4821
FAX 310-206-7744
http://www.bol.ucla.edu
e-mail: scislo@madnet.uclu.edu
*Sharon Cislo, Administrative Assistant*
*Kit Kehr, Executive Director*

Game board format where dinosaurs race each other home. Children press their switches to spin a spinner which randomly selects the color of the square. Children then move their dinosaurs by pressing their switches. Accommodates 1-4 players. *$35.00*

**1950 Early Discoveries: Size and Logic**

**Software to Go-Gallaudet University**
**800 Florida Avenue NE**
**Washington, DC 20002**      202-651-5705
FAX 202-651-5109
http://www.clerccenter.gallaudet.edu
e-mail: afbinfo@afb.net
*Ken Kurlychek, Project Coordinator*
*Karen Kauutz, Administrative Assistant*

**1951 Early Emerging Rules Series**

**Laureate Learning Systems**
**110 E Spring Street**
**Winooski, VT 05404**      802-655-4755
800-562-6801
FAX 802-655-4757
http://www.laureatelearning.com
e-mail: info@laureatelearning.com
*Mary Wilson, President*
*Bernard Fox, Vice President*

Three programs that introduce early developing grammatical constructions and facilitate the transition from single words to word combinations. *$175.00*

**1952 Early Learning I**

**MarbleSoft**
**12301 Central Avenue NE**
**Blaine, MN 55434**      763-755-1402
FAX 763-862-2920
http://www.marblesoft.com
e-mail: sales@marblesoft.com
*Valerie Reit, Sales*

Early Learning 2.0 includes four activities that teach prereading skills. Single and dual-switch scanning are built in and special prompts allow blind students to use all levels of difficulty. Includes Matching Colors, Learning Shapes, Counting Numbers and Letter Match. Runs on Macintosh and Windows computers. *$70.00*

**1953   Early Music Skills**

**Electronic Courseware Systems**
**1210 Lancaster Drive**
**Champaign, IL  61821**            **217-359-7099**
                                    **800-832-4965**
                            **FAX 217-359-6578**
                    **http://www.ecsmedica.com**
                    **e-mail: sales@ecsmedia.com**
*Jodie Varner, Director Education/Marketing*

Covers four basic music reading skills. *$39.95*

**1954   Early and Advanced Switch Games**

**RJ Cooper & Associates**
**27601 Forbes Road #39**
**Laguna Nigel, CA  92677**          **949-582-2572**
                                    **800-752-6673**
                            **FAX 949-582-3169**
                    **http://www.rjcooper.com**
                    **e-mail: info@rjcooper.com**
*RJ Cooper, Owner/Developer*

Thirteen single switch games that start at cause/effect, work through timing and selection and graduate with matching and manipulation tasks. *$75.00*

**1955   Edustar's Early Childhood Special Education Programs**

**Edustar America**
**6220 S Orange Blossom Trail**
**Orlando, FL  32809**               **561-638-8733**
                                    **800-952-3041**
                            **FAX 561-330-0849**
*David Zeldin, Marketing Manager*
*Stewart Holtz, Curriculum Director*

Integrated software program that incorporates manipulatives and special tables for learning early childhood subjects. Features include an illuminated six key keyboard. A special U-shaped touch table for the physically challenged and changeable mats and keys for different subject areas.

**1956   Electric Coloring Book**

**Heartsoft**
**3101 N Hemlock Circle**
**Broken Arrow, OK  74012**          **918-494-7878**
                                    **800-285-4018**
                            **FAX 800-285-3475**
                    **e-mail: sales@heartsoft.com**
Teaches young students the alphabet, numbers and basic keyboarding skills by using a graphic coloring concept. *$39.95*

**1957   If You're Happy and You Know It**

**UCLA Intervention Program for Handicapped Children**
**1000 Veteran Avenue**
**Los Angeles, CA  90095**           **310-825-4821**
                            **FAX 310-206-7744**
                    **http://www.bol.ucla.edu**
                    **e-mail: scislo@madnet.uclu.edu**
*Sharon Cislo, Administrative Assistant*
*Kit Kehr, Executive Director*

A nursery school song with five verses depicted in picture form. *$35.00*

**1958   Joystick Games**

**Technology for Language and Learning**
**PO Box 327**
**East Rockaway, NY  11518**         **516-625-4550**
                            **FAX 516-621-3321**
Five volumes of public domain joystick programs. *$28.50*

**1959   Kindercomp Gold**

**Software to Go-Gallaudet University**
**800 Florida Avenue NE**
**Washington, DC  20002**            **202-651-5705**
                            **FAX 202-651-5109**
                    **http://www.clerccenter.gallaudet.edu**
                    **e-mail: afbinfo@afb.net**
*Ken Kurlychek, Project Coordinator*
*Karen Kauutz, Administrative Assistant*

**1960   Old MacDonald's Farm**

**KidTECH**
**4181 Pinewood Lake Drive**
**Bakersfield, CA  93309**           **661-396-8676**
                            **FAX 661-396-8760**
Utilizes the all-time favorite children's song to teach vocabulary and animal sounds to young children. *$30.00*

**1961   Old MacDonald's Farm I**

**UCLA Intervention Program for Handicapped Children**
**1000 Veteran Avenue**
**Los Angeles, CA  90095**           **310-825-4821**
                            **FAX 310-206-7744**
                    **http://www.bol.ucla.edu**
                    **e-mail: scislo@madnet.uclu.edu**
*Sharon Cislo, Administrative Assistant*
*Kit Kehr, Executive Director*

Nursery School song depicting a farmer, his wife, and 6 farm animals — cow, sheep, rooster, pig, and duck — displayed on as overlay. Level I, the child selects any animal. Level II, the child selects an animal by name. Level III, the child selects an animal by its sound. *$35.00*

**1962 Optimum Resource**

18 Hunter Road
Hilton Head Island, SC 29926       843-689-8000
                                   888-784-2592
                              FAX 843-689-8008
                    http://www.stickybear.com
              e-mail: stickyb@stickybear.com
*Christopher Gintz, COO*
*Robert Stangroom, Product Manager*

An educational software publishing company for grades K-12. Our software titles are available in Consumer, School, Labpack or Site License versions. Please call for further details. Prices range from $59.95 for Consumer to $699.95 for Site Licenses.

**1963 Padded Vehicles**

UCLA Intervention Program for Handicapped
Children
1000 Veteran Avenue
Los Angeles, CA 90095              310-825-4821
                              FAX 310-206-7744
                       http://www.bol.ucla.edu
               e-mail: scislo@madnet.uclu.edu
*Sharon Cislo, Administrative Assistant*
*Kit Kehr, Executive Director*

Children identify 10 vehicles — airplane, helicopter, motorcycle, police car, truck, ambulance, garbage truck, school bus, fire engine, and tractor — which are depicted on an overlay. Level I, the child selects any vehicle. Level II, the child selects the vehicle by name. *$35.00*

**1964 Shape and Color Rodeo**

SRA Order Services
220 E Danieldale Road
DeSoto, TX 75115
                                   800-843-8855
                       http://www.sraonline.com
Children learn recognition and identification of common shapes and color discriminations. *$35.00*

**1965 Silly Sandwich**

UCLA Intervention Program for Handicapped
Children
1000 Veteran Avenue
Los Angeles, CA 90095              310-825-4821
                              FAX 310-206-7744
                       http://www.bol.ucla.edu
               e-mail: scislo@madnet.uclu.edu
*Sharon Cislo, Administrative Assistant*
*Kit Kehr, Executive Director*

Build a silly sandwich selecting from six to twelve different items depicted on a PowerPad overlay. *$35.00*

**1966 Switch It - Change It**

UCLA Intervention Program for Handicapped
Children
1000 Veteran Avenue
Los Angeles, CA 90095              310-825-4821
                              FAX 310-206-7744
                       http://www.bol.ucla.edu
               e-mail: scislo@madnet.uclu.edu
*Sharon Cislo, Administrative Assistant*
*Kit Kehr, Executive Director*

Cause and effect program presents color-animated common objects. *$35.00*

*Mac*

**1967 Trudy's Time and Place House**

Riverdeep
222 3rd Avenue SE
Cedar Rapids, IA 52401             888-242-6747
                                   800-362-2890
                              FAX 800-567-2714
                       http://www.riverdeep.net
In Trudy's Time and Place House, children enjoy exploring geography and time with Trudy's whimsical friends! Ann and Dan, Joe Crow and Nellie the Elephant invite kids to: build time-telling skills; develop mapping and direction skills; and travel the world learning about continents, oceans and landmarks. *$59.95*

**1968 Wheels on the Bus I: Intellipics Activity**

UCLA Intervention Program for Handicapped
Children
1000 Veteran Avenue
Los Angeles, CA 90095              310-825-4821
                                   800-899-6687
                              FAX 310-206-7744
                       http://www.bol.ucla.edu
               e-mail: scislo@madnet.uclu.edu
*Sharon Cislo, Administrative Assistant*
*Kit Kehr, Executive Director*

This native Macintosh activity requires Intellipics to run. It includes 6 verses (Baby, Bus, Doors, Horn, Kids, Mommy) with digitalized sound and color animations. It can be used with intellipics options such as color and a number selection, and includes both free choice and quiz options. *$25.00*

**1969 Wheels on the Bus II**

UCLA Intervention Program for Handicapped
Children
1000 Veteran Avenue
Los Angeles, CA 90095              310-825-4821
                              FAX 310-206-7744
                       http://www.bol.ucla.edu
               e-mail: scislo@madnet.uclu.edu
*Sharon Cislo, Administrative Assistant*
*Kit Kehr, Executive Director*

Popular nursery school song that is activated to sing 5 verses by pressing the corresponding picture on an overlay. Verses are driver, wheel, wiper, windows, daddy. *$36.00*

**1970 Wheels on the Bus III**

UCLA Intervention Program for Handicapped
Children
1000 Veteran Avenue
Los Angeles, CA 90095              310-825-4821
                              FAX 310-206-7744
                       http://www.bol.ucla.edu
               e-mail: scislo@madnet.uclu.edu
*Sharon Cislo, Administrative Assistant*
*Kit Kehr, Executive Director*

Popular nursery school song that is activated to sing 5 verses of the song by pressing the corresponding picture on an overlay. Verses are: People, money, brakes, seatbelt, wheelchair lift. *$36.00*

**1971 Where is Puff?**

**UCLA Intervention Program for Handicapped Children**
**1000 Veteran Avenue**
**Los Angeles, CA 90095**          310-825-4821
                                 FAX 310-206-7744
                          http://www.bol.ucla.edu
                    e-mail: scislo@madnet.uclu.edu
*Sharon Cislo, Administrative Assistant*
*Kit Kehr, Executive Director*

Early preposition program that includes six prepositions illustrated by Puff the cat: in, on, next to, under, in front of, in back of. Features include: scan speed selection and data collection. *$35.00*

**1972 Word Pieces**

**Software to Go-Gallaudet University**
**800 Florida Avenue NE**
**Washington, DC 20002**          202-651-5705
                                 FAX 202-651-5109
              http://www.clerccenter.gallaudet.edu
                       e-mail: afbinfo@afb.net
*Ken Kurlychek, Project Coordinator*
*Karen Kauutz, Administrative Assistant*

## Problem Solving

**1973 Captain's Log Cognitive Training System for Windows**

**BrainTrain**
**727 Twinridge Lane**
**Richmond, VA 23235**            804-320-0105
                                  800-822-0538
                            FAX 804-320-0242
                      http://www.braintrain.com
                      e-mail: info@braintrain.com
*Virginia Sandford, Vice President Sales/Marketing*

A comprehensive, multilevel computerized mental gym to help people with brain injuries, learning disabilities, developmental disabilities, ADD, ADHD and psychiatric disorders improve their cognitive skills. *$2695.00*

*ISBN 3-490019-95-0*

**1974 Changes Around Us CD-ROM**

**Steck-Vaughn Company**
**PO Box 690789**
**Orlando, FL 32819**             407-345-3800
                                  800-225-5425
                            FAX 800-269-5232
                     http://www.steck-vaughn.com
                    e-mail: info@steck-vaughn.com
*Connie Alden, Vice President of Human Resource*

Nature is the natural choice for observing change. By observing and researching dramatic visual sequences such as the stages of development of a butterfly, children develop a broad understanding of the concept of change. As they search this multimedia database for images and information about plant and animal life cycles and seasonal change, students strengthen their abilities in research, analysis, problem-solving, critical thinking and communication.

**1975 Factory Deluxe**

**Sunburst Technology**
**400 Columbus Avenue**
**Valhalla, NY 10595 1349**        914-747-3310
                                   800-321-7511
                             FAX 914-747-4109
                      http://www.sunburst.com
                    e-mail: support@sunburst.com
*Mark Sotir, President*

Five activities explore shapes, rotation, angles, geometric attributes, area formulas, and computation. Includes journal, record keeping, and on-screen help. This program helps sharpen geometry, visual thinking and problem solving skills.

**1976 Freddy's Puzzling Adventures**

**SRA Order Services**
**220 E Danieldale Road**
**DeSoto, TX 75115**
                                  800-262-4729
                      http://www.sraonline.com

Helps students acquire problem solving and logical thinking skills with three activities. *$34.00*

**1977 Guessing and Thinking**

**Software to Go-Gallaudet University**
**800 Florida Avenue NE**
**Washington, DC 20002**          202-651-5705
                                 FAX 202-651-5109
              http://www.clerccenter.gallaudet.edu
                       e-mail: afbinfo@afb.net
*Ken Kurlychek, Project Coordinator*
*Karen Kauutz, Administrative Assistant*

**1978 High School Math Bundle**

**Sunburst Technology**
**400 Columbus Avenue**
**Valhalla, NY 10595 1349**        914-747-3310
                                   800-321-7511
                             FAX 914-747-4109
                      http://www.sunburst.com
                    e-mail: support@sunburst.com
*Mark Sotir, President*

Each program in this bundle focuses on a specific area to ensure that your students master the math skills they need. This bundle allows students to master basics of Algebra, explore equations and graphs, practice learning with algebra graphs, use trigonometric functions, apply math concepts to practical situations and improve problem solving and data analysis skills.

**1979  Ice Cream Truck**

Sunburst Technology
400 Columbus Avenue
Valhalla, NY  10595 1349          914-747-3310
                                 800-321-7511
                          FAX 914-747-4109
                    http://www.sunburst.com
              e-mail: support@sunburst.com
*Mark Sotir, President*

Elementary students learn important problem solving, strategic planning and math operation skills, as they become owners of a busy ice cream truck.

**1980  Lesson Maker: Do-It-Yourself Computer Program**

Harris Communications
15155 Technology Drive
Eden Prairie, MN  55344          952-906-1180
                                 800-825-6758
                          FAX 952-906-1099
                            TDY:952-906-1198
                    http://www.harriscomm.com
               e-mail: mail@harriscomm.com
*Bill Williams, National Sales Manager*

For teachers, parents and students who want to create their own computer lessons. Choose any topic from Vocabulary to Volcanoes. For each lesson enter eight of your own questions or prompts with eight answers or desired responses. Lesson Maker automatically inputs information into 4 separate fun games for each lesson: Spinmeister; Matching; Paired Squares; and Pop Quiz. Up to 15 individual lessons can be made for one Unit. *$24.95*

*Diskettes*

**1981  Memory Match**

Software to Go-Gallaudet University
800 Florida Avenue NE
Washington, DC  20002            202-651-5705
                          FAX 202-651-5109
            http://www.clerccenter.gallaudet.edu
                      e-mail: afbinfo@afb.net
*Ken Kurlychek, Project Coordinator*
*Karen Kauutz, Administrative Assistant*

**1982  Memory: A First Step in Problem Solving**

Software to Go-Gallaudet University
800 Florida Avenue NE
Washington, DC  20002            202-651-5705
                          FAX 202-651-5109
            http://www.clerccenter.gallaudet.edu
                      e-mail: afbinfo@afb.net
*Ken Kurlychek, Project Coordinator*
*Karen Kauutz, Administrative Assistant*

**1983  Merit Software**

Merit Software
132 W 21 Street
New York, NY  10011              212-675-8567
                                 800-753-6488
                          FAX 212-675-8607
                    http://www.meritsoftware.com
             e-mail: sales@meritsoftware.com
*Ben Weintraub, Marketing Manager*

Deductive logic and problem solving are the primary skills developed in the variation of the game MASTERMIND. *$9.95*

**1984  Middle School Math Bundle**

Sunburst Technology
400 Columbus Avenue
Valhalla, NY  10595 1349          914-747-3310
                                 800-321-7511
                          FAX 914-747-4109
                    http://www.sunburst.com
              e-mail: support@sunburst.com
*Mark Sotir, President*

This bundle helps improve student's logical thinking, number sense and operation skills. This product comes with Math Arena, Building Perspective Deluxe, Equation Tile Teasers and Easy Sheet.

**1985  Nordic Software**

PO Box 5403
Lincoln, NE  68501               402-489-1557
                          FAX 402-489-1560
                    http://www.nordicsoftware.com
*Tammy Kear, Sales/Marketing*

Develops and publishes entertaining, educational software. Children ages three and up can build math skills, expand their vocabulary and increase proficiency in spelling, among other subjects. *$59.95*

**1986  Number Sense & Problem Solving CD-ROM**

Sunburst Technology
400 Columbus Avenue
Valhalla, NY  10595 1349          914-747-3310
                                 800-321-7511
                          FAX 914-747-4109
                    http://www.sunburst.com
              e-mail: support@sunburst.com
*Mark Sotir, President*

Build number and operation skills with these three programs: How the West Was One + Three x Four, Divide and Conquer and Puzzle Tank.

**1987  Problem Solving**

Psychological Software Services
6555 Carrollton Avenue
Indianapolis, IN  46220          317-257-9672
                          FAX 317-257-9674
                 http://www.neuroscience.cnter.com
                 e-mail: nsc@netdirect.net
*Odie Bracy MD, President*
*Nancy Bracy, Assistant Director*

Nine computer programs designed to challenge high functioning patients/students with tasks requiring logic. *$150.00*

**1988    Single Switch Games**

MarbleSoft
12301 Central Avenue NE
Blaine, MN 55434                    763-755-1402
                                   FAX 763-862-2920
                        http://www.marblesoft.com
                        e-mail: sales@marblesoft.com
*Valerie Reit, Sales*

There's a lot of educational software for single switch users, but how about something that's just for fun? We've taken some games similar to the ones you enjoyed as a kid and made them work just right for single switch users. Includes Single Switch Maze, A Frog's Life, Switching Lanes, Switch Invaders, Slingshot Gallery and Scurry. Runs on Macintosh and Windows computers. *$30.00*

**1989    Sliding Block**

Merit Software
132 W 21 Street
New York, NY 10011                 212-675-8567
                                   800-753-6488
                                   FAX 212-675-8607
                        http://www.meritsoftware.com
                        e-mail: sales@meritsoftware.com
*Ben Weintraub, Director*

Learners rearrange one of the four pictures which can be scrambled at five separate levels to test visual discrimination and problem solving skills. *$9.95*

**1990    SoundSmart**

BrainTrain
727 Twinridge Lane
Richmond, VA 23235                 804-320-0105
                                   800-822-0538
                                   FAX 804-320-0242
                        http://www.braintrain.com
                        e-mail: info@braintrain.com
*Virginia Sandford, Vice President Sales/Marketing*

Auditory Attention Building software to help improve phonenic awareness, listening skills, working memory, mental processing speech and self-control. *$549.00*

**1991    Strategy Challenges Collection: 1**

Riverdeep
222 3rd Ave SE
Cedar Rapids, IA 52401             888-242-6747
                                   800-362-2890
                                   FAX 800-567-2714
                        http://www.riverdeep.net

Play Mancala, Go-Muku and Nine Men's Morris- the three games in Strategy Challenges Collection 1 against Game Masters from around the world! Why? Because you'll learn important problem-solving and strategies thinking skills you can use throughout life in games, in school and in jobs. *$39.95*

**1992    Strategy Challenges Collection: 2**

Riverdeep
222 3rd Ave SE
Cedar Rapids, IA 52401             888-242-6747
                                   800-362-2890
                                   FAX 800-567-2714
                        http://www.riverdeep.net

Strategy Challenges Collection: 2 — featuring Jungle Chess, Surakarta and Tablut — boosts your thinking power! How does it work? Six diverse Opponents challenge you to build a repertoire of powerful problem-solving strategies and skills. You'll also meet Strategy Coaches who offer offensive and defensive tips that can improve your game and be applied throughout life. *$39.95*

**1993    Switch Arcade**

UCLA Intervention Program for Handicapped
Children
1000 Veteran Avenue
Los Angeles, CA 90095              310-825-4821
                                   FAX 310-206-7744
                        http://www.bol.ucla.edu
                        e-mail: scislo@madnet.uclu.edu
*Sharon Cislo, Administrative Assistant*
*Kit Kehr, Executive Director*

Three switch games are presented: Tug of War; Racing; Fishing. The racing game allows children to choose from several racers including cars, wheelchairs, and animals using a single switch. The game is designed for two players using two switches to play competitive, cooperative games together. Can be used to promote social interaction and eye-hand coordination. *$45.00*

   *Mac*

**1994    Thinkin' Things: All Around Frippletown**

Riverdeep
222 3rd Ave SE
Cedar Rapids, IA 52401             888-242-6747
                                   800-362-2890
                                   FAX 800-567-2714
                        http://www.riverdeep.net

Welcome to FrippleTown, where dozens of fun-loving Fripples will tickle your funny bone and challenge your brain. Discover and use the best of your creative thinking skills! Think through problems and explore solutions to furnish the Fripples with artful flags, crazy cookies, door-to-door surprises and more. Every visit to FrippleTown is a chance to discover something new.

**1995    Thinkin' Things: Collection 1**

Riverdeep
222 3rd Ave SE
Cedar Rapids, IA 52401             888-242-6747
                                   800-362-2890
                                   FAX 800-567-2714
                        http://www.riverdeep.net

Good thinkers learn quickly, adapt to change easily and accomplish remarkable things. That's why we created Thinkin' Things Collection 1, a powerful set of tools and toys to help children strengthen observation and memory, improve problem solving and encourage creativity. Thinkin' Things Collection 1 will help your child build a solid foundation for successful learning!

**1996 Thinkin' Things: Collection 2**

**Riverdeep**
**222 3rd Ave SE**
**Cedar Rapids, IA 52401**          **888-242-6747**
                                     **800-362-2890**
                          **FAX 800-567-2714**
                **http://www.riverdeep.net**

In this rapidly changing world, kids with strong thinking skills will thrive and excel. That's why the educators at Edmark developed Thinkin' Things Collection 2, a powerful set of tools and toys that strengthen observation and analysis, develop spatial awareness, improve memory and foster creativity. With a strong grasp of these skills, your child is ready to succeed!

**1997 Thinkin' Things: Collection 3**

**Riverdeep**
**222 3rd Ave SE**
**Cedar Rapids, IA 52401**          **888-242-6747**
                                     **800-362-2890**
                          **FAX 800-567-2714**
                **http://www.riverdeep.net**

Become a strong thinker with Thinkin' Things Collection 3 and build thinking skills you can use wherever you are in anything you do! Make trades with brokers from around the world, program a half-time show and solve the Case of the Empty Fripple House. You'll improve deductive and inductive reasoning, synthesis and analysis, while building problem-solving skills essential for success!

**1998 Thinkin' Things: Galactic Brain Benders**

**Riverdeep**
**222 3rd Ave SE**
**Cedar Rapids, IA 52401**          **888-242-6747**
                                     **800-362-2890**
                          **FAX 800-567-2714**
                **http://www.riverdeep.net**

Your brain power is needed all across the galaxy! Develop logic, sequencing and decision-making skills as you organize Fripples in space, experiment with special effects tools and program a half-time show at the Intergalactic Rocket Bowl.

**1999 Thinkin' Things: Sky Island Mysteries**

**Riverdeep**
**222 3rd Ave SE**
**Cedar Rapids, IA 52401**          **888-242-6747**
                                     **800-362-2890**
                          **FAX 800-567-2714**
                **http://www.riverdeep.net**

Inspector Cluestoe needs help cracking 14 zany mysteries to nab a slew of crafty culprits. Visit each island and put your best thinking skills to work to collect the clues! Prioritize tasks, apply your powers of observation and logic, and draw valid conclusions to solve the mysteries of the Sky Islands.

**2000 Thinkin' Things: Toony the Loon's Lagoon**

**Riverdeep**
**222 3rd Ave SE**
**Cedar Rapids, IA 52401**          **888-242-6747**
                                     **800-362-2890**
                          **FAX 800-567-2714**
                **http://www.riverdeep.net**

Toony the Loon's Lagoon sparkles with dozens of fun loving characters and activities that help kids learn how to be better thinkers. Toony, Oranga and other jungle friends guide your child toward success in six unique locations — plus there's a fun, new online puzzle each week.

# Professional Resources

**2001 Accurate Assessments**

**1823 Harney Street**
**Omaha, NE 68102**                  **402-341-8880**
                                     **800-324-7966**
                          **FAX 402-341-8911**
           **http://www.accurateassessments.com**
           **e-mail: info@accurateassessments.com**
*Bill Allen, Director*

Accurate Assessments offers a full range of superior innovative technological services and expertise to the behavioral health industry. Our premier product, AccuCare Behavioral Healthcare System, was developed by teams of experts in their respective fields, insuring our products are truly useful to clinicians and are easy to use. This innovative software program is a comprehensive and adaptable approach to the behavioral health practice environment.

**2002 Analytic Learning Disability Assessment Computer Report**

**Southern Micro Systems**
**203 Woodley Avenue**
**Pratville, AL 36066**              **334-365-6560**
                          **FAX 334-365-6464**
                   **http://www.smsi.net**

This software provides an interpretation of the ALDA assessment results. The report describes to the professional the most efficient method for this child to learn the basic subjects of Reading, Spelling, Math and Handwriting. The report can be given to the professional or parent and may be used to design remedial approaches and improve academic functioning. *$195.00*

**2003 Beyond Drill and Practice: Expanding the Computer Mainstream**

**Council for Exceptional Children**
**1110 N Glebe Road**
**Arlington, VA 22201**              **703-620-3660**
                                     **888-232-7733**
                          **FAX 703-264-9494**
                  **http://www.cec.sped.org/**
*Drew Albitran M.D., Executive Director*

Provides informative guidelines and examples for teachers who want to expand the use of the computer as a learning tool. *$10.00*

*120 pages*

**2004 CE Software**

**PO Box 65580**
**West Des Moines, IA 50265**        **515-221-1801**
                          **FAX 515-221-1806**
                   **http://www.cesoft.com**
                **e-mail: sales@cesoft.com**
*Eric Conrad, Director*

International software developer. Many products for adaptive technology.

**2005 CRISP**

National Institute of Health
6701 Rockledge Drive
Bethesda, MD 20892          301-435-0650
                           FAX 301-480-2845
http://www.commons.cit.nih.gov\crisp
e-mail: commons@od.nih.gov
*Dorrette Finch, Dir. Div. Research Documentation*

A major scientific information system containing data on the research programs supported by the US Public Health Service.

**2006 Claris Corporation**

5201 Patrick Henry Drive
Santa Clara, CA 95054
                           800-325-2747
                           FAX 408-987-3932
Company that produces a variety of Macintosh Documentation.

**2007 Classification Series**

Aquarius Instructional
13064 Indian Rocks Road
Indian Rocks Beach, FL 33774    727-595-7890
                                800-338-2644
                           FAX 727-595-2685
http://www.philliproy.com
*Ruth Bragman, President*
*Philip Padole, Vice President*

Curriculum-based programs are learning units containing matching, sorting, form and object, and familiar settings. *$75.00*

**2008 Compass Learning**

9920 Pacific Heights Boulevard
San Diego, CA 92121          858-587-0087
                             800-422-4339
                           FAX 858-587-1629
http://www.compasslearning.com
e-mail: lkrauss@compasslearning.com
*Lynn Krauss, Chief Executive Officer*

Educational software for teachers of K-12.

**2009 Conover Company**

2926 Hidden Hollow Road
Oshkosh, WI 54904            920-231-4667
                           FAX 920-231-4809
http://www.conovercompany.com
e-mail: conover@execpc.com
*Kris Volkman, Software Developer*

**2010 DC Health and Company**

222 Berckly Street
Lexington, MA 02116          617-351-5000
                           FAX 617-351-1110
http://www.hm.co.com
*Anthony Lucki, Chief Executive Officer*

Helping people with learning disabilities.

**2011 Edmark Corporation**

PO Box 97021
Redmond, WA 98073            425-556-8400
                             800-362-2890
                           FAX 425-556-8430
http://www.edmark.com
e-mail: edmarkteam@edmark.com
*Ellie McCormack, Director of Public Relations*

**2012 Filling Out Job Applications**

Lawrence Productions
1800 S 35th Street
Galesburg, MI 49053          269-665-7075
                             800-421-4157
                           FAX 269-665-7060
http://www.lpi.com
e-mail: sales@lpi.com
*Holly Argue, Author*
*Edwin Wright, President*

Designed for adolescents and adults in basic education classes providing one step analysis and completion of typical job applications. *$29.95*

**2013 HEATH Resource Center People with Handicaps**

HEATH Resource Center
2121 K Street NW
Washington, DC 20036         202-973-0904
                             800-544-3284
                           FAX 202-973-0908
http://www.heath.gwu.edu
e-mail: askheath@gwu.edu
*Dan Gardner, Publications Manager*

*$1.00*

**2014 IEP Companion Software**

LinguiSystems
3100 4th Avenue
East Moline, IL 61244        309-775-2300
                             800-776-4332
                           FAX 309-755-2377
                           TDY:800-933-8331
http://www.linguisystems.com
e-mail: service@linguisystems.com
*Carolyn Wilson, Janet Lanza, Jeannie Evans, Author*
*Linda Bowers, Owner*
*Rosemary Huisingh, Owner*

Get IEP goals from the best-selling book with the click of your mouse. Writing complete reports is easy! You'll get to choose from hundreds of individual and classroom goals and objectives for all the important speech and language areas. Just click on the specific goals you want to create your individualized report. *$69.95*

*Birth-Adult*

**2015  Interest Driven Learning**
383 DeSoto Drive
New Smyna Beach, FL  32169          386-427-4473
                                     800-245-5733
                                FAX 386-426-0100
                            http://www.drpeet.com
                       e-mail: drpeet@drpect.com
*Bill Peet MD, CEO*

Our mission is to provide affordable low and high-tech tools that will help people of all ages and abilities learn to read, write and communicate with support from assistive technology as needed.

**2016  International Society for Technology in Education**
University of Oregon
15th Avenue & Kincaid
Eugene, OR  97403                    541-346-4705
                                FAX 541-346-0987
                            http://www.uoregon.edu
                           e-mail: iste@iste.org
*Dave Frohnmayer, President*
*Lorraine Davis, Vice President*

A nonprofit professional organization dedicated to promoting appropriate uses of information technology to support and improve learning, teaching, and administration in K-12 education and teacher education.

**2017  KidDesk**
Riverdeep
222 3rd Ave SE
Cedar Rapids, IA  52401              888-242-6747
                                     800-362-2890
                                FAX 800-567-2714
                            http://www.riverdeep.net

A hard disk security program, KidDesk makes it easy for kids to launch their programs, but impossible for them to access adult programs. Includes interactive desktop accessories including desktop-to-desktop electronic mail, and voice mail. *$24.95*

**2018  KidDesk: Family Edition**
Riverdeep
222 3rd Ave SE
Cedar Rapids, IA  52401              888-242-6747
                                     800-362-2890
                                FAX 800-567-2714
                            http://www.riverdeep.net

Now kids can launch their programs, but can't access yours! With KidDesk Family Edition, you can give your children the keys to the computer without putting your programs and files at risk! The auto-start option provides constant hard drive security — any time your computer is turned on, KidDesk will appear. *$24.95*

**2019  LD Teacher's IEP Companion Software**
LinguiSystems
3100 4th Avenue
East Moline, IL  61244               309-775-2300
                                     800-776-4332
                                FAX 309-755-2377
                               TDY:800-933-8331
                         http://www.linguisystems.com
                      e-mail: service@linguisystems.com
*Molly Lyle, Author*
*Linda Bowers, Owner*
*Rosemary Huisingh, Owner*

Create customized, professional reports with these terrific academic goals and objectives. You'll have individual objectives from nine skill areas at the click of your mouse! Save time with the software version of the best-selling book! For both PC and Macintosh. *$69.95*

*Ages 5-18*

**2020  Laureate Learning Systems**
110 E Spring Street
Winooski, VT  05404                  802-655-4755
                                     800-652-6801
                                FAX 802-655-4757
                         http://www.laureatelearning.com
                     e-mail: info@laureatelearning.com
*Mary Wilson, President*
*Bernard Fox, Vice President*

Provides resources for people with learning disabilities.

**2021  Learning Company**
Riverdeep
100 Pine Street
San Francisco, CA  94111             415-659-2000
                                     800-852-2255
                            http://www.riverdeep.net

**2022  Microsoft Corporation**
11800 31st Court N
St Petersburg, FL  33716             800-444-4443
                            http://www.microsoft.com
Mission is to enable people and businesses throughout the world to realize their full potential.

**2023  Print Module**
Failure Free
140 Cabarrus Avenue W
Concord, NC  28025                   314-569-0211
                                     800-221-1274
                                FAX 314-569-2834
                        e-mail: ffsales@concord.nc.com

Includes teacher's manual, instructional readers, flashcards, independent activities and illustrated independent reading booklets. *$499.00*

**2024  PsycINFO Database**
American Psychological Association
750 1st Street NE
Washington, DC  20002                202-336-5650
                                     800-374-2722
                                FAX 202-336-5633
                               TDY:202-336-6123
                               http://www.apa.org
                        e-mail: psycinfo@apa.org
*Marion Harrell, Deport Manager*
*Norman Anderson, Director*

An online abstract database that provides access to citations to the international serial literature in psychology and related disciplines from 1887 to present. Available via PsycINFO Direct at www.psycinfo.com.

**2025 Public Domain Software**

Kentucky Special Ed TechTraining Center
229 Taylor Education Building
Lexington, KY 40506     859-257-4713
FAX 859-257-1325
TDY:859-257-4714
http://www.serc.gws.uky.edu

Entire collections of Macintosh, MS-DOS or Apple II software.

**2026 Pugliese, Davey and Associates**

Adaptive Technology Institutes
5 Bessom Street
Marblehead, MA 01945     781-639-1930
FAX 781-631-9928
TDY:781-224-2521

*Madelaine Pugliesc*

Offers computer lab courses for Apple IIGS and Macintosh LC.

**2027 Riverdeep**

222 3rd Ave SE
Cedar Rapids, IA 52401     888-242-6747
800-362-2890
FAX 800-567-2714
http://www.riverdeep.net
*Ellie McCormack, Director of Public Relations*

**2028 Scholastic**

2931 E McCarty Street
Jefferson City, MO 65102     573-636-5271
800-541-5513
FAX 573-632-5271
http://www.scholastic.com
e-mail: larryholland@scholastic.com
*Richard Jefferson, President*
*Larry Holland, Director of Human Resources*

**2029 Sunburst Communications**

101 Castleton Street
Pleasantville, NY 10570     914-747-3310
800-338-3457
FAX 914-747-4109
http://www.sunburst.com
e-mail: service@nysunburst.com
*Mark Sotir, President*

**2030 Testmaster**

Research Design Associates
5 Main Street
Freeville, NY 13068     607-844-4601
FAX 607-844-3310

A new concept in question and answer testing with an Exploratory Mode which allows students to explore a range of answers. *$199.95*

**2031 The Speech Bin**

1965 25th Avenue
Vero Beach, FL 32960     772-770-0007
800-477-3324
FAX 888-329-2246
http://www.speechbin.com
e-mail: info@speechbin.com
*Shane Peters, Product Coordinator*
*Jen Binney, Owner*

The Speech Bin offers materials to help persons of all ages who have special needs. We specialize in products for children and adults who have communication disorders.

**2032 WPS Automated IEP System**

Western Psychological Services
12031 Wilshire Boulevard
Los Angeles, CA 90025     310-478-2061
800-648-8857
FAX 310-478-7838
http://www.wpspublish.com
*Greg Gilmar, Director*

This computer program substantially reduces the time educators spend on preparing Individualized Educational Plans (IEPs). The system allows the user to use any IEP format. Simply type the format into the computer, and the program will customize the system to your district's specifications. *$115.00*

# Reading

**2033 Adaptive Technology Tools**

Freedom Scientific
11800 31st Court N
St. Petersburg, FL 33716     727-803-8000
800-444-4443
FAX 727-803-8001
http://www.freedomscientific.com
e-mail: lhamilton@freedomscientific.com
*Lee Hamilton, CEO*

A wide variety of adaptive technology tools for the visually or reading impaired person.

**2034 An Open Book**

Freedom Scientific
11800 31st Court N
St Petersburg, FL 33716     727-803-8000
800-444-4443
FAX 727-803-8001
http://www.freedomscientific.com
*James Fruchterman, President*

The stand-alone reading machine, An Open Book, is an easy-to-use appliance for noncomputer users that comes equipped with a Hewlett Packard ScanJet IIP scanner, DECtalk PC speech synthesizer and a 17 key keypad. An Open Book uses Calera WordScan optical character recognition (OCR) to convert pages into text, then reads it aloud with a speech synthesizer.

**2035  An Open Book Unbound**

**Freedom Scientific**
**11800 31st Court N**
**St Petersburg, FL  33716**          727-803-8000
                                      800-444-4443
                                      FAX 727-803-8001
                    http://www.freedomscientific.com
*James Fruchterman, President*

PC-based OCR and reading software. Together with a scanner and a speech synthesizer, this software provides everything needed to make an IBM-compatible PC into a talking reading machine. The system includes automatic page orientation, automatic contrast control, decolumnization of multicolumn documents and recognition of a wide variety of type fonts and sizes. *$995.00*

**2036  Bailey's Book House**

**Riverdeep**
**222 3rd Ave SE**
**Cedar Rapids, IA  52401**          888-242-6747
                                     800-362-2890
                                     FAX 800-567-2714
                         http://www.riverdeep.net
*Tina Martin, Education Marketing*

The award-winning Bailey's Book House now features 2 new activities! Bailey and his friends encourage young children to build important literacy skills while developing a love for reading. In seven activities, kids explore the sounds and meanings of letters, words, sentences, rhymes and stories. No reading skills are required: all directions and written words are spoken. *$59.95*

**2037  Banner Books**

**Queue**
**1 Controls Drive**
**Shelton, CT  06432**               203-335-0906
                                     800-232-2224
                                     FAX 203-336-2481
                         http://www.queueinc.com
                       e-mail: jck@queueine.com
*Monica Kantrowitz, President*
*Peter Uhrynowski, Controller*

This is a format students and teachers will love. Students select a variety of backgrounds and watch as they move by on the screen. Students then add clip art and text to create their own Banner Book pages. Offers various programs. *$49.95*

**2038  Basic Reading Skills**

**Phillip Roy**
**13064 Indian Rocks Road**
**Indian Rocks Beach, FL  33774**    727-593-2700
                                     800-255-9085
                                     FAX 727-595-2685
                         http://www.philliproy.com
                       e-mail: info@philliproy.com
*Ruth Bragman, President*
*Philip Padole, Vice President*

These programs are designed to encourage students to learn and use critical thinking skills. *$550.00*

*21 disks*

**2039  Boars in Camelot**

**Queue**
**1 Controls Drive**
**Shelton, CT  06432**               203-335-0906
                                     800-232-2224
                                     FAX 203-336-2481
                         http://www.queueinc.com
                       e-mail: jdk@queueinc.com
*Judith White, President*
*Peter Uhrynowski, Controller*

Written in an upbeat and amusing style to capture students' interest as they interact with the story by answering questions about what they have read. *$45.00*

**2040  Comprehension Connection**

**Milliken Publishing**
**11643 Lilburn Park Road**
**St. Louis, MO  63146**             314-991-4220
                                     800-325-4136
                                     FAX 314-991-4807
                         http://www.milikenpub.com
*Thomas Sr., President*

Comprehension Connection improves reading comprehension by stressing basic skills that combine the reading process with relevant activities and interesting, thought-provoking stories. This award-winning software package spans six reading levels that increase in difficulty. Passages range from 150-300 words. *$150.00*

**2041  Compu-Teach**

**Compu-Teach**
**PMB 137, 16541 Redmond Way**
**Redmond, WA  16541**               425-885-0517
                                     800-448-3224
                                     FAX 425-883-9169
                         http://www.compu-teach.com
                    e-mail: durban@compu-teach.com
*David Urban, President*

Higher resolution graphics, digitized voice, MIDI music, animation and sound effects make this program one of America's favorites. Children have never had so much fun learning the basics of reading, language and math! Includes letter recognition, counting, adding and sentence structure. This wonderful series will provide an exciting learning experience for any child between the ages of 2 and 7. The bonus pack contains six separate learning activities which have won many software awards. *$59.95*

*Ages 4-7*

**2042  Cosmic Reading Journey**

**Sunburst Technology**
**400 Columbus Avenue**
**Valhalla, NY  10595 1349**         914-747-3310
                                     800-321-7511
                                     FAX 914-747-4109
                         http://www.sunburst.com
                     e-mail: support@sunburst.com
*Mark Sotir, President*

This reading comprehension program provides meaningful summary and writing activities for the 100 books that early readers and their teachers love most.

**2043   Don Johnston Reading**

Don Johnston
26799 W Commerce Drive
Volo, IL  60073                    847-740-0749
                                   800-999-4660
                              FAX 847-740-7326
                        http://www.donjohnston.com
                        e-mail: info@donjohnston.com
*Angie Leboigh, Marketing Director*

Don Johnston Inc. is a provider of quality products and services that enable people with special needs to discover their potential and experience success. Products are developed for the areas of computer access and for those who struggle with reading and writing.

**2044   Failure Free Reading**

140 Cabarrus Avenue W
Concord, NC  28025                 314-569-0211
                                   800-221-1274
                              FAX 314-569-2834
*Bill Sedergren, Vice President*
*Bob Fowles, VP Sales*

Curriculum areas covered: reading for those with learning disabilities and moderate mentally disabled/emotionally disabled.

**2045   Judy Lynn Software**

PO Box 373
East Brunswick, NJ  08816          507-780-1859
                              FAX 732-390-8845
                          http://www.judylynn.com
                    e-mail: webmaster@judylynn.com
*Elliot Pludwinski, President*
*Myra Pludwinski, VP*

Offers switch computer programs for windows.The programs are geared towards children with a cognitive age level from 9 months to 4 years. Programs use bright colorful animation with captivating sounds to maintain attention span. Programs are reasonably priced from $20-$39. Recipient of a Parents' Choice Honor.

**2046   Kurzweil 3000**

Kurzweil Educational Systems
14 Crosby Drive
Bedford, MA  01730                 781-276-0600
                          http://www.kurzweiledu.com
                     e-mail: info@kurzweiledu.cc
*Christina Newman, Marketing Communications Manager*

Kurzweil Educational's flagship product for struggling readers and writers. It is widely recognized as the most comprehensive and integrated solution for addressing language and literacy difficulties. The software uses a multisensory approach — presenting printed or electronic text on the computer screen with added visual and audible accessibility. The product incorporates a host of dynamic features including powerful decoding, study skills tools and test taking tools.

**2047   Level II: Strategies for Older Students/Reading SOS**

Lexia Learning Systems
2 Lewis Street
Lincoln, MA  01773                 781-259-8752
                                   800-435-3942
                              FAX 781-259-1349
                        http://www.lexialearning.com
                     e-mail: info@lexialearning.com
*John Bower, President*

Five units with 65 branching activities and practice with 295 one-syllable words. *$250.00*

**2048   Level III: Phonics Based Reading-Grades 1, 2 & 3**

Lexia Learning Systems
2 Lewis Street
Lincoln, MA  01773                 781-259-8752
                                   800-435-3942
                              FAX 781-259-1349
                        http://www.lexialearning.com
                     e-mail: info@lexialearning.com
*John Bower, President*

Five activity areas with 64 branching units and practice with 535 one-syllable words and 90 two-syllable words. *$50.00*

**2049   Level IV: Reading Strategies for Older Students Grades 4, 5 & 6**

Lexia Learning Systems
2 Leis Street
Lincoln, MA  01773                 781-259-8752
                                   800-435-3942
                              FAX 781-259-1349
                        http://www.lexialearning.com
                     e-mail: info@lexialearning.com
*John Bower, President*

Four units with 60 branching activities focusing on two-syllable words with six syllable types, hard and soft c and g, construction of three-syllable words, reading comprehension with word attack strategies. *$250.00*

**2050   Lexia Early Reading: Lexia Phonics Based Reading, Reading Stategies for Older Students**

Lexia Learning Systems
PO Box 466
Lincoln, MA  01773                 781-259-8752
                                   800-435-3942
                              FAX 781-259-1349
                        http://www.lexialearning.com
                     e-mail: info@lexialearning.com
*John Bower, President*

Lexia's skill development assessment software helps children and adults with learning disabilities master their core reading skills. Based on the Orton-Gillingham method, Lexia Early reading, Phonics Based Reading and S.O.S. (Strategies for Older Students) apply phonics principles to help students learn essential sound-symbol correspondence and decoding skills.

**2051 Mike Mulligan & His Steam Shovel**
**Sunburst Technology**
**400 Columbus Avenue**
**Valhalla, NY 10595 1349**          **914-747-3310**
                                     **800-321-7511**
                               **FAX 914-747-4109**
                          **http://www.sunburst.com**
                    **e-mail: service@sunburst.com**
*Mark Sotir, President*

This CD-ROM version of the Caldecott classic lets students experience interactive book reading and participate in four skills-based extension activities that promote memory, matching, sequencing, listening, pattern recognition and map reading skills.

**2052 Optimum Resource**
**18 Hunter Road**
**Hilton Head Island, SC 29926**          **843-689-8000**
                                          **888-784-2592**
                                    **FAX 843-689-8008**
                          **http://www.stickybear.com**
                    **e-mail: stickyb@stickybear.com**
*Christopher Gintz, COO*
*Robert Stangroom, Product Manager*

An educational software publishing company for grades K-12. Our software titles are available in Consumer, School, Labpack or Site License versions. Please call for further details. Prices range from $59.95 for Consumer to $699.95 for Site Licenses.

**2053 Polar Express**
**Sunburst Technology**
**400 Columbus Avenue**
**Valhalla, NY 10595 1349**          **914-747-3310**
                                     **800-321-7511**
                               **FAX 914-747-4109**
                          **http://www.sunburst.com**
                    **e-mail: service@sunburst.com**
*Mark Sotir, President*

Share the magic and enchantment of the holiday season with this CD-ROM version of Chris Van Allsburg's Caldecott-winning picture book.

**2054 Prolexia**
**4726 13th Avenue NW**
**Rochester, MN 55901**          **507-780-1859**
                                 **888-776-5394**
                           **FAX 507-252-0131**
                      **http://www.prolexia.com**
                 **e-mail: info@prolexia.com**

Reading education softeare simulating actual Orton-Gillingham one-on-one tutoring.

**2055 Read On! Plus**
**Sunburst Technology**
**400 Columbus Avenue**
**Valhalla, NY 10595 1349**          **914-747-3310**
                                     **800-321-7511**
                               **FAX 914-747-4109**
                          **http://www.sunburst.com**
                    **e-mail: support@sunburst.com**
*Mark Sotir, President*

Promote skills and strategies that improve reading comprehension, and build appreciation for literature and the written word.

**2056 Read, Write and Type Learning System**
**Talking Fingers**
**1 Saint Vincent Drive**
**San Rafael, CA 94903**          **415-472-3104**
                                  **800-674-9126**
                            **FAX 415-472-7812**
                            **TDY:415-472-3106**
                      **http://www.readwritetype.com**
                 **e-mail: info@talkingfingers.com**
*Kris Kuedler, Chief Financial Officer*

A 40-level software adventure providing highly motivating instruction and practice in phonics, reading, writing, spelling and typing. This multisensory program includes 9 levels of assessment and reports. Classroom packs available.

**2057 Reading Power Modules Books**
**Steck-Vaughn Company**
**PO Box 690789**
**Orlando, FL 32819**          **407-345-3800**
                               **800-225-5425**
                         **FAX 800-269-5232**
                    **http://www.steck-vaughn.com**
               **e-mail: info@steck-vaughn.com**
*Connie Alden, Vice President of Human Resource*
*Michael Ruecker, Vice President of Human Resource*

Supplementary reading based on 4 decades of reading research. Companion books give students and teachers a choice of formats. High interest stories reinforce reading comprehension skills while building vocabulary, spelling skills, reading fluency, and speed.

**2058 Reading Realities Elementary Series**
**Teacher Support Software**
**3542 NW 97th Boulevard**
**Gainesville, FL 32606**          **352-332-6404**
                                   **800-228-2871**
                             **FAX 352-332-6779**
                        **http://www.tssoftware.com**
*Ruth Smith, Educational Software Consultant*

Students will read about topics that focus on issues they face in their everyday lives. Over 1000 students contributed stories that make up the program. Students will benefit from prereading, reading and follow-up activities in a directed reading-thinking format. The manager tracks reading ability and class and student progress. Vocabulary support and speech make this a nonthreatening atmosphere for sharing and learning.

**2059 Reading Skills Bundle**
**Sunburst Technology**
**400 Columbus Avenue**
**Valhalla, NY 10595 1349**          **914-747-3310**
                                     **800-321-7511**
                               **FAX 914-747-4109**
                          **http://www.sunburst.com**
                    **e-mail: support@sunburst.com**
*Mark Sotir, President*

Teach beginning reading with teacher-developed programs that sequentially present phonics, phonemic awareness, word recognition, and reading comprehension concepts.

**2060    Reading Who? Reading You!**

**Sunburst Technology**
**400 Columbus Avenue**
**Valhalla, NY  10595 1349**          **914-747-3310**
                                      **800-321-7511**
                              **FAX 914-747-4109**
                        **http://www.sunburst.com**
                     **e-mail: support@sunburst.com**
*Mark Sotir, President*

Teach beginning reading skills effectively with phonics instruction built into engaging games and puzzles that have children asking for more.

**2061    Roots, Prefixes & Suffixes**

**Sunburst Technology**
**400 Columbus Avenue**
**Valhalla, NY  10595 1349**          **914-747-3310**
                                      **800-321-7511**
                              **FAX 914-747-4109**
                        **http://www.sunburst.com**
                     **e-mail: support@sunburst.com**
*Mark Sotir, President*

Students learn to decode difficult and more complex words as they engage in six activities where they construct and dissect words with roots, prefixes and suffixes.

**2062    Sentence Master: Level 1, 2, 3, 4**

**Laureate Learning Systems**
**110 E Spring Street**
**Winooski, VT  05404**               **802-655-4755**
                                      **800-562-6801**
                              **FAX 802-655-4757**
              **e-mail: info@laureatelearning.com**
*Mary Wilson, President*
*Bernard Fox, VP*

A revolutionary way to teach beginning reading. Avoiding the confusing rules of phonics and the complexity of whole language, The Sentence Master focuses on the most frequently-used words of our language; i.e. the, is, but, and, etc., by truly teaching these little words, The Sentence Master gives students control over the majority of text they will ever encounter. *$475.00*

**2063    Simon Sounds It Out**

**Don Johnston**
**26799 W Commerce Dive**
**Volo, IL  60073**                   **847-740-0749**
                                      **800-999-4660**
                              **FAX 847-740-7326**
                     **http://www.donjohnston.com**
                   **e-mail: info@donjohnston.com**
*Angie Leboigh, Marketing Director*

Struggling students who can recite the alphabet and recognize letters on a page may still have trouble making connections between letters and sounds. This creates a barrier to recognizing and learning words which prevents your students from reading and writing successfully. Simon Sounds It Out provides the vital practice and repetition they need to overcome the letter-to-sound barrier. *$59.00*

**2064    Stickybear Software**

**Optimum Resource**
**18 Hunter Road**
**Hilton Head Island, SC  29926**     **843-689-8000**
                                      **888-784-2592**
                              **FAX 843-689-8008**
                        **http://www.stickybear.com**
                   **e-mail: stickyb@stickybear.com**
*Christopher Gintz, COO*
*Robert Stangroom, Product Manager*

An educational software publishing company for grades K-12. Our software titles are available in Consumer, School, Labpack or Site License versions. Please call for further details. Prices range from $59.95 for Consumer to $699.95 for Site Licenses.

**2065    Time for Teachers Online**

**Stern Center for Language and Learning**
**135 Allen Brook Lane**
**Williston, VT  05495**              **802-878-2332**
                                      **800-544-4863**
                              **FAX 802-878-0230**
                        **http://www.sterncenter.org**
                 **e-mail: learning@sterncenter.org**
*Blanch Podhajsk MD, President*
*Mary Stifler, Vice President*

A 45 hour course completed entirely on the internet, designed to help teachers implement research-based best practices in reading instruction. *$525.00*

## Science

**2066    Changes Around Us CD-ROM**

**Steck-Vaughn Company**
**PO Box 690789**
**Orlando, FL  32819**                **407-345-3800**
                                      **800-225-5425**
                              **FAX 800-269-5232**
                        **http://www.steck-vaughn.com**
                   **e-mail: info@steck-vaughn.com**
*Connie Alden, Vice President of Human Resource*
*Michael Ruecker, Vice President of Human Resource*

Nature is the natural choice for observing change. By observing and researching dramatic visual sequences such as the stages of development of a butterfly, children develop a broad understanding of the concept of change. As they search this multimedia database for images and information about plant and animal life cycles and seasonal change, students strengthen their abilities in research, analysis, problem-solving, critical thinking and communication.

**2067  Exploring Heat**
TERC
2067 Massachusetts Avenue
Cambridge, MA  02140          617-547-0430
                             FAX 617-349-3535
                   http://www.terc.edu
              e-mail: communications@terc.edu
*Dennis Partels, President*
*Sarah Glatt, Administrative Assistant*

A combination of lessons, software, temperature probes and activity sheets, specifically designed for the learning disabled child. *$160.00*

**2068  Field Trip Into the Sea**
Sunburst Technology
400 Columbus Avenue
Valhalla, NY  10595 1349      914-747-3310
                             800-321-7511
                       FAX 914-747-4109
                   http://www.sunburst.com
                   e-mail: service@sunburst
*Mark Sotir, President*

Visit a kelp forest and the rocky shore with this information packed guide that lets your students learn about the plants, animals and habitats of coastal environments.

**2069  Field Trip to the Rain Forest**
Sunburst Technology
400 Columbus Avenue
Valhalla, NY  10595 1349      914-747-3310
                             800-321-7511
                       FAX 914-747-4109
                   http://www.sunburst.com
                   e-mail: service@sunburst
*Mark Sotir, President*

Visit a Central American rainforest to learn more about its plants and animals with this dynamic research program that includes a useful information management tool.

**2070  Learn About Life Science: Animals**
Sunburst Technology
400 Columbus Avenue
Valhalla, NY  10595 1349      914-747-3310
                             800-321-7511
                       FAX 914-747-4109
                   http://www.sunburst.com
                   e-mail: service@sunburst.com
*Mark Sotir, President*

Learn about animal classification, adaptation to climate, domestication and special relationships between humans and animals.

**2071  Learn About Life Science: Plants**
Sunburst Technology
400 Columbus Avenue
Valhalla, NY  10595 1349      914-747-3310
                             800-321-7511
                       FAX 914-747-4109
                   http://www.sunburst.com
                   e-mail: service@sunburst.com
*Mark Sotir, President*

Students explore the world of plants. From small seeds to tall trees students learn what plants are and what they need to grow.

**2072  Milliken Science Series: Circulation and Digestion**
Milliken Publishing
11643 Liburn Park Raod
Saint Louis, MO  63146        314-991-4220
                             800-325-4136
                       FAX 314-991-4807
                   http://www.milikenpub.com
*Delores Boufard, Author*
*Thomas Moore, President*

A program designed to introduce students to two subsystems of the human body. Provides practice using the correct terms for the various organs that make up each system, illustrating how the parts of each subsystem work together, and ensuring that students can explain the functions of the subsystems and their parts.

**2073  NOMAD Graphics Packages**
American Printing House for the Blind
1839 Frankfort Avenue
Louisville, KY  40206         502-895-2405
                             800-223-1839
                       FAX 502-899-2274
                   http://www.aph.org
                   e-mail: info@aph.org
*Fred Gissoni, Customer Support*
*Kathy Smiddy, Executive Secretary*

Offers a variety of ready-made graphics as well as preprogrammed computer files, for use with NOMAD Talking Touch Pad. Topics include geography, orientation and mobility, and Star Trek.

**2074  Sammy's Science House**
Riverdeep
222 3rd Ave SE
Cedar Rapids, IA  52401       888-242-6747
                             800-362-2986
                       FAX 800-567-2714
                   http://www.riverdeep.net
*Tina Martin, Education Marketing*

Developed by early learning experts, the award-winning Sammy's Science House builds important early science skills, encourages wonder and joy as children discover the world of science around them. Five engaging activities help children practice sorting, sequencing, observing, predicting and constructing. They'll learn about plants, animals, minerals, fun seasons and weather, too! *$59.95*

**2075 Talking Walls**

**Riverdeep**
**500 Redmond Boulevard**
**Novato, CA 94947**          **415-763-4700**
                             **800-362-2890**
                      **FAX 415-763-4385**
                   **http://www.elmark.com**
                 **e-mail: info@riverdeep.net**
*Barry O'Callaghan, Chairman/CEO*
*Simon Calver, COO*
*John Rim, CFO*

The Talking Walls Software Series is a wonderful springboard for a student's journey of exploration and discovery. This comprehensive collection of researched resources and materials enables students to focus on learning while conducting a guided search for information.

**2076 Talking Walls: The Stories Continue**

**Riverdeep**
**500 Redmond Boulevard**
**Novato, CA 94947**          **415-763-4700**
                             **800-362-2890**
                      **FAX 415-763-4385**
                   **http://www.elmark.com**
                 **e-mail: info@riverdeep.net**
*Barry O'Callaghan, Chairman/CEO*
*Simon Calver, COO*
*John Rim, CFO*

Using the Talking Walls Software Series, students discover the stories behind some of the world's most fascinating walls. The award-winning books, interactive software, carefully chosen Web sites, and suggested classroom activities build upon each other, providing a rich learning experience that includes text, video, and hands-on projects.

## Social Studies

**2077 Discoveries: Explore the Desert Ecosystem**

**Sunburst Technology**
**400 Columbus Avenue**
**Valhalla, NY 10595 1349**       **914-747-3310**
                                 **800-321-7511**
                          **FAX 914-747-4109**
                       **http://www.sunburst.com**
                   **e-mail: service@sunburst.com**
*Mark Sotir, President*

This program invites students to explore the plants, animals, culture and georgraphy of the Sonoran Desert by day and by night.

**2078 Discoveries: Explore the Everglades Ecosystem**

**Sunburst Technology**
**400 Columbus Avenue**
**Valhalla, NY 10595 1349**       **914-747-3310**
                                 **800-321-7511**
                          **FAX 914-747-4109**
                       **http://www.sunburst.com**
                   **e-mail: service@sunburst.com**
*Mark Sotir, President*

This multi curricular research program takes students to the Everglades where they anchor their exploration photo realistic panaramas of the habitiat.

**2079 Discoveries: Explore the Forest Ecosystem**

**Sunburst Technology**
**400 Columbus Avenue**
**Valhalla, NY 10595 1349**       **914-747-3310**
                                 **800-321-7511**
                          **FAX 914-747-4109**
                       **http://www.sunburst.com**
                   **e-mail: service@sunburst.com**
*Mark Sotir, President*

This theme based CD-ROM enables students of all abilities to actively research a multitude of different forest ecosystems in the Appalachian National Park.

**2080 Imagination Express: Castle**

**Riverdeep**
**222 3rd Ave SE**
**Cedar Rapids, IA 52401**        **888-242-6747**
                                 **800-362-2986**
                          **FAX 800-567-2714**
                    **http://www.riverdeep.net**

Kids enter a medieval kingdom where knights, jesters, wild boars and falconers become actors in their own interactive stories. As kids cast characters, develop plots, narrate and write and record dialogue, they become enthusiastic writers, editors, producers and publishers! *$59.95*

**2081 Imagination Express: Neighborhood**

**Riverdeep**
**222 3rd Ave SE**
**Cedar Rapids, IA 52401**        **888-242-6747**
                                 **800-362-2986**
                          **FAX 800-567-2714**
                    **http://www.riverdeep.net**

In Destination: Neighborhood, familiar settings and characters encourage kids to write about actual or imagined adventures. Kids enjoy developing creativity, writing and communication skills as they explore the neighborhood and all the people who live there. As kids select scenes, choose and animate stickers, write, narrate, add music and record dialogue, their stories, journals, letters and poems come alive! *$59.95*

**2082 Imagination Express: Ocean**

**Riverdeep**
**222 3rd Ave SE**
**Cedar Rapids, IA 52401**        **888-242-6747**
                                 **800-362-2986**
                          **FAX 800-567-2714**
                    **http://www.riverdeep.net**

The fascinating shores and depths of Destination: Ocean inspire kids to create interactive stories and movies. Using exciting new technology, kids make stickers move across each scene: sharks swim through the sea kelp while dolphins leap above waves! With Destination: Ocean, your child's writing and creativity will soar! *$59.95*

**2083 Imagination Express: Pyramids**

Riverdeep
222 3rd Ave SE
Cedar Rapids, IA 52401          888-242-6747
                              800-362-2986
                         FAX 800-567-2714
                     http://www.riverdeep.net

Kids can create interactive electronic books and movies featuring pharaohs, mummies and life on the Nile. Builds writing, creativity and communication skills as they learn about and explore this captivating destination. Kids select scenes, choose and animate characters, plan plots, write stories, narrate pages and add music, dialogue and sound effects to make their own adventures. *$59.95*

**2084 Imagination Express: Rain Forest**

Riverdeep
222 3rd Ave SE
Cedar Rapids, IA 52401          888-242-6747
                              800-362-2986
                         FAX 800-567-2714
                     http://www.riverdeep.net

Rain Forest invities kids to step into a Panamanian rain forest, where they craft exciting, interactive adventures filled with exotic plants, insects, waterfalls and Kuna Indians. Kids build essential communication skills as they select scenes and characters, plan plots, write, narrate, animate and record dialogue to create remarkable adventures! *$59.95*

**2085 Imagination Express: Time Trip USA**

Riverdeep
222Box 97021
Cedar Rapids, IA 52401          888-242-6747
                              800-362-2986
                         FAX 800-567-2714
                     http://www.riverdeep.net

Children will love traveling through time to create interactive electronic books and movies set in a fictional New England town. As students select scenes, cast charcters, develop plots, narrate, write and record dialogue, they'll bring the town's history to life through their own exciting adventures. *$59.95*

**2086 NOMAD Graphics Packages**

American Printing House for the Blind
1839 Frankfort Avenue
Louisville, KY 40206            502-895-2405
                              800-223-1839
                         FAX 502-899-2274
                         http://www.aph.org
                       e-mail: info@aph.org
*Fred Gissoni, Customer Support*
*Kathy Smiddy, Executive Secretary*

Offers a variety of ready-made graphics as well as pre-programmed computer files, for use with NOMAD Talking Touch Pad. Topics include geography, orientation and mobility, and Star Trek.

## Speech

**2087 Eden Institute Curriculum: Speech and Language, Volume IV**

One Eden Way
Princeton, NJ 08540            609-987-0099
                         FAX 609-987-0243
                   http://www.edenservices.org
                   e-mail: info@edenservices.org
*David Holmes, Executive Director/President*
*Anne Holmes, Director Outreach Support*

Peceptive, expressive and pragmatic language skills programs for students with autism. *$170.00*

**2088 Spectral Speech Analysis: Software**

Speech Bin
1965 25th Avenue
Vero Beach, FL 32960           772-770-0007
                         FAX 772-770-0006
                    http://www.speechbin.com
                    e-mail: info@speechbin.com
*Shane Peter, Product Coordinator*
*Jenny Binney, Owner*

This exciting new software uses visual feedback as an effective speech treatment tool. Speech-language pathologists can record speech and corresponding visual displays for clients who then try to match either auditory or visual targets. These built-in visual patterns can be displayed as either sophisticated spectrograms or real-time waveforms. Item number P227. *$159.95*

## Word Processors

**2089 Braille' n Speak Classic**

American Printing House for the Blind
1839 Frankfort Avenue
Louisville, KY 40206           502-895-2405
                              800-223-1839
                         FAX 502-899-2274
                         http://www.aph.org
                       e-mail: info@aph.org
*Fred Gissoni, Customer Support*
*Kathy Smiddy, Executive Secretary*

This computerized, talking device has many features useful to student and adult braille users (word processors, print-to-braille translators, talking clocks/calculators and much more). *$929.95*

**2090 Kids Media Magic 2.0**

Sunburst Technology
400 Columbus Avenue
Valhalla, NY 10595             914-747-3310
                              800-321-7511
                         FAX 914-747-4109
                       http://www.sunburst.com
                    e-mail: service@sunburst.com
*Mark Sotir, President*

The first multimedia word processor designed for young children. Help your child become a fluent reader and writer. The Rebus Bar automatically scrolls over 45 vocabulary words as students type.

**2091  Media Weaver 3.5**
Sunburst Technology
400 Columbus Avenue
Valhalla, NY  10595 1349           914-747-3310
                                   800-321-7511
                              FAX 914-747-4109
                         http://www.sunburst.com
                    e-mail: support@sunburst.com
*Mark Sotir, President*

Publishing becomes a multimedia event with this dynamic word processor that contains hundreds of media elements and effective process writing resources.


**2092  Sunbuddy Writer**
Sunburst Technology
400 Columbus Avenue
Valhalla, NY  10595 1349           914-747-3310
                                   800-321-7511
                              FAX 914-747-4109
                         http://www.sunburst.com
                    e-mail: support@sunburst.com
*Mark Sotir, President*

An easy-to-use picture and word processor designed especially for young writers.


**2093  Write: Outloud**
Don Johnston
26799 W Commerce Drive
Volo, IL  60073                    847-740-0749
                                   800-999-4660
                              FAX 847-740-7326
                       http://www.donjohnston.com
                    e-mail: info@donjohnston.com
*Angie Leboigh, Marketing Director*

A flexible and user-friendly talking word processor that offers multisensory learning and positive reinforcement for writers of all ages and ability levels. Powerful features include a talking spell checker, on-screen speech and file management and color capabilities that allow for customization to meet individual needs or preferences. Requires Macintosh computer. Voted Best Special Needs Product by the Software Publishers Association. *$99.00*

---

## Writing

---

**2094  Abbreviation/Expansion**
Zygo Industries
PO Box 1008
Portland, OR  97207
                                   800-234-6006
                         http://www.zygo-usa.com
Allows the individual to define and store word/phrase abbreviations to achieve efficiency and accelerated entry rate of text. *$95.00*


**2095  Author's Toolkit**
Sunburst Technology
400 Columbus Avenue
Valhalla, NY  10595 1349           914-747-3310
                                   800-321-7511
                              FAX 914-747-4109
                         http://www.sunburst.com
                    e-mail: support@sunburst.com
*Mark Sotir, President*

Students can use this comprehensive tool to organize ideas, make outlines, rough drafts, edit and print all their written work.


**2096  Dr. Peet's Picture Writer**
Dr. Peet's Software
4241 Aldrich Avenue
Minneapolis, MN  55409             612-827-8060
                                   800-354-2950
                              FAX 386-426-0100
                          http://www.drpeet.com
                     e-mail: wpeet@drpeet.com
A talking picture-writer. It guides novice writers, regardless of age, motivation or ability, in creating simple talking picture sentences about things that are interesting and important to them. *$500.00*


**2097  Easybook Deluxe**
Sunburst Technology
400 Columbus Avenue
Valhalla, NY  10595 1349           914-747-3310
                                   800-321-7511
                              FAX 914-747-4109
                         http://www.sunburst.com
                    e-mail: service@sunburst.com
*Mark Sotir, President*

Designed to support the needs of a wide range of writers, this book publishing tool provides students with a creative environment to write, design and illustrate stories and reports, and to print their work in book formats.


**2098  Fonts 4 Teachers**
Therapro
225 Arlington Street
Framingham, MA  01702 8723         508-872-9494
                                   800-257-5376
                              FAX 508-875-2062
                      http://www.theraproducts.com
                   e-mail: info@theraproducts.com
*Karen Conrad, President*

A software collection of 31 True Type fonts for teachers, parents and students. Fonts include Tracing, lined and unlined Traditional Manuscript and Cursive (similar to Zaner Blouser and D'Nealian), math, clip art, decorative, time, American Sign Language symbols and more. The included manual is very informative, with great examples of lesson plans and educational goals. *$39.95*

*Windows/Mac*

**2099  Great Beginnings**

**Teacher Support Software**
**3542 NW 97th Boulevard**
**Gainesville, FL  32606**                    352-332-6404
                                              800-228-2871
                                         FAX 352-332-6779
                              http://www.tssoftware.com
                              e-mail: tssoftware.com
*Ruth Smith, Educational Software Consultant*

From a broad selection of topics and descriptive words, students may create their own stories and illustrate them with colorful graphics. *$69.95*

**2100  Language Experience Recorder**

**Teacher Support Software**
**3542 NW 97th Boulevard**
**Gainesville, FL  32606**                    352-332-6404
                                              800-228-2871
                                         FAX 352-332-6779
                              http://www.tssoftware.com
                              e-mail: tssoftware.com
*Ruth Smith, Educational Software Consultant*

This program provides students with the opportunity to read, write and hear their own experience stories. Analyzes student writing. Cumulative word list, word and sentence counts and readability estimate. *$99.95*

**2101  Once Upon a Time Volume I: Passport to Discovery**

**Compu-Teach**
**PMB 137, 16541 Redmond Way**
**Redmond, WA  98052**                        425-885-0517
                                              800-448-3224
                                         FAX 425-883-9169
                              http://www.compu-teach.com
                              e-mail: durban@compu-teach.com
*David Urban, President*
*Pat Donaven, Administrative Assistant*

Features familiar objects associated with three unique themes. These graphic images offer limitless possibilities for new stories and illustrations. As children author books from one to hundreds of pages, they can either display them on screen or print them out. Themes: Farm Life; Down Main Street; and On Safari. *$59.95*

*Ages 4-12*

**2102  Once Upon a Time Volume II: Worlds of Enchantment**

**Compu-Teach**
**PMB 137, 16541 Redmond Way**
**Redmond, WA  98052**                        425-885-0517
                                              800-448-3224
                                         FAX 425-883-9169
                              http://www.compu-teach.com
                              e-mail: durban@compu-teach.com
*David Urban, President*
*Pat Donaven, Administrative Assistant*

Makes writing, reading and vocabulary skills easy to learn. While building their illustrations, children experiment with perspective and other spatial relationships. This volume features familiar objects associated with three unique themes: Underwater; Dinosaur Age; and Forest Friends. *$59.95*

*Ages 4-12*

**2103  Once Upon a Time Volume III: Journey Through Time**

**Compu-Teach**
**PMB 137, 16541 Redmond Way**
**Redmond, WA  98052**                        425-885-0517
                                              800-448-3224
                                         FAX 425-883-9169
                              http://www.compu-teach.com
                              e-mail: durban@compu-teach.com
*David Urban, President*
*Pat Donaven, Administrative Assistant*

Makes writing, reading and vocabulary skills easy to learn. With imagination as a youngster's only guide, the important concepts of story creation and illustration are naturally discovered. Themes: Medieval Times, Wild West and Outer Space. *$59.95*

*Ages 4-12*

**2104  Once Upon a Time Volume IV: Exploring Nature**

**Compu-Teach**
**PMB 137, 16541 Redmond Way**
**Redmond, WA  98052**                        425-885-0517
                                              800-448-3224
                                         FAX 425-883-9169
                              http://www.compu-teach.com
                              e-mail: durban@compu-teach.com
*David Urban, President*
*Pat Donaven, Administrative Assistant*

The latest in award-winning creative writing series. Kids just hear, click and draw as the state of the art graphics and digitized voice make writing, reading and vocabulary skills easy to learn. Themes: Rain Forest; African Grasslands; Ocean; Desert; and Forest. *$59.95*

**2105  Raised Dot Computing Mega Dots**

**Duxbury Systems**
**270 Littleton Road**
**Westford, MA  01886**                       978-692-3000
                                              800-347-9594
                                         FAX 978-692-7912
                              http://www.buxyburdux.com
                              e-mail: joe@duxsys.com
*Joe Sullivan, President*

MegaDots is a mature DOS braille translator with powerful features for the volume transcriber and producer. Its straightforward, style based system and automated features let you create great braille with only a few keystrokes, yet it is sophisticated enough to please the fussiest braille producers. You can control each step MegaDots follows to format, translate and produce braille documents. *$540.00*

**2106  Read, Write and Type Learning System**

**Talking Fingers, California Neuropsych Services**
**1st Saint Vincents Drive**
**San Rafael, CA  94903**                     415-472-3104
                                              800-674-9126
                                         FAX 415-472-7812
                              http://www.readwritetype.com
                              e-mail: info@talkingfingers.com

A 40-level software adventure providing highly motivating instruction and practice in phonics, reading, writing, spelling and typing. This multisensory program includes 9 levels of assessment and reports. Classroom packs available.

**2107 StartWrite**

Therapro
225 Arlington Street
Framingham, MA  01702 8723          508-872-9494
                                     800-257-5376
                                  FAX 508-875-2062
                          http://www.theraproducts.com
                          e-mail: info@theraproducts.com
*Therapro Staff, Author*
*Karen Conrad, President*

With this easy-to-use software package, you can make
papers and handwriting worksheets to meet individual
student's needs. Type letters, words, or numbers and
they appear in a dot format on the triple line guide.
Change letter size, add shading, turn on or off guide
lines and arrow strokes and place provided clipart.
Fonts include Manuscript and Cursive, Modern Manuscript and Cursive and Italic Manuscript and Cursive.
Useful manual included. *$39.95*

*Windows/Mac*

**2108 Wish Writer**

Consultants for Communication Technology
508 Bellevue Terrace
Pittsburgh, PA  15202          412-761-6062
                            FAX 412-761-7336
              e-mail: 70272.1034@compuserve.com
*Kathleen Miller PhD, Partner/Speech Pathologist*
*Jaime Olivia, Partner*

Wish Writer is a word processing program designed to
be used by keyboard or single switch users. Word Prediction feature produces documents with fewer keystrokes. When used with the K, S, or multivoice
synthesizers, text typed into the PC can be spoken or
printed. *$300.00*

**2109 Writing Trek Grades 4-6**

Sunburst Technology
400 Columbus Avenue
Valhalla, NY  10595 1349          914-747-3310
                                   800-321-7511
                                FAX 914-747-4109
                          http://www.sunburst.com
                          e-mail: service@sunburst.com
*Mark Sotir, President*

Enhance your students' experience in your English
language arts classroom with twelve authentic writing
projects that build students' competence while encouraging creativity.

**2110 Writing Trek Grades 6-8**

Sunburst Technology
400 Columbus Avenue
Valhalla, NY  10595 1349          914-747-3310
                                   800-321-7511
                                FAX 914-747-4109
                          http://www.sunburst.com
                          e-mail: service@sunburst.com
*Mark Sotir, President*

Twelve authentic language arts projects, activities,
and assignments develop your students' writing confidence and ability.

**2111 Writing Trek Grades 8-10**

Sunburst Technology
400 Columbus Avenue
Valhalla, NY  10595 1349          914-747-3310
                                   800-321-7511
                                FAX 914-747-4109
                          http://www.sunburst.com
                          e-mail: service@sunburst.com
*Mark Sotir, President*

Help your students develop a concept of genre as they
become familiar with the writing elements and characteristics of a variety of writing forms.

## General

**2112** **American Institute for Foreign Study**
River Plaza
Stamford, CT  06902          203-399-5000
FAX 203-399-5590
http://www.aifs.com
e-mail: info@aifs.com
*William Gertz, President*

Provides summer travel programs overseas and in the US ranging from one week to a full academic year.

**2113** **American Universities International Program**
108 South Main St
Winterville, GA  30683          706-742-9285
http://www.auip.com
e-mail: info@auip.com

One hundred colleges and universities throughout the USA and Canada that participate in exchange programs.

**2114** **American-Scandinavian Foundation**
58 Park Avenue
New York, NY  10016          212-879-9779
FAX 212-686-2115
http://www.amscan.org
e-mail: info@amscan.org
*Jean Prahl, Director Training*

Offers young US citizens the opportunity to live in Scandinavia and train in their professional field.

**2115** **Association for International Practical Training**
10400 Little Patuxent Parkway
Columbia, MD  21044 3510          410-997-2200
FAX 410-992-3924
http://www.aipt.org
e-mail: aipt@aipt.org
*Jackson Janes MD, Executive Director*
*Cathleen , Associate Director*
*Lynn Van Norstrand, Financial Officer*

Be a leader in international human resource development by conducting high-quality international experiential training exchanges that enhance the ability of individual participants, employers, and host organizations to meet the opportunities and challenges of the global economy.

**2116** **Earthstewards Network**
PO Box 10697
Bainbridge Island, WA  98110          206-842-7986
800-561-2909
FAX 206-842-8918
http://www.earthstewards.org
e-mail: outreach@earthstewards.org
*Beverly Boos, Vice President*
*Chuck Meadows, Treasurer*

Hundreds of active, caring people in the US, Canada and other countries. Puts North American teenagers working alongside Northern Irish teenagers and more.

**2117** **Educational Foundation for Foreign Study**
1 Education Street
Cambridge, MA  02141          617-619-1000
800-447-4273
FAX 617-619-1401
http://www.effoundation.org
*Asa Fanelli, President*

Offers an opportunity to study and live for a year in a foreign country for students between the ages of 15 and 18.

**2118** **Higher Education Consortium for Urban Affairs**
2233 University Avenue W
Saint Paul, MN  55114          651-646-8831
800-554-1089
FAX 651-659-9421
http://www.hecua.org
e-mail: info@hecua.org
*Michael Eaton, Director of Enrollment Services*
*Judy , Assistant to Director*
*Phil Hatlie, Director of Operations*

Consortium of 15 Midwest colleges and universities offering undergraduate, academic programs, both international and domestic that incorporate field study and internships in the examination of urban and global issues.

**2119** **International Summerstays**
620 SW 5th Avenue
Portland, OR  97204          503-274-1776
800-274-6007
FAX 503-274-9004
http://www.summerstays.org
e-mail: info2summerstays.org
*Melinda Samis, Director*
*Patty Hayashi, Assistant Director*

Offers summer homestays in a different country for teenagers from Oregon only to Spain, Germany and France.

**2120** **Lisle Fellowship**
900 County Road
Leander, TX  78641          512-259-7621
800-477-1538
FAX 512-259-0392
http://www.lisleinternational.org
e-mail: lisle2@io.com
*Mark Kinney, Executive Director*

Educational organization which works toward world peace and a better quality of human life through increased understanding between persons of similar and different cultures.

**2121** **National Society for Experiential Education**
515 King Street
Alexandria, VA  22314          703-706-9552
FAX 703-684-6048
http://www.nsee.org
e-mail: info@nsee.org
*Linda Goff MD, Director*
*Albert Cabral, Vice President*
*Carole Rogin, Executive Director*

National nonprofit membership organization which supports the use of learning through experience for intellectual development, civic and social responsibility, career exploration and ethical development. Fosters the effective use of experience as an integral part of education.

**2122   No Barriers to Study**
**Lock Haven University**
**401 N Fairview Street**
**Lock Haven, PA  17745**               **570-893-2157**
                                        **800-223-8978**
                              **FAX 570-893-2659**
*Russell Jameson Jr, Resident Hall Director*
*Roger Johnson, Dean*

A regional consortium committed to facilitating study
abroad for college students with disabilities.

**2123   People to People International**
**501 E Armour Boulevard**
**Kansas City, MO  64109 2200**         **816-531-4701**
                              **FAX 816-561-7502**
                          **http://www.ptpi.org**
                      **e-mail: ptpi@ptpi.org**
*Mary Eisenhower, President*
*Marc Bright, Executive Vice President*
*Rosanne Rosen, Senior Vice President Operations*

Nonpolitical, nonprofit organization working outside
the government to advance the cause of international
understanding through international contact.

**2124   World Experience**
**2440 S Hacienda Boulevard**
**Hacienda Heights, CA  91745**         **626-336-3638**
                                        **800-633-6653**
                              **FAX 626-333-4914**
                  **http://www.worldexperience.org**
                  **e-mail: weworld@weworld.com**
*Bobby Fraker, President*
*Marje Archambault, Vice President*

Nonprofit organization which sponsors, develops and
carries out international student exchange programs
for study and service abroad.

**2125   Youth for Understanding USA**
**6400 Goldsboro Road**
**Bethesda, MD  20817**                 **240-235-2100**
                                        **866-493-8872**
                              **FAX 240-235-2104**
              **http://www.YouthForUnderstanding.org**
                      **e-mail: admissions@yfu.org**
*Mike Finnell, President*

Nonprofit international exchange program, prepares
young people for their responsibilities and opportunities in todays changing, interdependent world through
homestay exchange programs. Offers year, semester,
and summer study abroad and scholarship opportunities in 34 countries worldwide.

## Federal

**2126  Administration on Children, Youth and Families: US Department of Education**

330 C Street SW
Washington, DC  20447          202-205-8347
FAX 202-205-9721
http://www.acf.hhs.gov
*Frank Fuentes, Deputy Commissioner*

Programs under the Administration include the Children's Bureau, Head Start, Child Care Bureau, and The Family and Youth Services Bureau.

**2127  Civil Rights Division: US Department of Justice**

Coordination and Review Section
950 Pennsylvania Avenue NW
Washington, DC  20530          202-307-2222
800-848-5306
FAX 202-307-0595
TDY:800-514-0383
*R Costa, Assistant Attorney General*

Coordinates the reinforcement of Section 504 which prohibits discrimination on the basis of disability in all federally conducted programs and activities, and in the programs and activities that receive federal financial assistance.

**2128  Clearinghouse on Adult Education and Literacy**

US Department of Education
400 Maryland Avenue SW
Washington, DC  20202          202-401-2000
800-872-5327
FAX 202-401-0689
TDY:800-437- 083
http://www.ed.gov

The Clearinghouse was established in 1981 to link the adult education community with existing resources in adult education, provide information which deals with state administered adult education programs funded under the Adult Education and Family Literacy Act, and provide resources that support adult education activities.

**2129  Developmental Disability Services: US Department of Health & Human Services**

200 Independence Avenue SW
Washington, DC  20201          202-619-0257
877-696-6775
FAX 202-690-7203
http://www.hhs.gov
*Scott Whittaker, Chief of Staff*
*Andrew Knapp, Deputy Chief of Staff*

Councils in each state provide training and technical assistance to local and state agencies, employers and the public, improving services to people with developmental disabilities.

**2130  Employment Standards Administration: US Department of Labor**

Frances Perkins Building
Washington, DC  20210          202-693-5000
866-487-2365
FAX 202-693-0218
http://www.dol.gov
*Elaine Chao, Secretary of Labor*
*Steven Law, Deputy Secretary*

Develops policy and implements legislation for all workers in the nation.

**2131  Employment and Training Administration: US Department of Labor**

Frances Perkins Building
200 Constitution Avenue NW
Washington, DC  20210          202-693-2700
877-872-5627
FAX 202-693-2725
http://www.doleta.gov
*Grace Kilbane, Administrator*
*Sybil Hayes, Staff Assistant*

Through more than 1,700 state and local offices nationwide, provides employment services to job seekers, including employability assessments, job counseling, occupational training referral, job placement, and trained specialists to work with the specific needs of job-seekers with disabilities.

**2132  Equal Employment Opportunity Commission**

1801 L Street NW
Washington, DC  20507          202-663-4900
800-669-4000
FAX 202-663-4639
TDY:800-669-6820
http://www.eeoc.gov
*Cari Dominguez, Chair*
*Naomi Earp, Vice Chair*
*Paul Steven Miller, Commissioner*

Enforces Section 501 which prohibits discrimination on the basis of disability in Federal employment, and requires that all Federal agencies establish and implement affirmative action programs for hiring, placing and advancing individuals with disabilities. Also oversees Federal sector equal employment opportunity complaint processing system.

**2133  National Institute of Child Health and Human Development**

1 Center Drive
Bethesda, MD  20892          301-496-4000
800-370-2943
FAX 301-496-7101
http://www.nih.gov/nichd
e-mail: nihinfo@gov
*Elias Zerhouni MD, Director*

Its mission is science in pursuit of fundamental knowledge about the nature and behavior of living systems and the application of that knowledge to extend healthy life and reduce the burdens of illness and disability.

**2134 National Institute of Mental Health**

6001 Executive Boulevard
Bethesda, MD 20892 9663      301-443-4513
     866-615-6464
     FAX 310-443-4279
     TDY:301-443-8431
     http://www.nimh.nh.gov
     e-mail: nimhinfo@nih.gov

*Thomas Insel MD, Director*
*Richard Nakamura PhD, Deputy Director*
*William T Fitzsimmons, Executive Officer*

Mission is to diminish the burden of mental illness through research. This public health mandate demands that we harness powerful scientific tools to achieve better understanding, treatment and eventually prevention of mental illness.

**2135 National Institute on Disability and Rehabilitation Research**

US Department of Education
400 Maryland Avenue
Washington, DC 20202      202-205-5465
     FAX 202-205-9252
     http://www.ed.gov/offices

*Rod Paige, US Secretary Education*
*Anne Radice, Chief of Staff*
*Philip Link, Executive Secertariat Director*

Offers information about special education programs, vocational rehabilitation programs and information about national and international research regarding disabilities and rehabilitation.

**2136 National Library Services for the Blind and Physically Handicapped**

Library of Congress
1291 Taylor Street NW
Washington, DC 20011      202-707-5100
     800-424-8567
     FAX 202-707-0712
     TDY:202-707-0744
     http://www.nls@loc.gov
     e-mail: nls@loc.gov

*Frank Cylke, Director*
*Marvine Wanamaker, Assistant Director*

Administers a free program that loans recorded and braille books and magazines, music scores in braille and large print, and specially designed playback equipment to residents of the United States who are unable to read or use standard print materials because of visual or physical impairment.

**2137 National Technical Information Service**

US Department of Commerce
5285 Port Royal Road
Springfield, VA 22161      703-605-6000
     800-553-6847
     FAX 703-605-6900
     TDY:703-487-4639
     http://www.ntis.gov
     e-mail: info@ntis.fedworld.gov

*Wayne Gallant, Head Master*

Our mission supports the nation's economic growth by providing access to information that stimulates innovation and discovery.

**2138 National Technical Information Service: US Department of Commerce**

5285 Port Royal Road
Springfield, VA 22161      703-605-6000
     800-553-6847
     FAX 703-605-6900
     http://www.ntis.gov

*Wayne Gallant, Head Master*

Maintains a worldwide database for research, development and engineering reports on a range of topics, including architectural barrier removal, employing individuals with disabilities, alternative testing formats, job accommodations, school-to-work transition for students with disabilities, rehabilitation engineering, disability law and transportation.

**2139 Office of Civil Rights: US Department of Health and Human Services**

US Department of Health & Human Services
200 Independence Avenue SW
Washington, DC 20201      202-619-0403
     800-368-1019
     FAX 202-619-3437
     TDY:800-537-7697

*Richard Campanelli, Director*
*Robinsue Srohboese, Principal Deputy Director*

Responsible for investigating discrimination on the basis of race, color, national origin and religion in programs receiving financial assistance from the US Department of Health and Human Services.

**2140 Office of Civil Rights: US Department of Education**

400 Maryland Avenue, SW
Washington, DC 20202      800-872-5327
     FAX 202-401-0689
     TDY:877-521-2172
     http://www.ed.gov/ocr
     e-mail: ocr@ed.gov

*Rod Paige, US Secretary of Education*

Our mission is to ensure access to education and to promote educational excellence throughout the nation through vigorous enforecement of civil rights.

**2141 Office of Disability Employment Policy**

US Department of Labor
200 Constitution Avenue NW
Washington, DC 20210      202-693-7880
     866-487-2365
     FAX 202-693-7888
     http://www.dol.gov/odep
     e-mail: infoodep@dol.gov

*Elaine Chao, Secretary of Labor*
*Steven Law, Deputy Secretary*
*Ruth D Knouse, Executive Secretariat Director*

Provides national leadership to increase employment opportunities for adults and youth with disabilities, while striving to eliminate barriers to employment.

**2142 Office of Federal Contract Compliance Programs: US Department of Labor**

**Frances Perkins Building**
**Washington, DC 20210** 202-693-0101
866-487-2365
FAX 202-693-1304
http://www.dol.gov/esa/ofccp
*William Doyle Jr, Deputy Assistant Secretary*
*Shawn Hooper, Chief of Staff*

Administers a variety of federal labor laws including those that guarantee worker's rights to safe and healthful working conditions; a minimum hourly wage and overtime pay; freedom from employment discrimination; unemployment insurance; and other income support.

**2143 Office of Personnel Management**

**Office of Human Resources & EEO**
**1900 E Street NW**
**Washington, DC 20415 1000** 202-606-1800
FAX 202-606-1732
http://www.opm.gov
*Den Blair, Director*
*Ruth McGinn, Special Assistant to Director*
*Dan G Blair, Deputy Director*

The central personnel agency of the federal government. Provides information on the selective placement program for persons with disabilities.

**2144 Office of Program Operations: US Department of Education**

**400 Maryland Avenue SW**
**Washington, DC 20202** 202-205-5413
800-872-5327
FAX 202-401-0689
http://www.ed.gov
e-mail: customerservice@inet.ed.gov

Programs in each state provide information and assistance to individuals seeking or receiving services under the Rehabilitation Act of 1973.

**2145 Rehabilitation Services Administration State Vocational Program**

**US Department of Education**
**400 Maryland Avenue SW**
**Washington, DC 20202** 202-401-2000
800-872-5327
FAX 202-401-0689

State and local vocational rehabilitation agencies provide comprehensive services of rehabilitation, training and job-related assistance to people with disabilities and assist employers in recruiting, training, placing, accommodating and meeting other employment-related needs of people with disabilities.

**2146 Social Security Administration**

**Office of Public Inquiries**
**Windsor Park Building**
**Baltimore, MD 21235** 632-528-6300
800-772-1213
FAX 202-395-7298
http://www.ffagov
*Jo B Barnhart, Commissioner*

Provides financial assistance to those with disabilities who meet eligibility requirements.

**2147 US Bureau of the Census**

**4700 Silver Hill Road**
**Washington, DC 20233** 301-763-4748
http://www.census.gov
e-mail: pio@census.gov
*Charles Kincannon, Director*
*Betty , Executive Assistant*
*Herman Habermann, Deputy Director, COO*

The principal statistical agency of the federal government. It publishes data on persons with disabilities, as well as other demographic data derived from censuses and surveys.

## Alabama

**2148 Alabama Department of Industrial Relations**

**649 Monroe Street**
**Montgomery, AL 36130** 334-242-8003
FAX 334-242-8843
http://www.dir.state.al.us
e-mail: webmaster@dir.state.al.us

**2149 Alabama Disabilities Advocacy Program**

**University of Alabama**
**Tuscaloosa, AL 35487** 205-348-4928
800-826-1675
FAX 205-348-3909
TDY:205-348-9484
http://www.adap.net
e-mail: adap@adap.ua.edu
*Reuben Cook, Director*

**2150 Employment Service Division: Alabama**

**Department of Industrial Relations**
**649 Monroe Street**
**Montgomery, AL 36131** 334-242-8003
FAX 334-242-3960
e-mail: shorton@dir.state.al.us
*Thyllis Kennedy, Director*
*Michael , Assistant*

**2151 National Association for Developmental Dis**

**National Association For Council & Development of**
**100 N Union Street**
**Montgomery, AL 36130** 334-242-3973
800-232-2158
FAX 334-242-0797
http://www.acdd.org
e-mail: addpc@mh.state.al.us
*Elmyra Jones, Executive Director*
*Philip Young, Council Chairperson*

The council provides systems change, capacity building and advocacy efforts throughout the state for people with the most significant disabilities.

## Alaska

**2152 Alaska Department of Labor: Employment Security Division**

Department of Labor
PO Box 25509
Juneau, AK 99802      907-465-2712
FAX 907-465-4537
http://www.spaceaka.us
e-mail: frankmurkowski@spaceaka.us
*Frank Murkowski, Governor*

**2153 Assistive Technology: Metro Region**

State of Alaska
1251 Muldoon Road
Anchorage, AK 99504      907-269-3550
800-478-3387
FAX 907-269-3630
e-mail: mshiffer@educ.state.ak.us
*Kent Irenton, Manager*

Information and referral to Alaska residents with disabilities about adaptive aids and equipment that will better their lives.

**2154 Center for Community**

700 Katlian Street
Sitka, AK 99835      907-747-6960
800-478-6962
FAX 907-747-4868
*Margaret Andrews, Director Services*
*Connie Site, Executive Director*

Center for Community is a multiservice agency that provides early intervention, respite, futures planning, functional skills training, and vocational assistance for people with disabilities.

**2155 Correctional Education Division: Alaska**

Department of Corrections/Division of Institutions
4500 Diplomacy Drive
Anchorage, AK 99508      907-269-7416
FAX 907-269-7420
http://www.correct.state.ak.us/
e-mail: webmaster@correct.state.ak.us
*Rose Munago, Criminal Justice Planner*

**2156 Disability Law Center of Alaska**

3330 ArCourtic Boulevard
Anchorage, AK 99503      907-565-1002
800-478-1234
FAX 907-565-1000
http://www.dlcak.org
e-mail: akpa@dlcak.org
*David Fleurant, Executive Director*

**2157 Fair Employment Practice Agency**

Alaska State Commission for Human Rights
800 A Street
Anchorage, AK 99501      907-274-4692
800-478-4692
FAX 907-278-8588
TDY:907-276-3177
*Anne Kean, Administrative Assistant*
*Paula Haley, Executive Director*

**2158 State Department of Adult Education**

Department of Education
801 W 10th Street
Juneau, AK 99801      907-465-2800
FAX 907-465-4156
http://www.eed.state.ak.us/
e-mail: mpartlow@aduc.state.ak.us
*Roger Samson, Commissioner*
*Barbara Thompson, Director for TLS*

**2159 State Department of Education**

Department of Education
801 W 10th Street
Juneau, AK 99801      907-465-2800
FAX 907-465-3452
http://www.eed.state.ak.us/
*Roger Samson, Commissioner*
*Barbara Thompson, Director for TLS*

**2160 State GED Administration: GED Testing Program**

Alaska Department of Education
801 W 10th Street
Juneau, AK 99801      907-465-2800
FAX 907-465-3240
http://www.eed.state.ak.us/
*Roger Samson, Commissioner*
*Barbara Thompson, Director for TLS*

**2161 State of Alaska Community & Regional Affairs Department: Administrative Services**

150 3rd Street
Juneau, AK 99801      907-465-4708
FAX 907-465-3519

## Arizona

**2162 Adult & Family Literacy Education**

Arizona Department of Education
1535 W Jefferson Street
Phoenix, AZ 85007          602-364-4015
                    FAX 602-258-4986
                  http://www.ade.az.gov
              e-mail: kliersc@ade.az.gov
*Karen Liersch, State Director; Administrator*
*Rita Kenison, Parent Network/Child Find*

**2163 Arizona Center for Disability Law**

Arizona Center for Law in the Public Interest
100 N Stone Avenue
Tucson, AZ 85701          520-327-9547
                         800-922-1447
                    FAX 520-884-0992
                    TDY:520-327-9547
                   http://www.acdl.com
              e-mail: center@acdl.com
*Leslie Cohen, Executive Director*
*Lorraine Freyer, Executive Assistant*

**2164 Arizona Center for Law in the Public Interest**

18 E Ochoa
Tucson, AZ 85701          520-529-1798
                    FAX 520-529-2927
          http://www.NAU.edu\~ihd/acdl.html
              e-mail: info@aclpi.org
*Leslie Cohen, Executive Director*

**2165 Arizona Department of Economic Security**

Rehabilitation Services Administration
1789 W Jefferson Street 930-A
Phoenix, AZ 85007          602-542-3794
                         800-563-1221
                    FAX 602-542-3778
                http://www.azdes.gov/rsa
              e-mail: azrsa@azdes.gov
*Skip Dingham, Administrator*
*Joanne Steinman, Policy Specialist*

**2166 Arizona Department of Education**

Arizona Department of Education
1535 W Jefferson Street
Phoenix, AZ 85007          602-364-4015
                         800-352-8400
                    FAX 602-364-1532
                  http://www.ade.az.gov
              e-mail: rkeniso@ade.az.gov
*Adria Martinez, Director of Special Projects*
*Amy Koenig, Program Project Specialists*

**2167 Arizona Governor's Committee on Employment of the Handicapped**

ALS Association Arizona Chapter
5040 E Shea Boulevard
Scottsdale, AZ 85254          480-609-3888
                         FAX 480-556-9927
                       http://www.alsaz.org
                  e-mail: daniel@alsaz.org
*Elayne Achilles, Director*
*Frank Dinie, Patient Services Director*

**2168 Correctional Education**

Arizona Department of Corrections
1601 W Jefferson Street
Phoenix, AZ 85007          602-542-5810
                         FAX 602-364-0259
              e-mail: bkilian@adc.state.az.us
*Barbara MA NCC, Special Education Coordinator*

**2169 Fair Employment Practice Agency**

Office of the Arizona Attorney General
1275 W Washington Street
Phoenix, AZ 85007          602-542-5263
                         877-491-5742
                    FAX 602-542-8885
                    TDY:602-542-5002
                  http://www.azag.gov
*Terry Goddard, Attorney General*
*Jesse Cuilty, Compliance Officer*

**2170 GED Testing Services**

Arizona Department of Education
1535 W Jefferson Street
Phoenix, AZ 85007          602-364-4015
                         FAX 602 258 4986
                  http://www.ade.az.gov
              e-mail: rkeniso@ade.az.gov
*Karen Liersch, Administrator*

**2171 Governor's Council on Developmental Disabilities**

3839 N 3rd Street
Phoenix, AZ 85012          602-277-4986
                         800-889-5893
                    FAX 602-277-4454
                    TDY:602-277-4949
                  http://www.azgcdd.org
              e-mail: jsnyder@azdes.gov
*Jami Snyder, Executive Director*
*Sue Miller, Administrative Assistant*

## Arkansas

**2172  Arkansas Department of Education**

1401 W Capitol
Little Rock, AR  72201          501-682-2379
                               FAX 501-682-5159
                        http://www.arkedu.state.ar.us
                        e-mail: Mtolson@arkedu.k12.ar.us
*Marcia Harding, Associate Director*

**2173  Arkansas Department of Human Services:
Division of Rehabilitation Services**

PO Box 1437
Little Rock, AR  72203          501-682-8707
                               FAX 501-682-8679
                        http://www.state.ar.us/dhs

**2174  Arkansas Department of Special Education**

54 Capital Mall
Little Rock, AR  72201          501-682-4475
                        http://www.arkedu.state.ar.us
                        e-mail: dsydoriak@arkedu.k12.ar.us
*Diane Sydoriak MD, Associate Director*

**2175  Arkansas Department of Workforce Education**

3 Capitol Mall
Little Rock, AR  72201          501-682-1970
                               FAX 501-682-1509
                        http://www.work-ed.state.ar.us
                        e-mail: steve.franks@mial.state.ar.us
*Garland Hankins, Deputy Director*

**2176  Arkansas Employment Security Department**

1 Pershing Circle
North Little Rock, AR  72114    501-682-3105
                               FAX 501-682-3748
                               TDY:501-296-1669
                        http://www.state.ar.us/esd
                        e-mail: ed.rolle.aesd@mial.state.ar.us
*Albessie Thompson, Equal Opportunity Manager*

**2177  Arkansas Governor's Developmental Disabilities
Council**

5800 W 10th Street
Little Rock, AR  72204          501-661-2589
                               800-482-5400
                               FAX 501-661-2399
                               TDY:501-661-2736
                        http://www.ddcouncil.org
*Wilma Stewart, Director*
*Mary Edwards, Training and Service Coordinator*

**2178  Assistive Technology Project**

Increasing Capabilities Access Network
2201 Brookwood Drive
Little Rock, AR  72202          501-666-8868
                               800-828-2799
                               FAX 501-666-5319
                        e-mail: sgaskin@compuserve.com
*Sue Gaskin, Project Director*

A consumer responsive statewide program promoting
assistive technology devices and sources for persons
of all ages with disabilities.

**2179  Client Assistance Program (CAP): Arkansas
Division of Persons with Disabilities**

Disability Rights Center
1100 N University Avenue
Little Rock, AR  72207          501-296-1775
                               800-482-1174
                               FAX 501-296-1779
                               TDY:501-296-1775
                        http://www.arkdisabilityrights.org
                        e-mail: panda@arkdisabilityrights.org
*Eddie Miller, CAP Director*
*Nan Ellen East, Executive Director*

The Client Assistance Program is mandated by the
Federal Rehabilitation Act. It provides free services
to consumers and applicants for projects, programs,
and facilities funded under the Rehabilitation Act.
CAP analyzes issues a consumer/applicant may have
and provides advocacy services regarding Rehabilitation Act funded services.

**2180  Department of Correction School District**

8000 CorreCourtion Circle
Pine Bluff, AR  71603           870-267-6725
                               FAX 870-267-6731
                        e-mail: allenc@adcsd.k12.ar.us
*Charles Allen PhD, Superintendent*

**2181  Increasing Capabilities Access Network**

ACES Project
2201 Brookwood Drive
Little Rock, AR  72202          501-683-3014
                               FAX 501-666-5319
                               TDY:501-666-8868
                        http://www.arkansas-ICAN.org
                        e-mail: jswilson@ars.state.ar.us
*Barry Vuletich, Project Director*
*Leesa Frasier, Rehab Specialist*

**2182  Office of the Governor**

State Capitol
Little Rock, AR  72201          501-682-3642
                               FAX 501-682-1382
*Julie Rhodes, Director*

**2183  Protection & Advocacy Agency**
Advocacy Services
1100 N University Avenue
Little Rock, AR  72207          501-296-1775
                               800-482-1174
                          FAX 501-296-1779
                          TDY:501-296-1775
          http://www.arkdisabilityrights.org
          e-mail: panda@arkdisabilityrights.org
*Eddie Miller, CAP Director*
*Nan Ellen East, Executive Director*

**2184  State GED Administration**
Department of Workforce Education
3 Capitol Mall
Little Rock, AR  72201          501-682-1980
                          FAX 501-682-1982
             http://www.dwe.arkansa.gov
          e-mail: janice.hanlon@mail.state.ar.us
*Janice Hanlon, GED Test Administrator*

# California

**2185  California Department of Fair Employment and Housing**
2014 T Street
Sacramento, CA  95814          916-227-0551
                          FAX 916-227-2859
             http://www.dfeh.ca.gov

**2186  California Department of Rehabilitation**
PO Box 944222
Sacramento, CA  16541          916-263-7365
                          FAX 916-263-7474
                          TDY:916-263-7477
             http://www.rehab.cahwnet.gov
          e-mail: durban@compu-teach.com
*Catherine Campisi, Director*

The mission of the Department of Rehabilitation is to assist Californians with disabilities in obtaining and retaining employment and maximizing their ability to live independently in their communities.

**2187  California Department of Special Education**
721 Capitol Mall
Sacramento, CA  95814          916-323-4768
                          FAX 916-327-3516

**2188  California Employment Development Department**
800 Capitol Mall
Sacramento, CA  95814          916-654-8210
                          FAX 916-657-5294
             http://www.edd.ca.gov
*Karen Wall, Directors Secretary*

**2189  California State Board of Education**
1430 N Street
Sacramento, CA  95814          916-319-0827
                          FAX 916-319-0175
             http://www.cde.ca.gov/board
*Ruth Green, President*
*Glee Johnsen, Vice President*

**2190  California State Council on Developmental Disabilities**
2000 O Street
Sacramento, CA  95814          916-322-8481
                          FAX 916-443-4957
                          TDY:916-324-8420
             http://www.scdd.ca.gov
          e-mail: scdd@dss.ca.gov
*Edward Willis, Interim Director*
*Cynthia Fair, Deputy Director*

**2191  Career Assessment and Placement Center**
Whittier Union High School District
9401 S Painter Avenue
Whittier, CA  90602          562-698-8121
                          FAX 562-693-5354
*Daniel Hubert*

Provides job placement programs, remunerative work services and work adjustment training programs.

**2192  Clearinghouse for Specialized Media**
California Department of Education
560 J Street
Sacramento, CA  95814          916-445-5103
                          FAX 916-323-9732
             http://www.cde.ca.gov/re/pn/rc
          e-mail: rbrawley@cde.ca.gov
*Rod Brawley, Manager For Clearing House Media*
*Steven Parker, Accounting Technician*

Supports access to general education curriculum by students with disabilities. This unit of the state special schools and services division produces accessible versions of textbooks, workbooks, and literature books adopted for all public schools by the State Board of Education.

**2193  Education & Inmate Programs Unit**
1515 S Street
Sacramento, CA  94283          916-445-8035
                               800-952-5544
                          FAX 916-324-1416
             http://www.corr.ca.gov
*Gary Sutherland, Federal Grand Administrator*
*Adrianne Johnson, Secretary*

**2194** **Employment Development Department: Employment Services Woodland**

California Health and Human Services Agency
825 E Street
Woodland, CA 95776          530-661-2600
                            FAX 530-668-3152
                            http://www.edd.ca.gov

*Bill Burke, Contact*

**2195** **Employment Development Department: Employment Services W Sacramento**

California Health and Human Services Agency
500-A W Jefferson Boulevard
W Sacramento, CA 95605       916-375-6288
                            FAX 916-375-6310
                            http://www.edd.ca.gov

*Bill Burke, Contact*

**2196** **Pacific Disability and Business Technical Assistance Center**

555 12th Street
Oakland, CA 94607 4046       510-285-5600
                            FAX 510-285-5614
                            http://www.pacdbtac.org
                            e-mail: info@pdbtac.com

*Erica Jones, Program Director*

One of 10 federally funded regional resource centers of the Americans with Disabilities Act. We provide information, problem solving assistance and referrals for implementing the ADA.

**2197** **Region IX: Office of Federal Contract Compliance**

US Department of Labor
200 Constitution Avenue NW
Washington, DC 20210         888-376-3227
                            866-487-2365
                            FAX 202-693-1304
                            http://www.dol.gov/esa/ofccp

*Charles James, President*

These regional offices of agencies enforce laws prohibiting employment discrimination on the basis of disability.

**2198** **Region IX: US Department of Education-Office of Civil Rights**

US Department of Education
50 UN Plaza
San Francisco, CA 94012      415-556-4120
                            FAX 415-437-7540
                            http://www.ed.gov
                            e-mail: loni_hancock@ed.gov

*Mary T. Pearson, Secretary*
*Rick Latorre, Administrative Officer*

The Office of Federal Contract Compliance Programs is part of the US Department of Labor's Employment Standards Administration. It has a national network of six regional offices, each with district and area offices in major metropolitan centers.

**2199** **Region IX: US Department of Health and Human Services-Office of Civil Rights**

US Department of Health & Human Services
50 UN Plaza
San Francisco, CA 94102      415-437-8310
                            FAX 415-437-8329

These regional offices of agencies enforce laws prohibiting employment discrimination on the basis of disability.

**2200** **Sacramento County Office of Education**

10474 Mather Boulevard
Sacramento, CA 95827         916-228-2500
                            FAX 916-228-2403
                            TDY:958-259-003
                            http://www.scoe.net

*Carole Talan, Executive Director*

---

# Colorado

---

**2201** **Client Assistance Program (CAP): California Division of Persons with Disabilities**

PO Box 944222
Sacramento, CA 94244         916-263-7367
                            800-952-5544
                            FAX 916-263-7464
              http://www.dor.ca.gov/public/contacts
                            e-mail: capinfo@dor.ca.gov

*Sheila Mentkowski, Director*

The CAP is mandated by the Federal Rehabilitation Act. CAP provides free services to consumers and applicants for projects, programs, and facilities funded under the Rehabilitation Act. CAP services involve the analysis of issues a consumer/applicant may have and provision of advocacy services regarding Rehabilitation Act funded services.

**2202** **Colorado Assistive Technology Project**

1245 E Colfax
Denver, CO 80218             303-315-1280
                            FAX 303-837-1208
                            http://www.uchsc.edu/atp

*Cathy Bodine, Director*
*Miya Adams, Administrative Assistant*

Designed to support capacity building and advocacy activities, and to assist states in maintaining permanent, comprehensive statewide programs of technology related assistance for all people with disabilities living in Colorado.

**2203** **Colorado Civil Rights Division**

1560 Broadway
Denver, CO 80202             303-894-2997
                            FAX 303-894-7830

**2204  Colorado Department of Labor and Employment**
1515 Arapahoe
Denver, CO  80202                    303-318-8886
                                   FAX 303-318-8870
                              http://www.state.co.us
*Alexandra Hall, Executive Director*

**2205  Colorado Developmental Disabilities**
3824 W Princeton Circle
Denver, CO  80236                    303-866-7450
                                   FAX 303-866-7470
                                   TDY:303-866-7471
                           http://www.colorado.gov
                              e-mail: cddpc@aol.com
*Fred DeCrescentis, Executive Director*
*Lisa Vallejo, Assistant Director*

**2206  Correctional Education Division: Colorado**
Colorado Department of Corrections
2862 S Circle Drive
Colorado Springs, CO  80906       719-540-4862
                                   FAX 719-226-4565
                http://www.doc.state.co.us/programs.htm
                         e-mail: pio@doc.state.co.us
*Eric Brookens, Director Academic Education*

**2207  Increasing Capabilities Access Network (ICAN)**
2201 Brookwood Drive
Little Rock, AR  72202               501-683-3014
                                     800-828-2799
                                   FAX 501-666-5319
                                   TDY:501-666-8868
                          http://www.arkansas-ICAN.org
                         e-mail: sogaskin@ars.state.ar.us
*Barry Vuletich, Project Director*
*Leesa Frasier, Rehab Specialist*

ICAN is a federally funded program of the Arkansas
Rehabilitation Service, designed to make technology
information available and accessible for all who need
it. The program provides information on new and existing technology free to any person regardless of age
or disability.

**2208  Region VIII: US Department of Education**
Office of Civil Rights
1244 Spear Boulevard
Denver, CO  80204                    303-844-3544
                                   FAX 303-844-4303
                                   TDY:303-844-3417
                              http://www.ed.gov
*Lillan Gutierrez, Director of Civil Rights*
*Nancy Haberkorn, Office Assistant*

These regional offices of agencies enforce laws prohibiting employment discrimination on the basis of
disability.

**2209  Region VIII: US Department of Health
andHuman Services**
Office of Civil Rights
1961 Stout Street
Denver, CO  80294                    303-844-5101
                                   FAX 303-844-6665

These regional offices of agencies enforce laws prohibiting employment discrimination on the basis of
disability.

**2210  Region VIII: US Department of Labor-Office of
Federal Contract Compliance**
US Department of Labor
1809 California
Denver, CO  80202                    303-844-1600
                                   FAX 303-844-1616

These regional offices of agencies enforce laws prohibiting employment discrimination on the basis of
disability.

**2211  State Department of Education**
201 E Colfax Avenue
Denver, CO  80203                    303-866-6609
                                   FAX 303-830-0793
                   e-mail: howerter_c@cde.state.co.us
*Diane Bates, Contact*

## Connecticut

**2212  Assistive Technology Project**
Connecticut State Department of Social Services
25 Sigourney Street, 11th Floor
Hartford, CT  06106
                                     800-842-1508
                          http://www.techact.uconn.edu/
                              e-mail: cttap@aol.com
*John Ficarro, Project Director*

**2213  Bureau of Special Education & Pupil Services**
Department of Education
25 Industrial Park Road
Middletown, CT  06457                860-807-2025
                                   FAX 860-807-2047
                          http://www.stat.ct.us/sde/
                   e-mail: george.dowaliby@po.state.ct.us
Offers information on educational programs and services. The Complaint Resolution Process Office answers and processes parent complaints regarding
procedural violations by local educational agencies
and facilities. The Due Process Office is responsible
for the management of special education and due process proceedings which are available to parents and
school districts.

**2214  CHILD FIND of Connecticut**
275 Windsor Street
Hartford, CT  06120

800-632-1455
FAX 860-632-8870
http://www.serc.rh.edu

A service under the direction of The Connecticut State Department of Education and operated by the Special Education Resource Center. The primary goal is the identification, diagnosis and programming of all unserved disabled children.

**2215  Connecticut Bureau of Rehabilitation Services**
State of Connecticut
25 Sigourney Street
Hartford, CT  06106

860-424-5881
800-537-2549
FAX 860-424-4850
TDY:860-424-4839
http://www.brs.state.ct.us
e-mail: evelynknight@po.state.ct.us
*Patricia Coker, Commissioner*

Offers vocational rehabilitation and independent living services to individuals who are physically or mentally disabled.

**2216  Connecticut Department of Social Services**
25 Sigourney Street
Hartford, CT  06106

860-424-5881
800-842-1508
FAX 860-424-4952
TDY:860-424-4839
http://www.brs.state.ct.us
e-mail: mary.plaskonka@po.state.ct
*Patricia Coker, Commissioner*

**2217  Connecticut Office of Protection & Advocacecy for Handicapped & DD Persons**
Office of Protection & Advocacy
60 W Street
Hartford, CT  06120

860-297-4300
800-842-7303
FAX 860-566-8714
TDY:860-566-2102
http://www.state.ct.us/opapd
e-mail: james.mcgaughey@po.state.ct.us
*Jim McGaughey, Executive Director*

Supports families and individuals who are affected by developmental disabilities.

**2218  Connecticut State Department of Education**
Bureau of Adult and Education Training
165 Capital Avenue
Hartford, CT  06145

860-713-6740
FAX 860-713-7018
http://www.state.ct.us/sde/
e-mail: frances.rabimowitz@po.state.ct.us
*Barbara Westwater, Bureau Chief*
*Evanna Holloway, Administrative Assistant*

**2219  Correctional Education Division**
Unified School District #1
24 Wolcott Hill Road
Wethersfield, CT  06109

860-692-7536
FAX 860-692-7538
http://www.state.ct.us/doc/
e-mail: angela.jalbert@po.state.ct.us
*Angela Jalbert, Director of Academic Programs*
*William Barber, Superintendent of School*

**2220  Protection & Advocacy Agency**
Office of P&A for Persons with Disabilities
60B Weston Street
Hartford, CT  06120

860-297-4300
800-842-7303
FAX 860-566-8714
TDY:860-566-2102
http://www.state.ct.us/opapd
e-mail: linda.Mizzi@state.ct.us
*Jim McGaughey, Executive Director*

The mission of the Office of Protection and Advocacy is to advance the cause of equal rights for persons with disabilities and their families.

**2221  State GED Administration**
Bureau of Adult Education and Training
25 Industrial Park Road
Middletown, CT  06457

860-807-2110
FAX 860-807-2112
e-mail: roberta.pawloski@po.state.ct.us
*Carl Paternostro, Director*

**2222  State of Connecticut Board of Education & Services for the Blind**
184 Windsor Avenue
Windsor, CT  06095

860-602-4000
800-842-4510
FAX 860-602-4020
TDY:860-602-4002
http://www.besb.state.ct.us/
e-mail: besb@po.state.ct.us
*Brian Signan, Executive Director*
*Mary , Administrative Assistant*

Provides educational, vocational and communications services to legally blind persons of all ages. Services are free to registered clients

**2223  State of Connecticut: Board of Education for the Visually Impaired**
184 Windsor Avenue
Windsor, CT  06095

860-602-4000
800-842-4510
FAX 860-602-4020
TDY:860-602-4002
http://www.besb.state.ct.us/addresses.htm
e-mail: besb@po.state.ct.us
*Brian Signan, Executive Director*
*Mary , Administrative Assistant*

## Delaware

**2224 Client Assistance Program (CAP): Maryland Division of Persons with Disabilities**

254 E Camden Wyoming Avenue
Camden, DE 19934        302-698-9336
                              800-640-9336
                       FAX 302-698-9338
http://www.protectionandadvocacy.com
e-mail: info@magpage.com
*Melissa Shahun, Director*

Provides free services to consumers and applicants for projects, programs and facilities funded under the Rehabilitation Act.

**2225 Correctional Education Division**

Department of Corrections
245 McKee Road
Dover, DE 19904        302-739-5601
                       FAX 302-739-7215
http://www.state.de.us/correct/ddoc/default.htm
e-mail: johnj.ryan@state.de.us
*Bruce Hobler MD, Contact*
*John Ryan, Education Assistant*

**2226 Delaware Assistive Technology Initiative**

University of DE/duPont Hospital for Children
1600 Rockland Road
Wilmington, DE 19899        302-651-6790
                              800-870-DATI
                       FAX 302-651-6793
                       TDY:302-651-6794
http://www.asel.udel.edu/dati
e-mail: dati@asel.udel.edu
*Beth Mollica PhD, Project Director*
*Sonja Simowitz Rathel, Project Coordinator*

Focuses on improving public awareness, public access to information, funding for assistive technology devices and services, training and technical assistance, and coordination of statewide activities. The project has established Assistive Technology Resource Centers in each of Delaware's three counties. These barrier-free centers are open to the public and house assistive technology devices and materials that are available for demonstration and short-term loan.

**2227 Delaware Department of Labor**

4425 N Market Street
Wilmington, DE 19802        302-761-8000
                       FAX 302-761-6621
http://www.delaware.net
*Oliver Gumbs, Director*

**2228 Protection & Advocacy Agency**

Community Legal Aid/Disabilities Law Program
100 W 10th Street
Wilmington, DE 19801        302-575-0690
                              800-292-7980
                       FAX 302-575-0840
                       TDY:575-069-6302
http://www.declasi.org
*James Gissin, Director*

**2229 State Department of Adult & Community Education**

Department of Public Instruction
401 Federal Street
Dover, DE 19903        302-739-3340
                       FAX 302-739-1770
http://www.doe.state.de.us
e-mail: ftracymumf@state.de.us
*Fran Mumford, Director Adult Education*
*Valerie Woodruff, Education Secretary*

**2230 State GED Administration**

Department of Public Instruction
401 Federal Street
Dover, DE 19903        302-739-3340
                       FAX 302-739-1770
http://www.doe.state.de.us
e-mail: ftracymumf@state.de.us
*Fran Mumford, Director Adult Education*
*Valerie Woodruff, Education Secretary*

## District of Columbia

**2231 Client Assistance Program (CAP): District of Columbia**

University Legal Services
2001 Street NE
Washington, DC 20002        202-547-0198
                              877-211-4638
                       FAX 202-547-2083
                       TDY:202-547-2657
http://www.dcpanda.org
e-mail: info@napas.org
*Jane Brown, Executive Director*
*Kelly Bagby, Legal Director*
*Joseph Cooney, Information Ext 116*

Provides free services to consumers and applicants for projects, programs and facilities funded under the Rehabilitation Act.

**2232 District of Columbia Department of Employment Services**

77 P Street NE
Washington, DC 20002        202-671-1633
                              877-319-7346
                       FAX 202-673-3795
http://www.does.dc.gov
*Gregory Irish, Director*

**2233 District of Columbia Fair Employment Practice Agencies**

DC Office of Human Rights
1889 F Street NW
Washington, DC 20006          202-458-6002
                              FAX 202-458-3992

**2234 District of Columbia Office of Human Rights**

441 4th Street NW
Washington, DC 20001          202-727-3900
                              FAX 202-727-9589
                              http://www.ohr.dc.gov
                              e-mail: ohr@dc.gov
*Kenneth Saunders, Director*
*Brittney Matthews, Compliance Officer*

The DC Office of Human Rights is an agency of the District of Columbia government that seeks to eradicate discrimination, increase equal opportunity, and protect human rights in the city.

**2235 State Department of Adult Education**

University of The District of Columbia
4200 ConneCourticut Avenue NW
Washington, DC 20008          202-274-7181
                              FAX 202-274-7188
                              http://www.aceadultliteracy.org
                              e-mail: kbrisbane213@hotmail.com
*Sandra Lee Ande MD, State Director*
*Tracy Winston, Administrative Assistant*

## Florida

**2236 Client Assistance Program (CAP): Florida Division of Persons with Disabilities**

2671 Executive Center Circle W
Tallahassee, FL 32301          850-488-9071
                               800-342-0823
                               FAX 850-488-8640
                               TDY:800-346-4127
                        http://www.advocacycenter.org
*Elizabeth Holifield, Board President*

Provides free services to consumers and applicants for projects, programs and facilities funded under the rehabilitation act.

**2237 Florida Department of Labor and Employment Security**

2571 Executive Center
Tallahassee, FL 32399          850-921-1459
                               FAX 850-921-1459

**2238 Florida Fair Employment Practice Agency**

Florida Commission on Human Relations
2009 Apalachee Parkway
Tallahassee, FL 32301          850-488-7082
                               FAX 850-488-5291
                               http://www.fchr.state.fl.us
                               e-mail: fchrinfo@dmsstate.fl.us
*Derick Daniel, Executive Director*
*Nina Singleton, Assistant Executive Director*

## Georgia

**2239 Assistive Technology**

Tools for Life/Division of Rehabilitation Services
2 Peachtreet Street 35-415
Atlanta, GA 30303              404-657-0698
                               800-497-8665
                               FAX 404-657-3086
                               TDY:404-657-3085
*Christopher Lee, Contact*

**2240 Client Assistance Program (CAP): Georgia Division of Persons with Disabilities**

123 N McDonough Street
Decatur, GA 30030              404-373-2040
                               800-822-9727
                               FAX 404-373-4110
                       http://www.theombudsman.com/CAP
                e-mail: GaCAPDirector@dueOmbudsman.com
*Charles Martin, Director*
*Anil Lewis, Counselor*

Provides free services to consumers and applicants for projects, programs and facilities funded under the Rehabilitation Act.

**2241 Georgia Department of Technical & Adult Education**

1800 Century Place
Atlanta, GA 30345              404-679-1600
                               FAX 404-679-1710
                               http://www.dtae.org
                               e-mail: mdelaney@dtae.org
*Tony Bruehl, Director*
*Ron Jackson, Commissioner*

The Georgia Department of Technical and Adult Education oversees the state's system of technical colleges, the adult literacy program, and a host of economic and workforce development programs

**2242 Governor's Council on Developmental Disabilities**

2 Peachtree Street NW
Atlanta, GA 30303              404-657-2126
                               888-275-4633
                               FAX 404-657-2132
                               TDY:404-657-2133
                               http://www.dcdd.org
                               e-mail: tharris@dhr.state.ga.us
*Eric Jacobson, Executive Director*
*Kim Persons, Executive Assistant*
*Tonya L Harris, Executive Assistant*

Council collaborates with consumers, their families, advocacy organizations, and policymakers to promote public policies that enhance the quality of life for people with developmental disabilities and their families through advocacy and education, funding and project implementation, research and policy analysis.

**2243  Protection & Advocacy Center**

Georgia Advocacy Office
150 East Pounce Beleon Avenue
Atlanta, GA  30030          404-885-1234
                           800-537-2329
                       FAX 404-378-0031
                       http://www.thegov.org
*Ruby Moore, Director*
*Donna Champion, Executive Director*

**2244  Region IV: Office of Civil Rights**

US Department of Health & Human Services
61 Forsyth
Atlanta, GA  30323          404-562-7886
                       FAX 404-331-1807
                       TDY:404-562-7881
                       http://www.hhs.gov/ocr
*Roosevelt Freeman, Director*

These regional offices of agencies enforce laws prohibiting employment discrimination on the basis of disability.

**2245  State Department of Education**

Department of Technical and Adult Education
2051 Twin Towers E
Atlanta, GA  30334          404-657-7410
                           800-331-3627
                       FAX 404-657-6978
                       http://www.doe.k12.ga.us
                       e-mail: stateboard@doe.k12.ga.us
*Jean DeVard-Kem MD, Assistant Commissioner*

**2246  State GED Administration**

1800 Century Place NE
Atlanta, GA  30345          404-679-1621
                       FAX 404-679-4911
                       http://www.dtae.org
                       e-mail: klee@dtae.org
*Kim Lee, GED Director*

## Hawaii

**2247  Correctional Education**

Department of Public Safety
919 Ala Moana Boulevard
Honolulu, HI  96814          808-587-1279
                         FAX 808-587-1280
                       e-mail: maureen@smsii.com
*Maureen Tito, Program Manager*

**2248  Protection & Advocacy Agency**

1580 Makaloa Street
Honolulu, HI  96814          808-949-2922
                           800-882-1057
                       FAX 808-949-2928
                       http://www.dss.org/nta/states.HI.htm
*Gary Smith, Director*

**2249  State Council on Developmental Disabilities**

919 Ala Moana Boulevard
Honolulu, HI  96814          808-586-8100
                       FAX 808-586-7543
                       http://www.hiddc.org
                       e-mail: council@hiddc.org
*Waynette Cabral, Administrator*

**2250  State Department of Education**

Department of Adult Education
PO Box 2360
Honolulu, HI  96804          808-586-3230
                       FAX 808-586-3234
                       http://www.doe.k12.hi.us/
*Arthur Kaneshiro, Director*
*Grace Sebler, Secretary*

**2251  State GED Administration**

Building C-203
Honolulu, HI  96816          808-733-9124
*Paul Dan, Director*

## Idaho

**2252  Adult Education Office: Idaho Department of Education**

PO Box 83720
Boise, ID  83720          208-332-6931
                           800-432-4601
                       FAX 208-334-4664
                       http://www.sde.state.id.us
                       e-mail: stspence@sde.state.id.us
*Shirley Aker, Director Adult Education/ State*
*Virginia Banse, Administrative Assistant*

**2253  Division of Vocational Rehabilitation**

State of Idaho
650 W State
Boise, ID  83720-0096          208-334-3390
                       FAX 208-334-5305
                       http://www.state.id.us/idvr/
                       e-mail: scook@idvr.state.id.us
*Michael Graham, Administrator*
*Sue Payne, Chief Field Services*
*Sue Cook, Assistant Chief Field Services*

Helping individuals become more independent at home, in the community and at work. Direct services to people with disabilities, including learning disabilities. Services may include evaluation and diagnosis, counseling, guidance and referral services. Transportation to vocational training and assistive devices are available.

**2254    Idaho Center on Developmental Disabilities**

**ID Assistive Technology Project**
**129 W 3rd Street**
**Moscow, ID  83843**                 208-885-3559
                                      800-432-8324
                             FAX 208-885-3628
        http://www.educ.uidaho.edu/idatech
              e-mail: rseiler@uidaho.edu

*Ron Seiler, Director*
*Yvonne Write, Manager*

Assistive Technology Project at the University of Idaho, established 1994, offers alternatie financing (loan) programs for the purchase of assistive technology for the benefit of persons with disabilities in the state. The loan programs offer individuals with disabilities and their families low interest rates on loans for assistive technology and the option of securing a loan guarantee or a principle buy-down arrangement.

**2255    Idaho Fair Employment Practice Agency**

**Idaho Human Rights Commission**
**1109 Main Street**
**Boise, ID  83720**                  208-334-2873
                             FAX 208-334-2873
            http://www.state.id.us/ihrc

**2256    Idaho Human Rights Commission**

**1109 Main Street, 4th Floor**
**Boise, ID  83720**                  208-334-2873
                             FAX 208-334-2664
            http://www.state.id.us/ihrc

**2257    Protection & Advocacy Agency**

**4477 Emerald Street**
**Boise, ID  83706**                  208-336-5353
                                      866-262-3462
                             FAX 208-336-5396
                           TDY:208-336-5353
         http://www.coedinc.cableone.net
           e-mail: coadinc@mcleodusa.net

*James Baugh, Executive Director*

Gives assistance to incapacitated people to protect, promote and advance their legal rights.

**2258    State Department of Education: Special Education**

**650 W State Street**
**Boise, ID  83720**                  208-332-6917
                             FAX 208-334-4664

*Marilyn Howrds, Superintendent*

**2259    State GED Administration**

**PO Box 83720**
**Boise, ID  83720**                  208-332-6931
                                      800-432-4601
                             FAX 208-334-4664
              http://www.sde.state.id.us
       e-mail: etspence@sde.state.id.us

*Valerie Aker, State Director*
*Virginia Banse, Administrative Assistant*

---

# Illinois

**2260    Assistive Technology**

**1 W Old State Capitol Plaza**
**Springfield, IL  62701**            217-522-7985
                                      800-852-5110
                             FAX 217-522-8067
                    http://www.iltech.org

*Wilhelmina Gunther, Director*

**2261    Board of Education of Chicago**

**1819 W Pershing Road**
**Chicago, IL  60609**                773-553-1000
                             FAX 773-553-1501
             http://www.cps.k12.il.us/

*Michael Scott, President*
*Patricia Herman, Executive Assistant*

Offers instruction and information services, curriculum information and government relations advocacy.

**2262    Client Assistance Program (CAP): Illinois Division of Persons with Disabilities**

**100 N 1st Street**
**Springfield, IL  62702**            217-782-5374
                             FAX 217-524-1790
          http://www.dhs.state.IL.us/ors/CAP
            e-mail: cmeadows@dhs.state.il.us

*Cathy Meadows, Director*
*Tammy Davis, Office Support*

Provides free services to consumers and applicants for projects, programs and facilities funded under the Rehabilitation Act.

**2263    Correctional Education**

**Illinois Department of Corrections**
**1301 Concordia Court**
**Springfield, IL  62794**            217-522-2666
                                      800-546-0844
                             FAX 217-557-7902
               http://www.idoc.state.il.us/
          e-mail: webmaster@idoc.state.il.us

*Roger Walker, Director*

**2264 Great Lakes Disability and Business Technical Assistance Center**

**1640 W Roosevelt Road**
**Chicago, IL 60608**          312-413-1407
                               800-949-4232
                               FAX 312-413-1856
                               TDY:800-949-4232
                               http://www.greatlakes.org
                               e-mail: gldbtac@uic.edu
*Robin Jones, Project Director*
*Peter Berg, Technical Assistance*

Provides information, training and technical assistance to employers, people with disabilities and other entities with responsibilities under the ADA. These centers act as a one-stop central source of information, direct technical assistance, training and referral on ADA issues concerning employment, public accommodations, public services and communications.

**2265 Illinois Affiliation of Private Schools for Exceptional Children**

**Lawrence Hall Youth Services**
**4833 N Francisco Avenue**
**Chicago, IL 60625**          773-769-3500
                               FAX 773-769-0106
                               http://www.lawrencehall.org
*Sharri Demitrowicz, Director Education*

**2266 Illinois Council on Developmental Disabilities**

**830 S Spring Street**
**Springfield, IL 62704**      217-782-9696
                               FAX 217-524-5339
                               http://www.state.il.us
                               e-mail: sheila.romano@state.il.us
*Sheila Romano EdD, Director*
*Val Elzy, Office Coordinator*

**2267 Illinois Department of Commerce and Community Affairs**

**JTPA Programs Division**
**620 E Adams Street**
**Springfield, IL 62701**      217-782-7500
                               800-785-6055
                               FAX 800-785-6055
                               TDY:800-785-6055
                               http://www.commerce.state.il.us
*Jack Labin, Director*

**2268 Illinois Department of Employment Security**

**33 South State**
**Chicago, IL 60605**          312-793-5700
                               TDY:800-622-3943
                               http://www.ides.states.il.us
*Brenda Rassle, Director*
*Peggy Sander, Executive Assistant*

**2269 Illinois Department of Human Rights**

**James R Thompson Center**
**Chicago, IL 60601**          312-814-6201
                               FAX 312-814-6251
                               http://www.state.il.us/dhr
                               e-mail: David_Espionza@cms.state.il.us
*Roccko Claps, Director*
*Steven Kleen, Administrative Assistant*

**2270 Illinois Department of Rehabilitation Services**

**1200-1 W Jackson**
**McComb, IL 61455**           309-833-4573
                               FAX 309-833-5953
                               TDY:309-833-4573
                               http://www.dhs.state.il.us
                               e-mail: ors@dhs.state.il.us
*Robert Kilbury, Director*
*Lori Zenner, Administrative Assistant*

**2271 Illinois Fair Employment Practice Agency**

**Office of Discrimination and Hate Crimes**
**James R Thompson Center**
**Chicago, IL 60601**          312-814-6245
                               FAX 312-814-1436
                               TDY:312-263-1579
                               http://www.state.il.us/dhr
                               e-mail: David_Espionza@cms.state.il.us
*Roccko Claps, Director*
*Steven Kleen, Administrative Assistant*

**2272 Illinois Office of Rehabilitation Services**

**Illinois Department of Human Services**
**100 S Grand Avenue E**
**Springfield, IL 62762**      217-557-1601
                               e-mail: ors@dhs.state.il.us
*Teyonda Wertz, Chief of Staff*
*Rafael Diaz, Manager of Information Services*

DHS' Office of Rehabilitation Services is the state's lead agency serving individuals with disabilities.

**2273 Illinois State Board of Education: Division of Certificate Renewal**

**100 N 1st Street**
**Springfield, IL 62777**      866-262-6663
                               http://www.isbe.state.il.us/

**2274 Region V: Civil Rights Office**

**US Department of Health & Human Services**
**233 N Michidan Avenue**
**Chicago, IL 60601**          312-886-2359
                               FAX 312-866-1807
                               http://www.hhs.gov

These regional offices of agencies enforce laws prohibiting employment discrimination on the basis of disability.

**2275 Region V: US Department of Labor-Office of Federal Contract Compliance**

US Department of Labor
230 S Dearborn Street
Chicago, IL 60604     312-353-8927
FAX 312-886-0934
http://www.dol.gov
*Robert Jur, Director*

These regional offices of agencies enforce laws prohibiting employment discrimination on the basis of disability.

**2276 Region V: US Small Business Administration**

500 W Madison Street
Chicago, IL 60606     312-353-6070
FAX 312-353-3426

These regional offices of agencies enforce laws prohibiting employment discrimination on the basis of disability.

**2277 State Department of Adult Education**

State Board of Education
100 N 1st Street
Springfield, IL 62777     217-782-4321
FAX 217-782-9224
http://www.isbe.net
e-mail: jll.lit@isbe.net
*Randy Dunn MD, State Superintendent*

# Indiana

**2278 Assistive Technology**

32 East WA Street
Indianapolis, IN 46241     317-486-8808
800-528-8246
FAX 317-486-8809
http://www.attaininc.org
e-mail: attain@attaininc.org
*Gary Hand, Executive Director*
*Mary Duffer, Executive Assistant*

Assistive technology. To insure that all people with disabilities in Indiana have access to assistive technology.

**2279 Corrections Agency: Indiana Department of Correction**

302 W Washington Street
Indianapolis, IN 46204     317-232-5715
FAX 317-232-6798
TDY:317-232-5725
http://www.in.gov/indcorrection/
e-mail: ddonahue@coa.doc.state.in.us
*David Donahue, Commissioner*
*Ed Motley, Deputy Commissioner*

The mission of the Department of Correction is to protect the public by incarcerating offenders and complying with established means for preparing them for reentry into the community.

**2280 Indiana ATTAIN Project**

Indiana Family and Social Services Administration
402 West Washington Street
Indianapolis, IN 46207     317-233-0800
http://www.in.gov/fssa
*Mitch Robb, Director*
*John Clark, Secretary*

**2281 Indiana Employment Services and Job Training Program Liaison**

10 N Senate Avenue
Indianapolis, IN 46204     317-232-6702
FAX 317-233-1670
TDY:317-232-7560
http://www.in.gov/dwv/
e-mail: jhoward@dwd.state.in.us
*Darian Patterson, Director of Human Resources*
*Joy Howard, Administrative Assistant*

**2282 Protection & Advocacy Agency**

Indiana Advocacy Services
4701 N Keystone Avenue
Indianapolis, IN 46205     317-722-5555
800-622-4845
FAX 317-722-5564
http://www.ingov/ipas
e-mail: info@ipas.state.in.us
*Tomas Gallagher, Director*

**2283 State Department of Education**

State House
Indianapolis, IN 46204     317-232-0808
800-527-4931
FAX 317-233-6326
http://www.ideanet.doe.state.in.us/
e-mail: webmaster@doe.state.in.us
*Suellen Reed, Superintendent*
*Bob Merra, Associate Superintendent*

**2284 State GED Administration**

Indiana Department of Education
State House
Indianapolis, IN 46204     317-232-0522
FAX 317-233-0859
http://www.doe.state.in.us
e-mail: phelam@doe.state.in.us
*Paula Elam, GED State Administrator*
*Melinda , Alternate Administrator*

# Iowa

**2285  Client Assistance Program (CAP): Iowa Division of Persons with Disabilities**
321 E 12th Street
Des Moines, IA  50319          515-281-5969
                              888-219-0471
http://www.state.ia.us/government/dhr/pd
e-mail: harlietta.helland@dhr.state.ia.us
*Harlietta Helland, Director*
*Jill Fulitano-Avery, Administrator*

Designed to help people who are seeking or receiving rehabilitation services from an agency funded under the Rehabilitation Act. Provides information on all available services under the Act to any individual with disabilities in Iowa. This includes the Department for the Blind, the Division of Vocational Rehabilitation Services and seven centers for independent living.

**2286  Governor's Council on DevelopmentalDisabilities**
617 E 2nd Street
Des Moines, IA  50309          515-281-9082
                              800-452-1936
                          FAX 515-281-9087
http://www.state.ia.us/ddcouncil/
e-mail: akillin@dhs.state.ia.us
*Becky Harker, Director*
*Janet Shoeman, Manager*

The council identifies, develops and promotes public policy and support through capacity building, advocacy, and systems-changing activities. The purpose is to ensure that people with developmental disabilities and their families are included in planning, decision making, and development of policy related to services and supports that affect their quality of life and full participation in communities of their choice.

**2287  Iowa Employment Service**
1000 E Grand Avenue
Des Moines, IA  50319          515-281-9619
                          FAX 515-281-9650
http://www.state.ic.us/jobs/
e-mail: IWD.customerservice@iwd.state.ic.us

**2288  Iowa Welfare Programs**
Iowa Department of Human Services
Hoover State Building
Des Moines, IA  50319          515-281-5452
                          FAX 515-281-4940
                          TDY:800-735-2942
http://www.dhs.state.ia.us
e-mail: kconcan@dhs.state.ia.us
*Kevin Concannon, Executive Director*
*Sally Cunningham, Deputy Director*

To provide assistance to families in need in the Des Moines area.

**2289  Iowa Workforce Investment Act**
Department of Economic Development
200 E Grand Avenue
Des Moines, IA  50309          515-242-4700
                          FAX 515-242-4809
                          TDY:800-735-2934
http://www.iowalifechanging.com
e-mail: iowasmart@ided.state.ia.us
*Mike Blouin, Director*
*Deb Townsend, Web Specialist*

Job placement and training services. Especially for those workers who have been laid off, or have other barriers to steady employment.

**2290  Learning Disabilities Association of Iowa**
321 E 6th Street
Des Moines, IA  50329          515-280-8558
                              888-690-5324
                          FAX 515-243-1902
http://www.lda-ia.org
*Vicki Goshon, President*
*Kathy Specketer, Coordinator*

The Learning Disabilities Association of Iowa advances the education and general welfare of children and youth of normal, near-normal, and potentially normal intelligence who have learning disabilities.

**2291  Protection & Advocacy Agency**
NAPAS
950 Office Park Road
Des Moines, IA  50265          515-278-2502
                              800-779-2502
                          FAX 515-278-0539
                          TDY:515-278-0571
e-mail: info@ipna.org
*Silvia Piper, Director*

**2292  State Department of Adult Education**
Grimes State Office Building
Des Moines, IA  50319          515-281-3636
                          FAX 515-281-6544
http://www.state.ia.us/educate
e-mail: john.hartwig@ed.state.ia.us
*Miriam Temple, Director*
*Sally Schroeder, Assistant Director*

**2293  State Department of Education**
Grimms State Office Building
Des Moines, IA  50319          515-281-5294
                          FAX 515-242-5988
http://www.state.ia.us/educate/
e-mail: webmaster@ed.state.ia.us
*Judy Jeffrey, Director*
*Ted Stilwater, Director, Family Literacy*

# Kansas

**2294 Client Assistance Program (CAP):Kansas Division of Persons with Disabilities**

3745 SW Wanamaker Road
Topeka, KS 66610          785-266-8193
                         800-432-2326
                    FAX 785-273-9414
                    TDY:785-273-9661
              http://www.drckansas.org
              e-mail: info@drckansas.org

*Rocky Nichols, Director of Disability*

Provides free services to consumers and applicants for projects, programs and facilities funded under the rehabilitation act.

**2295 Kansas Adult Education Association**

Barton County Community College
245 NE 30th Road
Great Bend, KS 67530          620-792-2701
                              800-748-7594
                    http://www.barton.cc.ks.us

*Todd Moore, Director for Admission*
*Cassandra Montoya, Student Work Service*

The Kansas Adult Education Association has been the professional association for adult educators at community colleges, school districts, and non-profit organizations.

**2296 Kansas Advocacy Protective Services**

NAPAS
3745 SW Wanamaker Road
Topeka, KS 66610          785-273-9661
                         877-776-1541
                    FAX 785-273-9414

*Rocky Nichols, Executive Director*
*Michelle Rola, Director Operations*
*Tim Voth, Outreach Coordinator*

KAPS is the protection and advocacy system in Kansas. It provides legal, administrative and other advocacy services for Kansans with disabilities.

**2297 Kansas Department of Human Resources**

401 SW Topeka Boulevard
Topeka, KS 66603          785-296-5025
                    FAX 785-291-3425
              http://www.dol.ks.gov
              e-mail: uitax@dol.ks.gov

*Paul Bicknell, Chief of Contribution*
*Joe Vining, Assistant Chief of Contribution*

**2298 Kansas Department of Social and Rehabilitation Services**

State of Kansas
915 SW Harrison
Topeka, KS 66612          785-296-3959
                    FAX 785-296-2173
              http://www.srskansas.org
              e-mail: lkzh@srskansas.org

*Gary Daniels, Director*
*Laura Howard, Assistant Director*

**2299 Kansas Human Rights Commission**

Kansas Human Rights Commission
900 SW Jackson Street
Topeka, KS 66612          785-296-3206
                    FAX 785-296-0983
              http://www.khrc.net
              e-mail: khrc@ink.org

*William Minner, Director*
*Karen McDaneld, Office Manager*

**2300 Kansas State Department of Education of Education**

120 SE 10th Avenue
Topeka, KS 66612          785-296-4936
                    FAX 785-296-7933
                    TDY:785-296-6338
              http://www.ksde.org
              e-mail: pplamann@ksde.org

*Andy Tompkins, Commissioner*
*Penny Rice, Executive Assistant*

**2301 Kansas Welfare Programs: Kansas Social and Rehabilitative Services**

915 SLD Harrison
Topeka, KS 66612          785-296-3713
                    FAX 785-296-6960
              http://www.srskansas.org

*Kyle Kessler, Coordinator*
*Margaret Zillinger, Community Support Director*

To protect children and promote adult self-sufficiency.

**2302 Office of Disability Services**

Witchita State University
1845 Fairmont
Wichita, KS 67260          316-978-3309
                    FAX 316-978-3114
                    TDY:316-978-3309
              http://www.twsu.edu/~disserv
              e-mail: grady.landrum@witchita.edu

*Grady Landrum, Director*
*Ron Kopita, Vice President*

Serving students with learning disabilities, including ADD, ADHD, and dyslexia.

**2303 State Department of Adult Education**

Kansas Board of Regents
1000 SW Jackson Street
Topeka, KS 66612          785-296-7159
                    FAX 785-296-4526
              http://www.kansasregents.org
              e-mail: dglass@kasbor.org

*Dianne Glass, Director*
*Diane Whitley, Associate Director*

**2304 State GED Administration: Kansas State Department of Education**

Kansas Board of Regents
1000 SW Jackson Street
Topeka, KS 66612          785-296-7159
                         FAX 785-296-4526
                    http://www.kansasregents.org
                    e-mail: dglass@kasbor.org
*Dianne Glass, Director*
*Diane Whitley, Associate Director*

Promotes adult education.

**2305 Western Kansas Community Service Consortiuum**

348 NE SR
Pratt, KS 67124          620-672-6251
                    http://www.wkcsc.org
           e-mail: dedram@genmail.pcc.cc.ks.us
*Dedra Manes, Executive Director*

Mission is to provide cooperative community services to Western Kansas. Total service area includes 73 counties and nearly 3/4 of the state's geographic area.

# Kentucky

**2306 Assistive Technology Office**

8412 Westport Road
Louisville, KY 40242          502-327-0022
                              800-327-5287
                         FAX 502-327-9974
                         TDY:502-327-0022
                    http://www.katsnet.org
                    e-mail: katsnet@iglou.com
*Derrick Cox, Director*

**2307 Client Assistance Program (CAP): Kentucky Division of Persons with Disabilities**

209 Saint Clair Street
Frankfort, KY 40601          502-564-8035
                             800-633-6283
                        FAX 502-564-2951
                    http://www.kycwd.org
           e-mail: vickil.staggs@mail.state.ky.gov
*Gerry Gordon-Brown, Director*
*Vicki Staggs, Administrative Specialist III*

Provides advocacy for persons with disabilities who are clients or applicants of the Department of Vocational Rehabilitation or the Department for the Blind and are having problems receiving services.

**2308 Correctional Education**

Department of Corrections
PO Box 2400
Frankfort, KY 40242          502-564-4726
                        FAX 502-564-5037
                    http://www.correction.ky.gov
*Martha Slemp, Education Program Manager*

**2309 Kentucky Bureau of Education**

500 Mero Street
Frankfort, KY 40601          502-564-4770
                             800-533-5372
                        FAX 502-564-5680
                    http://www.education.ky.gov
*Gene Wilhoit, Commissioner*

**2310 Learning Disabilities Association of Kentucky**

2210 Goldsmith Lane
Louisville, KY 40218          502-473-1256
                              877-587-1256
                         FAX 502-473-4695
                    http://www.ldaofky.org
                    e-mail: LDAofky@aol.com
*Tim Woods, Director*

**2311 Protection & Advocacy Agency**

Department for Public Advocacy
100 Fair Oaks Lane
Frankfort, KY 40601          502-564-5967
                             800-372-2988
                        FAX 502-564-0848
                        TDY:502-372-2988
                    http://www.kypa.sky1.net
*Maureen Fitzgerald, Director*

**2312 State Department of Adult Education**

Department for Adult Education & Literacy
1024 Capital Cntr Dr
Frankfort, KY 40601          502-573-5114
                        FAX 502-573-5436
                    http://adulted.state.ky.us
           e-mail: reecied.stagnolia@mail.state.ky.us
*Sandy Degado, Contact*
*Harlan Stubbs, Director*

**2313 State Department of Education**

500 Mero Street
Frankfort, KY 40601          502-564-4770
                             800-533-5372
                        FAX 502-564-5680
                    http://www.education.ky.gov/
           e-mail: sdelgado@mail.state.ky.us
*Gene Wilhoit, Commissioner*

Promotes quality education.

## Louisiana

**2314  Client Assistance Program (CAP): Shreveport Division of Persons with Disabilities**

Advocacy Center
2620 Centenary Boulevard
Shreveport, LA  71104

318-227-6186
800-960-7703
FAX 318-227-1841
TDY:318-227-6186
http://www.advocacycenter@advocacyla.org
e-mail: dmirvis@advocacyla.org

*Diane Mirvis, Director*

Advocacy services for applicants and clients of Louisiana Rehabilitation Services (LRS) and American Indian Rehabilitation Services (AIRS). No fee.

**2315  Client Assistance Program (CAP): Louisiana HDQS Division of Persons with Disabilities**

Advocacy Center
225 Baronne Street
New Orleans, LA  70112 2112

504-522-2337
800-960-7705
http://www.advocacyla.org
e-mail: advocacycenter@advocacyla.org

*Lois Simpson, Director*

Advocacy services to applicants and clients of Louisiana Rehabilitation Services (LRS) and American Indian Rehabilitation Services (AIRS). No fee. Committed to the belief in the dignity of every life and the freedom of everyone to experience the highest degree of self-determination. Exists to protect and advocate for human and legal rights of the elderly and disabled. Umbrella organization for Advocacy Centers in Baton Rouge, Lafayette, Shreveport, Monroe, Pineville, Jackson, and Mandeville.

**2316  Correctional Education**

Louisiana Department of Education
PO Box 94064
Baton Rouge, LA  70804

225-342-3530
877-453-2721
FAX 225-342-0193
http://www.doe.state.la.us

*Cosby Joiner, Director*

Promotes quality correctional education.

**2317  Louisiana Assistive Technology Access Network**

3042 Old Forge Drive
Baton Rouge, LA  70808

225-952-9500
800-270-6185
FAX 225-925-9560
http://www.latan.org

*Julie Nesbit, Executive Director*

**2318  State Department of Adult Education**

Department of Education
PO Box 94064
Baton Rouge, LA  70804

225-342-3336
FAX 225-219-4439
http://www.doe.state.la.us
e-mail: customerservice@la.gov

*Cecil Picard, Superintendent*
*Rodney Watson, Confidential Assistant*

**2319  State GED Administration**

Louisiana Department of Education
PO Box 94604
Baton Rouge, LA  70804

225-342-3510
877-453-2721
FAX 225-342-0193
http://www.doe.state.la.us

*Glen Gosett, Director*

Promotes quality education.

## Maine

**2320  Adult Education Team**

Maine Department of Education
23 State House Station
Augusta, ME  04333

207-624-6730
FAX 207-624-6731
e-mail: andy.mcmahan@state.me.us

*Yvonne Davis, Director*

**2321  Consulting Advocacy Research Evaluation Services (CARES) and Client Assistance Program (CAP)**

47 Water Street
Hallowell, ME  04347

207-622-7055
800-773-7055
FAX 207-621-1869
TDY:800-773-7055
http://www.caresinc.org
e-mail: capsite@aol.com

*Steve Beam, Program Director*
*Dean Crocker, Executive Director*

Consulting, advocacy research and evaluation services.

**2322  Developmental Disabilities Council**

139 State House Station
Augusta, ME  04333

207-287-4213
800-244-3999
FAX 207-287-8001
TDY:800-244-3999
http://www.maine.ddc.org
e-mail: info@maineddc.org

*Julia Bell, Executive Director*
*Liza Collins, Research Analyst*

**2323 Maine Department of Labor: Bureau of Rehabilitation Services**

Department of Human Services
2 Anthony Avenue
Augusta, ME 04333-0150          207-624-5950
                                800-698-4440
                                FAX 207-624-5980
                                TDY:888-755-0023
                                http://www.maine.gov/labor
                                e-mail: webmaster_dhs@state.me.us
*Gil Duson, Director for Department of Labor*
*Penny Plourde, Director for Vocational Rehab*

**2324 Maine Department of Labor: Employment Services**

Bureau of Employment Security
20 Union Street
Augusta, ME 04330              207-287-2271
                               FAX 207-287-2947

**2325 Maine Human Rights Commission**

51 State House Station
Augusta, ME 04333              207-624-6050
                               FAX 207-624-6063
                               TDY:207-624-6064
                               http://www.state.me.us
                               e-mail: cheryl.foote@state.me.us
*Patricia Ryan, Director*
*John Kitredge, Support Staff*

The Commission investigates charges of unlawful discrimination in employment, housing, public accommodation, credit extension and education.

**2326 Protection & Advocacy Agency**

Disability Rights Center
24 Stone Street
Augusta, ME 04338              207-626-2774
                               800-452-1948
                               FAX 207-621-1419
                               e-mail: advocate@drcme.org
*Kim Moody, Executive Director*
*Leeann Mosley, Executive Assistant*

# Maryland

**2327 Client Assistance Program (CAP): Maryland Division of Persons with Disabilities**

Division of Rehabilitation Services
2301 Argonne Drive
Baltimore, MD 21218            410-554-9361
                               800-638-6243
                               FAX 410-554-9412
                               TDY:410-554-9360
                               http://www.dors.state.md.us
                               e-mail: cap@dors.state.md.us
*Beth Lash, Director*
*Robert Burns, Assistant Superintendent Rehab*

Provides free services for consumers and applicants of projects, programs and facilities funded under the Rehabilitation Act.

**2328 Correctional Education**

State Department of Education
200 W Baltimore Street
Baltimore, MD 21201            410-767-0100
                               888-246-0016
                               FAX 410-333-6033
                               TDY:410-333-6442
                               http://www.marylandpublicschools.org
*Nancy Garsmick MD, State Superintendent*
*Cindy Schaefer, Management Associate*

**2329 Maryland Developmental Disabilities Council**

300 W Lexington Street
Baltimore, MD 21201            410-333-3688
                               800-305-6441
                               FAX 410-333-3686
                               http://www.md-council.org
                               e-mail: info@md-council.org
*Brian Cox, Executive Director*

**2330 Maryland Technology Assistance Program**

Maryland Department of Disabilities
2301 Argonne Drive
Baltimore, MD 21218            410-554-9230
                               800-832-4827
                               FAX 410-554-9237
                               TDY:866-881-7488
                               http://www.mdtap.org
                               e-mail: mdtap@mdtap.org
*Jessica Vollmer, Office Manager*
*Lori Markland, Loan Program & IT*

Offers information and referrals, reduced rate loan program for assistive technology, five regional display centers, presentations and training on request.

**2331 State Department of Education**

200 W Baltimore Street
Baltimore, MD 21201            410-767-0100
                               888-246-0016
                               FAX 410-333-6033
                               TDY:410-333-6442
                               http://www.marylandpublicschools.org
*Nancy Garsmick MD, State Superintendent*
*Cindy Schaefer, Management Associate*

The mission of MSDE is to provide leadership, support, and accountabilty for effective systems of public education, library services, and rehabilitation services.

## Massachusetts

**2332  Assistive Technology Partnership Center**

MATP Center
1295 Boylston Street
Boston, MA  02215
617-355-7820
800-848-8867
FAX 617-355-6345
TDY:617-355-7301
http://www.matp.org
e-mail: info@matp.org

*Pat Hill, I&R Specialist*
*Marylyn Howe, Director of MATP Center*

Provides information and referral on assistive technology products and services for all Massachusetts residents.

**2333  Autism Support Center: Northshore Arc**

6 Southside Road
Danvers, MA  01923
978-777-9135
800-7-autism
FAX 978-762-3980
http://www2.primushost.com
e-mail: glcastorf@nsarc.org

*Gail Kastorf, Director*

Supports parents/professionals who need information and support about autism, PDD and Asperger's disorder. Directed by a Parent Advisory Policy Committee of parents of children with autism/PDD. Funded through Mass Department of Mental Retardation, we empower families by providing current, accurate and unbiased information about service referrals, resources, research trends and educational opportunities. We promote networking, increase community awareness and advocate for service and opportunity.

**2334  Client Assistance Program (CAP): Massachusetts Division of Persons with Disabilities**

1 Ashburton Place
Boston, MA  02108
617-727-7440
800-322-2020
FAX 617-727-0965
http://www.state.ma.us/mod
e-mail: barbara.lybarger@mod.state.ma.us

*Barbara Esq., Director*
*Phyllis Mitchell, Civil Rights Advocate*

If you have a disability and want to work but have trouble getting vocational rehabilitation services, or want a lifestyle which is more self-reliant but are having trouble getting independent living services, contact CAP. All dealings with us are confidential. CAP is independent of the vocational rehab and independent living agencies, run by Massachusetts Office of Disability, an indepedent state agency. MOD is responsible for promoting the rights of people with disability in Massachusetts.

**2335  Department of Corrections**

Inmate Training & Education
50 Maple Street
Milford, MA  01757
508-422-3314
FAX 508-422-3383
http://www.state.maus/doc/default.htm
e-mail: docinfo@doe.state.maus

*Carolyn Vicari, Director*

Protects the public by operating a safe corrections system.

**2336  Massachusetts Assistive Technology Partnership (MATP)**

MATP Children's Hospital
1295 Boylston Street
Boston, MA  02215
617-355-7820
http://www.matp.org
e-mail: mjackowitz@matp.org

*Judy Brewer, Project Director*
*Michael Jackowitz, Coordinator of Public Awareness*
*Howard Shane, PhD, Principal Investigator*

Funded under Tech Act/NIDRR to increase access to assistive technology for all ages and disabilities. Affiliated with Communication Enhancement Center, Dept of Otolaryngology, Children's Hospital. Conducts statewide project activities such as needs assessment, awareness, information referral, technical training/assistance and advocacy. Two peer programs are based at Stavros Center, Springfield (W Mass) and Cape Organization for Rights of the Disabled, Hyannis (E Mass).

**2337  Massachusetts Commission Against Discrimination**

1 Ashburton Place
Boston, MA  02108
617-994-6000
FAX 617-994-6024
TDY:617-994-6196
http://www.state.maus/mcad/

*Peter Piernan, Director*

Works for fair employment within Massachusetts.

**2338  Massachusetts GED Administration: Massachusetts Department of Education**

350 Main Street
Malden, MA  02148
781-338-6604
http://www.doe.mass.edu
e-mail: rderfler@doe.mass.edu

*Ruth Derfler, Director*

Thirty-three test centers operate state-wide to serve the needs of the adult population in need of a high school credential.

**2339  Massachusetts Rehabilitation Commission**

27 Wormwood Street
Boston, MA  02210
617-204-3600
800-245-6543
FAX 617-727-1354
http://www.state.ma.us/mrc

*Elmer Bartelz, Director*

**2340  Office of Federal Contract Compliance: Boston District Office**

US Department of Labor
JFK Federal Building
Boston, MA  02203
617-624-6780
FAX 617-624-6702
TDY:617-565-9869
http://www.dol.gov/dol/esa
e-mail: beatty.reba@dol.gov

*Reba Beatty, District Director*
*Rhonda Aubn-Smith, Assistant Director*

Enforces laws prohibiting employment discrimination on the basis of disability.

**2341  Protection & Advocacy Agency**

Disability Law Center
11 Beacon Street
Boston, MA  02108                617-723-8455
                                 800-872-9992
                            FAX 617-723-9125
                            TDY:617-227-9464
                            http://www.dlc-ma.org
                            e-mail: mail@dlc-ma.org
*Cristine Griffin, Director*

**2342  Region I: Office for Civil Rights**

US Department Health & Human Services
JF Kennedy Federal Building
Boston, MA  02203                617-565-1340
                                 800-368-1019
                            FAX 617-439-4482
                            TDY:617-165-1343
                            http://www.oca.gov
                            e-mail: daniel.steiner@oca.gov
*Daniel Steiner, President*

These regional offices of agencies enforce laws prohibiting employment discrimination on the basis of disability.

**2343  Region I: US Small Business Administration**

Massachusetts District Office
10 Causeway Street
Boston, MA  02222-1093           617-565-5590
                            FAX 617-565-5598
                            TDY:617-565-5797
                            http://www.sba.gov
                            e-mail: robert.coen@sba.gov
*Robert Coen, Deputy District Director*
*Ray Milano, Administrative Officer*

These regional offices of agencies enforce laws prohibiting employment discrimination on the basis of disability.

**2344  State Department of Adult Education**

Adult and Community Learning Services
350 Main Street
Malden, MA  02148                781-388-3300
                            FAX 781-388-3394
                            http://www.doe.mass.edu
                            e-mail: rbickerton@doe.mass.edu
*Bob Dickerton, Director*

## Michigan

**2345  Assistive Technology**

Michigan Jobs Commission
119 Pere Maegutte Drive
Lansing, MI  48917               517-485-4477
                            FAX 517-485-4488
                    http://www.publicpolicy.com/nyc.html
                            e-mail: ppa@publicpolicy.com
*Jeffrey Padden, President*
*Nancy Hewat, Executive Director*

**2346  Client Assistance Program (CAP): Michigan Department of Persons with Disabilities**

409 Legacy Parkway
Lansing, MI  48911               517-373-8193
                                 800-292-0827
                            FAX 517-373-0565
                            http://www.mpas.org
*Elmer Cerano, Executive Director*

Provides information and advocacy, without charge, to people with disabilities who are receiving, or want to receive, services under the Rehabilitation Act. CAP is operated by Michigan Protection and Advocacy Services, which receives money from the Michigan Department of Career Development to provide these services.

**2347  Correctional Education: Department of Corrections**

BCF Treatment & Education
PO Box 30003
Lansing, MI  48909               517-373-3605
                            FAX 517-335-0045
                            http://www.state.mi.us/mdoc
                            e-mail: spencede@state.mi.us
*Diane Spence, Director*

**2348  Michigan Assistive Technology: Michigan Rehabilitation Services**

Michigan Jobs Commission
119 Pere Marquette Drive
Lansing, MI  48912               517-485-4477
                            FAX 517-485-4488
                            http://www.publicpolicy.com
                            e-mail: ppa@publicpolicy.com
*Jeffrey Padden, President*
*Nancy Hewat, Executive Director*

**2349  Michigan Developmental Disabilities Council**

Lewis Cass Building, 320 Walnut St
Lansing, MI  48913               517-334-6123
                            FAX 517-334-7353
                            TDY:517-334-7354
                    http://www.michigan.gov/ddcouncil
                            e-mail: collinsve@state.mi.us
*Vendella Collins, Executive Director*
*Bud Kraft, Advocacy Director*
*Terry Hunt, Community Services Consultant*

An advocacy organization that engages in advocacy, capacity building and systemic change activities that promote self-determination, independence, productivity, integration and inclusion in all facets of community life for people with developmental disabilities.

**2350   Michigan Employment Security Commission**

7310 Woodward Avenue
Detroit, MI  48202                  313-876-5000
                                  FAX 313-876-5304

Brings people and jobs together.

**2351   Michigan Protection and Advocacy Service**

4095 Legacy Parkway
Lansing, MI  48911             517-487-1755
                              800-288-5923
                         FAX 517-487-0827
                      http://www.mpas.org
                   e-mail: tmassea@mpas.org
*Elmer Cerano, Executive Director*
*Michele Brand, Finance Administrator*

Advocates for people with disabilities and gives information and advice about their rights as a person with disabilities.

**2352   State Department of Adult Education**

Department of Education
608 W Allegan Street
Lansing, MI  48911             517-241-0162
                         FAX 517-335-0592
                         TDY:517-373-9434
                    http://www.michigan.gov/mde
                   e-mail: equity@ed.mde.state.mi.us
*Lindy Buch, Director*
*Renee , Coordinator*

Promotes quality adult education.

**2353   State GED Administration**

201 N Washington Square, 3rd Floor
Lansing, MI  48909             517-373-1692
                         FAX 517-335-3461
                    http://www.michigan.gov/mdcd
                   e-mail: williamsb4@michigan.gov
*Ben Williams, GED State Administrator*
*Amy Heckman, Administrative Assistant*

Promotes adult education.

## Minnesota

**2354   Assistive Technology**

Minnesota STAR Program
50 Sherburne Avenue
Saint Paul, MN  55155           651-296-2771
                               800-657-3862
                          FAX 651-282-6671
               http://www.admin.state.mn.us/AssistiveTech
                   e-mail: star.program@state.mn.us
*Chuck Rassbach, Executive Director*
*Carole Wiese, Project Coordinator*

Promotes independent living through technology.

**2355   Minnesota Department of Children, Families & Learning**

Department of Education
1500 Highway 36 W
Roseville, MN  55113            651-582-8200
                          FAX 651-582-8202
                    http://www.education.state.mn.us
                   e-mail: tammy.mcglone@state.mn.us
*Tammy McGlone, Director*
*Alice Seagren, Commissioner*

Works to help communities to improve the well-being of children through programs that focus on education.

**2356   Minnesota Department of Human Rights**

Army Corps of Engineers
190 E 5th Street
St. Paul, MN  55101             651-296-5663
                               800-657-3704
                          FAX 651-296-9064
                    http://www.humanrights.state.mn.us
                   e-mail: webmaster@therightsplace.net
*Thelma Korbel, Commissioner*

**2357   Minnesota Governor's Council on Developmental Disabilities**

370 Centennial Office Building
Saint Paul, MN  55155           651-296-9964
                               877-348-0505
                          FAX 651-297-7200
                          TDY:612-296-9962
           http://www.partnersinpolicymaking.com/mnddc.
                                              org
                   e-mail: admin.dd@state.mn.us
*Colleen PhD, Executive Director*

To teach best practices in disability, and to teach the competencies of influencing and communication.

**2358   Minnesota Life Work Center**

University of St. Thomas
1000 La Salle Avenue
Minneapolis, MN  55403          651-962-4763
                    http://www.stthomas.edu
                   e-mail: lifework@stthomas.edu
*Brian Dusbiber, Director*
*Mary Kernan, Career Counselor*

Supporting the educational goals, personal growth and career management needs of graduate students, education students, and alumni, through professional services and comprehensive resources.

**2359   Protection & Advocacy Agency**

Minnesota Disability Law Center
430 1st Avenue N
Minneapolis, MN  55401          612-332-1441
                               800-292-4150
                          FAX 612-334-5755
                          TDY:612-332-4668
                    http://www.mnlegalservices.org/mdlc
                   e-mail: lcohen@midmnlegal.org
*Pamela Huopes, Legal Director*
*Lisa Cohen, Administrator*

**2360  State Department of Adult Education**
Department of Children, Families & Learning
1500 Highway 36 W
Roseville, MN  55113          651-582-8200
FAX 651-582-8727
http://www.education.state.mn.us
e-mail: barry.shaffer@state.mn.us
*Barry Shaffer, Director Adult Education*

## Mississippi

**2361  Client Assistance Program (CAP): Mississippi Division of Persons with Disabilities**
Easter Seals Society
3226 N State Street
Jackson, MS  39216          601-982-7051
888-982-7051
FAX 601-982-1951
http://www.members.aol.com/msess1/cap.htm
*Presley Posey, Director*

Provides free services to consumers and applicants of projects, programs and facilities funded under the rehabilitation act.

**2362  Correctional Education**
PO Box A
Parchman, MS  38738          662-745-6611
FAX 601-745-3101
http://www.mdoc.state.ms.us
*Marjorie Dall, Acting Director*

**2363  Mississippi Employment Security Commission**
1235 Echelon Parkway
Jackson, MS  39215          601-321-6000
http://www.mesc.state.ms.us/
e-mail: lmi-info@mesc.state.ms.us
Brings people and jobs together.

**2364  Mississippi Project START**
MS Project START
PO Box 1698
Jackson, MS  39215          601-987-4872
800- 852-832
FAX 601-364-2349
*Stephen Power, Director*

The purpose of Project START is to expand the availability of assistive technology through a comprehensive, consumer-responsive, statewide program of technology-related services. The activities include providing technical assistance, conducting systems analysis, information and referral service, conducting training seminars, performing needs assessment and maintaining an equipment loan program.

**2365  State Department of Adult Education**
State Board for Community & Jr Colleges
359 NW Street
Jackson, MS  39205          601-359-3498
FAX 601-359-2198
http://www.mde.k12.ms.us
e-mail: dbowman@mdek12.state.ms.us
*Melody Bounds, Director*
*Paulette White, Bureau Director*

Promotes adult education.

**2366  State Department of Education**
359 NW Street
Jackson, MS  39205          601-359-3498
FAX 601-359-2198
http://www.mde.k12.ms.us
e-mail: dbowman@mdek12.state.ms.us
*Melody Bounds, Director*
*Paulette White, Bureau Director*

Promotes quality education.

## Missouri

**2367  Assistive Technology**
4731 S Cochnise
Independence, MO  64055          816-373-5193
800-647-8557
FAX 816-373-9314
http://www.dat.mo.gov
e-mail: matpmo@swbell.net
*Diane Golden, Director*

**2368  Assistive Technology Project**
University of Missouri-Kansas City
5100 Rockhill Road
Kansas City, MO  64110          816-235-2660
FAX 816-235-2662
http://www.umkc.edu
*Elson Floyd, President*

Promotes independent living through technology.

**2369  Correctional Education**
Department of Corrections
PO Box 236
Jefferson City, MO  65102          573-751-2389
888-877-2389
FAX 573-526-3009
TDY:575-522-1562
http://www.corrections.state.mo.us/divis
*Larry Crawford, Director*
*Judy Croker, Clerk*

**2370  Equal Employment Opportunity Commission**
1222 Spruce Street
St. Louis, MO  63103          314-539-5100
FAX 314-539-7895

These regional offices of agencies enforce laws prohibiting employment discrimination on the basis of disability.

**2371  Great Plains Disability and Business Technical Assistance Center (DBTAC)**

100 Corparte Lake Drive
Columbia, MO  65203                  573-882-3600
                                     800-949-4232
                                 FAX 573-884-4925
                            http://www.adaproject.org
                            e-mail: ada@missouri.edu
*Jim Dejong, Executive Director*
*Liza Hamburg, Office Manager*

Mission is to provide accurate, up-to-date technical information and links to resources regarding the Americans with Disabilities Act. The ADA Project has provided technical assistance since 1991 as one of ten regional Disability and Technical Assistance Centers (DBTAC) established by the National Institute for Disability and Rehabilitation Research (NIDDR)

**2372  Learning Disabilities Association of Missouri**

PO Box 3303
Springfield, MO  65808               417-864-5110
                                 FAX 417-864-7290
                              http://www.ldamo.org
                            e-mail: ldamo@cland.net
*Eleanor Scherff, Director*

**2373  Missouri Protection & Advocacy Services**

925 S Country Club Drive
Jefferson City, MO  65109            573-893-3333
                                     800-392-8667
                                 FAX 573-893-4231
                           http://www.moadvocacy.org
                        e-mail: mopasjc@earthlink.com
*Shawn Loyola, Executive Director*

Protects the rights of individuals with disabilities by providing advocacy and legal services. With branch offices in St. Louis 800-233-3958; Kansas City 800-233-3959; Cape Girardeau 800-356-3163; De Soto 877-321-4419; and Springfield 888-632-9551.

**2374  Protection & Advocacy Agency**

925 S Country Club Drive
Jefferson City, MO  65109            573-893-3333
                                     800-392-8667
                                 FAX 573-893-4231

*Shawn Deloyola, Director*
*Lymette Scott, Secretary*

Protects the rights of individuals with disabilities by providing advocacy and legal services.

**2375  Region VII: US Department of Health and Human Services**

Office of Civil Rights
601 E 12th Street
Kansas City, MO  64106               816-426-7278
                                     800-368-1019
                                 FAX 816-426-3686
                                 TDY:816-426-7065
                            http://www.hhs.gov/region7
*Sharie Last, Program Information Management*

The office for Civil Rights investigates complaints of discrimination against hospitals, nursing homes, social service agencies, mental health facilities, and other federally funded providers of health and social services. The office enforces Title II of the Americans with Disabilities Act with respect to all state and local government entities providing health and social services. This includes public medical and other health training schools and state-provided child care.

## Montana

**2376  Assistive Technology Project**

Rural Institute on Disabilities
52 Corbin Hall
Missoula, MT  59812                  406-243-5467
                                 FAX 406-243-4730
*William Lamb*

This statewide program at the University of Montana promotes assistive devices and services for persons of all ages with disabilities.

**2377  Correctional Education**

Department of Corrections & Human Services
1539 11th Avenue
Helena, MT  19620                    406-444-3930
                                 FAX 406-444-4920
                    http://www.cor.state.mt.us/css/default.csp
*Bill Slaughter, Director*
*Ted Ward, Administrative Support*

**2378  Developmental Disabilities Planning and Advisory Council**

111 N Last Chance Gulch, Unit 1C
Helena, MT  59624                    406-444-1334
                                     800-337-9942
                                 FAX 406-444-5999
                          e-mail: dswingley@state.mt.us
*Deborah Swingley, Executive Director*

**2379  MonTECH**

634 Eddy Avenue
Missoula, MT  59812                  406-243-5676
                                     800-732-0323
                                 FAX 406-243-4730
                          http://www.ruralinstitute.umt.edu
                          e-mail: montech@selway.umt.edu

**2380  Montana Department of Labor & Industry**

PO Box 1728
Helena, MT  59624                    406-444-3555
                                     800-922-2873
                                 FAX 406-444-1394
Promotes well being of Montana's workers, employees and citizens.

**2381 Montana Office of Public Instruction**

PO Box 202501
Helena, MT 59620          406-444-3680
                          888-231-9393
                          FAX 406-444-3924
http://www.asd.com/asd/edconn/tfrdoe.htm

Supports schools so that students acheive high standards.

**2382 Office of Adult Basic and Literacy Education**

Montana Office of Public Instruction
PO Box 202501
Helena, MT 59620          406-444-4443
                          FAX 406-444-1373
http://www.metnet.state.mt.us
*Becky Bird, Director*

---

# Nebraska

---

**2383 Answers4Families: Center on Children, Families, Law**

121 S 13th Street
Lincoln, NE 68588 0227     402-472-0844
http://www.answers4families.org/nrrs
e-mail: chayek@answers4families.org
*Connie Hayek, Director*
*Sharon Bloechle, Omaha Parent Coordinator*

A project of the Center on Children, Families and Law at University of Nebraska. Mission is to provide info, opportunities, education and support to Nebraskans through Internet resources. The Center serves individuals with special needs and mental health disorders, foster families, caregivers, assisted living, and school nurses.

**2384 Assistive Technology Project**

Department of Education
5143 S 48th Street
Lincoln, NE 68516          402-471-0734
                           888-806-6287
                           FAX 402-471-6052
http://www.nde.state.ne.us/ATP/TECHome.html
e-mail: mschultz@atp.state.ne.us
*Mark Schultz, Director*

**2385 Client Assistance Program (CAP): Nebraska Division of Persons with Disabilities**

Nebraska Department of Education
301 Centennial Mall S
Lincoln, NE 68509          402-471-3656
                           800-742-7594
                           FAX 402-471-0117
http://www.nde.state.ne.us
e-mail: victoria@cap.state.ne.us

The Client Assistance Program helps individuals who have concerns or difficulties when applying for or receiving rehabilitation services funded under the Rehabilitation Act.

**2386 Nebraska Department of Labor**

550 S 16th Street
Lincoln, NE 68508          402-471-2600
                           FAX 402-471-9867
http://www.dol.state.ne.us/
e-mail: lme_ne@dol.state.ne.us
*Phill Baker, Administrator*

**2387 Nebraska Equal Opportunity Commission**

1313 Farnam on the Mall
Omaha, NE 68102            402-595-2028
                           800-382-7820
                           FAX 402-595-1205
http://www.neoc.ne.gov.
e-mail: mclancy@ops.org
*Lend Frison, Acting Director*

**2388 State Department of Education**

301 Centennial Mall S
Lincoln, NE 68509          402-471-2295
                           FAX 402-471-0117
http://www.nde.state.ne.us
e-mail: joel.scherling@nde.state.ne.us
*Joel Scherling, Director of Human Resources*
*Frank Lloyd, Director of Rehab Services*

Mission to lead and support the preparation of all Nebraskans for learning, earning, and living.

**2389 State GED Administration**

Department of Education: Adult & Community
301 Centennial Mall S
Lincoln, NE 68509          402-471-4807
                           FAX 402-471-0117
*Vicki Bauer, Director*

Promotes adult education.

**2390 Vocational Rehabilitation Services for Central/East Nebraska**

3335 W Capital Avenue
Grand Island, NE 68803 0000     308-385-6200
                                FAX 402-471-0788
http://www.nchtm.okstate.edu
e-mail: Idaafneb@yahoo.com

Helps individuals with disabilites to secure employment through career planning, education and training, and restorative services as necessarsy to help secure employment. Other county offices are: Columbus 402-562-8065; North Platte 308-535-8100; Central East 308-385-6200; Omaha 402-595-2100; Kearney 308-865-5343; Scottsbluff 308-632-1321; Lincoln 402-471-2331; South Sioux City 402-494-2265; Norfolk 402-370-3200.

# Nevada

**2391** **Assistive Technology**

Office of Community Based Services
3636 56th Research Way
Carson City, NV 89706          775-687-4452
                              FAX 775-687-3292
                              TDY:701-687-3388
http://www.dol.ks.gov/index.html
e-mail: kvogel@gov.mail.state.nv.us
*Richard Weather, Head Director*
*Ken Vogel, Director*
*George Brown, Chairperson*

Promotes independent living through technology.

**2392** **Client Assistance Program (CAP): Nevada
Division of Persons with Disability**

2450 Wrondel Way
Reno, NV 89502               702-486-6888
                            800-633-9879
http://www.detr.state.nv.us/rehab/reh_cap
e-mail: detrcap@nvdtr.orgte.nv.us

Provides free services to consumers and applicants of
projects, programs and facilities funded under the rehabilitation act.

**2393** **Correctional Education**

State Department of Prisons
PO Box 607
Carson City, NV 89702        775-887-8588
                            FAX 775-887-3420
http://www.prisons.state.nu.us/
e-mail: ndopinfo@goumail.state.nu.us
*George Weeks, Director*

To continue and expand an educational training program which contains literacy, ESL, numeracy, community outreach, and vocational training that will
provide long-term benefits to both inmates and the
Nevada community in general.

**2394** **Nevada Bureau of Disability Adjudication**

1050 E Williams Street
Carson City, NV 89701        775-687-4430
http://www.detr.state.nv.us/rehab

Evaluates applications from individuals with permanent disabilities to determine if they are eligible for
federal Supplemental Security Income or Social Security Disability Insurance (SSDI).

**2395** **Nevada Employment Security Department**

500 E 3rd Street
Carson City, NV 89713        775-684-3909
                            FAX 775-684-3910
http://www.nncdetr.org
e-mail: bakeresd@govmail.state.nv.us
*Birgit Baker, Director*

**2396** **Nevada Employment Services: Department of
Employment, Training and Rehabilitation**

Employment Security Division
500 E 3rd Street
Carson City, NV 89713         775-687-4635
                             FAX 775-684-8681

**2397** **Nevada Equal Rights Commission: Fair
Employment Practice Agency**

1515 East Tropicana Avenue
Las Vegas, NV 89119          702-486-7161
                            FAX 702-486-7054
                            TDY:702-486-7164
http://www.detr.state.nu.us/nerc/
e-mail: detrnerc@goumail.state.nu.us
*Birgit Baker, Director*
*Norma Delaney, Management Assistant*

To foster the rights of all persons to seek, obtain and
maintain employment, and to access services in places
of public accommodation without discrimination, dis-
tinction, exclusion or restriction because of race, religion, creed, color, age, sex, disability, national origin
or ancestry.

**2398** **Nevada Governor's Council on Developmental
Disabilities**

3636 56th Research Way
Carson City, NV 89701         775-687-4452
                             FAX 775-687-3292
                             TDY:702-687-3388
http://www.dol.ks.gov/index.html
e-mail: kvogel@govmail.state.nv.us
*George Brown, Chairperson*
*Ken Vogel, Director*

**2399** **Nevada Governor's Council on Rehabilitation &
Employment of People with Disabilities**

505 East King Street
Reno, NV 89701               775-684-3200
                            FAX 775-684-4186
                            http://www.nv.gov
e-mail: mailto:kfbarth@nvdetr.org
*Donna Sanders, Executive Director*

To help insure vocational rehabilitation programs are
consumer oriented, driven and result in employment
outcomes for Nevadans with disabilities. Funding for
innovation and expansions grants

**2400** **Protection & Advocacy Agency**

State Disability and Law Center
6039 Eldora Avenue
Las Vegas, NV 89146          702-257-8150
                            888-349-3843
                            FAX 702-257-8170
                            http://www.ndalc.org
e-mail: ndalc@earthlink.net
*Jack Mayes, Executive Director*

Nevada's protection and advocacy system for individuals with disabilities.

**2401** **State Department of Adult Education**

Nevada Department of Education
700 E 5th Street
Carson City, NV 89701        775-687-9200
                            FAX 775-687-9101
http://www.nde.state.nv.us
e-mail: mkmoen@nsn.142.nu.us/
*Frankie Cave, Director for Special Education*

**2402  State Department of Education**
700 E 5th Street
Carson City, NV  89701          775-687-9200
                               FAX 775-687-9101
               http://www.nde.state.nu.us
*Frankie Cave, Director for Special Education*

## New Hampshire

**2403  Client Assistance Program: Governor's
Commission on Disability**
57 Regional Drive
Concord, NH  03301          603-271-2773
                            800-852-3405
                         FAX 603-271-2837
                         TDY:800-852-3405
             http://www.state.nh.us/disability
*Carole Nadeau, Executive Director*
*Maureen Stimpson, Project Specialist*

Provides information about vocational rehabilitation
services.

**2404  Granite State Independent Living Foundation**
21 Chennell Drive
Concord, NH  03301          603-228-9680
                         FAX 603-225-3304
                         TDY:888-396-3459
                http://www.gsil.org
*Clyde Terry, Executive Director*

A private, non-profit organization committed to
equality of opportunity for all people with disabilities.
GSIL is a statewide information, advocacy, and di-
rect-services organization run by and for people with
disabilities.

**2405  Institute on Disability**
**New Hampshire Technology Partnership Project**
62 College Road
Durham, NH  03824          603-862-0561
                        FAX 603-862-0034
                        TDY:603-862-4320
                http://www.iod.unh.edu
        e-mail: Twillkomm@NHATT.MV.com
*Jan Nisbet, Director*
*Maria Agorastov, Program Coordinator*

**2406  Institute on Disability at theUniversity of New
Hampshire**
105 Pleasant Street
Concord, NH  03301          603-271-8349
                         FAX 603-271-5265
                http://www.iod.unh.edu
*Jan Nisbet, Director*
*Mary Schuh, Associate Director*

Establishsed to provide a coherent university-based
focus for the improvement of knowledge, policy and
practice related to persons with disabilities. Our mission is to promote their full inclusion into their communities through areas of Early Childhood, High
School/Post Secondary, Adult Community Living,
Technology, Public Policy, Leadership Training/Pro-
fessional Development and publications. Work-
shops/seminars contact The Concord Center, Unit 14,
10 Ferry Street, Concord NY 03301, 800-238-2048

**2407  New Hampshire Commission for Human Rights**
2 Chenell Drive
Concord, NH  03301          603-271-2767
                         FAX 603-271-6339
                         TDY:800-735-2964
                http://www.state.nh.us
        e-mail: humanrights@nhsa.state.nh.us
*Katharine Daly, Executive Director*
*Roxanne Juliano, Assistant Director*

Investigates complaints of discrimination in employment, housing and public accommodations based on a
person's, race, color, religion, national origin, sex,
age, marital status, disability or sexual orientation.

**2408  New Hampshire Developmental Disabilities
Council**
21 South Fruit Street
Concord, NH  03301          603-271-3236
                            800-852-3345
                         FAX 603-271-1156
                         TDY:800-735-2964
                http://www.nhddc.com
        e-mail: nhddcncl@aol.com
*Gordon Allen, Executive Director*

**2409  New Hampshire Employment Security**
10 W Street
Concord, NH  03301          603-224-3311
                            800-852-3400
                         FAX 603-229-4353
                         TDY:800-735-2964
                http://www.nhes.state.nh.us
        e-mail: sdupree@nhes.state.nh.us
*Sandy Dupree, Public Information Officer*
*Doris Lachance, Director*

Refers individuals with disabilities to organizations
and agencies that assist people with disabilities without charge.

**2410  New Hampshire Governor's Commission on
Disability**
57 Regional Drive
Concord, NH  03301          603-271-2773
                            800-852-3405
                         FAX 603-271-2837
                         TDY:800-852-3405
             http://www.state.nh.us/disability
        e-mail: cnadeau@gov.state.nh.us
*Carole Nadeau, Executive Director*
*Maureen Stimpson, Project Specialist*

The goal is to remove the barriers, architectural or attitudinal, which bar persons with disabilities from participating in the mainstream of society. Formulates an integrated, comprehensive statewide plan to address the needs of individuals with disabilities. Responds to requests wtih answers to service providers, legislators, state and local officials and the many laws and regulations that affect disability issues. Weekly newpaper column, Beyond the Barriers, and newsletter, The Blue Sheet.

**2411  Parent Information Center: New Hampshire Coalition for Citizens With Disabilities**

151 A Manchester Street
Concord, NH  03302         603-224-7005
                          800-947-7005
                     FAX 603-224-4365
                     TDY:800-947-7005
http://www.parentinformationcenter.org
                          e-mail:
hthalheimer@parentinformationcenter.org
*Heather Thalheimer, Executive Director*
*Valerie Guy, Business Manager*

Works with families through parent training sessions, educational consultations about special ed needs and workshops, provides information, support, and an educational surrogate-parent training and mediation. Governed by a Board comprised of families with members with disability. Established Advisory Council to adsive the staff of community needs. Additional offices in Gorham, 800-286-3006, Mollie White; Manchester, 603-624-8082, Lynn Bolser; Nashua, 603-598-8012; Rochester, 603-330-0896.

**2412  Protection & Advocacy Agency**

18 Low Elf Avenue
Concord, NH  03302         603-228-0432
                          800-834-1721
                     FAX 603-225-2077
                http://www.drcnh.org
*Richard Cohen, Executive Director*

**2413  ServiceLink**

555 Auburn Street
Manchester, NH  03103      603-644-2240
                          866-634-9412
                     FAX 603-644-2361
http://www.servicelink.hailboroughcounty.org
*Dennis Hett, Executive Director*
*Wendi Aultman, Program Coordinator*

Provides community information and assistance to adults with disabilities in accessing services for caregiver support, financial and legal concerns, home care services, housing information, prescription drug options, recreational and social events, volunteer opportunities, wellness education. Offices in Laconia, Chocorua, Keene, Berlin, Littleton, Manchester, Lebanon, Nashua, Concord, Portsmouth, Rochester, Claremont and more satellites in each county, all reached through the toll-free number.

**2414  State Department of Education: Division of Vocational Rehabilitation and State GED Administration**

101 Pleasant Street
Concord, NH  03301         603-271-3759
                     FAX 603-271-1953
                     TDY:603-271-6698
                http://www.ed.state.nh.us
        e-mail: pleatuer@ed.state.nh.us
*Paul Leather, Administrator*

Provides assistance to eligible persons with disabilities in the State of New Hampshire to gain and retain employment outcomes through the provision of direct vocational rehabilitation services, as funded under the Rehabilitation Act Amendments of 1992.

---

## New Jersey

**2415  Assistive Technology**

State Technology Assisted Resource Program
210 S Broad Street
Trenton, NJ  08608         609-292-9742
                          800-382-7765
                     FAX 609-777-0187
*Larrissa Iwankiw, Director*

**2416  New Jersey Department of Education: Special Education**

Office of Special Education Programs
100 Riverview Plaza
Trenton, NJ  08625         609-292-0147
                          800-322-8174
                     FAX 609-984-8422
                     TDY:609-984-8432
                http://www.state.nj.us
e-mail: special.education@doe.state.nj.us
*Barbara Gantwerk, Director*
*Carol Kausman, Manager for Policy & Planning*

The office is resonsible for administering all federal funds received for educating people with disabilities ages 3 through 21. Also monitors the delivery of special education programs operated under state authority, provides mediation services to parents and school districts, processes hearings and conducts complaint investigations. Also funds four learning resource centers (LRCs) that provide information, circulate materials, offer technical assistance/consultation and production services.

**2417  New Jersey Department of Law and Public Safety**

New Jersey Division on Civil Rights
31 Clinton Street
Newark, NJ  07112          973-648-2700
                     FAX 973-648-4405
           http://www.njcivilrigths.org

The Division on Civil Rights enforces the New Jersey Law Against Discrimination which prohibits discrimination in employment, housing and public accommodations because of race, creed, color, national origin, ancestry, sex, affectional and sexual orientation, marital status, nationality or handicap.

**2418 New Jersey Programs for Children with Disabilities: Ages 3 - 5**

Office of Special Education Programs
100 Riverview Plaza
Trenton, NJ 08625          609-292-2912
                         FAX 609-984-8422
                         TDY:609-984-8432
          http://www.state.nj.us/education
      e-mail: special.education@doe.state.nj.us
*Barbara Gantwerk, Director*
*Carol Kausman, Manager for Policy & Planning*

Programs for young children with learning disabilities.

**2419 New Jersey Programs for Infants and Toddlers with Disabilities: Early Intervention System**

Division of Family Health Services
PO Box 364
Trenton, NJ 08625          609-777-7734
                         FAX 609-292-0296
      http://www.state.nj.us/health/fhs/eiphome.htm
*Celeste Wood, Assistant Commissioner*
*Terry Harrison, Coordinator*

Implements a statewide system of service for infants and toddlers, birth to age three, with developmental delays or disabilities. Maintains Services-Case Management in each county as entry into the system. Here a service coordinator talks with the family about their concerns and offers referral information if needed. If developmental evaluation is indicated, the coordinator will facilitate a multidisciplinary evaluation and assessment with no cost to the parents.

**2420 Northeast Disability & Business Technical Assistance Center (NeDBTAC)**

354 S Broad Street
Trenton, NJ 08608          510-285-5600
                         800-949-4232
                         FAX 609-392-3505
                         TDY:609-392-7044
          http://www.disabilityact.com
*Huntly Forester, Project Director*

Offers training and information on the Americans with Disabilities Act (ADA). The Center is a technical assistance program which provides important information and training to all businesses, employers, government agencies and persons with disabilities, plus tax incentive information. Free quarterly newsletter: EVERYBODY'S BUSINESS.

**2421 Protection & Advocacy Agency**

NJ Protection & Advocacy
210 S Broad Street
Trenton, NJ 08608          609-292-9742
                         800-922-7233
                         FAX 609-777-0187
                         TDY:800-852-7899
*Larrissa Iwankiw, Director*
*Marie Davis, Office Manager*

NJP&A is a private nonprofit consumer driven organization established to advocate for and protect the civil, human and leagal rights of citizens of New Jersey with disabilities.

**2422 State Department of Adult Education**

Department of Education
100 Riverview Plaza
Trenton, NJ 08625          609-292-4041
                         FAX 609-633-9825
          http://www.state.nj.us/education
*Arlene Roth, Director Adult Education*

**2423 State GED Administration: Office of Specialized Populations**

New Jersey Department of Education
100 River View Plaza
Trenton, NJ 08625          609-292-4041
                         FAX 609-633-9825
          http://www.state.nj.us/education
*Arlene Roth, Director*

# New Mexico

**2424 Client Assistance Program (CAP): New Mexico Protection and Advocacy System**

1720 Louisiana Boulevard NE
Albuquerque, NM 87110          505-256-3100
                             800-432-4682
                             FAX 505-256-3184
              http://www.nmpanda.org
*James Jackson, Executive Director*

Helps persons with disabilities who have concerns about agencies in New Mexico that provide rehabilitation or independent living services. The kind of help may be information or advocacy. For questions about Division of Vocational Rehabilitation, Commission for the Blind, Independent Living Centers and Preojects With Industsry CAP can help.

**2425 New Mexico Department of Labor: Employment Services and Job Training Programs**

PO Box 1928
Albuquerque, NM 87103          505-841-8409
                             FAX 505-841-8491
          http://www3.state.nm.us/dol/dol_esd.html

Currently composed of two bureaus and under the supervision of a Division Director responsible for the design, administration, management and implementation of the Workforce Investment Act in New Mexico and any successor legislation. Within this capacity, the Division serves on behalf of the Governor with respect to statewide oversight and compliance, and as the principle support staff to the State Workforce Development Board.

**2426 New Mexico Human Rights Commission Education Bureau**

1596 Pacheo Street
Santa Fe, NM 87505          505-827-6838
                          800-566-9471
                          FAX 505-827-6878
          http://www.user.gov/crd/cds_all.htm
*Francie Cordova, Director*

**2427 New Mexico Public Education Department**

300 Don Gaspar Avenue
Santa Fe, NM 87503      505-827-6788
FAX 505-827-6696
http://www.ped.state.nm.us
e-mail: dwatson@ped.state.nm.us
*Don Watson MD, Assistant Secretary*

**2428 New Mexico Technology-Related Assistance Program**

Department of Education
300 Don Gaspar Avenue
Santa Fe, NM 87503      505-954-8521
FAX 505-827-5066
e-mail: mlandazuri@ade.state.nm.us
*Andrew Winnegar, Project Director*

**2429 Protection & Advocacy System**

1720 Louisiana Boulevard
Albuquerque, NM 87110      505-256-3100
800-432-4682
FAX 505-256-3184
http://www.nmpanda.org
e-mail: nmpacurtiss@hotmail.com
*James Jackson, Executive Director*

**2430 State Department of Adult Education**

Department of Education
300 Don Gaspar Avenue
Santa Fe, NM 87501      505-827-6672
FAX 505-623-8220
http://www.sde.state.nm.us
*Patricia Chavez, Contact*

**2431 State GED Administration**

Assessment & Evaluation
300 Don Gaspar Avenue
Santa Fe, NM 87503      505-827-6788
FAX 505-827-6696
http://www.ped.state.nm.us
e-mail: dwatson@ped.state.nm.us
*Don Watson MD, Assistant Secretary*

# New York

**2432 Client Assistance Program**

CAP Director, NY Commission on Quality of Care
99 Washington Avenue
Albany, NY 12210      518-473-7378
FAX 800-624-4143

Provides free services to consumers and applicants for projects, programs and facilities funded under the rehabilitation act.

**2433 Department of Correctional Services**

1220 Washington Avenue
Albany, NY 12226      518-457-8126
FAX 518-457-7252
http://www.docs.state.ny.us/
*Glenn Goord, Commissioner*
*John Patterson, Executive Deputy Commissioner*

**2434 New York Department of Human Rights**

1 Fordham Plaza
Bronx, NY 10458      718-741-8400
FAX 718-741-3214
TDY:718-741-8304
http://www.nysdhr.com
*Michelle Donaldson, Head Commissioner*
*Arlene Williams, Key Board Specialist 1*

**2435 New York Department of Labor: Employment Services & Job Training**

State Office Building Campus 12
Albany, NY 12240      518-457-6369
FAX 518-485-1727
TDY:888-783-1370
http://www.labor.state.ny.us
e-mail: nysdol@labor.state.ny.us
*Robert Lillpopp, Director of Communications*
*Ruth Pillittere, Assistant Director*

**2436 New York Office of Advocates: TRAID Project**

1 Empire State Plaza
Albany, NY 12223      518-474-2825
800-522-4369
FAX 518-473-6005
http://www.oatwd.org
e-mail: oapwdinfo@advoc4disabled.state.ny.us
*Lisarah Rosano-Kackowski, Project Manager*

A statewide systems advocacy program promoting assistive technology devices and services to persons of all ages with all disabilities.

**2437 New York State Developmental Disabilities Council**

155 Washington Avenue
Albany, NY 12210      518-486-7505
800-395-3372
FAX 518-402-3505
TDY:800-395-3372
http://www.ddpc.state.ny.us
e-mail: grants@ddpc.state.ny.us
*Sheila Carey, Executive Director*
*George Fertal Sr., Chairperson*

**2438    New York State Office of Vocational &
Educational Services for Individuals with
Disabilities**

301 Manchester Road
Poughkeepsie, NY  12603                845-452-5325
                                    FAX 845-452-5336
                                    TDY:845-452-2910
                              http://www.nysad.gov
                        e-mail: doshea@mail.nysad.gov
*Bruce Solomkin, District Office Manager*
*Dan O'Shea, Senior Counselor/Manager*

The Office of Vocational and Educational Services for
Individuals with Disabilities (VESID), helps people
with disabilities find and maintain employment. Services include job placement, training at colleges, tuition assistance based on economic need, home and
vehicle modifications, vocational guidance and counseling.

**2439    Office of Advocacy for Persons with Disabilities**

One Empire State Plaza
Albany, NY  12223                     518-474-2825
                                    FAX 518-473-6005
                                    TDY:518-473-4231
*Lisarah Rosano-Kackowski, Project Manager*

**2440    Office of Curriculum & Instructional Support**

State Department of Adult Education
Washington Avenue
Albany, NY  12234                     518-474-8892
                                    FAX 518-474-0319
                        http://www.emsc.nysed.gov/workforce
                        e-mail: jstevens@mail.nysed.gov
*Jean Stevens, Assistant Commissioner*
*Tom Orsini, Team Leader of Adult Education*

Works with those seeking General Educational Development diplomas and technical training.

**2441    Programs for Children with Disabilities: Ages 3 - 5**

State Education Department
1 Commerce Plaza
Albany, NY  12234                     518-473-6108
                                    FAX 518-473-4057
                                    TDY:800-222-JOBS
                        http://www.vesid.nysed.gov/publications
                        e-mail: rmills@mail.nysed.gov
*Richard Mills, President /Commissioner*
*David Johnson, Secretary of Board of Regents*

**2442    Programs for Children with Special Health Care
Needs**

Bureau of Child & Adolescent Health
Corning Tower Building
Albany, NY  12237                     518-486-4966
                                    FAX 518-474-5445
                              http://www.health.state.ny.us
                        e-mail: rmdo7@health.state.ny.us
*Rachele long, Acting Director*
*Martha Riser, Assistant Director*

**2443    Programs for Infants and Toddlers with
Disabilities**

Bureau of Early Intervention
Bureau of Child & Adolescent Health
Albany, NY  12237                     518-473-7016
                                    FAX 518-486-1090
                              http://www.health.state.ny.us
                        e-mail: blm01@health.state.ny.us
*Barbara Tague, Acting Director*
*Donna Noyes, Director of Clinical Services*

**2444    Protection & Advocacy Agency**

NY Commission on Quality of Care
99 Washington Avenue
Albany, NY  12210                     518-473-7378
                                    FAX 800-624-4143

**2445    Region II: US Department of Health and Human
Services**

Office of Civil Rights
26 Federal Plaza
New York, NY  10278                   212-264-3313
                                    FAX 212-264-3039
                                    TDY:212-264-2355
                              http://www.hhs.gov\ocr
*Richard Campanelli, Director*
*Robinsue Frohboese, Principal Deputy Director*

These regional offices of agencies enforce laws prohibiting employment discrimination on the basis of
disability.

**2446    State Developmental Disabilities Planning Council**

NYS DD Planning Council
Tower Building
Albany, NY  12237                     518-474-2084
                                    FAX 518-473-8673
*Rachel long, Acting Director*

**2447    State GED Administration**

State Education Department
PO Box 7348
Albany, NY  12224 0348                518-474-3852
                                    FAX 518-474-3041
                        http://www.emsc.nysed.gov/workforce/ged
                        e-mail: ged@mail.nysed.gov
*Patricia Mooney, GED Administrator*

Instruction and testing for those over the age of 16 to
earn the General Educational Development diploma.

**2448    Vocational & Educational Services for Individuals
with Disabilities**

New York State Education Department
One Commerce Plaza
Albany, NY  12234                     518-474-7566
                                        800-222-5627
                                    FAX 518-473-9466
                                    TDY:800-222-5627
                              http://www.vesid.nysed.gov
                        e-mail: rmills@mail.nysed.gov
*Richard Mills, Commissioner*
*Rebecca Cort, Deputy Director*

Promotes educational equality and excellence for students with disabilities while ensuring that they receive the rights and protection to which they are entitled. Assures appropriate continuity between the child and adult services systems, and provides the highest quality vocational rehabilitation and independent living services to all eligible people.

## North Carolina

**2449** **Assistive Technology Program**

**Department of Human Resources**
**1110 Navaho Drive**
**Raleigh, NC 27609**          **919-850-2787**
                                  **FAX 919-850-2792**
                                  **TDY:919-850-2787**
                                  **http://www.ncatp.org**
*Carol William, Consumer Resource Specialist*
*Tina Daley, Administrative Assistant*

Provides free, statewide assistive technology services such as demonstration, loan, training, funding, resources, awareness and outreach presentations to persons of all ages and abilities.

**2450** **Client Assistance Program (CAP): North Carolina Division of Persons with Disabilities**

**2801 Mail Service Center**
**Raleigh, NC 27699**          **919-855-3600**
                                  **800-215-2772**
                                  **FAX 919-715-2456**
                **e-mail: kathy.brack@ncmail.net**
*Kathy Brack, Director*
*Tamy Andrews, Administrative Assistant*

The Client Assistance Program helps people understand and use rehabilitation services.

**2451** **North Carolina Council on Developmental Disabilities**

**1001 Navaho Drive**
**Raleigh, NC 27609**          **919-850-2833**
                                  **800-357-6916**
                                  **FAX 919-850-2895**
                                  **TDY:800-357-6916**
                          **http://www.nc-ddc.org**
          **e-mail: hriddle@ddc.dhr.state.nc.us**
*William Morris III, Council Chair*
*Holly , Executive Director*

**2452** **North Carolina Division of Employment and Training**

**313 Chapanoke Road**
**Raleigh, NC 27604**          **919-661-6010**
                                  **800-562-6333**
                                  **FAX 919-662-4770**
                          **http://www.ncdet.com**
*Alan Alexander, Director*
*Patricia Pate, Office Assistant*

**2453** **North Carolina Division of Vocational Rehabilitation**

**Department of Human Resources**
**2801 Mail Service Center**
**Raleigh, NC 27699 2801**          **919-855-3500**
                                  **FAX 919-733-7968**
                          **http://www.dvr.dhhs.state.nc.us**
                  **e-mail: gmccoy@dhr.state.nc.us**
*Carmen Hooker-Odom, Secretary Health/Human Services*
*George McCoy, Director*

Vocational rehabilitation counselors work with business and community agencies to help them prepare their worksites to accommodate employees who have physical or mental disabilities. The division also provides services that encourage and reinforce independent living for the disabled.

**2454** **North Carolina Employment Security Commission**

**PO Box 27625**
**Raleigh, NC 27605**          **919-733-7522**
                                  **FAX 919-733-0773**
                          **http://www.ncesc.com**
                  **e-mail: harry.payne@ncmail.net**
*Harry Payne, Chairman*
*Tom Whitaker, Assistant*

**2455** **North Carolina Office of Administrative Hearings: Civil Rights Division**

**PO Box 27447**
**Raleigh, NC 27611**          **919-733-0431**
                                  **FAX 919-733-4866**
*Ed Smith, Director*
*Arlo Lund, Personnel Officer*

**2456** **Office of the Governor**

**116 W Jones Street**
**Raleigh, NC 27603**          **919-733-7061**
                                  **FAX 919-733-0640**
                          **http://www.ncgov.com**
*Susan Rabon, Department Head*
*Margaret Johnson, Assistant*

**2457** **State Department of Adult Education**

**North Carolina Community College System**
**Caswell Building**
**Raleigh, NC 27699**          **919-807-7132**
                                  **FAX 919-807-7164**
                          **http://www.ncccs.cc.nc.us**
                  **e-mail: randyw@ncccs.cc.nc.us**
*Randy Whitfield MD, Associate Vice President*

## North Dakota

**2458    Client Assistance Program (CAP): Nebraska Division of Persons with Disabilities**

600 S 2nd Street
Bismarck, ND  58504          701-328-8947
800-207-6122
FAX 701-328-8969
TDY:701-328-8968
http://www.state.nd.us/cap/
e-mail: cap@state.nd.us

*Dennis Lyon, Director*
*Donna Nitschke, Administrative Assistant*

Provides free services to consumers and applicants for projects, programs and facilities funded under the rehabilitation act.

**2459    Department of Public Instruction**

Division of Adult Education
600 E Boulevard Avenue
Bismarck, ND  58505          701-328-2393
FAX 701-328-4770
http://www.dpi.state.nd.us
e-mail: dmassey@sendit.nodak.edu

*David Massey, Director Adult Education*
*Jolli Marcellais, Administrative Assistant*

**2460    North Dakota Department of Human Services**

Vocational Rehabilitation
600 S 2nd Street
Bismarck, ND  58504          701-328-8950
800-755-2745
FAX 701-328-8969
http://www.stae.nd.us/human services
e-mail: soperc@state.nd.us

*Jean Hyfjulien, Director*

**2461    North Dakota Department of Labor: Fair Employment Practice Agency**

600 E Boulevard Avenue
Bismarck, ND  58505          701-328-2660
800-582-8032
FAX 701-328-2031
TDY:800-366-688
http://www.state.nd.us/labor/
e-mail: labor@state.nd.us

*Leann Bertsch, Commissioner of Labor*
*Kathy kulesa, Human Rights Director*

Provides information and enforces laws related to labor standards and discrimination in employment, housing, public services, public accommodations and lending. The department also issues sub minimum wage certificates, verifies independent contractor status and licenses employment agencies.

**2462    North Dakota State Council on Developmental Disabilities**

ND Department of Human Services
600 E Boulevard Avenue
Bismarck, ND  58505          701-328-8953
FAX 701-328-8969
e-mail: sowalt@state.nd.us

*Tom Wallner, Executive Director*

## Ohio

**2463    Assistive Technology**

JL Camera Center
2050 Kenny Road
Columbus, OH  43212          614-292-3158
800-784-3425
FAX 614-292-5866
http://www.atohio.org
e-mail: huntt.1@osu.edu

*Douglas Hunt, Director*

**2464    Client Assistance Program (CAP): Ohio Division**

Gov Office of Advocacy for People w/Disabilities
8 E Long Street
Columbus, OH  43266          614-466-7264
800-282-9181
FAX 614-644-1888
http://www.olrs.ohio.gov

*Carolyn Knight, Director*
*Patt Brown, Secretary*

Provides free services to consumers and applicants for projects, programs and facilities funded under the Rehabilitation Act.

**2465    Correctional Education**

Department of Rehabilitation & Correction
1050 Freeway Drive
Columbus, OH  43229          614-752-1162
FAX 614-752-1086
http://www.drc.state.oh.us
e-mail: publicinfo@odrc.state.oh.us

*Jerry McGlone MD, Director*
*Amy Heckman, Administrative Assistant*

**2466    Ohio Adult Basic and Literacy Education**

Ohio Department of Education
25 S Front Street
Columbus, OH  43215          614-466-5015
FAX 614-728-8470
http://www.ode.state.oh.us/ctae/adult/able
e-mail: jim.bowling@ode.state.oh.us

*Denise Pottmyer, State Director*
*Joyce Sheets, Secretary*

**2467 Ohio Civil Rights Commission**
1111 E Broad Street
Columbus, OH 43205    614-466-5928
FAX 614-466-6250
TDY:614-752-2391
http://www.state.oh.us/crc/
e-mail: harringtonc@ocrc.state.oh.us
*Beleta Ebron, Regional Director*
*Michael Payton, Executive Director*

**2468 Ohio Developmental Disabilities Council**
8 E Long Street
Columbus, OH 43215    614-466-5205
800-766-7426
FAX 614-466-0298
TDY:614-644-5530
http://www.ohio.gov/ddc
*Kay Treanor, Children's Issues Committee*

A federal program under the DD Act which strives to develop innovative programs and services to support individuals with disabilities, and to make them more a part of their own communities.

**2469 Ohio Governor's Office of Advocacy for People With Disabilities**
8 E Long Street
Columbus, OH 43266    614-466-9956
FAX 614-644-1888
TDY:614-728-2553
http://www.olrs.ohio.gov
e-mail: webmaster@olrs.state.oh.us
*Carolyn Knight, Director*
*Jeffrey Folkerth, Administrative Services Director*

Helps children and adults with disabilities.

**2470 Ohio Office of Workforce Development Job Training Program Liaison**
Ohio Department of Job & Family Services
145 S Front Street
Columbus, OH 43215-4156    614-466-2100
FAX 614-995-1298
http://www.ohioworkforce.org
e-mail: workforce@odjfs.state.oh.us
*William Demidovich, Deputy Director*
*Mark Birnbrich, Assistant Deputy Director*

**2471 Protection & Advocacy Agency**
Ohio Legal Rights Service
8 E Long Street
Columbus, OH 43215    614-466-7264
800-282-9181
FAX 614-644-1888
http://www.olrs.ohio.gov
e-mail: hn7149@handsnet.org
*Carolyn Knight, Director*
*Patt Brown, Secretary*

Advocacy services.

**2472 State Department of Education**
65 S Front Street
Columbus, OH 43215    614-466-0224
877-644-6338
FAX 614-728-2338
http://www.ode.state.oh.us
e-mail: jeanne.Lance@ode.state.oh.us
*Frank New, Director*

**2473 State GED Administration**
State Department of Education
25 S Frontstreet Drive
Columbus, OH 43215    614-466-0224
FAX 614-728-2338
*David Fischer, GED Administrator*
*Susan , Officer In Charge*

## Oklahoma

**2474 Assistive Technology**
Seretean OSU-Wellness Center
1514 W Hall Of Fame
Stillwater, OK 74078    405-744-9864
800-257-1705
FAX 405-744-2487
TDY:888-885-5588
http://www.okabletech.okstate.edu
e-mail: mljwell@okstate.edu
*Linda Jaco, Program Manager*

**2475 Client Assistance Program (CAP): Oklahoma Division**
Office of Handicapped Concerns
2401 NW 23rd
Oklahoma City, OK 73107    405-521-3756
800-522-8224
FAX 405-522-6695
TDY:405-522-6706
http://www.ohc.state.ok.us
e-mail: CAP@ohc.state.ok.us
*Steven Stokes, Director*
*Dalene Barton, Office Manager*

The purpose of this program is to advise and inform clients and client applicants of all services and benefits available to them through programs authorized under the Rehabilitation Act of 1973. Assist and advocates for clients and client applicants in their relationships with projects, programs, and community rehabilitation programs providing services under the Act.

**2476 Correctional Education**
Department of Corrections
PO Box 11400
Oklahoma City, OK 73136    405-425-2500
FAX 405-425-2500
http://www.doc.state.ok.us
*Ron Ward, Director*

**2477 Oklahoma Disability Law Center**

Oklahoma City Office
2915 Classen Boulevard
Oklahoma City, OK 73106      405-525-7755
                            800-880-7755
                        FAX 405-525-7759
   http://www.oklahomadisabilitylaw.org
          e-mail: kbower1@flash.net
*Kayla Bower JD, Director*
*Janice Williams, Assistant*

Protection and advocacy system for people with disabilities.

**2478 Protection & Advocacy Agency**

Disability Law Center
2915 Classen Boulevard
Oklahoma City, OK 73106      405-525-7755
                            800-880-7755
                        FAX 405-525-7759
   http://www.oklahomadisabiltylaw.org
*Kayla Bower, Executive Director*
*Janice Williams, Assistant*

**2479 Secretary of Education**

2500 N Lincoln Boulevard
Oklahoma City, OK 73105      405-521-3311
                        FAX 405-521-2971
          http://www.sde.state.ok.us
*Sharon Lease MD, Assistant State Superintendent*

**2480 State Department of Adult Education**

Department of Education
2500 N Lincoln Boulevard
Oklahoma City, OK 73105      405-521-4873
                            800-405-0355
                        FAX 405-522-3503
          http://www.sde.state.ok.us
   e-mail: linda_young@mail.sde.state.ok.us
*Linda Young, Director*

**2481 State GED Administration**

State Department of Education
2500 N Lincoln Boulevard
Oklahoma City, OK 73105      405-521-4873
                        FAX 405-522-3503
          http://www.sde.state.ok.us
*Linda Young, Director*

## Oregon

**2482 Department of Community Colleges and Workforce Development**

255 Capitol Street NE
Salem, OR 97310              503-378-8648
                        FAX 503-378-8434
       http:// www.oregon.gov/ccwd
   e-mail: Sharlene.walker@odccwd.state.or.us
*Sharlene Walker, GED Administrator*

**2483 Oregon Advocacy Center**

620 SW 5th Avenue
Portland, OR 97204           503-243-2081
                            800-452-1694
                        FAX 503-243-1738
                        TDY:800-556-5351
          http://www.oradvocacy.org
     e-mail: welcome@oradvocacy.org
*Robert Joondeph, Director*
*Barbara Hergeth, Assistant Director*

**2484 Oregon Bureau of Labor and Industry: Fair Employment Practice Agency**

800 NE Oregon Street
Portland, OR 97232           503-731-4200
                        FAX 503-731-4208
          http://www.boli.state.or.us
   e-mail: dan.gardner@boli.state.or.us
*Dan Gardner, Commissioner*
*Annette Talbott, Deputy Commissioner*

**2485 Oregon Council on Developmental Disabilities**

540 24th Place NE
Salem, OR 97301              503-945-9941
                            800-292-4154
                        FAX 503-945-9947
          http://www.ocdd.org
       e-mail: oddc@aol.com
*Dill Lynch, Executive Director*

**2486 Oregon Department of Education: School-to-Work**

255 Capitol Street NE
Salem, OR 97310              503-378-3584
                        FAX 503-378-5156
                        TDY:503-378-3825
          http://www.ode.state.or.us
   e-mail: ode.frontdesk@ode.state.or.us
*Robert Larson, Policy & Research Director*
*Patrick Burk, Education Policy Deputy Director*

School-to-Work is a federally funded initiative that provides funding for state and local implementation of the Oregon Educational Act for the 21st Century.

**2487   Oregon Department of Human Resource Adult & Family Services Division**

500 Summer Street NE
Salem, OR  97310                    503-945-5733
                                   FAX 503-378-2897
                          http://www.dhs.state.or.us
                          e-mail: dhr.info@state.or.us
*Ramona Foley, Assistant Director*
*Gary Weeks, Director*

This group combines programs from the former Adult & Family Services Division and the State Office for Services to Children and Families.

**2488   Oregon Employment Department**

875 Union Street NE
Salem, OR  97311                    503-947-1394
                                   800-237-3710
                                   FAX 503-947-1668
                          http://www.workinoregon.org
*Deborah Lincoln, Director*
*Greg Hickman, Deputy Director*
*Odie Vogel, Assistant to Director*

Supports economic stability for Oregonians and communities during times of unemployment through the payment of unemployment benefits. Serves businesses by recruiting and referring the best qualified applicants to jobs, and provides resources to diverse job seekers in support of their employment needs.

**2489   State Department of Adult Education**

Department of Community Colleges
255 Capitol Street NE
Salem, OR  97310                    503-378-8648
                                   FAX 503-378-8434
                          http:// www.oregon.gov/ccwd
                          e-mail: sharlene.walker@state.or.us
*Sharlene Walker, GED Administrator*

**2490   Technology Access for Life Needs Project**

Access Technologies
3070 Lancaster Drive NE
Salem, OR  97305                    503-361-1201
                                   FAX 503-370-4530
                                   TDY:503-361-1201
                          http://www.taln.org
                          e-mail: info@accesstechnologiesinc.org
*Laurie Brooks, Executive Director*

A statewide program promoting services and assistive devices for people with disabilities.

**2491   Vocational Rehabilitation Division**

Department of Human Services
500 Summer Street NE
Salem, OR  97301 1098               503-945-5944
                                   877-277-0513
                                   FAX 503-378-2897
              http://www.dhs.state.or.us/vr/index.html
                          e-mail: info.vr@state.or.us
*Gary Weeks, Director Human Services*
*Stephanie Parrish-Taylor, Program Director*

Uses state and federal funds to assist Oregonians who have disabilities to achieve and maintain employment and independence.

## Pennsylvania

**2492   Client Assistance Program (CAP): Pennsylvania Division**

1617 JFK Boulevard
Philadelphia, PA  19103             215-557-7112
                                   888-745-2357
                                   FAX 215-557-7602
                                   TDY:215-577-7112
                          http://www.equalemployment.org
                          e-mail: info@equalemployment.org
*Steve Pennington, Director*

CAP is an advocacy program for people with disabilities administered by the Center for Disability Law and Policy. CAP helps people who are seeking services from the Office of Vocational Rehabilitation, Blindness and Visual Services, Centers for Independent Living and other programs funded under federal law. CAP services are provided at no charge.

**2493   Correctional Education**

Bureau of Correction Education
75 Utleg Drive
Camp Hill, PA  17011                717-731-7823
                                   FAX 717-731-7830
                          e-mail: bmaden@cor.state.pa.us
*Richard Bayer, Director*
*Janet Ring, Clerk*

**2494   Developmental Disabilities Council**

Commonwealth Avenue
Harrisburg, PA  17120               717-787-6057
                                   FAX 717-772-0738
                          http://www.paddc.org
                          e-mail: info@paddc.org
*Graham Mulholland, Executive Director*

**2495   Pennsylvania Human Rights Commission and Fair Employment Practice**

301 Chestnut Street
Harrisburg, PA  17101               717-787-4410
                                   FAX 715-214-0584
                                   TDY:717-783-9308
                          http://www.phrc.state.pa.us
*Homer Floyd, Executive Director*

The PHRC enforces the State's antidiscrimination laws in employment, housing, public accommodations and education. It receives, investigates, resolves and litigates formal complaints filed by aggrieved persons in three regional offices: Pittsburgh, Harrisburg and Philadelphia.

**2496   Pennsylvania Initiative on Assistive Technology**

1301 Cecil Moore Avenue
Philadelphia, PA  19122             215-204-1356
                                   FAX 215-204-6336
                                   TDY:215-204-1356
              http://www.temple.edu/ins_disabilities
              e-mail: dianeb@astro.ocis.temple.edu
*Amy Goldman, Director*

Mission to increase access to assistive technology for all Pennsylvanians with disabilities.

**2497  Pennsylvania's Initiative on Assistive Technology**

Institute on Disabilities at Temple University
423 Ritter Annex
Philadelphia, PA  19122          800-204-7428
                                 800-750-7428
                            FAX 215-204-9371
http://www.disabilities.temple/edu/piat
            e-mail: piat@temple.edu
*Carol Kann, Information Coordinator*


**2498  Protection & Advocacy Agency**

1414 N Cameron Street
Harrisburg, PA  17101           717-236-8110
                                800-692-7443
                           FAX 717-236-0192
                           TDY:877-375-7139
            http://www.ppainc.org
*Ilene Shane, Executive Director*
*Judy Banks, Deputy Director*

Provides information and referral to persons with disabilities and mental health issues.

**2499  Region III: US Department of Health and Human Services, Civil Rights Office**

US Department of Health & Human Services
150 S Independence Mall West
Philadelphia, PA  19106          215-861-4441
                                 800-368-1019
                            FAX 215-861-4431
                            TDY:215-861-4440

These regional offices of agencies enforce laws prohibiting employment discrimination on the basis of disability.

**2500  State Department of Adult Education**

333 Market Street
Harrisburg, PA  17101           570-722-3737
                           FAX 717-783-0583
http://www.pde.psu.edu/able/index.html
         e-mail: ckeenan@state.pa.us
*Cheryl Keenan, Director*


**2501  State Department of Education**

333 Market Street
Harrisburg, PA  01726           717-787-5820
                           FAX 717-787-7222
         http:// www.pde.state.pa.us
         e-mail: pde@psupen.psu.edu
*Donald Carroll, Secretary*


**2502  State GED Administration**

Pennsylvania Department of Education
333 Market Street
Harrisburg, PA  17101           717-787-5820
                           FAX 717-787-7222
         http://www.pde.state.pa.us
         e-mail: pde@psupen.psu.edu
*Lawrence Goodwin, Director*

## Rhode Island

**2503  Correctional Education**

Rhode Island Department of Corrections
PO Box 8312
Cranston, RI  02920             401-462-1000
                           FAX 401-464-2509
*Timothy Murphy, Administrator Education Services*


**2504  Protection & Advocacy Agency**

Rhode Island Disability Law Center
349 Eddy Street
Providence, RI  02903           401-831-3150
                                800-733-5332
                           FAX 401-274-5568
                           TDY:401-831-5335
            http://www.ridlc.org
*Raymond Bandusky, Executive Director*
*Jackie Johnson, Administrative Assistant*


**2505  Rhode Island Commission for Human Rights**

180 Westminster Stce
Providence, RI  02903           401-222-2661
                           FAX 401-222-2616


**2506  Rhode Island Department of Elementary and Secondary Education**

Rhode Island Department of Education
400 W Westminister Street
Providence, RI  02903           401-222-4600
                           FAX 401-222-6030
            http://www.ridoe.net
         e-mail: ccast@ride.ri.net
*Peter McWalters, Commissioner*
*Todd Flaherty, Deputy Commissioner*


**2507  Rhode Island Department of Employment Services & Job Training**

101 Friendship Street
Providence, RI  02903           401-277-3732
                           FAX 401-277-1473
         http://www.dlt.state.ri.us


**2508  Rhode Island Developmental Disabilities Council**

Rhode Island Department of Education
400 Bald Hill Road
Warwick, RI  02886              401-737-1238
                           FAX 401-737-3395
            http://www.riddc.org
         e-mail: riddc@riddc.org
*Marie Citrone, Executive Director*
*Mary Okero, Associate Director*
*Sylvia Klien, Secretary*

**2509  State Department of Adult Education**
400 W Westminster Street
Providence, RI  02903                    401-222-4600
                                         FAX 701-222-6030
                                         http://www.ridoe.net
*Robert Mason, Adult Education Specialist*

## South Carolina

**2510  Assistive Technology Program**
**South Carolina Developmental Disabilities Council**
**1205 Pendleton Street**
**Columbia, SC  29201**                  803-734-0465
                                         FAX 803-734-0241
                                         TDY:803-734-1147
                                         http://www.scddc.state.sc.us
                                         e-mail: jjenning@govoepp.state.sc.us
*Charles Lang, Director*
*Peggy Cannon, Administrative Assistant*

A statewide project established to provide an opportunity for individuals with disabilities to lead the fullest, most productive lives possible.

**2511  Protection & Advocacy Agency**
**3710 Landmark Drive**
**Columbia, SC  29204**                  803-782-0639
                                         866-275-7273
                                         FAX 803-790-1946
                                         TDY:866-275-7273
                                         http://www.protectionandadvocacy.org
                                         e-mail: scpa@sc-online.net
*Gloria Prevost, Executive Director*
*Anne Price, Administrative Director*

**2512  South Carolina Department of Corrections**
**4444 Broad River Road**
**Columbia, SC  29221**                  803-896-8555
                                         FAX 803-896-1220
                                         http://www.state.sc.us/scdc
                                         e-mail: corrections.info@doc.state.sc.us
*John Ozmint, Executive Director*
*Donna Hodges, Executive Assistant*

**2513  South Carolina Developmental Disabilities Council**
**South Carolina Developmental Disabilities Council**
**1205 Pendleton Street**
**Columbia, SC  29201**                  803-734-0465
                                         FAX 803-734-0241
                                         TDY:803-734-1147
                                         http://www.scddc.state.sc.us
                                         e-mail: jjenning@govoepp.state.sc.us
*Charles Lang, Executive Director*
*Peggy Cannon, Administrative Assistant*

**2514  South Carolina Employment Services and Job Training Services**
**PO Box 995**
**Columbia, SC  29202**                  803-737-2617
                                         FAX 803-737-2642
                                         http://www.sces.org
                                         e-mail: mmungo@sces.org
*Roosevelt Halley, Executive Director*
*Joey Tate, Executive Assistant*

**2515  South Carolina Human Affairs Commission**
**2611 Forest Drive**
**Columbia, SC  29204**                  803-737-7800
                                         800-521-0725
                                         FAX 803-253-4191
                                         http://www.schac.state.sc.us
                                         e-mail: information@schac.state.sc.us
*Jessie Washington, Commissioner*

**2516  State Department of Adult Education**
**1429 Senate Street**
**Columbia, SC  29201**                  803-734-8071
                                         FAX 803-734-2780
                                         http://www.myschools.com
                                         e-mail: cldaniel@sde.state.sc.us
*Cherry Daniel, Director*

**2517  State GED Administration**
**Department of Education**
**1429 Senate Street**
**Columbia, SC  29201**                  803-734-0322
                                         FAX 803-734-6142
*David Stout, GED Administrator*

## South Dakota

**2518  Client Assistance Program (CAP): South Dakota Division**
**South Dakota Advocacy Services**
**221 S Central Avenue**
**Pierre, SD  57501**                    605-224-8294
                                         800-658-4782
                                         FAX 605-224-5125
                                         TDY:605-224-8294
                                         http://www.sdadvocacy.com
                                         e-mail: sdas@sdadvocacy.com
*Robert Kean, Executive Director*
*Pam Middleton, Administrative Assistant*

Provides free services to consumers and applicants for projects, programs and facilities funded under the rehabilitation act.

**2519  Department of Correction: Education Coordinator**

Solem Public Safety Center
3200 E Highway 34
Pierre, SD  57501                    605-773-3478
FAX 605-773-3194
http://www.state.sd.us/
e-mail: DOCInternetinfo@state.sd.us
*Douglas Weber, Director*
*Joey Bjerae, Accounting Assistant*

**2520  South Dakota Council on DevelopmentalDisabilities**

Department of Human Services
Hillsview Plaza, E Highway 34
Pierre, SD  57501                    605-773-6339
FAX 605-773-5483
TDY:605-773-5990
http://www.state.sd.us/dhs/ddc
e-mail: info@DCC.dhs.state.sd.us
*Arlene Poncelet, Executive Director*

Established by the Developmental Disabilities Assistance Act, the council is made up of 21 members appointed by the Governor. The council works toward independence, productivity, integration and inclusion of individuals with developmental disabilities and their families.

**2521  South Dakota Department of Labor: Employment Services & Job Training**

700 Governors Drive
Pierre, SD  57501 2291               605-773-5071
FAX 605-773-4211
http://www.state.sd.us/dol/dol.htm
e-mail: miker@dol.pr.state.sd.us
*Michael Ryan, Administrator*

Job training programs provide an important framework for developing public-private sector partnerships. We help prepare South Dakotans of all ages for entry or re-entry into the labor force.

**2522  South Dakota Division of Human Rights**

118 W Capitol Avenue
Pierre, SD  57501                    605-773-4493
FAX 605-773-6893
http://www.state.sd.us/dor/hr/
e-mail: marianne.gabriel@state.sd.us

**2523  South Dakota Division of Special Education**

Department of Education
700 Governors Drive
Pierre, SD  57501                    605-773-3678
FAX 605-773-3782
http://www.state.sd.us/deca/special/special.htm
e-mail: michelle.powers@state.sd.us
*Deborah Barnett, Director*

The Office of Special Education advocates for the availability of the full range of personnel, programming, and placement options, including early intervention and transition services, required to assure that all individuals with disabilities are able to achieve maximum independence upon exiting from school.

**2524  State GED Administration**

Department of Labor
700 Governors Drive
Pierre, SD  57501                    605-773-5821
FAX 605-773-6184
e-mail: roxie.thielen@state.sd.us
*Marcia Hess, Adult Education/Literacy*

**2525  Youth Dakota Advocacy Services**

221 S Central Avenue
Pierre, SD  57501                    605-224-8294
800-658-4782
FAX 605-224-5125
TDY:605-224-8294
http://www.sdadvocacy.com
e-mail: sdas@iw.net
*Robert Kean, Executive Director*
*Pam Middleton, Administrative Assistant*

## Tennessee

**2526  Council on Developmental Disabilities**

500 Deadrick Street
Nashville, TN  37243-0228            615-532-6615
FAX 615-532-6964
TDY:615-741-4562
e-mail: wwillis@mail.state.tn.us
*Wanda Willis, Executive Director*
*Margaret Donald, Administrative Secretary*

**2527  Department of Human Services: Division of Rehabilitation Services**

400 Deaderick Street
Nashville, TN  37248 0060            615-313-4714
FAX 615-741-4165
TDY:800-270-1349
http://www.state.tn.us/humanserv/rehabilitation
e-mail: carlbrown@mail.state.tn.usa
*Carl Brown, Assistant Commissioner*
*Karen Wayson, Secretary*

Agency takes an active leadership role in removing the barriers to employment due to disabilities.

**2528  State Department of Education**

710 James Robertson Parkway
Nashville, TN  37243                 615-741-2731
800-531-1515
FAX 615-532-4791
http://www.state.tn.us
e-mail: phobbins@mail.state.tn.us
*Phil White, Director*

**2529 State GED Administration**

State Department of Education
710 James Robertson Parkway
Nashville, TN 37210          615-741-2731
                            800-531-1515
                       FAX 615-532-4791
                     http://www.state.tn.us
*Phil White, Director*

**2530 Tennessee Division of Rehabilitation Services**

Tennessee Department of Human Services
400 Deaderick Street
Nashville, TN 37248 6300     615-313-4918
                       FAX 615-741-6508
            http://www.state.tn.us/humanserv/
e-mail: Human-Services.Webmaster@state.tn.us
*Gina Lodge, Commissioner Human Services*
*Philip Wagster, Director Vocational Rehab*

Federal and state funded services to help individuals
with disabilities enter or return to employment.

**2531 Tennessee Technology Access Project**

400 Deadrick Street
Nashville, TN 37243          615-532-3122
                            800-732-5059
                       FAX 615-532-4685
                       TDY:615-741-4566
                     http://www.state.tn.us
            e-mail: ttap@mail.state.tn.us
*Kevin Wright, Project Director*

---

# Texas

---

**2532 Advocacy**

7800 Shoal Creek Boulevard
Austin, TX 78757            512-454-4816
                            800-252-9108
                       FAX 512-323-0902
            e-mail: hn2414@handsnet.org
*Mary Faithfull, Interim Executive Director*
*Karenh Stanfill, CAP Coordinator*

**2533 LAUNCH**

Department of Special Education
Commerce, TX 75428          903-886-5594
                       FAX 903-886-5510

An organization that provides resources for learning
disabled individuals, coordinates efforts of other local, state and national LD organizations.

**2534 Learning Disabilities Association**

1011 W 31st Street
Austin, TX 78705            512-458-8234
                            800-604-7500
                       FAX 512-458-3826
                       http://www.ldat.org
                     e-mail: contact@ldat.org
*Ann Robinson, State Coordinator*

Provides information, support and referrals.

**2535 Southwest Texas Disability & Business Technical
Assistance Center: Region VI**

2323 S Shepherd Drive
Houston, TX 77019           713-520-0232
                            800-949-4232
                       FAX 713-520-5785
                     http://www.dlrp.org
*Wendy Wilkinson, Project Director*
*Maria , Project Associate*

Southwest DBTA is the resource for trainings, technical assistance and materials on the ADA in Federal
Region VI. Authorized to provide training information, materials and technical assistance to individuals
and entities that are protected or have obligations under the Americans with Disabilities Act. Project staff
with expertise in all areas of the ADA are available.

**2536 State GED Administration**

Texas Education Agency
1701 Congress Avenue
Austin, TX 78701            512-463-9292
                       FAX 512-305-9493
                     http://www.tea.state.tx.us
            e-mail: proussos@mail.tea.state.tx.us
*Walter Tillman MD, Education Services*

**2537 Texas Commission on Human Rights**

6330 Highway 290 E
Austin, TX 78711            512-437-3450
                            888-452-4778
                       FAX 512-437-3478
                     http://www.tchr.state.tx.us
            e-mail: tchr.net@mail.carpnet.stste.tx.us
*Mary Bank, Chairman*
*Tom Anderson, Commissioner*

**2538 Texas Department of Commerce: Work Force
Development Division**

PO Box 12728
Austin, TX 78711            512-320-9439
                       FAX 512-320-0433

**2539 Texas Department of Criminal Justice**

Windham School District
PO Box 99
Huntsville, TX 77342        936-295-6371
                     http://www.tdcj.state.tx.us/
            e-mail: webmaster@tdcj.state.tx.us

**2540 Texas Education Agency**

1701 Congress Avenue
Austin, TX 78701            512-463-9734
                       FAX 512-463-9838
                     http://www.tea.state.tx.us
            e-mail: proussos@mail.tea.state.tx.us
*Walter Tillman MD, Education Services*

**2541  Texas Employment Services and Job Training Program Liaison**

15th & Congress Avenue
Austin, TX  78778          512-463-2652

**2542  Texas Planning Council for Developmental Disabilities**

6201 E. Oltorf
Austin, TX  78741          512-437-5432
                          800-262-0334
                     FAX 512-437-5434
                     TDY:512-437-5431
http://www.txddc.state.tx.us/menus/fset_cecl-1.
Roger Webb, Executive Director

The mission of the Texas Council for Developmental Disabilities is to create change so that all people are fully included in their communities and exercise control over their own lives.

**2543  Texas Rehabilitation Commission: Vocational Rehabilitation**

4800 N Lamar Boulevard
Austin, TX  78756
                          800-252-5204
http://www.dars.state.tx.us

**2544  University of Texas at Austin**

Sanchez Building
Austin, TX  78713          512-471-4161
                     FAX 512-471-2471
http://www.edb.utexas.edu/coe/depts
e-mail: heike@mail.utexas.edu
Penny Seay

# Utah

**2545  Assistive Technology Center**

1595 W 500 S
Salt Lake City, UT  84106          801-887-9500
                              FAX 801-485-8675
                              TDY:801-887-9503
http://www.usor.utah.org
Pete Miner, Director
Lynn Marcoux, Secretary

The fundamental goal is to improve the lives of children and adults with disabilities by introducing them and their families to the many ways in which microcomputer technology can enhance their jobs, careers and education.

**2546  Assistive Technology Program**

6588 Old Main Hill
Logan, UT  84322          435-797-3824
                     FAX 435-797-2355
http://www.uatpat.org/
e-mail: jmholt2@home.com
A program that helps ensure people with disabilities will be secure.

**2547  Center for Persons with Disabilities**

Utah State University
Logan, UT  84322          435-797-3681
                          866-284-2821
                     FAX 435-797-3944
http://www.cpd.usu.edu/
e-mail: sharon@cpd2.usu.edu
Sarah Rule, Director

A University Center for excellence in developmental disabilities education, research and services. The Center for Persons with Disabilities provides interdisciplinary training, research, exemplary services, and technical assistance to agencies related to people with disabilities.

**2548  Disability Law Center**

205 N 400 W
Salt Lake City, UT  84103          801-363-1347
                              800-662-9080
                         FAX 801-363-1437
                         TDY:800-550-4182
http://www.disabilitylawcenter.org
e-mail: info@disabilitylawcenter.org
Fraser Nelson, Legal Director

Nonprofit organization designated by the governor to protect the rights of people with disabilities in Utah.

**2549  State GED Administration**

1236 S State Street
Salt Lake City, UT  84101          801-578-8356
                              FAX 801-578-8198
Brent Gubler MD, State GED Administrator

Promotes adult education.

**2550  State Office of Education**

250 E 500 S
Salt Lake City, UT  84111          801-538-7894
                              800-451-9500
                         FAX 801-538-7882
http://www.school.utah.gov
e-mail: sgrant@usoe.k12.ut.us
Sandra Grant, Specialist
Dave Steele, State Director

**2551  Utah Governor's Council for People with Disabilities**

555 E 300 S
Salt Lake City, UT  84102          801-553-4128
                              FAX 801-533-5305
                              TDY:801-533-4128
http://www.gcpd.state.ut.us/images/default.htm
e-mail: cchamble@email.state.ut.us
Catherine Chambless, Executive Director

The mission of the Utah Governor's Council for People with Disabilities is to create an environment in which people with disabilities direct their own lives and participate in the community. The council achieves this through: facilitating interagency and citizen planning, identifying policy, promoting partnerships and more.

**2552 Utah Labor Commission: Utah Anti-discrimination and Labor Division**

160 E 300 S
Salt Lake City, UT 84111          801-530-6801
                                  800-222-1238
                           FAX 801-530-7609
                           TDY:801-530-7685
          http://www.laborcommission.utah.gov
                e-mail: shayashi@utah.gov
*Sherrie Hayashi, Program Director*
*Harold Stephens, Case Manager for Employment*

State agency responsible for enforcing laws which prohibit employment discrimination. The agency is also charged with enforcing laws which prohibit housing discrimination. Additionally, the agency is responsible for enforcing state laws which require the payment of wages, govern the employment of youth and establish Utah's minimum wage law.

**2553 Utah Work Force**

140 E Broadway
Salt Lake City, UT 84111          801-526-9675
                           FAX 801-526-9211
                    http://www.jobs.utah.gov
                 e-mail: tdowning@utah.gov
*Tani Downing, Executive Director*
*John Nixon, Deputy Director*

# Vermont

**2554 Assistive Technology Project**

Agency of Human Services
103 S Main Street Weeks Building
Waterbury, VT 05671               802-241-2620
                                  800-750-6355
                           FAX 802-241-2174
                           TDY:802-241-1464
                 http://www.dil.state.vt.us/atp
               e-mail: jtucker@dad.state.vt.us
*Julie Tucker, Project Director*
*Bettsie Ross, Administrative Assistant*

Provides a revolving loan fund for assistive technology, a used equipment recycling project, as well as training and technical assistance in computer and augmentative communications access.

**2555 Learning Disabilities Association of Vermont**

Learning Disabilities Association of America
PO Box 1041
Manchester Center, VT 05255    802-362-3127
                           FAX 802-362-3128
*Christina Thurston, President*

A nonprofit organization whose members are individuals with learning disabilities, their families, and the professionals who work with them.

**2556 Protection & Advocacy Agency**

141 Main Street
Montpelier, VT 05602              802-229-1355
                                  800-834-7890
                           FAX 802-229-1359
                           TDY:802-229-2603
                        http://www.vtpa.org
                    e-mail: info@vtpa.org
*Ed Paquin, Director*
*Jason Whitney, President of the Board*

Mission is to defend and advance the rights of people who have been labeled mentally ill.

**2557 REACH-UP Program: Department of Social Welfare**

State Office Building Division
103 S Main Street
Waterbury, VT 05671               802-241-2800
                           FAX 802-241-2830
*Karen Ryder*

**2558 State Department of Education**

120 State Street
Montpelier, VT 05620              802-828-3134
                           FAX 802-828-3146
              e-mail: srobinson@doe.state.vt.us
*Sandra Robinson, Director*
*Tracy Gallo, Director Life Long Learning*

Promotes quality education.

**2559 State GED Administration**

Department of Education,Career & Lifelong Learning
120 State Street
Montpelier, VT 05620              802-828-3134
                           FAX 802-828-3146
              e-mail: srobinson@doe.state.vt.us
*Tracy Gallo, Director Life Long Learning*

Promotes adult education.

**2560 Vermont Agency of Human Services**

Vocational Rehabilitation Division
103 S Main Street
Waterbury, VT 05671               866-879-6957
                http://www.vocrehabvermont.org

**2561 Vermont Assistive Technology Project: Department of Aging and Disabilities**

Agency of Human Services
103 S Main Street, Weeks Building
Waterbury, VT 05671               802-241-2620
                                  800-750-6355
                           FAX 802-241-2174
                           TDY:802-241-1464
                 http://www.dil.state.vt.us/atp
               e-mail: jtucker@dad.state.vt.us
*Julie Tucker, Project Director*
*Betsy Ross, Administrative Assistant*

**2562  Vermont Department of Employment & Training**
5 Green Mountain Drive
Montpelier, VT  05601 0488          802-828-4000
                                   FAX 802-828-4022
                     http://www.det.state.vt.us
                     e-mail: mcalcagni@det.state.vt.us
*Bob Ware, Director Jobs/Training*
*Mike Griffin, Labor Market Information*

Represents Vermont's efforts to provide services, information and support both to individuals to obtain and keep good jobs, and to employers to recruit and maintain a productive workforce.

**2563  Vermont Department of Welfare**
Economic Services Division
103 S Main Street
Waterbury, VT  05671          802-241-2834
                              800-287-0589
                         FAX 802-241-2830
                         TDY:888-834-7898
                     http://www.dcf.state.vtus
*James Forrset, Deputy Commissioner*
*Dianne Carmenti, Welfare Director*

**2564  Vermont Developmental Disabilities Council**
103 S Main Street
Waterbury, VT  05671          802-241-2612
                              888-317-2006
                         FAX 802-241-2989
            e-mail: vtddc@wpgate1.ahs.state.vt.us
*Karen Schwartz, Executive Director*

**2565  Vermont Disability Law Project**
Protection and Advocacy Agency
PO Box 1367
Burlington, VT  05402          802-863-2881
                               800-747-5022
                          FAX 802- 863- 7
*Judith Dickson, Project Director*

Works in partnership with persons with disabilities to protect, advocate for, and advance their human, legal, and service rights.

**2566  Vermont Governor's Office**
109 State Street
Montpelier, VT  05609          802-828-3333
                          FAX 802-828-3339
            http://www.vermont.gov\governor\
                     e-mail: jbagalio@state.vt.us
*Jim Douglas, Governor*
*Timothy Hayward, Chief of Staff*

**2567  Vermont Legal Aid Client Assistance Program and Disability Law Project**
PO Box 1367
Burlington, VT  05402          802-863-2881
                               800-747-5022
                          FAX 802- 863- 71
*Laura Philipps, Co-Director*
*Judy Dickson, Co-Director*

Program assists people with disabilities seeking information on vocational rehabilitation and independent living services from state agencies. Offers advisement of employment rights and services available under the ADA.

**2568  Vermont REACH-UP Program**
Department of Social Welfare
103 S Main Street
Waterbury, VT  05671          802-241-2800
                              800-775-0506
                         FAX 802-241-2830
*Karen Ryder*

**2569  Vermont Special Education**
120 State Street
Montpelier, VT  05620          802-828-3130
                          FAX 802-828-3140
                          TDY:802-828-2755
                     http://www.state.vt.us\educ
                     e-mail: edinfo@education.state.vt.us
*Karin Edward, Executive Director*
*Elaine Pickney, Deputy Director*

Promotes the quality of special education.

# Virginia

**2570  Adult and Employment Training: Virginia Department of Education**
Department of Education: Office of Adult Education

PO Box 2120
Richmond, VA  23218          804-225-2075
                        FAX 804-225-3352
                   http://www.pen.k12.va.us
                   e-mail: imclendo@pen.k12.va.us
*Elizabeth Hawa, Associate Director*
*Yvonne Theyer, Director*

Employment training for individuals in Virginia.

**2571  Assistive Technology System**
Department of Rehabilitative Services
8004 Franklin Farms Drive
Richmond, VA  23288          804-662-9998
                        FAX 804-622-9478
                   http://www.uats.org
Helps people with disabilities know that they will be secure.

**2572  Correctional Education**
Correctional Education
101 N 14th Street
Richmond, VA  23219          804-225-3310
                        FAX 804-225-3255
                   http://www.dce.state.va.us
                   e-mail: webmaster@dce.state.va.us
*Sharon Trimmer, Director of Special Education*

**2573  District of Columbia Department of Corrections**

1923 Vermont Ave, NW
Washington, DC  20001          202-673-7316
                              FAX 202-671-0169
                              http://www.dc.gov
*John Thomas, Deputy Director for Programs*

Protects the public by operating a safe, secure, humane and efficient corrections system.

**2574  State Department of Education**

Department of Education: Office of Adult Education
PO Box 2120
Richmond, VA  23218          804-225-2075
                              FAX 804-225-3352
                              http://www.pen.k12.va.us
*Lennox McLedon, Associate Director Adult Ed*

Promotes quality education.

**2575  State GED Administration**

Department of Education: Office of Adult Education
PO Box 2120
Richmond, VA  23218          804-225-2075
                              FAX 804-225-3352
                              http://www.pen.k12.va.us
*Patricia Ta'ani MD, Specialist*

Promotes quality education for adults.

**2576  Virginia Board for People with Disabilities**

202 N 9th Street
Richmond, VA  23219          804-786-0016
                              FAX 804-786-1118
                              TDY:800-846-4464
                              http://www.vaboard.org
                              e-mail: heidi.lawyer@vbpd.virginia.gov
*Heidi Lawyer, Director*
*Man Pemberton, Director of Administration*

---

## Washington

---

**2577  Client Assistance Program (CAP): Washington Division**

PO Box 22510
Seattle, WA  98144          206-721-5999
                            800-544-2121
                            FAX 206-721-4537
                            TDY:888-721-6072
                            e-mail: capseattle@adccomsys.net
*Jerry Johnsen, Director*

Provides information and advocacy for persons seeking services from the Department of Services for the Blind and the Division of Vocational Rehabilitation. Approximately 25 percent of cases involve assistive technology issues.

**2578  Correctional Education**

Department of Corrections
410 W 5th Avenue
Olympia, WA  98504          360-753-2500
                            FAX 360-586-6582
                            http://www.doc.wa.gov
                            e-mail: doccorrespondence@doc1.wa.gov
*Harold Clarke, Secretary of Department*
*Eldon Zail, Deputy Secretary*

Protects the public by operating a safe corrections system.

**2579  Department of Personnel & Human Services**

Department of Personnel & Human Services
614 Division Street
Port Orchard, WA  98366          360-337-4873
                                 FAX 360-337-7187
                                 TDY:360-337-7185
                                 http://www.kitsapgov.com
                                 e-mail: bpotter@co.kitsap.wa.us
*Bert Furuta, Director*
*Steve Frazier, Manager of Human Services*

**2580  Developmental Disabilities Council**

PO Box 48314
Olympia, WA  98504          360-586-3560
                            FAX 360-586-2424
                            TDY:800-634-4473
                            http://www.wa.gov/ddc
                            e-mail: cathyt@cted.wa.gov
*Edward Holen, Executive Director*
*Phil Rasmussen, Office Trainee*

**2581  Region X: US Department of Education Office for Civil Rights**

US Department of Education
915 2nd Avenue
Seattle, WA  98174          206-220-7800
                            FAX 206-220-7806
                            http://www.ed.gov
*Donna Foxley, Secretary Regional Rep*
*Linda Powley, Administrative Assistant*

These regional offices of agencies enforce laws prohibiting employment discrimination on the basis of disability.

**2582  Region X: US Department of Health and Human Services, Office of Civil Rights**

US Department of Health & Human Services
2201 6th Avenue
Seattle, WA  98121          206-615-2290
                            FAX 206-615-2297
                            http://www.hhs.gov/ocr/hipaa
These regional offices of agencies enforce laws prohibiting employment discrimination on the basis of disability.

## West Virginia

**2583 Region X: US Department of Labor Office of Federal Contract Compliance**

US Department of Labor
1111 3rd Avenue
Seattle, WA 98101          206-553-4543
                FAX 206-553-0098

These regional offices of agencies enforce laws prohibiting employment discrimination on the basis of disability.

**2584 State Department of Adult Education**

Board of Education
PO Box 47206
Olympia, WA 98504          360-725-6025
                FAX 360-586-2357
                TDY:360-664-3631
          http://www.sbe.wa.gov
     e-mail: imendozac@sbeta.ctc.edu
Larry Davis, Executive Director
Gene Thomas, Secretary

Promotes the quality of adult education.

**2585 State GED Administration**

State Board for Community & Technical Colleges
PO Box 47206
Olympia, WA 98504          360-725-6025
                FAX 360-586-2357
                TDY:360-664-3631
          http://www.sbe.wa.gov
Larry Davis, Executive Director
Gene Thomas, Secretary

Promotes adult education.

**2586 Washington Employment Services & Job Training Programs**

605 Wood Drive SE
Lacey, WA 98503          360-438-3168
                FAX 360-438-3208

Employment services and training programs provided to those working in Washington state.

**2587 Washington Human Rights Commission**

711 S Capitol Way Suite 402
Olympia, WA 98504          360-753-6770
                800-233-3247
          http://www.hum.wa.gov

**2588 Washington Protection and Advocacy System**

315-Fifth Ave South
Seattle, WA 98104          206-324-1521
                800-562-2702
                FAX 206-957-0729
          http://www.wpas-rights.org
          e-mail: wpas@wpas-rights.org
Mark Stroh, Director

Focuses on individuals with disabilities and mental illness. Services include information and referral, legal assistance, training and systemic advocacy. Investigates abuse and neglect at residential and treatment facilities.

**2589 Assistive Technology**

955 Hartman Run Road
Morgantown, WV 26505          304-293-4692
                800-841-8436
                FAX 304-293-7294
          http://www.cedwbu.org
          e-mail: jstweart@wuu.edu
Jack Stewart, Director
Jaime Haybeurst, Assistant Technology Coordinator

**2590 Client Assistance Program (CAP): West Virginia Division**

West Virginia Advocates
1207 Quarrier Street, Litton Bldg
Charleston, WV 25311          304-346-0867
                FAX 304-346-0867
          http://www.wvadvocates.org
Susan Edwards, Director

The Client Assistance Program (CAP), mandated in 1984 to provide advocacy to individuals seeking services from the State Division of Rehabilitation Services, Centers for Independent Living, supports employment programs and sheltered workshops under the federal Rehabilitation Act.

**2591 Correctional Education**

State Department of Education
1900 Kanawha Boulevard E
Charleston, WV 25305          304-558-8833
                FAX 304-558-5042
Frank Andrews, Superintendent
Tam Wright, Secretary

**2592 State Department of Adult Education**

Department of Education
1900 Kanawha Boulevard E
Charleston, WV 25305          304-558-6318
          e-mail: kpolis@access.k12.wv.us
Kathy Polis, Director

**2593 State Department of Education**

1900 Washington Street E
Charleston, WV 25305          304-558-2584
                FAX 304-558-0304
          http://www.wvde.state.wv.us
William Capehart, Director

Promotes quality education.

**2594 State GED Administration**

1900 Kanawha Boulevard E
Charleston, WV 25305          304-558-6315
                FAX 304-558-4874
          e-mail: pabston@access.k12.wv.us
Debra Kimbler, GED Administrator

Our organization's goal is to provide reasonable accommodations to qualifying GED candidates.

## Wisconsin

**2595  Assistive Technology Project**
State Grants Program
1 W Wilson Street, Room 450R
Madison, WI  53707                         608-266-1794
                                           FAX 608-267-3203
                                           TDY:608-267-9880
                                           http://www.wistech.org
                                           e-mail: abbeysu@dhfs.state.wi.us
*Susan Abbey, Manager*

A statewide program promoting assistive technology and services for people with disabilities.

**2596  Correctional Education**
Department of Corrections
3099 Washington Avenue
Madison, WI  53707-7925                    608-240-5000
                                           http://www.wi-doc.com
                                           e-mail: joh.brueggemann@doc.state.wi.us
*Tracy Bredeson, Director*

**2597  Protection & Advocacy Agency**
Coalition for Advocacy
16 N Carroll Street
Madison, WI  53703                         608-267-0214
                                           800-928-8778
                                           FAX 608-267-0368
                                           http://www.w-c-a-.org
                                           e-mail: lynnb@wca.org

*Lynn Breedlove, Director*
*Laurie Powers, Secretary*

**2598  State Capitol**
State of Wisconsin Department of Administration
Room 115 East
Madison, WI  53707                         608-266-7493
                                           FAX 608-267-8983
                                           http://www.wisgov.state.wi.us
                                           e-mail: governor@wisconsin.gov
*Claire Franz, Manager*
*Michael Stark, Bureau Director*

**2599  State Department of Education**
310 Price Place
Madison, WI  53707                         608-266-1770
                                           FAX 608-266-1285
                                           http://www.dpi.state.wi.us
                                           e-mail: webadmin@dpi.state.wi.us
*Edward Chin, Director*

Promotes quality education.

**2600  State GED Administration**
Department of Public Instruction
310 Price Place
Madison, WI  53707                         608-266-1770
                                           FAX 608-266-1285
*Kathleen Cole, Contact*

Promotes quality adult education.

**2601  Wisconsin Council on Developmental Disabilities**
201 West Washington Street
Madison, WI  53707                         608-266-7826
                                           FAX 608-267-3906
                                           TDY:608-266-6660
                                           http://www.wcdd.org
                                           e-mail: hfswiswcdd@dhfs.state.wi.us
*Jennifer Ondrejka, Executive Director*
*John Shaw, Supervisor*

A statewide advocacy organization working on system change for people with developmental disabilities.

**2602  Wisconsin Department of Workforce Development**
PO Box 7946
Madison, WI  53707                         608-267-4400
                                           FAX 608-266-1784
                                           http://www.dwd.state.wi.us
                                           e-mail: charlene.dwyer@dwd.state.wi.us
*Roberta Gassman, Secretary for the Workforce*
*Charlene Dwyer, Director for Division of Rehab*

Provides information on equal rights, employment and training programs, labor, market statistics, unemployment compensation and workers' compensation.

**2603  Wisconsin Equal Rights Division**
PO Box 8928
Madison, WI  53708-8928                    608-267-9678
                                           FAX 608-267-4592
                                           TDY:608-264-8752
                                           http://www.dwd.wisconsin.gov
                                           e-mail: lucianunez@dwd.state.wi.us
*Lucia Nunez, Administrator*
*Lynn Hendrickson, Executive Staff Assistant*

**2604  Wisconsin Governor's Commission for People with Disabilities**
1 West Wilson Street Room 1150
Madison, WI  53702-7851                    608-267-4896
                                           800-362-1290
                                           FAX 608-264-9832
                                           http://www.edhfs.state.wi.us
                                           e-mail: monge@edhfs.state.wi.us
*Malita Monger, Director*

## Wyoming

**2605  Adult Basic Education**
Wyoming Community College Commission
2020 Carey Avenue
Cheyenne, WY  82002                        307-777-3545
                                           FAX 307-777-6567
                                           http://www.commission.wcc.edu@wccc.ABE/
                                           e-mail: kmilmont@commission.wcc.edu
*Karen Milmont, Director*

**2606 Client Assistance Program (CAP): Wyoming Division**

320 W 25th Street
Cheyenne, WY 82001          307-638-7668
                           FAX 307-638-0815
                      e-mail: wypanda@vcn.com
*Kriss Smith, Director*

Provides free services to consumers and applicants for projects, programs and facilities funded under the rehabilitation act.

**2607 Correctional Education: Wyoming Women's Center**

1000 W Griffith
Lusk, WY 82225          307-334-3693
                       FAX 307-334-2254
                  e-mail: cthaye@state.wy.us
*Virginia Pullen, Educational Director*
*Melissa Bischner, Correctional Officer*

The Wyoming Women's Center is a full service, secure correctional facility for female offenders and the sole adult female facility in the State of Wyoming. In October 2000, WWC opened a self-contained 16 bed intensive addiction treatment unit, a is highly structured long term 7-9 month program based upon the therapeutic community treatment model. It is tailored to provide gender specific services and is funded with a combination of state and federal resources.

**2608 Protection & Advocacy Agency**

320 W 25th Street
Cheyenne, WY 82001          307-632-3496
                           800-624-7648
                       FAX 307-638-0815
              http://www.ucn.com/~wypan.da
                   e-mail: wypanda@ucn.com
*Jeanne Thobro, Director*

**2609 State Department of Education**

2300 Capitol Avenue
Cheyenne, WY 82002          307-777-7675
                       FAX 307-777-6234
                    http://www.k12.wy.us
            e-mail: nshels@educ.state.wy.us
*Trent Blankensh MD, Superintendent*
*Nance Shelsta, Director for Special Education*

**2610 State GED Administration**

State Department of Education
2300 Capitol Avenue
Cheyenne, WY 82002          307-777-7675
                       FAX 307-777-6234
                    http://www.k12.wy.us
            e-mail: nshels@educ.state.wy.us
*Trent Blankensh MD, Superintendent*
*Nance Shelsta, Director for Special Education*

Promotes quality adult education.

**2611 Wyoming Department of Employment and Job Training Programs**

Department of Employment
1510 E Pershing Boulevard
Cheyenne, WY 82002          307-777-7672
                           888-996-9226
                       FAX 307-777-5805
              http://www.wydoe.state.wy.us
               e-mail: cpomer@state.wy.us
*Cindy Pomeroy, Director*
*Charlie Rando, Administrator for Administration*

Employment training for persons working in Wyoming.

## National Programs

**2612  Academic Institute**
13400 NE 20th
Bellevue, WA  98005

888-385-2977
FAX 928-244-1315

*Sherrill O'Saughnessy*

Advising families and teens who have special needs.

**2613  Adaptive Environments**
Adaptive Environments
374 Congress Street
Boston, MA  02210

617-695-1225
800-949-4232
FAX 617-482-8099
TDY:617-695-1225
http://www.adaptiveenvironments.org
e-mail: info@adaptiveenvironments.org
*Valerie Fletcher, Executive Director*
*Andy Washburn, Information Specialist*

Adaptive Environments promotes design that works for everyone across the spectrum of ability and age and enhances human experience.

**2614  American Association for Adult and Continuing Education**
4380 Forbes Boulevard
Lanham, MD  20706

301-918-1913
FAX 301-918-1846
http://www.aaace.org
e-mail: aaace10@aol.com
*Marjean Buckner, President*
*Cle Anderson, Association Manager*

Mission is to provide leadership for the field of adult and continuing education: by expanding opportunities for adult growth and development; unifying adult educators; fostering the development and dissemination of theory, research, information and best practices; promoting identity and standards for the profession; and advocating relevant public policy and social change initiatives.

**2615  American Literacy Council**
148 W 117th Street
New York, NY  10026

800-781-9985
http://www.americanliteracy.com
e-mail: fyi@americanliteracy.com
*Edward Lias M.D., President*

Provides resources and assistance to persons and organizations who are involved in the literacy crisis in America. The organization provides software and publications that seek to promote solutions to the problem of illiteracy in English speaking countries. One primary product of the Council is Sound-Write (TM), a Windows-based writing program with instant audiovisual feedback and a 25,000 word vocabulary.

**2616  Association of Educational Therapists**
1804 W Burbank Boulevard
Burbank, CA  91506

800-286-4267
http://www.aetonline.org
e-mail: aetla@aol.com

A national professional organization dedicated to establishing ethical professional standards, defining the roles and responsibilities of the educational therapist, providing opportunities for professional growth, and to studying techniques and technologies, philosophies and research related to the practice of educational therapy.

**2617  Association on Higher Education and Disability**
100 Morrissey Boulevard
Waltham, MA  02454

781-788-0003
FAX 781-788-0033
http://www.AHEAD.org
e-mail: AHEAD@ahead.org
*Stephan Smith, Executive Director*
*Richard Allegra, Assistant Executive*

An international, muiticultural organization of professionals committed to full participation in higher education for persons with disabilities. The Association is a vital resource, promoting excellence through education, communication and training.

**2618  Career College Association (CCA)**
10 G Street NE
Washington, DC  20002

202-336-6700
FAX 202-336-6828
http://www.career.org
e-mail: cca@career.org
*Nick Glakas, President*

Represents more than 1,000 private for profit post secondary schools, institutes, colleges and universities.

**2619  Center for the Improvement of Early Reading Achievement CIERA**
University of Michigan School of Education
Rm 1600 SEB
Ann Arbor, MI  48109 1259

734-647-6940
FAX 734-615-4858
http://www.ciera.org
e-mail: ciera@umich.edu
*Karen Wixson, Director*
*Joanne Carlisle, Co Director*

CIERA is a national center for research on early reading, representing a consortium of educators from five universities.

**2620  Council for Educational Diagnostic Services**
Council for Exceptional Children
1110 N Glebe Road
Arlington, VA  22201

703-620-3660
800-224-6830
FAX 703-264-9494
http://www.cec.sped.org
e-mail: cathym@cec.sped.org
*Drew Albitran M.D., Executive Director*

The mission of the Council for Educational Diagnostic Services is: to promote the most appropriate education of children and youth through appraisal, diagnosis, educational intervention, implementation, and continuous evaluation of a prescribed educational program.

**2621 Distance Education and Training Council (DETC)**

1601 18th Street NW
Washington, DC 20009          202-234-5100
                              FAX 202-332-1386
                              http://www.detc.org
                              e-mail: detc@detc.org
*Michael Lambert, Executive Director*

Nonprofit educational association located in Washington, DC. DETC serves as a clearinghouse of information about the distance study/correspondence field and sponsors a nationally recognized accrediting agency called the Accrediting Commission of the Distance Education and Training Council.

**2622 Division for Children's Communication Development**

Council for Exceptional Children
1110 N Glebe Road
Arlington, VA 22201           703-620-3660
                              800-224-6830
                              FAX 703-264-9494
                              http://www.cec.sped.org
                              e-mail: service@cec.sped.org
*Drew Albitran M.D., Executive Director*

Dedicated to improving the education of children with communication delays and disorders and hearing loss. Members include professionals serving individuals with hearing, speech and language disorders in the areas of receptive and expressive, verbal and nonverbal spoken, written and sign communication. Members receive a quarterly journal and newsletter three times a year.

**2623 Division for Culturally and Linguistically Diverse Learners**

Council for Exceptional Children
1110 N Glebe Road
Arlington, VA 22201           703-620-3660
                              888-232-7733
                              FAX 703-620-2521
                              http://www.cec.sped.org
*Drew Albitran M.D., Executive Director*
*Gwendolyn Webb-Johnson, Division President*

Dedicated to advancing and improving educational opportunities for culturally and linguistically diverse learners with disabilites and/or who are gifted, their families and the professionals who serve them.

**2624 Division for Research**

Council for Exceptional Children
1110 N Glebe Road
Arlington, VA 22201           703-620-3660
                              888-232-7733
                              FAX 703-264-9494
                              http://www.cec.sped.org
                              e-mail: cathym@cec.sped.org
*Drew Albitran M.D., Executive Director*

Devoted to the advancement of research related to the education of individuals with disabilities and/or who are gifted. Members include university, public and private school teachers, researchers, administrators, psychologists, speech/language clinicians, parents of children with special learning needs and other related professionals and service personnel. Members receive quarterly journal and newsletter three times a year.

**2625 Educational Advisory Group**

2222 E Lake Avenue E
Seattle, WA 98102            206-323-1838
                             FAX 206-267-1325
                             http://www.eduadvisory.com
*Yvonne Jones, Associate*
*Paul Auchterlonie, Associate*

Specializes in matching children with the learning environments that are best for them and works with families to help them identify concerns and establish priorities about their child's education.

**2626 HEATH Resource Center: The George Washington University**

HEATH Resource Center
2121 K Street NW
Washington, DC 20037         202-973-0904
                             800-544-3284
                             FAX 202-973-0908
                             http://www.heath.gwu.edu
                             e-mail: askheath@heath.gwu.edu
*Pamela Ekpone MD, Director*
*Dan Gardner, Publication Manager*

Support from the US Department of Education enables the center to serve as an information exchange about educational services, policies, procedures, adaptations, and opportunities at American campuses, vocational-technical schools, and other postsecondary training entities.

**2627 Institute for Educational Leadership**

4455 Court Avenue NW
Washington, DC 20008         202-822-8405
                             FAX 202-872-4050
                             http://www.iel.org
                             e-mail: iel@iel.org
*Elizabeth Hale, President*
*Louise Clarke, Chief Administrator*
*Bert Berkley, Chairman of the Board*

Mission is to improve education and the lives of children and their families through positive and visionary change. Everyday, we face that challenge by bringing together diverse constituencies and empowering leaders with knowledge and applicable ideas.

**2628 Institute for the Study of Adult Literacy**

Pennsylvania State Univ. College of Education
102 Rackley Building
University Park, PA 16802     814-863-3777
                             FAX 814-863-6108
                             http://www.ed.psu.edu
                             e-mail: bdo1@psu.edu
*Eunice Askov M.D., Co-Director*

The Institute for the Study of Adult Literacy's goals include development and dissemination of sound conceptual and research base in the field of adult literacy; improvement of practice in the field of adult literacy; and leadership and coordination of a comprehensive approach to the delivery of adult literacy.

**2629 International Dyslexia Association: National Headquarters**

8600 Lasalle Road, Chester Building
Baltimore, MD 21286          410-296-0232
                             800-223-3123
                         FAX 410-321-5069
                     http://www.interdys.org
              e-mail: MBIDA4@hotmail.com
*Cathy Rosemond, President*
*Tom Biall, Director*

Nonprofit, scientific and educational organization dedicated to the study and treatment of dyslexia. Focus is educating parents, teachers and professionals in the field of dyslexia in effective teaching methodologies. Programs and services include: information and referral; public awareness; medical and educational research; governmental affairs; conferences and publications.

**2630 International Reading Association**

800 Barksdale Road
Newark, DE 19714-8139          302-731-1600
                               800-628-8508
                           FAX 302-737-0878
                       http://www.reading.org
                 e-mail: pubinfo@reading.org
*Alan Farstrup, Executive Director*
*Mark Mullen, Assistant Director*

A professional association with more than 80,000 members in nearly 100 countries dedicated to promoting higher achievement levels in literacy, reading and communications worldwide.

**2631 Learning Resource Network**

1130 Hostetler
Manhattan, KS 66502          785-539-5376
                             800-678-5376
                         FAX 785-539-7766
                     http://www.lern.org
                 e-mail: rebel@lern.org
*William Draves, Director*
*Greg Marcelo, Coordinator*

This network for educators provides resources to adult education and adult basic education service providers.

**2632 Literacy Volunteers of America**

Pro-Literacy Worldwide
1320 Jamesville Avenue
Syracuse, NY 13203          315-422-9121
                           888-528-2224
                       FAX 315-422-6369
                   http://www.proliteracy.org
               e-mail: info@proliteracy.org
*Robert Wedgeworth, President*

Literacy Volunteers of America is a fully integrated national network of local, state, and regional literacy providers that give adults and their families the opportunity to acquire skills to be effective in their roles as members of their families, communities, and workplaces.

**2633 National Adult Education Professional Development Consortium**

444 N Capitol Street NW
Washington, DC 20001          202-624-5250
                          FAX 202-624-1497
                      http://www.naepdc.org
                  e-mail: dc1@naepdc.org
*Patricia Bennett MD, Executive Director*

The Consortium, incorporated in 1990 by state adult education directors, provides professional development, policy analysis, and dissemination of information important to state staff in adult education.

**2634 National Adult Literacy & Learning Disabilities Center (NALLD)**

Academy for Educational Development
1825 ConneCourticut Avenue NW
Washington, DC 20009 5721          202-884-8178
                              FAX 202-884-8400
                          http://www.aed.org
                  e-mail: admindc@aed.org
*Stephen Mosley, President*
*Edward Russell, Chairman*

The center is a national resource for information on learning disabilities in adults and on the relationship between learning disabilities and low-level literacy skills.

**2635 National Association for Adults with Special Learning Needs**

PO Box 716
Bryn Mawr, PA 19010          610-525-8336
                             800-869-8336
                         FAX 610-446-6129
                     http://www.ldonline.org
           e-mail: 75250.1273@compuserv.com

A nonprofit organization designed to organize, establish, and promote an effective national and international coalition of professionals, advocates, and consumers of lifelong learning for the purpose of educating adults with special learning needs.

**2636 National Association of Private Special Education Centers**

NAPSEC
1522 K Street NW
Washington, DC 20005          202-408-3338
                          FAX 202-408-3340
                      http://www.napsec.com
                  e-mail: napsec@aol.com
*Sherry Kolbe, Executive Director/CEO*
*Alison Figi, Communications Coordinator*
*Dr. Mike Rice, President*

A nonprofit association whose mission is to ensure access for individuals to private special education as a vital component of the continuum of appropriate placement and services in American education. The association consists solely of private special education schools that serve both privately and publicly placed children with disabilities.

**2637  National Center for ESL Literacy Education (NCLE)**

4646 40th Street NW
Washington, DC  20016-1859          202-362-0700
                                     866-845-3378
                               FAX 202-363-7204
                               http://www.cal.org
                               e-mail: ncle@cal.org

*Donna Christian, President*
*Joy , Vice President*

A national organization focusing on literacy education for adults and out of school youth learning English as a second language. NCLE publishes many documents on its web site.

**2638  National Center for Family Literacy**

325 W Main Street
Louisville, KY  40202 4237          502-584-1133
                               FAX 502-584-0172
                               http://www.famlit.org
                               e-mail: ncfl@famlit.org

*Sharon Darling, President*
*Ken Middleton, Vice President*

Provides leadership for family literacy development nationwide; promotes policies at the national and state level to support family literacy; designs, develops and demostrates new family literacy practices that addresses the need of families in a changing social, economic and political landscape; delivers high quality, dynamic, research-based training, staff development and technical assistance; conducts research to expand the knowledge base of family literacy.

**2639  National Center for Learning Disabilities (NCLD)**

National Center for Learning Disabilities
381 Park Avenue S
New York, NY  10016-1401          212-545-7510
                                     888-575-7373
                               FAX 212-545-9665
                               http://www.ld.org
                               e-mail: help@ncld.org

*Fredrick Poses, Chairman of the Board*
*James Wendorf, Executive Director*

Increases opportunities for all individuals with learning disabilities to achive their potential. NCLD accomplishes its mission by increasing public awareness and understanding of learning disabilities, conducting educational programs and services that promote research-based knowledge, and providing national leadership in shaping public policy. Provides solutions that help people with LD participate fully in society.

**2640  National Center for the Study of Adult Learning & Literacy**

Harvard Graduate School of Education
Nichols House
Cambridge, MA  02138          617-495-4843
                         FAX 617-495-4811
                         http://www.gse.harvard.edu
                         e-mail: ncsall@gse.harvard.edu

*John P Comings MD, Director*
*Elizabeth Molle, Grant Administrator*

The National Center for the Study of Adult Learning & Literacy both informs and learns from practice. Its rigorous, high quality research increases knowledge and gives those teaching, managing, and setting policy in adult literacy education a sound basis for making decisions.

**2641  National Center on Adult Literacy (NCAL)**

University of Pennsylvania
3910 Chestnut Street
Philadelphia, PA  19104          215-898-2100
                         FAX 215-898-9804
                         http://www.literacyonline.org
                         e-mail: editor@literacy.upenn.edu

*Daniel A Wagner MD, Director*
*Denise Smiyth, Fiscal Coordinator*

NCAL's mission incorporates three primary goals: to improve understanding of youth and adult learning; to foster innovation and increase effectiveness in youth and adult basic education and literacy work; and to expand access to information and build capacity for literacy and basic skills service.

**2642  National Education Association (NEA)**

1201 16th Street NW
Washington, DC  20036 3290          202-833-4000
                               FAX 202-822-7974
                               http://www.nea.org

*Rug Weaver, President*

NEA is a volunteer-based organization supported by a network of staff at the local, state and national level. At the local level, NEA affiliates are active in a wide variety of activities, everything from conducting professional workshops on discipline and other issues that affect faculty and school support staff to bargaining contracts for school district employees. At the state level, NEA affiliate activities are equally wide-ranging.

**2643  National Institute for Literacy (NIFL)**

1775 I Street NW
Washington, DC  20006          202-233-2025
                         FAX 202-233-2050
                         TDY:877-576-7734
                         http://www.nifl.gov
                         e-mail: sbaxter@nifl.gov

*June Crawford, Program Director*
*Steve Langley, Staff Assistant*

NIFL's mission is to ensure that the highest quality of literacy services is available to adults. By fostering communication, collaboration, and innovation, NIFL works to build and strengthen a comprehensive, unified system for literacy in the US. NIFL maintains a database of over 7,000 literacy programs across the country and operates a hotline seven days a week.

**2644  National Lekotek Center**

3204 W Armitage Avenue
Chicago, IL  60647          773-276-5164
                                     800-366-7529
                               FAX 773-276-8644
                               http://www.lekotek.org
                               e-mail: lekotek@lekotek.org

*Dianna Nielander, Executive Director*

The mission of the National Lekotek Center is driven by the philosophy that children learn best when play is a family-centered activity that includes all children, regardless of their abilities or disabilities, in family and community activities. We offer play-centered services to children with disabilities and supportive services to their families. We also offer computer play, parent support and national resources for families and professionals.

**2645  Office of Special Education Programs**

US Department of Education
330 C Street SW
Washington, DC 20202          202-205-5507
http://www.ed.gov/offices/osers/osep/index.html

Administers programs and projects relating to the free appropriate public education of all children and young adults with disabilities, from birth through age 21; provides information and publications about disabilities and special education.

**2646  Reach for Learning**

1221 Marin Avenue
Albany, CA  94706          510-524-6455
                          FAX 510-524-5154
*Corinne Gustafson, Director*

Educational center providing diagnosis, instruction, consultation for children, youth, adults with learning disabilities or under achievement.

**2647  Thinking and Learning Connection**

239 Whitclem Court
Palo Alto, CA  94306          650-493-3497
                            FAX 650-494-3499

*Lynne Stietzel, Co-Director*
*Eric Stietzel, Co-Director*

A group of independent associates committed to teaching students to learn new paths of knowledge and understanding. Our primary focus is working with dyslexic and dyscalculia. Individualized educational programs utilize extensive multisensory approaches to teach reading, spelling, handwriting, composition, comprehension, and mathematics. The students are actively involved in learning processes that integrate visual, auditory, and tactile techniques.

## Alabama

**2648  Alabama Commission on Higher Education**

100 N Union Street
Montgomery, AL  36130          334-242-1998
                              FAX 334-242-0268
                    http://www.ache.state.al.us
                    e-mail: tvick@ache.state.al.us
*Michael Malone MD, Executive Director*
*Tim Vick, Associate Executive Director*

The Commission on Higher Education has the statutory responsibility for the overall statewide planning and coordination of higher education in Alabama, the administration of various student aid programs and the performance of designated regulatory functions.

## Alaska

**2649  Alaska Literacy Program**

Nine Star Enterprises
125 West 5th Avenue
Fairbanks, AK          907-279-7827
                      800-478-7587
                FAX 907-279-3299
                http://www.ninestar.com
                e-mail: amyy@ninestar.com
*Amy Young, Contact*
*Arva Carlson, Literacy Contact*

Evaluates student needs and addresses those needs through specialized lesson plans, private tutoring and personal attention.

**2650  Arkansas Adult Basic Education**

SERRC
210 Ferry Way
Juneau, AK  99801          907-586-5718
                          FAX 907-586-5971
                e-mail: carins@serrc.org
*Carin Smolin, Contact*

The mission of the Adult Basic Education program is to provide instruction in the basic skills of reading, writing, and mathematics to adult learners in order to prepare them for transitioning into the labor market or higher academic or vocational training.

**2651  Literacy Council of Alaska**

Pro Literacy America
823 3rd Avenue
Fairbanks, AK  99701          907-456-6212
                            FAX 907-456-4302
                http://www.literacycouncilofalaska.org
                e-mail: lca@literacycouncilofalaska.org
*Mike Donaldson, Director*

The Literacy Council of Alaska is a private, nonprofit educational agency. Our mission is to promote literacy for people of all ages in Fairbanks and the interior.

## Arizona

**2652  Adult Education Division of the Arizona Department of Education**

1535 W Jefferson Street
Phoenix, AZ  85007          602-542-3813
                          800-352-4558
                    FAX 602-258-4986
            http://www.ade.az.gov/adult-ed
            e-mail: kliersc@ade.az.gov
*Karen Liersch, State Director Adult Education*
*Wilda Theobald, Manager for Adult Education*

To ensure that learners 16 years of age and older have access to quality educational opportunities that will support them in their employment, job training, assist them in acquiring the knowledge and skills necessary for effective participation in society.

**2653  Literacy Volunteers of America: MaricopaCounty**

**Literacy Volunteers of Maricopa County**
**1500 E Thomas Road**
**Phoenix, AZ  85014**                602-274-3430
                                FAX 602-542-5440
http://www.literacyvolunteers-maricopa.org
                        e-mail: lvmc@lvmc.net
*Lynn Reed, Executive Director*
*Belinda Chron, Administrative Assistant*

To ensure that learners 16 years of age and older have access to quality educational opportunities that will support them in their employment, job training, assist them in acquiring the knowledge and skills necessary for effective participation in society.

**2654  Literacy Volunteers of America: Santa CruzCounty**

**Pro Literacy Worldwide**
**21 E Court Street**
**Nogales, AR  85621**                520-287-0111
                                FAX 520-287-0704
            e-mail: lruiz@co.santa-cruz.az.us
*Lizzette Ruiz, Director*
*Dora Rayon, Project Coordinator*

Literacy Volunteers of America is a national organization with over 1000 chapters teaching adult literacy throughout the United States. The Santa Cruz County Chapter is run out of the Nogales-Santa Cruz County Public Library, and relies on the work of local volunteer tutors and Americorps volunteers.

## Arkansas

**2655  Arkansas Adult Learning Resource Center**

**3905 Cooperative Way**
**Little Rock, AR  72209**                501-907-2490
                                    800-832-6242
                                FAX 501-907-2492
                            http://www.aalrc.org
                            e-mail: info@aalrc.org
*Marsha Taylor, Director*
*Klaus Neu, Media Coordinator*

The Arkansas Adult Learning Resource Center was established in 1990 to provide a source for identification, evaluation, and dissemination of materials and information to adult education/literacy programs within the state.

**2656  Arkansas Literacy Council: Laubach Literacy Action**

**Arkansas Literacy Council**
**4942 W Markham**
**Little Rock, AR  72205**                501-663-4321
                                    800-264-7323
                                FAX 501-663-3041
            http://www.arkansasliteracy.org
            e-mail: marie@arkansasliteracy.org
*Marie Bruno, Executive Director*
*Linda Bunda, Administrative Assistant*

Arkansas Literacy Council is a statewide 501 (c) (3) nonprofit agency on focusing strengthening learning efforts across Arkansas.

**2657  Literacy League of Craighead County**
**301 South Main**
**Jonesboro, AR  71401**                870-910-6511
                                    877-910-6511
                                FAX 870-910-0552
                    e-mail: llcc@newsources.net
*Thomas Templeton, Executive Director*

Offering information and resources on literacy throughout the area.

## California

**2658  Butte County Library Adult Reading Program**
**1820 Mitchell Avenue**
**Oroville, CA  95966**                530-538-7642
                                FAX 530-538-7235
            http://www.buttecounty.net/bclibrary
                e-mail: lib@buttecounty.net
*Nancy Brower, Library Director*
*Jean Lewis, Administrative Assistant*

Tutoring at no charge in reading, writing and math. Participants will learn the basics and more with one-on-one tutoring. A volunteer tutor will meet with participants at any branch library in Butte County.

**2659  California Association of Special Education & Services**

**CASES Executive Office**
**1722 J Street**
**Sacramento, CA  95814**                916-447-7061
                                FAX 916-447-1320
                            http://www.capses.com
                        e-mail: info@capses.com
*Janeth Serrano, Executive Director*
*Rita Celaya, Executive Administrative Assista*

The purposes are to serve as a liaison between the public and private sectors and to lend support for a continuum of programs and objectives which improve the delivery of services provided to the exceptional individual.

**2660  California Department of Education**

**Office of the Secretary for Education**
**1121 L Street**
**Sacramento, CA  95814**                916-323-0611
                                FAX 916-323-3753
                            http://www.ose.ca.gov
*Richard Riordan, Secretary for Education*
*Judy Tracy, Legislative Assistant*

The Office of the Secretary for Education is responsible for advising and making policy recommendations to the Governor on education issues.

**2661  California Literacy**

**133 N Altadena Drive**
**Pasadena, CA  91107 2379**                626-395-9989
                                    800-894-7323
                                FAX 626-395-9987
                            http://www.caliteracy.org
                        e-mail: office@caliteracy.org
*Lisa Bennett-Garrison, Executive Director*
*Archana Carey, Operations Director*

California Literacy was founded in 1956 and is the nation's oldest and largest statewide adult volunteer literacy organization. Its purpose is to establish literacy programs and to support them through tutor training, consulting, and ongoing education.

**2662  Lake County Literacy Coalition**

Pro Literacy Worldwide
1425 N High Street
Lakeport, CA  95422          707-263-7633
                             FAX 707-263-6796
                   http://www.co.lake.ca.us
                   e-mail: dianaf@co.lake.ca.us
*Ginn Devries, Director*
*Sookie Duncan, Administrative Assistant*

We provide free, basic literacy instruction to adult learners through confidential one-on-one study sessions that are geared to what the student wants to learn.

**2663  Literacy Program: County of Los AngelesPublic Library**

7400 East Imperial Highway
Downey, CA  90241            562-940-8511
                   http://www.colapublib.org
                   e-mail: hilda@colapl.org
*Margaret Donnellan, Librarian*
*Barbara Hirsch, Contact*

The Literacy Centers of the County of Los Angeles Public Library offer a variety of literacy services for adults and families at no charge. Literacy services include one-to-one basic literacy tutoring, English as a Second Language group instruction, Family Literacy and self-help instruction on audio cassettes, videocassettes and computer-based training. The literacy program is an affiliate of Literacy Volunteers of America, Inc.

**2664  Literacy Volunteers of America: ImperialValley**

Pro Literacy Worldwide
2695 S 4th Street
El Centro, CA  92243         760-352-8541
                             FAX 760-352-7812
                   e-mail: lva_ivy@icoet.org
*Norma Gomez, Director*
*MonaLisa Castleberry, Office Manager*

Literacy Volunteers of America is affiliated with ProLiteracy of America and provides the opportunity to acquire skills to be effective in their roles as members of their families, communities and workplaces.

**2665  Literacy Volunteers of America: WillitsPublic Library**

390 E Commercial Street
Willits, CA  95490           707-459-5098
                   http://www.mendolibrary.org/willits
                   e-mail: lvawillits@pacific.net
*Donna Kerr, Branch Librarian*
*Pamela Shilling, Contact*

The Literacy program offers one-on-one reading, writing and tutoring for adults in the area.

**2666  Marin Literacy Program**

San Rafael Public Library
1100 E Street
San Rafael, CA  94901        415-485-3318
                             FAX 415-485-3112
                   http://www.marinliteracy.org
                   e-mail: marinliteracy@marinliteracy.org
*Barbara Barwood, Director*
*Martha Haidet, Project Coordinator*

The Marin Literacy Program offers reading, writing and English conversation through professionally trained volunteers to Marin County adults who skills are too low to be helped by other services in the county.

**2667  Merced Adult School**

50 E 20th Street
Merced, CA  95344            209-385-6524
                             FAX 209-385-6430
                   e-mail: croberds@muhsd.k12.ca.us
*Carole Roberds, Principal*

To empower and educate our adult students to discover their own unique, productive place in our dynamic world and encourage them to be lifelong learners.

**2668  Metropolitan Adult Education Program**

760 Hillsdale Avenue
San Jose, CA  95136          408-723-6400
                   http://www.metroed.net
                   e-mail: jmondo@metroed.net
*Joyce Mondo, Public Information Officer*
*Nancy Arnold, Principal*

MetroED is the largest career-oriented educational organization in Santa Clara County. We provide vocational and adult education programs for the high school students and adults in their geographic areas.

**2669  Mid City Adult Learning Center**

Belmont Community Adult School
1510 Cambria Street
Los Angeles, CA  90017       213-483-8689
                             FAX 213-413-1356
                   e-mail: midcity@otan.dni.us
*Judy Griffin, Regional Center Manager*
*Helen Menke, Coordinator*

Provides adult education on ESL, basic reading, language and literacy programs.

**2670  Newport Beach Public Library LiteracyServices**

1000 Avocado Avenue
Newport Beach, CA  92660     949-717-3874
                   http://www.citynewportbeachlibrary.org
                   e-mail: literacy@city.newport-beach.ca.us
*Diane Moseley, Program Coordinator*
*Sheila Tierney, Program Assistant*

The mission of the Literacy Services Program is to help English-speaking adults improve their reading and writing skills.

**2671  Pomona Public Library Literacy Services**

Pro Literacy Worldwide
625 S Garey Avenue
Pomona, CA  91766                    909-620-2035
                                  FAX 909-620-3713
                                  TDY:909-620-3690
            http://www.youseemore.com/pomona
            e-mail: library@ci.pomona.ca.us
*Muriel Spill, Library Director*
*Verna English, Administrative Assistant*

The Pomona Literacy Service provides free adult literacy services to the City of Pomona. Volunteers provide tutorial programs to adults (16 years and older) who do not have basic literacy skills or whose literacy skills are so limited that they are not able to function independently in daily life or acquire employment or higher education.

**2672  Recording for the Blind & Dyslexic: Los Angeles**

Recording for the Blind & Dyslexic: New Jersey
5022 Hollywood Boulevard
Los Angeles, CA  90027               323-664-5525
                                     800-499-5525
                                  FAX 323-664-1881
                  http://www.rfbdla.org
                  e-mail: lea@rfbdla.org
*Carol Smith, Executive Director*
*Stacey Eubank, Outreach Director*

A national, nonprofit organization providing recorded textbooks, library services and other educational materials to students who cannot read standard print because of a visual, physical or learning disability. $50.00 registration fee and a $25.00 annual renewal fee. No fee for students whose schools are members.

**2673  Recording for the Blind & Dyslexic: Northern California Unit**

488 W Charleston Road
Palo Alto, CA  94306                 650-493-3717
                                     800-221-4792
                                  FAX 650-493-5513
                  http://www.rfbd.org
*John Stevenson, Executive Director*
*Valley Brown, Outreach Director*

A national network of thirty three studios with headquarters in Princeton, NJ. The sole purpose is to provide educational materials in recorded and computerized formats at every academic level. The materials are for all people unable to read standard print because of a visual, perceptual (dyslexia), or other physical disability.

**2674  Recording for the Blind & Dyslexic: Santa Barbara Chapter**

3970 La Colina Road
Golleta, CA  93110                   805-681-0532
                                  FAX 805-682-8197
                  http://www.rfbd.org
                  e-mail: jkarpenko@rfbd.org
*Tim Owens, Executive Director*

The Santa Barbara Unit was founded in 1976. Over 300 volunteers produce textbooks on tape for students at local schools and around the country.

**2675  Recording for the Blind and Dyslexic: Inland Empire-Orange County Unit**

1844 W 11th Street
Upland, CA  91786                    909-949-4316
                                  FAX 909-981-8457
                  http://www.rfbd.org
                  e-mail: mdavis@rfbd.org
*Sheri Weekes, Production Director*
*Mike Davis, Executive Director*
*Maggie Tupman, Educational Outreach Director*

Volunteers record texts on audio cassettes and computer disks for the visually, physically and perceptually disabled.

**2676  Regional Resource Center for San Diego: Imperial Counties**

6401 Linda Vista Road
San Diego, CA  92111                 858-292-3754
                                  FAX 858-268-9726
                                  TDY:858-571-7273
            http://wwww.aclpro-online.org
            e-mail: linda.carlton@suhsd.k12.ca.us
*Steve Niemeyer, Manager*
*Susan Yamate, Project Administrator*

The center assists regional adult education and literacy providers as they work to provide high quality and effective services to adult learners.

**2677  Sacramento Public Library Literacy Service**

828 I Street
Sacramento, CA  95814                916-264-2891
                                     800-561-4636
                                  FAX 916-264-2755
            http://www.saclibrary.org/literacy
            e-mail: contact@saclibrary.org
*Jackie Miller, Literacy Coordinator*
*Judith Alvi, Literacy Service Representative*
*Anne Marie Gold, Library Director*

The Literacy Service is committed to helping adults attain the skills they need to achieve their goals and develop their knowledge and potential. Free one-on-one tutoring is provided to English speaking adults who want to improve their basic reading and writing skills.

**2678  Sweetwater State Literacy Regional Resource Center**

Adult Resource Center
458 Moss Street
Chula Vista, CA  91911               619-691-5624
                                  FAX 619-425-8728
                  http://www.literacynet.org
                  e-mail: hurley@otan.dni.us
*Alice Hurley, Regional Manager*

The Sweetwater State Literacy Resource Center is located at the Adult and Continuing Education Division of the Sweetwater Union High School District. The Division is the fourth largest adult education program in the State of California, serving over 32,000 adult learners yearly.

**2679   Vision Literacy of California**

**Pro Literacy Worldwide**
**540 Valley Way**
**Milpitas, CA  95035**                   408-262-1349
                                    FAX 408-956-9384
                      http://www.visionliteracy.org
                      e-mail: info@visionliteracy.org
*Pat Lawson-North, Director*
*Brenda Eitemiller, Associate Manager of Operations*

Vision Literacy is dedicated to enriching the community in which we live by helping adults improve their literacy skills.

## Colorado

**2680   Colorado Adult Education and Family Literacy**

**Colorado Department of Education**
**201 East Colfax Avenue**
**Denver, CO  80203 1799**                303-866-6884
                                    FAX 303-830-0793
                      http://www.cde.state.co.us
                      e-mail: smith p@cde.state.co.us
*Pamela Smith, State Director*
*Debra Fawcett, Contact*

To assist adults to become literate in English and obtain the knowledge and skills necessary for employment and self-sufficiency.

**2681   Learning Disabilities Association of Colorado**

**4596 E Iliff Avenue**
**Denver, CO  80222**                     303-894-0992
                                    FAX 303-830-1645
                      http://www.ldanatl.org
                      e-mail: info@ldacolorado.com
*Tim Carroll, Public Relations*

A non-profit volunteer organization dedicated to advocacy and education of learning disabled children and adults.

**2682   Literacy Coalition of Jefferson County**

**10125 West 6th Avenue**
**Lakewood, CO  80215**                   303-271-6387
                                    FAX 303-854-4001
                      http://www.literacyjeffco.org
                      e-mail: marcie.hanson@judicial.state.co.us
*Marcie Hanson, Contact*

The purpose of the organization is to promote and foster increased literacy in Jefferson County, Colorado.

**2683   Literacy Volunteers of America: Colorado Literacy Outreach**

**Pro Literacy Worldwide**
**413 9th Avenue**
**Glenwood Springs, CO  81601**           970-945-5282
                                    FAX 970-945-7723
            http://www.literacyvolunteers.org/who/states
                      e-mail: mfred@coloradomtn.edu
*Martha Fredendall, Director*
*Bill Crymble, Coordinator*

Literacy Volunteers of America is a fully integrated national network of local, state and regional literacy providers that give adults and their families the opportunity to acquire skills to be effective in their roles as members of their families, communities, and workplaces.

## Connecticut

**2684   Connecticut Institute for Cultural Literacy and Wellness**

**60 Connolly Parkway, Building 12**
**Hamden, CT  06514**                     203-281-1347
                                    FAX 203-281-1386
*Fredrick Chappelle, Executive Director*

Offers adult education and literacy programs, as well as other programs that touch on other aspects of a well-rounded education.

**2685   Connecticut Literacy Resource Center**

**CREC/ATDW**
**111 Charter Oak Avenue**
**Hartford, CT  06106**                   860-247-2732
                                    FAX 860-246-3304
            http://www.crec.org/lc/index.shtml
                      e-mail: atyskiewicz@crec.org
*Bruce Douglas, Executive Director*
*Colleen Palmer, Assistant Executive Director*

The Literacy Center offers services that foster literacy development from early childhood to adult. Technical assistance and training are available in the following areas: School Readiness; k-12; and Family Literacy.

**2686   LEARN: Connecticut Reading Association**

**44 Hatchetts Hill Road**
**Old Lyme, CT  06371**                   860-434-4800
                                    FAX 860-434-4837
                      http://www.learn.k12.ct.us
                      e-mail: director@learn.k12.ct.us
*Virginia Seccom MD, Executive Director*

LEARN initiates, supports and provides a wide range of programs and services that enhance the quality and expand the opportunities for learning in the educational community.

**2687   Literacy Volunteers of Greater Hartford**

**30 Arbor Street**
**Hartford, CT  06106**                   860-233-3853
                                    http://www.lvgh.org
                      e-mail: susan.roman@lvgh.org
*Susan Roman, Executive Director*
*George Demetrion, Outreach Manager*

Literacy Volunteers of Greater Hartford has trained volunteers to provide free English literacy instruction to Hartford area adults.

## Delaware

**2688  Delaware Department of Education: AdultCommunity Education**

Department of Public Instruction
401 Federal Street
Dover, DE  19903                    302-739-3340
FAX 302-739-1770
http://www.doe.state.de.us
e-mail: ftracy-mumf@doe.k12.de.us
*Fran Mumford, Director Adult Education*
*Valerie Woodruff, Education Secretary*

Provides students with opportunities to develop skills needed to qualify for further education, job training, and better employment.

**2689  Literacy Volunteers of America: Wilmington Library**

10th and Market Street
Wilmington, DE  19899 2083          302-571-7400
http://www.wilmlib.org
e-mail: litvolunteers@aol.com
*Carmen Knox, Contact*

An organization of volunteers that provide a variety of services locally to enable people to achieve personal goals through literacy programs.

**2690  State of Delaware Adult and CommunityEducation Network**

516 West Loockermant Street
Dover, DE  19904                    302-739-5556
FAX 302-739-5565
http://www.acenetwork.org
e-mail: acedir@yahoo.com
*Joanne Heathy, Statewide Management Liaison*
*Meredith Mumford, Data Specialist*

The ACE Network is a service agency that supports adult education and literacy providers through training and resource development.

## District of Columbia

**2691  District of Columbia Department of Education: Vocational & Adult Education**

400 Maryland Avenue SW
Washington, DC  20202               202-205-5451
800-872-5327
FAX 202-205-8748
http://www.ed.gov/offices/OVAE
e-mail: ovae@ed.gov

To help all people achieve the knowledge and skills to be lifelong learners, to be successful in their chosen careers, and to be effective citizens.

**2692  District of Columbia Literacy Resource Center**

Martin Luther King Memorial Library
901 G Street NW
Washington, DC  20001               202-727-3157
FAX 202-727-1129
e-mail: marcia_harrington@csgi.com
*Marcia Harrington, ABE Specialist*

As part of the State Library, the State Resource Center provides electronic and print resources.

**2693  District of Columbia Public Schools**

825 N Capitol Street NE
Washington, DC  20202               202-442-4800
FAX 202-442-5517
http://www.k12.dc.us
e-mail: callcenter@k12.dc.us
*Elfreda Massie MD, Superintendent*

The public school system is committed to constant improvements in the achievement of all students today in preparation for their world tomorrow.

**2694  Literacy Volunteers of the NationalCapital Area**

PO Box 73275
Washington, DC  20056 3275          202-387-1772
http://www.lvanca.org
e-mail: dlewis@lvanca.org
*Connie Bombaugh, Executive Director*

Literacy Volunteers of the National Capital Area is an affiliate of ProLiteracy Network and provides free tutoring to illiterate adults in the Washington, D.C./National Capital Area.

## Florida

**2695  Florida Coalition**

Florida Literacy Coalition
934 N Magnolia Avenue
Orlando, FL  32803                  407-246-7110
800-237-5113
FAX 407-246-7104
http://www.floridaliteracy.org
e-mail: info@floridaliteracy.org
*Greg Smith, Executive Director*
*Kelley Jain, Education & Training Coordinator*

A nonprofit organization funded through private and corporate donations, state of Florida grants, and a diverse membership.

**2696  Florida Laubach Literacy Action**

52 E Main Street
Apopka, FL  32703                   407-889-0100
FAX 407-889-5576

*Teresa McElwee, President*

Laubach Literacy is a nonprofit educational corporation dedicated to helping adults of all ages improve their lives and their communities by learning reading, writing, math and problem solving skills.

**2697  Florida Literacy Coalition**

934 N Magnolia Avenue
Orlando, FL  32803                  407-246-7110
800-237-5113
FAX 407-246-7104
http://www.floridaliteracy.org
e-mail: info@floridaliteracy.org
*Kelley Jain, Education & Training Coordinator*
*Greg Smith, Executive Director*

A nonprofit organization funded through private and corporate donations, state of Florida grants, and a diverse membership.

**2698  Florida Literacy Resource Center**

**Adult & Community Educators of Florida**
**912 S Martin Luther King Jr**
**Tallahassee, FL  32301**          850-922-5343
                              FAX 850-922-5352
                      http://www.ace-leon.org
                      e-mail: ace@aceofflorida.org
*Veronica Sehrt, Project Manager*

As part of the State Library, the State Resource Center
provides electronic and print resources.

**2699  Florida Protection & Advocacy Agency for**
**Persons with Disabilities**

**2671 Executive Center Circle W**
**Tallahassee, FL  32301**          850-488-9071
                              800-342-0823
                              FAX 850-488-8640
                              TDY:800-346-4127
                      http://www.advocacycenter.org
                      e-mail: hubertg@advocacy.org
*Hubert Grissom, Interim Director*
*Sandy Evans, Administrative Assistant*

Offers help for people with disabilities.

**2700  Florida Vocational Rehabilitation Agency:**
**Division of Vocational Rehabilitation**

**Florida Department of Education**
**2002 Old Street Augustine Road**
**Tallahassee, FL  32399**          850-488-6210
                              FAX 850-921-7217
                      http://www.rehabworks.org
*Linda Parnell, Interim Director*
*Amanda Grimes, Assistant*

A statewide employment resource for businesses and
people with disabilities that enables individuals with
disabilities to obtain and keep employment.

**2701  Learning Disabilities Association of Florida**

**331 E Henry Street**
**Punta Gorda, FL  33950**          941-637-8957
                              FAX 941-637-0617
                      http://www.lda-fl.org
                      e-mail: ldaf00@sunline.net
*Cheryl Kron, Executive Secretary*

The Learning Disabilities Association of Florida is a
nonprofit volunteer organization of parents, professionals and LD adults.

## Georgia

**2702  Gainesville/Hall County Alliance for Literacy**

**PO Box 58**
**Gainesville, GA  30503**          770-531-4337
                              FAX 770-531-6406
                      http://www.northeastga.com
*Marci Hipp, Director*

A nonprofit agency designed to SUPPORT the literacy providers of Hall County. The Alliance for Literacy promotes education for adults, ages 16 and older.

**2703  Georgia Department of Education**

**Department of Technical & Adult Education**
**1800 Century Place**
**Atlanta, GA  30345**          404-679-1600
                              FAX 404-679-1710
                      http://www.dtae.org
                      e-mail: mdelaney@dtae.org
*Tony Bruehl, Director*
*Ron Jackson, Commissioner*

To oversee the state's system of technical colleges,
the adult literacy program, and a host of economic
workforce development programs.

**2704  Georgia Department of Technical & Adult**
**Education**

**Office of Adult Literacy**
**1800 Century Place**
**Atlanta, GA  30345**          404-679-1600
                              FAX 404-679-1710
                      http://www.dtae.org
                      e-mail: mdelaney@dtae.org
*Tony Bruehl, Director*
*Ron Jackson, Commissioner*

The Georgia Department of Technical and Adult Education oversees the state's system of technical colleges, the adult literacy program, and a host of
economic and workforce development programs

**2705  Georgia Literacy Resource Center: Office of**
**Adult Literacy**

**1800 Century Place NE**
**Atlanta, GA  30345**          404-679-1600
                              FAX 404-679-1630
                      http://www.dtae.org
                      e-mail: mdelaney@dtae.org
*Tony Bruehl, Director*
*Ron Jackson, Commissioner*

The mission of the adult literacy programs is to enable
every adult learner in Georgia to acquire the necessary
basic skills in reading, writing, computation, speaking, and listening to compete successfully in today's
workplace, strengthen family foundations, and exercise full citizenship.

**2706  Literacy Volunteers of America: Forsyth County**

**PO Box 1097**
**Cumming, GA  30028**          770-887-0074
                      http://www.litreacyforsyth.org
                      e-mail: focolit@sellsouth.net
*Eddith DeVeau, Executive Director*
*Dianne Anth, Director*

Dedicated to teaching adults to read in the Forsyth
County region.

**2707  Literacy Volunteers of America: Metropolitan**
**Atlanta**

**246 Sycamore Street**
**Decatur, GA  30030**          404-377-7323
                              FAX 404-377-8662
                      http://www.lvama.org
                      e-mail: lva_ma@mindspring.com
*Katie Wilson, Executive Director*

An organization dedicated to teaching adults to read
in the Atlanta area.

**2708 Literacy Volunteers of America: Tift County**

211 Chestnut Avenue
Tifton, GA 31794
229-382-0505
FAX 229-387-0442
e-mail: tiftlva@surfsouth.com
*Mary Laster, Director*

**2709 Literacy Volunteers of America: Troup County**

PO Box 1087
La Grange, GA 30241
706-883-7837
FAX 706-882-5114
e-mail: lvatc@mindspring.com
*Charlotte Anderson, Executive Director*

The Literacy Volunteers of America is a fully integrated national network of local, state and regional literacy providers that give adults and their families the opportunity to acquire skills to be effective in their roles as members of their families, communities and workplace.

**2710 Nancy Hart Literacy Council of Georgia**

150 Benson Street, Suite 2
Hartwell, GA 30643
706-376-5534
FAX 706-856-2655
*Emily Gunnells*

To organize volunteers for the purpose of improving literacy.

**2711 Toccoa/Stephens County Literacy Council**

409 West Waitman
Toccoa, GA 30577
706-282-5171
FAX 706-282-7633
e-mail: mwalters3@yahoo.com
*Maggie Walters, Tutor Coordinator*

## Hawaii

**2712 Hawaii Laubach Literacy Action**

Hawaii Literacy
200 N Vineyard Boulevard
Honolulu, HI 96817
808-537-6706
FAX 808-528-1690
http://www.literacynet.org/hilit
e-mail: hiliteracy@aol.com
*Millie Gorecki, Executive Director*

Laubach Literacy Action is a nonprofit educational corporation dedicated to helping adult of all ages improve their lives and their communities by learning reading, writing, math and problem-solving skills.

**2713 Hawaii Literacy Resource Center**

Office of State Libraries
3225 Salt Lake Boulevard
Honolulu, HI 96818
808-831-6878
FAX 808-831-6882
http://www.literacynet.org/hawaii/home
e-mail: susann@lib.state.hi.us
*Sue Berg, State Literacy Director*

As part of the state library, the state resource center provides electronic and print resources.

## Idaho

**2714 Idaho Adult Education Office**

Adult Education Office
650 W State Street
Boise, ID 83720-0027
208-332-6800
FAX 208-334-4664
http://www.sde.state.id.us
e-mail: Shoehler@sde.state.id.us
*Susan Oehler, Office Specialist*

**2715 Idaho Coalition for Adult Literacy**

325 W State Street
Boise, ID 83702
208-334-2150
800-458-3271
FAX 208-334-4016
http://www.lili.org
*Peggy McClendon, Literacy Coordinator*
*Ann Joslin, State Librarian*

An nonprofit organization which raise public awareness about the importance of a literate society.

**2716 Idaho Department of Corrections**

1299 N Orchard Street
Boise, ID 83706
208-658-2000
FAX 208-327-7496
http://www.corr.state.id.us
e-mail: inquiry@corr.state.id.us
*Gale Cushman, Education Bureau Chief*

The Education Bureau of the Idaho Department of Correction operates prison education programs in seven facilities across the state.

**2717 Idaho State Library**

325 W State Street
Boise, ID 83702
208-334-2150
800-458-3271
FAX 208-334-4016
http://www.lili.org
e-mail: lili@isL.state.id.us
*Stephanie Bailey-White, Public Information Officer*
*Ann Joslin, State Librarian*

Offers a history of pioneering new frontiers in library services.

**2718 Idaho Workforce Investment Act**

Idaho Department of Labor
317 Main Street
Boise, ID 83735
208-332-3570
FAX 208-334-6300
http://www.cl.idaho.gov
e-mail: cbrush@labor.state.id.us
*Cheryl Brush, Bureau Chief*
*Cherly Osment, Administrative Assistant*

Provides vocational training services for economically disadvantaged adults and youth, dislocated workers and others who face significant employment barriers.

**2719 Temporary Assistance for Needy Families: Idaho Department of Health and Welfare**

450 W State Street
Boise, ID 83720-0036          208-334-0606
                              FAX 208-334-6581
                              http://www.2.state.id.us
                              e-mail: BCEH@idhw.state.id.us
*Karl Kurtz, Director of Health and Welfare*
*Dian Prince, Administrative Assistant*

Provides assistance and work opportunities to needy families by granting states the federal funds and wide flexibility to develop and implement their own welfare programs.

## Illinois

**2720 Illinois Library Association**

33 W Grand Avenue
Chicago, IL 60610          312-644-1896
                           FAX 312-644-1899
                           e-mail: ila@ila.org
*Robert Doyle, Executive Director*

The Illinois Library Association is the voice for Illinois Libraries and the millions who depend on them. It provides leadership for the development, promotion, and improvement of library services in Illinois and for the library community.

**2721 Illinois Literacy Resource Center**

IL Network of Literacy/Adult Education Resources
431 S 4th Street
Springfield, IL 62701          217-785-6921
                               800-665-5576
                               FAX 217-785-6927
                               TDY:888-261-2709
*Cindy Colletti, Manager*

As part of the State Library, the State Resource Center provides electronic and print resources.

**2722 Illinois Literacy Resource Development Center**

209 W Clark Street
Champaign, IL 61820          217-355-6068
                             FAX 217-355-6347
                             http://www.ilrdc.org
                             e-mail: tbudz@ilrdc.org
*Suzanne Knell, Executive Director*
*Janet Scogins, Associate Director*

The Illinois Literacy Resource Development Center is dedicated to improving literacy policy and practice at the local, state, and national levels. It is a nonprofit organization supporting literacy and adult education efforts throughout Illinois and the nation. One key to its success has been its ability to build partnerships among the organizations, individuals and agencies working in the literacy arena from the local to the national level.

**2723 Illinois Office of Rehabilitation Services**

Illinois Department of Human Services
100 S Grand Avenue E
Springfield, IL 62762          217-557-1601
                               e-mail: ors@dhs.state.il.us
*Teyonda Wertz, Chief of Staff*
*Rafael Diaz, Manager of Information Services*

DHS' Office of Rehabilitation Services is the state's lead agency serving individuals with disabilities.

**2724 Illinois Protection & Advocacy Agency:Equip for Equality**

11 E Adams Street
Chicago, IL 60603          312-341-0022
                           800-537-2632
                           FAX 312-341-0295
                           TDY:800-610-2779
                           http://www.equipforequality.org
                           e-mail: hn6177@handsnet.org
*Peter Grosz, Developmental Director*

Equip for Equality is a not-for-profit Federally-funded organization that advocates for disability rights in the state of Illinois.

**2725 Literacy Chicago**

70 E Lake Street
Chicago, IL 60601          312-870-1100
                           FAX 312-870-4488
                           http://www.literacychicago.org
                           e-mail: info@literacychicago.org
*Susan Kidder, Executive Director*
*Judy Klikun, Program Director*

Literacy Chicago is dedicated to improving the literacy skills of Chicago-area adults and families.

**2726 Literacy Volunteers of America: Illinois**

30 E Adams Street
Chicago, IL 60603          312-857-1582
                           FAX 312-857-1586
                           http://www.literacyvolunteersillinois.org
                           e-mail: LVAILL@aol.com
*Dorothy Miaso, Executive Director*
*Dorish Rabinovitz, Program Coordinator*

Literacy Volunteers of Illinois is a statewide organization committed to developing and supporting volunteer literacy programs that help families, adults and out-of-school teens increase their literacy skills.

## Indiana

**2727 Indiana Literacy & Technical Education Resource Center**

Indiana State Library
140 N Senate Avenue
Indianapolis, IN 46204          317-232-3727
                                800-233-4572
                                FAX 317-232-3728
                                http://www.ciesck.in.us
                                e-mail: ilterc@statelib.lib.in.us
Provides literacy, technical, and career education resources to meet basic adult educational needs. Adult education materials include GED, learning disabilities and ESL resources. A thirty day loan period is provided to literacy, business and industry, goverment, schools and other adult education programs as well as to individual Indiana residents.

**2728  Indiana Literacy Foundation**
1920 W Morrison
Indianapolis, IN  46221          317-639-6106
                                 FAX 317-639-2782
                    http://www.indianaliteracy.org
                    e-mail: psiemant@indianaliteracy.org

Indiana Literacy Foundation is a non-profit organization dedicated to strengthening basic skills among children and adults working with and through volunteer literacy programs across Indiana.

**2729  Indiana Workforce Literacy**
10 N Senate Avenue
Indianapolis, IN  46204          317-232-4785
                                 FAX 317-232-1815
                    http://www.in.gov/dwd/information
                    e-mail: tmartin@dwd.state.in.us

The Office of Workforce Literacy is dedicated to strengthening the skills of Indiana's workforce and to increasing the competitive edge of Indiana employers. Workforce Literacy grants provide on-site, customized, specific job related training. Employers and workers alike report that knowledge, skills, work attitudes, and productivity improves as a result of job-specific training.

**2730  Indy Reads: Indianapolis/Marion County Public Library**
PO Box 211
Indianapolis, IN  46206          317-269-1700
                                 FAX 317-269-5220
                    http://www.imcpl.org
                    e-mail: lgabrielson@imcpl.org
*Linda Gabrielson, Manager*

Indy Reads, a nationally recognized not-for-profit affiliate of the Indianapolis-Marion County Public Library, exists to improve the reading and writing skills of adults in Marion County who read at or below the sixth grade level.

**2731  Literacy Volunteers of America: Cass County**
847 S Cicott Street
Logansport, IN  46947          219-722-6809
                               FAX 219-722-6810
*Jane Miller, Contact*

Literacy Volunteers of America is a fully integrated national network of local, state and regional literacy providers that gives adults and their families the opportunity to acquire skills to be effective in their roles as members of their families, communities, and workplaces.

**2732  Literacy Volunteers of America: White County**
1001 S Main
Monticello, IN  47960          574-583-0789
                               FAX 219-943-3533
*Judy Hickman, Contact*

A not-for-profit organization which provides a variety of free services to help people achieve personal goals through literacy.

**2733  Morrisson/Reeves Library Literacy Resource Center**
80 N 6th Street
Richmond, IN  47374          765-966-8291
                             FAX 765-962-1318
                    http://www.mrl.lib.org
                    e-mail: library@mrlinfo.org

The Literacy Resource Center provides free training for volunteers to tutor adults in Wayne County who want to learn to read, write and do basic math.

**2734  Steuben County Literacy Coalition**
Community Center
317 S Wayne
Angola, IN  46703          260-665-1414
                           FAX 260-665-1414
          http://www.steubencountyliteracycoalition.org
                           e-mail: sclc@locl.net
*Rebecca Fifer, President*
*Kathleen Armstrong, Director*

The Steuben County Literacy Coalition helps adults and families develop their potential through improved literacy, education, and training.

**2735  Three Rivers Literacy Alliance**
Pro Literacy Worldwide
709 Clay Street
Fort Wayne, IN  46802          260-426-7323
                               FAX 260-424-0371
                    http://www.tria.org
                    e-mail: trlafw@yahoo.com
*Kathleen Benson-Chaney, Literacy Coordinator*
*Judith Stabelli, Director*

Three Rivers Literacy Alliance addresses literacy issues with the adult population of Fort Wayne and the surrounding community.

# Iowa

**2736  Iowa Bureau of Community Colleges**
Department of Education
Grimes State Office Building
Des Moines, IA  50319          515-281-3125
                               FAX 515-281-6544
                    http://www.state.ia.us/educate/commcoll.html
                    e-mail: sally.schroeder@iowa.gov
*Sally Schroeder, Director*

**2737  Iowa Department of Education: Iowa Literacy Council Programs**
Grimes State Office Building
Des Moines, IA  50319          515-281-5294
                               FAX 515-242-5988
                    http://www.state.ia.us/educate/commcoll
                    e-mail: sally.schroeder@ed.state.ia.us
*Judy Jeffrey, Director*
*Ted Stilwater, Director, Family Literacy*

Helps adults and families develop their potential through improved literacy, education, and training.

**2738 Iowa JOBS Program: Division of Economic Assistance**

Department of Human Services
Hoover State Building
Des Moines, IA 50319     515-281-8629
FAX 515-281-4940
*Kevin Concannon, Executive Director*

**2739 Iowa Literacy Resource Center**

Iowa Literacy Resource Center
415 Commercial Street
Waterloo, IA 50701     319-233-1200
800-772-2023
FAX 319-233-1964
http://www.readiowa.org
e-mail: riesberg@neilsa.org
*Eunice Riesberg, Director*
*Denise Luppen, Administrative Assistant*

The Center provides a link to resource materials in Iowa and at a regional and national level for adult literacy practitioners and students.

**2740 Iowa Vocational Rehabilitation Agency**

Department of Education
Grimes State Office Building
Des Moines, IA 50319     515-281-5294
FAX 515-281-4703
TDY:515-242-5988
http://www.state.ia.us./educate/comcol
*Steve Wooderson, Administrator*
*Judy Jeffrey, Director*

**2741 Iowa Workforce Investment Act**

Department of Economic Development
200 E Grand Avenue
Des Moines, IA 50309     515-242-4700
FAX 515-242-4809
TDY:800-735-2934
http://www.iowalifechanging.com
e-mail: iowasmart@ided.state.ia.us
*Mike Blouin, Director*
*Deb Townsend, Web Specialist*

Job placement and training services. Especially for those workers who have been laid off, or have other barriers to steady employment.

**2742 Learning Disabilities Association of Iowa**

321 E 6th Street
Des Moines, IA 50329     515-280-8558
888-690-5324
FAX 515-243-1902
http://www.lda-ia.org
*Vicki Goshon, President*
*Kathy Specketer, Coordinator*

The Learning Disabilities Association of Iowa advances the education and general welfare of children and youth of normal, near-normal, and potentially normal intelligence who have learning disabilities.

**2743 Library Literacy Programs: State Library of Iowa**

1112 E Grand Avenue
Des Moines, IA 50319     515-281-4105
FAX 515-281-6171
http://www.silo.lib.ia.us
*Helen Dagley, Information Services*

---

# Kansas

**2744 Client Assistance Program (CAP):Kansas Division of Persons with Disabilities**

2914 SW Plass Court
Topeka, KS 66611     785-266-8193
800-432-2326
*Mary Reyer, Director*

Provides free services to consumers and applicants for projects, programs and facilities funded under the rehabilitation act.

**2745 Kansas Adult Education Association**

Barton County Community College
245 NE 30th Road
Great Bend, KS 67530     620-792-2701
800-748-7594
http://www.barton.cc.ks.us
*Todd Moore, Director for admission*
*Cassandra Montoya, Student Work Service*

The Kansas Adult Education Association has been the professional association for adult educators at community colleges, school districts, and non-profit organizations.

**2746 Kansas Correctional Education**

900 SW Jackson
Topeka, KS 66612     785-296-3317
888-317-8204
http://www.kdoc.dc.state.ks.us
*Roger Haden, Secretary of Programs & Staff*
*Margaret Murdock, Administrative Assistant*

The provision of correctional education programming to inmates.

**2747 Kansas Department of Corrections**

900 SW Jackson
Topeka, KS 66612     785-296-3317
888-317-8204
FAX 785-296-3317
http://www.kdoc.dc.state.ks.us
e-mail: jan.clausing@kdoc.dc.state.ks.us
*Jan Clausing, Human Resource Director*
*Bill Noll, Information Technology Director*

Correctional education programming to inmates.

**2748 Kansas Laubach Literacy Action**

120 E. Fifth Avenue
Arkansas City, KS 67005     316-442-1280

A non-profit educational corporation dedicated to helping adults of all ages improve their lives and their communities by learning reading, writing, math and problem-solving skills.

**2749 Kansas Library Literacy Programs: Kansas State Library**
200 Arco Place, Suite 309
Independence, KS 67301 620-331-8218
FAX 620-331-9087
e-mail: vikkijo@kslib.info
*Vikki Stewart, Management Coordinator*

The goal of the Kansas Library Literacy Program is to provide Kansans with current volunteer management information to assist in their effort to use volunteers to meet a mission, e.g., libraries, literacy programs, etc. and to provide Kansans with current literacy information to assist in their effort to help adults and youth to read better, e.g., community-based literacy programs, traditional adult education, etc.

**2750 Kansas Literacy Resource Center**
Kansas Board of Regents/Literacy Resource Center
1000 SW Jackson Street
Topeka, KS 66612 785-296-0175
800-296-4526
FAX 785-296-0983
http://www.literacy.kent.edu
e-mail: dglass@ksbor.org
*Dianne Glass, State Director Adult Education*
*Diane Whitley, Associate Director*

The Kansas Literacy Resource Center enhances systems, both private and public, that provide basic skills education across Kansas.

**2751 Kansas Literacy Volunteers of America**
Kansas State Library
State Capital Building
Topeka, KS 66612 1593 785-296-3296
800-432-3919
FAX 785-296-6650
http://www.skyways.org
e-mail: KSST15LB@INK.ORG
*Vikki Stewart, Literacy Program Director*
*Christie Brandau, Head of Library*

To give adults and their families the opportunity to acquire skills to be effective in their roles as members of their families, communities and workplaces.

**2752 Kansas State Department of Adult Education**
120 E 10th Street
Topeka, KS 66612 785-296-3201
FAX 785-296-7933
http://www.ksde.org
e-mail: atompkins@ksde.org
*Andy Tompkins, Commissioner*
*Dale Dennis, Deputy Commissioner*

To assist adults to become literate and obtain the knowledge and skills necessary for employment and self-sufficiency.

**2753 Kansas State Literacy Resource Center: Kansas State Department of Education**
1000 SW Jackson
Topeka, KS 66612-1368 785-296-0175
FAX 785-296-0983
*Janet Stotts, Co-Director*
*Dianne Glass, Co-Director*

The State Literacy Resource Center can assist adult education practitioners across the nation in locating and accessing the most current materials in their issue area.

**2754 Kansas Vocational Rehabilitation Agency**
300 SW Oakley, Biddle Building
Topeka, KS 66606 785-296-3911
FAX 785-368-6688
*Joyce Cussimanio, Commissioner*

To assist people with disabilities achieve suitable employment and independence.

**2755 Western Kansas Community Service Consortiuum**
348 NE SR
Pratt, KS 67124 620-672-6251
http://www.wkcsc.org
e-mail: dedram@genmail.pcc.cc.ks.us
*Dedra Manes, Executive Director*

Mission is to provide cooperative community services to Western Kansas. Total service area includes 73 counties and nearly 3/4 of the state's geographic area.

## Kentucky

**2756 Kentucky Laubach Literacy Action**
Department for Adult Education & Literacy
1024 Capital Center Dr
Frankfort, KY 40601 502-573-5114
FAX 502-573-5436
http://adulted.state.ky.us
e-mail: dvislisel@mail.state.ky.us
*Dave Vislisel, Director*

Dedicated to helping adults of all ages improve their lives and their communities by learning reading, writing, match and problem-solving skills.

**2757 Kentucky Literacy Resource Center**
Center for Adult Education & Literacy
1048 E. Chestnut St
Louisville, KY 40204 502-815-7000
800-win-net2
FAX 502-815-7001
http://www.win.net
e-mail: scallaway@mail.state.ky.us
*Sare Callaway, Contact*

As part of the State Library, the State Resource Center provides electronic and print resources.

**2758 Kentucky Literacy Volunteers of America**
1024 Capital Center Dr
Frankfort, KY 40601 502-573-5114
FAX 502-573-5436
http://adulted.state.ky.us
e-mail: dvislsel@mail.state.ky.us
*Dave Vislisel, Director*

Promotes literacy for people of all ages.

## Louisiana

**2759 Literacy Volunteers of America: Centenary College Program**

2911 Centenary Boulevard
Shreveport, LA  71134          318-869-2411
                              FAX 318-869-2474
                    e-mail: lvacent@bellsouth.net
*Sue Lee, Director*
*Garcy Balton, Office Secretary*

**2760 Louisiana State Literacy Resource Center: State Department of Education**

Office of School & Community Support
626 N 4th Street
Baton Rouge, LA  70804          225-342-3340
                               877-453-2721
                          FAX 225-219-4439
                http://www.louisianaschools.net
                    e-mail: mbryant@la.gov

The Center provides a link to resource materials in Louisiana and at a regional and national level for adult literacy, practitioners and students.

## Maine

**2761 Center for Adult Learning and Literacy: University of Maine**

Pro Literacy Worldwide
5749 Merrill Hall
Orono, ME  04469          207-581-2498
                         FAX 207-581-1517
                    http://www.umaine.edu
        e-mail: evelyn.beaulieu@umit.maine.edu
*Evelyn Beaulieu, Director*
*Carol Wynne, Project Coordinator*

The Center for Adult Learning and Literacy offers quality, research-based professional development and resources, based on funded initiatives to improve the quality of services within the Maine Adult Education System.

**2762 Maine Bureau of Applied Technical Adult Learning: Adult Career and Technical Education**

Maine Department of Education
23 State House Station
Augusta, ME  04333          207-624-6730
                           FAX 207-624-6731
                http://www.maine.gov/education
                e-mail: yvonne.davis@maine.gov
*Yvonne Davis, Director*

**2763 Maine Literacy Resource Center**

University of Maine
5749 Merrill Hall
Orono, ME  04469          207-581-2498
                         FAX 207-581-1517
                    http://www.umaine.edu
        e-mail: evelyn.beaulieu@umit.maine.edu
*Evelyn Beaulieu, Director*
*Carol Wynne, Project Coordinator*

As part of the State Library, the State Resource Center provides electronic and print resources.

**2764 Maine Literacy Volunteers of America**

142 High Street, Suite 514
Portland, ME  04103-8585          207-780-1352
                    http://www.lvaportland.org
                    e-mail: lvportland@gwi.net
*Kristian Stevens, Director*

A non-profit organization that provides free tutoring to adults who cannot read and to adults whose native language is not English.

## Maryland

**2765 Howard University School of Continuing Education**

1100 Wayne Avenue
Silver Spring, MD  20910          301-585-2295
                           FAX 301-585-8911
                http://www.con-ed.howard.edu
                e-mail: paberry@howard.edu

Howard University Continuing Education was established in April 1986 to meet the education and training needs of professionals, administrators, entrepreneurs, technical personnel, paraprofessionals and other adults on an individual or group basis.

**2766 Maryland Literacy Resource Center**

UMBC, Department of Education
1000 Hilltop Circle
Baltimore, MD  21250          410-455-1000
                             800-358-3010
                        FAX 410-455-1139
                    http://www.umbc.edu
                    e-mail: help@umbc.edu
*Katherine Ira, Director*

As part of the State Library, the State Resource Center provides resources and information for adult literacy providers and students in Maryland.

**2767 Maryland Project Literacy**

Howard County Library
10375 Little Patuxent Parkway
Columbia, MD  21044          410-313-7900
                            FAX 410-313-7811
                            TDY:410-313-7883
                    http://www.hclibrary.org
                e-mail: carsettj@hclibrary.org
*Janet Carsetti, Director*
*Yu-ching Ostendorp, Administrative Assistant*

## Massachusetts

**2768    Adult Center at PAL: Curry College**
1071 Blue Hill Avenue
Milton, MA  02186                              617-333-0500
                                          FAX 617-333-2114
                                  http://www.curry.edu/pal
                                   e-mail: pal@curry.edu
*Jane Adelizzi PhD, Contact*

The Adult Center at PAL (Program for Advancement of Learning) is the first program to offer academic and socio-emotional services to adults with LD/ADHD/Dyslexia in a college setting in the New England area. The ACD offers one-to-one academic tutorials; small support groups that meet weekly; and Saturday Seminars that explore issues that impact the lives of adults with LD/ADHD.

**2769    Eastern Massachusetts Literacy Council**
400 High Street
Medford, MA  02155                             781-395-2374
                                          FAX 781-395-3281
                                   http://www.emlc.org
                                e-mail: volunteer@emlc.org

The Eastern Massachusetts Literacy Council is a private non-profit affiliate of ProLiteracy Worldwide, the largest nonprofit volunteer adult literacy organization in the world. The EMLC trains volunteers to assist adults who are learning English as another language and adults who wish to strengthen their basic reading skills.

**2770    JOBS Program: Massachusetts Employment Services Program**
Dept of Transitional Assistance/Office of Health
600 Washington Street
Boston, MA  02111                              617-348-8400
                                          FAX 617-348-8575
                              http://www.state.ma.us/dta/index.htm
*John Wagner, Commissioner*
*Julie Noble, Assistant to the Assistant Direc*

The Employment Services Program is a joint federal and state funded program whose primary goal is to provide a way to self-sufficiency for TAFDC families ESP is an employment-oriented program that is based on a work-first approach.

**2771    Literacy Volunteers of Massachusetts**
15 Court Square
Boston, MA  02108                              617-367-1313
                                          FAX 617-367-8894
                              http://www.volunteerssolutions.org
                              e-mail: volunteers@uwmb.org
*Amy Todeschini, Coordinator*

The Literacy Volunteers of Massachusetts helps adults learn to read and write or speak English by matching them with trained volunteer tutors.

**2772    Massachusetts Correctional Education: Inmate Training & Education**
Department of Correction
MCI North Folk
Norfolk, MA  02056                             617-727-9170
                                          FAX 508-850-5214
                                   http://www.state.ma.us
*Carolyn Vicari, Director*
*Dianne Rice, Branch Manager*

To establish departmental policy regarding inmates' involvement in academic and vocational training programs.

**2773    Massachusetts Family Literacy Consortium**
State Government
350 Main Street
Malden, MA  02148                              781-338-3300
                                          FAX 781-338-3394
                                   http://www.doe.mass.edu
                                e-mail: MFLC@doe.mass.edu
*Kathy Rodriguez, MFLC Coordinator*
*Arlene Dale, State Coordinator*

The Massachusetts Family Literacy Consortium is a statewide initiative with the mission of forging effective partnerships among state agencies, community organizations, and other interested parties to expand and strengthen family literacy and support.

**2774    Massachusetts GED Administration: Massachusetts Department of Education**
350 Main Street
Malden, MA  02148                              781-338-6604
                                  http://www.doe.mass.edu
                              e-mail: rderfler@doe.mass.edu
*Ruth Derfler, Director*

Thirty-three test centers operate state-wide to serve the needs of the adult population in need of a high school credential.

**2775    Massachusetts Job Training Partnership Act: Department of Employment & Training**
CF Hurley Building, 3rd Floor
Boston, MA  02114                              617-626-6600
                                          FAX 617-727-0315
                                   http://www.detma.org
                                e-mail: mstonge@detma.org
*John O'Leary, Commissioner*

Supplies information on the local labor market and assists companies in locating employees.

## Michigan

**2776    Genesee County Literacy Coalition**
Zimmerman Center
2421 Corunna Road
Flint, MI  48503                               810-760-5182
                                          FAX 810-760-1215
                                   http://www.flint.lib.mi.us

The Genesee County Literacy Coalition is a non-profit organization dedicated to promoting literacy in Genesee County.

# Literacy & Learning Skills /Minnesota

**2777 Literacy Volunteers of America: Lansing Area Literacy Coalition**

1028 E Saginaw
Lansing, MI 48906        517-485-4949
FAX 517-485-1924
http://www.thereadingpeople.org
e-mail: mail@thereadingpeople.org
*Lois Bader, Executive Director*
*Di Clark, Assistant Director*

The Capital Area Literacy Coalition helps children and adults learn to read, write and speak English with an ultimate goal of helping individuals achieve self-sufficiency.

**2778 Literacy Volunteers of America: Sanilac Council**

Grace Temple
46 N Jackson Street
Sandusky, MI 48471        810-648-2200

Helps children and adults learn to read, write and speak English with self sufficiency as the ultimate goal.

**2779 Michigan Adult Learning & Technology Center**

Central Michigan University
219 Ronan Hall
Mount Pleasant, MI 48859        989-774-3337
FAX 989-714-7713
http://www.malt.cmich.edu
e-mail: malt@cmich.edu
*Michael Kent, Special Projects Coordinator*

A professional development center that extends support services and resources to adult education providers, volunteers, and students. These efforts include: disseminating research information; conducting and sponsoring training for tutors and educators; coordinating conferences; aiding in the utilization of technology in professional development and the classroom; providing grants or sponsoring research projects related to the field of education.

**2780 Michigan Assistive Technology: Michigan Rehabilitation Services**

Michigan Jobs Commission
119 Pere Marquette Drive
Lansing, MI 48912        517-485-4477
FAX 517-485-4488
http://www.publicpolicy.com
e-mail: ppa@publicpolicy.com
*Jeffrey Padden, President*
*Nancy Hewat, Executive Director*

**2781 Michigan Laubach Literacy Action**

2157 University Park Drive
Okemos, MI 48864        517-349-7511
FAX 517-349-6667
http://www.michiganliteracy.org
e-mail: mli@voyager.net
*Levona Whitaker, Contact*

Dedicated to advancing basic literacy skills throughout Michigan and beyond.

**2782 Michigan Libraries and Adult Literacy**

702 W Kalamazoo Street
Lansing, MI 48909-7507        517-373-1297
FAX 517-373-5853
TDY:517-373-1592
http://www.michigan.gov/libraryofmichigan
e-mail: librarian@michigan.gov
*Nancy Robertson, Acting State Librarian*
*Jenny Sipe, Administrative Assistant*

**2783 Michigan State Department of Adult Education: Office of Extended Learning Services**

Department of Education
608 W Allegan
Lansing, MI 48933        517-241-3946
FAX 517-335-0592
http://www.michigan.gov
e-mail: kingsleym@michigan.gov
*Maria Kingsley, Educational Consultant*
*Lindy Buch, Director*

**2784 Michigan Workforce Investment Act**

Michigan Jobs Commission
119 Pere Marquette Drive
Lansing, MI 48912        517-485-4477
FAX 517-485-4488
http://www.publicpolicy.com
e-mail: ppa@publicpolicy.com
*Jeffrey Padden, President*
*Nancy Hewat, Executive Officer*

## Minnesota

**2785 Minnesota Department of Adult Education: Adult Basic Education**

Department of Children, Families & Learning
1500 Highway 36 West
Rosevillel, MN 55113        651-582-8442
FAX 651-634-5154
*Brian Kanes, Coordinator*

**2786 Minnesota Department of Employment and Economic Development**

Minnesota Workforce Center
332 Minnesota street
St. Paul, MN 55101
800-657-3858
http://www.mnwfc.org
e-mail: mdes.customerservice@state.mn.us
*Bonnie Elsey, Director*

The Department of Employment and Economic Development is Minnesota's principal economic development agency, with programs promoting business expansion and retention, workforce development, international trade, community development and tourism.

**2787 Minnesota GED Administration**

997 Capitol Square Building
St. Paul, MN 55101        612-296-2704
FAX 612-668-3805
*Patrick Rupp, GED Director*

State of Minnesota General Educational Development.

**2788  Minnesota LDA Learning Disabilities Center**
4301 Highway 7
Minneapolis, MN  55416          952-922-8374
                                866-891-0601
                           FAX 952-922-8102
              http://www.ldaminnesota.org
              e-mail: kc@ldaminnesota.org
*Kitty Christiansen, Executive Director*
*Victoria Weinberg, Program Director*

The LDA Learning Center maximizes the potential of children, youth and adults with learning disabilities or related learning difficulties so that they and their families lead more productive and fulfilled lives.

**2789  Minnesota LINCS: Literacy Council**
756 Transfer Road
St. Paul, MN  55114 1404          651-645-2277
                                  800-225-7323
                             FAX 651-645-2272
                    http://www.mlc.org
*Cathy Grady, Program Director*
*Eric Nesheim, Executive Director*

Makes information available to literacy and other educators throughout Minnesota. The system is a result of cooperation between numerous agencies and organizations in Minnesota that realize the benefit of using the internet to provide information to the public. The system allows literacy and other educators to locate information at one central site or follow links to connect to wherever the information resides.

**2790  Minnesota Life Work Center**
University of St. Thomas
1000 La Salle Avenue
Minneapolis, MN  55403          651-962-4763
              http://www.stthomas.edu
              e-mail: lifework@stthomas.edu
*Brian Dusbiber, Director*
*Mary Kernan, Career Counselor*

Supporting the educational goals, personal growth and career management needs of graduate students, education students, and alumni, through professional services and comprehensive resources.

**2791  Minnesota Literacy Training Network**
University of St. Thomas
1000 La Salle
Minneapolis, MN  55403          651-962-4000
                                800-328-6819
                           FAX 651-962-4169
              http://www.stthomas.edu
*Deborah Simmons, Director*

Literacy Training Network offers noncredit learning opportunities for adult basic education and literacy training staff in Minnesota.

**2792  Minnesota Vocational Rehabilitation Agency: Rehabilitation Services Branch**
Department of Economic Security
390 N Robert Street
Saint Paul, MN  55101          651-296-5616
                               800-328-9095
                          FAX 651-297-5159
              http://www.mnworkforcecenter.org
              e-mail: Howard.Glad@state.mn.us
*Howard Glad, Contact*

Provides basic vocational rehabilitation services to consumers including vocational counseling, planning, guidance and placement, as well as certain special services based on individual circumstances.

## Missouri

**2793  Literacy Investment for Tomorrow: Missouri**
500 NW Plaza
Saint Louis, MO  63074          314-291-4443
                                800-729-4443
                           FAX 314-291-7385
              http://www.literacy.kent.edu
              e-mail: lift@icon-stl.net
*Sarah Beaman-Jones, Literacy Program Developer*
*Timothy , Executive Director*

LIFT develops and promotes resources to increase literacy skills of Missourians so all individuals can reach their personal and economic potential.

**2794  Literacy Kansas City**
Pro Literacy America
205 W 65th Street
Kansas City, MO  64113          816-333-9332
                           FAX 816-444-6628
              http://www.literacykc.org
              e-mail: info@literacykc.org
*Janis Doty, Program Director*
*Dianne Daldudrup, Executive Director*

Literacy Kansas City is a 501 (c) (3) not-for-profit organization that helps adults from greater metropolitan Kansas City improve their basic literacy skills.

## Montana

**2795  Literacy Volunteers of America: Montana**
Pro Literacy Worldwide
304 N Main Street
Butte, MT  59701          406-723-7905
                          888-606-7905
                     FAX 406-723-6196
              e-mail: lvabulit@in-tch.com
*Paula Anerson, Director*
*Vicki Mihelich, Assistant Director*

We provide adults and their families the opportunity to acquire skills to be effective in their roles as members of their families, communities, and workplaces.

**2796  Montana Literacy Resource Center**

Montana State Library
1515 E 6th Avenue
Helena, MT  59620-1800          406-444-3004
                               FAX 406-444-0266
                               TDY:406-444-3005
                               http://www.msl.mt.gov
                               e-mail: dstaffeldt@mt.gov
*Darlene Dstaffeldt, State Librarian*
*Kris Schmitz, Head of Administration*

A state-wide literacy support network.

## Nebraska

**2797  Answers4Families: Center on Children, Families, Law**

121 S 13th Street
Lincoln, NE  68588 0227          402-472-0844
            http://www.answers4families.org/nrrs
            e-mail: chayek@answers4families.org
*Connie Hayek, Director*
*Sharon Bloechle, Omaha Parent Coordinator*

A project of the Center on Children, Families and Law at University of Nebraska. Mission is to provide info, opportunities, education and support to Nebraskans through Internet resources. The Center serves individuals with special needs and mental health disorders, foster families, caregivers, assisted living, and school nurses.

**2798  Client Assistance Program (CAP): Nebraska Division of Persons with Disabilities**

Nebraska Department of Education
301 Centennial Mall S
Lincoln, NE  68509               402-471-3656
                                 800-742-7594
                            FAX 402-471-0117
                    http://www.nde.state.ne.us
                    e-mail: victoria@cap.state.ne.us

The Client Assistance Program helps individuals who have concerns or difficulties when applying for or receiving rehabilitation services funded under the Rehabilitation Act.

**2799  State Literacy Resource Center for Nebraska: Institute for the Study of Adult Literacy**

Department of Vocational and Adult Education
University of Nebraska-Lincoln
Lincoln, NE  68588               402-472-5924
                            FAX 402-472-5907
                    http://www.literacy.kent.edu
                    e-mail: bsparks1@unl.edu
*Barbara PhD, Director*
*Qian Geng, Coordinator*

As the State Literacy Resource Center for Nebraska, NISAL provides a central point of contact for researchers, decision makers and literacy providers in Nebraska and serves as a vital link between providers and user groups, community based organizations, state agencies and business and industry. The institute enhances existing practice by promoting and providing information and resources to enhance and encourage best practices.

## Nevada

**2800  Nevada Department of Adult Education**

Nevada Department of Education
700 E 5th Street
Carson City, NV  89701           775-687-9200
                            FAX 775-687-9101
                    http://www.nde.state.nv.us
*Frankie Cave, Director for Special Education*

Provides adult basic education and literacy services in order to assist adults to become literate and obtain the knowledge and skills necessary for employment and self-sufficiency.

**2801  Nevada Economic Opportunity Board: Community Action Partnership**

PO Box 270880
Las Vegas, NV  89127-4880        702-647-1510
                            FAX 702-647-6639
                    http://www.eobcap.org
*Mary Twitty, Executive Director*

Located in one of the fastest growing and most diverse communities in the United States, the Economic Opportunity Board of Clark County is a highly innovative Community Action Agency. Our mission is to eliminate poverty by providing programs, resources, services, and advocacy for self-sufficiency and economic empowerment.

**2802  Nevada Literacy Coalition: State Literacy Resource Center**

Pro Literacy Worldwide
100 N Stewart Street
Carson City, NV  89701-4285      775-684-3340
                                 800-445-9673
                            FAX 775-684-3344
http://www.nevadaculture.org/docs/nsla/literacy
                    e-mail: sfgraf@clan.lib.nv.us
*Susan Graf, Literacy Coordinator*
*Sara Jones, Library Administrator*

The Nevada State Literacy Resource Center has books, newsletters and a wide variety of multi-media resources such as videos, audiotapes and games for literacy instruction and programs for literacy students, trainers and tutors.

**2803  Northern Nevada Literacy Council**

680 Greenbrae Drive
Sparks, NV  89431                775-356-1007
                            FAX 775-356-1009
                    http://www.nnlc.org
                    e-mail: director@nnlc.org
*Vicki Newell, Executive Director*

Provides a framework that assists Nevada's communities in addressing their literacy needs at the local level.

## New Hampshire

**2804 New Hampshire Literacy Volunteers of America**
Manchester City Library
405 Pine Street
Manchester, NH 03104          603-624-6550
                               FAX 603-624-6559
                  http://www.manchesternh.gov
*Elizabeth Sabol, Program Director*
*Gwen Brown, Assistant Director*

This program is the only nationally accredited adult literacy program in New Hampshire. Provides free confidential one-to-one tutoring for adults who want to learn to write and read for lifelong learning.

**2805 New Hampshire Second Start Adult Education**
17 Knight Street
Concord, NH 03301          603-228-1341
                           FAX 603-228-3852
                http://www.second-start.org
             e-mail: ABE@second-start.org

Provides basic reading, writing and math skills for people who want to achieve educational goals, participate in the life of the community, gain independence and become lifelong learners.

## New Jersey

**2806 New Jersey Literacy Volunteers of America: Peoplecare Center**
Pro Literacy America
120 Finderne Avenue
Bridgewater, NJ 08807          908-203-4582
                               800-848-0048
                           FAX 908-203-4585
                    e-mail: lvanj@aol.com
*Elissa Director, Director*
*Mitch Heather, Administrative Assistant*

Literacy Volunteers of America-New Jersey (LVA-NJ) is a nonprofit, education organization providing training, technical assistance, communications, and program support to adult literacy organizations in New Jersey. It directs most of its services to its affiliated community based organizations located in twenty counties of the state.

## New Mexico

**2807 Deming Literacy Program**
2301 S Tin Street
Deming, NM 88030          505-546-7571
                          FAX 505-546-1356
                 e-mail: dlp@zianet.com
*Marisol Perez, Contact*

The Literacy Home Mentoring and After School Project will encourage parents to read to their children at home, as well as provide mentors to help children with their reading skills after school.

**2808 Literacy Center of Albuquerque**
PO Box 30393
Albuquerque, NM 87190 0393          505-266-7202
                                    FAX 505-884-3129
                       http://www.lcbq.org
                     e-mail: info@lcbq.org
*Kathleen Salas, Program Coordinator*

The Literacy Center of Albuquerque is a non-profit organization of students, tutors and supporters working together to enhance the lives of people with English as a Second Language and addresses literacy needs by providing programs through volunteers and community resources.

**2809 Literacy Volunteers of America: Cibola County**
Pro Literacy Worldwide
PO Box 306
Grants, NM 87020          505-285-5995
                          FAX 505-285-5995
                http://www.7cities.net
             e-mail: lvagrants@7cities.net
*Barbara Wesley, Executive Director*

Offers basic reading and ESL tutoring at no charge to adults in Cibola County.

**2810 Literacy Volunteers of America: Dona Ana County**
Dona Ana Branch Community College
3400 S Espina Street
Las Cruces, NM 88003          505-527-7640
                              800-903-7540
                          FAX 505-527-7515
               http://www.dabcc-www.nmsu.edu
*Larry Sharp, Coordinator*
*Patricia Moncoya, Secretary*

The Literacy Volunteers of America is designed to help people who cannot read or write the English language. This program gives adults a new opportunity to learn reading through the sixth-grade level.

**2811 Literacy Volunteers of America: Las Vegas, San Miguel**
PO Box 516
Las Vegas, NM 88701          505-454-8043
                   http://www.nmhu.edu
*Ann Costello, Director*

Las Vegas/San Miquel Literacy Volunteers are a part of the national non-profit organization Literacy Volunteers of America, which is dedicated to promoting literacy throughout the country.

**2812 Literacy Volunteers of America: Otero County**
New Mexico State University at Alamogordo
2400 N Scenic Drive
Alamogordo, NM 88310          505-439-3600
                              FAX 505-439-3643
                  http://www.alamo.nmsu.edu
             e-mail: reynolds@nmsua.nmsu.edu
*Anita Raynor, Director for Adult Basic Ed*
*Angie Gorgensen, Bookstore Manager*

Can provide volunteer tutors to work one-on-one with adult non-readers and non-English speaking adults. All these services are provided free of charge to adults.

**2813  Literacy Volunteers of America: Read West**

PO Box 44058
Rio Rancho, NM  87174            505-892-1131
                                FAX 505-892-1131
                        http://www.uwcnm.org
                  e-mail: readwest@hubwest.com
*Susan Markin-Ryerson, Executive Director*

Programs that assist adults in reading development.
English as a second language program offered. Family
literacy workshops for parents.

**2814  Literacy Volunteers of America: Santa Fe**

6401 Richards Avenue
Santa Fe, NM  87505              505-428-1353
                                FAX 505-428-1237
                        http://www.lvsf.net
                    e-mail: pete681@msn.com
*Letty Naranjo, Manager*
*Catherine Johnson, Program Coordinator*

Literacy Volunteers of Santa Fe was established to
provide free tutoring services for adults in the Santa
Fe area seeking to improve their reading skills or learn
English as a second language.

**2815  Literacy Volunteers of America: Socorro County**

PO Box 1431
Socorro, NM  87801               505-835-4659
                                FAX 505-835-1182
*Joyce Aguilar, Director*

Promotes literacy for people of Socorro County.

**2816  New Mexico Coalition for Literacy**

PO Box 6085
Sante Fe, NM  87502              505-982-3997
                                800-233-7587
                                FAX 505-982-4095
                        http://www.nmcl.org
                    e-mail: info@nmcl.org
*David Godsted, Executive Director*
*Rena Paradis, Training Coordinator*

The Coalition encourages and supports community-based literacy programs and is the New Mexico
affiliate and coordinator for the national program of
ProLiteracy America.

**2817  Valencia County Literacy Council**

Belen Public Library
280 LaEntrada
Los Lunas, NM  87031             505-925-8926
                                FAX 505-864-7798
             http://www.golibrary.org/vclc.htm
                  e-mail: joglesby@unm.edu
*Jill Oglesby, Executive Director*

Promotes and supports literacy in the area.

## New York

**2818  Literacy Volunteers of America: Middletown,
New York**

Literacy Volunteers of Western County Incorpo-
rated
70 Fulton Street
Middletown, NY  10940            845-341-5460
                                FAX 845-343-7191
                http://www.literacymiddletown.org
              e-mail: baclvamdtn@frontiernet.net
*Barbara Clifford, Executive Director*
*Rowena Reich, Program Coordinator*

An organization of volunteers which provides a variety of services to enable people to achieve personal
goals through literacy. We believe that the ability to
read is critical to personal freedom and maintenance
of a democratic society. These beliefs have led us to
make the following commitments: the personal
growth of our students; the effective use of our volunteers; the improvement of society and strengthening
and improving our organization.

**2819  New York Laubach Literacy International**

ProLiteracy Worldwide
1320 Jamesville Avenue
Syracuse, NY  13210              315-422-9121
                                888-528-2224
                                FAX 315-422-6369
                        http://www.proliteracy.org
                  e-mail: info@proliteracy.org
*Robert Wedgeworth, President*

The Syracuse chapters of the world's two largest adult
volunteer literacy organization merged and Laubach
Literacy International and Literacy Volunteers of
America became ProLiteracy Worldwide. This organization sponsors educational programs and services
for adults and their families. These programs assist
participants to acquire the literacy practices and skills
needed to function more effectively in their daily lives
and participate in their societies.

**2820  New York Literacy Assistance Center**

32 Broadway
New York, NY  10004              212-803-3300
                                FAX 212-785-3685
                        http://www.lacnyc.org
*Winston Lawrence, Coordinator of Adult Literacy*
*Ira Yankwitt, Director of Adult Literacy*

Founded in 1983, a not-for-profit organization that
provides essential referral, training information and
technical assistance services to hundreds of adult and
youth literacy programs in New York. Our mission is
to support and promote the expansion of quality literacy services in New York.

**2821  New York Literacy Partners**

30 E 33rd Street
New York, NY  10016              212-725-9200
                                FAX 212-725-9744
                        http://www.literacypartners.org
*Susan McLean, Executive Director*
*Doris Meister, Executive VP*

Literacy Partners, is a not-for-profit organization, providing free community-based adult and family literacy programs to ensure that all adults have the access to quality education needed to fully realize their potential as individuals, parents, and citizens.

**2822  New York Literacy Resource Center**

**State University of New York**
**135 Western Avenue**
**Albany, NY  12222**          518-442-5372
                              800-331-0931
                              FAX 518-442-5021
                    **http://www.albany.edu**
*Maritza Ramirez-Vallinas, Director*

State Literacy Resource Center is a statewide literacy information network throughout the state.

**2823  New York Literacy Volunteers of America**

**Literacy Volunteers of New York State**
**777 Maryvale Drive**
**Buffalo, NY  14225**          716-631-5282
                       FAX 716-631-0657
                  **http://www.lvanys.org**
              **e-mail: buffalo@lvanys.org**
*Janice Cuddahee, Associate Executive Director*
*Rosalinde Mecca, Program Director*

Literacy Volunteers of America in New York State is a nonprofit educational organization that provides training and technical assistance to 48 local, community-based literacy programs in New York. In addition, LVA-NYS offers consultation services and support to literacy organizations nationally.

**2824  Resources for Children with Special Needs**

**116 E 16th Street**
**New York, NY  10003**          212-677-4650
                         FAX 212-254-4070
                **http://www.resourcesnyc.org**
              **e-mail: info@resourcesnyc.org**
*Karen Schlesinger, Executive Director*
*Helene Crane, Associate Director*

An independent, nonprofit organization that provides information and referral, case management and support, individual and systemic advocacy, parent and professional training and library services to New York City parents and caregivers of children with disabilities and special needs and to professionals who work with them. Our publications include: Camps 2003; After School and more; The Comprehensive Directory; and Schools for Children with Autism Spectrum Disorders.

## North Carolina

**2825  Blue Ridge Literacy Council**

**PO Box 1728**
**Hendersonville, NC  28793**          828-696-3811
                             FAX 828-696-3887
                     **http://www.litcouncil.org**
                   **e-mail: info@litcouncil.org**

The Blue Ridge Literacy Council provides Henderson County adult students the English communication and literacy skills they need to reach their full potential as individuals, parents, workers and citizens.

**2826  Buncombe County Literacy Council**

**86 ViCourtoria Road**
**Asheville, NC  28801**          828-254-3442
                         FAX 828-254-1742
                  **http://www.main.nc.us/literacy**
          **e-mail: literacy@main.nc.buncombe.nc.us**
*Amanda Edwards, Executive Director*
*Irma Khasanoza, Office Manager*

Promotes increased adult literacy in Buncombe County through effective use of trained tutors; to provide support services for tutors and learners; and to collaborate with individuals, groups, or other community organizations desiring to foster increased adult literacy.

**2827  Durham County Literacy Council**

**1410 W Chapel Hill Street**
**Durham, NC  27701**          919-489-8383
                         800-562-2139
                   FAX 919-489-1456
          **http:// www.durhamliteracy.com**
             **e-mail: durhamlit@aol.com**
*Reginald Hodges, Executive Director*
*Cabaatha , Administration Coordinator*

The Durham County Literacy Council provides training in adult basic education (including reading, writing and mathematics), English for Speakers of Other Languages, GED examination preparation, Family Literacy, workplace literacy, and technology.

**2828  Gastonia Literacy Council**

**116 S Marietta**
**Gastonia, NC  28052**          704-868-4815
                       FAX 704-867-7796
                **http://www.gastonliteracy.org**
              **e-mail: literacy@gaston.org**
*Kaye Gribble, Executive Director*

The Gaston Literacy Council is dedicated to improving literacy throughout the Gastonia area.

**2829  Literacy Volunteers of America: Pitt County**

**504-A Dexter Street**
**Greenville, NC  27834**          252-353-6578
                         FAX 252-353-6868
              **e-mail: lva-pc@greenvillenc.com**
*Laura Smith, Executive Director*

The mission of LVA-PC is to teach adults to read or improve their reading, writing or English speaking skills through free, confidential, and small group instruction by trained volunteers.

**2830  North Carolina Literacy Resource Center**

**North Carolina Community College**
**200 W Jones Street**
**Raleigh, NC  27699**          919-807-7144
                       FAX 919-807-7164
               **http://www.ncccs.cc.nc.us**
            **e-mail: ALLENB@ncccs.cc.nc.us**
*Bob Allen, Coordinator*
*Marge Young, Assistant*

North Carolina Community College Literacy Resource Center collects and disseminates information about literacy resources and organizations.

**2831  Reading Connections of North Carolina**
122 N Elm Street
Greensboro, NC 27401          336-230-2223
                              FAX 336-230-2203
          http://www.Readingconnections.org
          e-mail: info@readingconnections.org
*Jenny Gore, Executive Director*
*Ira Williams, Program Coordinator*

The mission of Reading Connections is to help adults
live more independently by providing free and confidential basic literacy services, to increase community
awareness of adult literacy needs and to serve as a resource for the provision of basic literacy services.

# North Dakota

**2832  North Dakota Adult Education and Literacy
Resource Center**
1609 4th Avenue NW
Minot, ND  58703              701-857-4467
                              FAX 701-857-4489
          http://www.dpi.state.nd.us/adulted/
          e-mail: deb.sisco@sendit.nodex.edu
*Deb Sisco, Coordinator*
*Vicky Campbell, Director*

The purpose of the North Dakota Adult Education Resource Center is to provide training for adult education staff and volunteer personnel engaged in
programs designed to carry out the purposes of the National Literacy Act.

**2833  North Dakota Department of Career and
Technical Education**
600 E Boulevard Avenue
Bismarck, ND  58505           701-328-3180
                              FAX 701-328-1255
          http://www.state.nd.us
          e-mail: cte@state.nd.us
*Dwight Crabtree, State Director*
*Wayne Kutcer, Director*

The mission of the Board for Vocational and Technical Education is to work with others to provide all
North Dakota citizens with the technical skills,
knowledge, and attitudes necessary for successful
performance in a globally competitive workplace.

**2834  North Dakota Department of Corrections**
3100 Railroad Avenue
Bismarck, ND  58501           701-328-6390
                              FAX 701-328-6651
                              TDY:800-366-6888
          http://www.state.nd.us
          e-mail: elittle@state.nd.us
*Elaine Little, Director*
*Jeannine Piatz, Administrative Assistant*

Mission is to protect the public while providing a safe
and humane environment for both adults and juveniles
placed in the department's care and custody.

**2835  North Dakota Department of Human
Services:Welfare & Public Assistance**
State Capitol
600 E Boulevard Avenue
Bismarck, ND  58505           701-328-2310
                              800-472-2622
                              FAX 701-328-2359
          http://www.state.nd.us/humanservices
          e-mail: dhseo@state.nd.us
*Carol Olson, Executive Director*
*Yvonne Smith, Deputy Director*
*Tove Mandigo, Administrative Assistant*
To provide services and support for poor, disabled, ill,
elderly or juvenile clients in North Dakota.

**2836  North Dakota Department of Public Instruction**
Division of Adult Education and Literacy
600 E Boulevard Avenue
Bismarck, ND  58505           701-328-2393
                              FAX 701-328-4770
          http://www.dpi.state.nd.us/adulted
          e-mail: dmassey@mail.dpi.state.nd.us
*David Massey, Assistant State Superintendent*
*Jolli Marcellais, Administrative Assistant*

This unit provides funding and technical assistance to
local programs and monitors progress of each funded
project. This unit is also responsible for the administration of the GED Testing Program.

**2837  North Dakota Reading Association**
2420 2nd Avenue SW
Minot, ND  58701              701-857-4642
                              FAX 701-857-8761
          http://www.ndreading.utma.com
          e-mail: Paula.Rogers@sendit.nodak.edu
*Dina Laswoski, President*
*Paula Rogers, VP*

North Dakota Reading Association's mission is to
provide a variety of professional development opportunities.

**2838  North Dakota Workforce Development Council**
North Dakota Department of Commerce
1600 E Century Avenue, Suite 2
Bismarck, ND  58502           701-328-5300
                              FAX 701-328-5320
          http://www.growingnd.com
          e-mail: jhirsch@state.nd.us
*James Hirsch, Director Division of Workforce*
*Lee Peterson, Commissioner Department of Comme*

The role of the North Dakota Workforce Development
Council is to advise the Governor and the Public concerning the nature and extent of workforce development in the context of North Dakota's economic
development needs, and how to meet these needs effectively while maximizing the efficient use of available resources and avoiding unnecessary duplication
of effort.

**2839  Project Advancing Literacy in North Carolina**
2110 Library Circle
Grand Forks, ND  58201        701-772-6344
                              FAX 701-772-1379
          http://www.grandforksgov.com/readpal
          e-mail: info@grandforksgov.com
*Diane Bell, President*
*Dennis Page, Treasurer*

Project Advancing Literacy (PAL) is a basic literacy support program among adults in the Greater Grand Forks area. PAL provides one-to-one tutoring support to those who have identified a need to increase basic literacy.

## Ohio

**2840  Literacy Council of Medina County**

**Project Learn**
**222 S Broadway**
**Medina, OH  44256**            330-723-1314
                              FAX 330-722-6033
          http://www.projectlearnmedina.org
          e-mail: dmorawski@zoominternet.net
*Diane Morawski, Executive Director*

Our program helps individuals 14 and older improve basic reading, writing, spelling and comprehensive skills necessary to meet the challenges they encounter in the workplace and other aspects of their daily lives. It provides the only one-on-one tutoring available free of charge to anyone interested in improving basic skills.

**2841  Literacy Volunteers of America: Washington County**

**701 Wayne Street**
**Marietta, OH  45750**            740-374-6548
                              FAX 740-376-2457
          e-mail: ma_mkern@seovec.ohio.gov
*Rene Rudd*

Literacy Volunteers of America - Ohio provides training and technical assistance to literacy programs in Ohio. We offer consultation services and support to literacy organizations nationally.

**2842  Ohio Literacy Network**

**6161 Busch Blvd**
**Columbus, OH  43229**            614-505-0716
                              FAX 614-505-0718
          http://www.ohioliteracynetwork.org
          e-mail: KSOLN@cs.com
*Karen Scheid, Executive Director*

The Ohio Literacy Network is an association of organizations and individuals dedicated to helping adults achieve effectively in today's society, and to promote public awareness of adult literacy issues and needs.

**2843  Ohio Literacy Resource Center**

**Kent State University**
**Research 1-1100 Summit Street**
**Kent, OH  44242**            330-672-2007
                              800-765-2897
                              FAX 330-672-4841
          http://www.literacy.kent.edu/oasis/
          e-mail: olrc@literacy.kent.edu
*Marty Ropog, Director*

Mission is to stimulate joint planning and coordination of literacy services at the local, regional and state levels and to enhance the capacity of state and local organizations and services delivery systems.

**2844  Project LEARN of Summit County**

**Pro Literacy America**
**1040 E Tallmadge Avenue**
**Akron, OH  44310**            330-434-9461
                              FAX 330-643-9195
          http://www.projectlearnsummit.org
          e-mail: info@projectlearnsummit.org
*Rick McIntosh, Executive Director*
*Marqueita Mitchell, Program Coordinator*
*Doris Zene, Program Assistant*

Project LEARN is a nonprofit, community-based organization providing Summit County's nonreading adult population with free, confidential, small group classes and tutoring.

## Oklahoma

**2845  Creek County Literacy Program**

**Sapulpa Public Library**
**27 W Dewey Avenue**
**Sapulpa, OK  74066**            918-224-9647
                              FAX 918-224-3546
          http://www.cityofsapulpa.net
          e-mail: spl@oklahoma.net
*Barbara Belk, Executive Director*

Free one-on-one tutoring services for those residents of Creek County who wish to improve reading skills.

**2846  Literacy Volunteers of America: Tulsa City County Library**

**400 Civic Center**
**Tulsa, OK  74103**            918-596-7977
                              FAX 918-596-7907
          http://www.tulsalibrary.org/central
          e-mail: jgreb@tccl.lib.ok.us
*Linda Saferite, Executive Director*
*Richard Parker, Deputy Director*

We offer one-on-one tutoring to adults and young adults who wish to improve their reading and writing skills.

**2847  Northwest Oklahoma Literacy Council**

**1500 Main Street**
**Woodward, OK  73801**            580-254-8582
                              FAX 580-254-8546
          e-mail: nwoklitcouncil@woodward.lib.ok.us
*Cindy Colclasure, Coordinator*
*Patty McGuire, Contact*

Mission is to break the intergenerational cycle of illiteracy by broadening the learner and service base to include family members. Services include literacy and parenting instruction, as a compliment to ESL, adult basic education, and learning disabilities programs.

**2848  Oklahoma Literacy Resource Center**

**Oklahoma Department of Libraries**
**200 NE 18th Street**
**Oklahoma City, OK  73105**            405-522-3205
                              800-522-8116
                              FAX 405-525-7804
          http://www.state.ok.us/odl/literacy
          e-mail: lgelders@oltn.state.ok.us
*Leslie Gelders, Literacy Coordinator*
*Rebecca Barker, Literacy & ESL Consultant*
*Colleen Woolery, Family Literacy Coordinator*

Dedicated to supporting Oklahoma's library and community based literacy programs and their volunteer tutors. The office has been serving the literacy community in Oklahoma since 1983, first as the ODL Literacy Office, and now as the Oklahoma Literacy Resource Office.

## Oregon

**2849  Oregon Department of Corrections**

2575 Center Street NE
Salem, OR  97301 4667              503-945-9090
                              FAX 503-945-1173
                    http://www.doc.state.or.us
              e-mail: DOCinfo@doc.state.or.us
*Max Williams, Director*
*Mitch Morrow, Deputy Director*

The Oregon Department of Corrections is responsible for the management and administration of all adult correctional institutions and other functions related to state programs for adult corrections.

**2850  Oregon Department of Education: School-to-Work**

255 Capitol Street NE
Salem, OR  97310              503-378-3584
                        FAX 503-378-2892
                        TDY:503-378-2892
                 http://www.ode.state.or.us
              e-mail: rob.larson@state.or.us
*Robert Larson, Policy & Research Director*
*Patrick Burk, Education Policy Deputy*

School-to-Work is a federally funded initiative that provides funding for state and local implementation of the Oregon Educational Act for the 21st Century.

**2851  Oregon Department of Human Resource Adult & Family Services Division**

500 Summer Street NE
Salem, OR  97310              503-945-5733
                        FAX 503-378-2897
                 http://www.dhs.state.or.us
              e-mail: dhr.info@state.or.us
*Ramona Foley, Assistant Director*
*Gary Weeks, Director*

This group combines programs from the former Adult & Family Services Division and the State Office for Services to Children and Families.

**2852  Oregon Employment Department**

875 Union Street NE
Salem, OR  97311              503-947-1394
                              800-237-3710
                        FAX 503-947-1668
                 http://www.workinoregon.com
*Deborah Lincoln, Director*
*Greg Hickman, Deputy Director*
*Odie Vogel, Assistant to Director*

Supports economic stability for Oregonians and communities during times of unemployment through the payment of unemployment benefits. Serves businesses by recruiting and referring the best qualified applicants to jobs, and provides resources to diverse job seekers in support of their employment /needs.

**2853  Oregon GED Administrator: Office of Community College Services**

255 Capitol Street NE
Salem, OR  97310              503-378-8648
                        FAX 503-378-3365
                 http://www.oregon.gov/ccwd
              e-mail: Sharlene.WALKER@state.or.us
*Sharlene Walker, GED Administrator*

**2854  Oregon Literacy**

1001 SW 5th Avenue
Portland, OR  97204              503-244-3898
                              800-322-8715
                        FAX 503-244-9147
                 http://www.oregonliteracy.org
              e-mail: info@oregonliteracy.org
*John Toorock, Director For Community Developme*
*Elizabeth Raymond, Tutor Helpline Coordinator*

Mission is to increase the capacity and effectiveness of literacy services through partnerships with community-based programs across the state.

**2855  Oregon Office of Education and Workforce Policy**

State Capitol Building
Salem, OR  97301 4047              503-378-4582
                              FAX 503-378-4863
                 http://www.arcweb.sos.state.or.us
              e-mail: annette.talbott@state.or.us
*Annette Talbott, Workforce Policy Coordinator*
*Danny Santos, Education Policy Coordinator*

The Governor's Office of Education and Workforce Policy was established to assist the Governor in examining education and workforce efforts with a view to supporting and strengthening what is working well. The goal is to have Oregonians prepared to meet the education and workforce needs of Oregon businesses rather than having to recruit from outside the state to fill quality jobs.

**2856  Oregon State Library**

250 Winter Street NE
Salem, OR  97310              503-378-4243
                        FAX 503-588-7119
                        TDY:503-378-4334
                 http://www.oregon.gov/osl
              e-mail: leann.bromeland@state.or.us
*LeAnn Bromeland, Volunteer Coordinator*
*Mary , Program Manager*
*Jim Scheppke, State Librarian*

Mission is to provide quality information services to Oregon state government, to provide reading materials to blind and print-disabled Oregonians, and to provide leadership, grants, and other assistance to improve local library service for all Oregonians.

**2857  Oregon State Literacy Resource Center**

Department of Community Colleges & Workforce
255 Capitol Street NE
Salem, OR  97310              503-378-8648
                        FAX 503-378-8434
                 http://www.oregon.gov/ccwd
              e-mail: ric.latour@state.or.us
*Karen Madden, GED Administrator*
*Sharlene Walker, Unit Leader*

To contribute leadership and resources to increase the skills, knowledge and career opportunities of Oregonians.

**2858 Project Literacy Douglas County**

1034 SE Oak Avenue
Roseburg, OR 97470          541-957-9072
                           FAX 541-957-9072
                     e-mail: PLUR@rosenet.net
*Patricia Yeager*

**2859 Salem Literacy Council**

189 Liberty Street NE
Salem, OR 97301            503-588-0307
                          FAX 503-588-0307
http://www.angelfire.com/or/salemliteracy/

## Pennsylvania

**2860 Delaware County Literacy Council**

2217 Providence Avenue
Chester, PA 19013          610-876-4811
                          FAX 610-876-5414
                     http://www.dalit.org
*Patricia Gaul, Executive Director*

The Delaware County Literacy Council is a private, nonprofit, educational agency that provides one-on-one, free literacy instruction to non- and low-reading adults through a county-wide network of trained volunteer tutors. It is unique among the limited options available to adult residents of Delaware County who require help with their basic reading and writing skills in that it remains the only organization whose sole mission is adult literacy.

**2861 Learning Disabilities Association: Pennsylvania**

Toomey Building
Uwchland, PA 19480         610-458-8193
                          FAX 412-344-0224
                     http://www.ldanatl.org
*Anna McHugh, President*

LDAP is a nonprofit organization whose purpose is to advance the education and general well-being of persons with normal, potentially normal or above normal intelligence who have learning disabilities.

**2862 Literacy Council of Lancaster/Lebanon**

38 W King Street
Lancaster, PA 17603        717-295-5523
                          FAX 717-295-5342
                     http://www.adultlit.org
                e-mail: mary@adultlit.org
*Mary Hohensee, Executive Director*

Mission is to promote literacy for adults and children.

**2863 Pennsylvania Adult Literacy**

110 E Bald Eagle Street
Lock Haven, PA 17745       570-893-4038
                          FAX 570-748-1598
                http://www.wbtc.ciu10.com
                e-mail: vedmonst@lhup.edu
*Ginney Seay, Facilitator*
*Nancy Robbins, Executive Director*

**2864 Pennsylvania Literacy Resource Center**

ADVANCE Clearinghouse & Resource Center
333 Market Street
Harrisburg, PA 17126       717-783-9192
                           800-992-2283
                      FAX 717-783-5420
            http://www.cas.psu.edu/docs
*Evelyn Werner, Director*
*Leanne Stasiulatis, Librarian*

As part of the State Library, the State Resource Center provides electronic and print resources.

**2865 Project Literacy US (PLUS) in Pennsylvania**

4802 5th Avenue
Pittsburgh, PA 15213       412-622-1492
                          FAX 412-622-1492
            http://www.dyslexia-add.org/plus.htm
*Margot Woodwell, Project Director*
*Herb Stein, Assistant Director*

PLUS promotes adult literacy. A joint project of the Public Broadcasting Service and the American Broadcasting Corporation, PLUS uses media to increase awareness of literacy issues and to recruit individuals into literacy training programs.

**2866 York County Literacy Council**

800 E King Street
York, PA 17403             717-845-8719
                          FAX 717-843-4082
                http://www.yorkliteracy.org
                 e-mail: yclcpa@aol.com
*Joanne Olejowski, Director*

## Rhode Island

**2867 Family Independence Program of Rhode Island**

Department of Human Services
600 New London Avenue
Cranston, RI 02920         401-462-1300
                          FAX 401-462-6504
                          TDY:401-462-3363
                 http://www.dhs.ri.gov
*Ronald Label, Director*

**2868 Learning Disabilities Association: Rhode Island**

PO Box 6685
Providence, RI 02940       401-232-3822
*Norma Veresko, President*

**2869 Literacy Volunteers of America: Rhode Island**

260 W Exchange Street
Providence, RI 02903       401-861-0815
                          FAX 401-861-0863
            http://www.literacyvolunteers.org
                e-mail: lvaricindy@aol.com
*Yvette Kenner, Associate Director*

The mission of LVA-RI is to advance adult literacy in Rhode Island by: providing training and support services to local LVA-RI affiliates, volunteer tutors and adult literacy services; providing the state with information about adult literacy and with appropriate referral services; collaborating with other organizations to promote adult literacy in Rhode Island.

**2870 Literary Resources Rhode Island**

Brown University
PO Box 1974
Providence, RI 02912          401-863-2839
                              FAX 401-863-3094
                         http://www.brown.edu
              e-mail: janet_isserlis@brown .edu
*Howard Dooley Jr, Director*

Literacy Resources Rhode Island was established in 1997. Its goals include: expand existing professional capacity within the state's adult education community; increase educator and learner capacity to use and interact with online technology; and assist in improving delivery of services to adult learners, thereby strengthening adult education provision across the state.

**2871 Rhode Island Department of Employment and Training**

Center General Complex
Cranston, RI 02920          401-462-8000

**2872 Rhode Island Department of Human Services**

600 New London Avenue
Cranston, RI 02920          401-421-7005
                    http://www.dhs.state.ri.us
              e-mail: rcarroll@ors.state.ri.us
*Raymond Carroll, Acting Administrator*

**2873 Rhode Island Department of State Library Services**

1 Capitol Hill
Providence, RI 02903          401-222-1220
                              FAX 401-222-2083
*John O'Brien, Executive Director*

**2874 Rhode Island Human Resource Investment Council**

1511 Pontiac Avenue
Cranston, RI 02920          401-462-8860
                            FAX 401-462-8865
                        http://www.rihric.com
              e-mail: larnodd@dlt.state.ri.us
*Adelita Orefice, Director*
*Marshia , Administrative Assistant*

**2875 Rhode Island Vocational and Rehabilitation Agency**

Rhode Island Department of Human Services
40 Fountain Street
Providence, RI 02903          401-421-7005
                              FAX 401-222-3574
                            TDY:401-421-7016
                          http://www.ors.ri.gov
              e-mail: rcarroll@ors.state.ri.us
*Raymond Carroll, Administrator*
*Steven Brunero, Deputy Administrator*

Assists people with disabilities to become employed and to live independently in the community. In order to achieve this goal, we work in partnership with the State Rehabilitation Council, our customers, staff and community.

**2876 Rhode Island Workforce Literacy Collaborative**

Literacy Volunteers of Rhode Island
260 W Exchange Street
Providence, RI 02903          401-861-0815
                              FAX 401-861-0863
                    http://www.literacyvolunteers.org
                   e-mail: LVARIYVETT@aol.com
*Yvette Kenner, Associate Director*

Mission is to create a framework for an ongoing, comprehensive, seamless system for delivering adult workforce literacy services in Rhode Island.

---

# South Carolina

**2877 Greenwood Literacy Council**

2005 Kateway Building W
Greenwood, SC 29648          864-223-1303
                             FAX 864-223-0475
                   e-mail: sowens@greenwood.net
*Sandra Owens, Executive Director*

Provides ongoing, comprehensive adult literacy programs in Greenwood, for illiterate adults and their families.

**2878 Literacy Volunteers of the Lowcountry**

Pro Literacy America
9 Town Center Court
Hilton Head, SC 29928          843-686-6655
                               FAX 843-686-6949
                    e-mail: lvlhhi@hargray.com
*Nancy Williams, Executive Director*

**2879 Resource Center for Literacy Technology & Parenting**

South Carolina Department of Education
1429 Senate Street
Columbia, SC 29201          803-734-8500
                            FAX 803-734-8624
*Inez Tenenbaum, Superintendent*

Combines literacy programs with parenting instruction.

**2880 South Carolina Adult Literacy Educators**

PO Box 185
Blackville, SC 29817          803-284-4424
                              FAX 803-284-1444
                    http://www.barnwell19.k12.sc.us
*Lindsey Toomer, Contact*

**2881  South Carolina Department of Education**
1429 Senate Street
Columbia, SC  29201          803-734-8815
                              FAX 803-734-3389
          http://www.myscschools.com
          e-mail: tstokes@sde.state.sc.us
*Inez Tenenbaum, Superintendent*
*Terri Stokes, Administrative Assistant*

**2882  South Carolina Literacy Resource Center**
1722 Main Street
Columbia, SC  29201          803-929-2573
                              FAX 803-929-2571
       http://http://tlrc.tamu.edu/s.carolina
              e-mail: info@sclrc.org

The mission of the South Carolina Resource Center is to provide leadership in literacy to South Carolina's adults and their families, in conjunction with state and local public and private nonprofit efforts. The Center serves as a site for training for adult literacy providers, as a reciprocal link with the National Institute for Literacy for the purpose of sharing information to service providers, and as a clearinghouse for state-of-the-art literacy materials and technology.

## South Dakota

**2883  South Dakota GED: Literacy Department of Education & Cultural Affairs**
700 Governors Drive
Pierre, SD  57501          605-773-5017
                            FAX 605-773-6184
        http://www.state.sd.us/dol/abe/index.html
            e-mail: miken@dol.pr.state.sd.us
*Marcia Hess, State Administrator*

Adult Education & Literacy instruction is designed to teach persons 16 years of age or older to read and write English and to substantially raise their educational level. The purpose of the program is to expand the educational opportunities for adults and to establish programs that will enable all adults to acquire basic skills necessary to function in society and allow them to continue their education to at least the level of completion of secondary school.

**2884  South Dakota Literacy Council**
PO Box 219
Pierre, SD  57501          605-224-8212
                            800-484-6690
*Bonnie London*

**2885  South Dakota Literacy Resouce Center**
800 Governors Drive
Pierre, SD  57501          605-773-3101
                            800-423-6665
                          FAX 605-773-6969
        http://www.state.sd.us/deca/literacy/
            e-mail: dan.boyd@state.sd.us
*Marcia Hess, AEO & GED Program Specialist*

The mission of the SD Literary Resource Center is to establish a state wide on-line computer catalog of all existing literacy materials within South Dakota and a South Dakota Literacy Resource Center home page with links to other literacy sites within South Dakota, regionally and nationally.

## Tennessee

**2886  Center for Literary Studies Tennessee**
University of Tennessee: Knoxville
600 Henley Street
Knoxville, TN  37996          865-974-4109
                              FAX 865-974-3857
          http://www.cls.coc.utk.edu
          e-mail: mziegler@utk.edu
*Jean Stevens, Director*
*Peggy Robert, Administrative Assistant*

The Center for Literacy Studies strengthens adult literacy education in order to equip adults with the knowledge and skills they need to be lifelong learners and effective members of their families, communities and workplaces. The Center links theory and practice through research, professional development, partnerships, and building and sharing the knowledge of the field.

**2887  Claiborne County Adult Reading Experience**
Claiborne County Schools
PO Box 800
Tazewell, TN  37879          423-626-2273
                              FAX 423-626-5945
*Roger Hansard, Adult Education Supervisor*

**2888  Department of Human Services: Division of Rehabilitation Services**
400 Deaderick Street
Nashville, TN  37248 0060          615-313-4714
                                    FAX 615-741-4165
                                    TDY:800-270-1349
      http://www.state.tn.us/humanserv/rehabilitation
              e-mail: carlbrown@mail.state.tn.usa
*Carl Brown, Assistant Commissioner*
*Karen Wayson, Secretary*

Agency takes an active leadership role in removing the barriers to employment due to disabilities.

**2889  Nashville READ**
1701 W End Avenue
Nashville, TN  37203          615-255-4982
                              FAX 615-255-4783
          e-mail: literacy@nashvilleread.org
*Carol Thigpin, Contact*

**2890  Protection and Advocacy Agency: Tennessee**
PO Box 121257
Nashville, TN  37212          615-298-1080
                              800-342-1660
                              FAX 615-298-2046
                              TDY:901-343-4241
                          http://www.tpainc.org
*Shirley Shea, Executive Director*
*Gabriel Wood, Secretary*

**2891 Tennessee Department of Education**
710 James Robertson Parkway
Nashville, TN 37243                     615-741-2731
                                        800-531-1515
                                   FAX 615-532-4899
                              http://www.state.tn.us
                   e-mail: education.comments@state.tn.us
*Phil White, Director*

Mission is to take Tennessee to the top in education. Guides administration of the state's K-12 public schools.

**2892 Tennessee Department of Labor & Workforce Development: Office of Adult Education**
500 James Robertson Parkway
Nashville, TN 37243                     615-741-7054
                                   FAX 615-532-4899

*Phil White, Director*

**2893 Tennessee Literacy Coalition**
One Vantage Way
Nashville, TN 37228                     615-259-3700
                                        800-323-6986
                                   FAX 615-248-6545
                            http://www.tnliteracy.org
                      e-mail: mnugent@tnliteracy.org

**2894 Tennessee School-to-Work Office**
Department Of Education
Nashville, TN 37243                     615-741-2731
                              http://www.state.tn.us
                    e-mail: awilks@mail.state.tn.us
*Alberta Wilks, Consultant*

**2895 Tennessee State Library and Archives**
State Department of Education
403 7th Avenue North
Nashville, TN 37243                     615-741-3158
                                   FAX 615-741-6471
                      http://www.state.tn.us/sos/statelib
*Tricia Bengle, Special Projects Coordinator*

## Texas

**2896 Adult Literacy Council of the Tom Green County**
3111 SW Boulevard
San Angelo, TX 76904                    915-947-1536
                                   FAX 915-947-1875
                             e-mail: adlitl@gte.net
*Mary Cochran, Contact*

Promote adult literacy.

**2897 Commerce Library Literacy Program**
PO Box 308
Commerce, TX 75429                      903-886-5279
                                   FAX 903-886-7239
*Pricilla Donovan*

**2898 Greater Orange Area Literacy Services**
PO Box 221
Orange, TX 77631                        409-886-4311
                                   FAX 409-886-0149
                             e-mail: goals@pnx.com
*Joyce Corrati*

**2899 Irving Public Library Literacy Program**
440 S Nursery Rd
Irving, TX 75060                        972-721-3776
                             http://www.irvinglibrary.org
                   e-mail: mredburn@irvinglibrary.org
*Gwen Bates, Contact*

Promotes literacy among people of all ages.

**2900 Literacy Austin**
2002 A Manor Road
Austin, TX 78722                        512-478-7323
                                   FAX 512-479-7323
                                   TDY:512-478-7323
                            http://www.literacyaustin.org
                             e-mail: literacy@io.com
*Gil Harman, Director*
*Hector Hernandez, Office Manager*

**2901 Literacy Center of Marshall: Harrison County**
700 W Houston Street
Marshall, TX 75670                      903-935-0962
                                   FAX 903-935-2650
                   e-mail: joycehammer@hotmail.com
*Joyce Hammers, Executive Director*
*Patricia Jersild, Assistant Director*

**2902 Literacy Council of Bowie and Miller Counties**
600 Walnut Street
Texarkana, TX 75505                     903-838-8521
                                   FAX 870-774-2078
                        e-mail: RMagee@cableone.net
*Robbye Magee, Contact*

**2903 Literacy Volunteers of America: Bastrop**
1201 Church Street
Bastrop, TX 78602                       512-321-6686
                        e-mail: suemunster@aol.com
*Sue Steinbring*

Provides literacy training and pre-GED for students, English as a Second Language, tutoring and tutor training.

**2904 Literacy Volunteers of America: Bay City**
1921 5th Street
Bay City, TX 77414                      979-244-9544
                                   FAX 979-244-9566
                            e-mail: lvabc@wcnet.net
*Linda Brown, Contact*

Promotes literacy for people of all ages.

**2905 Literacy Volunteers of America: Beaumont Public Library**
PO Box 3827
Beaumont, TX 77704          409-835-7324
                           FAX 409-838-6734
              e-mail: bbeard@bpls.lib.tx.us
*Barbara Bear, Contact*

**2906 Literacy Volunteers of America: Brazos Valley**
Po Box 3387
Bryan, TX 77805          979-595-2801
          http://www.literacybrazosvalley.org
                   e-mail: lva@bvcog.org
*Bobbee Pennington, Contact*

Provides tutors for 18+ adults in reading, writing, math, and computer literacy. Lessons are one on one, free of charge.

**2907 Literacy Volunteers of America: Cleburne**
212 E Chambers
Cleburne, TX 76031          817-641-3187
                           FAX 817-556-3444
              e-mail: dlajean@juno.com
*Eduardo Ortiz, Education Manager*

Promotes literacy for people of all ages.

**2908 Literacy Volunteers of America: Houston**
Heights Learning Center
1111 Lawrence
Houston, TX 77008          713-868-9600
                           FAX 713-802-2527
*Sabrina Haselhorst, Contact*

Promotes literacy for people of all ages.

**2909 Literacy Volunteers of America: Laredo**
W End Washington Street
Laredo, TX 78042          956-724-5207
                          FAX 956-725-4253
          e-mail: lvlaredo@grandecom.net
*Terry Perez, President of the Board*

Promotes literacy for people of all ages.

**2910 Literacy Volunteers of America: Montgomery County**
Po Box 2704
Conroe, TX 77305          936-494-0635
*Twillia Liles*

As part of the national literacy organization, combats illiteracy in Montgomery County through volunteer tutoring.

**2911 Literacy Volunteers of America: Port Arthur Literacy Support**
4615 9th Avenue
Port Arthur, TX 77642          409-982-7257
*Deborah Campbell*

**2912 Literacy Volunteers of America: Wimberley Area**
PO Box 135
Wimberley, TX 78676          512-847-8953
          e-mail: johngray@wimberley-tx.com
*Jack Anderson, President*
*Linda Mueller, Accreditation Manager*
*Annette Harrington, Treasurer*

Nonprofit, volunteer organization which exists to improve the reading, writing, speaking, cultural and life skills of adults reading at or below the sixth grade level and/or those for whom English is not their native language. Provides GED instruction. All services are free.

**2913 Texas Center for Adult Literacy & Learning**
Texas A&M University
College Station, TX 77843          979-845-6615
                                   800-441-7323
                           FAX 979-845-0952
              http://www.cdlr.tamu.edu/tcall
*Victoria Hoffman, Director*

**2914 Texas Families and Literacy**
719 Hill Country Drive
Kerrville, TX 78028          830-896-8787
                           FAX 830-896-3639
          e-mail: famlit@maverickbbs.com
*Jimmy Sparks*

**2915 Victoria Adult Literacy**
Pro-literacy America
802 E Crestwood Drive
Victoria, TX 77901          361-573-7323
                           FAX 361-582-4348
              e-mail: valctx@yahoo.com
*Donna Bentley, Director*
*Patt Polley, Administrative Assistant*

**2916 Weslaco Public Library**
525 S Kansas Avenue
Weslaco, TX 78596          956-968-4533
                           FAX 956-969-4069
          e-mail: volcntr@ccwf.cc.utexas.edu
*Michael Fisher, Director*

## Utah

**2917 Literacy Volunteers of America: Wasatch Front**
175 N 600 W
Salt Lake City, UT 84116          801-328-5608
                                  FAX 801-328-5637
                           http://www.LVA2000.org
                       e-mail: erikaj29@yahoo.com
*Erika Johnson*

**2918 Utah Literacy Action Center**
3595 South Main St
Salt Lake City, UT 84115          801-265-9081
                                 FAX 801-265-9643
*Eileen Smart, Director*

**2919 Utah Literacy Resource Center**
State Office of Education
250 E 500 S
Salt Lake City, UT 84111         801-538-7824
                                 800-451-9500
                            FAX 801-538-7882
                     http://www.school.utah.gov
                  e-mail: dsteele@usoe.k12.ut.us
*David Steele, Coordinator*
*Sandra Grant, Specialist*
*Shauna South, Specialist*

As part of the State Library, the State Resource Center
provides electronic and print resources.

## Vermont

**2920 ABE Career and Lifelong Learning: Vermont
Department of Education**
120 State Street
Montpelier, VT 05620            802-828-3134
                           FAX 802-828-3146
              e-mail: srobinson@doe.state.vt.us
*Sandra Robinson, Director*
*Tracy Gallo, Director Life Long Learning*

Promotes quality education.

**2921 Learning Disabilities Association of Vermont**
PO Box 1041
Manchester Center, VT 05255     802-362-3127
                           FAX 802-362-3128
*Christina Thurston, President*

A nonprofit organization whose members are individuals with learning disabilities, their families, and the
professionals who work with them.

**2922 Vermont Assistive Technology Project:
Department of Aging and Disabilities**
Agency of Human Services
103 S Main Street, Weeks Building
Waterbury, VT 05671             802-241-2620
                                800-750-6355
                           FAX 802-241-2174
                           TDY:802-241-1464
                  http://www.dil.state.vt.us/atp
                  e-mail: jtucker@dad.state.vt.us
*Julie Tucker, Project Director*
*Betsy Ross, Administrative Assistant*

**2923 Vermont Department of Corrections**
103 S Main Street
Waterburry, VT 05671            802-241-2276
                           FAX 802-241-2565
                           TDY:800-241-1457
                     http://www.doc.state.vt.us
*Robert Lucenti, Superintendent Education Service*
*Robert Hofmann, Commissioner*

**2924 Vermont Department of Welfare**
Economics Services Division
103 S Main Street
Waterbury, VT 05671             802-241-2834
                                800-287-0589
                           FAX 802-241-2830
                           TDY:888-834-7898
                     http://www.dcf.state.vtus
*James Forrset, Deputy Commissioner*
*Dianne Carmenti, Welfare Director*

**2925 Vermont Human Resources Investment Council**
Vermont Department of Employment & Training
5 Green Mountain Drive
Montpelier, VT 05601 0488       802-828-4156
                           FAX 802-828-4022
                     http://www.det.state.vt.us
              e-mail: aevans@pop.det.state.vt.us
*Bob Ware, Director for Jobs and Training*
*Anne Ginevan, Commissioner*

**2926 Vermont Literacy Resource Center: Department
of Education**
120 State Street
Montpelier, VT 05602            802-828-5148
                           FAX 802-828-0573
              http://www.state.vt.us/educ/vlrc/
                  e-mail: wross@doe.state.vt.us
*Wendy Ross, Director Literacy Board*

The Vermont Literacy Resource Center links Vermont to national, regional, and state literacy organizations, provides staff development and serves as a
clearinghouse for the literacy community. The Vermont Literacy Resource Center is located at the Vermont Department of Education.

**2927 Vermont REACH-UP Program**
Department of Social Welfare
103 S Main Street
Waterbury, VT 05671             802-241-2800
                                800-775-0506
                           FAX 802-241-2830
*Karen Ryder*

**2928 Vermont Workforce Reinvestment Act**
Vermont Department of Employment & Training
5 Green Mountain Drive
Montpelier, VT 05601 0488       802-828-4000
                           FAX 802-828-4181
                     http://www.det.state.vt.us
              e-mail: mcalcagni@det.state.vt.us
*Anne Ginevan, Commissioner*
*Bob Ware, Director for Jobs and Training*

Vocational training and job listings for displaced
workers or others with difficulty finding regular employment.

**2929 VocRehab Vermont**
Agency of Human Services
103 S Main Street
Waterbury, VT  05671 2303          802-241-2186
866-879-6757
FAX 802-241-3359
TDY:802-241-2186
http://www.vocrehabvermont.org
e-mail: janetr@dad.state.vt.us
*Diana Dalmasse, Director*
*Wendy Hanifan, Administrative Assistant*

Works in close partnership with the Vermont Association of Business and Industry Rehabilitation to assist Vermonters with disabilities and maintain meaningful employment in their communities.

## Virginia

**2930 Charlotte County Literacy Program**
395 Thomas Jefferson Highway
Charlotte Court House, VA  23923  434-542-5782
e-mail: charcolit@hovac.com
*Mary Jones*

Offers basic and family literacy programs, ESL and computer, parenting and work skills.

**2931 DCE-LVA Virginia Institutions**
101 N 14th Street
Richmond, VA  23219          804-692-0282
FAX 804-786-0559
e-mail: sjoyner@saturn.vcu.edu

**2932 Highlands Educational Literacy Program**
334 Rose Street
Abingdon, VA  24212          276-676-4355
FAX 276-676-0677
e-mail: garretsj@jaxs.net
*Sallie Garrett, Executive Director*

**2933 Literacy Volunteers of America: Campbell County Public Library**
684 Village Highway
Lynchburg, VA  24588          434-332-9561
FAX 434-332-9697
http://www.tlc.library.net/campbell
e-mail: ccothrain@campbell.k12.us
*Carolyn Cothrain, Program Manager*
*Linda Owens, Director*

Provides tutoring for basic literacy and English as a second language.

**2934 Literacy Volunteers of America: Charlottsville/Albemarle**
PO Box 1156
Charlottesville, VA  22902          434-977-3838
FAX 434-979-7846
http://www.avenue.org/lva
e-mail: lva@avenue.org
*Anne Jellen, Administrative Director*
*Mary Mullen, Program Director*

Promotes literacy for people of all ages.

**2935 Literacy Volunteers of America: Fishersville**
26 John Lewis Road
Fishersville, VA  22939          540-949-6134
FAX 540-245-5115
e-mail: lvaaa.cfw.com
*Candida Clark*

Provides free and confidential one-to-one tutoring in basic reading and ESL to persons not in the school system.

**2936 Literacy Volunteers of America: Gloucester**
PO Box 981
Gloucester, VA  23061          804-693-1306
e-mail: jmes223@aol.com
*Shelby Friend*

**2937 Literacy Volunteers of America: Louisa County**
2128 S Lakeshore Drive
Louisa, VA  23093          540-967-1051
FAX 540-967-1051
*Terry McElhone*

**2938 Literacy Volunteers of America: Nelson County**
195 Callohill Drive
Lovingston, VA  22949          434-263-8228
FAX 434-263-4378
e-mail: grahame@cville.net
*Art Grahame*

**2939 Literacy Volunteers of America: New River Valley**
195 W Main Street
Christiansburg, VA  24073          540-382-7262
FAX 540-382-7262
e-mail: lvanrv@aol.com
*E Wertz, Executive Director*

The empowerment of every adult in the New River Valley through the provision of opportunities to achieve independence through literacy.

**2940 Literacy Volunteers of America: Northern Neck Chapter**
Northern Neck Adult Education Program
2172 Northumberland Highway
Lottsburg, VA  22511          804-580-3152
FAX 804-580-3152
*Tonya Creasy, Director*
*Rich Emery, Administrative Assistant*

**2941 Literacy Volunteers of America: Prince William**
4326 Dale Boulevard
Woodbridge, VA  22193          703-670-5702
FAX 703-583-0703
http://www.ivapw.org
e-mail: lvapw@aol.com
*Leticia Putney, Director*

Promotes literacy for people of all ages.

**2942  Literacy Volunteers of America: Shenandoah County**
PO Box 303
Woodstock, VA  22664          540-459-2446
*Terry Chambers*

**2943  One-on-One Literacy Program: Wythe and Grayson Counties**
PO Box 905
Independence, VA  24348          276-228-5225
e-mail: joanbolduc@ls.net
*Joan Bolduc, Director*

**2944  Skyline Literacy Coalition**
290 Mill Street
Dayton, VA  22821          540-879-2933
FAX 540-879-2033
http://www.home.rica.net/slc
e-mail: skylitjay@aol.com
*Jay Bungard, Director*

**2945  Virginia Adult Education Centers for Professional Development**
Adult Education and Literacy Resource Center
1015 W Main Street
Richmond, VA  23284          804-828-6521
800-237-0178
FAX 804-828-7539
http://www.vcv.edu/aelweb/
e-mail: vdesk@vcu.edu
*Barbara Gibson, Director*
*Danah Merrell, Staff*

We provide adult education and literacy resources, information, and professional development in Virginia.

**2946  Virginia Council of Administrators of Special Education**
Council for Exceptional Children
1110 N Glebe Road
Arlington, VA  22201          703-620-3660
800-224-6830
FAX 703-264-9494
TDY:703-620-3660
http://www.cec.sped.org
e-mail: service@cec.sped.org
*Drew Allbritten M.D., President*

The Virginia Council of Administrators of Special Education is organized to promote professional leadership, provide opportunity for the study of problems common to its members, and to communicate through discussions and publications information that will develop improved services for children with disabilities.

**2947  Virginia Literacy Coalition**
11503 Allecingie Parkway
Richmond, VA  23235          804-225-8777
FAX 804-225-1859
*Jean Proffitt, Organizational Liaison*

## Washington

**2948  Division of Vocational Rehabilitation**
Po Box 45340
Olympia, WA  98504          360-438-8045
FAX 360-407-8007
http://www.dshs.wa.gov
e-mail: ruddyl@dshs.wa.gov
*Michael O'Brien, Director*
*Lee Ruddy, Office Assistant*

**2949  Literacy Council of Kitsap**
612 5th Street
Bremerton, WA  98337          360-373-1539
FAX 360-373-6859
e-mail: literacy@krl.org
*Helen Robinson, Executive Director*

**2950  Mason County Literacy Council**
133 W Railraod
Shelton, WA  98557          360-426-9733
FAX 360-426-9789
e-mail: lbusacca@shelton.wednet.edu
*Lynn Busacca, Director*
*Angela Holley, Adult Service Coordinator*

**2951  Northwest Regional Literacy Resource Center**
State Board for Community Technical College
711 S Capitol Way Suite 708
Seattle, WA  98504-2496          360-586-3527
FAX 360-586-3529
http://www.literacynet.org
e-mail: nwrlrc@literacynet.org
*Israel Mendoza, Director*
*Nick d'Alonzo, Instructional Coordinator*

Provides resources and technical support to adult basic skills instructors in Alaska, Idaho, Oregon, Montana, Washington and Wyoming.

**2952  People's Learning Center of Seattle**
PO Box 28084
Seattle, WA  98198          206-325-8308
*Georgia Rogers*

**2953  South King County Multi-Service Center**
1200 S 336th Street
Federal Way, WA  98003          253-838-6810
FAX 253-874-7831
TDY:253-661-7827
http://www.multi-servicecenter.com
*Stephanie Boschee, Contact*

**2954  St. James ESL Program**
St. James Cathedral
804 9th Avenue
Seattle, WA  98104          206-382-4511
FAX 206-622-5303
http://www.stjames-cathedral.org/esl
e-mail: ckoehler@stjamescatherdral.org
*Christopher Koehler, Director*

Helps promote literacy among the community.

**2955**  **Washington Department of Corrections**
PO Box 41100
Olympia, WA  98504                          360-753-2500
FAX 360-586-3676

**2956**  **Washington Laubach Literacy Action**
Washington Literacy
220 Nickerson Street
Seattle, WA  98109                          206-284-4399
FAX 206-284-7895
http://www.waliteracy.org
e-mail: WALT@aol.com
*Brenda Gray, Executive Director*

---

## West Virginia

**2957**  **Division of Technical & Adult Education Services: West Virginia**
State Department of Education
1900 Kanawha Boulevard E, Bldg 6
Charleston, WV  25305                       304-558-6318
FAX 304-558-3946
http://wvabe.state.k12.wv.us
e-mail: cmoore@access.k12.wv.us
*Connie Moore, Secretary*
*Louise Miller, Coordinator*

Promotes the quality of adult education.

**2958**  **Laubach Literacy Action: West Virginia**
501 22nd Street
Dunbar, WV  25064                           304-766-7655
800-642-2670
FAX 304-766-7915
*David Coccari*

**2959**  **W Virginia Regional Education Services**
RESA III/Nitro-Putnam
501 22nd Street
Dunbar, WV  25064                           304-766-7655
800-642-2670
FAX 304-766-2824
http://www.nuemedia.net
e-mail: cshank@access.k12.wv.us
*Charles Nichols, Executive Director*
*Linda Andersen, Administrative Assistant*

Offers services for literacy and adult basic education including literacy hotline, networks newsletter, resources for English as a second language, beginning literacy, learning disabilities and other special learning needs.

**2960**  **West Virginia Department of Education**
1900 Kanawha Boulevard E, Bldg 6
Charleston, WV  26501                       304-558-6317
800-642-2670
FAX 304-558-3946
http://www.wvabe.state.k12.wv.us/
*Preston Browning, Assistant Director*

**2961**  **West Virginia Literacy Volunteers of America**
501 22nd Street
Dunbar, WV  25064                           304-766-7655
800-642-2670
FAX 304-766-7915
*David Greenstreet, Director*

---

## Wisconsin

**2962**  **Laubach Literacy Action: Wisconsin**
Literacy Plus-Grant County
PO Box 447
Lancaster, WI  53813                        608-723-2136
FAX 608-723-4834
*Arlene Siss, Co-Director*
*John Angelli, Co-Director*
*Leanne Smith, Office Assistant*
Includes Grant County.

**2963**  **Literacy Volunteers of America: Eau Claire**
221 W Madison Street
Eau Claire, WI  54703                       715-834-0222
FAX 715-834-2546
e-mail: info@lvacv.org
*Carol Gabler, Director*

Promotes literacy for people of all ages.

**2964**  **Literacy Volunteers of America: Marquette County**
PO Box 671
Montello, WI  53949                         608-297-8900
FAX 608-297-2673
e-mail: vjhawk@maqs.net
*Vicki Huffman, Executive Director*

Promotes literacy for people of all ages.

**2965**  **Literacy Volunteers of America: Wisconsin**
1118 South Park Street
Madison, WI  53715                          608-257-1655
http://www.wisconsinliteracy.org
e-mail: peggy.meyers@doc.state.wi.us
*Peggy Meyers, Contact*

Promotes literacy for people of all ages.

**2966**  **Price County Area Literacy Council**
211 N Lake Avenue
Phillips, WI  54555                         715-339-3939
FAX 715-339-3909
e-mail: rgstueber@yahoo.com
*Ruth Stueber*

**2967**  **Western Wisconsin Literacy Services**
113 Sillmore Street
Black River Falls, WI  54615               715-284-3361
FAX 715-284-9681
http://www.wwls.org
e-mail: jacksonlva@hotmail.com
*Sandy Quance, Director*

**2968  Wisconsin Literacy Resource Center**
**Board of Vocational, Technical & Adult Education**
**1118 S Park Street**
**Madison, WI  53715**                608-244-3899
                                                  FAX 608-257-1655
                        http://www.wisconsinliteracy.orgs
                        e-mail: mvellej@boardtec.wi.us
*Mark Johnson, Director*

As part of the state library, the State Resource Center provides electronic and print resources.

**2969  Wisconsin Literacy Services**
**1118 South Park St**
**Madison, WI  53715**                608-257-1655
                                                  FAX 920-294-6055
                        http://www.wisconsinliteracy.org
                        e-mail: glclc@hotmail.com
*Lisa Schubert, Contact*

## Wyoming

**2970  Literacy Volunteers of Casper**
**125 College Drive**
**Casper, WY  82601**                 307-268-2453
                                                  FAX 307-268-3021
                        e-mail: lmixer@caspercollege.edu
*Lisa Mixer, Director*

**2971  Literacy Volunteers of Douglas**
**203 N 6th Street**
**Douglas, WY  82633**                307-358-5622
                                                  FAX 307-358-5629
                        http://www.dwc.wy.edu
                        e-mail: slunsford@wewc.cc.wy.us
*Shannon Lunsford, Director*
*Carrie Frey, Administrative Assistant*

Promotes adult literacy among the people in the community.

**2972  Literacy Volunteers of Powell North College**
**231 W 6th Street**
**Powell, WY  82435**                 307-754-6280
                                                  FAX 307-754-6700
                        e-mail: bushnelr@nwc.cc.wy.us
*Rom Bushnell, Director*

Promotes literacy for people of all ages.

**2973  Literacy Volunteers of Sheridan/Northern Wyoming**
**102 S Connor Street**
**Sheridan, WY  82801**               307-673-2813
                                                  FAX 307-672-6157
                        e-mail: wa@fiberpipe.net
*Diane Marshall, Director*

Promotes literacy for people of all ages.

**2974  Wyoming Literacy Resource Center**
**Division of Lifelong Learning & Instruction**
**College of Education, Room 46**
**Laramie, WY  82071**                307-766-3970
                                                  FAX 307-766-6668
                        e-mail: dstithem@uwyo.edu
*Diana Stithem, Director*

As part of the state library, the State Resource Center provides electronic and print resources.

## Adults

**2975  A Miracle to Believe In**

**Option Indigo Press**
**2080 S Undermountain Road**
**Sheffield, MA  01257**                    413-229-8727
                                            800-562-7171
                                       FAX 413-229-8727
                         http://www.optionindio.com
                            e-mail: indigo@bcn.net
*Barry Neil Kaufman, Author*

A group of people from all walks of life come together and are transformed as they reach out, under the direction of Kaufman, to help a little boy the medical world had given up as hopeless. This heartwarming journey of loving a child back to life will not only inspire, but presents a compelling new way to deal with life's traumas and difficulties. *$7.99*

          *ISBN 0-449201-08-2*

**2976  All Kinds Of Minds: Young Student's BookAbout Learning Disabilities & Disorders**

**Educator's Publishing Service, Inc.**
**Po Box 9031**
**Cambridge, MA  02139**
                                            800-225-5750
                         http://www.epsbooks.com
Written by Melvin Levine, and published in 1992. Helps children with learning disabilities to come to terms with it. Shows them how to get around or just work out any problems with their disabilities.

**2977  Closer Look: Perspectives & Reflections on College Students with LD**

**Curry College Bookstore**
**1071 Blue Hill Avenue**
**Milton, MA  02186**                        617-333-2322
                                       FAX 617-333-2018
                         e-mail: dgoss@curry.edu
*Jane Adelizzi, Diane Goss, Author*
*Diane Goss, Editor*
*Jane Adelizzi, Editor*

This book is a collection of personal accounts by teachers and learners. It's a sensitive portrayal of the real world of teaching and learning, particularly as it impacts on those with learning differences. Topics include connections between theory and practice, emotions and learning disabilities, classroom trauma, learning disabilities and social deficits, metacognitive development, ESL and learning disabilities, models for inclusion and practical strategies. *$ 24.95*

          *240 pages*
          *ISBN 0-964975-20-3*

**2978  Dyslexia in Adults: Taking Charge of Your Life**

**Taylor Publishing**
**1550 W Mockingbird Lane**
**Dallas, TX  75235**                        214-637-2800
                                            800-677-2800
                                       FAX 214-819-8580
                         http://images.amazon.com
*Kathleen Nosek, Author*

Adult dyslexics are experts at hiding reading, writing, and spelling difficulties long after high school. Dyslexia in Adults is a perfect guidebook for adult dyslexias to use in coping with day-to-day problems that are complicated by their learning disability. *$12.95*

          *192 pages  Paperback*
          *ISBN 0-878339-48-5*

**2979  Faking It: A Look into the Mind of a Creative Learner**

**Heinemann/Boynton Cook Publishers**
**361 Hanover Street**
**Portsmouth, NH  03801**
                                            800-541-2086
                                       FAX 800-354-2004
                         http://www.heinemann.com
                      e-mail: custserv@heinemann.com
*Christopher Lee, Author*
*Rosemary Jackson, Author*

Engage in professional dialog with Heinemann's celebrated authors and colleagues!

          *181 pages  paperback*
          *ISBN 0-867092-96-3*

**2980  How to Get Services by Being Assertive**

**Family Resource Center on Disabilities**
**20 E Jackson Boulevard**
**Chicago, IL  60604**                       312-939-3513
                                            800-952-4199
                                       FAX 312-939-7297
                http://www.ameritech.net/users/frcdptiil
                   e-mail: FRCDPTIIL@ameritech.net
*Charlotte DesJardins, Executive Director*

A 100 page manual that demonstrates positive assertiveness techniques. Price includes postage & handling. *$12.00*

**2981  Language in Motion: Exploring the Nature of Sign**

**Harris Communications**
**15155 Technology Drive**
**Eden Prairie, MN  55344**                  952-906-1180
                                            800-825-6758
                                       FAX 952-906-1099
                                       TDY:952-906-1198
                         http://www.harriscomm.com
                      e-mail: mail@harriscomm.com
*David A Stewart, Author*
*Jerome D Schein, Author*
*Bill Williams, National Sales Manager*

Explore the nature of American Sign Language and its relationship to other sign languages and sign systems used around the world. An enlightening book about deaf people and their culture and a useful guide to interacting and communicating with deaf and hard-of-hearing people. *$24.95*

          *221 pages  Hardcover*

**2982  Myth Of Laziness**

Simon & Schuster
1230 Avenue Of The Americas
New York, NY  10020          212-698-7000
http://www.simonsays.com
e-mail: shop.feedback@simonsays.com

Written by Melvin Levine and published in 2003. It shows parents how to nurture their children's strength's and improve their classroom productivity. Also, it shows how correcting these problems early will help children live a fulfilling and productive adult life.

**2983  No Easy Answer**

Bantam Partners
1540 Broadway
New York, NY  10036          212-668-9852
http://www.randomhouse.com/bantamdell/index.htm

Written by Sally Smith, and published in 1995.

**2984  One Mind At A Time**

Simon & Schuster
1230 Avenue Of The Americas
New York, NY  10020          212-698-7000
http://www.simonsays.com
e-mail: shop.feedback@simonsays.com

Written by Melvin Levine, and published in 2003. It shows parents and others how to identify the individual learning patterns, explaining how to strenghten a child's abilities and either bypasss or overcome the child's weakness, producing positive results instead of reapeated frustration and failure.

**2985  Out of Darkness**

Connecticut Assoc. for Children and Adults with LD
25 Van Zant Street
East Norwalk, CT  06855          203-838-5010
FAX 203-866-6108
http://www.CACLD.org

Article by an adult who discovers at age 30 that he has ADD. *$1.00*

*4 pages*

**2986  Painting the Joy of the Soul**

Learning Disabilities Association of America
4156 Library Road
Pittsburgh, PA  15234          412-341-1515
FAX 412-344-0224
http://www.ldanatl.org
e-mail: ldanatl@usaor.net

The first comprehensively researched and written book on the art and life of America's beloved artist, P. Buckley Moss, whose passion for painting is equal only to her passion for people, especially those with learning disabilities. Inspirational book about a woman who succeeded not in spite of her disability, but because of it. Contains 168 full color pages, over 100 art images. *$50.00*

*168 pages  $5.00 postage*

**2987  Son-Rise: The Miracle Continues**

Option Indigo Press
2080 S Undermountain Road
Sheffield, MA  01257          413-229-8727
800-562-7171
FAX 413-229-8727
http://www.optionindio.com
e-mail: indigo@bcn.net

This book documents Raun Kaufman's astonishing development from a lifeless, autistic, retarded child into a highly verbal, lovable youngster with no traces of his former condition. It includes details of Raun's extraordinary progress from the age of four into young adulthood. It also shares moving accounts of five families that successfully used the Son-Rise Program to reach their own special children. An awe-inspiring reminder that love moves mountains. *$14.95*

*ISBN 0-915811-61-8*

**2988  Succeeding with LD**

Free Spirit Publishing
217 5th Avenue N
Minneapolis, MN  55401          612-338-2068
800-735-7323
FAX 612-337-5050
http://www.freespirit.com
e-mail: help4kids@freespirit.com
*Jill Lauren, MA, Author*
*Betsy Gabler, Sales Manager*

Twenty talented adults and children with LD share their stories, struggles, achievements, and tips for success. *$14.95*

*160 pages  Illustrated*
*ISBN 1-575420-12-0*

**2989  You Don't Outgrow It: Living with Learning Disabilities**

Academic Therapy Publications
20 Commercial Boulevard
Novato, CA  94949          415-883-3314
800-422-7249
FAX 415-883-3720
http://www.atpub.com
*Marnell L. Hayes, Author*

Offers information to help the learning disabled adult. Uses strengths creatively to work around learning disabilities to reach a goal, get and hold a job, etc. Comprehensive glossary, related readings and recommended resources. *$6.00*

*ISBN 0-878799-67-2*

## Children

**2990  123 Sign with Me**

**Harris Communications**
**15155 Technology Drive**
**Eden Prairie, MN  55344**        952-906-1180
                                   800-825-6758
                              FAX 952-906-1099
                              TDY:952-906-1198
                      http://www.harriscomm.com
                      e-mail: mail@harriscomm.com
*Bill Williams, National Sales Manager*

The Sign with Me number book is a book for all children. It is designed to teach basic counting skills, the numerals 1-10, and their manual counterparts in sign language. The book offers a unique opportunity to introduce sign language to young children through the natural process of reading. *$12.00*

*24 pages  Paperback*
*ISBN 0-939849-01-1*

**2991  ABC Sign with Me**

**Harris Communications**
**15155 Technology Drive**
**Eden Prairie, MN  55344**        952-906-1180
                                   800-825-6758
                              FAX 952-906-1099
                              TDY:952-906-1198
                      http://www.harriscomm.com
                      e-mail: mail@harriscomm.com
*Bill Williams, National Sales Manager*

The Sign with Me alphabet book is a book for all children. It is designed to teach the 26 letters of the alphabet and the corresponding manual alphabet in sign language. The book provides early exposure to letter recognition plus a unique opportunity to introduce sign language to young children. *$12.00*

*32 pages  Paperback*
*ISBN 0-939849-00-3*

**2992  Adam Zigzag**

**Bantam Doubleday Dell**
**1540 Broadway**
**New York, NY  10036**        212-782-9000
                               800-323-9872
                          FAX 212-302-7985
*Barbara Barrie, Author*

Dyslexia affects Adam's self-esteem and the lives of his family.

*ISBN 0-385311-72-9*

**2993  An Alphabet of Animal Signs**

**Harris Communications**
**15155 Technology Drive**
**Eden Prairie, MN  55344**        952-906-1180
                                   800-825-6758
                              FAX 952-906-1099
                              TDY:952-906-1198
                      http://www.harriscomm.com
                      e-mail: mail@harriscomm.com
*S Harold Collins, Author*
*Bill Williams, National Sales Manager*

A fun sign language starter book that presents an animal sign for each letter of the alphabet. *$5.95*

*13 pages  Paperback*

**2994  Basic Vocabulary: American Sign Language for Parents and Children**

**Harris Communications**
**15155 Technology Drive**
**Eden Prairie, MN  55344**        952-906-1180
                                   800-825-6758
                              FAX 952-906-1099
                              TDY:952-906-1198
                      http://www.harriscomm.com
                      e-mail: mail@harriscomm.com
*Terrence J O'Rourke, Author*
*Bill Williams, National Sales Manager*

A child's first dictionary of signs. Arranged alphabetically, this book incorporates developmental lists helpful to both deaf and hearing children with over 1,000 clear illustrations. *$8.95*

*228 pages  Paperback*
*ISBN 0-932666-00-0*

**2995  Beginning Signing Primer**

**Harris Communications**
**15155 Technology Drive**
**Eden Prairie, MN  55344**        952-906-1180
                                   800-825-6758
                              FAX 952-906-1099
                              TDY:952-906-1198
                      http://www.harriscomm.com
                      e-mail: mail@harriscomm.com
*Bill Williams, National Sales Manager*

A set of 100 cards designed especially for beginning signers. The cards present seven topics with words and signs. The topics: Color; Creatures; Family; Months; Days; Time and Weather. *$5.95*

**2996  Best Way Out**

**Harcourt Brace Jovanovich**
**6277 Sea Harbor Drive**
**Orlando, FL  32887**        407-345-2000
                         FAX 407-352-1318
                http://www.harcourtcollege.com
*Karyn Follis Cheatham, Author*
*John D Benson, VP*

A fictional story of thirteen-year-old Haywood Romby who faces the same real life academic and social problems faced daily by teenagers with learning disabilities.

*168 pages*

**2997  Christmas Bear**

**Teddy Bear Press**
**3639 Midway Drive**
**San Diego, CA  92110**        619-223-7311
                           FAX 619-255-2158
                 http://www.teddybearpress.net
                 e-mail: fparker@teddybearpress.net
*Fran Parker, President*

An 11x17 big book with color illustrations and a large print format uses the same simple sentence structure fount in I Can Read and Reading Is Fun programs. This story adds seasonal words to the developing sight vocabulary found in our reading programs. *$25.95*

*12 pages*
*ISBN 1-928876-11-0*

**2998  Don't Give Up Kid**

**Verbal Images Press**
**19 Fox Hill Drive**
**Fairport, NY  14450**                 585-377-3807
                                          800-888-4741
                                    FAX 716-377-5401
*Jeanne Gehret, MA, Author*
*Victoria Harmison, Marketing Director*

A picture book for children with dyslexia and other learning differences gives a clear understanding of their difficulties and the necessary courage to live with them. Young Alex finds in his hero, Thomas Edison, the strength to keep trying and to experiment with different ways to learn. Recommended by LDA and CHADD. *$9.95*

*40 pages  Paperback*
*ISBN 1-884281-10-9*

**2999  Fundamentals of Autism**

**Slosson Educational Publications**
**538 Buffalo Road**
**East Aurora, NY  14052**              888-756-7766
                                         800-828-4800
                                    FAX 800-655-3840
                               http://www.slosson.com
                          e-mail: slosson@slosson.com
*Georgina Moynihan, TTFM*

A handbook for those who work with children diagnosed as autistic.

**3000  Funny Bunny and Sunny Bunny**

**Teddy Bear Press**
**3639 Midway Drive**
**San Diego, CA  92110**                619-223-7311
                                    FAX 619-255-2158
                          http://www.teddybearpress.net
                      e-mail: fparker@teddybearpress.net
*Fran Parker, President*

An 11x17 big book with color illustrations and a large print format uses the same simple sentence structure fount in I Can Read and Reading Is Fun programs. This story adds seasonal words to the developing sight vocabulary found in our reading programs. *$25.95*

*17 pages*
*ISBN 1-928876-14-5*

**3001  Halloween Bear**

**Teddy Bear Press**
**3639 Midway Drive**
**San Diego, CA  92110**                619-223-7311
                                    FAX 619-255-2158
                          http://www.teddybearpress.net
                      e-mail: fparker@teddybearpress.net
*Fran Parker, President*

An 11x17 big book with color illustrations and a large print format uses the same simple sentence structure fount in I Can Read and Reading Is Fun programs. This story adds seasonal words to the developing sight vocabulary found in our reading programs. *$25.95*

*13 pages*
*ISBN 1-928876-15-3*

**3002  Handmade Alphabet**

**Harris Communications**
**15155 Technology Drive**
**Eden Prairie, MN  55344**             952-906-1180
                                         800-825-6758
                                    FAX 952-906-1099
                                    TDY:952-906-1198
                            http://www.harriscomm.com
                          e-mail: mail@harriscomm.com
*Laura Rankin, Author*
*Bill Williams, National Sales Manager*

An alphabet book which celebrates the beauty of the manual alphabet. Each illustration consists of the manual representation of the letter linked with an item beginning with that letter. *$16.99*

*32 pages  Hardcover*
*ISBN 0-803709-74-9*

**3003  I Can Read Charts**

**Teddy Bear Press**
**3639 Midway Drive**
**San Diego, CA  92110**                619-223-7311
                                    FAX 619-255-2158
                          http://www.teddybearpress.net
                      e-mail: fparker@teddybearpress.net
*Fran Parker, President*

Designed to accompany the I Can Read program is an 11x17 big book containing 54 charts which can be used to assist in introducing new words to students. These charts also provide review for previously taught words with either individual student or a small group. *$54.95*

*54 pages*

**3004  Josh: A Boy with Dyslexia**

**Waterfront Books**
**85 Crescent Road**
**Burlington, VT  05401**               802-658-7477
                                         800-639-6063
                                    FAX 802-860-1368
                          http://www.waterfrontbooks.com
                      e-mail: helpkids@waterfrontbooks.com
*Caroline Janover, Author*
*Sherrill N Musty, Owner/Publisher*

This is an adventure story for kids with a section in the back of facts about learning disabilities and a list of resources for parents and teachers. *$11.95*

*100 pages  Hardcover*
*ISBN 0-914525-18-2*

**3005  Jumpin' Johnny Get Back to Work: A Child's Guide to ADHD/Hyperactivity**

**Connecticut Association Children & Adults with LD**
**25 Van Zant Street**
**East Norwalk, CT  06855**          **203-838-5010**
                                      **FAX 203-866-6108**
                                      **http://www.CACLD.org**
                                      **e-mail: cacld@juno.com**
*Michael Gordon PhD, Author*
*Marie Armstrong, Information Specialist*

Written primarily for elementary age youngsters with ADHD, this book helps them to understand their disability. Also valuable as an educational tool for parents, siblings, friends and classmates. The author's text reflects his sensitivity toward children with ADHD. *$12.50*

*$2.50 shipping*

**3006  Leo the Late Bloomer**

**Connecticut Assoc. for Children and Adults with LD**
**25 Van Zant Street**
**East Norwalk, CT  06855**          **203-838-5010**
                                      **FAX 203-866-6108**
                                      **http://www.CACLD.org**
                                      **e-mail: cacld@juno.com**
*Robert Kraus, Author*
*Marie Armstrong, Information Specialist*

A wonderful book for the young child who is having problems learning. Children follow along with Leo as he finally blooms. *$6.50*

*$2.50 shipping*

**3007  Mandy**

**Harris Communications**
**15155 Technology Drive**
**Eden Prairie, MN  55344**          **952-906-1180**
                                      **800-825-6758**
                                      **FAX 952-906-1099**
                                      **TDY:952-906-1198**
                                      **http://www.harriscomm.com**
                                      **e-mail: mail@harriscomm.com**
*Barbar D Booth, Author*
*Jim La Marche, Illustrator*
*Bill Williams, National Sales Manager*

This book is presented in a lively, picture-book format and will give readers an understanding of the joys of sound and what it would be like not to be able to hear. Mandy, a young deaf girl, shares her perception of the world and her wonder of what sound actually is. Mandy is a fluent speechreader but also uses sign language occasionally in the text. *$5.35*

*32 pages  Hardcover*

**3008  My Brother Matthew**

**Woodbine House**
**6510 Bells Mill Road**
**Bethesda, MD  20817**          **301-897-3570**
                                  **800-843-7323**
                                  **FAX 301-897-5838**
                                  **http://www.woodbinehouse.com**
                                  **e-mail: info@woodbinehouse.com**
*Mary Thompson, Author*
*Mary Thompson, Illustrator*

Narrated by a young boy who describes the ups and downs of day-to-day life as he and his family adjust to his new brother, Matthew, who is born with a disability. *$14.95*

*28 pages  Hardcover*
*ISBN 0-933149-47-6*

**3009  My First Book of Sign**

**Harris Communications**
**15155 Technology Drive**
**Eden Prairie, MN  55344**          **952-906-1180**
                                      **800-825-6758**
                                      **FAX 952-906-1099**
                                      **TDY:952-906-1198**
                                      **http://www.harriscomm.com**
                                      **e-mail: mail@harriscomm.com**
*Pamela J Baker, Author*
*Patricia Bellan Gillen, Illustrator*

This book is an excellent source to teach children and even adults sign language. The illustrations are accurate in their representation of sign. It is colorful and visually attractive which makes it easy to read. The black and white manual alphabet, the fingerspelling, and aspects of sign provide exellent directions and pointers to signing correctly. The sign descriptions are a great supplement to the illustrations. *$11.96*

*76 pages  Hardcover*

**3010  My Signing Book of Numbers**

**Harris Communications**
**15155 Technology Drive**
**Eden Prairie, MN  55344**          **952-906-1180**
                                      **800-825-6758**
                                      **FAX 952-906-1099**
                                      **TDY:952-906-1198**
                                      **http://www.harriscomm.com**
                                      **e-mail: mail@harriscomm.com**
*Patricia Bellan Gillen, Author*
*Bill Williams, National Sales Manager*

Learn signs for numbers 0 through 20, and 30 through 100 by tens. *$14.95*

*56 pages  Hardcover*

**3011  Rosey: The Imperfect Angel**

**Special Needs Project**
**324 State Street**
**Santa Barbara, CA  93105**          **805-962-8087**
                                        **800-333-6867**
                                        **FAX 805-962-5087**
                                        **e-mail: books@specialneeds.com**
*Sandra Lee Peckinpah, Author*
*Trisha Moore, Illustrator*

Rosie, an angel with a cleft palate, works hard in her heavenly garden after the Boss Angel declares her disfigured mouth as lovely as a rose petal. Her reward is to be born on earth, as a baby with a cleft. *$15.95*

**3012  Scare Bear**

**Teddy Bear Press**
**3639 Midway Drive**
**San Diego, CA  92110**          **619-223-7311**
                                   **FAX 619-255-2158**
                                   **http://www.teddybearpress.net**
                                   **e-mail: fparker@teddybearpress.net**
*Fran Parker, President*

An 11x17 big book with color illustrations and a large print format uses the same simple sentence structure fount in I Can Read and Reading Is Fun programs. This story adds seasonal words to the developing sight vocabulary found in our reading programs. *$25.95*

*13 pages*
*ISBN 1-928876-16-1*

**3013  Signing is Fun: A Child's Introduction to the Basics of Sign Language**

**Harris Communications**
**15155 Technology Drive**
**Eden Prairie, MN  55344**          952-906-1180
                                      800-825-6758
                                FAX 952-906-1099
                                TDY:952-906-1198
**http://www.harriscomm.com**
*Mickey Flodin, Author*

The author of Signing for Kids offers children their first glimpse at a whole new world. Starting with the alphabet and working up to everyday phrases, this volume uses clear instructions on how to begin using American Sign Language and features an informative introduction to signing and its importance. One hundred and fifty illustrations. *$9.00*

*95 pages  Paperback*

**3014  Sixth Grade Can Really Kill You**

**Penquin Putnam Publishing Group**
**375 Hudson Street**
**New York, NY  10014**          212-366-2000
                                 800-788-6262
                            FAX 212-366-2666
*Barthe DeClements, Author*

Helen's learning difficulties cause her to act up and are threatening to keep her from passing sixth grade. *$4.60*

*Paperback*
*ISBN 0-670806-56-0*

**3015  Snowbear**

**Teddy Bear Press**
**3639 Midway Drive**
**San Diego, CA  92110**          619-223-7311
                            FAX 619-255-2158
            **http://www.teddybearpress.net**
            **e-mail: fparker@teddybearpress.net**
*Fran Parker, President*

An 11x17 big book with color illustrations and a large print format uses the same simple sentence structure fount in I Can Read and Reading Is Fun programs. This story adds seasonal words to the developing sight vocabulary found in our reading programs. *$25.95*

*13 pages*
*ISBN 1-928876-12-9*

**3016  Someone Special, Just Like You**

**Special Needs Project**
**324 State Street**
**Santa Barbara, CA  93105**          805-962-8087
                                      800-333-6867
                                 FAX 805-962-5087
            **e-mail: books@specialneeds.com**
*Tricia Brown, Author*
*Fran Ortiz, Photographer*

A handsome photo-essay including a range of youngsters with disabilities at four preschools in the San Francisco Bay area. *$6.25*

*19 pages*

**3017  Unicorns Are Real!**

**Learning Disabilities Association of America**
**4156 Library Road**
**Pittsburgh, PA  15234**          412-341-1515
                             FAX 412-344-0224
                          **http://www.ldanatl.org**
                          **e-mail: ldanatl@usaor.net**

This mega best-seller provides 65 practical, easy-to-follow-lessons to develop the much ignored right brain tendencies of children. These simple yet dramatically effective ideas and activities have helped thousands with learning difficulties. Includes an easy-to-administer screening checklist to determine hemisphere dominance, engaging instructional activities that draw on the intuitive, nonverbal abilities of the right brain, a list of skills associated with each brain hemisphere and more. *$14.95*

**3018  Valentine Bear**

**Teddy Bear Press**
**3639 Midway Drive**
**San Diego, CA  92110**          619-223-7311
                            FAX 619-255-2158
            **http://www.teddybearpress.net**
            **e-mail: fparker@teddybearpress.net**
*Fran Parker, President*

An 11x17 big book with color illustrations and a large print format uses the same simple sentence structure fount in I Can Read and Reading Is Fun programs. This story adds seasonal words to the developing sight vocabulary found in our reading programs. *$25.95*

*13 pages*
*ISBN 1-928876-13-7*

**3019  Zipper, the Kid with ADHD**

**Woodbine House**
**6510 Bells Mill Road**
**Bethesda, MD  20817**          301-897-3570
                                 800-843-7323
                            FAX 301-897-5838
            **http://www.woodbinehouse.com**
            **e-mail: info@Woodbinehouse.com**
*Caroline Janover, Author*
*Rick Powell, Illustrator*

Readers will enjoy this middle-grade novel's amusing but realistic portrayal of the effect of attention deficit hyperactivity disorder on a young person's life. Zipper, the Kid with ADHD will encourage other kids to find ways to manage their behavior, and give their friends a look at what it's like to have this disorder. *$11.95*

*108 pages  Paperback*
*ISBN 0-933149-95-6*

## Law

**3020   ADA Quiz Book: 3rd Edition**

Rocky Mountain Dis. & Bus. Technical Assistance
3630 Sinton Road
Colorado Springs, CO  80907          719-444-0268
                                     800-949-4232
                                 FAX 719-444-0269
http://www.adainformation.org
e-mail: regionviii@mtc-inc.com
*Jana Copeland, Editor*

A collection of puzzles, quizzes, questions and case
studies on the Americans with Disabilities Act of 1990
and accessible information technology. Features sections on ADA basics, employment, state and local
governments, public accommodations, architectural
accessibility, disability etiquette, effective communication, and electronic and information technology.
*$9.95*

*81 pages  4.00 shipping*

**3021   Americans with Disabilities Act Management
Training Program**

RPM Press
PO Box 31483
Tucson, AZ  85751               520-886-1990
                                888-810-1990
                            FAX 520-886-1990
http://www.rpmpress.com/
*Jan Stonebraker, Operations Manager*

Provides authoritative information on the Americans
with Disabilities Act and compliance requirements for
employers, schools and other entities which provide
employment, education or related opportunities to
persons with disabilities. *$142.95*

**3022   Approaching Equality: Education of the Deaf**

T-J Publishers
817 Silver Spring Avenue
Silver Spring, MD  20910        301-585-4440
                                800-999-1168
                            FAX 301-585-5930
                            TDY:301-585-4440
e-mail: tjpubinc@aol.com
*Frank Bowe, Author*
*Angela K Thames, President*
*Jerald A Murphy, VP*

Public education laws guarantee special education for
all deaf and learning disabled children, but many find
the special education system confusing, or are unsure
of their rights under current laws. For anyone with interest in education, advocacy and the disabled community, this book reviews dramatic developments in
education of special children, youth and adults.
*$12.95*

*112 pages*
*ISBN 0-932666-39-6*

**3023   Attention Deficit Disorder and the Law**

JKL Communications
PO Box 40157
Washington, DC  20016           202-223-5097
                            FAX 202-223-5096
http://www.lathamlaw.org
e-mail: plath3@his.com

*$29.00*

**3024   Discipline**

Special Education Resource Center
25 Industrial Park Road
Middletown, CT  06457           860-632-1485
                            FAX 860-632-8870
*JJ Jennings*
*CL Weatherly*

A general analysis of the problems encountered in the
discipline of students with disabilities. Discussion of
the legal principles of discipline that have evolved
pursuant to Public Law 94-142.

**3025   Dispute Resolution Journal**

American Arbitration Association
335 Madison Avenue
New York, NY  10017             212-716-3972
                            FAX 212-716-5906
e-mail: OConnorR@adr.org
*Ted Pons, Director of Publications*

Provides information on mediation, arbitration and
other dispute resolution alternatives. *$100.00*

*100 pages*

**3026   Documentation and the Law**

JKL Communications
PO Box 40157
Washington, DC  20016           202-223-5097
                            FAX 202-223-5096
http://www.lathamlaw.org
e-mail: plath3@his.com

*$29.00*

**3027   Education of the Handicapped: Laws**

William Hein & Company
1285 Main Street
Buffalo, NY  14209              716-882-2600
                                800-828-7871
                            FAX 716-883-8100
http://www.wshein.com/
*Bernard D Reams Jr, Author*

Focuses on elementary and secondary Education Act
of 1965 and its amendment, Education For All Handicapped Children Act of 1975 and its amendments and
acts providing services for the disabled.

**3028   Ethical and Legal Issues in School Counseling**

American School Counselor Association
801 N Fairfax Street
Alexandria, VA  22314           703-683-2722
                                800-306-4722
                            FAX 703-683-1619
http://www.schoolcounselor.org
e-mail: asca@schoolcounselor.org
*Stephanie Will, Office Manager*

Perhaps the increase in litigation involving educators and mental health practitioners is a factor. Certainly the laws are changing or at least are being interpreted differently, requiring counselors to stay up-to-date. The process of decision-making and some of the more complex issues in ethical and legal areas are summarized in this digest. *$40.50*

*ISBN 1-556200-55-2*

**3029  Individuals with Disabilities: Implementing the Newest Laws**

**Corwin Press**
**2455 Teller Road**
**Thousand Oaks, CA  91320**          805-499-9734
                                       800-818-7243
                                    FAX 805-499-5323
                           http://www.corwinpress.com
                          e-mail: order@corwinpress.com
*Patricia F First & Joan L Curcio, Author*
*Kimberly Gonzales, Marketing Director*
*Robb Clouse, Senior Acquisitions Editor*

Aimed at school administrators, this highly readable book covers the three major pieces of legislation: Americans with Disabilities Act of 1990; Individuals with Disabilities Education Act; and the Rehabilitation Act of 1973. Suitable for lay public use, anyone needing an overview of the laws affecting education and disabilities. *$12.95*

*64 pages*
*ISBN 0-803960-55-7*

**3030  Learning Disabilities and the Law**

**JKL Communications**
**PO Box 40157**
**Washington, DC  20016**          202-223-5097
                                 FAX 202-223-5096
                        http://www.lathamlaw.org
                        e-mail: plath3@his.com

*$29.00*

**3031  Least Restrictive Environment**

**Special Education Resource Center**
**25 Industrial Park Road**
**Middletown, CT  06457**          860-632-1485
                                 FAX 860-632-8870
*JJ Jennings*
*CL Weatherly*

A general discussion and analysis of the mandate to educate students with disabilities to the maximum extent appropriate with nondisabled students.

**3032  Legal Notes for Education**

**Oakstone Legal and Business Publishing**
**6801 Cahaba Valley Road**
**Burmingham, AL  35242**          205-991-5188
                                   800-365-4900
                                FAX 205-995-1926
                        e-mail: info@andrewspub.com
*Nancy McMeekin, CEO*

Summaries of court decisions dealing with education law. *$122.00*

**3033  Legal Rights of Persons with Disabilities: An Analysis of Federal Law**

**LRP Publications**
**747 Dresher Road**
**Horsham, PA  19044**          215-784-0941
                                800-341-7874
                            FAX 215-784-9639
                            TDY:215-658-0938
                         http://www.lrp.com
                       e-mail: custserv@lrp.com
*Bonnie P Tucker & Bruce A Goldstein, Author*
*Honora McDowell, Product Group Manager*

This book will provide professionals working with the disabled a comprehensive analysis of the rights accorded individuals with disabilities under federal law. *$185.00*

*2226 pages  +$7.50*
*ISBN 0-934753-46-6*

**3034  New Directions**

**Association of State Mental Health Program Direct.**
**66 Canal Center Plaza**
**Alexandria, VA  22314**          703-739-9333
                                 FAX 703-548-9517
                         http://www.nasddds.org
A newsletter offering information on laws, amendments, and legislation affecting the disabled. *$55.00*

**3035  New IDEA Amendments: Assistive Technology Devices and Services**

**Special Education Resource Center**
**25 Industrial Park Road**
**Middletown, CT  06457**          860-632-1485
                                 FAX 860-623-8870
*JJ Jennings*
*CL Weatherly*

A discussion of new mandates created by the 1990 Amendments to Public Law 94-142. An overview of the requirement for the provision of assistive technology devices and services as well as a discussion on the transition services that are to be provided to disabled adolescents.

**3036  Numbers That Add Up to Educational Rights for Children with Disabilities**

**Children's Defense Fund**
**25 E Street NW**
**Washington, DC  20001**          202-628-8787
                                 FAX 202-662-3510
                       http://www.childrensdefense.org
Information on the laws 94-142 and 504.

**3037  Opening Doors: Connecting Students to Curriculum, Classmate, and Learning**

**PEAK Parent Center**
**611 N Weber**
**Colorado Springs, CO  80903**          719-531-9400
                                          800-284-0251
                                       FAX 719-531-9452
                                       TDY:719-531-5403
                              http://www.peakparent.org
                            e-mail: info@peakparent.org
*Barbara Buswell, Editor*
*Beth Schaffner, Editor*
*Alison Seyler, Editor*

Written for educators and parents about including all students in general education classes and activities. Chapter topics, coauthored by leading education experts, include instructional strategies, curriculum modifications, behavior, standards, literacy, and providing supports. *$13.00*

*ISBN 0-884720-12-9*

**3038 Parent's Guide to the Social Security Administration**

**Eden Services**
**One Eden Way**
**Princeton, NJ 08540**          609-987-0099
          FAX 609-987-0243
     http://www.members.aol.com/edensvcs
          e-mail: info@edenservices.org
*David L Holmes EdD, Executive Director/President*
*Anne Holmes, Director Outreach Support Svcs*

A parents' guide to the Social Security Administration and Social Security Work Incentive Programs. *$16.00*

**3039 Procedural Due Process**

**Special Education Resource Center**
**25 Industrial Park Road**
**Middletown, CT 06457**          860-632-1485
          FAX 860-632-8870
*JJ Jennings*
*CL Weatherly*

Analyzes the importance of the procedural safeguards afforded to parents and their children with disabilities by the Public Law 94-142. Safeguards are discussed and possible legal implications are addressed.

**3040 Public Law 94-142: An Overview**

**Special Education Resource Center**
**25 Industrial Park Road**
**Middletown, CT 06457**          860-632-1485
          FAX 860-632-8870
*JJ Jennings*
*CL Weatherly*

An overview of the general provisions of the Individuals with Disabilities Education Act, commonly referred to as Public Law 94-142. Designed to provide the less-experienced viewer with a fundamental understanding of the Public Law and its significance.

**3041 Purposeful Integration: Inherently Equal**

**Federation for Children with Special Needs**
**1135 Tremont Street**
**Boston, MA 02120**          617-236-7210
          800-331-0688
          FAX 617-572-2094
          TDY:617-236-7210
          http://www.fcsn.org
          e-mail: fcsninfo@fcsn.org
*Richard J Robison, Executive Director*

This publication covers integration, mainstreaming, and least restrictive environments. *$8.00*

*55 pages*

**3042 Section 504 of the Rehabilitation Act**

**Special Education Resource Center**
**25 Industrial Park Road**
**Middletown, CT 06457**          860-632-1485
          FAX 860-632-8870
*JJ Jennings*
*CL Weatherly*

A general overview of the legal implications of the Rehabilitation Act and its implementing regulations, a law that is often forgotten in the process of appropriately educating children with disabilities.

**3043 Section 504: Help for the Learning Disabled College Student**

**Connecticut Assoc. for Children and Adults with LD**
**25 Van Zant Street**
**East Norwalk, CT 06855**          203-838-5010
          FAX 203-866-6108
          http://www.CACLD.org
          e-mail: cacld@juno.com
*Joan Sedita, Author*
*Marie Armstrong, Information Specialist*

Provides a review of Section 504 of the Vocational Rehabilitation Act as it relates specifically to the learning disabled. *$3.25*

*$2.50 shipping*

**3044 So You're Going to a Hearing: Preparing for Public Law 94-142**

**Learning Disabilities Association of America**
**4156 Library Road**
**Pittsburgh, PA 15234**          412-341-1515
          FAX 412-344-0224
          http://www.ldanatl.org
          e-mail: ldanatl@usaor.net
A public informational source offering legal advice to children and youth with learning disabilities. *$5.50*

**3045 Special Education Law Update**

**Data Research**
**4635 Nicols Road**
**Eagan, MN 55122**          651-452-8267
          800-365-4900
          FAX 651-452-8694
          http://www.dataresearchinc.com
*Bruce Montgomery*

Monthly newsletter service. Cases, legislation, administrative regulations and law review articles dealing with special education law. Annual index and binder included. *$159.00*

**3046 Special Education in Juvenile Corrections**

**Council for Exceptional Children**
**1110 N Glebe Road**
**Arlington, VA 22201**          703-620-3660
          888-232-7733
          FAX 703-264-9494
          http://www.cec.sped.org/
*Peter E Leone, Author*
*Robert B Rutherford Jr, Author*

This topic is of increasing concern. This book describes the demographics of incarcerated youth and suggests some promising practices that are being used. *$8.90*

> *26 pages*
> *ISBN 0-865862-03-6*

**3047  Special Law for Special People**

**Smith, Howard & Ajax**
**3333 Peachtree Road NE**
**Atlanta, GA  30326**
                                              **FAX 404-239-1930**

*Julie J Jennings, Contact*
*Charles L Weatherly, Contact*

A ten-tape video series that is designed to assist in educating regular education personnel as to the legal requirements of IDEA and Section 504.

**3048  Statutes, Regulations and Case LawProtecting Disabled Individuals**

**Data Research**
**4635 Nicols Road**
**Eagan, MN  55122**
                                              **651-452-8267**
                                              **800-365-4900**
                                        **FAX 651-452-8694**
                  **http://www.dataresearchinc.com**
*Bruce Montgomery*

Annum book presenting annotated statutes and regulations relevant to disability law issues. *$125.00*

**3049  Stories Behind Special Education Case Law**

**Special Needs Project**
**324 State Street**
**Santa Barbara, CA  93105**
                                              **805-962-8087**
                                              **800-333-6867**
                                        **FAX 805-962-5087**
                  **e-mail: books@specialneeds.com**
*Ree Martin, Author*

The personal stories behind ten leading court cases that shaped the basic principles of special education law. *$12.95*

> *150 pages*

**3050  Students with Disabilities and SpecialEducation**

**Data Research**
**4635 Nicols Road**
**Eagan, MN  55122**
                                              **651-452-8267**
                                              **800-365-4900**
                                        **FAX 651-452-8694**
                  **http://www.dataresearchinc.com**

Annual book presenting case summaries, citations, statutes and regulations relevant to special education. *$139.00*

> *500+ pages*
> *ISBN 0-939675-44-7*

**3051  Technology, Curriculum, and ProfessionalDevelopment**

**Corwin Press**
**2455 Teller Road**
**Thousand Oaks, CA  91320**
                                              **805-499-9734**
                                              **800-818-7243**
                                        **FAX 805-499-5323**
                  **http://www.corwinpress.com**
                  **e-mail: order@corwinpress.com**
*John Woodward, Larry Cuban, Author*
*Kimberly Gonzales, Marketing Director*
*Robb Clouse, Senior Acquisitions Editor*

Adapting schools to meet the needs of students with disabilities. The history of special education technologies, the requirements of IDEA'97, and the successes and obstacles for special education technology implementation. *$34.95*

> *264 pages*
> *ISBN 0-761977-43-0*

**3052  Testing Students with Disabilities**

**Corwin Press**
**2455 Teller Road**
**Thousand Oaks, CA  91320**
                                              **805-499-9734**
                                              **800-818-7243**
                                        **FAX 805-499-5323**
                  **http://www.corwinpress.com**
                  **e-mail: order@corwinpress.com**
*Martha Thurloiw, Judy Elliott, James Ysseldyke, Author*
*Kimberly Gonzales, Marketing Director*
*Robb Clouse, Senior Acquisitions Editor*

Practical strategies for complying with district and state requirements. Helps translate the issues surrounding state and district testing of students with disabilities, including IDEA, into what educators need to know and do. *$ 34.95*

> *296 pages*
> *ISBN 0-803965-52-4*

**3053  US Department of Justice: DisabilitiesRights Section**

**PO Box 66738**
**Washington, DC  20035**
                                              **800-514-0301**
                                        **FAX 202-307-1198**
              **http://www.usd.j.gov/crt/ada/adahoml.htm**

Information concerning the rights people with learning disabilities have under the Americans with Disabilities Act.

## Parents & Professionals

**3054  125 Brain Games for Babies**

**Therapro**
**225 Arlington Street**
**Framingham, MA  01702**
                                              **508-872-9494**
                                              **800-257-5376**
                                        **FAX 508-875-2062**
                  **http://www.theraproducts.com**
                  **e-mail: info@theraproducts.com**
*Jackie Silberg, Author*

Packed with everyday opportunities to enhance brain development of children from birth to 12 months. Each game includes notes on recent brain research in practical terms.

**3055  A Miracle to Believe In**

**Option Indigo Press**
**2080 S Undermountain Road**
**Sheffield, MA  01257**        413-229-8727
                            800-562-7171
                        FAX 413-229-8727
                    http://www.optionindio.com
                    e-mail: indigo@bcn.net
*Barry Neil Kaufman, Author*

A group of people from all walks of life come together and are transformed as they reach out, under the direction of Kaufman, to help a little boy the medical world had given up as hopeless. This heartwarming journey of loving a child back to life will not only inspire, but presents a compelling new way to deal with life's traumas and difficulties. *$7.99*

*ISBN 0-449201-08-2*

**3056  A Practical Parent's Handbook on TeachingChildren with Learning Disabilities**

**Charles C Thomas Publisher**
**2600 S 1st Street**
**Springfield, IL  62704**        217-789-8980
                            800-258-8980
                        FAX 217-789-9130
                    http://www.ccthomas.com
*Shelby Holley, Author*

Gives enough information for an adult with no previous teaching experience to design and implement an effective remedial program. Books sent on approval. *$68.95*

*308 pages  Paper $43.95*
*ISBN 0-398059-03-9*

**3057  ADHD in Adolescents: Diagnosis andTreatment**

**Guilford Publications**
**72 Spring Street**
**New York, NY  10012**        212-431-9800
                            800-365-7006
                        FAX 212-966-6708
                    http://www.guilford.com
                    e-mail: info@guilford.com
*Arthur L Robin, Author*

Here Dr. Robin teaches us not only about the facts of the disorder, but also about its nature and the proper means of clinically evaluating it. Includes numerous reproducible forms for clinicians and clients, among them rating scales and detailed checklists for psychological testing, interviewing, treatment planning, and school and family interventions. *$46.95*

*461 pages  Hardcover*
*ISBN 1-572303-91-3*

**3058  About Dyslexia: Unraveling the Myth**

**Connecticut Assoc. for Children and Adults with LD**
**25 Van Zant Street**
**East Norwalk, CT  06855**        203-838-5010
                        FAX 203-866-6108
                    http://www.CACLD.org
*Priscilla Vail, Author*

This book focuses on the communication patterns of strength and weaknesses in dyslexic people from early childhood through adulthood. *$7.95*

*49 pages*
*ISBN 0-935493-34-4*

**3059  Absudities of Special Education: The Best of Ants....Flying and Logs**

**Peytral Publicatons**
**PO Box 1162**
**Minnetonka, MN  55345**        952-949-8707
                            877-739-8725
                        FAX 952-906-9777
                    http://www.peytral.com
                    e-mail: help@peytral.com
*Michael F Giangreco, Author*

Now available in this full color edition. Create beautiful transperances or use in PowerPoint presentations for staff development. Also a great gift for parents of educators. *$39.95*

*114 pages*
*ISBN 1-890455-40-7*

**3060  Access Aware: Extending Your Reach to People with Disabilities**

**Alliance for Technology Access**
**1304 Southpoint Boulevard**
**Petaluma, CA  94954**        707-778-3011
                        FAX 707-765-2080
                    http://www.ataccess.org
                    e-mail: atainfo@ataccess.org
*Mary Lester, Executive Director*

This easy-to-use manual is designed to help any organization become more accessible for people with disabilities. *$45.00*

*219 pages*
*ISBN 0-897933-00-1*

**3061  Activity Schedules for Children with Autism: A Guide for Parents and Professionals**

**Woodbine House**
**6510 Bells Mill Road**
**Bethesda, MD  20817**        301-897-3570
                            800-843-7323
                        FAX 301-897-5838
                    http://www.woodbinehouse.com
                    e-mail: info@woodbinehouse.com
*Lynn E McClannahan PhD, Author*
*Patricia J Krantz PhD, Author*

Detailed instructions and examples help parents prepare their child's first activity schedule, then progress to more varied and sophisticated schedules. The goal of this system is for children with autism to make effective use of unstructured time, handle changes in routine, and help them choose among an established set of home, school, and leisure activities independently. *$14.95*

*117 pages  Paperback*
*ISBN 0-933149-93-X*

**3062  Alternate Assessments for Students with Disabilities**

**Corwin Press**
**2455 Teller Road**
**Thousand Oaks, CA  91320**          **805-499-9734**
                                      **800-818-7243**
                              **FAX 805-499-5323**
                  **http://www.corwinpress.com**
                  **e-mail: order@corwinpress.com**
*Sandra J Thompson, Rachel F Quenemoen, Author*
*Kimberly Gonzales, Marketing Director*
*Robb Clouse, Senior Acquisitions Editor*

Distinguished group of experts in a landmark book, co-published with the Council for Exceptional Children show you how to shift to high expectations for all learners, improve schooling for all. *$29.95*

*168 pages*
*ISBN 0-761977-74-0*

**3063  American Sign Language Concise Dictionary**

**Harris Communications**
**15155 Technology Drive**
**Eden Prairie, MN  55344**          **952-906-1180**
                                      **800-825-6758**
                              **FAX 952-906-1099**
                              **TDY:952-906-1198**
                  **http://www.harriscomm.com**
*Martin Sternberg, Author*

A portable version containing 2,000 of the most commonly used words and phrases in ASL. Illustrated with easy-to-follow hand, arm and facial movements. *$11.95*

*737 pages  Paperback*

**3064  American Sign Language Dictionary: A Comprehensive Abridgement**

**Harris Communications**
**15155 Technology Drive**
**Eden Prairie, MN  55344**          **952-906-1180**
                                      **800-825-6758**
                              **FAX 952-906-1099**
                              **TDY:952-906-1198**
                  **http://www.harriscomm.com**
*Martin Sternberg, Author*

An abridged version of American Sign Language. A comprehensive dictionary with 4,400 illustrated signs. It has 500 new signs and 1,500 new illustrations. Third edition. *$24.00*

*772 pages  Paperback*

**3065  American Sign Language: A Comprehensive Dictionary**

**Harris Communications**
**15155 Technology Drive**
**Eden Prairie, MN  55344**          **952-906-1180**
                                      **800-825-6758**
                              **FAX 952-906-1099**
                              **TDY:952-906-1198**
                  **http://www.harriscomm.com**
*Martin Sternberg, Author*

Contains over 5,000 entries and cross-references, an extensive bibliography and seven foreign language indexes. Contains clear illustrations and easily understood directions for forming and using each sign. *$75.00*

*1132 pages*

**3066  Another Door to Learning**

**Crossroad Publishing**
**481 8th Avenue**
**New York, NY  10001**          **212-868-1801**
                              **FAX 212-868-2171**
                  **e-mail: sales@crossroadpublishing.com**
*Judy Schwartz, Author*
*John Jones, Executive Manager*

Stories of eleven atypical learners who got the help they needed to make a lasting difference in their lives.

*ISBN 0-824513-85-1*

**3067  Answers to Distraction**

**Pantheon Books**
**201 E 50th Street**
**New York, NY  10022**          **212-751-2600**
                                      **800-638-6460**
                              **FAX 212-572-8700**
*Edward M Hallowell, Author*
*John Ratey, Author*

Responses to common questions the authors' audiences have asked, organized by topic.

*ISBN 0-679439-73-0*

**3068  Ants in His Pants: Absurdities and Realities of Special Education**

**Peytral Publication**
**PO Box 1162**
**Minnetonka, MN  55345**          **952-949-8707**
                                      **877-739-8725**
                              **FAX 612-906-9777**
                  **http://www.peytral.com**
                  **e-mail: help@peytral.com**
*Michael F Giangreco, Author*

With wit, humor, and profound one liners, this book will transform your thinking as you take a lighter look at the often comical and occcasionally harsh truth in the field of special education. This carefully crafted collection of 101 cartoons can be made into transparencies for staff development and training. *$19.95*

*128 pages*
*ISBN 1-890455-42-3*

**3069 Assessment & Instruction of Culturally & Linguistically Diverse Students**

Books on Special Children
PO Box 305
Congers, NY 10920          845-638-1236
FAX 845-638-0847
http://www.boscbooks.com/
e-mail: irene@boscbooks.com
*Sam Goldstein, PhD, Author*

Appropriate assessments and educational models and practices are discussed. Also, educational environment and how to help problems, understanding diversity and disability, legal aspects. *$49.00*

*254 pages  hardcover*
*ISBN 0-205156-29-0*

**3070 Attention-Deficit Hyperactivity Disorder**

Slosson Educational Publications
538 Buffalo Road
East Aurora, NY 14052          716-652-0930
800-828-4800
FAX 800-655-3840
http://www.slosson.com
e-mail: slosson@slosson.com
*Sue Larson, Author*

The book addresses issues of theory and practice quickly, with compassion and practicality and, most importantly, is very effective. Well-grounded answers and suggestions which would facilitate behavior, learning, social-emotional functioning, and other factors in preschool and adolescence are discussed.

**3071 Attention-Deficit Hyperactivity Disorder: A Handbook for Diagnosis and Treatment, 2nd Edition**

Guilford Publications
72 Spring Street
New York, NY 10012          212-431-9800
800-365-7006
FAX 212-966-6708
http://www.guilford.com
e-mail: info@guilford.com
*Russell A Barkley, Author*

Incorporates the latest findings on the nature, diagnosis, assessment, and treatment of ADHD. Clinicians, researchers, and students will find practical and richly referenced information on nearly every aspect of the disorder. *$ 55.00*

*628 pages*

**3072 Autism and the Family: Problems, Prospects and Coping with the Disorder**

Charles C Thomas Publisher
2600 S 1st Street
Springfield, IL 62704          217-789-8980
800-258-8980
FAX 217-789-9130
*David E Gray, Author*

Explores aspects of the family's experience of autism, offering a sociological account of what it is like to be parents of an autistic child. *$45.95*

*210 pages  Cloth*
*ISBN 0-398068-42-9*

**3073 Backyards & Butterflies: Ways to Include Children with Disabilities**

Brookline Books
300 Bedford Street
Manchester, NH 03101          617-734-6772
FAX 603-922-3348
http://www.brooklinebooks.com

*72 pages*

**3074 Behavior Management Applications for Teachers and Parents**

Prentice Hall Publishing Company
One Lake Street
Upper Saddle River, NJ 07458
800-382-3419
FAX 201-236-7141
http://www.prenhall.com
*Thomas J Zirpoli, Author*

A clear, extensive presentation of the technical basis and appropriate implementation strategies for managing behavior in classrooms, day care centers, even at home.

*ISBN 0-135205-37-9*

**3075 Behavior Technology Guide Book**

One Eden Way
Princeton, NJ 08540          609-987-0099
FAX 609-987-0243
http://www.edenservices.org
e-mail: info@edenservices.org
*David L Holmes, Executive Director/President*
*Anne Holmes, Director Outreach Support Svcs*

Techniques for increasing and decreasing behavior using the principles of applied behavior analysis and related teaching strategies — discrete trial, shaping, task analysis and chaining. *$50.00*

**3076 Beyond the Rainbow**

Learning Disabilities Association of America
4156 Library Road
Pittsburgh, PA 15234          412-341-1515
FAX 412-344-0224
http://www.ldanatl.org
e-mail: ldanatl@usaor.net
*Patricia Dodds, Author*

A guide for parents with children with dyslexia and other disabilities. *$16.00*

**3077 Bridges to Reading**

Parents & Educators Resource Center
PO Box 389
Brisbane, CA 94005          650-655-2410
800-471-9545
FAX 650-655-2411

Helps parents identify, understand, and address reading problems. Includes eight booklets, national resources, and information on tutoring and Attention Deficit/Hyperactivity Disorder. *$20.00*

**3078 Building Healthy Minds**

Perseus Publishing
5500 Central Avenue
Boulder, CO 80301

800-386-5656
FAX 800-822-4090

*Stanley Greenspan, MD, Author*

Explains what sorts of games, conversations and other interactions foster cognitive, emotional and moral development. *$17.00*

*398 pages Paperback*
*ISBN 0-738203-56-4*

**3079 Building a Child's Self-Image: A Guide for Parents**

Learning Disabilities Association of America
4156 Library Road
Pittsburgh, PA 15234
412-341-1515
FAX 412-344-0224
http://www.ldanatl.org
e-mail: ldanatl@usaor.net

*$9.25*

**3080 Care of the Neurologically Handicapped Child**

Special Needs Project
324 State Street
Santa Barbara, CA 93105
805-962-8087
800-333-6867
FAX 805-962-5087
e-mail: books@specialneeds.com

*Arthur Prensky, Author*

This book describes normal and abnormal development, what to expect from the various specialists parents may consult, and seven of the most common neurological disorders. *$32.95*

*331 pages*

**3081 Caring for Your Baby and Young Child: Birth to Age 5**

Bantam
400 Hahn Road
Westminster, MD 21157
800-726-0600
FAX 800-659-2436

*Sponsored by the American Academy of Pediatrics, Author*

Reliable information on child rearing, with particular emphasis on health issues. *$32.95*

*736 pages Hardcover*
*ISBN 0-553110-45-4*

**3082 Children with Autism**

Special Needs Project
324 State Street
Santa Barbara, CA 93105
805-962-8087
800-333-6867
FAX 805-962-5087
e-mail: books@specialneeds.com

*Michael Powers, Author*

Recommended as the first book that parents should read, this book provides a complete introduction to autism, while easing a family's fears and concerns as they adjust and cope with their child's disorder. *$14.95*

*368 pages*

**3083 Children with Cerebral Palsy: A Parent's Guide**

Therapro
225 Arlington Street
Framingham, MA 01702
508-872-9494
800-257-5376
FAX 508-875-2062
http://www.theraproducts.com
e-mail: info@theraproducts.com

*Elaine Geralis, Editor*

This book explains what cerebral palsy is, and discusses its diagnosis and treatment. It also offers information and advice concerning daily care, early intervention, therapy, educational options and family life.

**3084 Children with Special Needs: A Resource Guide for Parents, Educators, Social Workers...**

Charles C Thomas Publisher
2600 S 1st Street
Springfield, IL 62704
217-789-8980
800-258-8980
FAX 217-789-9130

*Karen L Lungu, Author*

Writing from her own experience as the parent of a special needs child and with the background of both a therapist and educator, the author presents a most readable text discussing developmental disabilities, emotional and intellectual challenges, neurological disabilities, communication and learning disorders, attention deficit disorders and more. *$49.95*

*234 pages Cloth*
*ISBN 0-398069-33-6*

**3085 Children with Tourette Syndrome**

Woodbine House
6510 Bells Mill Road
Bethesda, MD 20817
301-897-3570
800-843-7323
FAX 301-897-5838
http://www.woodbinehouse.com
e-mail: info@Woodbinehouse.com

*Tracy Haerle, Editor*

A guide for parents of children and teenagers with Tourette syndrome. Covers medical, educational, legal, family life, daily care, and emotional issues, as well as explanations of related conditions. *$14.95*

*352 pages Paperback*
*ISBN 0-933149-39-5*

**3086 Classroom Success for the LD and ADHD Child**

Therapro
225 Arlington Street
Framingham, MA 01702
508-872-9494
800-257-5376
FAX 508-875-2062
http://www.theraproducts.com
e-mail: info@theraproducts.com

*Suzanne H Stevens, Author*

Helpful book for parents and therapists who work with children with learning disabilities. It addresses specific issues such as organization, homework and concentration. Stevens offers practical suggestions on adjusting teaching techniques, adapting texts, adjusting classroom management procedures and testing and grading fairly.

*Revised*

**3087    Common Ground: Whole Language & Phonics Working Together**

**Modern Learning Press**
**PO Box 167**
**Rosemont, NJ  08556**                609-397-2214
                                       800-627-5867
                                  FAX 609-397-3467
*Priscilla L Vail, Author*

Offers guidelines for reading instruction in the primary grades that combines whole language with multisensory phonics instruction. *$9.95*

*ISBN 0-935493-27-1*

**3088    Common Sense About Dyslexia**

**Special Needs Project**
**324 State Street**
**Santa Barbara, CA  93105**           805-962-8087
                                       800-333-6867
                                  FAX 805-962-5087
                   e-mail: books@specialneeds.com
*Ann Marshall Huston, Author*

Offers important, need-to-know information about dyslexia. *$16.95*

*300 pages*

**3089    Communication Skills in Children with Down Syndrome**

**Woodbine House**
**6510 Bells Mill Road**
**Bethesda, MD  20817**                301-897-3570
                                       800-843-7323
                                  FAX 301-897-5838
                   http://www.woodbinehouse.com
                   e-mail: info@Woodbinehouse.com
*Libby Kumin, PhD, CCC-SLP, Author*

Accessible information, advice and practical home activities for children and adolescents with Down syndrome. *$14.95*

*256 pages  Paperback*
*ISBN 0-933149-53-0*

**3090    Complete IEP Guide: How to Advocate for Your Special Ed Child**

**NOLO**
**950 Parker Street**
**Berkeley, CA  94710**                510-549-1976
                                       800-955-4775
                                  FAX 510-548-5902
                         http://www.nolo.com
*Attorney Lawrence M Siegel, Author*
*Maira Dizgalvis, Trade Customer Service Manager*
*Susan McConnell, Director Sales*
*Natasha Kaluza, Sales Assistant*

This book has all the plain-English suggestions, strategies, resources and forms to develop an effective IEP. *$17.47*

*300 pages  paperback*
*ISBN 0-873376-07-2*

**3091    Complete Learning Disabilities Resource Library**

**Slosson Educational Publications**
**538 Buffalo Road**
**East Aurora, NY  14052**             888-756-7766
                                       800-828-4800
                                  FAX 800-655-3840
                          http://www.sloss.com
                   e-mail: slosson@slosson.com
*Joan M Harwell, Author*

These volumes provide easy-to-use tips, techniques, and activities to help students with learning disabilities at all grade levels. *$29.95*

**3092    Computer & Web Resources for People with Disabilities: A Guide to...**

**Alliance for Technology Access**
**1304 Southpoint Boulevard**
**Petaluma, CA  94954**                707-778-3011
                                  FAX 707-765-2080
                         http://www.ataccess.org
                   e-mail: atainfo@ataccess.org
*Mary Lester, President*

This highly acclaimed book includes detailed descriptions of software, hardware and communication aids, plus a gold mine of published and online resources. *$20.75*

*364 pages*

**3093    Conducting Individualized Education Program Meetings that Withstand Due Process**

**Charles C Thomas Publisher**
**2600 S 1st Street**
**Springfield, IL  62704**             217-789-8980
                                       800-258-8980
                                  FAX 217-789-9130
                         http://www.ccthomas.com
                   e-mail: books@ccthomas.com
*James N Hollis, Author*

Written to help parents, school administrators, teachers and assessment professionals meet basic requirements of conducting an IEP team meeting in a way that produces defensible IEP decisions in a litigious environment. *$41.95*

*180 pages  Cloth*

**3094    Contemporary Intellectual Assessment: Theories, Tests and Issues**

**Guilford Publications**
**72 Spring Street**
**New York, NY  10012**                212-431-9800
                                       800-365-7006
                                  FAX 212-966-6708
                         http://www.guilford.com
                   e-mail: info@guilford.com
*Dawn P Flanagan, Editor*
*Judy L Genshaft, Editor*
*Patti L Harrison, Editor*

This unique volume provides a comprehensive conceptual and practical overview of the current state of the art of intellectual assessment. The book covers major theories of intelligence, methods of assessing human cognitive abilities, and issues related to the validity of current intelligence test batteries. *$60.00*

*597 pages*

**3095  Controversial Issues Confronting Special Education**

**Books on Special Children**
**PO Box 305**
**Congers, NY  10920**                845-638-1236
                                      FAX 845-638-0847
                          http://www.boscbooks.com/
                          e-mail: irene@boscbooks.com
*William Stainback, Author*

The book has divergent perspectives from many contributors on twelve important controversial issues. Inclusive education, talented and gifted, classification and labeling, assessments, classroom management, research, adult services and more. *$59.00*

*314 pages softcover*
*ISBN 0-205182-66-6*

**3096  Deciding What to Teach and How to Teach It Connecting Students through Curriculum and Instruction**

**PEAK Parent Center**
**611 N Weber**
**Colorado Springs, CO  80903**       719-531-9400
                                      800-284-0251
                                      FAX 719-531-9452
                                      TDY:719-531-5403
                          http://www.peakparent.org
                          e-mail: info@peakparent.org
*E Castagnera, D Fisher, K Rodifer, C Sax, Author*

Provides exciting and practical resource tips to ensure that all students participate and learn successfully in secondary general education classrooms. Lead the reader through a step-by-step process for starting with general curriculum, making accommodations and modifications, and providing appropriate supports. Planning grids and concrete strategies make this an essential tool for both secondary educators and families. *$13.00*

**3097  Defiant Children**

**Guilford Publications**
**72 Spring Street**
**New York, NY  10012**               212-431-9800
                                      800-365-7006
                                      FAX 212-966-6708
                          http://www.guilford.com
                          e-mail: info@guilford.com
*Russell A Barkley, Author*
*Christine M Benton, Author*

This book is written expressly for parents who are struggling with an unyielding or combative child, helping them understand what causes defiance, when it becomes a problem, and how it can be resolved. Its clear eight-step program stresses consistency and cooperation, promoting changes through a system of praise, rewards, and mild punishment. Filled with helpful sidebars, charts, and checklists. *$35.00*

*255 pages  Hardcover*
*ISBN 1-572301-23-6*

**3098  Developing Fine and Gross Motor Skills**

**Therapro**
**225 Arlington Street**
**Framingham, MA  01702**             508-872-9494
                                      800-257-5376
                                      FAX 508-875-2062
                          http://www.theraproducts.com
                          e-mail: info@theraproducts.com
*Donna Staisiunas Hurley, Author*

This new home exercise program has dozens of beautifully illustrated, reproducible handouts for the parent, therapists, health care and child care workers. Each interval of 3 to 6 months in the child's development is divided into a fine motor and a gross motor section. Each section has several exercise sheets that guide parents in ways to develop specific motor skills that typically occur at that age level. Also includes practical information on how to guide parents when doing the exereices.

*Ages Birth-3*

**3099  Diamonds in the Rough**

**Slosson Educational Publications**
**538 Buffalo Road**
**East Aurora, NY  14052**            716-652-0930
                                      888-756-7766
                                      FAX 800-655-3840
                          http://www.slosson.com
                          e-mail: slosson@slosson.com
*Peggy Strass Dias, Author*
*Steven W Slosson, President*
*John Slosson, VP*

An invaluable multidisciplinary reference guide to learning disabilities. It is an indispensable resource for educators, health specialists, parents and librarians. The author has printed a clear picture of the archetypical learner with a step-by-step view of the learning disabled child. *$53.00*

**3100  Dictionary of Special Education & Rehabilitation: 4th Editon**

**Books on Special Children**
**PO Box 305**
**Congers, NY  10920**                845-638-1236
                                      FAX 845-638-0847
                          http://www.boscbooks.com/
                          e-mail: irene@boscbooks.com
*ML Anderegg, Author*

A reference of definitions of terminology and jargon in special education and rehabilitation fields. Latest language in the field clearly defined. For those new or inexperienced in special ed and rehabilitation. Includes abbreviations, acronyms, legal terms lists of associations and national centers, periodicals, journals and sources of legal assistance. *$32.95*

*210 pages  softcover*
*ISBN 0-891082-43-3*

**3101  Directive Group Play Therapy: 2nd Edtion**

**Books on Special Children**
**PO Box 305**
**Congers, NY  10920**                845-638-1236
                                      FAX 845-638-0847
                          http://www.boscbooks.com/
                          e-mail: irene@boscbooks.com
*N Leben, Author*

Morning Glory Treatment Center for Children is a licensed therapeutic foster group home of about 10 children of ages 5-17. These games are played as part of therapy milieu. Each game contains objectives, supplies used. *$28.00*

*96 pages  spiralbound*

**3102    Directory for Exceptional Children: 14th Edition**

**Porter Sargent Publishers**
**11 Beacon Street**
**Boston, MA  02108**                617-523-1670
                                      800-342-7470
                           FAX 617-523-1021
                  http://www.potersargent.com
                  e-mail: info@portersargent.com
*Dan McKeever, Senior Editor*
*John Yonce, General Manager*
*Leslie Weston, Production Editor*

A comprehensive survey of 3000 schools, facilities and organizations across the USA, serving children and young adults with developmental, emotional, physical and medical disabilities. An invaluable aid to parents and professionals. *$75.00*

*1056 pages  trienniel*
*ISBN 0-875581-41-2*

**3103    Dr. Larry Silver's Advice to Parents on AD-HD**

**Learning Disabilities Association of America**
**4156 Library Road**
**Pittsburgh, PA  15234**             412-341-1515
                           FAX 412-344-0224
                      http://www.ldanatl.org
                  e-mail: ldanatl@usaor.net
*Dr. Larry B Silver, Author*

Offers information on parenting children with Attention Deficit and Hyperactivity Disorders. *$19.95*

**3104    Early Childhood Special Education: Birth to Three**

**Connecticut Assoc. for Children and Adults with LD**
**25 Van Zant Street**
**East Norwalk, CT  06855**           203-838-5010
                           FAX 203-866-6108
                      http://www.CACLD.org
*J Jordan, Author*

Resources on early childhood education.

**3105    Educating Deaf Children Bilingually**

**Harris Communications**
**15155 Technology Drive**
**Eden Prairie, MN  55344**           952-906-1180
                                      800-825-9187
                           FAX 952-906-1099
                           TDY:952-906-1198
                  http://www.harriscomm.com
                  e-mail: mail@harriscomm.com
*Bill Williams, National Sales Manager*

Perspectives and practices in educating deaf children with the goal of grade-level achievement in fluency in the languages of the deaf community, general society and of the home are discussed in this book. *$19.95*

*262 pages*

**3106    Educating Students Who Have Visual Impairments with Other Disabilities**

**Brookes Publishing Company**
**PO Box 10624**
**Baltimore, MD  21285**              410-337-9580
                                      800-638-3775
                           FAX 410-337-8539
                  http://www.info@pbrookes.com
                  e-mail: sales@pbrookes.com
*Sharon Z Sacks PhD, Editor*
*Rosanne K Silberman EdD, Editor*

This text provides techniques for facilitating functional learning in students with a wide range of visual impairments and multiple disabilities. *$49.95*

*528 pages  Paperback*
*ISBN 1-557662-80-0*

**3107    Effective Instructions for Students withLearning Difficulties**

**Books on Special Children**
**PO Box 305**
**Congers, NY  10920**                845-638-1236
                           FAX 845-638-0847
                  http://www.boscbooks.com/
                  e-mail: irene@boscbooks.com
*PT Cegelka, Author*

The book is designed to help teach students and prevent academic failure. Overview of effective education: identify; measure; then manage behavior. Classroom structure to meet individual needs and teach reading, spelling written language skills, math. How to plan transition to adulthood. Each chapter has objectives outline and summary charts and forms. *$68.00*

*469 pages  softcover*
*ISBN 0-205162-68-1*

**3108    Effective Teaching Methods for Autistic Children**

**Charles C Thomas Publisher**
**2600 S 1st Street**
**Springfield, IL  62704**            217-789-8980
                                      800-258-8980
                           FAX 217-789-9130
                  e-mail: books@ccthomas.com
*Rosalind C Oppenheim, Author*

*124 pages  Hardcover  $30.95*
*ISBN 0-398028-58-3*

**3109    Emergence-Labeled Autistic**

**Therapro**
**225 Arlington Street**
**Framingham, MA  01702**             508-872-9494
                                      800-257-5376
                           FAX 508-875-2062
                  http://www.theraproducts.com
                  e-mail: info@theraproducts.com
*Temple Grandin, PhD as told by Margaret Scariano, Author*

In this autobiography, Temple tells the story of her emergence from her fear-gripped, autistic childhood to becoming a successful professional. This astonishing, true story will give new insight into autism and show it from the 'inside'.

*180 pages*

**3110   Emergence: Labeled Autistic**

Academic Therapy Publications
20 Commercial Boulevard
Novato, CA  94949                   415-883-3314
                                    800-422-7249
                               FAX 415-883-3720
               http://www.academictherapy.com
               e-mail: sales@academictherapy.com
*Temple Grandin and Margaret M. Scariano, Author*
*Anna Arena, President*

A recovered autistic individual shares her history, and
includes her own suggestions for parents and professionals. Technical Appendix, which overviews recent
treatment methods and more. *$13.00*

*184 pages*
*ISBN 0-878795-24-3*

**3111   Endangered Minds: Why Our Children Don't
Think**

Learning Disabilities Association of America
4156 Library Road
Pittsburgh, PA  15234               412-341-1515
                               FAX 412-344-0224
                    http://www.ldanatl.org
                    e-mail: ldanatl@usaor.net
*J Healy, Author*

*$13.00*

**3112   Essential ASL: The Fun, Fast, and Simple Way to
Learn American Sign Language**

Harris Communications
15155 Technology Drive
Eden Prairie, MN  55344             952-906-1180
                                    800-825-6758
                               FAX 952-906-1099
                               TDY:952-906-1198
*Martin LA Sternberg, EdD, Author*

This pocket version contains more than 700 frequently used signs with 2,000 easy-to-follow illustrations. Also, 50 common phrases. *$7.95*

*322 pages  Paperback*

**3113   Evaluation of the Association for Children with
Learning Disabilities**

National Center for State Courts
300 Newport Avenue
Williamsburg, VA  23185             757-253-2000
                               FAX 757-220-0449
                    http://www.ncsonline.org
                    e-mail: webmaster@ncsc.dni.us

Final report on children with learning disabilities
training institute. *$6.96*

**3114   Family Communication**

Harris Communications
15155 Technology Drive
Eden Prairie, MN  55344             952-906-1180
                                    800-825-6758
                               FAX 952-906-1099
                               TDY:952-906-1198
                    http://www.harriscomm.com

A broad range of topics that affect communication in
the home and classroom, including support for families, and ways parents and school can work together
toward language literacy development. *$10.95*

*62 pages*

**3115   Family Guide to Assistive Technology**

Federation for Children with Special Needs
1135 Tremont Street
Boston, MA  02120                   617-236 7210
                                    800-331-0688
                               FAX 617-572-2094
                    http://www.fcsn.org
                    e-mail: fcsninfo@fcsn.org
*Richard J Robison, Executive Director*

This guide is intended to help parents learn more
about assistive technology and how it can help their
children. Includes tips for getting started, ideas about
how and where to look for funding and contact information for software and equipment. *$10.00*

*143 pages*

**3116   Family Place in Cyberspace**

Alliance for Technology Access
1304 Southpoint Boulevard
Petaluma, CA  94954                 707-778-3011
                               FAX 707-765-2080
                    http://www.ataccess.org
                    e-mail: atainfo@ataccess.org
*Mary Lester, Executive Director*

Includes We Can Play, a variety of suggestions and
ideas for making play activities accessible to all.
Available in English and Spanish. Access in Transition. Information and resources for students with disabilities who are facing the transition from public
school to the next stage in life. Includes links and resources. Assistive Technology in K-12 Schools gives
a range of information about integrating assistive
technology into schools.

**3117   Fine Motor Skills in Children with Downs
Syndrome: A Guide for Parents and Professionals**

Therapro
225 Arlington Street
Framingham, MA  01702               508-872-9494
                                    800-257-5376
                               FAX 508-875-2062
                    http://www.theraproducts.com
                    e-mail: info@theraproducts.com
*Maryanne Bruni B.Sc., OT(C), Author*

Fine motor skills are the hand skills that allow us to do
the things like hold a pencil, cut with scissors, eat with
a fork, and use a computer. This practical guide shows
parents and professionals how to help children with
Downs syndrome from infancy to 12 years improve
fine motor functioning. Includes many age appropriate activities for home or school, with step by step instructions and photos. Invaluable for families and
professionals.

**3118  Fine Motor Skills in the Classroom: Screening & Remediation Strategies**

Therapro
225 Arlington Street
Framingham, MA  01702          508-872-9494
                                        800-257-5376
                              FAX 508-875-2062
                    http://www.theraproducts.com
                    e-mail: info@theraproducts.com
*Jayne Berry, OTR/L, Author*

The Give Yourself a Hand program, revised. Developed as a tool to facilitate consultation in the classroom. The manual consists of training modules, a screening to administer to an entire class, report formats for teachers and parents, and classroom and home remediation activities. The program is designed to include everyone involved in the education process and to make them aware of the opportunites offered by occupational therapy in the classroom.

*96 pages*

**3119  Flying By the Seat of Your Pants: More Absurdities and Realities of Special Education**

Peytral Publication
PO Box 1162
Minnetonka, MN  55345          952-949-8707
                                        877-739-8725
                              FAX 952-906-9777
                        http://www.peytral.com
                        e-mail: help@peytral.com
*Michael F Giangreco, Author*

In the sequel to Ants in His Pants, Giangreco continues to stimulate the reader to think differently about some of our current educational practices and raise questions about specific issues surrounding special education. Whether an educator, parent or advocate for persons with disabilities, you will smile, laugh aloud and ponder the hidden truths playfully captured in these carefully crafted cartoons. Transparencies may be created directly from the book. *$19.95*

*126 pages*
*ISBN 1-890455-41-5*

**3120  For Parents and Professionals: Down Syndrome**

LinguiSystems
3100 4th Avenue
East Moline, IL  61244
                              800-776-4332
                          FAX 800-577-4555
                    http://www.linguisystems.com
                    e-mail: service@linguisystems.com
*Linda Bowers, Owner*
*Rosemary Huisingh, Owner*

This comprehensive resource gives you valuable information, helpful tips, and great activities to share with parents, teachers, and other caregivers. Packed with examples and activities, chapters cover: getting to know the child with Down syndrome; applying teaching and learning strategies, oral-motor and feeding skills, impact on overall communication skills, getting through the school years and more.

**3121  Gross Motor Skills Children with Down Syndrome: A Guide For Parents and Professionals**

Therapro
225 Arlington Street
Framingham, MA  01702          508-872-9494
                                        800-257-5376
                              FAX 508-875-2062
                    http://www.theraproducts.com
                    e-mail: info@theraproducts.com
*Patricia C Winders, PT, Author*

Children with Down syndrome master basic gross motor skills, everything from rolling over to running, just as their peers do, but may need additional help. This guide describes and illustrates more than 100 easy to follow activities for parents and professionals to practice with infants and children from birth to age six. Checklists and statistics allow readers to track, plan and maximize a child's progress.

**3122  Guide for Parents on Hyperactivity in Children**

Learning Disabilities Association of America
4156 Library Road
Pittsburgh, PA  15234          412-341-1515
                              FAX 412-344-0224
                        http://www.ldanatl.org
                        e-mail: ldanatl@usaor.net
*Klaus K Minde, Author*

Describes difficulties faced by a child with ADHD. Elaborates on types of management and ends with a section called 'A Day With a Hyperactive Child: Possible Problems'. *$2.00*

*23 pages*

**3123  Guidelines and Recommended Practices for Individualized Family Service Plan**

Association for the Care of Children's Health
7910 Woodmont Avenue
Bethesda, MD  20814
                              FAX 301-986-4553
*B Johnson, Author*

Presents a growing consensus about best practices for comprehensive family-centered early intervention services as required by Part H of the Individuals with Disabilities Education Act. *$15.00*

*208 pages*

**3124  Handbook for Implementing Workshops for Siblings of Special Needs Children**

Special Needs Project
324 State Street
Santa Barbara, CA  93105          805-964-8087
                                        800-333-6867
                              FAX 805-962-5087
                    e-mail: books@specialneeds.com
*Donald Meyer, Author*

Based on three years of professional experience working with siblings ages 8 through 13 and their parents, this handbook provides guidelines and technologies for those who wish to start and conduct workshops for siblings. *$40.00*

*65 pages*

**3125 Handling the Young Child with Cerebral Palsy at Home**

Therapro
225 Arlington Street
Framingham, MA 01702          508-872-9494
                             800-257-5376
                       FAX 508-875-2062
           http://www.theraproducts.com
           e-mail: info@theraproducts.com
*Nancie R Finnie, Author*

This guide for parents remains a classic book on handling their cerebral palsied child during all activities of daily living. It has been said that its message is so important that it should be read by all those caring for such children including doctors, therapists, teachers and nurses. Many simple line drawings illustrate handling problems and solutions.

*3rd Edition*

**3126 Help Build a Brighter Future: Children at Risk for LD in Child Care Centers**

Learning Disabilities Association of America
4156 Library Road
Pittsburgh, PA 15234          412-341-1515
                       FAX 412-344-0224
                 http://www.ldanatl.org
                 e-mail: ldanatl@usaor.net

Offers information for parents and professionals caring for the learning disabled child. *$3.00*

**3127 Help Me to Help My Child**

Little Brown & Company
3 Center Plaza
Boston, MA 02108          617-227-0730
                     FAX 617-263-2871
*Jill Bloom, Author*

Contains nontechnical information on testing, advocacy, legal issues, instructional practices, and social-emotional development, as well as a resource list and bibliography.

*ISBN 0-316099-82-1*

**3128 Help for the Hyperactive Child: A Good Sense Guide for Parents**

Learning Disabilities Association of America
4156 Library Road
Pittsburgh, PA 15234          412-341-1515
                       FAX 412-344-0224
                 http://www.ldanatl.org
                 e-mail: ldanatl@usaor.net

A practical guide; offering parents of ADHD children alternatives to Ritalin. *$16.95*

**3129 Help for the Learning Disabled Child**

Slosson Educational Publications
538 Buffalo Road
East Aurora, NY 14052          888-756-7766
                             800-828-4800
                       FAX 800-655-3840
                 http://www.slosson.com
              e-mail: slosson@slosson.com
*Lou Stewart, Author*
*Steven W Slosson, President*
*John Slosson, VP*

An easy-to-read text describes observable behaviors, offers remediation techniques, materials, and specific test to assist in further diagnosis. *$38.00*

**3130 Helping Young Writers Master the Craft**

Brookline Books
300 Bedford Street
Manchester, NH 03101          617-734-6772
                        FAX 603-922-3348
              http://www.brooklinebooks.com
              e-mail: brooklinebks@delphi.com
*K Harris, Author*
*S Graham, Author*

Strategy instruction and self-regulation in the writing process.

**3131 Helping Your Child Achieve in School**

Academic Therapy Publications
20 Commercial Boulevard
Novato, CA 94949          415-883-3314
                        800-422-7249
                  FAX 415-883-3720
              http://www.apub.com
*Betty Lou Kratoville, Editor*

A wealth of simple and enjoyable at-home educational activities. Special emphasis is given to developing reading skills in primary-aged children and to building comprehension skills of middle-grade children. *$12.50*

*264 pages*
*ISBN 0-878794-65-4*

**3132 Helping Your Child with Attention-Deficit Hyperactivity Disorder**

Learning Disabilities Association of America
4156 Library Road
Pittsburgh, PA 15234          412-341-1515
                       FAX 412-344-0224
                 http://www.ldanatl.org
                 e-mail: ldanatl@usaor.net
*M Fowler, Author*

*$12.95*

**3133 Helping Your Hyperactive Child**

Connecticut Assoc. for Children and Adults with LD
25 Van Zant Street
East Norwalk, CT 06855          203-838-5010
                          FAX 203-866-6018
                    http://www.CACLD.org
*John Taylor, Author*

A large, comprehensive book for parents, covering everything from techniques pertaining to sibling rivalry to coping with marital stresses. Contains thorough discussions of various treatments: nutritional, medical and educational. Also is an excellent source of advice and information for parents of kids with ADHD. *$2195.00*

*483 pages*

**3134  Hidden Child: Linwood Method for Reaching the Autistic Child**

Therapro
225 Arlington Street
Framingham, MA  01702          508-872-9494
                                800-257-5376
                            FAX 508-875-2062
                        http://www.theraproducts.com
                        e-mail: info@theraproducts.com
*Jeanne Simmons and Sabine Oiski, PhD, Author*

This book provides an explanation of autism, then a step-by-step analysis of the Linwood method of establishing relationships, patterning good behavior, overcoming compulsions, developing skills, and fostering social and emotional development. This guidebook for teachers and therapists also has a message for parents.

**3135  Higher Education Services for Students with LD or ADD a Legal Guide**

JKL Communications
PO Box 40157
Washington, DC  20016          202-223-5097
                            FAX 202-223-5096
                        http://www.lathamlaw.org
                        e-mail: plath3@his.com

*$29.00*

**3136  How the Special Needs Brain Learns**

Corwin Press
2455 Teller Road
Thousand Oaks, CA  91320          805-499-9734
                                800-818-7243
                            FAX 805-499-5323
                        http://www.corwinpress.com
                        e-mail: order@corwinpress.com
*David A Sousa, Author*
*Kimberly Gonzales, Marketing Director*
*Robb Clouse, Senior Acquisitions Editor*

Research on the brain function of students with various learning challenges. Practical classroom activities and strategies, such as how to build self-esteem, how to work in groups, and strategies for engagement and retention. Focuses on the most commmon challenges to learning for many students. *$34.95*

*248 pages*
*ISBN 0-761978-51-8*

**3137  How to Get Services by Being Assertive**

Family Resource Center on Disabilities
20 E Jackson Boulevard
Chicago, IL  60604          312-939-3513
                            800-952-4199
                        FAX 312-939-7297
                        TDY:312-939-3519
*Family Resource Center on Disabilities, Author*

A manual that demonstrates positive assertiveness techniques for staffing, IEP meetings, due process hearings and other special education meetings. *$10.00*

*100 pages*

**3138  How to Organize Your Child and Save Your Sanity**

Learning Disabilities Association of America
4156 Library Road
Pittsburgh, PA  15234          412-341-1515
                            FAX 412-344-0224
                        http://www.ldanatl.org
                        e-mail: ldanatl@usaor.net
*Brown/Connelly, Author*

*$3.00*

**3139  How to Organize an Effective Parent-Advocacy Group and Move Bureaucracies**

Family Resource Center on Disabilities
20 E Jackson Boulevard
Chicago, IL  60604          312-939-3513
                            800-952-4199
                        FAX 312-939-7297
                        TDY:312-939-3519
*Charlotte Desjardins, Author*

A 100-page handbook that gives step-by-step directions for organizing parent support groups from scratch. *$10.00*

*100 pages*

**3140  How to Own and Operate an Attention Deficit Disorder**

Learning Disabilities Association of America
4156 Library Road
Pittsburgh, PA  15234          412-341-1515
                            FAX 412-344-0224
                        http://www.ldanatl.org
                        e-mail: ldanatl@usaor.net

Clear, informative and sensitive introduction to ADHD. Packed with practical things to do at home and school, the author offers her insight as a professional and mother of a son with ADHD. *$8.95*

*43 pages*

**3141  Hyperactive Children Grown Up**

Guilford Publications
72 Spring Street
New York, NY  10012          212-431-9800
                            800-365-7006
                        FAX 212-966-6708
                        http://www.guilford.com
                        e-mail: info@guilford.com
*Gabrielle Weiss, Author*
*Lily Trokenberg Hechtman, Author*

Long considered a standard in the field, this book explores what happens to hyperactive children when they grow into adulthood. Updated and expanded, this second edition describes new developments in ADHD, current psychological treatments of ADHD, contemporary perspectives on the use of medications, and assessment, diagnosis and treatment of ADHD adults. *$26.00*

*473 pages  Paperback*
*ISBN 0-898625-96-3*

**3142  Hyperactivity, Attention Deficits, and School Failure: Better Ways**

Learning Disabilities Association of America
4156 Library Road
Pittsburgh, PA  15234          412-341-1515
                              FAX 412-344-0224
                              http://www.ldanatl.org
                              e-mail: ldanatl@usaor.net
*WG Crook, Author*

*$6.00*

**3143  If it is to Be, It is Up to Me to Do it!**

AVKO Educational Research Foundation
3084 W Willard Road
Clio, MI  48420               810-686-9283
                              FAX 810-686-1101
                              http://www.avko.org/upto.htm
                              e-mail: DonMcCabe@aol.com
*Don McCabe, Author*
*Don McCabe, Research Director*

This is a tutors' book that can be used by anyone who can read this paragraph. It also contains the student's response pages. It is especially good to use to help an older child or adult. It uses the same basic format as Sequential Spelling I except it has the sentences to be read along with the word to be spelled. The students get to correct their own mistakes immediately. This way they quickly learn that mistakes are opportunities to learn. *$19.95*

*96 pages*
*ISBN 1-564007-42-1*

**3144  In Their Own Way: Discovering and Encouraging Your Child's Learning**

Special Needs Project
324 State Street
Santa Barbara, CA  93101      805-962-8087
                              800-333-6867
                              FAX 805-962-5087
                              e-mail: books@specialneeds.com
*Dr. Thomas Armstrong, Author*

An unconventional teacher has written a very popular book for a wide audience. It's customary to be categorical about youngsters who learn conventionally/are normal/are OK — and those who don't/who need special ed/are learning disabled. *$8.37*

*224 pages  Paperback*

**3145  In Time and with Love**

Special Needs Project
324 State Street
Santa Barbara, CA  93105      805-962-8087
                              800-333-6867
                              FAX 805-962-5087
                              e-mail: books@specialnedds.com
Play and parenting techniques for children with disabilities. *$12.95*

*19 pages*

**3146  In the Mind's Eye**

Prometheus Books
59 John Glenn Drive
Amherst, NY  14228            716-691-0133
                              800-421-0351
                              FAX 716-691-0137
                              http://www.prometheusbooks.com
                              e-mail: mrogers@prometheusmail.com
*TR West, Author*
*Marcia Rogers, Sales Manager*

Visual thinkers, gifted people with learning difficulties, computer images, and the ironies of creativity. Be concerned with results, not uniformity of learning style. *$28.00*

*397 pages*
*ISBN 1-573921-55-6*

**3147  Inclusion: 450 Strategies for Success**

Peytral Publication
PO Box 1162
Minnetonka, MN  55345         952-949-8707
                              877-739-8725
                              FAX 952-906-9777
                              http://www.peytral.com
                              e-mail: help@peytral.com
*Peggy A Hammeken, Author*

This perennial best seller is written for general and special educators in inclusive education settings. Topics include step-by-step guidelines to help develop and improve the inclusive setting, hundreds of practical teacher tested ideas, adaptations, and modifications covering both curriculum and instruction. Many reproducibles. General and special educators, ESL, Chapter one. *$23.95*

*190 pages*
*ISBN 1-890455-25-3*

**3148  Inclusion: A Practical Guide for Parents**

Peytral Publication
PO Box 1162
Minnetonka, MN  55345         952-949-8707
                              877-739-8725
                              FAX 952-906-9777
                              http://www.peytral.com
                              e-mail: help@peytral.com
*Lorraine O Moore, Author*

This comprehensive resource answers parent questions related to inclusive education and provides the tools to promote and enhance their child's learning. This publication includes practical strategies, exercises, questionnaires and do-it-yourself graphs to assist parents with their child's learning. Beneficial for parents, psychologists, social workers, and educators. *$19.95*

*192 pages*
*ISBN 0-964427-13-3*

**3149  Inclusion: An Essential Guide for the Paraprofessional**

Peytral Publication
PO Box 1162
Minnetonka, MN  55345                952-949-8707
                                     877-739-8725
                              FAX 952-906-9777
                              http://www.peytral.com
                              e-mail: help@peytral.com

*Peggy A Hammeken, Author*

This practical, simple, and easy-to-use resource provides ready-to-use information, ideas and strategies which can be put into practice immediately. Topics include special education background information, the paraprofessional's role, ideas to help with scheduling, communications, substitute lesson plans and monitoring of students. Hundreds of ideas and strategies for specific subject areas will help the paraprofessional in the classroom. Excellent training tool. *$21.95*

*142 pages*
*ISBN 0-964427-16-8*

**3150  Inclusion: Strategies for Working with Young Children**

Peytral Publication
PO Box 1162
Minnetonka, MN  55345                952-949-8707
                                     877-739-8725
                              FAX 952-906-9777
                              http://www.peytral.com
                              e-mail: help@peytral.com

*Lorraine O Moore, Author*

Developed for early childhood through grade two educators and parents, this comprehensive developmentally focused publication focuses on the whole child. Hundreds of developmentally-based strategies help young children learn about feelings, empathy, resolving conflicts, communication, large/small motor development, prereading, writing and math strategies are included, plus much more. Excellent training tool. *$21.95*

*185 pages*
*ISBN 0-964427-13-3*

**3151  Individual Education Plan: Involved Effective Parents**

PEAK Parent Center
611 N Weber
Colorado Springs, CO  80903          719-531-9400
                                     800-284-0251
                              FAX 719-531-9452
                              TDY:719-531-5403
                              http://www.peakparent.org
                              e-mail: info@peakparent.org

*Alison B Seyler, Barbara E Buswell, Author*

An essential tool for both families and educators as they develop and implement Individual Education plans. Explains what occurs before, during, and after the development of an IEP, and provides a continuity process for transferring information from year to year. Includes innovative forms for parents and educators. Complements the IEP video. *$10.00*

**3152  Innovations in Family Support for People with Learning Disabilities**

Brookes Publishing Company
PO Box 10624
Baltimore, MD  21285                 410-337-9580
                                     800-638-3775
                              FAX 410-337-8539
                              http://www.pbrookes.com
                              e-mail: custerv@pbrookes.com

*Barbara Coyne Cutler, EdD, Author*

*272 pages  Paperback $22.00*
*ISBN 1-870335-15-5*

**3153  Interventions for ADHD: Treatment in Developmental Context**

Guilford Publications
72 Spring Street
New York, NY  10012                  212-431-9800
                                     800-365-7006
                              FAX 212-966-6708
                              http://www.guilford.com
                              e-mail: info@guilford.com

*Phyllis Anne Teeter, Author*

This book takes a lifespan perspective on ADHD, dispelling the notion that it is only a disorder of childhood and enabling clinicians to develop effective and appropriate interventions for preschoolers, school-age children, adolescents, and adults. The author reviews empirically-and clinically-based treatment interventions including psychopharmacology, behavior management, parent/teacher training, and self-management techniques. *$40.00*

*378 pages  Hardcover*
*ISBN 1-572303-84-0*

**3154  Invisible Disability: Understanding Learning Disabilities in the Context of Health & Edu.**

Learning Disabilities Association of America
4156 Library Road
Pittsburgh, PA  15234                412-341-1515
                              FAX 412-344-0224
                              http://www.ldanatl.org
                              e-mail: ldanatl@usaor.net

*Pasquale Accardo, Author*

*$9.00*
*ISBN 0-937846-39-2*

**3155  It's Your Turn Now**

Harris Communications
15155 Technology Drive
Eden Prairie, MN  55344              952-906-1180
                                     800-825-6758
                              FAX 952-906-1099
                              TDY:952-906-1198
                              http://www.harriscomm.com
                              e-mail: mail@harriscomm.com

*Cindy Bailes, Author*
*Susan Searls, Author*
*Jean Slobodzian, Author*
*Jana Staton, Author*

Using dialogue journals with deaf students help the students learn to enjoy communicating ideas, information, and feelings through reading and writing. The book reviews teacher's questions and answers, frustrations and successes. *$14.95*

*130 pages*

**3156  Key Concepts in Personal Development**

**Marsh Media**
8082 Ward Parkway Plaza
Kansas City, MO  64114                     816-523-1059
                                           800-821-3303
                                       FAX 866-333-7421
                          http://www.marshmedia.com
                          e-mail: info@marshmedia.com
*Joan Marsh, President*
*Liz Sweeney, Editorial Assistant*

Our videos, books, and teaching guides bring character education to the classroom. These kits are invaluable aids in teaching everyday values like honesty, anger control, trustworthiness, perseverance, understanding and respect. They help you prepare youngsters to meet challenges and greet opportunities with skill and optimism.

**3157  Ladders to Literacy: A Kindergarten Activity Book**

**Brookes Publishing Company**
PO Box 10624
Baltimore, MD  21285                      410-337-9580
                                          800-638-3775
                                      FAX 410-337-8539
                          http://www.info@pbrookes.com
                          e-mail: sales@pbrookes.com
*Rollanda E O'Connor, PhD, et. al., Author*

The kindergarten activities are designed for higher developmental levels, focusing on preacademic skills, early literacy development, and early reading development. Goals and scaffolding are more intense as children learn to recognize letters, match sounds with letters, and develop phonological awareness and the alphabetic principle. *$32.16*

   *272 pages  Spiral bound*
   *ISBN 1-557663-18-1*

**3158  Ladders to Literacy: A Preschool Activity Book**

**Brookes Publishing Company**
PO Box 10624
Baltimore, MD  21285                      410-337-9580
                                          800-638-3775
                                      FAX 410-337-8539
                          http://www.info@pbrookes.com
                          e-mail: sales@pbrookes.com
*Angela Notari-Syverson, PhD, et. al., Author*

The preschool activity book targets basic preliteracy skills such as orienting children toward printed materials and teaching letter sounds. It also provides professionals (and parents) with developmentally appropriate and ecologically valid assessment procedures — informal observation guidelines, structured performance samples, and a checklist — for measuring children's learning. *$34.96*

   *352 pages  Spiral bound*
   *ISBN 1-557663-17-3*

**3159  Landmark Study Skills Guide**

**Landmark School**
429 Hale Street
Prides Crossing, MA  01965                978-236-3216
                                      FAX 978-927-7268
                          http://www.landmarkschool.org
                          e-mail: outreach@landmarkschool.org
*Joan Sedita, Author*
*Dan Ahearn, Program Director*
*Trish Newhall, Associate Director*
*Kathryn Frye, Administrative Assistant*

Provides practical teaching strategies for teachers and parents working with students who are unable to organize themselves, take adequate notes, use their textbooks efficiently or study on a regular basis. Includes chapters on organizing, main ideas, note-taking, summarizing, textbook skills, test preparation, and report-writing skills. Sample assignments and How To lists for students to follow are included throughout. *$30.00*

   *125 pages*
   *ISBN 0-962411-90-6*

**3160  Language-Related Learning Disabilities**

**Brookes Publishing Company**
PO Box 10624
Baltimore, MD  21285                      410-337-9580
                                          800-638-3775
                                      FAX 410-337-8539
                          http://www.pbrookes.com
                          e-mail: custerv@pbrookes.com
*Adele Gerber, MA, Author*

   *384 pages  Paperback  $47.00*
   *ISBN 1-557660-53-0*

**3161  Learning Difficulties and Emotional Problems**

**Temeron Books**
Bellingham, WA  98227
                                      FAX 360-738-4016
                          http://www.temerondetselig.com
                          e-mail: temeron@telusplanet.net
*Roy Brown and Maurice Chazan , Editors, Author*

International authorities shed light on recent research. *$18.95*

   *239 pages  Paperback*
   *ISBN 0-920490-89-1*

**3162  Learning Disabilities & ADHD: A Family Guide to Living and Learning Together**

**John Wiley & Sons**
10475 Crosspoint Road
Indianapolis, IN  46256                   201-748-6000
                                      FAX 800-597-3299
                          http://www.wiley.com
*Betty B Osman, Author*

   *228 pages  paperback  $14.95*
   *ISBN 0-471155-10-1*

**3163  Learning Disabilities A to Z**

Simon and Schuster
PO Box 11071
Des Moines, IA  50336                515-284-6751
                                     800-223-2348
                               FAX 515-284-2607
                  http://www.simonandschuster.com
*Smith, Corinne and Lisa Strick, Author*

Brings the best of recent research and educational experience to parents, teachers and caregivers who are responsible for children with information processing problems. Corinne Smith and Lisa Strick provide a comprehensive guide to the causes, indentification and treatment of learning disabilities. You will learn how these subtle neurological disorders can have a major impact on a child's development, both in and out of school. *$25.00*

*416 pages*
*ISBN 0-684827-38-7*

**3164  Learning Disabilities: Lifelong Issues**

Brookes Publishing Company
PO Box 10624
Baltimore, MD  21285                 410-337-9580
                                     800-638-3775
                               FAX 410-337-8539
                  http://www.info@pbrookes.com
                  e-mail: sales@pbrookes.com
*Shirley C Cramer, Editor*
*William Ellis, Editor*

Based on the diverse, representative viewpoints of educators, practitioners, policy makers, and adults with learning disabilities, this volume sets forth an agenda for improving the educational and ultimately, social and economic, futures of people with learning disabilities. *$36.00*

*352 pages  Paperback*
*ISBN 1-557662-40-1*

**3165  Learning Disabilities: Literacy, and Adult Education**

Brookes Publishing Company
PO Box 10624
Baltimore, MD  21285                 410-337-9580
                                     800-638-3775
                               FAX 410-337-8539
                  http://www.info@pbrookes.com
                  e-mail: sales@pbrookes.com
*Susan A Vogel PhD, Editor*
*Stephen Reder PhD, Editor*

This book focuses on adults with severe learning disabilities and the educators who work with them. *$49.95*

*400 pages  Paperback*
*ISBN 1-557663-47-5*

**3166  Learning Disabilities: Theories, Diagnosis and Teaching Strategies**

Houghton-Mifflin
222 Berkeley Street
Boston, MA  02116                    617-351-5468
                               FAX 617-351-1119
                  http://www.houghtonmifflinbooks.com
*J Lerner, Author*

Theories on learning disabilities.

*ISBN 0-395796-85-7*

**3167  Learning Journey**

Temeron Books
Bellingham, WA  98227
                               FAX 360-738-4016
                  http://www.temerondetselig.com
                  e-mail: temeron@telusplanet.net
*Malcom Jeffreys and Robert Gall, Author*

Enhancing lifelong learning and self-determination for people with special needs, this book presents a detailed view of emerging trends and models of service that promise a better future in terms of self-determination for the developmentally disabled. *$18.95*

*204 pages  Paperback*
*ISBN 1-550591-22-3*

**3168  Let's Learn About Deafness**

Harris Communications
15155 Technology Drive
Eden Prairie, MN  55344              952-906-1180
                                     800-825-6758
                               FAX 952-906-1099
                               TDY:952-906-1198
                  http://www.harriscomm.com
*Rachel Stone, Author*

Hands-on activities, games, bulletin board displays, surveys, quizzes, craft projects, and skits used to help teachers and their students become more aware of deafness and its implications are included in this book. *$16.95*

*82 pages*

**3169  Life Beyond the Classroom: Transition Strategies for Young People with Disabilities**

Books on Special Children
PO Box 305
Congers, NY  10920                   845-638-1236
                               FAX 845-638-0847
                  http://www.boscbooks.com/
                  e-mail: irene@boscbooks.com
*P Wehman, Author*

Community living, leisure activities, personal relationships as well as employment. Planning with community, individualized, state and local governments, curriculum for transition, job development and placement, independent living plans for people with mild MR, severe disabilities, LD, physical and health impairments, and traumatic brain injury. *$59.95*

*533 pages  softcover*
*ISBN 1-557662-48-7*

**3170  Living with a Learning Disability**

Southern Illinois University Press
PO Box 3697
Carbondale, IL  62902                618-453-2281
                                     800-346-2680
                               FAX 800-346-2681
                  http://www.siu.edu/nsiupress
                  e-mail: townsend@siu.edu
*Barbara Cordoni, Author*
*Larry Townsend, Director Sales/Marketing*

This book presents the kinds of adaptations needed for educating, communicating with, and parenting the child, the adolescent, and the young adult with learning disabilities. Deals with such issues as relationships, the legal process, implications for the professional, juvenile delinquency, and the future.

*17.5 pages*
*ISBN 0-809316-68-4*

**3171   Making Sense of Sensory Integration**

**Therapo**
**225 Arlington Street**
**Framingham, MA  01702**          508-872-9494
                                   800-257-5376
                              FAX 508-875-2062
                 **http://www.theraproducts.com**
                 **e-mail: info@theraproducts.com**
*Koomar, Szklut, Cermak and Silver, Author*

A discussion for parents and caregivers about sensory integration (SI), how it affects children throughout their lives, how diagnosis is made, appropriate treatment, recognizing red flags, and how SI difficulties affect child and family in their everyday lives. Informative 33 page book included. 75 minute audio tape.

*Audio Tape*

**3172   McGraw Hill Companies**

**2 Penn Plaza**
**New York, NY  10003**           212-904-5448
                              FAX 212-904-5974
                   **http://www.mcgraw-hill.com**
          **e-mail: elizabeth_schacht@mcgraw-hill.com**
Corrective reading program, helps students master the essential decoding and comprehension skills.

**3173   Me! A Curriculum for Teaching Self-Esteem Through an Interest Center**

**Connecticut Assoc. for Children and Adults with LD**
**25 Van Zant Street**
**East Norwalk, CT  06855**        203-838-5010
                              FAX 203-866-6108
                       **http://www.CACLD.org**
                       **e-mail: cacld@juno.com**
*Jo Ellen Hartline, Author*
*Marie Armstrong, Information Specialist*

A curriculum for the professional. *$18.50*

*$2.50 shipping*

**3174   Meeting the Needs of Students of ALL Abilities**

**Corwin Press**
**2455 Teller Road**
**Thousand Oaks, CA  91320**       805-499-9734
                                   800-818-7243
                              FAX 805-499-5323
                   **http://www.corwinpress.com**
                 **e-mail: order@corwinpress.com**
*Collleen Capper, Elise Frattura, Maureen Keyes, Author*
*Kimberly Gonzales, Marketing Director*
*Robb Clouse, Senior Acquisitions Editor*

Step-by-step handbook offers practical strategies for administrators, teachers, policymakers and parents who want to shift from costly special learning programs for a few students, to excellent educational services for all students and teachers, and adapting curriculum and instruction. *$32.95*

*224 pages*
*ISBN 0-761975-01-2*

**3175   Misunderstood Child**

**Connecticut Assoc. for Children and Adults with LD**
**25 Van Zant Street**
**East Norwalk, CT  06855**        203-838-5010
                              FAX 203-866-6108
                       **http://www.CACLD.org**
*LB Silver, Author*

A guide for parents of learning disabled children. *$8.95*

**3176   Moving Violations, A Memoir: War Zones, Wheelchairs, and Declarations of Independence**

**Books on Special Children**
**PO Box 305**
**Congers, NY  10920**            845-638-1236
                              FAX 845-638-0847
                   **http://www.boscbooks.com/**
                 **e-mail: irene@boscbooks.com**
*J Hockenberry, Author*

He is a newspaper man, out to get his story, wherever. What sets him apart is his inability to move his legs. He does what he must in a wheelchair. This is his remarkable story, told with humor and without self-pity. *$26.95*

*371 pages  hardcover*
*ISBN 0-786860-78-2*

**3177   Negotiating the Special Education Maze 3rd Edition**

**Woodbine House**
**6510 Bells Mill Road**
**Bethesda, MD  20817**           301-897-3570
                                   800-843-7323
                              FAX 301-897-5838
                 **http://www.woodbinehouse.com**
                 **e-mail: info@woodbinehouse.com**
*Winifred Anderson, Author*
*Stephen Chitwood, Author*
*Deidre Hayden, Author*

Now in its third edition, Negotiating the Special Education Maze is one of the best tools available to parents and teachers for developing an effective special education program for their child or student. Every step is explained, from eligibility and evaluation to the Individualized Education Program and beyond. *$16.95*

*264 pages  Paperback 7x10*
*ISBN 0-933149-72-7*

**3178** **New Language of Toys**

**Woodbine House**
**6510 Bells Mill Road**
**Bethesda, MD 20817**          **301-897-3570**
**800-843-7323**
**FAX 301-897-5838**
**http://www.woodbinehouse.com**
**e-mail: info@woodbinehouse.com**
*Sue Schwartz PhD, Author*
*Joan E Heller Miller EdM, Author*

This revised and updated edition presents a fun, hands-on approach to developing communication skills in children with disabilities using everyday toys. There's a fresh assortment of toys and books, as well as newe chapters on computer technology and language learning, videotapes and television. *$16.95*

*289 pages Paperback 7x10*
*ISBN 0-933149-73-5*

**3179** **No One to Play with: The Social Side of Learning Disabilities**

**Connecticut Assoc. for Children and Adults with LD**
**25 Van Zant Street**
**East Norwalk, CT 06855**          **203-838-5010**
**FAX 203-866-6108**
**http://www.CACLD.org**
**e-mail: cacld@juno.com**
*Betty Osman, Author*
*Marie Armstrong, Information Specialist*

Your child suffers from a learning disability and you have read reams on how to improve on her academic skills and now want to address his or her social needs. *$13.00*

*$2.50 shipping*

**3180** **Nobody's Perfect: Living and Growing with Children who Have Special Needs**

**Books on Special Children**
**PO Box 305**
**Congers, NY 10920**          **845-638-1236**
**FAX 845-638-0847**
**http://www.boscbooks.com/**
**e-mail: irene@boscbooks.com**
*NB Miller, Author*

Study of four families with children who have special needs. How they all adapted in surviving, how they care for the child, family, parents and siblings. How families react and relate. What it is like in community and extended family? Basic issues dicussed: self-esteem, separating parent from the adult with special needs and other issues. *$24.00*

*307 pages softcover*
*ISBN 1-557661-43-X*

**3181** **Optimizing Special Education: How Parents Can Make a Difference**

**Insight Books**
**233 Spring Street**
**New York, NY 10013**          **212-620-8000**
**800-221-9369**
**FAX 212-807-1047**
**http://www.plenum.com**
**e-mail: info@plenum.com**
*N Wilson, Author*

The author shows families how to use education laws to increase services or change services to suit a child's needs. Book contains personal anecdotes and balanced viewpoint of parent and professional relationships. *$26.50*

*300 pages*
*ISBN 0-306443-23-6*

**3182** **Out of Sync Child: Recognizing and Coping with Sensory Integration Dysfunction**

**Therapro**
**225 Arlington Street**
**Framingham, MA 01702**          **508-872-9494**
**800-257-5376**
**FAX 508-875-2062**
**http://www.theraproducts.com**
**e-mail: info@theraproducts.com**
*Carol Stock Kranowitz, MA, Author*

Finally, a parent-friendly book about sensory integration (SI) clearly written to explain SI dysfunction from the perspective of a teacher who has worked extensively with an OT. Part I deals with recognizing SI dysfunction. Part II addresses coping with SI dysfunction.

**3183** **Out of the Mouths of Babes: Discovering the Developmental Significance of the Mouth**

**Therapro**
**225 Arlington Street**
**Framingham, MA 01702**          **508-872-9494**
**800-257-5376**
**FAX 508-875-2062**
**http://www.theraproducts.com**
**e-mail: info@theraproducts.com**
*Frick, Frick, Oetter and Richter, Author*

Help children who have difficulty with focusing, staying alert, or being calm with these simple techniqes and activities. Learn how behavior is affected by suck/swallow/breathe (SSB) synchrony with suggestions for correcting specific problems. This informal writing style and many illustrations make it a great resource for parents, teachers and therapists.

**3184** **Parent Manual**

**Federation for Children with Special Needs**
**1135 Tremont Street**
**Boston, MA 02120**          **617-236-7210**
**800-331-0688**
**FAX 617-572-2094**
**TDY:617-236-7210**
**http://www.fcsn.org**
**e-mail: fcsninfo@fcsn.org**
*Richard J Robison, Executive Director*

Outlines parents' and children's rights in special education as guaranteed by Chapter 766, the Massachusetts special education law, and the Individuals with Disabilities Education Act (IDEA), the federal special education law *$ 25.00*

*75 pages*

**3185 Parenting Children with Special Needs**

AGC/United Learning
1560 Sherman Avenue
Evanston, IL 60201
800-328-6700
FAX 847-328-6706
http://www.agcunitedlearning.com
e-mail: info@agcunited.com
*Bill Wagonseller, Author*
*Jim McColl, VP Sales*

This program deals exclusively with the subject of parenting children with mental or physical disabilities. Particular emphasis is placed on children from infancy through early childhood. The content includes important topics such as: Birth and diagnosis of a child with disabilities Impact on the family system Psychological stages that most parents of children with disabilities will experience Importance of early intervention programs. *$95.00*

**3186 Parenting to Make a Difference: Your One to Four Year-Old**

Therapro
225 Arlington Street
Framingham, MA 01702
508-872-9494
800-257-5376
FAX 508-875-2062
http://www.theraproducts.com
e-mail: info@theraproducts.com
*Brenda Hussey-Gardner, MA, MPH, Author*

Covers twelve key topics to help parents foster the developmental growth of their young children.

**3187 Physical Side of Learning**

Therapro
225 Arlington Street
Framingham, MA 01702
508-872-9494
800-257-5376
FAX 508-875-2062
http://www.theraproducts.com
e-mail: info@theraproducts.com
*Leela C Zion, Author*

Assist preschool, elementary and special children with academic subjects by utilizing simple physical activities that are fun, easy to understand, and perform, all of which are clearly illustrated in this book. Explains the connection between movement/perception and learning, with special attention to promoting body awareness, directionality, balance, body concept, self-esteem and body mastery in general. Help prepare children for success in school through physical activities.

**3188 Play Therapy**

Books on Special Children
PO Box 305
Congers, NY 10920
845-638-1236
FAX 845-638-0847
http://www.boscbooks.com/
e-mail: irene@boscbooks.com
*KJ O'Connor, Author*

Leading authorities present various theoretical models of play therapy treatment and application. Case studies on how various treatments are applied. *$44.95*

*416 pages hardcover*
*ISBN 0-471106-38-0*

**3189 Positive Self-Talk for Children**

Books on Special Children
PO Box 305
Congers, NY 10920
845-638-1236
FAX 845-638-0847
http://www.boscbooks.com/
e-mail: irene@boscbooks.com
*D Bloch, Author*

This book teaches positive talk and ideas to achieve positive self-esteem. Use this as a rereference in specific situations: ie: fears on 1st day of school, doctor's visit. Covers cases, includes specific dialogue. *$12.95*

*331 pages softcover*
*ISBN 0-553351-98-2*

**3190 Practical Parent's Handbook on Teaching Children with Learning Disabilities**

Charles C Thomas Publisher
2600 S 1st Street
Springfield, IL 62704
217-789-8980
800-258-8980
FAX 217-789-9130
http://www.ccthomas.com
e-mail: books@ccthomas.com
*Shelby Holley, Author*

Helps children who learn differently and who have been failing or underachieving in school by enabling adults with no previous teaching experience to design and implement an effective remedial program. Helps parents make realistic changes in the physical and emotional environment at home and at school, gives simple objective tests that show what a child knows and what he needs to learn and shows how to use the test findings. *$65.95*

*308 pages Cloth*
*ISBN 0-398059-03-9*

**3191 Raising Your Child to be Gifted**

Brookline Books
300 Bedford Street
Manchester, NH 03101
617-734-6772
FAX 603-922-3348
http://www.brooklinebooks.com
*Dr. James R Campbell, Author*

Moving beyond the usual genetic eplanations for giftedness, Dr. James Campbell presents powerful evidence that it is parental involvement- very specific methods of working with and nurturing a child which increases the child's chances of being gifted. *$19.95*

*275 pages*
*ISBN 1-571290-00-1*

**3192** **Reading Writing & Rage: The Terrible Price Paid By Victims of School Failure**

RWR Press
16800 Adlon Road
Encino, CA 91436          818-784-6561
                          FAX 818-906-2158
             e-mail: dotrwr@earthlink.net
*Dorothy Ungerleider, Author*

Offers the story of seeking help through the words and perceptions of one learning disabled teen, his parents, teachers and professionals. It reveals an often over-looked source of potential violence: pent-up rage from feeling powerless and misunderstood, school failure and ineffective interventions. *$19.95*

*219 pages 2nd Ed. 1996*
*ISBN 0-965025-20-9*

**3193** **Right from the Start: Behavioral Intervention for Young Children with Autism: A Guide**

Therapro
225 Arlington Street
Framingham, MA 01702          508-872-9494
                              800-257-5376
                         FAX 508-875-2062
           http://www.theraproducts.com
            e-mail: info@theraproducts.com
*Mary Jane Weiss, PhD,BCBA & Sandra Harris, PhD, Author*

This informative and user-friendly guide helps parents and service providers explore programs that use early intensive behavioral intervention for young children with autism and related disorders. Within these programs, many children improve in intellectual, social and adaptive functioning, enabling them to move on to regular elementary and preschools. Benefits all children, but primarily useful for children age five and younger.

*215 pages*

**3194** **SMARTS: A Study Skills Resource Guide**

Connecticut Assoc. for Children and Adults with LD
25 Van Zant Street
East Norwalk, CT 06855          203-838-5010
                              FAX 203-866-6108
                http://www.CACLD.org
                e-mail: cacld@juno.com
*Susan Custer, Author*
*Marie Armstrong, Information Specialist*

A comprehensive teachers handbook of activities to help students develop study skills. *$20.50*

*$2.50 shipping*

**3195** **School-Based Home Developmental PE Program**

Therapro
225 Arlington Street
Framingham, MA 01702          508-872-9494
                              800-257-5376
                         FAX 508-875-2062
           http://www.theraproducts.com
            e-mail: info@theraproducts.com
*Barbara Wood, Author*

A wire bound flip book. Comprehensive developmental physical education program indentifies and improves motor ability right down to the specific sensory and perceptual motor areas for children. Has what you need: assessment; parent involvement; understandable directions; examples; and sample letters to parents. Includes fun sheets that parents/professionals can use with children. Activities are for vestibular integration, body awareness, eye-hand coordination, and fine motor manipulation.

**3196** **Seeing Clearly**

Therapro
225 Arlington Street
Framingham, MA 01702          508-872-9494
                              800-257-5376
                         FAX 508-875-2062
           http://www.theraproducts.com
            e-mail: info@theraproducts.com
*Lois Hickman, MS, OTR FAOTA & Rebecca Hutchins, OD, Author*

This booklet is chock-full of great information regarding vision andvisual perceptual problems and activities designed to improve visual skills of both adults and children. Begins with an overview of the development of vision with a checklist of warning signs of vision problems. 25 eye game activities are divided into those for Eye Movements, Suspended Ball, Chalkboard and Visualization (e.g. Pictures in your Mind, Spelling Comprehension, etc.)

**3197** **Sensory Defensiveness in Children Aged 2 to 12: An Intervention Guide for Parents/Caretakers**

Therapro
225 Arlington Street
Framingham, MA 01702          508-872-9494
                              800-257-5376
                         FAX 508-875-2062
           http://www.theraproducts.com
            e-mail: info@theraproducts.com
*Patricia Wilbarger and Julia Wilbarger, Author*

This booklet defines and describes the symptoms and behaviors related to sensory defensiveness, treatment approaches and the rationale behind treatment strategies. Recommended for everyone administering the Wilbarger Protocol Pressure Program.

**3198** **Sensory Integration and the Child**

Therapro
225 Arlington Street
Framingham, MA 01702          508-872-9494
                              800-257-5376
                         FAX 508-875-2062
           http://www.theraproducts.com
            e-mail: info@theraproducts.com
*A Jean Ayres, PhD, Author*

Designed to educate parents, students, and beginning therapists in sensory integration treatment.

**3199 Sensory Integration: Theory and Practice**
Therapro
225 Arlington Street
Framingham, MA 01702          508-872-9494
                              800-257-5376
                         FAX 508-875-2062
              http://www.theraproducts.com
              e-mail: info@theraproducts.com
*Fisher, Murray, and Bundy, Author*

This is the very latest in sensory integration theory and practice.The entire volume achieves an admirable balance between theory and practice, covering sensory integration theory, various kinds of sensory integrative dysfunction and comprehensive discussions of assessment, direct treatment, consultation and continuing research issues.

**3200 Siblings of Children with Autism: A Guide for Families**
Therapro
225 Arlington Street
Framingham, MA 01702          508-872-9494
                              800-257-5376
                         FAX 508-875-2062
              http://www.theraproducts.com
              e-mail: info@theraproducts.com
*Sandra Harris, PhD, Author*

An invaluable guide to understanding sibling relationships, how they are affected by autism, and what families can do to support their other children while coping with the intensive needs of the child with autism.

**3201 Simple Steps: Developmental Activities for Infants, Toddlers & Two Year Olds**
Therapro
225 Arlington Street
Framingham, MA 01702          508-872-9494
                              800-257-5376
                         FAX 508-875-2062
              http://www.theraproducts.com
              e-mail: info@theraproducts.com
*Karen Miller, Author*

300 activites linked to the latest research in brain development. Outlines a typical developmental sequence in 10 domains: social/emotional, fine motor, gross motor, language, cognition, sensory, nature, music & movement, creativity and dramatic play. Chapters on curriculum development and learning environment also included.

**3202 Social Perception of People with Disabilities in History**
Learning Disabilities Association of America
4156 Library Road
Pittsburgh, PA 15234          412-341-1515
                         FAX 412-344-0224
              http://www.ldanatl.org
              e-mail: ldanatl@usaor.net
*Herbert C Covey, Author*

Shows how historical factors shape some of our current perceptions about disability. Of interest to special educators, historians, students of the humanities and social scientists. *$62.95*

*324 pages  Cloth*
*ISBN 0-398068-37-2*

**3203 Son Rise: The Miracle Continues**
Option Indigo Press
2080 S Undermountain Road
Sheffield, MA 01257           413-229-8727
                              800-562-7171
                         FAX 413-229-8727
              http://www.optionindio.com
              e-mail: indigo@bcn.net
*Barry Neil Kaufman, Author*

This book documents Raun Kaufman's astonishing develpment from a lifeless, autistic, retarded child into a highly verbal, lovable youngster with no traces of his former condition. It details Raun's extraordinary progress from the age of four into young adulthood. It also shares moving accounts of five families that successfully used the Son-Rise Program to reach their own special children. An awe-inspiring reminder that love moves mountains. A must for any parent, professional or teacher. *$14.95*

*ISBN 0-915811-61-8*

**3204 Source for Dysarthria**
LinguiSystems
3100 4th Avenue
East Moline, IL 61244         800-776-4332
                         FAX 800-577-4555
              http://www.linguisystems.com
              e-mail: service@linguisystems.com
*Linda Bowers, Owner*
*Rosemary Huisingh, Owner*

You'll reach for this book as a therapy tool again and again. This outstanding manual gives you information on types of dysarthria, evaluation and treatment planning options, axamples of documentation, and much more.

*Adults*

**3205 Special-Needs Reading List**
Woodbine House
6510 Bells Mill Road
Bethesda, MD 20817            301-897-3570
                              800-843-7323
                         FAX 301-897-5838
              http://www.woodbinehouse.com
              e-mail: info@woodbinehouse.com
*Wilma Sweeney, Author*

In one easy-to-use volume, The Special-Needs reading List reviews and recommends the best books, journals, newsletters, organizations, and other information sources on children with disabilities. *$18.95*

*300 pages  Paperback*
*ISBN 0-933149-74-3*

**3206 Study Skills: A Landmark School Student Guide**
Landmark School
429 Hale Street
Prides Crossing, MA 01965     978-236-3216
                         FAX 978-927-7268
              http://www.landmarkschool.org
              e-mail: outreach@landmarkschool.org
*Diane Vener, Author*
*Dan Ahearn, Program Director*
*Trish Newhall, Associate Director*
*Kathryn Frye, Administrative Assistant*

Designed to help all students learn to comprehend and organize the information they must learn in school, Study Skills: A Landmark School Student Guide offers instruction in how to apply specific comprehension and study skills including multiple exercises to practice each skill. Intended for reading levels of middle school and beyond. *$30.00*

*187 pages*
*ISBN 0-962411-97-3*

**3207 Stuttering and Your Child: Questions and Answers**

**Stuttering Foundation of America**
**3100 Walnut Grove Road**
**Memphis, TN 38111**          901-452-7343
800-992-9392
FAX 901-452-3931
http://www.stutterSFA.org
e-mail: stutterSFA@vantek.net
*June Fraser, Director*
*Anne Edwards, Office Coordinator*

Provides help, information, and resources to those who stutter, their families, schools day care centers, and all others who need help for a stuttering problem. *$1.00*

**3208 Substance Use Among Children and Adolescents**

**Books on Special Children**
**PO Box 305**
**Congers, NY 10920**          845-638-1236
FAX 845-638-0847
http://www.boscbooks.com/
e-mail: irene@boscbooks.com
*AM Pagliaro, Author*

Exposure and use among infants, children and adolescents. Impact on mental and physical health. Ingestion of substances during pregnancy and effects on fetus and neonate. Drug abuse effects on learning, memory.. Preventing and treating children and adolescents. *$59.95*

*405 pages hardcover*
*ISBN 0-471580-42-2*

**3209 Supporting Children with Communication Difficulties In Inclusive Settings**

**Books on Special Children**
**PO Box 305**
**Congers, NY 10920**          845-638-1236
FAX 845-638-0847
http://www.boscbooks.com/
e-mail: irene@boscbooks.com
*L McCormick, Author*

A collaboration of professionals and parents can achieve language communication competence in classroom and other settings. Essential background material, assessment and intervention and needs of special populations are discussed. Contains sectional headings and marginal comments, chapter summary. *$55.95*

*530 pages softcover*
*ISBN 0-023792-72-8*

**3210 Surface Counseling**

**Edge Enterprises**
**PO Box 1304**
**Lawrence, KS 66044**          785-749-1473
FAX 785-749-0207
e-mail: edge@midusa.net
*Joe N Crank, Donald D Deshler, Jean B Schumaker, Author*
*Jacqueline Schafer, Managing Editor*

Details a set of relationship-building skills necessary for establishing a trusting, cooperative relationship between adults and youths and a problem-solving strategy that youths can learn to use by themselves. Includes study guide questions, model dialogues and role-play activities. Useful for any adult who has daily contact with children and adolescents. *$8.00*

*60 pages Paperback*

**3211 Survival Guide for Kids with LD**

**Therapro**
**225 Arlington Street**
**Framingham, MA 01702**          508-872-9494
800-257-5376
FAX 508-875-2062
http://www.theraproducts.com
e-mail: info@theraproducts.com
*Gary Fisher, PhD & Rhonda Cummings, EdD, Author*

Popular book that is highly reccommended. Contains vital information, practical advice, step-by-step strategies, and encouragement for children labeled Learning Disabled.

**3212 Tactics for Improving Parenting Skills (TIPS)**

**Sopris West**
**4093 Specialty Place**
**Longmont, CO 80504**
800-547-6747
FAX 303-776-5934
*Bob Algozzine, Author*
*Jim Ysseldyke, Author*

Perhaps best described as a compliation of one-page parenting brochures, this helpful resource represents volumes of ideas and suggestions on topics of concern in today's families.

*202 pages*
*ISBN 1-570350-35-3*

**3213 Tales from the Workplace ADD & LD**

**JKL Communications**
**PO Box 40157**
**Washington, DC 20016**          202-223-5097
FAX 202-223-5096
http://www.lathamlaw.org
e-mail: plath3@his.com

*$15.00*

# Media: Books /Parents & Professionals

**3214** **Teach Me Language**

**Slosson Educational Publications**
**538 Buffalo Road**
**East Aurora, NY 14052**          888-756-7766
                                   800-828-4800
                                   FAX 800-655-3840
                                   http://www.sloss.com
                                   e-mail: slosson@slosson.com
*Joan M Harwell, Author*

Teach Me Language is designed for teachers, therapists, and parents, and includes a step-by-step how to manual with 400 pages of instructions, explanations, examples, and games and cards to attack language weaknesses common to children with pervasive developmental disorders. *$29.95*

**3215** **Teaching Developmentally Disabled Children**

**Slosson Educational Publications**
**538 Buffalo Road**
**East Aurora, NY 14052**          716-652-0930
                                   800-828-4800
                                   FAX 800-655-3840
                                   http://www.slosson.com
                                   e-mail: slosson@slosson.com
*O Ivar Lovaas, Author*

This instructional program for teachers, nurses, and parents is clear and concisely shows how to help children who are developmentally disabled function more normally at home, in school, and in the community. *$34.00*

*250 pages*

**3216** **Teaching Old Logs New Tricks: Absurdities and Realities of Education**

**Peytral Publications**
**PO Box 1162**
**Minnetonka, MN 55345**          952-949-8707
                                  877-739-8725
                                  FAX 952-906-9777
                                  http://www.peytral.com
                                  e-mail: help@peytral.com
*Michael F Giangreco, Author*
*Kevin Ruelle, Illustrator*
*Peggy Hammeken, Owner/Publisher*

If you enjoyed Ants in His Pants and Flying by the Seat of your Pants - you'll love this book. This publication contains 100+ carefully crafted cartoons which may be reproduced as transparencies for staff development and training. This book is the third book in a series of three. *$19.95*

*112 pages  Educators*
*ISBN 1-890455-43-1*

**3217** **Teaching Reading to Children with Down Syndrome**

**Woodbine House**
**6510 Bells Mill Road**
**Bethesda, MD 20817**          301-897-3570
                                800-843-7323
                                FAX 301-897-5838
                                http://www.woodbinehouse.com
                                e-mail: info@woodbinehouse.com
*Patricia Logan Oelwein, Author*

Teach your child with Down syndrome to read using the author's nationally recognized, proven method. From introducing the alphabet to writing and spelling, the lessons are easy to follow. The many pictures and flash cards included appeal to visual learners and are easy to photocopy! *$16.95*

*392 pages  Paperback*
*ISBN 0-933149-55-7*

**3218** **Teaching Students with Mild Disabilities**

**Books on Special Children**
**PO Box 305**
**Congers, NY 10920**          845-638-1236
                               FAX 845-638-0847
                               http://www.boscbooks.com/
                               e-mail: irene@boscbooks.com
*William N Bender, Author*

Specific strategies for effective instruction in special ed. Basis for effective instruction, specialized instructional areas, strategies for curriculum content areas, information on indirect instructional responsibilities. Chapters have objectives, key words, chapter headings, interest boxes, tables, photos, sample questionaires. *$66.00*

*388 pages  softcover*
*ISBN 0-138927-20-0*

**3219** **Teaching of Reading: A Continuum from Kindergarten through College**

**AVKO Educational Research Foundation**
**3084 W Willard Road**
**Clio, MI 48420**          810-686-9283
                            FAX 810-686-1101
                            http://www.avko.org/teaching_of_reading.htm
                            e-mail: avkoemail@aol.com
*Don McCabe, Author*
*Don McCabe, Research Director*

This book covers concepts, techniques, and practical diagnostic tests not normally taught in regular college courses on reading. It is designed to be used by teachers, parents, tutors, and college reading instructors willing to try new approaches to old problems. *$49.95*

*364 pages*
*ISBN 1-564006-50-6*

**3220** **Teaching the Dyslexic Child**

**Slosson Educational Publications**
**538 Buffalo Road**
**East Aurora, NY 14052**          716-652-0930
                                   800-828-4800
                                   FAX 800-655-3840
                                   http://www.slosson.com
                                   e-mail: slosson@slosson.com
*Anita N Griffiths, Author*

Teaching the Dyslexic Child talks about the frustrations that the dyslexic youngsters and their parents encounter in the day to day collisions with life's demand. *$12.00*

*128 pages*

**3221** **Understanding Learning Disabilities: A Parent Guide and Workbook, Third Edition**

**York Press**
**PO Box 504**
**Timonium, MD  21094**          **410-560-1557**
                                **800-962-2763**
                          **FAX 410-560-6758**
                    **http://www.yorkpress.com**
                         **e-mail: york@abs.net**
*Mary Louise Trusdell & Inge Horowitz, Author*
*Elinor Hartwig, President*

An invaluable resource for parents who are new to the field of learning disabilities. Easy to read and overflowing with helpful information and advice. *$25.00*

   *380 pages*
   *ISBN 0-912752-67-X*

**3222** **Understanding and Teaching Children with Autism**

**Books on Special Children**
**PO Box 305**
**Congers, NY  10920**          **845-638-1236**
                          **FAX 845-638-0847**
                    **http://www.boscbooks.com/**
                   **e-mail: irene@boscbooks.com**
*R Jordan, Author*

The triad of impairment: social, language and communication and thought behavior aspects of development discussed. Difficulties in interacting, transfer of learning and bizarre behaviors are syndome. Many LD are associated with autism. *$57.00*

   *175 pages  hardcover*
   *ISBN 0-471958-88-3*

**3223** **Unlocking the Mysteries of Sensory Dysfunction**

**Therapro**
**225 Arlington Street**
**Framingham, MA  01702**          **508-872-9494**
                                **800-257-5376**
                          **FAX 508-875-2062**
                    **http://www.theraproducts.com**
                   **e-mail: info@theraproducts.com**
*Elizabeth Anderson & Pauline Emmons, Author*

A must-read for therapists, parents and educators. Written by parents, this book is informative and insightful regarding children with sensory integration problems. The autors offer practical suggestions dealing with the often complex realities of living with a child who has sensory issues. A good explanation of sensory integration therapy and advice about how to access it.

**3224** **What to Expect: The Toddler Years**

**Workman Publishing**
**708 Broadway**
**New York, NY  10003**
                                **800-722-7202**
                          **FAX 800-521-1832**
                    **http://www.workman.com**
*Arlene Eisenberg, et al., Author*
*Jerry Mandel, Special Markets Director*

They guided you through pregnancy, they guided you through baby's first year, and now they'll guide you through the toddler years. In a direct continuation of What to Expect When You're Expecting and What to Expect the Frist Year, American's bestselling pregnancy and childcare authors turn their uniquely comprehensive, lively, and reassuring coverage to years two and three. *$15.95*

   *928 pages  Paperback*

**3225** **When Your Child Has LD**

**Free Spirit Publishing**
**217 5th Avenue N**
**Minneapolis, MN  55401**          **612-338-2068**
                                **800-735-7323**
                          **FAX 612-337-5050**
                    **http://www.freespirit.com**
                 **e-mail: help4kids@freespirit.com**
*Rhoda Cummings and Gary Fisher, Author*
*Betsy Gabler, Sales Manager*

Clear, reassuring advice and essential information for parents of children ages five and up who have a learning difference. *$12.95*

   *160 pages*
   *ISBN 0-915793-87-3*

## Young Adults

**3226** **Assertive Option: Your Rights and Responsibilities**

**Research Press**
**PO Box 9177**
**Champaign, IL  61826**          **217-352-3273**
                                **800-519-2707**
                          **FAX 217-352-1221**
                    **http://www.researchpress.com**
                 **e-mail: rp@researchpress.com**
*Dr. Patricia Jakubowski, Dr. Arthur J Lange, Author*
*Ann Wendell, President*

A self instructional assertiveness book, with many exercises and self tests. *$24.95*

   *348 pages*
   *ISBN 0-878221-92-1*

**3227** **Education of Students with Disabilities: Where Do We Stand?**

**National Council on Disability**
**1331 F Street NW**
**Washington, DC  20591**          **202-272-2004**
                          **FAX 202-272-2022**
                    **http://www.ncd.gov**
                 **e-mail: mquigley@ncd.ogv**

**3228  Keeping Ahead in School: A Students Book About Learning Disabilities & Learning Disorders**
Educators Publishing Service
31 Smith Place
Cambridge, MA  02138          617-547-6706
                              800-225-5750
                          FAX 617-547-0412
                       http://www.epsbooks.com
                       e-mail: eps@epsbooks.com
*Mel Levine, Author*

Written for students 9 to 15 years of age with learning disorders. This book helps students gain important insights into their problems by combining realism with justifiable optimism. *$24.75*

        *ISBN 0-838820-09-7*

**3229  Modern Consumer Education: You and the Law**
Educational Design
345 Hudson Street
New York, NY  10014
                              800-221-9372
                          FAX 866-805-5723
                    http://www.triumphlearning.com
*Buz Traugot, Sales Representative*

An instructional program to teach independent living, with emphasis on legal resources and survival skills. *$59.00*

**3230  Phonemic Awareness: Lessons, Activities & Games**
Peytral Publicatons
PO Box 1162
Minnetonka, MN  55345          952-949-8707
                               877-739-8725
                           FAX 952-906-9777
                        http://www.peytral.com
                        e-mail: help@peytral.com
*Victoria Groves Scott, Author*

Help struggling readers with Phonemic Awareness training. This all inclusive book iuncludes 48 scripted lessons. May be used as a prerequisite to reading or for stuggling students. Includes 49 reproductible masters. May be used with individual students or with groups. *$27.95*

        *176 pages*

**3231  Reading Is Fun**
Teddy Bear Press
3639 Midway Drive
San Diego, CA  92110          619-223-7311
                          FAX 619-255-2158
                    http://www.teddybearpress.net
                    e-mail: fparker@teddybearpress.net
*Fran Parker, President*

Introduces 55 primer level words in six reading books and accompanting activity sheets. This easy to use reading program provides repition, visual motor, visual discrimination and word comprehension excersies. The manual and placement test. *$85.00*

        *ISBN 1-928876-01-3*

**3232  School Survival Guide for Kids with Learning Disabilities**
Free Spirit Publishing
217 5th Avenue N
Minneapolis, MN  55401          612-338-2068
                                800-735-7323
                            FAX 612-337-5050
                        http://www.freespirit.com
                        e-mail: help4kids@freespirit.com
*Rhoda Cummings & Gary Fisher, Author*
*Betsy Gabler, Sales Manager*

Strategies and tips for building confidence in reading, writing, spelling, and math, managing time, coping with testing, gtting help, and more. *$12.95*

        *176 pages*
        *ISBN 0-915793-32-6*

**3233  Succeeding in the Workplace**
JKL Communications
PO Box 40157
Washington, DC  20016          202-223-5097
                           FAX 202-223-5096
                       http://www.lathamlaw.org
                       e-mail: plath3@his.com

        *$29.00*

**3234  Survival Guide for Teenagers with LD**
Free Spirit Publishing
217 5th Avenue N
Minneapolis, MN  55401          612-338-2068
                                800-735-7323
                            FAX 612-337-5050
                        http://www.freespirit.com
                        e-mail: help4kids@freespirit.com
*Rhoda Cummings and Gary Fisher, Author*
*Betsy Gabler, Sales Manager*

A step-by-step handbook to help teens with LD succeed at school and prepare for life as adults. Also available in audio cassette format. *$12.95*

        *200 pages*
        *ISBN 0-915793-51-2*

**3235  Winning at Math: Your Guide to Learning Mathematics Through Successful Study Skills**
Academic Success Press
6023 26th Street
West Bradenton, FL  34207          941-359-2819
                                   800-444-2524
                               FAX 941-753-2882
                        http://www.academicsuccess.com
                        e-mail: academ@academicsuccess.com
*P Nolting, Author*

A guide that helps people with learning disabilities learn math easier.

**3236  Winning the Study Game**
Peytral Publicatons
PO Box 1162
Minnetonka, MN  55345          952-949-8707
                               877-739-8725
                           FAX 952-906-9777
                        http://www.peytral.com
*Lawrence J Greene, Author*

A comprehensive study skills program for students with learning differences in grades 6-11. The student book has 16 units which will help students learn to study better, take notes, advance their thinking skills while stregthening their reading and writing. The student version is available in a reproducible or consumable format. Teachers guide sold separately. *$34.95*

*2500 pages*
*ISBN 1-890455-48-2*

**3237 You Don't Have to be Dyslexic**

**Melvin-Smith Learning Center**
**7230 S Land Park Drive**
**Sacramento, CA 95831**        **916-392-6415**
                               **800-50L-EARN**
                               **FAX 916-392-6453**
*Joan M Smith, Author*

Dr. Smith has designed this user-friendly book to: Demystify the area of learning that is emotionally charged for many people, Provide teaching methods for teachers, professionals and parents. Depict actual case studies, describing various dyslexic learning styles. And use real-life cases which show excellent examples of how to remediate learning issues. *$19.95*

*205 pages*

## General

**3238  A Student's Guide to Jobs**
NICHCY
PO Box 1492
Washington, DC  20013          202-884-8200
800-695-0285
FAX 202-884-8441
http://www.nichcy.org
e-mail: nichcy@ace.org
*Susan Ripley, Information Specialist*

Young people with mental retardation speak freely about their job-related experiences. *$2.00*

*8 pages*

**3239  A Student's Guide to the IEP**
NICHCY
PO Box 1492
Washington, DC  20013          202-884-8200
800-695-0285
FAX 202-884-8441
http://www.nichcy.org
e-mail: nichcy@ace.org
*Susan Ripley, Information Specialist*

A guide for students that features other students discussing their experiences as active members on their IEP team. *$2.00*

*12 pages*

**3240  Accessing Parent Groups**
NICHCY
PO Box 1492
Washington, DC  20013          202-884-8200
800-695-0285
FAX 202-884-8441
http://www.nichcy.org
e-mail: nichcy@ace.org
*Susan Ripley, Information Specialist*

Helps parents locate support groups where they can share information, give and receive emotional support, and address common concerns. *$2.00*

*12 pages*

**3241  Accessing Programs for Infants, Toddlers and Preschoolers**
NICHCY
PO Box 1492
Washington, DC  20013          202-884-8200
800-695-0285
FAX 202-884-8441
http://www.nichcy.org
e-mail: nichcy@ace.org
*Susan Ripley, Information Specialist*

This guide helps locate intervention services for infants and toddlers with disabilities. Also answers questions about educational programs for preschoolers. *$2.00*

*20 pages*

**3242  Advocacy Services for Families of Children in Special Education**
Arizona Department of Education
1535 W Jefferson Street
Phoenix, AZ  85007          602-542-4361
800-352-4558
FAX 602-542-5440
http://www.ade.state.az.us
e-mail: ADE@ade.az.gov

Information provided to families that have children in special education.

**3243  Assessing Children for the Presence of a Disability**

NICHCY
PO Box 1492
Washington, DC  20013          202-884-8200
800-695-0285
FAX 202-884-8441
http://www.nichcy.org
e-mail: nichcy@ace.org
*Susan Ripley, Information Specialist*

Describes the criteria and process preformed by school systems to determine if a child has a learning disabilty. *$4.00*

*28 pages*

**3244  Assessing the ERIC Resource Collection**
NICHCY
PO Box 1492
Washington, DC  20013          202-884-8200
800-695-0285
FAX 202-884-8441
http://www.nichcy.org
e-mail: nichcy@ace.org
*Susan Ripley, Information Specialist*

A nationwide network that gives access to education literature, this document explains how to search and retrieve documents from ERIC. Also explains how to find information about children with disabilites. *$2.00*

*8 pages*

**3245  Can What a Child Eats Make Him Dull, Stupid or Hyperactive?**
Learning Disabilities Association of America
4156 Library Road
Pittsburgh, PA  15234          412-341-1515
FAX 412-344-0224
http://www.ldanatl.org
e-mail: ldanatl@usaor.net

*$2.00*

**3246  Children with Learning and Behavioral Disorders**

Learning Disabilities Association of America
4156 Library Road
Pittsburgh, PA  15234          412-341-1515
FAX 412-344-0224
http://www.ldanatl.org
e-mail: ldanatl@usaor.net

*$.50*

**3247 Complete Set of State Resource Sheets**

NICHCY
PO Box 1492
Washington, DC 20013          202-884-8200
800-695-0285
FAX 202-884-8441
http://www.nichcy.org
e-mail: nichcy@ace.org
*Susan Ripley, Information Specialist*

Provides a sheet for every state and territory in the United States. *$10.00*

*200 pages*

**3248 Directory of Organizations**

NICHCY
PO Box 1492
Washington, DC 20013          202-884-8200
800-695-0285
FAX 202-884-8441
http://www.nichcy.org
e-mail: nichcy@ace.org
*Susan Ripley, Information Specialist*

Lists many organizations and services *$4.00*

*28 pages*

**3249 Education of Children and Youth with Special Needs: What do the Laws Say?**

NICHCY
PO Box 1492
Washington, DC 20013          202-884-8200
800-695-0285
FAX 202-884-8441
http://www.nichcy.org
e-mail: nichcy@ace.org
*Susan Ripley, Information Specialist*

Provides an overview of 3 laws that aid disabled children; 1. Section 504 of the Rehabilitation Act of 1973, 2. the Individuals with Disabilities Education Act, and 3. the Carl P. Perkins Vocational Educational Act. *$4.00*

*16 pages*

**3250 Ethical and Legal Issues in School Counseling**

American School Counselor Association
801 N Fairfax Street
Alexandria, VA 22314          703-683-2722
800-306-4722
FAX 703-683-1619
http://www.schoolcounselor.org
e-mail: asca@schoolcounselor.org
*Stephanie Will, Office Manager*

Contains answers to many of the most controversial and challenging questions school counselors face every day. *$40.50*

*ISBN 1-556200-55-2*

**3251 Fact Sheet: Attention Deficit Hyperactivity Disorder**

Learning Disabilities Association of America
4156 Library Road
Pittsburgh, PA 15234          412-341-1515
FAX 412-344-0224
http://www.ldanatl.org
e-mail: ldanatl@usaor.net

A pamphlet offering factual information on ADHD.

**3252 Fundamentals of Autism**

Slosson Educational Publications
538 Buffalo Road
East Aurora, NY 14052          716-652-0930
800-828-4800
FAX 800-655-3840
http://www.slosson.com
e-mail: slosson@slosson.com
*Sue Larson, Author*
*Steven W Slosson, President*
*John Slosson, VP*

Provides a quick, user friendly effective and accurate approach to help in identifying and developing educationally related program objectives for children diagnosed as Autistic. These materials have been designed to be easily and functionally used by teachers, therapists, special education/learning disability resource specialists, psychologists, and others who work with children diagnosed with similar disabilites.

**3253 General Information about Autism**

NICHCY
PO Box 1492
Washington, DC 20013          202-884-8200
800-695-0285
FAX 202-884-8441
http://www.nichcy.org
e-mail: nichcy@ace.org
*Susan Ripley, Executive Director*

Offers information about autism.

**3254 General Information about Disabilities**

NICHCY
PO Box 1492
Washington, DC 20013          202-884-8200
800-695-0285
FAX 202-884-8841
http://www.nichcy.org
e-mail: nichcy@ace.org
*Susan Ripley, Information Specialist*

A fact sheet offering information on the Education of the Handicapped Act.

*2 pages*

**3255 General Information about Speech and Language Disorders**

NICHCY
PO Box 1492
Washington, DC 20013          202-884-8200
800-695-0285
FAX 202-884-8841
http://www.nichcy.org
e-mail: nichcy@ace.org
*Susan Ripley, Information Specialist*

Offers characteristics, educational implications and associations in the area of speech and language disorders.

**3256** **IDEA Amendments**
NICHCY
PO Box 1492
Washington, DC 20013          202-884-8200
                              800-695-0285
                         FAX 202-884-8441
                         http://www.nichcy.org
                         e-mail: nichcy@ace.org
*Susan Ripley, Information Specialist*

Examines the important changes that have occured in the Individuals Education Act, amended in June of 1997. *$4.00*

*40 pages*

**3257** **If Your Child Stutters: A Guide for Parents**
Stuttering Foundation of America
3100 Walnut Grove Road
Memphis, TN 38111            901-452-0995
                             800-992-9392
                        FAX 901-452-3931
                        http://www.stuttersfa.org
                        e-mail: stutter@vantek.net
*Anne Edwards, Coordinator*

A guide that enables parents to provide appropriate help to children who stutter. *$1.00*

**3258** **Individualized Education Programs**
NICHCY
PO Box 1492
Washington, DC 20013          202-884-8200
                              800-695-0285
                         FAX 202-884-8441
                         http://www.nichcy.org
                         e-mail: nichcy@ace.org
*Susan Ripley, Information Specialist*

Provides guidance regarding the legal requirement for beginning a student's IEP. *$2.00*

*32 pages*

**3259** **Interventions for Students with Learning Disabilities**
NICHCY
PO Box 1492
Washington, DC 20013          202-884-8200
                              800-695-0285
                         FAX 202-884-8441
                         http://www.nichcy.org
                         e-mail: nichcy@ace.org
*Susan Ripley, Information Specialist*

A document that examines 2 different interventions for students who have learning disabilities; the first deals with strategies and the second with phonological awareness. *$4.00*

*16 pages*

**3260** **National Resources**
NICHCY
PO Box 1492
Washington, DC 20013          202-884-8200
                              800-695-0285
                         FAX 202-884-8441
                         http://www.nichcy.org
                         e-mail: nichcy@ace.org
*Susan Ripley, Information Specialist*

Lists different organizations that provide information about different disabilities.

*6 pages*

**3261** **National Toll-free Numbers**
NICHCY
PO Box 1492
Washington, DC 20013          202-884-8200
                              800-695-0285
                         FAX 202-884-8441
                         http://www.nichcy.org
                         e-mail: nichcy@ace.org
*Susan Ripley, Information Specialist*

Gives the names of organizations with toll-free numbers who specialize in different disabilities.

*6 pages*

**3262** **Parenting a Child with Special Needs: A Guide to Reading and Resources**
NICHCY
PO Box 1492
Washington, DC 20013          202-884-8200
                              800-695-0285
                         FAX 202-884-8441
                         http://www.nichcy.org
                         e-mail: nichcy@ace.org
*Susan Ripley, Information Specialist*

Provides information to families whose child has been diagnosed with a disability. Also gives insight on how disabilities can in turn affect the family. *$4.00*

*24 pages*

**3263** **Parents Guide**
NICHCY
PO Box 1492
Washington, DC 20013          202-884-8200
                              800-695-0285
                         FAX 202-884-8841
                         http://www.nichcy.org
                         e-mail: nichcy@ace.org
*Lisa Kupper, Editor*
*Susan Ripley, Information Specialist*

Talks directly to parents about specific disability issues.

**3264** **Planning a Move: Mapping Your Strategy**
NICHCY
PO Box 1492
Washington, DC 20013          202-884-8200
                              800-695-0285
                         FAX 202-884-8441
                         http://www.nichcy.org
                         e-mail: nichcy@ace.org
*Susan Ripley, Information Specialist*

This guide helps to make moving to a new place easier for parents and their children by listing available services in the new area and compiling educational and medical records. *$2.00*

*12 pages*

**3265  Planning for Inclusion: News Digest**
**NICHCY**
**PO Box 1492**
**Washington, DC  20013**          **202-884-8200**
                                    **800-695-0285**
                              **FAX 202-884-8441**
                          **http://www.nichcy.org**
                          **e-mail: nichcy@ace.org**
*Susan Ripley, Information Specialist*

Provides a general guide to raising children with learning disabilities in an educational setting. *$4.00*

*32 pages*

**3266  Problem Sensitivity: A Qualitative Difference in the Learning Disabled**
**National Clearinghouse of Rehabilitation Materials**
**Oklahoma State University**
**Stillwater, OK  74078**          **405-744-2001**
                              **FAX 405-744-2000**
                    **http://www.nchrtm.okstate.edu**

Presenting information that can be used in modifying the cognitive structure at the Problem Sensitivity level, this paper looks at the learning disabled adult from the viewpoint of cognitive psychology. Behavior is considered significantly deviant when a person's approach to a task is at a qualitatively different level than expected at the person's age.

*21 pages*

**3267  Promising Practices and Future Directions for Special Education**
**NICHCY**
**PO Box 1492**
**Washington, DC  20013**          **202-884-8200**
                                    **800-695-0285**
                              **FAX 202-884-8441**
                          **http://www.nichcy.org**
                          **e-mail: nichcy@ace.org**
*Susan Ripley, Information Specialist*

Examines different research regarding the educational methods for children with learning disabilities. *$4.00*

*24 pages*

**3268  Public Agencies Fact Sheet**
**NICHCY**
**PO Box 1492**
**Washington, DC  20013**          **202-884-8200**
                                    **800-695-0285**
                              **FAX 202-884-8841**
                          **http://www.nichcy.org**
                          **e-mail: nichcy@ace.org**
*Susan Ripley, Information Specialist*

General information on public agencies that serve the disabled individual.

*2 pages*

**3269  Questions Often Asked about Special Education Services**
**NICHCY**
**PO Box 1492**
**Washington, DC  20013**          **202-884-8200**
                                    **800-695-0285**
                              **FAX 202-884-8841**
                          **http://www.nichcy.org**
                          **e-mail: nichcy@ace.org**
*Susan Ripley, Informaton Specialist*

Offers information regarding special education.

**3270  Questions Often Asked by Parents About Special Education Services**
**NICHCY**
**PO Box 1492**
**Washington, DC  20013**          **202-884-8200**
                                    **800-695-0285**
                              **FAX 202-884-8441**
                          **http://www.nichcy.org**
                          **e-mail: nichcy@ace.org**
*Susan Ripley, Information Specialist*

A publication to help parents learn about the Individuals with Disabilities Education Act. Also discusses how student access special education and other related services.

*12 pages*

**3271  Questions and Answers About the IDEA News Digest**
**NICHCY**
**PO Box 1492**
**Washington, DC  20013**          **202-884-8200**
                              **FAX 202-884-8441**
                          **http://www.nichcy.org**
                          **e-mail: nichcy@ace.org**
*Susan Ripley, Information Specialist*

Covers the more commonly asked questions from families and professionals about the IDEA. *$4.00*

*28 pages*

**3272  Related Services for School-Aged Children with Disabilities**
**NICHCY**
**PO Box 1492**
**Washington, DC  20013**          **202-884-8200**
                                    **800-695-0285**
                              **FAX 202-884-8441**
                          **http://www.nichcy.org**
                          **e-mail: nichcy@ace.org**
*Susan Ripley, Information Specialist*

Examines the different services offered to children with disabilities such as speech-language pathology, transportation, occupational and physical therapy and special health services. *$4.00*

*24 pages*

**3273  Resources for Adults with Disabilities**
NICHCY
PO Box 1492
Washington, DC  20013
202-884-8200
800-695-0285
FAX 202-884-8441
http://www.nichcy.org
e-mail: nichcy@ace.org
*Susan Ripley, Information Specialist*

Helps adults with disabilities find organizations that will help them find employment, education, recreation and independent living. *$2.00*

*16 pages*

**3274  Serving on Boards and Committees**
NICHCY
PO Box 1492
Washington, DC  20013
202-884-8200
800-695-0285
FAX 202-884-8441
http://www.nichcy.org
e-mail: nichcy@ace.org
*Susan Ripley, Information Specialist*

Part of the Parent's Guide series, this publication examines the different boards and committees on which parents of children with disabilities often serve. Also suggests ways to go about becoming involved with such organizations. *$2.00*

*8 pages*

**3275  Special Education and Related Services: Communicating Through Letterwriting**
NICHCY
PO Box 1492
Washington, DC  20013
202-884-8200
800-695-0285
FAX 202-884-8441
http://www.nichcy.org
e-mail: nichcy@ace.org
*Susan Ripley, Information Specialist*

Identifies the rights of parents and their children with disabilities and explains when and how to notify the school in writing about such conditions. *$2.00*

*20 pages*

**3276  State Capitals**
PO Box 7376
Alexandria, VA  22307
703-768-2545
800-876-2545
FAX 703-768-9690
http://www.statecapitals.com
e-mail: newsletters@statecapitals.com
Briefing on important selected state activities.

**3277  State Resource Sheet**
NICHCY
PO Box 1492
Washington, DC  20013
202-884-8200
800-695-0285
FAX 202-884-8441
http://www.nichcy.org
e-mail: nichcy@ace.org
*Susan Ripley, Information Specialist*

List numbers of different organizations that deal with disabilities by state.

**3278  Underachieving Gifted**
Council for Exceptional Children
1110 N Glebe Road
Arlington, VA  22201
703-620-3660
888-232-7733
FAX 703-264-9494
http://www.cec.sped.org/
*Gerard Hurley, Contact*

A collection of annotated references from the ERIC and Exceptional Child Evaluation Resources (171 abstracts). Note: Abstracts only. Not the complete research. *$1.00*

**3279  What Every Parent Should Know about Learning Disabilities**
Connecticut Assoc. for Children and Adults with LD
25 Van Zant Street
East Norwalk, CT  06855
203-838-5010
FAX 203-866-6108
http://www.CACLD.org
*CL Bete, Author*

What to do with a child with a learning disability.

**3280  When Pre-schoolers are Not on Target: Guide for Parents & Early Childhood Educators**
Learning Disabilities Association of America
LDA Literary Depository
Pittsburgh, PA  15234
412-341-1515
FAX 412-344-0224
http://www.ldanatl.org
e-mail: ldanatl@usaor.net
New booklet provides information on early identification of learning disabilities and appropriate intervention strategies to professionals who work with preschool children. Available in Spanish. Discounts for multiples. *$4.00*

**3281  Who's Teaching Our Children with Disabilities?**
NICHCY
PO Box 1492
Washington, DC  20013
202-884-8200
800-695-0285
FAX 202-884-8441
http://www.nichcy.org
e-mail: nichcy@ace.org
*Susan Ripley, Information Specialist*

Takes a detailed look at the people who are teaching children with disabilities. *$4.00*

*24 pages*

**3282  Your Child's Evaluation**
NICHCY
PO Box 1492
Washington, DC  20013
202-884-8200
800-695-0285
FAX 202-884-8441
http://www.nichcy.org
e-mail: nichcy@ace.org
*Susan Ripley, Information Specialist*

This document describes the steps that the school system will use to determine if you child has a learning disability. *$2.00*

*4 pages*

## Adults

**3283  Community Education Journal**

National Community Education Association
3929 Old Lee Highway
Fairfax, VA  22030          703-359-8973
                           FAX 703-359-0972
            e-mail: ncea@ids2.idsonline.com

A quarterly publication for people with disabilities.
$25.00

            *Quarterly*

**3284  Correctional Education Quarterly News: US
         Department of Education**

Office of Correctional Education
400 Maryland Avenue SW
Washington, DC  20202        202-205-5621
                           FAX 202-401-2615
            e-mail: oce@inet.ed.gov

Provides information about correctional education
and the activities of the Office of Correctional Education in the US Department of Education. Free.

**3285  International Dyslexia Association: Illinois Branch
         Newsletter**

751 Roosevelt Road
Glen Ellyn, IL  60137        630-469-6900
                           FAX 630-469-6810
            http://www.interdys.org
       e-mail: ilbranch_ida@ameritech.net

*Donna Rafanello, Executive Director*
*Gail Oliphant, Office Manager*

**3286  International Dyslexia Association: Louisiana
         Branch Newsletter**

2125 Coliseum Street
New Orleans, LA  70130        504-876-0034
                           FAX 504-595-8848

*Marqua Brunette, President*

**3287  Moving Forward**

1186 East Avenue
Napa, CA  94559              510-337-2460
                           FAX 510-934-9022
    http://www.iser.com/movingforward-CA.html
            e-mail: aia1@aol.com

*Paul Aziz, Publisher/Editor*
*Agena Aziz, Publisher/Business Manager*

A national newspaper for persons with disabilities offering convention information, book reviews,
assistive technology, law and legislation information
and more. *$11.50*

**3288  NAASLN Newsletter**

Nat'l Assn. of Adults with Special Learning Needs
PO Box 716
Bryn Mawr, PA  19010          610-525-8336
            http://www.ldonline.org

Newsletter focusing on issues related to teaching
adults with special learning needs.

**3289  NICHCY News DigestNat'l Dissemination Center
         For Children W/ Disabilities**

NICHCY
PO Box 1492
Washington, DC  20013        202-884-8200
                             800-695-0285
                       FAX 202-884-8841
            http://www.nichcy.org
            e-mail: nichcy@ace.org

*Lisa Kupper, Editor*

Addresses a single disability issue in depth.

**3290  Rural Education Forum**

161 College Court Building
Manhattan, KS  66506          785-532-5560
                           FAX 785-532-5637
            e-mail: wberryd@dce.ksu.edu

Provides information about rural education programs
resources, research and events.

**3291  Work America**

National Alliance of Business (NAB)
1201 New York Avenue NW
Washington, DC  20005
                             800-787-2848
                       FAX 202-289-1303
            http://www.nab.com
            e-mail: info@nab.com

A monthly newsletter focused on model programs and
information about employment and training.

            *Monthly*

## Children

**3292  Calliope**

Cobblestone Publishing Company
30 Grove Street
Peterborough, NH  03458        603-924-7209
                               800-821-0115
                         FAX 603-924-7380
       http://www.cobblestonepub.com
       e-mail: custsvc@cobblestone.mv.com

*Rosalie Baker, Editor*
*Malcom Jensen, Publisher*
*Charles Baker, Editor*

Winner of the coveted 1998 Educational Press Association's Golden Lamp Award. Calliope brings to the
classroom a fresh and exciting look at world history,
one theme at a time. *$29.95*

            *52 pages  9 times anually*
            ISSN 1050-7086

**3293  KIND News**

NAHEE
PO Box 362
East Haddam, CT  06423        860-434-8666
                           FAX 860-434-9579
            http://www.nahee.org
            e-mail: nahee@nahee.org

*Lesia Winiarskyj, Director Publications*
*Cathy Vincenti, Managing Editor*
*Jessica Vanase, Associate Editor*

Four-page color newspaper with games, puzzles and entertaining, informative articles designed to install kindness to people, animals, and the enviroment and to make reading fun. *$30.00*

*4 pages  9x school year*
*ISSN 1050-9542*

**3294   KIND News Jr: Kids in Nature's Defense**
**Kind News**
**PO Box 362**
**East Haddam, CT  06423**              860-434-8666
                                   FAX 860-434-6282
                          http://www.kindnews.org
                           e-mail: nahee@nahee.org
*Lesia Winiarsky, Director Publications*
*Cathy Vincenti, Managing Editor*
*Jessica Yanase, Associate Editor*

Short, easy-to-read items on the environment and animal world with puzzles, contests and cartoons. Many illustrations, pictures.

**3295   KIND News Primary: Kids in Nature's Defense**
**Kind News**
**PO Box 362**
**East Haddam, CT  06423**              860-434-8666
                                   FAX 860-434-6282
                          http://www.kindnews.org
                           e-mail: nahee@nahee.org
*Lesia Winiarsky, Director Publications*
*Cathy Vincenti, Managing Editor*
*Jessica Yanase, Associate Editor*

Short, easy-to-read items on the environment and animal world with puzzles, pictures to color and cartoons. Many illustrations, pictures.

**3296   KIND News Sr: Kids in Nature's Defense**
**NAHEE**
**PO Box 362**
**East Haddam, CT  06423**              860-434-8666
                                   FAX 860-434-6282
                          http://www.kindnews.org
                           e-mail: nahee@nahee.org
*Lesia Winiarsky, Director Publications*
*Cathy Vincenti, Managing Editor*
*Jessica Yanase, Associate Editor*

Publication put out by the National Association for Humane and Environmental Education, KIND News Sr. is intended for children between grades 5 through 6. The magazine covers different pet issues such as how to care for,feed and play with pets.

**3297   Koala Club News**
**San Diego Zoo Membership Department**
**PO Box 120551**
**San Diego, CA  92112**              619-231-1515
                                 FAX 619-231-0249
                        http://www.sandiegozoo.org
*Georgeanne Irvine, Editor*

A magazine about animals going to kids who are members of the Zoological Society of San Diego Koala Club. *$9.00*

**3298   Let's Find Out**
**Scholastic**
**555 Broadway**
**New York, NY  10012**
*Jean Marzollo, Editor*

Get your PreK and K classes off to a great start with Free-trail copies of Let's Find Out, and bring all this to your teaching program: monthly seasonal themes in 32 colorful weekly issues, activity pages to develop early reading and math skills. *$4.25*

**3299   National Association for Humane and Environmental Education**
**PO Box 362**
**East Haddam, CT  06423**              860-434-8666
                                   FAX 860-434-6282
                          http://www.nahee.org
                           e-mail: nahee@nahee.org
*Lesia Winiarsky, Director Publications*
*Cathy Vincenti, Managing Editor*
*Jesica Yanase, Associate Editor*

**3300   Ranger Rick**
**National Wildlife Foundation/Membership Services**
**11100 Wild Life Center Drive**
**Reston, VA  20190**
                                      800-822-9919
                                   FAX 703-438-6039
                          http://www.nuf.org
*Gerry Bishop, Editor*

A magazine for children ages 6-12 that is dedicated to helping students gain a greater understanding and appreciation of nature. *$15.00*

**3301   Sibling Forum**
**Family Resource Associates**
**35 Haddon Avenue**
**Shrewsbury, NJ  07702**              732-747-5310
                                   FAX 732-747-1896
*Susan Levine, Editor*

Newsletter for siblings aged 10 through teens with brothers or sisters with disabilities. Includes library information, special definitions and feedback from readers. Each issue also has a Focusing on Feelings discussion. A useful tool for siblings, parents, educators, and special workers. *$12.00*

*12 pages  4 Times/Sibling*

**3302   Stone Soup: The Magazine by Young Writers and Artists**
**PO Box 83**
**Santa Cruz, CA  95063**              831-426-5557
                                      800-447-4569
                                   FAX 831-426-1161
                          http://www.stonesoup.com
                           e-mail: editor@stonesoup.com
*Gerry Mandel, Editor*

A literary magazine publishing fiction, poetry, book reviews and art by children through age 13. *$32.00*

*6x/year*

## Parents & Professionals

**3303  ALL Points Bulletin: Department of Education**

**Division of Adult Education and Literacy**
**600 Independence Avenue SW**
**Washington, DC  20202**
                              **FAX 202-205-8973**

The quarterly newsletter of the division of adult education and literacy. Issues focus on selected areas of interest in the field of adult education, current research, new publications, and upcoming events. Special sections concentrate on ESL and workplace literacy issues.

**3304  Adult Basic Education: An Interdisciplinary Journal for Adult Literacy Educators**

**Commission on Adult Basic Education (COABE)**
**Piedmont College**
**Demorest, GA  30535**          **706-778-3000**
                              **FAX 706-778-2811**
        **http://www.206.75.28/journal/abe.html**
              **e-mail: kmelichar@piedmnt.edu**
*Ken Melichar, Editor*

Adult Basic Education: An Interdisciplinary Journal for Adult Literacy Educators is a double-blind, peer review, scholarly journal with a practical intent devoted to improving the efforts of adult educators working with low-literally disadvantaged, and educationally oppressed people. *$25.00*

                *3x/year*

**3305  Association of Higher Education Facilities Officers Newsletter**

**1643 Prince Street**
**Alexandria, VA  22314**          **703-684-1446**
                              **FAX 703-549-2772**
                   **http://www.appa.org**

A newsletter whose purpose is to promote excellence in the administration, care, operation, planning, and development of higher education facilities.

**3306  Children and Families**

**National Head Start Association**
**1651 Prince Street**
**Alexandria, VA  22314**          **703-739-0875**
                              **FAX 703-739-0878**

The magazine of the National Head Start Association.

**3307  Connections: A Journal of Adult Literacy**

**Adult Literacy Resource Institute**
**989 Commonwealth Avenue**
**Boston, MA  02215**              **617-782-8956**
                              **FAX 617-782-9011**
                   **http://www.alri.org**

Connections is primarily intended to provide an opportunity for adult educators in the Boston area to communicate with colleagues.

**3308  Council for Exceptional Children**
**1110 N Glebe Road**
**Arlington, VA  22201**              **703-620-3660**
                                   **888-232-7733**
                              **FAX 703-264-9494**
                   **http://www.cec.sped.org**
              **e-mail: cathym@cec.sped.org**
*Gerald Reynaud, President*
*Dave Edyburn, Editor*
*Nancy Safer, Executive Director*

**3309  Education Funding News**

**Education Funding Research Council**
**1725 K Street NW**
**Washington, DC  20006**          **202-872-4000**
                                   **800-876-0226**
                              **FAX 800-926-2012**
              **http://www.grantsandfunding.com**
*Emily Lechy, Editor*

Provides the latest details on funding opportunities in education. *$298.00*

                *50 pages*

**3310  Exceptional Children**

**Council for Exceptional Children**
**1110 N Glebe Road**
**Arlington, VA  22201**              **703-620-3660**
                                   **888-232-7733**
                              **FAX 703-264-9494**
                   **http://www.cec.sped.org**

Peer review journal publishing original research on the education and development of toddlers, infants, children and youth with exceptionality and articles on professional issues of concern to special educators. Published quarterly.

**3311  Federation for Children with Special Needs Newsletter**

**1135 Tremont Street**
**Boston, MA  02120**              **617-236-7210**
                              **FAX 617-572-2094**
                   **http://www.fcsn.org**
              **e-mail: fcsninfo@fcsn.org**
*Richard Robison, Executive Director*

The mission of the Federation is to provide information, support, and assistance to parents of children with disabilities, their professional partners, and their communities. Major services are information and referrals and parent and professional training.

**3312  International Dyslexia Association Quarterly Newsletter: Perspectives**

**IDA**
**8600 Lasalle Road**
**Baltimore, MD  21286**              **410-296-0232**
                                   **800-ABC-D123**
                              **FAX 410-321-5069**
                   **http://www.interdys.org**
              **e-mail: info@interdys.org**
*J Thomas Viall, Executive Director*

Nonprofit, scientific and educational organization dedicated to the study and treatment of dyslexia. Focus is educating parents, teachers and professionals in the field of dyslexia in effective teaching methodologies. Programs and services include: information and referral; public awareness; medical and educational research; governmental affairs; conferences and publications.

*50-56 pages  Free to Members*

**3313  International Dyslexia Association: Illinois Branch Newsletter**

751 Roosevelt Road
Glen Ellyn, IL  60137                    630-469-6900
                                    FAX 630-469-6810
                              http://www.interdys.org
                    e-mail: ilbranch_ida@ameritech.net
*Donna Rafanello, Executive Director*
*Gail Oliphant, Office Manager*

**3314  International Dyslexia Association: Louisiana Branch Newsletter**

2125 Coliseum Street
New Orleans, LA  70130                    504-876-0034
                                    FAX 504-595-8848

*Marqua Brunette, President*

**3315  International Dyslexia Association: Philadelphia Branch Newsletter**

PO Box 251
Bryn Mawr, PA  19010                    610-527-1548
                                    FAX 610-527-5011

*Jann Stuart Glider, President*

An international 501(c)(3) nonprofit, scientific and educational organization dedicated to the study and treatment of dyslexia. All branches hold at least one public meeting, workshop or conference per year.

**3316  International Reading Association Newspaper: Reading Today**

PO Box 8139
Newark, DE  19714                    302-731-1600
                                    FAX 302-731-1057
                              http://www.reading.org
                         e-mail: jbutler@reading.org
*Janet Butler, Public Information Associate*

The International Reading Association is a professional membership organization dedicated to promoting high levels of literacy for all by improving the quality of reading instruction, disseminating research and information about reading, and encouraging the lifetime reading habit. Our members include classroom teachers, reading specialistsss, consultants, administrators, supervisors, university faculty, researchers, psychologists, librarians, media specialists, and parents.

**3317  Journal of Physical Education, Recreation and Dance**

1900 Association Drive
Reston, VA  20191                    703-476-3475
                                    FAX 703-476-9537
                              http://www.aahpend.org

*80 pages  $9.00*

**3318  LDA Alabama Newsletter**

**Learning Disabilities Association Alabama**
PO Box 11588
Montgomery, AL  36111                    334-277-9151
                                    FAX 334-284-9357
                              http://www.ldaal.org
                         e-mail: alabama@ldaal.org
*Debbie Gibson, President*

Educational, support, and advocacy group for individuals with learning disabilities and ADD.

**3319  LDA Georgia Newsletter**

**Learning Disabilities Association Georgia**
PO Box 1337
Roswell, GA  30077                    678-461-4471
                                    FAX 678-461-4472
               http://www.accessatlanta.com/community/groups/
                         e-mail: ldaga@aol.com
*Vicki Hansberger, Executive Director*

Information and helpful articles on learning disabilities. Mailed free four times a year to members. Members also receive National Association newsletter four times a year *$40.00*

**3320  LDA Illinois Newsletter**

**Learning Disabilities Association Illinois**
10101 S Roberts Road
Palos Hills, IL  60465                    708-430-7532
                                    FAX 708-430-7592
                              http://www.idanatl.org/illinois
*Sharon Schussler, Administrative Assistant*

A non profit organization dedicated to the advancement of the education and general welfare of children and youth of normal or potentially normal intelligence who have perceptual, conceptual, coordinative or related learning disabilities.

**3321  Learning Disabilities Association of Texas Newsletter**

1011 W 31st Street
Austin, TX  78705                    512-458-8234
                                    800-604-7500
                                    FAX 512-458-3826
http://www.ourworld.compuserve.com/homepages/LD
                    e-mail: LDAT@compuserve.com
*Ann Robinson, State Coordinator*

Provides information, referral for services and support to those with learning disabilities.

**3322 Link Newsletter**

**Parent Information Center of Delaware**
**700 Barksdale Road**
**Newark, DE 19711**          302-366-0152
                             888-547-4412
                        FAX 302-366-0276
                          TDY:State Relay
            e-mail: picofdel@picofdel.org
*Marie-Anne Aghazadian, Director*

*20 pages quarterly $12.00*

**3323 Literacy News**

**National Institute for Literacy**
**1775 I Street NW**
**Washington, DC 20006**          202-233-2025
                             FAX 202-233-2050
                      http://www.novel.nifl.gov

Provides current information on what the Institute is
doing and its progress.

**3324 Louisiana State Planning Council on**
**Developmental Disabilities Newsletter**

**PO Box 3455**
**Baton Rouge, LA 70821**          225-342-6804
                             800-922-DIAL
                        FAX 225-342-1970
*Clarice Eichelberge, Executive Director*
*Shelia Bridgewater, DIAL Coordinator*

To improve circumstances, programs, and systems for
people with developmental disabilities.

**3325 OSERS Magazine**

**Office of Special Education & Rehabilitative Svcs.**
**303 C Street SW**
**Washington, DC 20202**          202-727-6436
                             800-433-3243
                       http://www.ed.gov

Provides information, research and resources in the
area of special learning needs.

*Quarterly*

**3326 Resources in Education**

**US Government Printing Office**
**710 N Capitol Street NW**
**Washington, DC 20401**          202-512-0132
                             FAX 202-512-1355
                   http://www.access.gpo.gov
                   e-mail: www.admine@gpo.gov

A monthly publication announcing education related
documents.

**3327 TASKS's Newsletter**

**100 W Cerritos Avenue**
**Anaheim, CA 92805**          714-533-8275
                          FAX 714-533-2533
               e-mail: taskca@yahoo.com
*Marta Anchondo, Executive Director*
*Brenda Smith, Deputy Director*

TASK's mission is to enable children with disabilities
to reach their maximum potential by providing them,
their families and the professionals whoserve them,
with training, support information resources and referrals. and by providing community awarness programs.

*28 pages TASK members*

**3328 TESOL Journal**

**Teachers of English to Speakers of Other Languages**
**706 S Washington Street**
**Alexandria, VA 22314**          703-836-0774
                             FAX 703-836-7864
                          http://www.tesol.org
                          e-mail: TJ@tesol.org

TESOL Journal articles focus on teaching and classroom research for classroom practitioners. The journal includes articles about adult education and
literacy in every volume year. Subscriptions available
to members only.

**3329 TESOL Newsletter**

**Teachers of English to Speakers of Other Languages**
**700 S Washington Street**
**Alexandria, VA 22314**          703-836-0774
                             FAX 703-836-7864
                          e-mail: info@tesol.org

TESOL produces the Adult Education Interest Section Newsletter and the Refugee Concerns Interest
Section Newsletter. They provide news, ideas, and activities for ESL instructors. Subscriptions are available to members only.

**3330 TESOL Quarterly**

**Teachers of English to Speakers of Other Languages**
**700 S Washington Street**
**Alexandria, VA 22314**          703-836-0774
                             FAX 703-836-7864
                          http://www.tesol.edu
                          e-mail: info@tesol.org

TESOL Quarterly is a referred interdisciplinary journal teachers of English to speakers of other languages.
Subscriptions available to members.

## Young Adults

**3331 Get Ready to Read!**

**National Center for Learning Disabilities**
**381 Park Avenue S**
**New York, NY 10016**          212-545-7510
                             888-575-7373
                        FAX 212-545-9665
                          http://www.ld.org
                          e-mail: help@ncld.org
*Amber Eden, Assistant Director Online Comm.*
*Hal Stucker, Managing Editor*

*Quarterly*

**3332 LD Advocate**

**National Center for Learning Disabilities**
**381 Park Avenue S**
**New York, NY 10016**          212-545-7510
                             888-575-7373
                        FAX 212-545-9665
                          http://www.ld.org
                          e-mail: help@ncld.org
*Amber Eden, Assistant Director Online Comm.*
*Hal Stucker, Managing Editor*

*Monthly*

**3333  LD News**

**National Center for Learning Disabilities**
**381 Park Avenue S**
**New York, NY  10016**          **212-545-7510**
                                 **888-575-7373**
                          **FAX 212-545-9665**
                           **http://www.ld.org**
                        **e-mail: help@ncld.org**
*Amber Eden, Assistant Director Online Comm.*
*Hal Stucker, Managing Editor*

*Monthly*

**3334  Literary Cavalcade**

**Scholastic**
**555 Broadway**
**New York, NY  10012**

Every issue makes literature come alive with captivating reading students will love, and skill-building activities that meet your teaching needs. *$8.95*

*48 pages*

**3335  National Geographic World**

**1145 17th Street NW**
**Washington, DC  20036**          **202-857-7000**
                                   **800-647-5463**
                            **FAX 202-429-5712**

*Susan M Tejada, Editor*

Features factual stories on outdoor adventures, natural history, sports, science and history. Special features include posters, games, crafts and mazes. *$17.95*

*32 pages*

**3336  Our World**

**National Center for Learning Disabilities**
**381 Park Avenue S**
**New York, NY  10016**          **212-545-7510**
                                 **888-575-7373**
                          **FAX 212-545-9665**
                           **http://www.ld.org**
                        **e-mail: help@ncld.org**
*Amber Eden, Assistant Director Online Comm.*
*Hal Stucker, Managing Editor*

*Quarterly*

**3337  Scholastic Action**

**Scholastic**
**555 Broadway**
**New York, NY  10012**

*Patrick Daley, Editor*

Motivate your grades 7-12 below-level readers to read and improve their language arts skills with FREE-trial copies of Scholastic Action. *$7.95*

*32 pages*

**3338  Sibling Forum**

**Family Resource Associates**
**35 Haddon Avenue**
**Shrewsbury, NJ  07702**          **732-747-5310**
                            **FAX 732-747-1896**

*Susan Levine, Editor*

Newsletter for siblings aged 10 through teens with brothers or sisters with disabilities. Includes library information, special definitions and feedback from readers. Each issue also has a Focusing on Feelings discussion. A useful tool for siblings, parents, educators, and special workers. *$12.00*

*12 pages  4 Times/Sibling*

## General

**3339  Academic Communication Associates**

Educational Book Division
4149 Avenida de la Plata
Oceanside, CA  92052          760-758-9593
                              888-758-9558
                         FAX 760-758-1604
                      http://www.acadcom.com
                    e-mail: acom@acadcom.com
*Dr. Larry Mattes, Founder/President*

Publishes hundreds of speech and language products, educational books and assessment materials for children and adults with speech, language, and hearing disorders, learning disabilities, developmental disabilities, and special learning needs. Products include books, software programs, learning games, augmentative communication materials, bilingual/multicultural materials, and special education resources.

**3340  Academic Success Press**

6023 26th Street W
PO Box 132
Bradenton, FL  34207
                              888-822-6657
                   http://www.academicsuccess.com
*Paul D Nolting PhD, Author*

Publishes books and materials in the interest of making the classroom learning experience less difficult, while improving student learning, to transform the classroom into a more successful environment where educators and students can use inventive learning techniques based on sound academic research.

**3341  Academic Therapy Publications**

20 Commercial Boulevard
Novato, CA  94949             415-883-3314
                              800-422-7249
                         FAX 888-287-9975
                   http://www.academictherapy.com
                e-mail: sales@academictherapy.com
*John Arena, Founder*

Publishes supplementary education materials for people with reading, learning and communication disabilities; features professional texts and reference books, curriculum materials, teacher/parent resources, and visual/perceptual training aids.

**3342  Active Parenting Publishers**

1955 Vaughn Road NW
Kennesaw, GA  30144           770-429-0565
                              800-825-0060
                         FAX 770-429-0334
                   http://www.activeparenting.com
                e-mail: cservice@activeparenting.com
*Michael H Popkin PhD, Founder/President*
*Harry Popkin, Secretary to the President*

Publishes materials that teach parenting skills. Offers video-based training and program packages that include videos, guidebooks, CD-ROMs and additional items.

**3343  Alexander Graham Bell Association for the Deaf and Hard of Hearing**

3417 Volta Place NW
Washington, DC  20007         202-337-5220
                         FAX 202-337-8270
                      http://www.agbell.org
                 e-mail: publications@agbell.org
*K Todd Houston PhD, Executive Director/CEO*
*Kathleen Daniel Sussman, President*
*Rachel Reed, Director Publication Projects*

Publishes and distributes books, brochures, instructional materials, videos, CDs and audiocassettes relating to hearing loss.

**3344  American Guidance Service**

4201 Woodland Road
Circle Pines, MN  55014       651-287-7220
                              800-328-2560
                         FAX 800-471-8457
                      http://www.agsnet.com
                    e-mail: agsmail@agsnet.com

Produces assessments, textbooks, and instructional materials for people with a wide range of needs; publishes individually administered tests to measure cognitive ability, achievement, behavior, speech and language skills, and personal and social adjustment.

**3345  American Printing House for the Blind**

1839 Frankfort Avenue
Louisville, KY  40206         502-895-2405
                              800-233-1839
                         FAX 502-899-2274
                      http://www.aph.org
                    e-mail: info@aph.org
*Tuck Tinsley III, President*
*Fred Gissoni, Customer Support*
*Tony Grantz, Business Development Manager*

Promotes independence of blind and visually impaired persons by providing specialized materials, products, and services needed for education and life.

**3346  American Psychological Association**

750 1st Street NE
Washington, DC  20002         202-336-5650
                              800-374-2722
                         FAX 202-336-5633
                   http://www.apa.org/psycinfo
                    e-mail: psycinfo@apa.org

Publishes periodicals, including PsycSCAN, a quarterly print abstract that provides citations to the journal literature on Learning Disorders and Mental Retardation, including theories, research, assessment, treatment, rehabilitation, and educational issues. Also publishes Psychological Abstracts, a monthly print reference tool containing summaries of journal articles, book chapters and books in the field of psychology and related disciplines.

**3347  Associated Services for the Blind**

919 Walnut Street
Philadelphia, PA  19107       215-627-0600
                         FAX 215-922-0692
                      http://www.asb.org
                    e-mail: asbinfo@asb.org
*Dolores Ferrara-Godzieba, Director*
*Patricia C Johnson, CEO*

Promotes self-esteem, independence and self-determination in blind and visually impaired people, providing educational materials, training and resources.

**3348  BOSC Books on Special Children**

BOSC Publishing
PO Box 3378
Amherst, MA  01004          413-256-8164
                           FAX 413-256-8896
           http://www.boscbooks.com
           e-mail: contact@boscbooks.com
*Irene Slovak, Founder/Owner*
*Marcia Young, President*

Offers books that cover all kinds of disabilities to librarians, other professionals and parents; publishes the BOSC Directory of programs, clinics, and centers for disabled individuals.

**3349  Bethany House Publishers**

11400 Hampshire Avenue S
Minneapolis, MN  55438        616-676-9185
                              800-877-2665
                           FAX 616-676-9576
           http://www.bethanyhouse.com
           e-mail: orders@bakerbooks.com
*Teresa Fogarty, General Publicist*

Publishes books in large-print format for the learning disabled.

**3350  Blackwell Publishing**

350 Main Street
Malden, MA  02148             781-388-8200
                           FAX 781-388-8210
           http://www.blackwellpublishing.com
       e-mail: dpeters@bos.blackwellpublishing.com
*Rene Olivieri, Chief Executive*
*Dawn Peters, Media Contact*

Publishes books and journals for the higher education, research and professional markets, including several journals on topics relating to learning disabilities.

**3351  Brookes Publishing**

PO Box 10624
Baltimore, MD  21285          410-337-9580
                              800-638-3775
                           FAX 410-337-8539
           http://www.brookespublishing.com
           e-mail: custserv@brookespublishing.com
*Paul H Brookes, President*
*Melissa A Behm, VP*

Publishes books, texts, curricula, videos, tools and a newsletter based on research in disabilities, education and child development, including learning disabilities, ADHD, communication and language, reading and literacy, and special education.

**3352  Brookline Books/Lumen Editions**

PO Box 97
Newton Upper Falls, MA  02464
                              800-666-2665
                           FAX 617-558-8011
           http://www.brooklinebooks.com
           e-mail: milt@brooklinebooks.com

Publishes books on education, learning and topics relating to disabilities.

**3353  Charles C Thomas Publisher**

2600 S 1st Street
Springfield, IL  62704        217-789-8980
                              800-258-8980
                           FAX 217-789-9130
           http://www.ccthomas.com
           e-mail: books@ccthomas.com

Publishes books on education and special education for the blind and visually impaired, the gifted and talented, the developmentally disabled, and people with learning disabilities.

**3354  City Creek Press**

1422 W Lake Street #202
Minneapolis, MN  55408        612-823-2500
                              800-585-6059
                           FAX 612-823-5380
           http://www.citycreek.com
*Judy Liautaud, Owner*

Publishes books and products offering a literature-based method of learning, such as books, clue cards, posters, magnetic math story boards, workbooks and audio tapes; the program is multisensory, interactive, and appeals to the visual, auditory and tactile learning styles.

**3355  Connecticut Association for Children and Adults with Learning Disabilities**

25 Van Zant Street
East Norwalk, CT  06855       203-838-5010
                           FAX 203-866-6108
           http://www.cacld.org
           e-mail: cacld@optonline.net

Offers over 300 books and titles to ensure access to the resources needed to help children and adults with learning disabilities and attention disorders achieve their full potential.

**3356  Corwin Press**

Sage Publications
2455 Teller Road
Thousand Oaks, CA  91320      805-499-9774
                              800-818-7243
                           FAX 800-583-2665
           http://www.corwinpress.com
           e-mail: webmaster@sagepub.com

Publishes books and products for all learners of all ages and their educators, including subjects such as classroom management, early childhood education, guidance and counseling, higher/adult education, inclusive education, exceptional students, student assessment, as well as behavior, motivation and discipline.

**3357  Edge Enterprises**

PO Box 1304
Lawrence, KS  66044           785-749-1473
                           FAX 785-749-0207
           e-mail: edgeenterprises@alltel.net
*Jean B Schumaker, President*
*Donald D Deshler, VP*
*Jacqueline Schafer, Managing Editor*

A research, development and publishing company addressing the needs of at-risk learners. Offers research-based instructor's manuals and videotapes for teachers and parents in the areas of learning strategies, math strategies, self advocacy, social skills, cooperative thinking strategies and community building. Catalogue available upon request. Training required associated with some products.

**3358   Educators Publishing Service**
PO Box 9031
Cambridge, MA  02139
800-435-7728
FAX 888-440-2665
http://www.epsbooks.com
e-mail: epsbooks@epsbooks.com
*Dr. Mel Levine, Author*

Publishes vocabulary, grammar and language arts materials for students from kindergarten through high school, and specializes in phonics and reading comprehension as well as materials for students with learning differences.

**3359   Federation for Children with Special Needs**
1135 Tremont Street
Boston, MA  02120
617-236-7210
800-331-0688
FAX 617-572-2094
http://www.fcsn.org
e-mail: fcsinfo@fcsn.org
*Pat Blake, Associate Executive Director*
*Sara Miranda, Associate Executive Director*
*Rich Robison, Executive Director*

Provides information to the parents of children with disabilities, their professional partners, and their communities, offering publications on school reform, inclusion, education laws, and advocacy.

**3360   Free Spirit Publishing**
217 Fifth Avenue N
Minneapolis, MN  55401
612-338-2068
800-735-7323
FAX 612-337-5050
http://www.freespirit.com
e-mail: help4kids@freespirit.com
*Judy Galbraith, Founder/President*

Publishes non-fiction materials which empower young people and promote self-esteem through improved social and learning skills. Topics include self-awareness, stress management, school success, creativity, friends and family, and special needs such as gifted and talented learners and children with learning differences.

**3361   GSI Publications**
PO Box 746
Dewitt, NY  13214
800-550-2343
FAX 315-446-2012
http://www.gsi-add.com
e-mail: addgsi@aol.com
*Dr. Gordon, Author*

Publishes books for parents, teachers, ADHD children and their siblings.

**3362   Great Potential Press**
PO Box 5057
Scottsdale, AZ  85261
602-954-4200
877-954-4200
FAX 602-954-0185
http://www.giftedpsychologypress.com
e-mail: info@giftedbooks.com
*James T Webb PhD, Founder/President/Publisher*

Specializes in education books for parents, teachers and educators of gifted, talented and creative children. Offers nearly forty products, including books and videos.

**3363   Guidance Channel**
135 Dupont Street
Plainview, NY  11803
800-999-6884
FAX 800-262-1886
http://www.guidancechannel.com
e-mail: info@guidancechannel.com
*Jennifer Brady, Editor*

Publishes educational products, media and resources available on the Internet and through direct mail catalogs. Offers multimedia programs, videos, curricula, information handouts, therapeutic games, prevention-awareness items, play therapy resources, newsletters and other publications.

**3364   Guilford Publications**
72 Spring Street
New York, NY  10012
212-431-9800
800-365-7006
FAX 212-966-6708
http://www.guilford.com
e-mail: info@guilford.com
*Seymour Weingarten, Editor-in-Chief*
*Chris Jennison, Senior Editor, Education*
*Robert Matloff, President*

Publishes books for education on the subjects of literacy, general education, school psychology and special education. Also offers books, videos, audio cassettes and software, as well as journals, newsletters, and AD/HD resources.

**3365   Harcourt Achieve**
PO Box 690789
Orlando, FL  32819
800-531-5015
FAX 800-699-9459
http://www.harcourtachieve.com
*Tim McEwen, President/CEO*
*Jeff Johnson, Director Marketing/Communication*

Produces learning solutions and materials to help young and adult learners, based on a development philosophy that assesses learner's skills, matches them to appropriate content, and accelerates the ability of learners to meet and exceed expectations.

**3366   Hazelden Publishing and Educational Services**
15251 Pleasant Valley Road
Center City, MN  55012
800-328-9000
FAX 651-213-4577
http://www.hazelden.org
e-mail: customersupport@hazelden.org
*Nick Motu, VP/Publisher*
*Christine Anderson, Media Specialist*

Publishes real-world resources that are accessible for all experience levels and learning styles, including audio and video formats, manuals for educators, workbooks for students, and a catalog of products.

**3367  Heinemann-Boynton/Cook**

361 Hanover Street
Portsmouth, NH  03801
603-431-7894
800-225-5800
FAX 603-431-2214
http://www.boyntoncook.com
e-mail: custserv@heinemann.com
*George Goldberg, VP Human Resources*

Publishes professional resources and provides educational services for teachers, and offers nearly 100 titles related to learning disabilities.

**3368  High Noon Books**

20 Commercial Boulevard
Novato, CA  94949
800-422-7249
FAX 888-287-9975
http://www.academictherapy.com
e-mail: sales@academictherapy.com

Features over 35 sets of high-interest, low-level books written on a first through fourth grade reading level, for people with reading difficulties, ages nine and up.

**3369  Holt, Rinehart and Winston**

Language Arts Catalog
6277 Sea Harbor Drive
Orlando, FL  32887
800-225-5425
FAX 800-269-5232
http://www.hrw.com
e-mail: holtinfo@hrw.com

Publishes secondary educational material including curriculum-based textbooks, CD-ROMs, videodiscs, and other support and reference materials.

**3370  JKL Communications**

2700 Virginia Avenue NW #707
Washington, DC  20037
202-333-1713
FAX 202-333-1735
http://www.lathamlaw.org
e-mail: plath@lathamlaw.org
*Peter S Latham JD, Director*
*Patricia Horan Latham JD, Director*

Publishes books and videos on learning disabilities and ADD with a focus on legal issues in school, higher education and employment.

**3371  Jewish Braille Institute of America**

110 E 30th Street
New York, NY  10016
212-889-2525
800-433-1531
FAX 212-689-3692
http://www.jewishbraille.org
e-mail: eisler@jbilibrary.org
*Dr. Ellen Isler, Executive VP*
*Israel Taub, Associate Director*
*Sandra Radinsky, Director of Development*

Publishes magazines, a newsletter, and special resources available to the reading disabled who are themselves print-handicapped in varying degrees. Seeks the integration of Jews who are blind, visually impaired and reading disabled into the Jewish community and society.

**3372  Learning Disabilities Association of America**

4156 Library Road
Pittsburgh, PA  15234
412-341-1515
FAX 412-344-0224
http://www.ldanatl.org
e-mail: info@ldaamerica.org
*Marianne Toombs, President*
*Suzanne Fornaro, First VP*
*Connie Parr, Second VP*

Maintains a large inventory of publications, videos and other materials related to learning disabilities, and publishes two periodicals available by subscription as well as various books, booklets, brochures, papers and pamphlets on topics related to learning disabilities.

**3373  Learning Disabilities Resources**

6 E Eagle Road
Havertown, PA  19083
610-446-6126
800-869-8336
FAX 610-446-6129
http://www.learningdifferences.com
e-mail: rcooper-ldr@comcast.net
*Dr. Richard Cooper, Executive Director*

Offers a variety of resources to help teach the learning disabled, including alternative ways to teach math, language, spelling, vocabulary, and also how to organize and study. Available in books, videos, and audio tapes.

**3374  Library Reproduction Service**

LRS
14214 S Figueroa Street
Los Angeles, CA  90061
310-354-2610
800-255-5002
FAX 310-354-2601
http://www.lrs-largeprint.com
e-mail: lrsprint@aol.com
*Joan Hudson-Miller, President*

Offers large print reproductions to special needs students in first grade through post-secondary, as well as adult basic and continuing education programs; also produces an extensive collection of large print classics for all ages as well as children's literature.

**3375  LinguiSystems**

3100 Fourth Avenue
East Moline, IL  61244
309-755-2300
800-776-4332
FAX 800-577-4555
TDY:800-933-8331
http://www.linguisystems.com
e-mail: service@linguisystems.com
*Linda Bowers, Co-Owner*
*Rosemary Huisingh, Co-Owner*

Publishes a newsletter and speech-language materials for learning disabilities, ADD/ADHD, auditory processing and listening, language skills, fluency and voice, reading and comprehension, social skills and pragmatics, vocabulary and concepts, writing, spelling, punctuation and other specialized subjects.

**3376 Love Publishing Company**

9101 E Kenyon Avenue
Denver, CO 80237              303-221-7333
                       FAX 303-221-7444
http://www.lovepublishing.com
e-mail: lpc@lovepublishing.com

Publishes titles for use in special education, counseling, social work, and individuals with learning differences.

**3377 Magination Press**

750 First Street NE
Washington, DC 20002
                       800-374-2721
                       FAX 202-336-5502
http://www.maginationpress.com
e-mail: magination@apa.org

Publishes special books for children's special concerns, including starting school, learning disabilities, and other topics in psychology, development and mental health.

**3378 Marsh Media**

8025 Ward Parkway Plaza
Kansas City, MO 64114
                       800-821-3303
                       FAX 866-333-7421
http://www.marshmedia.com
e-mail: info@marshmedia.com

Offers educational videos, storybooks and language-intensive teaching guides with a focus on key character-building concepts, health and guidance.

**3379 Mindworks Press**

4019 Westerly Place
Newport Beach, CA 92660        949-266-3730
                       FAX 949-266-3770
http://www.mindworkspress.com
e-mail: mindworkspress@aol.com
*Dr. Daniel Amen, Author*

Features books, audio, video, and CD-ROMs addressing a range of disorders, including anxiety, depression, obsessive-compulsiveness and ADD.

**3380 Modern Learning Press**

PO Box 9067
Cambridge, MA 02139
                       800-627-5867
                       FAX 888-558-7350
http://www.modlearn.com
e-mail: mlp@epsbooks.com

Publishes materials to help students, teachers and parents with literacy, school readiness and other important aspects of education and childhood.

**3381 Music Section: National Library Service for the Blind and Physically Handicapped**

Library of Congress
1291 Taylor Street NW
Washington, DC 20542           202-707-5100
                       800-424-8567
                   FAX 202-707-0712
                   TDY:202-707-0744
http://www.loc.gov/nls/music
e-mail: nlsm@loc.gov
*John Hanson, Department Head*

Offers a special music collection consisting of more than 30,000 braille and large print music scores, texts, and instructional recordings about music and musicians on cassette and audio disc.

**3382 National Association for Visually Handicapped**

22 W 21st Street
New York, NY 10010             212-889-3141
                       FAX 212-727-2931
http://www.navh.org
e-mail: staff@navh.org
*Lorraine H Marchi, Founder/CEO*

Publishes information about sight and sight problems for adults and children. Offers a product line of low-vision aids, a collection of articles about eye conditions, causes and treatment modalities, and a newsletter issued four times a year with information to assist people in dealing with low vision.

**3383 National Bible Association**

1865 Broadway
New York, NY 10023             212-408-1390
                       FAX 212-408-1448
http://www.nationalbible.org
e-mail: nba@nationalbible.org
*Thomas May, President*
*Tamara Collins, VP Reading Program*

Publishes Read it! A Journal for Bible Readers, which is issued three times a year. Also offers many versions of the Bible, including large-print editions and the easy-to-read Contemporary English Version.

**3384 Northwest Media**

326 W 12th Avenue
Eugene, OR 97401               541-343-6636
                       800-777-6636
                   FAX 541-343-0177
http://www.sociallearning.com
e-mail: nwm@northwestmedia.com
*Lee White, President*

Publishes material with a focus on independent living and foster care products.

**3385 Oxton House Publishers**

PO Box 209
Farmington, ME 04938
                       800-539-7323
                       FAX 207-779-0623
http://www.oxtonhouse.com
e-mail: oxtonhse@mainewest.com

Provides books and educational materials specializing in materials for teaching reading and mathematics and for dealing with learning disabilities.

**3386 Performance Resource Press**

1270 Rankin
Troy, MI 48083
                       800-453-7733
                       FAX 800-499-5718
http://www.prponline.net
e-mail: customerservice@prponline.net

Publishes over 600 products, including catalogs, journals, digests, newsletters, books, videos, posters and pamplets with a focus on behavioral health.

**3387  Peytral Publications**
PO Box 1162
Minnetonka, MN  55345          952-949-8707
                               877-739-8725
                          FAX 952-906-9777
                          http://www.peytral.com
                          e-mail: help@peytral.com

Publishes and distributes special education materials which promote success for all learners.

**3388  Phillip Roy**
The Roy Building
Largo, FL  33774               727-593-2700
                               800-255-9085
                          FAX 727-595-2685
                          http://www.philliproy.com
                          e-mail: info@philliproy.com
*Ruth Bragman PhD, President*

Publishes educational materials written for students of any age with different learning abilities. Offers an alternative approach to traditional education. Free catalog upon request.

**3389  Reader's Digest Partners for Sight Foundation**
Reader's Digest Road
Pleasantville, NY  10570
                               800-877-5293
                          http://www.rd.com
                          e-mail: partnersforsight@rd.com
*Susan Olivo, VP/General Manager*
*Dianna Kelly-Naghizadeh, Program Manager*

Offers large type editions of select books and large print editions of Readers Digest Magazines, as well as a foundation newsletter, Sightlines, which is published in large format with large type.

**3390  Riggs Institute**
4185 SW 102nd Avenue
Beaverton, OR  97005           503-646-9459
                               800-200-4840
                          FAX 503-644-5191
                          http://www.riggsinst.org
                          e-mail: riggs@riggsinst.org
*Myrna McCulloch, Founder/Director/Author*

Publishes materials to help remedial students using the Orton method, a multisensory approach to learning. Offers a catalog of products, including teacher's editions, phonogram cards, audio CDs for students, student materials and classroom materials.

**3391  Scholastic**
557 Broadway
New York, NY  10012            212-343-6100
                               800-246-2986
                          http://www.scholastic.com
*Richard Robinson, Chairman/President/CEO*
*Barbara A Marcus, VP/President Children's Books*
*Richard M Spaulding, Executive VP Marketing*

Produces educational materials to assist and inspire students of all ages, including a range of special education books, software, and other products.

**3392  Schwab Learning**
1650 S Amphlett Boulevard
San Mateo, CA  94402           650-655-2410
                               800-230-0988
                          FAX 650-655-2411
                          http://www.schwablearning.org
                          e-mail: media@schwablearning.org

Provides information, guidance, support and materials that address the emotional, social, practical and academic needs and concerns of children with learning difficulties, and their parents.

**3393  Slosson Educational Publications**
538 Buffalo Road
East Aurora, NY  14052         716-652-0930
                               888-756-7766
                          FAX 800-655-3840
                          http://www.slosson.com
                          e-mail: slosson@slosson.com

Publishes and distributes educational materials in the areas of intelligence, aptitude, developmental disabilities, school screening and achievement, speech-language and assessment therapy, emotional/behavior, and special needs. Offers a product line of testing and assessment materials, books, games, videos, cassettes and computer software intended for use by professionals, psychologists, teachers, counselors, students and parents.

**3394  Teddy Bear Press**
3639 Midway Drive
San Diego, CA  92110           619-223-7311
                          FAX 619-255-2158
                          http://www.teddybearpress.net
                          e-mail: fparker@teddybearpress.net
*Fran Parker, Author*

Publishes books and reading materials designed with the beginning reader in mind, written and illustrated by a special education teacher specializing in elementary education, learning disabilities, and education for the emotionally and mentally challenged.

**3395  Therapro**
225 Arlington Street
Framingham, MA  01702          508-872-9494
                               800-257-5376
                          FAX 508-875-2062
                          http://www.theraproducts.com
                          e-mail: info@theraproducts.com
*Karen Conrad ScD OTR/L, Co-Founder*
*Paul Weihrauch PhD, Co-Founder*

Offers specialty products and publications for all ages in the field of occupational therapy, including assistive technology, evaluations, handwriting programs, sensory-motor awareness and alerting products, oral motor products, early learning products, and perception, cognition and language resources.

**3396  Thomas Nelson Publishers**
PO Box 141000
Nashville, TN  37214           615-889-9000
                               800-889-9000
                          FAX 615-391-5225
                          http://www.thomasnelson.com
                          e-mail: publicity@thomasnelson.com
*Sam Moore, Chairman/CEO/President/Director*
*Michael S Hyatt, Executive VP/Group Publisher*
*Phil Stoner, Executive VP/Group Publisher*

Publishes books and other resources for the learning disabled.

**3397 Thomas T Beeler, Publisher**
PO Box 310
Rollinsford, NH 03869
603-794-0392
800-818-7574
FAX 888-222-3396
http://www.beelerpub.com
e-mail: tombeeler@beelerpub.com
*Thomas T Beeler, Publisher*
*David W O'Connor, President*
*Traci Watson, Editor*

Publishes and distributes hardcover, large print editions of popular titles for all ages, printed in 16-point type on acid-free paper and bound in sturdy, library-grade sewn binding with full color covers. Also offers audiobooks.

**3398 Thorndike Press**
295 Kennedy Memorial Drive
Waterville, ME 04901
800-223-1244
FAX 800-558-4676
http://www.galegroup.com/thorndike
*Debbie Ludden, Director Marketing*
*Jill Leckta, General Manager/Publisher*

Publishes and distributes over 900 new large-print editions per year, with an emphasis on bestsellers and genre fiction, as well as nonfiction titles.

**3399 Transaction Publishers**
Rutgers University
35 Berrue Circle
Piscataway, NJ 08854
732-445-2280
888-999-6778
FAX 732-445-3138
http://www.transactionpub.com
e-mail: trans@transactionpub.com
*Irving Louis Horowitz, Chairman*
*Mary E Curtis, President*
*Scott B Bramson, President Express Book Division*

Publishes over 70 books in large print, including new large print titles, as well as selections from the best of the company's backlist, with many classic titles from well-known American authors. The large print format makes selection easy for visually impaired readers.

**3400 Ulverscroft Large Print Books**
PO Box 1230
West Seneca, NY 14224
716-674-4270
800-955-9659
FAX 716-674-4195
http://www.ulverscroft.com
e-mail: enquiries@ulverscroft.co.uk
*Jan McGowan, Director*

Publishes large print books and audio products for people hard of seeing.

**3401 Wadsworth Publishing Company**
10 Davis Drive
Belmont, CA 94002
650-595-2350
800-354-9706
FAX 650-637-7544
http://www.wadworth.com
e-mail: dory.schaeffer@thomsonlearning.com
*Dan Alpert, Acquisitions Editor*
*Dory Schaeffer, Marketing Manager*

Publishes books on a wide range of topics in special education, including behavior modification, language disorders and development, and learning disabilities.

**3402 Waterfront Books**
85 Crescent Road
Burlington, VT 05401
800-639-6063
http://www.waterfrontbooks.com
e-mail: helpkids@waterfrontbooks.com
*Sherrill N Musty, President*

Publishes and distributes informative books and materials serving professionals and parents who are concerned with children at home, at school and in the workplace. Topics include overcoming barriers to learning, family support and parenting, personal safety, learning differences and special needs.

**3403 Woodbine House**
6510 Bells Mill Road
Bethesda, MD 20817
301-897-3570
800-843-7323
FAX 301-897-5838
http://www.woodbinehouse.com
e-mail: info@woodbinehouse.com
*Irv Shapell, Publisher*

Specializes in books about children with special needs; publishes sixty-five titles within the Special Needs Collection, covering AD/HD, learning disabilities, special education, communication skills, and other disabilities, for use by parents, children, therapists, health care providers and teachers.

**3404 Xavier Society for the Blind**
154 E 23rd Street
New York, NY 10010
212-473-7800
*Gina Ballero, Secretary to Director*

Provides resources for the visually impaired, including large-print, braille, and audio products.

**3405 York Press**
PO Box 504
Timonium, MD 21094
800-962-2763
FAX 410-560-6758
http://www.yorkpress.com
e-mail: info@yorkpress.com

Publishes books about language development and disabilities, especially dyslexia, and about hearing impairment.

## Classroom Resources

**3406  ADD From A to Z**

**Connecticut Assoc. for Children and Adults with LD**
**25 Van Zant Street**
**East Norwalk, CT 06855**          203-838-5010
                                    FAX 203-866-6108
                                    http://www.CACLD.org
                                    e-mail: cacld@juno.com
*Edward Hallowell MD, Presenter*

Dr. Hallowell, child and adult psychiatrist on the faculty of the Harvard Medical School, is widely regarded as a leading authority on the subject of Attention Deficit Disorder. This video version of one of his classic lectures provides a comprehensive overview of this complicated and often misunderstood subject. Topics include symptoms to look for, how to tell if it is not ADD, twenty steps to diagnosis, methods of treatment (medical and nonmedical) and the Ritalin controversy. *$34.95*

*$5.00 shipping*

**3407  ASCD Cooperative Learning Series**

**Assoc. for Supervision/Curriculum Development**
**1250 N Beauregard Street**
**Alexandria, VA 22311**          703-578-9600
                                  800-933-ASCD
                                  FAX 703-575-5400
                                  http://www.ascd.org
*RE Slavin, Author*

A facilitator's manual, book and five videotapes focusing on: providing a fundamental knowledge of cooperative learning and the benefits derived from its use, providing a basic understanding of how to plan and teach cooperative lessons and providing resources.

**3408  Arts Express**

**KET, The Kentucky Network Enterprise Division**
**600 Cooper Drive**
**Lexington, KY 40502**          859-258-7000
                                 800-354-9067
                                 FAX 859-258-7396

A delightful way to introduce elementary students to the visual arts, music and dance. Twenty 15 minute video programs available individually or onfive videotapes of four programs each. *$320.00*

*price/set*

**3409  Becoming a Proficient Cuer**

**Harris Communications**
**15155 Technology Drive**
**Eden Prairie, MN 55344**          952-906-1180
                                    800-825-6758
                                    FAX 952-906-1099
                                    TDY:952-906-1198
                                    http://www.harriscomm.com
*Melanie Metzger*
*Earl Fleetwood*

Video lessons are combined with workbook drills to describe and teach Cued Speech, and prevent and eliminate errors. Designed for hearing people at all levels of Cued Speech proficiency. *$49.95*

*19 pages  108-min. Video*

**3410  Collaboration in the Schools: The Problem-Solving Process**

**Pro-Ed**
**8700 Shoal Creek Boulevard**
**Austin, TX 78757**          512-451-3246
                              800-897-3202
                              FAX 512-451-8542
                              http://www.proedinc.com
*L Idol, Author*

An inservice/preservice video that demonstrates the stages of the consultative/collaborative process, as well as many of the various communicative/interactive skills and collaborative problem solving skills. *$106.00*

**3411  College Transition**

**Central Piedmont Community College**
**PO Box 35009**
**Charlotte, NC 28235**          704-330-2722
                                 FAX 704-330-6136
                                 http://www.cpcc.cc.nc.us

A video developed for facilitators to show to audiences of high school students, college transfer students and college freshman.

**3412  Cooperative Discipline: Classroom Management Promoting Self-Esteem**

**AGS**
**4201 Woodland Road**
**Circle Pines, MN 55014**          763-786-4343
                                    800-328-2560
                                    FAX 763-786-9077
                                    http://www.agsnet.com
                                    e-mail: agsmail@agsnet.com
*L Albert, Author*

A leader's guide, teacher's guide, set of 23 blackline masters, 2 scripts and 2 videotapes comprise this comprehensive discipline training program that helps teachers achieve control and order in their classroom. *$495.00*

**3413  Designing Clinical Strategies for Language Impaired Children**

**Purdue University Continuing Education**
**1586 Stewart Center**
**West Lafayette, IN 47907**          765-494-7231
                                      800-359-2968
                                      FAX 765-494-0567
*Jeanette S Leonard MS, Author*
*Laurence B Leonard, Author*

Discusses the application of single subject designs involving therapy with language-impaired children in day-to-day clinical practices; values of the designs for monitoring a child's progress and for assessing clinical effectiveness. *$81.00*

**3414 Educational Evaluation**

Stern Center for Language and Learning
135 Allen Brook Lane
Williston, VT 05495          802-878-2332
                            800-544-4863
                       FAX 802-878-0230
                  http://www.sterncenter.org
              e-mail: learning@sterncenter.org
*Andrea Brown*

The evaluation is an assessment of intelligence, academic achievement, language, and emotional and behavioral issues related to learning and includes pre- and post- evaluation conferences with parents and/ or students as well as an extensive written report detailing results and recommendations.

**3415 Fundamentals of Reading Success**

Educators Publishing Service
31 Smith Place
Cambridge, MA 02138          617-547-6706
                            800-225-5750
                       FAX 617-547-0412
                  http://www.epsbooks.com
              e-mail: eps@epsbooks.com
*Arlene W Sonday, Author*

This Orton-Gillingham-based video series teaches a phonic or code-emphasis approach to reading, spelling, and handwriting, and provides the foundation for a multisensory phonics curriculum. May be used by teachers and tutors. *$ 480.00*

*ISBN 0-838872-52-2*

**3416 Individual Instruction**

Stern Center for Language and Learning
135 Allen Brook Lane
Williston, VT 05495          802-878-2332
                            800-544-4863
                       FAX 802-878-0230
                  http://www.sterncenter.org
              e-mail: learning@sterncenter.org
*Stefanie Mitchell*

Individualized instruction to help students develop literacy skills and achieve academic success, building on learning strengths and compensating for areas of difficulty.

**3417 Instructional Strategies for Learning Disabled Community College Students**

Graduate School and University Center
365 5th Avenue
New York, NY 10036          212-817-7000
                       FAX 212-817-1503
                  http://www.gc.cuny.edu
For working with a cross-section of types of individuals with learning problems. *$47.50*

**3418 Key Concepts in Personal Development**

Marsh Media
8082 Ward Parkway Plaza
Kansas City, MO 64114          816-523-1059
                              800-821-3303
                         FAX 866-333-7421
                    http://www.marshmedia.com
                e-mail: info@marshmedia.com
*Joan Marsh, President*
*Liz Sweeney, Editorial Assistant*

Our videos, books, and teaching guides bring character education to the classrom. These kits are invaluable aids in teaching everyday values like honesty, anger control, trustworthiness, perseverance, understanding and respect. They help you prepare youngsters to meet challenges and greet opportunities with skill and optimism.

**3419 New Room Arrangement as a Teaching Strategy**

Teaching Strategies
PO Box 42243
Washington, DC 20015          202-362-7543
                              800-637-3652
                         FAX 202-364-7273
                http://www.TeachingStrategies.com
            e-mail: info@TeachingStrategies.com
*Diane Trister Dodge*

A manual and video present the impact of the early childhood classroom environment on how children learn, how they relate to others and how teachers teach. *$35.00*

**3420 Now You're Talking: Extend Conversation**

Educational Productions
9000 SW Gemini Drive
Beaverton, OR 97008          503-644-7000
                            800-950-4949
                       FAX 503-350-7000
                  http://www.edpro.com
              e-mail: custserv@edpro.com
*C Sharp, Author*
*Molly Krumm, Marketing Directror*

Video. Teachers in a language-based preschool and speech-language pathologists model effective techniques that focus and extend conversations of young children. *$295.00*

**3421 Phonemic Awareness: Lessons, Activities and Games**

Peytral Publication
PO Box 1162
Minnetonka, MN 55345          952-949-8707
                             877-739-8725
                        FAX 612-906-9777
                   http://www.peytral.com
               e-mail: help@peytral.com
*Victoria Groves Scott, Author*

Exceptional field tested guide to help educators who want to reach phonemic awareness as a prerequisite to reading, and/or to supplement the current curriculum. Special educators and speech clinicians will find this practical guide especially helpful as research indicates that deficits in phonemic awareness is often a major contributor to reading disabilities. This book contains fifty-eight scripted lessons, forty-nine reproducible blackline master and progress charts. Video also available *$27.95*

*176 pages*
*ISBN 1-890455-28-8*

**3422 Planning Individualized Education Programs for Language-Impaired Children**

**Purdue University Continuing Education**
**1586 Stewart Center**
**West Lafayette, IN 47907**          765-494-7231
                                       800-359-2968
                                  FAX 765-494-0567
*Nickola Wolf Nelson, PhD, Author*

Stresses the need to select different kinds of intervention strategies and content for different types of language disorders. Includes general consideration regarding the identification, writing and implementing of goals and short-term objectives. *$81.00*

**3423 Professional Development**

**Stern Center for Language and Learning**
**135 Allen Brook Lane**
**Williston, VT 05495**              802-878-2332
                                     800-544-4863
                                FAX 802-878-0230
                         http://www.sterncenter.org
                    e-mail: learning@sterncenter.org
*Jackie Earle Cruickshanks*

Staff development programs for preschool through grade 12 designed in response to requests from teachers and administrators for cutting-edge information about different kinds of learners and the teaching strategies most successful for them.

**3424 Restructuring America's Schools**

**Association for Supervision/Curriculum Development**
**1703 N Beaurguard Street**
**Alexandria, VA 22314**             703-578-9600
                                FAX 703-549-3891
                           http://www.ascd.org
*M D'Arcangelo, Author*

A leader's guide and videotape designed for administrators, teachers, parents, school board members, and community leaders.

**3425 Science Showtime! Videos**

**Steck-Vaughn Company**
**PO Box 690789**
**Orlando, FL 32819**
                                     800-531-5015
                                FAX 512-343-6854
                        http://www.steck-vaughn.com
                       e-mail: info@steck-vaughn.com

Interactive videos that bring science concepts to life. Programs of 6 to 12 minutes include Wonder Stops for classroom discussion. Additional Interactive Video Segments with activity sheets challenge listening, observing, and problem-solving skills.

**3426 Skillstreaming Video: How to Teach Students Prosocial Skills**

**Research Press**
**PO Box 9177**
**Champaign, IL 61826**              217-352-3273
                                     800-519-2707
                                FAX 217-352-1221
                          http://www.researchpress.com
                       e-mail: rp@researchpress.com
*Dr. AP Goldstein And Dr. Ellen McGinness, Author*
*Ann Wendell, President*

A video and two books providing an overview of a training procedure for teaching elementary and secondary level students the skills they need for coping with typical social and interpersonal problems. *$365.00*

**3427 Spelling Workbook Video**

**Learning Disabilities Resources**
**PO Box 716**
**Bryn Mawr, PA 19010**              610-525-8336
                                     800-869-8336
                                FAX 610-525-8337
                           http://www.ldonline.org
An instructional video which works through the spelling workbooks for teachers and students. *$16.00*

**3428 Strategic Planning and Leadership**

**Assoc. for Supervision/Curriculum Development**
**1703 N Beauregard Street**
**Alexandria, VA 22311**             703-578-9600
                                     800-933-2723
                                FAX 703-575-5400
                           http://www.ascd.org
Designed to explain and illustrate effective approaches to dealing with change through strategic planning.

**3429 Strategies Intervention Program**

**Special Education Resource Center**
**25 Industrial Park Road**
**Middletown, CT 06457**             860-632-1485
                                FAX 860-632-8870
*A Marks, Author*

A video illustrating through an interview with five eighth grade students, the effectiveness of a program designed to develop specific learning strategies for adolescents with learning disabilities.

**3430 Teaching Adults with Learning Disabilities**

**Stern Center for Language and Learning**
**135 Allen Brook Lane**
**Williston, VT 05495**              802-878-2332
                                     800-544-4863
                                FAX 802-878-0230
                         http://www.sterncenter.org
                    e-mail: bpodhajski@sterncenter.org
*Blanche Podhajski PhD, President/Editor*

A videotape training program and companion guide designed to help adult literacy teachers identify and instruct adults with learning disabilities. The focus of this five hour video series is on teaching basic reading and spelling skills. *$199.95*

**3431 Teaching Math**

Learning Disabilities Resources
PO Box 716
Bryn Mawr, PA 19010          610-525-8336
                             800-869-8336
                        FAX 610-525-8337
                  http://www.ldonline.org

A video for educational professionals teaching math to disabled children. *$12.00*

**3432 Teaching People with Developmental Disabilities**

Research Press
PO Box 9177
Champaign, IL 61826          217-352-3273
                             800-519-2707
                        FAX 217-352-1221
              http://www.researchpress.com
                 e-mail: rp@researchpress.com
*Ann Wendell, President*

A set of four videotapes and accompanying participant workbooks designed to help teachers, staff, volunteers, or family members master task analysis, prompting, reinforcement and error correction. *$595.00*

**3433 Teaching Strategies Library: Research Based Strategies for Teachers**

Assoc. for Supervision/Curriculum Development
1250 Pitt Street
Alexandria, VA 22314         703-549-9110
                        FAX 703-549-3891
                    http://www.ascd.org
*HF Silver, Author*

A trainer's manual and five videotapes designed for inservice education of teachers K-12 focusing on four different types of learning expected of students: mastery, understanding, synthesis and involvement.

**3434 Teaching Students Through Their Individual Learning Styles**

St. John's University, Learning Styles Network
8000 Utopia Parkway
Jamaica, NY 11439            718-990-6161
                        FAX 718-990-1882
                http://www.learningstyles.net
*R Dunn, Author*

A set of six videotapes introducing the Dunn and Dunn learning styles model. Explains the environmental, emotional, sociological, physical and psychological elements of style.

**3435 Technology in the Classroom Kit**

American Speech-Language-Hearing Association
10801 Rockville Pike
Bethesda, MD 20814           301-897-5700
                             888-498-6699
                        FAX 301-571-0457
                    http://www.asha.org
*Laurie Ward, Marketing Coordinator*

This kit includes a collection of four written modules and a videotape designed to help families and professionals implement assistive technology in the education programs of young children. Each module provides a brief background in assistive technology and covers specific topics in great detail. The technology is geared for children. *$104.00*

**3436 Telling Tales**

KET, The Kentucky Network Enterprise Division
600 Cooper Drive
Lexington, KY 40502          859-258-7000
                             800-354-9067
                        FAX 859-258-7396

Resource for teachers, librarians and drama departments at all levels of instruction. Telling Tales can be used to encourage creativity and self expression and help students understand their cultural and language arts skills, and develop openess to diverse cultures, build self confidence and leadership skills, improve communication and language arts skills and develop oral history projects. *$30.00*

**3437 Word Feathers**

KET, The Kentucky Network Enterprise Division
600 Cooper Drive
Lexington, KY 40502          859-258-7000
                             800-354-9067
                        FAX 859-258-7396

An activity-oriented language arts video series.

---

## Parents & Professionals

**3438 3 R'S for Special Education: Rights, Resources, Results**

Brookes Publishing Company
PO Box 10624
Baltimore, MD 21285          410-337-9580
                             800-638-3775
                        FAX 410-337-8539
                  http://www.pbrookes.com
                 e-mail: sales@pbrookes.com
*Grace Hanlon, Trevor*

This video helps parents navigate the steps of the special education system and work towards securing the best education and services for their children. *$49.95*

*Video*

**3439 A Mind of Your Own**

Fanlight Productions
4196 Washington Street
Boston, MA 02131             617-469-4999
                             800-937-4113
                        FAX 617-469-3379
                  http://www.fanlight.com
                 e-mail: fanlight@fanlight.com
*Sandy St. Louis, Contact*

New video on learning disabilities from the National Film Board of Canada, follows four learning disabled students through their struggles academically and socially as well as their successes in learning to cope with their disabilities and develop their own unique talents. Amtec Award of Merit. 37 minutes. *$199.00*

*Rental $60/day*
*ISSN DD29-0*

**3440  ABC's of ADD**

**JKL Communications**
PO Box 40157
**Washington, DC  20016**                    202-223-5097
                                   FAX 202-223-5096
                                http://www.lathamlaw.org
                                e-mail: plath3@his.com

*$29.00*

**3441  ABC's of Learning Disabilities**

**American Federation of Teachers**
555 New Jersey Avenue NW
**Washington, DC  20001**                    202-393-5674
                                   FAX 202-879-4597
                                   http://www.aft.org
                                e-mail: online@aft.org

This film illustrates the case histories of four learning disabled students with various learning disabilities.

**3442  ADHD**

**Brookes Publishing Company**
PO Box 10624
**Baltimore, MD  21285**                    410-337-9580
                                          800-638-3775
                                   FAX 410-337-8539
                                http://www.pbrookes.com
                                e-mail: custerv@pbrookes.com
*Sandra Rief, Presenter*

This video shows methods for helping students who have ADHD increase attention to tasks, improve listening skills, become better organized, and boost work production. *$99.00*

*Video*
*ISBN 1-557661-15-4*

**3443  ADHD in Adults**

**Guilford Publications**
72 Spring Street
**New York, NY  10012**                    212-431-9800
                                          800-365-7006
                                   FAX 212-966-6708
                                http://www.guilford.com
                                e-mail: info@guilford.com
*Russell A Barkley, Author*

This program integrates information on ADHD with the actual experiences of four adults who suffer from the disorder. Representing a range of professions, from a lawyer to a mother working at home, each candidly discusses the impact of ADHD on his or her daily life. These interviews are augmented by comments from family members and other clinicians who treat adults with ADHD. *$95.00*

*36-min VHS*

**3444  ADHD in the Classroom: Strategies for Teachers**

**Guilford Publications**
72 Spring Street
**New York, NY  10012**                    212-431-9800
                                          800-365-7006
                                   FAX 212-966-6708
                                http://www.guilford.com
                                e-mail: info@guilford.com
*Russell A Barkley, Author*

Viewers see the problems teachers encounter with children who suffer with ADHD, as well as instructive demonstrations of effective behavior management techniques including color charts and signs, point system, token economy, and turtle-control technique. Also includes a Leader's Guide and a 42-page Manual. *$95.00*

*36-min. VHS*

**3445  ADHD: What Can We Do?**

**Guilford Publications**
72 Spring Street
**New York, NY  10012**                    212-431-9800
                                          800-365-7006
                                   FAX 212-966-6708
                                http://www.guilford.com
                                e-mail: info@guilford.com
*Russell A Barkley, PhD, Author*

A video program that introduces teachers and parents to a variety of the most effective techniques for managing ADHD in the classroom, at home, andon family outings. Includes Leader's Guide and 30-page Manual. *$95.00*

*ISBN 0-898629-72-1*

**3446  ADHD: What Do We Know?**

**Guilford Publications**
72 Spring Street
**New York, NY  10012**                    212-431-9800
                                          800-365-7006
                                   FAX 212-966-6708
                                http://www.guilford.com
                                e-mail: info@guilford.com
*RA Barkley, Author*

An introduction for teachers and special education practitioners, school psychologists and parents of ADHD children. Topics outlined in this videoinclude the causes and prevalence of ADHD, ways children with ADHD behave, otherconditions that may accompany ADHD and long-term prospects for children with ADHD. *$95.00*

*Video*

**3447  Adults with Learning Problems**

**Learning Disabilities Resources**
PO Box 716
**Bryn Mawr, PA  19010**                    610-525-8336
                                          800-869-8336
                                   FAX 610-525-8337
                                http://www.ldonline.org

Educational materials for adults with a learning disability.

**3448** American Sign Language Phrase Book Videotape Series

Harris Communications
15155 Technology Drive
Eden Prairie, MN 55344     952-906-1180
800-825-6758
FAX 952-906-1099
TDY:952-906-1198
http://www.harriscomm.com

Includes book and three videotapes, each 60 minutes long. In Volume 1 you will find everyday expressions, signing and deafness, getting acquainted, health and water; in Volume 2 you will find family, school, food and drink, clothing, sports and recreation; and in Volume 3 you will find travel, animal, colors, civics, religion, numbers, time, dates and money. *$134.95*

**3449** Andreas: Outcomes of Inclusion

Center on Disability and Community Inclusion
499C Waterman Building
Burlington, VT 05401     802-656-4031
FAX 802-656-1357
http://www.uvm.edu/zvapvt/timfox
e-mail: syuan@zoo.uvm.edu

Video portrays the academic, occupational, and social inclusion of a high school student with severe disabilities. Includes commentary of parents, administrators, teachers, support personnel, classmates.

**3450** Anger Within Programs 1-4: Walking Through the Storm Life Space Crisis Intervention

NAK Production Associates
4304 E West Highway
Bethesda, MD 20814     301-654-4777
FAX 301-654-7772
e-mail: NAK@makprod.com

*NA Klotz, Author*
*Norman Klutz, Producer*

Videos focusing on parental and professional perspectives, understanding of children's feelings, treatment models and techniques and skills for working with students with emotional problems.

**3451** Around the Clock: Parenting the Delayed ADHD Child

Guilford Publications
72 Spring Street
New York, NY 10012     212-431-9800
800-365-7006
FAX 212-966-6708
http://www.guilford.com
e-mail: info@guilford.com

*Joan F Goodman*
*Susan Hoban*

This videotape provides both professionals and parents a helpful look at how the difficulties facing parents of ADHD children can be handled. *$150.00*

*45-min. VHS*

**3452** Art of Communication

United Learning
1560 Sherman Avenue
Evanston, IL 60201     847-647-0600
800-424-0362
FAX 847-647-0918
http://www.unitedlearning.com
e-mail: info@unitedlearning.com

*B Wagonseller, Author*
*Ronald Reed, VP Marketing*

Designed for parents and professionals, this video focuses on: effective parent-child communication; non-verbal communication in children; effective listening; effects of negative and critical messages; and deterrents limiting child/parent communication. *$99.00*

**3453** Attention Deficit Disorder

Pro-Ed
8700 Shoal Creek Boulevard
Austin, TX 78757     512-451-3246
800-897-3202
FAX 512-451-8542
http://www.proedinc.com

*DR Jordan, Author*

A video and book providing helpful suggestions for both home and classroom management of students with attention deficit disorder. *$19.00*

**3454** Augmentative Communication Without Limitations

Prentke Romich Company
1022 Heyl Road
Wooster, OH 44691     330-262-1984
800-262-1984
FAX 330-263-4829
http://www.prentrom.com

Looks at the issues one must consider in the selection process. These include hardware, software, service and support.

**3455** Avenues to Compliance

New England ADA Technical Assistance Center
374 Congress Street
Boston, MA 02210     617-695-1225
800-949-4232
FAX 617-482-8099
http://www.adaptenu.org/neada/defaultasp

This training video provides information on the requirements of a Title II entity to provide program access (as required by the Americans with Disabilities Act).

**3456** Behind the Glass Door: Hannah's Story

Fanlight Productions
4196 Washington Street
Boston, MA 02131     617-469-4999
800-937-4113
FAX 617-469-3379
http://www.fanlight.com
e-mail: fanlight@fanlight.com

*Karen Pascal, Producer*
*Sandy St. Louis, Contact*

New video, produced in association with Vision TV, follows the Shepard family through five years of struggle, hardship and bittersweet success in raising their child, Hannah, who was diagnosed with autism. Offers insight into the stress families and educators face as they tackle this mysterious disorder. Offers hope and inspiration to parents. Recipient of Silver Screen Award; US International Film and Video Festival. *$245.00*

> *Rental $50/day*
> *ISBN 1-572952-92-1*

**3457  Beyond the ADD Myth**
**Brookes Publishing Company**
PO Box 10624
**Baltimore, MD  21285**　　　　510-337-9580
　　　　　　　　　　　　　800-638-3775
　　　　　　　　　　FAX 410-337-8539
　　　　http://www.pbrookes.com
　　　e-mail: custerv@pbrookes.com
*Dr. Thomas Armstrong, Author*

This video builds on the theory that many of the behaviors associated with attention deficit disorder are not solely due to neurological dysfunction but actually result from a wide range of social, psychological, and educational causes. *$22.00*

> *Video*
> *ISBN 1-557661-15-4*

**3458  Characteristics of the Learning Disabled Adult**
**Special Education Nazareth**
**4245 E Avenue**
**Rochester, NY  14618**　　　　716-389-2860
　　　　　　　　　　　　　800-462-3944
　　　　　　　　　　FAX 585-389-2826

An awareness interactive video recognizing characteristics and instructional needs of learning disabled adults.

**3459  Child Management**
**AGC/United Learning**
**1560 Sherman Avenue**
**Evanston, IL  60201**
　　　　　　　　　　　　　800-328-6700
　　　　　　　　　　FAX 847-328-6706
　　　http://www.agcunitedlearning.com
　　　　e-mail: info@agcunited.com
*B Wagonseller, Author*
*Ronald Reed, VP Marketing*

For teachers, paraprofessionals, administrators, and special educators who deal with disruptive, inattentive, and hyperactive preschool and elementary age children. It gives teachers proven and practical strategies on how to manage these children, and importance of developing a network approach. *$99.00*

**3460  Child Who Appears Aloof: Module 5**
**Educational Productions**
**9000 SW Gemini Drive**
**Beaverton, OR  97008**　　　　503-644-7000
　　　　　　　　　　　　　800-950-4949
　　　　　　　　　　FAX 503-350-7000
　　　　http://www.edpro.com
　　　e-mail: custserv@edpro.com
*Molly Krumm, Marketing Directror*

A 30 minute video and 60 page facilitation packet focusing on children who pull back, who avoid social contact. Teaches strategies to understand and support these children. Part of the Hand-in-Hand Series. *$295.00*

**3461  Child Who Appears Anxious: Module 4**
**Educational Productions**
**9000 SW Gemini Drive**
**Beaverton, OR  97008**　　　　503-644-7000
　　　　　　　　　　　　　800-950-4949
　　　　　　　　　　FAX 503-350-7000
　　　　http://www.edpro.com
　　　e-mail: custserv@edpro.com
*Molly Krumm, Marketing Directror*

A 35 minute video and 60 page training facilitation packet examining the issues of anxious children and how a supporting adult can help bring them into play. Part of the Hand-in-Hand Series. *$295.00*

**3462  Child Who Dabbles: Module 3**
**Educational Productions**
**9000 SW Gemini Drive**
**Beaverton, OR  97008**　　　　503-644-7000
　　　　　　　　　　　　　800-950-4949
　　　　　　　　　　FAX 503-350-7000
　　　　http://www.edpro.com
　　　e-mail: custserv@edpro.com
*Molly Krumm, Marketing Directror*

A 30-minute video and 60-page training facilitation guide that compares dabbling to quality, invested play and offers various strategies for adultsto help children build play skills. Part of Hand-in-Hand Series. *$295.00*

**3463  Child Who Wanders: Module 2**
**Educational Productions**
**9000 SW Gemini Drive**
**Beaverton, OR  97008**　　　　503-644-7000
　　　　　　　　　　　　　800-950-4949
　　　　　　　　　　FAX 503-350-7000
　　　　http://www.edpro.com
　　　e-mail: custserv@edpro.com
*Molly Krumm, Marketing Directror*

A 30-minute video and 67-page training facilitation packet showing how to identify children who cannot engage in play so wander about the room. Shows creative interventions to help teach new skills. Part of Hand-in-Hand Series.

**3464  Child Who is Ignored: Module 6**
**Educational Productions**
**9000 SW Gemini Drive**
**Beaverton, OR  97008**　　　　503-644-7000
　　　　　　　　　　　　　800-950-4949
　　　　　　　　　　FAX 503-350-7000
　　　　http://www.edpro.vom
*Molly Krumm, Marketing Directror*

A 30 minute video and 60 page facilitation guide illustrating the children who are ignored by others and offering several interventions for them to learn social skills. Part of the Hand-in-Hand Series. *$295.00*

**3465  Child Who is Rejected: Module 7**

Educational Productions
9000 SW Gemini Drive
Beaverton, OR  97008          503-644-7000
                              800-950-4949
                          FAX 503-350-7000
                      http://www.edpro.com
                e-mail: custserv@edpro.com
*Molly Krumm, Marketing Directror*

A 35-minute video and 60-page facilitation packet
with strategies to help children whose behavior and/or
appearance causes them to be rejected by other children. Part of Hand-in-Hand Series.

**3466  Concentration Video**

Learning Disabilities Resources
PO Box 716
Bryn Mawr, PA  19010          610-525-8336
                              800-869-8336
                          FAX 610-525-8337
                      http://www.ldonline.org

A 53 minute instructional video provides an optimis-
tic perspective about attention problems ADD. Dr.
Cooper discusses different types of attention problems causes and solutions. The second part of the
video contains concentration exercises to help children and adults with attention problems. *$19.95*

*Video*

**3467  Degrees of Success: Conversations with College
Students with LD**

New York University
240 Green Street
New York, NY  10012           212-998-4980
                          FAX 212-995-4114
                   http://www.nyu.edu/osl/csd

A new video which features college students with
learning disabilities speaking in their own words
about: making the decision to attend college, developing effective learning strategies, coping with frustrations and utilizing college support services. Includes
resource packet with suggested discussion questions
and list of other resources. *$49.95*

**3468  Early Childhood STEP: Systematic Training for
Effective Parenting**

AGS
4201 Woodland Road
Circle Pines, MN  55014       763-786-4343
                              800-328-2560
                          FAX 763-786-9077
                      http://www.agsnet.com
                 e-mail: agsmail@agsnet.com

Parenting young children can be ususally rewarding,
occasionally difficult, and always a challenge. The
updated Early Childhood STEP can help parents meet
the challenge. It adapts and expands the proven principles and techniques of STEP while vividly illustrating
how they can be applied to babies, toddlers, and preschoolers. *$229.95*

**3469  Enhancing the Communicative Abilities of
Disabled Infants and Toddlers**

Purdue University Continuing Education
1586 Stewart Center
West Lafayette, IN  47907     765-494-7231
                              800-359-2968
                          FAX 765-494-0567
*M Jeanne Wilcox, PhD, Author*

Communication is a key need of most infants and toddlers with disabilities. This video provides: a brief
overview of specific communication difficulties encountered by young children, an overview of approaches to intervention, and strategies for using
children's interactive partners to enhance and facilitate communication skills. *$64.00*

**3470  FAT City**

Connecticut Assoc. for Children and Adults with LD
25 Van Zant Street
East Norwalk, CT  06855          203-838-5010
                             FAX 203-866-6108
                      http://www.CACLD.org
                    e-mail: cacld@juno.com
*Marie Armstrong, Information Specialist*

Nationally acclaimed video designed to sensitize
adults to the frustration, anxiety and tension that the
learning disabled child experiences daily. Add $5.00
for shipping and handling. *$49.95*

**3471  Getting Started with Facilitated Communication**

Syracuse University, Institute on Communication
370 Huntington Hall
Syracuse, NY  13244           315-443-9657
                          FAX 315-443-2274
             http://www.soeweb.syr.edu/thefair
                 e-mail: fcstaff@sued.syr.edu
*D Biklen, Author*

Describes in detail how to help individuals with autism and/or severe communication difficulties to get
started with facilitated communication.

**3472  Going to School with Facilitated Communication**

Syracuse University, School of Education
805 S Krouse
Syracuse, NY  13244           315-443-2693
                          FAX 315-443-2562
*D Biklen, Author*

A video in which students with autism and/or severe
disabilities illustrate the use of facilitated communication focusing on basic principles fostering facilitated communication.

**3473  Help! This Kid's Driving Me Crazy!**

Pro-Ed
8700 Shoal Creek Boulevard
Austin, TX  78757             512-451-3246
                              800-897-3202
                          FAX 512-451-8542
                      http://www.proedinc.com
*L Adkins, Author*

Designed for parents and professionals working with
children up to five years old, this videotape and booklet offers information about the nature, special needs,
and typical behavioral characteristics for young children with attention deficit disorder. *$5.00*

**3474** Helping Adults Learn: Learning Disabilities

Audio/Visual Services, PENN State University
1127 Fox Hill Road
University Park, PA 16803
800-826-0132
FAX 814-863-3102
*Thomas McKenna, Coordinator Media*

Intended for people who deal with adult learners. Focuses on the special needs of adults with learning disabilities. A printed guide accompanies this video package. *$28.00*

*140 pages*

**3475** How Difficult Can This Be?

Connecticut Assoc. for Children and Adults with LD
18 Marshall Street
Norwalk, CT 06854
203-838-5010
http://www.CACLD.org
*Rick Lavoie, Author*

This video for parents and professionals illustrates the frustration, anxiety and tension that learning disabled children face via simulations that recreate their experience firsthand. Video also comes with manual. *$49.95*

*70 min. Video*

**3476** I Want My Little Boy Back

Autism Treatment Center of America
2080 S Undermountain Road
Sheffield, MA 01257
413-229-2100
800-714-2779
FAX 413-229-8931
http://www.son-rise.org
e-mail: information@son-rise.org
*Lauren Astor, Public Relations Manager*

This BBC documentary follows an English family with a child with autism before, during, and after their time at the Son-Rise Program. It uniquely captures the heart of the Son-Rise Program and is extremely useful in understanding its techniques. *$20.00*

**3477** I'm Not Autistic on the Typewriter

Syracuse Univ./Facilitated Communication Institute
370 Huntington Hall
Syracuse, NY 13244
315-443-9657
FAX 315-443-2274
http://www.soeweb.syr.edu/thefci/
e-mail: fcstaff@sued.syr.edu
*Douglas Biklen, Director/Professor*

A video introducing facilitated communication, a method by which persons with autism express themselves. Focuses on the following elements: physical support; progression from initial training to practice, and finally to fluency; maintenance of focus on task; emotional support; and fading physical support. *$25.00*

**3478** I'm Not Stupid

Learning Disabilities Association of America
4156 Library Road
Pittsburgh, PA 15234
412-341-1515
FAX 412-344-0224
http://www.ldanatl.org
e-mail: ldanatl@usaor.net

This video depicts the constant battle of the learning disabled child in school. *$22.00*

**3479** IEP: A Tool for Realizing Possibilities (Video)

PEAK Parent Center
611 N Weber
Colorado Springs, CO 80903
719-531-9400
800-284-0251
FAX 719-531-9452
TDY:719-531-5403
http://www.peakparent.org
e-mail: info@peakparent.org
*PEAK/Partnership with San Diego State University, Author*

Highlights the importance and use of the IEP as the basic tool in designing and delivering supports and services for students with disabilities. Shows students successfully included in general education classrooms. Useful for building confidence in family members about their vital role in the IEP process. Available in English and Spanish. 20 minutes. *$15.00*

**3480** Identifying Learning Problems

Learning Disabilities Resources
PO Box 716
Bryn Mawr, PA 19010
610-525-8336
800-869-8336
FAX 610-525-8337
http://www.ldonline.org

Materials on how to identify a learning problem.

**3481** Inclusion Series

Comforty Mediaconcepts
2145 Pioneer Road
Evanston, IL 60201
847-475-0791
FAX 847-475-0793
e-mail: comforty@comforty.com

A series of video programs on inclusive education and community life. Titles include: Choices, providing instruction for all audiences to the inclusion process; Inclusion: Issues for Educators, focusing on particular teachers and administrators in Illinois schools; Families, Friends, Futures, emphasizing the need for early inclusion; and Together We're Better, providing an overview of this comprehensive program. Videos available separately or as a set.

**3482** Language Therapy

Purdue University Continuing Education
1586 Stewart Center
West Lafayette, IN 47907
765-494-7231
800-359-2968
FAX 765-494-0567
*Laura L Lee, MA, Author*

Discusses the clinical description of the typical preschool child manifesting a language disorder and observations that should be made by the clinician. *$64.00*

**3483  Language and the Retarded Child**

Purdue University Continuing Education
1586 Stewart Center
West Lafayette, IN  47907          765-494-7231
                                  800-359-2968
                                  FAX 765-494-0567
*Herold S Lillywhite, PhD, Author*

Describes the speech and language functions of the mentally retarded child; demonstrates problems in hearing, speech, language, cognition, and general motor development. *$64.00*

**3484  Latest Technology for Young Children**

Western Illinois University: Macomb Projects
27 Horrabin Hall
Macomb, IL  61455          309-298-1634
                          FAX 309-298-2305
                          http://www.mprojects.wiu.edu
                          e-mail: PL-Hutinger@wiu.edu
*Patricia Hutinger EdD, Director*
*Joyce Johanson, Coordinator*

This 25 minute videotape focuses on the Macintosh LC and adaptations for young children and includes a discussion of the features and advantages of the Macintosh LC, software demonstrations, footage of child applications, and ideas for off-computer activities. Videotape and written materials available. *$40.00*

*16-20 pages*

**3485  Learn to Read**

KET, The Kentucky Network Enterprise Division
600 Cooper Drive
Lexington, KY  40502          859-258-7000
                             800-354-9067
                             FAX 859-258-7396

Offers 30 half-hour programs tailored for the adult student.

**3486  Learning Disabilities and Discipline: Rick Lavoie's Guide to Improving Children's Behavior**

Connecticut Assoc. for Children and Adults with LD
25 Van Zant Street
East Norwalk, CT  06855          203-838-5010
                                FAX 203-866-6108
                                http://www.CACLD.org
                                e-mail: cacld@juno.com
*Rick Lavoie, Presenter*

In this video, Richard Lavoie, a nationally known expert on learning disabilities, offers practical advice on dealing with behavioral problems quickly and effectively. Shows how preventive discipline can anticipate many problems before they start. Explains how teachers and parents can create stable, predictable environments in which children with learning disabilities can flourish. 62 minutes. *$49.95*

*$5.00 shipping*

**3487  Learning Disabilities and Self-Esteem**

Connecticut Assoc. for Children and Adults with LD
25 Van Zant Street
East Norwalk, CT  06855          203-838-5010
                                FAX 203-866-6108
                                http://www.CACLD.org
                                e-mail: cacld@juno.com

The 60 minute Teacher video contains program material for building self-esteem in the classroom. The 60 minute Parent video contains program material for building self-esteem in the home. A 16 page Program Guide accompanies each video. Dr. Robert Brooks, a clinical psychologist, renowned speaker and nationally known expert on learning disabilities, is on the faculty at Harvard Medical School and is the author of The Self-Esteem Teacher. *$49.95*

*$5.00 shipping*

**3488  Learning Disabilities and Social Skills: Last One Picked..First One Picked On**

Connecticut Assoc. for Children and Adults with LD
25 Van Zant Street
East Norwalk, CT  06855          203-838-5010
                                FAX 203-866-6108
                                http://www.CACLD.org
                                e-mail: cacld@juno.com

Nationally recognized expert on learning disabilities, Richard Lavoie, gives examples on how to help LD children succeed in everyday social situations. Lavoie helps students dissect their social errors to learn correct behavior. Mistakes are seen as opportunities for learning. Available in parent (62 min.) or teacher (68 min.) version. *$49.95*

*$5.00 shipping*

**3489  Learning Problems in Language**

Learning Disabilities Resources
PO Box 716
Bryn Mawr, PA  19010          610-525-8336
                             800-869-8336
                             FAX 610-525-8337
                             http://www.ldonline.org

Identifying learning problems in speech.

**3490  Letting Go: Views on Integration**

Iowa University Affiliated Programs
University Hospital School
Iowa City, IA  52242          319-353-6390
                             FAX 319-356-8284

A video designed for parents and professionals involved in special education, illustrating the fears that parents of special needs children have of letting go, of allowing their children to experience life.

**3491  Lily Videos : A Longitudinel View of Lily with Down Syndrome**

Davidson Films
668 Marsh Street
Son Lois Obispo, CA  93401          805-594-0422
                                   888-437-4200
                                   FAX 805-594-0532
                                   http://www.davidsonfilms.com
                                   e-mail: dfi@davidsonfilms.com
*Elaine Taunt, Manager*

1. Lily: A Story About a Girl Like Me 2. Lily: A Sequal 3. Lily: At Thirty.

**3492  Lost Dreams & Growth: Parents' Concerns**

Resource Networks
Evanston, IL  60204          847-864-4522

*K Moses, Author*

A video designed for professionals and parents of children with developmental disabilities.

**3493  Motivation to Learn: How Parents and Teachers Can Help**

Assoc. for Supervision/Curriculum Development
1703 N Beauregard Street
Alexandria, VA  22311          703-578-9600
                              800-933-2723
                              FAX 703-575-5400
                              http://www.ascd.org

Two videos intended for all those concerned about how educators and families can develop student motivation to learn, solve motivational problems, and effectively participate in parent-teacher conferences.

**3494  Normal Growth and Development: Performance Prediction**

Love Publishing Company
PO Box 22353
Denver, CO  80222          303-221-7333
                           FAX 303-221-7444
                           http://www.lovepublishing.com
                           e-mail: lovepublishing@compuserve.com
*Dan Love, Director*

Teaches the age at which skills are normally achieved by children ages 0 to 48 months. *$140.00*

*Video*

**3495  Oh Say What They See: Language Stimulation**

Educational Productions
9000 SW Gemini Drive
Beaverton, OR  97008          503-644-7000
                             800-950-4949
                             FAX 503-350-7000
                             http://www.edpro.com
                             e-mail: custserv@edpro.com
*Molly Krumm, Marketing Directror*

A complete video training program illustrating indirect language stimulation techniques to teachers, parents, students, child care staff, and other adult caregivers working with children.

**3496  Parent Teacher Meeting**

Learning Disabilities Resources
PO Box 716
Bryn Mawr, PA  19010          610-525-8336
                             800-869-8336
                             FAX 610-525-8337
                             http://www.ldonline.org

Discusses learning differences and instructional techniques. *$12.00*

**3497  Phonemic Awareness: The Sounds of Reading**

Peytral Publicatons
PO Box 1162
Minnetonka, MN  55345          952-949-8707
                              877-739-8725
                              FAX 952-906-9777
                              http://www.peytral.com
                              e-mail: help@peytral.com
*Victoria Groves Scott, Author*

This staff development video may be used with paraprofessionals and teachers to learn the techniques of teaching pnomemic awareness. *$59.95*

*Video*
*ISBN 1-890455-29-6*

**3498  Regular Lives**

WETA-TV, Department of Educational Activities
2775 S Quincy Street
Arlington, VA  22206          703-998-2600
                             FAX 703-998-3401
                             http://www.weta.com
                             e-mail: info@weta.com
*DP Biklen, Author*

Designed to show the successful integration of handicapped students in school, work and community settings. Demonstrates that sharing the ordinary routines of learning and living is essential for people with disabilities.

**3499  STEP/Teen: Systematic Training for Effective Parenting of Teens**

AGS
4201 Woodland Road
Circle Pines, MN  55014          763-786-4343
                                800-328-2560
                                FAX 763-786-9077
                                http://www.agsnet.com
                                e-mail: agsmail@agsnet.com
*D Dinkmeyer, Author*

A parent training program designed to help parents of teenagers in the following areas: understanding misbehavior; improving communication and family relationships; understanding and expressing emotions and feelings and discipline. *$229.50*

**3500  Sign Songs: Fun Songs to Sign and Sing**

Harris Communications
15155 Technology Drive
Eden Prairie, MN  55344          952-906-1180
                                800-825-6758
                                FAX 952-906-1099
                                TDY:952-906-1198

Features performers John Kinstler, formerly with the National Theater of the Deaf, signing along to the lyrics of eleven kids' songs written and performed by Ken Lonnquist. Includes Public Performance rights and 10 lyric sheets for schools and public libraries. No captions. *$49.95*

*29-min. video*

**3501 Someday's Child: Special Needs Families**
**Educational Productions**
**9000 SW Gemini Drive**
**Beaverton, OR 97008**          503-644-7000
                                 800-950-4949
                                 FAX 503-350-7000
*LL Pletcher, Author*
*Molly Krumm, Marketing Directror*

A complete training video for parents and professionals working with young children with special needs: the personal accounts of three families with young children of their adjustment to and advocacy for their children. *$250.00*

**3502 Strengths and Weaknesses: College Students with Learning Disabilities**
**Altschul Group**
**2832 S Wentworth Avenue**
**Chicago, IL 60616**          312-326-6700
                               FAX 312-326-6793
Four students share their feelings and four professionals explore possible adjustment and compensation relative to learning disabilities.

**3503 Study Skills: How to Manage Your Time**
**Guidance Associates**
**100 S Bedford Road**
**Mount Kisco, NY 10549**      914-666-4100
                               800-431-1242
                               FAX 914-666-5319
                               http://www.guidanceassociates.com
                               e-mail: info@guidanceassociates.com
Describes how to create a personal schedule that will help users get more accomplished each day and waste less time. *$61.00*

*Video*

**3504 Teach an Adult to Read**
**KET, The Kentucky Network Enterprise Division**
**600 Cooper Drive**
**Lexington, KY 40502**        859-258-7000
                               800-354-9067
                               FAX 859-258-7396
A video series for reading tutors and tutor trainers that will help your program solve problems and give insight on how to teach an adult to read.

**3505 Time Together: Adults Supporting Play**
**Educational Productions**
**9000 SW Gemini Drive**
**Beaverton, OR 97008**        503-644-7000
                               800-950-4949
                               FAX 503-350-7000
                               http://www.edpro.com
                               e-mail: custserv@edpro.com
*Molly Krumm, Marketing Directror*

A complete video training program for beginning childhood teachers,aides and parents illustrating when to join a child's play, how to enhance and extend the play, and when to step back.

**3506 Tomorrow's Children**
**Vallejo City Unified School District**
**211 Valle Vista Avenue**
**Vallejo, CA 94590**          707-556-8950
                               FAX 707-556-8820
                               http://www.uallejo.k12.ca.us
*E Brower, Author*

Addresses the needs for early intervention and comprehensive services for high risk and handicapped infants and preschool children.

**3507 Treatment of Children's Grammatical Impairments in Naturalistic Context**
**Purdue University Continuing Education**
**1586 Stewart Center**
**West Lafayette, IN 47907**   765-494-7231
                               800-359-2968
                               FAX 765-494-0567
*Marc E Fey, PhD, Author*

The basic assumption is challenged that language intervention which takes place in naturalistic settings will be more effective than intervention that occurs in settings that are more heavily constrained by a clinician or other intervention agent. The concept of naturalness will be described as a continuum that is influenced by a number of factors that can be manipulated by clinicians. Several effective intervention approaches that reflect different levels of naturalness are presented. *$64.00*

**3508 Tutor Training Session**
**Learning Disabilities Resources**
**PO Box 716**
**Bryn Mawr, PA 19010**        610-525-8336
                               800-869-8336
                               FAX 610-525-8337
                               http://www.ldonline.org
Educational meterials on how to tutor someone with a learning disability.

**3509 Understanding Attention Deficit Disorder**
**Connecticut Assoc. for Children and Adults with LD**
**25 Van Zant Street**
**East Norwalk, CT 06855**     203-838-5010
                               FAX 203-866-6108
                               http://www.CACLD.org
                               e-mail: cacld@juno.com
*Simon Epstein MD*

A video in an interview format for parents and professionals providing the history, symptoms, methods of diagnosis and three approaches used to ease the effects of attention deficit disorder. A comprehensive general introduction to ADHD. 45 minutes. *$20.00*

*Video*

**3510 What About Me? Siblings Without Disabilities**
**Educational Productions**
**9000 SW Gemini Drive**
**Beaverton, OR 97008**        503-644-7000
                               800-950-4949
                               FAX 503-350-7000
                               http://www.edpro.com
                               e-mail: custserv@edpro.com
*S Butrille, Author*
*Molly Krumm, Marketing Directror*

Designed for siblings, parents, professionals, community members and students about pre-teens and two teenagers who share their perspectives, theirworries, concerns and histories about living with a sibling with a disability. *$ 250.00*

## 3511  What Every Parent Should Know About ADD

**AGC/United Learning**
**1560 Sherman Avenue**
**Evanston, IL  60201**          **800-328-6700**
**FAX 847-328-6706**
**http://www.agcunitedlearning.com**
**e-mail: info@agcunited.com**
*Bill Wagonseller, Author*
*Jim McColl, VP Sales*

Part 1: Identification and Diagnosis, clearly defines what Attention Deficit Disorder is and is not, giving parents a virtual behavioral road map to determine if their children exhibit any one of the leading symptoms of these conditions. Part 2: Causes and Strategies, explains the possible causes of ADD, and includes a step-by-step approach on what to do if parents suspect their children have the disorder. *$99.00*

*2/30 min Videos*

## 3512  What Every Teacher Should Know About ADD

**United Learning**
**6633 W Howard Street**
**Niles, IL  60714**          **847-647-0600**
**800-424-0362**
**FAX 847-647-0918**
**http://www.unitedlearning.com**
**e-mail: bistern@interaccess.com**
*Ronald Reed, VP Marketing*

This program is a must for teachers, para-professionals, administrators, and special educators. It is written for and about educators who deal with disruptive, inattentive, and hyperactive pre-school and elementary age children. It gives teachers proven and practical strategies on how to manage these children, and the importance of developing a teamwork approach.

*30-min. video*

## 3513  When a Child Doesn't Play: Module 1

**Educational Productions**
**9000 SW Gemini Drive**
**Beaverton, OR  97008**          **503-644-7000**
**800-950-4949**
**FAX 503-350-7000**
**http://www.edpro.com**
**e-mail: custserv@edpro.com**
*Molly Krumm, Marketing Directror*

A 30 minute video with 100 pages of facilitation materials presentsdramatic footage of children with play problems and how they miss critical opportunities to learn. Illustrates supportive strategies for adults. Foundation program for Hand-in-Hand Series. *$350.00*

## Vocational

## 3514  College: A Viable Option

**HEATH Resource Center**
**2121 K Street NW**
**Washington, DC  20036**          **202-973-0904**
**800-544-3284**
**FAX 202-973-0908**
**http://gopher://bobcat-ace.nche.edu**
**e-mail: heath@ace.nche.edu**
*Dan Gardner, Information Specialist*

A video discussing what a learning disability is, learning strategies and compensatory techniques. *$23.00*

## 3515  Different Way of Learning

**Brookes Publishing Company**
**PO Box 10624**
**Baltimore, MD  21285**          **410-337-9580**
**800-638-3775**
**FAX 410-337-8539**
**http://www.pbrookes.com**
**e-mail: custerv@pbrookes.com**
This video prepares students with learning disabilities for the transition from school to the workplace. *$49.00*

*Video*
*ISBN 1-557663-49-1*

## 3516  Direct Link, May I Help You?

**Direct Link for the Disabled**
**PO Box 1036**
**Solvang, CA  93464**          **805-688-1603**
**FAX 805-686-5285**

Introduces Direct Link and demonstrates practical ideas to include those with disabilities in the work force. *$25.00*

## 3517  Employment Initiatives Model: Job Coach Training Manual and Tape

**Young Adult Institute**
**460 W 34th Street**
**New York, NY  10001**          **212-273-6100**
**FAX 212-629-4113**
**http://www.yai.org**
**e-mail: ahorowitz@yai.org**
*Stephen E Freeman, Assoc. Executive Director*
*Thomas A Dern, Assoc. Executive Director*
*Aimee Horowitz, Project Specialist*

Video and manual providing an overview and orientation for staff members involved in transition services to ensure that they are well-grounded inthe concepts, responsibilities, and activities that are required to provide quality supported employment services.

## 3518  First Jobs: Entering the Job World

**Educational Design**
**345 Hudson Street**
**New York, NY  10014**
**800-221-9372**
**FAX 212-675-8922**

Career/vocational education with emphasis on job search skills, job interviews and survival skills. *$139.00*

**3519 How Not to Contact Employers**

Nat'l Clearinghouse of Rehab. Training Materials
Oklahoma State University
Stillwater, OK 74078    405-744-2000
FAX 405-744-2001
http://www.nchrtm.okstate.edu/
e-mail: index_3.html

A single vignette of what not to do when visiting perspective employers to secure positions for clients. *$10.00*

**3520 Job Coaching Video Training Series**

RPM Press
PO Box 31483
Tucson, AZ 85751    520-886-1990
888-810-1990
FAX 520-886-1990
*Jan Stonebraker, Operations Manager*

Multi-media professional training program designed for training educators, counselors, vocational rehabilitation personnel, employment specialists and paraprofessional staff in job coaching methods such as speed training, time sampling, fading, behavior observation and other methods. *$225.00*

**3521 Job Interview Reality Seminar**

Texas Commission for the Blind
4800 N Lamar Street
Austin, TX 78710    512-377-0500
FAX 512-459-2682
http://www.tcb.state.tx.us
e-mail: patw@tcb.state.tx.us

These tapes include job interview and feedback to the interviewee about his/her performance. *$20.00*

**3522 KET Basic Skills Series**

KET, The Kentucky Network Enterprise Division
600 Cooper Drive
Lexington, KY 40502    859-258-7000
800-354-9067
FAX 859-258-7396

Offers an independent learning system for workers who need retraining or help with basic skills.

**3523 KET Foundation Series**

KET, The Kentucky Network Enterprise Division
600 Cooper Drive
Lexington, KY 40502    859-258-7000
800-354-9067
FAX 859-258-7396

A highly effective basic skills series that is tailor-made for the needs of proprietary and vocational schools.

**3524 KET/GED Series**

KET, The Kentucky Network Enterprise Division
600 Cooper Drive
Lexington, KY 40502    859-258-7000
800-354-9067
FAX 859-258-7396

This nationally acclaimed instructional series helps adults prepare for the GED test.

**3525 KET/GED Series Transitional Spanish Edition**

KET, The Kentucky Network Enterprise Division
600 Cooper Drive
Lexington, KY 40502    859-258-7000
800-354-9067
FAX 859-258-7396

This award-winning series offers ESL students effective preparation for the GED test.

**3526 Life After High School for Students with Moderate and Severe Disabilities**

Beech Center on Families and Disability
3111 Haworth Hall
Lawrence, MA 66045    785-864-7600
FAX 785-864-7605

A set of three videotapes and a participant handbook document, and a teleconference in which family members, people with disabilities, teachers, rehabilitation specialists, program administrators and policy makers focus on improving the quality of services in high school and supported employment programs.

**3527 On Our Own Transition Series**

Young Adult Institute
460 W 34th Street
New York, NY 10001    212-273-6100
FAX 212-629-4113
http://www.yai.org
e-mail: ahorowitz@yai.org
*Stephen E Freemen, Assoc. Executive Director*
*Thomas A Dern, Assoc. Executive Director*
*Aimee Horowitz, Project Specialist*

Designed for parents and professionals, this series of 15 videotapes examines innovative transitional approaches that help create marketable skills, instill self-esteem and facilitate successful transition for individuals with developmental disabilities.

**3528 Social Skills on the Job: A Transition to the Workplace for Special Needs**

AGS
4201 Woodland Road
Circle Pines, MN 55014    763-786-4343
800-328-2560
FAX 763-786-9077
http://www.agsnet.com
e-mail: agsmail@agsnet.com

Presents 28 simulations to help students learn and practice 14 basic social skills that will allow them to compete successfully with their peers in the job market. *$299.95*

**3529 Succeeding in the Workplace**

JKL Communications
PO Box 40157
Washington, DC 20016    202-223-5097
FAX 202-223-5096
http://www.lathamlaw.org
e-mail: plath3@his.com

*$49.00*

**3530**  **Tools for Transition: Preparing Students with Learning Disabilities**

AGS
4201 Woodland Road
Circle Pines, MN  55014                763-786-4343
                                       800-328-2560
                                   FAX 763-786-9077
                              http://www.agsnet.com
                          e-mail: agsmail@agsnet.com

*EP Aune, Author*

Designed for learning disabled high school juniors and seniors, this program will prepare them for postsecondary education by focusing on: learningstyles, study skills, learning accommodations, self advocacy, career exploration, interpersonal relationships and choosing and applying to postsecondary schools. *$124.95*

## General

**3531  National Technical Information Service: US Department of Commerce**

5285 Port Royal Road
Springfield, VA  22161
703-487-4650
FAX 703-321-8547
http://www.ntis.gov

Maintains a worldwide database for research, development and engineering reports on a range of topics, including architectural barrier removal, employing individuals with disabilities, alternative testing formats, job accommodations, school-to-work transition for students with disabilities, rehabilitation engineering, disability law and transportation.

**3532  PsycINFO Database**

American Psychological Association
750 1st Street NE
Washington, DC  20002
202-336-5650
800-374-2722
FAX 202-336-5633
TDY:202-336-6123
http://www.apa.org/psycinfo
e-mail: psycinfo@apa.org

An online abstract database that provides access to citations to the international serial literature in psychology and related disciplines from 1887 to present. Available via PsycINFO Direct at www.psycinfo.com.

**3533  Special Needs Project**

http://www.specialneeds.com

A place to get books about disabilities.

**3534  www.abcparenting.com**

Information and resources related to learning disabilities.

**3535  www.adhdnews.com/sped.htm**

Guidance in writing IEPs, TIEPs for special education services.

**3536  www.ajb.dni.us**
**America's Job Bank**

Useful both for job seekers and employers; offers job announcements, talent banks and information about getting a job.

**3537  www.ala.org/roads**
**Roads to Learning**

Run by the American Library Association, this site works to raise public awareness about learning disabilities.

**3538  www.allaboutvision.com**
**All About Vision**

Vision information and resources, including articles on learning disabilities.

**3539  www.ataccess.org**
**Alliance for Technology Access**

Not sure where to begin your search for assistive technology information and tools? A wealth of information can be found here. ATA is a national network of assistive technology center, vendors, community based organizations, and individuals committed to increasing the use of technology by people with disabilities and junctioned invitations.

**3540  www.autismtreatment.com**
**Autism Treatment Center of America**

Since 1983, the Autism Treatment Center of America, has provided innovative training programs for parents and professionals caring for children challenged by Autism, Autism Spectrum Disorders, Pervasive Developmental Disorders (PDD) and other developmental difficulties. The Son-Rise Program teaches a specific yet comprehensive system of treatment and education designed to help families and caregivers enable their children to dramatically improve in all areas of learning.

**3541  www.babycenter.com**

Includes an easy-to-follow milestone chart, advice on when to call the doctor, chat rooms and an immunization scheduler.

**3542  www.career.com**
**Career Connections**

Posts a job announcement and an online application form, and hosts cyber job fairs.

**3543  www.childdevelopmentinfo.com**
**Child Development Institute**

Provides online information on child development, psychology, parenting, learning, health and safety as well as childhood disorders such as attention deficit disorder, dyslexia and autism. Provides comprehensive resources and practical suggestions for parents.

**3544  www.childparenting.about.com**

Information, research and resources for the learning disabled.

**3545** www.disabilityinfo.gov
**Disability Direct**

Provides one-stop online access to resources, services, and information available throughout the federal government to Americans with disabilities, their families, employers and service providers; also promotes awareness of disability issues to the general public.

**3546** www.disabilityresources.org

Information about learning disabilities and related subjects.

**3547** www.discoveryhealth.com

Information on conditions that impact learning.

**3548** www.dmoz.org
**DMOZ Open Directory Project**

Information on special education and learning disabilities.

**3549** www.doleta.gov/programs/adtrain.asp
**O'Net: Department of Labor's Occ. Information**

Useful for job seekers, employers and teachers; has career information and links to government resources.

**3550** www.drkoop.com
**Former Surgeon-General Dr. C Everett Koop**

Information on health and conditions that affect learning.

**3551** www.dyslexia.com
**Davis Dyslexia Association**

Links to internet resources for learning. Includes dyslexia, Autism and Asperger's Syndrome, ADD/ADHD and other learning disabilities.

**3552** www.familyvillage.wisc.edu
**University of Wisconsin-Madison**

A global community that integrates information, resources and communication opportunities on the Internet for all those involved with cognitive and other disabilities.

**3553** www.funbrain.com
**Quiz Lab**

Internet education site for teachers and kids. Access thousands of assessment quizzes online. Assign paperless quizzes that are graded automatically by email. Teaching tools are free and easy to use.

**3554** www.geocities.com

A site that informs and educates about common misconceptions associated with learning disabilities.

**3555** www.healthanswers.com

Health information, including learning disabilities, etc.

**3556** www.healthatoz.com
**Medical Network**

Health information, including ADD, ADHD, etc.

**3557** www.healthcentral.com

Information and products for a healthier life. Includes conditions that impact learning.

**3558** www.healthymind.com

Information on ADD and learning disabilities.

**3559** www.hood.edu/seri/serihome.htm
**Special Education Resources on the Internet**

Contains links to information about definitions, legal issues, and teaching and learning related to learning disabilities.

**3560** www.iamyourchild.org

From Rob Reiner's I Am Your Child Foundation, featuring information on child development.

**3561** www.icpac.indiana.edu/infoseries/is-50.htm
**Finding Your Career: Holland Interest Inventory**

Includes information on self-assessing one's skills and matching them to careers.

**3562** www.intelihealth.com

Includes information on learning disabilities.

**3563** www.irsc.org
**Internet Research for Special Children**

Attention deficit and hyperactivity disorder help website, created so information, support and ADD coaching are available without having to pour over all 531,136 links that come up on a net search.

**3564** www.jobhunt.org/slocareers/resources.html
**Online Career Resources**

Contains assessment tools, tutorials, labor market information, etc.

**3565  www.kidsdirect.net/pd**

Information on education and learning disabilities.

**3566  www.ld-add.com**
**Attention Deficit Disorder (ADD or ADHD)**

Do you think that you or your child has ADHD with or without learning disabilities? If the answer is yes, this webpage is for you.

**3567  www.ldonline.org**
**Learning Project at WETA**

Learning disabilities information and resources.

**3568  www.ldpride.net**
**LD Pride Online**

Inspired by Deaf Pride, a site developed as an interactive community resource for youth and adults with learning disabilities and ADD.

**3569  www.ldresources.com**

Resources for people with learning disabilities.

**3570  www.ldteens.org**
**Study Skills Web Site**

Run by the New York State Chapter of the International Dyslexia Association; a site for students, created by students; provides helpful tips and links.

**3571  www.marriottfoundation.org**
**Marriott Foundation**

Provides information on job opportunities for teenagers and young adults with disabilities.

**3572  www.my.webmd.com**
**Web MD Health**

Medical website with information which includes learning disabilities, ADD/ADHD, etc.

**3573  www.ocde.K12.ca.us/PAL/index2.html**
**Peer Assistance Leadership (PAL)**

A California-based outreach program for elementary, intermediate and high school students.

**3574  www.oneaddplace.com**
**One A D D Place**

A virtual neighborhood of information and resources relating to ADD, ADHD and learning disorders.

**3575  www.optimums.com**
**JR Mills, MS, MEd**

Information on learning disabilities.

**3576  www.pacer.org**
**Does My Child Have An Emotional Disorder**

Our mission is to expand opportunities and enhance the quality of life of children and young adults with disabilities and their families, based on the concept of parents helping parents.

**3577  www.parentpals.com**
**Ameri-Corp Speech and Hearing**

Offers parents and professionals special education support, teaching ideas and tips, special education continuing education, disability-specific information and more.

**3578  www.parentsplace.com**

Shares the adventure of parenting through articles, newsletters, questions and answers and polls.

**3579  www.peer.ca/peer.html**
**Peer Resources Network**

A Canadian organization that offers training, educational resources, and consultation to those interested in peer helping and education. Their resources section has information on books, articles and videos.

**3580  www.petersons.com**
**Peterson's Education and Career Center**

Contains postings for full-and part-time jobs as well as summer job opportunities.

**3581  www.schwablearnig.org**

A parent's guide to helping kids with learning differences.

**3582  www.son-rise.org**
**Autism Treatment Center of America**

Since 1983, the Autism Treatment Center of America, has provided innovative training programs for parents and professionals caring for children challenged by Autism, Autism Spectrum Disorders, Pervasive Developmental Disorders (PDD) and other developmental difficulties. The Son-Rise Program teaches a specific yet comprehensive system of treatment and education designed to help families and caregivers enable their children to dramatically improve in all areas of learning.

**3583**  www.specialchild.com
**Resource Foundation for Children with Challenges**

Variety of information for parents of children with disabilities, including actual stories, family and legal issues, diagnosis search, etc.

**3584**  www.specialneeds.comSpecial Needs Project

A place to get books about disabilities.

**3585**  www.therapistfinder.net

Locate psychologists, psychiatrists, social workers, family counselors, and more specializing in disorders.

**3586**  www.wrightlaw.com
**Wrightslaw**

Provides information about advocacy.

**3587**  www4.gvsu.edu
**Grand Valley State University**

Information and resources for the learning disabled.

## Counseling & Psychology

**3588** **American Psychologist**

American Psychological Association
750 1st Street NE
Washington, DC 20002                 202-336-5500
                                      800-374-2721
                             FAX 202-336-5500
                               TDY:202-336-6123
                               http://www.apa.org
                             e-mail: apeditor@apa.org

*Norman Anderson, Director*
*Marion Harrell, Deport Manager*

Contains articles of broad interest to all psychologists
that cut across all domains of the field of psychology.
The articles are theoretical in nature.

**3589** **Association of Educational Therapists**

1804 W Burbank Boulevard
Burbank, CA 91506                    818-843-1183
                             http://www.aetonline.org
                             e-mail: aetla@aol.com

*Janine Newell*

Contains articles on such topics as clinical practice,
current theory, research, reviews of testing methods
and assessments of materials. A legislative summary
is included. *$25.00*

**3590** **Case Manager**

Mosby
10801 Executive Center Drive
Little Rock, AR 72211                501-223-0183
                                      800-325-4177
                             FAX 501-223-0519
                             http://www.mosby.com/casemgr
                             e-mail: nathania.sawyer@mosby.com
*Nathania Sawyer, Associate Publisher*
*Catherine Mullahy, Editor*

Targeted to medical case managers and other related
professionals who create and manage patient care in
hospital, home, long-term care, rehabilitation, mental
health, and managed care settings. Articles, columns,
and departments provide the latest information in the
field though coverage of the profession's hottest topics, including outcomes management, guidelines and
standards of practice, reimbursement, trends in managed care, and ethical/ legal issues. *$45.00*

> *Bi-Monthly*
> *ISSN 1061-9259*

**3591** **Center Focus**

Nat'l Center for Research in Vocational Education
University Of California, Berkley
Berkeley, CA 94720                   510-642-348/
                             FAX 510-642-4803

Each issue provides a brief but thorough distillation of
research, development, evaluation and practice
knowledge about a specific topic.

> *Quarterly*

**3592** **Journal of Social and Clinical Psychology**

72 Spring Street
New York, NY 10012                   212-431-9800
                                      800-365-7006
                             FAX 212-966-6708

*Jody Falco, Managing Editor*

Examines and reports the burgeoning areas of theory,
research and practice. This journal was created to foster interdisciplinary communication and scholarship
among practitioners of social and clinical psychology. It concentrates on presenting solid clinical and
experimental reports on a wide range of topics crucial
to the practice and study of mental health. *$37.50*

> *ISSN 0736-7236*

**3593** **Learning Disabilities: Research and Practice**

Lawrence Erlbaum Associates
10 Industrial Avenue
Mahwah, NJ 07430                     201-236-9500
                                      800-926-6579
                             FAX 201-236-0072

*Margo Mastropieri, Co-Editor*
*Thomas Scruggs, Co-Editor*

Because learning disabilities is a multidisciplinary
field of study, this important journal publishes articles addressing the nature and characteristics of learning disabled students, promising research, program
development, assessment practices, and teaching
methodologies from different disciplines. In so doing,
LDRP provides information of great value to professionals involved in a variety of different disciplines
including school psychology, counseling, reading and
medicine. *$45.00*

> *ISSN 0938-8982*

**3594** **School Psychology Quarterly: Official Journal of
Div. 16 of the American Psychological Assoc**

Guilford Publications
72 Spring Street
New York, NY 10012                   212-431-9800
                                      800-365-7006
                             FAX 212-966-6708
                             http://www.guilford.com
                             e-mail: info@guilford.com

*Michael Gordon, Editor*
*Shelby Keiser, Editor*

This journal advances the latest research, theory, and
practice and features a new book review section.
Strengthening the relationship between school psychology and broad-based psychological science.
*$35.00*

> *4 issues/year*
> *ISSN 1045-3830*

## General

**3595  ASCD Update**

**Assoc. for Supervision/Curriculum Development**
**1703 N Beauregard Street**
**Alexandria, VA  22311**          703-578-9600
                                  800-933-2723
                              FAX 703-575-5400
                              http://www.ascd.org
*Ronald Brandt, Executive Editor*
*Marge Scherer, Managing Editor*

News on contemporary education issues and information on ASCD programs.

**3596  Adult Basic Education: An Interdisciplinary**
**Journal for Adult Literacy Educators**

**Commission on Adult Basic Education (COABE)**
**Piedmont College**
**Demorest, GA  30535**            706-778-3000
                              FAX 706-776-0133
                          http://www.piedmont.edu
                      e-mail: melichar@piedmnt.edu
*Ken Melichar, Editor*
*Denise Bamson, Secretary*

Adult Basic Education: An Interdisciplinary Journal for Adult Literacy Educators is a double blind, peer review, scholarly journal with a practical intent devoted to improving the efforts of adult educators working with low literally disadvantaged, and educationally oppressed people. *$25.00*

*3x/year*

**3597  American Journal of Occupational Therapy**

**American Occupational Therapy Association**
**4720 Montgomery Lane**
**Bethesda, MD  20824**            301-652-2682
                                  800-377-8555
                              FAX 301-652-7711
                              http://www.aota.org
                          e-mail: ajotsis@aota.org
*Liz Holcomb, Managing Editor*

An official publication of the American Occupational Therapy Association, inc. This peer reviewed journal focuses on research, practice, and health care issues in the field of occupational therapy. *$50.00*

**3598  American School Board Journal**

**National School Boards Association**
**1680 Duke Street**
**Alexandria, VA  22314**          703-838-6739
                              FAX 703-549-6719
                              http://www.asbj.com
                          e-mail: editor@asbj.com
*Sally Zakariya, Editor*
*Margaret Suslik, Magazine Coordinator*

American School Board Journal chronicles change, interprets issues, and offers readers — some 40,000 school board members and school administrators — practical advice on a broad range of topics pertinent to school go9vernance and management, policy making, student achievement, and the art of school leadership. In addition, regular departments cover education news, school law, research, and new books. *$54.00*

*Monthly*

**3599  Annals of Otology, Rhinology and Laryngology**

**Annals Publishing Company**
**4507 Laclede Avenue**
**Saint Louis, MO  63108**         314-367-4987
                              FAX 314-367-4988
                              http://www.annals.com
                          e-mail: manager@annals.com
*Edna Harrison, Chief Copy Editor*

Offers original manuscripts of clinical and research importance in otolaryngology - head and neck surgery, audiology, speech pathology, head and neck oncology and surgery, and related specialties. All papers are peer-reviewed *$ 179.00*

*112 pages  Monthly*

**3600  Autism Research Review International**

**Autism Research Institute**
**4182 Adams Avenue**
**San Diego, CA  92116**           619-281-7165
                              FAX 619-563-6840
                    http://www.autismresearchinstitute.com
*Matt Cobler, Assistant to the Director*
*Bernard Rimland, Director*

A quarterly newsletter that reviews current research pertaining to autism. *$16.00*

**3601  CABE Journal**

**Connecticut Association of Boards of Education**
**81 Wolcott Hill Road**
**Wethersfield, CT  06109**        860-571-7446
                                  800-317-0033
                              FAX 860-571-7452
                              http://www.cabe.org
                          e-mail: admin@cabe.org
*Bonnie Carney, Sr. Staff Associate*
*Robert Rader, Executive Director*

Published for school board members and deals with a wide range of issues such as: legal, teaching and learning, finances and resources, at-risk youth and more.

**3602  CEC Today**

**Council for Exceptional Children**
**1110 N Glebe Road**
**Arlington, VA  22201**           703-620-3660
                                  888-232-7733
                              FAX 703-264-9494
                              TDY:703-620-3660
                          http://www.cec.sped.org
                      e-mail: service@cec.sped.org
*Lynda Voyles, Editor*
*Drew Albritten M.D., President*

Newsletter of the Council for Exceptional Children. Available to members of the council.

*10x per year*

**3603  Chalk Talk**

**Fresno Teachers Association**
**5334 N Fresno Street**
**Fresno, CA  93710**              559-224-8430
                              FAX 559-224-1571
                          http://www.fresnoteacher.org
                          e-mail: garry@fresno.org
*Garry Alfred, Editor*
*Didi Case, Accountant*

Improvement in public education and the condition of the working environment of public school teachers. *$2.00*

*6 pages*

**3604    Child Assessment News**

**Guilford Publications**
**72 Spring Street**
**New York, NY  10012**                    **212-431-9800**
                                           **800-365-7006**
                              **FAX 212-966-6708**
                        **http://www.guilford.com**
                    **e-mail: info@guilford.com**
*Michael Gordon, Editor*
*Shelby Keiser, Editor*

Offers the easiest and most effective way possible for busy professionals to learn about: the hottest news in child assessment, brand new test materials, groundbreaking research developments, helpful clinical techniques, expertopinions of well-known and respected researchers and clinicians, important legislation, and software updates. *$75.00*

*Bimonthly*
*ISSN 1055-0518*

**3605    Classroom Computer Learning**

**Peter Li**
**2621 Dryden Rdoad**
**Dayton, OH  45439**
                                           **800-523-4625**
                              **FAX 800-370-4450**
                        **http://www.peterli.com**
An educational magazine geared toward teachers.

**3606    Creative Classroom Magazine**

**170 5th Avenue**
**New York, NY  10010**                    **212-243-5750**
                              **FAX 212-242-5628**
                **http://www.creativeclassroom.org**
                        **e-mail: ccmag@inch.com**
*Meg Bozzone, Editor*
*Robin Bromley, Associate Editor*

Classroom ideas, lesson suggestions, materials listings, advice and articles on teaching students current events such as environmental issues. Covers all subjects and includes a calendar of special events and suggestions for projects.

*Bimonthly*

**3607    Diagnostique**

**Council for Exceptional Children**
**1110 N Glebe Road**
**Arlington, VA  22201**                    **703-620-3660**
                                           **888-232-7733**
                              **FAX 703-264-9494**
                              **TDY:703-620-3660**
                    **http://www.cec.sped.org/**
                **e-mail: service@cec.sped.org**
*Gerard Hurley, Contact*

Offers information on preparation for postsecondary success. *$28.00*

**3608    Disability Compliance for Higher Education**

**LRP Publications**
**PO Box 24668**
**West Palm Beach, FL  33416**             **561-622-6520**
                                           **800-341-7874**
                              **FAX 561-622-0757**
                        **http://www.lfp.com**
                    **e-mail: custerve@lrp.com**
*Ed Fllo, Author*
*Anna McMahon, Product Group Manager*

This monthly newsletter combines analysis of disability law eith detaiols on innovative accommodations for students and staff. *$190.00*

*16 pages  Monthly*

**3609    Division for Children with Communication Disorders Newsletter**

**Council for Exceptional Children**
**1110 N Glebe Road**
**Arlington, VA  22201**                    **703-620-3660**
                                           **888-232-7733**
                              **FAX 703-264-9494**
                    **http://www.cec.sped.org/**
                **e-mail: service@cec.sped.org**
*Penny Griffith, Editor*
*Drew Albritten M.D., President*

Information concerning the education and welfare of children and youth with communication disorders; reports on division committee activities, highlights current research and programs.

*12 pages*

**3610    Education Digest**

**College of Education**
**University of Illinois**
**Urbana, IL  61801**                      **217-333-0260**
                              **FAX 217-244-7732**
                        **http://www.ed.uiuc.edu**

**3611    Education Technology News**

**Business Publishers**
**8737 Colesville Road**
**Silver Spring, MD  20910**               **301-587-6300**
                                           **800-274-0122**
                              **FAX 301-585-9075**
*Howard Fields, Editor*
*LA Eiserer, President*

Full coverage of innovations in technology that can be implemented in the classroom, including those which enhance learning for children with disabilities. Focus is on computer use in the classroom, and related subjects such as teacher training, new software, research findings, grants and other funding issues. *$267.00*

**3612    Education Week**

**4301 ConneCourticut Avenue NW**
**Washington, DC  20008**                  **202-364-4114**
                              **FAX 202-464-1039**
                        **http://www.edweek.org**
Offers articles of interest to educators, teachers, professionals and special educators on the latest developments, laws, issues and more in the various fields of education. *$69.94*

**3613 Educational Leadership**

Assoc. for Supervision/Curriculum Development
1703 N Beauregard Street
Alexandria, VA 22311        703-578-9600
                           800-933-2723
                      FAX 703-575-5400
                      http://www.ascd.org

**3614 Educational Researcher**

American Educational Research Association
1230 17th Street NW
Washington, DC 20036        202-223-9485
                       FAX 202-775-1824
                       http://www.aera.net
                  e-mail: flevine@aera.net
*Felize Levine, President*

**3615 Educational Staffing Program**

International Schools Services
15 Roszel Road
Princeton, NJ 08543          609-452-0990
                        FAX 609-452-2690
                        http://www.iss.adu
                        e-mail: iss@iss.edu
*John Nicklas, President*
*Dan Scinto, Vice President*

Opportunities for K-12 teachers and administrators exist in private American and international schools around the world. International Schools Services has placed over 15,000 K-12 educators in overseas schools since 1955. Interviews are conducted at one of our US-based international Recruitment Centers (IRCs). *$5.00*

**3616 Educational Technology**

Educational Technology
700 E Palisade Avenue
Englewood Cliffs, NJ 07632        201-871-4007
                             800-952-BOOK
                        FAX 201-871-4009
               http://www.bookstoread.com/ctp
                 e-mail: edtecpubls@aol.com
*L Lipsitz, Editor*

Leading magazine covering the field of educational technology, including devices for people with learning disabilities. 6x annually. *$119.00*

*64 pages*

**3617 Employment in the Mainstream**

Mainstream
3 Bethesda Metro Center
Bethesda, MD 20814          301-654-2400
                            800-424-8089
                       FAX 301-654-2403
               e-mail: info@mainstream.com
*Fritz Rumpel, Editor*

A magazine offering information on employment issues of interest to rehabilitation professionals and employers. *$25.00*

**3618 Faculty Inservice Education Kit**

Association on Higher Education and Disability
Po Box 540666
Waltham, MA 02454           781-788-0003
                       FAX 781-788-0033
                       http://www.ahead.org
        e-mail: ahead@postbox.acs.ohio-state.edu

Lists all the handouts and documentation necessary to conduct inservice training for the postsecondary community regarding the inclusion of students with disabilities in campus life. *$45.95*

**3619 GED Items**

GED Testing Services
1 Dupont Circle NW
Washington, DC 20036        202-939-9490
                            800-626-9433
                       FAX 202-775-8578
     http://www.acenet.edu/programs/calec/ged/home
                  e-mail: ged@ace.nche.edu
*Lisa Hone, Special Projects Manager*
*Lyn Schaeser, Project Manager/ Director*

A newsletter for GED examiners and teachers as well as other adult education professionals. It provides information about GED policies and best practices.

*5x/year*

**3620 Gander Publishing**

412 Higuera Street
San Luis Obispo, CA 93401        805-541-5523
                             800-554-1819
                        FAX 805-782-0488
                http://www.ganderpub.com
              e-mail: wcook@ganderpub.com
*Wendy Cook, Marketing Manager*

Books, kits, videos and CD-ROMs used to train educators and parents in specific programs for helping people with learning disabilities.

**3621 Gifted Child Today**

Prufrock Press
PO Box 8813
Waco, TX 76714              254-756-3337
                            800-998-2208
                       FAX 254-756-3339
*Joel McIntosh, Publisher*
*Susan Johnson, Editor*

Provides teachers accurate, current information about the education of gifted and talented children. *$29.95*

**3622 InfoTech Newsletter**

InfoTech
University of Iowa
Iowa City, IA 52242         319-353-8777
                            800-331-3027

A free publication covering topics relating to assistive technology, including announcements from Iowa's IPAT Program and from Minnesota's S.T.A.R. Program as well as Used Equipment Referral Service listing.

**3623  Information from HEATH**

HEATH Resource Center
2121 K Street NW
Washington, DC  20036          202-973-0904
                               800-544-3284
                          FAX 202-973-0908
                     http://www.heath.gwu.edu
                     e-mail: askheath@gwu.edu
*Dan Gardner, Publications Manager*

A newsletter offering information on postsecondary
education for individuals with disabilities. *$1.00*

**3624  Journal of Learning Disabilities**

Pro-Ed
8700 Shoal Creek Boulevard
Austin, TX  78757              512-451-3246
                               800-897-3202
                          FAX 512-451-8542
                     http://www.proedinc.com
*Judith Voress PhD, Periodicals Director*

Bimonthly, international publication containing articles on practice research, and theory related to learning disabilities.

*64 pages  Bimonthly*

**3625  Journal of Postsecondary Education and
Disability**

Association on Higher Education and Disability
PO Box 540666
Waltham, MA  02454             781-788-0003
                          FAX 781-788-0033
                       http://www.ahead.org
              e-mail: ahead@postbox.acs.ohio-state.edu
Provides in-depth examination of research, issues,
policies and programs in postsecondary education.

**3626  Journal of Rehabilitation**

National Rehabilitation Association
633 S Washington Street
Alexandria, VA  22314          703-836-0850
                               888-258-4295
                          FAX 703-836-0848
                   http://www.nationalrehab.org
                   e-mail: info@nationalrehab.org
*Michelle Vaughan, Executive Director*
*David Strauser, Editor*
*Carol Hamilla, Managing Editor*

The Journal of Rehabilitation publishes articles by
leaders in the fields of rehabilitation. The articles are
written for rehabilitation professionals and students
studying in the fields of rehabilitation *$18.00*

*ISSN 0022-4154*

**3627  Journal of School Health**

American School Health Association
7263 State Route 43
Kent, OH  44240                330-678-1601
                               800-445-2742
                          FAX 330-678-4526
                     http://www.ashaweb.org
                     e-mail: asha@ashaweb.org
*Susan Wooley, Executive Director*

**3628  Journal of Secondary Gifted Education**

Prufrock Press
PO Box 8813
Waco, TX  76714                254-756-3337
                               800-998-2208
                          FAX 254-756-3339
                 e-mail: periodical@prufrock.com
*Joel McIntosh, Publisher*
*Susan Johnsen, Editor*

Publishes research and critical theory related to the
education of adolescent gifted and talented students.
*$35.00*

**3629  Journal of Special Education Technology**

Peabody College, Box 328
Vanderbilt University
Nashville, TN  37203           615-322-7311
                          FAX 615-322-8236
                    http://www.vanderbilt.edu/
*Herbert Rieth, Editor*
*Paulette Jackson, Administrative Assistant*

*Quarterly $40.00*

**3630  KDDWB Variety Family Center**

University of Minnesota
200 Oak Street SE
Minneapolis, MN  55455         612-626-3087
                               800-276-8642
                          FAX 612-624-0997
                http://www.allaboutkids.umn.edu
                   e-mail: lib-web@tc.umn.edu
*Elizabeth MSW, Resource Coordinator*

A University Community partnership that provides
family-centered services that promote physical, emotional, psychological and social health and well-being
for children and youth at risk, including children and
youth with disabilities.

**3631  LDA Alabama Newsletter**

Learning Disabilities Association of Alabama
PO Box 11588
Montgomery, AL  36111          334-279-9324
                          FAX 334-284-9357
*Debbie Gibson, President*

Educational support and advocacy for those with
learning disabilities and Attention Deficit Disorder.

**3632  LDA Rhode Island Newsletter**

Learning Disabilities Association of Rhode Island
PO Box 8128
Cranston, RI  02920            401-946-6968
                          FAX 401-946-6968
                          TDY:401-946-6968
                       http://www.ldanatl.org
                    e-mail: lindixx@email.com
*Linda DiCecco, President*

A nonprofit, volunteer organization whose members
give their time and support to children with learning
disabilities as well as share information with other
parents, professionals and individuals with learning
disabilities.

**3633  Learning Disabilities Newsletter**

**Learning Disabilities Resources**
PO Box 716
Bryn Mawr, PA  19010              610-525-8336
                                 800-869-8336
                          FAX 610-525-8336
                    http://www.ldonline.org

Offers information on difficulties associated with
learning disabilities. *$10.00*

**3634  Learning Disabilities Quarterly**

**Council for Learning Disabilities**
PO Box 40303
Overland Park, KS  66204          913-492-8755
                          FAX 913-492-2546
               http://www1.winthrop.ecu/cld

Offers information to professionals on working with
learning disabled individuals.

**3635  Learning Disabilities Research & Practice**

**Council for Exceptional Children**
1110 N Glebe Road
Arlington, VA  22201              703-620-3660
                                 888-232-7733
                          FAX 703-264-9494
                 http://www.cec.sped.org/
             e-mail: service@cec.sped.org
*Gerard Hurley, Contact*
*Drew Albritten M.D., President*

Scholarly journal providing current research in the
field of learning disabilities of importance to teachers,
educators and researchers.

**3636  Learning Disabilities: A Multidisciplinary Journal**

**Learning Disabilities Association of America**
4156 Library Road
Pittsburgh, PA  15234             412-341-1515
                          FAX 412-344-0224
                    http://www.ldanatl.org
               e-mail: ldanatl@usaor.net
*Jane Browning, Editor-in-Chief*

A vehicle for disseminating the most current thinking
on learning disabilities and to provide information on
research, practice, theory, issues and trends regarding
learning disabilities. *$25.00*

         *Biannual*

**3637  Learning and Individual Differences**

**National Association of School Psychologists**
4340 E West Highway
Bethesda, MD  20814               301-657-0270
                                 866-331-6277
                          FAX 301-657-0275
                          TDY:301-657-4155
               http://www.nasponline.org
          e-mail: publications@naspweb.org
*Susan Gorin, Executive Director*

A multidisciplinary journal in education.

**3638  Mainstream**

**Johnson Press**
2973 Beech Street
San Diego, CA  92102              619-234-3138
                          FAX 619-234-3155

**3639  Media & Methods Magazine**
1429 Walnut Street
Philadelphia, PA  19102           215-563-6005
                                 800-555-5657
                          FAX 215-587-9706
               http://www.media-methods.com
*Michele Sokoloff, Publisher*
*Danielle Dunn, Office Assistant*

The education source magazine that features how to
use instructional technologies with all learning abilities. Practical and hands on teaching ideas and
expectional resources.

**3640  Mental Health Report**

**Business Publishers**
8737 Colesville Road
Silver Spring, MD  20910          301-587-6300
                                 800-274-6737
                          FAX 301-585-9075
                    http://www.dpinews.com
             e-mail: adodson@dpinews.com
*Ami Dodson, Editorial Director*

Covers issues of interest to mental health program administrators including treatment of children with
mental disorders and other special populations, tracks
federal agency regulation and funding for programs
nationwide, as well as court cases and state/federal
law. *$325.00*

**3641  National Dissemination Center for Children**

**Academy for the Educational Development**
PO Box 1492
Washington, DC  20013-149         202-884-8200
                                 800-695-0285
                          FAX 202-884-8841
                          TDY:800-695-0285
                    http://www.nichcy.org
               e-mail: nichcy@aed.org
*Susan Ripley, Executive Director*

A newsletter offering information, guides, books and
reference sources for the learning disabled.

**3642  National Organization on Disability**
910 16th Street NW
Washington, DC  20006             202-293-5960
                                 800-248-2253
                          FAX 202-293-7999
                          TDY:202-293-5968
*Alan Reich, President*

A newsletter offering information and articles on the
organization.

**3643  OT Practice**

**American Occupational Therapy Association**
4720 Montgomery Lane
Bethesda, MD  20824               301-652-2682
                                 800-SAY-AOTA
                          FAX 301-652-7711
                          TDY:800-377-8555
                    http://www.aota.org
               e-mail: lcollin@aota.org
*Laura Collins, Editor*
*Fred Somers, Executive Director*

The clinical and professional magazine of AOTA. It provides professional information and news on all aspects of practice and encourages a dialogue among our members on professional concerns and views.

*64 pages*

**3644 Occupational Outlook Quarterly**

**US Department of Labor**
**200 Constitution Avenue**
**Washington, DC 20212**     202-693-6000
                           FAX 202-693-6111
                           http://www.dol.gov

Information on new educational and training opportunities, emerging jobs, prospects for change in the work world and the latest research findings.

**3645 Ohio State Comparative Education Review**

**University Center for International Education**
**1712 Neil Avenue, Oxley Hall**
**Columbus, OH 43210**          614-292-8654
                              FAX 614-292-4273
                              http://www.osu.edu
*Erwin Epstein MD, Professor*

A scholarly journal that examines the application of social science theories and methods to international issues of education.

**3646 Rehabilitation Grants and Contracts Monitor**

**RPM Press**
**PO Box 31483**
**Tucson, AZ 85751**           520-886-1990
                             888-810-1990
                       FAX 520-886-1990
                  http://www.rpmpress.com
            e-mail: pmccray@theriver.com
*Jan Stonebraker, Operations Manager*
*Paul McCray, President*

Newsletter providing a listing of grants and contracts available in the areas of special education, education, voc-ed special needs, vocational rehabilitation, mental health, job training, housing, transportation and a variety of other human service fields. *$97.00*

**3647 Report on Disability Programs**

**Business Publishers**
**8737 Colesville Road**
**Silver Spring, MD 20910**     301-587-6300
                             800-274-6737
                       FAX 301-589-8463
                  http://www.bpinews.com
*L. Eiserer, President*

Public policy issues that affect people with disabilities, plus court cases, funding opportunities and national news. Focus is on laws including American with Disabilities Act, Rehabilitation Act, Fair Housing Amendments, Affirmative Action, Individuals with Disabilities Education Act, and other legislation. Also tracks education, housing, job training, rehabilitation, Social Security and SSI, Medicare, Medicaid, and more. Tracks court cases and news from 50 states as well as federal news. *$286.00*

**3648 Report on Education of the Disadvantaged**

**Business Publishers**
**951 Pershing Drive**
**Silver Spring, MD 20910**     301-587-6300
                             FAX 301-585-9075
*Clair Hill, Marketing Manager*

Covers federal aid to education programs affecting the disadvantaged, including children with special education needs. Covers funding programs, court cases and national/local news. *$273.00*

*8 pages*

**3649 Self-Advocacy Resources for Persons with Learning Disabilities**

**Learning Disabilities Association of America**
**4156 Library Road**
**Pittsburgh, PA 15234**        412-341-1515
                             FAX 412-344-0224
                       http://www.ldanatl.org
            e-mail: ldanatl@usaor.net
*Jane Browning, Editor-in-Chief*

A newsletter offering information on resources and programs for the learning disabled. *$1.50*

**3650 Teacher Magazine**

**Editorial Project in Education**
**6935 Arlington Road**
**Bethesda, MD 20814**          301-280-3100
                             FAX 301-280-3200
                       http://www.edweek.org
*Virginia Edwards, President*

Offers articles and information on the latest programs, software, books, classroom materials and more for the teaching professional. *$17.94*

**3651 Teaching Exceptional Children**

**Council for Exceptional Children**
**1110 N Glebe Road**
**Arlington, VA 22201**         703-620-3660
                             888-232-7733
                       FAX 703-264-9494
                       TDY:866-915-5000
                  http://www.cec.sped.org/
            e-mail: service@cec.sped.org
*Drew Albritten M.D., President*

Published specifically for teachers and administrators of children with disabilities and children who are gifted. Features practical articles that present methods and materials for classroom use as well as current issues in special education teaching and learning. Also provides the latest data on technology, assistive technology, procedures and techniques with applications to students with exceptionalities.

*6x per year*

**3652 Texas Key**

**Learning Disabilities Association of Texas**
**1011 W 31st Street**
**Austin, TX 78705**            512-458-8234
                             800-604-7500
                       FAX 512-458-3826
                       http://www.ldat.org
            e-mail: contact@ldat.org
*Ann Robinson, Editor*

Quarterly newsletter providing information of intrest to parents and professionals in the field of learning.

*16-24 pages*

## Language Arts

**3653  ASHA Leader**

**American Speech-Language-Hearing Association**
**10801 Rockville Pike**
**Bethesda, MD  20852**           **301-897-5700**
                              **888-498-6699**
                        **FAX 301-897-7358**
                        **TDY:301-897-5700**
                      **http://www.asha.org**
                **e-mail: epietrarton@asha.com**
*Laurie Ward, Marketing Coordinator*
*Arlene Pietranton, Executive Director*

Pertains to the professional and administrative activities in the fields of speech-language pathology, audiology and the American Speech-Language-Hearing Association.

*24X/year*

**3654  American Journal of Speech-Language Pathology: Clinical Practice**

**American Speech-Language-Hearing Association**
**10801 Rockville Pike**
**Bethesda, MD  20852**           **301-897-5700**
                              **888-498-6699**
                        **FAX 301-897-7358**
                        **TDY:301-897-5700**
                      **http://www.asha.org**
                **e-mail: epietrarton@asha.com**
*Laurie Ward, Marketing Coordinator*
*Arlene Pietranton, Executive Director*

Addresses all aspects of clinical practice in speech-language pathology. 3x annually.

**3655  Communication Outlook**

**Michigan University/Artificial Language Laboratory**

**405 Computer Center**
**East Lansing, MI  48824**          **517-353-0870**
                        **FAX 517-353-4766**
                  **http://www..msu.edu/~artlang**
                    **e-mail: artlang@msu.edu**
*John Eulenberg, Director*
*Julie Warren, Circulation/Advertising*

An international quarterly magazine which covers technological developments for persons who experience communication handicaps due to neurological, sensory or neuromuscular conditions. Communication Outlook provides clear and concise information about this emerging technology. Communication Outlook explains where and how communication aids are developed and where they may be purchased. Readers also learn how augmentative and alternative communication is expanding internationally.

*32 pages*

**3656  Journal of Speech, Language, and Hearing Research**

**American Speech-Language-Hearing Association**
**10801 Rockville Pike**
**Bethesda, MD  20852**           **301-897-5700**
                              **888-498-6699**
                        **FAX 301-897-7358**
                        **TDY:301-897-5700**
                      **http://www.asha.org**
                **e-mail: epietrarton@asha.com**
*Laurie Ward, Marketing Coordinator*
*Arlene Pietranton, Executive Director*

An archival research publication that includes papers pertaining to the processes and disorders of hearing, language, speech and to the diagnosis and treatment of these disorders.

**3657  Kaleidoscope, Exploring the Experience of Disability Through Literature and Fine Arts**

**701 S Main Street**
**Akron, OH  44311**               **330-762-9755**
                        **FAX 330-762-0912**
                        **TDY:330-379-3349**
                    **http://www.udsakron.org**
                **e-mail: mshiplett@udsakron.org**
*Gail Willmott, Senior Editor, Author*
*Phyllis Boerner, Publication Director*

Creatively focuses on the experience of disability through diverse forms of literature and the fine arts. An award-winning magazine unique to the field of disability studies, it is open to writers with or without disabilities. KALEIDOSCOPE strives to express how disability does or does not affect society and individuals feelings and reactions to disability. Its portrayals of disability reflect a conscious effort to challenge and overcome stereotypical and patronizing attitudes. *$6.00*

*64 pages  $10.00/year*

**3658  Language Arts**

**National Council of Teachers of English**
**1111 W Kenyon Road**
**Urbana, IL  61801**              **217-328-3870**
                              **800-369-6283**
                        **FAX 217-328-9645**
                      **http://www.ncte.org**
                **e-mail: lbianchini@ncte.org**
*Kent Williams, President*
*Bill Subick, Office Manager*

**3659  National Council of Teachers of English**

**National Council of Teachers of English**
**1111 W Kenyon Road**
**Urbana, IL  61801**              **217-328-3870**
                              **800-369-6283**
                        **FAX 217-278-3761**
                      **http://www.ncte.org**
                **e-mail: lbianchini@ncte.org**
*Lori Bianchini, Communications Specialist*

With 75,000 individual and institutional members worldwide, NCTE is dedicated to improving the teaching and learning of English and the language arts at all levels of education. Members include elementary, middle, and high school teachers, supervisors of English programs, college and university faculty, teacher educators, local and state agency English specialists, and professionals in related fields.

## College Guides

**3660 Assisting College Students with Learning Disabilities: A Tutor's Manual**

Association on Higher Education and Disability
PO Box 540666
Waltham, MA 02454        781-788-0003
                        FAX 781-788-0033
                        http://www.ahead.org
e-mail: ahead@postbox.acs.ohio-state.edu

This manual is designed for use by service providers and tutors working with students with learning disabilities. *$26.00*

**3661 Bridges to Career Success: A Model for Training Career Counselors**

National Clearinghouse of Rehabilitation Materials
206 W Sixth St
Stillwater, OK 74078        405-744-2000
                           FAX 405-744-2001
                           http://www.nchrtm.okstate.edu
*Jamie Satcher, Author*

This training package consists of materials for a one-day training program including an agenda outline, instructions and resource materials. Content encompasses services typically offered by college and university programs andresources to aid in career planning and placement. *$6.40*

*54 pages*

**3662 Guide for Delivering Faculty Inservice on the LD College Student**

HEATH Resource Center
2121 K Street NW
Washington, DC 20036        202-973-0904
                           800-544-3284
                           FAX 202-973-0908
                           http://www.heath.gwu.edu
e-mail: askheath@askheath.gwu.edu
*Dan Gardner, Publications Manager*

The guide focuses on providing faculty inservice and training on how to work with students with learning disabilities. *$15.00*

**3663 Guide to Community Colleges Serving Students with Learning Disabilities**

National Clearinghouse of Rehabilitation Materials
206 W Sixth Street
Stillwater, OK 74078        405-744-2000
                           FAX 405-744-2001
                           http://www.nchrtm.okstate.edu
                           e-mail: brookdj@okway.okstate.edu
*Sonja Burnhan and Jamie Satcher, Author*

The guide lists two-year community colleges in Mississippi, Alabama, Georgia, Tennessee, and Florida and describes services and accommodations provided for students with learning disabilities. *$2.80*

*18 pages  Item # 353.020*

**3664 Learning Disabilities Program at Family Service**

Children's Home Society
166 4th Street E
Saint Paul, MN 55101        651-222-0311
                           FAX 651-222-8920
                           TDY:651-222-0175
                           http://www.chsfs.org
e-mail: familyservice@familyinc.org
*Kristen Brown, LDP Educator*
*Renee Brekken, Manager*

The Learning Disabilities Program is committed to ensuring that people with challenges to learning are valued, contributing members of their community. This program assists individuals by providing individual consultation, educational presentations, information and referrals.

**3665 National Association of Colleges & Employe**

College Placement Council
62 Highland Avenue
Bethlehem, PA 18017        610-868-1421
                          800-544-5272
                          FAX 610-868-0208
                          http://www.naceweb.org
                          e-mail: cnader@naceweb.org
*Cecilia Nader, Administrative Assistant*

Gives hard data on practitioners, budgets, the college relations and recruitment function, entry-level hiring, on-campus recruitment, new hires and much much more. *$46.95*

*100+ pages*

**3666 Postsecondary Learning Disabilities Primer**

Carolina University
137 Killia Annex Western Carolina U
Cullowhee, NC 38723        828-227-7127
                          FAX 828-227-7078
*Carol Mellen, Student Support*

A collection of service options and handouts for students/service providers. *$20.50*

**3667 Project TAPE: Technical Assistance for Postsecondary Education**

Northern Illinois University
DeKalb, IL 60115        815-753-0659
                       FAX 815-753-0355
*Ernest Rose*

Includes intervention strategies for persons with learning disabilities attending two-year community colleges.

**3668 Service Operations Manual**

HEATH Resource Center
2121 K Street NW
Washington, DC 20036        202-973-0904
                           800-544-3284
                           FAX 202-973-0908
                           http://www.heath.gwu.edu
                           e-mail: askheath@askheath.gwu.edu
*Dan Gardner, Publications Manager*

This manual describes the system for delivering services to students with learning disabilities at community colleges. *$15.00*

**3669  Study of Job Clubs for Two-Year College Students with Learning Disabilities**

HEATH Resource Center
2121 K Street NW
Washington, DC  20036          202-973-0904
                              800-544-3284
                           FAX 202-973-0908
                      http://www.heath.gwu.edu
                  e-mail: askheath@askheath.gwu.edu
*Dan Gardner, Publications Manager*

This report describes the results of a study of how job clubs help two-year college students with learning disabilities improve their job-seeking skills. *$15.00*

## Counseling & Psychology

**3670  A Decision Making Model for Occupational Therapy in the Public Schools**

Therapro
225 Arlington Street
Framingham, MA  01702          508-872-9494
                              800-257-5376
                           FAX 508-875-2062
                      http://www.theraproducts.com
                   e-mail: info@theraproducts.com
*Wendy Drobnyk,MS,OTR/L & Sara Sicilliano,MS, OTR/L, Author*
*Paul Weirauch, Owner*
*Karen Conrad, President*

Designed to guide the often complex decision making process of initiating, continuing, and discontinuing occupational therapy in the public school. The first publication of its kind to describe entrance and exit criteria for students referred for occupational therapy services.

**3671  Accommodations in Higher Education under the Americans with Disabilities Act (ADA)**

Guilford Publications
72 Spring Street
New York, NY  10012          212-431-9800
                            800-365-7006
                         FAX 212-966-6708
                      http://www.guilford.com
                   e-mail: info@guilford.com
*Michael Gordon, Editor*
*Shelby Keiser, Editor*

Essential reading for any clinician evaluating students who are requesting educational accommodations under the ADA. It provides detailed information concerning how to conduct appropriate evaluations of mental disabilities, particularly attention-deficit/hyperactivity disorder and learning disabilities. Outlines a series of fundamental principles and actual clinical/administrative procedures, providing helpful diagnostic roadmaps, sample evaluations, and resource listings. *$35.00*

*236 pages*

**3672  Affect and Creativity**

Lawrence Erlbaum Associates
365 Broadway
Hillsdale, NJ  07642          201-666-4110
                              800-926-6579
                           FAX 201-666-2394
*Sandra Walker Russ, Author*
*Judy Nam, Owner*

This volume offers information on the role of affect and play in the creative process. Designed as a required or supplemental text in graduate level courses in creativity, children's play, child development, affective/cognitive development and psychodynamic theory. *$36.00*

*160 pages*
*ISBN 0-805809-86-4*

**3673  Behavior Analysis in Education**

Brooks/Cole Publishing Company
511 Forest Lodge Road
Pacific Grove, CA  93950          831-373-0728
                              FAX 831-375-6414
*Carolyn Crockett, Marketing Manager*
*Barbara Smallwood, Marketing Assistant*

Summarizes the major issues, trends, and findings found in behavior analysis in education literature. The contributors are leaders in the behavior analytic field, and their chapter-length treatment of topics, such as the Future of Behavior Analysis in Education, Early Childhood Interventions, and Promoting Applied Behavior Analysis, provides a volume that allows the professor to cover a range of topics which emphasize measurably superior instruction.

*512 pages*
*ISBN 0-534222-60-9*

**3674  Behavior Management System**

Connecticut Assoc. for Children and Adults with LD
25 Van Zant Street
East Norwalk, CT  06855          203-838-5010
                              FAX 203-866-6108
                          http://www.CACLD.org
                      e-mail: cacld@optonline.net
*Ethyl Papa, Author*
*Beryl Kaufman, Executive Director*
*Marie Armstrong, Information Specialist*

Offers information on behavior management for learning disabled students. *$5.95*

**3675  Behavioral Technology Guidebook**

Eden Services
One Eden Way
Princeton, NJ  08540          609-987-0099
                              FAX 609-987-0243
                      http://www.edenservices.org
                   e-mail: info@edenservices.org
*David Holmes EdD, Executive Director/President*
*Anne Holmes, Director Outreach Support*

Practical guide for behavior modification techniques. *$50.00*

**3676 Best Practice Occupational Therapy: Community Service with Children and Families**

Therapro
225 Arlington Street
Framingham, MA 01702      508-872-9494
800-257-5376
FAX 508-875-2062
http://www.theraproducts.com
e-mail: info@theraproducts.com

*Winnie Dunn, PhD, OTR, FAOTA, Author*
*Paul Weirauch, Owner*
*Karen Conrad, President*

An invaluable resource for sudents and practitioners interested in working with children and families in early intervention programs and public schools. Includes screening, pre-assessment, the referral process, best practice assessments, designing best paractice services and examples of IEPs and IFSPs. Many of the forms (screenings, checklists for teachers, referral forms assessment planning guide, etc.) are reproducible. The case studies give good examples of reports.

**3677 Cognitive-Behavioral Therapy for Impulsive Children: 2nd Edition**

Guilford Publications
72 Spring Street
New York, NY 10012      212-431-9800
800-365-7006
FAX 212-966-6708
http://www.guilford.com
e-mail: info@guilford.com

*Philip Kendall, Author*
*Lauren Braswell, Author*

The first edition of this book has been used successfully by thousands of clinicians to help children reduce impulsivity and improve their self-control. Building on the procedures reviewers call powerful tools and of great value to professionals who work with children. This second edition includes treatments, assessment issues and procedures and information on working with parents, teachers and groups of children. *$30.00*

*239 pages*

**3678 Collaborative Problem Solving**

Edge Enterprises
PO Box 1304
Lawrence, KS 66044      785-749-1473
FAX 785-749-0207
e-mail: eeinfo@edgeenterprises

*Knackendoffel, Robinson, Deshler and Schumaker, Author*
*Jacqueline Schafer, Managing Editor*

Outlines the communication skills necessary for establishing a cooperative relationship between two parties and then shows how to incorporate these skills within a problem-solving process that can be used to structure meetings between professionals and parents or students. This is especially useful for professionals who are consulting with teachers about problems they are having in their classrooms. *$10.00*

*74 pages Paperback*

**3679 Curriculum Based Activities in Occupational Therapy: An Inclusion Resource**

Therapro
225 Arlington Street
Framingham, MA 01702      508-872-9494
800-257-5376
FAX 508-875-2062
http://www.theraproducts.com
e-mail: info@theraproducts.com

*Paul Weirauch, Owner*
*Karen Conrad, President*

This book is a comprehensive guide to classroom based occupational therapy. The authors have compiled over 162 classroom activities developed to provide a strong linkage between educational and therapeutic goals. Each structured activity is categorized into standard curriculum subsections (reading, math, written language, etc.). Designed for a 3rd and 4th grade classroom, it can be modified for use in lower grades.

**3680 Disabled and Their Parents: A Counseling Challenge**

Slack Incorporated
6900 Grove Road
Thorofare, NJ 08086      856-848-1000
FAX 856-848-6091
http://www.slackinc.com
e-mail: rbellolio@slackinc.co

*Leo Buscaglia, Author*
*Robin Bellolio, Director*

Offers information on inclusion and counseling services for the learning disabled student. *$8.95*

**3681 Effective School Consultation: An Interactive Approach**

Brooks/Cole Publishing Company
511 Forest Lodge Road
Pacific Grove, CA 93950      831-373-0728
FAX 831-375-6414

*Sugai/Tindal, Author*
*Carolyn Crockett, Marketing Manager*
*Barbara Smallwood, Marketing Assistant*

This book provides special educators with strategies they can use to solve academic and social behavior problems in consultation with parents and professionals in planning, implementing and evaluating programs for students with learning and/or behavior difficulties. The authors' approach, prescriptive case consultation, emphasizes modifying teacher behavior and classroom environments using social learning principles to assist consultees.

*446 pages*
*ISBN 0-534193-02-1*

**3682  Emotional Disorders & Learning Disabilities in the Classroom**

Corwin Press
2455 Teller Road
Thousand Oaks, CA  91320　　　805-499-9734
　　　　　　　　　　　　　　　800-818-7243
　　　　　　　　　　　　FAX 805-499-5323
　　　　　　　http://www.corwinpress.com
　　　　　　e-mail: order@corwinpress.com

*Jean Cheng Gorman, Author*
*Kimberly Gonzales, Marketing Director*
*Robb Clouse, Senior Acquisitions Editor*

This unique book focuses on the interaction between learning disabilities and emotional disorders, fostering an understanding of how learning problems affect emotional well-being and vice-versa. This resource and practical classroom guide for all elementary school teachers includes an overview of common learning disabilities and emotional problems and a classroom-tested, research-based list of classroom interactions and interventions. *$27.95*

　　　*60 pages*
　　　*ISBN 0-761976-20-5*

**3683  Emotionally Abused & Neglected Child**

Books on Special Children
22 Webster Court
Amherst, MA  01002　　　　　845-638-1236
　　　　　　　　　　　　FAX 845-638-0847
　　　　　　　http://www.boscbooks.com
　　　　　　e-mail: irene@boscbooks.com

*D Iwaniec, Author*
*Marcia Young, President*

Describes emotional abuse and neglect and how it affects child's growth, development and well-being. Diagnosis, assessment and issues that should be addressed. *$31.95*

　　　*206 pages  softcover*
　　　*ISBN 0-471955-79-5*

**3684  Ethical Principles of Psychologists and Code of Conduct**

American Psychological Association
750 1st Street NE
Washington, DC  20002　　　　202-336-5650
　　　　　　　　　　　　　　　800-374-2722
　　　　　　　　　　　　FAX 202-336-5633
　　　　　　　　　　　TDY:202-336-6123
　　　　　　　　　http://www.apa.org
　　　　　　　e-mail: psycinfo@apa.org

*Marion Harrell, Deport Manager*
*Norman Anderson, Director*

General ethical principles of psychologists and enforceable ethical standards.

**3685  General Guidelines for Providers of Psychological Services**

American Psychological Association
750 1st Street NE
Washington, DC  20002　　　　202-336-5650
　　　　　　　　　　　　　　　800-374-2722
　　　　　　　　　　　　FAX 202-336-5633
　　　　　　　　　　　TDY:202-336-6123
　　　　　　　　　http://www.apa.org
　　　　　　　e-mail: psycinfo@apa.org

*Marion Harrell, Deport Manager*
*Norman Anderson, Director*

Offers information for the professional in the area of psychology.

**3686  HELP...at Home**

Therapro
225 Arlington Street
Framingham, MA  01702　　　　508-872-9494
　　　　　　　　　　　　　　　800-257-5376
　　　　　　　　　　　　FAX 508-875-2062
　　　　　　　http://www.theraproducts.com
　　　　　　e-mail: info@theraproducts.com

*Stephanie Parks, MA, Author*
*Paul Weirauch, Owner*
*Karen Conrad, President*

Practical and convenient format covers the 650 assesment skills from the Hawaii Early Learning Profile, with each page formatted as a separate, reproducible activity sheet. Therapist annotates, copies and hands out directly to parents to facilitate their involvement.

**3687  Handbook of Psychological and Educational Assessment of Children**

Guilford Publications
72 Spring Street
New York, NY  10012　　　　　212-431-9800
　　　　　　　　　　　　　　　800-365-7006
　　　　　　　　　　　　FAX 212-966-6708
　　　　　　　　http://www.guilford.com
　　　　　　　e-mail: info@guilford.com

*Cecil Reynolds, Editor*
*Randy Kamphaus, Editor*

Provides practitioners, researchers, professors, and students with an invaluable resource, this unique volume covers assessment of intelligence, learning styles, learning strategies, academic skills, and special populations, and discusses special topics in mental testing. Chapter contributions are by eminent psychologists and educators in the field of assessment with special expertise in research or practice in their topic areas. *$79.95*

　　　*814 pages*

**3688  Helping Students Become Strategic Learners**

Brookline Books
300 Bedford Street
Manchester, NH  03101　　　　617-734-6772
　　　　　　　　　　　　FAX 603-922-3348
　　　　　　　http://www.brooklinebooks.com

*Karen Scheid, Author*

The author demonstrates how teachers can implement cognitive theories of instruction in the classroom. *$26.95*

**3689  Helping Students Grow**

American College Testing Program
PO Box 168
Iowa City, IA  52243          319-337-1000
                              FAX 319-339-3021
                              TDY:319-337-1701
                              http://www.act.org
                      e-mail: sandy.schlote@act.org
*James Humphrey, Author*
*Richard Ferguson, Director*
*Sandy Schlote, Testing Coordinator*

Designed to assist counselors in using the wealth of information generated by the ACT assessment.

**3690  Overcoming Dyslexia in Children, Adolescents and Adults**

Connecticut Assoc. for Children and Adults with LD
25 Van Zant Street
East Norwalk, CT  06855        203-838-5010
                              FAX 203-866-6108
                          http://www.CACLD.org
                      e-mail: cacld@optonline.net
*Dale Jordan, Author*
*Beryl Kaufman, Executive Director*
*Marie Armstrong, Information Specialist*

This book describes some forms of dyslexia in detail and then relates those problems to the social, emotional and personal development of dyslexic individuals. *$30.25*

**3691  Pathways to Change: Brief Therapy Solutions with Difficult Adolescents**

Guilford Publications
72 Spring Street
New York, NY  10012            212-431-9800
                              800-365-7006
                          FAX 212-966-6708
                       http://www.guilford.com
                       e-mail: info@guilford.com
*Matthew D. Selekman, Author*
*Michael Gordon, Editor*
*Shelby Keiser, Editor*

Encouraging therapeutic improvisation and incorporating the use of humor, Selekman demonstrates how the clinican can capitalize on the strengths and resources of family members, peers, and other involved mental health professionhals to resolve the client's presenting problems rapidly. *$29.00*

*186 pages*
*ISBN 0-898620-15-5*

**3692  Practitioner's Guide to Dynamic Assessment**

Guilford Publications
72 Spring Street
New York, NY  10012            212-431-9800
                              800-365-7006
                          FAX 212-966-6708
                       http://www.guilford.com
                       e-mail: info@guilford.com
*Carol S. Lidz, Author*
*Michael Gordon, Editor*
*Shelby Keiser, Editor*

An excellent text aimed at general practitioners offering information on assessment and intervention techniques. *$20.95*

*210 pages  Paperback*

**3693  Prescriptions for Children with Learning and Adjustment Problems: A Consultant's Desk Reference**

Charles C Thomas Publisher
2600 S 1st Street
Springfield, IL  62704         217-789-8980
                              800-258-8980
                          FAX 217-789-9130
                       http://www.ccthomas.com
                     e-mail: books@ccthomas.com
*Ralph F Blanco, David F Bogacki, Author*
*Michael Thomas, President*

Third edition. Books sent on approval. Shipping charges: $5.50 US/6.50 Canada. Prices subject to change without notice.

*264 pages  Cloth*

**3694  Problems in Written Expression: Assessment and Remediation**

Guilford Publications
72 Spring Street
New York, NY  10012            212-431-9800
                              800-365-7006
                          FAX 212-966-6708
                       http://www.guilford.com
                       e-mail: info@guilford.com
*Sharon Bradley-Johnson, Author*
*Jusi Lesiak, Author*

A great resource for speech-language pathologists, counselors, resource specialists and other special educators. *$20.95*

*178 pages  Paperback*

**3695  Reading and Learning Disability: A Neuropsychological Approach to Evaluation & Instruction**

Charles C Thomas Publisher
2600 S 1st Street
Springfield, IL  62704         217-789-8980
                              800-258-8980
                          FAX 217-789-9130
                       http://www.ccthomas.com
                     e-mail: books@ccthomas.com
*Estelle L Fryburg, Author*
*Michael Thomas, President*

This text utilizes the current knowledge of neuropsychology (brain-behavior relationships) and the concepts of cognitive psychology to provide an understanding of reading and learning disability which has a practical application to education. The primary goal of the book is to provide teachers, psychologists, physicians, concerned professionals, and parents with an interdisciplinary view of learning and schooling. *$79.95*

*398 pages  Cloth*
*ISBN 0-398067-44-9*

**3696    Reflections Through the Looking Glass**

**Association on Higher Education and Disability**
**PO Box 540666**
**Waltham, MA  02454**            **781-788-0003**
**FAX 781-788-0033**
**http://www.ahead.org**
**e-mail: ahead@postbox.acs.ohio-state.edu**

A must for new professionals offering a philosophical review of the nature of the field written in first person by charter member and former Association President Richard Harris of Ball State University. *$5.50*

**3697    Revels in Madness: Insanity in Medicine and Literature**

**University of Michigan Press**
**839 Greene Street**
**Ann Arbor, MI  48104**            **734-615-6478**
**FAX 734-763-0456**
**http://www.press.umich.edu**
**e-mail: pgarner@umich.edu**

*Allen Thiher, Author*
*Mary Erwin, Assistant Director*

Revels in Madness offers a history of western culture's shifting understanding of insanity as evidenced in its literature and as influenced by medical knowledge. *$57.50*

*368 pages  cloth*
*ISBN 0-472110-35-7*

**3698    Self-Advocacy Handbook for High School Students**

**Utah Department of Special Education**
**250 E 500 S**
**Salt Lake City, UT  84114**            **801-538-7711**
**FAX 801-538-7991**
**http://www.usoe.k12.ut.us/sans/**
**e-mail: mtaylor@usoe.k12.ut.us**
*Ann Jepsen, Author*
*Travis Cook, Director*

This manual teaches the students to advocate for themselves.

**3699    Self-Advocacy for Junior High School Students**

**Utah Department of Special Education**
**250 E 500 S**
**Salt Lake City, UT  84114**            **801-538-7711**
**FAX 801-538-7991**
**http://www.usoe.k12.ut.us/sans/**
**e-mail: mtaylor@usoe.k12.ut.us**
*Travis Cook, Director*

A program designed to increase students' verbal expressive skills in discussing learning disabilities, ADD and related characteristics.

**3700    Self-Injurious Behavior: A Somatosensory Treatment Approach**

**Therapro**
**225 Arlington Street**
**Framingham, MA  01702**            **508-872-9494**
**800-257-5376**
**FAX 508-875-2062**
**http://www.theraproducts.com**
**e-mail: info@theraproducts.com**
*Haru Hirama, EdD, OTR/L, Author*
*Paul Weirauch, Owner*
*Karen Conrad, President*

Practical account of treatment. Stimulation is given to counteract the somatosensory deprivation experienced by the self-injurious individual. Includes reviews/illustrations of the treatment.

**3701    Teaching Students with Learning and Behavior Problems**

**Pro-Ed**
**8700 Shoal Creek Boulevard**
**Austin, TX  78757**            **512-451-3246**
**800-897-3202**
**FAX 512-451-8542**
**http://www.proedinc.com**
*Donald Hammill, Author*
*Judith Voress PhD, Periodicals Director*

This popular, classic text provides teachers with a comprehensive overview of the best practices in assessing and instructing students with mild-to-moderate learning and behavior problems. *$44.00*

*520 pages*
*ISBN 0-890796-10-6*

**3702    Treating Troubled Children and Their Families**

**Books on Special Children**
**22 Webster Court**
**Amherst, MA  01002**            **845-638-1236**
**FAX 845-638-0847**
**http://www.boscbooks.com**
**e-mail: irene@boscbooks.com**
*EF Wachtel, Author*
*Marcia Young, President*

In treating a child, learn about him or her as an individual, interview parents and family in separate units. Give caretaker various insights on treating this troubled child. Book has specific questions to ask, ways to interpret attitudes, explanations. Systemic and behavioral intervention formulated to specific needs of the child. *$38.00*

*303 pages  hardcover*
*ISBN 0-898620-07-4*

---

## General

**3703    A History of Disability**

**University of Michigan Press**
**839 Greene Street**
**Ann Arbor, MI  48104**            **734-764-4388**
**FAX 734-615-1540**
**http://www.press.umich.edu**
**e-mail: pgarner@umich.edu**
*Henri-Jacques Stiker, Author*
*Mary Erwin, Assistant Director*

Published in 1997 in France as Corps Infirms et Societes and available now in excellent English translation, the book traces the history of Western cultural responses to disability, from ancient times to the present. *$52.50*

*264 pages  cloth*
*ISBN 0-472110-63-2*

**3704    A Human Development View of Learning Disabilities: From Theory to Practice**

Charles C Thomas Publisher
2600 S 1st Street
Springfield, IL  62704          217-789-8980
                                800-258-8980
                           FAX 217-789-9130
                        http://www.ccthomas.com
                      e-mail: books@ccthomas.com
*Corrine E Kass and Cleborne D Maddux, Author*
*Michael Thomas, Owner*

Presents a strategy for designing day-to-day individualized lessons for learning disabled students from kindergarten through adulthood. Books sent on approval. Shipping charges: $5.50 US/&6.50 Canada. Prices subject to change without notice. *$50.95*

*222 pages  Cloth*
*ISBN 0-398058-86-5*

**3705    A Manual of Sequential Art Activities for Classified Children and Adolescents**

Charles C Thomas Publisher
2600 S 1st Street
Springfield, IL  62704          217-789-8980
                                800-258-8980
                           FAX 217-789-9130
                        http://www.ccthomas.com
                      e-mail: books@ccthomas.com
*Rocco AL Fugaro, Author*
*Michael Thomas, Owner*

*246 pages  Spiral (paper)  $41.95*
*ISBN 0-398050-85-6*

**3706    A Practical Approach to RSP: A Handbook for the Resource Specialist Program**

Charles C Thomas Publisher
2600 S 1st Street
Springfield, IL  62704          217-789-8980
                                800-258-8980
                           FAX 217-789-9130
                        http://www.ccthomas.com
                      e-mail: books@ccthomas.com
*Leslie A Williams and Lucile S Arntzen, Author*
*Michael Thomas, Owner*

Valuable to resource specialists in training and in service, administrators and related professionals. Books sent on approval. *$33.95*

*120 pages  Cloth*
*ISBN 0-398059-08-X*

**3707    Academic Skills Problems Workbook**

Guilford Publications
72 Spring Street
New York, NY  10012          212-431-9800
                             800-365-7006
                        FAX 212-966-6708
                     http://www.guilford.com
                   e-mail: info@guilford.com
*Edward S Shapiro, PhD, Author*
*Michael Gordon, Editor*
*Shelby Keiser, Editor*

This workbook is filled with reproducible forms, and features step-by-step instructions and practice exercises for school professionals that will facilitate observation, assessment, and intervention. *$19.95*

*135 pages*

**3708    Academic Skills Problems: Direct Assessment and Intervention, 2nd Edition**

Guilford Publications
72 Spring Street
New York, NY  10012          212-431-9800
                             800-365-7006
                        FAX 212-966-6708
                     http://www.guilford.com
                   e-mail: info@guilford.com
*Edward S Shapiro, PhD, Author*
*Barry Duncan, Author*
*Michael Gordon, Editor*

This book shows how to use direct methods for establishing clear links to intervention strategies and determining the success of remedial efforts. Contains reproducible forms and charts. *$32.00*

*315 pages*

**3709    Academic Therapy Publications**

Academic Therapy Publications
20 Commercial Boulevard
Novato, CA  94949            415-883-3314
                             888-287-9975
                        FAX 415-883-3720
                     http://www.atpub.com
                   e-mail: atpub@aol.com
*John Arena, Author*
*Debrah Akers, Editor*

What goes into an Individual Education Plan for a special education student? This book gives detailed information.

*ISBN 0-878790-72-1*

**3710    Academic and Developmental Learning Disabilities**

Love Publishing Company
PO Box 22353
Denver, CO  80222            303-221-7333
                        FAX 303-221-7444
                http://www.lovepublishing.com
              e-mail: lovepublishing@compuserve.com
*Samuel Kirk, Author*

This text is intended to serve as a basis for classifying children and to help teachers diagnose and remediate children who have major disabilities in the learning process. *$39.95*

*337 pages*

**3711  Accessing the General Curriculum Including Students with Disabilities in Standards-Based Reform**

**Corwin Press**
**2455 Teller Road**
**Thousand Oaks, CA  91320**                    805-499-9734
                                                800-818-7243
                                    FAX 805-499-5323
                        http://www.corwinpress.com
                    e-mail: order@corwinpress.com
*Victor Noiet, Margaret J McLaughlin, Author*
*Kimberly Gonzales, Marketing Director*
*Robb Clouse, Senior Acquisitions Editor*

Practical information and insight make it easier to design instruction that enables all students to access and make progress in inclusive K-12 environments. It also helps teachers, administrators, and curriculum development specialists design measures that can be used to assess the progress of special needs students, as well as develop effective collaborative relationships between general and special education instructors. *$29.95*

*152 pages*
*ISBN 0-761976-70-1*

**3712  Adapted Physical Education for Students**

**Exceptional Parent Press**
**2600 S 1st Street**
**Springfield, IL  62704**                      217-789-8980
                                                800-258-8980
                                    FAX 217-789-9130
                        http://www.ccthomas.com
                    e-mail: books@ccthomas.com
*Kimberly Davis, Author*
*Michael Thomas, President*

Focuses on the physical education needs and curriculum for autistic children. *$34.95*

*142 pages*

**3713  An Introduction to Learning Disabilities**

**Scott Foresman Addison Wesley**
**1900 E Lake Avenue**
**Glenview, IL  60025**                          847-729-3000
                                    FAX 847-729-8910
                        http://www.sf.aw.com
*Howard Adelman, Author*
*Paul McFall, President*

This text is designed to introduce learning disabilities in a way that clarifies both instructional options and large educational issues.

*354 pages*

**3714  An Introduction to the Nature and Needs of Students with Mild Disabilities**

**Charles C Thomas Publisher**
**2600 S 1st Street**
**Springfield, IL  62704**                      217-789-8980
                                                800-258-8980
                                    FAX 217-789-9130
                        http://www.ccthomas.com
                    e-mail: books@ccthomas.com
*Carroll J Jones, Author*
*Michael Thomas, Owner*

Mild mental retardation, behavior disorders, and learning disabilities are covered in this text. Designed as an introductory text for an undergraduate degree program in special education. Also included is information on the historical background of services in Europe, early-to-current services in the United States, landmark legislation, litigation relevant to each categorical area, with definitions and classification systems. *$50.95*

*300 pages  Cloth*
*ISBN 0-398067-11-2*

**3715  Annals of Dyslexia**

**International Dyslexia Association**
**8600 LaSalle Road, Chester Building**
**Baltimore, MD  21286**                        410-296-0232
                                                800-ABC-D123
                                    FAX 410-321-5069
                                    TDY:410-296-0232
                        http://www.interdys.org

The Society's scholarly journal contains updates on current research and selected proceedings from talks given at each ODS international conference. Issues of Annals are available from 1982 through the present year.

**3716  Art as a Language for the Learning Disabled Child**

**Learning Disabilities Association of America**
**4156 Library Road**
**Pittsburgh, PA  15234**                        412-341-1515
                                    FAX 412-344-0224
                        http://www.ldanatl.org
                    e-mail: ldanatl@usaor.net
*Jane Browning, Editor-in-Chief*

A guide promoting art therapy in the classroom for the learning disabled student. *$1.00*

**3717  Art for All the Children: Approaches to Art Therapy for Children with Disabilities**

**Charles C Thomas Publisher**
**2600 S 1st Street**
**Springfield, IL  62704**                      217-789-8980
                                                800-258-8980
                                    FAX 217-789-9130
                        http://www.ccthomas.com
                    e-mail: books@ccthomas.com
*Frances E Anderson, Author*
*Michael Thomas, Owner*

Tis edition is for art therapists in training and for in-service professionals in art therapy, art education and special education who have children with disabilities as a part of their case/class load. A major goal of this edition is to show the many ways that art can be adapted so that all children may have a meaningful encounter with art. The book will prepare the reader to understand children, their art, their disabilities and how to adapt art to meet their needs. *$ 69.95*

*398 pages  Cloth*
*ISBN 0-398057-97-4*

**3718  Art-Centered Education & Therapy for Children with Disabilities**

Charles C Thomas Publisher
2600 S 1st Street
Springfield, IL  62704                217-789-8980
                                      800-258-8980
                               FAX 217-789-9130
                           http://www.ccthomas.com
                         e-mail: books@ccthomas.com
*Frances E Anderson, Author*
*Michael homas, Owner*

To help both the regular education, and art and special education teachers, pre- and in-service, better understand the issues and realities of providing education and remediation to children with disabilities. Offers the concept that we must live, learn and develop through art - that art belongs at the core of the public school curriculum. *$49.95*

*284 pages  Cloth*
*ISBN 0-398058-96-2*

**3719  Assessment: The Special Educator's Role**

Brooks/Cole Publishing Company
511 Forest Lodge Road
Pacific Grove, CA  93950            831-373-0728
                               FAX 831-375-6414
*Cheri Hoy & Noel Gregg, Author*
*Carolyn Crockett, Marketing Manager*
*Barbara Smallwood, Marketing Assistant*

Hoy and Gregg, two well-known professionals in the field, highlight the process of assessment of mild to moderate disabilities for a wide age range (preschool to adult). Aimed at those with no classroom experience in assessment, this book focuses on the integration of dynamic, curriculum-based, and non-referenced data for diagnostic decisions and program planning.

*580 pages*
*ISBN 0-534211-32-1*

**3720  Attentional Deficit Disorder in Children and Adolescents**

Charles C Thomas Publisher
2600 S 1st Street
Springfield, IL  62704                217-789-8980
                                      800-258-8980
                               FAX 217-789-9130
                           http://www.ccthomas.com
                         e-mail: books@ccthomas.com
*Jack Fadely, Author*
*Virginia Hosler, Author*

This book presents an analysis of case studies of children and adolescents with attentional deficits and hyperactivity. The focus is to demonstrate CAUSAL factors in this disorder and to suggest treatment strategies both in psychological and medical practice. *$56.95*

*292 pages  Cloth*
*ISBN 0-398057-92-3*

**3721  Atypical Cognitive Deficits**

Lawrence Erlbaum Associates
365 Broadway
Hillsdale, NJ  07642                 201-666-4110
                                     800-926-6579
                               FAX 201-666-2394
*Sarah Broman, Author*
*Jordan Grafman, Author*

This volume is based on a conference held to examine what was known about cognitive behaviors and brain structure and function in three syndromes. *$29.95*

*352 pages*
*ISBN 0-805811-80-0*

**3722  Auditory Processes**

Academic Therapy Publications
20 Commercial Boulevard
Novato, CA  94949                    415-883-3314
                                     888-287-9975
                               FAX 415-883-3720
                           http://www.atpub.com
                         e-mail: atpub@aol.com
*Pamela Gillel, Author*
*Debrah Akers, Editor*
*Debrah Akers, Editor*

Explains how teachers, educational consultants and parents can identify auditory processing problems, understand their impact and implement appropriate instructional strategies to enhance learning. *$15.00*

*120 pages*
*ISBN 0-878790-94-2*

**3723  Auditory Processes: Revised Edition**

Therapro
225 Arlington Street
Framingham, MA  01702               508-872-9494
                                    800-257-5376
                               FAX 508-875-2062
                        http://www.theraproducts.com
                      e-mail: info@theraproducts.com
*Pamela Gillet, PhD, Author*
*Paul Weirauch, Owner*
*Karen Conrad, President*

This author clearly describes the sequence of auditory skill development as well as the symptomatic behavior of youngsters with auditory processing problems. Offers hundreds of tests and remedial exercises in areas such as auditory discrimination, auditory memory, auditiory perception deficit.

**3724  Auditory Training**

Harris Communications
15155 Technology Drive
Eden Prairie, MN  55344             952-906-1180
                                    800-825-6758
                               FAX 952-906-1099
                            TDY:952-906-1198
                         http://www.harriscmm.com
                       e-mail: info@harriscmm.com
*Norman P Erber, Author*
*Robert Harris, Owner*

Written for parents, educators, and rehabilitative audiologists, who are concerned with auditory development of hearing impaired children. Auditory instruction strategies encourage children to learn to hear through whatever type of amplification device they are using. Covers research and developments in auditory training, speech perception, speech production, screening, training and practical suggestions. *$23.95*

*197 pages Paperback*

**3725 BOSC Directory: Facilities for People with Learning Disabilities**
**4 Harkness Road**
**Pelham, MA 01002**          **845-638-1236**
                              **FAX 845-638-0847**
               **http://www.boscbooks.com**
            **e-mail: irene@boscbooks.com**
*Marcia Young, Owner*

Facilities that work with people with special needs; day and residential schools, independent living programs, centers and clinics, colleges and vocational training programs, agencies, and special consumer products. Specific and cumulative indexes with table of disabilities treated by the facility. *$70.00*

*300+ pages*
*ISBN 0-961386-07-0*

**3726 Bilingualism and Learning Disabilities**
**Learning Disabilities Association of America**
**4156 Library Road**
**Pittsburgh, PA 15234**        **412-341-1515**
                                **FAX 412-344-0224**
                **http://www.ldanatl.org**
              **e-mail: ldanatl@usaor.net**
*Jane Browning, Editor-in-Chief*

A comprehensive guide on bilingualism in the classroom and on the job for learning disabled adults. *$21.95*

**3727 Body and Physical Difference: Discourses of Disability**
**University of Michigan Press**
**839 Greene Street**
**Ann Arbor, MI 48104**        **734-764-4388**
                               **FAX 734-615-1540**
                **http://www.press.umich.edu**
              **e-mail: pgarner@umich.edu**
*David T Mitchell, Author*
*Mary Erwin, Assistant Director*

For years the subject of human disability has engaged those in the biological, social and cognitive sciences, while at the same time, it has been curiously neglected within the humanitites. The Body and Physical Difference seeks to introduce the field of disability studies into the humanities by exploring the fantasies and fictons that have crystallized around conceptions of physical and cognitive difference. *$52.50*

*320 pages cloth*
*ISBN 0-472096-59-1*

**3728 Bridging the Family-Professional Gap: Facilitating Interdisciplinary Services**
**Charles C Thomas Publisher**
**2600 S 1st Street**
**Springfield, IL 62704**       **217-789-8980**
                                **800-258-8980**
                           **FAX 217-789-9130**
                 **http://www.ccthomas.com**
              **e-mail: books@ccthomas.com**
*Billy Ogletree, Martin Fischer, Jane Schulz, Author*
*Michael Thomas, President*

Facilitates family preparedness for interdisciplinary team functioning and promotes interdisciplinary professionals' awareness of family members' concerns and priorities. *$49.95*

*300 pages Cloth*
*ISBN 0-398069-88-3*

**3729 Brief Intervention for School Problems: Collaborating for Practical Solutions**
**Guilford Publications**
**72 Spring Street**
**New York, NY 10012**          **212-431-9800**
                                **800-365-7006**
                           **FAX 212-966-6708**
                 **http://www.guilford.com**
               **e-mail: info@guilford.com**
*John Murphy, Author*
*Barry Duncan, Author*

This book focuses on what works and spells out a compelling rationale and practical blueprint for time-efficient, collaborative problem solving in the schools. Extensive case examples and sample dialogues guide school practitioners and trainees through the interview and intervention process and tables and figures help illustrate the approach. *$26.95*

*175 pages*

**3730 Case Studies of Exceptional Students: Handicapped and Gifted**
**Charles C Thomas Publisher**
**2600 S 1st Street**
**Springfield, IL 62704**       **217-789-8980**
                                **800-258-8980**
                           **FAX 217-789-9130**
                 **http://www.ccthomas.com**
              **e-mail: books@ccthomas.com**
*Carroll J. Jones, Author*
*Michael Thomas, President*

Clear, concise, educationally relevant case studies. *$56.95*

*272 pages Cloth*
*ISBN 0-398058-56-3*

**3731 Center Work**
**Center for Research in Vocational Education**
**2150 Shattuck Avenue**
**Berkeley, CA 94704**
                                **800-762-4093**

Profiles the center's current work and contains articles about policy issues, computer resources, NCRVE publications, and ERIC/ACVE digests.

*Quarterly-Free*

**3732 Children, Problems and Guidelines, Special Ed**

Slosson Educational Publications
538 Buffalo Road
East Aurora, NY 14052          888-756-7766
                              800-828-4800
                         FAX 800-655-3840
                        http://www.slosson.com
                        e-mail: slosson@slosson.com
*LaDeane Casey, Author*
*Steven Slosson, President*

A professional and responsible resource book which addresses many of the most common problems involving children and their homes or schools. *$45.00*

*99 pages Ages 6-16*

**3733 Classroom Management for Elementary Teachers: 4th Editon**

Books on Special Children
22 Webster Court
Amherst, MA 01002          845-638-1236
                      FAX 845-638-0847
                    http://www.boscbooks.com
                    e-mail: irene@boscbooks.com
*ET Emmer, Author*
*Marcia Young, President*

Good classroom management just doesn't happen, it takes good planning and effective teachers organizing classroom rules and procedures, planning and conducting instructions. Appropriate student behavior, managing problem behavior and special groups are discussed. *$34.95*

*228 pages softcover*
*ISBN 0-205264-27-1*

**3734 Classroom Management for Secondary Teachers: 4th Editon**

Books on Special Children
22 Webster Court
Amherst, MA 01002          845-638-1236
                      FAX 845-638-0847
                    http://www.boscbooks.com
                    e-mail: irene@boscbooks.com
*ET Emmer, Author*
*Marcia Young, President*

Good classroom management just doesn't happen, it takes good planning and effective teachers organizing classroom rules and procedures, planning and conducting instructions. Appropriate student behavior, managing problem behavior and special groups are discussed. *$34.95*

*216 pages softcover*
*ISBN 0-205264-28-X*

**3735 Classroom Notetaker: How to Organize a Program Serving Students with Hearing Impairments**

Harris Communications
15155 Technology Drive
Eden Prairie, MN 55344          952-906-1180
                              800-825-6758
                         FAX 952-906-1099
                         TDY:952-906-1198
                    http://www.harriscomm.com
                    e-mail: info@harriscmm.com
*Jimmie Joan Wilson, Author*
*Robert Harris, President*
*Patty Johnson, Office Manager*

Promotes classroom note taking and gives specifics on establishing a note taking program. Topics include proving the need for a note taking program, recruiting and training note takers, and the principles of note taking. *$25.95*

*127 pages Paperback*

**3736 Cognitive Approach to Learning Disabilities**

Pro-Ed
8700 Shoal Creek Boulevard
Austin, TX 78757          512-451-3246
                          800-897-3202
                     FAX 512-451-8542
                    http://www.proedinc.com
*D Kim Reid, Author*
*Judith Voress PhD, Periodicals Director*
*Barbara , Administrative Assistant*

This book is the first to bridge the gap between cognitive psychology and information processing theory in understanding learning disabilities. *$44.00*

*686 pages*
*ISBN 0-890796-85-8*

**3737 Cognitive Retraining Using Microcomputers**

Lawrence Erlbaum Associates
365 Broadway
Hillsdale, NJ 07642          201-666-4110
                              800-926-6579
                         FAX 201-666-2394
*Veronica Bradley, Author*
*John Welch, Author*

This text reviews representative examples from the literature relating to the training of cognitive systems with the emphasis on studies describing the use of computerized methods. *$69.95*

*304 pages*
*ISBN 0-863772-02-1*

**3738 Cognitive Strategy Instruction That Really Improves Children's Performance**

Brookline Books
300 Bedford Street
Manchester, NH 03101          617-734-6772
                         FAX 603-922-3348
                    http://www.brooklinebooks.com

A concise and focused work that summarily presents the few procedures for teaching strategies that aid academic subject matter learning that are empirically validated and fit well with the elementary school curriculum. *$27.95*

**3739 Competencies for Teachers of Students with Learning Disabilities**

Council for Exceptional Children
1110 N Glebe Road
Arlington, VA 22201          703-620-3660
                             888-232-7733
                          FAX 703-264-9494
                     http://www.cec.sped.org/
                     e-mail: service@cec.sped.org
*Amme Graves, Author*
*Mary Landers, Author*
*Jean Lockerson, Author*

Lists 209 specific professional competencies needed by teachers of students with learning disabilities and provides a conceptual framework for the ten areas in which the competencies are organized. *$5.00*

*25 pages*

**3740 Complete Learning Disabilities Handbook**

Learning Disabilities Association of America
4156 Library Road
Pittsburgh, PA 15234          412-341-1515
                           FAX 412-344-0224
                       http://www.ldanatl.org
                     e-mail: ldanatl@usaor.net
*JM Hartwell, Author*
*Jane Browning, Editor-in-Chief*

Offers complete coverage of persons with learning disabilities. *$29.95*

**3741 Comprehensive Assessment in Special Education: Approaches, Procedures and Concerns**

Charles C Thomas Publisher
2600 S 1st Street
Springfield, IL 62704          217-789-8980
                               800-258-8980
                          FAX 217-789-9130
                     http://www.ccthomas.com
                     e-mail: books@ccthomas.com
*Rotatori, Fox, Sexton and Miller, Author*
*Michael Thomas, President*

Books sent on approval. Shipping charges: $5.50, $6.50 Canada. Prices subject to change without notice. *$104.95*

*578 pages*
*ISBN 0-398056-45-5*

**3742 Cooperative Learning and Strategies for Inclusion**

Brookes Publishing Company
PO Box 10624
Baltimore, MD 21285          410-337-9580
                             800-638-3775
                          FAX 410-337-8539
                http://www.brookspublishing.com
                e-mail: custserv@brookespublishing.com
*JoAnne W Putnam, PhD, Author*

This book supplies educators, classroom support personnel, and administrators with numerous tools for creating positive, inclusive classroom environments for students from preschool through high school. *$37.00*

*288 pages Paperback*
*ISBN 1-557663-46-7*

**3743 Creating Positive Classroom Environments**

Brooks/Cole Publishing Company
511 Forest Lodge Road
Pacific Grove, CA 93950          831-373-0728
                              FAX 831-375-6414
*Epanchin/Stoddard/Townsend, Author*
*Carolyn Crockett, Marketing Manager*
*Barbara Smallwood, Marketing Assistant*

This book offers an approach to classroom management that encourages situation-specific decision-making. Presenting research-based information on how to establish an effective behavior management system in both regular and special education settings, this book centers on ways to help students manage their own behavior rather than on ways their behavior can be managed by others. Interventions focus on creating success.

*448 pages*
*ISBN 0-534222-54-4*

**3744 Creative Curriculum for Early Childhood**

Teaching Strategies
PO Box 42243
Washington, DC 20015          202-362-7543
                               800-637-3652
                          FAX 202-364-7273
                http://www.teachingstrategies.com
                e-mail: info@teachingstrategies.com
*DT Dodge And LJ Collier, Author*
*Angel White, President*

Focuses on the developmentally appropriate program in early childhood education. Illustrates how preschool and kindergarten teachers set the stage for learning, and how children and teachers interact and learn in various interest areas. *$39.95*

*390 pages*
*ISBN 1-879537-06-0*

**3745 Curriculum Development for Students with Mild Disabilities**

Charles C Thomas Publisher
2600 S 1st Street
Springfield, IL 62704          217-789-8980
                               800-258-8980
                          FAX 217-789-9130
                     http://www.ccthomas.com
                     e-mail: books@ccthomas.com
*Carroll J Jones, Author*
*Michael Thomas, President*

Many teachers of students with mild disabilities experience difficulty writing IEPs because they lack a foundation in the regular education curriculum of academic skills and sequences associated with each grade level. *$34.95*

*258 pages Spiral (paper)*
*ISBN 0-398070-18-0*

**3746 Curriculum Models and Strategies for Educating Individuals with Disabilities**

Charles C Thomas Publisher
2600 S 1st Street
Springfield, IL 62704          217-789-8980
                              800-258-8980
                          FAX 217-789-9130
                  http://www.ccthomas.com
              e-mail: books@ccthomas.com

*George Taylor, Author*
*Michael Thomas, Owner*
*Claire Slagler, Sales Manager*

Curriculum skills units developed as a guide to assist educators instructing disabled individuals in the areas of communication, math and science, socially effective and psychomotor skills, as well as morals and character. Also helpful to those working in community agencies with disabled individuals. *$48.95*

*260 pages  Cloth*
*ISBN 0-398069-75-1*

**3747 Curriculum-Based Assessment: A Primer**

Charles C Thomas Publisher
2600 S 1st Street
Springfield, IL 62704          217-789-8980
                              800-258-8980
                          FAX 217-789-9130
                  http://www.ccthomas.com
              e-mail: books@ccthomas.com

*Charles H Hargis, Author*
*Michael Thomas, President*

The use of curriculum-based assessment (CBA) to ensure learning disabled and low achieving students adequate educational opportunity is the focus of this book. CBA requires an intimate relationship between teaching and testing. The author presents examples and methods of implementation through reading and arithmetic activities and discusses at length the issues involved in test validity and grading. *$33.95*

*190 pages  Paperback*
*ISBN 0-398059-42-X*

**3748 Curriculum-Based Assessment: The Easy Way**

Charles C Thomas Publisher
2600 S 1st Street
Springfield, IL 62704          217-789-8980
                              800-258-8980
                          FAX 217-789-9130
                  http://www.ccthomas.com
              e-mail: books@ccthomas.com

*Carroll J Jones, Author*
*Michael Thomas, President*

Practical and specific methods for developing and using CBA's in an educational setting. *$27.95*

*176 pages  Spiral (paper)*

**3749 Curriculum-Based Evaluation: Teaching and Decision Making**

Brooks/Cole Publishing Company
511 Forest Lodge Road
Pacific Grove, CA 93950          831-373-0728
                            FAX 831-375-6414

*Howell/Fox/Morehead, Author*
*Carolyn Crockett, Marketing Manager*
*Barbara Smallwood, Marketing Assistant*

Focusing on effective instruction, instructional decision making, and the various evaluation models useful in curriculum-based assessment, this book examines teacher-made tests and curriculum as they relate to a child's success or failure. Using a step-by-step approach, the authors show teachers how to use the curriculum to meet the child's needs, how to assess in an ongoing way, and how to recognize when instructional change is warranted.

*526 pages*
*ISBN 0-534164-28-5*

**3750 Deal Me In: The Use of Playing Cards in Learning and Teaching**

CT Association for Children and Adults with LD
25 Van Zant Street
East Norwalk, CT 06855          203-838-5010
                          FAX 203-866-6108
                     http://www.CACLD.org
              e-mail: cacld@optonline.net

*M Golick, Author*
*Marie Armstrong, Information Specialist*
*Beryl Kaufman, Executive Director*

A book of how to play cards with your learning disabled child. *$10.95*

*$2.50 shipping*

**3751 Defects: Engendering the Modern Body**

University of Michigan Press
839 Greene Street
Ann Arbor, MI 48104          734-764-4388
                          FAX 734-615-1540
                  http://www.press.umich.edu
              e-mail: pgarner@umich.edu

*Helen Deutsch, Author*
*Mary Erwin, Assistant Director*

Defects brings together essays on the emergence of the concept of monstrosity in the eighteenth century and the ways it paralleled the emergence of notions of sexual difference. *$57.50*

*344 pages  cloth*
*ISBN 0-472096-98-2*

**3752 Developmental Variation and Learning Disorders**

Educators Publishing Service
31 Smith Place
Cambridge, MA 02139          617-547-6706
                              800-225-5750
                          FAX 617-547-0412
                  http://www.epsbooks.com
              e-mail: eps@epsbooks.com

*Dr. Melvin Levine, Author*
*Steven Courtes, President*

Unique in its approach to learning disorders, this Second Edition combines what is known about normal child development during the school years with insights into the nature of variation and dysfunction. *$69.00*

*ISBN 0-838819-92-3*

**3753 Dictionary of Special Education and Rehabilitation**

Love Publishing Company
PO Box 22353
Denver, CO 80222
303-221-7333
FAX 303-221-7444
http://www.lovepublishing.com
e-mail: lovepublishing@compuserve.com
*Glenn A Vergason, Author*

A valuable basic resource in the field. It incorporates hundreds of additions and changes. *$32.00*

**3754 Directory for Exceptional Children**

Porter Sargent Publishers
11 Beacon Street
Boston, MA 02108
617-523-1670
800-342-7870
FAX 617-523-1021
http://www.portersargent.com
e-mail: info@portersargent.com
*Daniel McKeever, Senior Editor*
*John Yonce, General Manager*
*Leslie Weston, Production Editor*

A comprehensive survey of 3000 schools, facilities, and organizations across the USA. Serving children and yound adults with developmental, physical, medical, and emotional disabilities. Aide to parents, consultants, educators, and other professionals. *$64.00*

*1312 pages*
*ISBN 0-875581-31-5*

**3755 Disability Awareness in the Classroom: A Resource Tool for Teachers and Students**

Charles C Thomas Publisher
2600 S 1st Street
Springfield, IL 62704
217-789-8980
800-258-8980
FAX 217-789-9130
http://www.ccthomas.com
e-mail: books@ccthomas.com
*Lorie and Isabelle St. Onge Levison, Author*
*Michael Thomas, President*

Dispels misconceptions that contribute to stereotyping. Provides training for general education teachers and students preparing for inclusion or wanting to enhance their inclusion experiences. *$38.95*

*230 pages Spiral (paper)*
*ISBN 0-398069-53-0*

**3756 Early Adolescence Perspectives on Research, Policy and Intervention**

Lawrence Erlbaum Associates
10 Industrial Avenue
Mahwah, NJ 07430
201-236-9500
800-926-6579
FAX 201-236-0072
http://www.erlbaum.com
*Richard M Lerner, Author*

This forthcoming volume brings together a diverse group of scholars to write integratively about cutting-edge research issues pertinent to the study of early adolescence. *$99.95*

*528 pages*
*ISBN 0-805811-64-8*

**3757 Eden Institute Curriculum: Adaptive Physical Education, Volume V**

Eden Services
One Eden Way
Princeton, NJ 08540
609-987-0099
FAX 609-987-0243
http://www.edenservices.org
e-mail: info@edenservices.org
*David Holmes EdD, Executive Director/President*
*Anne Holmes, Director Outreach Support*

Teaching programs in the areas of sensory integration and adaptive physical education for students with autism. *$50.00*

**3758 Eden Institute Curriculum: Classroom Orienation, Volume II**

Eden Services
One Eden Way
Princeton, NJ 08540
609-987-0099
FAX 609-987-0243
http://www.edenservices.org
e-mail: info@edenservices.org
*David Holmes EdD, Executive Director/President*
*Anne Holmes, Director Outreach Support*

Academic and social skills programs for students with autism. *$100.00*

**3759 Eden Institute Curriculum: Core**

Eden Services
One eden Way
Princeton, NJ 08540
609-987-0099
FAX 609-987-0243
http://www.edenservices.org
e-mail: info@edenservices.org
*David Holmes EdD, Executive Director/President*
*Anne Holmes, Director Outreach Support*

Teaching programs for students with autism. *$200.00*

**3760 Eden Institute Curriculum: Speech and Language, Volume IV**

Eden Services
One Eden Way
Princeton, NJ 08540
609-987-0099
FAX 609-987-0243
http://www.edenservices.org
e-mail: info@edenservices.org
*David Holmes EdD, Executive Director/President*
*Anne Holmes, Director Outreach Support*

Speech and language development programs for students with autism. *$170.00*

**3761 Educating All Students Together**

Corwin Press
2455 Teller Road
Thousand Oaks, CA 91320
805-499-9734
800-818-7243
FAX 805-499-5323
http://www.corwinpress.com
e-mail: order@corwinpress.com
*Leonard C Burrello, Carl Lashley, Edith Beatty, Author*
*Kimberly Gonzales, Marketing Director*
*Robb Clouse, Senior Acquisitions Editor*

A plan for unifying the separate and parallel systems of special and general education. Key concepts include: schools embracing special services personnel; the role of the community; program evaluation and incentives; brain and holographic design; collaboration between school administrators and teachers; and adapting curriculum; and instruction. *$32.95*

*264 pages*
*ISBN 0-761976-98-1*

**3762  Educating Children with Multiple Disabilities, A Transdisciplinary Approach**

Books on Special Children
22 Webster Court
Amherst, MA  01002               845-638-1236
                                 FAX 845-638-0847
                        http://www.boscbooks.com
                        e-mail: irene@boscbooks.com
*FP Orelove, Author*
*Marcia Young, President*

Contributors discuss inclusive education for severely disabled students. Examines teamwork, needs of special students, designs curriculum needs, and special strategies for intervention. Discusses sensory disabilities, including new technology, and the need for working with family. *$42.00*

*494 pages  softcover*
*ISBN 1-557662-46-0*

**3763  Educator's Guide to Students with Epilepsy**

Charles C Thomas Publisher
2600 S 1st Street
Springfield, IL  62704          217-789-8980
                                800-258-8980
                           FAX 217-789-9130
                        http://www.ccthomas.com
                        e-mail: books@ccthomas.com
*Robert J Michael, Author*
*Michael Thomas, President*

The purposes of the book are to: present relevant knowledge about epilepsy for the educator; create an awareness of and sensitivity to students with epilepsy; focus on the role of education with students with epilepsy; present the major educational issues associated with epilepsy; define the educator's responsibility to students with epilepsy; and present useful resources. *$44.95*

*174 pages  Cloth*
*ISBN 0-398065-37-3*

**3764  Educator's Publishing Service**

Delta Corporation
31 Smith Place
Cambridge, MA  09031            617-547-6706
                                800-225-5750
                           FAX 617-547-0412
                        http://www.epsbooks.com
                        e-mail: eps@epsbooks.com
*Steven Courtes, President*

Written for both parents and teachers, this is based on the view that education should be a system of care that looks after the specific needs of individual students. Using case studies, it identifies and illustrates twenty-six common behaviors or phenomena that often inhibit or interfere with school performance. These are arranged according to six different themes and include behaviors related to poorly regulated attention, reduced remembering. *$28.00*

*340 pages*
*ISBN 0-838814-87-7*

**3765  Ending Discrimination in Special Education**

Charles C Thomas Publisher
2600 S 1st Street
Springfield, IL  62704          217-789-8980
                                800-258-8980
                           FAX 217-789-9130
                        http://www.ccthomas.com
                        e-mail: books@ccthomas.com
*Herbert Grossman, Author*
*Michael Thomas, President*

For special educators, school administrators, pychologists and regular education teachers who need to acquire the competencies necessary to succeed with all disabled, gifted and talented students who will be included in their classrooms. Books sent on approval. Shipping charges: $5.50 US/&6.50 Canada. Prices subject to change without notice. *$18.95*

*104 pages  Paper*

**3766  Enhancing Self-Concepts & Achievement of Mildly Handicapped Students**

Charles C Thomas Publisher
2600 S 1st Street
Springfield, IL  62704          217-789-8980
                                800-258-8980
                           FAX 217-789-9130
                        http://www.ccthomas.com
                        e-mail: books@ccthomas.com
*Carroll J Jones, Author*
*Michael Thomas, President*

The self-concept theory is reviewed and examined from a chronological and developmental perspective, relating the impact of self concept on academic functioning. Includes approaches and techniques a teacher might choose, including interventions which are metacognitive, behavioral, social, or academic in nature. A valuable review of current best practices for understanding and intervening on behalf of mildly handicapped learners with emotionally fragile self-concepts. *$ 39.95*

*294 pages  Cloth*
*ISBN 0-398057-60-5*

**3767  Exceptional Child: An Introduction to Special Education**

University of Sydney/School Educational Psychology
2011 New S Wales
Australia, NY

*Susan Ruth Butler, PhD, Author*
*Susan*

This comprehensive text, the first in Australia, covers all major special education topics. It features special contributions from professionals working with special disabilities. It has been edited to achieve a balance of substantive text (with medical and educational implications for each special need) as well as practical illustrative components and first-hand commentary from professionals and organizations in the field. *$36.95*

*800 pages*
*ISBN 0-729503-72-0*

**3768 Exceptional Individuals: An Introduction**

**Brooks/Cole Publishing Company**
**60 Garden court**
**Pacific Grove, CA 93950**            831-373-0728
                                  FAX 831-375-6414
*Gearhart/Mullen/Gearhart, Author*
*Carolyn Crockett, Marketing Manager*
*Barbara Smallwood, Marketing Assistant*

This book provides a direct, compassionate, and positive introduction to the characteristics and needs of exceptional individuals with disabilities and those who are gifted and talented. It looks at the role technology plays in meeting the needs of exceptional students, as well as the importance of early intervention, the impact of cultural and linguistic background and the role of the family as key factors in educational and social development.

*548 pages*

**3769 Exceptional Teacher's Handbook: First Year Special Education Teacher's Guide for Success**

**Corwin Press**
**2455 Teller Road**
**Thousand Oaks, CA 91320**           805-499-9734
                                     800-818-7243
                                  FAX 805-499-5323
                           http://www.corwinpress.com
                          e-mail: order@corwinpress.com
*Carla F Shelton, Alice B Pollingue, Author*
*Kimberly Gonzales, Marketing Director*
*Robb Clouse, Senior Acquisitions Editor*

This guide provides teachers with easily referenced tools for any situation and skill level, including skill development categories and icons showing which abilities are needed for each activity. An essential resource for both new and veteran teachers of students with special needs. *$32.95*

*208 pages*
*ISBN 0-761977-40-6*

**3770 Exceptionality**

**Lawrence Erlbaum Associates**
**365 Broadway**
**Hillsdale, NJ 07642**               201-666-4110
                                     800-926-6579
                                  FAX 201-666-2394
*Edward J Sabornie, Author*
*Susan Osborne, Co-Editor*
*Judy Nam, Owner*

Dedicated to the publication of original research and research reviews pertaining to individuals of all ages and disabilities as well as those who are gifted and talented. *$40.00*

*ISSN 0936-2835*

**3771 Faculty Guidebook: Working with Students with Learning Disabilities**

**HEATH Resource Center**
**2121 K Street NW**
**Washington, DC 20036**              202-973-0904
                                     800-544-3284
                                  FAX 202-973-0908
                           http://www.heath.gwu.edu
                        e-mail: askheath@askheath.gwu.edu
*Dan Gardner, Publications Manager*

A compilation of articles written by various faculty members of New River Community College. Among others, topics addressed include suggestions for teaching general academic subjects, options for instruction in the social sciences, strategies and suggestions for math and data processing teachers and electrical/electronic technologies. *$7.50*

**3772 Fawcett Book Group on Learning Disabilities**

**Fawcett Book Group**
**1745 Broadway**
**New York, NY 10022**                212-751-2600
                                  FAX 212-572-8700
                           http://www.randomhouse.com
*Lawrence Greene, Author*
*Betsy Czajka, Human Resource Associate*

Case studies, anecdotal material and educational data are used to tell parents of children with learning disabilities how to recognize the symptoms of a learning problem and what steps to take to see that their children receive the remediation needed. *$12.00*

*255 pages*

**3773 Focus on Exceptional Children**

**Love Publishing Company**
**PO Box 22353**
**Denver, CO 80222**                  303-221-7333
                                  FAX 303-221-7444
                           http://www.lovepublishing.com
                        e-mail: lovepublishing@compuserve.com

Journal containing research and theory-based articles on special education topics, with an emphasis on application and intervention of interest to teachers, professors and administrators. *$30.00*

**3774 Frames of Reference for the Assessment of Learning Disabilities**

**Brookes Publishing Company**
**PO Box 10624**
**Baltimore, MD 21285**               410-337-9580
                                     800-638-3775
                                  FAX 410-337-8539
                           http://www.pbrookes.com
                      e-mail: custserv@brookespublishing.com
*G Lyon PhD, Editor*

This valuable reference offers an in-depth look at the fundamental concerns facing those who work with children with learning disabilities — assessment and identification.

*672 pages  Hardcover*
*ISBN 1-557661-38-3*

### 3775 General Educators Guide to Special Education

**Peytral Publications**
**PO Box 1162**
**Minnetonka, MN  55345**          **952-949-8707**
                                   **877-739-8725**
                          **FAX 952-906-9777**
                  **http://www.peytral.com**
                  **e-mail: help@peytral.com**
*Jody L Maanun, Author*
*Peggy Hammeken, Owner/Publisher*

This valuable new resource is essential for educators who teach students with special needs or may refer students for special education placement. This new release is appropriate for educators at all levels. Very useful and practical. *$23.95*

*192 pages  Educators*
*ISBN 1-890455-32-6*

### 3776 HELP Activity Guide

**Therapro**
**225 Arlington Street**
**Framingham, MA  01702**          **508-872-9494**
                                   **800-257-5376**
                          **FAX 508-875-2062**
                  **http://www.theraproducts.com**
                  **e-mail: info@theraproducts.com**
*Setan Furuns, PhD, Author*
*Paul Weirauch, Owner*
*Karen Conrad, President*

Takes you easily beyond assesment to offer the important next step, thousands of practical, task-analyzed curriculum activities and intervention strategies indexed by the 650 HELP skills. With up to ten activities and strategies per skill, this valuable resource includes definitions for each skill, illustrations, cross-references to skills in other developmental areas and a glossary. *$28.00*

*190 pages*

### 3777 HELP for Preschoolers Assessment and Curriculum Guide

**Therapro**
**225 Arlington Street**
**Framingham, MA  01702**          **508-872-9494**
                                   **800-257-5376**
                          **FAX 508-875-2062**
                  **http://www.theraproducts.com**
                  **e-mail: info@theraproducts.com**
*Paul Weirauch, Owner*
*Karen Conrad, President*

Assessment procedure and instructional activities in one easy to use reference. Offers 6 sections of key information for each of the 622 skills: Definition, Materials, Assesment Procedures, Adaptions, Instructional Materials, and Instructional Activities.

### 3778 Handbook for Volunteer Tutors

**HEATH Resource Center**
**1 Dupont Circle NW**
**Washington, DC  20036**          **202-939-9320**
                                   **800-544-3284**
                          **FAX 202-833-4760**
                  **http://www.gwu.edu**
                  **e-mail: askheath@askheath.gwu.edu**
*Dan Gardner, Publications Manager*

Filled with tips for both students and tutors, as well as materials to increase awareness and understanding of learning disabilities. *$25.00*

### 3779 Handwriting: Not Just in the Hands

**Therapro**
**225 Arlington Street**
**Framingham, MA  01702 8723**          **508-872-9494**
                                        **800-257-5376**
                               **FAX 508-875-2062**
                       **http://www.theraproducts.com**
                       **e-mail: info@theraproducts.com**
*Eileen Vreeland MS OTR/L, Author*
*Karen Conrad, President*
*Paul Weirauch, Owner*

Save time and provide professional services with this comprehensive resource and presentation manual! Reviews current literature and research providing an excellent knowledge base. Covers pre-writing skills, handwriting skills, handwriting instruction, ergonomics and informal assessment in the classroom, remedial and compensatory exercises. Compatible with any handwriting program, it includes reproducible handouts, ready-to-make overheads, group activities and more. *$ 80.00*

*3 ring binder*

### 3780 Helping Learning Disabled Gifted Children Learn Through Compensatory Active Play

**Charles C Thomas Publisher**
**2600 S 1st Street**
**Springfield, IL  62704**          **217-789-8980**
                                    **800-258-8980**
                           **FAX 217-789-9130**
                   **http://www.ccthomas.com**
                   **e-mail: books@ccthomas.com**
*James H Humphrey, Author*
*Michael Thomas, President*

About three percent of the school population is gifted and 5-8 percent suffer from learning disabilities. These children experience a great deal more trauma than the normal child. This text will help educators deal with learning disabilities more effectively. *$36.95*

*164 pages  Cloth*
*ISBN 0-398056-95-1*

### 3781 Helping Students Succeed in the Regular Classroom

**Jossey-Bass**
**989 Market Street**
**San Francisco, CA  94104**          **415-433-1740**
                           **FAX 415-433-0499**
                   **http://www.josseybass.com**
                   **e-mail: dhunter@josseybass.com**
*Joseph Zins, Author*
*Debrah Hunter, President*

The first book in a series from Jossey-Bass on psychoeducational interventions. Shows how to develop programs to help the learning disabled students integrate within the regular classroom situation and avoid costly and often ineffective special education classes. *$26.95*

**3782    Hidden Youth: Dropouts from Special Education**

**Council for Exceptional Children**
**1110 N Glebe Road**
**Arlington, VA  22201**            **703-620-3660**
                                     **888-232-7733**
                               **FAX 703-264-9494**
                          **http://www.cec.sped.org/**
                       **e-mail: service@cec.sped.org**
*Donald L MacMillan, Author*
*Drew Albritten M.D., President*

Examines the characteristics of students and schools that place students at risk for early school leaving. Discusses the accounting procedures used by different agencies for estimating graduation and dropout rates and cautions educators about using these rates as indicators of educational quality. *$8.90*

> *37 pages*
> *ISBN 0-865862-11-7*

**3783    How Difficult Can This Be?**

**CT Association for Children and Adults with LD**
**25 Van Zant Street**
**East Norwalk, CT  06855**          **203-838-5010**
                               **FAX 203-866-6108**
                          **http://www.CACLD.org**
                       **e-mail: caccld@optonline.net**
*Rick Lavoie, Presenter*
*Beryl Kaufman, Executive Director*

FAT City Workshop video and discussion guide. Looks at the world through the eyes of a learning disabled child. Features a unique workshop attended by educators, psychologists, social workers, parents, siblings and a student with LD. They participate in a series of classroom activities which cause Frustration, Anxiety, and Tension-emotions all too familiar to the student with a learning disability. A discussion of topics ranging from school/home communication to social skills follows. *$49.95*

> *$5.00 shipping*

**3784    How Does Your Engine Run? A Leaders Guide to the Alert Program for Self Regulation**

**Therapro**
**225 Arlington Street**
**Framingham, MA  01702**            **508-872-9494**
                                     **800-257-5376**
                               **FAX 508-875-2062**
                          **http://www.theraproducts.com**
                       **e-mail: info@theraproducts.com**
*Mary Sue Williams,OTR & Sherry*
*Schellenberge,OTR, Author*
*Karen Conrad, President*
*Paul Weirauch, Owner*

Introduces the entire Alert Program. Explains how we regulate our arousal states and describes the use of sensorimotor strategies to manage levels of alertness. This program is fun for students and the adults working with them, and translates easily into real life.

**3785    How Significant is Significant? A Personal Glimpse of Life with LD**

**Association on Higher Education and Disability**
**PO Box 540666**
**Waltham, MA  02454**               **781-788-0003**
                               **FAX 781-788-0033**
                          **http://www.ahead.org**
                  **e-mail: ahead@postbox.acs.ohio-state.edu**
*Carolee Reiling, Author*

Provides a perspective not usually found in learning disability research material. *$3.50*

**3786    Human Development View of Learning Disabilities: From Theory to Practice**

**Charles C Thomas Publisher**
**2600 S 1st Street**
**Springfield, IL  62704**           **217-789-8980**
                                     **800-258-8980**
                               **FAX 217-789-9130**
                          **http://www.ccthomas.com**
                       **e-mail: books@ccthomas.com**
*Michael Thomas, Owner*
*Cleborne Maddux, Author*

The ultimate purpose of this book is to present a strategy for designing day-to-day, individualized lessons for learning disabled students from kindergarten through adulthood. The book will have great appeal to teachers, clinicians, researchers, and graduate students who are interested in considering the field from a particular point of view for a holistic approach to the task of identifying and educating persons with learning disabilities. *$50.95*

> *222 pages  Cloth*
> *ISBN 0-398058-86-5*

**3787    Implementing Cognitive Strategy Instruction Across the School**

**Brookline Books**
**300 Bedford Street**
**Manchester, NH  03101**            **617-734-6772**
                               **FAX 603-922-3348**
                          **http://www.brooklinebooks.com**
*Irene Gaskins, Author*

Describes a classroom based program planned and executed by teachers to focus and guide students with serious reading problems to be goal oriented, planful, strategic and self-assessing. *$24.95*

**3788    Improving Test Performance of Students with Disabilities in the Classroom**

**Corwin Press**
**2455 Teller Road**
**Thousand Oaks, CA  91320**         **805-499-9734**
                                     **800-818-7243**
                               **FAX 805-499-5323**
                          **http://www.corwinpress.com**
                       **e-mail: order@corwinpress.com**
*Judy L Elliott, Martha L Thurlow, Author*
*Kimberly Gonzales, Marketing Director*
*Robb Clouse, Senior Acquisitions Editor*

Elliott and Thurlow, long-time colleagues at the National Center on Educational Outcomes build on their highly respected work in accountability and assessment of students with disabilities to focus now on improving test performance — with an emphasis throughout on practical application. Common learning disabilities and emotional problems and a classroom-tested, research-based list of classroom interventions. *$39.95*

*360 pages*
*ISBN 0-761975-59-4*

**3789 Including Students with Severe and Multiple Disabilities in Typical Classrooms**

Brookes Publishing Company
PO Box 10624
Baltimore, MD 21285          410-337-9580
                            800-638-3775
                       FAX 410-337-8539
                   http://www.pbrookes.com
        e-mail: custserv@brookespublishing.com
*Mary A Favey, PhD, Author*
*Reid Lyon PhD, Editor*

This straightforward and jargon-free resource gives instructors the guidance needed to educate learners who have one or more sensory impairments in addition to cognitive and physical disabilities. *$32.95*

*224 pages  Paperback*
*ISBN 1-557662-39-8*

**3790 Inclusion: 450 Strategies for Success**

Peytral Publications
PO Box 1162
Minnetonka, MN  55345        952-949-8707
                            877-739-8725
                       FAX 952-906-9777
                   http://www.peytral.com
                e-mail: help@peytral.com
*Peggy Hammeken, Owner/Publisher*

Commences with step-by-step guidelines to help develop, expand and improve the existing inclusive education setting. Hundreds of practical teacher tested ideas and accommodations are conveniently listed by topic and numbered for quick, easy reference. *$23.95*

*192 pages  Educators*
*ISBN 1-890455-25-3*

**3791 Inclusion: An Annotated Bibliography**

National Clearinghouse of Rehabilitation Materials
206 W. Sixth St.
Stillwater, OK  74078-4080    405-744-2000
                             800-223-5219
                        FAX 405-744-2001
                       TDY:405-624-3156
                http://www.nchrtm.okstate.edu
                   e-mail: brookdj@okstate.edu
*Caroline Moore, Susanne Carter, Author*

This annotated bibliography is an initial compilation of recently published literature about what the special education community calls inclusion rather than mainstreaming. *$57.30*

*563 pages  Item # 262.007A*

**3792 Inclusion: An Essential Guide for the Paraprofessional**

Peytral Publications
PO Box 1162
Minnetonka, MN  55345        952-949-8707
                            877-739-8725
                       FAX 952-906-9777
                   http://www.peytral.com
                e-mail: help@peytral.com
*Peggy Hammeken, Owner/Publisher*

This best-selling publication is developed specifically for paraprofessionals and classroom assistants. The book commences with a simplified introduction to inclusive education, handicapping conditions, due process, communication, collaboration, confidentiality and types of adaptations. Used by many schools and universities as a training tool for staff development. *$23.95*

*205 pages  Assistants*
*ISBN 1-890455-34-2*

**3793 Inclusive Elementary Schools: Recipes for Success**

PEAK Parent Center
611 N Weber
Colorado Springs, CO  80903    719-531-9400
                              800-284-0251
                         FAX 719-531-9452
                         TDY:719-531-5403
                   http://www.peakparent.org
                    e-mail: info@peakparent.org
*Douglas Fisher, Nancy Frey, Caren Sax, Author*
*Barbara Buswell, Executive Director*
*Amy Schaub, Administrative Assistant*

State-of-the-art step process to determine what and how to teach elementary students with disabilities in inclusive classrooms. This breakthrough publication highlights strategies for accommodating and modifying assignments and activities by using core curriculum. *$13.00*

**3794 Individualizing Instruction for the Educationally Handicapped: Teaching Strategies**

Charles C Thomas Publisher
2600 S 1st Street
Springfield, IL  62704        217-789-8980
                             800-258-8980
                        FAX 217-789-9130
                   http://www.ccthomas.com
                  e-mail: books@ccthomas.com
*Jack Campbell, Author*
*Michael Thomas, President*

Covers children that qualify for special education as well as those that are just on the cusp and do not. The author advocates that by clinically analyzing the child's learning ecology and modifying the instructional plan based on student performance, the teacher is able to design instruction appropriate for the unique needs of each child.

*186 pages  Cloth*
*ISBN 0-398069-01-8*

**3795  Instructional Methods for Students**

Allyn & Bacon
160 Gould Street
Needham Heights, MA  02494          781-455-1250
                                   800-852-8024
                              FAX 781-455-1220
*Patrick Joseph Schloss, Author*

Instructional methods for students with learning and behavior problems.

**3796  Intervention in School and Clinic**

Pro-Ed
8700 Shoal Creek Boulevard
Austin, TX  78757                  512-451-3246
                                   800-897-3202
                              FAX 512-451-8542
                     http://www.proedinc.com
*Judith Voress PhD, Periodicals Director*

Features articles and instructional ideas to help teachers and therapists work with students with learning and behavior problems. *$20.00*

**3797  KDES Health Curriculum Guide**

Harris Communications
15155 Technology Drive
Eden Prairie, MN  55344            952-906-1180
                                   800-825-6758
                              FAX 952-906-1099
                              TDY:952-906-1198
                     http://www.harriscomm.com
                     e-mail: info@harriscmm.com
*Sara Gillespie, Author*
*Robert Harris, Owner*
*Bill Williams, National Sales Manager*

Provides students with the information they need to make wise choices for healthy living. Divided into age-appropriate sections, there are four main areas covered: Health and Fitness, Safety and First Aid, Drugs, and Family Life.

*125 pages*

**3798  LD Teacher's IDEA Companion (2BK Set)**

LinguiSystems
3100 4th Avenue
East Moline, IL  61244             309-755-2300
                                   800-776-4332
                              FAX 309-755-2377
                              TDY:800-933-8331
                     http://www.linguisystems.com
                     e-mail: service@linguisystems.com
*Linda Bowers, Owner*
*Rosemary Huisingh, Owner*

Help your special education students succeed in the regular classroom! Each book gives you page after page of goals and strategies to comply with current IDEA regulations. You'll get content standards, goals, benchmarks, and instructional modifications for several academic areas. You'll also get information on life skills and transition beyond high school.

*Ages 5-18*

**3799  LD Teacher's IEP Companion**

LinguiSystems
3100 4th Avenue
East Moline, IL  61244             309-755-2300
                                   800-776-4332
                              FAX 309-755-2377
                              TDY:800-933-8331
                     http://www.linguisystems.com
                     e-mail: service@linguisystems.com
*Molly Lyle, Author*
*Linda Bowers, Owner*
*Rosemary Huisingh, Owner*

These IEP goals are organized developmentally by skill area with individual objectives and classroom activity suggestions. Goals and objectives cover these academic areas: math; reading; writing; literacy concepts; attention skills; study skills; classroom behavior; social interaction; and transition skills. *$39.95*

*169 pages  Ages 5-18*

**3800  Landmark School Resources**

Landmark Foundation
PO Box 227
Prides Crossing, MA  01965         978-236-3216
                              FAX 978-927-7268
                     http://www.landmarkschool.org
                     e-mail: outreach@landmarkschool.com
*Joan Steinberg, Editor*
*Robert Broudo, President*

A compilation of 28 of the best articles available on learning disabilities and a collection of resources for parents and educators, including an annotated bibliography, sources for video and audio material, government resources, and parent/professional organizations. *$25.00*

*150 pages*
*ISBN 0-962411-94-9*

**3801  Learning Disabilities Materials Guide: Secondary Level**

Learning Disabilities Association of America
4156 Library Road
Pittsburgh, PA  15234              412-341-1515
                              FAX 412-344-0224
                     http://www.ldanatl.org
                     e-mail: ldanatl@usaor.net
*Jane Browning, Editor-in-Chief*

*$3.00*

**3802  Learning Disabilities in High School**

Learning Disabilities Association of America
4156 Library Road
Pittsburgh, PA  15234              412-341-1515
                              FAX 412-344-0224
                     http://www.ldanatl.org
                     e-mail: ldanatl@usaor.net
*Jane Browning, Editor-in-Chief*

*$3.00*

**3803 Learning Disabilities: The Interaction of Learner, Task and Setting**

Learning Disabilities Association of America
4156 Library Road
Pittsburgh, PA 15234          412-341-1515
                              FAX 412-344-0224
                              http://www.ldanatl.org
                              e-mail: ldanatl@usaor.net
*CR Smith, Author*
*Jane Browning, Editor-in-Chief*

$62.00

**3804 Learning Disabilities: Theoretical and Research Issues**

Lawrence Erlbaum Associates
365 Broadway
Hillsdale, NJ 07642          201-666-4110
                             800-926-6579
                        FAX 201-666-2394
*H Swanson, Author*
*Judy Nam, Owner*

This volume has been developed as a direct result of a conference sponsored by the International Academy for Research in Learning Disabilities, held at the University of California at Los Angeles. The test provides a review and critique achievement, and subtyping as they relate to learning disabilities. *$79.95*

*384 pages*
*ISBN 0-805803-92-0*

**3805 Learning Disability: Social Class and the Construction of Inequality in American Education**

Bergin & Gravey Greenwood
88 Post Road W
Westport, CT 06881           203-226-3571
                             800-225-5800
                        FAX 203-222-1502
                    http://www.greenwood.com
                    e-mail: dgoss@curry.edu
*Diane Goss, Author*
*George Goldberg, Head of Human Resources*
*James Deegan, Facility Manager*

In straightforward, empathic tones, authors sensitively offer support to parents of children with LD/ADD. *$22.50*

*248 pages*
*ISBN 0-964975-20-3*

**3806 Learning Problems & Learning Disabilities: Moving Forward**

Brooks/Cole Publishing Company
511 Forest Lodge Road
Pacific Grove, CA 93950      831-373-0728
                        FAX 831-375-6414
*Adelman/Taylor, Author*
*Carolyn Crockett, Marketing Manager*
*Barbara Smallwood, Marketing Assistant*

Current trends and new ideas for improving practice and research are covered in this exploration of learning problems and learning disabilities. This book's broad scope and futuristic outlook emphasizes current and evolving assessment and intervention approaches, discussing motivational as well as developmental differences, deficiencies, and dysfunctions. In addition to key references, twenty specialized readings stimulate thought of critical issues and re-emphasize the need to move forward.

*480 pages*
*ISBN 0-534187-56-0*

**3807 Mainstreaming Exceptional Students: A Guide for Classroom Teachers**

Allyn & Bacon
160 Gould Street
Needham Heights, MA 02494    781-455-1250
                             800-852-8024
                        FAX 781-455-1220
                    http://www.ablongman.com
                e-mail: exam.copies@ablongman.com
*Schultz & Carpenter, Author*
*Bill Parke, President*

Provides a clear overview of mainstreaming and public law.

**3808 Making School Inclusion Work**

Brookline Books
300 Bedford Street
Manchester, NH 03101         617-734-6772
                        FAX 603-922-3348
                    http://www.brooklinebooks.com
The authors explain true inclusion at the preschool/elementary level. *$24.95*

*264 pages*

**3809 Meeting the Needs of Special Students: Legal, Ethical, and Practical Ramifications**

Corwin Press
2455 Teller Road
Thousand Oaks, CA 91320      805-499-9734
                             800-818-7243
                        FAX 805-499-5323
                        TDY:805-499-0721
                http://www.corwinpress.com
                e-mail: order@corwinpress.com
*Lawrence J Johnson & Anne M Bauer, Author*
*Kimberly Gonzales, Marketing Director*
*Robb Clouse, Senior Acquisitions Editor*

The author gives administrators the information they need about the rights of students, federal guidelines and case law and precedents. *$17.00*

*96 pages*
*ISBN 0-803960-21-2*

**3810 Mentoring Students at Risk: An Underutilized Alternative Education Strategy...**

Charles C Thomas Publisher
2600 S 1st Street
Springfield, IL 62704        217-789-8980
                             800-258-8980
                        FAX 217-789-9130
                    http://www.ccthomas.com
                e-mail: books@ccthomas.com
*Gary Reglin, Author*
*Michael Thomas, President*

For K-12 teachers. Books sent on approval. Shipping charges: $5.50 US, $6.50 Canada. Prices subject to change without notice. *$17.95*

*110 pages  Paper*

### 3811  Myofascial Release and Its Application to Neuro-Developmental Treatment

**Therapro**
**225 Arlington Street**
**Framingham, MA  01702**          **508-872-9494**
**800-257-5376**
**FAX 508-875-2062**
**http://www.theraproducts.com**
**e-mail: info@theraproducts.com**
*Regi Boehme, OTR, Author*
*Karen Conrad, President*
*Paul Weirauch, Owner*

This fully illustrated resource provides the therapist with techniques to approach myofascial restrictions which are secondary to tonal dysfunction in children and adults with neurological deficits. The Neuro-Developmental Treatment approach is included in the illustrated treatment rationale.

### 3812  Narrative Prosthesis: Disability and the Dependencies of Discourse

**University of Michigan Press**
**839 Greene Street**
**Ann Arbor, MI  48104**          **734-764-4388**
**FAX 734-615-1540**
**http://www.press.umich.edu**
**e-mail: pgarner@umich.edu**
*David T Mitchell, Author*
*Mary Erwin, Assistant Director*

This book develops a narrative theory of the pervasive use of disability as a device of characterization in literature and film. It argues that, while other marginalized identities have suffered cultural exclusion due to dearth of images reflecting their experience, the marginality of disabled people has occurred in the midst of the perpetual circulation of images of disability in print and visual media. *$49.50*

*264 pages cloth*
*ISBN 0-472097-48-2*

### 3813  Otitis Media: Coping with the Effects in the Classroom

**Harris Communications**
**15155 Technology Drive**
**Eden Prairie, MN  55344**          **952-906-1180**
**800-825-6758**
**FAX 952-906-1099**
**TDY:952-906-1198**
**http://www.harriscomm.com**
**e-mail: info@harriscmm.com**
*Dorinne S Davis, MA, CCC-A, Author*
*Robert Harris, Owner*

Designed to alert teachers and specialists to the potential for communication difficulties associated with children who are prone to recurrent middle ear infections. Ideas are provided to be used to assist children toward appropriate language skill development. *$28.95*

*137 pages Paperback*

### 3814  Peytral Publications Strategies for Effective Communication

**Peytral Publication**
**PO Box 1162**
**Minnetonka, MN  55345**          **952-949-8707**
**877-739-8725**
**FAX 612-906-9777**
**http://www.peytral.com**
**e-mail: help@peytral.com**
*Patty Lee, EdD, Author*

With inclusive education, general and special educators are expected to collaborate in ways never anticipated in the educational system. With more than sixty strategies and 180 practice activities from which to chose, you and your colleagues will be able to focus on specific areas or several areas simultaneously. Includes tip cards for effective communication. *$19.95*

*85 pages*
*ISBN 0-964427-13-3*

### 3815  Points of Contact: Disability, Art, and Culture

**University of Michigan Press**
**839 Greene Street**
**Ann Arbor, MI  48104**          **734-764-4388**
**FAX 734-615-1540**
**http://www.press.umich.edu**
**e-mail: pgarner@umich.edu**
*Susan Crutchfield and Marcy Epstein, Author*
*Mary Erwin, Assistant Director*

This book brings together contributions by leading writers, artistis, scholars, and critics to provide a remarkably broad and consistently engaging look at the intersection of disability and the arts. *$47.50*

*36 pages  cloth*
*ISBN 0-472097-11-3*

### 3816  Prescriptions for Children with Learning and Adjustment Problems: A Consultant's Desk Reference

**Charles C Thomas Publisher**
**2600 S 1st Street**
**Springfield, IL  62704**          **217-789-8980**
**800-258-8980**
**FAX 217-789-9130**
**http://www.ccthomas.com**
**e-mail: books@ccthomas.com**
*Ralph F Blanco, David F Bogacki, Author*
*Michael Thomas, President*

Third edition. Books sent on approval. Shipping charges: $5.50 US, $6.50 Canada. Prices subject to change without notice. *$37.95*

*264 pages Cloth*

### 3817  Preventing Academic Failure

**Educators Publishing Service**
**31 Smith Place**
**Cambridge, MA  02138**          **617-573-6706**
**800-225-5750**
**FAX 617-547-0412**
*Phyllis Bertin, Eileen Perlman, Author*
*Phyllis Bertin,*

This multisensory curriculum meets the needs of children with learning disabilities in regular classrooms by providing a four-year sequence of written language skills (reading, writing and spelling). PAF has a handwriting and numerical program. *$42.00*

*ISBN 0-838852-71-8*

**3818    Project Success: Meeting the Diverse Needs of Learning Disabled Adults**

Richland College of the Dallas Community College
12800 Abrams Road
Dallas, TX  75243                           972-238-6106
                                        FAX 972-238-3799
                                  http://www.rlc.dcocd.edu
*Marcy Duarte, Secretary*

**3819    Project Upgrade: Working with Adults Who Have Learning Disabilities**

Manhattan Adult Learning and Resource Center
801 Poyntz Ave
Manhattan, KS  66502                        785-587-2820

**3820    Promoting Postsecondary Education for Students with Learning Disabilities**

Pro-Ed
8700 Shoal Creek Boulevard
Austin, TX  78757                           512-451-3246
                                             800-897-3202
                                        FAX 512-451-8542
                                   http://www.proedinc.com
*Loring Brinckerhoff, Author*
*Judith Voress PhD, Periodicals Director*
*Joan McGuire, Author*

This handbook is made up of comprehensive and practical chapters designed for the service provider. Contains an extensive reference section as well as 18 useful appendices. *$45.00*

*440 pages*
*ISBN 0-890795-89-4*

**3821    Reach Them All: Adapting Curriculum & Instruction with Technology in Inclusive Classrooms**

Indiana Institute on Disability and Community
2853 E 10th Street
Bloomington, IN  47408                      812-855-6508
                                        FAX 812-855-9630
                                        TDY:812-855-9396
                                http://www.iidc.indiana.edu
                                   e-mail: iidc@indiana.edu
*David Mank, Director*

Manual designed as a resource tool to help teachers use technology appropriately to meet individual student learning needs. Contents include technology information and tips, learning styles and adaptations, a 12-step process for making adaptations, 10 types of adaptations, strategies for technology use with simple adaptations and reproducible lesson and recording forms. *$12.00*

**3822    Rehabilitation of Clients with Specific Learning Disabilities**

National Clearinghouse of Rehabilitation Materials
206 W Sixth Street
Stillwater, OK  74078                       405-744-2000
                                        FAX 405-744-2001
                                  http://www.nchrtm.okstate.edu
                                  e-mail: brookdj@okstate.edu
*A Kansas RRTC, Author*

Functional definitions on SLD that made adults eligible for vocational rehabilitation services are given. Three types of populations are examined and the implications for vocational rehabilitation are considered. Administrative issues are addressed to encourage rehabilitation professionals to think ahead and to develop policies for SLD. *$11.00*

*100 pages  Item # 353.019*

**3823    Relationship of Learning Problems and Classroom Performance to Sensory Integration**

Therapro
225 Arlington Street
Framingham, MA  01702                       508-872-9494
                                             800-257-5376
                                        FAX 508-875-2062
                                  http://www.theraproducts.com
                                  e-mail: info@theraproducts.com
*Norma Quirk, MS, OTR and Marie DiMatties, MS, OTR, Author*
*Karen Conrad, President*
*Paul Weirauch, Owner*

This is an invaluable resource written for therapists and teachers to explain how sensory integration deficits impact classroom performance.

**3824    Resourcing: Handbook for Special Education Resource Teachers**

Council for Exceptional Children
1110 N Glebe Road
Arlington, VA  22201                        703-620-3660
                                             888-232-7733
                                        FAX 703-264-9494
                                  http://www.cec.sped.org/
                                  e-mail: service@cec.sped.org
*Mary Yeomans Jackson, Author*
*Drew Albritten M.D., President*

Everything you need to know about how to be a resource for other teachers and support personnel who work with special education students. This book will teach how to be a resource to yourself, how to be a resource to others and how to access resources: people; telephone; parents; instructional materials; and national resources. *$11.40*

*64 pages*
*ISBN 0-865862-19-2*

**3825    School Age Children with Special Needs**

Special Needs Project
324 State Street
Santa Barbara, CA  93105                    805-962-8087
                                             800-333-6867
                                        FAX 805-962-5087
                                  e-mail: books@specialneeds.com
*Dale Borman Fink, Author*
*Loraine Gray, Conference Coordinator*

The most comprehensive survey to date of child care practice for school aged children with a wide range of disabilities. *$12.95*

*148 pages*

**3826  School-Home Notes: Promoting Children's Classroom Success**

**Guilford Publications**
**72 Spring Street**
**New York, NY  10012**                    212-431-9800
                                           800-365-7006
                                      FAX 212-966-6708
                               http://www.guilford.com
                               e-mail: info@guilford.com
*Mary Lou Kelley, Author*
*Barry Duncan, Author*
*Shelby Keiser, Editor*

A comprehensive guide to establish and maintain a regular school-home contact. *$20.95*

*198 pages  Paperback*

**3827  Scissors, Glue, and Concepts, Too!**

**LinguiSystems**
**3100 4th Avenue**
**East Moline, IL  61244**                 309-755-2300
                                           800-776-4332
                                      FAX 309-755-2377
                                    TDY:800-933-8331
                          http://www.linguisystems.com
                          e-mail: service@linguisystems.com
*Linda Bowers, Owner*
*Rosemary Huisingh, Owner*

Your young students will learn to follow directions and understand basic concepts in context. Concepts for each activity are grouped as they naturally occur in our language. Teach over 50 concepts including right/left, above/below, empty/full, and more.

*Ages 5-8*

**3828  Segregated and Second-Rate: Special Education in New York**

**Advocates for Children of New York**
**151 W 30th Street**
**New York, NY  10001**                    212-947-3089
                                      FAX 212-947-9790
                        http://www.advocatesforchildren.org
                        e-mail: info@advocatesforchildren.org
*Diane K Autin Esq., Author*

Highlights the fact that New York rates last among all states in inclusive education. *$15.00*

**3829  Self-Advocacy Strategy for Education and Transition Planning**

**Edge Enterprises**
**PO Box 1304**
**Lawrence, KS  66044**                    785-749-1473
                                      FAX 785-749-0207
                          e-mail: eeinfo@edgeenterprises
*A Van Reusen, C Bos, J Schumaker, D Deshler, Author*
*Jacqueline Schafer, Managing Editor*

This research-based instructor's manual features step-by-step instructions on how to teach students to advocate for themselves within the context of meetings with adults. Covered are the instruction of basic social skills, creating a personal inventory of strengths and weaknesses, creating a list of goals and using a strategy to communicate at the meeting. Individual Education Planning Conferences, Transition Planning conferences as well as other types of meetings are covered. *$15.00*

*204 pages  Paperback*

**3830  Sensory Integration: Theory and Practice**

**Therapro**
**225 Arlington Street**
**Framingham, MA  01702**                  508-872-9494
                                           800-257-5376
                                      FAX 508-875-2062
                          http://www.theraproducts.com
                          e-mail: info@theraproducts.com
*Anne Fisher, Ann Bundy, Elizabeth Murray, Author*
*Karen Conrad, President*
*Paul Weirauch, Owner*

The very latest in sensory integration theory and practice. *$45.00*

*418 pages*

**3831  Social and Emotional Development of Exceptional Students**

**Charles C Thomas Publisher**
**2600 S 1st Street**
**Springfield, IL  62704**                 217-789-8980
                                           800-258-8980
                                      FAX 217-789-9130
                              http://www.ccthomas.com
                              e-mail: books@ccthomas.com
*Carroll J Jones, Author*
*Michael Thomas, President*

Provides teachers with understandable information regarding the social and emotional development of exceptional students. *$41.95*

*218 pages  Cloth*
*ISBN 0-398057-81-8*

**3832  Sopris West**

**Cambium Learning**
**4093 Specialty Place**
**Longmont, CO  80504**                    303-651-2829
                                      FAX 303-776-5934
                             http://www.sopriswest.com
*Dave Cabalucci, President*

IEP connections, IEP Tracker, Better IEP's, Self Directed IEP's

**3833  Source for Down Syndrome**

**LinguiSystems**
**3100 4th Avenue**
**East Moline, IL  61244**                 309-755-2300
                                           800-776-4332
                                      FAX 309-755-2377
                                    TDY:800-933-8331
                          http://www.linguisystems.com
                          e-mail: service@linguisystems.com
*Linda Bowers, Owner*
*Rosemary Huisingh, Owner*

Get in-depth information on working with students with Down sydrome. Packed with helpful tips and therapy techniques, chapters cover characteristics of Down syndrome, feeding and oral motor skills, language development and intervention, augmentative communication, motor and sensorimotor skills, and much more.

**3834 Source for Learning Disabilities**

**LinguiSystems**
**3100 4th Avenue**
**East Moline, IL 61244**　　　　**309-755-2300**
　　　　　　　　　　　　　　**800-776-4332**
　　　　　　　　　　　**FAX 309-755-2377**
　　　　　　　　　　　**TDY:800-933-8331**
　　　　　　**http://www.linguisystems.com**
　　　　**e-mail: service@linguisystems.com**
*Linda Bowers, Owner*
*Rosemary Huisingh, Owner*

This is the definitive source for information on learning disabilities. Get new information about federal mandates, teaming, transitioning, and involving parents. You'll also have a thorough discussion of the social and emotional aspects of LD and a glossary of terms.

**3835 Source for Nonverbal Learning Disorders**

**LinguiSystems**
**3100 4th Avenue**
**East Moline, IL 61244**　　　　**309-755-2300**
　　　　　　　　　　　　　　**800-776-4332**
　　　　　　　　　　　**FAX 309-755-2377**
　　　　　　　　　　　**TDY:800-933-8331**
　　　　　　**http://www.linguisystems.com**
　　　　**e-mail: service@linguisystems.com**
*Sue Thompson, Author*
*Linda Bowers, Owner*
*Rosemary Huisingh, Owner*

Not sure if you have a student with nonverbal learning disorder? See if this description sounds familiar: ignores nonverbal cues such as facial expressions; is clumsy for no apparent reason; makes inappropriate social remarks; and has difficulty with visual-spatial-organizational tasks. This resource provides you with useful checklists, anecdotes, and methods for dealing with this little understood disorder through the lifespan. *$41.95*

*Birth-Adult*

**3836 Source for Treatment Methodologies in Autism**

**LinguiSystems**
**3100 4th Avenue**
**East Moline, IL 61244**　　　　**309-755-2300**
　　　　　　　　　　　　　　**800-776-4332**
　　　　　　　　　　　**FAX 309-755-2377**
　　　　　　　　　　　**TDY:800-933-8331**
　　　　　　**http://www.linguisystems.com**
　　　　**e-mail: service@linguisystems.com**
*Linda Bowers, Owner*
*Rosemary Huisingh, Owner*

Get basic, factual information on the leading treatment methodologies for autism in one handy resource. You'll get clear, helpful information to share with parents and other professionals faced with treatment decisions.

*Ages Birth-18*

**3837 Special Education Technology: Classroom Applications**

**Brooks/Cole Publishing Company**
**511 Forest Lodge Road**
**Pacific Grove, CA 93950**　　　**831-373-0728**
　　　　　　　　　　　**FAX 831-375-6414**
*Carolyn Crockett, Marketing Manager*
*Barbara Smallwood, Marketing Assistant*

This exciting text helps pre- and in-service teachers understand how they can use technology to benefit individuals with disabilities in the classroom. Addressing the needs of a variety of populations, Lewis focuses on methods for adapting computers, as well as technologies such as environmental control devices; augmentative communication devices, mobility devices, systems that translate print for the blind and assistive listening devices.

*552 pages*
*ISBN 0-534202-86-1*

**3838 Special Educators Guide to Regular Education**

**CT Association for Children and Adults with LD**
**25 Van Zant Street**
**East Norwalk, CT 06855**　　　**203-838-5010**
　　　　　　　　　　　**FAX 203-866-6108**
　　　　　　　　　　**http://www.CACLD.org**
　　　　　　**e-mail: cacld@optonline.net**
*L Lieberman, Author*
*Beryl Kaufman, Executive Director*
*Marie Armstrong, Information Specialist*

Offers information on special education for learning disabled students. *$10.50*

**3839 Strategy Assessment and Instruction for Students with Learning Disabilities**

**Pro-Ed**
**8700 Shoal Creek Boulevard**
**Austin, TX 78757**　　　　　**512-451-3246**
　　　　　　　　　　　　　　**800-897-3202**
　　　　　　　　　　　**FAX 512-451-8542**
　　　　　　　　　**http://www.proedinc.com**
*Lynn Meltzer, Author*
*Judith Voress PhD, Periodicals Director*

The unifying theme of this volume is the view that strategic learning is a critical component of academic success and that inefficient strategy use characterizes many learning disabled students and prevents them from functioning at the level of their potential. *$41.00*

*424 pages*
*ISBN 0-890795-40-1*

**3840 Subtypes of Learning Disabilities**

**Lawrence Erlbaum Associates**
**365 Broadway**
**Hillsdale, NJ 07642**　　　　**201-666-4110**
　　　　　　　　　　　　　　**800-926-6579**
　　　　　　　　　　　**FAX 201-666-2394**
*Lynne Feagans, Author*
*Judy Nam, Owner*
*Lynn Meltzer, Author*

Although experts agree that various types of learning disabilities do exist, few attempts have been made to classify learning disabled children into subtypes. The editors of this collection feel that the lack of subcategorization has frustrated previous research efforts to obtain a generalizable body of knowledge in the field. *$59.95*

*288 pages*
*ISBN 0-805806-02-4*

**3841  Survival Guide with Kids with LD**

**Free Spirit Publishing**
**217 5th Avenue N**
**Minneapolis, MN  55401**            **612-338-2068**
                                      **866-703-7322**
                              **FAX 612-337-5050**
                      **http://www.freespirit.com**
                **e-mail: help4kids@freespirit.com**
*Gary Fisher & Rhoda Cummings, Author*
*Judy Galbraith, President*

Vital information, practical advice, step-by-step strategies, and encouragement for children labeled learning disabled. *$9.95*

*104 pages*
*ISBN 0-915793-18-0*

**3842  Take Part Art**

**CT Association for Children and Adults with LD**
**25 Van Zant Street**
**East Norwalk, CT  06855**          **203-838-5010**
                              **FAX 203-866-6108**
                      **http://www.CACLD.org**
                **e-mail: caccld@optonline.net**
*Bob Gregson, Author*
*Marie Armstrong, Information Specialist*
*Beryl Kaufman, Executive Director*

Offers information on art therapies and their inclusion in learning disabled environments. *$19.50*

*$2.50 shipping*

**3843  Teachers Ask About Sensory Integration**

**Therapro**
**225 Arlington Street**
**Framingham, MA  01702**            **508-872-9494**
                                      **800-257-5376**
                              **FAX 508-875-2062**
                      **http://www.theraproducts.com**
                **e-mail: info@theraproducts.com**
*Carol Kranowitz, Stacey Szkult and David Silver,*
*Author*
*Karen Conrad, President*
*Paul Weirauch, Owner*

A narration and discussion for teachers and school professionals about how to teach children with sensory integration problems. 60 page book included, filled with checklists, idea sheets, sensory profiles and resorces. 86 minute audio tape.

*Audio Tape*

**3844  Teaching Kids with LD in the Regular Classroom**

**Free Spirit Publishing**
**217 5th Avenue N**
**Minneapolis, MN  55401**            **612-338-2068**
                                      **866-703-7322**
                              **FAX 612-337-5050**
                      **http://www.freespirit.com**
                **e-mail: help4kids@freespirit.com**
*Susan Winebrenner, Author*
*Judy Galbraith, President*

Proven, classroom-tested, curriculum specific ways to help teachers help special ed, slow and remedial students in their mixed ability classroom. *$27.95*

*248 pages*
*ISBN 1-575420-04-X*

**3845  Teaching Learners with Mild Disabilities**

**Brooks/Cole Publishing Company**
**511 Forest Lodge Road**
**Pacific Grove, CA  93950**          **831-373-0728**
                              **FAX 831-375-6414**
*Meese/Overton/Whitfield, Author*
*Carolyn Crockett, Marketing Manager*
*Barbara Smallwood, Marketing Assistant*

This very applied text introduces preservice teachers to best practices for teaching learners with mild disabilities. The authors illustrate interactions among regular teachers, special education teachers and students with mild disabilities through the use of eight hypothetical case studies of students and teachers.

*496 pages*
*ISBN 0-534211-01-0*

**3846  Teaching Students Ways to Remember**

**Brookline Books**
**300 Bedford Street**
**Manchester, NH  03101**            **617-734-6772**
                              **FAX 603-922-3348**
                      **http://www.brooklinebooks.com**
*Margo Mastropie MD, Author*
*Thomas Scruggs, Author*

This book was written in response to the enormous interest in mnemonic instruction by teachers and administrators, telling them how it can be used with their students. *$21.95*

**3847  Teaching Visually Impaired Children**

**Charles C Thomas Publisher**
**2600 S 1st Street**
**Springfield, IL  62704**            **217-789-8980**
                                      **800-258-8980**
                              **FAX 217-789-9130**
                      **http://www.ccthomas.com**
                **e-mail: books@ccthomas.com**
*Virginia E. Bishop, Author*
*Michael Thomas, President*

This book provides a comprehensive resource for the classroom teacher who is working with a visually impaired child for the first time, as well as a systematic overview of education for the specialist in visual disabilities. It approaches instructional challenges with clear explanations and practical suggestions, and it addresses common concerns of teachers in a reassuring and positive manner. The book is organized into three sections: Vision, Learning, and Testing & Transitions. *$51.95*

*274 pages  Cloth*
*ISBN 0-398065-95-0*

**3848    Teaching the Learning Disabled Adolescent: Strategies and Methods**

**Learning Disabilities Association of America**
**4156 Library Road**
**Pittsburgh, PA   15234**          412-341-1515
                                    FAX 412-344-0224
                          http://www.ldanatl.org
                          e-mail: ldanatl@usaor.net
*Jane Browning, Editor-in-Chief*

This book gives expert strategies and methods for teaching learning disabled adolescents. *$58.00*

**3849    Technology in the Classroom: Communication Module**

**American Speech-Language-Hearing Association**
**10801 Rockville Pike**
**Bethesda, MD   20852**          301-897-5700
                                 888-498-6699
                          FAX 301-897-7358
                          TDY:301-897-5700
                          http://www.asha.org
                          e-mail: epietrarton@asha.com
*Laurie Ward, Marketing Coordinator*
*Arlene Pietranton, Executive Director*

Provides a brief background of assistive technology and a detailed discussion on augmentative communication. Contains technology and strategies aimed at giving children who have disabilities, another way to communicate when speaking is difficult or impossible. *$40.00*

**3850    Technology in the Classroom: Education Module**

**American Speech-Language-Hearing Association**
**10801 Rockville Pike**
**Bethesda, MD   20852**          301-897-5700
                                 888-498-6699
                          FAX 301-897-7358
                          TDY:301-897-5700
                          http://www.asha.org
                          e-mail: randerson@asha.org
*Laurie Ward, Marketing Coordinator*
*Rick Anderson, Marketing Director*

Offers in-depth discussion as to how assistive technology can be used in educational settings. The technology is geared for children who have severe disabilities and provides a discussion of how to assess a child's needs for assistive technology in order to perform both pre-academic and academic tasks. *$40.00*

**3851    Technology in the Classroom: Positioning, Access and Mobility Module**

**American Speech-Language-Hearing Association-ASHA**
**10801 Rockville Pike**
**Bethesda, MD   20852**          301-897-5700
                                 888-498-6699
                          FAX 301-897-7358
                          TDY:301-897-5700
                          http://www.asha.org
                          e-mail: randerson@asha.org
*Laurie Ward, Marketing Coordinator*
*Rick Anderson, Marketing Director*

This manual emphasizes the importance of proper positioning that comfortably enables a child to perform activities of everyday life, and the technology which is available to help children move about when they are physically unable to do so. *$35.00*

**3852    Test Accommodations for Students with Disabilities**

**Charles C Thomas Publisher**
**2600 S 1st Street**
**Springfield, IL   62704**          217-789-8980
                                     800-258-8980
                            FAX 217-789-9130
                          http://www.ccthomas.com
                          e-mail: books@ccthomas.com
*Edward Burns, Author*
*Michael Thomas, President*

The purpose here is to consider legal questions, theoretical issues, and practical methods for meeting the assessment needs of students with disabilities. The ultimate goal of this book is to consider a variety of concerns and to provide several ideas for conceptualizing and implementing valid test accommodations. *$66.95*

*340 pages  Cloth*
*ISBN 0-398068-44-5*

**3853    To Be Gifted and Learning Disabled: From Definitions to Practical Intervention Strategies**

**Creative Learning Press**
**PO Box 320**
**Mansfield Center, CT   06250**          860-429-8118
                                          888-518-8004
                                FAX 860-429-7783
                    http://www.creativelearningpress.com
                          e-mail: clp@neca.com
*Susan M Baum, Steven V Owen, John Dixon, Author*
*Kristina Morgan, Executive Director*
*Steven Owen*

The gifted and learning disabled child exhibits remarkable talents in some areas and disabling weakness in others. Covers everything a classroom or enrichment teacher must know in order to address the needs of gifted learning disabled youngsters, including identification, learning styles, and more. *$16.95*

*149 pages*
*ISBN 0-936386-59-2*

**3854 To Teach a Dyslexic**

AVKO Educational Research Foundation
3084 W Willard Road
Clio, MI 48420                    810-686-9283
                                 FAX 810-686-1101
                        http://www.avko.org/upto.htm
                        e-mail: avkoemail@aol.com
*Don McCabe, Author*
*Don McCabe, Research Director*

Just as it takes a thief to catch a thief, this is an autobiography of a dyslexic who discovered how to teach dyslexics. Common sense, logical approach, valuable to all who teach in our nation's classrooms. *$14.95*

*ISBN 1-564000-04-4*

**3855 Tools for Transition**

AGS
4201 Woodland Road
Circle Pines, MN 55014            763-786-4343
                                  800-328-2560
                                 FAX 763-786-9077
                        http://www.agsnet.com
                        e-mail: agsmail@agsnet.com
*Kevin Brueggenan, President*

The materials in this kit offer a curriculum that is not always included in learning disabled programs. Comes with a teacher's manual, complete with instructions for each unit and a Student Workbook filled with skill-building activities. The accompanying video presents a variety of sciences to demonstrate plus an interview with college students who have learning disabilities.

**3856 Understanding & Management of Health Problems in Schools**

Temeron Books
Bellingham, WA 98227              403-283-0900
                                 FAX 360-738-4016
                        http://www.temerondetselig.com
                        e-mail: temeron@telusplanet.net
*H Moghadam, Author*

A guide for teachers of students with problems which are an obstacle to learning, this book offers information and suggestions teachers can use to help students learn. *$13.95*

*152 pages  Paperback*
*ISBN 1-550591-21-5*

**3857 Understanding and Managing Vision Deficits**

Therapro
225 Arlington Street
Framingham, MA 01702              508-872-9494
                                  800-257-5376
                                 FAX 508-875-2062
                        http://www.theraproducts.com
                        e-mail: info@theraproducts.com
*Mitchell Scheiman, OD, Author*
*Karen Conrad, President*
*Paul Weirauch, Owner*

This book is a unique and comprehensive collaboration from OT's and optometrists developed to increase the understanding of vision. Learn to screen for common visual deficits and effectively manage patients with vision disorders. Provides recommendations for direct intervention techniques for a variety of vision problems and supportive and compensatory stratagies for visual field deficits and visual neglect.

**3858 Vision and Learning Disabilities**

Learning Disabilities Association of America
4156 Library Road
Pittsburgh, PA 15234              412-341-1515
                                 FAX 412-344-0224
                        http://www.ldanatl.org
                        e-mail: ldanatl@usaor.net
*Jane Browning, Editor-in-Chief*

*$1.25*

**3859 Working Memory and Severe Learning Difficulties**

Lawrence Erlbaum Associates
365 Broadway
Hillsdale, NJ 07642               201-666-4110
                                  800-926-6579
                                 FAX 201-666-2394
*Charles Hulme, Author*
*Judy Nam, Owner*

This monograph considers the development of working memory skills in children with severe learning difficulties. These children have marked difficulties with a wide range of cognitive tasks. The studies reported show that they also experience profound difficulties on verbal working memory tasks. *$29.95*

*160 pages*
*ISBN 0-863770-75-4*

**3860 Working with Visually Impaired Young Students: A Curriculum Guide for 3 to 5 Year-Olds**

Charles C Thomas Publisher
2600 S 1st Street
Springfield, IL 62704             217-789-8980
                                  800-258-8980
                                 FAX 217-789-9130
                        http://www.ccthomas.com
                        e-mail: books@ccthomas.com
*Ellen Trief, Author*
*Michael Thomas, President*

The purpose of this guide is to offer a curriculum model to preschool programs that provides services to visually impaired 3 to 5 year olds with emphasis on the need for psychological evaluations to establish the preschooler's cognitive and intellectual level of functioning, basic pre-braille concepts, orientation and mobility, activities that help facilitate speech and language learning, art therapy methods, and the application of music therapy to improve motor, language, and social skills.

*218 pages  Paperback*
*ISBN 0-398068-75-5*

## Language Arts

**3861 Clinical Interview: A Guide for Speech-Language Pathologists/Audiologists**

**American Speech-Language-Hearing Association**
10801 Rockville Pike
Bethesda, MD 20852          301-897-5700
                           888-498-6699
                           FAX 301-897-7358
                           TDY:301-897-5700
                           http://www.asha.org
                           e-mail: randerson@asha.org
*Laurie Ward, Marketing Coordinator*
*Rick Anderson, Marketing Director*

Integrates the components of the clinical interview within the context of the speech-language pathology and audiology helping process. *$9.00*

**3862 Closer Look: The English Program at the Model Secondary School for the Deaf**

**Harris Communications**
15155 Technology Drive
Eden Prairie, MN 55344          952-906-1180
                               800-825-6758
                           FAX 952-906-1099
                           TDY:952-906-1198
                           http://www.harriscomm.com
                           e-mail: info@harriscmm.com
*MSSD English Teachers, Author*
*Robert Harris, Owner*

Features research-supported principles for incorporating the whole language philosophy into classroom routines, highlighting student-centered activities. Strategies are outlined for determining student levels based largely on the degree of teacher guidance needed. Reading and writing objectives are provided for grades 8-12. *$9.95*

*67 pages*

**3863 Communication Skills for Visually Impaired Learners**

**Charles C Thomas Publisher**
2600 S 1st Street
Springfield, IL 62704          217-789-8980
                               800-258-8980
                           FAX 217-789-9130
                           http://www.ccthomas.com
                           e-mail: books@ccthomas.com
*Randall Harley, Mila B. Truan & LaRhea D. Sanford, Author*
*Michael Thomas, President*

Designed to provide a better understanding of teaching reading, writing, and listening skills to students with visual impairments. Intended for use by teachers who have a basic knowledge of the communication skills needed to teach students with normal vision and who have proficiencies in reading and writing the braille code, using large print, optical aids, and current technology such as microcomputers, access equipment, and closed caption TV. *$69.95*

*322 pages Cloth*
*ISBN 0-398066-92-2*

**3864 First Start in Sign Language**

**Harris Communications**
15155 Technology Drive
Eden Prairie, MN 55344          952-906-1180
                               800-825-6758
                           FAX 952-906-1099
                           TDY:952-906-1198
                           http://www.harriscomm.com
                           e-mail: info@harriscmm.com
*Amy J Strommer, Author*
*Robert Harris, Owner*

Fun pictures, stories, and activities are included in this book. Students first learn to sign words for people, animals, objects and actions. Then they learn to produce simple ententes and to sign stories. Reproducible activity pages included. *$32.00*

*190 pages Paperback*

**3865 From Talking to Writing: Strategies for Scaffolding Expository Expression**

**Landmark School**
429 Hale Street
Prides Crossing, MA 01965          978-236-3216
                               FAX 978-927-7268
                           http://www.landmarkschool.org
                           e-mail: outreach@landmarkschool.org
*Terrill Jennings and Charles Haynes, Author*
*Dan Ahearn, Program Director*
*Trish Newhall, Associate Director*
*Kathryn Frye, Administrative Assistant*

Designed for teachers who work with students who have difficulty with writing and/or expressive language skills, this book provides practical strategies for teaching expository expression at the word, sentence, paragraph, and short essay levels. *$40.00*

*191 pages*
*ISBN 0-962411-98-1*

**3866 Helping Young Writers Master the Craft**

**Brookline Books**
300 Bedford Street
Manchester, NH 03101          617-734-6772
                           FAX 603-922-3348
                           http://www.brooklinebooks.com
*Karen R Harris, Author*

This text for teachers will help the beginning writer, the unmotivated student and the learning disabled student to learn writing. *$24.95*

**3867 Landmark Method for Teaching Writing**

**Landmark School**
429 Hale Street
Prides Crossing, MA 01965          978-236-3216
                               FAX 978-927-7268
                           http://www.landmarkschool.org
                           e-mail: outreach@landmarkschool.org
*Jean Gudaitis Tarricone, Author*
*Dan Ahearn, Program Director*
*Trish Newhall, Associate Director*
*Kathryn Frye, Administrative Assistant*

This book provides practical strategies for teaching writing in the classroom. It emphasizes the integration of language and critical thinking skills within a five-step writing process. Paragraph framing, graphic organizing, multiparagraph writing, sample templates, and exercises that teachers can use in their classrooms are included. *$30.00*

*92 pages*
*ISBN 0-962411-93-0*

## 3868  Language Learning Everywhere We Go

**Harris Communications**
**15155 Technology Drive**
**Eden Prairie, MN  55344**          952-906-1180
                                     800-825-6758
                              FAX 952-906-1099
                              TDY:952-906-1198
                    http://www.harriscomm.com
                    e-mail: info@harriscmm.com
*Cecilia Casas, Author*
*Robert Harris, Owner*

Students learn the vocabulary associated with each situation that they encounter on their travels with Bernardo Bear. Questions and vocabulary lists are included in English and Spanish for each picture. The 103 situational pictures may all be reproduced. *$34.00*

*209 pages  Paperback*

## 3869  Multisensory Teaching Approach

**Deta Corporation**
**31 Smith Place**
**Cambridge, MA  02139**          617-547-6706
                                  800-225-5750
                           FAX 617-547-0412
                  http://www.epsbooks.com
                  e-mail: eps@epsbooks.com
*Margaret Taylor Smith, Author*
*Steven Courtes, President*

MTA is a comprehensive, multisensory program in reading, spelling, cursive handwriting, and alphabet and dictionary skills for both regular and remedial instruction. Ungraded, MTA is based on the Orton-Gillingham techniques and Alphabetic Phonics.

## 3870  Problems in Written Expression: Assessment and Remediation

**Guilford Publications**
**72 Spring Street**
**New York, NY  10012**          212-431-9800
                                 800-365-7006
                          FAX 212-966-6708
                  http://www.guilford.com
                  e-mail: info@guilford.com
*Sharon Bradley-Johnson, Author*
*Jusi Lesiak, Author*

A great resource for speech-language pathologists, counselors, resource specialists and other special educators. *$20.95*

*178 pages  Paperback*

## 3871  Report Writing in the Field of Communication Disorders

**American Speech-Language-Hearing Association**
**10801 Rockville Pike**
**Bethesda, MD  20852**          301-897-5700
                                 888-498-6699
                          FAX 301-897-7358
                          TDY:301-897-5700
                    http://www.asha.org
                    e-mail: randerson@asha.org
*Laurie Ward, Marketing Coordinator*
*Rick Anderson, Marketing Director*

Stresses the summarization and interpretation of vital information and highlights matters of ethics, privacy and more. *$7.00*

## 3872  Signs of the Times

**Harris Communications**
**15155 Technology Drive**
**Eden Prairie, MN  55344**          952-906-1180
                                     800-825-6758
                              FAX 952-906-1099
                              TDY:952-906-1198
                    http://www.harriscomm.com
                    e-mail: info@harriscmm.com
*Robert Harris, President*
*Patty Johnson, Administrative Assistant*

Contains 1,185 signs in 41 lessons. Each lesson contains clearly illustrated vocabulary, English glosses and synonyms, sample sentences to define vocabulary context, and sentences for practice. *$24.95*

*433 pages  Paperback*

## 3873  Slingerland-Multisensory Approach to Language Arts for Specific Language Disability Children

**Deta Corporation**
**31 Smith Place**
**Cambridge, MA  02139**          617-547-6706
                                  800-225-5750
                           FAX 617-547-0412
                  http://www.epsbooks.com
                  e-mail: eps@epsbooks.com
*Beth H Slingerland, Author*
*Steven Courtes, President*

This adaptation of the Orton-Gillingham approach for classroom teachers provides a phonetically structured introduction to reading, writing and spelling. Books 1 and 2 are for first and second grade, Book 3 for primary classrooms and older students. Numerous supplementary materials are available.

## 3874  Source for Processing Disorders

**LinguiSystems**
**3100 4th Avenue**
**East Moline, IL  61244**          309-755-2300
                                    800-776-4332
                             FAX 309-755-2377
                             TDY:800-933-8331
                    http://www.linguisystems.com
                    e-mail: service@linguisystems.com
*Linda Bowers, Owner*
*Rosemary Huisingh, Owner*

This great resource helps you differentiate between language processing disorders and auditory processing disorders. Chapters cover: the neurology of processing and learning; the central auditory processing model; the language processing model; and a lot more!

*Ages 5-Adult*

**3875 Source for Syndromes**

**LinguiSystems**
**3100 4th Avenue**
**East Moline, IL 61244**          **309-755-2300**
                                   **800-776-4332**
                            **FAX 309-755-2377**
                            **TDY:800-933-8331**
            **http://www.linguisystems.com**
            **e-mail: service@linguisystems.com**
*Gail J Richard, Debra Reichert Hoge, Author*
*Linda Bowers, Owner*
*Rosemary Huisingh, Owner*

Do you often wish someone would just tell you what to do with a specific youngster on your caseload? The Source for Syndromes can do just that. Learn about the speech-language characteristics for each sydrome with a focus on communication issues. This resource covers pertinent information for such sydromes such as Angelman, Asperger's, Autism, Rett's, Tourette's, Williams, and more. *$41.95*

*117 pages Ages Birth-18*

**3876 Teaching Language-Deficient Children: Theory and Application of the Association Method**

**Educators Publishing Service**
**31 Smith Place**
**Cambridge, MA 02139**          **617-547-6706**
                                  **800-225-5750**
                            **FAX 617-547-0412**
            **http://www.epsbooks.com**
            **e-mail: eps@epsbooks.com**
*N Etoile duBard and Maureen K Martin, Author*
*Steven Courtes, President*

This revised and expanded edition of Teaching Aphasics and Other Language Deficient Children offers information on its theory, implementation of the method and sample curriculum. *$42.00*

*360 pages*
*ISBN 0-838823-40-8*

**3877 Thematic Instruction: Teacher's Primer for Developing Speaking & Writing Skill**

**Landmark Foundation**
**PO Box 227**
**Prides Crossing, MA 01965**          **978-236-3216**
                            **FAX 978-927-7268**
            **http://www.landmarkschool.org**
            **e-mail: outreach@landmarkschool.org**
*Terrill Jennings, Author*
*Charles Haynes, Author*
*Joan Sedita, Outreach Program*

This book introduces teachers to a theme-centered approach to expressive language skills instruction. It is designed for classroom teachers who are teaching speaking and writing skills. It combines a structured, skills-based approach with thematic orientation. *$20.00*

**3878 Visualizing and Verbalizing for Language Comprehension/Thinking**

**Academy of Reading**
**416 Higuera Street**
**San Luis Obispo, CA 93401**          **805-541-3836**
                                       **800-233-1819**
                            **FAX 805-541-8756**
*Nanci Bell, Author*

This book identifies the important sensory connection that imagery provides and teaches specific techniques. Specific steps and sample dialog are presented. Summary pages after each step make it easy to implement the program in the classroom.

*284 pages*
*ISBN 0-945856-01-6*

# Math

**3879 Landmark Method for Teaching Arithmetic**

**Landmark School**
**429 Hale Street**
**Prides Crossing, MA 01965**          **978-236-3216**
                            **FAX 978-927-7268**
            **http://www.landmarkschool.org**
            **e-mail: outreach@landmarkschool.org**
*Christopher Woodin, Author*
*Dan Ahearn, Program Director*
*Trish Newhall, Associate Director*
*Kathryn Frye, Administrative Assistant*

This book is written for teachers who work with students having difficulty learning math. It includes practical strategies for teaching multiplication, division, word problems, and math facts. It also introduces the reader to two learning tools developed at Landmark — Woodin Ladders and Woodmark Icons. Sample templates and exercises that teachers can copy and use in their classrooms are included. *$30.00*

*145 pages*
*ISBN 0-962411-92-2*

**3880 Math and the Learning Disabled Student: A Practical Guide for Accommodations**

**Academic Success Press**
**6023 26th Strete**
**West Bradenton, FL 34206**          **941-359-2819**
                                      **800-444-2524**
                            **FAX 800-777-2525**
*P Nolting, Author*
*Mary Liscio, Editor*

More and more learning disabled students are experiencing difficulty passing mathematics. The book is especially written for counselors and mathematics instructors of learning disabled students, and provides information on accommodations for students with different types of learning disabilities.

*91 pages*
*ISBN 0-940287-23-4*

**3881 Moving Toward the Standards: A National Action Plan for Math Education Reform for the Deaf**

Harris Communications
15155 Technology Drive
Eden Prairie, MN 55344      952-906-1180
800-825-6758
FAX 952-906-1099
TDY:952-906-1198
http://www.harriscomm.com
e-mail: info@harriscmm.com
*Robert Harris, Owner*

Offers help for teachers working with students who are deaf and hard of hearing by presenting the most current, practical approaches to math instruction.

*750 pages*

**3882 Teaching Mathematics to Students with Learning Disabilities**

Pro-Ed
8700 Shoal Creek Boulevard
Austin, TX 78757      512-451-3246
800-897-3202
FAX 512-451-8542
http://www.proedinc.com
*Nancy Bley, Author*
*Judith Voress PhD, Periodicals Director*

Offers information on problem-solving, estimation and the use of computers in teaching mathematics to the child with learning disabilities. *$38.00*

*486 pages*
*ISBN 0-890796-03-3*

## Preschool

**3883 Access for All: Integrating Deaf, Hard of Hearing, and Hearing Preschoolers**

Harris Communications
15155 Technology Drive
Eden Prairie, MN 55344      952-906-1180
800-825-6758
FAX 952-906-1099
TDY:952-906-1198
http://www.harriscomm.com
e-mail: info@harriscmm.com
*Gail Solit, Author*
*Robert Harris, Owner*
*Maral Taylor, Author*

Covers basic information needed to establish a successful preschool program for deaf and hearing children; interagency cooperation, staff training, and parental involvement. *$29.95*

*169 pages Video-90 min.*

**3884 Administrator's Policy Handbook for Preschool Mainstreaming**

Brookline Books
300 Bedford Street
Manchester, NH 03101      617-734-6772
FAX 603-922-3348
http://www.brooklinebooks.com
*Barbara J Smith, Author*

Prepared specifically for the public school administrator who is developing the policies and procedures to place young children with disabilities in mainstreamed settings. *$39.95*

**3885 Early Intervention in Natural Environments**

Brooks/Cole Publishing Company
511 Forest Lodge Road
Pacific Grove, CA 93950      831-373-0728
FAX 831-375-6414
*Noonan and McCormick, Author*
*Carolyn Crockett, Marketing Manager*
*Barbara Smallwood, Marketing Assistant*

Organized by topical area, this text offers the skills to adapt assessment and intervention methods to the needs of the child as well as the wishes of the parent. While emphasizing child independence, support, empowerment, and family enablement, the authors explore issues such as early intervention methods, procedures for infants, toddlers, preschoolers and their families, and the role of play as learning opportunities.

*412 pages*
*ISBN 0-534144-42-0*

**3886 KDES Preschool Curriculum Guide**

Harris Communications
15155 Technology Drive
Eden Prairie, MN 55344      952-906-1180
800-825-6758
FAX 952-906-1099
TDY:952-906-1198
http://www.harriscomm.com
e-mail: info@harriscmm.com
*Robert Harris, Owner*

A complete, four-year program developed for preschool children who are deaf or hard of hearing. The guide offers a comprehensive scope and sequence of objectives, resource units and evaluation tools: a sample instructional unit; a bibliography; and a record-keeping system for student progress. Also contains general information for teachers and administrators, including how to modify the program for children with special needs.

*327 pages*

**3887 When Slow Is Fast Enough: Educating the Delayed Preschool Child**

Guilford Publications
72 Spring Street
New York, NY 10012      212-431-9800
800-365-7006
FAX 212-966-6708
http://www.guilford.com
e-mail: info@guilford.com
*Joan F Goodman, Author*
*Robert Coles, Foreword*
*Barry Duncan, Author*

Bold and controversial book critiques early intervention programs that attempt to accelerate development in delayed young children. Goodman suggests that in pressuring these children to perform more, and sooner, we are undermining their capacity for independent development and depriving them of the freedom we insist upon for the nondelayed. *$18.95*

*306 pages Paperback*

## Reading

**3888  Dyslogic Syndrome**

Learning Disabilities Association of America
4156 Library Road
Pittsburgh, PA  15234          412-341-1515
                              FAX 412-344-0224
                           http://www.ldanatl.org
                        e-mail: ldanatl@usaor.net
*Jane Browning, Editor-in-Chief*

  *$2.00*

**3889  Gillingham Manual**

Educators Publishing Service
31 Smith Place
Cambridge, MA  02139          617-547-6706
                              800-225-5750
                           FAX 617-547-0412
                         http://www.epsbooks.com
                        e-mail: eps@epsbooks.com
*Anna Gillingham Bessie W Stillman, Author*
*Steven Courtes, President*

This classic in the field of specific language disability
has now been completely revised and updated. The
manual covers reading, spelling, writing and dictionary technique. It may be used with individuals or
small groups. *$60.00*

  *352 pages*
  *ISBN 0-838802-00-1*

**3890  Phonic Remedial Reading Lessons**

Academic Therapy Publications
20 Commercial Boulevard
Novato, CA  94949          415-883-3314
                          888-287-9975
                       FAX 415-883-3720
                     http://www.atpub.com
                    e-mail: atpub@aol.com
*Debrah Akers, Editor*

A step-by-step program for teaching reading to children who failed to learn by conventional methods.
Consistent sound-symbol relationships are presented
and reinforced using a grapho-vocal method. *$15.00*

  *144 pages*
  *ISBN 0-878795-08-1*

**3891  Phonology and Reading Disability**

University of Michigan Press
839 Greene Street
Ann Arbor, MI  48104          734-764-4388
                              FAX 734-615-1540
                         http://www.press.umich.edu
                   e-mail: umpress_orders@umich.edu
*Donald Shankweiler, Author*
*Mary Erwin, Assistant Director*

Argues the association of words with the sounds they
represent is crucial to the learning process. *$47.50*

  *ISBN 1-472101-33-1*

**3892  Preventing Reading Difficulties in Young
       Children**

National Academies Press
500 Fifth NW
Washington, DC  20055          202-334-3313
                               800-624-6242
                            FAX 202-334-1891
                            http://www.nap.edu
*National Research Council, Author*
*Barbara Klein-Pope, Executive Director*

Examines factors that put children at risk of poor reading. Explores in detail how literacy can be fostered
from birth through kindergarten and the primary
grades including evaluation of philosophies, systems
and materials commonly used to teach reading.

**3893  Readability Revisited: The New Dale-Chall
       Readability Formula**

Brookline Books
300 Bedford Street
Manchester, NH  03101          617-734-6772
                               FAX 603-922-3348
                        http://www.brooklinebooks.com
Information is given on reading difficulties in children with learning disabilities and how to overcome
them.

  *168 pages*
  *ISBN 1-571290-08-7*

**3894  Reading Brain: The Biological Basis of Dyslexia**

Learning Disabilities Association of America
4156 Library Road
Pittsburgh, PA  15234          412-341-1515
                               FAX 412-344-0224
                            http://www.ldanatl.org
                         e-mail: ldanatl@usaor.net
*Jane Browning, Editor-in-Chief*

  *$35.00*

**3895  Reading Disabilities in College and High School**

Learning Disabilities Association of America
4156 Library Road
Pittsburgh, PA  15234          412-341-1515
                               FAX 412-344-0224
                            http://www.ldanatl.org
                         e-mail: ldanatl@usaor.net
*Aaron and Baker, Author*
*Jane Browning, Editor-in-Chief*

Offers a comprehensive guide to information on reading disabled students in the college and high school
arenas. *$23.00*

**3896  Reading Problems: Consultation and Remediation**

Guilford Publications
72 Spring Street
New York, NY  10012          212-431-9800
                             800-365-7006
                          FAX 212-966-6708
                        http://www.guilford.com
                      e-mail: info@guilford.com
*PG Aaron, Author*
*R Joshi, Author*

Offers information to educators on consultation and remediation programs. *$30.00*

*285 pages*

**3897 Reading Programs that Work: A Review of Programs From Pre-K to 4th Grade**

Milken Family Foundation
1250 Fourth Street
Santa Monica, CA 90401 1353      310-570-4800
FAX 310-570-4801
http://www.mff.org
*Dr. John Schacter, Author*
*Richard Sandler, Executive Vice President*
*Lowell Milken, President*

This 72 page publication tackles two questions, why are some students failing to learn to read and what reading programs are proven to be effective? Included in this reading report are analyses of 35 different reading programs and their impact on student achievement.

**3898 Reading and Learning Disabilities: A Resource Guide**

NICHCY
PO Box 1492
Washington, DC 20013-149      202-884-8200
800-695-0285
FAX 202-884-8841
TDY:800-695-0285
http://www.nichcy.org
e-mail: nichcy@aed.org
*Donna Waghorn, Assistant Executive*
*Susan Ripley, Executive Director*

*12 pages*

**3899 Reading and Learning Disability: A Neuropsychological Approach to Evaluation & Instruction**

Charles C Thomas Publisher
2600 S 1st Street
Springfield, IL 62704      217-789-8980
800-258-8980
FAX 217-789-9130
http://www.ccthomas.com
e-mail: books@ccthomas.com
*Estelle L Fryburg, Author*
*Michael Thomas, Owner*
*Claire Slagler, Sales Manager*

This text utilizes the current knowledge of neuropsychology (brain-behavior relationships) and the concepts of cognitive psychology to provide an understanding of reading and learning disability which has a practical application to education. The primary goal of the book is to provide teachers, psychologists, physicians, concerned professionals, and parents with an interdisciplinary view of learning and schooling. *$79.95*

*398 pages Cloth*
*ISBN 0-398067-44-9*

**3900 Reading-Writing-Rage: The Terrible Price Paid by Victims of School Failure**

Jalmar Press
24426 South Main Street
Carson, CA 90745      310-816-3085
FAX 310-816-3092
http://www.jalmarpress.com
*DF Ungerleider, Author*

**3901 Reading/Learning Disability: An Ecological Approach**

Learning Disabilities Association of America
4156 Library Road
Pittsburgh, PA 15234      412-341-1515
FAX 412-344-0224
http://www.ldanatl.org
e-mail: ldanatl@usaor.net
*Bartoli & Botel, Author*
*Jane Browning, Editor-in-Chief*

*$9.00*

**3902 Starting Out Right: A Guide to Promoting Children's Reading Success**

National Academies Press
500 Fifth NW
Washington, DC 20055      202-334-3313
800-624-6242
FAX 202-334-1891
http://www.nap.edu
*National Research Council, Author*
*Barbara Klein-Pope, Executive Director*

Discusses how best to help children succeed in reading. The book identifies the important questions and explores the authoritative answers on the topic of how children can grow into readers. A resource for any adult who wants to lay down a solid language and literacy foundation for every child.

**3903 Teaching Reading to Disabled and Handicapped Learners**

Charles C Thomas Publisher
2600 S 1st Street
Springfield, IL 62704      217-789-8980
800-258-8980
FAX 217-789-9130
http://www.ccthomas.com
e-mail: books@ccthomas.com
*Harold D Love and Freddie W Litton, Author*
*Michael Thomas, President*

Guides prospective and present special education teachers in assisting and teaching handicapped learners to read. Integrates traditional methods with newer perspectives. Books sent on approval. Shipping charges: $5.50 US, $6.50 Canada. Prices subject to change without notice. *$54.95*

*260 pages Cloth*
*ISBN 0-398059-09-8*

**3904 Teaching the Dyslexic Child**

Academic Therapy Publications
20 Commercial Boulevard
Novato, CA 94949
415-883-3314
888-287-9975
FAX 415-883-3720
http://www.atpub.com
e-mail: atpub@aol.com

*Anita Griffiths, Author*
*Debrah Akers, Editor*

Dyslexia can be crushing to a child's self-image. The author shows teachers and parents how to focus on the child's ability and become a partner inlearning to help restore a positive self-image. *$13.00*

*128 pages*
*ISBN 0-878792-05-8*

**3905 Textbooks and the Students Who Can't Read Them**

Brookline Books
300 Bedford Street
Manchester, NH 03101
617-734-6772
FAX 603-922-3348
http://www.brooklinebooks.com

*Jean Ciborowski, Author*

Based on a careful analysis of 10 textbook programs, 5 science and 5 social studies, the author concisely and sensibly indicates the procedure that facilitates teacher's use of regular grade level textbooks with low-reading students. *$21.95*

**3906 Visual Processes in Reading and Reading Disabilities**

Lawrence Erlbaum Associates
365 Broadway
Hillsdale, NJ 07642
201-666-4110
800-926-6579
FAX 201-666-2394

*Dale Willows, Author*
*Judy Nam, Owner*
*Evely Corcos, Author*

The purpose of this book is to bring together a broad range of evidence that concerns the role of visual information in reading and reading disabilities. Because reading processes are of central interest to cognitive scientists, neuropsychologists, psycholinguists, clinicians, and educators, this book should draw a very broad readership. *$89.95*

*504 pages*
*ISBN 0-805809-00-7*

**3907 Why Wait for a Criterion of Failure?**

Educators Publishing Service
31 Smith Place
Cambridge, MA 02139
617-547-6706
800-225-5750
FAX 617-547-0412
http://www.epsbooks.com
e-mail: eps@epsbooks.com

*B Slingerland, Author*
*Steven Courtes, President*

A monograph concerning the teaching of reading to learning disabled students using the multi-sensory approach, which is the crux of the Orton-Gillingham approach. This book describes structured lessons, with sample word lists, and reading lessons. *$6.00*

*48 pages*
*ISBN 0-838802-43-5*

## Social Skills

**3908 ADHD in the Schools: Assessment andIntervention Strategies**

Guilford Publications
72 Spring Street
New York, NY 10012
212-431-9800
800-365-7006
FAX 212-966-6708
http://www.guilford.com
e-mail: info@guilford.com

*George DuPaul, Author*
*Gary Stoner, Author*

For psychologists, educators, and others who are involved in the treatment of children with ADD. Addresses such problems as academic under achievement, noncompliance with classroom rules, and problematic peer relationships. Tells school professionals how to identify and assess students who might have ADHD and how to develop and implement classroom-based programs. *$30.00*

*269 pages*

**3909 Behavior Change in the Classroom: Self-Management Interventions**

Guilford Publications
72 Spring Street
New York, NY 10012
212-431-9800
800-365-7006
FAX 212-966-6708
http://www.guilford.com
e-mail: info@guilford.com

*Edward Shapiro, Author*
*Christine Cole, Author*

This book presents practical approaches for designing and implementing self-management interventions in school settings. An excellent resource for school-based practitioners who wish to address the needs of all school-age children and adolescents. *$26.95*

*204 pages*

**3910 Group Activities to Include Students with Special Needs**

Corwin Press
2455 Teller Road
Thousand Oaks, CA 91320
805-499-9734
800-818-7243
FAX 805-499-5323
http://www.corwinpress.com
e-mail: order@corwinpress.com

*Julia Wilkins, Author*
*Kimberly Gonzales, Marketing Director*
*Robb Clouse, Senior Acquisitions Editor*

This guide provides teachers with easily referenced tools for any situation and skill level, including skill development categories and icons showing which abilities are needed for each activity. An essential resource for both new and veteran teachers of students with special needs. *$34.95*

*240 pages*

*ISBN 0-761977-26-0*

## 3911 Joy of Listening

**Harris Communications**
**15155 Technology Drive**
**Eden Prairie, MN 55344**          952-906-1180
                                    800-825-6758
                        FAX 952-906-1099
                        TDY:952-906-1198
                http://www.harriscomm.com
                e-mail: info@harriscmm.com
*Janice Baliker Light, Author*
*Robert Harris, Owner*

Includes lessons that improve listening skills, auditory discrimination, attention span, and memory in hearing-impaired children and adults. Also recommended for learning-disabled children with auditory weaknesses. Many of the sections may be used for teaching lipreading skills. *$12.95*

*148 pages Paperback*

## 3912 Key Concepts in Personal Development

**Marsh Media**
**8082 Ward Parkway Plaza**
**Kansas City, MO 64114**          816-523-1059
                                    800-821-3303
                        FAX 866-333-7421
                http://www.marshmedia.com
                e-mail: info@marshmedia.com
*Joan Marsh, President*
*Liz Sweeney, Editorial Assistant*

Our videos, books, and teaching guides bring character education to the classroom. These kits are invaluable aids in teaching everyday values like honesty, anger control, trustworthiness, perseverance, understanding and respect. They help you prepare youngsters to meet challenges and greet opportunities with skill and optimism.

## 3913 Progress Program

**Edge Enterprises**
**PO Box 1304**
**Lawrence, KS 66044**          785-749-1473
                        FAX 785-749-0207
                e-mail: eeinfo@edgeenterprises
*Jean Schumaker, Melbourne Hovell, James Sherman, Author*
*Jacqueline Schafer, Managing Editor*

Describes how teachers, administrators and parents can work together to use a Daily Report Card Program to control disruptive student behavior and improve the academic and social performance of students who are at-risk for failure. This program is carefully sequenced to move from extrinsic control to student (intrinsic) control of behavior. *$10.00*

*96 pages Paperback*

## 3914 Social Perception and Learning Disabilities

**Learning Disabilities Association of America**
**4156 Library Road**
**Pittsburgh, PA 15234**          412-341-1515
                        FAX 412-344-0224
                http://www.ldanatl.org
                e-mail: ldanatl@usaor.net
*Jane Browning, Editor-in-Chief*

*$6.00*

## 3915 Teaching Social Skills to Hearing Impaired Students

**Harris Communications**
**15155 Technology Drive**
**Eden Prairie, MN 55344**          952-906-1180
                                    800-825-6758
                        FAX 952-906-1099
                        TDY:952-906-1198
                http://www.harriscomm.com
                e-mail: info@harriscmm.com
*Robert Harris, Owner*
*Maureen Smith MA, Author*

Provides teachers and parents with a comprehensive, hands-on program to develop important social skills in hearing-impaired children and young adults. *$24.95*

*203 pages Paperback*

## 3916 Training for Independent Living Curriculum

**RPM Press**
**PO Box 31483**
**Tucson, AZ 85751**          520-886-1990
                                888-810-1990
                        FAX 520-886-1990
*Jan Stonebraker, Operations Manager*

Provides educators and rehabilitation personnel with a 400 page curriculum designed to help teach developmentally disabled and other severely challenged persons essential independent living skills including personal and social adjustment, money management, meal preparation, money handling, personal safety, grooming and more. *$79.95*

## Publications

**3917 Above and Beyond**

AASCU
1 Dupont Circle NW
Washington, DC 20036          202-293-7070
                             FAX 202-833-4760

*Jade Ann Gingerich, Author*

Describes college services for students with learning disabilities. *$8.00*

*32 pages*

**3918 Assisting College Students with Learning Disabilities: A Tutor's Manual**

Association on Higher Education and Disability
PO Box 540666
Waltham, MA 02454          781-788-0003
                          FAX 781-788-0033
                          http://www.ahead.org
e-mail: ahead@postbox.acs.ohio-state.edu

This resource manual is for service providers who want to take concrete action toward integrating women with disabilities into the mainstream of college life. *$9.95*

**3919 Campus Opportunities for Students with Learning Differences**

Octameron Associates
PO Box 2748
Alexandria, VA 22301          703-836-5480
                             FAX 703-836-5650
                    http://www.octameron.com

*J Katz, Public Relations Director*

A book about going to college for young adults with various types of learning disabilities. Details questions to ask in selecting a college. CAMPUS OPPORTUNITIES teaches how to be a self-advocate. *$7.00*

*48 pages Biannual*
*ISBN 1-575090-52-X*

**3920 Chronicle Financial Aid Guide**

Chronicle Guidance Publications
66 Aurora Street
Moravia, NY 13118          315-497-0330
                          800-622-7284
                    FAX 315-497-3359
        http://www.chronicleguidance.com
    e-mail: janet@chronicleguidance.com

*Janet Seemann, Managing Editor*

Offers information on more than 1,950 financial aid programs, offering over 400,000 awards from current, verified sources. *$24.98*

*424 pages Annual*
*ISBN 1-556312-91-1*

**3921 College Placement Council Directory**

College Placement Council
62 Highland Avenue
Bethlehem, PA 18017          610-868-1421
                            800-544-5272
                    http://www.naceweb.org

Offers the who's who in the college placement/recruitment field. *$47.95*

**3922 Colleges/Universities that Accept Students with Learning Disabilities**

Learning Disabilities Association of America
4156 Library Road
Pittsburgh, PA 15234          412-341-1515
                             FAX 412-344-0224
                    http://www.ldanatl.org
            e-mail: ldanatl@usaor.net

*Jane Browning, Editor-in-Chief*

List of colleges by state. *$4.00*

**3923 Directory of Catholic Special Education Programs and Facilities**

National Catholic Education Association
1077 30th Street NW
Washington, DC 20007          202-337-6232
                             FAX 202-333-6706
                    http://www.ncea.org
            e-mail: nceadmin@ncea.org

A valuable resource for anyone seeking appropriate placements in Catholic settings. *$8.00*

*100 pages*
*ISBN 1-558330-11-9*

**3924 Directory of Educational Facilities for Learning Disabled Students**

Learning Disabilities Association of America
4156 Library Road
Pittsburgh, PA 15234          412-341-1515
                             FAX 412-344-0224
                    http://www.ldanatl.org
            e-mail: ldanatl@usaor.net

*Jane Browning, Editor-in-Chief*

A large directory offering information on educational facilities nationwide accepting and schooling learning disabled students. *$4.00*

**3925 Dispelling the Myths: College Students and Learning Disabilities**

National Center for Learning Disabilities
381 Park Avenue S
New York, NY 10016          212-545-7510
                           888-575-7373
                    FAX 212-545-9665
                    http://www..ld.org
            e-mail: help@ncld.org

*James Wendors, Director*
*Marcia Pauyo, Executive Assistant*

A monograph for students and educators that explains what learning disabilities are and what faculty members can do to help students with learning disabilities achieve success in college.

**3926  Four-Year College Databook**

Chronicle Guidance Publications
66 Aurora Street
Moravia, NY  13118          315-497-0330
                                       800-622-7284
                           FAX 315-497-3359
http://www.ChronicleGuidance.com
e-mail: janet@chronicleguidance.com
*Janet Seemann, Managing Editor*
*Nancy Carmody, Marketing*

Chronicle Four-Year College Databook contains two sections: The Four-Year College Majors section lists 2,160 institutions offering 790 four-year graduate and professional majors. *$24.99*

*487 pages  Annual*
*ISBN 1-556312-92-X*

**3927  From Access to Equity**

Association on Higher Education and Disability
PO Box 540666
Waltham, MA  02454          781-788-0003
                           FAX 781-788-0033
http://www.ahead.org
e-mail: ahead@postbox.acs.ohio-state.edu
This resource manual is for service providers who want to take concrete action toward integrating women with disabilities into the mainstream of college life. *$9.95*

**3928  Getting LD Students Ready for College**

HEATH Resource Center
2121 K Street NW
Washington, DC  20036          202-973-0904
                                       800-544-3284
                           FAX 202-973-0908
http://www.heath.gwu.edu
e-mail: askheath@askheath.gwu.edu
*Carol Sullivan, Counselor*
*Dan Gardner, Publications Manager*

List offering parents, counselors, teachers and learning disabled students a reminder of helpful skills and necessary steps to take as a high school student with a learning disability moves toward college.

**3929  Guide to Colleges for Learning Disabled Students**

Academic Success Press
6023 26th Strete
West Bradenton, FL  34206          941-359-2819
                                       800-444-2524
                           FAX 800-777-2525
*Mary Liscio, Editor*

**3930  Guide to Community Colleges Serving Students with Learning Disabilities**

Mississippi State University/ Student Services
01 Montgomery
University, MS  38677          662-325-3335
                           FAX 662-325-8190
http://www.ms.state.edu
e-mail: dbaker@saffairs.ms.state.edu
*Sonja Burnham, Author*
*Debbie Baker, Executive Director*
*Julie Berry, Assistant Director*

A list by state of two-year community colleges in Mississippi, Alabama, Georgia, Tennessee and Florida, describing services and accommodations provided for students with learning disabilities. *$1.50*

**3931  HEATH Resource Directory**

National Clearinghouse on Postsecondary Education
1 Dupont Circle NW
Washington, DC  20036          202-939-9300
                           FAX 202-833-4760
e-mail: askheath@askheath.gwu.edu
*Dan Gardner, Publications Manager*

Annotated listings of over 150 national organizations which can provide additional information about postsecondary education and individuals with disabilities. *$1.00*

*30 pages*

**3932  Higher Education Information Center**

Boston Public Library
700 Boylston Street
Boston, MA  02116          617-536-0200
                                       800-442-1171
                           FAX 617-266-4673
http://www.bpl.org
e-mail: hr@bpl.org
*Willis Hulings, President*
*Ann Coles, Vice President*

Offers information on colleges and universities, vocational/technical schools, financial aid and careers, counseling on school selection and paying for educational costs.

**3933  How the Student with Hearing Loss Can Succeed in College**

Harris Communications
15155 Technology Drive
Eden Prairie, MN  55344          952-906-1180
                                       800-825-6758
                           FAX 952-906-1099
                           TDY:952-906-1198
http://www.harriscomm.com
e-mail: info@harriscmm.com
*Carol PhD, Editor*
*Robert Harris, Owner*
*Ron Leavitt MS, Editor*

A handbook for students families and professionals. Includes information on academic, financial, technological, and support services. *$28.95*

*278 pages  Paperback*

**3934  How to Succeed in College with Dyslexia**

Learning Disabilities Association of America
4156 Library Road
Pittsburgh, PA  15234          412-341-1515
                           FAX 412-344-0224
http://www.ldanatl.org
e-mail: ldanatl@usaor.net
*J Woods, Author*
*Jane Browning, Editor-in-Chief*

Offers information on college education for children with dyslexia. *$19.95*

**3935 How to Succeed in College: A Handbook for Students with Learning Disabilities**

National Center on Employment and Disability
201 IU Willets Road
Albertson, NY 11507                    516-747-5400
                                    FAX 516-747-5378
                                    TDY:516-746-5355
                                    http://www.ncds.org
*Jennifer Neft, Assistant Director*

These two volumes demonstrate the advantages of co-operation between vocational rehabilitation and education. *$15.00*

**3936 ISS Directory of International Schools**

International Schools Services
15 Roszel Road
Princeton, NJ 08540                    609-452-0990
                                    FAX 609-452-2690
                                    http://www.iss.edu
                                    e-mail: iss@iss.edu
*John Nicklas, President*

Comprehensive guide to over 550 American and international schools worldwide. *$45.95*

*550 pages  Plus S&H*
*ISBN 0-913663-17-5*

**3937 K&W Guide to Colleges for the Learning Disabled**

HarperCollins Publishers
10 E 53rd Street
New York, NY 10022                    212-207-7000
                                    800-242-8192
                                    FAX 212-207-7145
                                    http://www.harpercollins.com
*Marybeth Kravets, Author*
*Imy Wax, Author*

Offers information on support services for learning disabled college students. Includes learning disability services available, programs offered, college graduation requirements, admissions policies, costs, housing, tutorial help, learning resource centers and athletics.

**3938 Learning to Care**

Incorporation For National & Community Service
1201 New York Avenue NW
Washington, DC 20525                    202-606-5000
                                    FAX 202-565-2777

A national directory of student community service programs.

**3939 National Association of Private Schools for Exceptional Children**

NAPSEC
1522 K Street NW
Washington, DC 20005                    202-408-3338
                                    FAX 202-408-3340
                                    http://www.napsec.com
                                    e-mail: napsec@aol.com
*Sherry Kolbe, Executive Director*
*Alison Figi, Communications Coordinator*

A membership directory listing NAPSEC'S members. Information given includes: disabilities served, program descriptions, school profiles, admissions procedures and funding approval. *$32.00*

*300 pages*

**3940 Peterson's Colleges with Programs for Students with Learning Disabilities or ADD**

Peterson's
2000 Lenox Drive
Lawrenceville, NJ 08648                    609-896-1800
                                    800-338-3282
                                    FAX 609-896-1811
                                    http://www.petersons.com
                                    e-mail: custsvce@petersons.com
*Charles Mangrum II, Author*
*Mary Gatsch, Officer In Charge*

Directs special-needs students to educational programs and services at 1,000 two-and four-year colleges and universities in the US and Canada. *$29.95*

*672 pages  Sixth Edition*
*ISBN 0-768904-55-2*

**3941 Questions to Aid in Selecting an Appropriate College Program for LD**

CT Association for Children and Adults with LD
25 Van Zant Street
East Norwalk, CT 06855                    203-838-5010
                                    FAX 203-866-6108
                                    http://www.CACLD.org
                                    e-mail: caccld@optonline.net
*Marie Armstrong, Information Specialist*
*Beryl Kaufman, Executive Director*

A collection of five one page information sheets, each from a different source. *$2.00*

*$1.00 shipping*

**3942 Schoolsearch Guide to Colleges with Programs & Services for Students with LD**

Schoolsearch Press
127 Marsh Street
Belmont, MA 02478                    617-489-5785
                                    FAX 617-489-5641
                                    http://schoolsearch.com
                                    e-mail: mlipkin@schoolsearch.com
*Midge Lipkin, President*

Lists more than 770 colleges and universities that offer programs and services to high school graduates with learning disabilities. *$39.95*

*1660 pages  3rd Edition*
*ISBN 0-962032-67-0*

**3943 Shopper's Guide to Colleges Serving the Learning Disabled College Student**

Learning Disabilities Association of America
4156 Library Road
Pittsburgh, PA 15234                    412-341-1515
                                    FAX 412-344-0224
                                    http://www.ldanatl.org
                                    e-mail: ldanatl@usaor.net
*Fred Barbaro, Author*
*Jane Browning, Editor-in-Chief*

*$3.00*

**3944   Two-Year College Databook**

Chronicle Guidance Publications
66 Aurora Street
Moravia, NY  13118                    315-497-0330
                                      800-899-0454
                                  FAX 315-497-3359
                http://www.chronicleguidance.com
                e-mail: janet@chronicleguidance.com
*Janet Seemann, Managing Editor*

Comprehensive package offers students and counselors up-to-date information for selection colleges. The Chronical Two-Year Databook contains information on college majors, and on 2,432 institutions offering 760 occupational-career, associate, and transfer programs. *$24.97*

*385 pages  Annual*
*ISBN 1-556312-93-8*

**3945   Vocational School Manual**

Chronicle Guidance Publications
66 Aurora Street
Moravia, NY  13118                    315-497-0330
                                      800-899-0454
                                  FAX 315-497-3359
                http://www.chronicleguidance.com
                e-mail: janet@chronicleguidance.com
*Janet Seemann, Managing Editor*

Offers information on occupational education programs currently available in the United States, Guam, and Puerto Rico. Programs consist of study or training leading to definite occupations. Prepares people for employment in recognized occupations, helps people make educated occupational choices, and upgrade and update their occupational skills. Includes data on vocational schools offering postsecondary occupational education. Accrediting associations are listed with contact information. *$24.96*

*260 pages  Annual*
*ISBN 1-556312-90-8*

**3946   World of Options: A Guide to International Education**

Mobility International USA
PO Box 10767
Eugene, OR  97440                     541-343-1284
                                  FAX 541-343-6812
                              http://www.miusa.org
                              e-mail: info@miusa.org
*Christa Bucks, Editor*

Offers information on a wide variety of opportunities available to disabled participants including travel and international programs, and personal experience stories from people with disabilities who have had successful international experiences. *$35.00*

*600 pages*

## Alabama

**3947   Alabama Aviation and Technical College**

Enterprise Ozark Community College
3405 South US Highway 231
Ozark, AL  36360                      334-774-5113
                                      800-624-3468
                                  FAX 334-774-6399
                              http://www.eocc.edu
*Stafford Thompson, President*
*Terry Spicer, Vice President*

A public two-year college with 15 special education students out of a total of 600. Certified by the Federal Aviation Administration, and offers the only comprehensive aviation maintenance training program in the state of Alabama, with instruction in airframe, powerplant and avionics.

**3948   Alabama Southern Community College**

PO Box 2000
Monroeville, AL  36461                251-575-3156
                              http://www.ascc.edu
*Theada Samuel*

A public two-year college with 21 special education students out of a total of 1,127.

**3949   Auburn University**

Program for Students with Disabilities
1244 Haley Center
Auburn, AL  36849                     334-844-2096
                                  FAX 334-844-2099
                             http://www.auburn.edu
*Kelly Haynas, Director*
*Tonia Barron, Administrative Assistant*

Four year college offering services to students with learning disabilities.

**3950   Auburn University at Montgomery**

Center for Special Services
Library Tower, 7th Floor
Montgomery, AL  36124                 334-244-3468
                                  FAX 334-244-3907
                                 TDY:334-244-3754
                                http://www.aum.edu
                          e-mail: tmassey@mickey.aum.edu
*Holly Brown, Acting Director*
*Tamara Massey-Garret, Student Services Coordinator*

Offers a variety of services to students with disabilities including equipment, extended testing time, interpreting services, counseling services, and special accommodations.

**3951   Birmingham-Southern College**

900 Arkadelphia Road
Birmingham, AL  35254                 205-226-4672
                                      800-523-5793
                                  FAX 205-226-4627
                                http://www.bsc.edu
*Judith Cox, Director Academic Advising*
*Sara Hoover, Director Personal Counseling*

Offers a variety of services to students with disabilities including notetakers, extended testing time, counseling services, and special accommodations.

**3952** **Bishop State Community College**
414 Stanton Street
Mobile, AL 36617 250-690-6801
http://www.bscc.cc.al.us
e-mail: info@bscc.cc.al.us
*Carrie Moore, Counselor*

A public two-year college with 2 special education students out of a total of 2144.

**3953** **Chattahoochee Valley State Community College**
2602 College Drive
Pheonix City, AL 36867 334-291-4900
FAX 334-291-4944
http://www.cvcc.cc.al.us
*Jacquie Thacker, ADA Coordinator*

Offers a variety of services to students with disabilities including note takers, extended testing time, counseling services and special accommodations.

**3954** **George County Wallace State Community College**
300 E Goodwin Parkway
Selma, AL 36702 334-876-9227
FAX 334-876-9250
http://www.wccs.edu
*Gail May, Dean*
*James Mitchell, President*

Offers a variety of services to students with disabilities including note takers, extended testing time, counseling services and special accommodations.

**3955** **Horizons School**
2111 University Boulevard
Birmingham, AL 35233 205-322-6606
800-822-6242
FAX 205-322-6605
http://www.horizonsschool.org
e-mail: mcelheny@horizonsschool.org
*Jade Carter MD, Director*
*Marie McElheny, Assistant Director*

Serves students age 19-26 with specific learning disabilities and other mild learning problems. Gives students the opportunity to establish friendships, prepares students for successful transition to the community and offers courses in career, life and social skills.

**3956** **Jacksonville State University**
700 Pelham Road N
Jacksonville, AL 36265 256-782-5400
FAX 256-782-5121
http://www.jsu.edu
e-mail: lbedford@jsucc.jsu.edu
*Daniel Miller, Director*
*William Maham, President*

Offers a variety of services to students with disabilities including notetakers, extended testing time, counseling services, and special accommodations.

**3957** **James H Faulkner State Community College**
1900 US Highway 31 S
Bay Minette, AL 36507 251-580-2100
800-231-3752
FAX 251-580-2226
http://www.faulknerstate.edu
e-mail: bkennedy@faulknerstate.edu
*Brenda Kennedy MD, Dean Student Development*
*Nancy Williams, College Receptionist*

A public two-year community college with approximately 125 students with disabilities out of a total student population of 4,350. Committed to the professional and cultural growth of each student without regard to race, color, qualified disability, gender, religion, creed, national origin, or age. Attempts to provide an educational environment that promotes development and learning through a wide variety of educational programs, adequate and comfortable facilities, and flexible scheduling.

**3958** **John M Patterson State Technical College**
H Council Tren Holn State Tech
3920 Troy Highway
Montgomery, AL 36116 334-288-1080
FAX 334-284-9357
http://www.trenholntech.cc.us
e-mail: jjoyce@trenhontech.cc.al.us
*Jerry Joyce, Coordinator*

A public two-year college with 101 special education students out of a total of 800.

**3959** **Lureen B Wallace Community College**
1708 N Main Street
Opp, AL 36467 334-493-3573
FAX 334-493-7003
http://www.lbwcc.edu
*Edward Meadows, President*

A public two-year college with 102 special education students out of a total of 630. Provides postsecondary occupational education on a nondiscriminatory basis for individuals who desire to prepare for entry level employment, advancement, or retraining in a career field.

**3960** **Marion Military Institute**
1101 Washington Street
Marion, AL 36756 334-683-2306
800-664-1842
FAX 334-683-2383
http://www.mairon-institue.org
*Col. P Carruthers, Admissions Director*

An independent two-year college with an academic advantage program for students with learning difficulties and for a limited number with diagnosed learning disabilities.

**3961** **Northeast Alabama Community College**
138 Alabama Highway 35 E
Rainsville, AL 35986 256-638-4418
FAX 256-228-6861
http://www.nacc.cc.al.us
*Elaine Hayden, Assistant Dean Instruction*

A public two-year college with support services for students with special needs that is consistant with the mission of the Alambama College System: to provide accessible quality educational opportunities, promote economic growth, and enhance the quality of life for people in Alabama.

**3962   Troy State University Dothan**
PO Box 8368
Dothan, AL  36304              334-983-6556
                               FAX 334-983-6322
                               http://www.tsud.edu
                               e-mail: kseagle@tsud.edu
*Keith Seagle, Director Counseling Services*

Offers a variety of services to students with disabilities including notetakers, extended testing time, counseling services, and special accommodations.

**3963   University of Alabama**
PO Box 870132
Tuscaloosa, AL  35487          205-348-4285
                               FAX 205-348-9046
                               http://www.ua.edu
*Cathy Hitt, Counselor*
*Karen Clayton, Manager Physical Disabilities*

A public four-year college with approximately 650 students identified with disabilities out of a total of 19,200.

**3964   University of Alabama: Huntsville**
301 Sparkman Drive
Huntsville, AL  35899          256-824-6070
                               FAX 256-824-6073
                               http://www.uah.edu
                               e-mail: admitme@email.uah.edu
*Delois Smith, Director*
*Frank , President*

Offers a variety of services and accommodations to assist students with disabilities in eliminating barriers they encounter in pursuing higher education.

**3965   University of Montevallo**
Station 6030
Montevallo, AL  35115          205-665-6000
                               FAX 205-665-6042
                               http://www.montevallo.edu
*Elaine Elledge, Special Services*
*Robert , President*

Offers a variety of services to students with disabilities including notetakers, extended testing time, counseling services, and special accommodations.

**3966   University of North Alabama**
Box 5008
Florence, AL  35630            256-765-4248
                               FAX 256-765-4904
                               http://www.una.edu
                               e-mail: jadams@unanov.una.edu
*Jennifer Adams, Associate Director*
*Kim Greenway, Director*

Developmental services of UNA provides accommodation and supportive services to assist students with disabilities throughout their college expirence.

**3967   University of South Alabama**
182 Adminstration Building
Mobile, AL  36688              251-460-6211
                               FAX 251-460-7827
                               http://www.usouthal.edu
                               e-mail: admiss@jaguarl.usouthal.edu
*Keith Ayers, Director*
*Diane Agee, Administrative Assistant*

Offers a variety of services to students with disabilities including note takers, extended testing time, counseling services, and special accommodations.

# Alaska

**3968   Alaska Pacific University**
**Disabled Student Services**
**4101 University Drive**
Anchorage, AK  99508           907-564-8345
                               FAX 907-564-8806
                               http://www.alaskapacific.edu
                               e-mail: tamera@alaskapacific.edu
*Tamera Randolph, Coordinator Disability Support*

Four-year college offering special services to students that are learning disabled.

**3969   Juneau Campus: University of Alaska Southeast**
**11120 Glacier Highway**
Juneau, AK  99801              907-465-6462
                               877-465-4827
                               FAX 907-465-6365
                               http://www.uas.alaska.edu
                               e-mail: uas.info@uas.alaska.edu
*Dolores Graver, Administrative Assistant*
*Joel Milsat, Director*

Offers a variety of services to students with disabilities including notetakers, extended testing time, counseling services, and special accommodations.

**3970   Ketchikan Campus: University of Alaska Southeast**
**2600 7th Avenue**
Ketchikan, AK  99901           907-225-6177
                               FAX 907-225-3624
                               http://www.ketch.alaska.edu
                               e-mail: info@uas.alaska.edu
*L Naugen, Assistant Professor*

Offers a variety of services to students with disabilities including note takers, extended testing time, counseling services and special accommodations.

**3971   University of Alaska Anchorage: Disability Support Services**
**3211 Providence Drive**
Anchorage, AK  99508           907-786-1480
                               FAX 907-786-4888
                               http://www.uaa.alaska.edu
                               e-mail: ayenrol@alaska.edu
*Lyn Stoller, Director*

Provides equal opportunites for students who experience disabilities.

**3972  University of Alaska: Fairbanks**
PO Box 757480
Fairbanks, AK  99775                907-474-7500
FAX 907-474-5379
http://www.uaf.edu
e-mail: fyadmission@uaf.edu
*Stacey Howdeshell, Administrative Assistant*
*Nancy Dix, President*

A public four-year college. Services provided to students with learning disabilities include: assistance determining accommodations, advocacy, testing accommodations, books on tape, peer support groups and individual counseling.

## Arizona

**3973  Arizona State University**
Box 870112
Tempe, AZ  85287                480-965-7788
FAX 480-965-3610
TDY:480-965-1234
http://www.asu.edu
e-mail: upgradingones@asu.edu
*Tedde Scharf, Director*

Four-year college that offers support to students with learning disabilities.

**3974  Eastern Arizona College**
615 N. Stadium Ave.
Thatcher, AZ  85552
800-678-3808
http://www.eac.edu
*Beverly Teague, Student Services*

Offers a variety of services to students with disabilities including note takers, extended testing time, counseling services and special accommodations.

**3975  Glendale Community College**
6000 W Olive Avenue
Glendale, AZ  85302                603-845-3000
FAX 623-845-3329
http://www.gc.maricopa.edu
*Mark Ferris, Coordinator Disability Service*
*Nancy Oreshack, LD Specialist*

A public two-year college with 212 special education students out of a total of 15,200.

**3976  Grand Canyon University**
3300 W Camelback Road
Phoenix, AZ  85061                602-589-2855
800-800-9776
FAX 602-589-2580
http://www.gcu.edu
e-mail: admiss@gcu.edu
*Jane Castillo MD, Instructor Education*
*Brent Richardson, President*

Offers a variety of services to students with disabilities including note takers, extended testing time, counseling services, and special accommodations.

**3977  Mesa Community College**
1833 W Southern Avenue
Mesa, AZ  85202                480-461-7870
FAX 480-461-7139
http://www.mc.maricopa.edu
*Judith Taussig, Special Services*

Offers a variety of services to students with disabilities including note takers, extended testing time, counseling services and special accommodations.

**3978  Northern Arizona University**
PO Box 4084
Flagstaff, AZ  86011                928-523-2223
FAX 928-523-7486
http://www.nau.edu
e-mail: undergraduate.admissions@nau.edu
*Marsha Fields, Director*

A public four-year college.

**3979  Phoenix College**
1202 W Thomas Road
Phoenix, AZ  85013                602-285-7476
FAX 602-285-7700
TDY:602-285-7477
http://www.pc.maricopa.edu
*Mitra Mehraban, Special Services*

A public two-year college with 23 special education students out of a total of 14,327.

**3980  Pima Community College**
2202 W Anklam Road
Tucson, AZ  85709                520-206-3139
FAX 520-206-6071
http://www.pima.edu
*Eric Morrison, Facility Advisor*
*Carolyn Reynolds, Administrator*

A public two-year college offering special education classes for students with disabilities.

**3981  Scottsdale Community College**
9000 E Chaparral Road
Scottsdale, AZ  85256                480-423-6517
FAX 480-423-6200
TDY:480-423-6377
http://www.scc.maricopa.edu
e-mail: donna.young@sccmail.maricopa.edu
*Donna Young, director*
*Becky Jaco, Program Adviser*

Student Services office works closely with learning disabled students to provide the best accommodations possible.

**3982  South Mountain Community College**
7050 S 24th Street
Phoenix, AZ  85040                602-243-8119
FAX 602-243-8118
http://www.smc.maricopa.edu
e-mail: winkharnar@smcmail.maricopa.edu
*Wink Harnar, Special Service Director*
*Janet Denson, Student Cooperative Director*

Offers a variety of services to students with disabilities including note takers, extended testing time, counseling services and special accommodations.

**3983   Spring Ridge Academy**
13690 S Burton Road
Spring Valley, AZ 86333          928-632-4602
                                 FAX 928-632-7661
         http://www.springridgeacademy.edu
         e-mail: sraemail@northlink.com
*Joe Gubbins, Principal*

**3984   University of Advancing Computer Technology**
2625 W Baseline Road
Tempe, AZ 85283                  602-383-8228
                                 800-658-5744
                                 FAX 602-383-8222
              http://www.uact.edu
              e-mail: admissions@uat.edu
*Daniel Edwards, National Admissions Director*

The University of Advancing Computer Technology
has a program for you. Areas of study include digital
animation production, game design, digital video production, interactive media, web design, graphic design, application development, computer
programming, database programming, Internet development and administration, network engineering,
game programming, network security, web site production, technology management, e-commerce marketing or internet database management.

**3985   University of Arizona**
PO Box 210040
Tucson, AZ 85721                 520-621-3237
                                 FAX 520-621-9799
              http://www.arizona.edu
              e-mail: appinfo@arizona.edu
*Sue Kroeger MD, Director*

The Strategic Alternative Learning Techniques
(SALT) Center values the achievement of individuals
with learning disabilities and provides an array of services to maximize student success.

**3986   Yavapai College**
Student Support Services
1100 E Sheldon Street
Prescott, AZ 86301               928-776-2117
                                 800-922-6787
                                 FAX 928-776-2030
              http://www.yc.edu
*Patricia Quinn-Kane, Learning Specialist*
*Carol Clayton, Director*

A public two-year college that offers a variety of services for students with disabilities.

## Arkansas

**3987   Arkansas Baptist College**
1600 Bishop Street
Little Rock, AR 72202            501-374-7856
                                 FAX 501-374-7856
              http://www.anicbapcol.edu
              e-mail: fredie.fox@arkbap.col
*Fredie Fox, registrar*
*Mrs. Williams, Administrative Assistant*

An independent four-year college with 44 special education students out of a total of 418.

**3988   Arkansas Northeastern College**
Student Support Services
PO Box 1109
Blytheville, AR 72316            870-762-1020
                                 FAX 870-763-1654
              http://www.anc.edu
              e-mail: mjeffers@anc.edu
*Myles Jeffers, Director*
*Tracy Jones, Office Assistant*

Offers a variety of services to students with disabilities including note takers, extended testing time,
counseling services and special accommodations.

**3989   Arkansas State University**
Disability Services
2105 E Aggie Road
Jonesboro, AR 72467              870-972-3964
                                 FAX 870-910-8048
                                 TDY:870-972-3965
              http://www.astate.edu
              e-mail: lglover@astate.edu
*Philip Hestand, Director for Counseling*
*Jennifer Ricemason, President*

Arranges for academic adjustments and auxiliary aids
to be provided to qualified students and coordinates
workplace accommodations.Will provide auxiliary
aids, without cost, to those students with verified disabilities who require such services.

**3990   Arkansas Tech University**
1605 Coliseum Drive
Russellville, AR 72801           479-968-0389
                                 FAX 479-968-0208
              http://www.atu.edu
*Janet Jones, Disabilities Coordinator*

Provides equal opportunities for higher education to
academically qualified individuals who are disabled.
Students are integrated as completely as possible into
the university community.

**3991   Garland County Community College**
101 College Drive
Hot Springs, AR 71913            501-760-4222
                                 888-671-1229
                                 FAX 501-760-4100
              http://www.gccc.cc.ar.us
              e-mail: tspencer@npcc.edu
*Tom Spencer, President*
*Luke , Vice President*

Offers a variety of services to students with disabilities including note takers, extended testing time,
counseling services and special accommodations.

**3992   Harding University**
900 E Center
Searcy, AR 72149                 501-279-4028
                                 800-477-4407
                                 FAX 501-279-4217
              http://www.harding.edu
              e-mail: admission@harding.edu
*Jim Johnston MD, Dir. Student Support Services*
*Teresa McLead, Disabilities Specialist*

Strives to deliver a program of services that will result
in increasing the college retention and graduation
rates of these students.

**3993  Jones Learning Center**
University of the Ozarks
415 N College Avenue
Clarksville, AR 72830        479-979-1403
                            800-264-8636
                       FAX 479-979-1429
                    http://www.ozarks.edu
                    e-mail: jlc@ozarks.edu
*Julia Frost, Director*
*Debby Mooney, Assistant Director Center*

An academic support unit that offers enhanced services to college students with diagnosed learning disabililites or attention deficit disorder. Services are individualized and focus on the development of strategies and skills to build upon strengths and circumvent deficits. The ratio of professional full time staff to students is 1:4.

**3994  Philander Smith College**
1 Trudy Kibbe Reed Drive
Little Rock, AR 72202         501-370-5221
                             800-446-6772
                        FAX 501-370-5225
                    http://www.philander.edu
            e-mail: administrator@philander.edu
*Arnella Hayes, Director*

Offers a variety of services to students with disabilities including notetakers, extended testing time, counseling services, and special accommodations.

**3995  Sheldon Jackson College**
801 Lincoln Street
Sitka, AK 99835              907-747-5208
                            800-478-4556
                       FAX 907-747-6366
                   http://www.sj-alaska.edu
           e-mail: yukonjohn@sj-alaska.edu
*Alice Smith, Director*

Seeks to help students find their forte, best learning modes, and best modes of expression; and seeks to help students prepare to find the greatest possible joy in vocation and service to others.

**3996  Southern Arkansas University**
Disabled Student Programs & Services
PO Box 9371
Magnolia, AR 71753          870-235-5262
                            800-332-7286
                       FAX 870-235-4931
                    http://www.saumag.edu
               e-mail: pwwoods@saumag.edu
*Paula Washington-Woods, Disability Support Services Dire*
*Beverly Rowden, Office Assistant*

Offers a variety of services to students with disabilities including notetakers, extended testing time, counseling services, and special accommodations.

**3997  University of Arkansas**
232 Silas Hunt Hall
Fayetteville, AR 72701       479-575-5346
                            800-377-8632
                       FAX 479-575-7515
                      http://www.uark.edu
            e-mail: uafadmis@comp.uark.edu
*Dawn Medley, Director Admissions*

Offers a variety of services to students with disabilities including note takers, extended testing time, counseling services, and special accommodations.

**3998  University of the Ozarks**
415 College Avenue
Clarksville, AR 72830
                            800-264-8636
                      http://www.ozarks.edu
             e-mail: jdecker@ozarks.edu
*Julia Frost, Director*

A four-year college that provides a learning center for students with learning disabilities.

## California

**3999  Academy of Art College**
Academy Resource Center
180 New Montgomery
San Francisco, CA 94015      415-263-8895
                     http://www.academyart.edu
           e-mail: nhaughnes@academyart.edu
*Natasha Haugnes, Academy Resource Director*
*Ryan Kashmir, Director of Student Support*

**4000  Allan Hancock College**
800 S College Drive
Santa Maria, CA 93454        805-922-6966
                        FAX 805-922-3556
                 http://www.hancockcollege.edu
             e-mail: malangko@hancock.edu
*Mark Malangko, LAP Director*
*Odette Tinhiro, Administrative Assistant*

Students with mobility, visual, hearing and speech impairments, learning disabilities, acquired brain injury, developmental disabilities, psychological and other disabilities are eligible to receive special services which enable them to fully participate in the community college experience at Allan Hancock College.

**4001  Antelope Valley College**
3041 W Avenue K
Lancaster, CA 93536          661-722-6300
                        FAX 661-722-6361
                       http://www.avc.edu
                   e-mail: info@avc.edu
*David Greenleaf, Learning Disability Specialist*

A public two-year college with 228 learning disabled students out of a total of 11,105.

**4002  Bakersfield College**
1801 Panorama Drive
Bakersfield, CA 93305        661-395-4011
                        FAX 661-395-4500
                     http://www.bc.cc.ca.us
*Tim Bohan, Director*

A public two-year college with 207 special education students out of a total of 12,312.

**4003 Barstow Community College**
Disabled Student Programs & Services
2700 Barstow Road
Barstow, CA 92311          619-252-2411
FAX 619-252-1875
http://www.barstow.cc.ca.us
e-mail: dsps@barstow.cc.ca.us
*Gene Pfeifer, Counselor*
*Gordon Smith, LD Specialist*

Educational support program for disabled students including special classes and support services for all disabled students.

**4004 Bethany College**
Special Advising
800 Bethany Drive
Scott Valley, CA 95066          831-438-3800
800-843-9410
FAX 408-438-4517
http://www.bethany.edu
*Kathy Tagg, Director*
*Barbara , Special Advising Counselor*

An independent four-year college with support services for special education students.

**4005 Biola University**
13800 Biola Avenue
La Mirada, CA 90639          562-903-6000
800-OKBIOLA
FAX 562-903-4709
http://www.biola.edu
e-mail: tom-engle@peter.biola.edu
*Tim Engle, Coordinator*
*Michelle Masterson, Staff*

Christian liberal arts university responsible for all programs related to students with disabilities.

**4006 Butte College**
3536 Butte Campus Drive
Oroville, CA 95965          530-895-2511
FAX 530-895-2345
http://www.butte.edu
*Richard Dunn, LD Specialist*

A public two-year college with 223 special education students out of a total of 12,848.

**4007 Cabrillo College**
3500 Soquel Drive
Aptos, CA 95003          831-479-6390
FAX 831-479-6393
http://www.cabrillo.cc.ca.us
e-mail: frlynch@cabrillo.cc.ca.us
*Frank Lynch, Director*

A two-year college that offers services and programs to disabled students.

**4008 California Lutheran University**
60 W Olsen Road
Thousand Oaks, CA 91360          805-493-3260
FAX 805-493-3472
TDY:800-735-2929
http://www.clunet.edu
e-mail: cluadm@clunet.edu
*Damian Pena, Director*
*Lisa Spreen, Administrative Assistant*

Offers a variety of services to students with disabilities including notetakers, extended testing time, counseling services, and special accommodations.

**4009 California Polytechnic State University: San Luis Obispo**
Disability Resource Center
1 Grand Avenue
San Luis Obispo, CA 93407          805-756-1111
FAX 805-756-5400
TDY:805-756-1395
http://www.calpoly.edu
e-mail: admissions@calpoly.edu
*William Bailey, Director*
*Warren Baker, President*

Comprehensive program of academic advisement, disability management, and support services, including peer mentors; currently providing services to more than 350 students with learning disabilities, 700 students with various disabilities total.

**4010 California State Polytechnic University: Pomona**
3801 W Temple Avenue
Pomona, CA 91768          909-468-5020
FAX 909-869-4529
http://www.csupomona.edu
e-mail: cppadmit@csupomona.edu
*Fred Henderson, Director*

Offers a variety of services to students with disabilities including notetakers, extended testing time, counseling services, and special accommodations.

**4011 California State University: Bakersfield**
Services for Students with Disabilities
9001 Stockdale Highway
Bakersfield, CA 93311          661-664-3360
FAX 661-664-2171
TDY:661-665-6288
http://www.csubak.edu
e-mail: jclausen@csub.edu
*Janice Clausen, Director*
*Patrick Choi, Assistant Director*

Four year college which provides services to the learning disabled.

**4012 California State University: Chico**
400 W 1st Street
Chico, CA 95929          530-898-4428
800-542-4426
FAX 530-898-6456
http://www.csuchico.edu
*Billie Jackson, Director*

To facilitate accommodation requests and provide the support services necessary to ensure equal access to university programs for students with disabilities.

**4013 California State University: Dominguez Hills**
1000 E ViCourtoria Street
Carson, CA 90747                        310-243-3660
                                        FAX 310-516-4247
                                        http://www.csudh.edu
                                        e-mail: pwells@csudh.edu
*Patricia Wells, Director*
*Mark Smith, Counselor*

The purpose of the Disabled Student Services (DSS) program is to make all of the University's educational, cultural social and physical facilities available to students with disabilities. The program serves as a centralized source of information for students with disabilities and those who work with them. By providing support services, DSS assists students with disabilities in the enhancement of their academic, career and personal development.

**4014 California State University: Fresno**
Services for Students with Disabilities
5200 N Barton
Fresno, CA 93740                        559-278-6511
                                        FAX 559-278-4214
                                        http://ww.csufresno.edu
                                        e-mail: pat_blore@csufresno.edu
*Pat Blore, Coordinator*

Four year college that provides students with services for the learning disabled.

**4015 California State University: Fullerton**
Disabled Student Services
University Hall 101
Fullerton, CA 92834                     714-278-3117
                                        FAX 714-278-2408
                                        TDY:714-278-2786
                                        http://www.fullerton.edu
                                        e-mail: smyr@fullerton.edu
*Doug Liverpool, Counselor*
*Debra Fletcher, Learning Disabilities Specialist*

A public four-year college with 500 special education students out of a total of 29,000. The Office of Disabled Student Services aims to increase access and retention for students with permanent and temporary disabilities by ensuring equitable treatment in all aspects of campus life. Provides co-curricular and academically related services which empower students with disabilities to achieve academic and personal self-determination.

**4016 California State University: Hayward**
Student with Disability Resource Center
25800 Carlos Bee Boulevard
Hayward, CA 94542                       520-885-3868
                                        FAX 510-885-7400
                                        http://www.csuhayward.edu
                                        e-mail: rwong@csuhayward.edu
*Russell Wong, Learning Resources Counselor*

**4017 California State University: Long Beach**
Stephen Benson Program
1250 Bellflower Boulevard
Long Beach, CA 90840                    562-985-4430
                                        FAX 562-985-7183
                                        http://www.csulb.edu
                                        e-mail: bcarey@csulb.edu
*Brian MFT, Learning Disability Specialist*

Four-year college offers a program for the learning disabled.

**4018 California State University: Northridge**
PO Box 1286
Northridge, CA 91328                    818-677-3773
                                        FAX 818-677-4665
                                        http://www.csun.edu
                                        e-mail: lorraine.newlon@csun.edu
*Lee Axelrod, Learning Disability Director*

To assist students with learning disabilities in reaching their full potential, the program offers a comprehensive and well-coordinated system of educational support services that allow students to be judged on the basis of their ability rather than disability.

**4019 California State University: Sacramento**
Services to Students with Disabilities
6000 J Street
Sacramento, CA 95819-0642              916-278-6955
                                        FAX 916-248-7825
                                        TDY:916-278-7239
                                        http://www.csus.edu
                                        e-mail: cronink@csus.edu
*Kathleen Cronin-Brown, Learning Disabilities Specialist*
*Jennifer Schmidt, Director*

Offers a variety of services to students with disabilities including notetakers, extended testing time, counseling services, and special accommodations.

**4020 California State University: San Bernardino**
Disability Services
5500 University Parkway
San Bernardino, CA 92407               909-880-5000
                                        FAX 909-880-5200
                                        TDY:880-500-0000
                                        http://www.csusb.edu
                                        e-mail: cppadmit@csupomona.edu
*Laurie Flynn, Director*

Dedicated to assuring each student an opportunity to experience equity in education .

**4021 California State University: San Marcos**
Disabled Student Services
333 South Twinox Valley
San Marcos, CA 92096                   760-750-4905
                                        FAX 760-750-3445
                                        http://www2.csusm.edu
                                        e-mail: kkornher@csusm.edu
*Kara Kornher MD, Psychologist*
*Brenda Manning, Office Assistant*

Four year college that offers its learning disabled student support and services.

**4022 California State University: Stanislaus**
Disability Resource Center
801 W Monte Vista Avenue
Turlock, CA 95382                      209-667-3159
                                        FAX 209-667-3585
                                        TDY:209-667-3044
                                        http://www.csustan.edu
                                        e-mail: lbettencourt@csustan.edu
*Lee Bettencourt, Director*
*Marlene Hughes, President*

A public four-year college with 31 special education students out of a total of 4,293.

**4023  Canada College**

**4200 Farm Hill Boulevard**
**Redwood City, CA  94061**      650-306-3100
FAX 650-306-3457
TDY:650-306-3161
http://www.canadacollege.edu
e-mail: hetrick@smccd.net
*Regina Blok, Program Coordinator*
*Jinney Gross, Dean*

Three unique programs that serve eligible students with disabilities: the Physically Challenged Program, the Learning Achievement Program and the Adaptive P.E. Program.

**4024  Cerritos College**

**Learning Disability Services**
**11110 Alondra Boulevard**
**Norwalk, CA  90650**      562-860-2451
FAX 562-467-5071
http://www.cerritos.edu
*Al Spetrino, Program Head*

A public two-year college with 63 special education students out of a total of 20,679.

**4025  Chaffey Community College District**

**Disabled Students Programs and Services**
**5885 Haven Avenue**
**Rancho Cucamonga, CA  91737**    909-941-2379
FAX 909-466-2834
TDY:909-466-2829
http://www.chaffey.cc.ca.us
e-mail: sharlenesmith@jc.edu
*Sharlene Smith, Director*
*Marie Kane, President*

Chaffey College's Disabled Student Programs and Services (DSP&S) offer instruction and support services to students with developmental, learning, physical, psychological disabilities or aquired brain injury. Students can recieve a variety of services such as: test facilitation, note taking, tutoring, adaptive physical education, pre-vocational training, career preparation, and job placement.

**4026  Chapman University**

**One University Drive**
**Orange, CA  92666**      714-997-6828
FAX 714-532-6079
http://www.chapman.edu
*Anthony Garcia*

Offers a variety of services to students with disabilities including note takers, extended testing time, counseling services and special accommodations.

**4027  College of Alameda**

**555 Atlantic Avenue**
**Alameda, CA  94501**      510-522-7221
FAX 510-748-2339
TDY:510-748-2330
http://www.peralta.edu
e-mail: ndarcey@peralta.edu
*Nancy Darcey, LD Specialist*
*Dennise Massett, Administrative Assistant*

Accommodations, assessment and special classes are provided for learning disabled students enrolled at College Alameda, a 2 year college located by San Francisco Bay.

**4028  College of Marin**

**Disabled Students Program**
**Kentfield, CA  94904**      415-485-9406
FAX 415-457-4791
TDY:415-721-0736
http://www.marin.cc.ca.us
e-mail: rfb@marin.cc.ca.us
*Marie McCarthy, Coordinator*
*Ellen Tollen, Co-Coordinator*

Offers a variety of services to students with disabilities including note takers, extended testing time, counseling services, and special accommodations. Also offers diagnostic testing and remedial classes for learning disabled students.

**4029  College of San Mateo**

**1700 W Hillsdale Boulevard**
**San Mateo, CA  94402**      650-574-6433
FAX 650-358-6803
TDY:650-574-6230
http://www.collegesanmateo.edu
e-mail: paparelli@smccd.net
*Marie Paparelli, LD Specialist*
*Laura Skaff, Program Service Coordinator*

Primary objective of the Disabled Students Program-Learning Disabilities Center is to assist the student in achieving academic, vocational, personal and social success. This is best accomplished by integration into the mainstream of college classes and services. The learning disabilities program provides support services in the following areas: assessment and evaluation, specialized tutoring, test accommodations, computer access and more.

**4030  College of the Canyons**

**26455 Rockwell Canyon Road**
**Santa Clarita, CA  91355**      661-259-7800
FAX 661-259-8302
http://www.coc.cc.ca.us
*Nina Nashur MD, Coordinator*

A public two-year college with 45 special education students out of a total of 6,255.

**4031  College of the Desert**

**Center for Training and Development**
**43500 Monterey Avenue**
**Palm Desert, CA  92260**      760-773-2596
FAX 760-776-0128
TDY:760-674-0266
http://www.desert.cc.ca.us/
*Mike O'Neill, LD Specialist*

Offers a variety of services to students with disabilities including note takers, extended testing time, counseling services and special accommodations.

**4032 College of the Redwoods: Learning Skills Center**
7351 Tompkins Hill Road
Eureka, CA 95501 707-476-4280
800-641-0400
FAX 707-476-4418
TDY:707-476-4284
http://www.redwoods.edu
e-mail: trish-blaire@redwoods.edu
*Trish Blair, LD Specialist*
*Susan Mindus, Program Assistant*

Mission is to assist individual students in the development of a realistic self-concept, assist in the development of educational interests and employment goals, provide the advice, counseling, and equipment necessary to facilitate success, starting with specialized assistance in the registration process.

**4033 College of the Sequoias**
Disability Resource Center
915 S Mooney Boulevard
Visalia, CA 93277 559-730-3805
FAX 559-730-3803
TDY:559-730-3913
http://www.cos.edu
*Don Mast, Dean*
*David Maciel, Director*

A public two-year college with approximately 600 special education students out of a total of 10,300.

**4034 College of the Siskiyous**
800 College Avenue
Weed, CA 96094 530-938-4461
FAX 530-938-5367
http://www.siskiyous.edu
e-mail: ar@siskiyous.edu
*Karen Zeigler, Director*
*David Pelham, President*

Dedicated to meeting the needs of students with disabilities.

**4035 Columbia College**
11600 Columbia College Drive
Sonora, CA 95370 209-588-5100
FAX 209-588-5104
http://www.columbia.yosemite.cc.ca.us.
*Suzanne Patterson, LD Specialist*

Offers a variety of services to students with disabilities including note takers, extended testing time, counseling services and special accommodations.

**4036 Contra Costa College**
2600 Mission Bell Drive
San Pablo, CA 94806 510-235-7800
FAX 510-236-6768
http://www.contracosta.cc.ca.us/
*Peggy Fleming, Learning Specialist*

Offers a variety of services to students with disabilities including notetakers, extended testing time, counseling services, and special accommodations.

**4037 Cosumnes River College**
1410 Ethan Allan Way
Sacramento, CA 95823 916-563-3241
FAX 916-563-3264
http://www.crc.bsrios.cc.ca.us
e-mail: rebrac@losrois.org
*Paris Greenlee, Director*

A public two-year college with 150 learning disabled students out of a total of 10,000.

**4038 Crafton Hills College**
11711 Sand Canyon Road
Yucaipa, CA 92399 909-389-3209
FAX 909-794-7881
http://www.elac.cc.ca.us
*Kristen Colvey, LD Specialist*

A public two-year college with 52 special education students out of a total of 5,732.

**4039 Cuesta College**
Disabled Student Programs & Services
PO Box 8106
San Luis Obispo, CA 93403 805-546-3148
FAX 805-546-3930
TDY:805-546-3148
http://www.cuesta.cc.ca.us
e-mail: llong@bass.cuesta.cc.ca.us
*Pat Scwab, Director*

A public, two-year community college, offering instruction and services to students with learning disabilities since 1973. A comprehensive set of services and special classes are available. Contact the program for further information.

**4040 De Anza College: Special Education Divisio**
21250 Stevens Creek Boulevard
Cupertino, CA 95014 408-864-5300
http://www.deanza.fhda.edu
*Suzanne Caillat, Office Manager*
*Pauline Waathiq, Director*

A public two-year college with 300 special education students out of a total of 20,000.

**4041 Diablo Valley College**
Disability Support Services
321 Golf Club Road
Plesant Hill, CA 94523 925-685-1230
FAX 925-687-1829
http://www.dvc.edu
*Terry Armstrong, Dean of Counseling*
*Mark Edelstein, President*

Disabled Student Program & Services (DSPS) is a program that is designed to ensure that students with disabilities have equal access to all of the educational offerings at Diablo Valley College. We facilitate equal opportunity through the provision of appropriate support services, curriculum, instruction and adaptive technology.

**4042 East Los Angeles College**

1301 Avenida Cesar Chavez
Monterey Park, CA 91754        323-265-8758
                               FAX 323-265-8759
            http://www.elac.cc.ca.us

*Marilyn Hutchens, Contact*
*Ram Gust, Librarian*

A public two-year college with 44 special education students out of a total of 14587. There is a an additional fee for the special education program in addition to the regular tuition.

**4043 Educational Psychology Clinic**

California State University, Long Beach
1250 N Bellflower Boulevard
Long Beach, CA 90840        562-985-4111
                            FAX 562-985-5804
            e-mail: magaddin@csulb.edu

*Tami Shirron, Graduate Assistant*
*Michael , Clinic Director*

A primary training site for the school psychology, counseling, and special education programs while providing comprehensive educational and psychological services to school age children and their families at a moderate cost. Services at the clinic are provided by graduate students under supervision by faculty in the college of education.

**4044 El Camino Community College**

16007 Crenshaw Boulevard
Torrance, CA 90506        310-532-3670
                          FAX 310-660-3818
            http://www.elcamino.edu
            e-mail: tfallo@elcamino.edu

*Dave Snowden, Admissions/Records*
*Thomas Fallo, President*

Offers a variety of services to students with disabilities including note takers, extended testing time, counseling services, and special accommodations.

**4045 Evergreen Valley College**

3095 Yerba Buena Road
San Jose, CA 95135        408-274-7900
                          FAX 408-432-1962
            http://www.euc.edu
            e-mail: bonnie.clark@euc.edu

*Bonnie Clark, LD Specialist*
*Nacy Tung, Instruction Assistant*

A public two-year college with 82 learning disabled students out of a total of 9,000.

**4046 Excelsior Academy**

7202 Princess View Drive
San Diego, CA 92120        619-583-6762
                           FAX 619-583-6764
            http://www.excelsioracademy.com
            e-mail: nanmag@earthlink.net

**4047 Feather River College**

570 Golden Eagle Avenue
Quincy, CA 95971        530-283-0202
                        FAX 530-283-3757
            http://www.frcc.cc.ca.us

*Maureen McPhee, Contact*

Offers a variety of services to students with disabilities including note takers, extended testing time, counseling services and special accommodations.

**4048 Foothill College**

Disabilities Services/ AHEAD
12345 El Monte Road
Los Altos Hills, CA 94022        650-949-7017
                                 FAX 650-917-1064
                                 TDY:650-948-6025
            http://www.foothill.fhda.edu
            e-mail: dobbinsmargo@foothill.edu

*Margo Dobbins, Coordinator DSP*
*Beatrix Cashmore, Counselor*

Offers a variety of services to students with disabilities including note takers, extended testing time, counseling services and special accommodations.

**4049 Fresno City College**

1101 E University Avenue
Fresno, CA 93741        559-442-4602
                        FAX 559-265-5784
            http://www.fcc.cc.ca.us
            e-mail: pio571@sccd.com

*Jeanette Imperatrice, LD Specialist*
*Ned Doffoney, President*

A public two-year college with 259 special education students out of a total of 17,949.

**4050 Fullerton College**

Learning Resource Services
321 E Chapman Avenue
Fullerton, CA 92832        714-992-7542
                           FAX 714-992-7551
            http://www.fullcoll.edu

*Thomas Cantrell, Contact*
*Ricardo Perez, Director*

A public two-year college with 281 special education students out of a total of 20,731.

**4051 Gavilan College**

5055 Santa Teresa Boulevard
Gilroy, CA 95020        408-848-4755
                        FAX 408-846-4914
            http://www.gavilan..edu

*Susan Swaney, Coordinator*

Offers a variety of services to students with disabilities including note takers, extended testing time, counseling services and special accommodations.

**4052 Hartnell College**

Learning Disability Services
156 Homestead Avenue
Salinas, CA 93901        831-755-6721
            http://www.hartnell.cc.ca.us

*Deborah Shulman, Enabler*

A public two-year college with 72 special education students out of a total of 7,593.

**4053  Humboldt State University**

Disability Resource Center
Arcata, CA  95521 707-826-4678
FAX 707-826-5397
TDY:707-826-5392
http://www.sdrc.humboldt.edu
e-mail: rdm7001@humbolde.edu
*Ralph McFarland, Director*

A public four-year university which provides necessary services and assistance to students with disabilities, through their Disabled Students Services Program. Services are intended to offset the intrusiveness of the disability on a student's academic experience.

**4054  Imperial Valley College**

PO Box 158
Imperial, CA  92251 760-352-8320
FAX 760-355-2663
http://www.imperial.edu
*Norma Nava-Pinuleas, Instructional Specialist*
*David Poor, Staff*

A public two-year college with 44 special education students out of a total of 5,230.

**4055  Institute for the Redesign of Learning**

Almansor Center, The
1137 Huntington Drive
South Pasadena, CA  91030 323-341-5580
FAX 323-257-0284
http://www.redesignlearning.org
*Nancy Lavelle, Contact*
*Greg Cohen, Administrative Assistant*

A full day school serving 100 boys and girls, at-risk infants and children. Vocational Program serves adults and includes Supported Employment Services and an Independent Living Program.

**4056  Irvine Valley College**

Learning Disabilities
5500 Irvine Center Drive
Irvine, CA  92618 949-451-5630
FAX 949-451-5386
http://www.ivc.edu
*Julie Willard, LD Specialist*
*Bill Hewitt, Director*

The goal is to effectivly provide assistance to all students with disabilities to achieve academic success while at Irvine Valley. The primary function is to accommodate a student's disability, whether it is a physical, communication, learning or psychological disability.

**4057  Laney College**

Disability Resource Center
900 Fallon Street
Oakland, CA  94607 510-464-3162
FAX 510-986-6906
http://www.laney.parita.cc.ca.us
*Sondra Neiman, LD Specialist*
*Odell Johnson, President*

A public two-year college with 58 special education students out of a total of 11,808.

**4058  Long Beach City College Pacific Coast Campus**

4351 Faculty Avenue
Long Beach, CA  90806 562-938-4558
FAX 562-938-4457
TDY:562-938-4833
http://www.dsps.lbcc.cc.ca.us
e-mail: dhansch@lbcc.ca.us
*Mark Matsui, Director for Disability*
*Dan Hansch, LD Specialist*

Disabled Student Services (DSPS) is a program within Student Services at LBCC. DSPS provides many support services that enable students with disability related limitations to participate in the college's programs and activities. DSPS offers a wide range of services that compensate for a students limitations, like note taking assistance, interpretive services, alternative media, etc.

**4059  Los Angeles City College**

Learning Disabilities Program
855 N Vermont Avenue
Los Angeles, CA  90029 323-953-4000
FAX 323-953-4526
http://www.lacc.cc.ca.us
*Susan Matranga, LD Specialist*

A public two-year college with 175 students with learning disabilities; total student body is 16,000. The Learning Disabilities Program provides assessment for eligibility in the program, support services, accommodations, and special classes in study skills and problem solving.

**4060  Los Angeles Mission College: Disabled Student Programs and Services**

13356 Eldridge Avenue
Sylmar, CA  91342 818-364-7732
FAX 818-364-7755
TDY:818-364-7861
http://www.lamission.cc.ca.us/front/dsps#
*Rick Scuderi MD, Director*

A support system that enables students to fully participate in the college's regular programs and activities. We provide a variety of services from academic and vocational support to assistance with finacial aid. All services are individulalized according to specific needs. They do not replace regular programs, but rather, accommodate students special requirements.

**4061  Los Angeles Pierce College**

6201 Winnetka Avenue
Woodland Hills, CA  91371 818-719-6401
http://www.piercecollege.com
*David Phoenix, Contact*

A public two-year college with 257 special education students out of a total of 19,207.

**4062  Los Angeles Valley College**

Disabled Student Programs & Services
5800 Fulton Avenue
Van Nuys, CA  91401 818-947-2600
FAX 818-947-2680
http://www.lavc.edu
*Kathleen Sullivan, Coordinator*

Provides specialized support services to students with disabilities which are in addition to the regular services provided to all students. Special accommodations and services are determined by the nature and extent of the disability related educational limitations of the student and are provided based upon the recommendation of DSPS.

**4063 Los Medanos College**
**2700 E Leland Road**
**Pittsburg, CA 94565** 925-439-2181
FAX 925-427-1599
http://www.losmedanos.net
*Dorrie Fisher, Contact*

A public two-year college with 177 special education students out of a total of 7,784.

**4064 Loyola Marymount University**
**7900 Loyola Boulevard**
**Los Angeles, CA 90045** 310-338-2750
FAX 310-338-2797
http://www.lmu.edu
e-mail: admissns@lmumail.lmu.edu
*Matthew Fissinger, Director*
*Elena Williams, Admission Assistant*

Provides specialized assistance and resources that enable students with physical, perceptual, emotional and learning disabilities to achieve maximum independence while they pursue their educational goals.

**4065 Master's College**
**ELS Care College of Canyon**
**26455 Rockwell Canyon Road**
**Santa Clarita, CA 91321** 661-362-5554
FAX 661-362-5555
http://www.els.edu
e-mail: greyes@els.edu
*Gina Reyes, Center Director*
*Mary Hernandez, Academic Director*

An independent two-year college with 5 special education students out of a total of 850. There is an additional fee for the special education program in addition to the regular tuition.

**4066 Mendocino College**
**PO Box 3000**
**Ukiah, CA 95482** 707-468-3151
FAX 707-468-3120
http://www.mendocino.cc.ca.us
*Kathleen Daigle, Specialist*

A two-year public college that offers programs for the disabled.

**4067 Menlo College**
**Academic Success Program**
**1000 El Camino Real**
**Atherton, CA 94027**
800-556-3656
http://www.menlo.edu
e-mail: admissions@menlo.edu
*Mark Hager, Director*

Four year college that offers a program for learning disabled students.

**4068 Merced College**
**3600 M Street**
**Merced, CA 95348** 209-384-6155
FAX 209-384-6103
TDY:209-384-6311
http://www.merced.cc.ca.us
*Ben Duran MD, President*
*Richard Marashlian, Director*

Students with physical, communicative, learning, and or psychological disabilities are encouraged to contact the Disabled Student Services Office. Students with verified disabilities are provided with services to meet their particular needs. These include, but are not limited to, counseling, instructional aids, interpeters for the deaf, registration assistance, computer access through the High Tech Center, learning strategies instruction, and test proctoring.

**4069 Merritt College**
**Disabled Student Programs & Services**
**12500 Campus Drive**
**Oakland, CA 94619** 510-436-2429
FAX 510-436-2503
http://www.merritt.edu
e-mail: ctissot@merrit.edu
*Cristana Tissot, LD Specialist*
*Susan Wilhite, Administrative Assistant*

A public two-year college with 78 special education students out of a total of 6,688.

**4070 Mills College**
**5000 MacArthur Boulevard**
**Oakland, CA 94613** 510-430-2264
FAX 510-430-3235
http://www.mills.edu
e-mail: kennedyg@mills.edu
*Kennedy Golden, Director*
*Janet Holgram, President*

Services provided to disabled students.

**4071 Miracosta College**
**1 Barnard Drive**
**Oceanside, CA 92056** 760-795-6658
888-201-8480
FAX 760-795-6604
TDY:760-439-1060
http://www.maricosta.edu
e-mail: nschafer@maricosta.edu
*Nancy Schafer, LD Specialist*
*Angela Degirolamo, Assistant*

A community college which provides in-class academic accommodations to students with verified disabilities.

**4072 Modesto Junior College**
**435 College Avenue**
**Modesto, CA 95350** 209-575-6225
FAX 209-575-6852
TDY:209-575-6863
*John Martinez, Dean Special Services*

The primary purposes of the Disability Services Center at Modesto Junior College are to provide students with disabilities access to post-secondary education and educational development opportunities, through supportive service and or instruction, depending on individual needs; and to improve campus and community understanding of the needs of students who have disabilities.

**4073  Monterey Peninsula College**

980 Fremont Street
Monterey, CA  93940          831-645-1357
                             FAX 831-645-1390
                             http://www.mpc.edu

Bill Jones, LD Coordinator
Kirk Avery, President

A public two-year college with 202 special education students out of a total of 8,502.

**4074  Moorpark College**

7075 Campus Road
Moorpark, CA 93021          805-378-1434
                            FAX 805-378-1563
             http://www.moorpark.cc.ca.us
Joanna Dillon, Contact

A public two-year college with 154 special education students out of a total of 12,414.

**4075  Mt. San Antonio Community College**

Disabled Student Programs & Services
1100 N Grand Avenue
Walnut, CA  91789           909-594-5611
                            FAX 909-468-3943
                            TDY:909-594-3447
                   http://www.dsps.mtsac.edu
                   e-mail: ghanson@mtsac.edu
Grace Hanson, Director
James Andrews, Counselor LD Specialist
Clifford Stewart, LD Specialist

A public two-year college with 1,300 students with disabilities who receive special services. Total population of students is approximately 40,000.

**4076  Mt. San Jacinto College**

1499 N State Street
San Jacinto, CA  92583      951-487-6752
                   http://www.msjc.edu
Milly Douthit, LD Specialist

A public two-year college with 98 special education students out of a total of 9,000 students.

**4077  Napa Valley College**

2277 Napa Valley Highway
Napa, CA  94558             707-253-3117
                            800-826-1077
                            FAX 707-253-3116
                   http://www.nuc.cc.ca.us
Gwynne Katz MD, LD Specialist

Offers a variety of services to students with disabilities including note takers, extended testing time, counseling services and special accommodations.

**4078  Ohlone College**

43600 Mission Boulevard
Fremont, CA  94539          510-659-7362
                            FAX 510-659-6032
                   http://www.ohlone.edu
Fred Hilke, Special Services Director
Doug Threadway, President

The Ohlone College Disabled Student Services Program is designed to open doors to educational and occupational opportunities for students with physical or medical disabilities. Our primary purpose is to provide an opportuninty for all individuals to gain maximun benefit from their educational experience. Ohlone College encourages students with physical or medical disabilities to participate within the limits of their disabilities in the same activies and courses as other students.

**4079  Orange Coast College**

2701 Fairview Road
Costa Mesa, CA  92626       714-432-5047
                            FAX 714-432-5609
                   http://www.occ.cccd.edu
                   e-mail: mcucurny@cccd.edu
Ken Ortiz MD, Associate Dean

A public two-year college with 350 special education students out of a total of 27,960. There is a an additional fee for the special education program in addition to the regular tuition.

**4080  Oxnard College**

4000 S Rose Avenue
Oxnard, CA  93033           805-986-5800
                            FAX 805-986-5806
                   http://www.oxnard.edu
                   e-mail: ocinfo@vcccd.net
Carole Frick, LD Specialist
Ellen Young, Coordinator

Offers a complete repertoire of support services for students with disabilities, including linkage with the local department of rehabilitation. Special instruction and high tech center available.

**4081  Pacific Union College**

One Angwin Avenue
Angwin, CA  94508           707-965-7364
                            FAX 707-965-6797
                   http://www.puc.edu
                   e-mail: njacobo@puc.edu
Nancy Jacobo, Director Enrollment Services

Services provided to students with learning disabilities.

**4082  Palomar College**

1140 W Mission Road
San Marcos, CA  92069       760-744-1150
                            FAX 706-761-3509
                            TDY:760-471-8506
                   http://www.palomar.edu
                   e-mail: dsts@palomar.edu
Ronald Haines, Disabled Student Programs
Mary Tuttle, Staff

A public two-year college with 993 special education students out of a total of 23,909.

**4083 Pasadena City College**

1570 E Colorado Boulevard
Pasadena, CA 91106        626-585-7127
FAX 626-585-7566
TDY:626-585-7052
http://www.pasadena.edu
e-mail: elweller@paccd.cc.ca.us
*Emy Lu Weller MD, Teacher Specialist/Professor*
*Bianca Richards, Counselor*

A public two-year college with over 500 students with learning disabilities of over 24,000 credit students.

**4084 Pepperdine University**

24255 Paific Coast Highway
Malibu, CA 90263        310-456-4269
FAX 310-456-4827

**4085 Porterville College**

100 E College Avenue
Porterville, CA 93257        559-791-2200
FAX 559-784-4779
http://www.pc.cc.ca.us
e-mail: dallen@pc.cc.ca.us
*Diane Allen, LD Specialist*

A public two-year college with 90 learning disabled students. Services include assessment, special counseling, liaison with campus and community, notetakers, readers, registration assistance, test taking assistance, transcription and tutoring.

**4086 Rancho Santiago College**

2323 N. Broadway
Santa Ana, CA 92706        714-480-7300
http://www.rsccd.org
*Mary Kobane, LD Specialist*

A public two-year college with 319 special education students out of a total of 26,393.

**4087 Rancho Santiago Community College**

1530 West 17th Street
Santa Ana, CA 92706        714-564-6000
FAX 714-564-6455
http://www.rsccd.org
*Ann Vescial, Coordinator*
*Linda Miscovic, Director*

The mission of Rancho Santiago Community College District is to respond to the educational needs of an everchanging community and to provide programs and services that reflect academic excellence. The district's two colleges promote open access and celebrate the diversity of both its students and staff, as well as the community.

**4088 Raskob Learning Institute and Day School**

3520 Mountain Boulevard
Oakland, CA 94619        510-436-1275
FAX 510-436-1106
http://www.rascobinstitute.com
e-mail: raskobinstitute@hnu.edu
*Rachel Wylde, Executive Director*
*Rachel Hallanger, Head Teacher*

A nonprofit, nondenominational service for children and adults with learning problems in the areas of reading, spelling, writing, language and mathematics. Diagnostic evaluation, remedial instruction, full-time comprehensive educational program. On the campus of Holy Names College in the Oakland Hills.

*9-14 years old*

**4089 Reedley College**

995 N Reed Avenue
Reedley, CA 93654        559-638-3641
FAX 559-638-5040
http://www.reedleycollege.com
e-mail: janice.emerzian@reedleycollege.edu
*Janice Emerzian MD, District Director*

Offer various services including: academic advising; adapted computer equipment; adapted physical education; books-on-tape and other educational aids; cooperative accommodations with instructors; educational limitations and accommodation notices to instructors; interpreters; learning disability assessment; liaison and referral to on-campus and off-campus resources; mobility assistance; notetakers; personal counseling and typing services.

**4090 Roosevelt Center at Cypress College**

9200 Valley View Street
Cypress, CA 90630        714-484-7104
FAX 714-826-4042
TDY:714-761-0961
http://www.cypresscollege.edu
*Cindy Owens, LD Specialist*

The Roosevelt Center provides testing to determine eligibility for LD services. For those students with verified learning disabilities, services including tutoring, test accommodations, and adapted software.

**4091 Saint Mary's College of California**

1928 Saint Mary's Road
Morago, CA 94575        925-631-4358
FAX 925-631-4835
http://www.stmarys-ca.edu
e-mail: jparfitt@stmarys-ca.edu
*Jeannie Chavez-Parfitt, Director*
*Ron Gallager, President*

Four year college that provides support and services to its disabled students.

**4092 San Diego City College**

1313 12th Avenue
San Diego, CA 92101        619-388-3400
FAX 619-388-3501
http://www.city.sdccd.cc.ca.us
*Ken Mayer, Counselor*

Offers a variety of services to students with disabilities including note takers, extended testing time, counseling services, and special accommodations.

**4093   San Diego Miramar College**

Disabled Students Programs & Services
10440 Black Mountain Road
San Diego, CA  92126          858-536-7212
                              FAX 858-536-4302
                              TDY:858-536-4301
                    http://www.intergate.miramar
                    e-mail: kdoorly@sdccd.com
*Kathleen Doorly, Program Coordinator*
*Sandra Smith, DSPS Counselor/LD Specialist*
*Kandice Walker, DSPS Counselor*

A public two-year college with 500 learning disabled students. These students receive services and accommodations appropriate for their success in college. Individual counseling, class advising and LD assessments are also available. Special classes are offered to support college courses.

**4094   San Diego State University**

5500 Campanile Dr
San Diego, CA  92182          619-594-6871
                    http://www.sdsu.edu
                    e-mail: admissions@sdsu.edu
*Margo Behr, Director*
*Sandra Cook, Admissions Director*

A public four-year college with 520 disabled students out of a total of 25,658.

**4095   San Francisco State University**

Disability Resource Center
1600 Holloway Avenue
San Francisco, CA  94132       415-338-6356
                              FAX 415-338-1041
                    http://www.sfsu.edu
                    e-mail: defreese@sfsu.edu
*Deidre Defreese, Director*

A public four-year college with 400 special education students out of a total of 21,044.

**4096   San Jose City College**

2100 Moorpark Avenue
San Jose, CA  95128            408-288-3746
                              FAX 408-971-8201
                              TDY:408-294-3447
                    http://www.sjcc.edu
                    e-mail: donna.wirt@sjcc.edu
*Donna Wirt, LD Specialist*
*Merdith Matos, Program Assistant*

Offers a variety of services to students with disabilities including note takers, extended testing time, counseling services and special accommodations.

**4097   San Jose State University**

Disability Resource Center
1 Washington Square
San Jose, CA  95192            408-924-6000
                              FAX 408-924-5999
                              TDY:408-924-5990
                    http://www.sjsu.edu
                    e-mail: marty@drc.sjsu.edu
*Martin Schulter, Director*
*John Bradbury, Admissions Director*

A four-year public university with 600 out of 20,679 receiving disability services.

**4098   Santa Ana College**

1530 West 17th Street
Santa Ana, CA  92706           714-564-6265
                              FAX 714-836-6696
                    http://www.sacollege.org
*Cheryl Dunn-Hoanzl, Director*

Offers a variety of services to students with disabilities including note takers, extended testing time, counseling services and special accommodations.

**4099   Santa Barbara City College**

721 Cliff Drive
Santa Barbara, CA  93109       805-965-0581
                              FAX 805-884-4966
                              TDY:805-962-4084
                    http://www.sbcc.net
                    e-mail: dspshelp@sbcc.edu
*Mary Lawson, LD Specialist*
*Gerry Lewin, LD Specialist*

Offers complete repertoire of support services for students with disabilities, including linkage with local department of rehabilitation. Special instruction available. High tech center.

**4100   Santa Clara University**

Disability Resources
500 El Camino Real
Santa Clara, CA  95053         408-554-4111
                              FAX 408-554-2709
                    http://www.scu.edu
                    e-mail: eravenscroft@scu.edu
*Ann Ravenscroft, Director*
*Sandra Hayes, Admissions Director*

Designated by the University to ensure access for all students with disabilities to all academic programs and University resources. Types of disabilities include medical, physical, psychological, attention deficit and learning disabilities. Reasonable accommodations are provided to minimize the effects of a student's disability and to maximize the potential for success.

**4101   Santa Monica College**

1900 Pico Boulevard
Santa Monica, CA  90405        310-434-4684
                              FAX 310-434-3694
                    http://www.smc.edu
                    e-mail: gmarcopulos@smc.edu
*George Marcopulos, Learning Specialist*
*Audrey Morris, Coordinator*

A public two-year college with 300 students with learning disabilities out of a total of 26,361.

**4102   Santa Rosa Junior College**

Disability Resource Department
1501 Mendocino Avenue
Santa Rosa, CA  95401          707-527-4278
                              800-564-7752
                              FAX 707-527-4798
                    http://www.santarosa.edu
                    e-mail: kvigeland@santarosa.edu
*Kari Vigeland, Director*
*Ricardo Navarrette, Admissions Director*

A public two-year college with 300 special education students out of a total of 28,223.

**4103 Shasta College**

11555 Old Oregon Trail
Redding, CA 96003 530-225-4912
FAX 530-225-4952
http://www.shasta.cc.ca.us
e-mail: info@shastacollege.edu
*Parker Pollock, Handicapped Director*
*Jaime Larson, Professor*

A public two-year college with 104 special education students out of a total of 12,822.

**4104 Sierra College**

Learning Opportunities Center
5000 Rocklin Road
Rocklin, CA 95677 916-781-0599
FAX 916-789-2967
http://www.sierra.cc.ca.us
e-mail: jhirschinger@scmail.sierra.cc.ca.us
*Jim Hirschinger, Director*
*Mandy Davis, Admissions Director*

A public two-year college with 400 special education students out of a total of 17,000.

**4105 Skyline College**

Developmental Skills Program
3300 College Drive
San Bruno, CA 94066 650-738-4193
FAX 650-738-4299
http://www.skylinecollege.net
*Linda Sciver, Coordinator*

A public two-year college with 103 special education students out of a total of 9,023.

**4106 Solano Community College**

4000 Suisun Valley Road
Flaire Field, CA 94585 707-864-7136
FAX 707-863-7810
http://www.solano.edu
*Ron Nelson, coordinator*

The LD Center offers eligibility assessment (students with average to above average intelligence with severe processing deficit(s) and severe aptitude-achievement discrepancies), and instruction in strategies and interventions to help the student become more successful in regular college classes. Academic and personal counseling from Disabled Student Programs Counselors are available. Support services such as notetaking, extended test time and other modifications are available.

**4107 Sonoma State University**

Disabled Student Services
1801 E Cotati Avenue
Rohnert Park, CA 94928 707-664-2677
FAX 707-664-2505
TDY:707-664-2958
http://www.sonoma.edu
e-mail: bill.clopton@sonoma.edu
*Linda Lipps, Director*
*Katharyn Crabbe, Admissions Director*

A public four-year college with 230 disabled students out of a total of 6,211.

**4108 Southwestern College**

Diagnostic Learning Center
900 Otay Lakes Road
Chula Vista, CA 91910 619-482-6327
FAX 619-482-6435
http://www.swc.cc.ca.us
*Diane Branman, Contact*
*Irma Alvarez, Dean*

A public two-year college with 99 special education students out of a total of 17,083.

**4109 Springall Academy**

6550 Soledad Mountain Road
La Jolla, CA 92037 858-459-9047
FAX 858-459-4660
http://www.springall.org
*Arlene Baker MD, Executive Director*
*Sally McNamara, Curriculum Director*

Offers a variety of services to students with disabilities including note takers, extended testing time, counseling services, and special accommodations. The academy is a nonprofit school for learning and behaviorally challenged students.

**4110 Stanbridge Academy**

515 E Poplar Avenue
San Mateo, CA 94401 650-375-5860
FAX 650-375-5861
http://www.stanbridgeacademy.org
e-mail: info@stanbridgeacademy.org
*Sanford Shapiro, Executive Director*

**4111 Stanford University**

123 Meyer Library
Stanford, CA 94305 650-723-2273
FAX 650-725-7411
http://www.stanford.edu
*Molly Sandperl, Special Services*

An independent four-year college with 102 special education students out of a total of 6,527.

**4112 Sterne School**

2690 Jackson Street
San Francisco, CA 94115 415-922-6081
FAX 415-922-1598
http://www.sterneschool.org/
e-mail: office@sterneschool.org
*Liza Graham, Director*
*Cindy Weingard, Development Director*

A private school serving students in 6-12 grade who have specific learning disabilities. Established in 1976.

**4113 Taft College**

29 Emmons Park Drive
Taft, CA 93268 661-763-7700
FAX 661-763-7705
TDY:661-763-7801
http://www.taft.cc.ca.us/
e-mail: jross@taft.org
*Jeff Ross, Coordinator Program Services*
*Abel Nunec, Executive Director*

A public two-year college with 56 special education students out of a total of 952.

**4114  UCLA Office for Students with Disabilities**
405 Hilgard Avenue
Los Angeles, CA 90095          310-825-4321
                              FAX 310-825-9656
                              TDY:310-206-6083
                              http://www.ucla.edu
                              e-mail: jmorris@saonet.ucla.edu
*Julie Morris, LD Program Coordinator*
*Kathy Molini, Director*

Offers a variety of services to students with disabilities including notetakers, accommodated testing, counseling services, assistive technology, support groups, advocacy to faculty, strategies, workshops and counseling.

**4115  USC University Affiliated Program: Childrens Hospital at Los Angeles**
University of Southern California
Mailstop #53
Los Angeles, CA 90054          323-669-2300
                              FAX 323-663-6707
                              http://www.usc.edu
*Robert Jacobs, Director*
*Connie Nickelson, Administrative Assistant*

The primary mission of the USC UAP is the continued improvement of the health and welfare of children and families who are affected by disabling conditions, chronic illness, or other special health care needs.

**4116  United States International University**
10455 Pomerado Road
San Diego, CA 92131          858-635-4598
                              FAX 858-635-4690
                              http://www.alliance.edu
*Lorna Reese, Assistant Dean*
*Geoffrey Cox, President*

Four year college offering services to disabled students.

**4117  University of California-Davis: Student Disability Resource Center**
One Shields Avenue
Davis, CA 95616          530-752-3184
                          FAX 530-752-0161
                          TDY:530-752-6833
                          http://http://sdc.ucdavis.edu/
                          e-mail: caodell@ucdavis.edu
*Christine O'Dell, LD Specialist*
*Tina Morton, Administrative Assistant*

Committed to ensuring equal educational opportunities for students with disabilities. Promotes independence and integrated participation in campus life for students with disabilities.

**4118  University of California: Berkeley**
Disabled Student's Program
260 Ceasar Chavez
Berkeley, CA 94720-4250          510-642-0518
                                  FAX 510-643-9686
                                  TDY:510-642-6376
                                  http://www.dsp.berkeley.edu
                                  e-mail: erogers@berkeley.edu
*Ed Rogers, Director*

A four-year public university.

**4119  University of California: Irvine**
Office for Disability Services
105 Administration Building
Irvine, CA 92697          949-824-7494
                          FAX 949-824-3083
                          TDY:949-824-6272
                          http://www.disability.uci.edu
                          e-mail: ods@uci.edu
*Ron Blosser MD, Special Services*

Our mission is to provide effective and reasonable academic accommodations and related disability services to UCI students, Extension and Summer Session students, and other program participants. Consults with and educates faculty about reasonable academic accommodations. Strives to improve access to UCI programs, activities, and facilities for students with disabilities. Advises and educates academic and administrative departments about access issues to programs or facilities.

**4120  University of California: Irvine Campus**
105 Administration Building
Irvine, CA 92717          949-824-7494
                          FAX 949-824-8566
                          http://www.uci.edu
*Ron Blosser MD, Director*

Offers a variety of services to students with disabilities including note takers, extended testing time, counseling services and special accommodations.

**4121  University of California: Los Angeles**
Office for Students with Disabilities
405 Hilgard Avenue
Los Angeles, CA 90095          310-825-1501
                              FAX 310-825-9656
                              TDY:310-206-6083
                              http://www.ucla.edu
                              e-mail: kmolini@saonet.ucla.edu
*Kathy Molini, Director*
*Vu Tran, Admissions Director*

Served by a TWP learning disabilities specialist, UCLA offers a full range of accommodations and services. Services are individually designed, and include disability- related counseling, special test arrangements, notetaker services, readers, priority enrollment, adaptive technology, and individual small group and individual content area tutoring. An active support group and peer-mentor program provides opportunities for students to discuss mutual concerns and enhance learning strategies.

**4122  University of California: Riverside**
Disabled Student Services
900 University Avenue
Riverside, CA 92521          951-827-1012
                              http://www.ucr.edu
*Marcia Schiffer, Director DSS*

A public four-year college with 25 learning disabled students out of a total of 8,000.

**4123 University of California: San Diego**

Office for Students with Disabilities
9500 Gilman Drive
La Jolla, CA 92093          858-534-4382
                           FAX 858-534-4650
                    http://www.osd.ucsd.edu
              e-mail: rgimblett@ucsd.edu
*Roberta Gimblett, Director*
*Mae Brown, Admissions Director*
*Naomi Levoy, Outreach Assistant*

A public four-year college with 150 students receiving disability services out of 15,840.

**4124 University of California: San Francisco**

Office of Student Relations
500 Paranassus Avenue
San Francisco, CA 94143       415-476-4318
                           FAX 415-476-7295
                           TDY:415-476-4318
              http://http://student.ucsf.edu/
            e-mail: ekoenig@osl.uscsf.edu
*Eric Koenig, Director*
*Barbara Smith, Operations Manager*
*Candy Clemens, Adminstrative Assistant*

The Office of Student Relations is responsible for co-ordinating Services for Students with Disabilities at UCSF.

**4125 University of California: Santa Barbara**

Disabled Student Program
1210 Cheadle Hall
Santa Barbara, CA 93106       805-893-2182
                           FAX 805-893-7127
                           TDY:805-893-2668
                    http://www.ucsb.edu
              e-mail: batty-c@sa.ucsb.edu
*Diane Glenn, Director*
*Gary White, Director*

Works to increase the retention and graduation rates of students with disabilities and to foster student independence.

**4126 University of California: Santa Cruz**

146 Hahn
Santa Cruz, CA 95064         831-459-2089
                           FAX 831-459-5064
                           TDY:831-459-4806
                    http://www.ucsc.edu
              e-mail: drc@ucsc.edu
*Sharyn Martin, Director Special Services*
*Barbara Duron, Assistant Director*

A public four-year college with 87 special education students out of a total of 9,162.

**4127 University of Redlands**

Academic Support Services/Disabled Student Service

1200 E Colton Avenue
Redlands, CA 92373           909-335-4079
                           FAX 909-335-5297
                    http://www.redlands.edu
            e-mail: judy.bowman@redlands.edu
*Judy Bowman, Academic Support/Disabled Svcs.*
*Paul Driscoll, Admissions Director*

Offers a variety of services to students with disabilities including notetakers, extended testing time, counseling services, and special accommodations.

**4128 University of San Diego**

9500 Gilman Drive
La Jolla, CA 92093           858-534-5149
                           FAX 858-822-5407
                    http://www.ucsd.edu
*Tyler Gabriel MD, Academic Counseling*

An independent four-year college with 35 special education students out of a total of 3,904.

**4129 University of San Francisco**

Learning Disability Services
2130 Fulton Street
San Francisco, CA 94117       415-422-6876
                           FAX 415-422-5906
                           TDY:415-422-2613
                    http://www.usfca.edu
              e-mail: ongt@usfca.edu
*Tom Merrell, Director*

A four-year private college with 190 students recieving LD/ADHD services.

**4130 University of Southern California**

Disability Services and Programs
3601 Trousdale Parkway
Los Angeles, CA 90089        213-740-0776
                           FAX 213-740-8216
                           TDY:213-740-6948
                    http://www.usc.edu
              e-mail: jeddy@usc.edu
*Eddie Roth MD, LD Consultant*
*Laurel Tews, Admissions Director*

An independent four-year university with 350 LD students out of a total of 15,705. The support structure for students with documented learning disabilities at USC is one that is totally individualized. Offers support at the student's request for such things as extended time for exams, proofreading papers and reports, and advocacy with faculty. There is no special admission process.

**4131 University of the Pacific**

Office of Special Services for Students with Dis.
3601 Pacific Avenue
Stockton, CA 95211           209-946-3221
                           FAX 209-946-2278
              http://www.pacific.edu/education/ssd
              e-mail: hhouck@uop.edu
*Lisa Cooper, Coordinator*

Offers a variety of services to qualified students with disabilities on a case-by-case basis such as test proctoring services, note-taking assistance, priority registration or referrals to other campus services such as counseling and tuturial support.

**4132 Vanguard University of Southern California**

55 Fair Drive
Costa Mesa, CA 92626         714-556-3610
                             800-722-6279
                           FAX 714-966-5471
                    http://www.vanguard.edu
              e-mail: jmireles@vanguard.edu
*Jessica Mireles, Director*

Four year college offers support for its disabled students.

**4133 Ventura College**
4667 Telegraph Road
Ventura, CA 93003      805-654-6400
     FAX 805-648-8915
     TDY:805-642-4583
     http://www.ventura.cc.ca.us
*Jeff Barsch MD, LD Director*
*Nancy Latham, Coordinator*

A public two-year college with 424 special education students out of a total of 12,153.

**4134 Victor Valley College**
18422 Bear Valley Road
Victorville, CA 92392      760-245-4271
     FAX 760-245-9744
     http://www.victor.cc.ca.us
*Susan Tillman, LD Specialist*

Offers a variety of services to students with disabilities including note takers, extended testing time, counseling services and special accommodations.

**4135 West Hills College**
300 W Cherry Lane
Coalinga, CA 93210      559-934-2000
     FAX 559-935-5655
     http://www.westhills.cc.ca.us
*Tom Winters, Contact*

A public two-year college with 63 special education students out of a total of 3,530.

**4136 West Los Angeles College**
9000 Overland Avenue
Culver City, CA 90230      310-287-4200
     FAX 310-287-4317
     http://www.ulac.edu
     e-mail: regalaba@lacitycollege.edu
*Frances Israel, Learning Specialist*
*Casandra Brown, Program Assistant*

A public two-year college with 104 special education students out of a total of 8,952.

**4137 West Valley College**
14000 Fruitvale Avenue
Saratoga, CA 95070      408-741-2000
     http://www.westvalley.edu
*Susan Bunch, LD Specialist*

A public two-year college with 209 special education students out of a total of 1,429.

**4138 Westmark School**
5461 Louise Avenue
Encino, CA 91316      818-986-5045
     FAX 818-986-2605
     http://www.westmarkschool.org
     e-mail: sshenkin@westmarkschool.org
*Saray Shenkin, Director*
*Sylvia Lopez, Office Assistant*

**4139 Whittier College**
Learning Support Services
13406 Philadelphia Street
Whittier, CA 90608      562-907-4233
     FAX 562-907-4980
     http://www.whittier.edu
     e-mail: tthomsen@whittier.edu
*Joan Smith, Director*
*Tina Thomsen, Administrative Assistant*

A four-year private college with 30 students recieving disability services out of 1,297.

## Colorado

**4140 Aims Community College**
5401 W 20th Street
Greeley, CO 80632      970-330-8008
     800-301-5388
     FAX 970-339-6682
     http://www.aims.edu
*Donna Wright, LD Center*

Offers a variety of services to students with disabilities including note takers, extended testing time, counseling services, and special accommodations.

**4141 Arapahoe Community College**
5900 S Santa Fe Drive
Littleton, CO 80160      303-797-4222
     FAX 303-797-0127
     http://www.arcpahoe.edu
*Alex Labak MD, Contact*

Offers a variety of services to students with disabilities including note takers, extended testing time, counseling services, and special accommodations.

**4142 Colorado Christian University**
Academic Support
160 S Garrison Street
Lakewood, CO 80226      303-963-3266
     FAX 303-274-7560
     http://www.ccu.edu
     e-mail: jlambert@ccu.edu
*Joanne Lambert, Assistance Coordinator*

Four-year college that offers support to learning disabled students.

**4143 Colorado Mountain College**
Central Admissions Office
3000 County Road
Glenwood Springs, CO 81602      970-947-8253
     800-621-8559
     FAX 970-928-9668

The Disability Service Program at Colorado Mountain College is designed to assist students with disabilities to be successful in their programs. The program design offers students enhancement of basic skills, completion in a chosen area of study and removal of barriers in the classroom while preserving the integrity of the course objectives.

**4144 Colorado Northwestern Community College**
**500 Kennedy Drive**
**Rangely, CO 81648**          970-675-2261
                              800-562-1105
                              FAX 970-675-3330
                              http://www.cncc.edu
                              e-mail: jim.hoganson@cncc.edu
*Jim Hoganson, LD Director*
*Robert Rizzudo, President*

A public two-year college with 11 special education students out of a total of 502.

**4145 Colorado State University**
**Resources for Disabled Students**
**100 General Services**
**Fort Collins, CO 80523**      970-491-6385
                              FAX 970-491-3457
                              TDY:970-491-6385
                              http://www.colostate.edu
                              e-mail: kivy@lamar.edu
*Chelsea Duncan, Staff Assistant*
*Rosemary Creston, Director*

The mission of Resources for Disabled Students (RDS) is to assist Colorado State University in ensuring that qualified students with disabilities are afforded and given access to the same, or equal, educational opportunities available to other university students.

**4146 Community College of Aurora**
**16000 E Centre Tech Parkway**
**Aurora, CO 80011**           303-360-4700
                              FAX 303-631-7432
                              http://www.cco.edu
                              e-mail: reniece.jones@cco.edu
*Reniece Jones, Coordinator*

Offers a variety of services to students with disabilities including note takers, extended testing time, counseling services, and special accommodations.

**4147 Community College of Denver**
**Students Disabilities Services**
**1111 West Coalfax**
**Denver, CO 80217**           303-556-2600
                              FAX 303-556-4563
                              TDY:303-556-3300
                              http://www.ccd.edu
*Michael Rusk, Director*
*Connie Trujillo, Office Manager*

A public two-year college with 100 special education students out of a total of 6,000. There is an additional fee for the special education program in addition to the regular tuition.

**4148 Denver Academy**
**1101 S Race Street**
**Denver, CO 80210**           303-777-5870
                              FAX 303-777-5893
                              http://www.denveracadamy.org
*Lori Richardson, Dean*
*Jim Loan, President*

Denver Acadmy was founded in 1972 and is internationally recognized for the quality of its program. Our mission is to be a center of excellence for the education of students with learning differences in order to help them fully develop their intellectual, social, physical and moral potential thereby providing them with the necessary skill to be successful in life.

**4149 Disability Services**
**University of Colorado at Colorado Springs**
**Main Hall 105**
**Colorado Springs, CO 80933**   719-262-3354
                              FAX 719-262-3354
                              http://www.uccs.edu/dss
                              e-mail: disbserv@uccs.edu
*Kaye MA, Coordinator Disability*

Provides services and accommodations to students with disabilities, works closely with faculty and staff in an advisory capacity, assists in the development of reasonable accommodations for students and provides equal access for otherwise qualified individuals with disabilities.

**4150 Fort Lewis College**
**1000 Rim Drive**
**Durango, CO 81301**          970-247-7263
                              FAX 970-247-2703
                              http://www.fortlewis.edu
                              e-mail: admission@fortlewis.edu
*Tim Slane, Disabled Student Director*

Coordinates services at Fort Lewis for those students with disabilities, acts as liaison between students and faculty programs. Advises and directs those students to the appropriate services and academic advisors.

**4151 Front Range Community College Progressive Learning**
**3645 W 112th Avenue**
**Westminster, CO 80031**       303-460-1032
                              FAX 303-469-7143
                              http://www.frontrange.edu
*Janeth Gullick, President*
*Karen Hossack, Faculty*

A public two-year college with a unique remedial program for all adults with learning disabilities. Enrollment is not necessary to attend Progressive Learning Program.

**4152 John F Kennedy Child Development Center**
**University of Colorado Health Sciences Center**
**4200 E 9th Avenue**
**Denver, CO 80262**           303-315-6511
                              FAX 303-315-6844
                              TDY:303-864-5266
                              http://www.uchsc.edu/sm/jfk/
                              e-mail: robinson.cordelia@tchden.org
*Cordelia Robinson, Director*
*Beverly Murdock, Administrative Assistant*

**4153  Lamar Community College**
2401 S Main Street
Lamar, CO  81052
719-336-2248
800-968-6920
FAX 719-336-2448
http://www.Icc.cccoes.edu
e-mail: gary.hammar@lcc.ccoes.edu
*Garry Hammar, Director of Financial*
*Dr , Director of Disability*

Offers a variety of services to students with disabilities including notetakers, extended testing time, counseling services, and special accommodations.

**4154  Morgan Community College**
300 Main Street
Fort Morgan, CO  80701
970-867-3351
800-622-0216
FAX 970-867-3352
http://www.mcc.cccoes.edu
*Maxine Weimer, Developmental Education*

A public two-year college with 11 special education students out of a total of 887.

**4155  Northeastern Junior College**
100 College Drive
Sterling, CO  80751
970-522-6600
800-626-4637
FAX 970-521-6672
http://www.nejc.edu
e-mail: lgill@nejc.edu
*Lori Gill, Special Services Director*
*Judy Giacgomini, President*

A public two-year college with 36 special education students out of a total of 2,042.

**4156  Pikes Peak Community College**
5675 S Academy Boulevard
Colorado Springs, CO  80906
719-540-7128
800-456-6847
FAX 719-540-7254
TDY:719-540-7128
http://www.ppcc.edu
*Michael Nusen, Coordinator*

A public two-year college with 108 special education students out of a total of 6,517.

**4157  Pueblo Community College**
900 W Orman Avenue
Pueblo, CO  81004
719-549-3228
888-642-6017
FAX 719-544-1179
http://www.pueblocc.edu
*Bob Alstyne, Contact*
*Mike , President*

Offers a variety of services to students with disabilities including note takers, extended testing time, counseling services, and special accommodations.

**4158  Red Rocks Community College**
13300 W 6th Avenue
Lakewood, CO  80228
303-914-6600
FAX 303-914-6666
http://www.rrcc.edu
*Theona Hammond-Harns, Special Services*

A public two-year college with 33 special education students out of a total of 6,300.

**4159  Regis University**
Disability Services
3333 Regis Boulevard
Denver, CO  80221
303-458-4941
FAX 303-964-3647
http://www.regis.edu
e-mail: mbwillia@regis.edu
*Joie Williams, Director*

A four-year private university with 110 students recieving disability services out of 1,022.

**4160  Trinidad State Junior College**
136 Main Street
Trinidad, CO  81082
719-846-5644
FAX 719-846-4550
http://www.tsjc.cccoes.edu/
*John Giron, Special Services*

Offers a variety of services to students with disabilities including note takers, extended testing time, counseling services, and special accommodations.

**4161  University of Colorado at Boulder Disability Services**
Academic Access and Resource Program (AAR)
107 UCB
Boulder, CO  80309
303-492-8671
FAX 303-492-5601
TDY:303-492-8671
http://www.colorado.edu/disabilityservices
e-mail: dsinfo@colorado.edu
*Jayne MacArthur, Supervisor*
*Cindy Donahue, Director*
*Barbara Schneider, Admissions Director*

Provides a variety of services to individuals with nonvisible disabilities, including individualized strategy sessions with a disability specialist, an assistive technology lab, a writing lab and a career program for students with disabilities. Disability specialists also assist with obtaining reasonable accommodations if documentation meets disability services requirements and supports the need for them.

**4162  University of Colorado: Colorado Springs**
Disability Services
Main Hall 105
Colorado Springs, CO  80933
719-262-3354
FAX 719-262-3354
http://www.uccs.edu
e-mail: disbserv@uccs.edu
*Kaye Simonton, Director*
*Randy Kouba, Admissions Director*

A four-year public university with 200 students receiving disability services out of 5,054.

**4163  University of Denver**
Learning Effectiveness Program
2199 S University Boulevard
Denver, CO  80208
303-871-2372
FAX 303-871-3938
http://www.du.edu
e-mail: tmay@du.edu
*Ted May, Director*
*John Dolan, Admissions Director*

A fee for service program offering comprehensive, individualized services to University of Denver Students with learning disabilities and or ADHD. The LEP is part of a larger organization called University Disability Services.

**4164 University of Northern Colorado**

**Disability Access Center**
**UNC Admissions Office**
Greeley, CO  80639          970-351-2289
FAX 970-351-4166
http://www.unco.edu/dss
e-mail: nlkauff@unco.edu
*Nancy Kauffman, Director*
*Gary Gulickson, Admissions Director*

Offers a variety of services to students with disabilities including notetakers, extended testing time, counseling services, and special accommodations.

**4165 University of Southern Colorado**

**2200 Bonforte Boulevard**
Pueblo, CO  81001          719-549-2581
877-872-9653
FAX 719-549-2195
http://www.colostate-pueblo.edu
e-mail: joe.marshall@colostate-pueblo.edu
*Joe Marshall, Director*
*John Valdez, Office Manager*

Support services for special needs students are provided on an individual basis. The student must provide documentation of disability with a formal request for specific support services needed.

**4166 Western State College of Colorado**

**600 N Adams Street**
**Gunnison, CO  81231**
800-876-5309
http://www.western.edu
*Jill Martinez, Advisor*

A public four-year college with 59 special education students out of a total of 2,450.

## Connecticut

**4167 Albertus Magnus College**

**Director of the Academic Development Center**
**700 ProspeCourt Street**
New Haven, CT  06511          203-773-8590
FAX 203-773-3119
http://www.albertus.edu
e-mail: jmcnamera@albertus.edu
*Julia McNamera, President*
*William Schuz, Vice President*

Offers a variety of services to students with disabilities including note takers, extended testing time, counseling services, and special accommodations.

**4168 Asnuntuck Community Technical College**

**170 Elm Street**
Enfield, CT  06082          860-253-3000
FAX 860-253-3063
http://www.acc.commnet.edu
e-mail: mmcleod@acc.commnet.edu
*Martha McLeod, President*
*Vince Fulginity, Vice President*

The Academic Skills Center is offered to students with learning disabilities.

**4169 Ben Bronz Academy**

**139 N Main Street**
West Hartford, CT  06107          860-236-5807
FAX 860-233-9945
http://www.tli.com
e-mail: bba@tli.com
*Aileen Stan-Spence, Director*
*Mary Austin, Staff*

Ben Bronz Acadamy is a day school for bright disabled students. Guides 60 students through an intensive school day that includes writing, mathematics, literature, science and social studies. Oral language is developed and stressed in all classes.

**4170 Briarwood College**

**2279 Mount Vernon Road**
Southington, CT  06489          860-628-4751
800-952-2444
FAX 860-628-6444
http://www.briarwood.edu
*Cynthia Clarky, Disabilities Coordinator*
*Lyn , President*

Briarwood College is accredited by the New England Association of Schools and Colleges and the Connecticut State Board for Higher Education. Indiviual progams are also accredited by organizations within their specific professions.

**4171 Capitol Community-Tech College**

**61 Woodland Street**
Hartford, CT  06105          860-520-7800
*Virginia Foley-Psillas*

Offers a variety of services to students with disabilities including note takers, extended testing time, counseling services, and special accommodations.

**4172 Central Connecticut State University**

**1615 Stanley Street**
New Britain, CT  06050          860-832-2278
FAX 860-832-2522
http://www.ccsu.edu
*George Tenney, Director*
*Myrna Garcia-Bowen, Director for Admissions*

Offers services and supports that promote educational equity for students with disabilities. Assistance includes arranging accommodations and auxillary aids that are necessary for students with disabilities to pursue their academic careers.

**4173 Connecticut College**

Office of Disability Services
270 Mohegan Avenue
New London, CT 06320          860-439-5428
FAX 860-439-5430
http://www.conncoll.edu
e-mail: slduq@conncoll.edu
*Susan Duques PhD, Director*
*Lee Coffin, Admissions Director*

Offers a variety of services to students with disabilities including notetakers, extended testing time, counseling services, and special accommodations.

**4174 Eastern Connecticut State University**

Support Services Center
Willimantic, CT 06226          860-465-5573
FAX 860-465-0136
TDY:860-465-5799
http://www.ecsu.ctstateu.edu
e-mail: starrp@easternct.edu
*Pamela Starr, Coordinator/Counselor*

Academic support services are designed to provide equal access to the educational program. Each service must be approved by the OAS Coordinator and can be accessed by completing the appropriate service request form.

**4175 Fairfield University**

Office of Student Support Services
1073 N Benson Road
Fairfield, CT 06824          203-254-4000
FAX 203-254-4000
http://www.fairfield.edu
*David Ryan-Soderlund, Assistant Director*
*Aloysius Kelley, President*

Provides students with disabilities an equal opportunity to access the benefits, rights and privileges of Fairfield University's services, programs and activities in an accessible setting.

**4176 Gateway Community-Tech College**

60 Sargent Drive
New Haven, CT 06511          203-285-2000
800-390-7723
http://www.gwcc.commnet.edu
*Shelley RN, ADA Coordinator*

Offers a variety of services to students with disabilities including extended testing time, counseling services, and special accommodations.

**4177 Hartford College for Women**

University of Hartford
1265 Asylum Avenue
Hartford, CT 06105          860-236-1215
FAX 860-768-5622
http://www.hartford.edu
e-mail: hcwinfo@mail.hartford.edu
*Walter Harrisson, President*
*Lee Peterson, Vice President*

Offers a variety of services to students with disabilities including note takers, extended testing time, counseling services, and special accommodations.

**4178 Housatonic Community Technical College**

900 Lafayette Boulevard
Bridgeport, CT 06604          203-332-5000
FAX 203-332-5123
http://www.hctc.commnet.edu
*Peter Anderheggen, Director*

The Federally-funded Special Services Program works to help students do well at Housatonic, stay in college, and graduate. Students are eligible for the Special Services Program based on criteria which include placement test scores, income levels, physical handicap, limited English ability, or first generation college student (neither parent has a bachelor's degree).

**4179 Learning Disability Center**

University of Connecticut
Box U-64
Storrs, CT 06269          860-486-0178
FAX 860-486-0210
http://www.ucimt.uconn.edu/
*David Praker, Director*
*Carol Wayde, Project assistant*

Membership organization specializing in the education of people with special needs through technology and media.

**4180 Manchester Community Technical College**

Great Path
Manchester, CT 06045          860-512-3000
http://www.mctc.commnet.edu
*Mary White-Edge MD, LD Director*

A public two-year college with 60 special education students out of a total of 6,134.

**4181 Mitchell College**

Learning Resource Center
437 Pequot Avenue
New London, CT 06320          860-701-5141
800-443-2811
FAX 860-701-5099
http://www.mitchell.edu
*Peter Troiano, Director LRC*
*Mary , President*

An independent two-year or four-year college with 275 special education students out of a total of 621. There is a an additional fee for the special education program in addition to the regular tuition.

**4182 Naugatuck Community College**

750 Chase Parkway
Waterbury, CT 06708          203-575-8040
FAX 203-575-8001
http://www.nvcc.commnet.edu
*Louise Meyers, Coordinator LD Program*
*Laurie Novi, Coordinator LD Services*

Committed to providing equal educational opportunity and full participation for qualified students with disabilities in accordance with the Americans with Disabilities Act of 1990 (ADA). This includes equality of access, accommodations, auxiliary aids and services determined to be appropriate to address those functional limitations of the disability that adversely affects educational opportunity.

**4183  Northwestern Connecticut Community College**
Park Place E
Winsted, CT  06098                          860-738-6307
                                     FAX 860-379-4465
                                     TDY:860-738-6307
                    http://www.nwctc.commnet.edu
                 e-mail: rdennelien@nwcc.commnet.edu
*Roseann Dennerlein, Counselor*
*Barbara , President*

Offers a variety of services to students with disabilities including notetakers, extended testing time, counseling services, and special accommodations.

**4184  Norwalk Community-Technical College**
188 Richards Avenue
Norwalk, CT  06854                          203-857-7000
                                     FAX 203-857-3339
                    http://www.nctc.commnet.edu
*Lori Orvetti, Developmental Studies Counselor*

NCC is accessible to students with disabilites. Students who require accommodations are advised to notify the coodinator at least 6 weeks in advance.

**4185  Paier College of Art**
20 Gorham Avenue
Hamden, CT  06514                          203-287-3031
                                     FAX 203-287-3021
                    http://www.paiercollegeofart.edu
*Francis Cooley, Dean*

Offers a variety of services to students with disabilities including notetakers, extended testing time, counseling services, and special accommodations.

**4186  Quinebaug Valley Community Technical College**
742 Upper Maple Street
Danielson, CT  06239              860-774-1130
                    http://www.qvctc.commnet.edu
*Gary Hottinger, Director LD Center*
*Pam Abel, Learning Specialist*

The Learning Assistance Center provides academic support for students with disabilities. Such support may include untimed tests, readers, proctors, note-takers, tape recorders and so on. There is a Peer Advocate for Students with Disabilities to assist disabled students; there is also a Learning Specialist available ten hours a week to counsel and tutor disabled students.

**4187  Quinnipiac University**
275 Mount Carmel Avenue
Hamden, CT  06518                          203-582-8200
                                     800-462-1944
                                     FAX 203-582-8970
                 e-mail: John.Jarvis@Quinnipiac.edu
*John Jarvis, Coordinator Learning Services*

Provides reasonable accommodations to those students who have self-disclosed and provided documentation of a disability.

**4188  Sacred Heart University**
5151 Park Avenue
Fairfield, CT  06432                          203-365-4730
                                     FAX 203-396-8049
                    http://www.sacredheart.edu
                 e-mail: angottaj@sacredheart.edu
*Jill Angotta, Director*

Four year college that provides services to the learning disabled.

**4189  Southern Connecticut State University**
Disability Resource Office
501 Crescent Street
New Haven, CT  06515                          203-392-6828
                                     888-500-7278
                                     FAX 203-392-6829
                    http://www.southernct.edu
                 e-mail: TuckerSl@southernct.edu
*Suzanne Tucker, Director*
*Sharon Brennan, Admissions Director*

Provides students, faculty and staff with assistance and information on issues of access and full participation for persons with disabilities. The major responsibility of the Disability Resource Office is to provide services and supports that promote educational equality for students with documented disabilities.

**4190  St. Joseph College**
Academic Resource Center
1678 Asylum Avenue
West Hartford, CT  06117                          860-232-4571
                                     866-442-8752
                                     FAX 860-233-5695
                                     http://www.sjc.edu
                 e-mail: judyarzt@sjc.edu
*Judy Arzt, Director*
*Evelyn , President*

Offers a variety of services to students with disabilities including notetakers, extended testing time, counseling services, and special accommodations.

**4191  Thames Valley Campus of Three Rivers Community College**
574 New London Turnpike
Norwich, CT  06360                          860-885-2612
                                     800-886-4960
                                     FAX 860-886-6670
*Linda Jacobsen MD, Counselor*
*Chris Scarborough, Learning Specialist*

Offers associate degrees in computers, and engineering technologies (architectural, civil, electrical, general, manufacturing, mechanical and nuclear, business, general studies, liberal arts and sciences, nursing and others) and one-year certificates in architectural and CADD drafting and data processing.

**4192  Trinity College**
300 Summit Street
Hartford, CT  06106                          860-297-2000
                                     860-297-2272
                                     FAX 860-297-5140
                                     http://www.trincoll.edu
*Frederick Alford, Dean Student*
*James , President*

Offers a variety of services to students with disabilities including notetakers, extended testing time, counseling services, and special accommodations.

**4193   Tunxis Community College**

271 Scott Swamp Road
Farmington, CT  06032          860-255-3500
                               FAX 860-676-8906
        http://www.tunxis.commnet.edu
*David Smith MD, LD Director*
*Alison Iovanna, Director*

Offers a variety of services to students with disabilities including note takers, extended testing time, counseling services, and special accommodations.

**4194   University of Bridgeport**

**Office of Special Services**
**60 Lafayette Street**
**Bridgeport, CT  06604**          203-576-4454
                                   800-392-3582
                              FAX 203-576-4455
           http://www.bridgeport.edu
*Barbara Maryak, Dean of Admissions*
*Solomon Darko, Counselor*

Committted to the development of all students. An advocate and liaison for the students with disabilities, as defined by the American with Disabilities Act. The goal is to provide supportive services for those students with special needs in order to promote sensitivity and equality for the entire University of Bridgeport community.

**4195   University of Connecticut**

**University Program for College Students with LD**
**249 Glen Brook Road**
**Storrs, CT  06269 2064**          860-486-2020
                               FAX 860-486-5794
           http://www.apld.uconn.edu
           e-mail: j.madaus@uconn.edu
*David Parker, Director*

Committed to assuring equal educational opportunity for students with learning disabilities who have the potential for success in a highly competitive university setting. Since 1984, a comprehensive program has been available to assist qualified students with learning disabilities to become independent and successful learners within the regular University curriculum.

**4196   University of Hartford**

**Learning Plus**
**200 Bloomfield Avenue**
**W Hartford, CT  06117**          860-768-4312
                                   860-768-4312
                               FAX 860-768-4183
           http://www.hartford.edu
           e-mail: LDsupport@hartford.edu
*Lynne Goldman, Director*

An academic support service available to any University of Hartford student who has submitted appropriate documentation showing evidence of a specific learning disability and/or attention disability.

**4197   University of New Haven**

300 Boston Post Road
W Haven, CT  06516          203-932-7331
                            800-324-5864
                       FAX 203-932-6082
                       TDY:203-932-7409
           http://www.newhaven.edu
           e-mail: lcokeke@newhaven.edu
*Linda Cupney-Okeke, Director Disability Services*
*Jane Sangeloty, Admissions Director*

Persons who have special needs requiring accommodation should notify the Office for Students with Disabilities. The office handles all referrals regarding any student with a disability. The director provides guidance, assistance and information for students with disabilities and oversees the University's compliance with the Americans with Disabilities Act and the HEW Rehabilitation Act of 1973.

**4198   VISTA Vocational & Life Skills Center**

1356 Old Clinton Road
Westbrook, CT  06498          860-399-8080
                          FAX 860-399-3103
        http://www.vistavocational.org
        e-mail: hbosch@vistavocational.org
*Helen Bosch, Executive Director*

Building self-esteem and confidence in the lives of adults with disabilities through work, independence and friendship. Offers a post-secondary program for young adults with learning disabilities providing individualized training and support in career development, independent living skills, social skills development and community involvement.

**4199   Wesleyan University**

237 High Street
Middletown, CT  06459          860-685-2000
                           FAX 860-685-2201
          http://www.wesleyan.edu
          e-mail: vrutherford@wesleyan.edu
*Vancenia Rutherford, Associate Dean*
*Richard Culliton, Associate Dean*

Wesleyan University is committed to supporting all students in their academic and co-curricular endeavors. Although Wesleyan does not offer special academic programs for individuals with disabilities, the University does provide services and reasonable accommodations to all students who need and have a legal entitlement to such accommodations.

**4200   Western Connecticut State University**

**Students with Disabilities Services**
**181 White Street**
**Danbury, CT  06810**          203-837-8210
                                877-837-WCSU
                            FAX 203-837-9337
                            TDY:203-837-8284
           http://www.wcsu.edu
           e-mail: admissions@wcsu.edu
*James Roach, President*
*Amy Thuston, Administrative Assistant*

Offers a variety of services to students with disabilities including notetakers, extended testing time, counseling services, and special accommodations.

**4201  Yale University**
PO Box 208305
New Haven, CT  06520 8305          203-432-2324
                                   FAX 203-432-7884
                                   TDY:203-432-8250
                          http://www.yale.edu
                    e-mail: judith.york@yale.edu
*Judith York, LD Director*
*Caroline Barrett, Assistant Director*

Offers a variety of services to students with disabilities including notetakers, extended testing time, counseling services, and special accommodations.

## Delaware

**4202  Atlantic Coast Special Educational Services**
49 W Avenue
Ocean View, DE  19970          302-537-7263
                               877-785-7774
                    http://www.atlanticcoast.org
                    e-mail: lelling111@aol.com
*Lloyd Elling, President/Owner*

Full year, summer and respite care. Ages 18 and older.

**4203  Delaware Technical and Community College: Terry Campus**
100 Campus Drive
Dover, DE  19904          302-857-1000
                          FAX 302-857-1296
                    http://www.dtcc.edu
*Orlando George MD, President*

Offers a variety of services to students with disabilities including advocacy, readers, note takers, extended testing time, counseling services, and special accommodations.

**4204  University Affiliated Program for Families & Individuals with Developmental Disabilities**
University of Delaware
101 Alison Hall
Newark, DE  19716          302-831-6974
                           FAX 302-831-4690
                    e-mail: dkoch@udel.edu
*Michael Gamel-McCormick, Director*

Supports families and individuals who are affected by developmental disabilities.

**4205  University of Delaware**
Academic Services Center
5 W Main Street
Newark, DE  19716          302-831-1639
                           FAX 302-831-4128
                    http://www.aec.udel.edu
                    e-mail: lysbet@udel.edu
*Lysbet Murray, Associate Director*
*David Roselle, President*

Provides accommodations for eligible students with disabilities or ADHD.

## District of Columbia

**4206  American University: Academic Support Center**
Learning Services Program
4400 Massachusetts Avenue NW
Washington, DC  20016          202-885-3360
                               FAX 202-885-1042
                    http://www.american.edu
                    e-mail: asc@american.edu
*Melissa Scarfone, Learning Services Program Coordi*
*Kathy Schwartz, Director Academic Support Center*

Focuses on assisting students with their transition from high school to college during their freshman year. It is a small, mainstream program offering weekly individual meetings with the coordinator of the Learning Services Program throughout the student's first year.

**4207  Catholic University of America**
Distict Support Services
620 Michigan Avenue NE
Washington, DC  20064          202-319-5211
                               FAX 202-319-5126
                    http://disabilityservices.cua.edu
                    e-mail: mcclellan@cua.edu
*Bonnie McClellan, Director Disability Support*
*Christine Mica, Director Undergraduate Admission*

Four-year college that has support services for students with learning disabilities.

**4208  George Washington University**
Disability Support Services
2121 Eye St NW
Washington, DC  20052          202-994-1000
                          http://www.gwu.edu
                    e-mail: cwillis@gwu.edu
*Christy Willis, Director*
*Kathryn Napper, Admissions Director*

An independent four-year college with 260 students with disabilities out of a total of 8,837.

**4209  Georgetown University**
Disability Support Services/Learning Services
37th & O Streets NW
Washington, DC  20057          202-687-6985
                               FAX 202-687-6158
                    http://www.georgetown.edu
                    e-mail: gwr@georgetown.edu
*Marcia Fulk, Director*
*Dean , Admissions Director*

A four-year private university with a total enrollment of 6,418.

**4210  Howard University**
2400 6th Street NW
Washington, DC  20059          202-806-6100
                          http://www.howard.edu
*Vincent Johns, Dean Special Services*

Howard University is committed to compliance with the Americans with Disabilities Act, including providing special services to its disabled students such that they are able to achieve their academic goals. The Office of the Dean for Special Student Services (ODSSS)Æhas been delegated the responsibility of providing reasonable accommodations for students with disabilities.

**4211 Trinity College**

125 Michigan Avenue
Washington, DC 20017          202-884-9647
                             FAX 202-884-9229
                    http://www.trinitydc.edu
               e-mail: harrisk@trinitydc.edu
*Kimberly Harris, Director*
*Lynne Israel, Owner*

Four year college that provides services to students with a learning disability.

**4212 University of the District of Columbia**

4200 ConneCourticut Avenue NW
Washington, DC 20008          202-274-5336
                             FAX 202-274-6334
                    http://www.udc.edu
*Madhuck Ohal MD, Senior Director*

Offers a variety of services to students with disabilities including note takers, extended testing time, counseling services, and special accommodations.

# Florida

**4213 Barry University**

Center for Advanced Learning
11300 NE 2nd Avenue
Miami Shores, FL 33161          305-899-3461
                             FAX 305-899-3778
                    http://www.barry.edu
              e-mail: vcastro@mail.barry.edu
*Vivian Castro, CAL Program Director*

A comprehensive support program for students with learning disabilities and attention deficit disorders.

**4214 Beacon College**

105 E Main Street
Leesburg, FL 34748          352-787-7660
                             FAX 352-787-0721
                    http://www.beaconcollege.edu
            e-mail: admissions@beaconcollege.edu
*Shirley Smith, Assistant to the Vice President*
*Stephanie Knight, Admissions Counselor*

Offering BA and AA degree programs exclusively for students with learning disabilities.

**4215 Brevard Community College**

1519 Clearlake Road
Cocoa, FL 32922          321-632-1111
                             FAX 321-634-3779
                    http://www.brevard.cc.fl.us
*Brenda Fettrow, Director*

A public two-year college with 602 students with disabilities out of a total of 15,033.

**4216 Broward Community College**

111 East Olas Blvd
Fort Lauderdale, FL 33301          954-201-7400
                    http://www.broward.edu

Offers a variety of services to students with disabilities including note takers, extended testing time, counseling services, and special accommodations.

**4217 Central Florida Community College**

3001 SW College Road
Ocala, FL 34474          352-237-2111
                             FAX 352-237-0510
                    http://www.gocfcc.com
*Charles Vassance, President*

A public two-year college with 19 special education students out of a total of 5,616.

**4218 Chipola College**

3094 Indian Circle
Marianna, FL 32446          850-526-2761
                             FAX 850-718-2240
                    http://www.chipola.edu
*Gayle Duncan, Disabled Student Counselor*
*Gene , President*

A public two-year college.

**4219 DePaul School for Dyslexia**

701 Orange Avenue
Clearwater, FL 33756          727-443-2711
                             FAX 727-443-2604
                    http://www.webcoast.com/depaul/
              e-mail: mandroclese@earthlink.net
*Mary Hercher, Principal*

**4220 Disabled Student Services**

Miami Dade Community College
11011 SW 104th Street
Miami, FL 33176          305-237-2767
                             FAX 305-237-0880
                    http://www.mdc.edu
*Dianne Rossman, Coordinator*

A public two-year college with 307 special education students out of a total of 30,013.

**4221 Eckerd College**

4200 54th Avenue S
Saint Petersburg, FL 33711          727-864-8331
                                   800-456-9009
                             FAX 727-866-2304
                    http://www.eckerd.edu
              e-mail: admissions@ecker.edu
*Laura Schlack, Director*

Offers a variety of services to students with disabilities including notetakers, extended testing time, counseling services, and special accommodations.

**4222 Edison Community College**

8099 College Parkway SW
Fort Myers, FL 33919          239-489-9300
                    http://www.edison.edu
              e-mail: inquiry@edison.edu
*Andrea Anderson, Contact*

Offers a variety of services to students with disabilities including note takers, extended testing time, counseling services, and special accommodations.

**4223 Embry-Riddle Aeronautical University**
600 S Clyde Morris Boulevard
Daytona Beach, FL 32114      386-226-6000
800-862-2416
FAX 386-226-7070
http://www.embyriddle.edu
*Jim Hampton, Director*
*Richard Clark, Director for Admissions*

An independent four-year college with 19 special education students out of a total of 4,643.

**4224 Florida Agricultural & Mechanical University**
Learning Development & Evaluation Center
Foote-Hilyer Administration Center
Tallahassee, FL 32307      850-599-3000
http://www.famu.edu
e-mail: n.saabirjohnson@famu.edu
*Sharon Wooten, Director*
*Barbara Cox, Admissions Director*

A four-year public school with 275 students receiving disability services out of 10,691.

**4225 Florida Atlantic University**
Office for Students with Disabilities
777 Glades Road
Boca Raton, FL 33431      561-297-3880
FAX 561-297-2184
http://www.osd.fau.edu
e-mail: nrokoi@fau.edu
*Nicole MEd, Director*
*Albert Colom, Admissions Director*

Offers a variety of services to students with disabilities including notetakers, extended testing time, counseling services, and special accommodations.

**4226 Florida Community College at Jacksonville**
501 W State Street
Jacksonville, FL 32202      904-766-6769
FAX 904-646-2204
http://www.fccj.org
e-mail: lchilders@fccj.org
*Lucretia Childers, Disabled Student Coordinator*

A public two-year college with 80 special education students out of a total of 19,878.

**4227 Florida Gulf Coast University**
Office of Multi Access Services
10501 FGCU Boulevard
Fory Meyers, FL 33965      239-590-7956
FAX 239-590-7975
http://www.fgcu.edu
e-mail: cbright@fgcu.edu
*Cori Bright, Coordinator*

Four year college that offers students services for the disabled.

**4228 Florida International University**
Office of Disability Services
University Park GC 190
Miami, FL 33199      305-348-3532
FAX 305-348-3850
http://www.fiu.edu
e-mail: drcupgl@fiu.edu
*Julio Garcia, Director*
*Kathy Trionfo, Associate Director*
*Diane Russell, Assistant Director*

A public four-year university with a north campus office, serving more than 30,000 students. Students with disabilities seeking assistance number about 500. Tuition is $63.73 per credit for undergraduate and $138.08 for graduate students.

**4229 Florida State University**
Student Disability Resource Center
2249 University Center
Tallahassee, FL 32306      850-644-9566
FAX 850-644-7164
http://www.fsu.edu
e-mail: sdrc@fsu.edu
*Lauren Kennedy, Director*
*John Burnhill, Admissions Director*

A public four-year college with 500 students with learning disabilities out of a total of 27,014.

**4230 Gulf Coast Community College**
5230 W Highway 98
Panama City, FL 32401      850-769-1551
FAX 850-679-1556
http://www.gc.cc.fl.us
*Linda Dalen, Coordinator*

A public two-year college with 65 special education students out of a total of 7,374.

**4231 Hillsborough Community College**
10414 E Columbus Drive
Tampa, FL 33567      813-253-7914
FAX 813-253-7910
http://www.hccfl.edu
e-mail: dgiarrusso@hccfl.edu
*Denise Giarrusso, Coordinator*

A two-year college that provides services to the learning disabled.

**4232 Indian River Community College**
3209 Virginia Avenue
Fort Pierce, FL 34981      772-462-4700
*Rhoda Brant, Counselor*

Two-year community college providing services for learning disabled students (i.e., unlimited tests, notetakers, etc.).

**4233 Jacksonville University**
2800 University Boulevard N
Jacksonville, FL 32211      904-256-7000
FAX 904-256-7012
http://www.ju.edu
*Kerry D. Romesb MD, President*
*Dolores Star, Executive Secretary*

Offers a variety of services to students with disabilities including note takers, extended testing time, counseling services, and special accommodations.

**4234 Johnson & Wales University: Florida**

Student Success
1701 NE 127th Street
N Miami, FL 33181      305-892-7568
800-232-2433
FAX 305-892-5399
http://www.jwu.edu
e-mail: martha_saccks@jwu.edu
*Martha Sacks, Director*
*Sharmaine Beckford, Administrative Assistant*

**4235 Lake City Community College**

Disability Services
Route 19
Lake City, FL 32025      386-752-1822
FAX 386-754-4594
http://www.lakecity.cc.fl.us
e-mail: mitchelln@mail.lakecity.cc.fl.us
*Janice Irwin, Coordinator*
*Charles Hall, President*

A public two-year college with 31 special education students out of a total of 2,553.

**4236 Learning Development and Evaluation Center**

Florida A&M University
677 Ardelia Court
Tallahassee, FL 32307      850-599-3180
FAX 850-561-2513
http://www.famu.edu
*Sharon Wooten MD, Director*
*Donna Shell, Associate Director*

Assists the students by providing a variety of supportive services for example counseling, academic advisement, learning strategies.

**4237 Lynn University**

Advancement Program
3601 N Military Trail
Boca Raton, FL 33431      561-237-7239
800-888-5966
FAX 561-237-7873
http://www.lynn.edu
e-mail: melglines@lynn.edu
*Gary LMCH, Director*
*Allen Mullen, Admissions Director*

Independent four-year college with 268 special education students out of a total of 1,633 full time undergraduates. There is an additional special education fee.

**4238 Office of Disabled Students at Manatee Community College**

5840 26th Street W
Bradenton, FL 34206      941-752-5000
FAX 941-727-6380
http://www.mcc.fl.edu
*Paul Nolting, Adult Services Coordinator*
*Yvon Wills, Director*

Provides reasonable accommodations to ensure the inclusive and total access of disabled students to credit courses at the college while, at the same time, maintaining the integrity and quality of the college's academic programs. Offers a variety of services to students with disabilities including note takers, extended testing time, counseling services and special accommodations.

**4239 Okaloosa-Walton College**

100 College Boulevard
Niceville, FL 32578      850-729-6079
FAX 850-729-5323
http://www.owcc.edu
e-mail: swensonj@owcc.net
*Jody Swenson, Coordinator Services*

Offers a variety of services to students with disabilities including note takers, extended testing time, counseling services, and special accommodations.

**4240 PACE-Brantley Hall School**

3221 Sand Lake Road
Longwood, FL 32779      407-869-8882
FAX 407-869-8717
http://www.pacebrantleyhall.org/
*Kathleen Shatlock, Principal*
*Debbie Langran, Office Assistant*

**4241 Pensacola Junior College**

1000 College Boulevard
Pensacola, FL 32504      850-484-1637
FAX 850-484-2049
TDY:850-484-2093
http://www.pjc.cc.fl.us
e-mail: jnickles@pjc.edu
*James Nickles MD, Director*
*Linda Sheppard, Coordinator*
*Becky Adkins, Sign Language Interpretor*

Provide services accommodations to students with disabilities enrolled in community college programs.

**4242 Polk Community College**

999 Avenue H NE
Winter Haven, FL 33881      863-297-1000
http://www.polk.edu
*James Dowdy, Special Services*

Offers a variety of services to students with disabilities including note takers, extended testing time, counseling services, and special accommodations.

**4243 Saint Leo University**

Office for Students with Disabilities
PO Box 6665
Saint Leo, FL 33574      352-588-8464
FAX 352-588-8605
http://www.saintleo.edu
e-mail: karen.hahn@saintleo.edu
*Karen Hahn, Director*

Four year college that offers services to the disabled.

**4244 Santa Fe Community College: Florida**
3000 NW 83rd Street
Gainesville, FL  32606      352-395-5000
FAX 352-395-4100
http://www.sfcc.edu
e-mail: drc@sfcc.edu
*Larry Kiser, Disability Resource Counselor*
*Claudia Munnis, Disability Resource Counselor*
*Michael Hutley, Disability Resource Counselor*

Located on the first floor of the Student Services Building in S-112. If you have a disability that impacts your academic success, please visit us.

**4245 Seminole Community College**
100 Weldon Boulevard
Sanford, FL  32773      407-328-4722
FAX 407-328-2139
http://www.seminole.cc.fl.us
e-mail: admissions@scc-fl.edu
*Dorothy Paishon, Coordinator*
*Ann McGee, President*

Disability Support Services can be reached at 407-328-2109. We provide learning aids, course substitutions, instructor notification and support, referral to area agencies and college services, interpreters, notetakers, talking texts and tutors. We also have workshops on identifying and creating positive learning environments for disabled students.

**4246 Southeastern College of the Assemblies of God**
1000 Longfellow Boulevard
Lakeland, FL  33801      863-667-5157
FAX 863-667-5200
http://www.secollege.edu
*Misty Mancini, Director*
*Kristin Green, Assistant to the Director*

Offers a variety of services to students with disabilities including note takers, extended testing time, counseling services, and special accommodations.

**4247 St. Johns River Community College**
5001 Saint Johns Avenue
Palatka, FL  32177      386-312-4200
FAX 386-312-4283
http://www.sjrcc.cc.us
*Paula Sheppard, Special Services Director*
*Robert McLendon, President*

Students with disabilities are welcome at SJRCC, and are encouraged to contact the Counseling Center on their campus where special assistance is available with orientation, registration, academic planning, special supplies, and equipment. In addition, specialized services are available to students whose disability prevents them from participating fully in classroom activities.

**4248 St. Petersburg Junior College**
PO Box 13489
Saint Petersburg, FL  33733      727-341-3721
http://www.spjc.edu
e-mail: duncand@spcollege.edu
*Susan Blanchard MD, Learning Specialist*

A public two-year college with 890 special education students out of a total of 20,000+.

**4249 Tallahassee Community College**
444 Appleyard Drive
Tallahassee, FL  32304      850-201-6200
FAX 850-201-8518
http://www.tallahassee.cc.fl.us/
*Mark Linehan, Counselor*
*Margaret Handee, Educational Specialist*

A public two-year college with 584 special education students out of a total of 10,400.

**4250 Tampa Bay Academy**
12012 Boyette Road
Riverview, FL  33569      813-677-6700
800-678-3838
FAX 813-671-3145
TDY:813-677-2502
http://www.tampabay-acadamy.com
e-mail: ed.hoefle@tampa.yfcs.com
*Ed Hoefle, President*
*Cathy Black, Executive Secretary*

Offers a variety of services to students with disabilities including note takers, extended testing time, counseling services, and special accommodations.

**4251 University of Florida**
Office for Students with Disabilities
202 Peabody Hall
Gainsville, FL  32611      352-392-1261
FAX 352-392-5566
TDY:352-392-3008
http://www.ufl.edu
e-mail: johnpd@dfl.uso.edu
*John Denny, Director*
*William Kolb, Admissions Director*

A four-year public university with 100 students receiving disability services out of 32,680.

**4252 University of Miami**
PO Box 248106
Coral Gables, FL  33124      305-284-2374
FAX 305-284-1999
http://www.miami.edu
*Judith Antinarella, Director*
*Noemi Berrios, Senior Staff Assistant*

Offers a variety of services to students with disabilities including note takers, extended testing time, counseling services, and special accommodations.

**4253 University of North Florida**
4567 Saint Johns Bluff Road S
Jacksonville, FL  32216      904-620-2624
FAX 904-620-2414
TDY:904-620-2969
http://www.unf.edu
*John Delaney, President*
*Pam McCuheon, Admissions Coordinator*

Offers a variety of services to students with disabilities including notetakers, extended testing time, counseling services, and special accommodations.

**4254 University of Tampa**

401 W Kennedy Boulevard
Tampa, FL 33606          813-253-3333
                        FAX 813-258-7208
                        http://www.ut.edu
                        e-mail: disability.services@ut.edu
Cheri Kittrell, Assistant Director Academic Cent
Ronald , President

A private, comprehensive university with an international reputation for excellence.

**4255 University of West Florida**

11000 University Parkway
Pensacola, FL 32514          850-474-2387
                             FAX 850-857-6188
                             TDY:850-474-2000
                             http://www.uwf.edu
                             e-mail: bfitzpat@uwf.edu
Barbara Fitzpatrick, Assistant Director
John , President

A public four-year college with 8 special education students out of a total of 6793.

**4256 Valencia Community College**

PO Box 3028
Orlando, FL 32825          407-299-5000
                           FAX 407-293-8839
                           http://www.ualencia.cc.fl.us
Walter Johnson, Counselor
Peg Edmonds, Counselor

A public two-year college with 1,200 students with disabilities out of a total of 25,000.

**4257 Webber College**

PO Box 96
Babson Park, FL 33827          863-638-1431
                               800-741-1844
                               FAX 863-638-1591
                               http://www.webber.edu
                               e-mail: jragans@hotmail.com
Julie Ragans, Director Admissions
Patty Beaslie, Coordinator

An independent four-year college with 39 special education students out of a total of 354.

**4258 Woodland Hall Academy-Dyslexia Research Institute**

5746 Centerville Road
Tallahassee, FL 32309          850-893-2216
                               FAX 850-893-2440
                               http://www.dyslexia-add.org
                               e-mail: dri@talstar.com
Robyn Rennick, Program Coordinator

Participates in field research and offers testing materials for dyslexia, ADD, SLD children and adults.

*6-20 years old*

---

# Georgia

**4259 Albany State University**

504 College Drive
Albany, GA 31705          229-430-4600
                          FAX 229-430-3936
                          http://www.asurams.edu
Portia Shields, President
Kenneth Dyer, Vice President

Four-year college offering services and support to students with learning disabilities.

**4260 Andrew College**

413 College Street
Cuthbert, GA 39840
                          800-664-9250
                          FAX 229-732-5991
                          http://www.andrewcollege.edu
                          e-mail: focus@andrewcollege.edu
Sherri Taylor, Director

The FOCUS program offers an intensive level of academic support designed for and limited to documented learning disabilities or attention deficit disorder. While FOCUS supplements and complements the tutorial and advising to all students, the program also provides an additional level of professional assistance and mentoring. Those accepted into FOCUS are charged regular tuition andd fees, plus a FOCUS laboratory fee.

**4261 Atlanta Speech School**

Wardlaw School for Children with LD
3160 Northside Parkway NW
Atlanta, GA 30327          404-233-5332
                           FAX 404-266-2175
                           http://www.atlantaspeechschool.org
                           e-mail: jkroese@atlantaspeechschool.org
Judy Kroese, Director Professional Service
Sandra Mims, Coordinator Lower School
Maureen Demku, Coordinator, Upper School

Wardlaw School is for children with mild to moderate language and learning disabilities.

**4262 Berry College**

PO Box 490159
Rome, GA 30149          706-236-2215
                        FAX 706-236-2248
                        http://www.berry.edu
Marshall Jenkin MD, Director

Offers a variety of services to students with disabilities including notetakers, extended testing time, counseling services, and special accommodations.

**4263 Brandon Hall School**

1701 Brandon Hall Drive
Atlanta, GA 30350          770-394-8177
                           FAX 770-804-8821
                           http://www.brandonhall.org
                           e-mail: pstockhammer@brandonhall.org
Paul Stockhammer, President
Marcia Shearer, Admissions Director

College preparatory, co-ed day and boys' boarding school for students in grades 4-12. Designed for academic underachievers and students with minor learning disabilities, attention deficit disorders and dyslexia. Enrollment 150 students; faculty 40, with 100% college acceptances. Interscholastic sports and numerous co-curriculum activities and summer programs.

**4264  Brenau University**

Learning Center
1 Centennial Circle
Gainesville, GA  30501          770-534-6134
                               800-252-5119
                          FAX 770-534-6221
                      http://www.brenau.edu
          e-mail: vyamilkoski@lib.brenau.edu
*Vincent EdD, Learning Center Director*
*Christina Chocran, Women's College Admissions*

Program for students with a diagnosed learning disability and who have average to above average intellectual potential. This program is designed to provide support services for learning disabled students as they attend regular college courses. Offers a more structured learning environment, as well as the freedom associated with college living.

**4265  Brewton-Parker College**

PO Box 2124
Mount Vernon, GA  30445         912-583-3222
                                800-342-1087
                           FAX 912-583-4498
                        http://www.bpc.edu
              e-mail: jkissell@bpc.edu
*Juanita Kissell, Director Counseling Service*

An independent four-year college with 15 special education students out of a total of 1,942.

**4266  Clayton College & State University**

Disability Services
5900 N Lee Street
Morrow, GA  30260               770-961-3500
                           FAX 770-961-3752
                      http://www.clayton.edu
*Thomas Harden MD, President*

Four-year college that offers programs for learning disabled students.

**4267  Columbus State University**

4225 University Avenue
Columbus, GA  31907             706-568-2330
                           FAX 706-569-3096
                     http://www.colstate.edu
       e-mail: willliams_aracelis@colstate.edu
*Yolanda Jackson, Staff*

Offers a variety of services to students with disabilities including note takers, extended testing time, counseling services, and special accommodations.

**4268  DeVry Institute of Technology**

250 N Arcadia Avenue
Decatur, GA  30030              404-292-2645
                           FAX 404-292-7011
                    http://www.atl.devry.edu
*Andrea Rutherford, Academic Support Director*
*Donna Loraine, President*

Offers a variety of services to students with disabilities including notetakers, extended testing time, counseling services, and special accommodations.

**4269  East Georgia College**

131 College Circle
Swainsboro, GA  30401           478-289-2017
                        http://www.ega.edu
         e-mail: rlosser@ega.peachnet.edu
*Bennie Brinson, Student Services*

Offers a variety of services to students with disabilities including note takers, extended testing time, counseling services, and special accommodations.

**4270  Emory University**

Office of Disability Services
201 Dowman Drive
Atlanta, GA  30322              404-727-6016
                           FAX 404-727-1126
                       http://www.emory.edu
              e-mail: gweaver@emory.edu
*Gloria McCord, Director*
*Jane Jordon, Admissions Director*

An independent four-year college with 150 special education students out of a total of 6,316.

**4271  Fort Valley State University**

Counseling & Career Development Center
1005 State University Dr
Fort Valley, GA  31030          478-825-6211
                        http://www.fvsu.edu
          e-mail: asmissap@mail.fvsu.edu
*Myldred Hill MD, Director*

Four-year college that provides counseling for learning disabled students.

**4272  Gables Academy**

811 Gordon Street
Stone Mountain, GA  30083       770-465-7500
                                877-465-7500
                           FAX 770-465-7700
                  http://www.gablesacademy.com
            e-mail: info@gablesacademy.com
*Jim Meffen, President*
*Carol Clark, Administrative Assistant*

Offers a variety of services to students with disabilities including notetakers, extended testing time, counseling services, and special accommodations.

**4273  Georgia Affiliated Program for Persons with Developmental Disabilities**

University of Georgia
Dawson Hall
Athens, GA  30602               706-542-3457
                           FAX 706-542-4815
*Zolinda Stoneman, Director*

For students with developmental disabilities.

# Schools & Colleges /Georgia

**4274 Georgia College**
Georgia College & State University
Milledgeville, GA 31061      478-445-5004
                             800-342-0471
                http://www.gcsu.edu
         e-mail: dcsmith@mail.gcsu.edu
*Craig Smith MD, Chair*

Offers a variety of services to students with disabilities including note takers, extended testing time, counseling services, and special accommodations.

**4275 Georgia Institute of Technology**
225 N Avenue
Atlanta, GA 30332      404-894-2564
                       FAX 404-894-9928
                http://www.gatech.edu
*RoseMary Watkins, Director*
*Wayne Clough, President*

A public four-year college with 6 special education students out of a total of 9,587.

**4276 Georgia Southern University**
Student Disability Resource Center
PO Box 8037
Statesboro, GA 30460      912-871-1566
                          FAX 912-871-1419
                http://www.gasou.edu
       e-mail: cwatkins@gsix2.cc.gasou.edu
*Wayne Akins, Director*
*Teresa Thompsen, Admissions Director*

Offers a variety of services to students with disabilities including note takers, extended testing time, counseling services, and special accommodations.

**4277 Georgia State University**
Disability Services
33 Gilmer Street, Unit 3
Atlanta, GA 30303      404-463-9044
                       FAX 404-463-9049
                http://www.gsu.edu/disability
         e-mail: disleb@langate.gsu.edu
*Louise Bedrossian, Cognitive Disability Specialist*
*Rodney Penamon, Director*

An accessible campus with 149 students with disabilities. Support services include a staff of professionals and student aides who provide tutors, mobility assistance, test proctoring, extended time for exams, interpreters, transcribing, readers, reading machines, taped textbooks and class materials. Technology includes computers with voice output and zoom text, print magnification systems, Arkenstone and Kurzweil Readers, assistive listening devices, and specialized software programs.

**4278 Life University**
1269 Barclay Circle
Marietta, GA 30075      770-426-2725
                        FAX 770-426-2728
                http://www.life.edu
         e-mail: adrake@life.edu
*Ann Drake MD, Director*
*Lisa Rubin, Director*

Four-year college offers academic support to students with disabilities.

**4279 Macon State College**
100 College Station Drive
Macon, GA 31206      478-471-2700
         e-mail: sloyd@mail.maconstate.edu
Four-year college that provides services to those students who are disabled.

**4280 Mercer University: Atlanta**
Teaching Learning Center
Atlanta, GA 30341-4155      678-547-6000
                http://www.mercer,edu
*Dorothy Roberts, Director*

Offers a variety of services to students with disabilities including note takers, extended testing time, counseling services, and special accommodations.

**4281 Mill Springs Academy**
13660 New Providence Road
Alpharetta, GA 30004      770-360-1336
                          FAX 770-360-1341
                http://www.millsprings.org/
*Robert Moore, President*

**4282 North Georgia College & State University**
122 Barnes Hall
Dahlonega, GA 30597      706-867-2782
                         FAX 706-867-2882
                http://www.ngcsu.edu
         e-mail: emcintosh@ngcsu.edu
*Elizabeth McIntosh, Coordinator*

Four-year college that provides resources and programs for learning disabled students.

**4283 Piedmont College**
PO Box 10
Demorest, GA 30535
                         800-277-7020
                http://www.piedmont.edu
*Nancy Adams, Special Services*

Offers a variety of services to students with disabilities including notetakers, extended testing time, counseling services, and special accommodations.

**4284 Reinhardt College**
Academic Support Office
7300 Reinhardt College Circle
Waleska, GA 30183      770-720-5567
                       FAX 770-720-5602
                http://www.reinhardt.edu
         e-mail: srr@reinhardt.edu
*Sylvia Robertson, Director Academic Support Office*

An independent four-year college with 80 learning disabled students out of a total of 1,190 being served in academic support. There is an additional fee for the tutorial program in addition to the regular tuition.

**4285 Savannah State University**
Comprehensive Counseling Center
PO Box 20376
Savannah, GA 31404          912-356-2202
                        FAX 912-356-2464
                    http://www.savstate.edu
                e-mail: akoredea@savstate.edu
*Orlando Spencer, Coordinator*

Four-year college has a comprehensive counseling center for students that are learning disabled.

**4286 Shorter College**
315 Shorter Avenue SW
Rome, GA 30165          706-291-2121
                        800-868-6980
                    FAX 706-236-1515
                    http://www.shorter.edu
*Ed Schroeder MD, President*

Offers a variety of services to students with disabilities including note takers, extended testing time, counseling services, and special accommodations.

**4287 South Georgia College**
100 W College Park Drive
Douglas, GA 31533          912-389-4220
                        800-342-6364
                    FAX 912-389-4392
                    http://www.sga.edu
                e-mail: calott@sga.edu
*Edward Jackson, President*
*Glenda Clark, Interim Vice President*

The Office of Disability Services, a division of Academic Affairs, is committed to providing an equal educational opportunity for all qualified students with disabilities. The Office of Disability Services is responsible for initiating and coordinating services for students with disabilities at South Georgia College.

**4288 Southern College of Technology**
1100 S Marietta Parkway
Marietta, GA 30060          678-915-7778
                        800-635-3204
                    http://www.spsu.edu
*Patricia Soper MD, Special Services*

Offers a variety of services to students with disabilities including note takers, extended testing time, counseling services, and special accommodations.

**4289 Southern Polytechnic State University**
1100 S Marietta Parkway
Marietta, GA 30060          678-915-7778
                        800-635-3204
                    http://www.spsu.edu
                e-mail: tcordle@spsu.edu
*Terri Cordle, Counselor*

Four-year college that offers counseling services to learning disabled students.

**4290 State University of West Georgia**
1601 Maple Street
Carrollton, GA 30118          678-839-5000
                    http://www.westga.edu
                e-mail: speacock@westga.edu
*Shannon Peacock, Coordinator*

Four-year college that provides services to disabled students.

**4291 Toccoa Falls College**
PO Box 777
Toccoa Falls, GA 30598          706-886-6831
                        888-785-5624
                    FAX 706-886-6412
                    http://www.toccoafalls.edu
                e-mail: wgardner@tfc.edu
*Wayne Gardner, President*
*Christy Meadows, Department Head of Admissions*

Four-year college that provides services to the learning disabled.

**4292 University of Georgia**
Learning Disabilities Center
Clark Howell
Athens, GA 30602          706-542-7034
                    FAX 706-542-7719
                    TDY:705-542-8778
                    http://www.drc.uda.edu
*Karen Kaloboda, Director*
*Elaine Manglitz, Service Head*
*Nancy McBuss, Admissions Director*

A public four-year university with 276 students with learning disabilities out of a total of 24,213. There is no fee for the comprehensive service program. To be eligible for services, students must submit recent documentation which meets evaluation standards.

**4293 Valdosta State University**
1500 N Patterson Street
Valdosta, GA 31698          229-333-5800
                        800-618-1878
                    http://www.valdosta.edu
                e-mail: kgadden@valdosta.edu
*Kimberly Gadden, Special Services Coordinator*

A public four-year university with 90 learning disabled students out of a total of 9,000.

**4294 West Georgia College**
303 Fort Dr
LaGrange, GA 30240          706-845-4323
                    http://www.westga.tec.ga.us
*Ann Phillips MD, Special Services*

A public four-year college with 34 special education students out of a total of 5,528.

# Hawaii

**4295 Brigham Young University: Hawaii**
55-220 Kulanui Street
Laie, HI 96762          808-293-3211
                    FAX 808-293-3741
                    http://www.byuh.edu
*Eric Scumway, President*

Offers a variety of services to students with disabilities including note takers, extended testing time, counseling services, and special accommodations.

**4296 Center on Disability Studies, University Affiliated Program: University of Hawaii**
University of Hawaii at Manoa
1776 University Avenue
Honolulu, HI 96822          808-956-6914
          FAX 808-956-7878
http://www.cds.hawaii.edu
e-mail: juana@hawaii.edu
*Robert Stodden, Director/Professor*

Dedicated to supporting the quality of life, inclusion, and empowerment of all persons with disabilities and their families through partnerships in training, service, evaluation, research, dissemination, and technical assistance. Nurtures, sustains, and expands promising practices for people with disabilities.

**4297 University of Hawaii: Honolulu Community College**
874 Dillingham Boulevard
Honolulu, HI 96817          808-845-9282
          FAX 808-847-9836
http://www.honolulu.hawaii.edu
e-mail: acess@hcc.hawaii.edu
*Lorri Taniguchi, Disability Services Provider*
*Sheryl Legaspi, Disability Services Provider*

Academic support provided for students with documented disabilities. Intake interview required to determine appropriate accommodations which may include taped books, testing accommodations, note takers, etc. Early notification requested.

**4298 University of Hawaii: Kapiolani Community College**
4303 Diamond Head Road
Honolulu, HI 96816          808-734-9552
          FAX 808-734-9447
http://www.kcc.hawaii.edu
*Joselyn Yoshimura, Director*

A public two-year college with 28 special education students out of a total of 6,529.

**4299 University of Hawaii: Kauai Community College**
3-1901iKaumualii Highway
Lihue, HI 96766          808-245-8210
http://www.kauaicc.hawaii.edu
*Frances Dinnan, Special Services*

Offers a variety of services to students with disabilities including note takers, extended testing time, counseling services, and special accommodations.

**4300 University of Hawaii: Leeward Community College**
Program for Adult Achievement
96-045 Ala Ike Street
Pearl City, HI 96782          808-455-0421
          FAX 808-455-0471
http://www.lcc.hawaii.edu
e-mail: kprogram@hawaii.edu
*Mark Silliman, Chancellor*

A public two-year college with 153 special education students out of a total of 6,345.

## Idaho

**4301 Boise State University**
1910 University Drive
Boise, ID 83725          208-426-1156
          FAX 208-426-3765
http://www.boisestate.edu
*Charles Ruch, President*

A public four-year college with 31 special education students out of a total of 12,812.

**4302 College of Southern Idaho**
315 Falls Avenue
Twin Falls, ID 83303          208-733-9554
          800-680-0274
          FAX 208-736-3015
          TDY:208-734-9929
http://www.csi.cc.id.us/
e-mail: marrossa@csi.edu
*Jerry Meybrhoeffer, President*
*Monty Arrossa, Director of Human Resources*

Offers a variety of services to students with disabilities including note takers, extended testing time, counseling services, and special accommodations.

**4303 Idaho State University**
ADA Disabilities Resource Center
Campus Box 8121
Pocatello, ID 83209          208-282-3242
          http://www.isu.edu
          e-mail: lawsjona@isu.edu
*Robert Campbell, Director*

Four-year college that provides information and resources to students with a learning disability.

**4304 North Idaho College**
1000 W Garden Avenue
Coeur d'Alene, ID 83814          208-769-7794
          FAX 208-769-3300
          http://www.nic.edu
*Kristine Wold, Special Services*
*Sharon Folic, Coordinator*

Offers a variety of services to students with disabilities including note takers, extended testing time, counseling services, and special accommodations.

**4305 University of Idaho**
Student Disability Services
UI Admissions Office
Moscow, ID 83844
          888-884-3246
          http://www.uidaho.edu
          e-mail: sds@widaho.edu
*Diane Milhullin, Student Disability Services*
*Dan Davenport, Admissions Director*

Provides disability support services for students with temporary or permanent disabilities, in accordance with the Americans with Disabilities Act, and the Rehabilitation Act. The Campus Guide for People with Disabilities describes some of these services. About 100 people are served annually.

**4306 University of Idaho: Idaho Center on Development**

College of Education
129 W 3rd Street
Moscow, ID 83843          208-885-3559
                          800-393-7290
                          FAX 208-885-3628
                          http://www.idahocdhd.org
*Julie Fodor, Director*
*Jennifer Magelky, Administrative Assistant*

Positive behavioral supports.

## Illinois

**4307 Acacia Academy**

6425 Willow Springs Road
La Grange Highlands, IL 60525   708-579-9040
                                FAX 708-579-5872
        e-mail: kfouks@acaciaacademy.com
*Kathryn Fouks, Principal*
*Eileen Petzold, Dean*

A school for grades K-12 for children with learning disabilities. NCA accredited and approved for out of district students in special education in the state of Illinois.

**4308 Aurora University**

347 S Gladstone Avenue
Aurora, IL 60506          630-892-6431
                          800-742-5281
                          FAX 630-844-5463
                          http://www.aurora.edu
                          e-mail: inquiry@aurora.edu
*Eric Schwaerze, Co-Director Learning Center*
*Patsy Mahoney, Director Learning Center*

An independent four-year college with an enrollment near 2,000 students. The University Learning Center provides accommodations, tutoring and support for all students with physical or learning disabilities.

**4309 Barat College of DePaul University**

Learning Opportunities Program
700 E Westleigh Road
Lake Forest, IL 60045     847-234-3000
                          FAX 847-574-6000
                          http://www.barat.edu
                          e-mail: dwitikka@barat.edu
*Debbie Sheade, Director*

A four-year college with small classes and personalized education. There is a separate fee for the special education program in addition to the regular tuition. There is also a separate admissions procedure.

**4310 Blackburn College**

700 College Avenue
Carlinville, IL 62626     217-854-3231
                          FAX 217-854-3713
                          http://www.blackburn.edu
*Patricia Kowal, Director*

Offers a variety of services to students with disabilities including notetakers, extended testing time, counseling services, and special accommodations.

**4311 Brehm Preparatory School**

1245 E Grand Avenue
Carbondale, IL 62901      618-457-0371
                          FAX 618-529-1248
                          http://www.brehm.org
                          e-mail: everhart@bayou.com
*Richard PhD, Executive Director*
*Donna Collins, Director Admissions*

A coeducational boarding school for students with learning differences. Services are provided for students in grades 6-12. A post-secondary program, OPTIONS, is also available.

**4312 Center for Academic Development: National College of Education**

2840 Sheridan Road
Evanston, IL 60201        847-905-2356
*Annol Kim, Assistant Professor*
*Evanston Cad, Coordinator*

Peer tutoring available- hours per week per course for documented Learning disability students who were regularly admitted and meet college entrance criteria.

**4313 Chicago State University**

Office of Student Development, Adm. 303
9501 South King Drive
Chicago, IL 60628         773-995-2000
                          http://www.csu.edu
*Sandra Westbroo MD, Assistant Provost*
*Bridget Mason, Research Assistant*

The Office of Student Development maintains a Student Support Services Program for the disabled students on the campus. Seeks to meet the needs and concerns of the disabled. Services, sources and suggestions are welcomed.

**4314 College of DuPage**

425 Fawell Boulevardt
Glen Ellyn, IL 60136      630-942-4259
                          FAX 630-858-5409
                          http://www.cod.edu
                          e-mail: ryanth@cdnet.cod.edu
*Sunil Chand, President*
*Tom Ryan, Vice President*

Offers a variety of services to students with disabilities including note takers, extended testing time, counseling services, and special accommodations.

**4315 College of Health & Human Development: Department of Disability & Human Development**

University of Illinois at Chicago
1640 W Roosevelt Road
Chicago, IL 60608         312-413-1647
                          FAX 312-413-2918
                          TDY:312-413-0453
                          http://www.uic.edu/depts/idhd
                          e-mail: DHD@uic.edu
*David PhD, Professor*
*Maita Obligado, Office Assistant*

Dedicated to the scholarly, interdisciplinary study of disability and related aspects of human development. It critically examines current and prospective disability policies, conceptual models, and intervention strategies in terms of their historical development and their present merits.

**4316 Columbia College Chicago**

Student Support Services
600 S Michigan Avenue
Chicago, IL 60605      312-344-8132
FAX 312-344-8005
http://www.colum.edu
e-mail: banderson@popmail.colum.edu
*Beverly Anderson, Director*
*Gabriel Watkins, Administrative Assistant*

Four-year college that offers support and services to special needs students.

**4317 Danville Area Community College**

2000 E Main Street
Danville, IL 61832      217-443-8747
FAX 217-431-0751
TDY:217-443-8853
http://www.dacc.ccil.us
e-mail: pmcconn@dacc.cc.il.us
*Penny McConnell, Assessment Center Coordinator*

The college offers the associate's degree in 59 occupational programs and 36 transfer prgrams. DACC also offers 10 baccalaureate degree programs through cooperative agreements with Eastern Illinois University, Southern Illinois University, University at Carbondale, and Franklin University in Columbus, Ohio. Six of these four-year degree programs are offered online. Accommodations for students with disabilities.

**4318 Eastern Illinois University**

Office of Disability Services
600 Lincoln Avenue
Charleston, IL 61920      217-581-6583
FAX 217-581-7208
http://www.eiu.edu
e-mail: cfmpj@eiu.edu
*Kathy Waggoner, Director*
*Julie Walters, Office Assistant*

A public four-year university with 90 students receiving disability services out of 9,346.

**4319 Elgin Community College**

1700 Spartan Drive
Elgin, IL 60123      847-697-1000
888-545-7222
FAX 847-669-9105
http://www.elgin.cc.il.us/
*Annabelle Rhoades, Director LD*

Offers a variety of services to students with disabilities including note takers, extended testing time, counseling services, and special accommodations.

**4320 Governors State University**

1 University Parkway
University Park, IL 60466-0975      708-534-5000
http://www.govst.edu
e-mail: gsunow@govst.edu
*Pamela Bax, Outreach Counselor*

Provides assistance to GSU students with disabilities. Assistance includes coordination of untimed tests, notetakers, test readers, computerized testing and other assistance that will allow students equal access to the learning environment.

**4321 Highland Community College**

2998 W Pearl City Road
Freeport, IL 61032      815-599-3403
FAX 815-235-6130
*Sue Wilson, Director*

A public two-year college with 23 special education students out of a total of 3,262.

**4322 Illinois Central College**

1 College Drive E
Peoria, IL 61635      309-999-4582
800-422-2293
FAX 309-999-4549
http://www.icc.edu
e-mail: tingles@icc.edu
*Denise Cioni, Special Needs Coordinator*
*Terri Ingles, Director*

A public two-year college with approximately 100 students with learning disabilities and/or attention deficit disorder. Students may borrow tape recorders, use note takers, access books on tape, request test accommodations and utilize tutorial labs and/or individual tutoring.

**4323 Illinois Eastern Community College/LincolnTrail College**

11220 State Highway I
Robinson, IL 62454      618-544-8657
FAX 618-544-7423
http://www.iecc.edu
e-mail: ltcadmissions@iecc.cc.il.us
*Searoba Haskin, Learning Skills*
*Deanna Chysler, Administrative Assistant*

A public two-year college with 4 special education students out of a total of 1,040.

**4324 Illinois Eastern Community College/OlneyCentral College**

305 NW Street
Olney, IL 62450      618-395-4351
866-622-4322
FAX 618-392-5212
http://www.iecc.edu
e-mail: occadmissions.iecc.cc.il.us
*Teresa Tagler, Business Instructor*
*Peggy King, Secretary*

Offers a variety of services to students with disabilities including note takers, extended testing time, counseling services, and special accommodations.

**4325 Illinois Eastern Community College/WabashValley College**

2200 College Drive
Mount Carmel, IL 62863      618-262-8641
866-982-4322
FAX 618-262-8962
http://www.iecc.cc.edu
e-mail: wwvcadmissions@iecc.cc.il.us
*Marj Doty, Learning Skills*

Offers a variety of services to students with disabilities including note takers, extended testing time, counseling services, and special accommodations.

**4326 Illinois Eastern Community Colleges/Frontier Community College**

2 Frontier Drive
Fairfield, IL  62837          618-842-3711
877-464-3687
FAX 618-842-4425
http://www.iecc.cc.il.us
e-mail: fccadmissions@iecc.cc.il.us
*Beverly Fisher, Contact*
*Dennise Hilliard, Administrative Assistant*

Offers a variety of services to students with disabilities including note takers, extended testing time, counseling services, and special accommodations.

**4327 Illinois State University**

Disability Concerns
350 Fell Hall
Normal, IL  61790          309-438-5853
FAX 309-438-7713
TDY:309-438-8620
http://www.ilstu.edu
e-mail: ableisu@ilstu.edu
*Ann Caldwell, Director*
*Steven Adams, Admissions Director*

A public four-year university with 130 students with learning disabilities and/or attention deficit (hyperactivity) disorder. Students may be eligible for services such as notetakers, testing accommodations, books on tape and e-text.

**4328 John A Logan College**

700 Logan College Road
Carterville, IL  62918          618-985-3741
800-851-4720
FAX 618-985-2867
http://www.jal.cc.il.us
e-mail: logan@jal.cc.il.us
*Judy Zineyard, Director*

A public two-year college with 47 special education students out of a total of 4,642.

**4329 Joliet Junior College**

1215 Houbolt Road
Joliet, IL  60431          815-729-9020
FAX 815-744-5507
http://www.jjc.edu
e-mail: carol_smith@jjc.edu
*Carol Smith, Special Needs Coordinator*
*JD Ross, President*

Student Accommodations and Resources (StAR) is the academic support department which provides support services to students with disabilities and students enrolled in career and technical majors.

**4330 Kaskaskia College**

27210 College Road
Centralia, IL  62801          618-545-3011
800-642-0859
FAX 618-532-5313
http://www.kc.cc.il.us
e-mail: smartin@kaskaskia.edu
*Lisa Oelze, SNAP Coordinator*
*Shirley Martin, Executive Assistant to the Presi*

Offers a variety of services to students with disabilities including note takers, extended testing time, counseling services, and special accommodations.

**4331 Kendall College**

900 N Branch Street
Chicago, IL  60622          877-588-8860
http://www.kendal.edu
*Peter Pauletti, Admissions*

An independent four-year college with 50 special education students out of a total of 400.

**4332 Kishwaukee College**

21193 Malta Road
Malta, IL  60150          815-825-2086
FAX 815-825-2072
http://www.kishwaukee.edu
*Frances Loubere, Coordinator*
*Dave Louis, President*

Community college services for students with special needs. Students will be counseled and appropriate accommodations made on an individual basis.

**4333 Knox College**

2 ES Street
Galesburg, IL  61401          309-341-7151
FAX 309-341-7718
http://www.knox.edu
*John Haslem, Director*

Offers a variety of services to students with disabilities including note takers, extended testing time, counseling services, and special accommodations.

**4334 Lake Land College**

5001 Lakeland Boulevard
Mattoon, IL  61938          217-234-5232
800-252-4121
FAX 217-234-5390
TDY:217-234-5371
http://www.lakeland.cc.il.us
e-mail: dbeno@lakeland.cc.il.us
*Donna Beno, Perkins/Title III Coordinator*
*Emily Hartke, Counselor*

A public two-year college with 180 students with disabilities out of a total enrollment of approximately 5,000.

**4335 Lewis and Clark Community College**

5800 Godfrey Road
Godfrey, IL  62035          618-466-3411
FAX 618-466-1294
http://www.lc.cc.il.us
*Patricia Dunn-Horn, Coordinator*

Offers a variety of services to students with disabilities including note takers, extended testing time, counseling services, and special accommodations.

**4336 Lincoln College**

**Supportive Educational Services**
**300 Keokuk**
**Lincoln, IL  62656**          217-732-3155
                              800-569-0556
                          FAX 207-732-7715
           **http://www.lincolncollege.com**
            **e-mail: rumler@lincolncollege.com**
*Rod Rumler, Director*

A private two-year college with 180 special education students out of a total of 725.

**4337 Lincoln Land Community College**

**5250 Shepherd Road**
**Springfield, IL  62794**          217-786-2267
                                 800-727-4161
                            FAX 217-786-2866
                            TDY:217-786-2798
               **http://www.llcc.edu**
*Linda Chriswell, Special Needs*
*Jack , President*

A public two-year college with 75 special education students out of a total of 7,880.

**4338 McHenry County College**

**8900 US Highway 14**
**Crystal Lake, IL  60012**          815-455-3700
                             FAX 815-455-0718
                             TDY:815-455-8614
              **http://www.mchenry.edu**
*Walter Packard, President*
*Debrah Tatton, Executive Officer*

Offers a variety of services to students with disabilities including note takers, extended testing time, counseling services, and special accommodations.

**4339 Millikin University**

**1184 W Main Street**
**Decatur, IL  62522**          217-424-3511
                            FAX 217-362-6497
               **http://www.millikin.edu**
            **e-mail: webmaster@mail.millikin.edu**
*Elizabeth Abrahamson, Director*
*Doug Zemky, President*

Four-year college that provides programs for the learning disabled.

**4340 Moraine Valley Community College**

**88th Avenue**
**Palos Hills, IL  60465**          708-974-5469
                             FAX 708-974-0078
                             TDY:708-974-9556
              **http://www.moraine.cc.il.us**
            **e-mail: moraine@moraine.valley.edu**
*Laura Vonborstel, Director*

A public two-year college with 128 special education students out of a total of 13,958.

**4341 Morton College**

**3801 S Central Avenue**
**Cicero, IL  60804**          708-656-8000
                          FAX 708-656-3924
                          TDY:708-656-0389
             **http://www.morton.cc.il.us**
*Brent Knight, President*
*Patti Demopoulos, Learning Assistant Specialist*

A public two-year community college with 75 special education students out of a total of 5,044. Support services and accommodations are provided for students with disabilities. Tutoring is also available.

**4342 National-Louis University**

**Center for Academic Devlopment**
**2840 Sheridan Road**
**Evanston, IL  60201**          847-465-5829
                             FAX 847-465-5610
                **http://www.nl.edu**
             **e-mail: aneukranz-butler@nl.edu**
*Andreen Neukranz-Butler, Diversity Director*
*Pat Patillo, Admissions Director*

An independent four-year university with 10 special education students out of a total of 3,539. Two hours of tutoring per course per week available for documented LD Students.

**4343 North Central College**

**30 N Brainard Street**
**Naperville, IL  60540**          630-637-5100
                             FAX 630-637-5521
                **http://www.noctrl.edu**
*Mary Lynch, Associate Dean*

Offers a variety of services to students with disabilities including note takers, extended testing time, counseling services, and special accommodations.

**4344 Northeastern Illinois University**

**Disability Resource Center**
**5500 NS Louis Avenue**
**Chicago, IL  60625**          773-583-4050
                            FAX 773-442-5499
                            TDY:773-442-5499
                **http://www.neiu.edu**
             **e-mail: v-amey-flippin@neiu.edu**
*Victoria Amey-Flippin, Director*
*Effie Sturdivant, Administrative Assistant*

A public four-year college with 38 special education students out of a total of 7,715.

**4345 Northern Illinois University**

**Center for Access Ability Resources**
**Williston Hall 101, NIU**
**DeKalb, IL  60115**          815-753-9734
                           FAX 815-753-9599
                **http://www.reg.niu.edu**
             **e-mail: admissions-info@niu.edu**
*Nancy Kasinski, Director*
*Robert Burk, Admissions Director*

A public four-year university with 150 students receiving disability services out of 16,893.

**4346 Northwestern University**
Services for Students with Disabilities
1801 Hinman Avenue
Evanston, IL 60204          847-467-5530
                            FAX 847-467-5531
          http://www.northwestern.edu
          e-mail: sst@northwestern.edu
*Margee Roe, Coordinator*
*Henry Bienen, President*
*Carol Lunkenheimer, Admissions Director*

Offers a variety of services to students with disabilities including notetakers, extended testing time, counseling services and special accommodations.

**4347 Northwestern University Communicative Disorders**
2240 N Campus Drive
Evanston, IL 60208          847-491-2416
                            FAX 847-467-2776
          http://www.northwestern.edu
          e-mail: ckthom@casbah.acns.nwu.edu
*Cindy Thompson, Professor*

Offers speech/language and voice services, learning disabilities center and a hearing service.

**4348 Oakton Community College**
1600 E Golf Road
Des Plaines, IL 60016          847-635-1700
                               FAX 847-635-1764
                               TDY:847-635-1944
          http://www.oakton.edu
          e-mail: tbers@oakton.edu
*Margaret Lee MD, President*
*Irene Kovala, Vice President*

Students at Oakton Community College have the right to: Equal opportunity to participate; work and learn; reasonable accommodations; appropriate confidentiality; information about available services and accommodations; information about decisions made by the college regarding appropriate accommodations; accessible campus facilities and advocacy within the college community.

**4349 Parkland College**
2400 W Bradley Avenue
Champaign, IL 61821          217-351-2200
                             800-346-8089
                        FAX 217-351-2581
          http://www.parkland.cc.il.us
*Evelyn Brown, LD Specialist*
*Norm Lambert, Counselor*

Services for students with disability is a part of the counseling department. These services are coordinated by a full-time counselor. Under the umbrella of these services is a targeted program (Learning Resource Services) for students with learning disabilities (LD) administered by an LD Specialist with type 10 LD certification. Provides accommodations for students with learning disabilities including extended test time, one-on-one tutoring, tape recorders, note takers and individual sessions.

**4350 Productive Learning Strategies Program**
DePaul University
2320 N Kenmore Avenue
Chicago, IL 60614          773-325-4239
                          FAX 773-325-4673
          http://www.condor.depaul.edu
          e-mail: smiras@depaul.edu
*Stamatios Miras, Director*
*Dennis Holtschnieder, President*

PLuS is a comprehensive program designed to assist students with specific learning disabilities and/or attention deficit disorders in experiencing academic success at DePaul University. Please visit PLuS' website for a description of services and application forms.

**4351 Quincy University**
1800 College Avenue
Quincy, IL 62301          217-228-5210
                          800-688-4295
                     FAX 217-228-5479
          http://www.quincy.com
          e-mail: admissions@quincy.edu
*Kevin Brown, Admissions Director*
*Linda Godley, Dean Academic/Support Service*

Offers a variety of services to students with disabilities including notetakers, extended testing time, counseling services, and special accommodations.

**4352 Richland Community College**
One College Park
Decatur, IL 62521          217-875-7200
                           FAX 217-875-6965
          http://www.richland.edu
          e-mail: rcchelp@richland.edu
*Mary Atkins, Coordinator*
*Margaret Swaim, Secretary/DAS*

Richland Community College is committed to providing accommodations to students with disabilities. Each individual has a basic right to an education in accordance with his/her aspirations, talents, and skills. Support services ensure students with disabilities an equal opportunity to participate fully in the total college experience.

**4353 Robert Morris College**
401 S State Street
Chicago, IL 60605          312-935-6892
                           FAX 312-935-6861
          http://www.rmcil.edu
          e-mail: bmylott@smtp.rmcil.edu
*Brittany Mylott, Director*

Four-year college offering programs to students who are disabled.

**4354 Rockford College**
5050 E State Street
Rockford, IL 61108          815-226-4000
                            800-892-2984
                       FAX 815-226-4119
          http://www.rockford.edu
          e-mail: jgrey@rockford.edu
*Jeanne Grey, Director*
*Paul Tribbenow, President*

The L.R.C. is a nonprofit, educational resource center offering diagnostic testing, remedial tutoring in reading, writing, and mathematics, and enrichment workshops to enhance the learning experience.

**4355  Roosevelt University**

**Learning and Support Services Program**
430 S Michigan Avenue
Chicago, IL  60605          312-341-3810
                            FAX 312-341-3735
                     http://www.roosevelt.edu
          e-mail: dessimm@admvsbk.roosevelt.edu
*Nancy Litke, Director*
*Charles Middleton, President*

The Disabled Student Services office serves all students with special needs. The use of services is voluntary and confidential. This office is a resource for students and faculty. The goal of this office is to ensure educational opportunity for all students with special needs by providing access to full participation in all aspects of campus life and increase awareness of disability issues on campus.

**4356  Rosary College**

7900 W Division Street
River Forest, IL  60305          708-366-2490
                                 FAX 708-524-6939
                          http://www.business.dom.edu
                          e-mail: gradbus@dom.edu
*Molly Burke MD, Special Services*
*Grace Whiting, Recruitment Director*

Offers a variety of services to students with disabilities including note takers, extended testing time, counseling services, and special accommodations.

**4357  Saint Xavier University**

3700 W 103rd Street
Chicago, IL  60655          773-298-3540
                            FAX 773-779-3066
*Mary Sansore, LD Director*

Offers a variety of services to students with disabilities including notetakers, extended testing time, counseling services, and special accommodations.

**4358  School of the Art Institute of Chicago**

37 S Wabash Avenue
Chicago, IL  60603          312-899-5100
                            800-232-7242
                            FAX 312-263-0141
              http://www.artic.edu/said/life/sdd.html
                     e-mail: swhitlow@artic.edu
*Susan Whitlow, Coordinator of Services*

The Office of Services for Students with Disabilities attempts to ensure that students with disabilities have equal access to all programs and activities offered at the School of the Art Institute of Chicago. This can be accomplished by setting up needed accommodations and working to eliminate both attudinal and architectural barriers that exist at the school.

**4359  Services for Students with Learning Disabilities at the University of Illinois at Urbana**

1207 S Oak Street
Champaign, IL  61820          217-333-8705
                              FAX 217-333-0248
                              TDY:217-333-4603
                       http://www.disability.uci.edu
                       e-mail: kwold2@uiuc.edu
*Karen Wold, Learning Disabilities Specialist*

Available accommodations may include, but are not restricted to: notetakers; alternate ways of completing exams and assignments; text conversion to an accessible format; access to assistive computer technologies; and consultation regarding learning strategies and disability management skills.

**4360  Shawnee College**

8364 Shawnee College Road
Ullin, IL  62992          618-634-3200
                          800-481-2242
                          FAX 618-634-3300
                   http://www.shawnee.cc.il.us
*Don Slayter, Special Services*

Offers a variety of services to students with disabilities including notetakers, extended testing time, counseling services, and special accommodations.

**4361  Shimer College**

PO Box 500
Waukegan, IL  60079          847-623-8400
                             800-215-7173
                             FAX 847-249-8798
                      http://www.shimer.edu
                      e-mail: b.paterson@shimer.edu
*Bill Paterson, Director Admissions*
*William Rice, President*

A private four-year college with 3 special education students out of 100.

**4362  Southeastern Illinois College**

3575 College Road
Harrisburg, IL  62946          618-252-5400
                               866-338-2742
                               FAX 618-252-3062
                        http://www.sic.edu
                        e-mail: lraymer@sic.cc.il.us
*Rey Cummiskey, President*

A public two-year college with more than 50 special education and other special needs students out of a total of over 4,000.

**4363  Southern Illinois University: Carbondale**

**Clinical Center Achieve Program**
Carbondale, IL  62901          618-453-2369
                               FAX 618-453-3711
                        http://www.siu.edu/~achieve
                        e-mail: admrec@siu.edu
*Sally Decker MS, Director*
*Walker Allen, Admissions Director*

The Achieve Program is a comprehensive academic support service for students with LD and/or ADHD. Students must apply to both Achieve and the University.

**4364  Southern Illinois University: Edwardsville**
Disability Support Services
PO Box 1047
Edwardsville, IL  62026          618-650-3782
                                 FAX 618-650-5691
                                 http://www.siue.edu
                                 e-mail: jfloydh@siue.edu
*Jane Floyd-Hendey, Director*
*Boyd Bradshaw, Admissions Director*

A public four-year college with 50 special education students out of a total of 9,576.

**4365  Spoon River College**
23235 N Co 22
Canton, IL  61520                309-647-4645
                                 800-334-7337
                                 FAX 309-649-6393
                                 http://www.spoonrivercollege.edu
                                 e-mail: info@src.edu
*Tom Hines, President*
*Mickey Decker, Admission officer*

A public two-year college with 61 special education students out of a total of 2,312.

**4366  Springfield College in Illinois**
1500 N 5th Street
Springfield, IL  62702           217-525-1420
                                 FAX 217-789-1698
                                 http://www.sci.edu
*Karen Anderson, Dean*
*Nereida Avendano, Director*

Offers a variety of services to students with disabilities including note takers, extended testing time, counseling services, and special accommodations.

**4367  University of Illinois at Springfield**
1 University Plaza
Springfield, IL  62703           217-206-6600
                                 888-977-4847
                                 FAX 217-206-6511
                                 http://www.uis.edu
*Chris Miller, Dean Students*

A public four-year college with 26 special education students out of a total of 2,644.

**4368  Waubonsee Community College**
Route 47 Waubonsee Drive
Sugar Grove, IL  60554           630-466-7900
                                 FAX 630-466-4649
                                 TDY:630-466-4649
                                 http://www.waubonsee.edu
                                 e-mail: ihansen@waubonsee.edu
*Iris Hansen, Manager ACSD*

A public two-year college with 400 special education students out of a total 10,000.

**4369  Western Illinois University**
Disability Support Services
1 University Circle
Macomb, IL  61455                309-298-2512
                                 FAX 309-298-2361
                                 http://www.wiu.edu
                                 e-mail: joan_grren@ccmail.wiu.edu
*Joan Green, Director*
*Karen Helmers, Admissions Director*

A public four-year college with 135 special education students out of a total of 10,652.

**4370  William Rainey Harper College**
1200 W Algonquin Road
Palatine, IL  60067              847-925-6266
                                 FAX 847-925-6267
                                 TDY:847-397-7600
                                 http://www.harpercollege.edu
                                 e-mail: pherrera@harpercollege.edu
*Pascuala Herrera, LD Coordinator*
*Tom Thompson, Director*

A public two-year college with 550 students with disabilities out of a total of 24,00. Offer a special instructional program for students with LD or ADD for an additional fee. Offers a TRIO/SSS project for degree-seeking students (150 involved annually).

# Indiana

**4371  Ancilla College**
9601 S Union Road
Donaldson, IN  46513             574-936-8898
                                 http://www.ancilla.edu
*Kathryn Bigley, Director*

An independent two-year college with three special education students out of a total of 667.

**4372  Anderson University**
Disabled Student Services
1100 E 5th Street
Anderson, IN  46012              765-641-4226
                                 FAX 765-641-3851
                                 http://www.anderson.edu
                                 e-mail: rsvogel@anderson.edu
*Rinda Vogelgesang, Director*
*Jim King, Admissions Director*

An independent four-year college with 78 special education students out of a total of 1,977.

**4373  Ball State University**
Disability Services
Muncie, IN  47306                765-285-5293
                                 800-482-4278
                                 FAX 765-285-5295
                                 http://www.bsu.edu
*Richard Harris, Director*

Offers a variety of services to students with disabilities including note takers, extended testing time, counseling services, and special accommodations.

**4374  Bethel College: Indiana**
1001 W McKinley Avenue
Mishawaka, IN  46545          574-259-8511
                              800-422-4101
                http://www.bethel-in.edu

Offers a variety of services to students with disabilities including note takers, extended testing time, counseling services, and special accommodations.

**4375  Butler University**
4600 Sunset Avenue
Indianapolis, IN  46208
                              800-368-6852
                          FAX 317-940-9930
                   http://www.butler.edu
                   e-mail: info@butler.edu
*Rick Tirman*

Offers a variety of services to students with disabilities including notetakers, extended testing time, counseling services, and special accommodations.

**4376  Earlham College**
801 National Road W
Richmond, IN  47374          765-983-1341
                             800-327-5426
                         FAX 765-973-2120
                  http://www.earlham.edu
                  e-mail: keesldo@earlham.edu
*Donna Keesling, Executive Director*

Offers a variety of services to students with disabilities including note takers, extended testing time, counseling services, and special accommodations.

**4377  Franklin College of Indiana**
501 E Monroe Street
Franklin, IN  46131          317-738-8000
                             800-522-0232
                         FAX 317-738-8234
                  http://www.franklincoll.edu
                  e-mail: webmaster@franklincoll.edu
*Dana Giles, Assistant Director*

An independent four-year college with six special education students out of a total of 914.

**4378  Goshen College**
1700 S Main Street
Goshen, IN  46526            574-535-7535
                             800-348-7422
                         FAX 574-535-7660
                   http://www.goshen.edu
                   e-mail: mhooley@goshen.edu
*Marty Hooley, Director*

An independent four-year college with 23 special education students out of a total of 1,042.

**4379  Holy Cross College**
54515 State Road
Notre Dame, IN  46556        574-239-8400
                         FAX 574-239-8323
                   http://www.hcc-nd.edu
                   e-mail: uduke@hcc-nd.edu

A two-year colege that provides programs for learning disabled students.

**4380  Indiana Institute of Technology**
Student Support Services
1600 E Washington Boulevard
Fort Wayne, IN  46803        260-422-5561
                             800-937-2448
                         FAX 260-422-1518
                   http://www.indtech.edu
                   e-mail: scudder@indtech.edu
*Mary Scudder, Director Student Services*

A program of academic support services, including appropriate tutoring, peer mentoring and academic assistance, which is provided to students meeting specific federal eligibility guidelines.

**4381  Indiana Institute on Disability and Community at Indiana University**
2853 E Tenth Street
Bloomington, IN  47408 2696    812-855-6508
                               800-437-7924
                           FAX 812-855-9630
                           TDY:812-835-9396
                   http://www.iidc.indiana.edu
                   e-mail: iidc@indiana.edu
*David Mank PhD, Director*
*Joel Fosha, Coordinator Office Marketing*

The Indiana Institute on Disability and Community (IIDC) at Indiana University, Bloomington is committed to providing Hoosiers with disability-related information and services that touch the entire life span, from birth through older adulthood. Through its collaborative efforts with institutions of higher education, state and local government agencies, community service providers, persons with disabilities and their families, and advocacy organizations.

**4382  Indiana State University**
210 N 7th Street
Terre Haute, IN  47809       812-237-4000
                         FAX 812-237-7948
                   http://www.web.indstate.edu
                   e-mail: oprasay@usugw.indstate.edu
*Lloyd Benjamin III, President*
*Barbara Asay, Assistant to the President*

Offers a variety of services to students with disabilities including note takers, extended testing time, counseling services, and special accommodations.

**4383  Indiana University East**
Student Support Services
2325 Chester Boulevard
Richmond, IN  47374          765-973-8200
                             800-959-3278
                         FAX 765-973-8388
                   http://www.iue.indiana.edu
*Sherryl Stafford, Director*
*Sally Sayre, Secretary*

A public four-year college with 21 special education students out of a total of 2,249.

**4384  Indiana University Northwest**
3400 Broadway
Gary, IN  46408              219-980-6500
                             888-YOUR-IUN
                   http://www.iun.edu
*Ronald Thornton, Student Coordinator*

A public four-year college with 34 special education students out of a total of 5,000.

**4385  Indiana University Southeast**

4201 Grant Line Road
New Albany, IN  47150          812-941-2579
                               FAX 812-941-2589
                               http://www.ius.edu
                               e-mail: jojames@ius.edu
*Jodi James, Coordinator*

Offers a variety of services to students with disabilities including note takers, extended testing time, counseling services, and special accommodations.

**4386  Indiana University: Bloomington**

Disabled Student Services
601 East Kirkwood Avenue
Bloomington, IN  47405          812-855-7578
                                FAX 812-855-7650
                                http://www.indiana.edu
                                e-mail: dsscoord@indiana.edu
*Martha Jacques, Director*
*Mary , Admissions Director*

A public four-year college with 225 special education students out of a total of 29,383.

**4387  Indiana University: Kokomo**

3102 S Lasountain
Kokomo, IN  46902               765-455-2000
                                FAX 765-455-2020
                                http://www.iuk.edu
*Jeremy Lipinski, Director*
*Sherry Stone, Office Staff*

A combination of attitudes assistance, accommodations, classroom arrangements and technological aids that make it possible for learning disabled and physically disabled students to succeed in a degree program for which they are qualified.

**4388  Indiana University: Purdue**

425 University Boulevard
Indianapolis, IN  46202          317-274-4591
                                 FAX 317-274-4493
                                 http://www.iupui.edu
*Pamela King, Director*

A public four-year college with 154 special education students out of a total of 21,165.

**4389  Indiana Vocational Technical: Southeast Campus**

Ivy Tech Drive
Madison, IN  47250               812-265-2580
                                 800-403-2190
                                 FAX 812-265-4028
                                 http://www.ivytech.edu
*Kevin Bradley, registrar*
*Don Heiderman, President*

Offers a variety of services to students with disabilities including notetakers, extended testing time, counseling services, and special accommodations.

**4390  Indiana Wesleyan University**

Student Support Services
4201 South Washington Street
Marion, IN  46953                765-677-2257
                                 FAX 765-677-2140
                                 http://www.indwes.edu
                                 e-mail: todd.ream@indwes.edu
*Todd Ream, Director*
*Nan Turner, Assistant*

Offers a variety of services to students with disabilities including notetakers, extended testing time, counseling services and special accommodations.

**4391  Ivy Tech State College Southwest**

3501 N 1st Avenue
Evansville, IN  47710            812-429-1386
                                 FAX 812-429-1483
                                 TDY:812-429-9803
                                 http://www.ivytech.edu
                                 e-mail: pehlen@ivytech.edu
*Peg Ehlen, Disability Services Coordinator*
*Sherry Pejarano, Administrative Assistant*

Provides reasonable and effective accommodations to qualified students with learning disabilities.

**4392  Ivy Tech State College: Northcentral**

220 Dean Johnson Boulevard
South Bend, IN  46601            574-289-7001
                                 888-489-3478
                                 FAX 574-236-7178
                                 http://www.ivytech.edu
                                 e-mail: amatthew@ivy.tec.in.us
*Amy Cassa, Coordinator Disabilities Service*
*Gail Craker, Support Services Coordinator*

Accommodations based on individual needs.

**4393  Manchester College**

Services for Students with Disabilities
604 E College Ave
North Manchester, IN  46962      260-982-5000
                                 http://www.manchester.edu
                                 e-mail: dshowe@manchester.edu
*Denise Howe, Director*
*JoLane Rohr, Admissions Director*

An independent four-year college with 50 special education students out of a total of 1,091.

**4394  Purdue University**

Educational Studies
Beering Hall 100 N University Stree
West Lafayette, IN  47907        765-494-9170
                                 FAX 765-496-1228
                                 http://www.purdue.edu
*Sarah Templin, Special Services*

A public four-year college with 232 special education students out of a total of 29,673.

**4395  Riley Child Development Center**
Indiana University School of Medicine
702 Barnhill Drive
Indianapolis, IN  46202          317-274-8167
                                FAX 317-274-9760
                      http://www.child-dev.com
                         e-mail: jrau@iupui.edu
*John Rau, Director*
*Linda Newton, Administrative Assistant*

The Child Development Center provides interdisciplinary assessment for academics, communication, motor, behavior, medical concerns, for children and their families.

**4396  Rose-Hulman Institute of Technology**
5500 Wabash Avenue
Terre Haute, IN  47803          812-877-1511
                                FAX 812-877-8175
                      http://www.rose-hulman.edu
*Susan Smith, Director*
*Jody Doughrty, Administrative Assistant*

Offers a variety of services to students with disabilities including note takers, extended testing time, counseling services, and special accommodations.

**4397  Saint Joseph's College**
Highway 231
Rensselaer, IN  47978          219-866-6000
                               800-447-8781
                           FAX 219-866-6355
                      http://www.saintjoe.edu
*David Weed, Director*
*Joan Cramer, Secretary of the Director*

Offers a variety of services to students with disabilities including note takers, extended testing time, counseling services, and special accommodations.

**4398  Saint Mary-of-the-Woods College**
3301 Saint Mary-of-the-Woods
St. Mary-of-the-Woods, IN  47876   812-535-5151
                                FAX 812-535-4900
                      http://www.smwc.edu
                      e-mail: smwc@smwc.edu
*Kate Satchwill, Vice President*

Offers a variety of services to students with disabilities including note takers, extended testing time, counseling services, and special accommodations.

**4399  Southcentral Indiana Vocational Technical College**
8204 Highway 311
Sellersburg, IN  47172          812-246-3301
                                FAX 765-973-8383
*Jack Womack, Contact*

Offers a variety of services to students with disabilities including note takers, extended testing time, counseling services, and special accommodations.

**4400  Taylor University**
236 W Reade Avenue
Upland, IN  46989          765-998-5523
                           FAX 765-998-5569
                      http://www.tayloru.edu
                      e-mail: edwelch@tayloru.edu
*R Edwin Welch MD, Coordinator*

Four-year college that provides academic support to students with disabilities.

**4401  University of Evansville**
1800 Lincoln Avenue
Evansville, IN  47722          812-479-2500
                               800-423-8633
                           FAX 812-475-6429
                      http://www.evansville.edu
*Nealon Gaskey MD, Professor*
*Steven Jennings, President*

An independent four-year college with 60 special education students out of a total of 2,500.

**4402  University of Indianapolis**
Baccalaureate for University of Indianapolis
1400 E Hanna Avenue
Indianapolis, IN  46227          317-788-2140
                                 800-232-8634
                             FAX 317-788-3300
                        http://www.uindy.edu
                        e-mail: dspinney@uindy.edu
*Deborah Spinney, Director BUILD Program*
*Deb Kelly, Tutorial Coordinator*
*Ron Wilks, Admissions Director*

A private four-year university with a comprehensive program for students with learning disabilities. The BUILD Program offers a variety of services including private tutoring, specialized college courses, course substitutions, testing accommodations and assistive technology. There is a fee for this specialized program in addition to the university tuition.

**4403  University of Notre Dame**
Office for Students with Disabilities
220 Main Building
Notre Dame, IN  46556          574-631-5000
                          http://www.nd.edu
                  e-mail: margaret.spitzer@uncu.edu
*Scott Howland, Director*
*Dan Saracino, Admissions Director*

An independent four-year college with 20 special education students out of a total of 8,038.

**4404  University of Saint Francis**
Student Learning Center
2701 Spring Street
Fort Wayne, IN  46808
                               800-729-4732
                          http://www.sfc.edu
                          e-mail: mkruyer@sf.edu
*Michelle Kruyer, Director*
*John Arruza, Director*

Through the Student Learning Center, University of Saint Francis offers a support program providing comprehensive services for student with diagnosed disabilities in the university setting. Students who present appropriate documentation and qualify for support services will receive modifications and accommodations to facilitate academic success. These services are provided at no cost to the student.

**4405    University of Southern Indiana**

**Counseling Center**
**8600 University Boulevard**
**Evansville, IN  47712**                    **812-464-1867**
                                        **FAX 812-461-5288**
                                        **TDY:812-465-7072**
                                        **http://www.usi.edu**
                              **e-mail: lmsmith@usi.edu**
*Leslie Smith, Assistant Director Counseling*
*James Browning, Director Counseling*
*Eric Otto, Admissions Director*

Offers a variety of services to students with disabilities including notetaker supplies, tutor referral, extended testing time, counseling services, advocacy, sign language services and special accommodations.

**4406    Vincennes University**

**Students Transition into Education Program**
**1002 N 1st Street**
**Vincennes, IN  47591**                     **812-888-4485**
                                             **800-742-9198**
                                        **FAX 812-888-5707**
                                        **http://www.vinu.edu**
                      **e-mail: jkavanaugh@vinu.edu**
*Jane Kavanaugh, Education Director*
*Susan Laue, Associate Professor*
*Ann Skuce, Admissions Director*

A public two-year college with 200 learning disabled students in the STEP Program. Total student enrollment is 6,000. There is a fee for the special education program.

# Iowa

**4407    Central College: Student Support Services**

**812 University Avenue**
**Pella, IA  50219**                         **641-628-9000**
                                        **FAX 641-628-7647**
                                        **http://www.central.edu**
                      **e-mail: krosen@central.edu**
*Nancy Kroese, Director*

Four-year college that provides student support for those with learning disabilities.

**4408    Clinton Community College**

**1000 Lincoln Boulevard**
**Clinton, IA  52732**                       **563-244-7183**
                                             **800-637-0559**
                                        **FAX 563-244-7005**
                                        **http://www.eicc.edu**
                      **e-mail: bkunau@eicc.edu**
*Karen Vickers, President*
*Ron Erpliss, Dean College*

Offers a variety of services to students with disabilities including note takers, extended testing time, counseling services, and special accommodations.

**4409    Coe College**

**1220 1st Avenue NE**
**Cedar Rapids, IA  52402**                  **319-399-8547**
                                        **FAX 319-399-8503**
                                        **http://www.coe.edu**
                      **e-mail: lkabela@coe.edu**
*Lois Kabela-Coates, Director*
*Nancy Carberry, Administrative Assistant*

Services include: tutors, note takers, test proctoring for untimed and oral tests, assistance with accessing textbooks on tape, study skills and time management assistance, reading and writing assistance, personal and academic counseling, and assistance with course and instructor selection.

**4410    Cornell College**

**600 1st Street W**
**Mount Vernon, IA  52314**                  **319-895-4000**
                                        **FAX 319-896-5188**
                                  **http://www.cornell-iowa.edu**
                  **e-mail: admissions@cornell-iowa.edu**
*Leslie Garner, President*

An independent four-year college with 11 special education students out of a total of 1,114.

**4411    DesMoines Area Community College**

**2006 S Ankeny Boulevard**
**Ankeny, IA  50021**                        **515-964-6250**
                                             **800-362-2127**
                                        **FAX 515-964-7022**
                                        **TDY:964-381-1551**
                                  **http://www.dmacc.cc.ia.us**
                  **e-mail: webmaster@dmacc.cc.ia.us**
*Jim Barron, Director*

DMACC is committed to providing an accessible environment that supports students with disabilities in reaching their full potential. Support services are available for students with disabilities to ensure equal access to educational opportunities.

**4412    Dordt College**

**Academic Skills Center**
**498 4th Avenue NE**
**Sioux Center, IA  51250**                  **712-722-6490**
                                        **FAX 712-722-4498**
                                        **http://www.dordt.edu**
                      **e-mail: admissions@dordt.edu**
*Marliss Vanderzwaag, Coordinator*
*Pam DeJong, Director*

Four-year college that offers academic services to students.

**4413    Drake University**

**Student Disability Services**
**3116 Carpenter Avenue**
**Des Moines, IA  50311**                    **515-271-3100**
                                             **800-443-7253**
                                        **FAX 515-712-1855**
                                        **TDY:515-271-2825**
                                        **http://www.drake.edu**
                  **e-mail: christal.stanley@drake.edu**
*Chrystal Stanley, Director*
*Thomas Willoughby, Admissions Director*

Offers a variety of services to students with disabilities including formal academic accommodations and support services.

**4414  Ellsworth Community College**
1100 College Avenue
Iowa Falls, IA  50126            641-648-3128
http://www.iavalley.cc.ia.us
e-mail: lmulford@iavalley.cc.ia.us
*Lori Mulford, Coordinator*

Offers a variety of services to students with disabilities including note takers, extended testing time, counseling services and special accommodations.

**4415  Graceland College**
1 University Place
Lamoni, IA  50140            641-784-5000
FAX 641-784-5698
http://www2.graceland.edu
*JR Smith, Director*

An independent four-year college with 27 special education students out of a total of 968. There is an additional fee for the special education program in addition to the regular tuition.

**4416  Grand View College**
1200 Grandview Avenue
Des Moines, IA  50316            515-263-2871
FAX 515-263-2840
http://www.gvc.edu
e-mail: cwassenaar@gve.edu
*Carolyn Wassenaar, Director*
*Debbie Borger, Admissions Director*

An independent four-year college with 15 special education students out of a total of 1,419.

**4417  Grinnell College**
Academic Advising Office
PO Box 805
Grinnell, IA  50112            641-269-3702
FAX 641-269-3710
http://www.grinnell.edu
e-mail: sternjm@grinnell.edu
*Joyce Stern, Associate Dean*
*Jim Sumner, Admissions Director*

An independent four-year college which currently provides academic accommodations to students with learning disabilities and 15 students with ADHD out of a total of 1,344.

**4418  Hawkeye Community College**
1501 E Orange Road
Waterloo, IA  50704            319-296-2320
FAX 319-296-4018
*Kathy Linda, Developmental Studies Department*
*Ruben Carrion, Student Development Director*

Offers a variety of services to students with disabilities including notetakers, extended testing time, tutoring, counseling services, and special accommodations.

**4419  Indian Hills Community College**
Success Center
525 Grandview Avenue
Ottumwa, IA  52501            641-683-5155
800-726-2585
FAX 641-683-5184
http://www.ihec.cc.ia.us
e-mail: successcenter@ihcc.cc
*Mary Stewart, Dean Academic Services*
*Marva Chilipsen, Disability Service Provider*
*Sally Harris, Admissions Director*

A public two-year college with 400 special education students out of a total of 3,166. There is a fee for the special education program in addition to the regular tuition.

**4420  Iowa Central Community College**
330 Avenue M
Fort Dodge, IA  50501            515-576-7201
800-362-2793
FAX 515-576-7206
http://www.iccc.cc.ia.us/icc/home/default.htm
e-mail: lundeen@triton.iccc.cc.ia.us
*Shelly Lundeen, Student Success Teacher*
*Carol Koettlin, Desk Coordinator*

A public two-year college with approximately 50 special needs students out of a total of 3,003.

**4421  Iowa Lakes Community College: Emmetsburg Campus**
3200 College Drive
Emmetsburg, IA  50536            712-852-3554
800-242-5108
FAX 712-852-2152
http://www.iowalake.edu
e-mail: sjnait@iowalake.edu
*Ann Petersen, Special Needs*
*Elizabeth Ankeny, SAVE Coordinator*

Offers a variety of services to students with disabilities including notetakers, extended testing time, counseling services, and special accommodations, including secondary programs at post-secondary institutions.

**4422  Iowa Lakes Community College: Success Centers**
300 S 18th Street
Estherville, IA  51334            712-362-2604
800-521-5054
FAX 712-362-3969
http://www.iowalakes.edu
e-mail: info@iowalakes.edu
*Colleen Peltz, Professor Developmental Educatio*
*Lynn Dodge, Assistant Professor Dev. Educ.*
*Linda Helmers, Counselor*

Offers a variety of services to students with disabilities including note takers, extended testing time, counseling services, and special accommodations.

**4423  Iowa State University**
Disability Resources
1076 Student Services Bldg.
Ames, IA  50011            515-294-0644
FAX 515-294-2397
TDY:515-294-6635
http://www.dso.iastate.edu/dett/ascl/disability
e-mail: accomodation@iastate.edu
*Bea Awoniyi, Director*
*Marc Harding, Admissions Director*

A public four-year university that has 80 students receiving disability services out of 21,503.

**4424  Iowa Wesleyan College**
601 N Main Street
Mount Pleasant, IA  52641         319-385-8021
                                  FAX 319-385-6384
*Linda Widmer, Director*

An independent four-year college with four special education students out of a total of 1,000.

**4425  Iowa Western Community College: Council Bluffs Campus**
2700 College Road
Council Bluffs, IA  51502         712-325-3390
                                  800-432-5852
                        FAX 712-388-0123
            http://www.iwcc.cc.ia.us
            e-mail: cholst@iwcc.cc.ia.us
*Chris Holst, Coordinator*

IWCC is committed to making individuals with disabilities full participants in its programs, services and activities. It is the policy of IWCC that no otherwise qualified individual with a disability shall be denied access to or participation in any program, service or activity offered by the college.

**4426  Loras College**
Learning Disabilities Program
1450 Alta Vista
Dubuque, IA  52004                563-588-7100
                                  800-245-6727
            http://www.loras.edu
            e-mail: dgibson@loras.edu
*Dianne Gibson, Director*
*Tim Hauber, Admissions Director*

Private Catholic four-year college with 40 learning disabled students out of a total of 1,626. The Learning Disabilities Program charges a fee for the Enhanced program. Mandated services are free.

**4427  Luther College**
700 College Drive
Decorah, IA  52101                563-387-2000
                                  800-458-8437
                        FAX 563-387-2158
            http://www.luther.edu
            e-mail: equalaccess@luther.edu
*G Rosales, Director*
*Janice Halsne, Services Director*

In keeping with the mission of Luther College, the Student Academic Support Center (SASC) exists to support all students as they pursue a liberal arts education, and specifically to be an advocate for students with disabilities. SASC processes all student requests for accommodations to provide each student with a suitable learning environment. The accommodations provided are not remedial in nature, nor do they change or reduce the academic standard.

**4428  Marshalltown Community College**
3700 S Center Street
Marshalltown, IA  50158           641-752-7106
                        FAX 641-752-8149
            http://www.iavalley.cc.ia.us
*Regina West, Coordinator*

A two-year community college that offers programs for its learning disabled students.

**4429  Morningside College**
Achievement Center
Sioux City, IA  51106             712-274-5104
                                  800-831-0806
                        FAX 712-274-5101
            http://www.morningside.edu
            e-mail: rohlena@morningside.edu
*Robbie Rohlena, Director*
*Karmen Jucht, LD Specialist*

A comprehensive learning disabilities program which offers academic advisement accommodations, subject area tutoring, and supportive services.

**4430  Mount Mercy College**
1330 Elmhurst Drive NE
Cedar Rapids, IA  52402           319-363-8213
                        FAX 319-363-6341
            http://www.mt mercy.edu
            e-mail: nbrauhn@mmc.mtmercy.edu
*Mary Stanton, Director*
*Robert , President*

Four-year college offering support and services to learning disabled students.

**4431  Mount Saint Clare College**
400 N Bluff Boulevard
Clinton, IA  52732                563-242-4023
                                  800-242-4153
            http://www.clare.edu
*Diane Cornilsen, Director*

Offers a variety of services to students with disabilities including notetakers, extended testing time, counseling services, and special accommodations.

**4432  Muscatine Community College**
152 Colorado Street
Muscatine, IA  52761              563-288-6166
                                  800-351-4669
                        FAX 563-288-6104
            http://www.eiccd.cc.ia.us
            e-mail: smewwiam@eicc.edu
*Kathryn Trosen, Retention Specialist*

A public two-year college with 29 special education students out of a total of 1,192.

**4433  North Iowa Area Community College**
500 College Drive
Mason City, IA  50401             614-422-4106
                                  888-466-4222
                        FAX 614-422-4150
            e-mail: ewerster@niaccicc.ia.us
*Terri Ewers, Director of Counseling*

Offers a variety of services to students with disabilities including notetakers, extended testing time, counseling services, and special accommodations.

**4434  Northwestern College**
3003 Snelling Ave, North
St Paul, MN  55113                651-631-5100
            http://www.nwc.nwc.edu
*Marcia Olson, Special Services*

Offers a variety of services to students with disabilities including note takers, extended testing time, counseling services, and special accommodations.

**4435  Saint Ambrose College**

**Services for Students with Disabilities**
**518 W Locus Street**
**Davenport, IA  52803**                    563-333-6000
                              http://www.sau.edu
                   e-mail: aaqustin@saunix.sau.edu
*Ann Austin, LD Specialist*
*Meg Flagherty, Admissions Director*

An independent four-year college with 63 special education students out of a total of 2,022.

**4436  Scott Community College**

**500 Belmont Road**
**Bettendorf, IA  52722**                    563-441-4000
                              FAX 563-441-4066
                       http://www.eiccd.cc.ia.us
*Jerri Crabtree, Director*

A public two-year college with 59 special education students out of a total of 3,611.

**4437  Southeastern Community College: North Campus**

**1500 West Agency Road.**
**West Burlington, IA  52655**              319-752-2731
                                     866-727-4692
                              FAX 319-752-4995
                        http://www.scciowa.edu
*Chris Man, Admissions Coordinator*
*Stacy White, Admissions Coordinator*

Offers special services and student services to the learning disabled.

**4438  Southwestern Community College**

**Services for Students with Disabilities**
**1501 Townline Road**
**Creston, IA  50801**                       641-782-7081
                              FAX 641-782-1334
                        http://www.swcc.iowa.edu
                   e-mail: pantini@swcc.iowa.edu
*Deb Pantini, Special Needs Coordinator*
*Bill Taylor, Director for Student Services*

Offers a variety of services to students with disabilities including note takers, extended testing time, counseling services, and special accommodations.

**4439  University of Iowa**

**Student Disability Services**
**107 Calvin Hall**
**Iowa City, IA  52242**                     319-335-1462
                              FAX 319-335-3973
                        http://www.uiowa.edu
                 e-mail: mary-richard@uiowa.edu
*Mary Richard, Disability Services Coordinator*
*Michael Barron, Admissions Director*

A public four-year college with 301 learning disabled students out of a total of 19,284.

**4440  University of Northern Iowa**

**Disability Services**
**213 SSC**
**Cedar Falls, IA  50614**                   319-273-2676
                              FAX 319-273-6884
                              TDY:319-273-3011
                          http://www.uni.edu
                 e-mail: jane.slykhuis@uni.edu
*Jane Slykhuis, Coordinator*
*David , Director*
*Clark Elmer, Admissions Director*

Four-year college that provides services to students with a learning disability.

**4441  Waldorf College**

**Learning Disabilities Program**
**106 S 6th Street**
**Forest City, IA  50436**
                                     800-292-1903
                              http://www.waldorf.edu
                       e-mail: hillb@waldorf.edu
*Rebecca Hill, Director*
*Steve Lovick, Admissions Director*

An independent two-year college with 20 learning disabled students out of a total of 599. There is an additional fee for the learning disabled program in addition to the regular tuition.

**4442  Wartburg College**

**100 Wartburg Boulevard**
**Waverly, IA  50677**                       319-352-8260
                                     800-772-2085
                              FAX 319-352-8568
                        http://www.wartburg.edu
*Alexander Smith, Vice President*
*Jack Ohley, President*

An independent four-year college with 11 special education students out of a total of 1,454.

# Kansas

**4443  Allen County Community College**

**1801 N Cottonwood Street**
**Iola, KS  66749**                          620-365-5116
                              http://www.allen.cc.ks.us
*Rochelle Smith, Contact*

Offers a variety of services to students with disabilities including note takers, extended testing time, counseling services, and special accommodations.

**4444  Baker University**

**Learning Resource Center**
**Po Box 65**
**Baldwin City, KS  66006**                  785-594-6451
                              http://www.bakeru.edu
                 e-mail: marian@harvey.bakeru.edu
*Kathy Marian, Director*
*Paige Illum, Admissions Director*

A private four-year college with a total of 923 students.

**4445  Barton County Community College**
245 NE 30th Road
Great Bend, KS  67530         620-792-2701
http://www.barton.cc.ks.us
*Todd Moore, Director for admission*
*Cassandra Montoya, Student Work Service*

A public two-year college with 12 special education students out of a total of 4,462.

**4446  Bethel College**
300 E 27th Street
North Newton, KS  67117        316-283-2500
800-522-1887
FAX 316-284-5286
http://www.bethelks.edu
*Laberne Epp, President*
*Mary Enz, Bookstore Coordinator*

Offers a variety of services to students with disabilities including notetakers, extended testing time, counseling services, and special accommodations.

**4447  Butler County Community College**
College Drive
El Dorado, KS  16003           724-287-8711
800-826-2829
FAX 724-287-4961
*Lora Rozeboom, Special Needs*

A public two-year college with 93 special education students out of a total of 5,601.

**4448  Center for Research on Learning**
University of Kansas
1122 W Campus Road
Lawrence, KS  66045            785-864-4780
FAX 785-864-5728
http://www.ku-crl.org
e-mail: cre@ku.edu
*Don Deshler, Director*
*Jamin Dreasher, Office Assistant*

All of the research undertaken at the center adheres to a single mission that has been crafted to respond to these educational challenges: an information explosion in all content areas; a limited amount of instructional time; and increased expectations for student achievement.

**4449  Colby Community College**
1255 S Range Avenue
Colby, KS  67701               785-462-3984
FAX 785-462-4600
http://www.colby.cc.edu
e-mail: joyce@colby.cc.edu
*Joyce Washburn, Academic Services*
*Mikel , President*

Offers a variety of services to students with disabilities including note takers, extended testing time, counseling services, and special accommodations.

**4450  Cowley County Community College**
125 S 2nd Street
Arkansas City, KS  67005       620-442-0430
http://www.cowleycollege.com
e-mail: watson@cowleycollege.com
*Bruce Watson, ADA Coordinator*

Offers a variety of services to students with disabilities including notetakers, extended testing time, counseling services, and special accommodations.

**4451  Donnelly College**
608 N 18th Street
Kansas City, KS  66102         913-621-8764
FAX 913-621-8719
http://www.donnelly.edu
e-mail: stephens@donnelly.edu
*Lee Stephenson, Director Student Services*

An independent two-year college with 10 special education students out of a total of 381.

**4452  Emporia State University**
1200 Commercial Street
Emporia, KS  66801             620-341-5374
FAX 620-341-5918
http://www.emporia.edu
*Keith Frank MD, Coordinator*

Offers a variety of services to students with disabilities including note takers, extended testing time, counseling services, and special accommodations.

**4453  Fort Scott Community College**
2108 S Horton
Fort Scott, KS  66701          620-223-2700
800-874-3722
http://www.fortscott.edu
e-mail: beckyw@ftscott.cc.ks.us
*Becky Weddle, Director CE/ETC/Mill*

A public two-year college with 34 special education students out of a total of 1,928.

**4454  Hutchinson Community College**
1300 N Plum Street
Hutchinson, KS  67501          620-665-3500
800-289-3501
FAX 620-665-3310
http://www.hutchcc.edu
e-mail: info@hutchcc.edu
*Mary Coplen, Director*

Offers a variety of services to students with disabilities including notetakers, extended testing time, counseling services, and special accommodations.

**4455  Kansas Community College: Kansas City**
7250 State Avenue
Kansas City, KS  66112         913-334-1100
FAX 913-596-9606
http://www.kckcc.cc.ks.us
*Valarie Webb, Disability Resource Center Coord*

A public two-year college with an enrollment of approximately 6,000 students. Thirty-five LD students request services each semester. Developmental courses and accommodations are offered for students with learning disabilities.

**4456 Kansas State University**

Disability Support Services
Holton Hall
Manhattan, KS 66506
785-532-6441
FAX 785-532-6457
http://www.ksu.edu
e-mail: dss@ksu.edu

*Gretchen Holden, Director*
*Andrea Blair, LD Specialist*
*Larry Moeder, Admissions Director*

Dedicated to providing equal opportunity and access for every student. The staff provides a broad range of supportive services in an effort to ensure that the individual needs of each student are met. In addition, the staff functions as an advocate for students with disabilities on the K-State campus.

**4457 Kansas University Center for Developmental Disabilities (KUCDD)**

1000 Sunnyside Avenue
Lawrence, KS 66045
785-864-4950
FAX 785-864-5323
http://www.lsi.ku.edu
e-mail: schroeder@ku.edu

*Stephen Schrander, Director*

KUCDD develops alternatives to institutional care for persons with developmental disabilities. Helps families of persons with disabilities define their needs and find resources and plan and evaluate services on a cost-performance basis. Also provides in-service trainig to service providers.

**4458 Labette Community College**

200 S 14th Street
Parsons, KS 67357
620-421-6700
FAX 620-421-0921
http://www.labette.cc.ks.us

*Viv Metcalf, Director*

A public two-year college with 80 special education students out of a total of 2,598.

**4459 Neosho County Community College**

800 W 14th Street
Chanute, KS 66720
620-431-2820
FAX 620-235-4030
http://www.neosho.cc.ks.us

*John Messenger, Instructor*

Offers a variety of services to students with disabilities including note takers, extended testing time, counseling services, and special accommodations.

**4460 Newman University**

3100 McCormick Street
Wichita, KS 67213
316-942-4291
FAX 316-942-4483
http://www.newmanu.edu
e-mail: niedensr@newmanu.edu

*Rosemary Niedens, Dean of Students*
*Julie , ADA Coordinator*

Offers a variety of services to students with disabilities including notetakers, extended testing time, counseling services, and special accommodations.

**4461 North Central Kansas Technical College**

Nursing Department
2205 Wheatland Drive
Hays, KS 67601
785-623-6155
800-658-4655
FAX 785-623-6152
http://www.ncktc.tec.ks.us

*George Mihel, President*

**4462 Ottawa University**

1001 S Cedar Street
Ottawa, KS 66067
785-242-5200
800-755-5200
FAX 785-242-1008
http://www.ottawa.edu

*Karen Ohnesorge-Fick, Academic Achievement*

An independent four-year college with 11 special education students out of a total of 546.

**4463 Pittsburg State University**

Learning Center
1701 S Broadway Street
Pittsburg, KS 66762
620-231-7000
http://www.pittstate.edu
e-mail: nhenry@pittstate.edu

*Nick Henry, Special Services*
*Ange Peterson, Admissions Director*

A public four-year college with 74 special education students out of a total of 5,222.

**4464 Saint Mary College**

4100 S 4th Street
Leavenworth, KS 66048
913-682-5151
800-752-7043
FAX 913-758-6140
http://www.stmary.edu
e-mail: admiss@hub.smcks.edu

*Sandra Hoose, Academic Dean*
*Sandra , Academic Dean*

Offers a variety of services to students with disabilities including note takers, extended testing time, counseling services, and special accommodations.

**4465 Seward County Community College**

1801 N Kansas Avenue
Liberal, KS 67905
316-624-1951
800-373-9951
FAX 316-629-2715
http://www.scc.cc.ks.us/

*Larry Philbeck, Academic Achievement*

A public two-year college with 13 special education students out of a total of 1,522.

**4466 Tabor College**

400 S Jefferson
Hillsboro, KS 67063
620-947-3121
800-TABOR-99
FAX 620-947-2607
http://www.tabor.edu
e-mail: larryn@tabor.edu

*Larry Nikkel, President*
*Karol Hunt, Vice President*

Offers a variety of services to students with disabilities including note takers, extended testing time, counseling services, and special accommodations.

**4467  University Affiliated Program**

**Kansas University**
**2601 Gabriel Avenue**
**Parsons, KS  67357**                   **620-421-6550**
**FAX 602-421-6550**
**http://www.parsons.lsi.ku.edu**
**e-mail: dmoody@ku.edu**
*David Lindeman, Director*
*Debbie Moody, Administrative Assistant*

Mission is optimize the quality of life and extend the concept of independence, productivity, integration and inclusion of individuals with disabilities in all aspects of life. This can be accomplished by providing new options, meaningful choices, independence, self-reliance, dignity of risk, and the means to achieve enhanced personal productivity.

**4468  University of Kansas**

**1450 Jay Hawk**
**Lawrence, KS  66045**                   **785-864-2620**
**FAX 785-864-2817**
**TDY:785-864-2620**
**http://www.ku.edu**
**e-mail: disability@ku.edu**
*Mary Rasnack, Director*
*Melissa Manning, Associate Director*

Accommodates students with a learning disability by understanding the students ability.

**4469  Washburn University of Topeka**

**University of Topeka**
**1700 SW College Avenue**
**Topeka, KS  66621**                   **785-231-1010**
**FAX 785-234-3813**
**http://www.washburn.edu**
*Greg Moore, Contact*

Offers a variety of services to students with disabilities including note takers, extended testing time, counseling services, and special accommodations.

**4470  Wichita State University**

**1845 Fairmount Street**
**Wichita, KS  67260**                   **316-978-3085**
**800-362-2594**
**FAX 316-978-3016**
**http://www.wichita.edu**
*Grady Landrum, Special Services*

A public four-year college with 11 special education students out of a total of 13,103.

## Kentucky

**4471  Bellarmine College**

**Disability Services**
**2001 Newburg Road**
**Louisville, KY  40205**                   **502-452-8131**
**800-274-4723**
**http://www.bellarmine.edu**
**e-mail: rgarveynix@bellarmine.edu**
Four-year college that provides services for the disabled.

**4472  Berea College**

**CPO 2190 College Station**
**Berea, KY  40404**                   **859-985-3500**
**FAX 859-985-3917**
**http://www.berea.edu**
**e-mail: webresponse@berea.edu**
*John Cook*

Offers a variety of services to students with disabilities including note takers, extended testing time, counseling services, and special accommodations.

**4473  Brescia University**

**717 Frederica Street**
**Owensboro, KY  42301**                   **270-686-4259**
**877-273-7242**
**FAX 270-686-4266**
**http://www.bresciu.edu**
**e-mail: maustin@bresciu.edu**
*Mary Austin, Director Admissions*
*Dolores Kisler, Director for Student Support*

Provides the following for students with learning disabilities: developmental courses (English, mathematics and study skills); individual tutoring for all areas; and academic and career counseling.

**4474  Clear Creek Baptist Bible College**

**300 Clear Creek Road**
**Pineville, KY  40977**                   **606-337-3196**
**FAX 606-337-2372**
**http://www.ccbbc.edu**
**e-mail: ccbbc@ccbbc.edu**
*Georgia Mink*

An independent four-year college with 11 special education students out of a total of 141.

**4475  Eastern Kentucky University**

**Students Services Building**
**Richmond, KY  40475**                   **859-622-1500**
**FAX 859-622-6395**
**TDY:859-622-2937**
**http://www.eku.edu**
**e-mail: teresa.belluscio@eku.edu**
*Teresa Belluscio, Director*
*Joan Glasser, President*

Mission of project SUCCESS is to respond effectively and efficiently to the individual's educational needs.

**4476  Jefferson Technical College**
727 W Chestnut Street
Louisville, KY 40203          502-213-4100
                             FAX 502-213-4500
                             http://www.kcts.edu
*Robert Silliman, Director*

Offers a variety of services to students with disabilities including note takers, extended testing time, counseling services, and special accommodations.

**4477  Kentucky State University**
103 Jackson Hall
Frankfort, KY 40601          502-597-6000
                             FAX 502-597-6407
                             http://www.kysu.edu
            e-mail: bmorelock@gwmail.kysu.edu
*Patricia Jones, Director*
*Mary Fias, President*

Offers a variety of services to students with disabilities including note takers, extended testing time, counseling services, and special accommodations.

**4478  Lexington Community College**
103 Oswald Building
Lexington, KY 40506          859-257-4872
                             866-774-4872
                             FAX 859-323-7136
                             TDY:849-257-6068
                             http://www.uky.edu
                             e-mail: lccinfo@lsv.uky.edu
*Veronica Miller, Director*
*Regina Johnson, SS Associate*

Comprehensive community college on campus of University of Kentucky.

**4479  Lindsey Wilson College**
210 Lindsey Wilson Street
Columbia, KY 42728          270-384-8080
                            800-264-0138
                            FAX 270-384-8050
                            http://www.lindsey.edu
                            e-mail: luddend@lindsey.edu
*Lilian Roland, Learning Disabilities Coordinato*

Offers a variety of services to students with disabilities including notetakers, extended testing time, counseling services, and special accommodations.

**4480  Madisonville Community College: Universityof Kentucky**
2000 College Drive
Madisonville, KY 42431          270-821-2250
                               FAX 270-821-1555
                               http://www.madcc.kctcs.edu
                               e-mail: aimee.bullock@kctcs.edu
*Aimee Bullock, Coordinator*
*Lydia Wilson, Office Assistant*

Offers a variety of services to students with disabilities including note takers, extended testing time, counseling services, and special accommodations.

**4481  Murray State University**
Lowry Center
Delamare, KY 42071          270-762-2018
                            FAX 270-762-4339
                            http://www.murraystate.edu
            e-mail: donna.harris@murraystate.edu
*Cindy Clemson, Coordinator*
*Alexander King, President*

Services and programs provided to the learning disabled.

**4482  Northern Kentucky University**
Nunn Drive
Highland Heights, KY 41099          859-572-5220
                                   800-637-9948
                                   http://www.nku.edu
                                   e-mail: admitnku@nku.edu
*A Adams, Special Services*

Offers a variety of services to students with disabilities including note takers, extended testing time, counseling services, and special accommodations.

**4483  Pikeville College**
147 Sycamore Street
Pikeville, KY 41501          606-218-5250
                             FAX 606-218-5269
                             http://www.pc.edu
                             e-mail: webmaster@pc.edu
*William Little*

Offers a variety of services to students with disabilities including notetakers, extended testing time, counseling services, and special accommodations.

**4484  Thomas More College**
333 Thomas More Parkway
Crestview Hills, KY 41017          606-344-3521
                                  FAX 606-344-3342
                                  http://www.thomasmore.edu
                                  e-mail: barb.davis@thomasmore.edu
*Dale Meyers MD, Dean of Academic Affairs*
*Barbara Davis, Director Student Services*

An independent four-year college with 50 special education students out of a total of 1,272.

**4485  University of Kentucky: Interdisciplinary Human Development Institute**
University of Kentucky
126 Mineral Industries Building
Lexington, KY 40506          859-257-1714
                             FAX 859-323-1901
                             http://www.ihdi.uky.edu
                             e-mail: mafar101@uky.edu
*Harold Klinert, Director*
*Jay Chaney, Staff Assistant*

Mission is to promote independence, productivity, and integration of all people through numerous research, training and outreach activities.

**4486 University of Louisville**
Robbins Hall
Louisville, KY 40292          502-852-6938
                             FAX 502-852-0924
                             TDY:502-852-6938
                             http://www.louisville.edu
*Cathy Patus, Director*
*James Ransey, President*

A public four-year college with 60 learning disabled
students out of a total of 22,000.

**4487 Western Kentucky University**
Student Disability Services
1 Big Red Way
Bowling Green, KY 42101          270-745-5004
                                FAX 270-745-6289
                                TDY:270-745-3030
                                http://www.wku.edu
                                e-mail: disabilityservices@wku.edu
*Matt Davis, Coordinator for Student Disabili*
*Huda Melky, Director for Equal Opportunity*

The goal of the program is to foster the participation of
persons with disabilities.

## Louisiana

**4488 Human Development Center**
Louisiana State University
1100 Florida Avenue
New Orleans, LA 70119          504-942-8202
                              FAX 504-942-8305
                              TDY:504-942-7801
                              http://www.hdc.lsuhsc.edu
                              e-mail: rcrow@hcdc.lsuhsc.edu
*Robert Crow, Director*
*Cathy Dwyer, Administrative Manager*

**4489 Learning Disabilities Association of Louisiana**
Northwestern State University
Teacher Education Center
Natchitoches, LA 71497          318-357-5154
                               FAX 318-357-3275
                               e-mail: duchardt@nsula.edu
*Barbara Duchard MD, Associate Professor*

**4490 Louisiana College**
Program to Assist Student Success
1140 College Drive
Pineville, LA 71360          318-487-7629
                            FAX 318-487-7285
                            http://www.lacollege.edu
                            e-mail: pass@lacollege.edu
*Betty Matthews, Director*
*Betty Morris, Assistant Director*

This highly individualized, limited enrollment program provides support services and personal attention
to students who may need special academic guidance,
tutoring, and classroom assistance.

**4491 Louisiana State University Agricultural and
Mechanical College**
110 Thomas Boyd Hall
Baton Rouge, LA 70803          225-578-1175
                              http://www.lsu.edu
*Tina Schultz*

A public four-year college with 88 special education
students out of a total of 21,245.

**4492 Louisiana State University: Alexandria**
8100 Highway 71 S
Alexandria, LA 71302          318-473-6545
                             888-473-6417
                             FAX 318-473-6580
                             http://www.lsua.edu
*Dee Slavant MD, Director Student Services*
*Donna Roberts, Administrative Assistant*

Offers a variety of services to students with disabilities including extended testing time, counseling services, and special accommodations.

**4493 Louisiana State University: Eunice**
2048 Johnson Highway
Eunice, LA 70535          337-457-7311
                         888-367-5783
                         FAX 337-550-1445
                         http://www.lsue.edu
*Marvette Thomas, Director TRIO*
*William Nunez, President*

A public two-year college with 31 special education
students out of a total of 2,595.

**4494 Loyola University New Orleans**
6363 St. Charles Avenue
New Orleans, LA 70118          504-865-2990
                              FAX 504-865-3543
                              http://www.loyno.edu
                              e-mail: ssmith@loyno.edu
*Sarah Smith, Director*
*Kacey McNaloy, Counselor*

Four year college that provides services to disabled
students.

**4495 McNeese State University**
4205 Ryan Street
Lake Charles, LA 70609          337-475-5000
                               800-622-3352
                               http://www.mcneese.edu
*Sena Theall, Director Special Project*
*Denise Leiato, Coordinator*

Provides academic advising, arrangements for individual accommodations for disabilities, tutoring and
computers and word processing equipment. All services are available to the students at no charge.

**4496 Nicholls State University**
PO Box 2050
Thibodaux, LA 70310          985-448-4214
                            FAX 985-448-4423
                            http://www.nich.edu
                            e-mail: nicholls@nich-nsunet.nich.edu
*Carol Ronka, Director*
*Ronda Zeringue, Administrative Assistant*

Students with dyslexia are offered individual tutoring assistance and communicators.

**4497 Southeastern Louisiana University**

SLU 752
Hammond, LA 70402          985-549-2000
FAX 985-549-3640
http://www.selu.edu
e-mail: mhall@selu.edu
*Michelle Hall MD, Interim Director*

Four-year college that offers programs for students whom are disabled.

**4498 Tulane University**

6823 St. Charles Avenue
New Orleans, LA 70118          504-865-5113
FAX 504-862-8148
TDY:504-862-8433
http://www.tulane.edu
e-mail: dtylicki@tulane.edu
*David Tylicki, Director*
*Pam Ernst, Administrative Assistant*

Four-year college that provides services to those students who are learning disabled.

**4499 University of Louisiana at Lafayette: Services of Students with Disabilities**

PO Drawer 41650
Lafayette, LA 70504          337-482-5252
FAX 337-482-0195
http://www.ull.edu
*Srisharsha Ogoti, Office Assistant*
*Edward Pratt, Dean*

The Mission of Services for Students with Disabilities is to provide extensive post secondary services for emotionally, physically and learning impaired students. Our goals are to facilitate the transition from high school to college, to assist students developing the necessary skills to succeed in college; and to provide counseling, including career counseling, and to assist in successful transition from college to employment.

**4500 University of New Orleans**

2000 Lakeshore Drive
New Orleans, LA 70148          504-280-6595
800-514-4275
http://www.uno.edu
*Amy King, Coordinator*

A public four-year college with 45 special education students out of a total of 12,441.

## Maine

**4501 ALLTech**

University of Southern Maine
Lewiston Hall
New Gloucester, ME 04260          207-688-4573
http://www.alltech-tsi.org
e-mail: info@alltech-tsi.org
*Deb Dimmick, Director*

**4502 Bates College**

102 Lane Hall
Lewiston, ME 04240          207-786-6219
FAX 207-786-6219
http://www.bates.edu
e-mail: tgoundie@bates.edu
*Tedd Goundie, Dean*
*Mary Gravel, Assistant to the Dean*

An independent four-year college with 17 special education students out of a total of 1,501.

**4503 Bowdoin College**

5000 College Station
Brunswick, ME 04011          207-725-3958
FAX 207-725-3764
http://www.bowdoin.edu
e-mail: help3030@bowdoin.edu
*Mary McCann, Contact*

Offers a variety of services to students with disabilities including note takers, extended testing time, counseling services, and special accommodations.

**4504 Center for Community Inclusion (CCI): Maine's University Center for Excellence**

University of Maine
5717 Corbett Hall
Orono, ME 04469          207-581-1084
800-203-6957
FAX 207-581-1231
http://www.ume.maine.edu/cci
e-mail: ccimail@umit.maine.edu
*Lucille Zeph, Director*
*Marge Zubik, Administrative Assistant*

CCI has four core functions: interdisciplinary education; community services, outreach education and technical assistance; research and evaluation; and dissemination.

**4505 Eastern Maine Vocational-Technical Institute**

354 Hogan Road
Bangor, ME 04401          207-974-4600
800-286-9357
http://www.emtc.org
e-mail: admissions@emtc.org
*Phillip Pratt*

Offers a variety of services to students with disabilities including notetakers, extended testing time, counseling services, and special accommodations.

**4506 Kennebee Valley Technical College**

92 Western Avenue
Fairfield, ME 04937          207-453-5000
http://www.kvtc.net
e-mail: jhood@kvtc.net
*Pat Ross, Students Services*
*Julie Hood, Coordinator*

A public two-year college with 13 special education students out of a total of 1,086.

**4507 Mid-State College**

411 West Northmoor Rd
Peoria, IL 61614

800-251-4299
http://www.midstatecollege.com
e-mail: info@midstatecollege.com

*Richard Gross, Special Services*

Offers a variety of services to students with disabilities including notetakers, extended testing time, counseling services, and special accommodations.

**4508 Northern Maine Community College**

33 Edgemont Drive
Presque Isle, ME 04769

207-768-2787
800-535-NMTC
FAX 207-768-2831
http://www.nmcc.edu
e-mail: lflag@nmcc.edu

*Laura Flagg, Special Services coordinator*
*Kristen Lloyd, Staff*

A public two-year college with 33 special education students out of a total of 817.

**4509 Southern Maine Technical College**

2 Fort Road
South Portland, ME 04106

207-741-5500
http://www.smtc.net

*Mark Krogman, Disability Services Provider*

Southern Maine Technical College is committed to helping qualified students with disabilities achieve their educational goals. Upon request and verification of the disability, SMTC will provide service coordination and reasonable accommodations to remediate the competitive disadvantage that a disability can create in the educational setting.

**4510 Unity College**

Unity, ME 04988

207-948-3131
FAX 207-948-6277
http://www.unity.edu
e-mail: jhoran@unity.edu

*James Horan, Special Services*
*David Glenn-Lewin, President*

Offers a variety of services to students with disabilities including notetakers, extended testing time, counseling services, and special accommodations.

**4511 University of Maine**

Disability Support Services
Onward Building
Orono, ME 04469

207-581-2319
FAX 207-581-2969
http://www.umaine.edu
e-mail: ann.smith@umit.maine.edu

*Ann Smith, Director*
*Sara Henry, Disability Counselor*

The primary goal of the University of Maine Disability Support Services is to create educational access for students with disabilities at UMaine by providing a point of coordination, information and education for those students and the campus community.

**4512 University of Maine: Fort Kent**

Academic and Counseling Services
23 University Drive
Fort Kent, ME 04743

207-834-7500
888-879-8635
FAX 207-834-7503
TDY:207-834-7466
http://www.umfk.maine.edu

*George Diaz, Director of Counseling Svcs.*
*Garland Caron, Counselor*

Students with a documented disability, who need academic accommodations, are encouraged to meet with an Academic and Counseling Services representative to develop a plan for their accommodations.

**4513 University of Maine: Machias**

9 O'Brien Avenue
Machias, ME 04654

207-255-1200
800-468-6866
http://www.umm.maine.edu
e-mail: admissions@acd.umm.maine.edu

*Jean Schild, Coordinator*

Prepared to assist students with disabilities with reasonable accommodations to qualified individuals with disabilities upon request.

**4514 University of New England: University Campus**

Disability Services
11 Hills Beach Road
Biddeford, ME 04005

207-283-0171
800-477-4863
FAX 207-294-5931
http://www.une.edu
e-mail: schurch@une.edu

*Susan Church, Coordinator*

The Office for Students with Disabilities exists to ensure that the University fulfills the part of its mission that seeks to promote respect for individual differences and to ensure that no person who meets the academic and technical standards requisite for admisssion to, and continued enrollment at, the University is denied benefits or subjected to discrimination at UNE solely by reason of his or her disability.

**4515 University of New England: Westbrook College Campus**

716 Stevens Avenue
Portland, ME 04103

207-797-7261
FAX 207-282-6379
e-mail: Cehringhaus@mailbox.une.edu

*Carolyn Ehringh MD, Director*

Offers academic accommodations, as mandated under federal and state law, through the Office for Students with Disabilities (free of charge). General academic support services, such as tutoring and study strategies instruction, are available through the Learning Assistance Center. (Note: The Individual Learning Program is offered only on the Biddeford Campus).

**4516 University of Southern Maine: Office of Academic Support for Students with Disabilities**

96 Falmouth Street, Room 242
Portland, ME 04104 9300      207-780-4706
800-800-4USM
FAX 207-780-4403
http://www.usm.maine.edu
*Joyce Branaman, Coordinator*

OASSD affirms the commitment of the University of Southern Maine to provide equal access to higher education for qualified students with disabilities. All services are provided with a philosophical framework that stresses student independence and self-reliance.

## Maryland

**4517 Baltimore City Community College**

2901 Liberty Heights Avenue
Baltimore, MD 21215      410-462-8000
888-203-1261
FAX 412-462-8556
TDY:410-333-5802
http://www.bccc.edu
*Nicole Hoke-Wilson, Director*
*Michelle Reynold, Counselor*

Offers a variety of services to students with disabilities including notetakers, extended testing time, counseling services, and special accommodations.

**4518 Charles County Community College**

PO Box 910
La Plata, MD 20646      301-934-2251
800-933-9177
FAX 301-934-7838
TDY:301-934-1188
http://www.csmd.edu
e-mail: bonnien@charles.cc.md.us
*Elaine Ryan, President*
*Steven Goldman, Vice President*

A public two-year college with 600+ students with disabilities out of a total of 6,055.

**4519 Chelsea School**

711 Pershing Drive
Silver Spring, MD 20910      301-585-1430
FAX 301-585-5865
http://www.chelseaschool.edu
e-mail: tocannor@chelseaschool.edu
*Linda A Handy MD, Academic Head of School*
*Timothy Hall, Director*

Chelsea is a co-educational, residential or day school for bright, dyslexic students in grade K-12.

**4520 Chesapeake College**

Routes 50 and 213
Wye Mills, MD 21679      410-822-5400
FAX 410-822-9466
TDY:410-827-9164
http://www.chesapeake.edu
e-mail: mhickey__@chesapeake.edu
*Stewart Bounds, President*
*Maurice Hicky, Vice President*

Offers a variety of services to students with disabilities including notetakers, extended testing time, counseling services, and special accommodations.

**4521 College of Notre Dame of Maryland**

Disability Services
4701 N Charles Street
Baltimore, MD 21210      410-532-5379
FAX 410-532-5167
http://www.ndm.edu
e-mail: wdaisley@ndm.edu
*Theresa Cannone, Marketing Manager*
*Winifred Daisley, Director*

Disability Services attends to students' physical, emotional, and learning disabilities by ensuring that students with disabilities are afforded the accommodations that they need to help them succeed at the College of Notre Dame.

**4522 Columbia Union College**

7600 Flower Avenue
Takoma Park, MD 20912      301-891-4080
800-835-4212
FAX 301-891-4167
http://www.cuc.edu
e-mail: jmcfarla@cuc.edu
*Betty Howard, Assistant Dean*
*Mickaela Davis, Office Assistant*

Offers a variety of services to students with disabilities including note takers, extended testing time, counseling services, and special accommodations.

**4523 Community College of Baltimore County**

800 S Rolling Road
Catonsville, MD 21228      410-455-4382
FAX 410-455-4504
http://www.ccbc.cc.md.us/campuses/cat/htm
*Mark Lieberman, Counselor*
*Jill Hodge, Counselor*

Offers a variety of services to students with disabilities including notetakers, extended testing time, counseling services, and special accommodations.

**4524 Frostburg State University**

101 Braddock Road
Frostburg, MD 21532      301-687-4000
FAX 301-687-7049
http://www.frostburg.edu
e-mail: fsuadmission@frostburg.edu
*Catherine Gira MD, President*
*Alice , Vice President*

A public four-year college with 153 special education students out of a total of 4,472.

**4525 Hagerstown Junior College**

11400 Robinwood Drive
Hagerstown, MD 21742      301-790-2800
866-422-2468
FAX 301-791-9165
http://www.hagerstowncc.edu
e-mail: admission@hagerstowncc.edu
*Guy Altieri MD, President*
*Julian , Dean of Academic Affairs*

A public two-year college with 22 special education students out of a total of 3,364.

**4526  Harford Community College**
401 Thomas Run Road
Bel Air, MD  21015                          410-836-4000
                                            FAX 410-836-4200
                                            TDY:410-836-4402
                          http://www.harford.edu
                          e-mail: lpenisto@harford.edu
*Lorraine Peniston, Coordinator*
*Cindy Conroy, Administrative Specialist*

An open enrollment two-year college, with reasonable accommodations provided for students with documented disabilities through disability support services. Students may also receive academic advising, personal and career counseling, and study skills instruction.

**4527  Hood College**
**Disabilities Services Office**
**401 Rosemont Avenue**
**Frederick, MD  21701**                     301-663-3131
                                            FAX 301-694-7653
                          http://www.hood.edu
                          e-mail: webmaster@hood.edu
*Ron Bolpe, President*

Four-year college that provides services to disabled students.

**4528  Howard Community College**
**10901 Little Patuxent Parkway**
**Columbia, MD  21044**                      410-772-4822
                                            FAX 410-772-4803
                          http://www.howardcc.edu
                          e-mail: jmarks@howardcc.edu
*Janice Marks, Director*
*Mary , President*

A public two-year college with 225 students with disabilities using services out of a total of 5,500.

**4529  Ivymount School**
**11614 Seven Locks Road**
**Rockville, MD  20854**                     301-469-0223
                                            FAX 301-469-0778
                          e-mail: lpender@ivymount.org
*Janet Wintrol, Director*
*Stephanie deSibour, Assistant Director*

Independent day-school serving students, 3-21, with disabilities including developmental delays, communication deficits, learning disabilities, and autism.

**4530  James E Duckworth School**
**11201 Evans Trail**
**Beltsville, MD  20705**                    301-572-0620
                                            FAX 301-572-0628
                http://www.pgcps.pg.k12.md.us/~duckw/
                          e-mail: jedworth@pgcps.org
*Trinell Bowman, Principal*

**4531  Johns Hopkins Institution**
**3400 N Charles Hall**
**Baltimore, MD  21218**                     410-516-8000
                                            FAX 410-614-7251
                          http://www.jhi.edu
*Martha Rosemann, Associate Dean*

Once a student with disabilities has been admitted to The Johns Hopkins School of Public Health it is important that he/she submits disability documentation to the school's disability services coordinator. This applies to both new students as well as current/continuing students who are requesting accommodation for the first time.

**4532  Prince George's Community College**
**301 Largo Road**
**Largo, MD  20772**
                          http://www.pgweb.pg.cc.md.us
                          e-mail: enrollmetnservices@pg.cc.md.us
*Carrier Johnson, Special Services*

Offers a variety of services to students with disabilities including note takers, extended testing time, counseling services, and special accommodations.

**4533  Summit School**
**664 E Central Avenue**
**Edgewater, MD  21037**                     410-798-0005
                                            FAX 410-798-0008
                          http://www.thesummitschool.org
*Jane R Snider MD, Founding Director*

A school for children with language-based reading difficulties, particularly in the area of decoding, with average to above average cognitive ability, who are ultimately planning to attend a college-prep high school with limited support.

**4534  Towson State University**
**8000 York Road**
**Towson, MD  21252**                        410-704-2000
                                            800-225-5878
                                            FAX 410-704-4247
                          http://www.towson.edu
                          e-mail: ruhland@towson.edu
*Ronni Uhland, Director*

A public four-year college with 134 special education students out of a total of 13,761.

**4535  Towson University**
**8000 York Road**
**Towson, MD  21252**                        410-704-2000
                                            800-225-5878
                                            FAX 410-704-4247
                          http://www.towson.edu
                          e-mail: ruhland@towson.edu
*Ronnie Uhland, Learning Disabilities Specialist*

A four-year college that provides services to the learning disabled.

**4536  University of Maryland: Baltimore County**
**1000 Hilltop Circle**
**Baltimore, MD  21250**                     410-455-2459
                                            FAX 410-455-1028
                          http://www.umbc.edu
                          e-mail: chill@umbc.edu
*Patty Wilson, Office Manager*
*Cynthia Hill, Director*

The Office of Student Support Services provides services that are designed to improve the educational and personal development of disabled and returning students.

**4537  University of Maryland: College Park**

2111 Shoemaker Building
College Park, MD  20742          301-405-9969
                                 FAX 301-314-9206
                                 http://www.maryland.edu
                                 e-mail: mh185@umail.umd.edu
*William Scales MD, Director Disability Support*
*Peggy Hayestrip, LD Coordinator*

The mission of the Disability Support Service is to ensure individuals with disabilities equal access to the University of Maryland College Park programs.

**4538  University of Maryland: Eastern Shore**

Blackbone Road
Princess Anne, MD  21853          410-651-6456
                                  FAX 410-651-6322
                                  http://www.umes.edu
                                  e-mail: dshowellhighcherry@mail.umes.edu
*Diann Showell MD, Director*

Offers a variety of services to students with disabilities including note takers, extended testing time, counseling services, and special accommodations.

**4539  Valley Academy**

301 W Chesapeake Avenue
Towson, MD  21204                 410-828-0620
                                  FAX 410-828-0438
                                  http://www.jemicyschool.org
                                  e-mail: bshisrin@jemicyschool.org
*Ben Shisrin, Principal*
*Mark Westervelt, Assistant Principal*

**4540  West Nottingham Academy**

1079 Firetower Road
Colora, MD  21917                 410-658-5556
                                  800-962-1744
                                  FAX 410-658-6790
                                  http://www.wna.org
                                  e-mail: admissions@wna.org
*Heidi Sprinkle, Director, Admissions*
*Tom Sorci, Director, Learning Center*
*Dr. John Watson, Headmaster*

A college preparatory school dedicated to the intellectual, spiritual and social growth of each student. The academy equips students to become successful in all aspects of life through individual attention within a diverse community and a safe and caring environment.

**4541  Western Maryland College: Academic Skills Center**

2 College Hill
Westminster, MD  21157            410-857-2504
                                  800-638-5005
                                  FAX 410-857-2729
                                  http://www.wmdc.edu
                                  e-mail: dmarjaru@wmdc.edu
*Denise Marjarum, Academic Skills Center*
*Susan Dorsey, Co-Director*

The Academic Skills Center (ASC) provides reasonable accommodations and a range of services to meet the academic needs of students with learning disabilities or some type of documented learning problem.

**4542  Wor-Wic Community College**

32000 Campus Drive
Salisbury, MD  21801              410-334-2800
                                  FAX 410-334-2952
                                  http:// www.worwic.edu
                                  e-mail: suzannea@worwic.edu
*Suzanne Alexander, Counseling Director*

A comprehensive two-year institution located on Maryland's eastern shore. The faculty and staff are dedicated to serving the unique needs of each student with a learning disability.

## Massachusetts

**4543  American International College: Supportive Learning Services Program**

1000 State Street
Springfield, MA  01109            413-737-7000
                                  800-242-3142
                                  FAX 413-205-3908
                                  http://www.aic.edu
                                  e-mail: inquiry@www.aic.edu
*Mary Saltus, Coordinator of Supportive Learni*
*Anne Midura, Office Manager*

An independent four-year college with 95 special education students out of a total of 1,433. There is an additional fee for the special education program in addition to the regular tuition.

**4544  Amherst College**

PO Box 2206
Amherst, MA  01004                413-542-2529
                                  FAX 413-542-2223
                                  http://www.amherst.edu
                                  e-mail: info@amherst.edu
*Frances Tuleja, Director*

Offers a variety of services to students with disabilities including note takers, extended testing time, counseling services, and special accommodations.

**4545  Anna Maria College**

50 Sunset Lane
Paxton, MA  01612                 508-849-3300
                                  800-344-4586
                                  FAX 508-849-3319
                                  http://www.annamaria.edu
*Olivia Tarleton, Director*

An independent four-year college with 12 special education students out of a total of 691.

**4546  Atlantic Union College**

Center for Academic Success
PO Box 1000
S Lancaster, MA  01561            978-368-2416
                                  FAX 978-368-2015
                                  http://www.atlanticuc.edu
                                  e-mail: info@atlanticuc.edu
*Elizabeth Anderson, Center Academic Success Director*

**4547  Babson College**
**Disability Services**
**Hollister Hall Babson College**
**Babson Park, MA  02457**          781-239-4075
                                    800-488-3696
                              FAX 781-239-5567
                              TDY:781-239-4017
            http://www.babson.edu\callssdeans
*Erin Evans, Manager*

An independent four-year business-based college with 110 undergraduate and graduate students with disabilities. Accommodations are individualized for students presenting documentation and may include notetaking assistance, extended time, separate location for testing, books-on-tape and other special accommodations. Adaptive equipment, academic advising, counseling services and teaching of organizational and time management skills, study skills and test taking strategies are offered.

**4548  Bentley College**
**175 Forest Street**
**Waltham, MA  02452**              781-891-2000
                              FAX 781-891-247
                              TDY:781-891-2280
                        http://www.bentley.edu
              e-mail: jgorgone@bentley.edu
*Brenda Hawks MD, Associate Director*
*Lansche Stalmon, Administrator*

An independent four-year college with 13 special education students out of a total of 5181.

**4549  Berkshire Center**
**College Internship Program**
**18 Park Street**
**Lee, MA  01238**                  413-243-2576
                              FAX 413-243-3351
                http://www.berkshirecenter.org
            e-mail: gshaw@berkshirecenter.org
*Mike McManmon MD, Executive Director*
*Grey Shaw, Program Director*

A post secondary college business school or vocational program for young adults 18-27 with learning disabilities. A co-ed population from four countries and all regions of the United States. Students have individual academic tutorials, and courses in money management and vocational counseling. Students live in apartments and learn life skills.

**4550  Boston College**
**140 Commonwealth Avenue**
**Chestnut Hill, MA  02467**        617-552-8000
                                    800-294-0294
                              FAX 617-552-2097
                        http://www.bc.edu
                  e-mail: ugadmis@bc.edu
*Kathleen Duggan MD, Assistant Director*

An independent four-year college with 195 special education students out of a total of 14,230. There is an additional fee for the special education program in addition to the regular tuition.

**4551  Boston University**
**Office of Disability Services**
**Martin Luther King Jr Center**
**Boston, MA  02215**               617-353-3658
                              FAX 617-353-9646
                              TDY:617-353-3658
                        http://www.bu.edu
              e-mail: lwolf@bu.edu/disability
*Lorraine Wolf, Clinical Director*

Provides basic support services such as test taking accommodations, note taking assistance, etc. Provides comprehensive services that include learning strategies instruction for an additional fee. LDSS offers a six-week summer program, The Summer Transition Program, for high school graduates.

**4552  Brandeis University**
**415 S Street**
**Waltham, MA  02454**              781-736-4464
                              FAX 781-736-4466
                        http://www.brandeis.edu
              e-mail: ddgratto@brandeis.edu
*Laura Lyndon, Assist Dean/Student Disability*

An independent four-year college with 67 special education students out of a total of 2,901. Brandeis is committed to providing reasonable accommodation/s to individuals with appropriately documented physical, learning and psychological disabilities.

**4553  Bridgewater State College**
**Bridgewater, MA  02325**          508-531-1276
                              FAX 508-531-6107
                        http://www.bridgew.edu
*Martha Jones, Dean Studies*

Offers a variety of programs and services to students with disabilities including pre-college workshop, notetakers, extended testing time, counseling services, adaptive computing, peer tutors, supplemental instruction and special accommodations.

**4554  Bristol Community College**
**777 Elsbree Street**
**Fall River, MA  02720**           508-678-2811
                              FAX 508-730-3297
                        http://www.bristol.mass.edu
*Susan Boissonneault*

Located in Southeastern New England, serves the residents of Bristol County and Rhode Island, in offering Associate of Art Degrees and Associate of Science Degrees in career and transfer programs, as well as certificates in other programs. Offers the QUEST Project which is an academic support program for learning disabled students as they begin their college education. Builds academic skills and confidence in the student's ability to do college work. Advises students on career choices.

**4555  Cape Cod Community College**
**2240 Lyanough Road**
**West Barnstable, MA  02668**      503-362-2131
                                    877-846-3672
                              FAX 508-362-3988
                        http://www.capecod.mass.edu
              e-mail: info@capecod.mass.edu
*Richard Sommers MD, LD Specialist*

A public two-year college with 165 special education students out of a total of 2,141. A full range of accommodations are available to students with disabilities.

**4556 Clark University**
950 Main Street
Worcester, MA 01610
508-793-7431
800-GO-CLARK
FAX 508-793-8821
http://www.clarku.edu
e-mail: admissions@clarku.edu
*Sharon Klerk, Director Special Services*

An independent four-year college with 84 special education students out of a total of 2151.

**4557 Curry College**
**Program For Advancement of Learning**
1071 Blue Hill Avenue
Milton, MA 02186
617-333-2250
800-669-0686
FAX 617-333-2018
TDY:617-333-2250
http://www.curry.edu
e-mail: spratt@curry.edu
*Lisa Ijiri, Director*
*Susan Pratt, PAL Coordinator*
*Joan Manchester, Program Administrator*

PAL is a program within Curry College, a co-educational, four-year liberal arts institution serving 2,000 students and located in the Boston suburb of Milton, Massachusetts. For over 25 years, PAL has both shaped and been shaped by Curry's distinctive philosophy of education. Serves college age students with specific learning disabilities.

**4558 Dean College**
99 Main Street
Franklin, MA 02038
508-541-1764
FAX 508-541-1918
http://www.dean.edu

Committed to maintaining a caring and nurturing environment for its students.

**4559 Dearborn Academy**
**School for Children**
34 Winter Street
Arlington, MA 02474
781-641-5992
FAX 781-641-5997
http://www.spedschools.com
e-mail: twalton@sscinc.org
*Tucker Walton, Associate Director*
*Milliy Foaugei, Administrative Assistant*

**4560 Eagle Hill School**
242 Old Petersham Road
Hardwick, MA 01037
413-477-6000
FAX 413-477-6837
http://www.ehs1.org
e-mail: admission@ehs1.org
*Dana Harbert, Director for Admission*

Since 1967 has offered premier services to the special needs community. This co-educational, college preparatory, boarding program is designed to meet academic and social needs of students diagnosed with learning disabilities (LD) and Attention Deficit Disorder (ADD). Offers a success-oriented atmosphere, and a consistently structured and socially supportive environment. The program is ungraded and serves students ages 11-19.

**4561 Eastern Nazarene College**
**Student Affairs Office**
23 E Elm Avenue
Quincy, MA 02170
617-745-3000
800-883-6288
FAX 617-984-4901
http://www.enc.edu
e-mail: klitticj@enc.edu
*Joyce Klittich, Director Academic Services*

Offers a variety of services to students with disabilities including note takers, extended testing time, counseling services, and special accommodations.

**4562 Endicott College**
376 Hale Street
Beverly, MA 01915
978-927-0585
800-325-1114
FAX 978-232-2600
http://www.endicott.edu
e-mail: bpierima@endicott.edu
*Eloise Knowlton, Head of Disability Department*
*Barbara Pierimarchi, Administrative Assistant*

An independent two-year college with 48 special education students out of a total of 793.

**4563 Essex Agricultural and Technical Institute**
562 Maple Street
Hawthorne, MA 01937
978-774-0050
FAX 978-774-6530
http://www.agtech.org
e-mail: rraucci@agtech.org
*Helen Keyes, Secretary to the Superintended*

A public two-year college with 74 special education students out of a total of 533.

**4564 Fitchburg State College**
**Disability Services**
160 Pearl Street
Fitchburg, MA 01420
978-665-4020
FAX 978-665-3021
http://www.fsc.edu
e-mail: jperkins@fsc.edu
*Julie Maky, Staff Assistant*

**4565 Framingham State College**
100 State Street
Framingham, MA 01701
508-620-1220
http://www.framingham.edu

Offers a variety of services to students with disabilities including note takers, extended testing time, counseling services, and special accommodations.

**4566  Hampshire College**
Learning Disabilities Support Services
893 W Street
Amherst, MA  01002            413-559-5458
FAX 413-559-5695
http://www.hampshire.edu
*Joel Dansky, Associate Dean*

Four year college that offers students with learning disabilities services and support.

**4567  Harvard School of Public Health**
677 Huntington Avenue
Boston, MA  02115            617-432-1032
FAX 617-432-2009
http://www/hsph.harvard.edu
e-mail: hsph@harvard.edu
*Marie Trottier, Disability Coordinator*
*Kelly Teixeyra, Assistant*

An independent four-year college with 45 special education students out of a total of 6,621. Disabled students are encouraged to take advantage of opportunities available to help them achieve their educational goals.

**4568  Institute for Community Inclusion (ICI)**
UMass Boston
100 Morrissey Boulevard
Boston, MA  02115            617-287-4300
FAX 617-287-4352
http://www.communityinclusion.org
e-mail: ici@umb.edu
*William Kiernan, Director*
*Rachael Webb, Administrative Assistant*

ICI promotes the inclusion of people with disabilities in their communities through training, consultation, clinical and employment services and research.

**4569  Landmark School Elementary and Middle School Program**
429 Hale Street
Prides Crossing, MA  01965            978-236-3000
FAX 978-927-7268
http://www.landmarkoutreach.org
e-mail: jtruslow@landmarkschool.org
*Carolyn Orsini, Director Admission*

For students entering grades 2-8, of average to above average intelligence, who have a history of healthy emotional development, and who've been diagnosed with a specific language-based learning disability. Ten month programs include 1:1 daily tutorials.

**4570  Landmark School High School Program**
429 Hale Street
Prides Crossing, MA  01965            978-236-3000
FAX 978-927-7268
http://www.landmarkoutreach.org
e-mail: jtruslow@landmarkschool.org
*Carolyn Orsini, Director Admission*

For students entering grades 9-12, of average to above average intelligence, who have a history of healthy emotional development, and who've been diagnosed with a specific language-based learning disability. Ten month programs include 1:1 daily tutorials.

**4571  Landmark School Preparatory Program**
429 Hale Street
Prides Crossing, MA  01965            978-236-3000
FAX 978-927-7268
http://www.landmarkoutreach.org
e-mail: jtruslow@landmarkschool.org
*Carolyn Orsini, Director Admission*

Offers a secondary school level curriculum emphasizing organizational and study skills development in a traditional classroom setting, and is designed for college bound boys and girls who have progressed to within one year of expected grade level performance.

**4572  Linden Hill School**
154 S Mountain Road
Northfield, MA            413-498-2906
866-498-2906
FAX 413-498-2908
http://www.lindenhs.org
e-mail: office@lindenhs.org
*Vanessa Towne, Office Secretary*

An ungraded boarding school for boys between the ages of 9-15 with dyslexia or specific learning/language differences. Linden Hill also offers a formal freshman year program. The school's primary objective is to provide a comprehensive language training program in reading, spelling, and writing. The language program provides an alternative to the traditional approach by using the sight-recognition (whole word) method of learning.

**4573  Massachusetts Bay Community College**
50 Oakland Street
Wellesley, MA  02481            781-239-3000
FAX 781-239-1047
http://www.mbcc.mass.edu
e-mail: Josepho@mbcc.edu
*Joseph O'Niel, LD Specialist*

A public two-year college with 44 special education students out of a total of 4,684.

**4574  Massachusetts College of Liberal Arts**
375 Church Street
North Adams, MA  01247            413-662-5308
FAX 413-662-5319
*Claire Smith, Coordinator Academic Support*

Academic support services for students with disabilities.

**4575 Massasoit Community College**

1 Massasoit Boulevard
Brockton, MA 02302      508-588-9100
800-CAREERS
FAX 508-427-1250
TDY:508-427-1240
http://www.massasoit.mass.edu
e-mail: pjohnston@massasoit.mass.edu
*Peter Johnston, Dean of Humanities*
*Richard Cronin, Director of Marketing*

A public two-year college with 164 special education students out of a total of 6,423.

**4576 Middlesex Community College**

591 Springs Road
Bedford, MA 01730      732-906-2546
800-818-3434
FAX 732-906-2506

A public two-year college with 298 special education students out of a total of 4,028.

**4577 Mount Ida College**

777 Dedham Street
Newton, MA 02459      617-928-4535
FAX 617-928-4760
http://www.mountida.edu
e-mail: admissions@mountida.edu
*Maya Evans, Associate Director*
*Brian Stuart, Associate Director of Communicat*

Designed and developed to provide additional support for students with learning disabilities. Services include individual tutoring by professional learning specialists, reduced course load, credit study skills course, specialized accommodations and community functions.

**4578 Mount Wachusett Community College**

444 Green Street
Gardner, MA 01440      978-632-6600
FAX 978-630-9559
http://www.mwce.mass.edu
e-mail: dasquino@mwcc.nass.edu
*Daniel Asquino, President*
*Edward Terceiro, Vice President*

A public two-year college with 177 special education students out of a total of 2,202.

**4579 Newbury College**

129 Fisher Avenue
Brookline, MA 02445      617-730-7072
FAX 617-232-5139
http://www.newbury.edu/
e-mail: brookline@newbury.edu
*Sara d'Anjou, Academic Services*

An independent four-year college with 35 self identified special education students out of a total of 800.

**4580 North Shore Community College**

One Ferncroft Road
Danvers, MA 01923      978-762-4000
FAX 978-762-4038
TDY:781-477-2136
http://www.northshore.edu
e-mail: hheineman@northshore.edu
*Helen Heineman, President*
*Philip , Vice President*

A public two-year college with 280 special education students out of a total of 3,301.

**4581 Northeastern University**

Disability Resource Center
360 Huntington Avenue
Boston, MA 02115      617-373-2675
FAX 617-373-7800
TDY:617-373-2730
http://www.neu.edu
e-mail: drcinfo@neu.edu
*G Kukiela Bork, Dean/Director*
*Laura havans, Secretary*

Offers a variety of services to students with disabilities including note takers, extended testing time, counseling services, and special accommodations.

**4582 Pine Manor College**

400 Heath Street
Chestnut Hill, MA 02467      617-731-7000
800-762-1357
FAX 617-731-7199
http://www.pmc.edu
e-mail: admissions@pmc.edu
*Bill nichols, Dean of Admissions*
*Mary Walsh, Center Director*

For students with learning disabilities, Pine Manor College offers the Learning Resource Center. The LRC supports and challenges students to realize their maximum academic potential in the way that best suits their individual learning styles.

**4583 Regis College: Massachusetts**

235 Wellesley Street
Weston, MA 02493      781-768-7000
866-438-7344
FAX 781-768-8339
http://www.regiscollege.edu
e-mail: admission@regiscollege.edu
*Emily Keily, Director Admissions*

Offers a variety of services to students with disabilities including notetakers, extended testing time, counseling services, and special accommodations.

**4584 Riverview School**

551 Route 6A
East Sandwich, MA 02537      508-888-0489
FAX 508-888-1315
http://www.riverviewschool.org
e-mail: admissions@riverviewschool.org
*Jeanne Pachero, Director Admissions/Placement*
*Maureen Brenner, Head School*

An independent, residential school of international reputation and service enrolling 183 male and female students in its secondary and post-secondary programs. Students share a common history of lifelong difficulty with academic achievement and the development of friendships. On measures of intellectual ability, most students score within the 70-100 range and have a primary diagnosis of learning disability and/or complex language or learning disorder.

**4585 Salem State College**

325 Lafayeete Street
Salem, MA 01970      **978-542-6217**
**FAX 978-542-6753**
**http://www.salem.mass.edu**
**e-mail: admissions@salemstate.edu**
*Eileen Berger, Director*

Four year college offering a learning disabilities program for students.

**4586 Simmons College**

300 Fenway
Boston, MA 02115      **617-521-2000**
**FAX 617-521-3190**
**http://www.simmons.edu**
**e-mail: daniel.cheever@simmons.edu**
*Daniel Cheever, President*
*Kathleen Rogers, Vice President*

An independent four-year college with 44 special education students out of a total of 1,399.

**4587 Smith College**

College Hall 7
Northampton, MA 01063      **413-584-2700**
**FAX 413-585-4498**
**TDY:413-585-2072**
**http://www.smith.edu**
**e-mail: admission@smith.edu**
*Laura Rausher, Director Disability Services*
*Anna Megill, Administrator*

An independent four-year college with 42 special education students out of a total of 2,613.

**4588 Springfield College**

263 Alden Street
Springfield, MA 01109      **413-748-3768**
**FAX 413-748-3937**
**http://www.spfldcol.edu**
**e-mail: ddickens@spfldcol.edu**
*Deb Dickins, Director*
*Lynn Vlinn, Administrative Assistant*

Four-year college that offers student support to students with learning disabilities.

**4589 Springfield Technical Community College**

One Armory Square
Springfield, MA 01105      **413-781-7822**
**FAX 413-733-8403**
**http://www.stcc.edu**
**e-mail: deena.shriver@stcc.edu**
*Deena Shriver, Special Services*
*Liza Herbert, Operator*

Offers a variety of services to students with disabilities including note takers, extended testing time, counseling services, and special accommodations.

**4590 Stonehill College**

320 Washington Street
Easton, MA 02357      **508-565-1000**
**FAX 508-565-1500**
**TDY:508-565-1425**
**http://www.stonehill.edu**
**e-mail: academicservices@stonehill.edu**
*Richard Grant, Assistant Dean Academic Services*
*David , Learning Disabilities Specialist*

A small liberal arts-based college of 2000 students set in a quiet suburb of Boston sponsored by the Holy Cross Fathers. This Catholic college offers programs in the liberal arts, business, and the sciences and is committed to providing reasonable accommodations to students with disabilities.

**4591 Suffolk University**

8 Ashburton Place
Boston, MA 02108      **617-573-8239**
**FAX 617-742-2582**
**TDY:617-557-4875**
**http://www.suffolk.edu**
**e-mail: jatkinso@admin.suffolk.edu**
*Nancy Stoll, Dean Students*
*Beth Tiomgson, Administrator*

Offers a variety of services to students with disabilities including note takers, extended testing time, counseling services, special accommodations, assistive technology, and tutorial assistance.

**4592 Threshold Program at Lesley University**

Lesley University
29 Everett Street
Cambridge, MA 02138      **617-349-8181**
**800-999-1959**
**FAX 617-349-8189**
**http://www.lesley.edu**
**e-mail: jwilbur@lesley.edu**
*James Wilbur, Director*

The Threshold Program is a comprehensive, nondegree campus-based program at Lesley University for highly motivated young adults with diverse learning disabilities and other special needs.

**4593 Tufts University**

419 Boston Avenue
Medford, MA 02155      **617-627-2000**
**FAX 617-627-3971**
**http://www.tufts.edu**
**e-mail: studentservices@ase.tufts.edu**
*Nadia Medina, Director ARC*
*Sandra Baer, Coordinator*

Offers a variety of services to students with disabilities including note takers, extended testing time, counseling services, and special accommodations.

**4594 University of Massachusetts: Amherst**

Disabilities Services
231 Whitmore Administration Bldg
Amherst, MA 01003 0892      **413-545-0892**
**FAX 413-577-0691**
**TDY:413-545-0892**
**http://www.umass.edu**
**e-mail: zygmont@acad.umass.edu/**
**ds@educ.umass.edu**
*Madeline Peters, Director*

A public four-year college with 192 special education students out of a total of 17,207.

**4595 University of Massachusetts: Boston**
Ross Center
Boston, MA 02125          617-287-7430
                         FAX 617-287-7436
                         http://www.umb.edu
                         e-mail: rosscenter.umb.edu
*Sheila Petruccelli, Director*

A public four-year college with 151 special education students out of a total of 8,598. Committed to the goal of providing equal access to its education programs, so that its students may achieve their academic potential.

**4596 University of Massachusetts: Lowell**
Office of Disability Services
McGauvran 363
Lowell, MA 01854 3092        978-934-4338
                            FAX 508-934-3011
                            http://www.uml.edu
                            e-mail: noelc@uml.edu
*Noel PhD, Director Disabilities*
*Chandrika , Assistant Director*
*Kerry Donohoe, Disabilities Coordinator*

Office of Disability Services has responsibility for assuring reasonable accommodations, program access and support to qualified physically and learning disabled students and students with psychiatric disabilities.

**4597 Wellesley College**
106 Central Street
Wellesley, MA 02481         781-283-1000
                           FAX 781-283-3644

An independent four-year college with 41 special education students out of a total of 2,325.

**4598 Wheaton College**
Norton, MA 02766           508-286-8215
                          FAX 508-286-5621
                          TDY:508-286-5682
                          http://www.wheatoncollege.edu
                          e-mail: mbleadsoe@wheaton,edu
*Martha Bredsu, Assistant Dean College Skills*
*Victoria McGillin, Dean*

An independent four-year college with 200 students with learning disabilities out of a total of 1450.

## Michigan

**4599 Adrian College**
Academic Services Program
110 S Madison Street
Adrian, MI 49221           517-265-5161
                          800-877-2246
                          FAX 517-264-3181
                          TDY:517-265-5161
                          http://www.adrian.edu
                          e-mail: ctapp@adrian.edu
*Carol Tapp, Learning Specialist*
*Mike Balllard, Campus Safety*

A private, co-educational liberal arts and sciences undergraduate college. The college strives to enroll a student body that reflects the wealth and diversity of our society and is committed to providing appropriate services to all students. There are 35 academic majors and 9 preprofessional programs.

**4600 Alma College**
614 W Superior Street
Alma, MI 48801             989-463-7111
                          FAX 989-463-7353
                          http://www.alma.edu
                          e-mail: perkins@alma.edu
*Mindy Sargent, Interim Director*
*Julie Liz, Contact*

An independent four-year college with 5 special education students out of a total of 1,222.

**4601 Andrews University**
Old US 31
Berrien Springs, MI 49104
                          800-253-2874
                          FAX 269-471-6900
                          http://www.andrews.edu
*Marion Swanpoel, Director*

Offers a variety of services to students with disabilities including notetakers, extended testing time, counseling services, and special accommodations.

**4602 Aquinas College**
Aquinas College
1607 Robinson Road SE
Grand Rapids, MI 49506      616-459-8281
                           800-678-9593
                           FAX 616-732-4431
                           http://www.aquinas.edu
                           e-mail: admissions@aquinas.edu
*Tom Mikowski, Director of Admissions*
*Harry Konoke, President*

An independent four-year college with 32 special education students out of a total of 2,141.

**4603 Augmentative Communication Technology**
Central Michigan University
441 Moore Hall
Mount Pleasant, MI 48859    989-774-4000
                           FAX 989-774-1727
                           http://www.chp.cmich.edu/aac
*Anne Ratcliffe MD, Director*

Maintains a clinic for assessment and consultation for individuals needing special communication technology and/or augmentative communication strategies. Provides personnel preparation and in-servicing for professionals in practice.

**4604 Bay De Noc Community College**
2001 N Lincoln Road
Escanaba, MI 49829         906-786-5802
                          800-221-2001
                          FAX 906-789-6912
                          http://www.baydenoc.com
                          e-mail: paavilam@baydenoc.cc.mi.us
*Marlene Paavilainen, Special Populations Director*

A community college with 30 learning disabled students out of 2,500.

**4605  Calvin College**
Services to Students with Disabilities
3201 Burton Street SE
Grand Rapids, MI  49546          616-526-6077
FAX 616-526-7066
http://www.calvin.edu
e-mail: vriend@calvin.edu
*Margaret Vriend, Coordinator*

**4606  Central Michigan University**
120 Park Library
Mount Pleasant, MI  48859          989-774-3018
FAX 989-774-1326
http://www.cmich.edu/student-disability
e-mail: sds@cmich.edu
*Carol Wojcik, Director Student Services*

Public four-year university offering students a choice of 24 degrees. Academic accommodations are available for students with documented learning disabilities.

**4607  Charles Stewart Mott Community College**
1401 E Court Street
Flint, MI  48503          810-762-0241
FAX 810-762-0159
http://www.mcc.edu
*Delores Williams, Contact*

Offers a variety of services to students with disabilities including note takers, extended testing time, counseling services, and special accommodations.

**4608  College of Art and Design: Center for Creative Studies**
201 E Kirby Street
Detroit, MI  48202          313-664-7400
FAX 313-872-2739
*Rochana Koach*

Offers a variety of services to students with disabilities including notetakers, extended testing time, counseling services, and special accommodations.

**4609  Delta College**
Office of Disability Services
1961 Delta Road
University Center, MI  48710          989-686-9000
FAX 989-667-2228
http://www.delta.edu
e-mail: michaelcooper2@delta.edu
*Michael Cooper, Special Needs Director*

Offers a variety of services to students with disabilities including note takers, extended testing time, counseling services, and special accommodations.

**4610  Detroit College of Business**
3488 N Jennings Road
Flint, MI  48504          810-789-2200
FAX 810-789-2266
http://www.dcb.edu
*Fran Jarvis, Director*

Offers a variety of services to students with disabilities including notetakers, extended testing time, counseling services, and special accommodations.

**4611  Detroit College of Business: Warren Campus**
27650 Dequindre Road
Warren, MI  48092          586-558-8700
http://www.dcb.edu
*Mary Cross, Associate Dean*

Offers a variety of services to students with disabilities including note takers, extended testing time, counseling services, and special accommodations.

**4612  Developmental Disabilities Institute: Wayne State University**
4809 Woodward Avenue
Detroit, MI  48202          313-577-2654
FAX 313-577-3770
http://www.wayne.edu.DDI
e-mail: B_Le_Roy@wayne.edu
*Barbara LeRoy, Director*

Contributes to the development of inclusive communities and quality of life for people with disabilities and their families through a culturally sensitive statewide program of interdisciplinary education, community support and services, research and dissemination of information.

**4613  Eastern Michigan University**
Access Services Office
203 King Hall
Ypsilanti, MI  48197          734-487-2470
FAX 734-487-5784
TDY:734-487-2470
http://www.emich.edu
e-mail: danderson1@emich.edu
*Don Anderson, Director*

Four year college that offers students with learning disabilities support and services.

**4614  Eton Academy**
Eton Academy
1755 Melton Road
Birmingham, MI  48009          248-642-1150
FAX 248-642-3670
http://www.etonacademy.org
e-mail: webmaster@etonacademy.org
*Pete Pullen, Head Master*
*Sharon Morey, Admissions Director*

A special purpose school dedicated to educating 1st through 12th grade students of average and above average academic potential who are experiencing specific learning disabilities.

**4615  Ferris State University**
420 Oak Street
Big Rapids, MI  49307          231-591-3772
FAX 231-591-3686
http://www.ferris.edu
e-mail: eunicemerwin@ferris.edu
*Eunice Merwin, Director*

Committed to a policy of equal opportunity for qualified students. Mission is to serve and advocate students with disabilities.

**4616** **Finlandia University**

**Program for Students with Learning Disabilities**
**601 Quincy Street**
**Hancock, MI 49930**          906-487-7258
                              FAX 906-487-7567
                              http://www.suomi.edu
*Carol Bates, Associate Professor/Director*

**4617** **Glen Oaks Community College**

**Special Services Office**
**62249 Shimmel Road**
**Centreville, MI 49032**          269 467-9945
                                  888-994-7818
                              FAX 269-467-9068
                          http://www.glenoaks.edu
                      e-mail: lraven@glenoaks.edu
*Lyle Raven, Special Populations Counselor*
*Barbara Clouse, Secretary*

A public two-year college with 50 special education
students out of a total of 1,416.

**4618** **Henry Ford Community College**

**5101 Evergreen Road**
**Dearborn, MI 48128**          313-845-9600
                                800-585-4322
                            FAX 313-845-9700
                            http://www.hfcc.edu
                          e-mail: hfcc@hfcc.edu
*Theodore Jr, Program Manager*
*Bunny Monroe, Human Resource Secretary*

A public two-year college with 36 special education
students out of a total of 15,514.

**4619** **Hope College**

**Hope College**
**35 E 12th Street**
**Holland, MI 49422**          616-395-7860
                            FAX 616-395-7118
                            http://www.hope.edu

*Jacqueline Heisler, Director*
*James Bultman, President*

An independent four-year liberal arts college recognized for its strong academics (it is a Phi Beta Kappa
School), excellent facilities and supportive Christian
dimension. Students with learning disabilities are admitted according to regular admission criteria. Admitted students must then determine whether Hope's
support services are adequate for their needs.

**4620** **Jackson Community College**

**2111 Emmons Road**
**Jackson, MI 49201**          517-787-0800
                            FAX 517-796-8632
                          http://www.jccmi.edu
                  e-mail: Chris.kane@jccmi.edu
*Chris Kane, Faculty Member*
*Melissa Weatherwax, Employment Specialist*

Offers a variety of services to students with disabilities including notetakers, extended testing time, counseling services, and special accommodations.

**4621** **Kalamazoo College**

**1200 Academy Street**
**Kalamazoo, MI 49006**          269-337-7000
                                  800-253-3602
                              FAX 269-337-7390
                            http://www.kzoo.edu
                      e-mail: admission@kzoo.edu
*Vaughn Maatman, Dean Students*
*Bernard Palchick, Acting President*

A selective, independent and undergraduate liberal
arts college. The unique curricular plan weaves career
development internships, study abroad programs and
senior independent research projects with traditional
liberal arts on campus programs.

**4622** **Kellogg Community College**

**Support Services**
**450 N Avenue**
**Battle Creek, MI 49017**          269-965-3931
                              http://www.kellogg.edu
                  e-mail: webmaster@kellogg.cc.mi.us
*Janice McNearney, Support Services*

Offers a variety of services to students with disabilities including notetakers, extended testing time, counseling services, and special accommodations.

**4623** **Kendall College of Art and Design**

**17 Fountain Street NW**
**Grand Rapids, MI 49503**          616-451-2787
                              FAX 616-451-9867
                            http://www.kcad.edu
                e-mail: kathy_jordan@ferris.edu
*Kathy Jordan, Counselor*
*Barbara Boldman, Executive Assistant*

An independent four-year college with 11 special education students out of a total of 657.

**4624** **Lake Michigan College**

**Lake Michigan College**
**2755 E Napier Avenue**
**Benton Harbor, MI 49022**          269-927-8100
                                    800-252-1562
                                FAX 269-927-6874
                                TDY:269-927-8100
                  http://www.lakemichigancollege.edu
*Zomar Peter, Manager of Records Department*

A two-year community college offering students vo-
cational/technical programs in business, health science, technology and the first two years of college
credit toward transfer in a baccalaureate program. Tutors, readers, note takers and other support services
are available to eligible disabled students.

**4625** **Lansing Community College**

**PO Box 40010**
**Lansing, MI 48901**          517-483-1207
                            FAX 517-483-1170
                            TDY:517-483-1207
                            http://www.lcc.edu
                      e-mail: eadvising@lcc.edu
*Pam Davis, Disability Specialist*
*Daniel Snider, Student Staff*

Offers a variety of services to students with disabilities including tutoring, extended testing time, counseling services, special services such as priority
registration and classroom accommodations.

**4626  Madonna University**
36600 Schoolcraft
Livonia, MI  48150          734-432-5639
FAX 734-432-5393
http://www.madonna.edu
e-mail: sherron@madonna.edu
*Michael Meldrum, Director*
*Jamie Dewitt, Office Manager*

Four-year college that offers services to disabled students.

**4627  Michigan State University**
105b W Fee Hall
East Lansing, MI  48824          517-353-6654
FAX 517-355-6473
http://www.msu.edu
e-mail: jad.megen@msu.edu

Offers a variety of services to students with disabilities including note takers, extended testing time, counseling services, and special accommodations.

**4628  Michigan Technological University**
1400 Townsend Drive
Houghton, MI  49931          906-487-2212
FAX 906-487-3060
http://www.mtu.edu
e-mail: gbmelton@mtu.edu
*Gloria Melton, Dean*
*Jeanne Meyers, Office Assistant*

A public undergraduate and graduate university with programs in engineering, sciences, business, technology, forestry, social sciences, and humanities. In 2000/01, there were requests for services from 50 individuals with physical or learning disabilities. Services include extended testing time, books on tape, and counseling. Total student enrollment 6,336.

**4629  Mid-Michigan Community College**
1375 S Clare Avenue
Harrison, MI  48625          989-386-6622
FAX 989-386-2411
http://www.midmich.cc.mi.us
e-mail: mmiller@midmich.edu
*Sandy Clark, Counselor Special Populations*

Tutoring, note taking, readers, writers, interpreters, text-on-tape, counseling, advising and career exploration available. Support services funded under the Carl D Perkins Vocational and Applied Technology Education Act for eligible students enrolled in vocational technical programs. Services for all other programs provided through college resources. Writing center and math lab available to students. Liaison with community services.

**4630  Monroe County Community College**
1555 S Rainesville Road
Monroe, MI  48161          734-242-7300
FAX 734-242-9711
http://www.monroeccc.edu
e-mail: criedel@monroeccc.edu
*Cindy Riedel, Special Services*
*David , President*

Offers a variety of services to students with disabilities including notetakers, extended testing time, counseling services, and special accommodations.

**4631  Montcalm Community College**
2800 College Drive
Sidney, MI  48885          989-328-2111
FAX 517-328-2950
http://www.montcalm.edu
*Donald Burns, President*
*Jim Lantz, Vice President*

Offers a variety of services to students with disabilities including note takers, extended testing time, counseling services, and special accommodations.

**4632  Northern Michigan University**
1401 Presque Isle Avenue
Marquette, MI  49855          906-227-1737
FAX 906-227-1714
TDY:906-227-1543
http://www.nmu.edu/disserve
e-mail: disserve@nmu.edu
*Lynn Walden, Coordinator*
*Linda Row, Office Assistant*

Disability services provides assistance for students who are qualified under the Americans with Disabilities Act to receive accommodations.

**4633  Northwestern Michigan College**
Instructional Support Center
1701 E Front Street
Traverse City, MI  49686          231-995-1000
FAX 231-995-1138
TDY:231-995-1929
http://www.nmc.edu/tss
e-mail: deverett@mnc.edu
*Denny Everett, Disability Specialist*
*Michelle Poertner, Tutoring Program Manager*

Offers a wide range of services for students that have disabilities and need accommodations in order to achieve their academic goals.

**4634  Northwood University**
4000 Whitting Drive
Midland, MI  48640          989-837-4200
FAX 989-837-4111
http://www.northwood.edu
*Michael Sullivan, Counselor*

Four-year college that offers services to disabled students.

**4635  Oakland Community College: Orchard Ridge Campus**
27055 Orchard Lake Road
Farmington Hills, MI  48334          248-522-3400
FAX 248-471-7767
http://www.occ.cc.mi.us
*Lawrence Gage MD, Learning Program*
*David , Academic Dean*

Offers comprehensive services to students with learning disabilities including note takers, extended testing time, counseling services, special accommodations and advocacy support.

**4636  Oakland University**
2200 North Squirrel Road
Rochester, MI  48309-4401          248-370-2100
800-OAK-UNIV
FAX 218-370-4989
TDY:248-370-3268
http://www.oakland.edu
*Gary Russi, President*
*Sheila Carpenter, Office Assistant*

Offers a variety of services to students with disabilities including notetakers, extended testing time, priority registration, assistance with sign language interpreter services, assistive technology, and assistance with general needs and concerns.

**4637  Office of Services for Students with Disabilities**
**University of Michigan**
G-664 Haven Hall 505 S State St.
Ann Arbor, MI  48109-1045          734-763-3000
FAX 734-936-3947
TDY:734-763-3000
http://www.umich.edu/~sswd
e-mail: djhansdu@umich.edu
*Sam Goodin, Director*
*Stuart Segal, Coordinator LD Services*
*Joan E Smith, Coordinator Deaf Services*

Offers selected student services, free of charge, which are not provided by other University offices or outside organizations. Assists students in negotiating disability-related barriers to the pursuit of their education. Strives to improve access to University programs, activities and facilities for students with disabilities. Promotes increased awareness of disability issues on campus.

**4638  Saginaw Valley State University**
7400 Bay Road
University Center, MI  48710          989-964-4000
800-968-9500
FAX 989-964-7838

**4639  St. Clair County Community College**
PO Box 5015
Port Huron, MI  48061          810-989-5555
FAX 810-984-4730
http://www.sc4.cc
*Nancy Pecorilli, Counselor*
*Gerri Barber, Learning Center Coordinator*

The learning center's supportive services are provided free of charge. These services include counseling, outreach and referrals, handicapped services, tutoring and study skills assistance, share information and financial aid assistance.

**4640  University of Michigan: Dearborn**
2157 University Center
Dearborn, MI  48128          313-593-5430
FAX 313-593-3263
http://www.umd.michigan.edu
e-mail: counseling@umd.umesh.edu
*Mary Ann Zawada MD, Counseling Director*
*Dennis Underwood, Coordinator*

A public four-year college with 300 special education students out of a total of 8,000.

**4641  University of Michigan: Flint**
Student Development Center
264 University Center
Flint, MI  48502          810-762-3456
FAX 810-762-3498
TDY:810-766-6727
http://www.flint.umich.edu
e-mail: papolla@umflint.edu
*Paola Pollander, Accessibility Coordinator*
*Virginia July, Office Manager*

Provides support services and auxiliary aids for students with a variety of disabilities.

**4642  Washtenaw Community College**
4800 E Huron River Drive
Ann Arbor, MI  48106          734-973-3300
http://www.wccnet.edu
*Francie Helm Mo MD, Special Services*

A public two-year college with 78 special education students out of a total of 10,765.

**4643  Western Michigan University**
Western Michigan University
W Michigan Avenue
Kalamazoo, MI  49008          269-387-4440
FAX 269-387-0633
http://www.dsrs.umich.edu
*Beth Hartigh, LD Director*

A public four-year college with 79 special education students out of a total of 20,951.

# Minnesota

**4644  Alexandria Technical College**
1601 Jefferson Street
Alexandria, MN  56308          320-762-0221
888-234-1222
FAX 320-762-4634
TDY:320-762-4623
http://www.alextech.edu
e-mail: marya@alextech.edu
*Renee Larson, Counselor*
*Mary Ackerman, Support Services*

Offers a variety of services to students with disabilities including note takers, extended testing time, counseling services, and special accommodations.

**4645  Anoka-Ramsey Community College**
MNSCU
11200 Mississippi Boulevard NW
Coon Rapids, MN  55433          763-427-2600
FAX 763-422-3341
TDY:763-576-5949
http://www.anokaramsey.edu
e-mail: scott.bay@anokaramsey.edu
*Scott Bay, Director Disabilities*

A public two-year college with 55 special education students out of a total of 6,900.

**4646 Augsburg College**
Center for Learning and Adaptive Student Services
2211 Riverside Avenue
Minneapolis, MN 55454          612-330-1648
                              FAX 612-330-1137
                              TDY:612-330-1749
                        http://www.augsburg.edu
                   e-mail: doljanac@augsburg.edu
*Robert Doljanac, Director*
*Karina Jones, Disability Specialist*
*Anne Lynd, Disability Specialist*

The Center for Learning and Adaptive Student Services coordinates academics accommodations and services for students with learning, attentional and psychiatric disabilities.

**4647 Bemidji State University**
12 Sanford Hall
Bemidji, MN 56601          218-755-2595
                           FAX 218-755-3788
*Ann Austad, Coordinator*

Offers a variety of services to students with disabilities including note takers, extended testing time, counseling services, and special accommodations.

**4648 Bethel College: Minnesota**
Disability Services Department
3900 Bethel Drive
Saint Paul, MN 55112          651-635-8759
                              800-255-8706
                              FAX 651-635-8695
*Lucie Johnson, LD Program Director*
*Kathleen , Director*

An independent Christian four-year college with LD Program serving 30 students out of a total of 1,800.

**4649 Calvin Academy and Special Education Day School**
Calvin Academy and Special Education Day School
2574 Highway 10
Moudsview, MN 55112          763-717-0609
                             FAX 763-786-9535
                       http://www.calvinacademy.com/
                       e-mail: info@CalvinAcademy.com
*Stafford Calvin, Founder*
*Susan Johnson, Headmaster*

**4650 Century College**
3300 Century Avenue N
White Bear Lake, MN 55110          651-779-3200
                         http://www.century.cc.mn.us
*Vicki Johnson, Coordinator Disabled Center*
*Willie Nesbit, Dean Students*

The disabilities access center provided by the college is a liaison service for students with disabilities to provide access to educational and student programs at the college.

**4651 College of Associated Arts**
344 Summit Avenue
Saint Paul, MN 55102          612-226-3416
                              FAX 612-224-8854
*Barbara Davis, Associate Professor*

Offers a variety of services to students with disabilities including note takers, extended testing time, counseling services, and special accommodations.

**4652 College of Saint Scholastica**
1200 Kenwood Avenue
Duluth, MN 55811          218-723-6552
                          FAX 218-723-6482
                          http://www.css.edu
                     e-mail: njewcomb@css.edu
*Jay Newcomb, Director*

Offers a variety of services to students with disabilities including note takers, extended testing time, counseling services, and special accommodations.

**4653 College of St. Catherine: Minneapolis**
Learning Disabilities Department
2004 Randolph Avenue
St.Paul, MN 55105          651-690-6000
                           800-945-4599
                           FAX 651-690-6064
                           TDY:651-690-8145
                     http://www.stkate.edu
                e-mail: tgockenbach@stkate.edu
*Teri Gockenbach, LD Specialist*
*Annette Caupenter, Disability Specialist*

Services for students with disabilities are coordinated through the learning Center. There is a support group for students with disabilities that meets bimonthly. Other services include testing accommodations, note taking, computers, and reading course materials.

**4654 College of St. Catherine: St. Paul Campus**
O'Neill Learning Center
2004 Randolph Avenue
Saint Paul, MN 55105          651-690-6563
                              800-945-4599
                        http://www.stkate.edu
*Elaine McDonough, Assistant Director*
*Vera Mandel, Director*

Academic support services for students with disabilities of the College.

**4655 Concordia College**
901 8th Street S
Moorhead, MN 56562          218-299-4000
                            FAX 218-299-3345
                            http://www.cord.edu
                     e-mail: forde@gloria.cord.edu
*Joli Coeur, Development Director*

An independent four-year college with 13 special education students out of a total of 602.

**4656 Gustavus Adolphus College**
800 W College Avenue
St Peter, MN 56082          507-933-6286
                            FAX 507-933-6277
                            http://www.gac.edu
*Laurie Bickett, Disability Services Coordinator*

Gustavus Adolphus College is dedicated to providing for the needs of enrolled students who have disabilities. Reasonable modifications in the classroom and auxiliary aids will be provided for students with appropriately documented disabilities.

**4657 Hamline College**
Study Resource Center
1536 Hewitt Avenue
St. Paul, MN 55104          651-523-2417
                      FAX 651-523-2809
                http://www.hamline.edu
          e-mail: cla-admins@gw.hamline.edu
*Barbara Simmons, Assistant Dean*
*Matt Derby, Director*

Four-year college that offers services to its disabled students.

**4658 Hibbing Community College**
Hibbing Community College
1515 E 25th
Hibbing, MN 55746          218-262-7200
                           800-224-4422
                      FAX 218-262-6717
          http://www.hibbing.tec.mn.us
          e-mail: admissions@hcc.mnscu.edu
*Ken Simberg, Provost*
*Sandra Seppala, Assistant Provost*

The College is committed to serving students with special needs. If you need an accommodation for a disability, please contact our disabilities staff to make arragements. HCC is completely accessible to students with physical disabilities.

**4659 Inver Hills Community College**
2500 80th Street E
Inver Grove Heights, MN 55076    651-450-8500
                            FAX 651-450-8677
                    http://www.ih.cc.mn.us
*Gini Spurr*

A public two-year college with 177 special education students out of a total of 5,450.

**4660 Itasca Community College**
Itasca Community College
1851 E Highway 169
Grand Rapids, MN 55744        218-327-4460
                              800-996-6422
                         FAX 218-327-4350
            http://www.itasca.mnscu.edu
         e-mail: svelzen@itasca.mnscu.edu
*Sally Velzen, Learning Skills*

Itasca Community College is committed to providing equal opportunity to qualified persons with physical or learning disabilities.

**4661 Lake Superior College**
Lake Superior College
2101 Trinity Road
Duluth, MN 55811              218-733-7650
                         FAX 218-733-5945
            http://www.lsc.cc.mn.us
         e-mail: enroll@lsc.mnscu.edu
*Giorgia Robillard, Coordinator*
*Erin White, Disability Assistant*

A two-year college that provides a selection of programs for its disabled students.

**4662 Macalester College**
Disability Services
1600 Grand Avenue
Saint Paul, MN 55105          651-696-6534
                         FAX 651-696-6687
                http://www.macalester.edu
          e-mail: admissions@macalstr.edu
*Bob Brandt, Health Services Director*

**4663 Mankato State University**
PO Box 42
Mankato, MN 56002             507-389-6767
                              800-722-0544
                         FAX 507-389-2227
            http://www.mankato.msus.edu
*Daniel Beebe MD*

This office houses documentation of disability for students, provides verification of disability for faculty, provides accommodations, offers direct services to students such as taped texts, notetaker and more.

**4664 Mesabi Range Community & Technical College**
1001 W Chestnut Street
Virginia, MN 55792            218-749-0325
                              800-657-3860
                         FAX 218-748-2419
                         TDY:218-749-7783
            http://www.mr.mnscu.edu
         e-mail: c.thomas@mr.mnscu.edu
*Carrie Thomas, Student Life Director*
*Tina Royer, Provost*

Students with a documented disability are offered assistance and the opportunity to succeed.

**4665 Minneapolis Community College**
1501 Hennepin Avenue S
Minneapolis, MN 55403         612-341-7000
                              800-247-0911
                         FAX 612-659-6732
                         TDY:612-659-6731
            http://www.minneapolis.edu
*Carol Udstrand, LD Specialist*
*Jane Larson, Center Director*

A public two-year college with 104 special education students out of a total of 4,155.

**4666 Minnesota Life College**
7501 Logan Avenue S
Richfield, MN 55423           612-869-4008
                         FAX 612-869-0443
          http://www.minnesotalifecollege.com
          e-mail: info@minnesotalifecollege.com
*Kathryn Thomas, Executive Director*
*Marlyn Wisberg, Manager*

A college-like apartment living program for young adults with learning disabilities who need an intermediate level of support. Students must be at least 18 years of age and have a documented diagnosis of a learning disability or related condition such as attention deficit disorder. The program focuses on independent living skills, social skills, vocational readiness, career exploration, post secondary education, jobs placement, decision-making, fitness, health, leisure and recreation.

**4667  Minnesota State Community & Technology Col**

Minnesota State Community & Technical College
1414 College Way
Fergus Falls, MN  56537                    218-739-7500
                                           877-450-3322
                                    FAX 218-736-1510
                                    TDY:218-736-1537
                        http://www.minnesota.edu
                e-mail: dave.seyfried@minnesota.edu
*David Seyfried MD, Director of Disability Services*
*Karen Gabrielson, Secretary*

The students with disabilities bring a unique dynamic
and special needs to the classroom. Fegus Falls Community College recognizes that many students require
assistance. These students often need modifications in
programs, services, and activities to succeed in a
changing, technology-based curriculum.

**4668  Minnesota State University Moorehead**

1104 7th Avenue
Moorhead, MN  56560                        218-299-5859
                                    FAX 218-287-5050
                                    TDY:218-299-5859
                        e-mail: toutges@mnstate.edu
*Greg Toutges, Coordinator*
*Lisa Therson, Assistant Secretary*

A public four-year university serving approximately
60-80 students with learning disabilities out of a total
of 7,200. Services, such as notetaking, alternate testing, taped textbooks, and more, are provided through
the office of Disability Services to students with documented learning disabilities.

**4669  Minnesota University Affiliated Program on
       Developmental Disabilities**

University of Minnesota
102 Pattee Hall
Minneapolis, MN  55455                     612-624-6300
                                    FAX 612-624-9344
                        http://www.ici.umn.edu/wel-
                        come/theuapnetwork.ht
*Scott McConnell, Director*

The Institute on Community Integration is the Minnesota University Affiliated Program on Developmental
Disabilities (UAP). We are one of a national network
of over 60 similar programs in major universities and
teaching hospitals in the country, known as the American Association of University Affiliated Programs.

**4670  Minnesota West Community & Technical College**

344 W Main Street
Marshall, MN  56258                        507-537-7051
                                           800-576-6728
                                    FAX 507-537-7081
                        http://www.mnwest.edu
                e-mail: debra.carrow@mnwest.edu
*Debra Carrow, Director Support Services*
*Linda Degriselles, Coordinator*

Minnesota West offers a variety of services to students with disabilities including notetakers, academic
counseling services, alternative testing, referral services, advocacy/support and special accommodations.

**4671  Normandale Community College**

9700 France Avenue S
Bloomington, MN  55431                     952-487-8200
                                           866-880-8740
                        http://www.nr.cc.mn.us
*Mary Jibben, DEEDS Coordinator*

A public two-year college with 169 special education
students out of a total of 9,327.

**4672  North Hennepin Community College**

7411 85th Avenue N
Brooklyn Park, MN  55445                   763-424-0702
                                    FAX 763-424-0929
                        http://www.nh.cc.mn.us
*Sue Smith, Special Services*

Works to promote program and physical access while
helping to ensure the rights of students with disabilities and meeting federal and state statutes.

**4673  Northwestern College**

3003 Snelling Avenue N
Saint Paul, MN  55113                      651-631-5221
                                    FAX 651-631-5124
                        http://www.nwc.edu
*Yvonne Redmond- MD, Assistant Professor*

Four-year college that offers disabled students support and services.

**4674  Pillsbury Baptist Bible College**

Admissions Office
315 S Grove Avenue
Owatonna, MN  55060                        507-451-2710
                                    FAX 507-451-6459
                        http://www.pillsbury.edu
*Stephen Seidler, Admissions Director*
*Connie Seidler, Admissions Coordinator*

An independent four-year college with two special education students out of a total of 350.

**4675  Rainy River Community College**

Rainy River Community College
1501 Highway 71
International Falls, MN  56649             218-285-7722
                                           800-456-3996
                                    FAX 218-285-2239
                                    TDY:218-285-2261
                        http://www.rrcc.mnscu.edu
                e-mail: admissions@rrcc.mnscu.edu
*Carol Grim, Disability Services*
*Tammy Wood, Advisor*

The campus program provides services to students
with disabilities to ensure their equal access to the college and its programs.

**4676  Riverland Community College Student Success
       Center**

1900 8th Avenue NW
Austin, MN  55912                          507-433-0569
                                           800-247-5039
                                    FAX 507-433-0515
                        http://www.riverland.cc
                e-mail: maskelso@river.cc.mn.us
*Mindi Askelson, Director Student Support Svcs.*

A two-year comprehensive technical and community college offering. 4000 students outstanding opportunities in carrer and transfer education. Facilites are located in Albert Lea, Austin, and Owatonna, Minnesota.

**4677 Rochester Community and Technical College**

851 30th Avenue SE
Rochester, MN 55904 507-280-2968
800-247-1296
FAX 507-285-7496
http://www.roch.edu
e-mail: travis.kromminga@roch.edu
*Travis MA, Director*

To provide academic support and advising services to assist disabled persons in achieving their educational goals.

**4678 Saint John's School of Theology & Seminary**

Collegeville, MN 56321 320-363-2102
800-361-8318
FAX 320-363-3145
http://www.csbsju.edu/sot/
e-mail: mbanken@csbsju.edu
*Mary Banken OSB*

An independent four-year college with 36 special education students out of a total of 1,880.

**4679 Saint Mary's University of Minnesota**

700 Terrace Heights
Winona, MN 55987 507-457-1465
800-635-5987
FAX 507-457-1633
http://www.smumn.edu
e-mail: bsmith@smumn.edu
*Bonnie Smith, Support Services*
*Jane Ochrymowycz, Center Director*

Accommodations and support services based on recent positive assessment and recommendations of evaluator.

**4680 Southwest Minnesota State University: Learning Resources**

1501 State Street
Marshall, MN 56258 507-537-6169
800-642-0684
FAX 507-537-6027
http://www.southwestmsu.edu
e-mail: Leach@southwest.msus.edu
*Marilyn Leach, Learning Resource Director*
*Pam Ekstrom, Accommodations Coordinator*

Offers a variety of services to students with disabilities including test accommodations, notetakers, academic counseling services, 504/ADA advocacy, taped texts, computers with assistive/access technology and software. The department also offers skills development courses, tutoring services and student mentors.

**4681 St. Cloud State University**

Student Disability Services
720 4th Avenue S
St. Cloud, MN 56301 320-255-0121
FAX 320-654-5139
http://www.stcloudstate.edu/
e-mail: webteam@stcloudstate.edu
*Lee Bird MD, Disability Services*

A public comprehensive university that provides services for students with learning disabilities and other needs: alternative testing, note taking, referrals to campus resources and advocacy/support.

**4682 St. Olaf College**

Student Disability Services
1520 St. Olaf Avenue
Northfield, MN 55057 507-646-3288
800-800-3025
FAX 507-663-3459
http://www.stolaf.edu
e-mail: asc@stolaf.edu
*Ruth Bolstad, Director Special Services*
*Linne Jensen, Associate Director*

Offers a variety of services to students with disabilities including note takers, extended testing time, counseling services, and special accommodations.

**4683 St. Paul Technical College**

235 Marshall Avenue
Saint Paul, MN 55102 651-846-1600
FAX 651-221-1416
http://www.saintpaul.edu
*Margie Warrington, Transition Director*

A public two-year college with 79 special education students out of a total of 3,574.

**4684 University of Minnesota Disability Services**

University of Minnesota
180 Mahamara Allimai Center
Minneapolis, MN 55455 612-626-1333
FAX 612-625-5572
TDY:612-626-1333
http://www.disserv3.stu.umn.edu
e-mail: dstest@umn.edu
*Robert Bruininks, President*
*E , Senior Vice President*

Disability Services is a University Resource Promotion barrier free environment (physical program, information, attitude) which means expressing the rights of people with disabilities and assisting the university with meeting its responsibilities under federal and state statues. Disability Services works to ensure access to University employment, courses, programs, facilities, services and activities by documenting disabilities.

**4685 University of Minnesota: Crookston**

Student Disability Services
270 Owen Hall
Crookston, MN 56716 218-281-8587
800-232-6466
FAX 218-281-8584
TDY:800-627-3529
http://www.crk.umn.edu
e-mail: lwilson@umn.edu
*Laurie Wilson, Coordinator*

A public four-year college with 40-70 students with disabilities out of a total of 1,341.

**4686   University of Minnesota: Duluth**
*Learning Disabilities Program*
10 University Drive
Duluth, MN  55812
218-726-7500
800-232-1339
FAX 218-726-6394
TDY:218-726-7380
http://www.d.umn.edu
e-mail: jbromen@d.umn.edu
*Judy Bromen, LD Coordinator*
*Katheryn Martin, Chancellor*

UMD is committed to providing equal opportunities in higher education to academically qualified students with disabilities who demonstrate a reasonable expectation of college success.

**4687   University of Minnesota: Morris**
**Student Disability Services**
600 E 4th Street
Morris, MN  56267
320-589-6178
FAX 320-589-1673
TDY:320-589-6035
http://www.morris.umn.edu
e-mail: angfa@morris.umn.edu
*Ferolyn Angell, Director Academic Assistance*
*Kathryn , Coordinator*

Offers a variety of services to students with disabilities including note takers, extended testing time, counseling services, and special accommodations.

**4688   University of Minnesota: Twin Cities Campus**
200 Oaks Street SE Mc Nanara Alumni
Minneapolis, MN  55455
612-624-4037
FAX 612-626-9654
TDY:612-626-1333
http://www.d.umn.edu
*Lynn Dhitao, Senior Officer Specialist*
*Robert Bruininks, President*

The goals of the university are: to create equal opportunities for students, faculty, and staff with disabilities to learn and work; to increase the visibility and awareness of Disability Services and enhance the quality, effectiveness, and efficiency of its operations.

**4689   University of St. Thomas**
2115 Summit Avenue
Saint Paul, MN  55105
651-962-5000
FAX 651-962-5910
http://www.stthomas.edu
*Stephanie Zurek, Coordinator*

An independent four-year college with 52 special education students out of a total of 5,283.

**4690   Worthington Community College**
1450 College Way
Worthington, MN  56187
507-372-3485
800-657-3966
FAX 507-372-5801
*Pam Sieve, Coordinator*

A public two-year college with 18 special education students out of a total of 868.

## Mississippi

**4691   Hinds Community College**
505 E Main Street
Raymond, MS  39154
601-857-3359
FAX 601-857-3539
http://www.hinds.cc.edu
*Michael Handle, Director*

Offers a variety of services to students with disabilities including note takers, extended testing time, counseling services, and special accommodations.

**4692   Holmes Community College**
**Student Affairs Office**
PO Box 369
Goodman, MS  39079
662-472-2312
FAX 662-472-9076
http://www.holmescc.edu
*Fran Cox, Dean for Student Affairs*

Offers a variety of services to students with disabilities including note takers, extended testing time, counseling services, and special accommodations.

**4693   Itawamba Community College**
**Learning Disabilities Department**
602 W Hill Street
Fulton, MS  38843
662-862-8000
FAX 662-862-8273
http://www.icc.cc.ms.us
e-mail: mleaton@iccms.edu
*Sarah Johnson, Vice President*
*Marcia Eaton, Coordinator*

Offers a variety of services to students with disabilities including note takers, extended testing time, counseling services, and special accommodations.

**4694   Mississippi State University**
**Student Affairs Office**
PO Box 806
Mississippi State, MS  39762
662-325-3335
FAX 662-325-8190
http://www.msstate.edu
e-mail: dbaker@saffairs.msstate.edu
*Debbie Baker, Director*
*Carlene Pylate, Office Assistant*

Four-year college that provides student support to learning disabled students.

**4695   Mississippi University Affiliated Program**
**University of Southern Mississippi**
118 College Drive
Hattiesburg, MS  39406-0001
601-266-5163
888-671-0051
FAX 601-266-5114
TDY:888-671-0051
http://www.usm.edu
e-mail: latouisha.wilson@usm.edu
*Jane PhD, Executive Director*
*Shelby Thames, President*

**4696  Northeast Mississippi Community College**

Special Populations Office
101 Cunningham Boulevard
Booneville, MS  38829
662-728-7751
FAX 662-728-2428
http://www.nemcc.edu
e-mail: twalker@nemcc.edu
*Tommye Walker, Director*
*Liz Ketchum, Special Populations Councilor*

A public two-year college with 5 special education students out of a total of 3,047.

**4697  University of Mississippi**

PO Box 187
University, MS  38677
662-915-7236
FAX 662-915-7211
e-mail: abroad@olemiss.edu
*Ardessa Milor, Special Services*

A public four-year college with 76 special education students out of a total of 8,804.

**4698  University of Southern Mississippi**

Box 8586
Hattiesburg, MS  39406
601-266-5024
FAX 601-266-6035
TDY:601-266-6837
http://www.usm.edu
e-mail: latouisha.wilson@usm.edu
*Jane PhD, Executive Director*
*Shelby Thames, President*

Four year college that provides students with support and resources whom are disabled.

**4699  William Carey College**

498 Tuscan Avenue
Hattiesburg, MS  39401
601-318-6195
FAX 601-318-6196
*Brenda Waldrip, Special Services*

Offers a variety of services to students with disabilities including note takers, extended testing time, counseling services, and special accommodations.

# Missouri

**4700  Central Methodist College**

Disability Support Department
411 CMC Square
Fayette, MO  65248
660-248-3391
877-268-1854
FAX 660-248-2622
TDY:660-248-6223
http://www.centralmethodist.edu
e-mail: koliver@centralmethodist.edu
*Ken Oliver, Special Education Director*
*Shawn Baker, Student Affairs Office*

Offers a variety of services to students with disabilities including note takers, extended testing time, counseling services, and special accommodations.

**4701  Central Missouri State University**

Office of Accessibility Services
Union 222
Warrensburg, MO  64093
660-543-4421
FAX 660-543-4724
TDY:660-543-4421
http://www.cmsu.edu\access
e-mail: mayfield@cmsu1.cmsu.edu
*Barbara Mayfiel MD, Director*
*Linda Persing, Office Assistant*

Provider of equal opportunity to education for students with disabilities through notetakers, extended testing time, interpreters and other accommodations.

**4702  East Central College**

Special Services Office
1964 Prairie Dell Road
Union, MO  63084
636-583-5193
FAX 636-583-1011
TDY:636-583-4851
http://www.eastcentral.edu
e-mail: peckaw@eastcentral.edu
*Michael Knight, Assessment Director*
*Wendy Peckaw, Access Director*

Offers a variety of services to students with disabilities including note takers, extended testing time, counseling services, and special accommodations.

**4703  Evangel University**

1111 N Glenstone Avenue
Springfield, MO  65802
417-865-2811
FAX 417-865-9599
http://www.evangel.edu
*Laynah Rogers MD, Associate Professor*

An independent four-year college with 23 special education students out of a total of 1,449.

**4704  Fontbonne College**

Kinkel Center
6800 Wydown Boulevard
St. Louis, MO  63105
314-889-4571
FAX 314-889-1451
http://www.fontbonne.edu
e-mail: jsnyder@fontbonne.edu
*Jane D Synder MD, Director*

Four-year college provides services through the Kinkel Center for students with learning disabilities.

**4705  Jefferson College**

1000 Viking Drive
Hillsboro, MO  63050
636-789-3000
FAX 636-789-4012
TDY:636-789-5772
http://www.jeffco.edu
*Tom Burke, Director*

Offers a variety of services to students with disabilities including notetakers, extended testing time, counseling services, and special accommodations.

**4706 Kansas City Art Institute**

Kansas City Art Institute
4415 Warwick Boulevard
Kansas City, MO 64111
816-802-3376
800-522-5224
FAX 816-802-3480
http://www.kcai.edu
e-mail: arc@kcai.edu
*Bambi PhD, Assistant Dean Academic Affairs*

Offers a variety of services to students with disabilities including notetakers, extended testing time, counseling services, and special accommodations.

**4707 Lindenwood College**

209 S Kingshighway
St. Charles, MO 63301
636-949-2000
FAX 314-949-4910
http://www.lindenwood.edu
e-mail: lindenwood@lindenwood.edu
*V Pitts, Director*

Offers a variety of services to students with disabilities including note takers, extended testing time, counseling services, and special accommodations.

**4708 Longview Community College: ABLE Program-Academic Bridges to Learning Effectiveness**

500 SW Longview Road
Lees Summit, MO 64081
816-672-2366
FAX 816-672-2417
TDY:816-672-2144
http://www.kcmetro.edu
e-mail: maryellen.jenison@kcmetro.edu
*Mary Jenison, ABLE Program Director*

ABLE is an intensive support services program, designed to empower individuals with learning disabilities or brain injuries with the skills needed to gain control of their own lives and learning, so that they can make a successful transition to regular college courses, vocational programs, or the workplace. In addition to courses especially designed for this population, students take basic skills courses (if needed), regular college courses with study support, and attend weekly support groups.

**4709 Maple Woods Community College**

Learning Disabilities Department
2601 NE Barry Road
Kansas City, MO 64156
816-437-3000
FAX 816-437-3483
TDY:816-437-3318
http://www.kcmetro.edu/maplewoods
e-mail: kim.fernandes@kcmetro.edu
*Kim Fernandes, Coordinator*
*Janet Weaver, Outreach Counselor*

A public two-year college with 30 special education students out of a total of 5,007.

**4710 Missouri Southern State College**

Learning Center
3950 E Newton Road
Joplin, MO 64801
417-625-9373
800-606-MSSC
FAX 417-659-4456
TDY:800-766-3776
http://www.mssu.edu
e-mail: locher-m@mssu.edu
*Melissa Locher, Coordinator*
*Eillen Godsey, Director*

Offers a variety of services to students with disabilities including note takers, extended testing time, and counseling services.

**4711 Missouri Valley College**

500 E College Street
Marshall, MO 65340
660-886-6924
FAX 660-831-4039
http://www.moval.edu
e-mail: admissions@moval.edu
*Virginia Zank, Director*
*Linda Kanagawa, Coordinator*

An independent four-year college with 5 special education students out of a total of 1,132.

**4712 North Central Missouri College**

1301 Main Street
Trenton, MO 64683
660-359-3948
FAX 660-359-2899
http://www.ncmc.cc.mo.us
e-mail: webmaster@mail.ncmc.cc.mo.us
*Ginny Wickoff, Counselor*

Offers a variety of services to students with disabilities including note takers, extended testing time, counseling services, and special accommodations.

**4713 Northwest Missouri State University**

Special Services Department
800 University Drive
Maryville, MO 64468
660-562-1219
FAX 660-562-1121
http://www.nwmissouri.edu
e-mail: admissions@mail.nwmissouri.edu
*WC Dizney, Special Services*

Offers a variety of services to students with disabilities including notetakers, extended testing time, counseling services, and special accommodations.

**4714 Saint Louis University**

Student Educational Services
3840 Lindell Boulevard
St. Louis, MO 63108
314-977-2930
FAX 314-977-3315
TDY:314-977-3499
http://www.slu.edu
e-mail: meyerah@slu.edu
*Adam Meyer, Disabilities Coordinator*

Four year college offering comprehensive programs for the learning disabled.

**4715** **Southwest Missouri State University**
Office of Disability Services
901 S National Avenue
Springfield, MO 65804 417-836-4192
FAX 417-836-4134
TDY:417-836-6792
http://www.smsu.edu/disability
e-mail: ksw2780@msu.edu
*Steager -Wilson, Director*
*Tabatha Haynes, Assistant Director*

At Southwest Missouri State University, we believe
all students should have equal access to higher education and university life. Disability Services helps ensure an equitable college experience for SMS
Students with disabilities.

**4716** **St. Louis Community College at Florissant Valley:
Access Office**
3400 Pershall Road
Saint Louis, MO 63135 314-595-4551
FAX 314-513-4876
TDY:314-595-4552
http://www.stlcc.edu/access
e-mail: smatthews@stlcc.edu
*Suelaine Matthews, Manager*
*Mary Wagner, Access Specialist*

A public two-year college with 200 students with disabilities, out of a total of 7,000.

**4717** **St. Louis Community College at Forest Park:
Access Office**
5600 Oakland Avenue
Saint Louis, MO 63110 314-644-9100
FAX 314-644-9752
http://www.stlcc.edu
e-mail: stlcc@stlcc.edu
*Glenn Marshall, Manager ACCESS*
*Karen Lerch, Administrative Registrar Assista*

The St. Louis Community College ACCESS OFFICE
collaborates with faculty, staff, students, and the community to encourage a college environment where individuals are viewed on the basis of ability, not
disability.

**4718** **St. Louis Community College at Meramec**
11333 Big Bend Boulevard
Kirkwood, MO 63122 314-984-7704
FAX 314-984-7117
TDY:314-984-7127
http://www.stlcc.edu
e-mail: stlcc@stlcc.edu
*Lynn E Suydam MD, President*
*Ann , Executive Dean*

The Access office offers support services to students
who have documented disabilities of a permanent or
temporary nature. The staff is available to provide the
following services: individual counseling and advising; coordination of needed accommodations such as
interpreters and more.

**4719** **University Affiliated Program for Developmental
Disabilities**
University of Missouri at Kansas City
2220 Holmes Street
Kansas City, MO 64108 816-235-1755
800-444-0821
FAX 816-235-1762
TDY:800-452-1185
http://www.iht.umck.edu
e-mail: calkinsc@umkc.edu
*Carl Calkins PhD, Director*

**4720** **University of Missouri**
Office of Disability Services
A38 Brady Commons
Columbia, MO 65201 573-882-4696
FAX 573-884-9272
TDY:573-882-8054
http://www.missouri.edu
e-mail: weavers@missouri.edu
*Sarah Colby-Wea MD, Director*
*Laura Durham, Office Support Staff*

Four-year independent college offering support for
learning disabled students.

**4721** **University of Missouri: Kansas City**
Department of Disability Services
5100 Rockhill Road
Kansas City, MO 64110 816-235-5696
FAX 816-235-6537
http://www.umkc.edu
e-mail: disability@umkc.edu
*Scott Laurent, Coordinator*

Offers a variety of services to students with disabilities including note takers, extended testing time,
counseling services, and special accommodations.

**4722** **University of Missouri: Rolla**
University of Missouri Systems
1870 Miner Circle
Rolla, MO 65409 573-341-4211
800-522-0938
FAX 573-341-6333
TDY:573-341-4205
http://www.umr.edu
e-mail: webmaster@umr.edu
*Debra Robinson MD, Vice Chancellor Student Af-
fairs*
*Gary Thomas, Chancellor*

Offers a variety of services to students with disabilities including note takers, extended testing time,
counseling services, and special accommodations.

**4723** **Washington University**
1 Brookings Drive
Saint Louis, MO 63130 314-935-4062
FAX 314-935-8272
TDY:314-935-4062
http://www. wustl.edu
e-mail: vachary@wustl.edu
*Vachary McBbe, Office Manager*

Offers a variety of services to students with disabilities including note takers, extended testing time,
counseling services, and special accommodations.

**4724  Westminster College**
Learning Disabilities Program
501 Westminster Avenue
Fulton, MO  65251                  573-592-5304
                                   800-475-3361
                              FAX 573-592-5180
          http://www.westminster-mo.edu
   e-mail: ottingh@jaynet.westminster-mo.edu
*Hank Ottinger, Director*
*Fletcher , President*

Four year college that offers a program for students with learning disabilities.

## Montana

**4725  Dull Knife Memorial College**
Office of Disabilities Services
1 College Drive
Lame Deer, MT  59043              406-477-6215
                             FAX 406-477-6219
          http://www.dkmc.cc.mt.us
          e-mail: alderson@cdkc.edu
*Juanita Lonebear, GED Director*

Offers a variety of services to students with disabilities including notetakers, extended testing time, counseling services, and special accommodations.

**4726  Flathead Valley Community College**
777 Grandview Drive
Kalispell, MT  59901              406-756-3880
                             FAX 406-756-3911
                             TDY:406-756-3881
          http://www.fvcc.edu
          e-mail: edavis@fvcc.edu
*Elaine Davis, Disability Specialist*
*Lynn Farris, Director*

GED testing and learning styles assessment is available in the Learning Center. Advocates for Students with Disabilities work with faculty and staff to provide appropriate accommodations for students with learning disabilities.

**4727  Montana State University**
Disabled Student Services
1555 Strand Union Building
Bozeman, MT  59717                406-994-2824
                             FAX 406-994-3943
                             TDY:406-994-6701
          http://www.montana.edu
          e-mail: byork@montana.edu
*Brenda York, Director*
*Deidre Manry, Administrative Assistant*

Disabled Student Services (DSS) is committed to facilitating Montana State goal of making its programs, services and activities accessible to students with disabilities. We provide a variety of services to students with disabilities, including note taking assistance, exam accommodations, adaptive technology, and advice and advocacy.

**4728  Montana Tech College**
Disabled Student Services
1300 W Park Street
Butte, MT  59701                  406-496-3730
                             FAX 406-496-3710
          http://www.mtech.edu
          e-mail: lbarnett@mtech.edu
*Lee Barnett, Director*
*Margie Pascoe, Counseling Services*

Committed to making the appropriate accommodations for students with disabilities.

**4729  Montana University Affiliated Program**
University of Montana/ Office of Disability
154 Lommasson Center
Missoula, MT  59812               406-243-5467
                                  888-268-2743
                             FAX 406-243-2349
                             TDY:406-243-5467
          http://www.ruralinstitute.umt.edu
          e-mail: dss@umt.edu
*Jim Burke, Director*
*Dan Burke, Coordinator*

The Rura Institute works on behalf of people with disabilities of all ages to support full participation in community life. We train professionals, provide services directly to people with disabilities, share our knowledge with others, and conduct research to develop solutions.

**4730  Northern Montana College**
PO Box 77511
Havre, MT  59501                  406-265-3783
                                  800-662-6132
                             FAX 406-265-3597
*Linda Hoines, Learning Specialist*

To provide college students with support and skills needed to remain in college and complete a degree program.

**4731  Rocky Mountain College**
Services for Academic Success
1511 Poly Drive
Billings, MT  59102               406-657-1128
                                  800-877-6259
                             FAX 406-259-9751
          http://www.rocky.edu/campus/sas
          e-mail: vandykj@rocky.edu
*Jane Van Dyk MD, Director*

An independent four-year college with 20-30 students with learning disabilities out of a total of 850.

**4732  University of Great Falls**
1301 20th Street S
Great Falls, MT  59405            406-761-8210
                                  800-848-3431
                             FAX 406-791-5214
          http://www.ugf.edu
*Sue Romas, Head Academic Excellence*

An independent four-year college with 25 special education students out of a total of 1,038.

**4733  University of Montana**

032 Corbin Hall
Missoula, MT 59812          406-243-2243
                           FAX 406-243-5330
                           http://www.umt.edu
                e-mail: marks@selway.umt.edu
*Jim Marks, Director*

Four year college that provides programs for students
with a learning disabilities.

**4734  Western Montana College**

710 S Atlantic Street
Dillon, MT 59725

                           800-WMC-MONT
                           http://www.wmc.edu
*Clarence Kostelecky, Special Services*

A public four-year college with 6 special education
students out of a total of 1,100.

# Nebraska

**4735  Chadron State College**

1000 Main Street
Chadron, NE 69337          308-432-6461
                           888-461-4461
                           FAX 308-432-6395
                           http://www.csc.edu
                    e-mail: jcassady@csc.edu
*Jerry Cassady, Counselor*
*Frances Gonzalez, Tutor Coordinator*

Offer a variety of services to students with disabilities
including tutoring, counseling, and special accommodations as appropriate. Students are mentored in self
understanding and self-advocacy.

**4736  Creighton University**

2500 California Plaza
Omaha, NE 68178            402-280-2749
                           800-282-5835
                           FAX 402-280-5579
                           TDY:402-280-5733
                  http://www.creighton.edu
              e-mail: chess@creighton.edu
*Wade Pearson, Director*
*Fr. , President*

An independent four-year college with 73 special education students out of a total of 4,123.

**4737  Doane College**

1014 Boswell Avenue
Crete, NE 68333            402-826-8554
                           FAX 402-826-8278
                           http://www.doane.edu
               e-mail: shanigan@doane.edu
*Sherri Hanigan, Director Student Support Svcs*

An independent four-year college with 12 special education students out of a total of 950.

**4738  Hastings College**

710 N Turner Avenue
Hastings, NE 68901-7621    402-461-7386
                           800-LEA-RNHC
                           FAX 402-461-7480
                           http://www.hastings.edu
                e-mail: khaverly@hastings.edu
*Kathleen Haverly, Center Director*
*Mary Molliconi, Admissions Director*

Learning disabled students are provided with a personalized accommodation plan. Students must be verified prior to enrollment and submit a psychological
review profile prior to being served. Services include:
study skills instruction, academic, career and vocational counseling services, note takers, tutors, professionals and testing accommodations.

**4739  Midland Lutheran College**

Academic Support Services
900 N Clarkson
Fremont, NE 68025          402-721-5480
                           FAX 402-721-0250
                           http://www.mlc.edu
                e-mail: moseman@mlc.edu
*Mose Man, Director*
*Connie Stewart, Administrative Assistant*

Four-year college that provides academic support for
students who have a learning disability.

**4740  Munroe-Meyer Institute for Genetics and
Rehabilitation**

University Affiliated Program
444 S 44th Street
Omaha, NE 68131            402-559-6402
                           FAX 402-559-5737
                  http://www.unmc.edu/mmi
               e-mail: mfbennie@unmc.edu
*Bruce Buehler, Director*
*Thelma Roberts, Billing Representative*

Diagnostic, evaluation, therapy, speech, physical, occupational, behavioral therapies, pediatrics, dentistry, nursing, psychology, social work, genetics,
Media Resource Center, education, nutrition. Adult
services for developmentally disabled, Genetic evaluation and counseling, adaptive equipment, motion
analysis laboratory, recreational therapy.

**4741  Southeast Community College: Beatrice Campus**

Career and Advising Program
4771 W Scott
Beatrice, NE 68310         402-228-3468
                           800-233-5027
                           FAX 402-228-2218
                           http://www.southeast.edu
               e-mail: tcardwell@southeast.edu
*Tom Cardwell MD, Dean Students*
*Robert Kluge, Career Counselor*

A public two-year college with 7 special education
students out of a total of 941.

**4742    Southeast Community College: Lincoln Campus**

**Career and Advising Program**
**8800 O Street**
**Lincoln, NE  68520**                  402-437-2620
                                        800-642-4075
                                        FAX 402-437-2404
                        http://www.college.sccm.cc.ne.us
                              e-mail: smiller@southeast.ed
*Sherine Miller, Director*
*Greg Peters, Career Adviser*

A two year vocational/technical/academic transfer college with approximately 4,000 full/part time students. Accommodations for students with disabilities are made through the Counselors.

**4743    Union College**

**3800 S 48th Street**
**Lincoln, NE  68506**                  402-486-2506
                                        800-228-4600
                                        FAX 402-486-2895
                              http://www.ucollege.edu
                              e-mail: jeforbes@ucollege.edu
*Jennifer Forbes, Director*
*Anne Ballard, Academic Support*

For students with disabilities The Learning Center offers support services to students with learning disabilities, such as dyselexia, and accommodations are made for all students with disabilities.

**4744    University of Nebraska: Lincoln**

**132 Administration Building**
**Lincoln, NE  68588**                  402-472-3787
                                        800-742-8800
                                        FAX 402-472-0080
                                        TDY:402-472-0054
                              http://www.unl.edu
                              e-mail: vcheney2@unl.edu
*Veva Cheney, Director for Special Services*

A public four-year college with 141 special education students out of a total of 19,888.

**4745    University of Nebraska: Omaha**

**6001 Dodge Street**
**Omaha, NE  68182**                    402-554-2393
                                        800-858-8648
                                        FAX 402-554-3555
                              http://www.unomaha.edu
*John Hill MD*

Offers a variety of services to students with disabilities including notetakers, extended testing time, counseling services, and special accommodations.

**4746    Wayne State College**

**Office of Differing Disabilities**
**1111 Main Street**
**Wayne, NE  68787**                    402-375-7213
                                        FAX 402-375-7079
                              http://www.wsc.edu
                              e-mail: jecarst1@wsc.edu
*Jeff Carsten MD, Assistant Dean of Students*
*Richard Collings, President*

Offers a variety of services to students with disabilities including LD diagnosis, academic accommodations, and advocacy.

**4747    Western Nebraska Community College: Scotts Bluff Campus**

**1601 E 27th Street**
**Scottsbluff, NE  69361**              308-635-3606
                                        800-348-4435
                                        FAX 308-635-6100
                              http://www.wncc.net
*Norman Stephenson, Counseling Director*

Offers a variety of services to students with disabilities including notetakers, extended testing time, counseling services, and special accommodations.

---

# Nevada

**4748    Community College of Southern Nevada**

**Disability Resource Center**
**3200 E Cheyenne**
**North Las Vegas, NV  89030**          702-651-4000
                                        FAX 702-651-4179
                                        TDY:702-651-4328
                              http://www.ccsn.nevada.edu
                              e-mail: cipriano_chavez@ccsn.edu
*Cip Chavez, Director Student Services*
*Tracy , Disabilities Specialist*

Note takers, test proctors, books on tape, enlarged books, lab assistants, scribes, interpreters, special accommodations, etc.

**4749    Sierra Nevada College**

**999 Tahoe Boulevard**
**Incline Village, NV  89450**          775-831-1314
                                        FAX 775-831-1347
                              http://www.sierranevada.edu
                              e-mail: bsolomon@sierranevada.edu
*Ben Solomon, Director*

Four year college that provides services to disabled students.

**4750    Truckee Meadows Community College**

**Disability Resource Center**
**7000 Dandini Boulevard**
**Reno, NV  89512**                     775-673-7286
                                        FAX 775-673-7207
                              http://www.tmcc.edu
                              e-mail: lgeldmacher@tmcc.edu
*Michelle Glazier, Director*
*Lee Geldmacher, Adviser*

A public two-year college with 142 special education students out of a total of 9,813.

**4751    University Affiliated Program: University of Nevada**

**College of Education**
**REPC-285**
**Reno, NV  89557**                     775-784-4921
                                        FAX 775-784-4997
                              http://www.unr.edu
                              e-mail: joannj@unr.edu

*Jo Johnson, Director*

**4752 University of Nevada: Las Vegas**

Disability Support Services
4505 Maryland Parkway
Las Vegas, NV 89154          702-895-0866
                            FAX 702-895-0651
                            TDY:702-895-0652
                            http://www.unlv.edu
                    e-mail: les@ccmail.nevada.edu
*Jane Jones, Director*

The Disability Resource Center provides academic accommodations for students with documented disabilities who are otherwise qualified for university programs. The DRC has been designated as the official office for housing records as specified by Section 504 of the Rehabilitation Act of 1973.

**4753 University of Nevada: Reno**

1664 W Virginia Street
Reno, NV 89557                 775-784-6000
                            FAX 775-784-6955
                            TDY:775-327-5131
                            http://www.unr.edu
*Mary Zabel, Director*
*Kristina Wearne, Administrative Assistant*

Offers a variety of services to students with disabilities including notetakers, extended testing time, counseling services, and special accommodations.

**4754 Western Nevada Community College**

2201 W College Parkway
Carson City, NV 89703          775-445-3271
                            FAX 775-887-3105
                       http://www.wncc.nevada.edu
*Susan Hannah, Coordinator DSS*

Offers a variety of services to students with disabilities including note takers, extended testing time, counseling services, and special accommodations.

## New Hampshire

**4755 Colby-Sawyer College**

541 Main Street
New London, NH 03257           603-526-3711
                               800-272-1015
                            FAX 603-526-3452
                       http://www.colby-sawyer.edu
                    e-mail: mmar@colby-sawyer.edu
*Mary Mar MD, Director Learning Services*
*Ann Chalker, Learning Specialist*

An independent four-year college with 100 LD education students out of a total of 800.

**4756 Daniel Webster College**

Academic Support Services
20 University Drive
Nashua, NH 03063               603-577-6612
                               800-325-6876
                            FAX 603-577-6001
                            http://www.dwc.edu
                       e-mail: admissions@dwc.edu
*Lorraine Sylvester, Admissions Specialist*
*Sean Ryan, Dean of Admissions*

Four-year college that offers academic support services to the learning disabled students.

**4757 Dartmouth College**

301 Collis Center
Hanover, NH 03755              603-646-2014
                            FAX 603-646-1629
                            TDY:603-646-1564
                       http://www.dartmouth.edu
              e-mail: admissions.office@dartmouth.edu
*Nancy Pompian, Director of Student Services*
*James Wright, President*

Offers a variety of services to students with disabilities including note takers, extended testing time, counseling services, and special accommodations.

**4758 Franklin Pierce College**

Office Differing Disabilities
College Road
Rindge, NH 03461               603-899-4107
                               800-437-0048
                            FAX 603-899-4395
                            http://www.fpc.edu
                 e-mail: academicservices@fpc.edu
*Patricia Moore, Coordinator*

An independent four-year college with 56 special education students out of a total of 1321.

**4759 Hampshire Country School**

122 Hampshire Road
Rindge, NH 03461               603-899-3325
                            FAX 603-899-6521
                http://www.hampshirecountryschool.com
              e-mail: hampshirecountry@monad.net
*William Dickerman, Headmaster/Admissions Director*

Twenty-five student boarding school for high ability boys, mostly 10-15 years old, needing an unusual amount of adult attention, structure and guidance.

**4760 Institute on Disability: A University Center for Excellence on Disability**

University of New Hampshire
10 W Edge Drive
Durham, NH 03824               603-862-4320
                            FAX 603-862-0555
                       http://www.iod.unh.edu
              e-mail: institute.disability@unh.edu
*Jan PhD, Director*
*Mary , Associate Director*

Promotes the inclusion of people with disabilities into their schools and communities.

**4761 Keene State College**

229 Main Street
Keene, NH 03435                603-358-2353
                               800-KSC-1909
                            FAX 603-358-2257
                            http://www.keene.edu
*Dwight Fischer, Director*
*Stanley Yarosewick, President*

A public four-year college with 105 special education students out of a total of 3,800.

**4762  Learning Skills Academy**
1247 Washington Road
Rye, NH  03870                                     603-964-4903
                                            FAX 603-964-3838
                              http://www.lsa.pvt.k12.nh.us
                           e-mail: marcus@lsa.pvt.k12.nh.us
*Marcus Mann, Director*
*Lisa McManus, Education Director*

**4763  New England College**
24 Bridge Street
Henniker, NH  03242                                603-428-2218
                                            FAX 603-428-3155
                                       http://www.nec.edu
*Anna Carlson, Academic Advising/Support*
*Heidi Hamel, Events Coordinator*

An independent four-year college with 140 students
with learning differences out of a total undergraduate
enrollement of 750.

**4764  New Hampshire Community Technical College at
Stratham/Pease**

Disabilities Support Services
277 Portsmouth Avenue
Stratham, NH  03885                                603-772-1194
                                                   800-522-1194
                                            FAX 603-772-1198
                              http://www.ms.nhctc.edu/caps/
                                 e-mail: scronin@nhctc.edu
*Sharon Cronin, Coordinator*
*Patsy Golinski, Admissions*

A public two-year college with support services for
students with disabilities that include classroom accommodations, assistive technology, self advocacy,
counseling, and one-on-one tutoring.

**4765  New Hampshire Vocational Technical College**
379 Belmont Road
Laconia, NH  03246                                 603-524-3207
                                                   800-357-2992
                                            FAX 603-524-8084
                                            TDY:603-524-3207
                              http://www.laconia.nactc.edu
                              e-mail: laconow@nactc.edu
*Maureen Baldwin-Lamper, Special Services*

Offers a variety of services to students with disabilities including notetakers, extended testing time, counseling services, and special accommodations.

**4766  Rivier College**
420 Main Street
Nashua, NH  03060                                  603-888-0906
                                                   800-447-4843
                                            FAX 603-897-8807
                                            TDY:800-735-2964
                                      http://www.rivier.edu
                                 e-mail: kricci@rivier.edu
*Kate Ricci, Coordinator of Special Services*
*Williams , President*

An independent four-year college with 17 special education students out of a total of 1,651.

**4767  Southern New Hampshire University**
Office of Disability Services
Exeter Hall, CLASS Suite
Manchester, NH  03106-1045                         603-668-2211
                                                   800-642-4968
                                            FAX 603-645-9693
                                      http://www.snhu.edu
                              e-mail: h.jaffe@snhu.edu
*Hyla Jaffe, Disability Services Coordinator*
*Paul Leblanc, President*

Offers services to students with disabilities based on
recommendations from documentaion supporting a
disability. Accommodations are made for specific
needs.

**4768  University of New Hampshire**
ACCESS Office
118 Memorial Union Building
Durham, NH  03824                                  603-862-2648
                                            FAX 603-862-4043
                                      http://www.unh.edu
                              e-mail: parkerman@maple.unh.edu
*Maxine Little, Director*

The University believes each student has the right and
also the responsibility to determine whether or not to
take advantage of support services.

---

# New Jersey

**4769  Banyan School**
Banyan School
12 Hollywood Avenue
Fairfield, NJ  07004                               973-439-1919
                                            FAX 973-439-1396
                              http://www.banyanschool.com
                           e-mail: msaunders@banyanschool.com
*Mary Saunders, Director*

**4770  Caldwell College**
Office of Disability Services
9 Ryerson Avenue
Caldwell, NJ  07006                                973-618-3645
                                            FAX 973-618-3488
                                  http://www.caldwell.edu
                              e-mail: ebenowitz@caldwell.edu
*Abbe Benowitz, Coordinator*

Four-year college that provides disability services to
those students who are learnig disabled.

**4771  Camden County College**
PO Box 200
Blackwood, NJ  08012                               856-227-7200
                                            FAX 856-374-4975
                                  http://www.camdencc.edu
                              e-mail: jkinzy@camdencc.edu
*Joanne Kinzy, Coordinator*

A two-year college that provides services to the learning disabled.

**4772  Centenary College: Office of Disability**

Project ABLE
400 Jefferson Street
Hackettstown, NJ  07840          908-852-1400
FAX 908-813-1984
http://www.centenarycollege.edu
e-mail: zimdahj@centenarycollege.edu
*Jeffery Zimdahl, Disability Services Director*

**4773  College of New Jersey**

Office of Differing Disabilities
2000 Pennington Road
Ewing, NJ  08628          609-771-2571
FAX 609-637-5131
http://www.tcnj.edu/~wellness/disability/
e-mail: degennar@tcnj.edu
*An DeGennaro, Director for Wellness*
*Terri Yamiolkowski, Coordinator*

Four-year college provides services to students with
disabilities.

**4774  College of Saint Elizabeth**

2 Convent Road
Morristown, NJ  07960-6989          973-290-4000
http://www.cse.edu
*Sr. MacNamee, Dean Studies*

Offers a variety of services to students with disabilities including notetakers, extended testing time, counseling services, and special accommodations.

**4775  Community High School**

1135 Teaneck Road
Teaneck, NJ  07666          201-862-1796
FAX 201-862-1791
http://www.communityschool.org
e-mail: office@communityschool.us
*Toby Barnstein, Director Education*
*Dennis Cohen, Program Director*

Complete college prep HS program for LD/ADD adolescent grades 9-12.

**4776  Community School**

11 W Forest Avenue
Teaneck, NJ  07666          201-837-8070
FAX 201-837-6799
http://www.communityschool.org
e-mail: office@communityschool.us
*Rita Rowan, Executive Director*
*Dennis Cohen, Program Director*

Comprehensive academic program for LD/ADD children grades K-8; NY and NJ funding available.

**4777  Craig School**

200 Comly Road
Lincoln Park, NJ  07035          973-305-8085
FAX 973-305-8086
http://www.craigschool.org
e-mail: jday@craigschool.org
*Eric Caparulo, Director Upper School*

A school for children with learning differences such
as dyslexia, auditory processing issues and ADD.

**4778  Cumberland County College**

Project Assist
3322 College Drive
Vineland, NJ  08362          856-691-8600
FAX 856-690-0059
http://www.cccnj.net
e-mail: ssherd@cccnj.edu
*Sandy Sherd, Director*

A two-year college that offers services to its learning
disabled students.

**4779  Fairleigh Dickinson University: Metropolitan
Campus**

1000 River Road T-RH5-02
Teaneck, NJ  07666          201-692-2087
800-SDU-8803
FAX 201-692-2813
http://www.fdu.edu
*Vincent Varrassi, Campus Director*
*Grace Hottinger, Admissions Coordinator*
*Dr. Mary Farrell PhD, University Director*

Comprehensive support services to students with language based LD.

**4780  Forum School**

107 Wyckoff Avenue
Waldwick, NJ  07463          201-444-5882
FAX 201-444-4003
http://www.theforumschool.com
e-mail: forum@ultradsl.net
/info@theforumschool.com
*Steven Krapes, Director*
*Linda Oliver, Office Manager*

Day school for children through age 16 who have neurologically based developmental disabilities, including autism, ADHD, LD, and asperger syndrome.
Services include extended year, speech, adaptive
physical education, music, art therapy, and parent
program.

**4781  Georgian Court College**

Learning Center
900 Lakewood Avenue
Lakewood, NJ  08701          732-364-2200
800-458-8422
FAX 732-987-2026
http://www.georgian.edu
*Patricia Cohen, Director*
*Sister , President*

Four-year college that offers services through the
school learning center to students with disabilities.

**4782  Gloucester County College**

1400 Tanyard Road
Sewell, NJ  08080          856-468-5000
FAX 856-468-9462
TDY:856-468-8452
http://www.gccnj.edu
e-mail: dcook@gccnj.edu
*Dennis Cook, Director for Special Needs Ser*

The Office of Special Needs Services addresses supportive needs toward academic achievement for those
students with documented disabilties such as learning
disabled, visually impaired, hard of hearing and mobility impaired individuals.

**4783 Hudson County Community College**
25 Journal Square
Jersey City, NJ 07306      201-714-4497
FAX 201-963-0789
http://www.hudson.cc.nj.us
*Ellen O'Shea, Coordinator*

Offers a variety of services to students with disabilities including note takers, extended testing time, counseling services, and special accommodations.

**4784 Jersey City State College**
2039 Kennedy Boulevard
Jersey City, NJ 07305
888-441-NJCU
*Myrna Ehrlich MD, Director Project Mentor*

Offers a variety of services to students with disabilities including notetakers, extended testing time, counseling services, and special accommodations.

**4785 Kean College of New Jersey**
Community Disabilities Services
1000 Morris Avenue
Union, NJ 07803      908-527-2000
FAX 908-737-5155
TDY:908-737-5156
http://www.kean.edu
e-mail: mpitts@coger.kean.edu
*Roye-Ann Wallace, Director*
*Maria Pitts, Office Assistant*

Operates a number of clinics, each of which may function interdisciplinarily to provide services, such as speech, audiology, psychology, reading, learning, social work and special education.

**4786 Kean University**
Community Disabilities Services
1000 Morris Avenue
Union, NJ 07803      908-527-2000
FAX 908-737-5155
TDY:908-737-5156
http://www.kean.edu
e-mail: mpitts@coger.kean.edu
*Roye-Ann Wallace, Director*
*Maria Pitts, Office Assistant*

Provides services to disabled students.

**4787 New Jersey City University**
2039 Kennedy Boulevard
Jersey City, NJ 07305      201-200-2091
877-652-8472
FAX 201-200-3141
http://www.njcu.edu
*Jason Hand, Director*

Provides students with learning disabilities a mentor, a teacher, advisor or a faculty member.

**4788 New Jersey Institute of Technology**
Office for Students with Learning Disabilities
University Heights
Newark, NJ 07102      973-596-3420
FAX 973-596-3419
http://www.njit.edu
e-mail: phyllis.colling@njit.edu
*Phyllis Bolling MD, Coordinator for Disability Servi*

A public four-year college with 24 special education students out of a total of 4,906.

**4789 Ocean County College**
College Drive
Toms River, NJ 08754      732-255-0456
FAX 732-255-0458
TDY:732-255-0424
http://www.ocean.edu
e-mail: mreustle@ocean.edu
*Maureen Reustle, Director PASS*
*Anne Hammond, Counselor PASS*

A regional resource center and comprehensive support center for college students with learning disabilities, offering a range of services including psycho-educational assessments, faculty/staff in-service training, program development assistance and consultation, and technical support. Individual and/or small group counseling is available, and vocational/career counseling on transition issues is also offered.

**4790 Princeton University**
303 W College
Princeton, NJ 08544      609-258-3054
FAX 609-258-1020
http://www.princeton.edu
*Stephen Cochrane, Special Services*

Offers a variety of services to students with disabilities including note takers, extended testing time, counseling services, and special accommodations.

**4791 Project Connections**
Middlesex County College
2600 Woodbridge
Edison, NJ 08818      732-906-2506
FAX 732-906-7767
http://www.middlesex.cc.nj.us
e-mail: elizabeth_lowe@middlesex.edu
*Elizabeth Lowe, Director LD Services*
*Elaine Weir-Daidone, Counselor*

Project Connections is a comprehensive academic and counseling service for students with learning disabilities who are enrolled in mainstream programs at Middlesex County College.

**4792 Ramapo College of New Jersey**
Office of Specialized Services
505 Ramapo Valley Road
Mahwah, NJ 07430      201-684-7514
FAX 201-684-7004
http://www.ramapo.edu/content/student.resources
e-mail: oss@ramapo.edu
*Jean Balutanski, Director*

Ramapo College demostated a strong commitment to providing equal access to all students through the removal of architectural and attitudinal barriers. Integration of qualified students with disabilities into college community has been the Ramapo way since the College opened in 1971.

**4793  Raritan Valley Community College**

**Route 28 and Lamington Road**
**Somerville, NJ  08876**          908-526-1200
                                   FAX 908-704-3442
                            http://www.raritanval.edu
*Linda Baum, LD Specialist*

A public two-year college with 180 special education students out of a total of 5,634.

**4794  Richard Stockton College of New Jersey**

**PO Box 195**
**Pomona, NJ  08240**             609-652-4400
                                  FAX 609-626-5550
                          http://www2.stockton.edu
                   e-mail: webmaster@stockton.edu
*Thomasa Gonzale MD, Director Wellness Center*

Offers a variety of services to students with disabilities including note takers, extended testing time, counseling services, and special accommodations.

**4795  Rider University**

**2083 Lawrenceville Road**
**Lawrenceville, NJ  08648**        609-896-5000
                                    800-257-9026
                                   FAX 609-895-6645
                               http://www.rider.edu
                           e-mail: dfox@rider.edu
*Derek Fox, Assistant Director*
*Mordechai Rozanski, President*

Four-year college that provides resources, programs and support for students with learning disabilities.

**4796  Robert Wood Johnson Medical School**

**University Affiliated Program, Brookwood II**
**45 Knightsbridge Road**
**Piscataway, NJ  08854**          732-235-5600
                                   FAX 732-235-9330
                          http://www.rwjms.umdnj.edu
*Deborah Spitalink, Director*

An academic unit of the University of Medicine and Dentistry of New Jersey which is the state's University of the Health Sciences. The medical school is dedicated to the pursuit of excellence in the education of health professionals, in the conduct of biomedical, clinical, and public health research, in the delivery of health care and in the promotion of community health for the residents of our state.

**4797  Rutgers Center for Cognitive Science**

**152 Frelinghuysen Road**
**Piscataway, NJ  08854**          732-445-0635
                                   FAX 732-445-6715
                        http://www.ruccs.rutgers.edu
                   e-mail: admin@ruccs.rutgers.edu
*Rochel Gelman, Co-Director*
*Charles Gallistel, Co-Director*

A public four-year college with 2 special education students out of a total of 437.

**4798  Salem Community College**

**460 Hollywood Avenue**
**Carneys Point, NJ  08069**        856-299-2100
                                    FAX 856-299-9193
                                http://www.salemcc.org
                        e-mail: SCCinfo@salemcc.org
*Teresa Haman, Admissions Coordinator*

Offers a variety of services to students with disabilities including extended testing time, counseling services, and special accommodations.

**4799  Seton Hall University**

**Seton Hall University**
**400 S Orange Avenue**
**South Orange, NJ  07079**         973-761-9166
                                    FAX 973-275-2040
                                http://www.shu.edu
                         e-mail: fraziera@shu.edu
*Ray Frazier, Director*

Student Support Services is an academic program that addresses the needs of students with disabilities.

**4800  Trenton State College**

**2000 Pennington Road**
**Ewing, NJ  08628**               609-771-1855
                                   FAX 609-637-5174
                               http://www.tcnj.edu
                        e-mail: webmaster@tcnj.edu
*Juneau Gary MD, Special Services*

A public four-year college with 24 special education students out of a total of 6,118.

**4801  William Paterson College of New Jersey**

**Special Education Services**
**300 Pompton Road**
**Wayne, NJ  07470**               973-720-2000
                                   FAX 973-720-2910
                               http://www.wpunj.edu
                        e-mail: BOONES@wpunj.edu
*Barbara Milne, Special Services Director*
*Sharon Lowry, Secretary*

Offers a variety of services to students with disabilities including notetakers, extended testing time, counseling services, and special accommodations.

# New Mexico

**4802  Albuquerque Technical Vocational Institute**

**Special Services**
**525 Buena Vista SE**
**Albuquerque, NM  87106-4096**     505-224-3259
                                    FAX 505-224-3261
                                    TDY:505-224-3262
                                http://www.tvi.edu
                             e-mail: pauls@tvi.edu
*A Smarrella, Director Special Services*
*Yolanda Striplings, Administrative Support Specialis*

Provides or coordinates services for students with all disabilities. For students with learning disabilities can arrange for special testing situations, notetaker/scribes, tape recorders, use of wordprocessors or other accommodations based on individual needs.

**4803 Brush Ranch School**
**HC 73**
**Terrero, NM 87573**          505-757-6114
FAX 505-757-6118
http://www.brushranchschool.org
e-mail: kaycrice@hotmail.com
*Kay Rice MA, Head School*
*Ms. , Head Master*
*Suzie Weisman, Admissions Director*

A co-educational boarding school for teens with learning differences. The school is fully licensed and accredited by both the New Mexico Board of Education and the North Central Association of Colleges and Schools. Situated on 283 acres in the Santa Fe National Forest, the school offers a wide range of educational and recreational opportunities.

**4804 Center for Development & Disability (CDD)**
**University of New Mexico/School of Medicine**
**2300 Menaul Boulevard NE**
**Albuquerque, NM 87107**          505-272-3000
FAX 505-272-5280
TDY:505-272-0321
http://www.cdd.unm.edu
e-mail: cdd@unm.edu
*Cate McClain, Director*
*Melody Smith, Assistant Director*

The mission of the CDD is the full inclusion of people with disabilities and their families in their community by: engaging individuals in making life choices; partnering with communities to build resources; and improving systems of care.

**4805 College of Santa Fe**
**1600 St. Michaels Drive**
**Santa Fe, NM 87505**          505-473-6447
FAX 505-473-6124
http://www.csf.edu
*Tom Baumgartel, Director*

Provides services to the learning disabled.

**4806 Eastern New Mexico University**
**Highway 70 Station 34**
**Portales, NM 88130**          505-562-2280
FAX 505-562-2998
TDY:505-562-2280
http://www.enmu.edu
e-mail: bernita.davis@enmu.edu
*Bernita Davis, Director*
*John Prater, Outreach Specialist*

Four year college that provides programs for the learning disabled.

**4807 Eastern New Mexico University: Roswell**
**52 University Boulevard Suite 100**
**Roswell, NM 88202**          505-624-7000
FAX 505-624-7350
http://www.roswell.enmu.edu
e-mail: linda.green@roswell.enmu.edu
*Linda Green, Director for Special Services*
*Vicky Anderson, Assistant Director*

A public two-year college with a total of 2500 students. Accommodations provided include tutoring, instruction, notetaking, recorded text books, testing and registration accommodations.

**4808 Institute of American Indian Arts**
**PO Box 20007**
**Santa Fe, NM 87504**          505-424-2300
FAX 505-988-6446
*Karen Strong, Learning Resources*

A public two-year college with 8 special education students out of a total of 237.

**4809 New Mexico Institute of Mining and Technology**
**801 Leroy Place**
**Socorro, NM 87801**          505-835-5100
800-428-8324
FAX 505-835-5989
http://www.nmt.edu
*Judith Raymond MD, Special Services*

A public four-year college with 5 special education students out of a total of 1,128.

**4810 New Mexico Junior College**
**5317 Lovington Highway**
**Hobbs, NM 88240**          505-392-5410
800-657-6260
FAX 505-392-3668
http://www.nmjc.cc.nm.us
*Marilyn Jackson, Dean Transitional Studies*

A public two-year college with 170 special education students out of a total of 2,438.

**4811 New Mexico State University**
**PO Box 30001**
**Las Cruces, NM 88003**          505-646-6840
800-662-6678
FAX 505-646-5222
http://www.nmsu.edu
e-mail: admissions@nmsu.edu
*John Irvin, Director*
*Michael Armendarez, Coordinator*

A public four-year college with 230 registered students with disabilities out of a total of 12,922.

**4812 Northern New Mexico Community College**
**1002 N Onate Street**
**Espanola, NM 87532**          505-747-2100
FAX 505-747-2180
http://nnm.cc.nm.us
*Millie Lowry, Special Services*

If you have a learning disability, support services include: reading class, readers of tests, notetakers, taped texts, tutoring, math class, recorders for classroom use, library assistance, extra time for tests, self-esteem counseling, resume assistance and kurzweil reading computers.

**4813  San Juan College**

4601 College Boulevard
Farmington, NM  87402          505-326-3311
FAX 505-566-3500
http://www.sjc.ccnm.us

*Sandra Conner, Counselor*
*Ken Kernagis, Counseling Director*

A public two-year college with 28 special education students out of a total of 3,654.

**4814  University of New Mexico**

Main Campus
Albuquerque, NM  87131          505-277-8291
FAX 505-277-7224
http://www.unm.edu
e-mail: lssunm@unm.edu

*Patricia Useem, Manager*

Offers a variety of services to students with disabilities including notetakers, extended testing time, counseling services, and special accommodations.

**4815  University of New Mexico: Los Alamos Branch**

4000 University Drive
Los Alamos, NM  87544          505-662-5919
800-894-5919
FAX 505-662-0344
http://www.la.unm.edu

*Jay Ruybalid, Public Affairs Representative*

Offers a variety of services to students with disabilities including notetakers, extended testing time, counseling services, and special accommodations.

**4816  University of New Mexico: Valencia Campus**

280 La Entrada
Los Lunas, NM  87031          505-925-8500
FAX 505-925-8501
http://www.unm.edu/~vc

*Sharon DiMaria, Coordinator*

A public two-year college with 57 special services students out of a total of 1,400.

**4817  Western New Mexico University**

PO Box 680
Silver City, NM  88062          505-538-6336
800-872-9668
FAX 505-538-6492
http://www.wnmu.edu

*Karen Correa, Director*

Offers a variety of services to students with disabilities including notetakers, extended testing time, counseling services, and special accommodations.

# New York

**4818  Academic Support Services for Students with Disabilities**

Ithaca College
322A Smiddy Hall
Ithaca, NY  14850          607-274-1257
FAX 607-274-3957
TDY:607-274-7319
http://www.ithaca.edu/acssd
e-mail: acssd@ithaca.edu

*Leslie Schettino, Director*
*Linda Uhll, Assistant Director*

**4819  Adirondack Community College**

640 Bay Raod
Queensbury, NY  12804          518-743-2282
FAX 517-745-1433
http://www.crisny.org
e-mail: guyd@acc.sunyacc.edu

*Deborah Guy, Director*

A two-year community college that provides services to the learning disabled.

**4820  Albert Einstein College of Medicine**

1165 Morris Park Avenue
Bronx, NY  10461          718-430-3900
FAX 718-430-3989

*Mary Kelly PhD, Director*
*Mary Kelly PhD, Associate Director*

Provides evaluation and psychoeducational treatment to children and adults of normal intelligence, 21 years or older, who have serious reading difficulties.

**4821  Alfred University**

Special Academic Services
Crandall Hall
Alfred, NY  14802          607-871-2148
800-425-3733
FAX 607-871-3014
http://www.alfred.edu
e-mail: sdstagg@alfred.edu

*Terry Taggart, Director*
*Beth Niles, Secretary*

Special Academic Services provides support services, consultation and advocacy for students with learning, physical and/or psychological disabilities. Services for persons with disabilities shall complement and support, but not duplicate, the University's regular existing services and programs.

**4822  Bank Street College: Graduate School of Education**

610 W 1112th Street
New York, NY  10025          212-875-4404
FAX 212-875-4678
http://www.bnkst.edu/html/grad_ad/
e-mail: GradCourses@bnkst.edu

*Augusta Kappner, President*
*Frank Naura, Vice President*

For learning disabled college students who are highly motivated to become teachers of children and youth with learning problems and who wish to earn a masters degree in Special Education.

**4823  Binghamton University**

**Vestal Parkway E**
**Binghamton, NY 13902 6000**          607-777-2686
                                        FAX 607-777-6893
                                        TDY:607-777-2686
                              http://www.binghamton.edu
                          e-mail: bjfairba@binghamton.edu
*B Fairbairn, Director Students with Disabilit*
*Bethany Beecher, LD Specialist*

Provides assistance to students with physical or learning disabilities.

**4824  Bramson Ort Technical Institute**

**69-30 Austin Street**
**Forest Hills, NY 11375**             718-261-5800
                                        FAX 718-575-5118
                              http://www.bramsonort.org
                          e-mail: rbaskin@bramsonort.org
*Rivka Burkos, Librarian*
*Aron Reznikoss, Job Placement*

Offers a variety of services to students with disabilities including notetakers, extended testing time, counseling services, and special accommodations.

**4825  Broome Community College**

**PO Box 1017**
**Binghamton, NY 13905**               607-778-5000
                                        FAX 607-778-5662
                              http://www.sunybroome.edu
                          e-mail: bpomeroy@sunybroome.edu
*Bruce Pomeroy, Director*

A public two-year college providing services to approximately 75-125 students with learning disabilities per school year. Services include note taking, tutoring, an LD specialist, adaptive educational equipment, testing services, and other appropriate support as based on documentation of need.

**4826  CUNY Queensborough Community College**

**56th Avenue & Springfield Boulevard**
**Bayside, NY 11364**                  718-281-5000
                                        FAX 718-229-1733
                              http://www.qcc.cuny.edu
*Barbara Bookman, Director*

The Office of Services for Students with Disabilities (Science Building, Room 132) offers special assistance and couseling to students with specific needs. The services offered include academic, vocational, psychological and rehabilitation counseling, as well as liasion with community social agencies.

**4827  Canisius College**

**Disability Support Service**
**2001 Main Street**
**Buffalo, NY 14208**                  716-888-3748
                                        FAX 716-888-3747
                                        TDY:716-888-3748
                              http://www.canisius.edu
                          e-mail: dobies@canisius.edu
*Anne Dobies, Director*
*Dan Norton, Graduate Assistant*

Four-year college offering services to students with physical and cognitive disabilities.

**4828  Cazenovia College**

**22 Sullivan Street**
**Cazenovia, NY 13035**                315-655-7208
                                        800-654-3210
                                        FAX 315-655-4860
                              http://www.cazenovia.edu
                          e-mail: cazenovia@cazenovia.edu
*Cyndi Pratt, Special Services*
*Jesse Lott, Director*

An independent college with a significant number of special education students.

**4829  Colgate University**

**Office Disabilities Services**
**13 Oak Drive**
**Hamilton, NY 13346**                 315-228-7225
                                        FAX 315-228-7831
                              http://www.colgate.edu
                          e-mail: admission@mail.colgate.edu
*Lynn Waldman, Director*

Provides for a small body of liberal arts education that will expand individual potential and ability to particpate effectively in the society.

**4830  College of Aeronautics**

**Academic Support Services**
**8601 23rd Avenue**
**East Elmhurst, NY 11369**            718-429-6600
                                        FAX 718-505-0667
                              http://www.aero.edu
                          e-mail: mcpartland@aero.edu
*Sharon McPartland, Coordinator*

College offering support services to its learning disabled students.

**4831  College of New Rochelle: New Resources Division**

**Student Services**
**29 Castle Place**
**New Rochelle, NY 10805**             914-654-5000
                                        800-933-5923
                                        FAX 914-654-5866
                              http://www.cnr.edu
                          e-mail: info@cnr.edu
*Joan Bristol, Vice President for Student Servi*
*Steven Sweeny, College President*

Offers a variety of services to students with disabilities including notetakers, extended testing time, counseling services, and special accommodations.

**4832  College of Saint Rose**

**432 Western Avenue**
**Albany, NY 12203 1490**              518-337-2335
                                        FAX 518-458-5330
                              http://www.strose.edu
                          e-mail: hermannk@strose.edu
*Kelly Hermann, Coordinator Special Services*

Four year college that provides disabled students with services and support.

# Schools & Colleges /New York

**4833 College of Staten Island of the City University of New York**

2800 Victory Boulevard
Staten Island, NY 10314     718-982-2513
FAX 718-982-2117
TDY:718-982-2515
http://www.csi.cuny.edu
e-mail: venditti@postbox.csi.cuny.edu
*Margaret Venditti, Director*
*Margaret Venditti, Coordinator*

A public four-year college with 33 special education students out of a total of 11,136. Priority registration, test accommodations and tutoring.

**4834 Columbia College**

Disability Services
2920 Broadway
New York, NY 10027     212-854-2388
FAX 212-854-3448
http://www.columbia.edu
e-mail: disability@columbia.edu
*Susan Cheer, Director*
*Colleen Lewis, Program Coordinator*

Four-year college that offers disability services to its students.

**4835 Columbia-Greene Community College**

4400 Route 23
Hudson, NY 12534     518-828-4181
FAX 518-822-2015
http://www3.sunycgcc.edu
*Sheri Bolevice, LD Specialist*
*Pat Nobes, Alternative Learning*

A public two-year college in upstate New York with an enrollment of about 1,800. Services available to students with a documented learning disability include various academic accommodations, peer tutoring and academic counselling. Six developmental courses are offered in reading, math, English, and study skills.

**4836 Concordia College: New York**

Connections
171 White Plains Road
Bronxville, NY 10708     914-337-9300
FAX 914-395-4500
http://www.concordia-ny.edu
e-mail: ghg@concordia-ny.edu
*George Groth, Connection Program Director*
*Michael Weschler, Assistant Director*

**4837 Cornell University**

Student Disability Services
420 CCC
Ithaca, NY 14853     607-255-6310
FAX 607-255-1562
TDY:607-255-7665
http://www.cornell.edu
e-mail: cornell-clt@cornell.edu
*Helene Selco, Director*
*Nancy Jerabek, Office Manager*

Cornell University is committed to ensuring that students with disabilities have equal access to all university programs and activities. Policy and procedures have been developed to provide students with as much independence as possible, to preserve confidentiality, and to provide students with disabilities the same exceptional opportunities available to all Cornell students.

**4838 Corning Community College**

1 Academic Drive
Corning, NY 14830     607-962-9459
800-358-7171
FAX 607-962-9006
TDY:607-962-9459
http://www.corning-cc.edu
e-mail: northop@corning-cc.edu
*Judy Northrop, Coordinator Student Disability*
*Sheery White, Typist*

A public two-year community college. There are approximately 100 LD students out of a student body of 4,500. A variety of services are available to students with LD, including specialized advising and registration, individualized tutoring, academic advisoring, and accommodations. Also on campus: Kurzweil reading machines, voice activated word processing, etc.

**4839 Dowling College**

Program for Potentially Gifted College Students
150 Idle Hour Boulevard
Oakdale, NY 11769     631-244-3306
FAX 631-244-5036
http://www.dowling.edu
e-mail: strached@dowling.edu
*Dorothy Stracher, Program Director*
*MK Schneid, Assistant Director*

Academic program to help college students with LD develop strategies for success. They work one-on-one with graduate students.

**4840 Dutchess Community College**

53 Pendell Road
Poughkeepsie, NY 12603     845-431-8000
800-378-9707
FAX 845-471-4869
http://www.sunydutchess.edu
e-mail: webmaster@sunydutchess.edu

A public two-year college with 45 special education students out of a total of 7,511.

**4841 Erie Community College: South Campus**

Special Education Department
4041 Southwestern Boulevard
Orchard Park, NY 14127     716-648-5400
FAX 716-851-1629
TDY:716-851-1831
http://www.ecc.edu
e-mail: adamsjm@ecc.edu
*Nancy Bailey, Counselor*

A public two-year college with 200 special education students out of a total of 3,455.

**4842 Fashion Institute of Technology**

7th Avenue and 27th Street
New York, NY 10001          212-217-7522
                          FAX 212-217-7192
                      http://www.fitnyc.suny.edu
               e-mail: fitinfo@sfitva.cc.fitsuny.edu
*Gail Ballard, Program Coordinator*
*Joyce Brown, President*

A public four-year college with 106 special education
students out of a total of 12,011.

**4843 Finger Lakes Community College**

4355 Lakeshore Drive
Canandaigua, NY 14424          585-394-3500
                             FAX 585-394-5005
                        http://www.fingerlakes.edu
                     e-mail: admissions@flcc.edu
*Patricia Malinowski, Chairperson of The Developmental*
*Daniel Hayes, President*

Provides services such as pre-admission counseling,
academic advisement, tutorials, computer assistance,
workshops, peer counseling and support groups. The
college does not offer a formal program but aids students
in arranging appropriate accommodations.

**4844 Fordham University**

Disabled Student Services
Keating Hall
Bronx, NY 10458          718-817-4700
                       FAX 718-817-3735
                       TDY:718-817-0655
                   http://www.fordham.edu
            e-mail: disabilityservices@fordham.edu
*Cristina Bertisch, Director*

The Office of Disability Services collaborates with
students, faculty and staff to ensure appropriate services for students with disabilities. The University
will make reasonable acccommodations, and provide
appropriate aids.

**4845 Fulton-Montgomery Community College**

2805 State Highway 67
Johnstown, NY 12095          518-762-4651
                           FAX 518-762-4334
                      http://www.fmcc.suny.edu
                e-mail: efosmire@fmcc.suny.edu
*Ellie Fosmire, Coordinator*

A public two-year college with 76 special education
students out of a total of 1,748.

**4846 Genesee Community College**

SUNY (State University of New York) Systems
1 College Road
Batavia, NY 14020          585-343-0055
                         FAX 716-343-4541
                    http://www.genessee.edu
              e-mail: admissions@genesee.suny.edu
*Karol Shallowhorn, Director*
*Stephanie Smythe, Counselor*

A public two-year college with 78 special education
students out of a total of 3,212.

**4847 Gow School**

Gow School
Emery Road
South Wales, NY 14139          716-652-3450
                             FAX 716-687-2003
                          http://www.gow.org
                   e-mail: admissions@gow.org
*M Rogers Jr, Headmaster*
*Robert Garcia, Admissions Director*

The nation's oldest college preparatory school for
young men (grades 7-12) with dyslexia/language
based learning differences. The 100 acre residential
campus is located in upstate New York. Co-Ed summer program for ages 8-16.

**4848 Hamilton College**

198 College Hill Road
Clinton, NY 13323          315-859-4022
                         FAX 315-859-4077
                         TDY:315-859-4294
                    http://www.hamilton.edu
               e-mail: rbellmay@hamilton.edu
*Roxanne Bellmay-Campdell, Associate Dean*
*Louise Peckingham, Compliance Officer*

Four year college that offfers services for learning
disabled students.

**4849 Herkimer County Community College**

100 Reservior Road
Herkimer, NY 13350          315-866-0300
                          FAX 315-866-7253
                          TDY:888- GO4HCCC
                    http://www.hccc.ntcnet.com
               e-mail: coylemf@hcc.suny.edu
*Michele Weaver, LD Specialist*
*Suzanne Paddock, Counselor*

A public two-year college with approximately 200
documented disabled students. Tuition and fees:
$2,450 (annual basis); overall enrollment 95-96:
$2,445 (1,857 full time/588 part-time).

**4850 Hofstra University**

Program of the Higher Education of the Disabled
101 Memorial Hall
Hempstead, NY 11549 1000          516-463-6972
                                FAX 516-463-6674
                           http://www.hofstra.edu
                    e-mail: nucizg@hofstra.edu
*Karin Spencer, Associate Dean*
*Kelly Timko, Graduate Assistant*

Provides the support services which allow students to
compete on an equal level with their classmates, but
also to foster the growth of independent living skills
necessary for survival at Hofstra University and beyond.

**4851 Houghton College**

Student Academic Services
1 Willard Avenue
Houghton, NY 14744          585-567-9239
                          FAX 585-567-9570
                     http://www.houghton.edu
               e-mail: shice@houghton.edu
*Susan Hice MD, Director*
*Irene Willis, Student Academic Services Direct*

Four year college that provides academic support to disabled students.

**4852 Hudson Valley Community College**

Disabilities Resource Center
80 Vandenburgh Avenue
Troy, NY 12180                         518-629-7154
                                        FAX 518-629-4831
                                        TDY:518-629-7596
                                        http://www.hvcc.edu
                                        e-mail: editor@hvcc.edu
*Pablo Negron, Director*

A public two-year college with 28 special education students out of a total of 10,106.

**4853 Hunter College of the City University of New York**

Office for Students with Disabilities
New York, NY 10021                      212-772-4824
                                        FAX 212-650-3456
                                        http://www.hunter.cuny.edu
*Sandra LaPorta, Director*

Provides services to over 250 students with learning disabilities. A learning disability is a disorder in one or more of the basic psychological processes involved in understanding or in using spoken or written language.

**4854 Iona College: College Assistance Program**

715 N Avenue
New Rochelle, NY 10801                   914-633-2582
                                         800-231-4662
                                         FAX 914-633-2011
                                         http://www.iona.edu
                                         e-mail: lrobertello@iona.edu
*Linda Robertello, Director*
*Regina Carlo, Assistant Director*

Offers a comprehensive support program for students with learning disabilities. CAP is designed to encourage success by providing instruction tailored to individual strenghts and needs.

**4855 Ithaca College: Speech and Hearing Clinic**

Smiddy Hall
Ithaca, NY 14850                         607-274-3714
                                         FAX 607-274-1137
                http://www.ir.tompkins.ny.us/beOra7du.htm
*Richard Schissel*

Offers a variety of services to students with disabilities including notetakers, extended testing time, counseling services, and special accommodations.

**4856 Jamestown Community College**

State University of New York Systems
525 Falconer Street
Jamestown, NY 14701                      716-665-5220
                                         800-388-8557
                                         FAX 716-665-9110
                                         http://www.sunyjcc.edu
                                         e-mail: admissions@mail.sunyjcc.edu
*Nancy Callahan, Disability Support*
*Gregory Decinque, President*

A public two-year college with 41 special education students out of a total of 4,541.

**4857 Jefferson Community College**

Jefferson Community College
Coffeen Street
Watertown, NY 13601                      315-786-2277
                                         888-435-6522
                                         FAX 315-786-2459
                                         http://www.sunyjefferson.edu
                                         e-mail: straingham@sunyjefferson.edu
*Sheree Trainham, Learning Skills/Disability*
*Rosanne Weir, Director*

A public two-year college with 44 special education students out of a total of 2,121.

**4858 John Jay College of Criminal Justice of the City University of New York**

445 W 59th Street
New York, NY 10019                       212-237-8122
                                         FAX 212-237-8777
                                         TDY:212-237-8233
                                         http://www.jjay.cuny.edu
                                         e-mail: admiss@jjay.cuny.edu
*Farris Forsythe, Coordinator*
*John Teravis, President*

An independent two-year college with 67 special education students out of a total of 7,912.

**4859 Kildonan School**

425 Morse Hill Road
Amenia, NY 12501                         845-373-8111
                                         FAX 845-373-9793
                                         http://www.kildonan.org
                                         e-mail: rwilson@kildonan.org
*Ronald Wilson, Headmaster*
*Joseph Ruggiero, Academic Dean*

Offers a fully accredited college preparatory curriculum. The school is co-educational, enrolling boarding students in Grades 6-Postgraduate and day students in Grade 2-Postgraduate. Provides daily one-on-one Orton-Gillingham tutoring to build skills in reading, writing, and spelling. Daily independent reading and writing work reinforces skills and improves study habits. Interscholastic sports, horseback riding, clubs and community service enhance self-confidence.

**4860 Learning Disabilities Program**

ADELPHI UNIVERSITY
Chapman Hall
Garden City, NY 11530                    516-877-4710
                                         800-233-5144
                                         FAX 516-877-4711
                http://www.academics.adelphi.edu/ldprog
                e-mail: LDprogram@adelphi.com
                                         /Ldprogram@adelphi.edu
*Susan Spencer, Assistant Dean/Director*
*Janet Cohen, Assistant Director*

The programs professional staff, all with advanced degrees, provide individual tutoring and counseling to learning disabled students who are completely mainstream in the University.

**4861 Long Island University: CW Post Campus**
Academic Resource Center
720 Northern Boulevard
Brookville, NY 11548          516-299-2937
                              FAX 516-299-2126
          http://www.cspost.liunet.edu
              e-mail: crundlet@liu.edu
*Carol Rundlett, Academic Resource Center Dir*

**4862 Manhattan College**
4513 Manhattan College Parkway
Riverdale, NY 10471          718-862-7101
                             FAX 718-862-7808
   http://www.manhattan.edu/sprscent/index.html
              e-mail: rpollack@manhattan.edu
*Ross EdD, Director*

The Specialized Resource Center serves all students with special needs including individuals with temporary disabilities, such as those resulting from injury or surgery. The mission of the center is to ensure educational opportunity for all students with special needs by providing access to full participation in all aspects of the campus life.

**4863 Manhattanville College**
Higher Education Learning Program
2900 Purchase Street
Purchase, NY 10577          914-323-5313
                            FAX 914-323-5493
          http://www.mville.edu
      e-mail: admissions@manhattanville.edu
*Eleanor Shwortz, Coordinator*

Students preparing for a career in Special Education learns the full spectrum of physical, emotional, and mental challenges faced by people.

**4864 Maria College**
700 New Scotland Avenue
Albany, NY 12208          518-438-3111
                          FAX 518-438-7170
          http://www.mariacollege.edu
      e-mail: laurieg@mariacollege.edu
*Margie Byrd, Dean*
*Mary Riker, Contact*

An independent two-year college with 13 special education students out of a total of 875.

**4865 Marist College**
Learning Disabilities Support Program
3399 N Road
Poughkeepsie, NY 12601          845-575-3000
                                800-436-5483
                                FAX 845-575-3011
          http://www.marist.edu
      e-mail: specserv@marist.edu
*Linda Cooper, Director*
*Deborah Reeves-Duncan, Councilor*

Provides a comprehensive range of academic support services and accommodations which promote the full integration of students with disabilities into the mainstream college environment.

**4866 Marymount Manhattan College**
221 E 71st Street
New York, NY 10021          212-774-0724
                            FAX 212-517-0541
          http://www.marymount.mmm.edu
              e-mail: jbonomo@mmm.edu
*Jaquelyn Bonomo MD, Assistant Director*
*Ann Jablon, Director*

An independent four-year college with 25 learning disabled students out of a total of 1,700. There is an additional fee for the learning disabled education program in addition to the regular tuition.

**4867 Medaille College**
Disability Services Department
18 Agassiz Circle
Buffalo, NY 14214          716-884-3281
                           800-292-1582
                           FAX 716-884-0291
          http://www.medaille.edu
              e-mail: jmatheny@medaille.edu
*Lisa Morisson, Director*

Offers a variety of services to students with disabilities including notetakers, extended testing time, counseling services, and special accommodations.

**4868 Mercy College**
Star Program
555 Broadway
Dobbs Ferry, NY 10522          914-674-7218
                               FAX 914-674-7410
          http://www.mercynet.edu
      e-mail: admissions@merlin.mercynet.edu
*Terry Rich, Director*

Helps people with learning disabilities.

**4869 Mohawk Valley Community College**
1101 Sherman Drive
Utica, NY 13501          315-731-5702
                         FAX 315-731-5868
                         TDY:315-792-5413
          http://www.mvcc.edu
              e-mail: dowsland@mvcc.edu
*Wendy Dowsland, Learning Disabilities Specialist*
*Lynn Igoe, Students w/Disabilities Coordina*

MVCC'S LD program is staffed by a half time LD specialist. Service provided to students with learning disabilities include advocacy, information and referral to on and off campus services, testing accommodations, taped materials, loaner tape recorders and note takers.

**4870 Molloy College**
1000 Hempstead Avenue
Rockville Centre, NY 11571          516-678-5000
                                    888-4MALLOY
                                    FAX 516-678-2284
          http://www.molloy.edu
              e-mail: tforker@molloy.edu
*Therese Forker, Director STEEP*
*Barbara Nirrengarten, Assistant Director*

STEEP (Success Through Expanded Education), is a program specifically designed to assist students with learning disabilities and enable them to become successful students. The program offers the student the opportunities to learn techniques which alleviate some of their problems. Special emphasis is directed toward the development of positive self-esteem.

**4871 Nassau Community College**

**Disabled Support Department**
**One Education Drive**
**Garden City, NY 11530**           516-572-7241
                                FAX 516-572-9874
                          http://www.sunynassau.edu
                         e-mail: schimsj@sunynassau.edu
*Victor Margolis MD, Coordinator Disabled Services*

Our goal is to help students achieve success while they are attending Nassau Community College by learning to become their own advocates through talking with their professors about their disability and the accommodations they need for the course.

**4872 Nazareth College of Rochester**

**Disability Support Services**
**4245 E Avenue**
**Rochester, NY 14618**              585-586-2452
                                FAX 716-586-2452
                             http://www.naz.edu
                           e-mail: avhouse@naz.edu
*Annemarie House, Counselor*

Four-year college that offers students with a learning disability support and services.

**4873 New York City Technical College of the City University of New York**

**Special Education Department**
**300 Jay Street**
**Brooklyn, NY 11201**               718-260-5000
                                FAX 718-254-8539
                                TDY:718-260-5443
                http://www.citytech.cuny.edu\studentsupport
                  e-mail: studentsupport@citytech.cuny.edu
*Faith Sogelman, Director*

The student support services program, located in A237, provides comprehensive services to students with physical, health and learning disabilities. These services include counseling, tutorial, computers and specially designed technology, testing accommodations, and appropriate reasonable accommodations, as per students individual needs and documentation of disabilitiy.

**4874 New York Institute of Technology: OldWestbury**

**Northern Boulevard**
**Old Westbury, NY 11568**           516-686-7516
                                  800-345-NYIT
                                FAX 516-686-7613
                             http://www.nyit.edu
                          e-mail: eguillano@nyit.edu
*Edward PhD, President*
*Alexandra Logue PhD, VP Academic Affairs*

Offers the Vocational Independence Progran for students who have significant learning disabilities.

**4875 New York University**

**Henry and Lucy Moses Center**
**240 Green Street**
**New York, NY 10012**               212-998-4980
                                FAX 212-995-4114
                             http://www.nyu.edu
                           e-mail: lc83@nyu.edu
*Lakshmi MA, CSD Coordinator*
*Scott Hornack, Contact*

The staff of the Center for Students with Disabilities provides a wide range of services. Each student's needs are assessed prior to enrolling at the University, and the resulting written accommodation plan may include taking tests and exams with extended time, use of a computer or word processor, in-class note taker, permission to audi-tape class lectures.

**4876 New York University Medical Center: Learning Diagnostic Program**

**400 E 34th Street**
**New York, NY 10016**               212-263-7753
                                FAX 212-263-7721
*Ruth MD, Professor Clinical Neurology*
*Becky Chow, Assistant Professor*

Assessment team, neurology, neuro-psychology, psychiatry services are offered.

**4877 Niagara County Community College**

**3111 Saunders Settlement Road**
**Sanborn, NY 14132**                716-614-6222
                                FAX 716-614-6700
                          http://www.niagaracc.suny.edu
*Karen Drilling, Disabled Student Services*

The College provides reasonable accommodations for students with disabilties, including those with specific learning disabilities. Students with learning disabilities must provide documentation by a qualified professional that proves thry are eligible for accommodations.

**4878 Niagara University**

**Support Services Department**
**Seton Hall First Floor**
**Niagara University, NY 14109**     716-286-8076
                                  800-462-2111
                                FAX 716-286-8063
                             http://www.niagara.edu
                           e-mail: ds@niagara.edu
*Diane Stoelting, Specialized Support Services*

Reasonable accommodations are provided to students with disabilities based on documentation of disability. Depending on how the disability impacts the individual, reasonable accommodations may include extended time on tests taken in a separate location with appropriate assistance, notetakes or use of a tape recorder in class, interpreter, textbooks and course materials in alternative format, as well as other academic and non-academic accommodations.

**4879 Norman Howard School**

275 Pinnacle Road
Rochester, NY 14623          585-334-8010
              FAX 585-334-8073
              http://www.normanhoward.org
              e-mail: info@normanhoward.org
*Marcie Roberts, Executive Director*

**4880 North Country Community College**

State University Of New York SUNY Systems
23 Santanoni Avenue
Saranac Lake, NY 12983          518-891-2915
              888-879-6222
              FAX 518-891-0898
              http://www.nccc.edu
              e-mail: admissions@nccc.edu
*Jeannine Golden, Learning Lab/Malone*
*Scott Lambert, Enrollment & Financial Aid Couns*

Located in the Adirondack Olympic Region of northern New York, NCCC is committed to providing a challenging and supportive environment where the aspirations of all can be realized. The college provides a variety of services for students with special needs which includes: specialized advisement, tutors and supplemental instruction, specialized accommodations, technology and equipment to accommodate learning disabilities and other resources.

**4881 Onondaga Community College**

Services for Students with Special Needs
4941 Onondaga Road
Syracuse, NY 13215          315-498-2622
              FAX 315-498-2107
              http://www.sunyocc.edu
              e-mail: occinfo@sunyocc.edu
*Linda Koslowsky, Administrative Aids*

A public two-year college with 203 special education students out of a total of 8,393.

**4882 Orange County Community College**

115 S Street
Middletown, NY 10940          845-341-4030
              FAX 845-342-8662
              http://www.sunyorange.edu
*Marilynn Brake, Special Services Coordinator*

The Office of Special Services for the Disabled provides support services to meet the individual needs of students with disabilities. Such accommodations include oral testing, extended time testing, tape recorded textbooks, writing lab, note-takers and others. Pre-admission counseling ensures accessibility for the qualified student.

**4883 Purchase College State University of New York**

Special Services Office
735 Anderson Hill
Purchase, NY 10577          914-251-6390
              FAX 914-251-6399
              http://www.purchase.edu
*Ronnie Mait, Coordinator Office Special Svcs*
*Donna Siegmann, Coordinator Supported Education*

Offers a variety of services to students with disabilities including note takers, extended testing time, counseling services, and special accommodations.

**4884 Queens College City University of New York**

Special Services Office
65-30 Kissena Boulevard
Flushing, NY 11367          718-997-5000
              FAX 718-997-5895
              TDY:718-997-5870
              http://www.qc.edu
              e-mail: christopher_rosa@qc.edu
*Christopher Rosa, Office Director*

Services include tutoring and notetaking, accommodating testing alternatives, counseling, academic and vocational advisement, as well as diagnostic assessments in order to pinpoint specific deficits.

**4885 Rensselaer Polytechnic Institute**

110 8th Street
Troy, NY 12180          518-276-2746
              800-448-6562
              FAX 518-276-4839
              http://www.rpi.edu
              e-mail: hamild@rpi.edu
*Debra Hamilton, Disabled Student Services*

An independent four-year college with 53 learning disabled students out of a total of 6,000.

**4886 Rochester Business Institute**

1630 Portland Avenue
Rochester, NY 14621          585-266-0430
              888-741-4271
              FAX 585-266-8243
              http://www.rochester-institute.com
              e-mail: dpfluke@cci.edu
*Deanna Fluke, Admissions Director*
*Jim Rodriguez, Admissions Representative*

An independent two-year college with 12 special education students out of a total of 528.

**4887 Rochester Institute of Technology**

28 Lomb Memorial Drive
Rochester, NY 14623          585-475-7804
              FAX 585-475-5832
              http://www.rit.edu
              e-mail: palldc@rit.edu
*Carla Katz, Chair Learning Support Services*
*Pamela Lloyd, Coordinator Disability Services*

An independent four-year college serving 600 students with disabilities out of a total of 14,000 students. Offers a wide variety of accommodations and support services to students with documented disabilities.

**4888 Rockland Community College**

145 College Road
Suffern, NY 10901          845-574-4316
              FAX 845-574-4462
*Marge Zemek, Learning Disabilities Specialist*

A public two-year college with 300 special education students out of a total of 5,500. The office of Disability Services provides a variety of support services tailored to meet the individual needs and learning styles of students with documented learning disabilities.

**4889   Rose F Kennedy Center**
Albert Einstein College of Medicine
1410 Pelham Parkway S
Bronx, NY  10461                     718-430-8500
                                  FAX 718-904-1162
              http://www.aecom.yu.edu/cerc
              e-mail: cerc@aecom.yu.edu
*Herbert Cohen MD, Director*

Mission is to help children with disabilities reach their
full potential and to support parents in their efforts to
get the best care, education, and treatment for their
children.

**4890   STAC Exchange: St.Thomas Aquinas College**
Pathways
125 Route 340
Sparkill, NY  10976                  845-398-4230
                                  FAX 845-398-4229
                    http://www.stac.edu
              e-mail: stacexch@stac.edu
*Richard Heath, Director*
*Amelia DeMarco, Assistant Director*

Comprehensive support program for selected college
students with learning disabilites and/or ADHD. Services include individual professional mentoring,
study groups, workshops, academic counseling, priority registration, assistive technology, and a specialized summer program prior to the first semester.

**4891   SUNY Canton**
34 Cornell Drive
Canton, NY  13617                    315-386-7392
                                  FAX 315-379-3877
                                  TDY:315-386-7943
                    http://www.canton.edu
              e-mail: leev@canton.edu
*Veigh Lee, DSS Coordinator*
*Heather Lauzon, Office Assistant*

Four year state college that provides resources and
services to learning disabled students.

**4892   SUNY Cobleskill**
Disability Support Center
Route 7
Cobleskill, NY  12043                518-255-5282
                                     800-295-8988
                                  FAX 518-255-6430
                                  TDY:518-255-5454
                    http://www.cobleskill.edu
              e-mail: Johnsok@Cobleskill.edu /
*Lynn Abarno, Coordinator Support Services*

A public two-year college with a Bachelor of Technology component in agriculture. Approximately 170
students identify themselves as having a learning disability out of the 2,000 total population. Tuition
$3,500 in state/$8,300 out of state. Academic support
services and accommodations for documented LD students.

**4893   SUNY Institute of Technology: Utica/Rome**
PO Box 3050
Utica, NY  13504                     315-792-7500
                                     866-278-6948
                                  FAX 315-792-7837
                    http://www.sunyit.edu
              e-mail: admissions@sunyit.edu
*Marybeth Lyonsvan, Interim Director Admissions*
*Tat Saranr, Business Office Secretary*

Upper division bachelor's degree in a variety of professional and technical majors; masters degree and
continuing educational coursework is also available.

**4894   Sage College**
140 New Scotland Avenue
Albany, NY  12214                    518-292-8624
                                  FAX 578-292-1910
                    http://www.sage.edu
              e-mail: chowed@sage.edu
*David Chowenhill, Director*

Four year college that offers services to students with
a learning disability.

**4895   Schenectady County Community College**
Disability Services Department
78 Washington Avenue
Schenectady, NY  12305               518-381-1366
                                  FAX 518-346-0379
                    http://www.sunysccc.edu
*Tom Dotson, Coordinator*

Access for All program is designed to make programs
and facilities accessible to all students in pursuit of
their academic goals. Disabled Student Services seeks
to ensure accessible educational opportunities in accordance with individual needs. Offers general support services and program services such as: exam
assistance, special scheduling, adaptive equipment,
readers, taping assistance and more.

**4896   Services for Students with Disabilities**
Binghamton University
PO Box 6000
Binghamton, NY  13902                607-777-2686
                                  FAX 607-777-6893
                                  TDY:607-777-2686
                    http://www.binghamton.edu
              e-mail: bjfairba@binghamton.edu
*B Fairbairn, Director*
*Janice Beecher, LD Specialist*

Provides a wide range of support services to
Binghamton University students with physical learning or other disabilities.

**4897   Siena College**
515 Loudon Road
Loudonville, NY  12211               518-783-4239
                                     888-ATSIENA
                                  FAX 518-782-6770
                    http://www.siena.edu
              e-mail: jpellegrini@siena.edu
*Juliet Pellegrini, Director of Services For Student*

Four year college that offers programs for the learning
disabled.

**4898  St. Bonaventure University**

Teaching & Learning Center
Room 26, Doyle Hall
St. Bonaventure, NY  14778          716-375-2066
                                   800-462-5050
                                   FAX 716-375-2072
                                   http://www.sbu.edu
                                   e-mail: nmatthew@sbu.edu
*Nancy Matthews, Coordinator*

Catholic University in the Franciscan tradition. Independent coeducational institution offering programs through its schools of arts and sciences, business administration, education and journalism and mass communication. 2500 students, tuition $16,210, room and board $6,190.

**4899  St. Lawrence University**

23 Romoda Drive
Canton, NY  13617                  315-229-5104
                                   FAX 315-229-7453
                                   http://www.stlawu.edu
                                   e-mail: jmeagher@mail.stlawu.edu
*John Meagher, Director*
*Liv Regosin, Director of Advising*

The Office of Special Needs is here to ensure that all students with disabilities can freely and actively participate in all facets of University life, to coordinate support services and programs that enable students with disabilities to reach their educational potential, and to increase the level of awareness among all members of the University so that students with disabilites are able to perform at a level limited only by their abilities, not their disabilities.

**4900  State University of New York College Technology at Delhi**

2 Main Street
Delhi, NY  13753                   607-746-4593
                                   800-96-DELHI
                                   FAX 607-746-4004
                                   http://www.delhi.edu
                                   e-mail: weinbell@delhi.edu
*Linda Weinberg, Disabilities Coordinator*
*Candace , President*

Provide services for students with disabilities. Alternate test-taking arrangements, adapted equipment, assistive technology, accessibility information, note taking services, reading services, tutorial assistance, interpreting services, accessble parking and elevators, sounseling, guidance and support, refferral information and advocacy services, workshops and support groups.

**4901  State University of New York College at Brockport**

State University Of New York SUNY Systems
350 New Campus Drive
Brockport, NY  14420               585-395-5409
                                   800-382-8447
                                   FAX 585-395-5291
                                   TDY:585-395-5409
                                   http://www.brockport.edu
                                   e-mail: osdoffic@brockport.edu
*Maryellen Post, Coordinator*

Provides support and assistance to students with medical, physical, emotional or learning disabilities, specially those experiencing problems in areas such as academic environment.

**4902  State University of New York College of Agriculture and Technology**

Cobleskill, NY  12043              518-255-5282
                                   800-295-8988
                                   FAX 518-255-6430
                                   TDY:518-255-5454
                                   http://www.cobleskill.edu
                                   e-mail: labarno@cobleskill.edu
*Lynn Abarno, Coordinator of Support Services*
*Pat Sprage, Assistant*

The primary objective is to develop and maintain a supportive campus environment that promotes academic achievement and personal growth for students with disabilities. Services provide by the office are based on each student's documentation and are tailored to each student's unique individual needs.

**4903  State University of New York: Albany**

1400 Washington Avenue
Albany, NY  12222                  518-442-5566
                                   FAX 518-442-5589
                                   TDY:518-442-3366
                                   http://www.albany.edu
                                   e-mail: cmalloch@uamail.albany.edu
*Carolyn Malloch, Learning Disabilities Specialist*

The University at Albany offers a wide array of advocacy and support services for students with learning disabilities. We also have a Writing Center, a Center for Computing and Disability, Comprehensive Academic Support Services (tutors, study groups, academic mentoring, study skills workshops). These are excellent resources for LD students. Services include extended time on testing, advocacy with faculty, diagnostic testing, advising and consultation. One week summer transition program offered.

**4904  State University of New York: Buffalo**

Special Services Department
1300 Elmwood Avenue
Buffalo, NY  14260                 716-645-4500
                                   FAX 716-645-3473
                                   http://www.buffalostate.edu
                                   e-mail: savinomr@buffalostate.edu
*Marianne Savino, Coordinator Special Services*

The Office of Disability Services (ODS) is the University at Buffalo's center for coordinating services and accommodations to ensure accessiblity and usability of all programs, services and activities of UB by people with disabilities, and is a resource for information and advocacy toward their full participation in all aspects of campus life.

**4905  State University of New York: College of Technology**

SUNY Farmingdale
Farmingdale, NY  11735             631-420-2000
                                   FAX 631-420-2689
                                   http://www.farmingdale.edu
                                   e-mail: webmaster@farmingdale.edu
*Malka NCC, CRC, MC, Director Support Services*
*Kimberly , Counselor*

Dedicated to the principle that equal opportunity be afforded each student to realize his/her fullest potential. The goal is to assist students with disabilities to function as independently as possible, and to ensure a comprehensively accessible university experience where individuals with disabilities have the same access to programs, opportunities and activities as all other students at the university.

**4906 State University of New York: College at Buffalo**

**Disability Services Department**
**1300 Elmwood Avenue**
**Buffalo, NY 14222**　716-878-4500
FAX 716-878-3804
http://www.buffalostate.edu
e-mail: savinomr@buffalostate.edu
*Marianne Savino, Coordinator*
*Amy Rosenbrand, Accommodations Specialist*

Services provided to approximately 400 students per year with a variety of disabilities, the majority of whom have learning disabilities. All support is determined on a case-by-case basis with a goal toward careers and independence as much as possible in the worksite.

**4907 State University of New York: Fredonia**

**Disabilities Services Office**
**SUNY Fredonia**
**Fredonia, NY 14063**　716-673-3251
800-252-1212
FAX 716-673-3801
TDY:716-673-4763
http://www.fredonia.edu
e-mail: disabilityservices@fredonia.edu
*Carolyn Boone, Coordinator. Disabled Student Se*

Offers a variety of services to students with disabilities including notetakers, extended testing time, counseling services, and special accommodations.

**4908 State University of New York: Geneseo College**

**Office of Disability Services**
**1 College Circle**
**Geneseo, NY 14454**　585-245-5112
FAX 585-245-5032
http://www.admissions.geneseo.edu
e-mail: admissions@geneseo.edu
*Tabitha Buggie-Hunt, Director Disability Services*
*Janet Jackson, Support Staff*

To provide qualified students with disabilities, whether temporary or permanent, equal and comprehensive access to college-wide programs, services, and campus facilities by offering academic support, advisement, and removal of architectural and attitudinal barriers.

**4909 State University of New York: Oneonta**

**State University of New York**
**209 Alumni Hall**
**Oneonta, NY 13820**　607-436-2137
800-SUNY123
FAX 607-436-3167
http://www.oneonta.edu
e-mail: sds@oneonta.edu
*Craig MA, Coordinator*
*Heather Bussy, Keyboard Specialist*

To work with both students and college faculty/staff to ensure that compliance with disability laws is being upheld throughout the institution. SDS is also a resource to students diagnosed with a disability to assist in coordinating services which will lead the student toward receiving and equitable oppportunity at the College at Oneonta.

**4910 State University of New York: Oswego**

**Disability Services Office**
**210 Swetman Hall**
**Oswego, NY 13126**　315-312-3358
FAX 315-312-2943
http://www.oswego.edu
e-mail: dss@oswego.edu
*Starr Knapp, Interim Coordinator*

A public four-year college of arts and sciences currently serving 140 students identified with disabling conditions. Total enrollment is approximately 8,000. Full time coordinator of academic support services for students with disabilities works with students on an individual basis.

**4911 State University of New York: Plattsburgh**

**Student Support Services**
**Angell College Center 110**
**Plattsburgh, NY 12901**　518-564-2810
FAX 518-564-2807
http://www.plattsburgh.edu
e-mail: michele.carpentier@plattsburgh.edu
*Michele Carpentier, Director*

Academic support program funded by the United States Department of Education. Staffed by caring and commited professional whose mission is to provide services for students with disabilities.

**4912 State University of New York: Potsdam**

**Sisson Hall**
**Potsdam, NY 13676**　315-267-3267
FAX 315-267-3268
TDY:315-267-2071
http://www.potsdam.edu
e-mail: housese@potsdam.edu
*Sharon House, Academic Coordinator*

A public four-year college with approximately 200 students with disabilities out of a total of 4,000.

**4913 State University of New York: Stony Brook**

**Disability Support Services**
**128 Educational Communications Cour**
**Stony Brook, NY 11794 2662**　631-632-6748
FAX 631-632-6747
http://www.sunysb.edu
e-mail: dss@notes.cc.sunysb.edu
*Joanna Harris, Director Disability Services*
*Donna Molley, Assistant Director*

Assist students with disabilities in accessing the many resources of the University. Individuals with disabilities are invited to make use of the services and equipment available.

**4914 Suffolk County Community College: Eastern Campus**

Speonk-Riverhead Road
Riverhead, NY 11901　　　631-548-2500
http://www.sunysuffolk.edu
*Judith Koodin, Counselor*

The Eastern Campus is an accessible, open admissions institution. Services are provided to learning disabled students to allow them the same or equivalent educational experiences as nondisabled students.

**4915 Suffolk County Community College: Selden Campus**

533 College Road
Selden, NY 11784　　　631-451-4045
FAX 631-451-4473
http://www.sunysuffolk.edu
*Marlene Boyce, Assistant Director*
*Arlene Zink, Office Manager*
*Harriet Friedheim, Specialist*

Equalizes educational opportunities by minimizing physical, psychological and learning barriers. Attempt to provide as typical a college experience as possible, encouraging students to achieve academically through the provision of special services, support aids, or reasonable program accommodations.

**4916 Suffolk County Community College: Western Campus**

Crooked Hill Road
Brentwood, NY 11717　　　631-451-4045
FAX 631-451-4473
http://www.sunysuffolk.edu
*Judith Taxier-Reinauer, Counselor*
*Cheryl Every-Wartz, Counselor*

The goal of Suffolk Community College with regard to students with disabilities is to equalize educational opportunities by minimizing physical, psychological and learning barriers. We attempt to provide as typical a college experience as is possible, encouraging students to achieve academically through the provision of special services, auxillary aids, or reasonable program modifications.

**4917 Sullivan County Community College**

Learning & Student Development Services
112 College Road
Loch Sheldrake, NY 12759　　　845-434-5750
800-577-5243
FAX 845-434-4806
http://www.sullivan.suny.edu
*Helene Laurenti, Director*

SCCC is fully committed to institutions accessability for individuals with disabilities. Students who wish to obtain particular services or accommodations should communicate their needs and concerns as early as possible. These may include, but are not limited to, extended time for tests, oral examinations,reader and notetaker services, campus maps, and elevator privileges. Books on tape may be ordered through recordings for the blind. Appropriate documentation needed.

**4918 Syracuse University**

Services For Students with Disabilities
804 University Avenue
Syracuse, NY 13244　　　315-443-4498
FAX 315-443-2583
TDY:315-443-1312
http://www.syracuse.edu
e-mail: dtwillia@syr.edu
*Dana Williams, Coordinator Academic Services*
*Cesar Reyes, Administrative Assistant*

The office of disability services provides and coordinates services for students with documented disabilities. Students must provide current documentation of their disability in order to receive disability services and reasonable accommodations.

**4919 Trocaire College**

360 Choate Avenue
Buffalo, NY 14220　　　716-826-1200
FAX 716-828-6107
http://www.trocaire.edu
*Norine Truax, Coordinator*

An independent two-year college with 3 special education students out of a total of 1,056.

**4920 Ulster County Community College**

Student Support Services
Cottekill Road
Stone Ridge, NY 12484　　　845-687-5000
800-724-0833
FAX 845-687-5090
http://www.sunyulster.edu
*James Quirk, Associate Dean*

The Student Support Services program promotes student success for students who are academically disadvantaged, economically disadvantaged, first-generation college students, and or students with disabilities. The goals of the program are to increase the retention, graduation, and transfer rates of those enrolled.

**4921 University of Albany**

Campus Center 130
Albany, NY 12222　　　518-442-5566
FAX 518-442-5589
TDY:518-442-3366
http://www.albany.edu
e-mail: cmalloch@uamail.albany.edu
*Carolyn Malloch, Learning Disability Specialist*

Offers a full time Learning Disability Specialist to work with students that have learning disabilities and or attention deficit disorder. The specialist offers individual appointments to develop study and advocacy skills.

**4922 Utica College of Syracuse University**

1600 Burrstone Road
Utica, NY 13502　　　315-792-3032
800-782-8884
FAX 315-792-3292
http://www.utica.edu
e-mail: KHenkel@utica.edu
*Kateri Henkel, Coordinator Learning Services*
*Stephen Pattarini, Director*

Provides students with disabilities individualized learning accommodations designed to meet the academic needs of the student. Counseling support and the development of new strategies for the learning challenges posed by college level work are an integral part of the services offered through Academic Support Services.

**4923 Vassar College**
124 Raymond Avenue
Poughkeepsie, NY 12604     845-452-7000
FAX 845-437-5715
http://www.assar.edu
e-mail: guthrie@vassar.edu
*Belinda Guthrie, Director*

Offers a variety of services to students with disabilities including note takers, extended testing time, counseling services, and special accommodations.

**4924 Wagner College**
One Campus Road
Staten Island, NY 10301     718-390-3411
800-221-1010
FAX 718-390-3105
http://www.wagner.edu
*Ruth Perri, Director*
*Chris Davis, Administrative Assistant Counsel*

An independent four-year college with 25 special education students out of a total of 1,272. There is an additional fee for the special education program in addition to the regular tuition.

**4925 Westchester Community College**
75 Grasslands Road
Valhalla, NY 10595     914-785-6600
FAX 914-785-6540
http://www.sunywcc.edu
*Alan Seidman MD, Special Services*

Students with Disabilities parallels the mission of WCC to be accessible, community centered, comprehensive, adaptable and dedicated to lifelong learning for all students. Full participation for students with disabilities is encouraged.

## North Carolina

**4926 Appalachian State University**
Learning Disability Program
ASU Box 32087
Boone, NC 28608     828-262-2291
FAX 828-262-6834
http://www.ods.appstate.edu
e-mail: wehnerst@appstate.edu
*Suzanne Wehner, Director*
*Joy Clawson, Director for Learning Assistance*

Disabled Student Services assists students with indentified learning disabilities by providing the support they need to become successful college graduates. Disabled Student Services provides academic advising, alternative testing, assistance with technology, tutoring, practical solutions to learning problems, counseling, self-concept building and career exploration.

**4927 Bennett College**
900 E Washington Street
Greensboro, NC 27401     336-273-4431
800-413-5323
FAX 336-273-4431
http://www.bennett.edu
*Mary Stuart, Support Services*

An independent four-year college with 10 special education students out of a total of 568.

**4928 Brevard College**
Office for Students with Special Needs
400 N Broad Street
Brevard, NC 28712     828-883-8292
FAX 828-884-3790
http://www.brevard.edu
e-mail: skuehn@brevard.edu
*Susan Keen, Director*

Four year college provides services to special needs students.

**4929 Caldwell Community College and Technical Institute**
Basic Skills Department
2855 Hickory Boulvard
Hudson, NC 28638     828-726-2200
FAX 828-726-2216
http://www.cccti.edu
e-mail: ccrump@cccti.edu
*Christie Crump, Director*
*Cindy Richards, Administrative Assistant*

A public two-year college with 18 special education students out of a total of 2,744.

**4930 Catawba College**
Learning Disability Department
2300 W Innes Street
Salisbury, NC 28144     704-637-4259
800-228-2922
FAX 704-637-4401
http://www.catawba.edu
e-mail: ekgross@catawba.edu
*Emily Gross, Director*
*Julie Baranski, Office Assistant*

An independent four-year liberal arts college with an enrollment of 1,400.

**4931 Catawba Valley Community College**
Student Services Office
2550 Highway 70 SE
Hickory, NC 28602     828-327-7000
FAX 828-327-7276
http://www.cvcc.edu
e-mail: dulin@cvcc.edu
*William Dulin, Dean*

The following is a partial list of accommodations provided by the college: counseling services, tutors, note-takers and carbonless duplication paper, recorded textbooks, tape recorders for taping lecture classes, interpeters, computer with voice software, and extended time for texts. Catawba Valley Community College provides services for students with disabilities.

**4932  Central Carolina Community College**
1105 Kelly Drive
Sanford, NC  27330                         919-775-5401
                                           FAX 919-718-7380
http://www.ccarolina.cc.nc.us
*Frances Andrews MD, Associate Dean*

Adopted to guide its delivery of services to students with disabilities that states that no otherwise qualified individual shall by reason of disability be excluded from the participation in, be denied benefits of, or be subjected to discrimination under any program at Central Carolina Community College. The college will make program modification adjustments in instructional delivery and provide supplemental services.

**4933  Central Piedmont Community College**
Learning Disability Department
PO Box 35009
Charlotte, NC  28235                        704-330-6556
                                           FAX 704-330-4020
                                           TDY:704-330-6421
http://www.cpcc.cc.nc.us
e-mail: patricia.adams@cpcc.edu
*Pat Goings-Adams, Learning Disabilities Counselor*

A public two-year college with 300 special education students out of a total of 60,000.

**4934  Craven Community College**
Craven Community College
800 College Court
New Bern, NC  28562                         252-638-7274
                                           FAX 252-672-8020
                                           TDY:252-638-8634
http://www.craven.cc.nc.us
e-mail: harris@cravencc.edu
*Charles Tfautz, Director*
*Opal Harris, Desk Assistant*

Offers a variety of services to students with disabilities including notetakers, extended testing time, counseling services, and special accommodations.

**4935  Davidson County Community College**
PO Box 1287
Lexington, NC  27293                        336-249-8186
                                           FAX 336-249-0088
http://www.davidsonccc.edu
e-mail: emorse@davidsonccc.edu
*Ed Morse MD, Dean*
*Mary , President*

Offers a variety of services to students with disabilities including notetakers, extended testing time, counseling services, and special accommodations.

**4936  Dore Academy**
Dore Academy
1727 Providence Road
Charlotte, NC  28207                        704-365-5490
                                           FAX 704-365-3240
http://www.doreacademy.org
e-mail: ecommendatore@doreacademy.org
*Mary Dore, Founder*
*Erin Commendatore, Admissions Director*

Dore Academy is Charlotte's oldest college-prep school for students with learning differences. A private, non-profit, independent day school for students in grades 1-12, it is approved by the state of North Carolina, Division of Exceptional children. All teachers are certified by the state and trained in the theory and treatment of dyslexia and attention disorders. With a maximum of 10 students per class ( 5 in reading classes), the teacher student ratio is 1 to 7.

**4937  East Carolina University**
E 5th Street
Greenville, NC  27858                       252-328-6131
http://www.ecu.edu
*CC Rowe, Coordinator*

A public four-year college with 47 special education students out of a total of 13,903.

**4938  Forsyth Technical Community College**
2100 Silas Creek Parkway
Winston-Salem, NC  27103                    336-734-7248
                                           FAX 336-761-2399
                                           TDY:336-723-3411
http://www.forsyth.tec.edu
e-mail: pcompton@forsyth.tec.edu
*Van Wilson, Vice President*
*Paula Compton, Director*

Offers a variety of services to students with disabilities including notetakers, extended testing time, counseling services, and special accommodations.

**4939  Gardner-Webb University**
Noel Program
PO Box 997
Boiling Springs, NC  28017                  704-406-4000
                                           FAX 704-406-3524
http://www.gardner-webb.edu
e-mail: sjennings@gardner-webb.edu
*Sharon Jennings, Director*

Four year college that provides a program for disabled students.

**4940  Guilford Technical Community College**
601 High Point Road
Jamestown, NC  27282                        336-454-1126
                                           FAX 336-454-2510
http://www.gtcc.cc.nc.us
e-mail: dcameron@gtcc.cc.nc.us
*Don Cameron, President*
*Sonny White, Vice President*

The purpose of disability access services is to provide equal access and comprehensive, quality services to all students who experience barriers to academic, personal and social success.

**4941  Isothermal Community College**
Department of Disability Services
PO Box 804
Spindale, NC  28160                         828-286-3636
                                           FAX 828-286-8109
                                           TDY:828-286-3636
http://www.isothermal.cc.nc.us
e-mail: kharris@isothermal.cc.nc.us
*Karen Harris, Director*

Isothermal Community College, in compliance with the Americans with Disabilities Act, makes every effort to provide accommodations for students with disabilities. It is our goal to integrate students with disabilities into the college and help them participate and benefit from programs and activities enjoyed by all students. We at Isothermal are committed to improving life through learning.

**4942 Johnson C Smith University**

**Disability Support Services Department**
**100 Beatties Ford Road**
**Charlotte, NC 28216**          **704-378-1282**
                            **FAX 704-330-1336**
                      **http://www.jcsu.edu**
                **e-mail: jcuthbertson@jcsu.edu**
*James Cuthbertson, Coordinator*
*James Saunders, Director*

Four year college that provides support to those who are disabled.

**4943 Lenoir Community College**

**North Carolina Community College System**
**231 Highway 58 S**
**Kinston, NC 28502**          **252-527-6223**
                            **FAX 252-527-1199**
                      **http://www.lenoir.cc.edu**
                **e-mail: bsanders@lenoircc.edu**
*Joy Tucker, Evening Counselor*
*Bertie Sanders, Director of Human Resource*

Lenoir Community College is committed to serving the needs of students with disabilities. If special assistance is needed, please give the college prior notice by contacting the ADA Coordinator.

**4944 Lenoir-Rhyne College**

**PO Box 7470**
**Hickory, NC 28603**          **828-328-7296**
                            **FAX 828-328-7329**
                      **http://www.lrc.edu**
                **e-mail: kirbydr@lrc.edu**
*Donavon Kirby, Coordinator*

Four year college that provides services for those students that are learning disabled.

**4945 Louisburg College**

**501 N Main Street**
**Louisburg, NC 27587**          **919-497-3216**
                            **FAX 919-496-1788**
                      **http://www.louisburg.edu**
*Jayne Davis, Director*

A two-year college that offers programs for the learning disabled.

**4946 Mars Hill College**

**124 Cascade Street**
**Mars Hill, NC 28754**          **828-689-1201**
                                  **800-543-1514**
                            **FAX 828-689-1274**
                      **http://www.mhc.edu**
                **e-mail: ccain@mhc.edu**
*Chris Cain, Director*
*Coorny Wood, Assistant Director*

An independent four-year college with 15 special education students out of a total of 1,321.

**4947 Mayland Community College**

**Support Options for Achievement and Retention**
**PO Box 547**
**Spruce Pine, NC 28777**          **828-765-7351**
                                  **800-462-9526**
                      **http://www.mayland.edu**
                **e-mail: dcagle@mayland.edu**
*Nancy Godwin, Director*
*Debra Cagle, Administrative Assistant*

Offers a variety of services to students with disabilities including notetakers, extended testing time, counseling services, and special accommodations.

**4948 McDowell Technical Community College**

**Student Enrichment Center**
**54 Universal Drive**
**Marion, NC 28752**          **828-652-6021**
                            **FAX 828-652-1014**
                  **http://www.mcdowelltech.cc.nc.us**
                **e-mail: donnashort@cc.nc.us**
*Donna Short, Admissions Director*

A public two-year college with 15 special education students out of a total of 857. Free auxiliary services for LD students include: tutors, books on tape, unlimited testing, oral testing, notetakers and counseling. All faculty are trained in working with the LD student.

**4949 Meredith College**

**Disability Counseling Office**
**Disability Services**
**Raleigh, NC 27607**          **919-760-8427**
                                  **800-637-3348**
                            **FAX 919-760-2383**
                      **http://www.meredith.edu**
                **e-mail: disabilityservices@meredith.edu**
*Betty Prevatt, Coordinator/Assistant Director*
*Beth Meier, Director*

The college goal is to create an accessible community where people are judged on their abilities not their disabilities. The Disability Services staff strives to provide individuals with the tools by which they can better accomplish their educational goals.

**4950 Montgomery Community College: North Carolina**

**1011 Page Street**
**Troy, NC 27371**          **910-576-6222**
                            **FAX 910-576-2176**
                      **http://www.montgomery.cc.nc.us**
*Virginia Morgan MD, Chairperson*

Offers a variety of services to students with disabilities including note takers, extended testing time, counseling services, and special accommodations.

**4951 North Carolina State University**

**Box 7509**
**Raleigh, NC 27695**          **919-515-7653**
                            **FAX 919-513-2840**
                            **TDY:919-515-8830**
                      **http://www.ncsu.edu/dss**
                **e-mail: cheryl_branker@ncsu.edu**
*Cheryl Branker, Director*

Academic accommodations and services are provided for students at the university who have documented learning disabilities. Admission to the university is based on academic qualifications and learning disabled students are considered in the same manner as any other student. Special assistance is available to accommodate the needs of these students, including courses in accessible locations when appropriate.

**4952  North Carolina Wesleyan College**

**North Carolina Wesleyan College
3400 N Wesleyan Boulevard
Rocky Mount, NC  27804**          252-985-5269
800-488-6292
FAX 252-985-5284
http://www.ncwc.edu
e-mail: albunn.infowc@edu
*Elizabeth Lanchaster, Assistant Registrar
Cliff Sullivan, Registrar*

The Center provides support to students interested in achieving academic success. The staff works to provide you with information about academic matters and serves as an advocate for you. Services focus on pre-major advising, tutoring, mentoring, skills enrichment, disabilities assistance, self-assessment and retention.

**4953  Peace College**

**15 E Peace Street
Raleigh, NC  29604**          919-508-2293
FAX 919-508-2326
http://www.peace.edu
e-mail: amann@peace.edu
*Ann F Mann MD, Director*

Four year college offering programs to disabled students.

**4954  Piedmont Baptist College**

**716 Franklin Street
Winston-Salem, NC  27101**          336-725-8344
FAX 336-725-5522
http://www.pbc.edu
e-mail: cpetitt@pbc.edu
*Charles Petitt MD, President
Paul Holrtic, Vice President*

A four year college offering comprehensive programs for students with learning disabilities.

**4955  Pitt Community College**

**Pitt Community College
Highway 11 S
Greenville, NC  27835**          252-321-4294
FAX 252-321-4401
http://www.pitt.cc.edu
e-mail: mbribg@email.pittcc.edu
*Mike Bridgers, Coordinator Disability Services*

The staff of Disability Servics looks forward to working with you to achieve your immediate academic and long range career goals. Our office is designed to provide academic, personal and technical support services to students with disabilities who qualify for post secondary education, but whose deficits are such that they are unlikely to succeed in college without thoses services.

**4956  Randolph Community College**

**629 Industrial Park Avenue
Asheboro, NC  27204**          336-633-0227
FAX 336-629-4695
http://www.randolf.edu
e-mail: jbranch@randolf.edu
*Joyce Branch, Director Special Services
Rebekah Megerian, Basic Skills*

A public two-year college with 23 special education students out of a total of 1,487. Applicants with disabilities who wish to request accommodations in compliance with the ADA must identify themselves to the admissions counselor before placement testing.

**4957  Rockingham Community College**

**Highway 65 West and County Home Ro
Wentworth, NC  27375**          336-342-4261
FAX 336-349-9986
TDY:336-634-0132
http://www.rcc.cc.nc.us
e-mail: rkeys@rcc.cc.nc.us
*Robert C Keys MD, President
William , Vice President*

Offers a variety of services to students with disabilities including notetakers, extended testing time, counseling services, and special accommodations.

**4958  Salem College**

**S Church Street
Winston-Salem, NC  27108**          336-721-2600
FAX 336-721-2683
http://www.salem.edu
e-mail: smith@salem.edu
*Micha Jeffries, Teacher Education Director*

Offers a variety of services to students with disabilities including notetakers, extended testing time, counseling services, and special accommodations.

**4959  Sandhills Community College**

**3395 Airport Road
Pinehurst, NC  28374**          910-695-3733
800-338-3944
FAX 910-695-1823
http://www.sandhills.cc.nc.us
*Peggie Chavis, Disabilities Coordinator*

Offers a variety of services to students with disabilities including notetakers, extended testing time, counseling services, and special accommodations.

**4960  Southwestern Community College: North Carolina**

**447 College Drive
Sylva, NC  28779**          828-586-4091
800-447-4091
FAX 828-586-3129
http://www.southwesterncc.edu
e-mail: cheryl@southwest.cc.nc.us
*Cheryl Conner, Director*

Southwestern Community College provides equal access to education for persons with disabilities. It is the responsibility of the student to make their disability known and to request academic adjustments. Requests should be made in a timely manner and submitted to the Director of Student Support Services. Every reasonable effort will be made to provide service, however, not requesting services prior to registration may delay implementation.

**4961 St Andrews Presbyterian College**

1700 Dogwood Mile
Laurinburg, NC 28387      910-277-5331
                         FAX 910-277-5020
                         http://www.sapc.edu
                         e-mail: info@sapc.edu

Four year college that supports and provides services to the learning disabled students.

**4962 Stone Mountain School**

126 Camp Elliott Road
Black Mountain, NC 28711      828-669-8639
                              FAX 828-669-2521
        http://www.stonemountainschool.org
        e-mail: smoore@stonemountainschool.com
*Sam Moore, Executive Director*
*Paige Thomas, Admissions Director*

**4963 Surry Community College**

630 S Main Street
Dobson, NC 27017      336-386-8121
                      FAX 336-386-8951
        http://www.surry.cc.nc.us
        e-mail: riggsj@surry.edu
*Laura Bracken, Special Programs*
*Judy Riggs, Dean of Continuing Education*

Offers a variety of services to students with disabilities including notetakers, extended testing time, counseling services, and special accommodations.

**4964 Tri-County Community College**

4600 E US 64
Murphy, NC 28906      828-837-6810
                      FAX 828-837-3266
                      TDY:724-228-4028
        http://www.tccc.cc.nc.us
*Sarah Harper, Executive Director*

Offers a variety of services to students with disabilities including notetakers, extended testing time, counseling services, and special accommodations.

**4965 University of North Carolina: Chapel Hill**

Learning Disabilities Services
137 E Franklin Street
Chapel Hill, NC 27514      919-962-7227
                           FAX 919-962-3674
                           http://www.unc.edu
                           e-mail: lds@email.unc.edu
*Theresa Maitlan MD, Learning Disabilities Specialist*

Promotes learning by providing academic support to meet the individual needs of students diagnosed with specific learning disabilities. Strives to ensure the independence of participating students so that they may succeed during and beyond their university years.

**4966 University of North Carolina: Charlotte**

Special Education Department
9201 University Boulevard
Charlotte, NC 28223      704-687-2213
                         FAX 704-687-3353
                         http://www.uncc.edu
                         e-mail: abennett@email.uncc.edu
*Gail Honeycutt, Accounting Technician*
*Ann Bennett, Office Manager*

Introduction to Students with Special Needs. Characteristics of students with special learning needs, including those who are gifted and those who experience academic, social, emotional, physical and developmental disabilities. Legal, historical and philosophical foudations of special education and current issues in providing appropriate educational services to students with special needs.

**4967 University of North Carolina: Greensboro**

Disability Services
215 Elliott University Center
Greensboro, NC 27402      336-334-5440
                          FAX 336-334-4412
                          TDY:336-334-5440
                          http://www.uncg.edu/ods
                          e-mail: ods@uncg.edu
*Mary Culkin, Director*
*Laura Ripplinger, Office Manager*

A public four-year university with over 300 students with disabilities out of a total of 12,000.

**4968 University of North Carolina: Wilmington**

Disability Services Department
601 S College Road
Wilmington, NC 28403-5942      910-962-3746
                               FAX 910-962-7556
                               TDY:910-962-3853
        http://www.uncw.edu/stuaff/sds\disability
                               e-mail: stonec@uncw.edu
*Margaret PhD, Disability Services*
*Chris Stone, Office Manager*

Offer accommodative services, consultation, counseling and advocacy for Disabled Students enrolled at UNCW.

**4969 Wake Forest University**

1834 Wake Forest Road
Winston-Salem, NC 27109      336-758-5000
                             FAX 336-758-6074
                             http://www.wfu.edu
*Thomas Hearn, President*
*John Anderson, Vice President*

Offers a variety of services to students with disabilities including notetakers, extended testing time, counseling services, and special accommodations.

**4970 Wake Technical Community College**

Disabilities Support Department
9101 Fayetteville Road
Raleigh, NC 27603      919-662-3405
                       FAX 919-662-3564
                       TDY:919-779-0668
                       http://www.waketech.edu
                       e-mail: jtkillen@waketech.edu
*Janet Killen, Director*
*Elaine Sardi, Coordinator*

If you are a person with a documented disability who requires accommodations to achieve equal access to Wake Tech facilities, academic programs or other activities, you may request reasonable accommodations.

**4971 Western Carolina University**

Student Support Services
137 Killian Annex
Cullowhee, NC 28723          828-227-7127
FAX 828-227-7078
http://www.wcu.edu
e-mail: mellen@wcu.edu

*Carol Mellen, Director*
*Suzanne Baker, Adviser*

Students with a documented disability may be provided with appropriate academic accommodations such as, note takers, testing accomadations, books on tape, readers/scribes, use of adaptive equipment and priority registration.

**4972 Wilkes Community College**

Student Support Services
PO Box 120
Wilkesboro, NC 28697          336-838-6560
FAX 336-838-6277
http://www.wilkes.cc.nc.us
e-mail: nancy.sizemore@wilkescc.edu

*Kim Faw, Director*
*Nancy Sizemore, Disability Coordinator*

A public two-year community college. Special services include: testing and individualized education plans; oral and extended time testing; individual and small group tutoring; study skills; readers and proctors and specialized equipment.

**4973 Wilson County Technical College**

North Carolina Community College System
902 Herring Avenue
Wilson, NC 27893          252-246-1261
FAX 252-243-7148
TDY:252-246-1362
http://www.wilsontech.edu

*William James, Student Support Services*
*Thelma McAllister, Secretary*

Offers a variety of services to students with disabilities including notetakers, extended testing time, counseling services, and special accommodations.

**4974 Wingate University**

Disability Services Department
220 N Camden Street
Wingate, NC 28174          704-233-8000
800-755-5550
FAX 704-233-8290
http://www.wingate.edu

*Linda Stedje-Larsen, Director*

An independent four-year college with 50 special education students out of a total of 1,372. There is an additional fee for the special education program in addition to the regular tuition.

**4975 Winston-Salem State University**

302 Hauser Building
Winston-Salem, NC 27110          336-750-2000
FAX 336-750-2392
http://www.wssu.edu\fyc

*Myra Watdell, Director*

Offers a variety of services to students with disabilities including notetakers, extended testing time, counseling services, and special accommodations.

# North Dakota

**4976 Bismarck State College**

1500 Edwards Avenue
Bismarck, ND 58506          701-224-5426
800-445-5073
FAX 701-224-5550
http://www.bsc.nodak.edu
e-mail: lschlafm@gwmail.nodak.edu
*Lisa Schlafman, Coordinator/Disability Support*

Offers a variety of services to students with disabilities including notetakers, extended testing time, counseling services, and special accommodations.

**4977 Dickinson State University**

Student Support Services
291 Campus Drive
Dickinson, ND 58601          701-483-2029
FAX 701-783-2006
http://www.dsu.nodak.edu
e-mail: richardpadilla@dickinsonstate.edu
*Richard Padilla, Planner/Coordinator*

Four year college offers support services to learning disabled students.

**4978 Fort Berthold Community College**

PO Box 490
New Town, ND 58763          701-627-3665
FAX 701-627-3609
http://www.spcc.bia.edu
e-mail: lgwin@spcc.bia.edu
*Susan Paulson, Academic Dean of Students*

An independent two-year college with 3 special education students out of a total of 279.

**4979 Mayville State University**

Learning Disabilities Department
330 3rd Street NE
Mayville, ND 58257          701-788-2301
800-437-4104
FAX 701-788-4748
http://www.mayvillestate.edu
e-mail: kyllo@mayvillestate.edu
*Greta Kyllo, Academic Support Director*

Offers a variety of services to students with disabilities including notetakers, extended testing time, counseling services, and special accommodations.

**4980  Minot State University: Bottineau Campus**

Special Services Office
105 Simrall Boulevard
Bottineau, ND  58318            701-228-5487
                                800-542-6866
                            FAX 701-228-5499
                    http://www.misu-b.nodak.edu
                e-mail: jan.nahinurk@misu.nodak.edu
*Jan Nahinurk, Director*

Offers a variety of services to students with disabilities including notetakers, extended testing time, counseling services, and special accommodations.

**4981  North Dakota Center for Persons with Disabilities (NDCPD)**

Minot State University
500 University Avenue W
Minot, ND  58707                701-858-3580
                                800-233-1737
                            FAX 701-858-3483
                            TDY:701-858-3580
                         http://www.ndcpd.org
                 e-mail: ndcpd@minotstateu.edu
*Bryce Fifield, Director*
*Susie Mack, Office Manager*

NDCPD works with the disability community, university, faculty and researchers, policy makers and service providers to identify emerging needs in the disability community and how to obtain resources to address them.

**4982  North Dakota State College of Science**

Disabilities Services Office
800 N 6th Street
Wahpeton, ND  58076             701-671-2623
                                800-342-4325
                            FAX 701-671-2440
                    http://www.ndscs.nodak.edu
                e-mail: joy.eichhorn@ndscs.nodak.edu
*Joy Eichhorn, Disability Services Director*

A public two-year comprehensive college with a student population of 2400. Students with disabilites comprise seven percent of the population. Tuition $2025.

**4983  North Dakota State University**

Counseling & Disability Services
212 Ceres Hall
Fargo, ND  58105                701-231-7671
                            FAX 701-231-6318
                            TDY:800-366-6888
                    http://www.ndsu.edu/counselling
                e-mail: jennifer.erickson@ndsu.edu
*Jennifer Erickson, LD Specialist*
*Tiffany Bendixon, Coordinator*

Provides comprehensive services for students who have learning disabilities. Staff can explain how to access services, provide initial consultation regarding the possible presence of learning, emotional or physical disabilities that hinder academic performance. Consult with students, faculty and staff to determine and provide appropriate accommodations. Assist in arranging for accommodations.

**4984  Standing Rock College**

1341 92nd Street
Fort Yates, ND  58538           701-854-3861
                            FAX 701-854-3403
                    http://www.sittingbull.edu
*Linda Ivan, Special Services*

Offers a variety of services to students with disabilities including notetakers, extended testing time, counseling services, and special accommodations.

# Ohio

**4985  Antioch College**

Academic Support Center
795 Livermore Street
Yellow Springs, OH  45387           937-769-1166
                                    800-543-9436
                                FAX 937-769-1163
                    http://www.antioch-college.edu
                e-mail: lizek@antioch-college.edu
*Elizabeth Kennedy, Director*
*John Smith, Assistant Director*

Comprehensive integrated support, including tutoring, time management and organization support, software, accommodations for our academic and cooperative education programs.

**4986  Art Academy of Cincinnati**

1125 Saint Gregory Street
Cincinnati, OH  45202               513-721-5205
                                    800-323-5692
                                FAX 513-562-8778
                        http://www.artacadamy.edu
*Jane Stanton, Dean of Students*
*Sarah Mulhauser, Director of Student Services*

Offers a variety of services to students with disabilities including notetakers, extended testing time, counseling services, and special accommodations.

**4987  Baldwin-Wallace College**

275 Eastland Road
Berea, OH  44017                    440-826-2900
                                FAX 440-826-3830
                            http://www.bw.edu
*Mark Collier, President*
*Obobie Brender, Executive Assistant*

Offers a variety of services to students with disabilities including notetakers, extended testing time, counseling services, and special accommodations.

**4988  Bluffton College**

Special Student Services
280 W College Avenue
Bluffton, OH  45817                 419-358-3458
                                FAX 419-358-3323
                            http://www.bluffton.edu
                    e-mail: bergerd@bluffton.edu
*Timothy Byers, Program Contact*

Four year college offers special programs to learninig disabled students.

**4989  Bowling Green State University**

413 S Hall
Bowling Green, OH  43403          419-372-8495
                                  FAX 419-372-8496
                      http://www.bgsu.edu
              e-mail: rcunnin@bgnet.bgsu.edu
*Robert Cunningham, Director*

The Disability Services Office is evidence of Bowling Green State University's commitment to provide a support system which assists in conquering obstacles that persons with disabilities may encounter as they pursue their educational goals and activities. Our hope is to facilitate mainstream mobility and recognize the diverse talents that persons with disabilities have to offer to our university and our community.

**4990  Case Western Reserve University**

10900 Euclid Avenue
Cleveland, OH  44106              216-368-2000
                                  FAX 216-368-8826
                      http://www.cwru.edu
*Susan Sampson, Coordinator Disability Services*

While all students will have preferences for learning, students with physical or learning disabilities have different actual needs as well. Students with physical disabilities such as visual impairments, hearing impairments, or temporary or permanent motor impairments may need guide dogs, interpeters, note-takers, wheelchair accessible rooms, or other types of assistance to help them attend and participate in class. Also available, extra time or a separate room for exams, tutoring and more.

**4991  Center for the Advancement of Learning**

PLUS Program/Muskingum College
Montgomery Hall
New Concord, OH  43762            740-826-8280
                                  800-752-6082
                                  FAX 740-826-8285
                      http://www.muskingum.edu
              e-mail: butler@muskingum.edu
*Jen Navicky, Director*

A professional, adult staff provides two levels of academic support and currently serves 150 learning disabled students. Support includes all reasonable accommodations and intensive one-on-one and small group tutoring. Learning Strategy instruction is embedded within course contents. Full services include a minimum of one hour of tutoring each week and students average 3-5 hours. Maintenance level services are flexibly arranged for half that amount. The Program has excellent faculty.

**4992  Central Ohio Technical College**

Developmental Education
1179 University Drive
Newark, OH  43055                 740-366-1351
                                  800-963-9275
                                  FAX 740-364-9641
                      http://www.cotc.edu
*Phyllis Thompso MD, Coordinator*
*Bunnie , President*

Learning Assitance Center and Disability Services (LAC/DS) is the academic support unit in Student Support Services. LAC/DS provides FREE programs and services designed to help students sharpen skills necessary to succeed in college.

**4993  Central State University**

Office of Disability Services
1400 Brush Row Road
Wilberforce, OH  45384            937-376-6411
                                  FAX 937-376-6661
                      http://www.centralstate.edu
              e-mail: info@csu.ces.edu
*John Garland, President*
*Carlos Vargas-Aburto, Vice President*

Four year college that provides services for the learning disabled students.

**4994  Cincinnati State Technical and Community College**

3520 Central Parkway
Cincinnati, OH  45223             513-569-1613
                                  FAX 516-569-1562
                      http://www.cinstate.cc.oh.us
              e-mail: dcover@cinstate.cc.oh.us
*David Cover, Counselor of Special Needs*
*Ron , President*

Services include assistance and support services for students with permanent and temporary disabilities, test proctoring, readers/scribes, taping, tape recording loan, reading machines, assistance with locating interpeters, mediating between student and faculty to overcome specific disability issues; also offers braille access.

**4995  Clark State Community College**

Disability Retention Center
570 E Leffel Lane
Springfield, OH  45505            937-328-6019
                                  FAX 937-328-6142
                      http://www.clark.cc.oh.us
*Deborah Titus, Counselor*
*Mary , Disability Retention Specialist*

In accordance with the Americans with Disabilities Act, it is the policy of Clark State Community College to provide reasonable accommodations to persons with disabilities. The office of disability services offers a variety of services to Clark State students who have documented physical, mental or learning disabilities.

**4996  Cleveland Institute of Art**

Academic Services
11141 E Boulevard
Cleveland, OH  44106              216-421-7462
                                  800-278-6446
                                  FAX 216-754-2557
                      http://www.cia.edu
              e-mail: jmilenski@gate.cia.edu
*Jill Milenski, Associate Director*
*Rachel Browner, Director*

No student should be discouraged from attending CIA because of a learning disability. A student working on their BFA degree at the Institute of Art can get academic support from the tutoring director in the Office of Academic Services. Services include books-on-tape, one-on-one tutoring, alternative curriculum advising, notetaking services, alternative test taking and assignment arrangements. Services outside the scope of the program can be arranged at the student's expense.

## 4997 Cleveland State University

**1983 E 24th Street**
**Cleveland, OH 44115**            216-687-2000
                                   888-278-6446
                               FAX 216-687-9366
                          http://www.csuohio.edu
                    e-mail: m.zuccaro@csuohio.edu
*Michael Zuccaro, Disability Services*

CSU aims to provide equal opportunity to all of its students. Services are available to those who might need some extra help because of a physical disability, communication impairment or learning disability. This program is designed to address the personal and academic issues of the physically handicapped students as they become oriented to campus. A full range of services is offered.

## 4998 College of Mount Saint Joeseph

**Project EXCEL**
**5701 Delhi Road**
**Cincinnati, OH 45233**           513-244-4623
                                   800-654-9314
                               FAX 513-244-4222
                            http://www.msj.edu
               e-mail: jane_pohlman@mail.msj.edu
*Jane Pohlman, Director*

Learning disabled staff offers intensive instruction in reading, writing and study skills.

## 4999 College of Wooster

**1189 Beall Avenue**
**Wooster, OH 44691**              330-263-2000
                          http://www.wooster.edu
*Carol Roose MD*

Offers a variety of services to students with disabilities including notetakers, extended testing time, counseling services, and special accommodations.

## 5000 Columbus State Community College: Department of Disability Services

**550 E Spring Street**
**Columbus, OH 43215**             614-287-2570
                                   800-621-6407
                               FAX 614-287-6054
                            TDY:614-287-2570
     http://www.cscc.edu/docs/disability/intro.html
                     e-mail: wcocchi@cscc.edu
*Wayne Cocchi, Director*
*Val Moeller, President*

A public two-year college serving qualified students with disabilities, including learning disabilities. Support services are provided based on disability documentation and can include, books, tapes, alternative testing, notetaking, counseling, equipment use, reader, scribe, and peer tutoring.

## 5001 Cuyahoga Community College: Eastern Campus

**Government Funded College**
**4250 Richmond Road**
**Highland Hills, OH 44122**       216-987-2034
                               FAX 216-987-2423
                            TDY:216-987-2230
         http://www.tri-c.edu/home/default.htm
           e-mail: Maryann.Syarto@tri-c.cc.oh.us
*Mary Sender, LD Director*
*Charlotte Burgin, Tutor*

The ACCESS Programs strive to assist Tri-C students with disabilities to realize their learning potential, bring them into the mainstream of the College community, enhance their self-sufficiency, and enable them to achieve academic success. Services include tuoring, test proctoring, interpreters, adaptive equipment, readers and/or scribes for exams, alternative test taking arrangements, alternative format for printed materials and textbooks on tape.

## 5002 Cuyahoga Community College: Western Campus

**1000 W Pleasant Valley Road**
**Parma, OH 44130**                216-987-5077
                               FAX 516-987-5050
                            TDY:516-987-5117
                          http://www.tri-c.edu
                 e-mail: rose.kolovrat@tri-c.edu
*Rose Kolovrat, Director*

The ACCESS programs strive to assist Tri-C students with disabilities to realize their learning potential, bring them into the mainstream of the College community, enhance their self-suffciency and enable them to achieve academic success. Services provided include tutoring, test proctoring, interpeters, adaptive equipment, readers/scribes for exams, alternative testing arrangements, alternative format for printed material and textbooks on tape.

## 5003 Defiance College

**701 N Clinton Street**
**Defiance, OH 43512**             419-784-4010
                                   800-520-4632
                               FAX 419-784-0426
                          http://www.defiance.edu
                 e-mail: admissions@defiance.edu
*Debbie Stevens, Assistant Director*
*Mark Thompson, Dean*

Offers a variety of services to students with disabilities including notetakers, extended testing time, counseling services, and special accommodations.

## 5004 Denison University

**Denison University**
**104 Doane Hall**
**Granville, OH 43023**            740-587-6666
                                   800-336-4766
                               FAX 740-587-5629
                          http://www.denison.edu
                   e-mail: vestal@denison.edu
*Jennifer Vestal, Associate Dean*
*Abby Ghering, Assistant Dean*

The Office of Academic Support (OAS) offers a wide range of services for students with disabilities. In supporting our students as they move forward toward graduation and the world of work beyond, we strongly encourage and promote self advocacy regarding disability related issues.

**5005 Franklin University**
201 S Grant Avenue
Columbus, OH 43215      614-341-6237
877-341-6300
FAX 614-224-0434
http://www.franklin.edu
*Carla Marshall, Adviser Disabilities Services*
*Paul , President*

Students who have disabilities may notify the University of their status by checking the appropriate space on the registration form each trimester. Then the Coordinator of Disability Services will help them file proper documentation so that accommodations can be made for their learning needs.

**5006 Hiram College**
Hiram College
Hiram, OH 44234      330-569-3211
FAX 330-569-5398
http://www.hiram.edu
*Lynn Taylor, Counseling Director*

Offers a variety of services to students with disabilities including notetakers, extended testing time, counseling services, and special accommodations.

**5007 Hocking College**
Hocking College
3301 Hocking Parkway
Nelsonville, OH 45764      740-753-3591
800-282-4163
FAX 740-753-4097
http://www.hocking.edu
e-mail: forbes_k@hocking.edu
*Kim Powell, Coordinator*
*Rosie Smith, Director*

The Access Center Office of Disability Support Services is dedicated to serving the various needs of individuals with disabilities and promoting their participation in college life.

**5008 Hocking Technical College**
Hocking Technical College
3301 Hocking Parkway
Nelsonville, OH 45764      740-753-3591
800-282-4163
FAX 740-753-1452
http://www.hocking.edu
e-mail: forbes_k@hocking.edu
*Kim Powell, Coordinator*
*Rosie Smith, Director*

Offers a variety of services to students with disabilities including notetakers, extended testing time, counseling services, and special accommodations.

**5009 ITT Technical Institute**
1030 N Meridian Road
Youngstown, OH 44509-4098      330-270-1600
800-832-5001
*Frank Quartini, Educational Director*

Offers a variety of services to students with disabilities including note takers, extended testing time, counseling services, and special accommodations.

**5010 Kent State University**
Student Disability Services
181 MSC
Kent, OH 44242      330-672-3391
FAX 330-672-3763
http://www.kent.edu/sds
e-mail: ajannaro@kent.edu
*Anne Jannarone, Director*

Student Disability Services (SDS) provides assistance to students with varying degrees and types of disabilities in order to maximize educational opportunity and academic potential. Types of disabilities that students have who are served by SDS include mobility impairments, visual, hearing or speech impairments, specific learning disabilities, attention deficit disorder, chronic health disorders, psychological disabilities and temporary disabilities.

**5011 Kent State University: Tuscarawas Academic Services**
330 University Drive NE
New Philadelphia, OH 44663      330-339-3391
FAX 330-308-7575
TDY:330-339-7888
http://www.tusc.kent.edu
e-mail: www@tusc.kent.edu
*Fran Haldar MD, Assistant Dean*
*Gregg , Dean*

Offers a variety of services to students with disabilities including notetakers, extended testing time and special accommodations.

**5012 Lorain County Community College**
1005 N Abbe Road
Elyria, OH 44035      440-365-4191
800-955-5222
FAX 440-366-4127
http://www.lorainccc.edu
*Ruth Porter, Coordinator*

LCCC serves over 80 learning disabled students per year out of a total student population of about 7,000. Services include readers/testers, scribes, notetaking accommodations, assistive technology, advocacy training and personal counseling. Free tutoring is available to all students at the college. No diagnostic testing is available.

**5013 Malone College**
515 25th Street NW
Canton, OH 44709      330-471-8100
800-521-1146
FAX 330-471-8478
TDY:330-471-8359
http://www.malone.edu
e-mail: pplittle@malone.edu
*Patty Little, Director Retention/Special Needs*

An independent four-year college with about 40 special education students out of a total of almost 2,000.

**5014  Marburn Academy**
1860 Walden Drive
Columbus, OH  43229          614-433-0822
                             FAX 614-433-0812
              http://www.marburnacademy.org
                                     e-mail:
         marburnadmission@marburnacademy.org
*Scott Burton, Director Admission*
*Barbara Davidson, Director Auxiliary Programs*

Marburn Academy is a small, independent day school offering the finest education for bright children who learn differently. Our entire program is deisgned to meet the academic and social needs of children who have learning differences such as dyslexia, learning disabilities or ADHD. Marburn Academy's program is accredited by the Academy of Orton-Gillingham Practitioners and Educators.

**5015  Marietta College**
Marietta College
215 5th Street
Marietta, OH  45750          740-376-4643
                             FAX 740-376-4901
              http://www.marietta.edu
              e-mail: williams@marietta.edu
*Bruce Peterson, Resident Director*
*Jen , President*

An independent four-year college with a special education student population of about 5%.

**5016  Marion Technical College**
Marion Technical College
1467 Mount Vernon Avenue
Marion, OH  43302            740-389-4636
                             FAX 740-389-6136
              http://www.mtc.edu
*Mike Stuckey, Coordinator of Disability Servic*
*Jay Richard , President*

The Student Resource Center also houses the Office of Disabilities. The SRC director will advocate on student's behalf for resonable accommodations for those with physical, mental and or emotional disabilities.

**5017  Miami University**
301 S Campus Avenue
Oxford, OH  45056            513-529-8741
                             FAX 513-529-3841
              http://www.mid.muohio.edu
              e-mail: greendw@muohio.edu
*James Garland, President*
*John Skillings, Interim Provost*

A public four-year college with approximately 5% of its students with LD/ADHD.

**5018  Miami University: Middletown Campus**
4200 E University Boulevard
Middletown, OH  45042        513-727-3431
                             800-662-2262
                             FAX 513-727-3223
                             TDY:513-727-3308
              http://www.mid.muohio.edu
              e-mail: nferguson@mid.muohio.edu
*Nancy Ferguson, Coordinator Disability Services*
*Margir Perkins, Academic Services*

Offers a variety of services to students with disabilities including notetakers, extended testing time, counseling services, and special accommodations.

**5019  Mount Vernon Nazarene College**
800 Martinsburg Road
Mount Vernon, OH  43050      740-397-9000
                             FAX 740-393-0511
              http://www.mvnu.edu
              e-mail: amy.stemen@mvnu.edu
*Carol Matthews MD, Director*
*Amy Stemen, Office Manager*

Four year college that provides programs for learning diabled students.

**5020  Muskingum College**
163 Stormont Street
New Concord, OH  43762       740-826-8284
                             FAX 740-826-8285
              http://www.muskingum.edu
              e-mail: adminfo@muskingum.edu
*Ann Steele, President*
*George Sims, Vice President of Academic Affai*

Center for Advancement of Learning houses the PLUS Program, a full service for students with LD.

**5021  Northwest Technical College**
1900 28th Avenue S
Moorehead, OH  56560         218-236-6277
                             800-426-5603
                             FAX 218-236-0342
              http://www.minnesota.edu
              e-mail: jerome.migler@minnesota.edu
*Dr Migler, President*
*John Centko, Dean of Academics*

Offers a variety of services to students with disabilities including notetakers, extended testing time, counseling services, and special accommodations.

**5022  Notre Dame College of Ohio**
4545 College Road
South Euclid, OH  44121      216-381-1680
                             FAX 216-381-3802
              http://www.ndc.edu
              e-mail: ekadlec@ndc.edu
*Elizabeth Kaldec, Director*
*Andrew Roth, President*

Four year college that offers support and services to students with learning disabilities.

**5023  Oberlin College**
Academic Support for Students with Disabilities
118 N Professor Street
Oberlin, OH  44074           440-775-8121
                             FAX 440-775-8886
              http://www.oberlin.edu
              e-mail: jane.boomer@oberlin.edu
*Jane Boomer, Coordinator*
*Phyllis Hogan, Office Manager*

An independent four-year college with small percentage of education students.

**5024 Ohio State University Agricultural Technical Institute**
1382 Dover Road
Wooster, OH 44691          330-264-3911
                          800-647-8283
                          FAX 330-202-3579
          http://www.ati.ag.ohio-state.edu
*Gerri Wolfe, LD Specialist*

A public two-year college with nearly 10% special education students. There is no fee for the special education program in addition to the regular tuition.

**5025 Ohio State University: Lima Campus**
**Disability Services**
**4240 Campus Drive**
**Lima, OH 45804**          419-995-8453
                          FAX 419-995-8483
          http://www.lima.ohio-state.edu
          e-mail: meyer.193@osu.edu
*Karen Meyer, Coordinator/Disability Services*

A public four-year college providing services to learning disabled students including extended test time, counseling, notetakers and other special accommodations.

**5026 Ohio State University: Mansfield Campus, Disability Services**
**1680 University Drive**
**Mansfield, OH 44906**          419-755-4234
                              FAX 419-755-4243
          http://www.mansfield.ohio-state.edu
          e-mail: corso.1@osu.edu
*Ginny Corso, Learning Disabilities Liaison*

A public four-year college providing services to learning disabled students including peer tutoring, extended test time, quiet rooms and other special accommodations.

**5027 Ohio State University: Marion Campus**
**1465 Mount Vernon Avenue**
**Marion, OH 43302**          740-389-6786
                          FAX 614-292-5817
          http://www.marion.ohio-state.edu
*Margaret Hazelett, LD Specialist*

A public four-year college providing a full range of services for students with disabilities.

**5028 Ohio State University: Newark Campus**
**1179 University Drive**
**Newark, OH 43055**          740-366-3321
                          FAX 740-366-5047
          http://www.newark.ohio-state.edu
*Barbara Deutschle, Learning Disability Specialist*

A public four-year college providing services to learning disabled students including peer tutoring, extended test time, quiet rooms and other special accommodations. There is no separate fee for these services.

**5029 Ohio State University: Nisonger Center**
**1581 Dodd Drive**
**Columbus, OH 43210**          614-292-8365
                            FAX 614-292-3727
                            TDY:614-688-8040
          http://www.nisonger.osu.edu
*Stephen Reiss MD, Director*

The Ohio State University Nisonger Center for Mental Retardation and Developmental Disabilities provides interdisciplinary training, research and exemplary services pertaining to people with developmental disabilities. The center, which is a part of a national network of activities called University Afffiliated Programs, was founded in 1968. Training is provided in medicine (pediatrics and psychiatry), dentistry, education, physical therapy, psychology and other relevant disciplines.

**5030 Ohio State University: Office for Disability Services**
**1760 Neil Avenue**
**Columbus, OH 43210**          614-292-3307
                            FAX 614-292-4190
                            TDY:614-292-0901
          http://www.osu.ohio-state.edu
          e-mail: frontliner@ods.ohio-state.edu
*Patty Carlton, Director*
*Lois Burke, Counselor*

ODS offers academic accommodations for students with documented disabilities including but not limited to students who are deaf or hard of hearing, visually impaired, mobilty impaired or have ADHD, learning disabilities, psychiatric disabilities or medical disabilities. ODS also provides auxiliary aids which include access to class notes, print materials in alternate format, interpreters and/or closed captioning for deaf students, and a variety of adaptive technology.

**5031 Ohio University**
**Ohio University**
**101 Crewson House**
**Athens, OH 45701**          740-593-1000
                          FAX 740-593-2708
          http://www.ohiou.edu
*William Smith, Director*
*Ruth Blickle, Administrative Associate*

A public four-year college with a small percentage of special education students.

**5032 Ohio University Chillicothe**
**Ohio University Chillicothe**
**571 W 5th Street**
**Chillicothe, OH 45601**          740-774-7245
                              877-462-6824
                              FAX 740-774-7290
          http://www.ohiou.edu/~childept
          e-mail: diekroge@ohio.edu
*Diane Diekroger MD, Coordinator of Student Support*
*Richard Bebee, Dean*

Offers a variety of services to students with disabilities including note takers, extended testing time, counseling services, and special accommodations.

**5033  Otterbein College**
102 W College Avenue
Westerville, OH  43081            614-890-3000
800-488-8144
FAX 614-823-1200
http://www.otterbein.edu
e-mail: uotterb@otterbein.edu
*Ellen Kasualis, Director of Academic Support Ser*
*Brent Devore, President*

An independent four-year college with a small percentage of special education students.

**5034  Owens Community College**
**Disability Resources Department**
**PO Box 10000**
**Toledo, OH  43699**            419-661-7230
800-466-9367
FAX 419-661-7607
http://www.owens.cc.oh.us
e-mail: bscheffert@owens.cc.oh.us
*Beth Scheffert, Director*

A comprehensive Community College that offers educational programs in over 50 technical areas of study leading to the Associate of Applied Science, Associate of Applied Business or Associate of Technical Studies degree. Provides programs designed for college transfer and leads to the Associate of Arts or Associate of Science degree. Finally, a number of certificate programs as well as short term credit and non-credit programs are available.

**5035  Shawnee State University**
**940 2nd Street**
**Portsmouth, OH  45662**         740-354-3205
800-959-4778
FAX 740-351-3111
http://www.shawnee.edu
e-mail: rlattimore@shawnee.edu
*Bob Trusz, Coordinator*
*Rita , President*

Offers a variety of services to students with disabilities including notetakers, extended testing time, counseling services, and special accommodations.

**5036  Sinclair Community College**
**Learning Disability Support Services**
**444 W 3rd Street**
**Dayton, OH  45402**             937-512-3550
FAX 937-512-4521
TDY:937-512-3096
http://www.sinclair.edu
*Robin Moore-Cooper, Program Coordinator/Director*
*Robin More-Cooper, Counselor*

Funded by the Federal Department of Education, Student Support Services is an organization devoted to helping students meet the challenges of college life. Our goals are to help students stay in school, then eventually graduate and/or transfer to a four-year college or university. We strive to develop new ways of helping students achieve their educational, career and professional goals.

**5037  Southern Ohio College: Northeast Campus**
Brown Mackie College
2791 Mogadore Road
Akron, OH  44312                  330-733-8766
FAX 330-733-5853
http://www.brownmackie.edu
*Jannette Mason, Administrative Assistant*
*Kim Cook, Dean of Academic Services*

Offers a variety of services to students with disabilities including notetakers, extended testing time, counseling services, and special accommodations.

**5038  Southern State Community College**
**100 Hobart Drive**
**Hillsboro, OH  45133**          937-393-3431
FAX 937-393-9370
*Carl Vertona, Special Services*

Offers a variety of services to students with disabilities including notetakers, extended testing time, counseling services, and special accommodations.

**5039  Terra State Community College**
**Special Education Services**
**2830 Napoleon Road**
**Fremont, OH  43420**            419-334-8400
866-AT-TERRA
FAX 419-334-9035
http://www.terra.cc.us/terra2.html
e-mail: info@terra.cc.oh.us
*Richard Newman, Coordinator*
*Gina Staccone-Smeal, Coordinator*

Provides quality learning experiences which are accessible and affordable. Terra is actively committed to excellence in learning and offers associate degrees in various technologies as well as in arts and sciences, applied business, and applied science. Our office of student support services works with students with learning disabilities and other disabilities.

**5040  University of Akron Wayne College**
1901 Smucker Road
Orrville, OH  44667               330-683-2010
800-221-8308
FAX 330-684-8989
http://www.wayne.uakron.edu/
e-mail: juliabeyeler@uakron.edu
*Julia Beyeler, Director Learning Support Servic*

A public two-year college with a small percentage of special education students.

**5041  University of Cincinnati: Raymond Walters General and Technical College**
9555 Plainfield Road
Cincinnati, OH  45236            513-745-5600
FAX 513-792-8624
TDY:513-745-8300
http://www.rwc.uc.edu
e-mail: john.kraimer@uc.edu
*John Kraimer, Director Disability Services*

Offers a variety of services to students with disabilities including notetakers, extended testing time, counseling services, and special accommodations.

**5042  University of Dayton**

Special Education Services
300 College Park Drive
Dayton, OH  45469                    937-229-3684
                                FAX 937-229-3270
                                TDY:937-229-3837
                        http://www.udayton.edu
            e-mail: timothy.king@notes.udayton.edu
*Timothy King, Director*
*Erin Courtney, Office Manager*

An independent four-year college with about 5% special education students.

**5043  University of Findlay**

Disability Services Office
1000 N Main Street
Findlay, OH  45840                    419-434-5532
                                     800-472-9502
                                FAX 419-434-5748
                                TDY:419-434-5532
                        http://www.findlay.edu
                e-mail: ods@mail.findlay.edu
*Lori Colchdgoff, Director Disability Services*

An independent four-year college with a small percentage of special needs students.

**5044  University of Toledo**

Toledo, OH  43606                    419-530-4636
                        http://www.utoledo.edu
*Carl Earwood, Office Director*

A public four-year college whose mission is to provide the support services and accommodations necessary for all students to succeed.

**5045  Urbana University**

Student Affairs Office
597 College Way
Urbana, OH  43078                    937-484-1301
                                FAX 937-484-1322
                        http://www.urbana.edu

*Sheri Holmes, Director*

An independent four-year college with a small percentage of special education students.

**5046  Ursuline College**

Program for Students with Learning Disabilities
2500 Lander Road
Peper Pike, OH  44124                 440-449-2046
                                FAX 440-646-8318
                        http://www.ursuline.edu
                e-mail: agromada@ursuline.edu
*Annette Gromada, Learning Disabilities Specialist*

A four year college that offers programs to students with learning disabilities.

**5047  Walsh University**

2020 East Maple
North Canton, OH  44720              330-499-7090
                                     800-362-9846
                                FAX 330-490-7165
                        http://www.walsh.edu
                e-mail: bfreshour@walsh.edu
*Francie Morrow, Director*
*Joni Hendricks, Secretary*

An independent four-year college. The Office of Student Support Services maintains an early warning system for students in academic, financial, social and/or emtional difficulty. The Office proudly communicates regularly with students regarding their general well being, and assists in the students' academic and financial concerns with referals to appropriate offices.

**5048  Washington State Community College**

710 Colegate Drive
Marietta, OH  45750                  740-374-8716
                                FAX 740-376-0257
                        http://www.wscc.edu/

*Ann Hontz, Director*

A public two-year college with a small percentage of special education students.

**5049  Wilmington College of Ohio**

251 Ludovic Street
Wilmington, OH  45177
                                     800-341-9318
                        http://www.wilmington.edu
*Laurel Eckels, Special Services*

Offers a variety of services to students with disabilities including notetakers, extended testing time, counseling services, and special accommodations.

**5050  Wright State University**

Disability Department
3640 Colonel Glenn Highway
Dayton, OH  45435                    937-775-5680
                                FAX 937-775-5795
                        http://www.wright.edu
                e-mail: judith.roberts@wright.edu
*Jeffrey Vernooy, Assistant Director*

A public university with over 14,000 undergraduated and graduated students. The Office of Disability Services offers programs to promote each student's academic, personal, physical, and vocational growth so that people with physical and learning disabilities can learn their full potential.

**5051  Xavier University**

3800 ViCourtory Parkway
Cincinnati, OH  45207                513-745-2800
                                     800-344-4698
                                FAX 513-745-3387
                        http://www.xu.edu
*Ann PhD, Director Learning Assistance*

We seek to ensure that all students with disabilities can freely and actively participate in all facets of university life.

## Oklahoma

**5052  Bacone College**
2299 Old Bacone Road
Muskogee, OK  74403          918-683-4581
                             888-682-5514
                        FAX 918-682-5514
                     http://www.bacone.edu
                 e-mail: stewarta@bacone.edu
*Rhonda Cambiano, Director*
*Ann Stewart, Coordinator*

Offers a variety of services to students with disabilities including notetakers, extended testing time, counseling services, and special accommodations.

**5053  East Central University**
1100 E 14th Street
Ada, OK  74820               580-310-5294
                        FAX 580-310-5654
                      http://www.ecok.edu/
*Dwain West, Student Support Services*
*Pamela Armstrong, Registrar*

A public four-year college with a small percentage of special education of students.

**5054  Moore-Norman Vo-Tech**
4701 12th Avenue NW
Norman, OK  73069            405-364-5763
                        FAX 405-360-9989
                http://www.mntechnology.com
*Bill Henderson*

Offers a variety of services to students with disabilities including notetakers, extended testing time, counseling services, and special accommodations.

**5055  Northeastern State University**
600 N Grand Avenue
Tahlequah, OK  74464         918-458-2120
                        FAX 918-458-2340
                     http://www.nsuok.edu
*Jan Smith-Clayton, Assistant to Dean*

Four year college that offers programs and services to disabled students.

**5056  Oklahoma City Community College**
Department of Student Support Services
7777 S May Avenue
Oklahoma City, OK  73159     405-682-7520
                        FAX 405-682-7545
                        TDY:405-682-7520
                     http://www.okccc.edu
                e-mail: jhoward@okccc.edu
*Jenna Howard, Students w/Disabilities Advisor*
*Pat Stowe, Disabled Students Services Direc*

Comprehensive community college with individualized services and accommodations for students with disabilities arranged by the Office of Student Support Services. Services include Deaf Program, and accommodations as described by section 504 & ADA. Five tutoring labs are available on campus and assistive technology including voice synthesizers and voice recognition for computer based word processing.

**5057  Oklahoma Panhandle State University**
Box 430
Goodwell, OK  73939          580-349-2611
                        FAX 580-349-2302
                        TDY:580-349-1559
                     http://www.opsu.edu
                 e-mail: opsu@opsu.edu
*David Bryan MD, President*
*Wayne , Vice President*

Four year college that offers programs to the learning disabled.

**5058  Oklahoma State University: Tech Branch-Oklahoma City**
900 N Portalnd
Oklahoma City, OK  73107     405-945-3385
                        FAX 405-945-8656
                     http://www.osuokc.edu
                e-mail: crainet@osuokc.edu
*Tiffany Craine, Director*

Offers access to students with disabilities based upon the diagnostic documentation which is provided by the student and the functional impact of the disability.

**5059  Oklahoma State University: Technical Branch-Okmulgee**
1801 E 4th
Okmulgee, OK  74447          918-293-4678
                  http://www.osu-okmulgee.edu
*Billie Coakley, Special Services*

Offers a variety of services to students with disabilities including notetakers, extended testing time, counseling services, and special accommodations.

**5060  Oral Roberts University**
7777 S Lewis Avenue
Tulsa, OK  74171             918-495-7018
                        FAX 918-495-7879
                     http://www.oru.edu
                e-mail: droberson@oru.edu
*Don Roberson, Director*

Four year college that offers resources to students with a learning disability.

**5061  Rogers State University**
1701 W Will Rogers Boulevard
Claremore, OK  74017         918-341-7777
                             800-256-7511
                        FAX 918-343-7712
                     http://www.rsu.edu
                e-mail: llawless@rsu.edu
*Lennette Lawless, Student Development Coordinator*

A public four-year university with several special education students out of a total of approximately 3,300.

**5062 Rose State College**

**Academic Support Department**
**6420 SE 15th Street**
**Midwest City, OK 73110** 405-733-7311
FAX 405-736-0372
TDY:405-736-7308
http://www.rose.cc.ok.us
e-mail: rjones@rose.edu

*James Cook, President*
*Terry Britton, President*

Services and facilities include academic advisement, referal and liaison with other community agencies, recorded textbooks and individual testing for qualified students.

**5063 Seminole Junior College**

**2701 Boren Boulevard**
**Seminole, OK 74818-0351** 405-382-9950
FAX 405-382-3122
TDY:405-382-9950
http://www.ssc.cc.ok.us
e-mail: downey_m@ssc.cc.ok.us

*James Utterback MD, President*
*Tracey Woods, Academic Counselor*

Provides free peer tutoring, study skill workshops, computer programs, (CAI) and videos, alternative textbooks and workbooks, classnotes/test files and other support materials to all students. A learning disabilities specialist works closely with learning disabled students, instructors and counselors to identify and implement useful and appropriate support services. Students meeting ADA guidelines can request other academic assistance services (notetakers, readers, adapted testing, etc.).

**5064 Southeastern Oklahoma State University**

**Box 4112**
**Durant, OK 74701** 580-745-2394
FAX 580-745-7470
TDY:580-745-2704
http://www.sosu.edu
e-mail: sdodson@sosu.edu

*Susan Dodson, Director*
*Glen , President*

Four year college that provides services to the learning disabled students.

**5065 Southwestern Oklahoma State University**

**100 Campus Drive**
**Weatherford, OK 73096** 580-772-6611
FAX 580-774-3795
http://www.swosu.edu

*Kim Liebscher, Student Development*
*John , President*

Offers a variety of services to students with disabilities including notetakers, extended testing time, counseling services, and special accommodations.

**5066 St. Gregory's University**

**Partners in Learning**
**1900 W MacArthur Drive**
**Shawnee, OK 74804** 405-878-5398
FAX 405-878-5198
TDY:405-878-5103
http://www.sgc.edu
e-mail: ajwood@stgregory.edu

*Anita Wood, Director Partners in Learning*
*Melody Harrington, Assistant Director for Partners*

Four-year college offering programs for students with learning disabilities.

**5067 Tulsa Community College**

**Disabled Student Resource Center**
**909 S Boston Avenue**
**Tulsa, OK 74119** 918-595-7115
FAX 918-595-8398
TDY:918-595-7287
http://www.tulsacc.edu
e-mail: info@tulsacc.edu

*Yolanda Williams, Director*

Offers a variety of services to students with disabilities including note takers, extended testing time, counseling services, and special accommodations.

**5068 Tulsa University Student Support Center**

**Center for Student Academic Support**
**600 S College Avenue**
**Tulsa, OK 74104** 918-631-2315
FAX 918-631-3459
TDY:918-631-3329
http://www.utulsa.edu
e-mail: jcorso@utulsa.edu

*Jane Corso MD, Director*
*Ruby Wile, Coordinator*
*Julana Boyett, Adminstrative Secretary*

**5069 University of Oklahoma**

**620 Elm Avenue**
**Norman, OK 73019** 405-325-3852
800-522-0772
FAX 405-325-4491
TDY:405-325-4173
http://www.dsa.ou.edu/ods/
e-mail: sdyer@ou.edu

*Suzette Dyer, Director Disability Services*

A public doctoral degree-granting research university. The University of Oklahoma is an equal opportunity institution.

**5070 University of Tulsa**

**Center for Student Academic Support**
**600 S College**
**Tulsa, OK 74104** 918-631-2334
FAX 918-631-3459
http://www.utulsa.edu
e-mail: jcorso@utulsa.edu

*Jane Corso, Director*
*Ruby Wile, Coordinator*

Four year college that offers services to disabled students. The small class size and individual attention that students recive make this institution an excellent choice for the students with disabilities.

# Oregon

**5071  Blue Mountain Community College**

Services for Students with Learning Disabilities
2411 NW Carden
Pendleton, OR  97801                 541-278-5807
                                    FAX 541-278-5888
                                    http://www.bluecc.edu
                                    e-mail: aspiegel@bluecc.edu
*Amy Spiegel, Coordinator*

A rural community college that offers both lower division transfer and professional technical degrees. Accommodations and academic adjustments for students with learning disabilities are determined and provided on an individual basis. Diagnostic testing for learning disabilities is available. 1,200 full-time students.

**5072  Cascade College**

9101 E Burnside Street
Portland, OR  97216                  503-255-7060
                                    FAX 503-257-1222
                                    http://www.cascade.edu
                                    e-mail: sjones@cascade.edu
*Dennis Lynn, President*
*Shawn Jones, Academic Dean*

Offers a variety of services to students with disabilities including note takers, extended testing time, counseling services, and special accommodations.

**5073  Central Oregon Community College**

2600 NW College Way
Bend, OR  97701                      541-383-7580
                                    FAX 541-383-7506
                                    http://www.cocc.edu
                                    e-mail: DisabilityServices@cocc.edu
*Alicia Moore, Registrar*
*Jim , President*

COCC is committed to making physical facilities and instructional programs accessible to students with disabilities.

**5074  Clackamas Community College**

Disability Resource Center
19600 S Molalla Avenue
Oregon City, OR  97045               503-657-6958
                                    FAX 503-650-6654
                                    TDY:503-650-6649
                                    http://www.clackamas.edu
                                    e-mail: caseys@clackamas.edu
*Casey Sims, Director*

A public two-year college. Special education services are designed to support student success by creating full access and providing appropriate accommodations for all students with disabilities.

**5075  George Fox College**

Academic Resource Center
414 N Meridian Street
Newberg, OR  97132                   503-538-8383
                                    800-765-4369
                                    FAX 503-554-3834
                                    http://www.georgefox.edu
                                    e-mail: rmuthiah@georgefox.edu
*Rick Muthiah, Director*

An independent four-year college with a small percentage of special education students.

**5076  Lane Community College**

4000 E 30th Avenue
Eugene, OR  97405                    541-463-5150
                                    FAX 541-563-4739
                                    TDY:541-463-3079
                                    http://www.lanecc.edu
                                    e-mail: moretd@lanecc.edu
*Nancy Hart, Director*
*Mary Stilde, President*

We provide accommodations, technology, advising, support systems, training and education.

**5077  Linfield College**

Learning Support Services
900 SE Baker Street
McMinnville, OR  97128               503-883-2444
                                    FAX 503-883-2647
                                    TDY:503-883-2396
                                    http://www.linfield.edu
                                    e-mail: jhaynes@linfield.edu
*Judith Haynes, Learning Support Services Dir.*
*Eileen Dowty, Learning Support Services Asst.*

An independent four-year college. Services include tutoring, extended time for testing, assistance with advising and counseling. Student needs are considered in customizing individual programs of support for documented special needs.

**5078  Linn-Benton Community College**

Learning Disabilities Support Services
Learning Resource Center
Albany, OR  97321                    541-917-4683
                                    FAX 541-917-4808
                                    TDY:541-917-4703
                                    http://www.linnbenton.edu
                                    e-mail: ods@linnbenton.edu
*Lynne Cox, Coordinator*

A public two-year college. LBCC provides a number of services and programs for students with disabilities including classes, supportive services and aids.

**5079  Mount Bachelor Academy**

33051 NE Ochoco Highway
Prineville, OR  97754                541-462-3404
                                    800-462-3404
                                    FAX 541-462-3430
                                    http://www.mtba.com/

**5080  Mt. Hood Community College**

Learning Disabilities Department
26000 SE Stark Street
Gresham, OR  97030                   503-491-6923
                                    FAX 503-491-6090
                                    TDY:503-491-7670
                                    http://www.mhcc.edu
                                    e-mail: dsoweb@mhcc.edu
*Elizabeth Johnson, Director*
*Laurie Clarke, Program Adviser*

A commitment to providing educational opportunities for all students forms the foundation of the disability services program. If you are a student with a disability, disability services will help you overcome potential obstacles so that you may be successful in your area of study. Disability services gives you the needed support to help you meet your goals without separating you and other students with disabilities from existing programs.

**5081 Oregon Institute of Technology**

**Oregon State University Systems**
**3201 Campus Drive**
**Klamath Falls, OR 97601**          **541-885-1031**
                                     **800-422-2017**
                                     **FAX 541-885-1520**
                                     **TDY:541-885-1072**
                                     **http://www.oit.edu**
                                     **e-mail: access@oit.edu**
*Ron McCutcheon, Director-Campus Access*
*Martha Dow, President*

A public four-year college enrolling about 3,000 students. Accommodations are tailored to the needs of individual students on a case-by-case basis for those self-identified as having learning disabilities.

**5082 Oregon State University**

**Services for Students with Disabilities**
**A202 Kerr Administration Building**
**Corvallis, OR 97331**          **541-737-4098**
                                 **FAX 541-737-7354**
                                 **TDY:541-737-3666**
                          **http://www.ssd.oregonstate.edu**
                   **e-mail: disabilty.services@oregonstate.edu**
*Tracy Bentley-Towlin, Director*
*Rani Jeannette, Administrative Assistant*

A public four-year college with a small percentage of students.

**5083 Portland Community College**

**Science and Technology Building**
**Portland, OR 97280**          **503-977-4341**
                                **FAX 503-977-4882**
                                **http://www.pcc.edu**
*Carolee Schmeer, LD Specialist*

Our team includes rehabilitation guidance counselors, learning disability specialists, sign language interpreters, a technology specialist, vocational progarm and special needs coordinatiors.

**5084 Reed College**

**3203 SE Woodstock Boulevard**
**Portland, OR 97202 3203**          **503-771-1112**
                                     **FAX 503-777-7234**
                                     **http://www.reed.edu**
                                 **e-mail: admissions@reed.edu**
*Betsy Emerick, Associate Dean Students*
*Burel Clayton, Administrative Officer*

Offers a variety of services to students with disabilities including notetakers, extended testing time, counseling services, and special accommodations.

**5085 Southern Oregon State College**

**Counseling Center, Britt 205**
**Ashland, OR 97520**          **541-552-6425**
                               **FAX 541-552-6329**
                               **http://www.sou.edu**

Offers a variety of services to students with disabilities including note takers, extended testing time, counseling services, and special accommodations.

**5086 Southwestern Oregon Community College**

**1988 Newmark Avenue**
**Coos Bay, OR 97420**          **541-888-2525**
                                **800-962-2838**
                                **FAX 541-888-7247**
                                **http://www.socc.edu**
*Tom Nickels, Director*
*Steve Kridelbaugh, President*

The college will provide reasonable accommodation for students with learning disabilities. Some instructors in academic skills have special training in working with learning disabled students.

**5087 Treasure Valley Community College**

**650 College Boulevard**
**Ontario, OR 97914**          **503-889-6493**
                               **FAX 541-881-2717**
                               **http://www.tvcc.cc.or.us**
*Royo Spurgeon, Director*

Offers a variety of services to students with disabilities including notetakers, extended testing time, counseling services, and special accommodations.

**5088 Umpqua Community College**

**PO Box 967**
**Roseburg, OR 97470**          **541-440-4600**
                                **FAX 541-440-4612**
                                **http://www.umpqua.edu**
*Barbara Stoner, Coordinator of Disability Servic*
*Blaine , President*

A public two-year college with a small percentage of special education students.

**5089 University of Oregon**

**164 Oregon Hall**
**Eugene, OR 97403**          **541-346-1155**
                              **FAX 541-346-6013**
                              **TDY:541-346-1083**
                              **http://www.ds.uoregon.edu**
*Steve Pickett, Director*
*Molly Sirois, Counselor Disability Services*

A public four-year college with about 5% of students with disabilities.

**5090 Warner Pacific College**

**2219 SE 68th Avenue**
**Portland, OR 97215**          **503-517-1000**
                                **800-582-7885**
                                **FAX 503-517-1350**
                                **http://www.warnerpacific.edu**
                         **e-mail: webmaster@warnerpacific.edu**
*Jay Barber, President*
*Wayne Peterson, Vice President*

Offers a variety of services to students with disabilities including notetakers, extended testing time, counseling services, and special accommodations.

**5091 Western Baptist College**
500 Deer Park Drive
Salem, OR 97301        503-375-7012
                      FAX 503-585-4316
                      http://www.wbc.edu
                      e-mail: dmiliones@wbc.edu
*Darren Miliones, Director*

Four year college that offers programs for learning
disabled students.

**5092 Western Oregon University**
345 N Monmouth Avenue
Monmouth, OR 97361        503-838-8000
                         877-877-1593
                         FAX 503838-8474
                         http://www.wou.edu
*Joseph Sendelba MD, Quality Services*

A public four-year college. Strives to provide and promote a supportive, accessible, non-discriminatory
learning and working environment for students, faculty, staff and community members with disabilities.
These goals are realized through the provision of individualized support services, advocacy and the identification of current technology and information.

**5093 Willamette University**
Learning Disabilities Department
900 State Street
Salem, OR 97301        503-370-6471
                      FAX 503-375-5420
                      TDY:503-375-5383
http://www.willamette.edu/dept/disability/main.
                      e-mail: jhill@willamette.edu
*Jo Hill, Director Disability/Learning*
*Lyn Breen, Office Manager*

Offers a variety of services to students with disabilities including notetakers, extended testing time, counseling services, and special accommodations.
Provides services for all students on campus, including graduate schools.

## Pennsylvania

**5094 Albright College**
13th and Bern Street
Reading, PA 19612        610-921-7662
                         FAX 610-921-7530
                         http://www.albright.edu
                         e-mail: albright@alb.edu
*Sue Miller, Administrative Assistant*
*David , Interim President*

An independent four-year college with a small percentage of special education students. There is an additional fee for the education program in addition to
the regular tuition.

**5095 Bloomsburg University**
400 E 2nd Street
Bloomsburg, PA 17815        570-389-4000
                           FAX 570-389-3700
                           http://www.bloomu.edu
*Jessica Kozloff MD, President*

Offers a variety of services to students with disabilities including notetakers, extended testing time, counseling services, and special accommodations.

**5096 Boyce Campus of the Community College of
Allegheny County**
595 Beatty Road
Monroeville, PA 15146        724-325-6620
                            FAX 724-325-6797
                            http://www.ccac.edu
                            e-mail: mailto:Pflorent@ccac.edu
*Renee Clark MD, Director*

Offers a variety of services to students with disabilities including notetakers, extended testing time, counseling services, and special accommodations.

**5097 Bryn Mawr College**
Educational Support Services
101 N Meroin Avenue
Bryn Mawr, PA 19010        610-526-5375
                          FAX 610-526-7450
                          http://www.brynmawr.edu
                          e-mail: lmendez@brynmawr.edu
Bryn Mawr is a private liberal arts college located in
Bryn Mawr, Pennsylvania not far from Philadelphia.
The College provides support services for qualified
students with documented learning, physical, and
psychological disabilities. For additional information
visit www.brynmawr.edu/access_services .

**5098 Cabrini College**
Disability Support Services
610 King of Prussia Road
Radnor, PA 19087        610-902-8572
                       FAX 610-902-8441
                       TDY:610-902-8582
                       http://www.cabrini.edu
                       e-mail: ama722@cabrini.edu
*Anne Abbuhl, Director*

Offers support services and appropriate accommodations to students with documented learning disabilities.

**5099 California University of Pennsylvania**
Center for Academic Research and Enhancement
250 University Avenue
California, PA 15419        724-938-4404
                          FAX 724-938-4564
                          http://www.cup.edu
*Cheryl Bilitski, Director*
*Charles Williamson, Administrative Assistant Coun-
sel*

One of fourteen universities in the Pennsylvania State
System of Higher Education. The CARE Project provides services to students with learning disabilities
through two programs. The Specialized Support Service Program is a fee-for-service program which provides services beyond those mandated by 504/ADA
and has a cap of 40 students each semester. The Modified Basic Support Program provides basic services
at no cost and enrollment is unlimited.

**5100 Carnegie Mellon University**
Equal Opportunity Services
143 N Craig Street
Pittsburgh, PA 15213          412-268-2012
                             FAX 412-268-7472
                             http://www.cmu.edu
                  e-mail: ly2t@andrew.cmu.edu
*Lisa Zamperini, Coordinator*

Four year college that offers its students services for the learning disabled.

**5101 Clarion University**
840 Wood Street
Clarion, PA 16214            814-393-2000
                             FAX 814-393-2039
                             TDY:814-393-1601
                             http://www.clarion.edu/
                          e-mail: info@clarion.edu
*Jennifer May, Director Disability Support Serv*

Offers a variety of services to students with disabilities including note taking assistance, extended testing time, and special accommodations.

**5102 College Misericordia**
Alternative Learners Project
301 Lake Street
Dallas, PA 18612             570-674-6347
                             800-852-7675
                             FAX 570-675-2441
                             http://www.miseri.edu
                       e-mail: jrogan@miseri.edu
*Joseph Rogan, Director/Professor*

An independent four-year college with about 5% special education students.

**5103 Community College of Allegheny County: College Center, North Campus**
Learning Disabilities Services
8701 Perry Highway
Pittsburgh, PA 15237         412-369-3686
                             FAX 412-369-3635
                             TDY:412-369-4110
                             http://www.ccac.edu
                       e-mail: kwhite@ccac.edu
*Kathleen White, Director*

Support services for students with disabilities are provided according to individual needs. Services include assistance with testing, advisement, registration, classroom accommodations, professor and agency contact.

**5104 Community College of Allegheny County: Allegheny Campus**
Learning Disabilities Services
808 Ridge Avenue
Pittsburgh, PA 15212         412-237-4612
                             FAX 412-237-2721
                             http://www.ccac.edu
                  e-mail: mailto:Mdoyle@ccac.edu
*Marilyn Gleser, LD Coordinator*
*Mary , Director*

A public two-year college with a small percentage of special education students.

**5105 Community College of Philadelphia**
Center on Disability
1700 Spring Garden Street
Philadelphia, PA 19130       215-751-8050
                             FAX 215-751-8001
                             http://www.ccp.edu
                       e-mail: fdirosa@ccp.edu
*Francesca DiRosa, Center Director*
*Jackie Williams, Administrative Assistant*

**5106 Delaware County Community**
901 Media Line Road
Media, PA 19063              610-325-2748
                             FAX 610-355-7162
                             TDY:610-359-5020
                             http://www.dccc.edu
                       e-mail: abinder@dccc.edu
*Ann Binder, Director Special Needs*
*Jerome Parker, President*

Delaware County Community College, the ninth largest college in the Philadelphia metropolitan area, is a public, two year institution offering more than 60 programs of study. Its open-door policy, and affordable tuition make it accessible to all. Services to physically and learning disabled students include counseling services, tutoring, extended testing, tape recorded lectures, spelling allowances, assistive equipment, notes copied and study skills workshops.

**5107 Delaware Valley College of Science and Agriculture**
Delaware Valley College of Science and Agriculture
700 E Butler Avenue
Doylestown, PA 18901         215-345-1500
                             FAX 215-230-2964
                             http://www.devalcol.edu
                    e-mail: karen.kay@devalcol.edu
*Karen Kay, Counseling Director*

Offers a variety of services to students with disabilities including notetakers, extended testing time, counseling services, and special accommodations.

**5108 Delaware Valley Friends School**
19 E Central Avenue
Paoli, PA 19301              610-640-4150
                             FAX 610-296-9970
                             http://www.dvfs.org
                       e-mail: pilln@fc.dvfs.org
*Katherine Schantz, School Head*
*Pritchard Garret, Assistant Head*

**5109 Dickinson College**
Services for Students with Disabilities
PO Box 1773
Carlisle, PA 17013           717-245-1485
                             FAX 717-245-1534
                             TDY:717-245-1080
                             http://www.dickenson.edu
                    e-mail: jervis@dickinson.edu
*Keith Jervis, Coordinator*

The Office of Counseling and Disability Services is dedicated to the enhancement of healthy student development. Professional and paraprofessional staff offer confidential individual and group counseling sessions and outreach services which help students with both general developmental issues and with specific personal or interpersonal difficulties.

**5110  Drexel University**

**Office of Disability Services**
**3141 Chestnut Street**
**Philadelphia, PA  19104**          215-895-2506
                                     800-237-3935
                              FAX 215-895-1402
                              TDY:215-895-2299
                         http://www.drexel.edu
                    e-mail: mmp46@drexel.edu
*Michelle Peters, Director*
*Maren Farris, Disability Specialist*

An independent four-year college with a small percentage of special education students.

**5111  East Stroudsburg University of Pennsyslvania**

**200 Prospect Street**
**East Stroudsburg, PA  18301**       570-422-3954
                                      877-230-5547
                              FAX 570-422-3898
                              TDY:570-422-3543
                           http://www.esu.edu
               e-mail: emiller@po-box.esu.edu
*Edith Miller MD, Director Disability Services*
*Robert J , President*

Four year college that offers services to disabled students.

**5112  Edinboro University of Pennsylvania**

**Office for Students with Disabilities**
**Crawford Center**
**Edinboro, PA  16444**               814-732-2462
                              FAX 814-732-2866
                              TDY:814-732-2462
                        http://www.edinboro.edu
                e-mail: strodder@edinboro.edu
*Kathleen Strosser, Assistant Director*
*Janet Jenkins, LD Coordinator*

Specific documentation required. Focuses on the needs of college capable students with learning disabilities.

**5113  Gannon Universtiy**

**Program for Students with Learning Disabilities**
**University Square**
**Erie, PA  16541**                   814-871-5326
                              FAX 814-871-7499
                         http://www.gannon.edu
                 e-mail: lowreyool@gannon.edu
*Joyce SSJ, Director*
*Jane Kanter, Assistant Director*

**5114  Gettysburg College**

**300 N Washington**
**Gettysburg, PA  17325**             717-337-6100
                                      800-431-0803
                              FAX 717-337-6145
*Tim Dodd, Associate Dean*

Offers a variety of services to students with disabilities including notetakers, extended testing time, counseling services, and special accommodations.

**5115  Gwynedd: Mercy College**

**1325 Sumneytown Pike**
**Gwynedd Valley, PA  19437**         215-646-7300
                              FAX 215-641-5598
                         http://www.gmc.edu
                   e-mail: gcassidy@gmc.edu
*Barbara RN, Director Services/ADA*

Recognizing the diversity of our student population and the challenges and needs this brings to the educational enterprise, Gwynedd-Mercy College, within the bounds of its resources, intends to provide reasonable accommodations for students with disabilities. Requests for specific accommodations are processed on an individual basis.

**5116  Harcum Junior College**

**750 Montgomery Avenue**
**Bryn Mawr, PA  19010**              610-525-4100
                         http://www.harcum.edu
*Kathy King, Director*

An independent two-year college. There is an additional fee for the special education program in addition to the regular tuition.

**5117  Harrisburg Area Community College**

**Disability Services Office**
**1 HACC Drive**
**Harrisburg, PA  17110**             717-780-2410
                                      800-222-4222
                              FAX 717-780-3285
                         http://www.hacc.edu
                   e-mail: admit@hacc.edu
*AL Jackson, Affairs & Enrollment Management*
*Carol Keeper, Director*

A public two-year college with a small percentage of special needs students.

**5118  Indiana University of Pennsylvania**

**106 Pratt Hall**
**Indiana, PA  15705**                724-357-4067
                              FAX 724-357-2889
                              TDY:724-357-4067
                         http://www.iup.edu
          e-mail: advising-testing@grove.iup.edu
*Catherine Dugan, Director*
*Todd Banwier, Assistant Director*

Disability Support Services is a component of the Advising and Testing Center. The mission of DSS is to ensure that students with disabilities who attend Indiana University of Pennsylvainia receive an integrated, quality education.

**5119  Keystone Junior College**

**One College Green**
**LaPlume, PA  18440**

                                      877-4college
                         http://www.keystone.edu
*Dan Rosenfield, Contact*

Offers a variety of services to students with disabilities including notetakers, extended testing time, counseling services, and special accommodations.

**5120  King's College**
Academic Skills Center
133 N River Street
Wilkes-Barre, PA  18711          570-208-5800
                                 FAX 570-825-9049
                                 http://www.kings.edu
                                 e-mail: jaburke@kings.edu
*Jacintha Burke, Academic Skills Center Director*

**5121  Kutztown University of Pennsylvania**
220 Administration Building
Kutztown, PA  19530              610-683-4060
                                 FAX 610-683-1520
                                 TDY:610-683-4499
                                 http://www.kutztown.edu
                                 e-mail: sutherla@kutztown.edu
*Patricia Richter, Director*

Kutztown University of Pennsylvania, a member of the Pennsylvania State System of Higher Education, was founded in 1856 as Keystone Normal School, and achieved University status in 1983. Today Kutztown University is a modern, comprehensive University. There are approximately 7,900 full and part time undergraduate and graduate students.

**5122  Lebanon Valley College**
101 N College Avenue
Annville, PA  17003              717-867-6158
                                 FAX 717-867-6979
                                 http://www.lvc.edu
                                 e-mail: perry@lvc.edu
*Anne Hohenwarter, Coordinator*

Four year college that offers learning disabled students support and services.

**5123  Lehigh Carbon Community College**
4525 Education Park Drive
Schnecksville, PA  18078         610-799-1156
                                 800-414-3975
                                 FAX 610-799-1527
                                 http://www.Iccc.edu
                                 e-mail: wschappell@Icc.edu
*Karen Goode-Ferguson, Director*

General services include assistance with the admission and registration process. Access and academic accommodation requests will be reviewed on a case by case basis. Additional learning support is available through Learning Assistance Services.

**5124  Lock Haven University of Pennsylvania**
Learning Disabilities Office
401 N Fairview Street
Lock Haven, PA  17745            570-893-2027
                                 800-332-8900
                                 FAX 570-893-2201
                                 http://www.lhup.edu
                                 e-mail: rjunco@lhup.edu
*Rey Junco MD, Director*

A public four-year college with a small percentage of students with disabilities.

**5125  Lycoming College**
Admissions House
Williamsport, PA  17745          570-321-4000
                                 800-345-3920
                                 FAX 570-321-4337
                                 http://www.lycoming.edu
*Diane Bonner MD, Director*

An independent four-year college with a small percentage of special education students.

**5126  Manor Junior College**
Manor Junior College
700 Fox Chase Road
Jenkintown, PA  19046            215-884-2216
                                 FAX 215-576-6564
                                 http://www.manor.edu
                                 e-mail: ftadmiss@manor.edu
*Mary Jurasinski, President*
*Sally Mydlowec, Vice President*

Offers a variety of services to students with disabilities including notetakers, extended testing time, counseling services, and special accommodations.

**5127  Mansfield University of Pennsylvania**
Services for Students with Learning Disabilities
213 S Hall Academy Street
Mansfield, PA  16933             570-662-4798
                                 800-577-6826
                                 FAX 570-662-4121
                                 http://www.mansfield.edu
                                 e-mail: wchabala@mansfield.edu
*William Chabala, Director*

Offers a variety of services to students with disabilities including, extended testing time, counseling services, and special accommodations.

**5128  Marywood University**
Special Education Department
2300 Adams Avenue
Scranton, PA  18509              570-961-4731
                                 FAX 570-961-4744
                                 http://www.marywood.edu
                                 e-mail: russo@es.marywood.edu
*Anthony Russo MD, Director*

Four year college that offers programs that are for the learning disabled.

**5129  Mercyhurst College**
Learning Disabilities Program
501 E 38th Street
Erie, PA  16546                  814-824-2573
                                 800-825-1926
                                 FAX 814-824-2071
                                 http://www.mercyhurst.edu
                                 e-mail: admug@paradise.mercy.edu
*Jim Breckenridge, Director Admissions*
*Dianne Rogers, Director LD Program*

Mercyhurst provides a comprehensive program of academic accommodations and support services to students with documented learning disabilities. Accommodations may include audiotaped textbooks, extended time for tests, a test reader and use of a computer to complete essay tests.

**5130 Messiah College**
One College Avenue
Grantham, PA 17027    717-796-5358
800-233-4220
FAX 717-796-5217
http://www.messiah.edu
e-mail: kdrahn@messiah.edu
*Keith PhD, Director*
*Carol Wickey, Assistant to Director*

A private Christian college of the liberal and applied arts and sciences located in Central Pennsylvania.

**5131 Millersville University of Pennsylvania**
Disability Support Department
348 Lyle Hall
Millersville, PA 17551    717-872-3178
FAX 717-871-2129
http://www.millersv.edu
*Sherilynn Bessick, Director*
*Terry Asche, Office Manager*

Four year college that provides services to learning disabled students.

**5132 Moravian College**
1132 Monocacy Street
Bethlehem, PA 18018    610-861-1510
FAX 610-861-1577
http://www.moravian.edu
e-mail: memld02@moravian.edu
*M Davenport, Director*

Four year college that offers programs for the learning disabled.

**5133 Northampton Community College**
Disability Support Services
3835 Green Pond Road
Bethlehem, PA 18020    610-861-5342
FAX 610-861-5075
TDY:610-861-5351
http://www.northampton.edu/disabilityservices
e-mail: LDemshock@northampton.edu
*Laraine Demshock, Disability Service Coordinator*

Encourages academically qualified students with disabilities to take advantage of educational programs. Services and accommodations are offered to facilitate accessiblity to both college programs and facilities. Services provided to students with disabilities are based upon each student individual needs.

**5134 Pennsylvania Institute of Technology**
800 Manchester Avenue
Media, PA 19063    610-892-1500
800-422-0025
FAX 610-892-1510
http://www.pit.edu
*Paul Smith, President*

Offers a variety of services to students with disabilities including notetakers, extended testing time, counseling services, and special accommodations.

**5135 Pennsylvania State University: Mont Alto**
1 Campus Drive
Mont Alto, PA 17237    717-749-6046
FAX 717-749-6116
http://www.ma.psu.edu
e-mail: nmhz@psu.edu
*Nanette Hatzef, Learning Center Director*

It is the intention of Penn State University to provide equal access to students with disabilities as mandated by the Americans with Disabilities Act, and the Rehabilitiation Act. Students with disabilities are encouraged to take advantage of the support services provided to help them successfully meet the high academic standards of the university.

**5136 Pennsylvania State University: Schuylkill Campus**

Disability Services
200 University Drive
Schuylkill Haven, PA 17972    570-385-6000
FAX 570-385-3672
http://www.sl.psu.edu
*Sylvester Kohut, Assistant Provost*
*Melinda , Coordinator*

Offers a variety of services to students with disabilities including notetakers, extended testing time, counseling services, and special accommodations.

**5137 Pennsylvania State University: Shenango Valley Campus**
Office for Disability Services
116 Boucke Building
University Park, PA 16802    814-863-1807
FAX 814-863-2217
TDY:814-863-1807
http://www.equity.psu.edu/ods
e-mail: william.welsh@equity.psu.edu/ods
*William Welsh, Director*
*Karen Port, Exam Coordinator*

Penn State encourages academically qualified students with disabilities to take advantage of its educational programs. To be eligible for disability related accommodations, individuals must have a documented disability as defined by the Americans with Disabilities Act. A disability is defined by the physical or mental impairment that substantially limits a major life function. Individuals seeking accommodations are required to provided documentation.

**5138 Pennsylvania State University: Worthington Scranton Campus**
120 Ridgeview Drive
Dunmore, PA 18512    570-963-2500
FAX 570-963-2535
http://www.sn.psu.edu
*Michele Steele, Special Services*

Penn State encourages academically qualified students with disabilities to take advantage of its educational programs. It is the policy of the university not to discriminate against persons with disabilities in its admissions policies or procedures or its educational programs, services and activities.

**5139 Point Park College**

Program for Academic Success
201 Wood Street
Pittsburgh, PA 15222     412-391-4100
800-321-0129
FAX 412-261-5303
http://www.pointpark.edu
e-mail: pboykin@pointpark.edu
*Patricia Boykin, Director*

Provides appropriate, reasonable accommodations for students who are disabled in accordance with the Americans with Disabilities Act. All campus accommodations are coordinated through the Program for Academic Success (PAS).

**5140 Reading Area Community College**

10 S 2nd Street
Reading, PA 19603     610-372-4721
800-626-1665
FAX 610-607-6264
http://www.racc.edu
*Richard Kratz, President*
*David Adams, Director of Admissions*

A public two-year college with a small percentage of special education students.

**5141 Seton Hill University**

Seton Hill Drive
Greensburg, PA 15601     724-838-4255
800-826-6234
FAX 724-830-1294
http://www.setonhill.edu
e-mail: bassi@setonhill.edu
*Teresa Bassi, Director Counseling Center*
*Mary , Director Admissions*

Offers programs to those who are eligible and learning disabled.

**5142 Shippensburg University of Pennsylvania**

1871 Old Main Drive
Shippensburg, PA 17257     717-477-1161
FAX 717-477-4001
http://www.ship.edu
e-mail: lawate@wharf.ship.edu
*Lois Waters MD, Director*

Four year college that offers services to the learning disabled students.

**5143 Solebury School**

Phillips Mill Road
New Hope, PA 18938     215-862-5261
FAX 215-862-3366
http://www.solebury.com/
*Annette Miller, Dean*

**5144 Support Services for Students with Learning Disabilities**

Pennsylvania State University
116 Boucke Building
University Park, PA 16802     814-863-1807
FAX 814-863-2217
TDY:814-863-1807
http://www.equity.psu.edu/ods
e-mail: william.welsh@equity.psu.edu/ods
*William Welsh, Director*
*Ann Ette, Secretary*

Penn State provides academic accommodations and support services to students with documented learning disabilities. Accommodations may include audiotaped textbooks, extended time for tests, a test reader and use of a computer to complete essay tests.

**5145 Temple University**

Temple University
1301 Cecil B Moore Avenue
Philadelphia, PA 19122     215-204-1280
FAX 215-204-6794
http://www.temple.edu/disability
e-mail: drs@temple.edu
*Wendy Kohler, LD Coordinator*
*Brian Seidel, Administrative Assistant*

Offers a variety of services to students with disabilities including proctoring, interpreting and academic accommodations.

**5146 Thiel College**

Office of Special Needs
75 College Avenue
Greenville, PA 16125     724-589-2063
800-248-4435
FAX 724-589-2092
http://www.thiel.edu
e-mail: scowan@thiel.edu
*Susan Cowan MSN RN, Office of Special Needs Coordina*

Four year college that provides an Office of Special Needs for those students with disabilities.

**5147 University of Pennsylvania**

34th and Spruce Streets
Philadelphia, PA 19104     215-898-6993
FAX 215-898-5756
http://www.upenn.edu
e-mail: lrcmail@pobox.upenn.edu
*Alice Nagle, Special Services*
*Myrna Cohen, Director*

Services for People with Disabilities coordinates academic support services for students with disabilities; services include readers, notetakers, library research assistants, tutors or transcribers.

**5148 University of Pittsburgh at Bradford**

Learning Development Department
300 Campus Drive
Bradford, PA 16701     814-362-7609
800-872-1787
FAX 814-362-7684
http://www.upb.pitt.edu
*Gillian Boyce MD, Director*
*Kara Kennedy, Learning Development Specialist*

Offers a variety of services to students with disabilities including extended testing time, counseling services, and special accommodations.

**5149  University of Pittsburgh: Greensburg**
Disabilities Services Office
1150 Mount Pleasant Road
Greensburg, PA  15601          724-836-9880
FAX 724-836-7134
http://www.pitt.edu/~upg
e-mail: upgadmit@pitt.edu
*Lou Sears, Disability Services Provider*
*Helen Connors, Counselor*

The Learning Resources Center is an important place for students with disabilities at Pitt Greensburg. Students are encouraged to register with Lou Ann Sears to recieve any accommodations they are entitled to.

**5150  University of Scranton**
Memorial Hall
Scranton, PA  18510          570-941-7400
FAX 570-941-7899
http://http://matrix.scranton.edu
e-mail: addmissions@scranton.edu
*Mary McAndrew, Assistant Director*

Four year college that offers programs for learning disabled students.

**5151  University of the Arts**
320 S Broad Street
Philadelphia, PA  19102          215-875-2254
800-616-2787
FAX 215-717-6045
http://www.uarts.edu
*Lois Elman, Learning Specialist*
*Migule Cruso, President*

The University is committed to supporting students with learning disabilities to ensure that they have an equal opportunity to participate in the university programs. The Learning Specialist provides individual support to students with documented learning disabilities and serves as a liaision between students and faculty when needed.

**5152  Ursinus College**
Box 1000 Main Street
Collegeville, PA  19426          610-409-3000
FAX 610-489-0627
http://www.ursinus.edu
*Richard DiFeliciantonio, Director of Admissions*

Offers a variety of services to students with disabilities including notetakers, extended testing time, counseling services, and special accommodations.

**5153  Villanova University**
800 Lancaster Avenue
Villanova, PA  19085          610-519-5636
FAX 610-519-8015
http://www.villanova.edu
e-mail: nancy.mott@villanova.edu
*Nancy Mott, Coordinator*
*Fr. , President*

Four year college that provides services to learning disabled students.

**5154  Washington and Jefferson College**
60 S Lincoln Street
Washington, PA  15301          724-222-4400
888-926-3529
FAX 724-223-5271
http://www.washjeff.edu
*Catherine Sherman, Assistant Dean*
*Denny Trelka, Dean*

An independent four-year college with a small percentage of special education students.

**5155  Westmoreland County Community College**
400 Armbrust Road
Youngwood, PA  15697          724-925-4000
800-262-2103
FAX 724-925-5802
TDY:724-925-4297
http://www.wccc-pa.edu
e-mail: bbresm@wccc-ta.edu
*Mary Beres, Student Support Services*
*Sandra Zelenak, Director Student Development*

Offers a variety of services to students with disabilities including notetakers, extended testing time, counseling services, and special accommodations. All services are based on a review of a current evaluation presented by the student. Appropriate services are then arranged by the student support service counselor.

**5156  Widener University**
Enable
1 University Place
Chester, PA  19013          610-499-1266
FAX 610-499-1192
http://www.widener.edu/sss/ssmain.html
e-mail: rebecca.a.corsey@widener.edu
*Rebecca Corsey MD, Director of Enable*
*James Harris, President*

An independent four-year college with comprehensive support services.

# Rhode Island

**5157  Brown University**
Disability Support Services
20 Benevolents Street
Providence, RI  02912          401-863-9588
FAX 401-863-1999
TDY:401-863-9588
http://www.brown.edu
e-mail: catherine_axe@brown.edu
*Elyse Chaplin MA, Assistant Dean*
*Catherine Axe, Director*

Brown University has as its primary aim the education of a highly qualified and diverse student body and respects each student's dignity, capacity to contribute, and desire for personal growth and accomplishment. Brown's commitment to students with disabilities is based on awareness of what students require for success. The University desires to foster both intellectual and physical independence to the greatest extent possible in all of its students.

**5158   Bryant College**
Academic Services
1150 Douglas Pike
Smithfield, RI  02917          401-232-6000
                              FAX 401-232-6038
                        http://www.bryant.edu
                    e-mail: lhazard@bryant.edu
*Laurie Hazard MD, Director*
*Sharon Doyle, Office Manager*

An independent four-year Business and Liberal Arts
College. A learning specialist is on campus to provide
services for students with learning disabilities.

**5159   Community College of Rhode Island-Knight
Campus**
400 E Avenue
Warwick, RI  02886          401-825-2164
                            FAX 401-333-7113
                       http://www.ccri.cc.ri.us
*Elizabeth Dalton*

Academic accommodations are available to students
with disabilities who demonstrate a documented need
for the requested accommodation. Accommodations
include but are not limited to adapted equipment, alternative testing, course accommodations, sign language interpreters, reader/audio taping services,
scribes and peer note-takers.

**5160   Johnson & Wales University**
8 Abbott Park Place
Providence, RI  02903          401-598-4689
                               800-343-2565
                           FAX 401-598-4657
                      e-mail: mberstein@swu.edu
*Meryl Berstein, Center Academic Support Director*

An independent four-year university servicing about
5% special education students. Accommodations are
individualized to students presenting documentation
and may include extended time testing, tape recorders
in class, notetaking assistance, reduced course load,
preferential scheduling and tutorial assistance.

**5161   Providence College**
Disability Services Office
549 River Avenue
Providence, RI  02918          401-865-2494
                               FAX 401-865-1219
                               TDY:401-865-2494
                        http://www.providence.edu
                     e-mail: oas@providence.edu
*Nicole Kudarauskas, Coordinator*
*Dan Kwash, Interim*

Offers a variety of services to students with disabilities including note takers, extended testing time,
counseling services, and special accommodations.

**5162   Rhode Island College**
600 Mount Pleasant Avenue
Providence, RI  02908          401-456-8061
                               FAX 401-456-8702
                          http://www.ric.edu
*Ann Roccio, Director*
*Barbara Kingston, Administrative Assistant*

Four-year college with support and services for
learnig disabled students.

**5163   Roger Williams University**
Old Ferry Road
Bristol, RI  02809          401-253-3038
                            800-458-7144
                        FAX 401-254-3302
                       http://www.rwu.edu
An independent comprehensive four-year university
with about 5% special education students.

**5164   Sherlock Center Island College**
600 Mount Pleasant Avenue
Providence, RI  02908          401-456-8072
                               FAX 401-456-8150
                               TDY:401-456-8773
                    http://www.sherlockcenter.org
                     e-mail: aantosh@ric.edu
*A Antosh, Director*
*Erika Tuttle, Administrative Assistant*

The University Affiliated Program (UAP) of Rhode
Island is a member of a national network of UAPs. The
UAP is charged with four core functions: 1. Providing
pre-service training to prepare quality service providers. 2. Providing community outreach training and
technical assistance. 3. Disseminating information
about research and exemplary practice. 4. Research.

**5165   University of Rhode Island**
Disability Services
330 Memorial Union
Kingston, RI  02881          401-874-2098
                             FAX 401-874-5574
                         http://www.uri.edu
*Pamela Rohland, Director*

Disability Service for Students fosters a barrier free
environment to individuals with disabilities through
education that focuses on inclusion, awareness, and
knowledge of ADA/504 compliance. Our mission is
two fold: 1. To encourage a sense of empowerment for
students with disabilities by providing a process that
involves the student. 2. To be an information resource
to the University faculty and staff regarding disability
awareness and academic services.

## South Carolina

**5166   Aiken Technical College**
Student Services
Granite Ville
Aiken, SC  29829          803-593-9231
                          FAX 803-593-6641
                        http://www.atc.edu
                     e-mail: weldon@atc.edu
*Richard Weldon, Counselor*

A public two-year college offering services to the
learning disabled.

**5167   Citadel-Military College of South Carolina**
171 Moultrie Street
Charleston, SC  29409          843-953-5000
                               FAX 843-953-7036
                          http://www.citadel.edu
*Gordon Wallace*

Offers a variety of services to students with disabilities including notetakers, extended testing time, counseling services, and special accommodations.

**5168 Clemson University**
Student Development Services
707 University Union
Clemson, SC 29634 864-656-0515
FAX 864-656-0514
http://www.clemson.edu
e-mail: bmartin@clemson.edu
*Bonnie Martin, Director*

Four-year college offers services to learning disabled students.

**5169 Coastal Carolina University**
Disability Services Department
PO Box 261954
Conway, SC 29528 843-347-3161
FAX 843-349-2990
http://www.coastal.edu
*Monica Yates, Director*
*Vonna Gengo, Coordinator Disability Services*

Coastal Carolina University provides a program of assistance to students with disabilities. Upon acceptance to the University, students will become eligible for support services by providing documentation of their disability. Accommodations include academic labs, tutorial referral, study skills, counseling, auxillary aids, coordination with other agencies and classroom accommodations.

**5170 College of Charleston**
Special Needs Advising Plan
66 George Street
Charleston, SC 29424 843-953-1431
FAX 843-953-7731
TDY:843-953-8284
http://www.cofc.edu/~cds
e-mail: SNAP@cofc.edu
*Ann Lacy, Coordinator SNAP Services*

Provides reasonable and appropriate accommodations specific to individual needs based on the psycho-educational assessment, communication with instructors as needed to heighten awareness of individual needs, alternative coursesin math and foreign language, if need, is documented by assessment.

**5171 Erskine College**
Due West, SC 29639 864-379-2131
FAX 864-379-2167
http://www.erskine.edu
*Katharine Chandler*

Offers a variety of services to students with disabilities including notetakers, extended testing time, counseling services, and special accommodations.

**5172 Francis Marion University**
PO Box 100547
Florence, SC 29501 843-661-1362
800-368-7551
http://www.fmarion.edu
*Kenneth Dye*

A public four-year college with services for special education students.

**5173 Greenville Technical College**
PO Box 5616
Greenville, SC 29606 864-250-8176
800-922-1183
FAX 864-250-8580
http://www.greenvilletech.com
*Owen Perkins, Associate Dean*

Committed to providing equal access for all students and assisting students in making their college experience successful in accordance with ADA/504 and the Rehabilitation Act. The Office of Special Needs for Students with Disabilities has counselors available to assist in the planning and implementation of appropriate accommodations.

**5174 Limestone College**
Program for Alternative Learning Styles
1115 College Drive
Gaffney, SC 29340 864-489-7151
http://www.limestone.edu
e-mail: jpitts@saint.limestone.edu
*Joseph Pitt, Director*

Independent four-year college with a program designed to serve students with learning disabilities. There is an additional fee for the first year in the program in addition to the regular tuition. However, that additional cost is reduced by 50% after the freshman year depending on the grade point average.

**5175 Midlands Technical College**
PO Box 2408
Columbia, SC 29202 803-738-1400
FAX 803-822-3290
http://www.midlandstech.edu
e-mail: brussell@midland.tec.edu
*Barry Russell, President*
*Gina Mounsield, Vice President*

Services to Students with Disabilities counselors support and assist students with disabilities in meeting their personal, educational and career goals. Services include academic and career planning, faculty/student liasion, assistive technology, readers, writers, interpeters, closed circuit television in libraries, TDD, testing services, orientation sessions and a support group.

**5176 North Greenville College**
Learning Disabilities Services
PO Box 1892
Tigerville, SC 29688 864-977-7000
800-468-6642
FAX 864-977-2089
http://www.ngc.edu
e-mail: nisgett@ngc.edu
*Nancy Isgett, Learning Disabilities Liaison*

Offers a variety of services to students with disabilities including notetakers, extended testing time, counseling services, and special accommodations.

**5177 South Carolina State University**
PO Box 7508
Orangeburg, SC 29115 803-536-8670
FAX 803-536-8702
http://www.scsu.edu
e-mail: gouveia@scsu.edu
*Imogene Gouveia MD, Chief Psychologist*

Four-year college that provides information and resources for the learning disabled.

**5178  Spartanburg Methodist College**
1200 Textile Road
Spartanburg, SC  29301          864-587-4000
FAX 864-587-4355
http://www.smcsc.edu
*Sharon Porter, Student Support Director*

An independent two-year college with services for special education students.

**5179  Technical College of Lowcountry: Beaufort**
921 Ribaut Road
Beaufort, SC  29902          843-525-8324
FAX 843-521-4142
*Carolyn Banner, Career Development*

Offers a variety of services to students with disabilities including note takers, extended testing time, counseling services, and special accommodations.

**5180  Trident Academy**
1455 Wakendaw Road
Mt Pleasant, SC  29464          843-884-7046
FAX 843-881-8320
http://www.tridentacademy.com/
e-mail: admissions@tridentacademy.com
Trident Academy is an internationally known independent school for children with diagnosed learning disabilities such as dyslexia and attention deficit disorder serving students in grades K-12.

**5181  Trident Technical College**
PO Box 118067
Charleston, SC  29423          843-574-6111
877-349-7184
FAX 843-574-6484
http://www.trident.tec.sc.us
*Vincent Jr, Special Services*

Recognizes its responsibility to identify and maintain the standards (academic, admissions, scores, etc.) that are necessary to provide quality academic programs while ensuring the rights of students with disabilities.

**5182  University of South Carolina**
Disability Services
Room 106 LeConte
Columbia, SC  29208          803-777-6742
FAX 803-777-6741
TDY:803-777-6744
http://www.sc.edu
e-mail: kpettus@sc.edu
*Dorothy Prioleau, Office Manager*
*Andrea Bullock, Office Assistant*

The Office of Disability Services provides accommodations for students with documented physical, emotional, and learning disabilities. The professionally trained staff works toward accessiblity for all university programs, services, and activities in compliance with ADA/504. Services include orientation,priority registration, library access, classroom adaptions, interpeters, and access to adapted housing.

**5183  University of South Carolina: Aiken**
171 University Parkway
Aiken, SC  29801          803-648-6851
FAX 803-641-3362
http://www.usca.sc.edu/ds
e-mail: kayb@aiken.sc.edu
*Randy Duckett, Special Services*

The mission of Disability Services (DS) is to facilitate the transition of students with disabilities into the University enviroment and to provide appropriate accommodations for each student's special needs in order to ensure equal access to all programs, activities and services at USCA.

**5184  University of South Carolina: Beaufort**
801 Carteret Street
Beaufort, SC  29902          843-521-4100
FAX 843-521-4194
http://www.sc.edu/beaufort
*Joan Lemoine MD, Associate Dean*

A public two-year college with services for special education students.

**5185  University of South Carolina: Lancaster**
Admissions Office
PO Box 889
Lancaster, SC  29721          803-313-7000
FAX 803-313-7106
http://www.lancaster.sc.edu
e-mail: ksaile@gwm.sc.edu
*John Catalano, Dean*
*Rebecca Parker, Director*

Offers a variety of services to students with disabilities including notetakers, extended testing time, counseling services, and special accommodations.

**5186  Voorhees College**
PO Box 678
Denmark, SC  29042          803-703-7131
FAX 803-793-4584
*Adeleri Onisegu MD, Director*

Four-year college that offers programs to learning disabled students.

**5187  Winthrop University**
Student Disabilities Department
701 Oakland Avenue
Rock Hill, SC  29733          803-323-2211
FAX 803-328-2855
TDY:803-323-2233
http://www.winthrop.edu
e-mail: smithg@winthrop.edu
*Gina Smith, Director*

Since each student has a unique set of special needs, the Counselor for Students with Disabilities makes every effort to provide the student with full access to programs and services. Reasonable accommodations are provided based on needs assessed through proper documentation and an intake interview with the couselor. The majority of buildings on campus are accessible.

## South Dakota

**5188  Black Hills State College**
1200 University
Spearfish, SD  09078                 605-642-6099
                                     800-255-2478
                            FAX 605-642-6391
                    http://www.bhsu.edu/disability
                    e-mail: larryvrooman@bhsu.edu
*Larry Vrooman, Coordinator of Disability Servic*
*Thomas , President*

Provide the comprehensive supports necessary in
meeting the individual needs of students with disabilities.

**5189  Northern State University**
1200 S Jay Street
Aberdeen, SD  57401                  605-626-2371
                            FAX 605-626-3399
                      http://www.northern.edu
                    e-mail: diagle@northern.edu
*Kay Diagle, Director*

Four-year college that provides services to students
with a learning disability.

**5190  South Dakota School of Mines & Technology**
501 E Saint Joseph Street
Rapid City, SD  57701                605-394-2414
                                     800-544-8162
                            FAX 605-394-1268
                       http://www.sdsmt.edu
                    e-mail: fcampone@sdsmt.edu
*Francine Campon MD, Associate Dean*

Four-year college that offers support services to those
students whom are disabled.

**5191  South Dakota State University**
Box 2201
Brookings, SD  57007                 605-688-4496
                                     800-952-3541
                            FAX 605-688-6891
                            TDY:605-688-4394
                       http://www.sdstate.edu
          e-mail: SDSU_Admissions@sdstate.edu
*Nancy Hartenhoff-Crookf, Coordinator*
*Dana Dykhouse, President&Chief Executive Office*

Committed to providing equal opportunities for
higher education for learning disabled students.

**5192  Yankton College**
1801 Summit Street
Yankton, SD  57078                   605-665-3661
                                     866-665-3661
                            FAX 605-665-0541
                    http://www.yanktoncollege.org
                       e-mail: yc@byelectric
*Elizabeth Elbe, Executive Director*
*Charles , President*

Offers a variety of services to students with disabilities including note takers, extended testing time,
counseling services, and special accommodations.

## Tennessee

**5193  Austin Peay State University: Office of Disability Services**
Office of Disabilities Services
PO Box 4567
Clarksville, TN  37044               931-221-6230
                            FAX 931-221-7102
                            TDY:931-221-6278
                      http://www.apsu.edu/disability
                    e-mail: oldhamb@apsu.edu
*Beulah Oldham, Director*
*Bryan Kleusner, Assistant Director*

The Office of Disability Services is dedicated to providing academic assistance for students with disabilities enrolled at Austin Peay State University. We
provide information to students, faculty, staff and administrators about the needs of students with disabilities. We ensure the accessiblity of programs, services,
and activities to students having a disability. We are a
resource of information pertaining to disability issues
and advocate participation in campus life.

**5194  Boling Center for Developmental Disabilities**
University of Tennessee
711 Jefferson Avenue
Memphis, TN  38105                   901-448-6511
                                     888-572-2249
                            FAX 901-448-7097
                      http://www.utmem.edu/bcdd
                    e-mail: wwilson@utmem.edu
*Fredrick Palmer MD, Director*
*William , Clinical Services Coordinator*

Interdisciplinary or focused evaluation of learning,
behavioral and developmental problems in infants,
toddlers, children and young adults. Treatment of
some conditions offered.

**5195  Brookhaven College**
Special Services Office
3939 Valley View Lane
Farmers Branch, TN  75244            972-860-4847
                      http://www.dcccd.edu.bhc
*Amadeo Ledesma, Grants Manager*

Physically challenged and learning disabled special
services office offers advisement, additional diagnostic evaluations, mobility assistance, note taking, textbook taping, interpreters for the deaf and assistance in
test taking.

**5196  Bryan College: Dayton**
PO Box 7000
Dayton, TN  37321                    423-775-7207
                                     800-277-9522
                            FAX 423-775-7199
                       http://www.bryan.edu
*Mark Craver, Director of Admissions*
*Peter Held, VP Student Life*

Committed to providing quality education for those who meet admission standards but learn differently from others. Modifications are made in the learning environment to enable LD students to succeed. Some of the modifications made require documentation of the specific disability while other adaptations do not. In addition to modifications the small teacher-student ratio allows the school to provide much individual attention to those with learning difficulties.

**5197  Carson-Newman College**

**1646 Russell Avenue**
**Jefferson City, TN  37760**          **865-417-2000**
**800-678-9061**
**FAX 865-471-3502**
**http://www.cn.edu**
*John Gibson, Associate Professor*

An independent four-year college with support services for special education students.

**5198  DHH Outreach**

**East Tennessee State University**
**Box 70605**
**Johnson City, TN  37614**          **423-439-8346**
**FAX 423-439-8489**
**TDY:423-439-8370**
**http://www.etsu.edu**
**e-mail: storey@mail.etsu.edu /gibson@etsu.edu**
*Linda MEd, Disability Services Director*
*Martha Edde-Adams, Disability Services Asst Dir*
*Elizabeth Tipton, Lead Deaf Interpreter*

The Deaf and Hard of Hearing Outreach program provides coordination of interpreting services for student needs related to classroom and university events.

**5199  East Tennessee State University Disability Services**

**Box 70605**
**Johnson City, TN  37614**          **423-439-8346**
**FAX 423-439-8489**
**TDY:423-439-8370**
**http://www.etsu.edu**
**e-mail: storey@mail.etsu.edu /gibson@etsu.edu**
*Linda MEd, Disability Services Director*
*Martha Edde-Adams, Disability Services Asst Dir*
*Elizabeth Tipton, Lead Deaf Interpreter*

The Disability Services Office works to provide services to give students with disabilities equal opportunities at ETSU through the provision of resonable accommodations, coordination of auxiliary aids, and support services.

**5200  Knoxville Business College**

**720 N 5th Avenue**
**Knoxville, TN  37917**          **865-524-6511**
**FAX 423-637-0127**
**http://www.kbcollege.edu**
*Judy Ferguson, Dean Students*

Offers a variety of services to students with disabilities including notetakers, extended testing time, counseling services, and special accommodations.

**5201  Lambuth College**

**705 Lambuth Boulevard**
**Jackson, TN  38301**          **731-425-2500**
**800-526-2884**
**FAX 731-988-4600**
**http://www.lambuth.edu**
*Becky Sadowski, School Education Head*

Offers a variety of services to students with disabilities including notetakers, extended testing time, counseling services, and special accommodations.

**5202  Leap Program**

**East Tennessee State University**
**Box 70605**
**Johnson City, TN  37614**          **423-439-8346**
**FAX 423-439-8489**
**TDY:423-439-8370**
**http://www.etsu.edu**
**e-mail: storey@mail.etsu.edu /gibson@etsu.edu**
*Linda MEd, Disability Services Director*
*Martha Edde-Adams, Disability Services Asst Dir*
*Elizabeth Tipton, Lead Deaf Interpreter*

The Learning Empowerment for Academic Performance Program is a grant funded program sponsored by Tennessee Department of Human Services, Division of Vocational Rehabilitation.

**5203  Learning Disabilities Program: University of Memphis**

**Learning Disabilities Program**
**215 Scates Hall**
**Memphis, TN  38152**          **901-678-2880**
**FAX 901-678-3070**
**TDY:901-678-2880**
**http://www.people.memphis.edu/~sds/**
**e-mail: stepaske@memphis.edu**
*Susan TePaske, Director*
*Dona Sparger, Director*
*Stephen Shaver, Learning Specialist*

Emphasizes individual responsibility for learning by offering a developmentally oriented program of college survival skills, learning strategies, and individualized planning and counseling based on the students strengths and weaknesses. The program also coordinates comprehensive support services, including test accommodations, tutoring, books on tape, assistive technology and peer mentoring. The program serves approximately 500 students with learning disabilities and ADHD per year.

**5204  Lee University: Cleveland**

**Academic Support Program**
**1120 N Ocoee Street**
**Cleveland, TN  37320**          **423-614-8181**
**800-533-9930**
**FAX 423-614-8179**
**http://www.leeuniversity.edu**
**e-mail: ggallher@leeuniversity.edu**
*Gayle Gallaher MD, Director*
*Paul Conn, President*

An independent four-year college with services for special education students.

**5205 Middle Tennessee State University**

Middle Tennessee State University
1301 E Main Street
Murfreesboro, TN 37132          615-898-2783
                                FAX 615-898-4893
                                http://www.mtsu.edu
                                e-mail: dssemail@mtsu.edu
*John Harris, Disabled Student Services*
*Sidney McPhee, President*

We offer a wide variety of services to students with disabilities including assisting in registration, providing readers and attendants, maintaining an inventory of auxillary aids, offering testing accommodations, providing access to the latest in adaptive computer technologies and acting as a liaison to Uuniversity departments.

**5206 Motlow State Community College**

6051 Ledford Mill Road
Lynchburg, TN 37352          931-455-8511
                             800-654-4877
                             FAX 931-393-1764
                             http://www.mscc.cc.tn.us
                             e-mail: asimmons@mscc.cc.tn.us
*A Simmons, Dean Student Development*

A public two-year college with support services for special education students.

**5207 Northeast State Technical Community College**

Learning Disabilities Department
2425 Highway 75
Blountville, TN 37617          423-354-2476
                              800-836-7822
                              FAX 423-279-7649
                              TDY:423-279-7640
                              http://www.nstcc.cc.tn.us
                              e-mail: kafoulk@northeaststate.edu
*Betty Mask, Director*
*Tonya Cassell, Office Manager*

To assure equal educational opportunities for individuals with disabilities.

**5208 Pellissippi State Technical Community College**

10915 Hardin Valley Road
Knoxville, TN 37932          865-694-6411
                            FAX 865-539-7217
                            http://www.pstcc.cc.tn.us
                            e-mail: semcmurray@pstcc.cc.tn.us
*Joan Newman, Director Academic Assess*

Services for Students with Disabilities develops individual educational support plans, provides priority registration and advisement, furnishes volunteer notetakers, provides readers, scribes, tutor bank, provides interpeter services and publishes a newsletter. The office acts as a liaison, and assists students in location of resources appropriate to their needs.

**5209 Scenic Land School**

1130 Mountain Creek Road
Chattanooga, TN 37405          423-877-9711
                               FAX 423-876-0398
                               http://www.sceniclandschool.org
                               e-mail: ecard@sceniclandschool.org
*Eileen Card, Head of School*
*Mary Brown, Director IEP & Assessment*
*Michele McRae, Dean of Students*

Scenic Land School is a private nonprofit school for students with learning disabilities. The school primarily serves students with dyslexia and ADHD. Average class size is 8 students and a 1:4 teacher:student ratio.

**5210 Shelby State Community College**

737 Union Avenue
Memphis, TN 38174          901-333-5087
                           FAX 901-333-5711
                           http://www.sscc.cc.tn.us
*Jimmy Wiley, Director*

A two-year college providing information and resources to disabled students.

**5211 Southern Adventist University**

Academic Support
PO Box 370
Collegedale, TN 37315          423-236-2779
                               800-768-8437
                               FAX 423-238-1765
                               http://www.ldpsych.southern.edu
                               e-mail: adossant@southern.edu
*Alberto Santos, Dean*
*Mikhaile Spence, Graduate School Coordinator*

A private university offering undergraduate degrees in education designed for K-8, 1-8, 7-12, and K-12 certification plus graduate degrees designed for inclusion (special needs in the regular classroom), multiage/multigrade teaching, outdoor education, and psychology and counseling of exceptional individuals. College age students with special needs and those desiring to teach students with special needs are welcome to apply.

**5212 Southwest Tennessee Community College**

5983 Macon Cove
Memphis, TN 38134          901-333-4193
                           888-832-4937
                           FAX 901-333-4458
                           http://www.southwest.tn.edu
*Maxine Ford*

Offers a variety of services to students with disabilities including note takers, extended testing time, counseling services, and special accommodations.

**5213 Tennessee State University**

Office of Disabled Student Services
3500 John Merritt Boulevard
Nashville, TN 37209          615-963-7400
                             888-536-7655
                             FAX 615-963-2176
                             TDY:615-963-7440
                             http://www.tnstate.edu
                             e-mail: jcade@picard.tnstate.edu
*Patricia Scudder, Director*
*Monique Mitchell, Secretary*

Four year college offers services for learning disabled students.

**5214  University of Tennessee: Knoxville**

**Disability Services Office**
**191 Hoskins Library**
**Knoxville, TN 37996**                    **865-974-6087**
                                        **FAX 865-974-9552**
                                        **TDY:865-974-6087**
                            **http://www. ods.utk.edu**
                            **e-mail: esinger1@utk.edu**
*Emily Singer, Director*

Offers a variety of services to students with disabilities including note takers, extended testing time, counseling services, and special accommodations.

**5215  University of Tennessee: Martin**

**Program Access for College Enhancement**
**209 Clement**
**Martin, TN 38238**                    **731-881-7000**
                                        **FAX 731-881-7702**
                                **http://www.utm.edu**
                                **e-mail: sroberts@utm.edu**
*Sharon Robertson, Coordinator*
*George Daniel, Director*

A four-year independent college that offers a program called Program Access for College Enhancement for students with learning disabilities.

**5216  Vanderbilt University**

**Vanderbilt University**
**VU Station V # 351809**
**Nashville, TN 37203**                    **615-322-4705**
                                        **FAX 615-343-0671**
                                        **TDY:615-322-4705**
                        **http://www.vanderbilt.edu**
                        **e-mail: sara.s.ezell@vanderbilt.edu**
*Sara Ezell, Assistant Director*
*Gordon Gee, Chancellor*

An independent four-year college with support services for special education students.

**5217  William Jennings Bryan College**

**HEATH Resource Center**
**2121 K Street NW**
**Washington, DC 20036**                    **202-973-0904**
                                            **800-544-3284**
                                        **FAX 202-973-0908**
                            **http://www.heath.gwu.edu**
                            **e-mail: askheath@heath.gwu.edu**
*Dan Gardner, Publications Manager*

A public four-year college. The HEALTH Resource Center operates the national clearinghouse on postsecondary education for individuals with disabilities.

## Texas

**5218  Abilene Christian University**

**Alpha Academic Services**
**ACU Box 29204**
**Abilene, TX 79699**                    **915-674-2750**
                                    **FAX 915-674-6847**
                                **http://www.acu.edu**
                                **e-mail: dodda@acu.edu**
*Ada Dodd, Counselor*

A four year college that offers services to students who are learning disabled.

**5219  Alvin Community College**

**Alvin Community College**
**3110 Mustang Road**
**Alvin, TX 77511**                        **281-331-6111**
                                        **FAX 281-756-3843**
                            **http://www.alvin.cc.tx.us**
*Eileen Cross, Counselor*
*Alyssa Reeves, Admission Specialist*

A public two-year college with support services for special education students.

**5220  Amarillo College: Department of Disabilities**

**Department of Disabilities**
**PO Box 447**
**Amarillo, TX 79178**                    **806-371-5000**
                                        **FAX 806-371-5771**
                                        **TDY:806-345-5506**
                                **http://www.actx.edu**
                                **e-mail: wilkes-bj@actx.edu**
*Brenda Wilkes, Coordinator*

Offers a variety of services to students with disabilities including note takers, extended testing time, counseling services, and special accommodations.

**5221  Angelina College**

**Student Services Office**
**PO Box 1768**
**Lufkin, TX 75902**                    **936-639-1301**
                                    **FAX 936-633-5455**
                            **http://www.angelina.edu**
                            **e-mail: jtwohig@angelina.edu**
*James Twohig, Dean*

A public two-year college with support services for special education students.

**5222  Baylor University**

**Office of Access & Learning Accommodation**
**PO Box 97204**
**Waco, TX 76798**                        **254-710-3605**
                                        **FAX 254-710-3608**
                                **http://www.baylor.edu**
                                **e-mail: ahelia_graham@baylor.edu**
*Shelia Graham MD, Director*

Four-year college that offers support and services to students who are learning disabled.

**5223  Briarwood School**

**12207 Whittington Drive**
**Houston, TX 77077**                        **281-493-1070**
                                            **FAX 281-493-1343**
                            **http://www.briarwoodschool.org**
                            **e-mail: info@briarwoodschool.org**
*Carole Wills, Head of School*
*Priscilla Mitchell, Director Admissions*

Briarwood has been serving students with diagnosed learning differences for 35 years. A co-ed private day school offering small classes, remedial and college prep curriculum for its 300 K-12 students. Briarwood believes that every child can learn and has the right to be taught in the way that he or she learns best.

**5224 Cedar Valley College**
Special Support Services
3030 N Dallas Avenue
Lancaster, TX 75134　972-860-8199
FAX 972-860-8014
http://www.dcccd.edu
e-mail: gcf787@dcccd.edu
*Grenna Fynn, Director*
*Michelle Quinn, Special Support Services*

A two-year college that provides special services to its disabled students.

**5225 Central Texas College**
6200 W Central Texas Expressway
Killeen, TX 76542　254-526-7161
800-792-3348
FAX 254-526-1700
TDY:254-526-1378
http://www.ctcd.edu
e-mail: jose.apotte@ctcd.edu
*Jose Apotte, Counselor*
*James , Chancellor*

Offers a variety of services to students with disabilities including notetakers, extended testing time, counseling services, and special accommodations.

**5226 Cisco Junior College**
Cisco Junior College
101 College Heights
Cisco, TX 76437　254-442-2567
FAX 254-442-5100
http://www.cisco.cc.tx.us
*Link Harris, Counselor*
*Elaine Lee, Executive Secretary*

A public two-year college with support services for special education students.

**5227 College of the Mainland**
Student Support Services
1200 Amburn Road
Texas City, TX 77591　409-938-1211
888-258-8859
FAX 409-938-1306
http://www.com.edu
e-mail: kkimbark@com.edu
*Kris Kimbark, Director*

Offers a variety of services to students with disabilities including notetakers, extended testing time, counseling services, and special accommodations. The mission of services for students with disabilities is to provide each student with the resources needed to register, enroll and complete their course work and/or degree plan.

**5228 Collin County Community College**
2200 W University
McKinney, TX 75069　972-881-5790
FAX 972-548-6702
http://www.ccccd.edu
*Norma Johnson, Director*

A public two-year college. ACCESS provides resonable accommodations, individual attention and support for students with disabilities who need assistance with any aspect of their campus experience such as accessibility, academics and testing.

**5229 Concordia University at Austin**
3400 IH 35 N
Austin, TX 78705　512-486-2000
FAX 512-486-1155
http://www.concordia.com
e-mail: admissionj@concordia.edu
*Beryl Dunsmoir MD, Chair*

Four year college offers services to disabled students.

**5230 Dallas Academy**
950 Tiffany Way
Dallas, TX 75218　214-342-1481
FAX 214-327-8537
http://www.dallas-academy.com
e-mail: mail@dallas-academy.com
*Karen Kinsella, Assistant Director*
*Ronda Criss, Development Director*

Offers a variety of services to students with disabilities including notetakers, extended testing time, counseling services, and special accommodations.

**5231 Dallas Academy: Coed High School**
950 Tiffany Way
Dallas, TX 75218　214-324-1481
FAX 214-327-8537
http://www.dallas-academy.com
e-mail: mail@dallas-academy.com
*Karen Kinsella, Assistant Director*
*Ronda Criss, Development Director*

Coed Day School for bright children grades 7-12 with diagnosed learning differences. Curriculum includes sports, art, music, and photography programs.

**5232 Dallas County Community College**
3737 Motley Drive
Mesquite, TX 75150　972-86+0-768
FAX 972-860-7227
http://www.dcccd.edu/
Offers a variety of services to students with disabilities including note takers, extended testing time, counseling services, and special accommodations.

**5233 East Texas Baptist University**
1209 N Grove
Marshall, TX 75670　903-935-7963
800-804-3828
FAX 903-938-7798
http://www.etbu.edu
*Charles Taylor, Director*

Offers a variety of services to students with disabilities including notetakers, extended testing time, counseling services, and special accommodations.

**5234 East Texas State University**
E Texas Station
Commerce, TX 75428　903-886-5000
FAX 903-886-5702
*Tom Lynch, Contact*

Offers a variety of services to students with disabilities including note takers, extended testing time, counseling services, and special accommodations.

**5235 Eastfield College**

3737 Motley Drive
Mesquite, TX 75150     972-860-7100
FAX 972-860-8342
http://www.efc.dcccd.edu
e-mail: mds4420@dcccd.edu
*Reva Rattan, Coordinator*

Offers a variety of services to students with disabilities including note takers, extended testing time, counseling services, and special accommodations.

**5236 El Centro College**

El Centro College
Main and Lamar Streets
Dallas, TX 75202     214-860-207
FAX 214-860-2335
http://www.ecc.dcccd.edu
e-mail: kir5341@dcccd.edu
*Jim Handy, Director Counseling*
*Karen Reed, Assistant Director*

A public two-year college with support services for special education students.

**5237 El Paso Community College: Valle Verde Campus**

Center for Students with Disabilities
PO Box 20500
El Paso, TX 79998     915-831-3722
FAX 915-831-2244
http://www.epcc.edu
e-mail: janlc@epcc.edu
*Jan Lockhart, Director*

A support service for students enrolled at the college who have a verified temporary or permanent disability. Support services offered include advising, tutoring, note taking, test assistance and more.

**5238 Frank Phillips College**

Special Populations Department
PO Box 5118
Borger, TX 79008     806-457-4200
800-687-2056
FAX 806-457-4226
http://www.fpc.cc.tx.us
*S Orand, Special Populations Coordinator*

Offers a variety of services to students with disabilities including notetakers, extended testing time, counseling services, and special accommodations.

**5239 Galveston College**

4015 Avenue Q
Galveston, TX 77550     409-763-6551
FAX 409-762-9367
http://www.gc.edu
*Gaynelle Hayes MD, Vice President*

A public two-year college. A variety of services and programs are available to assist students with disabilities, those who are academically and/or economically disadvantaged and those with limited English proficiency.

**5240 Hill College of the Hill Junior College District**

112 Lamar Drive
Hillsboro, TX 76645     254-582-2555
FAX 254-582-7591
http://www.hillcollege.edu
e-mail: bknelson@hillcollege.edu
*Bill Gilker, Dean Students*
*Belinda Nelson, Admissions Coordinator*

Offers a variety of services to students with disabilities including note takers, extended testing time, counseling services, and special accommodations.

**5241 Houston Community College System**

Houston Community College System
3100 Holman
Houston, TX 77004     713-718-6164
FAX 713-718-2111
TDY:713-718-6166
http://www.hccs.edu
e-mail: welbert@hccs.edu
*John Reno, Director*
*Cherry Caraway, Office Manager*

Offers a variety of services to students with disabilities including note takers, extended testing time, counseling services, and special accommodations.

**5242 Jarvis Christian College**

Highway 80 E
Hawkins, TX 75765     903-769-5700
800-292-9517
FAX 903-769-5005
http://www.jarvis.edu
e-mail: florine_white@jarvis.edu
*Florine White MD, Dir Student Support Services*
*Johnnye , VP*

Student Support Services is a federally funded program whose purpose is to improve the retention and graduate rate of program participants. Eligible program participants include low income, first generation college students and students with learning and physical disabilities. A variety of support services are provided.

**5243 Lamar University: Port Arthur**

Special Populations
1500 ProspeCourt Street
Port Arthur, TX 77641     409-983-4921
800-477-5872
FAX 409-984-6000
TDY:409-984-6242
http://www.pa.lamar.edu
e-mail: andrea.munoz@lamarpa.edu
*Andrea Munoz, Director*
*Stephanie Bucanan, Administrative Assistant*

A public two-year college with support services for special education students.

**5244 Laredo Community College: Special Populations Office**

Special Populations Office
W End Washington Street
Laredo, TX 78040     956-721-5137
FAX 956-721-5838
e-mail: sylviat@laredo.cc.tx.us
*Sylvia LMSW, Counselor/Coordinator*

Offers a variety of services to students with disabilities including notetakers, extended testing time, counseling services, and special accommodations.

**5245  Lubbock Christian University**

5601 19th Street
Lubbock, TX  79407                806-796-8800
                                  800-933-7601
                             FAX 806-720-7162
                          http://www.lcu.edu
                    e-mail: admissions@lcu.edu
*Ken Jones, President*
*Rod Blackwood, Vice President*

Offers a variety of services to students with disabilities including notetakers, extended testing time, counseling services, and special accommodations.

**5246  McLennen Community College**

McLennan Community College
1400 College Drive
Waco, TX  76708                   254-299-8790
                             FAX 254-299-8556
                       http://www.mclennan.edu
*Anitra Cooton, Director*
*Mickey Reyes, Desktop Publishing Technician*

A public two-year college with support services for special education students.

**5247  Midwestern State University**

Disability Counseling Office
3410 Taft Boulevard
Wichita Falls, TX  76308          940-397-4618
                             FAX 940-397-4934
                             TDY:940-397-4515
                          http://www.mwsu.edu
                    e-mail: counselling@mwsu.edu
*Debra Higginbotham, Director*

A public four-year college with support services for special education students.

**5248  North Harris County College**

North Harris County College
2700 WW Thorne Drive
Houston, TX  77073                281-618-5400
                             FAX 281-618-5706
                             TDY:281-765-7938
                http://www.northharriscollege.com
           e-mail: spatton@northharriscollege.com
*Sandi Patton, Special Services*
*David Sam, President*

Offers a variety of services to students with disabilities including note takers, extended testing time, counseling services, and special accommodations. We train students in the use of specialized software and hardware.

**5249  North Lake College**

Disabilities Services Office
5001 N Macarthur Boulevard
Irving, TX  75038                 972-273-3165
                             FAX 972-273-3164
                             TDY:972-273-3169
                          http://www.dcccd.edu
*Carole Gray, Disability Services Coordinator*
*Sherry Beal, Office Manager*

A public two-year college. Our mission is to provide a variety of support services to empower students, foster independence, promote achievement of realistic career and educational goals and assist students in discovering, developing and demonstrating full potential and abilities.

**5250  Odyssey School**

831 Houston Street
Austin, TX  78756                 512-472-2262
                             FAX 512-236-9385
                    http://www.odysseyschool.com/
                    e-mail: nelsonchase@dpsk12.org

**5251  Office of Disability Services**

Stephen F Austin State University
1936 North Street
Nacogdoches, TX  75961            936-468-3401
                             FAX 936-468-5810
                          http://www.sfasu.edu
*Margie Franklin, Director*

Offers a variety of services to students with disabilities including note takers, extended testing time, counseling services, and special accommodations.

**5252  Pan American University**

Office of Disability Services
1201 W University Drive
Edinburg, TX  78541               956-381-2011
                             FAX 956-316-7034
                             TDY:956-316-7092
                          http://www.panam.edu
*Rick Gray, Director*
*Esperanza Cavazos, Associate Director*

Offers a variety of services to students with disabilities including note takers, extended testing time, counseling services, and special accommodations.

**5253  Rawson-Saunders School**

2600 Exposition Boulevard
Austin, TX  78703                 512-476-8382
                             FAX 512-476-1132
                    http://www.rawson-saunders.org
*Harriett Choffel, Head School*
*Luann Hargrave, Office Manager*

**5254  Richland College**

12800 Abrams Road
Dallas, TX  75243                 972-238-6180
                             FAX 972-238-6957
                       http://www.rlc.dcccd.edu
                    e-mail: stevem@dcccd.edu
*Jeanne Brewer, LD Director*

Offers a variety of services to students with disabilities including note takers, extended testing time, counseling services, and special accommodations.

**5255  Sam Houston State University**

1700 Sam Houston Avenue
Huntsville, TX  77341             936-294-1111
                             FAX 936-294-3970
                          http://www.shsu.edu
*James Gaertner MD, President*

Offers a variety of services to students with disabilities including note takers, extended testing time, counseling services, and special accommodations.

**5256 San Antonio College**

Programs for the Handicapped
1300 San Pedro Avenue
San Antonio, TX 78212     210-733-2000
FAX 210-733-2202
http://www.accd.edu/sac/sacmain/sac.htm
*Maria Gomez, Coordinator*
*Regina Pino, Assistant Coordinator*

A public two-year college with support services for special education students.

**5257 San Jacinto College: Central Campus**

8060 Spencer Hwy
Pasadena, TX 77501     281-476-1501
FAX 281-476-1892
http://www.sjcd.cc.tx.us
*Judy Ellison, Special Populations*

Offers a variety of services to students with disabilities including notetakers, extended testing time, counseling services, and special accommodations such as test readers and writers.

**5258 San Jacinto College: South Campus**

San Jacinto College: South Campus
13735 Beamer Road
Houston, TX 77089     281-922-3431
FAX 281-922-3485
http://www.sjcd.edu
e-mail: tmontgomery@sjcd.edu
*Tina Montgomery, Registrar*
*Joan Rondot, Administrative Assistant*

A public two-year college with support services for special education students.

**5259 San Marcos Texas State University: Office of Disability Services**

Office of Disability Services
601 University Drive
San Marcos, TX 78666     512-245-3451
FAX 512-245-3452
TDY:512-245-3451
http://www.swt.edu
e-mail: rp16@swt.edu
*Richard Poe, Learning Disability Specialist*

Provides support services and coordinates academic accommodations based on the individual students disibility-based need.

**5260 Schreiner University**

2100 Memorial Boulevard
Kerrville, TX 78028     830-896-5411
800-343-4919
FAX 830-792-7226
http://www.schreiner.edu
e-mail: ctait@scheiner.edu
*Charles Tait, Admissions Counselor*

An independent four-year university with about 10% of students in the Learning Support Services Program. There is a fee for the LSS program in addition to the regular tuition.

**5261 South Plains College**

1401 S College Avenue
Levelland, TX 79336     806-894-9611
FAX 806-894-5274
http://www.spc.cc.tx.us
*Bill Powell, Studies Program*

Offers a variety of services to students with disabilities including notetakers, extended testing time, counseling services, and special accommodations.

**5262 Southern Methodist University**

6425 Boaz Street
Dallas, TX 75275     214-768-4563
FAX 214-768-4572
http://www.smu.edu
e-mail: rmarin@mail.smu.edu
*Rebecca Marin, Coordinator*
*Carolyn Hamby, Assistant*

An independent four-year college with support services for special education students.

**5263 Southwestern Assemblies of God University**

Southwestern Assemblies of God university
1200 Sycamore Street
Waxahachie, TX 75165     972-937-4010
888-YES-SAGU
FAX 972-923-0488
http://www.sagu.edu
e-mail: sagu@sagu.edu
*Kermit Bridges, President*

Offers a variety of services to students with disabilities including notetakers, extended testing time, counseling services, and special accommodations.

**5264 St. Edwards University**

Learning Disabilities Services
3001 S Congress Avenue
Austin, TX 78704     512-448-8400
FAX 512-448-8492
http://www.stedwards.edu
*Lorraine Prea, Director*

An independent four-year college. Students with disabilities meet with a counselor from academic planning and support and they work together to ensure equal access to all academic services.

**5265 St. Mary's University of San Antonio**

One Camino Santa Maria
San Antonio, TX 78228     210-436-3203
FAX 210-436-3782
http://www.stmarytx.edu
*Barbara Biassiolli, Center Director*
*Lisa Seller, Assistant Director*

Offers a variety of services to students with disabilities including tutoring, extended testing time, and academic counseling services.

**5266  Tarleton State University**

Tarleton State University
Box T-0010
Stephenville, TX  76401                254-968-9103
                                  FAX 254-968-9703
                          http://www.tarleton.edu
*L Dwayne Snider MD, Associate Vice President For Aca*
*Lisa Howe, Administrative Assistant For Aca*

Four year college that provides students with learning disabilities support and services.

**5267  Tarrant County College DSS-NE: Disability Support Services**

Disability Support Services
828 Harwood Road
Hurst, TX  76054                       817-515-6333
                                  FAX 817-515-6112
                                  TDY:817-515-6812
                            http://www.tccd.edu
                    e-mail: judy.kelly@tccd.edu
*Judy Kelley, Director*
*Dorotha McDonnell, Secretary*

Offers a variety of services to students with disabilities including notetakers, extended testing time, tutors, counseling services, special accommodations, and registration assistance.

**5268  Texas A&M University**

1265 TAMU
College Station, TX  77843             979-845-3471
                                  FAX 979-847-8737
                            http://www.tamu.edu
                  e-mail: anne@stulife2.tamu.edu
*Anne Reber MD, Coordinator*

A public four-year college with support services for special education students.

**5269  Texas A&M University: Commerce**

PO Box 3011
Commerce, TX  75429                    903-886-5835
                                  FAX 903-468-3220
                    http://www.tamu-commerce.edu
            e-mail: frank_perez@tamu-commerce.edu
*Frank Perez, Assistant Director*

Four-year college that provides student support services and programs to those students who are learning disabled.

**5270  Texas A&M University: Kingsville**

1210 Retama Drive
Kingsville, TX  78363                  361-593-3024
                                  FAX 361-593-2006
                            http://www.tamuk.edu
                e-mail: adrain.garcia@tamuk.edu
*Rachel Cox, Assistant Coordinator*

Four-year college that provides an academic support center for students who are disabled.

**5271  Texas Southern University**

3100 Cleburne Street
Houston, TX  77004                     713-313-7011
                                  FAX 713-313-7539
                              http://www.tsu.edu
*Minnine Simmons, Counselor*

A public four-year college with support services for special education students.

**5272  Texas State Technical Institute: Sweetwater Campus**

300 College Drive
Sweetwater, TX  79556                  325-235-7300
                                       800-592-8784
                      http://www.sweetwater.tstc.edu
*Phyllis Morris, Special Services*

Offers a variety of services to students with disabilities including notetakers, extended testing time, counseling services, and special accommodations.

**5273  Texas Tech University**

AccessTECH & TECHniques Center
143 Wiggins West
Lubbock, TX  79409                     806-742-2405
                                  FAX 806-742-4837
                                  TDY:806-742-2092
                   http://www.accesstech.dsa.ttu.edu
                    e-mail: accesstech@ttu.edu
*Frank Silvas, Director*
*Leann DiAndreth-Elkins, Assistant Director of Technique*

AccessTECH is a place for students with disabilities to register in order to receive reasonable academic accommodations. TECHniques Center is a fee-for-service program that provides supplemental academic support for college students with documented learning disabilities and attention deficit disorders.

**5274  Texas Tech University: AccessTECH**

143 Wiggins West
Lubbock, TX  79409                     806-742-2405
                                  FAX 806-742-4837
                                  TDY:806-742-2092
                   http://www.accesstech.dsa.ttu.edu
                    e-mail: accesstech@ttu.edu
*Frank Silvas, Director*
*Leann DiAndreth-Elkins, Assistant Director of Technique*

A place for students with disabilities to register in order to receive reasonable academic accommodations.

**5275  Texas Tech University: TECHniques Center**

TECHniques Center
100 Wiggins West
Lubbock, TX  79409                     806-742-1822
                                  FAX 806-742-0295
                                  TDY:806-742-2092
                     http://www.techniques.ttu.edu
                e-mail: techniques.center@ttu.edu
*Leann DiAndreth-Elkins, Techniques Center Director*

The TECHniques Center is a fee-for-service program that provides supplemental academic support for college students with documented learning disabilities and attention deficit disorders.

**5276 Texas Woman's University**
Disability Support Services
PO Box 425966
Denton, TX 76204
940-898-3626
FAX 940-898-3965
TDY:940-898-3830
http://www.twu.edu
e-mail: dss@twu.edu
*Jo-ann Nunnelly, Director*

A public four-year college with support services for special education students.

**5277 Tyler Junior College**
PO Box 9020
Tyler, TX 75711
903-510-2458
FAX 903-510-2434
http://www.tyler.cc.tx.us
*Vickie Geisel, Special Services*

Offers a variety of services to students with disabilities including note takers, extended testing time, counseling services, and special accommodations.

**5278 University Affiliated Program: University of Austin, Texas**
Education Building 306
Austin, TX 78712
512-471-7621
FAX 512-471-0577
*Penny Seay, Director*

**5279 University of Houston**
Disability Support Services
CSD Building
Houston, TX 77204
713-743-5400
FAX 713-743-5396
TDY:713-749-1527
http://www.uh.edu
e-mail: wscrain@mail.uhe.edu
*Scott Crain, Counselor*
*Dr , Assistant Director*
*Cheryl Amotuso, Director*

A public four-year college with support services for students with disabilities.

**5280 University of North Texas**
Office of Disability Accommodation
Union 322, 400 Avenue A
Denton, TX 76203
940-565-4323
FAX 940-369-7969
TDY:940-369-8652
http://www.unt.edu/oda
e-mail: undergrad@unt.edu
*Ron Venable, Director*

A public four-year college with a small percentage of learning disabled students.

**5281 University of Texas: Arlington**
Disability Support Office
300 W 1st Street
Arlington, TX 76019
817-272-3364
FAX 817-272-1447
TDY:817-272-1520
http://www.uta.edu/disability
*Dianne Hengst, Director*
*Penny Acrey, Assistant Director*
*Amber Mitchell, Interpeting Services Coodinator*

A public four-year university. There is no specific LD program, but comprehensive support services are available. Total enrollment 20,000+.

**5282 University of Texas: Dallas**
PO Box 830688
Richardson, TX 75083
972-883-2221
FAX 972-883-2156
http://www.utdallas.edu
*Tracy Cole, Disability Services*

Offers a variety of services to students with disabilities including notetakers, extended testing time, counseling services, and special accommodations.

**5283 University of Texas: Pan American**
1201 W University Drive
Edinburg, TX 78541
956-381-UTPA
866-441-UTPA
http://www.panam.edu
*Arturo Ramos, Assistant Director*

Offers a variety of services to students with disabilities including notetakers, extended testing time, counseling services, and special accommodations.

**5284 University of Texas: San Antonio**
1604 W Loop
San Antonio, TX 78249
210-458-4157
800-669-0919
FAX 210-458-4980
TDY:210-458-4981
http://www.utsa.edu
e-mail: nestor.reyes@utsa.edu
*Lorraine Harrison, Director*
*Nestor Reyes, Assistant Director*

Disability Services provides support services, accommodations and equipment for UTSA students with temporary or permanent disabilities. Goals of DS are to promote a barrier free environment, to encourage students to become as independent and self-reliant as possible and to provide information and consultation about specific disabilities to the entire community.

**5285 University of the Incarnate Word**
4301 Broadway
San Antonio, TX 78209
210-829-6005
800-749-WORD
FAX 210-283-5021
http://www.uiw.edu
e-mail: uiwhr@universe.uiwtx.edu
*Lorena Novak, Coordinator*

Four year college that provides services to learning disabled students.

**5286 Wharton County Junior College**
911 Boling Highway
Wharton, TX 77488
979-532-4560
800-561-9252
FAX 979-532-6587
http://www.wcjc.cc.tx.us/

Offers a variety of services to students with disabilities including note takers, extended testing time, counseling services, and special accommodations.

**5287** Wiley College
711 Wiley Avenue
Marshall, TX 75670
903-927-3300
800-658-6889
FAX 903-938-8100
http://www.wilec.edu
e-mail: vdavis@wileyc.edu

Offers a variety of services to students with disabilities including notetakers, extended testing time, counseling services, and special accommodations.

# Utah

**5288** Brigham Young University
1520 Wilkinson Center
Provo, UT 84602
801-378-4636
FAX 801-422-0174
TDY:801-422-0436
http://www.byu.edu
e-mail: UAC@BYU.EDU
*Paul Bird, Director*
*John Call, Acting Director*

Offers a variety of services to students with disabilities including note takers, extended testing time, counseling services, and special accommodations.

**5289** Center for Persons with Disabilities
Utah State University
6800 Old Main Hill
Logan, UT 84322
435-797-1981
866-284-2821
FAX 435-797-3944
TDY:435-797-1981
http://www.cpd.usu.edu
e-mail: info@cpd2.usu.edu
*Sarah Rule, Director*

A University Center for Excellence in Developmental Disabilities Education, Research and Services. The Center for Persons with Disabilities provides interdisciplinary training, research, exemplary services, and technical assistance to agencies related to people with disabilities.

**5290** College of Eastern Utah
451 E 400 N
Price, UT 84501
435-637-2120
FAX 435-613-5112
http://www.ceu.edu
*Dee Howa, DRC Director*
*Ryan Thomas, President*

The DRC at CEU provides academic accommodations for the learning disabled.

**5291** Latter-Day Saints Business College
411 E South Temple
Salt Lake City, UT 84111
801-524-8100
FAX 801-524-1900
http://www.ldsbc.edu
*Tina Orden, Dean Students*

Offers a variety of services to students with disabilities including notetakers, extended testing time, counseling services, and special accommodations.

**5292** Salt Lake Community College: Disability Resource Center
4600 S Redwood Road
Salt Lake City, UT 84123
801-957-4659
FAX 801-957-4947
TDY:801-957-4646
http://www.slcc.edu
e-mail: linda.bennett@slcc.edu
*Rod Romboy, Director*
*Linda Bennett, Office Manager*

A program to assist students with disabilities in obtaining equal access to college facilities and programs. The resource center serves all disabilities and provides services and accommodations such as testing, adaptive equipment, text on tape, readers, scribes, note takers, and interpreters for the deaf.

**5293** Snow College
150 E College Avenue
Ephraim, UT 84627
435-283-7000
800-848-3399
FAX 435-283-7449
http://www.snow.edu
*Cyndi Crabb, Special Services*

A public two-year college with support services for special education students.

**5294** Southern Utah University
351 W Center Street
Cedar City, UT 84720
435-586-7710
FAX 435-865-8393
http://www.suu.edu
e-mail: thompson@suu.edu
*Georgia Thompson, Coordinator*
*Steven Bennion, President*

A public four-year University with support services for special education students.

**5295** University of Utah
110 Park
Salt Lake City, UT 84112
801-581-5020
800-444-8638
FAX 801-581-5487
TDY:801-581-5020
http://www.utah.edu
e-mail: onadeau@saun.saff.utah.edu
*Olga Nadeau, Director*

A public four-year college. Services include admissions requirements modification, testing accommodations, priority registration, advisement on course selection and number, adaptive technology, support group. Documentation of learning disability is required.

**5296** Utah State University
0101 Old Main Hall
Logan, UT 84322
435-797-2444
FAX 435-797-0130
TDY:435-797-0740
http://www.usu.edu
e-mail: dhardman@addmissions.usu.edu
*Diane Hardman, Director*

A public four-year college with support services for students with learning disabilities.

**5297  Utah Valley State College**

Accessibility Services Department
800 West University Pkwy
Orem, UT  84058                      801-863-INFO
                                     FAX 801-226-5207
                                     http://www.uvsc.edu
                                     e-mail: info@uvsc.edu
*Curtis Pendleton, Disabled Services*
*Michelle Lundell, Department Director*
*Ann Lickey, Secretary*

The mission for Accessibility Services at Utah Valley
State College is to ensure, in compliance with federal
and state laws, that no qualified individual with a disability be excluded from participation in or be denied
the benefits of a quality education at UVSC or be subjected to discrimination by the college or its personnel. UVSC offers a large variety of support services,
accommodative services and assistive technology for
individuals with learning disabilities.

**5298  Weber State University**

Disabilities Support Office
1103 University Circle
Ogden, UT  84408                      801-626-6000
                                      FAX 801-626-6744
                                      TDY:801-626-7283
                                      http://www.weber.edu

*Jeff Morris, Director*

Offers a variety of services to students with disabilities including notetakers, extended testing time, counseling services, and special accommodations.

**5299  Westminster College of Salt Lake City**

Learning Disability Program
1840 S 1300 E
Salt Lake City, UT  84105             801-832-2280
                                      800-748-4753
                                      FAX 801-832-3101
                                      TDY:801-832-2286
                            http://www.westminstercollege.edu
                    e-mail: gdewitt@westminstercollege.edu
*Ginny DeWitt, Director*
*Amy Gordon, Office Manager*

Offers a variety of services to students with disabilities including notetakers, extended testing time, counseling services, and special accommodations.

## Vermont

**5300  Burlington College**

95 N Avenue
Burlington, VT  05401                 802-862-9616
                                      800-862-9616
                                      FAX 802-660-4331
                                      http://www.burlcol.edu
                                      e-mail: jsanders@burlcol.edu
*Jane Sanders, President*
*Jillian McMahon, Office Manager*

Education process vs test and grades. Small classes.
Learning specialist available.

**5301  Champlain College**

Support Services
163 S Willard Street
Burlington, VT  05401                 802-865-6425
                                      FAX 802-860-2764
                                      http://www.champlain.edu
                                      e-mail: peterson@champlain.edu
*Rebecca Peterson, Coordinator*

Four year college that supports students with a learning disability.

**5302  College of St. Joseph**

71 Clement Road
Rutland, VT  05701-3899               802-773-5900
                                      FAX 802-773-5900
                                      http://www.csj.edu
                                      e-mail: fmiglorie@csj.edu
*Frank Miglorie, President*
*Gary , Vice President*

Offers a variety of services to students with disabilities including note takers, extended testing time,
counseling services, and special accommodations.

**5303  Community College of Vermont**

Student Services Office
PO Box 120
Waterbury, VT  05676                  802-241-3535
                                      FAX 802-241-3526
                                      http://www.ccv.edu
                                      e-mail: ccvinfo@ccv.vsc.edu
*Mel Donovan, Director for  Student Services*
*Joyce Judy, Provost*

A public two-year college offering courses, certificates and associate degrees.

**5304  Green Mountain College**

Calhoun Learning Center
One College Circle
Poultney, VT  05764                   802-287-8232
                                      FAX 802-287-8099
                                      http://www.greenmtn.edu
                                      e-mail: admiss@greenmtn.edu
*Nancy Ruby, Director*
*Becky Eno, Assistant Director*

Four-year college that offers support through the
school's Calhoun Learning center to students with
disabilities.

**5305  Johnson State College**

Learning Disabilities Department
337 College Hill
Johnson, VT  05656                    802-635-1259
                                      800-635-2356
                                      FAX 802-635-1454
                                      TDY:802-635-1456
                                      http://www.jsc.vsc.edu
                                      e-mail: dian.duranleau@jsc.vsc.edu
*Dr Madden, Director*
*Dian Duranleau, Learning Specialist / Director*

A public four-year college with support services for
special education students.

**5306** **Landmark College**
River Road S
Putney, VT 05346
                                    802-387-6718
                                    FAX 802-387-6868
                    http://www.landmarkcollege.org
                    e-mail: admissions@landmarkcollege.org
*Ed Parker, Associate Dean Admissions*
*Christopher Ken, Assistant Dean of Admissions*

Landmark College provides ambitious and motivated students with learning disabilities or ADHD with the skills needed for academic success. Every Landmark student receives personalized instruction and attention. All students are provided with intense one-on-one tutorials, which help them identify their individual learning styles. Students develop the critical language and study skills that will allow them to work within the expectations of academia and the work force.

**5307** **Norwich University**
**Learning Support Center**
**158 Harron Drive**
**Northfield, VT 05663**
                                    802-485-2132
                                    800-468-6679
                    FAX 802-485-2032
                    http://www.norwich.edu
                    e-mail: gills@norwich.edu
*Paula Gills, Special Services*

The Learning Center offers an opportunity for individualized assistance with many aspects of academic life in a supportive, personalized atmosphere. Students may voluntarily choose from a wide variety of service options.

**5308** **Southern Vermont College**
**978 Mansion Drive**
**Bennington, VT 05201**
                                    802-447-6360
                                    800-378-2782
                    FAX 802-447-4695
                    http://www.svc.edu
                    e-mail: tgerson@svc.edu
*Todd Gerson, Coordinator*

Offers students with documented learning disabilities a highly supportive environment and a wide range of support services which include basic skills tutoring, content area academic support, study techniques, notetaking and more.

**5309** **University of Vermont**
**ACCESS**
**633 Main Street**
**Burlington, VT 05405**
                                    802-656-7753
                    FAX 802-656-0739
                    TDY:802-656-3865
                    http://www.uvm.edu/access
                    e-mail: access@uvm.edu
*Donna Panko, Learning Specialist*
*Nick Ogrizovich, Information Specialist*
*Joe Wilson, Learning Specialist*

Provides accommodation, consultation, collaboration and educational support services as a means to foster opportunities for students with disabilities to participate in a barrier free learning environment.

**5310** **Vermont Technical College**
**Main Street**
**Randolph Center, VT 05061**
                                    802-728-1000
                                    800-442-8821
                    FAX 802-728-1390
                    TDY:802-728-1278
                    http://www.vtc.vsc.edu
                    e-mail: rgoodall@vtc.edu
*Robin Goodall, Learning Specialists*
*Eileen Haddon, Assistive Technology Project*

Offers a variety of services to students with disabilities including individualized accommodations, counseling services, academic counseling.

---

# Virginia

---

**5311** **Averett College**
**Support Services for Students**
**428 Firth Hall**
**Danville, VA 24541**
                                    434-791-5744
                    FAX 804-791-4392
                    http://www.averett.edu
                    e-mail: priedel@averett.edu
*Pamela Riedel MD, Support Services Coordinator*

Four-year college that offers services for the learning disabled.

**5312** **Blue Ridge Community College**
**Virginia Community College System**
**Houff Student Center Room 103 B**
**Weyers Cave, VA 24486**
                                    540-234-9261
                                    888-750-2722
                    FAX 540-234-9598
                    http://www.brcc.edu
                    e-mail: khardy@brcc.edu
*Kathy Hardy, Academic Adviser*
*Liell Hern, Administrative Assistant*

A public two-year college. The Office of Disability Services is part of the Blue Ridge Community Counseling Center. Its mission is to provide disabled students with the support services needed to be successful in college.

**5313** **College of William and Mary**
**College of William and Mary**
**Williamsburg, VA 23187**
                                    757-221-4000
                    FAX 757-221-2749
                    TDY:757-221-1154
                    http://www.wm.edu
*Carroll Hardy MD, Director*
*Timothy Sullivan, President*

Offers a variety of services to students with disabilities including notetakers, extended testing time, counseling services, and special accommodations.

**5314 Eastern Mennonite University**

Academic Support Center - Student Disability Svcs.
1200 Park Road
Harrisonburg, VA 22802     540-432-4233
    800-368-2665
    FAX 540-432-4977
    TDY:540-432-4631
    http://www.emu.edu
    e-mail: hedrickj@emu.edu
*Joyce Hedrick, Coordinator*

EMU is committed to working out reasonable accommodations for students with documented disabilities to ensure equal access to the University and its related programs.

**5315 Emory & Henry College**

One Garnand Drive
Emory, VA 24327     276-944-4121
    800-848-5493
    FAX 276-944-6934
    http://www.ehc.edu
*Jill Smeltzer, Director of Counseling Services*
*Judy Jarnes, Administrative Assistant to the*

A private four-year liberal arts college located in the foothills of southwest Virginia. Student enrollment of appox. 1,000, almost equally divided between men and women. The Paul Adrian Powell III resource center offers a variety of services to students with disabilities including extended testing time, counseling services, and special accommodations, as well as tutorial services.

**5316 Ferrum College**

PO Box 1000
Ferrum, VA 24088     540-365-2121
    800-868-9797
    FAX 540-365-4203
    http://www.ferrum.edu
*Dr Braaten, President*

An independent four-year college with support services for special education students.

**5317 GW Community School**

GW Community School
9001 Braddock Road
Springfield, VA 22151     703-978-7208
    FAX 703-978-7226
    http://www.gwcommunityschool.com
    e-mail: info@gwcommunityschool.com
*Alexa Warden, School Director*

The GW Community School is owned and operated by teachers who understand the learning process and the students' needs, and who genuinely enjoy teaching adolesents. They work closely with students and their families to maximize learning. The GW School for Divergent Learners embodies a vision shared by teachers, parents, and students. A school committed to developing and optimizing the giftedness and intellegence of each student and fostering a sense of social awareness and civic responsibility

**5318 Hampden-Sydney College**

Box 685
Hampden-Sydney, VA 23943     434-223-6000
    FAX 434-223-6346
    http://www.hsc.edu
*Elizabeth Ford, Associate Dean of Academic Suppo*
*Wlalter Bortz, President*

Offers a variety of services to students with disabilities including note takers, extended testing time, counseling services, and special accommodations.

**5319 James Madison University**

Office of Disabilities Services
Wilson Learning Center, Room 107
Harrisonburg, VA 22807     540-568-6705
    FAX 540-568-3780
    TDY:540-568-6705
    http://www.jmu.edu/disabilityser/
    e-mail: gotojmu@jmu.edu /disability-svcs@jmu.edu
*Lou Hedrick, Director*

The Office of Disability Services at James Madison University provides support services for students with documented learning disabilities. The program ensures equal access to education by providing the appropriate accommodations. Documentation must be current (within the last four years). Students with learning disabilities must go through the standard admissions process.

**5320 John Tyler Community College**

Office of Disability Services
13101 Jefferson Davis Highway
Chester, VA 23831     804-706-5225
    800-552-3490
    FAX 804-796-4163
    http://www.jtcc.edu
*Robert Tutton, Counselor*
*Betsy , Director*

A public two-year college with support services for special education students.

**5321 Learning Needs & Evaluation Center: Elson Student Health Center**

University of Virginia
400 Brandon Avenue
Charlottesville, VA 22908     434-924-3601
    FAX 434-243-5188
    http://www.virginia.edu/studenthealth/
*Jennifer Maedge MD, Director*

Full range of support services for students admitted to any of the ten schools of the university, including graduate/professional schools. Including, not limited to, taped texts, writing support, learning strategies, exam accommodation, liaison with faculty.

**5322 Liberty University**

Office of Academic Disability Support
1971 University Boulevard
Lynchburg, VA 24502     434-582-2000
    FAX 804-582-2468
    TDY:434-522-0420
    http://www.liberty.edu
    e-mail: wdmchane@liberty.edu
*W McHaney, Academic Disability Support Dir.*
*Jerry , President*

Religiously oriented, private, coeducational, comprehensive four year institution. Students who have documented learning disabilities are eligible to receive support services. These would include academic advising, priority class registration, tutoring and testing accommodations.

**5323    Little Keswick School**

PO Box 24
Keswick, VA  22947                    434-295-0457
                                       FAX 434-977-1892
                          http://www.avenue.org/lks
*Terry Columbus, Director*

Little Keswick School is a therapeutic boarding school for 30 learning disabled and/or emotionally disturbed boys between the ages of 10 to 15 at acceptance and served through 17. IQ range accepted ti sbelow average to superior structured routine in a small, nurturing environment services include psychotherapy, occupational therapy, speech therapy and art therapy. Five week summer session.

**5324    Longwood College**

201 High Street
Farmville, VA  23919                   434-395-2391
                                        800-281-4677
                                  FAX 434-395-2434
                                  TDY:800-281-4677
                        http://www.longwood.edu
                      e-mail: roodse@longwood.edu
*Susan Rood, Disability Support Services*
*Nathan Fortener, Administrative Support*

A public four-year college with support services for special education students.

**5325    Lord Fairfax Community College**

173 Skirmisher Lane
Middletown, VA  22645                  540-868-7000
                                        800-906-5322
                                  FAX 540-868-7100
                             http://www.lfcc.edu
*Paula Dean, Coordinator of Testing Center*

A public two-year college. Students are encouraged to identify special needs during the admissions process and to request support services, such as individualized placement testing, developmental studies, learning assistance programs, and study skills. A 504 faculty team recommends accommodations to academic programs, and communicates with area service providers.

**5326    Mary Washington College**

University of Mary Washington Disability Services
1301 College Avenue
Fredericksburg, VA  22401              540-654-1010
                                  FAX 540-654-1063
                                  TDY:540-654-1102
                            http://www.umw.edu
                        e-mail: ssmith@umw.edu
*Stephanie Smith, Director*
*Cathy Payne, Office Manager*

A public four-year college with support services for special education students.

**5327    New River Community College**

PO Box 1127
Dublin, VA  24084                      540-674-3600
                                        866-462-6722
                                  FAX 540-674-3644
                                  TDY:540-674-3619
                             http://www.nr.edu
                   e-mail: nrdixoj@nr.ca.cc.va.us
*Jeananne Dixon, Coordinator of Learning Disabili*
*Bonnie Hall, Information Center*

A public two-year college with support services for special education students.

**5328    Norfolk State University**

Norfolk State University
700 Park Avenue
Norfolk, VA  23464                     757-823-8173
                                  FAX 757-823-2237
                             http://www.nsu.edu
                        e-mail: bbharris@nsu.du
*Beverly Harris, Director*
*Marie McDemmond, President*

Four year college that offers programs for the students with learning disabilities.

**5329    Northern Virginia Community College**

Disability Support Department
4001 Wakefield Chapel Road
Annandale, VA  22003                   703-323-3000
                                  FAX 703-323-3559
                             http://www.nvcc.edu
                   e-mail: jthrash@nv.cc.va.us
*Robert Tentlin, President*
*Steven Sachs, Vice President*

A public two-year college.

**5330    Old Dominion University**

Old Dominion University
2228 Webb Center
Norfolk, VA  23529                     757-683-4655
                                  FAX 757-683-5356
                                  TDY:757-683-5356
                e-mail: disabilityservices@odu.edu
*Sheron Ynmilton, Coordinator Disability Services*
*Roseann Runte, President*

Works with students to provide access to higher education. Reasonable accommodations are identified to address specific individual needs. Accommodations may include extended testing time, permission to tape record classes, distraction-free test setting, etc.

**5331    Patrick Henry Community College**

645 Patriot Avenue
Martinsville, VA  24115                276-656-0296
                                        800-232-7997
                                  FAX 276-656-0327
                                  TDY:276-638-2433
                        http://www.ph.vccs.edu
                      e-mail: sss@ph.vccs.edu
*Scott Guebert, Dir Student Support Services*
*Mary McAlexander, Disability Counselor*

Offers a variety of services to students with disabilities including note takers, adaptive testing, counseling services, peer tutoring and adaptive equipment, and accessible transportation.

**5332** **Paul D Camp Community College**
100 N College Drive
Franklin, VA 23857     757-569-6700
FAX 757-569-6795
http://www.pc.vccs.edu
*Douglas Boyce MD, President*

A public two-year institution with two campuses. Students with learning disabilities are eligible for special services provided by the Student Support Service Program. Learning-disabled students may take advantage of tutors (outside of class time and during class labs), notetakers, and taped textbooks. A counselor serves as student advocate and helps students arrange for classroom accommodations with instructors.

**5333** **Piedmont Virginia Community College**
501 College Drive
Charlottesville, VA 22902     434-977-3900
FAX 434-961-5251
http://www.pvcc.edu
e-mail: pbuck@pvcc.edu
*Wendy Bolt, Counselor*

A two-year comprehensive community college dedicated to the belief that individuals should have equal opportunity to develop and extend their skills and knowledge. Consistent with this philosophy and in compliance with the Americans with Disabilities Act, we encourage persons with disabilities to apply.

**5334** **Randolph-Macon Woman's College**
2500 Rivermont Avenue
Lynchburg, VA 24503     434-947-8000
800-745-RMWC
FAX 434-947-8996
TDY:434-947-8608
http://www.rmwc.edu
e-mail: admissions@rmwc.edu
*Tina Barnes, Dir Learning Resources Center*
*Kathleen Bowman, President*

An independent four-year college with support services for students with disabilities.

**5335** **Rappahannock Community College**
12745 College Drive
Glenns, VA 23149     804-758-6700
FAX 804-758-3852
http://www.rcc.vccs.edu
e-mail: pfisher@rcc.vccs.edu
*Paula Fisher, Director*

Offers a variety of services to students with disabilities including notetakers, extended testing time, counseling services, and special accommodations.

**5336** **Southern Seminary College**
One College Hill Drive
Buena Vista, VA 24416     703-761-8420
*Jack Turregano, Special Services*

Offers a variety of services to students with disabilities including note takers, extended testing time, counseling services, and special accommodations.

**5337** **Southern Virginia College**
One College Hill Drive
Buena Vista, VA 24416     540-261-8420
800-229-8420
http://www.southernvirginia.edu
*Jack Turregano, Special Services*

Offers a variety of services to students with disabilities including note takers, extended testing time, counseling services, and special accommodations.

**5338** **Southside Virginia Community College**
109 Campus Drive
Alberta, VA 23821     434-949-1000
FAX 434-949-7863
http://www.sv.vccs.edu
*John Sykes, Provost*

Offers a variety of services to students with disabilities including notetakers, extended testing time, counseling services, and special accommodations.

**5339** **Southwest Virginia Community College**
PO Box 5UCC
Richlands, VA 24641     276-964-2555
FAX 540-964-7259
http://www.sw.edu
e-mail: admissions@sw.edu
*Dr King, President*
*Gaynalle Harman, Admissions Coordinator*

Offers a variety of services to students with disabilities including note takers, extended testing time, counseling services, and special accommodations.

**5340** **Thomas Nelson Community College**
Thomas Nelson Community College
99 Thomas Nelson Drive
Hampton, VA 23666     757-825-2700
FAX 757-825-2763
http://www.tncc.edu
*Thomas Kellen, Advisor of Admissions*
*Charles Taylor, President*

A public two-year college with support services for students with disabilities.

**5341** **Tidewater Community College**
Tidewater Community College
300 Granby Street
Norfolk, VA 23510     757-822-1213
FAX 757-822-1214
http://www.tcc.edu
e-mail: tcharro@tcc.edu
*Linda Harris, District Coordinator*
*Deborah , President*

This public two-year college offers transfer and occupational/technical degrees on four campuses and a visual arts center in the Hampton Roads area of Virginia. TCC offers students evaluations, all reasonable accommodations, and a wide array of assistive technology.

**5342 University of Virginia**
PO Box 400160
Charlottesville, VA 22904          434-924-0311
                                   FAX 434-243-5188
                                   TDY:804-982-HEAR
                                   http://www.virginia.edu
*Jennifer Maedgen, Director*

Diagnostic services and educational planning for students and adults in the workplace who have a history or who suspect learning difficulties may stem from the Specific Learning Disabilities condition.

**5343 Virginia Commonwealth University**
Services for Students with Disabilities
901 W Franklin Street
Richmond, VA 23284          804-828-0100
                            800-841-3638
                            FAX 804-828-1323
                            http://www.vcu.edu
                            e-mail: jbknight@vcu.edu
*Joyce Knight, Director*

Offers a variety of services to students with disabilities including note takers, extended testing time, counseling services, and special accommodations.

**5344 Virginia Highlands Community College**
Route 372
Abingdon, VA 24212          540-628-6094
                            FAX 540-628-7576
                            http://www.vh.cc.va.us
                            e-mail: cfaris@vh.cc.va.us
*Charlotte Faris, Director*

A public two-year college. Strives to assist students with disabilities in successfully responding to challenges of academic study and job training.

**5345 Virginia Intermont College**
1013 Moore Street
Bristol, VA 24201          276-669-6101
                           800-451-1842
                           FAX 540-669-5763
                           http://www.vic.edu
                           e-mail: bholbroo@vic.edu
*Steve Greiner MD, President*
*Michael Cugalisi, Vice President*

Virginia Intermont College is a private, four-year Baptist affiliated liberal arts college located near the Appalachian Mountains of Southwest Virginia. Intermont has an enrollment of 850 men and women students. Accommodations, such as notetakers, extended time on tests, transcribers, oral testing, tutors and other services, are provided based on documentiation of disabilities.

**5346 Virginia Polytechnic Institute and State University**

150 Henderson Hall
Blacksburg, VA 02461          540-231-6000
                              FAX 540-231-3232
                              TDY:540-231-1740
                              http://www.ssd.vt.edu
                              e-mail: ssd@vt.edu
*Susan Angle MD, Director For Disability Services*
*Charles Steger, President*

A public four-year college with support services for special education students.

**5347 Virginia Wesleyan College**
Disabilities Services Office
1584 Wesleyan Drive
Norfolk, VA 23502          757-455-3200
                           800-737-8684
                           http://www.vwc.edu
                           e-mail: fpearson@vwc.edu
*Fayne Pearson, Disabilities Coordinator*

Four year college that offers support to students with a learning disability.

**5348 Virginia Western Community College**
3095 Colonial Avenue SW
Roanoke, VA 24038          540-857-7319
                           FAX 540-857-6102
                           TDY:540-857-6351
                           http://www.vw.cc.va.us
*Michael Henderson, Special Services*
*Dana Asciolla, Admissions Staff*

A public two-year college with support services for special education students.

# Washington

**5349 Bellevue Community College**
3000 Landerholm Circle SE
Bellevue, WA 98007          425-564-2498
                            FAX 425-641-2230
                            http://www.bcc.ctc.edu
*Susan Gjolmesli, Director*
*Carol Jones-Watkins, Coordinator*

Disability Support Services provides accommodations for people with disabilities to make their academic careers a success. There is no separate fee for these services.

**5350 Central Washington University**
Disability Support Services
400 E University Way
Ellensburg, WA 98926          509-963-2171
                              FAX 509-963-3235
                              TDY:509-963-2143
                              http://www.cwu.edu
                              e-mail: campbelr@cwu.edu
*Bob Campbell, Director*
*Pamela Wilson, Accommodations Specialist*
*Ian Campbell, Coord. Adaptive Tech Services*

A public four-year college with disability support services for students with disabilities.

**5351 Centralia College**
600 W Locust Street
Centralia, WA 98531          360-736-9391
                             FAX 360-330-7503
                             http://www.centralia.edu
                             e-mail: demerson@centralia.ctc.edu
*Lucretia Folks, Director*
*Donna Emerson, Administrative Assistant*

The Special Services Office offers a variety of services to students with disabilities including notetakers, extended testing time, counseling services, and special accommodations.

**5352 Children's Institute for Learning Differences: New Heights School**

4030 86th Avenue SE, Campus F
Mercer Island, WA 98040　　206-232-8680
　　　　　　　　　　　　　FAX 206-232-9377
http://www.childrensinstitute.com
e-mail: robbo@childrensinstitute.com /
　　　　　　　　　　　　bevdchildrenis
*Fristine Frost, Admissions/Public Relations Dir.*
*Trina Westerlund, Executive Director/Founder*

A middle school program serving children ages 11-14.

**5353 Children's Institute for Learning Differences: Child School**

4030 86th Avenue SE, Campus F
Mercer Island, WA 98040　　206-232-8680
　　　　　　　　　　　　　FAX 206-232-9377
http://www.childrensinstitute.com
e-mail: robbo@childrensinstitute.com /
　　　　　　　　　　　　bevdchildrenis
*Fristine Frost, Admissions/Public Relations Dir.*
*Trina Westerlund, Executive Director/Founder*

A pre-elementary school program serving children ages 3-11.

**5354 Clark College**

1800 E McLoughlin Boulevard
Vancouver, WA 98663　　360-992-2000
　　　　　　　　　　　FAX 360-992-2879
　　　　　　　　　　　TDY:360-992-2835
　　　　　　　http://www.clark.edu/dss
*Tami Jacobs, Program Manager*

Offers a variety of services to students with disabilities including note takers, extended testing time, counseling services, and special accommodations.

**5355 Columbia Basin College**

2600 N 20th Avenue
Pasco, WA 99301　　509-547-0511
　　　　　　　　　FAX 509-546-0401
　　　　　　　　　TDY:509-547-0400
　　　　　　　http://www.cbc2.org
　　　　e-mail: pbuchmiller@cbc2.org
*Peggy Buchmiller, Director*
*Kathy Freeman, Program Coordinator*

The Education Access Disability Resource Center provides a range of services for diagnosed learning disabled students, including alternate educational media, test accommodations, notetaking, priority registration, scribe services, books on tape and specialized computer software.

**5356 Cornish College of the Arts**

Cornish College of the Arts
1000 Lenora Street
Seattle, WA 98121　　206-726-5098
　　　　　　　　　　800-726-ARTS
　　　　　　　　FAX 206-726-5097
　　　　　　http://www.cornish.edu
　　　e-mail: studentaffairs@cornish.edu
*George Sedano, Director*

Through the Student Affairs Office, appropriate accommodations are provided for students with learning disabilities.

**5357 Dartmoor School**

13401 Bel Red Road
Bellevue, WA 98005　　425-649-8976
　　　　　　　　　　FAX 425-603-0038

**5358 ETC Preparatory Academy**

8005 SE 28th
Mercer Island, WA 98040　　206-236-1095
　　　　　　　　　　　　FAX 206-236-0998
*Meredith Ouellette, Director*
*Jan Bleakney, Director*

Assessment, referral, tutorial, courses for credit, advocacy, dissertation, adults and students that are school age.

**5359 Eastern Washington University: Disability Support Services**

124 Tawaka
Cheney, WA 99004　　509-359-6871
　　　　　　　　　FAX 509-359-7458
　　　　　　　　　TDY:509-359-6261
　　　　　　　http://www.ewu.edu
　　　e-mail: KRAVER@mail.EWU.EDU
*Karen Raver, Director*
*Kevin Hills, Accommodations Specialist*
*Pam McDermott, Program Assistant*

Although the University does not offer a specialized program specifically for learning disabled students, the disability support services office works with students on a case by case basis.

**5360 Edmonds Community College**

20000 68th Avenue W
Lynnwood, WA 98036　　425-640-1320
　　　　　　　　　　FAX 425-640-1622
　　　　　　　　　　TDY:425-774-8669
　　　　　　　http://www.edcc.edu/ssd
　　　　　e-mail: ssdmail@edcc.edu
*Dee Olson, Director*
*Tania Kulikov, Assistant Director*

Offers a variety of services to students with disabilities including notetakers, extended testing time, and special accommodations.

**5361 Epiphany School**

3710 E Howell Street
Seattle, WA 98122　　206-323-9011
　　　　　　　　　FAX 206-324-2127

**5362 Everett Community College**

Center for Disabilities Services
2000 Tower Street
Everett, WA 98201　　425-388-9272
　　　　　　　　　FAX 425-388-9109
　　　　　　　　　TDY:425-388-9438
　　　　　　　http://www.everettcc.edu
　　　　e-mail: cds@everettcc.edu
*Kathy Cook, Director*
*Kristine Grimsby, Program Assistant*

Offers a variety of services to students with disabilities including notetakers, extended testing time, adaptive software and individual accommodations.

**5363  Evergreen Academy**
16017 118th Place NE
Bothell, WA 98011          425-488-8000
                          FAX 425-488-0994
*Arlene Vixie, Contact*

**5364  Evergreen State College**
2700 Evergreen Parkway NW
Olympia, WA 98505          360-867-6348
                          877-787-9721
                          FAX 360-867-6360
                          TDY:360-867-6834
                          http://www.evergreen.edu
                          e-mail: pickeril@evergreen.edu
*Linda Pickering, Director*
*Meredith Inocencio, Program Assistant*

Academic adjustments and auxiliary aids are provided
for students with documented disabilties.

**5365  Green River Community College**
Green River Community College
12401 SE 320th Street
Auburn, WA 98092          253-833-9111
                          FAX 253-288-3467
                          TDY:253-288-3359
                          http://www.greenriver.edu
                          e-mail: rblosser@greenriver.edu
*Ron Blosser, Coordinator/Disability Services*
*Jennifer Nelson, Program Assistant*

Support services for students with disabilities to ensure that our programs and facilities are accessible.
Our campus is organized to provide reasonable accommodations, including core services, to qualified
students with dissabilities.

**5366  Heritage Christian School**
Heritage Christian School
10310 NE 195th
Bothell, WA 98011          425-485-2585
                          FAX 425-486-2895
                          http://www.acseagles.org
                          e-mail: randyn@fbcbothell.org
*Randy Nadine, Business Manager*
*Dave Rehnberg, Principal*

**5367  Highline Community College**
2400 S 240th Street
Des Moines, WA 98198          206-878-3710
                          FAX 206-870-3773
                          TDY:206-870-4853
                          http://www.highline.edu
                          e-mail: cjones@highline.edu
*Carol Jones, Coordinator for Disability Servi*
*Priscilla , President*

Offers a variety of services to students with disabilities including note takers, extended testing time,
counseling services, and special accommodations.

**5368  Morningside Academy**
201 Westlake Avenue N
Seattle, WA 98109          206-329-9412
                          FAX 206-709-4611
                          http://www.morningsideacademy.org
                          e-mail: info@morningsideacademy.org
*Joanne Robbins MA, Principal*
*Beth Bartter, Office Manager*

**5369  North Seattle Community College**
Educational Access Center
9600 College Way N
Seattle, WA 98103          206-527-3697
                          FAX 206-527-3635
                          http://www.nsccux.sccd.ctc.edu
*Suzanne Sewell, Manager*

The Educational Access Center offers a variety of services to students with disabilities including
notetakers, extended testing time, counseling services, and special accommodations.

**5370  Northwest School**
NAIS ( National Association of Independents School
1415 Summit Avenue
Seattle, WA 98122          206-682-7309
                          FAX 206-467-7353
                          http://www.northwestschool.org
*Ellen Taussig, School Head*
*Jonathan Hochberg, Project Manager*

**5371  Pacific School of Academics**
11105 Homestead Road
Arlington, WA 98223          360-403-8885
                          FAX 360-403-7607
*Nola Smith*

**5372  Paladin Academy**
5660 Federal Highway
Boca Raton, FL 33487          561-998-2343
*Rhonda Jalali, Contact*

**5373  Pierce Community College**
Pierce Community College
9401 Farwest Drive SW
Lakewood, WA 98498          253-964-6500
                          FAX 253-964-6713
                          http://www.pierce.ctc.edu
*Michele Johnson, President*

A federally funded TRIO progrm providing academic
support services to low income students, first generation college students and students with disabilities in
order to improve their retention, academic
proformance, graduation and transfer to four-year institutions.

**5374  Seattle Academy of Arts and Sciences**
1432 15th Avenue
Seattle, WA 98122          206-323-6600
                          FAX 206-676-6881
                          http://www.seattleacademy.org
*Jean Orvis, Director*
*Barbara Burk, Administrative Assistant*

**5375  Seattle Central Community College**
Seattle Community College District
1701 Broadway
Seattle, WA  98122                  206-587-3800
                                    FAX 206-344-4390
                                    TDY:206-344-4395
                    http://www.seattlecentral.org
*Dr Ollee, President*
*Ronald , Vice President*

Offers a variety of services to students with disabilities including notetakers, extended testing time, counseling services, and special accommodations.

**5376  Seattle Christian Schools**
18301 Military Road S
Sea Tac, WA  98188                  206-246-8241
                                    FAX 206-246-9066
                    http://www.seattlechristian.org
                    e-mail: jjennings@seattlechristian.org
*Judy Jennings, Superintendent*
*Bryan Peterson, Principal*

Independent, interdenominational Christian Day School established in 1946, serving 750+ students.

**5377  Seattle Pacific University**
3307 3rd Avenue W
Seattle, WA  98119                  206-281-2475
                                    FAX 206-286-7348
                                    TDY:206-281-2475
          http://www.spu.edu/departs/cfl/dsshome.asp
                    e-mail: centerforlearning3@spu.edu
*Bethany Anderson, Program Coordinator*
*Linda Wagner, Director*

Offers a variety of services to students with disabilities including notetakers, extended testing time, books on tape, interpreters and special accommodations.

**5378  Shoreline Christian School**
Shoreline Christian School
2400 NE 147th
Shoreline, WA  98155                206-364-7777
                                    FAX 206-364-0349
                    http://www.shorelinechristian.org
                    e-mail: admin@shorelinechristian.org
*Timothy Visser, Principal*

**5379  Snohomish County Christian**
17931 64th Avenue W
Lynnwood, WA  98037                 425-742-9518
                                    FAX 425-745-9306
                    http://www.sccslions.org
*Debbie Schindler, Administrator*
*Mary , Principal*

**5380  South Puget Sound Community College**
2011 Mottman Road SW
Olympia, WA  98512                  360-754-7711
                                    FAX 360-596-5709
                    http://www.spscc.ctc.edu
                    e-mail: jshowalter@spscc.ctc.edu
*Christy James, Disability Support Coordinator*

Offers a variety of services to students with disabilities including notetakers, extended testing time, books on tape, readers, scribes, interpreters, assistance with registration.

**5381  South Seattle Community College**
6000 16th Avenue SW
Seattle, WA  98106                  206-763-5137
                                    FAX 206-768-6649
                                    TDY:206-764-5845
                    http://www.sccd.ctc.edu/south
                    e-mail: rtillman@sccd.ctc.edu
*Roxanne Tillman, Director/Special Student Service*

Offers a variety of services to students with disabilities including notetakers, extended testing time, counseling services and special accommodations.

**5382  Spokane Community College**
1810 N Greene Street
Spokane, WA  99217                  509-533-7000
                                    800-248-5644
                                    FAX 509-533-8839
                                    TDY:509-533-7482
                    http://www.scc.spokane.edu
                    e-mail: shanson@scc.spokane.edu
*Steve Hanson, President*

Offers a variety of services to students with disabilities including notetakers, extended testing time, counseling services, and special accommodations.

**5383  Spokane Falls Community College**
3410 W Fort George Wright Drive
Spokane, WA  99224 5288             509-533-4166
                                    888-509-7944
                                    FAX 509-533-3547
                                    TDY:509-533-3838
                    http://www.spokanefalls.edu
*Ben Webinger, Dir Disability Support Services*

Offers a variety of services to students with disabilities including notetakers, extended testing time, counseling services, and special accommodations.

**5384  St. Alphonsus**
St. Alphonsus
5816 15th NW
Seattle, WA  98107                  206-782-4363
                                    FAX 206-789-5709
                    http://www.st-alphonsus-sea.org
                    e-mail: stalphons@aol.com
*Robert Rutledge, President*
*Charlene Sweet, School Secretary*

**5385  St. Matthew's**
1230 NE 127th
Seattle, WA  98125                  206-362-2785
                                    FAX 206-362-4863

**5386  St. Thomas School**
PO Box 124
Medina, WA  98039                   425-454-5880
                                    FAX 425-454-1921
                    http://www.stthomasschool.org
                    e-mail: info@stthomasschool.org
*David Selby, Head of School*

**5387  University Preparatory Academy**

NAIS ( National Association of Independents School
8000 25th NE
Seattle, WA  98115                    206-525-2714
                                  FAX 206-525-9659
                     http://www.universityprep.org
*Erica Hamlin, Headmaster*
*Linda Smith, Main Office Coordinator*

**5388  University of Puget Sound**

University of Puget Sound
1500 N Warner Street
Tacoma, WA  98416                    253-879-3100
                                  FAX 253-879-3500
                                  TDY:253-879-3399
                              http://www.ups.edu
                        e-mail: iwest@ups.edu
*Sherry Kennedy, Administrative Assistant*
*Ivey West, Coordinator of Disability Servic*

Support services and accommodations are individually tailored depending upon a student's disability, its
severity, the students academic environment and
courses, housing situation, activities, etc. Accommodations include instruction in study strategies, free tutoring, assistance in note taking, sign language and
additional academic advising.

**5389  University of Washington**

448 Schmitz Hall
Seattle, WA  98195                    206-543-8925
                                  FAX 206-616-8379
                                  TDY:206-543-8925
                http://www.washington.edu/stu-
                              dents/gencat/front
          e-mail: uwdss@u.washington.edu
*Dyane Haynes, Director*
*Sally Green, Secretary*

Provides services and academic accommodations to
students with documented permanent and temporary
disabilities to ensure equal access to the university's
educational programs and facilities. Services may include but are not limited to exam accommodations,
notetaking, audio-taped class texts/materials, sign
language interpreters, auxilary aids (assistive listening devices, and accessible furniture).

**5390  University of Washington: Center on Human
        Development and Disability**

PO Box 357920
Seattle, WA  98195                    206-543-7701
                                  FAX 206-543-3417
             http://www.depts.washington.edu/chdd
*Michael Guralnick, Director*
*Carolyn Hamby, Assistant to the Director*

The Center on Human Development and Disability
(CHDD) at the University of Washington makes important contributions to the lives of people with developmental disabilities and their families, through a
comprehensive array of research, clinical services,
training, community outreach and dissemination activities.

**5391  WSU/Disability Resource Center**

Administration Annex #206
Pullman, WA  99164                    509-335-3564
                                  FAX 509-335-8511
                                  TDY:509-335-3421
                         http://www.wsu.edu/-drc/
                      e-mail: schaeff@wsu.edu
*Susan Schaeffer, Executive Director*

Goals are: to assist students with disabilities to receive reasonable accommodations in academic and
non-academic programs that provide them with an
equal opportunity to fully participate in all aspects of
student life at WSU: to increase awareness of issues
and abilities of people with disabilities among the
WSU students, faculty and staff.

**5392  Walla Walla Community College**

500 Tausick Way
Walla Walla, WA  99362                509-522-2500
                                      877-992-9922
                                  FAX 509-527-4249
                                  TDY:509-527-4412
                              http://www.wwcc.edu
*La Smelcer, Coordinator of Disability Servic*

The Special Services Office offers a variety of services to students with disabilities including
notetakers, extended testing time, counseling services, and special accommodations.

**5393  Washington State University**

AD Annex 206
Pullamn, WA  99164                    509-335-1566
                                  FAX 509-335-8511
                              http://www.wsu.edu
                      e-mail: schaeff@wsu.edu /
*Jane Carter, Disability Specialist*

Four year college that helps students and has programs for students with learning disabilities.

**5394  Western Washington University**

516 High Street
Bellingham, WA  98225                 360-650-3083
                                  FAX 360-650-2810
                              http://www.wwu.edu
*David Brunnemer, Associate Director*

Disabled Student Services offers a variety of services
to students with disabilities including note takers, extended testing time, counseling services and special
accommodations.

**5395  Whatcom Community College**

237 W Kellogg Road
Bellingham, WA  98226                 360-676-2170
                                  FAX 360-676-2171
                         http://www.whatcom.ctc.edu
*Bill Culwell, Coordinator Disability Services*

A public two-year college with support services for
special education students.

**5396   Whitworth College**

W 300 Hawthorne Drive
Spokane, WA  99251                509-777-1000
                                 FAX 509-777-3758
                                 http://www.whitworth.edu
                                 e-mail: joannnielsen@whitworth.edu
*Diane Thomas, Contact*

Offers a variety of services to students with disabilities including note takers, extended testing time, counseling services, and special accommodations.

**5397   Yakima Valley Community College**

16th Avenue & Nob Hill Boulevard
Yakima, WA  98907                 509-574-4600
                                 FAX 509-574-6860
                                 http://www.yvcc.cc.wa.us/
*Robert Chavez*

Offers a variety of services to students with disabilities including notetakers, extended testing time, counseling services, and special accommodations.

# West Virginia

**5398   Bethany College West Virginia**

Special Advising Office
Morlan Hall
Bethany, WV  26032               304-829-7400
                                 FAX 304-829-7108
                                 http://www.bethanywv.edu
                                 e-mail: bpauls@bethanywv.edu
*Becky Pauls, Director*

**5399   Center for Excellence in Disabilities (CED)**

West Virginia University
959 Hartman Run Road
Morgantown, WV  26505            304-293-4692
                                 FAX 304-293-7294
                                 TDY:304-293-4692

*Ashok Dey, Director*
*Kim Michael, Secretary*

The mission of the West Virginia University Center for Excellence in Disabilities (WVUCED) is to enhance the quality of life of individuals of all ages with developmental and other disabilities so that they and their families can experience independence and inclusion in society through informed choices and self-determination.

**5400   Davis & Elkins College**

Learning Disability Program
100 Campus Drive
Elkins, WV  26241                304-637-1229
                                 800-624-3157
                                 FAX 304-637-1413
                                 http://www.dne.edu
                                 e-mail: mccaulj@dne.wvnet.edu
*Judith McCauley, Director*

Offers a program to provide individual support to college students with specific learning disabilities. This comprehensive program includes regular sessions with one of the three full-time learning disabilities instructors and specialized assistance and technology not available elsewhere on campus.

**5401   Fairmont State College**

Student Disabilities Services
1201 Locust Avenue
Fairmont, WV  26554              304-367-4686
                                 FAX 304-366-4870
*Lynn McMullen, Coordinator*

Four year college provides services to learning disabled students.

**5402   Glenville State College**

Student Disability Services
200 High Street
Glenville, WV  26351             304-462-4118
                                 800-924-2010
                                 FAX 304-462-8619
                                 TDY:304-462-4136
                                 http://www.glenville.wvnet.edu
                                 e-mail: cottrill@GLENVILLE.WVNET.EDU
*Daniel Reed, Student Disability Services Coor*

**5403   Marshall University**

Higher Education for Learning Problems Program
520-18th Street
Huntington, WV  25755            304-696-6252
                                 FAX 304-696-3231
                                 http://www.marshall.edu/help
                                 e-mail: weston@marshall.edu
*Lynne Weston, Assistant Director*
*Dr , Director*
*K Renna Moore, Administrative Assistant*

Offers the following services: individual tutoring to assist with coursework, studying for tests, administration of oral tests when appropriate; assistance with improvement of memory, assistance with note taking; assistance to determine presence of learning problems.

**5404   Marshall University: HELP Program**

520-18th Street
Huntington, WV  25755            304-696-6252
                                 FAX 304-6963231
                                 http://www.marshall.edu/help
                                 e-mail: weston@marshall.edu
*Lynne Weston, Assistant Director*

A remedial program for LD medical students/physicians offering 5 week programs in January, March, June and September. Individual sessions by appointment. Assistance with reading comprehension, memory strategies, study skills, test-taking strategies and self esteem. Improvement of board scores.

**5405   Parkersburg Community College**

300 Campus Drive
Parkersburg, WV  26101           304-424-8000
                                 FAX 304-424-8332
                                 TDY:304-424-8337
                                 http://www.wvup.wvnet.edu
                                 e-mail: pam.clevenger@mail.wvu.edu
*Cathy Mutz, Director*
*Pam Clevenger, Office Manager*

Offers a variety of services to students with disabilities including notetakers, extended testing time, counseling services, and special accommodations.

**5406 Salem International University**
233 W Main Street
Salem, WV 26426         304-782-5011
800-283-4562
FAX 304-782-5395
TDY:304-782-5011
http://www.salemiu.edu
e-mail: admissions@salemiu.edu
*Debra Jocwick, Director Student Support*

Student Support Services grant program funded by the US Dept of Education for 125 college students who are identified as disadvantaged and/or disabled. On staff are a counselor, a learning disabled specialist in math and science and a learning specialist in reading and writing.

**5407 Southern West Virginia Community College & Technical College**
PO Box 2900
Mount Gay, WV 25637       304-792-7160
FAX 304-792-7096
http://www.southern.wvnet.edu
e-mail: sherryd@southern.wvnet.edu
*Sherry Dempsey, Program Manager*

Southern has made reasonable modifications in its policies, practices and procedures to ensure that qualified individuals with disabilities enjoy equal opportunities services. Our facilities are compliant with Section 504 of the Rahabilitation Act of 1973 and the Americans with Disabilities Act of 1990. Offers a variety of services to students with disabilities including note takers, extended testing time, counseling services, and special accommodations.

**5408 West Virginia Northern Community College**
1704 Market Street
Wheeling, WV 26003       304-233-5900
FAX 304-232-8187
http://www.northern.wvnet.edu
*Debbie Cresap, Special Services*

A public two-year college with support services for special education students.

**5409 West Virginia State College**
Campus Box 197
Institute, WV 25112       304-766-3000
800-987-2112
FAX 304-766-4100
http://www.wvsc.edu
*Kellie Dunlap, Disability Services*

A public four-year college. Accommodations are individualized to meet student's needs.

**5410 West Virginia University: Department of Speech Pathology & Audiology**
PO Box 6122
Morgantown, WV 26506       304-293-4242
FAX 304-293-7565
http://www.wvu.edu/~speechpa
e-mail: lcartwri@wvu.edu
*Lynn Cartwright, Department Chair*
*Barbara Brown, Administrative Secretary*

Offers clinic services for people with speech, language, and/or hearing disorders.

**5411 West Virginia Wesleyan College**
Student Academic Support Services
59 College Avenue
Buckhannon, WV 26201       800-722-9933
http://www.wvwc.edu
e-mail: admission@wvwc.edu
*Robert Skinner II, Director Admissions/Finance*
*Shawn Kuba, Director Academic Support*
*Carolyn Baisden, Administrative Assistant*

Offers an individually structured program to accommodate college students with varying needs. Master level professionals in the fields of learning disabilities, reading, education, and counseling work to help each student design strategies for academic success. Accommodation plans are determined through a review of the documentation provided by the student and the recommendations of the student's comprehensive advisor, who works closely with each individual.

# Wisconsin

**5412 Alverno College**
3400 S 43rd Street
Milwaukee, WI 53215       414-382-6026
800-933-3401
FAX 414-382-6354
http://www.alverno.edu
e-mail: colleen.barnett@alverno.edu
*Nancy Bornstein, Director Instructional Services*
*Colleen Barnett, Coordinator Disability Services*

An independent liberal arts college with 2,000 students in its weekday and weekend degree programs. Support services for students with learning disabilities include appropriate classroom accommodations, assistance in developing self advocacy skills, instructor assistance, peer tutoring, study groups, study strategies workshops, a communication resource center and math resource center.

**5413 Beloit College**
700 College Street
Beloit, WI 53511       608-363-2572
FAX 608-363-2670
http://www.beloit.edu/~stuaff/disability.html
*Diane Arnzen, Director*
*John Burris, President*

Offers a variety of services to students with disabilities such as self advocacy training, study skills and time management guidance, couseling services, and special accommodations.

**5414 Blackhawk Technical College**
6004 Prairie Road
Janesville, WI 53547       608-758-6900
800-498-1282
FAX 608-758-6418
TDY:608-743-4422
http://www.blackhawk.edu
*Christine Flottum, Project Manger*

A public two-year college with support services for special education students.

**5415   Cardinal Stritch College**
Academic Support
6801 N Yates Road
Milwaukee, WI  53217          414-410-4168
                             800-347-8822
                             FAX 414-410-4239
                             http://www.stritch.edu
*Marica Laskey, Director Academic Support*

An independent four-year college with support services for special education students.

**5416   Carthage College**
Academic Support Program
2001 Alford Park Drive
Kenosha, WI  53140            262-551-8500
                             FAX 262-551-6208
                             http://www.carthage.edu
*Laura Busch, Director*

An independent four-year college with support services for special education students.

**5417   Chippewa Valley Technical College**
Chippewa Valley Technical College
620 W Clairemount Avenue
Eau Claire, WI  54701         715-833-6200
                             800-547-2882
                             FAX 715-833-6470
                             http://www.cvtc.edu
                             e-mail: jhegge@cvtc.edu
*Bill Ihlenfeldt, President*
*Joe Hegge, Vice President*

A public two-year college with support services for special education students.

**5418   Edgewood College**
1000 Edgewood College Drive
Madison, WI  53711            608-257-4861
                             800-444-4861
                             FAX 608-663-3291
                             http://www. edgewood.edu
                             e-mail: admissions@edgewood.edu
*Daniel Carey, President*

An independent four-year college with support services for students with learning disabilities.

**5419   Fox Valley Technical College**
1825 N Bluemound Drive
Appleton, WI  54913           920-735-5600
                             800-735-3882
                             FAX 920-831-4396
                             http://www.foxvalley.tec.wi.us
*Lori Weyers, Dean General Studies*

A public two-year college with support services for special education students.

**5420   Gateway Technical College**
Gateway Technical College
3520 30th Avenue
Kenosha, WI  53144            262-564-2200
                             800-353-3152
                             FAX 262-656-6909
                             http://www.gtc.edu
*Samuel Borden, President*

In accordance with Section 504 of the Vocational Rehabilitation Act, Gateway provides a wide range of services that assist special needs students in developing independence and sel-reliance within the Gateway campus community. Reasonable accommodations will be made for students with learning disabilities or physical limitations.

**5421   Lakeshore Technical College**
Office For Special Needs
1290 N Avenue
Cleveland, WI  53015          920-693-8213
                             FAX 920-693-3561
                             http://www.gotoltc.edu
                             e-mail: viwi@ltc.tec.wi.us
*Rivi Hatt, Director*

A two-year college that provides comprehensive programs to students with learning disablities.

**5422   Lawrence University**
PO Box 599
Appleton, WI  54912           920-832-6530
                             FAX 920-832-6884
                             http://www.lawrence.edu
                             e-mail: excel@lawrence.edu
*Geoff Gajawski, Assoc. Dean Student Academic Svc*

Four year college that offers services to the learning disabled.

**5423   Maranatha Baptist Bible College**
Maranatha Baptist Bible College
745 W Main Street
Watertown, WI  53094          920-206-2341
                             FAX 920-261-9109
                             http://www.mbbc.edu
                             e-mail: cmidcalf@mbbc.edu
*Cynthia Midcalf, Director*

Four year college that offers programs for the learning disabled.

**5424   Marian College of Fond Du Lac**
45 S National Avenue
Fond Du Lac, WI  54935        920-923-7600
                             FAX 920-923-8755
                             http://www.mariancollege.edu
*Ellen Mercer, Counselor*

Offers a variety of services to students with disabilities including note takers, extended testing time, counseling services, and special accommodations.

**5425   Marquette University**
Disability Services Department
PO Box 1881
Milwaukee, WI  53201          414-288-7302
                             800-222-6544
                             FAX 414-288-3764
                             http://www.marquette.edu
                             e-mail: patriciaalmon@marquette.edu
*Patricia Almon, Director*

An independent four-year university with support services for students with learning disabilities.

**5426 Mid-State Technical College**

Mid-State Technical College
500 32nd Street N
Wisconsin Rapids, WI 54494          715-422-5300
                                    888-575-MSTC
                                    FAX 715-422-5345
                                    http://www.mstc.edu
                                    e-mail: webmaster@midstate.tec.wi.us
*Patti Lloyd, Coordinator of Disability Servic*
*John , President*

Offers a variety of services to students with disabilities including notetakers, extended testing time, counseling services, and special accommodations.

**5427 Milwaukee Area Technical College**

700 W State Street
Milwaukee, WI 53233          414-297-6594
                             FAX 414-297-7990
                             http://www.milwaukee.tec.wi.us
*Brenda Benton, Guidance Counselor*
*Robert Bullock, Manager*

A public two-year college with support services for disabled students.

**5428 Nicolet Area Technical College: Special Needs Support Program**

Nicolet Area Technical College: Special Needs Sup
PO Box 518
Rhinelander, WI 54501          715-365-4410
                               800-544-3039
                               FAX 715-365-4445
                               http://www.nicolet.tec.wi.us
                               e-mail: inquire@nicolet.tec.wi.us
*Bobert Steber, Special Needs*
*Sandy Jenkins, Case Manager*

In support of the Nicolet Area Technical College Student services mission, the Special Needs Support Program provides appropriate accommodations empowering students with disabilities to identify and develop abilities for successful educational and life experiences.

**5429 Northcentral Technical College**

1000 W Campus Drive
Wausau, WI 54401          715-675-3331
                          FAX 715-675-9776
*Lois Gilliland, Special Services*

Offers a variety of services to students with disabilities including notetakers, extended testing time, counseling services, and special accommodations.

**5430 Northeast Wisconsin Technical College**

Special Services Program
2740 W Mason Street
Green Bay, WI 54307
                          800-272-2740
                          FAX 920-498-5618
                          http://www.nwtc.edu
                          e-mail: moreinfo@nwtc.edu
*Jerome Miller, Special Services*

The Special Needs Office of NWTC offers assistance to individuals with disabilities when choosing educational and vocational goals, building self-steem and increasing their occupational potential. We offer a wide range of support services and accommodations which increases the potential of individuals with exceptional education needs to successfully complete Associate Degree and Technical Diploma programs.

**5431 Northland College**

Northland College
1411 Ellis Avenue
Ashland, WI 54806          715-682-1224
                           FAX 715-682-1258
                           http://www.northland.edu
                           e-mail: admit@northland.edu
*Anissa Cram, Office Manager*
*Jason Turley, Director*

Four year college that provides students with learning disabilities with support and services.

**5432 Ripon College: Student Support Services**

300 Seward Street
Ripon, WI 54971          920-748-8107
                         FAX 920-748-8335
                         http://www.ripon.edu
                         e-mail: krhin@ripon.edu
*Dan Krhin, Director*

Program provides support services for disabled college students including an array of reasonable accommodations.

**5433 St. Norbert College**

Academic Support Services
100 Grant Street
DePere, WI 54115          920-403-1326
                          800-236-4878
                          FAX 920-403-4021
                          http://www.snc.edu
                          e-mail: karen.gooa-bartholomew@snc.edu
*Karen Goode-Bartholomew, Director*

Provides reasonable accommodations for documented disabilities.

**5434 University of Wisconsin Center: Marshfield Wood County**

University of Wisconsin Center
2000 W 5th Street
Marshfield, WI 54449          715-387-1147
                              http://www.marshfield.uwc.edu
*Linda Gleason, Associate Director*

A public two-year college with support services for special education students.

**5435 University of Wisconsin: Eau Claire**

105 Garfield Avenue
Eau Claire, WI 54701          715-836-4542
                              FAX 715-836-3712
                              http://www.uwec.edu
*Thomas Bouchard, Director*

Offers a variety of services to students with disabilities including note takers, extended testing time, counseling services, and special accommodations.

**5436 University of Wisconsin: La Crosse**

1725 State Street
La Crosse, WI 54601          608-785-6900
                              FAX 608-785-6910
                              TDY:608-785-6900
                              http://www.uwlax.edu
              e-mail: reinert.june@uwlax.edu
*June Reinert, Disability Services*
*Ashley Reiser, Work Study*

Offers a variety of services to students with disabilities including note takers, extended testing time, counseling services, and special accommodations.

**5437 University of Wisconsin: Madison**

905 University Avenue
Madison, WI 53715          608-263-2741
                            FAX 608-265-2998
                            TDY:608-263-6393
              http://www.mcburney.wisc.edu
e-mail: mcburney@uwmadmail.services.wisc.edu

*Cathleen Trueba, LD Coordinator*
*Trey Duffy, Director For Disability Services*

Offers a variety of services to students with disabilities including notetakers, extended testing time, counseling services, and special accommodations.

**5438 University of Wisconsin: Milwaukee**

Exceptional Education Department
PO Box 413
Milwaukee, WI 53201          414-229-5251
                              FAX 414-229-5500
                              TDY:414-229-4764
              http://www.exed.soe.uwm.edu
                   e-mail: exed@uwm.edu
*Ann Haines, Chairperson*
*Yolanda Rivera, Office Manager*

A public four-year college with support services for special education students.

**5439 University of Wisconsin: Oshkosh**

800 Algoma Boulevard
Oshkosh, WI 54901          920-424-1033
                            FAX 920-424-0858
              http://www.uwosh.edu
*William Kitz, Associate Professor*

Disability Services of the Dean of Students Office desires to coordinate reasonable accommodations for students with disabilities. To offer the fullest opportunity for ademic potential while integrating into the vibrant extra-curricular life of the University.

**5440 University of Wisconsin: Platteville**

114 Warner Hall
Platteville, WI 53818          608-342-1818
                                FAX 608-342-1918
                   http://www.uwplatte.edu
              e-mail: petersre@uwplatt.edu
*Rebecca Peters, Coordinator*
*Priscilla Hahn, Disabilities Specialist*
*Vicki Chase, Disabilities Assistant*

Coordinates academic accommodations, provides an advocacy resource center for students with disabilities.

**5441 University of Wisconsin: River Falls**

University of Wisconsin: River Falls
410 S 3rd Street
River Falls, WI 54022          715-425-3531
                                FAX 715-425-3277
                   http://www.uwrf.edu
*Mark Johnson, Coordinator*
*Ruth Taoford, Contract Manager*

Offers a variety of services to students with disabilities including note takers, extended testing time, counseling services, and special accommodations.

**5442 University of Wisconsin: Whitewater**

University of Wisconsin: Whitewater
2021 Roseman Building
Whitewater, WI 53190          262-472-4788
                                FAX 262-472-5210
                   http://www.uww.edu
              e-mail: amachern@uww.edu
*Nancy Amacher, Director*
*Jamie Leurquin, Assistant Director*

A public four-year college. There is an additional fee for the special education program in addition to the regular tuition.

**5443 Viterbo University**

900 Viterbo Drive
La Crosse, WI 54601          608-796-3060
                              800-VITERBO
                              FAX 608-796-3050
                   http://www.viterbo.edu
*Jane Eddy, Director of Learning Center*
*Nicki Robinson, Administrative Assistant*

An independent four-year college with special services for special education students.

**5444 Waisman Center: University of Wisconsin-Madison**

1500 Highland Avenue
Madison, WI 53705          608-263-5776
                            FAX 608-263-0529
                            TDY:608-263-0802
              http://www.waisman.wisc.edu
         e-mail: webmaster@waisman.wisc.edu
*Marsha Mailick-Seltzer, Acting Director*
*Ruby Chew, Program Assistant 1*

To advance knowledge about human development, developmental disabilities, and neurodegenerative diseases.

**5445 Waukesha County Technical College**

Special Services Department
800 Main Street
Pewaukee, WI 53072          262-691-5210
                              877-892-9282
                              FAX 262-691-5089
                              TDY:262-691-5293
                   http://www.wctc.edu
              e-mail: djilbert@wctc.edu
*Deb Jilbert, Director*

Offers technical and associate degree programs. Services for students with a documented disability may include academic support services, transition services, assistance with the admissions process, testing accommodations, interpreting services, note taking and assistance with RFB&D.

**5446 Western Wisconsin Technical College**
304 N 6th Street
La Crosse, WI 54602          608-785-9200
FAX 608-785-9205
http://www.wwtc.edu
e-mail: lee.rusch@wwtc.edu
*Keith Valiquette, Special Services*
*Lee Rusch, President*

Offers a variety of services to students with disabilities including notetakers, extended testing time, counseling services, and special accommodations.

**5447 Wisconsin Indianhead Tech College: Ashland Campus**
Wisconsin Indianhead Tech College: Ashland Campus
2100 Beaser Avenue
Ashland, WI 54806          715-682-4591
800-243-9482
FAX 715-682-8040
TDY:715-468-7755
http://www.witc.edu
*Cindy Utities-Heart, Special Services*
*Don Marcouiller, Administrator*

A public two-year college with support services for special education students.

**5448 Wisconsin Indianhead Tech College: Rice Lake Campus**
Wisconsin Indianhead Tech College: Rice Lake Campu
1900 College Drive
Rice Lake, WI 54868          715-234-7082
800-243-WITC
FAX 715-234-5172
http://www.witc.edu
*Patricia Peters, Special Needs*
*Dr , President*

A public two-year college with support services for special education students.

# Wyoming

**5449 Laramie County Community College: Disability Resource Center**
Disability Resource Center
1400 E College Drive
Cheyenne, WY 82007          307-778-1359
800-522-2993
FAX 307-778-1262
TDY:307-778-1266
http://www.lccc.wy.edu
e-mail: ldignan@lccc.wy.edu
*Lisa Dignan, DRC Coordinator*
*Patty Pratz, ADA Compliance Officer*

Students with disabilities will find services and adaptive equipment to reducce mobility, sensory, and perceptual problems in the Disability Resource Center.

**5450 Northwest College**
231 W Sixth Street
Powell, WY 82435          307-754-6695
FAX 307-754-6700
http://www.nwc.cc.wy.us
e-mail: tiffany.self@ncag.edu
*Lyn Pizor, Director*

A two-year college that provides comprehensive programs to learning disabled students.

**5451 Sheridan College**
3059 Cofeen Avenue
Sheridan, WY 82801          307-674-6446
800-913-9139
FAX 307-674-7205
http://www.sheridan.edu
*Zane Garstard, Director Advising*
*Theresa Miller, Student Service Specialist*

A public two-year college with support services for special education students.

**5452 University of Wyoming**
Po Box 3434
Laramie, WY 82071          307-766-1121
FAX 307-766-4010
TDY:307-766-3073
http://www.uwyo.edu
e-mail: dur@uwyo.edu
*Chris Primus, Associate Director*
*Barbara Moeller, Office Associate*

An independent four-year college with support services for special education students.

**5453 University of Wyoming: Division of Social Work and Wyoming Institute for Disabilities (WIND)**
1000 E University
Laramie, WY 82071          307-766-2761
FAX 307-766-2763
TDY:307-766-2720
http://www.wind.uwyo.edu/
e-mail: kamiller@uwyo.edu
*Keith PhD, Executive Director WIND*
*Ken Heinlein, Director*

## Alabama

**5454 Good Will Easter Seals**
2448 Gordon Smith Drive
Mobile, AL 36617     251-471-1581
800-411-0068
FAX 251-476-4303
http://www.alabama.easterseals.com
*Tina Robinson, Human Resource Manager*

Children and adults with disabilities and special needs find highest-quality services designed to meet their individual needs.

**5455 Special Education Action Committee**
Special Education Action Committee
576 Azalea Road
Mobile, AL 36616     251-478-1208
800-222-7322
FAX 251-473-7877
http://www.seacparentassistancecenter.com
e-mail: seacofmobile@zebra.net
*Mavis Smith, Director*
*Ramona Smith, Parents Information Resource Cen*

Parent Training and Information Program views parents as full partners in the educational process and a significant source of support and assistance to each other. Funded by the Division of Personnel Preparation, Office of Special Education Programs, these programs provide training and information to parents to enable such individuals to participate more effectively with professionals in meeting the educational needs of disabled children.

**5456 Three Springs**
Three Springs
1131 Eagletree Lane
Huntsville, AL 35801     256-880-3339
888-758-4356
FAX 256-880-7026
http://www.threesprings.com
e-mail: info@threesprings.com
*Brooke Blach, President*

The mission of Three Springs is the healing and restoration of children and their families. Every resource at our disposal, be it financial, human or operational, is directed toward this purpose. Our efforts will always be governed by the principles of honor, respect, teamwork, reponsibilities, accountability and honesty.

**5457 Wireglass Rehabilitation Center**
795 Ross Clark Circle
Dothan, AL 36302     334-792-0022
800-395-7044
FAX 334-712-7632
*Jack Sasser, Administrator*
*Tracy Zurran, Program Services*

Provides services to individuals with disabilities in order to render them employable.

**5458 Workshops**
4244 3rd Avenue S
Birmingham, AL 35222     205-592-9683
888-805-9683
FAX 205-592-9687
http://www.workshopsinc.com
*James Crim, Executive Director*
*Debbie Richards, Director*

Funded by the public, community chest and workshop sales this center provides evaluation, employment, pre-vocational training and sheltered workshops to the disabled areas of Birmingham, Jefferson County, Northern Alabama and Shelby County.

## Alaska

**5459 Center for Community**
700 Katlian Street
Sitka, AK 99835     907-747-6960
800-478-6970
FAX 907-747-4868
*Tracy Hodges, Program/Care Coordinator*

A private, nonprofit corporation provides comprehensive and individualized support and training services for people of all ages who have a developmental delay or disability. Programs include assistive technology services and vocational assessment, training and placement, as well as other residential and respite services.

## Arizona

**5460 Academy of Tucson**
10720 E 22nd
Tucson, AZ 85748     520-749-1413
FAX 520-733-0097
e-mail: hari@at.tuccoxmail.com
*Holly Leeman, Dean*
*Shari Stewart, Assistant Superintendent*

A state charted, nonprofit co-ed school serving grades 9-12. Founded in 1986, accredited by North Central Association, it is a college preparatory school for students who learn best in a small, personalized setting. Teachers hold Arizona certificates, and class ratios are 1:20. The curriculum meets college entrance requirements. Charter sponsored by Arizona Stats Board of Education. Tuition free.

**5461 Devereux Arizona Treatment Network**
11000 N Scottsdale Road
Scottsdale, AZ 85254     480-998-2920
800-345-1292
FAX 480-443-5589
http://www.devereuxaz.org
*Jim Cole, Executive Director*
*Diane Mark, Clinical Coordinator*

Provides a wide array of behavioral health and social welfare services for persons with emotional and behavioral disorders or who are victims of physical or sexual abuse and neglect.

**5462  LATCH School**
10251 N 35th Avenue
Phoenix, AZ  85051                    602-995-7366
                                     FAX 602-995-0867
                         http://www.latchschool.org
                         e-mail: latchinc@aol.com
*Connie Laird, Executive Director*
*Marge Cook, Education Director*
*Stephanie Denning, Development Coordinator*

LATCH School is a private school, non-profit, special
education school providing educational, behavioral
and therapeutic services to over 200 students, ages
3-21, with cognitive, emotional, orthopedic, and/or
behavioral disabilities.

**5463  Life Development Institute (LDI)**
18001 N 79th Avenue
Glendale, AZ  85308                   623-773-2774
                                     FAX 623-773-2788
                    http://www.life-development-inst.org
                    e-mail: LDIinARIZ@aol.com
*Robert Crawford, President*

A program service for older adoloscents and young
adults with learning disabilities, AD/HD and other related disorders.

**5464  New Way Learning Academy**
1300 N 77th Street
Scottsdale, AZ  85257                 480-946-9112
                                     FAX 480-946-2657
                       http://www.newwayacademy.org
                       e-mail: newway@phnx.uswest.net
*Anita Marinelli, Executive Assistant*
*Dawn Gutierrez, Principal*

Serving children with learning disabilities, attention
deficit disorder and underachievers in grades K-12 for
34 years. New Way is approved by the Arizona State
Department of Special Education to serve students
with learning disabilities and meets state mandated
standards and guidelines. Our enrollment is approximately 120 students, and we have 35 staff members.

**5465  Raising Special Kids**
2400 N Central Avenue
Phoenix, AZ  85004-1313               602-242-4366
                                     800-237-3007
                                     FAX 602-242-4306
                     http://www.raisingspecialkids.org
                     e-mail: info@raisingspecialkids.org
*Joyce Millard, Executive Director*
*Jennie Figueroa, Administrative Assistant*

A parent training and information center providing information, resources and support to families of children with disabilities.

**5466  Turning Point School**
Turning Point School
200 E Yavapai Road
Tucson, AZ  85705                     520-292-9300
                                     FAX 520-292-9075
                      http://www.turningpointschool.com
*Nancy Wald, Director, President*

For dyslexics, attention deficit disorder children who
have difficulties in reading, writing, spelling and
math. Summer and regular school students return to
public school in 1-3 years, with secure skills.

## Arkansas

**5467  Arkansas Disability Coalition**
1123 S University Avenue
Little Rock, AR  72204                501-614-7020
                                     800-223-1330
                                     FAX 501-614-9082
                         http://www.adcpti.org
                         e-mail: adcoalition@earthlink.net
*Wanda Stovall, Director*

Our mission is to work for equal rights and opportunities for Arkansans with disabilities through public
policy change, cross-disability collaboration, and empowerment of people with disabilities and their families.

## California

**5468  Ann Martin Children's Center**
1250 Grand Avenue
Piedmont, CA  94610                   510-655-7880
                                     FAX 510-655-3379
                         http://www.annmartin.org

A private, nonprofit community center that helps children with special educational needs become more
confident and independent learners.

**5469  Brislain Learning Center**
1550 Humboldt Road
Chico, CA  95928                      530-342-2567
                                     FAX 530-342-2573
*Judy EdD*

Assists children of all ages who have learning disabilities. Offers a diagnostic program and tutoring program for ADD and learning disabilities. Provides
counseling and support groups for children and
adults.

**5470  Center for Adaptive Learning**
3227 Clayton Road
Concord, CA  94519                    925-827-3863
                                     FAX 925-827-4080
                    http://www.centerforadaptivelearning.org
                    e-mail: info@centerforadaptivelearning.org
*Genevieve Stolarz, Executive Director*
*Nancy Perry, Clinical Neurophysiologist*

The center provides a comprehsive program that is designed to address many needs; physical, social, emotional and vocational. To empower adults with a
developmental neurological disability to realize their
own potential.

**5471  Charles Armstrong School**
1405 Solana Drive
Belmont, CA  94002          650-592-7570
                           FAX 650-592-0780
        http://www.charlesarmstrong.org
        e-mail: info@charlesarmstrong.org
*Lisa Shupp-Mules, President*
*Wilbur Mattison, Chairman*
*Rosalie Whitlock, Headmaster*

The mission of the Charles Armstrong School is to serve the dyslexic learner by providing an appropriate educational experience which not only enables the students to acquire language skills, but also instills a joy of learning, enhances self-worth, and allows each the right to identify, understand and fulfill personal potential.

**5472  Children's Therapy Center**
Children's Therapy Center
1000 Paseo Camarillo
Camarillo, CA  93010          805-383-1501
                             FAX 805-383-1504
*Beth Maulhardt, Director*

The Children's Therapy Center is a private evaluation and treatment center for children who show delays in motor development, speech/language development, play and social development and/or learning problems. We offer occupational therapy, physical therapy, speech/language therapy, counseling and psychological testing.

**5473  Devereux Santa Barbara**
PO Box 6784
Santa Barbara, CA  93160          805-968-2525
                                 FAX 805-968-3247
        http://www.devereux.org
        e-mail: info@devereux.org
*Alec Bruice, Director*

To provide quality services to children, adults and families with special needs which derive from behavioral, psychological, intellectual or neurological impairments.

**5474  Dyslexia Awareness and Resource Center**
Dyslexia Awareness and Resource Center
928 Carpinteria Street
Santa Barbara, CA  93103          805-963-7339
                                 FAX 805-963-6581
        http://www.dyslexiacenter.org
        e-mail: info@dyslexiacenter.org
*Leslie Esposito, Executive Development Director*
*Joan Esposito, Founder/Program Director*
*Valerie Allen, Center Coordinator*

The Dyslexia Awareness and Resource Center is here to help students and adults with dyslexia and ADD, as well as their parents, teachers and professionals who work with them.

**5475  Eye Care Center**
Southern California College of Optometry
2575 Yorba Linda Boulevard
Fullerton, CA  92831          714-449-7400
                             FAX 714-992-7811
        http://www.scco.edu
        e-mail: mrouse@scco.edu
*Troy Allred, Instructor*
*Tal Barak, Instructor*
*Eric Borsing, Professor*

The Center offers comprehensive primary vision care for patients of all ages. The Vision Therapy Service specializes in complete diagnostic and therapeutic care of both children and adults presenting with visual and related learning problems. The primary goal is the diagnosis and management of visual and visual perceptual-motor difficulties that may interfere with efficient learning. Testing services are also available for the diagnosis of specific dyslexia. A sliding fee scale is available.

**5476  Frostig Center**
971 N Altadena Drive
Pasadena, CA  91107          626-791-1255
                            FAX 626-798-1801
        http://www.frostig.org
        e-mail: helpline@frostig.org
*Bennett PhD, Executive Director*

A non profit organization that specializes in helping children who have learning disabilities. Offers parent training, consulting and direct instructional services to learning disabled children.

*6-18 years old*

**5477  Full Circle Programs**
70 Skyview Terrace San Rafael
San Rafael, CA  94903          415-499-3320
                              FAX 415-499-1542
        http://www.fullcircleprograms.org
        e-mail: info@fullcircleprograms.org
*Brian Weele, Executive Director*
*Deborah Riggins, Associate Director*

Full Circle has been actively caring for children and their families in need. Full Circle offers a continuum of care ranging from residential treatment for several emotionally disturbed boys, to outpatient counseling for children and their families.

**5478  Help for Brain Injured Children**
Cleta Harder Developmental School
981 N Euclid Street
La Habra, CA  90631          562-694-5655
                            FAX 562-694-5657
        http://www.hbic.org
        e-mail: hbiccleta@aol.com
*Cleta Harder, Executive Director*
*Sylvia Conde, Administrative Director*

Offers home rehabilitation programs. We also offer an after school developmental motor program for elementary students K-5th grade.

**5479  Kayne-ERAS Center**
5350 Machado Road
Culver City, CA  90230          310-737-9393
                               FAX 310-737-9344
        http://www.erascenter.com
        e-mail: erascenter@aol.com
*Joni Berry, President*
*Shelby Arnold, Vice President*

Kayne-ERAS accomplishes its mission by offering educational resources, direct service, and a professional training center. Kayne-ERAS provides personalized programming to children and young adults from at risk conditions and those challenged by emotional, learning, developmental and/or chronic neurological and/or medical disabilities.

**5480  Marina Psychological Services**
4640 Admiralty Way
Marina Del Rey, CA  90292        310-822-0109
                                 FAX 310-822-1240
        e-mail: marinapsych@hotmail.com
*Bruce Hirsch, Psychologist*
*Stuart , Psychologist*

Psychological evaluations, psychotherapy and counseling, parent education and counseling, consultation to schools and employers.

**5481  Melvin-Smith Learning Center**
EDU-Therapeutics
775 Kimball Avenue
Seaside, CA  93955              831-620-1908
                                800-505-3276
                            FAX 831-620-1907
        http://www.edu-therapeutics.com
                e-mail: edu-t@erc1.com
*Joan EdD, Director*
*Mark Wolinski, Administrator*

Nonprofit corporation that provides assistance for children and adults with dyslexia, attention deficit, learning handicaps, or reading challenges through a wide range of services, publications, and training programs.

**5482  NAWA Academy**
17351 Trinity Mountain Road
French Gulch, CA  96033         530-359-2215
                                800-358-6292
                            FAX 530-359-2229
        http://www.nawa-academy.com
        e-mail: nawamain@hotmail.com
*David Hull, President*
*Sandy Gilliam, Secretary*

A boarding school located in a remote valley of the Trinity Alps that provides individual curriculum, theory and structure for 7-9 grade students, many of who have learning disabilities. ÆServices include individual counseling, small academic classes, behavior modification programs and numerous after school activities.

**5483  New Vistas Christian School**
68 Morello Avenue
Martinez, CA  94553             925-370-7767
                            FAX 925-370-6395
        http://www.nvcs.info
*Maria Zablah, Principal*
*Linda Scott, Chief Executive Officer*

A non-profit 5th-12th school for students of average or above average intelligence with learning disabilities offering a non-traditional approach to multiple learning styles.

**5484  Newport Language: Speech and Audiology Center**

Newport Speech and Audiologist Center
26137 La Paz Road
Mission Viejo, CA  92691        949-581-5206
                            FAX 949-599-0247
        http://www.newportaudiology.com
            e-mail: info@newaud.com
*Sharlene Goodman, President/Chief Executive Office*

We aim to enhance the quality of people's lives by improving their ability to communicate. We provide the highest level of audiological services possible, through our highly efficient staff, informative education programs, community services, high quality products, and true spirit of customer service.

**5485  One To One Reading & Educational Center**
One to One Reading and Educational Center
11971 Salem Drive
Granada Hills, CA  91344        818-368-1801
                            FAX 818-368-9345
*Paul Klinger, Owner/Director*
*Julie Klinger, Assistant/Associate*

Educational therapy for students with reading and math problems and tutoring for many subjects all one on one.

**5486  Park Century School**
2040 Stoner Avenue
Los Angeles, CA  90025          310-478-5065
                            FAX 310-473-9260
        http://www.parkcenturyschool.org
        e-mail: nbley@parkcenturyschool.org
*Genny Shain, Co-Director*
*Gail Splindler, Co-Director*
*Nancy Bley, Academic Coordinator*

An independent school for average and above average intellect children with learning disabilities. The program emphasizes developing the skills and strategies necessary to return to a traditional program. With a 2:1 student-staff ratio.

*7-14 years old*

**5487  Prentice School**
Prentice School
18341 Lassen Drive
Santa Ana, CA  92705-2012       714-538-4511
                            FAX 714-538-7023
        http://www.prentice.org
        e-mail: pdadmin@prentice.org
*Debra Jarvis, Executive Director*
*Carol Clark, Director Education*
*Diana Wilhite, Assistant to Executive Director*

The Prentice School is an independent, nonprofit, coeducational day school dedicated to the needs of Specific Language Disabled Students.

**5488  Providence Speech and Hearing Center**
Providence Speech and Hearing Center
1301 W Providence Avenue
Orange, CA  92868               714-639-4990
                            FAX 714-744-3841
        http://www.pshc.org
        e-mail: psqc@pshc.org
*Margaret Inman, Founder*
*Mary , Executive Director*

Comprehensive services for testing and treatment of all speech, language and hearing problems. Individual and group therapy beginning with parent/infant programs.

**5489  REACH for Learning**
1221 Marin Avenue
Albany, CA  94706          510-524-6455
                          FAX 510-524-5154
*Corinne Gustafson, Director*

Educational services for children and adults including: diagnostic assessment, individual remediation/tutoring, small group workshops, and consultation for parents and professionals.

**5490  Reading Center of Bruno**
4952 Warner Avenue
Huntington Beach, CA  92649     714-377-7910
                          FAX 562-436-4428
                     e-mail: Readingct.@aol.com
*Walter Waid, Director*

We work with children, teens and adults with dyslexia, auditory and visual perceptual confusions through our specialized training program. Diagnostic testing is available, as well.

**5491  Rincon Learning Center**
594 N Westwind Drive
El Cajon, CA  92020          619-442-2722
                          FAX 619-442-1011
             http://www.rinconlearningcenter.com
*Lois Dotson, Director*

Diagnostic and therapy services for a wide range of learning disabilities. Offers one on one tutoring.

**5492  Santa Barbara Center for Educational Therapy**
1811 State Street
Santa Barbara, CA  93101     805-687-3711
                          FAX 805-569-6882
*Susan Hamilton, Director, Education*
*Joyce Tolle, Director Education*

Provides educational assessment to determine learning style and document learning disabilities. Also provided are one-to-one remedial or tutorial services for individuals specializing in dyslexia.

**5493  Santa Cruz Learning Center**
720 Fairmount Avenue
Santa Cruz, CA  95062          831-427-2753
                     e-mail: sclrngcntr@yahoo.com
*Eleanor Stitt, Director*

Individualized one-to-one tutoring for individuals aged 5 to adult. Specializes in dyslexia, learning difficulties and gifted persons. Includes test preparation, math, reading, self confidence, study skills, time organization and related services.

**5494  Second Start: Pine Hill School**
3002 Leigh Avenue
San Jose, CA  95124          408-979-8210
                          FAX 408-979-8223
                   http://www.pinehillschool.com
              e-mail: blancan@secondstart.org
*Greg Zieman, Executive Director*
*David Gerster, Principal*
*Terry Reynolds, Registrar*

A private school that provides special education and alternative services to students with a wide range of learning and behavior disabilities.

**5495  Stockdale Learning Center**
Stockdale Learning Center
1701 Westwind Drive
Bakersfield, CA  93301          661-326-8084
                          FAX 661-327-4752
          http://www.stockdalelearningcenter.net
                   e-mail: slc@igalaxy.net
*Andrew Barling MA CET, Owner/Director*

Stockdale Learning Center is a professional State Certified Educational Therapy clinic designed to collaboratively diagnose and assess individuals 5 years of age through adult.

**5496  Stowell Learning Center**
20955 Pathfinder Road
Diamond Bar, CA  91765          909-598-2482
                          FAX 909-598-3442
              http://www.learningdisability.com
           e-mail: info@learningdisability.com
*Jill Stowell, Director*

A diagnostic and teaching center for learning and attention disorders. Specializes in instruction for dyslexic or learning disabled children and adults. Our services include diagnostic evaluation, developmental evaluation, cognitive and educational therapy which is provided on a one-to-one basis, and a full day class for elementary age students with reading disabilities.

**5497  Switzer Center**
1110 Sartori Avenue
Torrance, CA  90501          310-328-3611
                          FAX 310-328-5648
                   http://www.switzercenter.org
*Rebecca Foo MD, Executive Director*
*Larry Brugnatelli, Associate Director*

Improving lives of those challenged by learning, social and emotional difficulties by maximizing educational competence and psychological well being.

**5498  Team of Advocates for Special Kids (TASK)**
Team of Advocates for Special Kids
100 W Cerritos Avenue
Anaheim, CA  92805          714-533-8275
                          FAX 714-533-2533
                   http://www.taskca.org
              e-mail: taskca@yahoo.com
*Marta Anchondo, Executive Director*
*Brenda Smith, Deputy Director*

Team of Advocates for Special Kids (TASK) is a Parent Training and Information Center that Parents and Professionals can turn to for assistance in seeking and obtaining needed early intervention and educational, medical or therapeutic support service for children.

**5499  Total Education Solutions**

**1137 Huntington Drive**
**South Pasadena, CA  91030**          323-341-5580
                                      FAX 323-257-0284
        **http://www.redesignlearning.org**
*Nancy Lavelle, Executive Director*

Committed to serving children, youth and young adults with learning, developmental and emotional disabilities.

**5500  Vision Care Clinic of Santa Clara Valley**

**2730 Union Avenue**
**San Jose, CA  95124**              408-377-1150
                                    FAX 408-377-1152
        **http://www.visiondiva.com**
        **e-mail: rice@visiondiva.com**
*Liane Rice MD, Director*

Diagnostic and training for those with visual disabilities.

## Colorado

**5501  Developmental Disabilities Resource Center**

**Developmental Disabilities Resource Center**
**11177 W 8th Avenue**
**Lakewood, CO  80215**              303-233-3363
                                     800-649-8815
                                FAX 303-233-4622
                                TDY:303-462-6606
            **http://www.ddrcco.com**
            **e-mail: ahogling@ddrcco.com**
*Arthur Hogling, Executive Director*
*Robert Arnold, Associate Executive Director*

The Center's mission is to provide leading-edge services that create opportunities for people with developmental disabilities and their families to participate fully in the community.

**5502  Havern Center**

**4000 S Wadsworth Boulevard**
**Littleton, CO  80123**             303-986-4587
                                 FAX 303-986-0590
        **http://www.haverncenter.org**
        **e-mail: agoyette@haverncenter.org**
*Cathy Pasquariello, Executive Director*
*Denise Ensslin, Staff/Curriculum Consultant*

School for children with learning disabilities. Educational programs, special language programs and occupational therapy is available.

*6-13 years old*

**5503  PEAK Parent Center**

**PEAK Parent Center**
**611 N Weber**
**Colorado Springs, CO  80903**       719-531-9400
                                      800-284-0251
                                  FAX 719-531-9452
                                  TDY:719-531-9403
            **http://www.peakparent.org**
            **e-mail: info@peakparent.org**
*Barbara Bushwell, Executive Director*

PEAK Parent Center is Colorado's Parent Training and information center. PEAK is a statewide organization of parents of children with disabilities reaching out to assist other parents and professionals.

## Connecticut

**5504  American School for the Deaf**

**139 N Main Street**
**West Hartford, CT  06107**          860-570-2300
            **http://www.asd-1817.org**
        **e-mail: chris.thorkelson@asd-1817.org**
*Fern Reisinger, Interim Director*
*Edward Peltier, Assistant Executive Director*
*Chris Thorkelson, Public Information Officer*

The American School for the Deaf is a residential/day program operating as a state-aided private school and governed by a board of directors. It is the oldest permanent school for the deaf in America, offering a comprehensive educational program for the deaf and hard of hearing students, infants, preschoolers, primary, elementary, junior high school, high school, and post-secondary students.

**5505  Boys and Girls Village**

**528 Wheelers Farms Road**
**Milford, CT  06460**                203-877-0300
                                  FAX 203-876-0076
            **http://www.boysvillage.org**
            **e-mail: trottac@boysvill.org**
*Reverend Fellenbaum, CEO*
*Steven Kant, Medical Director*
*Carmine Trotta, Support Services Director*

The agency through the years has evolved into a leading therapeutic and learning facility offering residential shelter, counseling, educational, foster and adoptive training, family support services, and day programs for children and their families.

**5506  COPE Center of Progressive Education**

**Residential Services Division**
**425 Grant Street**
**Bridgeport, CT  06610**             203-426-3344
                                  FAX 203-781-4792
            **e-mail: info@aptfoundation.org**
*Gretchen Celestino, Principal*

COPE is an alternative, special education school serving substance abusing adolescents placed at the Alpha House Residential Treatment Facility.

**5507  Candee Hill**

122 Candee Hill Road
Watertown, CT  06795               860-274-8332
                                  FAX 860-828-3912

*Frank Popkiewicz, Director*

Emphasis on increasing client's self-sufficiency in areas of daily skills, community awareness and social interaction.

**5508  Community Child Guidance Clinic School**

317 N Main Street
Manchester, CT  06040             860-643-2101
                                  FAX 860-645-1470
                                  http://www.ccgcinc.org
                                  e-mail: clinic@ccgcinc.org
*Clifford Johnson, Executive Director*
*Lynn Helman, Medical Director*

The Community Child Guidance Clinic is a private, non-profit mental health agency offering diagnostic, treatment and consultation services to children up to the age of 18 and their families.

**5509  Connecticut Center for Augmentative Communication**

St. Vincent's Special Needs Center
95 Merritt Boulevard
Trumbull, CT  06611               203-386-2728
                                  FAX 203-380-1190
        http://www.saintvincentsspecialneeds.org
               e-mail: feroleto.child.dev@snet.net
*Virginia Smith, Director Marketing*
*Harry Schaffer, Program Director*

Provides persons of all ages with evaluation/training in augmentative aids/systems to facilitate communication, writing and computer access.

**5510  Connecticut Center for Children and Families**

8 Titus Road
Washington Depot, CT  06794       860-868-1155
                                  FAX 860-868-1288
*Patricia Thomas*
*Janet Bloch*

The Connecticut Center is a group of affiliated professionals with a diversity of talent but with a common vision. We believe that collaborative intervention is often the most clinically and financially effective way to solve learning and educational problems. The Center offers the services of psychiatrists, psychologists, learning specialists and tutors.

**5511  Connecticut College Children's Program**

270 Mohegan Avenue
New London, CT  06320             860-439-2920
                                  FAX 860-439-5317
        http://www.conncoll.edu/academics/department/
                         e-mail: bldem@conncoll.edu
*Sarah Radlinski, Program Director*

The mission of the Connecticut College Children's Program is to provide, within a community context, a model child and family-focused early childhood program for infants and young children of diverse backgrounds and abilities in Southeastern Connecticut.

**5512  Connecticut Institute for the Blind**

120 Holcomb Street
Hartford, CT  06112               860-242-2274
                                  FAX 860-242-3103
                                  http://www.ciboakhill.org
                                  e-mail: info@ciboakhill.org
*Suzanne Heise, Vice President Development*
*Marion Jones, Assistant Director*

Providing children and adults with disabilities the opportunity to live, learn and work in the community.

**5513  Curtis Home**

380 Crown Street
Meriden, CT  06450                203-237-4338
                                  FAX 203-630-1127
                                  http://www.thecurtishome.org
                                  e-mail: info@thecurtishome.org
*Robert Flyntz, President*
*Ronald Stempien, Vice President*
*Mary Lyons, Secretary*

Now managed by the Hartford Healthcare System, the Children's Program continues to provide support in the following service areas: Residential Treatment, Day Treatment, The Cheshire School, Family Placement Program, and Safe Harbors. The Curtis Home still owns a majority of the facilities housing the Children's Program.

**5514  Devereux Glenholme School**

81 Sabbaday Lane
Washington, CT  06793 0138        860-868-7377
                                  FAX 860-868-7894
                                  http://www.theglenholmeschool.org
                                  e-mail: info@theglenholmeschool.org
*Kathi Fitzherbert, Admissions Director*
*Christine Sulborski, Admissions Assistant*

The Glendholme School is a boarding school for special needs students situated on over 100 idyllic acres of Connecticut countryside.

**5515  Eagle Hill School**

45 Glenville Road
Greenwich, CT  06831              203-622-9240
                                  FAX 203-622-0914
                                  http://www.eaglehillschool.org
                                  e-mail: info@eaglehillschool.org
*Mark Griffin, Director Admissions*
*Abby Hanrahan, Teacher Camp*

Eagle Hill is a languaged-based, remedial program committed to educating children with learning disabilities. The curriculum is individualized, interdisciplinary, and transitional in nature.

**5516  Elmcrest Schools**

25 Marlborough Street
Portland, CT  06480  860-342-6266
FAX 860-342-5106
*Elaine Green, Director*

Offers short-term treatment, long-term treatment and a day treatment program for the learning disabled and children with substance abuse problems.

**5517  Focus Alternative Learning Center, Inc.**

126 Dowd Ave
Po box 452
Canton, CT  06019  860-693-8809
FAX 860-693-0141
*Donna Swanson, Executive Director*
*Yvonne Gardner, Program Coordinator*

Private, nonprofit, licensed, clinical program, and learning center specialized in the treatment of creative, wired and socially challenged children. Trusts children on the autism spectrum who suffer from high anxiety, processing diffculties, learning problems, etc.

**5518  Forman School**

Forman School
12 Norfolk Road
Litchfield, CT  06759  860-567-1802
FAX 860-567-8317
http://www.formanschool.org
e-mail: admissions@formanschool.org
*Mark Perkins, School Head*
*Beth Rainey, Admissions Director*

Forman offers students with learning differences the opportunity to achieve academic excellence in a traditional college preparatory setting. A coeducational boarding school of 180 students, we maintain a 3:1 student:teacher ratio. Daily remedial instruction balanced with course offerings rich in content provide each student with a flexible program that is tailored to his or her unique learning style and needs.

**5519  Foundation School**

719 Derby Milford Road
Orange, CT  06477  203-795-6075
FAX 203-876-7531
*Walter Bell, Director*

Basic developmental skills address speech/language and perceptual/motor areas. Academic skills are reading, writing and arithmetic with social studies, science and career studies.

**5520  Founders' Respite Care**

PO Box 470
Norwalk, CT  06852 0470  203-847-6760
FAX 203-847-0545
http://www.starinc-lightingtheway.org
*Jackie Leniart, Family Support Manager*

Facility-based respite care is provided by STAR at Founders Cottage. A lovely home, is co-ed, and can accomodate four individuals at a time. It is for people with development disabilities who are 16 years or older and who reside within the Southwest Region. All persons must be registered with the Connecticut Department of Mental Retardation and have a DMR number assigned.

**5521  Gengras Center**

Saint Joseph College
1678 Asylum Avenue
West Hartford, CT  06117 2791  860-232-4571
FAX 860-231-8396
http://www.sjc.edu
e-mail: blindauer@sjc.edu
*Bernard Lindauer, Director*

A highly structured special education program providing academic, vocational evaluation training, and related service, in combination with behavioral, social, and emotional support tailored to the need of the student.

**5522  Intensive Education Center**

840 N Main Street
West Hartford, CT  06117  860-236-2049
FAX 860-231-2843
*Helen CSJ, Director*
*Carol Devlen, Intake Coordinator*

A non-profit, non sectarian school for children 6 to 21 years with different learning styles. Individualized program with a 5:1 student teacher ratio. Program strives to help each student reach their potential by gaining confidence, recognizing their strengths and limitations, setting realistic goals and attaining satisfaction by achieving these goals. State accredited. Full-day curriculum is offered.

**5523  Klingberg Family Centers**

370 Linwood Street
New Britain, CT  06052  860-224-9113
FAX 860-832-8221
http://www.klingberg.com
e-mail: information@klingberg.com
*Lynne Roe, Intake Coordinator*
*David Lawrence-Hawley, Community Services Director*

The Klingber Family Centers provide structured programs for residential, day treatment and day school students in a therapeutic environment. We are a private, nonprofit organization serving children and families from across Connecticut.

**5524  Lake Grove Durham**

459R Wallingford Road
Durham, CT  06422  860-349-3467
888-525-9007
FAX 860-349-1382
e-mail: www.lgstc.org
*Robert Ruggiero, Director*

Lake Grove at Durham serves its clients in eight expanded split-level homes in a rural community atmosphere. Support facilities include a school building, administration building, dining hall, horse stables and pasture, clubhouse, and several staff homes.

**5525  Learning Center**

**Children's Home, The**
**60 Hicksville Road**
**Cromwell, CT  06416**　　　　860-635-6010
　　　　　　　　　　　　FAX 860-635-3425
　　　　http://www.childrenshome-ct.org
　　　　e-mail: info@childhome.org
*David Tompkins, Program Administrative Officer*
*Cindy Sarnowski, Education Director*

The Learning Center at The Children's Home is accredited by the Connecticut State Department of Education as an educational institution for children and adolescents with emotional and learning difficulties.

**5526  Learning Clinic**

**PO Box 324**
**Brooklyn, CT  06234 0324**　　　860-774-1036
　　　　　　　　　　　　FAX 860-774-1037
　　　　http://www.thelearningclinic.org
　　　e-mail: admissions@thelearningclinic.org
*Raymond DuCharme, Executive Director*
*Beth Jardin, Office Manager*

A private, nonprofit educational program that provides day and residential school focused on ADHD and learning and emotional issues. The program is coeducational and serves sixty students. The faculty is 50 in number including special and regular education certified staff. Academic, Young Apprentice and Wilderness programs are individualized and self-paced. College bound and vocationally oriented students are welcome.

**5527  Lorraine D Foster Day School**

**1861 Whitney Avenue**
**Hamden, CT  06517**　　　　203-230-4877
　　　　　　　　　　　　FAX 203-288-5749
　　　　http://www.ldfds.com
　　　　e-mail: ldfds@snet.net
*Dominique Fontaine, Director*
*Christine Kirschenbaum, Assistant Director*

Lorraine D Foster Day School is a psycho-educational day school for students who are identified as seriously emotionally disturbed and/or learning disabled. We accept students between the ages of 8 and 18 and it is our mission to prepare students for successful re-intergration to the public school.

**5528  Mount Saint John**

**135 Kirtland Street**
**Deep River, CT  06417**　　　　860-526-5391
　　　　　　　　　　　　FAX 860-526-1636
　　　　http://www.mtstjohn.org
　　　　e-mail: info@mtstjohn.org
*Cathi Coridan, Executive Director*
*Arthur Avitabile, Associate Director*
*Sandra Easton, Treatment Services Director*

This special education program offers individualized and small group instruction for boys who are socially/emotionally disabled and/or learning disabled.

**5529  Natchaug Hospital School Program**

**189 Storrs Road**
**Mansfield Center, CT  06250**　　860-456-1311
　　　　　　　　　　　　800-426-7792
　　　　　　　　　　　　FAX 860-423-6114
　　　　http://www.natchaug.org
*Stephen Larcen, President/CEO*
*Craig Martin, Medical Director*
*David Klein, Clinical Services Director*

The hospital's 54-bed facility in Mansfield Center, provides inpatient care for over 400 seriously emotionally disturbed children and adolescents as well as 1,000 adults in crisis each year.

**5530  Northwest Village School: Wheeler Clinic**

**91 NW Drive**
**Plainville, CT  06062**　　　　860-793-3500
　　　　　　　　　　　　888-793-3500
　　　　　　　　　　　　FAX 860-793-3520
　　　　http://www.wheelerclinic.org
　　　　e-mail: eap@wheelerclinic.org
*David Berkowitz, Executive Director*
*John Mattas, Education Services Director*
*Elaine Couture, Human Resources Director*

The Northwest Village School is designed especially for special education students, preschool to age 21, whose social and emotional adjustment, speech and language impairments, learning problems and/or other disabilities have resulted in public school's selection of a specialized program. The Wheeler Clinic provides human services which will prevent problems and which enhance knowledge, skills and attitudes.

**5531  OPTIONS**

**Easter Seals Rehabilitation Center**
**158 State Street**
**Meriden, CT  06450**　　　　203-237-1448
　　　　　　　　　　　　FAX 203-237-9187
　　　　http://www.eastersealsct.org
*Beverly Malinowski, Vice President*
*John Quinn, President*

A program developed for children ages birth to three with developmental delays. Children may receive therapy, education, and/or social work services in their homes, day cares or our family classroom. Emphasis is on teaching children in natural settings to experience and develop social, communication, motor and learning skills.

**5532  Rensselaer Learning Institute**

**275 Windsor Street**
**Hartford, CT  06120**　　　　860-548-2470
　　　　　　　　　　　　800-306-7778
　　　　　　　　　　　　FAX 860-548-7999
　　　　http://www.rh.edu
　　　　e-mail: rli-info@rh.edu
*Rebecca Danchak, Admissions Director*

The Rensselaer Learning Institute is a department within Rensselaer at Hartford, a branch campus of the Rensselaer Polytechnic Institute. RLI offers corporate training and professional development programs in the areas of Leadership & Executive Development, Computer Information Technology, and Technical & Professional Development. RLI's vision is to deliver the best training and education solutions for working professionals anytime.

**5533 Saint Francis Home for Children: Highland Heights**

**651 ProspeCourt Street**
**New Haven, CT 06511**     **203-777-5513**
                        **FAX 203-777-0644**
*Peter Solerno, Executive Director*

A component of the residential treatment program which offers residential treatment, special education and day treatment programs.

**5534 University School**

**160 Iranistan Avenue**
**Bridgeport, CT 06604**     **203-579-0434**
                        **FAX 203-330-9075**
*Nicholas Macol, Director*
*Lynn Ford, Principal*

Located at the University of Bridgeport campus at Seaside Park, the center has access to U.B. facilities as part of its program to serve the socially/emotionally maladjusted and the learning disabled students.

**5535 VISTA Vocational & Life Skills Center**

**1356 Old Clinton Road**
**Westbrook, CT 06498**     **860-399-8080**
                        **FAX 860-399-3103**
         **http://www.vistavocational.org**
         **e-mail: info@vistavocational.org**
*Elena Patterson, President*
*Helen Bosch, Executive Director*

VISTA opened its doors in 1989 to young adults with neurological disabilities who completed their secondary academic education yet require additional residential training to transition to adulthood. VISTA's central mission is to provide experiential, hands-on training in vocational and life skills.

**5536 Villa Maria Education Center**

**161 SkyMeadow Drive**
**Stamford, CT 06903**     **203-322-5886**
                        **FAX 203-322-0228**
         **http://www.villamariaedu.org**
         **e-mail: ecassidy@villamariaedu.org**
*Eileen Cassidy, Admissions Director*
*Sister , Executive Director*

Villa Maria Education Center affirms the dignity and giftedness of each person. We reach out to embrace children whose learning styles are different because they are learning disabled. We offer personalized and specialized instruction in an environment sufficiently varied for students of widely different personalities, interests and levels of learning.

**5537 Waterford Country Schools**

**78 Hunts Brook Road**
**Quaker Hill, CT 06375**     **860-442-9454**
                        **FAX 860-442-2228**
         **http://www.waterfordcountryschool.org**
         **e-mail: PHaqqlund@waterfordcs.org**
*David Moorehead, Executive Director*
*Lynn Morey, Executive Assistant*
*Anna Kemper, Residential Treatment Director*

Waterford Country School is a non-profit, human services agency located on a beautiful 350 acre campus in rural Southeastern Connecticut. We are dedicated to doing whatever it takes to enrich the lives of children and strengthen families through specialized programs, resources, and community services.

**5538 Wheeler Clinic**

**Northwest Village School**
**91 NW Drive**
**Plainville, CT 06062**     **860-793-3717**
                        **888-793-3717**
                        **FAX 860-793-3521**
         **http://www.wheelerclinic.org**
         **e-mail: nvs@wheelerclinic.org**
*David Berkowitz, Executive Director*
*John Mattas, Education Director*

Provides special education programs for students with severe behavior and learning problems. Services include speech and language, occupational therapy, individual, group and family counseling.

**5539 Wilderness School**

**240 N Hollow Road**
**East Hartland, CT 06027**     **860-653-8059**
                        **800-273-2293**
                        **FAX 860-653-8120**
         **http://www.state.ct.us**
         **e-mail: Tom.Dyer@po.state.ct.us**
*Thomas Dyer, Director*
*David Czaja, Assistant Director*

The Wilderness School is a prevention, intervention, and transition program for troubled youth from Connecticut. The school offers high impact wilderness programs intended to foster positive youth development.

**5540 Yale Child Study Center**

**230 S Frontage Road**
**New Haven, CT 06520 7900**     **203-785-2513**
                        **FAX 203-737-4197**
         **http://www.info.med.yale.edu**
         **e-mail: lori.klein@yale.edu**
*Allan Kazdin MD, Director*
*Fred , Director*

The Yale Child Study Center is a department at Yale University School of Medicine that brings together multiple disciplines to further the understanding of the problems of children and families. The mission of the Center is to understand child development, social, behavioral, and emotional adjustment, and psychiatric disorders and to help children and families in need of care.

## Delaware

**5541 AdvoServ**
4185 Kirkwood St. Georges Road
Bear, DE 19701          302-834-7018
                          800-593-4959
                     FAX 302-834-6999
             http://www.advoserv.com
        e-mail: dreardon@advoserv.com
*Greg Harrison, Director*
*Fran Ryan, Contact*

Private residential and educational treatment facilities for children and adults with developmental and emotional disturbances.

**5542 Centreville School**
6201 Kennett Pike
Wilmington, DE 19807          302-571-0230
                          FAX 302-571-0270
          http://www.centrevilleschool.org
   e-mail: information@centrevilleschool.org
*Victoria Yatzus, School Head*
*Ida Donegan, School Secretary*

Centreville School is motivated by two fundamental goals; to provide learning disabled children a vibrant and challenging curriculum comparable to those found at any primary or intermediate level school, and to offer each student the specialized and focused support he or she needs.

**5543 Meadows Consulting**
506 New Castle Street Extended
Rehoboth, DE 19971          302-227-9327
                          FAX 302-227-9327
*Nancy Meadows, President*

Comprehensive educational services include testing, consultations and remedial, supportive, enrichment, and instructional suggestions. Pre-school through adults.

**5544 Parent Information Center of Delaware**
700 Barksdale Road
Newark, DE 19711          302-366-0152
                          888-547-4412
                     FAX 302-366-0276
             http://www.picofdel.org
        e-mail: picofdel@picofdel.org
*Marie-Anne Aghazadian, Director*

Assists individuals with disabilities and special needs and those who serve them; also provides information and referral to other agencies.

**5545 Pilot School**
100 Garden of Eden Road
Wilmington, DE 19803          302-478-1740
                          FAX 302-478-1746
             http://www.pilotschool.com
        e-mail: kcraven@pilotschool.com
*Kathleen Craven, Director*

Pilot School provides a creative, nurturing environment for children with special learning needs. We work with each child to discover his or her unique learning strengths.

## District of Columbia

**5546 Kingsbury Center**
5000 14th Street NW
Washington, DC 20011          202-722-5555
                          FAX 202-722-5533
             http://www.kingsbury.org
        e-mail: center@kingsbury.org
*Peter Engebretson, COO*
*Cherryl Smith, Psychological Services Director*

Kingsbury Center is the oldest nonprofit educational organization to address the needs of children and adults with learning disabilities and differences in the Washington, DC area.

**5547 Lab School of Washington**
4759 Reservoir Road NW
Washington, DC 20007          202-965-6600
                          FAX 202-965-5105
             http://www.labschool.org
*Sally Smith, Founder/Director*

The Lab School of Washington is internationally recognized for its innovative programs for children and adults with learning disabilities. The Lab School offers individualized instruction to students in kindergarten through 12 grade.

**5548 Paul Robeson School for Growth and Development**
3700 10th Street NW
Washington, DC 20010          202-576-5151
                          FAX 202-576-8804
*Harriet Crawley, Program Manager*

Offers a variety of diagnostic and therapy services.

**5549 Scottish Rite Center for Childhood Language Disorders**
1630 Columbia Road NW
Washington, DC 20009          202-939-4703
                          FAX 202-939-4717
                          TDY:202-939-4703
             e-mail: trobinso@cnmc.org
*Tommie Robinson MD, Director*

Speech and language services provided for children birth to 21 years of age. Services include: speech-language evaluations; language learning disabilities evaluations; individual and group therapy consultations; insurance training; and advocacy training. Bilingual speech-language pathologists are also available.

## Florida

**5550 Academic Achievement Center**
313 Pruett Road
Seffner, FL 33584          813-654-4198
                          FAX 813-871-7468
             e-mail: ALSofAAC@aol.com
*Lillian Stark PhD, Executive Administrator*
*Arnold Stark PhD, Education Director*

A private program for bright and gifted children with LD and/or ADD, in grades 2-12, which offers multisensory-based instruction, remediation of basic skills, academic challenge in science, social science, and literature, plus award-winning art and drama, and curriculum-enhancing field trips and travel. Maximum student body is 22 and it is coeducational. After school tutoring and phonelogical awareness training are also available.

**5551  Assistive Technology Network**

**Orange County Public School**
**434 N Tampa Avenue**
**Orlando, FL  32805**        407-317-3504
                             FAX 407-317-3526
                             http://www.ese.ocps.net
                             e-mail: folkst@ocps.k12fl.us
*Tami Folks, Director*
*Dianne Mathews, Assistant Director*

Our mission is to provide assistive technology intervention strategies, tools and training to maximize learning outcomes of students with disabilities.

**5552  Barbara King's Center for Educational Services**

**5005 W Laurel Street**
**Tampa, FL  33607**         813-874-3918
                             FAX 813-874-3575
*Barbara King, Director*

Educational therapy services offered.

**5553  Beach Learning Center**

**105 S Riverside Drive**
**Indialantic, FL  32903**   321-725-7437
*Peggy Christ, Contact*

Diagnostic and therapy services for the learning disabled.

**5554  Brevard Learning Clinic**

**1900 S Harbor City Boulevard**
**Melbourne, FL  32901**     321-676-3024
                             FAX 321-676-3064
                             http://www.hbrandon.com
                             e-mail: blcmelfl@hbrandon.com
*Mary Kellogg, Consultant*
*Mary Kellogg, Director*

A full time learning clinic for evaluation and remediation featuring trained multisensory clinicians.

**5555  Kurtz Center for Cognitive Development**

**1201 Louisiana Avenue**
**Winter Park, FL  32789**   407-740-5678
                             FAX 407-629-6886
                             http://www.learningdisabilities.com
                             e-mail: ld-request@learningdisabilities.com
*Gail Kurtz, Owner*
*Denton Kurtz, Psychologist*

Provides a full diagnostic testing and cognitive therapy for reading, comprehension of oral and written language, written expression and motor output for those with learning difficulties, language difficulties, processing difficulties and ADHD or ADD.

**5556  Matlock Precollegiate Academy**

**2491 Homewood Road**
**West Palm Beach, FL  33416**   561-687-0327
                                 FAX 561-684-3935
                                 http://www.matlockacademy.com
                                 e-mail: info@matlockacademy.com
*Daphne Grad, Founder*

Designs its program to meet the specific needs of the students who are underachievers, seeking to fulfill their needs through a comprehensive student centered philosophy and offering a very successful educational program.

**5557  McGlannan School**

**10770 SW 84th Street**
**Miami, FL  33173**         305-274-2208
                             FAX 305-274-0337
                             TDY:305-274-2208
*Frances McGlannan, Director*
*Arlene , Assistant Director*

A day school for students with dyslexia 6-14 years old. Diagnostic, multidisciplinary, prescriptive, research-based and individualized to reach the whole child.

**5558  Mental Health and Educational Services**

**Mental Health and Educational Services**
**5251 Emerson Street**
**Jacksonville, FL  32207**   904-399-0324
                              FAX 904-399-0420
                              http://www.psydoc.com
*Ruth Klein PhD, Director*

Diagnostic and therapy services for a wide range of emotional and behavioral disabilities.

**5559  Morning Star School**

**Morning Star School**
**210 E Linebaugh Avenue**
**Tampa, FL  33612**         813-935-0232
                             FAX 813-932-2321
                             http://www.tampa-morningstar.org
                             e-mail: jfriedheim@tampa-morningstar.org
*Jeanette Friedheim, Principal*
*Eileen Daly, Assistant Administrator*

Morning Star School is a Catholic Diocesan school dedicated to meeting the needs of students with learning disabilities and related difficulties. It is a non-graded school for children from the ages of 6 to 16. The student's self-esteem is enhanced in an atmosphere that is both challenging and nurturing.

**5560  New Lifestyles**

**1210 Gateway Road**
**Lake Park, FL  33403**     561-848-5537
                             FAX 954-797-2813
                             e-mail: theoptions@aol.com

New Lifestyles provides comprehensive life management services including assessment, programming, residential placement at various locations in Palm Beach County, Florida and Winchester, Virginia. Programs focus on issues such as self-esteem, interpersonal skills and adjustments, vocational placement, independent living, time management, organizational skills, and decision-making skills.

**5561  PACE: Brantley Hall School**

3221 Sand Lake Road
Longwood, FL  32779          407-869-8882
                             FAX 407-869-8717
http://www.pacebrantleyhall.org
e-mail: bw@mypbhs.org

*Barbara Winter, Admissions Director*
*Kathleen Shatlock, Principal*

PACE-Brantley Hall School is an independent, non-profit Elementary - 12 grade school for children with learning differences. The PACE program has been specifically designed for students who have been diagnosed with learning disabilities, attention deficit disorder, dyslexia and similar challenges.

**5562  PEAC: South**

1501 Venera Avenue
Coral Gables, FL  33146          305-667-5011
http://www.susanmaynardphd.com

*Susan PhD*

Administers a complete Psycho-Educational Test battery to determine if clients have learning disabilities. Marriage and family therapy and therapy for individuals available.

**5563  Palm Beach Gardens Prep School**

10350 Riverside Drive
Palm Beach Gardens, FL  33410     561-622-0401
                                  FAX 561-622-0402

*Philip T Rosen MD, Director*

Grades 1-12 day school, coed, college preparatory curriculum, including art, physical education etc., diagnostic prescriptive methodologies, SLD mainstreamed, small classes (6-10), non-residential, founded in 1977.

**5564  Progressive School**

Educational Services of America
1950 Prairie Road
West Palm Beach, FL  33406        561-642-3100
                                  FAX 561-969-1950
http://www.progressiveschool.org
e-mail: Progsch@FDN.com

*Jennifer Glynn, Admissions Director*
*Sandra Arroyo, Headmaster*

A small, private, highly individualized program, K-8, for children with attention disorders, dyslexia and other academic learning problems. Day students only.

**5565  Ralph J Baudhuin Oral School of Nova University**

Baudhin Pre-school
3375 SW 75th Avenue
Fort Lauderdale, FL  33314        954-262-7100
                                  FAX 954-262-3936
http://www.nova.edu/msi

*Debra Abolassa, Executive Director*
*Ronni , Director*

Preschool for autistic children.

**5566  Tampa Day School and Reading Clinic**

12606 Henderson Road
Tampa, FL  33625          813-269-2100
                          FAX 813-963-7843
http://www.tampadayschool.com
e-mail: tds@tampadayschool.com

*Lois Delaney, School Head*
*Andrea Mowatt, Assistant Principal*
*Lisa Guffey, Learning Solutions Director*

At Tampa Day School we provide a learning environment that promotes that individual feeling of success for each child and to meet each child's needs. The Reading Clinic has been helping children become better readers for over 30 years. Once we have targeted the problem, and provide exactly the kind of help your child needs, the gains are immediate and long lasting.

**5567  Vanguard School**

Vanguard School
22000 Highway 27
Lake Wales, FL  33859 6858        863-676-6091
                                  FAX 863-676-8297
http://www.vanguardschool.org
e-mail: vanadmin@vanguardschool.org

*James Moon PhD, President*
*Ray Borglund, Vice President*

The Vanguard School program is designed for students age 10 through high school who are experiencing academic difficulties due to learning disability such as dyslexia or dyscalculia or an attention deficit.

*11-20 years old*

## Georgia

**5568  Achievement Academy**

Achievement Academy
5700 River Road
Columbus, GA  31904          706-660-0050
                             FAX 706-660-0056
e-mail: bnzysawyer@mindspring.com

*Beth Sawyer, Coordinator*

Offers diagnostic and educational services for a variety of learning disabilities.

**5569  Atlanta Speech School**

3160 Northside Parkway NW
Atlanta, GA  30327          404-233-5332
                            FAX 404-266-2175
http://www.atlantaspeechschool.org
e-mail: cyates@atlspsch.org

*Tony Aeck, Chairman*
*Paula Ford, Director of Communications*

The Atlanta Speech School is one of the Southeast's oldest therapeutic educational centers for children and adults with hearing, speech, language, or learning disabilities. We help children and adults with communication disorders realize their full potential.

**5570  Bedford School**

5665 Milam Road
Fairburn, GA  30213                      770-774-8001
                                        FAX 770-774-8005
http://www.thebedfordschool.org
e-mail: bbox@thebedfordschool.org
*Betsy Box, Founder/Director*
*Jess James, Assistant Director*

The Bedford School is a nine-month day program specifically designed to meet the needs of children with learning disabilities. We are certified through the Georgia Accrediting Commission.

**5571  Brandon Hall School**

1701 Brandon Hall Drive
Atlanta, GA  30350-3706              770-394-8177
                                    FAX 770-804-8821
http://www.brandonhall.org
e-mail: pstockhammer@brandonhall.org
*Paul Stockhammer, President*
*Marcia Shearer, Admissions Director*

College preparatory, co-ed day and boys' boarding school for students in grades 4-12. Designed for academic underachievers and students with minor learning disabilities, attention deficit disorders and dyslexia. Enrollment 150 students; faculty 40, with 100% college acceptances. Interscholastic sports and numerous co-curriculum activities and summer programs.

**5572  Chatham Academy**

Royce Learning Center
4 Oglethorpe Professional Boulevard
Savannah, GA  31406                  912-354-4047
                                    FAX 912-354-4633
http://www.roycelearningcenter.com
e-mail: info@roycelearningcenter.com
*Carolyn Hannaford, Assistant Director/Principal*
*Cindy Hamilton, Assistant Principal*

Chatham Academy provides a specialized curriculum and individualized instruction for students with diagnosed learning disabilities and/or attention deficit disorder. Chatham's goal is to improve students' functioning to levels commensurate with their potential in all areas so that they may return to and succeed in regular educational programs.

**5573  Creative Community Services**

1543 Lilburn-Stone Mountain Road
Stone Mountain, GA  30087            770-469-6226
                                    866-618-2823
                                    FAX 770-469-6210
http://www.ccsgeorgia.org
e-mail: info@ccsgeorgia.org
*Sally Buchanan, Executive Director*
*Sandy Corbin, Clinical Director*

Creative Community Services Inc. provides therapeutic foster care for kids and home-based support services for children and adults with mental retardation and developmental disabilities.

**5574  Horizons School**

Georgia Accrediting Commission
1900 DeKalb Avenue NE
Atlanta, GA  30307                   404-378-2219
                                     800-822-6242
                                    FAX 404-378-8946
http://www.horizonsschool.com
e-mail: HorizonsSchool@horizonschsool.com
*Les Garber, Principal*
*Martha Rummel, Administrative Assistant*

The intent is to develop in students those values and skills which assure maximum opportunities. Students learn real-life skills through active participation in the classroom, as well as in other aspects of the school. They learn responsibility, decision-making, and problem-solving skills through active involvement in the management of the community. Such a leadership role empowers students, giving them the knowledge that they have control of personal decisions and interpersonal interactions.

**5575  Howard School Central Campus**

1246 Ponce De Leon Avenue NE
Atlanta, GA  30306                   404-377-7436
                                    FAX 404-377-0884
http://www.howardschool.org
e-mail: kerens@howardschool.org
*Sandra Kleinman, Executive Director*
*Keren Schuller, Admissions Director*

At Howard School we believe that every child should have the opportunity to succeed. We serve students whose personal learning style may not be complemented in traditional teaching and learning environments, compromising the student's ability to reach his or her full potential.

**5576  Howard School North Campus**

Disability Support Department
9415 Willeo Road
Roswell, GA  30075                   707-642-9644
                                    FAX 707-998-1398
http://www.howardschool.org
e-mail: KerenS@howardschool.org
*Sandra Kleinman MD, Executive Director*
*Keren Schuller, Admissions Director*

At the Howard School we understand that every child can learn. We believe that every child should have the opportunity to succeed. Our mission is to successfully teach each student in the unique way that student learns.

**5577  Mill Springs Academy**

Special Education Systems
13660 New Providence Road
Alpharetta, GA  30004                770-360-1336
                                    FAX 770-360-1341
http://www.millsprings.org
*Tweetie Moore, Executive Director*
*Robert Moore, Administrator*

A small, structured, accredited day school combining learning disability teaching techniques within the therapeutic milieu. Integral components include supportive services for parents and consistent communication with other professionals working with our students. The K-12 program includes an after school program for younger students and an athletic program for older students. Mark Trail Camp is a 7 week summer program for K-7th grades which includes academics and camp activities.

**5578  New School**

13660 New Providence Road
Alpharetta, GA  30004          770-360-1336
                               FAX 770-360-1341

*Tweetie Moore*

**5579  Reading Success**

Reading Success
4434 Columbia Road
Martinez, GA  30907            706-863-8173
                               FAX 706-863-4523
http://www.readingsuccess.com
e-mail: tutorme@readingsuccess.com
*Sandra Mashburn, Founder/Director*

Reading Success, Inc. is a locally owned and operated program, serving the CSRA for over 30 years and providing professional help to students with all kinds of learning problems. Our guarantee is; if one year of improvement has not been made in the 48 lessons, the student receives instruction free of charge for 18 lessons.

**5580  Wardlaw School: A Division of the Atlanta Speech School**

3160 Northside Parkway NW
Atlanta, GA  30327             404-233-5332
                               FAX 404-266-2175
http://www.atlantaspeechschool.org/wardlaw
e-mail: cyates@atlspsch.org
*Tony Aeck, Chairman*
*Paula Ford, Director of Communications*

The mission of the Wardlaw School is to help children with average to very superior intelligence and mild to moderate learning disabilities learn how to become self-confident, independent learners. Placement at the school is intended to be short term; however, ongoing support for the child and his/her family is available throughout the child's educational experience.

## Hawaii

**5581  Center on Disability Studies**

University of Hawaii Manoa
1776 University Avenue
Honolulu, HI  96822            808-956-9142
                               FAX 808-956-5713
http://www.cds.hawaii.edu
e-mail: Robert.Stodden@cds.hawaii.edu
*Robert PhD, Executive Director*
*Tom Conway, Media Coordinator*

The Center for Disability Studies is a Hawaii University Affiliated Program at the University of Hawaii at Manoa. The mission of the CDS is to support the quality of life, community inclusion, and self-determination of all persons with disabilities and their families.

**5582  Hawaii Parents Unlimited**

200 N Vineyard Boulevard
Honolulu, HI  96817            808-536-2280
                               800-533-9684
                               FAX 808-537-6780
http://www.ldahawaii.org
e-mail: ldah@ldahawaiii.org
*Jennifer Schember-Lang, Executive Director*

Parent Training and Information Program views parents as full partners in the educational process and a significant source of support and assistance to each other. Funded by the Division of Personnel Preparation, Office of Special Education Programs, these programs provide training and information to parents to enable such individuals to participate more effectively with professionals in meeting the educational needs of disabled children.

**5583  Variety School of Hawaii**

Variety School of Hawaii
710 Palekaua Street
Honolulu, HI  96816            808-732-2835
                               FAX 808-732-4334
e-mail: yeevariety@inets.com
*Alexi K Dankeit MD, Executive Director*

The mission of Variety School of Hawaii is to educate children with learning disabilities, attention deficit disorder, and/or autism, and to assist these children in achieving their maximum potential through a multidisciplinary approach. To this end, the school offers children ages five through thirteen a wide variety of programs and experiences in a warm, nurturing, intimate environment that truly makes a difference in their lives - and in their families' lives as well.

*5-13 years old*

## Idaho

**5584  Idaho Parents Unlimited**

Idaho Parents Unlimited
600 N Curtis Road
Boise, ID  83706               208-342-5884
                               800-242-4785
                               FAX 208-342-1408
http://www.ipulidaho.org
e-mail: ipui@rmci.net
*Evelyn Mason, Executive Director*
*Kathy Hall, Bookkeeper Administrative Assist*

Idaho Parents Unlimited (IPUL) is a statewide organization founded to provide support, information and technical assistance to parents of children and youth with disabilities.

## Illinois

#### 5585  Achievement Centers
6425 Willow Springs Road
La Grange Highlands, IL  60525    708-579-9040
                                FAX 708-579-5872
                        http://www.acaciaacademy.com
                        e-mail: kfouks@acaciaacademy.com
*Kathie Fouks, Principal/Director*
*Eileen Bybee, Dean of Students*

A Tradition of Nurturing Minds, Enriching Lives, and
Building Self-Esteem. Offering a variety of
year-round and summer programs designed to meet
each student's learning objectives in terms of his/her
learning capacities.

*Ages 5-Adult*

#### 5586  Allendale Association
PO Box 1088
Lake Villa, IL  60046            847-356-2351
                                888-255-3631
                            FAX 847-356-0289
                    http://www.allendale4kids.org
                    e-mail: development@allendale4kids.org
*Mary Shahbazian, President*
*Ron Howard, Vice President*

The Allendale Association is a private, not-for-profit
organization dedicated to excellence and innovation
in the care, education, treatment and advocacy for
troubled children, youth and their families.

#### 5587  Att-P'tach Special Education Program
P'tach
2828 W Pratt Avenue
Chicago, IL  60645               773-973-2828
                            FAX 773-973-6666
                        http://www.att.org
                        e-mail: mantanky@att.org
*Rabbi Well, Superintendent*
*Susan Feuer, Director*

Offers mainstreaming, independent skills, therapeutic
swim classes and psychological services.

#### 5588  Brehm Preparatory School
1245 E Grand Avenue
Carbondale, IL  62901            618-457-0371
                            FAX 618-529-1248
                        http://www.brehm.org
                        e-mail: brehm1@brehm.org
*Richard Collins PhD, Executive Director*
*Brian Brown, Associate Executive Director*

Brehm Preparatory School is a not-for-profit corporation, with a mission to empower students with complex learning disabilities to recognize and optimize
their full potential.

#### 5589  Camelot Care Center: Illinois
1502 N NW Highway
Palatine, IL  60067              847-359-5600
                            FAX 847-359-2759
*Katherine Lau, Principal*

A psychiatric residential treatment center using a developmentally based treatment model called Process
Therapy.

#### 5590  Catholic Children's Home
Special Education School
1400 State Street
Alton, IL  62002                 618-465-3594
                            FAX 618-465-1083
                        http://www.altoncch.org
                        e-mail: cch1400@ezl.com
*Steven Roach, Executive Director*
*Laura Ballard, Educational Director*

The Catholic Children's Home is sponsored and primarily supported by the Catholic Diocese in Springfield, Illinois, and serves to promote and care for the
needs, education and welfare of dependent, neglected
or otherwise needy children and youths who need
structured care away from their own homes.

#### 5591  Center for Learning
National Louis University
2840 Sheridan Road
Evanston, IL  60201              847-256-5150
                            FAX 847-256-6542
                        http://www.nl.edu
                        e-mail: kadamle@nc.edu
*Kim Adamle, Director*
*Curtis , President*

Offers psychological, educational and neuro psychological evaluations, testing of gifted children and remedial tutoring for children with learning disabilities.

#### 5592  Center for Speech and Language Disorders
Center for Speech and Language Disorders
195 Spangler
Elmhurst, IL  60126              630-530-8551
                            FAX 630-530-5909
                        http://www.csld.org
                        e-mail: info@csld.org
*Mary Brady, Operations Manager*
*Phyllis Kupperman, Founder*
*Christina R Rees, Co-Clinical Manager*

Our mission is to help children with speech and language disorders reach their full potential. CSLD is an
internationally recognized leader in the diagnosis and
treatment of hyperlexia and other language disorders.

#### 5593  Chicago Urban Day School
1248 W 69th Street
Chicago, IL  60636               773-483-3555
                            FAX 773-483-9758
*Georgia Jordan, Executive Director*

**5594 Children's Center for Behavioral Development**

Children's Center for Behavioral Development
353 N 88th Street
East Saint Louis, IL  62203          618-398-1152
                                     FAX 618-398-6977
                        e-mail: ccbd@mvp.net
*Carolyn Birth, Executive Director*

A special education program for children and adolescents with emotional disturbances, behavioral disorders and learning disabilities.

**5595 Cove School**

350 Lee Road
Northbrook, IL  60062              847-562-2100
                                   FAX 847-562-2112
                    http://www.coveschool.org
                    e-mail: ssover@coveschool.org
*Sally Sover, Executive Director*
*Carol Sward, Principal*
*Mark Wall, Dean of Students*

The Cove School was established in 1947, to educate students with learning disabilities and to facilitate their return to their neighborhood schools in the shortest possible time. The heart of Cove's educational philosophy is to design a program that pulls out the child's skills.

**5596 Early Achievement Center Preschool & Kindergarten**

6425 Willow Springs Road
La Grange Highlands, IL  60525    708-579-9040
                                  FAX 708-579-5872
                   http://www.acaciaacademy.com
                   e-mail: info@acaciaacademy.com
*Kathie Fouks, Principal/Director*
*Eileen Bybee, Dean of Students*

The Early Achievement Center Program encourages growth of the total child in social, intellectual, physical, and emotional abilities.

*Ages 2-6*

**5597 Educational Services of Glen Ellyn**

364 Pennsylvania
Glen Ellyn, IL  60137              630-469-1479
                                   FAX 630-469-1265
                 e-mail: educationalservices@juno.com
*Beth Sievens, Owner*

Tutoring for all ages in all subject areas. Diagnostic testing, specializing in learning disabilities and career counseling for learning disabled adults.

**5598 Elim Christian Services**

Learning Disability Program
13020 S Central Avenue
Palos Heights, IL  60463           708-389-0555
                                   FAX 708-389-2488
                     http://www.elimcs.org
                     e-mail: info@elimcs.org
*Bill Lodewyk, President/Executive Director*
*Pam Connolly, Programs Supervisor*

Elim Christian Services is a non-profit corporation that seeks to equip persons with special needs to achieve to their highest God-given potential.

**5599 Esperanza School**

520 N Marshfield Avenue
Chicago, IL  60622                 312-243-6097
                                   FAX 312-243-2076
                                   TDY:800-526-0844
                   http://www.esperanzaservices.org
*Barbara Fields, Executive Director*
*Myra Rodas, Secretary*

Self-help educational services offered to children who are autistic or mentally disabled.

**5600 Family Resource Center on Disabilities**

20 E Jackson Boulevard
Chicago, IL  60604                 312-939-3513
                                   800-952-4199
                                   FAX 312-939-7297
                                   TDY:312-939-3519
                     http://www.frcd.org
                  e-mail: info@frcd.ptiil.americom.net
*Charlotte Jardins, Executive Director*

The Family Resource Center on Disabilities was formerly known as the Coordinating Council for Handicapped Children. FRCD was organized in 1969 by parents, professionals, and volunteers who sought to improve services for all children with disabilities.

**5601 Hammit School: The Baby Fold**

108 E Willow Street
Normal, IL  61761                  309-452-1170
                                   FAX 309-452-0115
                    http://www.thebabyfold.org
                    e-mail: info@thebabyfold.org
*Dale Strssheim, Executive Director*
*Rebeca Haremaker, Office Assistant*

The Baby Fold is a multi-service agency that provides Residential, Special Education, Child Welfare, and Family Support Services to children and families in central Illinois.

**5602 Hope School**

50 Hazel Lane
Springfield, IL  62716             217-585-5437
                                   FAX 217-786-3356
                                   TDY:217-585-5105
                   http://www.thehopeschool.org
                   e-mail: info@thehopeschool.org
*Clinton Conway, Day Education Contact*
*Judy Bukowski, Administrator*

The Hope School is a private, not-for-profit educational and residential center, that has been serving children with multiple disabilities and their families since 1957.

**5603 Illinois Center for Autism**

Illinois Center for Autism
548 S Ruby Lane
Fairview Heights, IL  62208        618-398-7500
                                   FAX 618-394-9869
                  http://www.illinoiscenterforautism.org
*Susan Szekeoy, Executive Director*

A not-for-profit, community based, mental health treatment, and educational agency dedicated to serving people with autism. Referrals for possible student placement are made through local school districts, hospitals, regional special education centers, and doctors.

**5604  Joseph Academy**

7530 N Natchez
Niles, IL  60714                       847-588-2990
                                       FAX 847-588-2950
                   http://www.josephacademy.org
              e-mail: information@josephacademy.org
*Michael Schack, Executive Director*
*Heather Elliott, Principal*

Founded in 1983, Joseph Academy provides a nurturing and challenging environment for young people. Our mission is to serve children and adolescents with behavioral, emotional and learning disorders by helping them develop the social, academic and vocational skills they need to function in society.

**5605  LEARN Center**

Illinois Masonic Medical Center
836 W Nelson Street
Chicago, IL  60657                     773-296-7065
                                       FAX 773-296-5885
                   http://www.iser.com/LEARN.html
*Bethany Graham*

**5606  La Grange Area Department of Special Education**

La Grange Area Department of Special Education
1301 W Cossitt Avenue
La Grange, IL  60525                   708-354-5730
                                       FAX 708-354-0733
                                       TDY:708-352-5994
                                       http://www.ladse.org
                   e-mail: JimSurber@ladse.org
*James M Surber MD, Executive Director*
*Lois Miller, Executive Assistant Director*

Offers programs for students with moderate to severe mental retardation, learning disabilities or behavior disorders.

**5607  Professional Assistance Center for Education (PACE)**

National-Louis University
2840 Sheridan Road
Evanston, IL  60201                    847-256-5150
                                       800-443-5522
                                       FAX 847-256-5190
            http://www.3.nl.edu/academics/nce/programs/pace
                   e-mail: cburns@nl.edu
*Carol Burns, Director*
*Curtis , President*

Founded in 1986 PACE is a two-year noncredit postsecondary certificate program located on the campus of National-Louis University. The PACE program is designed especially to meet the transitional needs of students with multiple learning disabilities in a university setting.

**5608  South Central Community Services**

8316 S Ellis Avenue
Chicago, IL  60619                     773-483-0900
                                       FAX 773-483-5701
                   http://www.sccsinc.org
*Felicia Blasingame, President/CEO*
*Felicia Blasingame, Executive Director*

South Central Community Services, Inc. is a grassroots, not-for-profit organization established in 1970 by a group of community residents concerned about the absence of human service facilities and programs in the community.

**5609  St. Joseph's Carondelet Child Center**

739 E 35th Street
Chicago, IL  60616                     773-624-7443
                                       FAX 773-624-7676
                   http://www.stjccc.org
                   e-mail: jwhite@stjccc.org
*D Black, Administrative Assistant*

St. Joseph's Carondelet Child Center is a residential, day and outpatient treatment center for 180 boys and girls (ages 6-21) who are orphaned by neglect, substance abuse, physical and sexual abuse, violence and despair. In 1989 we opened a second program facility (Solace Place in Englewood community), extending its service to older boys and girls (ages 14-21) deemed to be at high risk for delinquency.

**5610  Summit School**

611 E Main Street
Dundee, IL  60118                      847-428-6451
                                       FAX 847-428-6419
                   http://www.summitdundee.org
                   e-mail: scarl@summitdundee.org
*Sharon Carl, Principal*
*George Phelan, President*

Summit School is a private, non-profit organization dedicated to fulfilling the needs of children with learning problems that prevent them from achieving in a standard classroom situation.

*6-21 years old*

# Indiana

**5611  Clearinghouse on Reading, English andCommunications**

Indiana University of Bloomington
107 S Indiana Avenue
Bloomington, IN  47405                 812-855-5847
                                       FAX 812-856-5512
                   http://www.reading.indiana.edu
                   e-mail: iuadmit@indiana.edu
*Stephen Stroup, Associate Director*
*Kenneth , Chancellor*

Offers information on reading, English and communication skills, preschool through college.

**5612  Educational Enrichment Center**
1450 Bellemeade Avenue
Evansville, IN  47714                    812-473-0651
                                         FAX 812-471-1145
*Janet Dill, Coordinator*

The center provides the following services: educational assessment; personal development; tutoring; psychological testing and therapy; neuropsychological evaluation; and cognitive therapy. The center offers tutors who are qualified teachers with a broad area of training including Orton-Gillingham multisensory techniques. Many services for head injured individuals with Halstead-Reitan Neuropsychological evaluation and comprehensive cognitive retraining are available.

**5613  IN*SOURCE**
809 N Michigan Street
South Bend, IN  46601                    574-234-7101
                                         800-332-4433
                                         FAX 574-234-7279
                                         http://www.insource.org
                                         e-mail: insource@insource.org
*Richard Burden, Executive Director*
*Scott Carson, Assistant Director*

The mission of IN*SOURCE is to provide parents, families and service providers in Indiana the information and training necessary to assure effective educational programs and appropriate services for children and young adults with disabilities.

## Iowa

**5614  Iowa Compass**
Center for Disabilities and Development
100 Hawkins Drive
Iowa City, IA  52242                     319-353-8777
                                         800-779-2001
                                         FAX 319-384-5139
                                         TDY:319-353-8777
                                         http://www.medicine.uiowa.edu
                                         e-mail: iowa-compass@uiowa.edu
*Jane Gay, Director*
*Amy Mikelson, Outreach/Training Coordinator*

A free information and referral service on assistive technology, product information, the used equipment referral service, funding options, and referral to free legal advocacy. Also publishes a newsletter.

## Kansas

**5615  Families Together**
501 Jackson Street
Topeka, KS  66603                        785-233-4777
                                         800-264-6343
                                         FAX 785-233-4787
                                         http://www.familiestogetherinc.org
                                         e-mail: topeka@familiestogetherinc.org
*Lesli Girard, Center Coordinator*
*Karen Snell, Regional Center Coordinator*

Families Together is a statewide non-profit organization assisting Kansas families which include sons and/or daughters who have any form of disability.

**5616  Heartspring School**
8700 E 29th Street N
Wichita, KS  67226                       316-634-8700
                                         800-835-1043
                                         FAX 316-634-0555
                                         http://www.heartspring.org
                                         e-mail: rappe@heartspring.org
*Cara Rapp, Admissions Director*
*Kendra Conard, Accounting Assistant*

Heartspring School has earned an international reputation for improving the lives of children. Heartspring is a not-for-profit private residential school that serves children 5-21. We serve children with disabilities such as autism, asperger's, communication disorders, developmental disabilities, dual diagnosed, behavoir disorders, hearing or vision impaired.

**5617  Menninger Center for Learning Disabilities**
Menninger Clinic
5800 SW Sixth Street
Topeka, KS  66606
                                         800-351-9058
                                         http://www.iser.com/menninger.html
*Michele PhD, Director*

The Center offers the following services for children and adults: 1) educational evaluations for learning disabilities, dyslexia, learning problems and other special needs 2) gifted evaluations 3) workshops for parents and educators 4) reading assessments 5) training for teachers in multisensory remedial approaches and 6) group and individual tutoring.

## Kentucky

**5618  De Paul School**
1925 Duker Avenue
Louisville, KY  40205                    502-459-6131
                                         FAX 502-458-0827
                                         http://www.depaulschool.org
                                         e-mail: dpinfo@depaulschool.org
*Peggy Woolley, Admissions Director*
*Anthony Kemper, School Head*

Teachs students with dyslexia and other specific learning differences how to learn. Grades 1-8.

**5619  KY-SPIN**
10301-B Deering Road
Louisville, KY  40272                    502-937-6894
                                         800-525-7746
                                         FAX 502-937-6464
                                         TDY:502-937-6894
                                         http://www.kyspin.com
                                         e-mail: spininc@kyspin.com
*Paulette Olgsdon, Director*
*Tara Becker, Office Assistant*

Parent Training and Information Project views parents as full partners in the educational process and a significant source of support and assistance to each other. Funded by the Division of Personnel Preparation, Office of Special Education Programs, these programs provide training and information and support to parents and families of children of all ages with all types of disabilities. We empower parents to recognize and use all available resources.

**5620  Meredith-Dunn School**

3023 Melbourne Avenue
Louisville, KY 40220                       502-456-5819
FAX 502-456-5953
http://www.meredith-dunn-school.org
e-mail: mdschool@bellsouth.net
*Cindy Bunnell, Admissions Director*
*Kathy Beam, Principal*

The Meredith-Dunn School was founded in 1971 as a non-profit institution to provide educational assistance for children with learning difficulties. We admit only children of average to above average IQ who possess learning difficulties, whether or not these difficulties are recognized as such by federal or public definition.

**5621  Shedd Academy**

401 S 7th Street
Mayfield, KY 42066                        270-247-8007
FAX 270-247-0637
http://www.sheddacademy.org
e-mail: paulthompson@sheddacademy.org
*Paul Thompson MD, Executive Director*
*Debbie Craven, Admissions Office*

The mission of the Shedd Academy is to prepare dyslexia and ADD students for college or vocational training and for their future by helping them to understand their unique learning styles; fulfill their intellectual, academic, physical, artistic, creative, social, spiritual, and emotional potential; develop a sense of self responsibility; assume a value system so that they can become contributing members of society and increase their skills to ensure they are armed with a variety of abilities.

## Louisiana

**5622  Crescent Academy**

821 General Pershing Street
New Orleans, LA 70115                     504-895-3952
FAX 504-895-3964
*Barbara Leggett*

Offers a variety of services to students with disabilities including note takers, extended testing time, counseling services, and special accommodations.

**5623  Project PROMPT**

Families Helping Families
4323 Division Street
Metairie, LA 70002                        504-888-9111
800-766-7736
FAX 504-888-0246
http://www.projectprompt.com
e-mail: info@projectprompt.com
*Cindy Arceneaux, Project Director*
*Mary Jacob, Project Coordinator*

Parent Training and Information Program views parents as full partners in the educational process and a significant source of support and assistance to each other. Funded by the Division of Personnel Preparation, Office of Special Education Programs, these programs provide training and information to parents to enable such individuals to participate more effectively with professionals in meeting the educational needs of disabled children.

## Maryland

**5624  Academic Resource Center at the Gunston Day School**

PO Box 200
Centreville, MD 21617                     410-758-0620
FAX 410-758-0628
http://www.gunstondayschool.org
*Jeffrey Woodworth, President*
*Reid Henry, Office Assistant*

Provides tutoring for individuals K through adult. Also offers limited and brief educational testing.

**5625  Behavioral Directions**

Behavioral Directions
7945 MacArthur Boulevard
Cabin John, MD 20818                      703-855-4032
FAX 571-333-0292
http://www.BehavioralDirections.com
e-mail:
behavioraldirections@smartneighborhood.net
*Jane PhD, Coordinator*

Specializing in services to individuals (children and adults) with autism and developmental disabilities and their families. Services are provided by licensed psychologists utilizing Applied Behavior Analysis (ABA) as the treatment approach. Services, including behavioral assessment, functional analysis, educational assessment, parent/staff training, and program evaluation, are provided in home, school, and community settings.

**5626  Chelsea School**

711 Pershing Drive
Silver Spring, MD 20910                   301-585-1430
FAX 301-585-9621
http://www.chelseaschool.edu
e-mail: dfrengel@chelseaschool.edu
*Dave Frengel, Admissions Director*
*Timothy Hall, President*

At Chelsea School, we shatter the stigma of learning disabilities and prepare our students for a lifetime of intellectual exploration, personal growth and social responsibility. Because our students have language-based learning disabilities, we strongly focus on teaching reading and language arts.

**5627  Children's Developmental Clinic**

**Prince George's Community College
301 Largo Road
Largo, MD  20774**                     301-322-0151
                                        FAX 301-322-0519
                                        TDY:301-322-0122
                                        http://www.pgcc.edu
                                        e-mail: advising@pgcc.edu
*Paul H Hahn MD, Director*
*Kathy Hinkel, Coordinator*

The Children's Development Clinic is a continuing education program conducted in cooperation with the Department of Health and Human Performance at Prince George's Community College. The clinic provides special services to children, birth and up, who are experiencing various development difficulties such as learning problems, developmental delays, physical fitness and coordination problems, brain injury, mental retardation, emotional problems, or orthopedic challenges.

**5628  Developmental School Foundation**

**Broschart School
14901 Broschart Road
Rockville, MD  20850**                  301-251-4624
                                        FAX 301-251-4588
                                        http://www.broschartschool.edu
*Mary Kennelly, Executive Director*

Provides a therapeutic day setting with a full school program that addresses the children's social/emotional and learning needs.

**5629  Edgemeade: Raymond A Rogers Jr School**

**13101 Croom Road
Upper Marlboro, MD  20772**             301-888-1333
                                        800-486-3343
                                        FAX 301-579-2342
                                        http://www.gildlearningdisable.org
*Cindy Spiller, Executive Director*

Edgemeade provides residential and day treatment services with a special education school program for kids with disabilities. The facility is licensed by the DHMH and accredited by JCAHO, and the education program is accredited by the MSDE. The therapeutic environment is structured to provide supervision and direction and an opportunity for each child to express himself.

**5630  Forbush School**

**Sheppard and Enoch Pratt Hospital
6501 N Charles Street
Towson, MD  21204**                     410-938-4400
                                        FAX 410-938-4421
                                        http://www.sheppardpratt.org
                                        e-mail: blohnes@sheppardpratt.org
*Burt PhD, Program Director*
*Alania Foster, Office Assistant*

Pre-school to high school, offers programs for the emotionally disturbed and learning disabled.

**5631  Frost Center**

**4915 Aspen Hill Road
Rockville, MD  20853**                  301-933-3451
                                        FAX 301-933-3330
                                        http://www.frostcenter.com
                                        e-mail: chobbes@frostcenter.com
*Carol Hobbes, Admissions Staff*
*Sean McLaughlin, Director*

The Frost school established in 1976, is a school and therapeutic day program that serves emotionally troubled adolescents and their families. Our 12 month school program serves students from ages 7 to 21 who need a supportive and structured environment.

*5-20 years old*

**5632  Group for the Independent Learning Disabled (GILD)**

**PO Box 322
Brooklandville, MD  21022**             410-363-4300
                                        FAX 410-363-7919
                                        http://www.gildlearningdisable.org
*Leith Herrmann, President*
*Harriet Wolf, Membership Chair*

The Group for the Independent Learning Disabled provides support services for adults 18 years and older with a learning disability.

**5633  Hannah More School**

**12039 Reistertown Road
Reistertown, MD  21136**                410-526-5000
                                        FAX 410-526-7631
                                        http://www.HannahMore.org
                                        e-mail: hmsinfo@hannahmore.org
*Carolyn Martin, Admissions Director*
*Mark Waldman, President*

Educates emotionally disabled students and children with a pervasive development disorder and provides therapeutic services so that the student may develop responsible patterns of behavior. A psychoeducational approach consisting of a comprehensive combination of academic subjects, a technology program, counseling programs and a behavioral management systems is designed to meet the individual needs of each student.

**5634  Kennedy Krieger Institute for Handicapped Children**

**University Affiliated Program
707 N Broadway
Baltimore, MD  21205**                  443-923-9200
                                        800-873-3377
                                        FAX 443-923-9405
                                        http://www.kennedykrieger.org
*Gary Goldstien, President/CEO*
*Jim Anders, Vice President*

The Kennedy Krieger Institute is an internationally recognized facility dedicated to improving the lives of children and adolescents with pediatric developmental disabilities through patient care, special education, research and professional training.

**5635 Parents' Place of Maryland**

801 Cromwell Park Drive
Glenn Burnie, MD 21061     410-768-9100
FAX 410-768-0830
http://www.ppmd.org
e-mail: info@ppmd.org
*Suzie Shannon, Office Administrator*
*Josie Thomas, Director*

We are here to serve the parents of children with disabilities throughout Maryland, regardless of the nature of their child's disability or the age of their child.

**5636 Phillips School: Programs for Children andFamilies**

8920 Whiskey Bottom Road
Laurel, MD 20723     301-470-1620
FAX 301-470-1624
http://www.phillipsprograms.org
e-mail: Gary.Behrens@phillipsprograms.org
*Sally Sibley, President/CEO*
*Gavin Behrens, Program Director*

Phillips is a non-profit, private organization serving the needs of individuals with emotional and behavioral problems and their families through education, family support services, community education and advocacy.

**5637 Sensory Integration & Vision Therapy Specialists**

**Vision Help Network**
6509 Democracy Boulevard
Bethesda, MD 20817     301-897-8484
FAX 301-897-8486
http://www.visionhelp.com
e-mail: info@visionhelp.com
*S Appelbaum MD, Owner*
*Barbara Bassin, Co-owner*

Dr. Appelbaum's practice, established in 1977, offers a full range of family vision care and eye services, specializing in the treatment of children and adults with behavioral, sensorimotor or learning-related vision problems such as those previously diagnosed with add-adhd, dyslexia, acquired brain injury, stroke, learning disabilities, and/or avoidance of reading.

**5638 Sensory Integration & Vision Therapy Specialists**

**Georgetown Plaza Bridges Learning Center**
914 Bay Ridge Road
Annapolis, MD 21403     301-897-8484
FAX 301-897-8486
http://www.visionhelp.com
e-mail: Drstrab@erols.com
*S Appelbaum MD, Owner*
*Barbara Bassin, Co-owner*

Dr. Appelbaum's practice, established in 1977, offers a full range of family vision care services, specializing in the treatment of children and adults with behavioral, sensorimotor or learning-related vision problems such as those previously diagnosed and-adhd, dyslexia, and/or avoidance reading.

**5639 The Nora School**

955 Sligo Avenue
Silver Spring, MD 20910     301-495-6672
FAX 301-495-7829
http://www.nora-school.org
e-mail: dave@nora-school.org
*David Mullen, Headmaster*
*Elaine Mack, Admissions Director*

A small, progressive, college preparatory high school that nurtures and empowers bright students who have been frustrated in larger, more traditional school settings.

## Massachusetts

**5640 Adult Center at PAL: Curry College**

1071 Blue Hill Avenue
Milton, MA 02186     617-333-0500
FAX 617-333-2114
TDY:617-333-2250
http://www.curry.edu/pal
e-mail: pal@curry.edu
*Jane Adelizzi PhD, Contact*

The Adult Center at PAL (Program for Advancement of Learning) is the first program to offer academic and socio-emotional services to adults with LD/ADHD/Dyslexia in a college setting in the New England area. The ACD offers one-to-one academic tutorials; small support groups that meet weekly; and Saturday Seminars that explore issues that impact the lives of adults with LD/ADHD.

**5641 Berkshire Meadow**

249 N Plain Road
Housatonic, MA 01236     413-528-2523
FAX 413-528-0293
http://www.berkshiremeadows.org
e-mail: berkshiremeadows@jri.org
*Gail Charpentier, Executive Director*

Residential school for children and adolescents who have severe developmental disabilities.

**5642 Brightside for Families and Children**

2112 Riverdale Street
West Springfield, MA 01089     413-788-7366
800-660-4673
FAX 413-747-0182
http://www.mercycares.com
e-mail: lora.davis-allen@sghs.com
*Lora Davis-Allen, Educational Administrator*
*Rose Marceau, Executive Secretary*

Brightside for Families and Children is a non-profit, social service organization dedicated to strengthening, supporting and preserving all children and families. Brightside is especially focused on those children and families in Western Massachusetts who are most vulnerable and disavantaged regardless of race, creed or color.

**5643 College Internship Program at the Berkshire Center**

Berkshire Center
18 Park Street
Lee, MA  01238          413-243-2576
                        FAX 413-243-3351
              http://www.berkshirecenter.org
         e-mail: gshaw@berkshirecenter.org
*Michael McManmo MD, Director*
*Gary Shaw, Program Director*

A post secondary program for young adults with learning disabilities, ages 18-26. Half of the students attend Berkshire Community College and business school while the others may go directly into the world of work. Services include vocational/academic preparation, tutoring, college liaison, life skills instruction, driver's education, money management, psychotherapy and more.

**5644 Commonwealth Learning Center**

Commonwealth Learning Center
123 Highland Avenue
Needham, MA  02494          781-444-5193
                           800-461-6671
                      FAX 781-444-6916
              http://www.commlearn.com
              e-mail: info@commlearn.com
*Lisa Brooks, Director*
*Jerri Murray, Office Manager*

Nonprofit learning center offering one-to-one tutorial for kindergarten through adult students. Programs in reading, spelling, writing, comprehension, math, study skills. Teacher training in multisensory methodologies. Educational evaluations available. Also centers in Danvers, MA and Sudbury, MA.

**5645 Cotting School**

453 Concord Avenue
Lexington, MA  02173          617-862-7323
                            FAX 617-861-1179
                http://www.cotting.org.
                e-mail: dnewark@cotting.org
*Janine Brown-Smith, Admissions Director*

A chapter 766 approved day school in Lexington, MA for boys & girls ages 3-22 with physical, communication and other challenges to learning.

*6-21 years old*

**5646 Devereux Massachusetts**

60 Miles Road
Rutland, MA  01543          508-886-4746
                          FAX 508-886-4773
                http://www.devereux.org
            e-mail: ddaunais@devereux.org
*Donna Daunais, Chief Administrative Officer*

A residential program for children, adolescents and young adults who have emotional and behavioral disorders with developmental and learning disabilities.

*6-21 years old*

**5647 Doctor Franklin Perkins School**

971 Main Street
Lancaster, MA  01523          978-365-7376
                            FAX 978-368-8861
                http://www.perkinschool.org
            e-mail: blossom@perkinschool.org
*Michelle Brady, Admissions Director*
*Sharon Lowry, Day School Program Director*

The Doctor Franklin Perkins School is a comprehensive human service agency operating at several sites in the Central Massachusetts towns of Lancaster and Clinton. Perkins provides a variety of services to several specialized populations of children, adolescents, adults and senior citizens.

**5648 Evergreen Center**

345 Fortune Boulevard
Milford, MA  01757          508-478-5597
                          FAX 508-634-3251
                http://www.evergreenctr.org
            e-mail: services@evergreenctr.org
*Robert Littleton Jr, Executive Director*

The Evergreen Center is a residential school serving children and adolescents with severe developmental disabilities.

**5649 Frederic L Chamberlain School**

1 Pleasant Street
Middleboro, MA  02346          508-947-7825
                             FAX 508-947-0944
              http://www.chamberlainschool.org
        e-mail: admissions@chamberlainschool.org
*William Doherty, Executive Director*
*Lawrence Mutty, Admissions Director*

The Frederic L Chamberlain School is more than a small New England boarding school. Chamberlain is a community of adolescents who have experienced significant diffulties at home, in the community and/or in traditional schools.

**5650 Getting Ready for the Outside World**

Riverview School
551 Route 6A
East Sandwich, MA  02537          508-888-0489
                                FAX 508-888-1315
              http://www.riverviewschool.org
        e-mail: admissions@riverviewschool.org
*Diana , Events Coordinator*

The GROW Program (Getting Ready for the Outside World) is a unique 10 month transitional program (1-3 years) for students who have graduated from Riverview (or a similar program), designed to provide students with the skills that will assist them in functioning more independently within the adult world.

**5651 Landmark Preparatory Program**

Landmark School
429 Hale Street
Prides Crossing, MA  01965          978-236-3010
                                  FAX 978-927-7268
              http://www.landmarkoutreach.org
        e-mail: jtruslow@landmarkschool.org
*Carolyn Orsini, Admissions Director*
*Robert Broudo, Headmaster*

Offers a secondary school level curriculum emphasizing organizational and study skills development in a traditional classroom setting, and is designed for college bound boys and girls who have progressed to within one year of expected grade level performance.

**5652 Landmark School and Summer Programs**
429 Hale Street
Prides Crossing, MA 01965        978-236-3010
FAX 978-927-7268
http://www.landmarkoutreach.org
e-mail: jtruslow@landmarkschool.org
*Carolyn Orsini, Admissions Director*
*Robert Broudo, Headmaster*

Landmark is a coeducational, residential, and day school for emotionally stable students who have been diagnosed with a language-based learning disability. We individualize instruction for each of our students, providing an appropriate program emphasizing the development of language and learning skills within a highly structured learning environment. We also offer an intensive six-week summer program for students who wish to explore the beneficial effects of short-term remediation.

**5653 League School of Greater Boston**
300 Boston Providence Turnpike
Walpole, MA 02032        508-850-3900
FAX 617-964-3264
http://www.leagueschool.com
e-mail: admin@leagueschool.com

To provide social, academic, and vocational programs for children with Autism/Asperger Spectrum Disorders who need a specialized alternative to public school, preparing them to transfer into an environment offering greater independence.

**5654 Learning Center of Massachusetts**
411 Waverley Oaks Road
Waltham, MA 02452        781-893-6000
FAX 781-893-1171
http://www.protestantguild.org
e-mail: admissions@protestantguild.org
*Debrah Rosser, Director*

The Learning Center is an educational program of the Protestant Guild for Human Services, Inc. The 365 community-based school is for students with mental retardation, autism and other developmental disabilities.

**5655 Linden Hill School**
154 S Mountain Road
Northfield, MA 01360        413-498-2906
866-498-2906
FAX 413-498-2908
http://www.lindenhs.org
e-mail: office@lindenhs.org
*James Daniel, Headmaster*
*Vanessa Towne, Office Secretary*

The Linden Hill School enrolls bright, inquisitive, boys who have language based disorders and/or dyslexia.

*9-16 years old*

**5656 Living Independently Forever (LIFE)**
550 Lincoln Road Extention
Hyannis, MA 02601        508-790-3600
FAX 508-778-4919
http://www.lifecapcod.org
e-mail: groupmashpee@lifecapcod.org
*Mary Matthews, President*
*Barry Schwartz, Executive Director*

Living Independently Forever, Inc. is dedicated to serving the life-long needs of adults with significant learning disabilities within our residential communities. LIFE is committed to providing these men and women with the adult education and the opportunities to develop their personal and vocational / occupational skills to their maximum potential, and to supporting them appropriately in independent and group living.

**5657 May Institute**
One Commerce Way
Norwood, MA 02062        781-440-0400
800-778-7601
TDY:781-440-0461
http://www.mayinstitute.org
e-mail: info@mayinstitute.org
*Walter PhD, President/CEO*
*Dennis Russo PhD, Chief Clinical Officer*

Provides educational and rehabilitative services for individuals with autism, developmental disabilities, neurological disorders and mental illness.

**5658 New England Center for Children**
33 Turnpike Road
Southborough, MA 01772        508-481-1015
FAX 508-485-3421
http://www.necc.org
e-mail: info@necc.org
*Vincent Strully, Executive Director*
*Katherine Foster, Associate Executive Director*

The New England Center for Children is a private, nonprofit organization serving children with autism and other related disabilities.

**5659 Regis College**
235 Wellesley Street
Weston, MA 02493        781-768-7000
FAX 781-768-7071
http://www.regiscollege.edu
e-mail: admissions@regiscollege.edu
*MaryJane England, President*
*Emily Keily, Admissions Director*

The college encourages student self-advocacy, the coordination of appropriate academic accommodations and the promotion of disability awareness.

**5660 Riverbrook Residence**
4 Ice Glen Road
Stockbridge, MA 01262        413-298-4926
FAX 413-298-5166
http://www.riverbrook.org
e-mail: riverbro@berkshire.net
*Joan Burkhard, Executive Director*
*Patty Morris, Program Coordinator*

A residence in western Massachusetts, providing supported living to developmentally disabled women, with therapy and treatment focused on the arts.

**5661   Seven Hills at Groton**

22 Hillsdale Avenue
Groton, MA  01450
978-448-3388
FAX 978-448-9695
http://www.sevenhills.org
e-mail: hjarek@sevenhills.org
*Holly Jarek, Vice President*

Our Seven Hills at Groton program provides residential care for children and young adults with multiple disabilities.

**5662   Son-Rise Program: Autism Treatment Center of America**

Option Institute, The
2080 S Undermountain Road
Sheffield, MA  01257
413-229-2100
FAX 413-229-3202
http://www.son-rise.org
e-mail: correspondence@option.org
*Neil Kaufman, Sun-Rise Co-Founder*

The Son-Rise Program, a powerful and effective treatment for children and adults challenged by Autism, Autism Spectrum Disorders, Pervasive Developmental Disorder, Asperger's and all other developmental difficulties. The Sun-Rise Program teaches a specific yet comprehensive system of treatment and education designed to help families and caregivers enable their children to dramatically improve in all areas of learning, development, communication and skill acquisition.

**5663   Stetson School**

Stetson School
455 S Street
Barre, MA  01005
978-355-4541
FAX 978-355-6335
http://www.stetsonschool.org
e-mail: kathyoconnor@yahoo.com
*Kathleen O'Connor, Admissions Coordinator*
*Robert Fitzgerald, Deputy Executive*

A nonprofit residential treatment and special education program for adolescent boys that are sex offenders.

**5664   Threshold Program**

29 Everett Street
Cambridge, MA  02138
617-868-9600
800-999-1959
http://www.lesley.edu/threshold
e-mail: threshld@mail.lesley.edu
*James Wilbur, Director*
*Helen McDonald, Admissions Director*
*Jen Benway, Admissions Coordinator*

The Threshold Program is a comprehensive, non-degree campus based program at Lesley University for highly motivated adults with diverse learning disabilities and other special needs.

**5665   Unity College Learning Resource**

Center Quaker Hill Road
Unity, ME  04988
207-948-3131
800-624-1024
FAX 207-948-2928
http://www.unity.edu
e-mail: admissions@unity.edu
*Jim Horan, Director of Learning Resource Ce*
*Kay Fiedler, Director*

**5666   Valleyhead**

79 Reservoir Road
Lenox, MA  01240
413-637-3635
FAX 413-637-3501
http://www.valleyhead.org
e-mail: cmacbeth@valleyhead.org
*Christine MacBeth, Executive Director*
*Ellen Merrit, Admissions Director*

Valleyhead was founded in 1969. It is a residential school for for girls in the scenic Berkshire Hills of Lenox, Massachusetts. We provide a home and education for girls ages 12-22 with emotional needs. Most of our girls come from abusive and traumatic backgrounds. Many do not have intact families.

**5667   Willow Hill School**

98 Haynes Road
Sudbury, MA  01776
978-443-2581
FAX 978-443-7560
http://www.willowhillschool.org
e-mail: info@willowhillschool.org
*Nancy Brody, Admissions Director*

Willow Hill School provides supportive and individualized educational programs for middle and high school students who are capable of advancing along a strong academic curriculum, but have experienced frustration in earlier school settings.

*11-21 years old*

## Michigan

**5668   Center for Human Development**

Berkley Medical Center
1695 W 12 Mile Road
Berkley, MI  48072
248-691-4744
FAX 248-691-4745
http://www.beaumonthospitals.com
e-mail: ekrug@beaumonthospital.com
*Ernest Krug III MD FAAP, Director*
*Ann Ekola, Office Assistant*

The Center for Human Development evaluates and treats infants, children and adolescents who are showing evidence of, or are at risk for, problems in their behavioral, psychological or learning development.

**5669 Eton Academy**

Eton Academy
1755 Melton Road
Birmingham, MI 48009     248-642-1150
                         FAX 248-642-3670
                    http://www.etonacademy.org
                    e-mail: smorey@etonacademy.org
*Peggy Pattison, Development Director*
*Sharon Morey, Admissions Director*
*Pete Pullen, Head of School*

The Eton Academy is dedicated to educating students of average and above average intelligence with specific learning disabilities. The mission of Eton Academy is to help students understand their learning styles and practice strategies that will prepare them for responsible independence, lifelong learning and participation in school, family and community.

**5670 Lake Michigan Academy**

2428 Burton SE
Grand Rapids, MI 49546     616-464-3330
                           FAX 616-285-1935
                        http://www.wmldf.org
                        e-mail: execdir@wmldf.org
*Jerry Mack, Executive Director*

Lake Michigan Academy is a state-certified, non-profit school for learning disabled children in grades 1 through 12 with average or above average intelligence. The learning disabilities of the children here vary. Some are dyslexic and have difficulty with decoding or comprehending written language. Some are dyscalculic and experience difficulty with mathematical computations and concepts. Many are dysgraphic and exhibit difficulties with writing skills. Our mission is to build self esteem.

**5671 SLD Learning Center**

525 Cheshire NE
Grand Rapids, MI 49505     616-361-1182
                           888-271-8881
                           FAX 616-361-3648
                        http://www.sldread.org
                        e-mail: sldlc@iserv.net
*Pat Harter, President*
*Anne Baird, Vice President*

The SLD Learning Center is a non-profit educational service institute established in 1974 to provide one-to-one instruction for people of all ages who exhibit dyslexia tendencies or who have not succeeded with traditional teaching methods.

## Minnesota

**5672 Groves Academy**

Groves Academy
3200 Highway 100 S
Saint Louis Park, MN 55416     952-920-6377
                               FAX 952-920-2068
                        http://www.grovesacademy.org
                        e-mail: information@grovesadacemy.org
*Michael Mongeau, President*

A day school for children who have learning difficulties.

**5673 LDA Learning Center**

4301 Highway 7
Minneapolis, MN 55416     952-922-8374
                          FAX 952-922-8102
                    http://www.ldalearningcenter.com
                    e-mail: info@ldalearningcenter.com
*Kitty Christiansen, Executive Director*
*Victoria Weinberg, Program Director*

Maximizes the potential of children, youths, adults and families, especially those with learning disabilities and other learning difficulties so that they can lead more productive and fulfilled lives. Provides consultations, tutoring, assessments, parent workshops, training and outreach on sliding fee scale.

## Mississippi

**5674 Heritage School**

550 Sunnybrook Road
Ridgeland, MS 39157     601-853-7163
                        FAX 601-853-7163
*Jeanie Muirhead, Contact*

**5675 Millcreek Schools**

PO Box 1160
Magee, MS 39111     601-849-4221
                    800-372-1994
                    FAX 601-849-6107
                    http://www.yfcs.com
                    e-mail: info.mc-ms@yfcs.com
*Margaret Tedford, Chief Operations Officer*
*Anne Russum, President*

A residential treatment center for children with emotional disturbances and an intensive care facility for children with mental retardation.

## Missouri

**5676 Churchill School**

1035 Price School Lane
Saint Louis, MO 63124     514-997-4343
                          FAX 314-997-2760
                    http://www.churchillschool.org
                    e-mail: churchill@churchillschool.org
*Sandra Gilligan, Director*
*Deborah Warden, Assistant Director*
*Jenny Hyde Carney, Outreach Coordinator*

The Churchill School is a private, not-for-profit, coeducational day school. It is designed to serve children between the ages of 8-16 with diagnosed learning disabilities. The goal is to help each child reach his or her full potential and prepare for a successful return to a traditional classroom in as short a period of time as possible.

**5677  Gillis Center**
8150 Wornall Road
Kansas City, MO  64114          816-363-1414
                                FAX 816-363-4782
*Barbara O'Toole, Executive Director*

**5678  Metropolitan School**
7281 Sarah Street
Saint Louis, MO  63143          314-644-0850
                                FAX 314-644-3363
                        http://www.metroschool.org
                        e-mail: info@metroschool.org
*Rita Buckley, Executive Director*
*Cindy Keitel, Executive Assistant*
*Moriel Maston, Program Assistant*

The mission of Metropolitan School is to lead our community in providing effective, comprehensive educational services for adolescents who have atypical learning styles.

**5679  Miriam School**
501 Bacon Avenue
St. Louis, MO  63119-1512       314-962-6059
                                FAX 314-962-0482
                        http://www.miriamsfoundation.org
                        e-mail: info@miriamfoundation.org
*Joan Holland, Director*
*Michael Robinson, Executive Director*

A nonprofit day school for children between four and twelve years of age who are learning disabled and/or behaviorally disabled. Speech and language services and occupational therapy are integral components of the program. The focus of all the activities is to increase children's self-esteem and help them acquire the coping skills needed to successfully meet future challenges.

*4-12 years old*

**5680  Missouri Parents Act (MPACT)**
One W Armour Boulevard
Kansas, MO  64111               816-531-7070
                                800-743-7634
                                FAX 417-882-8413
                        http://www.ptimpact.com
                        e-mail: msavage@ptimpact.com
*Mary Savage, Executive Director*
*Diana Biere, Associate Director*
*Marcella Galapo, Parent Advisor*

MPACT assists parents to effectively advocate for their children's educational rights and services. MPACT is a statewide parent training and information center serving all disabilities. Our mission is to ensure that all children with special needs receive an education that allows them to achieve their personal goals.

## Montana

**5681  Parents Let's Unite for Kids**
516 N 32nd Street
Billings, MT  59101             406-255-0540
                                800-222-7585
                                FAX 406-255-0523
                        http://www.pluk.org
                        e-mail: plukinfo@pluk.org
*Dennis Moore, Director*
*Maegan Parks, Office Assistant*

PLUK is a private, nonprofit organization formed in 1984 by parents and children with disabilities and chronic illnesses in the state of Montana for the purpose of information, support, training and assistance to aid their children at home, school and as adults.

## Nebraska

**5682  Nebraska Parents Training and Information Center**
PTI (Parent Training & Information) Nebraska
3135 N 93rd Street
Omaha, NE  68134                402-346-0525
                                800-284-8520
                                FAX 402-934-1479
                                TDY:800-284-8520
                        http://www.pti-nebraska.org
                        e-mail: info@pti-nebraska.org
*Cathy Heinen, Office Manager*
*Glenda Davis, Executive Director*

Parent Training and Information Program views parents as full partners in the educational process and a significant source of support and assistance to each other. Funded by the Division of Personnel Preparation, Office of Special Education Programs, these programs provide training and information to parents to enable such individuals to participate more effectively with professionals in meeting the educational needs of disabled children.

## New Hampshire

**5683  Becket School**
PO Box 101
Haverhill, NH  03765            603-989-5100
                                FAX 603-989-5488
                        http://www.becket.org
                        e-mail: beck@becket.org
*Kerry Beck, Executive Director*
*Sharon Edwards, Special Ed Director*

Becket guides and inspires adolescents having difficulties at home, in school or in the community.

**5684    Cardigan Mt. School**

62 Alumni Drive
Canaan, NH  03741                          603-523-4321
                                       FAX 603-523-7227
                               http://www.cardigan.org
                          e-mail: rryerson@cardigan.org
*Tom Needham, Headmaster*
*Jamie Funnell, President*

**5685    Cedarcrest**

91 Maple Avenue
Keene, NH  03431                           603-358-3384
                                       FAX 603-358-6485
                           http://www.cedarcrest4kids.org
                          e-mail: info@cedarcrest4kids.org
*Catherine Gray, President/CEO*
*Peg Knox, Nursing Director*

A nonprofit home, school and medical support facility
for children with complex medical needs and multiple
disabilities. Cedarcrest serves up to 25 children, without regard to race, color, religious affiliation or financial standing. As a State Department of
Education-approved school, Cedarcrest also serves as
a placement option for any school district in the state.

**5686    Hampshire Country School**

122 Hampshire Road
Rindge, NH  03461                          603-899-3325
                                       FAX 603-899-6521
                       http://www.hampshirecountryschool.com
                       e-mail: hampshirecountry@monad.net
*William Dickerman, Headmaster/Admission Direc-
tor*

Hampshire Country School is a small boarding school
for 25 boys of high ability who need a personal environment with an unusual amount of adult attention and
structure. It is primarily a junior school, suited particularly to students from 9 to 15 years old; but some
younger students may be accepted and some students
may remain through high school.

**5687    Parent Information Center**

151-A Manchester Street
Concord, NH  03301                         603-224-7005
                                           800-947-7005
                                       FAX 603-224-4365
                                       TDY:603-224-7005
                       http://www.parentinformationcenter.org
                   e-mail: picinfo@parentinformationcenter.org
*Heather Thalheimer, Executive Director*
*Bonnie Dunham, Project Director*

Parent Training and Information Program views parents as full partners in the educational process and a
significant source of support and assistance to each
other. Funded by the Division of Personnel Preparation, Office of Special Education Programs, these programs provide training and information to parents to
enable such individuals to participate more effectively with professionals in meeting the educational
needs of children with disabilities.

## New Jersey

**5688    Bancroft Neurohealth**

Hopkins Lane
Haddonfield, NJ  08033-0018               856-429-0010
                                           800-774-5516
                                       FAX 856-429-1613
                       http://www.bancroftneurohealth.org
                          e-mail: adestefa@bnh.org
*Arleen DeStefano, Admissions Director*
*Paul Healy, Public Relations Director*

Nonprofit organization offering educational/voca-
tional programs, therapeutic support services and full
range of community living opportunities for children
and adults with brain injury in Maine, New Jersey,
Delaware, and Louisiana. Residential options include
community living supervised apartments, specialized
supervised apartments, group homes and supported
living models.

**5689    Center School**

319 N 3rd Avenue
Highland Park, NJ  08904                  732-249-3355
                                       FAX 732-249-1928
                           http://www.thecenterschool.com
*Jeanne Prial, Director*
*Joanne Jordan, Office Assistant*

The Center School is a school designed for bright students in grades 1-12 with learning and behavioral difficulties. The Center School offers counseling, speech
and language, and occupational therapy. Our school is
committed to helping each student become as self-suf-
ficient and successful as possible.

**5690    Children's Institute**

1 Sunset Avenue
Verona, NJ  07044                         973-509-3050
                                       FAX 973-740-0369
                               http://www.tcischool.org
                          e-mail: webmaster@tcischool.org
*Bruce Ettinger, Executive Director*
*Carole Spiro, Volunteer Coordinator*

The Children's Institute is a private, non-profit school
approved by the New Jersey State Board of Education,
serving children facing learning, language and social
challenges, ages 3-21.

**5691    Craig School**

Craig School
10 Tower Hill Road
Mountain Lake, NJ  07046                  973-334-1295
                                       FAX 973-334-1299
                               http://www.craigschool.org
                          e-mail: jday@craigschool.org
*Julie Day, Director of Advancement*
*David Blanchard, Headmaster*

The Craig School is an independent, nonprofit school serving children who have difficulty succeeding in the traditional classroom environment. We specialize in a language-based curriculum for children of average or above average intelligence with such disorders as dyslexia, auditory processing and attention deficit.

**5692  Devereux Center for Autism**

**198 Roadstown Road**
**Bridgeton, NJ  08302**       856-455-7200
                              FAX 856-455-2765
*James Gill Jr, Executive Director*

A residential and educational program for individuals with autism and/or developmental disabilities.

**5693  Devereux Deerhaven**

**901 Mantua Pike**
**Woodbury, NJ  08096**       856-384-9680
                             FAX 856-384-6742
                       http://www.devereux.org
*Kristy Hartman, Admissions Director*

Residential and day programs for females who have emotional and behavioral disorders and learning disabilities.

*5-21 years old*

**5694  ECLC of New Jersey**

**Ho-Ho-Kus Campus**
**302 N Franklin Turnpike**
**Ho Ho Kus, NJ  07423**      201-670-7880
                             FAX 201-670-6675
                        e-mail: eclc@nac.net
*Bruce Litinger, Executive Director*
*Vicki Lindorff, Principal*
*Dan Mullen, Assistant Director*

A private school for individuals with disabilities between the ages of 5-21. Our mission is to help disabled students discover how they fit into the world and guide them towards becoming independent and employed adults.

**5695  Eden Services**

**One Eden Way**
**Princeton, NJ  08540**      609-987-0099
                             FAX 609-987-0243
                     http://www.edenservices.org
                    e-mail: info@edenservices.org
*David Holmes, President/Executive*
*Joani Truch, Administrator of Communications*

Nonprofit organization founded in 1975 to provide a comprehensive continuum of lifespan services for individuals with autism and their families.

**5696  Family Resource Associates**

**35 Haddon Avenue**
**Shrewsbury, NJ  07702**     732-747-5310
                             FAX 732-747-1896
              http://www.familyresourceassociates.org
*Nancy Thalanukorn, Executive Director*

We are a New Jersey non-profit agency dedicated to helping individuals with disabilities and their families.

**5697  Forum School**

**107 Wyckoff Avenue**
**Waldwick, NJ  07463**       201-444-5882
                             FAX 201-444-4003
                     http://www.theforumschool.com
                    e-mail: info@theforumschool.com
*Steven Krapes, Director*
*Linda Oliver, Office Manager*

Special education day school for developmentally atypical children ages 3-16 years. The Forum School offers a therapeutic education environment for children who cannot be accommodated in a public school setting.

**5698  High Road Schools**

**10-G Auer Court**
**East Brunswick, NJ  08816**  732-390-0303
                              FAX 732-390-5577
                        http://www.kids1inc.com
                       e-mail: kids1@kids1inc.com
*Ellyn PhD, President*

Offers programs serving the educational, social and emotional needs of children with specific learning disabilities, communication disorders and/or behavioral difficulties.

**5699  Kingsway Learning Center**

**144 Kings Highway W**
**Haddonfield, NJ  08033**    856-428-8108
                             FAX 856-428-7520
                       http://www.kingswaylc.com
                    e-mail: dpanner@kingswaylc.com
*Donna Thorpe, Program Specialist*
*David Panner, Executive Director*

Kingsway is a private, non-profit special education school devoted to the academic and therapeutic needs of children with developmental and learning disabilities. We serve children from birth to 16 years of age with multiple handicaps.

**5700  Lewis Clinic and School**

**53 Bayard Lane**
**Princeton, NJ  08540**      609-924-8120
                             FAX 609-924-5512
                       http://www.lewisschool.org
*Marsha Gaynor-Lewis, Director*
*Kerry Roche, Administrative Assistant*

The Clinic and School integrate teaching and diagnostic perspective of multisensory educational practices in the classrooms, and the perspective of clinical research into the brain's learning process.

**5701  Matheny School and Hospital**

**Main Street**
**Peapack, NJ  07977**        908-234-0011
                             FAX 908-719-2137
                        http://www.matheny.org
                    e-mail: development@matheny.org
*Steven Proctor, President*

Matheny School and Hospital is a teaching hospital and a premier facility for people of all ages with developmental disabilities. Matheny specializes in the care of children and adults with cerebral palsy, muscular dystrophy, spina bifida and Lesch-Nyhan Disease.

**5702  Metropolitan Speech and Language Center**

Metropolitan Speech and Language Center
66 W Mount Present
Livingston, NJ  07039           973-994-4468
                               FAX 973-994-4412
                               e-mail: lillyok@aol.com
*Lilian Dollinger, Executive Director*

Provides diagnostics and therapy for children and adults with speech, language, voice and stuttering problems.

**5703  Midland School**

94 Readington Road
North Branch, NJ  08876        908-722-8222
                               FAX 908-722-6203
                               http://www.midlandschool.org
                               e-mail: info@midlandschool.org
*Edward Scagliotta, Founder*

The mission of Midland School is a comprehensive special education program serving the individual social, emotional, academic, and career education needs of children with developmental disabilities.

**5704  Newgrange School**

530 S Olden Avenue
Hamilton, NJ  08629            609-584-1800
                               FAX 609-584-6166
                               http://www.thenewgrange.org
                               e-mail: info@thenewgrange.org
*Gordon PhD, Executive Director*
*Cindy Ege, Administrative Officer*

Newgrange is a non-profit organization established in 1977 to provide specialized educational programs for people with learning disabilities.

**5705  SEARCH Day Program**

73 Wickapecko Drive
Ocean, NJ  07712               201-531-0454
                               FAX 732-531-5934
                               http://www.members.aol.com/SEARCHDay
                               e-mail: SEARCHDay@aol.com
*Katherine Solana, Executive Director*

SEARCH Day Program is a private, non-profit, New Jersey State certified school for individuals ages three through twenty-one with autism.

**5706  Statewide Parent Advocacy Network**

Central Office
35 Halsey Street
Newark, NJ  07102              973-642-8100
                               800-654-7726
                               FAX 973-642-8080
                               http://www.spannj.org
                               e-mail: span@spannj.org
*Diana Autin, Co-Executive Director*
*Debra Jennings, Co-Executive Director*

A nonprofit educational and advocacy center for parents of children from birth to 21 years of age. Assists families of infants, toddlers, children and youth with and without disabilities. Serves as a vehicle for the exchange of ideas, promoting awareness of the abilities and needs of the children and youth and improves services for children and families in the state of NJ.

---

# New Mexico

---

**5707  Brush Ranch School**

North Highway 63
Terrero, NM  87573             505-757-6114
                               FAX 505-757-6118
                               http://www.brushranchschool.org
                               e-mail: kaycrice@hotmail.com
*Kay Rice MA, School Head*
*Eve Bowen, Health Director*
*Suzanne Weisman, Admissions Director*

A co-educational boarding school for teens with learning differences. The school is fully licensed and accredited by both the New Mexico Board of Education and the North Central Association of Colleges and Schools. Situated on 283 acres in the Santa Fe National Forest, the school offers a wide range of educational and recreational opportunities.

**5708  Designs for Learning Differences School**

8600 Academy Road
Albuquerque, NM  87111         505-822-0476
                               FAX 505-858-4427
                               http://www.dldsycamoreschool.org
                               e-mail: lern@dldsycamoreschool.org
*Linda Murry, Director*
*Benita Kernodle, Administrative Assistant*

**5709  EPICS Parent Project**

Abrazos Family Support Services
412 Camino Don Tomas
Bernalillo, NM  87004          505-867-3396
                               FAX 505-867-3398
                               http://www.swcr.org
                               e-mail: info@swcr.org
*Martha Gorospe, Director*

EPICS - Education for Parents of Indian Children with Special Needs Project is a service for parents of American Indian children and young adults with disabilities and other special needs.

**5710  New Mexico Speech & Language Consultants**

1000 W 4th Street
Roswell, NM  88201             505-623-8319
                               FAX 505-623-8220
*Eileen Grooms, President*

Provides diagnostic and therapy services for communicatively impaired individuals.

**5711  Parents Reaching Out To Help (PRO)**
1920 B Columbia Drive SE
Albuquerque, NM  87106          505-247-0192
                               800-524-5176
                          FAX 505-247-1345
     http://www.parentsreachingout.org
*Sally VanCuren, Executive Director*
*Larry Fuller, Program Manager*

PRO views parents as full partners in the educational process and a significant source of support and assistance to each other. Programs provide training and information to parents to enable such individuals to participate more effectively with professionals in meeting the educational needs of disabled children.

## New York

**5712  Advocates for Children of New York**
151 W 30th Street
New York, NY  10001          212-947-9779
                        FAX 718-729-8931
     http://www.advocatesforchildren.org
     e-mail: info@advocatesforchildren.org
*Jill Chaifetz, Executive Director*
*Elisa Hyman, Deputy Director*

For over 25 years Advocates for Children of New York, Inc. has worked in partnership with New York City's most impoverished and vulnerable families to secure quality and equal public education services. AFC works on behalf of children from infancy to age 21 who have disabilites, ethnic minorities, immigrants, homeless children, foster care children, limited English proficient children and those living in poverty.

**5713  Anderson School**
4885 Route 9
Staatsburg, NY  12580          845-889-4034
                          FAX 845-889-3104
     http://www.andersonschool.org
     e-mail: info@andersonschool.org
*Neil Pollack, Executive Director*

Anderson School provides a vast array of educational, residential, clinical, and support services to children and adults with autism and other developmental disabilities.

**5714  Baker Hall School**
777 Ridge Road
Lackawanna, NY  14218          716-828-9737
                          FAX 716-828-9798
*Nancy Pancow, Executive Director*

Offers a certified special education program and a full range of classroom options; in-house, pre-vocational training and BOCES school placements are available to students depending on need.

**5715  Behavioral Arts**
58 W 88th Street
New York, NY  10024          212-799-9388
                             888-497-3722
                        FAX 212-799-4403
*Enid PhD, Executive Director*
*Nancy Morales, Office Manager*

Behavioral Arts is an outpatient psychotherapy clinic dedicated to helping individuals and families develop the mental and physical well-being that lends itself to healthy relationships and effective functioning. The Center's staff consists of warm, dedicated, professionals who specialize in such issues as Attention Deficit Disorder, anxiety, depression, co-dependency, substance abuse, chronic illness, learning disabilities and self-esteem.

**5716  Center for Discovery**
PO Box 840
Harris, NY  12742          845-794-1400
                        FAX 845-794-1474
     http://www.thecenterfordiscovery.org
     e-mail: admissions@thecenterfordiscovery.org
*Kerri Muzurik, Director for Education*
*Patrick Dollard, Chief Executive Officer*

Programs for children with multiple disabilities. Creative classes, beautiful residences, totally accessible country campus.

**5717  Child Center for Developmental Service**
251 Manetto Hill Road
Plainview, NY  11803          516-938-3788
*Iris Lesser, Director*

**5718  Community Based Services**
3 Fields Lane
North Salem, NY  10560          914-277-4771
                          FAX 914-277-8956
*Vick Sylvester PhD, Chief Executive Officer*
*Paulette Sladkus, Chief Operations Officer*

Six intermediate care facilities for people with autism and developmental disabilities, and one individual residential alternative.

**5719  Diagnostic Learning Center**
505 Ridge Road
Queensbury, NY  12804          518-793-0668
                               800-338-3781
                          FAX 518-793-0668
     http://www.learningproblems.com
     e-mail: janb@capital.net
*Jan Bishop, Director*

Offers diagnosis and remediation of learning problems, cognitive remediation for the head injured. In-services for teachers and parent groups. Tutorials only; no day or stay programs.

**5720  EAC Developmental Program**

382 Main Street
Port Washington, NY  11050        516-883-3006
                                  FAX 516-883-0412

*Gerald Stone, Program Director*
*Patricia Dely, Secretary*

**5721  Eden II School for Autistic Children**

Eden II School for Autistic Children
150 Granite Avenue
Staten Island, NY  10303          718-816-1422
                                  FAX 718-816-1428
                                  http://www.eden2.org
                          e-mail: jgerenser@eden2.org

*Joanne Gerenser, Executive Director*

Offers programs for children with autism and an adult day training program.

**5722  Environmental Science and Forestry**

State University of New York College
110 Bray Hall
Syracuse, NY  13210               315-470-6660
                                  FAX 315-470-4728
                                  http://www.esf.edu
                          e-mail: toslocum@esf.edu

*Thomas Slocum, Special Services*

**5723  Gow School**

Gow School
Emery Road
South Wales, NY  14139            716-652-3450
                                  FAX 716-687-2003
                                  http://www.gow.org
                          e-mail: admissions@gow.org

*M Rogers Jr, Headmaster*
*Robert Garcia, Admissions Director*

The nation's oldest college preparatory school for young men (grades 7-12) with dyslexia/language based learning differences. The 100 acre residential campus is located in upstate New York. Co-Ed summer program for ages 8-16.

**5724  Hallen School**

97 Centre Avenue
New Rochelle, NY  10801           914-636-6600
                                  FAX 914-636-2844
                                  http://www.hallenschool.com

*Carol LoCascio, Executive Director*
*Michelle Bonelli, Office Assistant*

A special education school offering a sound academic program in a therapeutic setting.

**5725  International Center for the Disabled**

340 E 24th Street
New York, NY  10010               212-585-6083
                                  FAX 212-585-6161
                                  http://www.icdrehab.org
                          e-mail: ssegal@icdrehab.org

*Sondra Segal, Director Development*
*Arnold Shapiro, Director Center for Speech/Lang.*

ICD is the nation's oldest outpatient rehabilitation center offering comprehensive medical, vocational, and mental health services. The Center for Speech/Language, Learning and Hearing includes a learning disabilities section providing diagnostic and individualized remedial services for both children and adults who are experiencing difficulty with reading, writing, spelling and/or math.

**5726  Julia Dyckman Andrus Memorial**

1156 N Broadway
Yonkers, NY  10701                914-965-3700
                                  FAX 914-965-3883
                                  http://www.andruschildren.org
                          e-mail: nment@jdam.org

*Nancy Ment, Executive Director*

Residential treatment for youngsters who have moderate to severe emotional problems.

**5727  Just Kids: Early Childhood Learning Center**

Just Kids: Early Childhood Learning Center
PO Box 12
Middle Island, NY  11953          631-924-0008
                                  FAX 631-924-4602
                          e-mail: jkschool@aol.com

*Steven Held, Executive Director*

A family focused early intervention program for young children with disabilities.

**5728  Karafin School**

40 Radio Circle Drive
Mount Kisco, NY  10549            914-666-9211
                                  FAX 914-666-9868
                                  http://www.Bestwes.net/~karafin

*John Greenfeldt MD, Executive Director*
*Bart , Associate Director*

**5729  Kildonan School**

425 Morse Hill Road
Amenia, NY  12501                 845-373-8111
                                  FAX 845-373-9793
                                  http://www.kildonan.org
                          e-mail: admissions@kildonan.org

*Ronald Wilson, Headmaster*
*Robert Lane, Academic Dean*

Offers a fully accredited College Preparatory curriculum. The school is co-educational, enrolling boarding students in Grades 6-Postgraduate and day students in Grade 2-Postgraduate. Provides daily one-on-one Orton-Gillingham tutoring to build skills in reading, writing, and spelling. Daily independent reading and writing work reinforces skills and improves study habits. Interscholastic sports, horseback riding, clubs and community service enhance self-confidence.

**5730  Learning Diagnostic Center**
**Schneider Children's Hospital**
**26901 76th Avenue**
**New Hyde Park, NY  11040**           **718-470-3140**
                                        **FAX 718-343-3578**
*Sheldon Horowitz EdD, Associate Director*

Committed to helping each child maximize his/her potential for academic, social and emotional development. The Center's staff uses a broad range of standardized and informal diagnostic tools as part of the evaluation process and provides comprehensive written reports including recommendations to improve functioning both in school and at home.

**5731  Manhattan Center for Learning**
**590 W End Avenue**
**New York, NY  10024**                **212-787-5712**
                                        **FAX 212-787-5323**
*Judith PhD, Director*

Services for the learning disabled include tutoring, remediation, cognitive therapy, psycho-educational testing, parent counseling and neuropsychological testing provided by a very qualified staff including a licensed psychologist certified as a learning disabilities specialist.

**5732  Maplebrook School**
**Maplebrook School**
**5142 Route 22**
**Amenia, NY  12501**                  **845-373-8191**
                                        **FAX 845-373-7029**
                    **http://www.maplebrookschool.org**
                    **e-mail: mbsecho@aol.com**
*Roger Fazzone, CEO*
*Jennifer Scully, Dean of Admissions*
*Donna M Konkolics, Head of School*

A traditional boarding school enrolling students with learning differences and ADD. Offers strong academics and character development. The Responsibility Increases Self Esteem (RISE) Program provides the structure and support to awaken the learner in each student, promote responsibility and develop character, foster independence and growth and enhance social development.

**5733  Maplebrook School Learning Centerry Studies (CAP)**
**Division of Maplebrook School**
**5142 Route 22**
**Amenia, NY  12501**                  **845-373-8191**
                                        **FAX 845-373-7029**
                    **http://www.maplebrookschool.org**
                    **e-mail: mbsecho@aol.com**
*Jennifer Scully, Dean of Admissions*
*Jenny Hill, Assistant Director Of Admissions*

CAPS offers a vocational program with employment skills and training, as well as a collegiate program with courses taken at the local community college and other support services.

**5734  Mary McDowell Center for Learning**
**20 Bergen Street**
**Brooklyn, NY  11201**                **718-625-3939**
                                        **FAX 718-625-1456**
                    **http://www.marymcdowell.org**
                    **e-mail: debbiez@marymcdowell.org**
*Debbie Zlotowitz, School Head*
*Stephanie Lazzara, School Administrator*

An elementary school for children with learning disabilities ages 5-12.

**5735  New Interdisciplinary School**
**430 Sills Road**
**Yaphank, NY  11980**                 **631-924-5583**
                                        **FAX 631-924-5687**
                    **e-mail: nis1977@aol.com**
*Helen Wilder, Director*
*Betsy Kapian, Assistant Director*

As the name suggests, the school offers the integration of services into the classroom and at home from a variety of disiplines: special education; speech and language development; gross and fine motor; sensory integration; psychological; social work audiology; and nursing for children form birth to five.

**5736  New York Institute for Special Education**
**New York Institute for Special Education**
**999 Pelham Parkway**
**Bronx, NY  10469**                   **718-519-7000**
                                        **FAX 718-231-9314**
                    **http://www.nyise.org/**
*Kim Benisatto, Operations Manager*

**5737  Niagra Frontier Center for Independent Living**
**National Independent Living Council**
**1522 Main Street**
**Niagra Falls, NY  14305**            **716-284-2452**
                                        **866-306-6245**
                                        **FAX 716-284-0829**
                                        **TDY:866-306-6245**
                    **http://www.md-nfeil.org**
                    **e-mail: info@nfeil.org**
*Michael DeVinney, Director Programs/Services*
*Amanda Banes, Office Manager*

**5738  Norman Howard School**
**Norman Howard School**
**275 Pinnacle Road**
**Rochester, NY  14623**               **585-334-8010**
                                        **FAX 585-334-8073**
                    **http://www.normanhoward.org**
                    **e-mail: info@normanhoward.org**
*Marcie Roberts, Executive Director*
*Julie Murray, Associate Director of Admissions*

**5739    Parent Network Center**

1000 Main Street
Buffalo, NY  14202                    716-332-4170
                                      866-277-4PNC
                                  FAX 716-332-4171
                        http://www.parentnetworkwny.org
*Joan Watkins, Executive Director*
*Maria Kerber, Director Training*

Views parents as full partners in the educational process and a significant source of support and assistance
to each other. These programs provide training and information to parents to enable such individuals to participate more effectively with professionals in
meeting the educational needs of disabled children,
and ongoing needs as they age out of mandated services and require independent help to live inclusive
lives and experience full citizenship.

**5740    Program for Learning Disabled College Students:
Adelphi University**

Eddy Hall-Lower Level
Garden City, NY  11530              516-877-4850
                                    800-ADELPHI
                                 FAX 516-877-4711
                                 TDY:516-877-4777
                             http://www.adelphi.edu
*Robert Scott, President*

**5741    Robert Louis Stevenson School**

24 W 74th Street
New York, NY  10023                 212-787-6400
                                 FAX 212-873-1872
          e-mail: stevensonschool@stevensonschool.org
*Bud Henrichsen, Headmaster*
*Rick Couchman, Dean*

                *12-18 years old*

**5742    Stephen Gaynor School**

22 W 74th Street
New York, NY  10023                 212-787-7070
                                 FAX 212-787-3312
                             http://www.sgaynor.com
*Lilli Friedman, Director Admissions*
*Scott Gaynor, Director Operations*
*Yvette Siegel, Director Education*

Our guiding principle is to provide a nurturing environment in which students with learning differences
can acquire the skills they need to achieve success in
their educational pursuits.

**5743    Vocational Independence Program (VIP)**

New York Institute of Technology
Central Campus
Central Islip, NY  11722            631-348-3354
                                 FAX 631-348-0437
                           http://www.vip-at-nyit.org
*David Finkelstein, Director*
*Jim Rein, Dean*

VIP is a three year certificate program for students
with moderate to severe learning disabilities. Emphasizes independent living, social and vocational skills,
as well as individual academic support, with a college
support program called Track II for students who can
take college credit courses or pursue a degree.

**5744    Windward School**

Windward Avenue
White Plains, NY  10605             914-949-6968
                                 FAX 914-949-8220
*Maureen Sweeney, Admissions Director*
*James , Head Master*

---

# North Carolina

---

**5745    Comprehensive Educational Services (CES)**

Manus Academy
6401 Carmel Road
Charlotte, NC  28226                704-542-6471
                                 FAX 704-541-2858
*Rosanne MA, President*
*Stan Covelski, Center Director*

School for students with learning disabilties.

**5746    Eastern Associates Speech and Language Services**

2501B Wayne Memorial Drive
Goldsboro, NC  27534                919-731-2234
                                 FAX 919-731-2306
*Rhonda Sutton-Merritt, Director*

A private practice clinic providing diagnosis and
treatment of speech and language disorders/differ-
ences. All speech pathologists hold a master's degree,
are licensed by the NC Board of Examiners for Speech
Pathologists and Audiologists and hold a Certificate
of Clinical Competence issued by the American
Speech-Language and Hearing Association.

**5747    Exceptional Children's Assistance Center**

Exceptional Children's Assistance Center
907 Barra Row
Davidson, NC  28036                 704-892-1321
                                    800-962-6817
                                 FAX 704-892-5028
                      http://www.ecac-parentcenter.org
               e-mail: information@ecac-parentcenter.org
*Connie Hawkins, Chairman*
*Mary Lacorte, Manager*

Parent Training and Information Program views parents as full partners in the educational process and a
significant source of support and assistance to each
other. Funded by the Division of Personnel Preparation, Office of Special Education Programs, these programs provide training and information to parents to
enable such individuals to participate more effectively with professionals in meeting the educational
needs of disabled children.

**5748    Hill Center**

3200 Pickett Road
Durham, NC  27705                   919-489-7464
                                 FAX 919-489-7466
                             http://www.hillcenter.org
                     e-mail: smaskel@hillcenter.org
*Sharon Maskel, Director*
*Wendy Speir, Director Admissions*
*Jean Neville, Dir. Professional Development*

Offers a unique half-day program to students in grades K-12 with diagnosed learning disabilities and attention deficit disorders. Also offers a comprehensive teacher program.

**5749  Joy A Shabazz Center for Independent Living**

235 N Green Street
Greenboro, NC  27406          336-272-0501
                              FAX 336-272-0575
                              TDY:336-272-0501
        http://www.advocacyproject.org
        e-mail: marlene@advocacyproject.org
*Aaron Shabazz, Executive Director*
*Benita Williams, Deputy Director*
*Marlene Mesot, Information Resources*

A nonprofit, consumer oriented, independent living center providing advocacy, peer counseling, independent living training, information and referral, with other related services for persons with disabilities. We currently serve five counties.

**5750  Piedmont School**

815 Old Mill Road
High Point, NC  27265          336-883-0992
                               FAX 336-883-4752
        http://www.thepiedmontschool.com
        e-mail: info@piedmontschool.com
*Pam Garner, Administrative Assistant*
*Dorie Sturgill, Director*

Nonprofit private school for 1st-8th grade students diagnosed with a specific learning disability and/or an attention deficit disorder.

**5751  Raleigh Learning and Language Clinic**

7101 Creedmoor Road
Raleigh, NC  27609          919-676-5477
        http://www.huntinglearning.com
*Stan Kant, Contact*

# North Dakota

**5752  Anne Carlsen Center for Children**

Anne Carlsen Center for Children
701 3rd Street NW
Jamestown, ND  58401          701-252-3850
                              800-568-5175
                              FAX 701-952-5154
        http://www.annecenter.org
*Dan Howell, Chief Executive Officer*

Offers education, therapy, medical care and social and psychological services for children and young adults with special needs.

# Ohio

**5753  Akron Reading and Speech Center**

700 Ghent Road
Akron, OH  44333          330-666-1161
                          FAX 330-665-1862
*Ardath PhD, Director*
*Lora Spencer, Secretary*

Remedial, developmental and enrichment reading and speech therapy services.

**5754  Bellefaire JCB**

22001 Fairmount Boulevard
Shaker Heights, OH  44118          216-932-2800
                                   800-879-2522
                                   FAX 216-932-6704
        http://www.bellefairjcb.org
*Jill Yulish, Intake Coordinator*
*Debra Mundell, Associate Director*

Residential treatment center for adolescents, offering foster care, an adoption center, Monarch School for Children with Autism.

**5755  Child Advocacy Center**

131 N High Street
Columbus, OH  43215          614-221-7994
                             FAX 614-221-8442
        http://www.oncac.org
        e-mail: cadcenter@aol.com
*Ben Murray, Executive Director*

A training and information center for parents of children with special needs. It is funded by various federal, state, and local grants and is managed by parents of disabled children. Its goals are to assure that disabled children receive quality educational services in natural, age-appropriate settings and to help parents and other community members understand their rights and responsibilities under federal and state educational law.

**5756  Cincinnati Center for Developmental Disorders**

3333 Burnet Avenue
Cincinnati, OH  45229          513-636-4688
                               800-344-2462
                               FAX 513-636-7361
                               TDY:513-636-4623
        http://www.cincinnatichildrens.org
        e-mail: johnb0@chmcc.org
*Sonya MD, Director*
*Judy Neubacher, Accountant*

**5757  Cincinnati Occupational Therapy Institute for Services and Study**

4440 Carver Woods Drive
Cincinnati, OH  45242          513-791-5688
                               FAX 513-791-0023
        http://www.cintiotinstitute.com
        e-mail: coti@cintiotinstitute.com
*Joan Dostal, Pediatric Coordinator*
*Elaine Mullin, Executive Director*

Pediatric occupational therapy services specializing in sensory integration.

**5758 Ohio Coalition for the Education of Children with Learning Disabilities**

165 West Center Street
Marion, OH 43302      740-382-5452
     800-374-2806
     FAX 740-382-6421
     http://www.ocecd.org

Funded by the Division of Personnel Preparation, Office of Special Education Programs, these programs provide training and information to parents to enable such individuals to participate more effectively with professionals in meeting the educational needs of disabled children.

**5759 Olympus Center: Unlocking Learning Potential**

2230 Park Avenue
Cincinnati, OH 45206      513-559-0404
     FAX 513-559-0008
     http://www.olympuscenter.org
     e-mail: olympus@fuse.net
*Sandy Martin, Director*
*Pat Wideamn, Secretary*

A nonprofit agency provides evaluations and consultations for children and adults by learning issues.

**5760 RICHARDS READ Systematic Language**

North Coast Tutoring Services
120 N Main Street
Chagrin Falls, OH 44022      440-247-1622
     FAX 440-247-9049
     http://www.northcoastad.com
     e-mail: info@northcoastad.com
*Carole Richards, President*
*John Kusik, Vice President*

North Coast Tutoring Services strives to provide on-site education services to individual learners or groups. Uppermost in the delivery of these services is the development of self-esteem, expanding learner potential and utilizing problem-solving to identify strengths and weaknesses. We specialize in working with at-risk learners which include learning disabled students. Our systematic language program is extremely successful with language learning difficulties from age 5 to adult.

**5761 Springer School and Center**

2121 Madison Road
Cincinnati, OH 45208      513-871-6080
     FAX 513-871-6218
     http://www.springerschoolandcenter.org
     e-mail: info@springer.hccanet.org
*Jan Annette, Admissions Director*
*Susan Blanger, School Secretary*

Empowering students with learning disabilities to lead successful lives (Grades 1-8). Center serves teachers, parents and students.

## Oklahoma

**5762 Pro-Oklahoma**

UCP of Oklahoma
5208 West Reno
Oklahoma City, OK 73127      405-917-7080
     FAX 405-917-7082
     http://www.ucpok.org
     e-mail: PROOK1@aol.com
*Sharon Bishop, Director*
*Marilynn Alexander, Coordinator*

Views parents as full partners in the educational process and a significant source of support and assistance to each other. Funded by the Division of Personnel Preparation, Office of Special Education Programs, these programs provide training and information to parents to enable such individuals to participate more effectively with professionals in meeting the educational needs of disabled children.

**5763 Town and Country School**

5150 E. 101st Street
Tulsa, OK 74137      918-296-3113
*Frances Day MA, Executive Director*

A private school for learning disabled students, with or without attention deficit disorder. Class size limited to 12 persons, a certified teacher and an aide.

## Oregon

**5764 Chemetka Community College**

Services for Students with Disabilities
4000 Lancaster Drive NE
Salem, OR 97309      503-399-5142
     FAX 503-399-2519
     TDY:503-399-5192
*Michael Duggan, Disabilities Specialist*

Chemetka Community College provides a wide variety of services for students including individualized tutoring, testing accommodations, books on tape, and adaptive technology to name a few.

**5765 Cornell Vision Center**

1010 NE Cornell Road
Hillsboro, OR 97124      503-640-3333
     FAX 503-681-9459
     e-mail: dianaeye@aol.com
*Diana Ludlam, Vision Therapist*
*Debbie Mish, Office Manager*

Learning realted vision problems, visual aspects of cerebral palsy, head trauma, syndromes involving visual function.

**5766 Learning Unlimited Network of Oregon**

31960 SE Chin Street
Boring, OR 97009      503-663-5153
     e-mail: luno@cse.com
*Gene Lehman, Contact*

Offers programs for home, group, business or institution, serving any number of students. These materials and programs can quickly change the habits, attitudes and performances of students mastering basic language skills, from elementary to adult levels.

**5767 Thomas A Edison Program**

**Thomas A Edison High School**
**9020 SW Beaverton Hillsdale Highway**
**Portland, OR 97225**          503-297-2336
                    FAX 503-297-2527
            http://www.taedisonhs.org
        e-mail: thomasedison@taedisonhs.org
*Patrick Maguire, Director*
*Fram Dalby, Office Manager*

The goal of this program is to help learning disabled students transfer into a larger high school setting after 1 to 2 years. Counselors play a strong role in helping students make that transition. The program offers parent involvement programs, transition programs, counseling, and affordable tuition.

**5768 Tree of Learning High School**

**9000 SW Beaverton Hillsdale Highway**
**Portland, OR 97225**          503-297-2336
                    FAX 503-297-2527
            http://www.taedisonhs.org
        e-mail: thomasedison@taedisonhs.org
*Fram Dalby, Office Manager*

# Pennsylvania

**5769 Center for Alternative Learning**

**PO Box 716**
**Bryn Mawr, PA 19010**          610-525-8336
                    800-869-8336
                FAX 610-525-8337
            http://www.ldonline.org
*Richard Cooper MD, Contact*

A nonprofit organization designed to provide direct services to learning disabled adults and teacher training to adult learning disabled practitioners.

**5770 Center for Psychological Services**

**125 Coulter Avenue**
**Ardmore, PA 19003**          610-642-4873
                FAX 610-642-4886
            http://www.centerpsych.com
        e-mail: ctrpsychsv@aol.com
*Moss Jackson MD, Director*
*Bruce , Director*
*Channa Oxelrod, Director*

Individual, family and group therapy psychoeducational evaluation and school consultation.

**5771 Cornell Abraxas I**

**PO Box 59**
**Marienville, PA 16239**          814-927-6615
                    800-227-2927
                FAX 814-927-8560
*Jamesl Nawsome, Facility Director*

**5772 Devereux Brandywine**

**PO Box 69**
**Glenmoore, PA 19343**          610-942-5900
                    866-532-2209
                FAX 610-942-9572
            http://www.devereux.org
*Gary Bilski, Director of Operations*
*Sue Schofield, Administrative Support*

Residential treatment for emotionally disturbed males consisting of five distinct programs based upon age and diagnostic criteria. Includes program for the deaf. Services provided include: psychiatric; therapeutic; milieu with integrated behavior management system; intermediate; high school with 12-month educational program and more. Offers a 350 acre campus, including stocked lake, swimming pool, playing fields and more.

**5773 Devereux Foundation**

**444 Devereux Drive**
**Villanova, PA 19085**          610-542-3090
                    800-935-6789
                FAX 610-25124150
Offers residential and community-based treatment centers nationwide. Provides comprehensive services to individuals of all ages.

**5774 Devereux Mapleton**

**Devereux Foundation**
**655 Sugartown Road**
**Malvern, PA 19355**          610-296-6973
                    800-935-6789
                FAX 610-296-5866
            http://www.devereux.org
*Walter Grono, Executive Director*
*Howard Jarden, Assistant Executive Director*

Residential and in-patient program for children, adolescents and young adults with emotional disorders and learning disabilities.

*13-21 years old*

**5775 Dr. Gertrude A Barber Center**

**Dr.Gertrude A Barber Center**
**136 E Avenue**
**Erie, PA 16507**          814-453-7661
                FAX 814-455-1132
        http://www.barbernationalinstitute.org
*John Barber, President/CEO*
*Bob Will, Senior Vice President*

An individualized educational program designed for preschool and school-aged students.

**5776 Hill Top Preparatory School**

**737 S Ithan Avenue**
**Rosemont, PA 19010**          610-527-3230
                FAX 610-527-7683
            http://www.hilltopprep.org
        e-mail: headmaster@hilltopprep.org
*Les McLean MD, Head Master*
*Anne Scali, Associate Admissions Director*

A fully-accredited, state-licensed, private, secondary, diploma-granting school for the learning disabled adolescent combining academic and clinical components to provide a preparatory program.

**5777 Hillside School**

2697 Brookside Road
Macungie, PA 18062          610-967-5449
                           FAX 610-965-7683
          http://www.hillsideschool.org
          e-mail: office@hillsideschool.org
*Linda Whitney, Director*

A day school for children with learning disabilities. One hundred and twenty-eight children in grades K-6 attend the school. Scholarships are available.

*5-13 years old*

**5778 KidsPeace**

5300 Kidspeace Drive
Orefield, PA 18069
                           800-8KID-123
          http://www.kidspeace.org
          e-mail: admissions@kidspeace.org
*John Peter, President*

Offers various programs including community residential care, specialized group homes, child and family guidance center and student assistance programs.

**5779 Melmark**

2600 Wayland Road
Berwyn, PA 19312           610-325-4969
                           888-635-6275
                           FAX 610-353-4956
          http://www.melmark.org
          e-mail: pjm@melmark.org
*Peter McGuiness, Director Admissions*
*Joanne , President*

Provides residential, educational, therapeutic and recreational services for children and adults with mild to severe developmental disabilities.

**5780 New Castle School of Trades**

RR 1
Pulaski, PA 16143          724-964-8811
                           FAX 724-964-8177
*Rex Spaulding, Director*

**5781 Parent Education Network**

Parent Education Network
2107 Industrial Highway
York, PA 17402             717-600-0100
                           800-522-5827
                           FAX 717-600-8101
                           TDY:800-522-5827
          http://www.parentednet.org
          e-mail: pen@parentednet.org
*Louise Phieme, Director*

Parent training and information center of Pennsylvania. Serves parents of all special needs children, birth to adulthood, to attain appropriate educational and support services by providing specific knowledge of state and federal laws and regulations; develops and disseminates material explaining the special education process and its relationship to other systems.

**5782 Parents Union for Public Schools**

228 W Chelten Avenue
Philadelphia, PA 11944     215-991-9724
                           FAX 215-991-9943
          e-mail: ParentsU@aol.com

Parent Training and Information Program views parents as full partners in the educational process and a significant source of support and assistance to each other. Funded by the Division of Personnel Preparation, Office of Special Education Programs, these programs provide training and information to parents to enable such individuals to participate more effectively with professionals in meeting the educational needs of disabled children.

**5783 Pathway School**

162 Egypt Road
Norristown, PA 19403       610-277-0660
                           FAX 610-539-1493
          http://www.pathwayschool.org
          e-mail: louiser@pathwayschool.org
*Louise Robertson, Admissions Director*
*William Rennekemt, Education Director*
*William O'Flanagan PhD, Executive Director*

Provides day and residential programming for individuals ages 5-21, who have learning disabilities, neurological impairments and neuropsychiatric disorder. Special education, counseling, speech and language therapy, reading therapy, and other specialized services are provided in a small, warm and supportive atmosphere.

**5784 Rehabilitation Institute of Pittsburgh**

1405 Shady Avenue
Pittsburgh, PA 15217       412-521-9000
                           FAX 412-521-0570

Offers quality services to young people with moderate to severe disabilities with different levels of physical, cognitive and emotional functioning.

**5785 Rosemont College**

1400 Montgomery Avenue
Rosemont, PA 19010         610-527-0200
                           FAX 610-527-0341
          http://www.rosemont.edu
*Linda Simone, Admissions Director*

Offers a variety of services to students with disabilities including notetakers, extended testing time, counseling services, and special accommodations.

**5786 Stratford Friends School**

5 Llandillo Road
Havertown, PA 19083        610-446-3144
                           FAX 610-446-6381
          http://www.stratfordfriends.org
*Sandra Howzwe, Director*
*Nancy D'Angelo, Admissions*

A Quaker elementary school for children with learning differences with average to above average intelligence.

**5787 Thaddeus Stevens College of Technology**

Special Needs Department
750 E King Street
Lancaster, PA 17602
717-299-7408
800-THAD-TEC
FAX 717-391-6929
http://www.stevenscollege.edu
e-mail: schuch@stevenscollege.edu
*Deb Schuch, Special Needs Coordinator*

Two year trade and technical college, with dormitories, state of the art field house, and intercollegiate sports such as football, basketball, wrestling, track and field, volleyball, and archery. Full time AST Degree Programs in Collision Repair, Automotive, Architecture, Mechanical Engineering and etc.

**5788 Vanguard School**

1777 N Valley Road
Paoli, PA 19301
610-296-6700
FAX 610-640-0132
http://www.vanguardschool-pa.org
*Bratt Strom, Head of School*
*Tim Lanshe, Director Education*
*Donna Annechino-Jiore, Director Admissions*

State licensed and approved private, non-profit, non-sectarian day school serving children from three to twenty-one years of age who have been diagnosed with neurological disorders, emotional disturbance or autism/PDD.

**5789 Woods Schools**

Residential Center
PO Box 36
Langhorne, PA 19047
215-750-4000
FAX 215-750-4229
http://www.woods.org
*Robert Griffith, President*
*Mary Knudson, Administrative Assistant*

Provides a full range of residential, special education, rehabilitation, recreation and vocational training.

## Rhode Island

**5790 Harmony Hill School**

63 Harmony Hill Road
Chepachet, RI 02814
401-949-0690
FAX 401-949-2060
TDY:401-949-4130
http://www.harmonyhillschool.org
e-mail: gmiranda@hhs.org
*Terrence Leary, President/CEO*

A private residential and day treatment center for behaviorally disordered and learning disabled boys, age eight through eighteen, who cannot be treated within their local educational system or community based mental health programs. Individual, group and family psychotherapy and 24-hour crisis intervention are available. Other programs include: Extended Day, Sex Offender, Diagnostic Day, Transition Programming, Summer Day, Career Education Center, and a Formalized Life Skills Program.

**5791 Rhode Island Parent Information Network**

175 Main Street
Pawtucket, RI 02860
401-727-4144
800-464-3399
FAX 401-727-4040
TDY:800-464-3399
http://www.ripin.org
e-mail: ripin@ripin.org
*Vivian Wiseman, Executive Director*
*Matthew Cox, Associate Director*

Parent Training and Information Program views parents as full partners in the educational process and a significant source of support and assistance to each other. Funded by the US Department of Education under the Individuals with Disabilities Education Act, these programs provide training and information to parents to enable such individuals to participate more effectively with professionals in meeting the educational needs of disabled children.

## South Carolina

**5792 Gateway School**

353 Lawrence Street NW
Aiken, SC 29801
803-642-5067
*Nancy Elliot, Executive Director*

School geared for grades K-8 for children with learning disabilities.

**5793 Parents Reaching Out to Parents of South Carolina**

652 Bush River Road
Columbia, SC 29210
803-772-5688
800-759-4776
FAX 803-772-5341
http://www.proparents.org
e-mail: PROParents@proparents.org
*Mary Eaddy, Executive Director*

Private nonprofit parent oriented organization providing information, individual assistance and workshops to parents of children with disabilities ages birth-21. Services focus on enabling parents to have a better understanding of special education to participate more effectively with professionals in meeting the educational needs of disabled children. Funded by a grant from the US Department of Education and tax deductible contributions.

**5794 Pine Grove**
1500 Chestnut Road
Elgin, SC 29045 803-438-3011
FAX 803-438-8611
e-mail: carlmets@aol.com
*Carl Herring, Executive Director*
*Melanie Stevens, Office Assistant*

Offers an intensive academic, social skills and behavior modification program designed to return the child to his/her home area as soon as possible.

**5795 Sandhills Academy**
1500 Hallbrook Dr
Columbia, SC 29209 803-695-1400
http://http://sandhillsacademy.com
*Joan Hathaway, Director*

A private, nonprofit school for children with learning disabilities. Serves students from grades 1-8 and also offers diagnostic evaluations, summer school and educational therapy for all ages. Boarding with local families is also available.

**5796 Trident Academy**
1455 Wakendaw Road
Mt. Pleasant, SC 29464 843-884-7046
FAX 843-881-8320
http://www.tridentacademy.com
e-mail: admissions@tridentacademy.com
*Myron Harrington Jr, Headmaster*
*Betsy Fanning, Admissions Director*

Private school for children with learning disabilities grades K through 12th, day students accepted with limited boarding. Offers an intensive, effective, multisensory program to remediate learning differences, tailored to each students unique needs.

## Tennessee

**5797 Bodine School**
2432 Yester Oaks Drive
Germantown, TN 38139 901-754-1800
FAX 901-751-8595
http://bodineschool.org
e-mail: info@bodineschool.org
*Rene Lee, Executive Director*

**5798 Camelot Care Center**
183 Fiddlers Lane
Kingston, TN 37763 865-376-2296
FAX 865-376-1950
*James Spicer, Executive Director*

A psychiatric residential treatment center serving children with emotional disturbances and learning disabilities.

**5799 Devereux Genesis Learning Centers**
Genesis Learning Centers
430 Allied Drive
Nashville, TN 37211 615-832-4222
FAX 615-832-4577
http://www.genesislearn.org
*Terry Adams, President*
*Melissa Adams, Vice President*

Day school and treatment programs for adolescents and young adults who have emotional disorders and learning disabilities.

## Texas

**5800 Bridges Academy**
901 Arizona Avenue
El Paso, TX 79902 915-532-6647
FAX 915-532-8767
*Irma Keys, Director*

Private School for students with learning disabilities.

**5801 Bright Students Who Learn Differently**
Winston School
5707 Royal Lane
Dallas, TX 75229 214-691-6950
FAX 214-691-1509
http://www.winston-school.org
e-mail: amy_smith@winston-school.org
*Pamela Murfin PhD, Head of School*
*Amy Smith, Admission Director*

The Winston School is a co-educational day college preparatory school, grades 1-12. Winston provides individualized programs for students with learning differences, including problems in reading, writing, language and mathematics, as well as attention-deficit/hyperactivity disorder. Student teacher ratio of 8:1. Founded in 1975 in a suburban 6-acre campus, 4 buildings on campus. Winston is accredited by the Independent Schools Association of the Southwest (ISAS) and a member of NAIS.

**5802 Crisman Preparatory School**
2455 N Eastman Road
Longview, TX 75605 903-758-9741
FAX 903-758-9767
*Lucy Peacock, Director*

**5803 Diagnostic and Remedial Reading Clinic**
622 Isom Road
San Antonio, TX 78216 210-341-7417
FAX 210-341-7417
*Margo PhD*

This clinic provides: complete psychological and educational evaluations; diagnostic and remedial services for academic problems; one-on-one instruction in all academic subjects; and consultation and evaluation services to public and private schools.

**5804 Gateway School**

Gateway School
2570 N W Green Oaks Boulevard
Arlington, TX 76011          817-226-6222
                        FAX 817-226-6225
          http://www.gatewayschool.com
*Harriet Walber, Executive Director*
*Marsha Godfrey, Administrative Assistant*

An alternative school for students designed for the student who has average or above average intelligence yet has experienced little or no success previously in school.

**5805 Gateway School: Arlington**

Gateway School
2570 N W Green Oaks Boulevard
Arlington, TX 76011          817-226-6222
                        FAX 817-226-6225
          http://www.gatewayschool.com
*Harriet Walber, Executive Director*
*Marsha Godfrey, Administrative Assistant*

The only nonprofit accredited secondary school in the Forth Worth/Arlington area addressing academic and social challenges of students. Students who successfully complete the program earn a high school diploma.

**5806 Houston Learning Academy**

Houston Learning Academy
3333 Bering Drive
Houston, TX 77057          713-974-6658
                        FAX 713-975-6666
*Susan McKinney, Executive Director*
*Shari Schiftman, Operations Controller*

Offers high schools, grades 9-12. Six locations in Houston. Teachers work with special learning needs, including ADHD and classes are small. Established in 1983.

**5807 Keystone Academy**

6506 Frankford Road
Dallas, TX 75252          972-250-4455
                        FAX 972-250-4960
          http://www.keystoneacademy.com
              e-mail: kacademy@juno.com
*Helen Werner, Founder/Director*

A private, nonprofit school accommodating the learning differences of children in K-7th grade.

**5808 Lane Learning Center**

230 W Main Street
Lewisville, TX 75057          972-221-2564
                          888-412-5263
                     FAX 972-436-6964
       http://www.lanelearningcenter.com/
          e-mail: info@lanelearningcenter.com
*Kenneth Lane, Owner*

**5809 Neuhaus Education Center**

Neuhaus Education Center
4433 Bissonnet Street
Bellaire, TX 77401          713-664-7676
                        FAX 713-664-4744
              http://www.neuhaus.org
              e-mail: info@neuhaus.org
*Kay Allen, Director*
*Suzanne Carraker, Director Teacher Development*

Dyslexia specialist training courses and workshops for regular education teaching, parent consultation and adult literacy classes.

**5810 Overton Speech and Language Center**

Overton Speech and Language Center
4763 Barwick Drive
Fort Worth, TX 76132          817-294-8408
                        FAX 817-294-8411
          http://www.overtonspeech.net
          e-mail: info@overtonspeech.net
*Valerie Johnston, Director*

Provides speech and language therapy.

**5811 Parish School**

Parish School
11059 Timberline Road
Houston, TX 77043          713-467-4696
                        FAX 713-467-8341
          http://www.parishschool.org
*Robbin MA CCC-SLP, Director/Founder*
*Margaret , Academic Coordinator*
*Melanie Siegle, Clinical Coordinator*

Private school with a language based curriculum for children 18 months through nine years of age with language and learning differences.

**5812 Partners Resource Network**

1090 Longfellow Drive
Beaumont, TX 77706          409-898-4684
                          800-866-4726
                     FAX 409-898-4869
          http://www.partnerstx.org
          e-mail: txprnpath@sbcglobal.net
*Janice Meyer, Executive Director*
*Alice Robertson, Training Coordinator*

Views parents as full partners in the educational process and a significant source of support and assistance to each other. Funded by the Division of Personnel Preparation, Office of Special Education Programs and the US Department of Education, these programs provide training and information to parents to enable such individuals to participate more effectively with professionals in meeting the educational needs of children with disabilities.

**5813 Psychoeducational Diagnostic Services**

7233 Brentfield Drive
Dallas, TX 75248          972-931-5299
                        FAX 972-392-7155
*Harrian Stern PhD, Educator Diagnostician*

Psychoeducational diagnostic assessment of intellectual and academic ability, including assessing the ability of students with various learning styles. Offers consultations with parents, schools, etc.

# Learning Centers /Utah

**5814 Psychology Clinic of Fort Worth**
4200 S Hulen Street
Fort Worth, TX 76109          817-731-0888
*William Norman PhD, Contact*

**5815 SHIP Resource Center**
University United Methodist Church
5084 De Zavala Road
San Antonio, TX 78249          210-696-1033
http://www.uumcsatx.org
e-mail: uumcsatx@uumcsatx.org
*Vicki Spangler, Special Needs Director*
*Karen Andrews, Assistant Director*

**5816 Scottish Rite Learning Center**
Scottish Rite Mason
PO Box 10135
Lubbock, TX 79408          806-765-9150
FAX 806-765-9564
e-mail: srlcwt@nts-online.net
*Doris Haney, Director*
*Linda Stringer, Associate Director*

Language training for students at risk for dyslexia.

**5817 Shelton School and Evaluation Center**
Special Services Office
15720 Hillcrest Road
Dallas, TX 75248          972-774-1772
FAX 972-991-3977
http://www.shelton.org
e-mail: jdodd@shelton.org
*Joyce Pickering, Executive Director*
*Sandy Ritchie, Special Support Services*
*Anne Thomas, Director Public Relations*

A coeducational day school serving 780 students in grades Pre-K-12. The school focuses on the development of learning disabled students of average to above average intelligence, enabling them to succeed in conventional classroom settings. Services include on-site Evaluation Center for diagnostic testing, a Speech, Language and Hearing Clinic, an Early Childhood Program, open summer school and more.

**5818 Star Ranch**
Star Programs
149 Cant Scenic Loop
Ingram, TX 78025          830-367-4868
FAX 830-367-2814
http://www.starranch.org
e-mail: 1southhard@starranch.org
*Colline Southhard, Co-Director*
*Rand Southard, Director Child Services*

Operates two programs at Star Ranch. One is a recreational/educational summer camp for children with learning difficulties. Boys and girls ages 7-18 attend one or two week sessions during the summer. Traditional summer camp activities as well as academic tutoring are offered. The second is a residential treatment center for boys ages 7-17 who are diagnosed as learning disabled and emotionally disturbed. Preference is given to younger boys as placement is long term.

**5819 Starpoint School**
Texas Christian University
TCU School Of Education
Fort Worth, TX 76129          817-257-7660
FAX 817-257-7466
http://www.sofe.tcu.edu
e-mail: education@tcu.edu
*Kathleen Williams, Director*
*Barbara Trice, School Secretary*

**5820 VIP Educational Services**
3921 Steck Avenue
Austin, TX 78759          512-345-9274
FAX 512-345-0314
http://www.learnatvip.com
e-mail: vip_educational@hotmail.com
*Roberta Rosen, Owner/Educational Consultant*

A diagnostic and tutoring service providing help to children and adults with learning disabilities, dyslexia, ADHD, and underachievement. Enrichment, organization, time management, study skills, and test taking strategies are also addressed. An assessment process identifies learning strengths and weaknesses. Advocacy for parents and students is provided.

**5821 Vickery Meadow Learning Center**
6329 Ridgecrest
Dallas, TX 75231          214-265-5057
FAX 214-265-1666
e-mail: vmlcforliteracy@aol.com
*Patrice Doerries*

## Utah

**5822 Mountain Plains Regional Resource Center**
Utah State University
1780 N Research Parkway
Logan, UT 84341          435-752-0238
FAX 435-753-9750
TDY:435-753-9750
http://www.usu.edu/mprrc
e-mail: cope@cc.usu.edu
*John Copenhaver, Director*
*Carol Massanari, Co-Director*

A federally funded project at Utah State University which provides technical assistance to CO, AZ, KS, MT, NE, ND, NM, SD, UT and WY on how to serve disabled infants, toddlers, children, youth and their families. Learning disabled children constitute a large block of our service population. A major component of our technical assistance is in the form of information drawn from thousands of documents ranging from published research studies to newsletters.

**5823  Reid School**

Reid School
3310 S 2700 E
Salt Lake City, UT  84109          801-486-5083
                                  800-468-3274
                              FAX 801-485-0661
                          http://www.reidschool.com
                          e-mail: ereid@xmission.com
*Ethna Reid, Director*
*Angela Burke, Office Manager*

Private school for all students.

**5824  SEPS Center for Learning**

SEPS Center for Learning
1924 S 1100 E
Salt Lake City, UT  84105          801-467-2122
                              FAX 801-467-2148
                          http://www.sepslc.com
                       e-mail: dvd.eva.seps@sepslc.com
*Abe Packinger MD, Director*

Designs educational programs that help adults and children succeed in school and life. Specializing in one-on-one tutoring in all areas for all age levels, assessment, day school and preschool programs, computer assisted cognitive and academic therapy, reading programs, summer recreation and academic programs, consultation for schools and businesses.

**5825  Utah Parent Center**

Utah Parent Center
2290 E 4500 S
Salt Lake City, UT  84117          801-272-1051
                                  800-468-1160
                              FAX 801-272-8907
                       http://www.utahparentcenter.org
                    e-mail: upcinfo@utahparentcenter.org
*Helen Post, Director*
*Jeanne Gibson, Associate Director*

Parent Training and Information Program views parents as full partners in the educational process and a significant source of support and assistance to each other. Funded by the Division of Personnel Preparation, Office of Special Education Programs, these programs provide training and information to parents to enable such individuals to participate more effectively with professionals in meeting the educational needs of disabled children.

## Vermont

**5826  Pine Ridge School**

Pine Ridge School
9505 Williston Road
Williston, VT  05495               802-434-2161
                              FAX 802-434-5512
                          http://www.pineridgeschool.com
                          e-mail: prs@pineridgeschool.com
*Josh Doyle, Director Admissions*
*Shannon Dixon, Assistant Director for Admission*

Serves students who have been diagnosed with a primary, specific language disability or a non-verbal learning disability. They are in the average range of intelligence and want to use those strengths in their remediation of their language weaknesses.

**5827  Stern Center for Language and Learning**

Stern Center for Language and Learning
135 Allen Brook Lane
Williston, VT  05495               802-878-2332
                              FAX 802-878-0230
                          http://www.sterncenter.org
*Blanche PhD, President*

Founded in 1983, the center is a nonprofit organization providing comprehensive services for children and adults with learning disabilities. The Center is also an educational resource serving all of Northern New England and Northern New York State. Programs include educational testing, individual instruction, psychotherapy, school consultation, professional training for educators and a parent/professional resource library.

## Virginia

**5828  Accolink Academy**

8519 Tuttle Road
Springfield, VA  22152             703-451-8041
                              FAX 703-569-5365
                          http://www.accolink.com
*Julia Warden, Director Education*
*Nesrin Elbannen, Administrative Assistant*

**5829  Achievment Center, The**

615 N Jefferson Street
Roanoke, VA  24016                 540-366-7399
                              FAX 540-982-3629
                          http://www.achievementcenter.org
                          e-mail: info@achievementcenter.org
*Rebecca Clendenin, Director*

A private day school for children with learning disabilities.

**5830  Chesapeake Bay Academy**

821 Baker Road
Virginia Beach, VA  23462          757-497-6200
                              FAX 757-497-6304
                          http://www.chesapeake.bayacademy.org
                          e-mail: contact@chespeakebayacademy.net
*MaryAnne Dukas, Head of School*
*Hunter Wortham, Admissions Director*

Chesapeake Bay Academy is the only accredited independent school in Southeastern Virginia specifically dedicated to providing a strong academic program and individualized instruction for bright students in grade K-12 with LD and ADHD. With a student/teacher ratio of 5:1 a student:computer ratio of 2:1, qualified professionals tailor their techniques to individual needs, allowing students who have difficulty learning in traditional settings to finally succed.

**5831  Fairfax House**

3300 Woodburn Road
Annandale, VA  22003          703-560-6116
                             FAX 703-560-6592
*Bruce Wyman, Program Director*

**5832  Grafton School**

PO Box 2500
Winchester, VA  22604          540-542-0280
                             FAX 540-542-1722
                             http://www.grafton.org
                             e-mail: admis@grafton.org
*Don Davis, Admissions Supervisor*
*Jean McIntyre, Admissions Supervisor*

Grafton provides individualized educational and residential services and in-community supports for children, youth and adults with severe emotional disturbance, learning disabilities, mental retardation, autistic disorder, behavioral disorders, and other complex challenges, including physical disabilities.

**5833  Learning Center of Charlottesville**

2132 Ivy Road
Charlottesville, VA  22903          434-977-6006
                             FAX 434-977-6009
                             http://www.cvillelearning.org
*Linda Harding, Executive Director*
*Eileen Perrino, Assistant Director*

Individualized one-on-one tutoring for children and adults year round. Consultations. Educational and psychological evaluations.

**5834  Learning Resource Center**

909 1st Colonial Road
Virginia Beach, VA  23454          757-428-3367
                             FAX 757-428-1630
*Nancy Harris-Kroll, Executive Director*

One-on-one remedial and tutorial sessions after school during the school year and all day and evening during the summer with specialists who have masters degrees. Advocacy services for parents of students with special needs. Psychoeducational testing is available. Special study skills and SAT courses given. Gifted, average, and learning disabled students attend.

**5835  Leary School of Virginia**

Special Services Department
6349 Lincolnia Road
Alexandria, VA  22312          703-941-8150
                             FAX 703-941-4237
                             http://www.learyschool.org
                             e-mail: learyschool@bellatlantic.net
*Ed Schultze, Executive Director*
*Gene Meale, Director of Admissions*
*Francesca Creo, Director Programs*

A private, day, co-educational, special education facility. Currently serves 130 students, ages six to 21, with emotional, learning and behavioral problems. Along with individualized academic instruction, Leary School of Virginia offers a range of supportive and therapeutic services, including physical education, recreation therapy, group counseling, individual psychotherapy and art therapy.

**5836  Little Keswick School**

PO Box 24
Keswick, VA  22947          434-295-0457
                             FAX 434-977-1892
                             http://www.avenue.org/oks
*Marc Columbus, Headmaster*

A residential special education school for 30 boys with emotional disturbances, learning disabilities and educable mental retardation with highly structured academic and behavioral programs.

**5837  New Community School**

4211 Hermitage Road
Richmond, VA  23227          804-266-2494
                             FAX 804-264-3281
                             http://www.tncs.org
                             e-mail: admissions@tncs.org
*Julia Greenwood, School Head*
*Gita Morris, Admissions Chair*

The New Community School is an independent school specializing in college preparatory instruction and intensive remediation for dyslexic students in grades 6-12.

**5838  New Vistas School**

520 Eldon Street
Lynchburg, VA  24501          434-846-0301
                             FAX 434-528-1004
                             http://www.newvistasschool.org
*Lucy Ross, Executive Director*

**5839  Oakwood School**

Oakwood School
7210 Braddock Road
Annandale, VA  22003          703-941-5788
                             FAX 703-941-4186
                             http://www.oakwoodschool.com
                             e-mail: rporter@oakwoodschool.com
*Robert McIntyre, Executive Director*
*Muriel Jedlicka, Admissions Specialist*

A coeducational day school of 110 elementary and middle school students with mild to moderate learning disabilities.

**5840  Parent Resource Center**

Harry James Elementary School
1807 Arlington Road
Hopewell, VA  23860          804-541-6443
                             FAX 804-541-6409
*Brenda Atkins, Parent Coordinator*
*Joni Hunphries, Educator*
*Anna Noland, Educator*

Purpose of this center is to provide training and information for teachers and parents of children with special needs. The goals are to help parents understand the special education process, and promote cooperation/communication between home, school and community.

**5841    Pines Residential Treatment Center**

Pines Residential Treatment Center
825 Crawford Parkway
Portsmouth, VA  23704                    757-398-0300
                                         877-227-7000
                              FAX 877-846-6237
                         http://www.absfirst.com
                         e-mail: info@absfirst.com
*Lenard Lexier, Executive Medical Director*

**5842    Riverside School for Dyslexia**

Riverside School for Dyslexia
2110 McRae Road
Richmond, VA 23235                       804-320-3465
                              FAX 804-320-6146
                    http://www.riversideschool.org
                    e-mail: info@riversideschool.org
*Patricia DeOrio, Director*
*Julie , Principal*

Day school for dyslexic students average to gifted; certified to operate by the Virginia Board of Education. Gillingham Academy accredited training site.

**5843    StoneBridge Schools: Riverview Learning Center**

4225 Portsmouth Boulevard
Chesapeake, VA  23321                    757-488-7586
                              FAX 757-465-8995
*Trudy Webb, Director of Riverview Learning C*
*Jim Arcieri, Head Master*

Centers on stimulating each student's area of weakness in perception, language and cognition. We also work with each student's problem-solving and organizational skills.

# Washington

**5844    Children's Institute for Learning Differences: Consultation and Training**

4030 86th Avenue SE, Campus F
Mercer Island, WA  98040                 206-232-8680
                              FAX 206-232-9377
                    http://www.childrensinstitute.com
                    e-mail: robbo@bevdchildrenistitute.com
*Kristine Frost, Admissions/PR Director*
*Trina Westerlund, Executive Director/Founder*

Providing a wide array of consultation services and training opportunities to parents and community professionals, as well as ongoing teacher training for our staff.

**5845    Children's Institute for Learning Differences: Developmental Therapy Services**

4030 86th Avenue SE, Campus F
Mercer Island, WA  98040                 206-232-8680
                              FAX 206-232-9377
                    http://www.childrensinstitute.com
                    e-mail: robbo@bevdchildrenistitute.com
*Kristine Frost, Admissions/PR Director*
*Trina Westerlund, Executive Director/Founder*

A pediatric clinic providing occupational therapy services with emphasis on motor planning problems and/or significant sensory processing problems.

**5846    Glen Eden Institute**

19351 8th Avenue
Poulsbo, WA  98370                       360-697-0125
                              FAX 360-697-4712
                    http://www.glenedeninstitute.com
                    e-mail: director@glenedeninstitute.com
*A Seifert, Co-Director*
*FV Brennan, Co-Director*

Offers a unique educational alternative to meet the needs of those students who have been unable to reach their academic potential.

**5847    Hamlin Robinson School**

10211 12th Avenue S
Seattle, WA  98168                       206-763-1167
                              FAX 206-762-2419
                    http://www.hamlinrobinson.org
                    e-mail: hamlinrobinson@aol.com
*Barbara Bradshaw, Director*

A nonprofit, state approved elementary day school for children with specific language disability (dyslexia), providing a positive learning environment, meeting individual needs to nurture the whole child. Small classes use the Slingerland multi-sensory classroom approach in reading, writing, spelling and all instructional areas. It helps students discover the joy of learning, build positive self-esteem, and explore their full creative potential while preparing them for the classroom.

**5848    Specialized Training for Military Parents**

10209 Bridgeport Way SW
Tacoma, WA  98499                        253-588-1741
                                         800-298-3543
                              FAX 263-984-7520
                              TDY:283-588-1741
*Heather Hebdon, Project Coordinator*
*Toni Salato, Parent Resource Coordinator*
*Sandy Grove, Parent Resource Coordinator*

Parent Training and Information Program views parents as full partners in the educational process and a significant source of support and assistance to each other. Funded by the Division of Personnel Preparation, Office of Special Education Programs, these programs provide training and information to parents to enable such individuals to participate more effectively with professionals in meeting the educational needs of disabled children.

**5849    St. Christopher Academy**

Jevne Academy
140 S 140th Street
Seattle, WA  98168                       206-246-9751
                              FAX 253-639-3466
                    http://www.stchristopheracademy.com
                    e-mail: jevne@stchristopheracademy.com
*Darlene Jevne, Director*

High school program for learning disabled, ADD/ADHD students. Non-religious state approved since 1982. SCA also has a working ranch program near Sun Valley for children ages 13-18 with learning disabilities.

## West Virginia

**5850** **Parent Training and Information**
1701 Hamil Avenue
Clarksburg, WV 26301       304-624-1436
800-281-1436
FAX 304-624-1438
TDY:304-624-1436
http://www.wvpti.org
e-mail: wvpti@aol.com
*Pat Haberbosch, Project Director*
*Ed Barrett, Bookkeeper*

Provides information to parents and to professionals
who work with children with disabilities.

## Wisconsin

**5851** **Chileda Institute**
1020 Mississippi Street
La Crosse, WI 54601       608-782-6480
FAX 608-782-6481
http://www.chileda.org
*Kirby Lentz, Vice President*

Educators for youth with developmental disabilities.
Residential treatment center provides complete training and intensive therapy for children with severe
mental and physical disabilities, closed head injuries
and challenging behaviors.

    *6-17 years old*

## Wyoming

**5852** **Wyoming Parent Information Center**
5 N Lobban
Buffalo, WY 82834       307-684-2277
800-660-9742
FAX 307-684-5314
TDY:307-684-2277
http://www.wpic.org
e-mail: tdawson@wpic.org
*Terry Dawson, Director*

Parent Training and Information Program views parents as full partners in the educational process and a
significant source of support and assistance to each
other. Funded by the Division of Personnel Preparation, Office of Special Education Programs, these programs provide training and information to parents to
enable such individuals to participate more effectively with professionals in meeting the educational
needs of disabled children.

## Centers

**5853 American College Testing Program**

ACT Universal Testing
PO Box 168
Iowa City, IA 52243 0168
319-337-1000
FAX 319-339-3021
TDY:319-337-1701
http://www.act.org
e-mail: sandy.schlote@act.org
*Sandy Schlote, Testing Coordinator*
*Ed Colby, Public Relations*
*Richard J Ferguson, CEO*

Helps individuals and organizations make informed decisions about education and work. We provide information for life's transitions.

**5854 Diagnostic and Educational Resources**

Traveling Tutors
6832 Old Dominion Drive
McLean, VA 22101-3827
703-883-2009
FAX 703-734-0910
http://www.der-online.com
e-mail: aspector@DER-online.com
*Annette Spector, Executive Director*
*Elisabeth Wester, Course Coordinator*

Focuses on what the child can do and builds self-esteem. Provides a full range of psychoeducational testing, parent advocacy, case management, and tutoring services. Diagnostic testing determines individual needs, which are addressed in one-on-one tutoring sessions in the child's home or school. Staff trained in LD/ADHD methodologies remediate learning disabilities and offer practical suggestions for home programs and for working with school systems.

**5855 Educational Diagnostic Center at Curry College**

Curry College
1071 Blue Hill Avenue
Milton, MA 02186
617-333-2250
FAX 617-333-2018
TDY:617-333-2250
http://www.curry.edu
e-mail: curryadm@curry.edu
*Dr Winbury, Coordinator/Professor*

A comprehensive evaluation and testing center specializing in the learning needs of adolescents and adults. The Diagnostic Center welcomes adolescents and adults in need of learning strategies, long term educational plans, and better understanding of their learning profiles.

**5856 Educational Testing Service**

Test Collection
Rosedale Road
Princeton, NJ 08541
609-921-9000
FAX 609-734-5410
TDY:800-877-2540
http://www.ets.org
e-mail: etsinfo@ets.org
*Kurt Landgraf, President/CEO*
*Rosie Oliver, Strategic Workforce Solutions As*

Our mission is to help advance quality and equity in education by providing fair and valid assessments, research and related services.

**5857 Educational Testing Service: SAT Services for Students with Disabilities**

College Board SAT Program
PO Box 6200
Princeton, NJ 08541
609-771-7137
FAX 609-771-7944
http://www.collegeboard.org
e-mail: ssd@info.collegeboard.org

Offers testing accommodations to attempt to minimize the effect of disabilities on test performance. The SAT Program tests eligible students with documented visual, physical, hearing, or learning disabilities who require testing accommodations for SAT.

**5858 GED Test Accommodations for Candidates with Specific Learning Disabilities**

American Council on Education
1 Dupont Circle NW
Washington, DC 20036
202-939-9490
800-626-9433
FAX 202-775-8578
http://www.gedtest.org
e-mail: ged@ace.nche.edu
*Joan Auchter, Executive Director*
*Charles Bedore, Director Program Operations*

The American Council on Education, founded in 1918, is the nation's coordinating higher education association. ACE is dedicated to the belief that equal educational opportunity and a strong higher education system are essential cornerstones of a democratic society.

**5859 Georgetown University Child Development Center**

3307 M Street NW
Washington, DC 20007
202-687-8635
FAX 202-687-8899
http://www.gucdc.georgetown.edu
e-mail: gucdc.georgetown.edu
*Norio MD, Chief of Hospital Pathology*
*Judith Areen, Dean/Executive Vice President*

To improve the quality of life for all children and youth, especially those with, or at risk for, special needs and their families.

**5860 Law School Admission Council**

Law School Admission Council
PO Box 2001
Newtown, PA 18940 0981
215-968-1001
FAX 215-968-1119
TDY:215-968-1128
http://www.lsac.org
e-mail: sschreiber@lsab.org
*Bill Shelton, President*
*Stephen Schreiber, Vice President*

Students with documented learning disabilities can apply for test accommodations as appropriate.

**5861 Munroe-Meyer Institute for Genetics and Rehabilitation**

University Affiliated Program
444 S 44th Street
Omaha, NE 68131
402-559-6402
FAX 402-559-5737
http://www.unmc.edu/mmi
e-mail: mfbennie@unmc.edu
*Bruce Buehler, Director*
*Thelma Roberts, Billing Representative*

Diagnostic evaluation therapy, speech, physical, occupational, behavioral therapies, pediatrics, dentistry, nursing, psychology, social work, genetics, Media Resource Center, education, nutrition. Adult services for developmentally disabled, genetic evaluation and counseling, adaptive equipment, motion analysis laboratory, recreational therapy.

**5862 National Center for Fair & Open Testing**

National Center for Fair and Open Testing
342 Broadway
Cambridge, MA 02139
617-864-4810
FAX 617-497-2224
http://www.fairtest.org
e-mail: info@fairtest.org
*Monty Neill, Executive Director*
*Larry Wood, K-12 Assessment Reform Organizer*

Dedicated to ensuring that America's students and workers are assessed using fair, accurate, relevant and open tests.

**5863 Plano Child Development Center**

5401 S Wentworth Avenue
Chicago, IL 60609-6300
773-924-5297
FAX 773-373-3548
e-mail: drjj@worldnet.att.net
*Stephanie Johnson, Executive Director*
*Mrs. David, Manager*

Surveys children with visually related learning disabilities and offers vision education seminars geared to learning disabilities.

**5864 Providence Speech and Hearing Center**

Providence Speech and Hearing Center
1301 W Providence Avenue
Orange, CA 92868
714-639-4990
FAX 714-744-3841
http://www.pshc.org
e-mail: psqc@pshc.org
*Margaret Inman, Founder*
*Mary , Executive Director*

Comprehensive services for testing and treatment of all speech, language and hearing problems. Individual and group therapy beginning with parent/infant programs.

**5865 Reading Assessment System**

Harcourt Achieve
6277 Sea Harbor Drive
Orlando, FL 32887
252-480-3200
800-531-5015
FAX 800-699-9459
http://www.steckvaughn.com
e-mail: info@steckvaughn.com
*Steck-Vaughn Staff, Author*
*Tim McEwen, President/CEO*
*Jeff Johnson, Dir Marketing Communications*
*Chris Lehmann, Team Coordinator*

The Reading Assessment System provides an ongoing meaure of specific student's skills and offers detailed directions for individual instruction and remediation. Up to eight reports are available. This popular program generates individual scores, class scores, school scores, and district reports.

**5866 Reading Group**

#6 Lincoln Square
Urbana, IL 61801
217-367-0914
FAX 217-367-0500
http://www.readinggroup.org
e-mail: info@readinggroup.org
*Marilyn Kay, Executive Director*
*Rita Young, Early Childhood Coordinator*

One on one testing instruction and therapy for children and adults with dyslexia, ADD, Asperger Syndrome and gifted students with puzzling learning differences.

**5867 Rehabilitation Resource**

University Of Wisconsin-Stout Vocational Rehabilit
University of Wisconsin-Stout
Menomonie, WI 54751 0790
715-232-1232
800-447-8688
FAX 715-232-2356
http://www.chd.uwstout.edu/svri/twi
e-mail: admissions@uwstout.edu
*Bob Peters, Program Director*
*Marilyn Mars, Director of Purchasing Departmen*

Develops, publishes, and distributes a variety of rehabilitation related materials. Also makes referrals to other sources on rehabilitation.

**5868 Riley Child Development Center**

Indiana University School of Medicine
702 Barnhill Drive
Indianapolis, IN 46202
317-274-8167
FAX 317-274-9760
http://www.child-dev.com
e-mail: child-dev@child-dev.com
*John Rau, Director*

The Child Development Center provides interdisciplinary assessment for academics, communication, motor, behavior, medical concerns, for children and their families.

**5869 Rose F Kennedy Center**
**Albert Einstein College of Medicine**
**1410 Pelham Parkway S**
**Bronx, NY 10461**                    **718-430-8500**
                        **FAX 718-904-1162**
        **http://www.aecom.yu.edu/cerc**
            **e-mail: cerc@aecom.yu.edu**
*Herbert Cohen, Director*

Provides comprehensive diagnostic services and intervention services for children and adults with learning disabilities.

**5870 Scholastic Testing Service**
**480 Meyer Road**
**Bensenville, IL 60106**              **630-766-7150**
                        **800-642-6787**
                    **FAX 630-766-8054**
        **http://www.ststesting.com**
        **e-mail: sts@mail.ststesting.com**
*John Kauffman, Vice President Marketing*

Publisher of assessment materials from birth to adulthood, ability and achievement tests for kindergarten through grade twelve. Publishes the Torrance Tests of Creative Thinking, Thinking Creatively in Action and Movement, the STS High School Placement Test and Educational Development Series.

## Behavior & Self Esteem

**5871 A Day in the Life: Assessment and Instruction**
**Curriculum Associates**
**PO Box 2001**
**North Billerica, MA 01862 9914**    **978-667-8000**
                        **800-225-0248**
                    **FAX 800-366-1158**
        **http://www.curriculumassociates.com**
    **e-mail: ca@infocurriculumassociates.com**
*Frank Ferguson, President*
*Fred Ferguson, VP Corporate Development/CIO*

Embeds basic reading, writing, math and problem-solving skills in simulated job tasks. Two programs provide the activities that help students master these basic skills.

**5872 AAMR Adaptive Behavior Scale: School Edition**
**Pro-Ed**
**8700 Shoal Creek Boulevard**
**Austin, TX 78757**                  **512-451-3246**
                        **800-897-3202**
                    **FAX 512-451-8542**
        **http://www.proedinc.com**
            **e-mail: info@proedinc.com**
*Nadine Lambert, Author*
*Don Hamhill, President*

Assesses children whose behavior indicates possible mental retardation, emotional disturbances or other learning difficulties.

**5873 Autism Screening Instrument for Educational Planning**
**Slosson Educational Publications**
**538 Buffalo Road**
**East Aurora, NY 14052-0280**        **716-652-0930**
                        **800-828-4800**
                    **FAX 800-655-3840**
        **http://www.slosson.com**
            **e-mail: slosson@slosson.com**
*Bradley Erford, Edward Kelly, Sue Larson, Author*
*Steven Slosson, President*
*John Slosson, Vice President*

Publishes materials on aptitude, developmental disabilities, school screening, speech language assessment, therapy, behavior conduct, special needs; also electronic teaching tapes and testing items.

**5874 BASC Monitor for ADHD**
**AGS**
**4201 Woodland Road**
**Circle Pines, MN 55014 1796**       **651-287-7220**
                        **800-328-2560**
                    **FAX 800-471-8457**
        **http://www.agsnet.com**
            **e-mail: agsmail@agsnet.com**
*Randy W Kamphaus and Cecil R Reynolds, Author*
*Kevin Brueggman, President*

The BASC Monitor for ADHD is a powerful new tool to help evaluate the effectiveness of ADHD treatments using teacher and parent rating scales, and database software for tracking behavior changes.

**5875 Behavior Assessment System for Children**
**AGS**
**4201 Woodland Road**
**Circle Pines, MN 55014 1796**       **651-287-7220**
                        **800-328-2560**
                    **FAX 800-471-8457**
        **http://www.agsnet.com**
            **e-mail: agsmail@agsnet.com**
*Randy W Kamphaus and Cecil R Reynolds, Author*
*Kevin Brueggman, President*

A powerful assessment to evaluate child and adolescent behavior. Includes a self-report form for describing the behaviors and emotions of children and adolescents. Administration time: 10 - 20 minutes (TRS & PRS) 30 - 45 minutes for SRP.

**5876 Behavior Rating Instrument for Autistic and Other Atypical Children**
**Slosson Educational Publications**
**538 Buffalo Road**
**East Aurora, NY 14052**             **716-652-0930**
                        **800-828-4800**
                    **FAX 800-655-3840**
        **http://www.slosson.com**
            **e-mail: slosson@slosson.com**
*Sue Larson, Author*
*Steven Slosson, President*
*John Slosson, Vice President*

This instrument assesses: Relationship to an Adult; Communication; Drive for Mastery; Vocalization and Expressive Speech; Sound and Speech Reception; Social Responsiveness; and Psychobiological Development. Each of the seven scales begins with the most severe autistic behavior, and progresses to behavior roughly comparable to that of a normal 3 1/2 to 4 1/2 year-old. Also available for nonvocal communication. Administration is untimed and observational.

**5877   Behavior Rating Profile**

**Pro-Ed**
**8700 Shoal Creek Boulevard**
**Austin, TX   78757**               **512-451-3246**
                                      **800-897-3202**
                              **FAX 512-451-8542**
                        **http://www.proedinc.com**
                        **e-mail: info@proedinc.com**
*Linda Brown, Author*
*Don Hamhill, President*

A global measure of behavior providing student, parent, teacher and peer scales. It helps to identify behaviors that may cause a student's learning problems.

**5878   Child Behavior Checklist**

**University of Vermont**
**1 S ProspeCourt Street**
**Burlington, VT  05401 3456**        **802-656-8313**
                              **FAX 802-264-6433**
                          **http://www.aseba.org**
                          **e-mail: mail@aseba.org**
*Thomas M Achenbach PhD, Author*
*Thomas M. Achen MD, Department Head/Psychiatrist*
*Mark Wanner, Manager*

A standardized form for obtaining parents' reports of children's behavioral/emotional problems and competencies. Related forms obtain teacher, interviewer, observer and self-reports.

**5879   Children's Apperceptive Story-Telling Test**

**Pro-Ed**
**8700 Shoal Creek Boulevard**
**Austin, TX  78757**                 **512-451-3246**
                                      **800-897-3202**
                              **FAX 512-451-8542**
                        **http://www.proedinc.com**
                        **e-mail: info@proedinc.com**
*Mary Schneider, Author*
*Don Hamhill, President*

Employs apperceptive stories to evaluate the emotional functioning of school-age children.

*Ages 6-13*

**5880   Culture-Free Self-Esteem Inventories**

**Pro-Ed**
**7700 Shoal Creek Boulevard**
**Austin, TX  78757**                 **512-451-3246**
                                      **800-897-3202**
                              **FAX 512-451-8542**
                        **http://www.proedinc.com**
                        **e-mail: info@proedinc.com**
*James Battle, Author*
*Don Hamhill, President*

A series of self-report scales used to determine the level of self-esteem in children and adults.

*Ages 5-Adult*

**5881   Devereux Early Childhood Assessment Program**

**Kaplan**
**1310 Lewisville-Clemmons Road**
**Lewisville, NC  27023**             **336-766-7374**
                                      **800-334-2014**
                              **FAX 800-452-7526**
                        **http://www.kaplanco.com**
*Devereux, Author*

Easy-to-use, standardized assessment system that enhances social and emotional growth in children from 2-5 years. Encourages parent involvement, helps teachers with classroom planning and takes just 10 minutes to administer. Meets Head Start and IDEA requirements for strength-based assessment, as well as APA and NAEYC assessment guidelines.

**5882   Disruptive Behavior Rating Scale**

**Slosson Educational Publications**
**538 Buffalo Road**
**East Aurora, NY  14052**            **716-652-0930**
                                      **800-828-4800**
                              **FAX 800-655-3840**
                        **http://www.slosson.com**
                        **e-mail: slosson@slosson.com**
*Georgina Moynihan, TTFM*
*Steven Slosson, President*

Identifies common behavior problems such as attention deficit disorder, attention deficit hyperactivity disorder, oppositional disorders and anti-social conduct problems. *$39.00*

**5883   Draw a Person: Screening Procedure for Emotional Disturbance**

**Pro-Ed**
**8700 Shoal Creek Boulevard**
**Austin, TX  78757**                 **512-451-3246**
                                      **800-897-3202**
                              **FAX 512-451-8542**
                        **http://www.proedinc.com**
                        **e-mail: info@proedinc.com**
*Jack Naglieri, Timothy McNeish, Achilles Bandos, Author*
*Don Hamhill, President*

A screening test that helps identify children and adolescents who have emotional problems and require further evaluation.

**5884   Fundamentals of Autism**

**Slosson Educational Publications**
**538 Buffalo Road**
**East Aurora, NY  14052**            **716-652-0930**
                                      **800-828-4800**
                              **FAX 800-655-3840**
                        **http://www.slosson.com**
                        **e-mail: slosson@slosson.com**
*Sue Larson, Author*
*Steven Slosson, President*
*John Slosson, Vice President*

The handbook and two accompanying checklists provide a quick, user-friendly approach to help in identifying and developing educationally related program objectives for the child diagnosed as Autistic.

**5885  Multidimensional Self Concept Scale**

**Pro-Ed**
**8700 Shoal Creek Boulevard**
**Austin, TX  78757**                   512-451-3246
                                         800-897-3202
                                   FAX 512-451-8542
                      http://www.proedinc.com
                      e-mail: info@proedinc.com
*Bruce Bracken, Author*
*Don Hamhill, President*

A thoroughly researched, developed and standardized clinical instrument. It assesses global self-concept and six context-dependent self-concept domains that are functionally important in the social-emotional adjustment of youth and adolescents.

*Ages 9-19*

**5886  Psychoeducational Assessment of Preschool Children**

**Western Psychological Services**
**12031 Wilshire Boulevard**
**Los Angeles, CA  90025**               310-478-2061
                                         800-648-8857
                                   FAX 310-478-7838
                  http://www.wpspublishing.com
                  e-mail: help@wpspublising.com
*Bruce A Bracken PhD, Author*
*Greg Gilnar, President*
*David Nemor, Office Assistant*

Comprehensive, multidisciplinary presentation by nationally recognized contributors is based upon the concept that preschool assessment is a vibrant entity of its own - qualitatively and quantitatively different from the assessment of infants and toddlers. For professionals in pre-school assessment, early childhood education, and psycoeducational diagnostics.

*573 pages*
*ISBN 0-205290-21-3*

**5887  Revised Behavior Problem Checklist**

**Psychological Assement Resources**
**16204 N Florida Avenue**
**Lutz, FL  33549**                      813-968-3003
                                         800-331-8378
                                   FAX 800-727-9329
                     http://www.parinc.com
                  e-mail: chairman@parinc.com
*Bob III, Chairman/Chief Executive Officer*
*Kay Cunningham, Director*

Psychological test products and software designed by mental health professionals.

**5888  SSRS: Social Skills**

**AGS**
**4201 Woodland Road**
**Circle Pines, MN  55014 1796**         651-287-7220
                                         800-328-2560
                                   FAX 800-471-8457
                      http://www.agsnet.com
                  e-mail: agsmail@agsnet.com
*Frank M Gresham and Stephen N Elliot, Author*
*Kevin Brueggman, President*

A nationally standardized series of questionnaires that obtain information on the social behaviors of children and adolescents from teachers, parents and the students themselves. Administration time is 10-15 minutes per questionnaire.

*Ages 3 - 18*

**5889  School Behaviors and Organization Skills**

**Curriculum Associates**
**PO Box 2001**
**North Billerica, MA  01862 9914**      978-667-8000
                                         800-225-0248
                                   FAX 800-366-1158
                http://www.curriculumassociates.com
           e-mail: ca@infocurriculumassociates.com
*Frank Ferguson, President*
*Fred Ferguson, VP Corporate Development/CIO*

Introduces school behaviors for before, during, and after class. Critical organization and time management skills are key elements of this module.

**5890  Self-Esteem Index**

**Pro-Ed**
**8700 Shoal Creek Boulevard**
**Austin, TX  78757 6897**               512-451-3246
                                         800-897-3202
                                   FAX 512-451-8542
                      http://www.proedinc.com
                      e-mail: info@proedinc.com
*Linda Brown, Jacquelyn Alexander, Author*
*Don Hamhill, President*

A new, multidimensional, norm-referenced measure of the way that individuals perceive and value themselves.

*Ages 0-11*

**5891  Social-Emotional Dimension Scale**

**Pro-Ed**
**8700 Shoal Creek Boulevard**
**Austin, TX  78757 6897**               512-451-3246
                                         800-897-3202
                                   FAX 512-451-8542
                      http://www.proedinc.com
                      e-mail: info@proedinc.com
*Jerry Hutton, Timothy Roberts, Author*
*Don Hamhill, President*

A quick, well-standardized rating scale that can be used by teachers, counselors and psychologists to screen students who are at risk for conduct disorders or emotional disturbances.

*Ages 6-11*

**5892  System of Multicultural Pluralistic Assessment (SOMPA)**

**Harcourt Assessment**
**19500 Bulverde Road**
**San Antonio, TX  78259**               210-339-5000
                                         800-211-8378
                                   FAX 210-949-4475
                http://www.harcourtassessment.com
*Jeff Galt, Chief Executive Officer*

This comprehensive test determines the cognitive abilities, sensory/motor abilities and adaptive behavior of children ages 5-11 years of age. SOMPA provides nine different measures and a way of estimating learning potential through sociocultural and health factors.

*C-level product*

## LD Screening

**5893  ADD-H Comprehensive Teacher's Rating Scale: 2nd Edition**

**Slosson Educational Publications**
**538 Buffalo Road**
**East Aurora, NY 14052**            716-652-0930
                                     800-828-4800
                               FAX 800-655-3840
                          http://www.slosson.com
                       e-mail: slosson@slosson.com
*Rina Ullmann, Robert Sprague, Author*
*Steven Slosson, President*
*John Slosson, Vice President*

This brief checklist assesses one of the most prevalent childhood behavior problems: attention-deficit disorder, with or without hyperactivity. Because this disorder manifests itself primarily in the classroom, it is best evaluated by teacher ratings. Also available in a Spanish translation; please indicate when ordering. *$54.00*

**5894  Attention-Deficit/Hyperactivity Disorder Test**

**Slosson Educational Publications**
**538 Buffalo Road**
**East Aurora, NY 14052-0280**        716-652-0930
                                      800-828-4800
                                FAX 800-655-3840
                           http://www.slosson.com
                        e-mail: slosson@slosson.com
*James E Gilliam, Author*
*Steven Slosson, President*
*John Slosson, Vice President*

An effective instrument for identifying and evaluating ADHD. Contains 36 items that describe characteristic behaviors of persons with ADHD. These items comprise three subtests representing the core symptoms necessary for the diagnosis of ADHD: hyperactivity, impulsivity, and inattention. *$95.00*

**5895  BRIGANCE Screens: Early Preschool**

**Curriculum Associates**
**PO Box 2001**
**North Billerica, MA 01862 9914**    978-667-8000
                                      800-225-0248
                                FAX 800-366-1158
                   http://www.curriculumassociates.com
                e-mail: ca@infocurriculumassociates.com
*Albert Brigance, Author*
*Frank Ferguson, President*
*Fred Ferguson, VP Corporate Development/CIO*

An affordable, easy-to-administer, all-purpose solution. Accurately screen key developmental and early academic skills in just 10-15 minutes per child. Widely used in Early Head Start programs, it meets IDEA requirements and provides consistent results that support early childhood educator's observations and judgement. *$89.00*

**5896  BRIGANCE Screens: Infants and Toddler**

**Curriculum Associates**
**PO Box 2001**
**North Billerica, MA 01862 9914**    978-667-8000
                                      800-225-0248
                                FAX 800-366-1158
                   http://www.curriculumassociates.com
                e-mail: ca@infocurriculumassociates.com
*Albert Brigance, Author*
*Frank Ferguson, President*
*Fred Ferguson, VP Corporate Development/CIO*

An affordable, easy-to-administer, all-purpose solution. The Infant and Toddler Screen accurately assesses key developmental skills, and observes caregivers involvement and interactions. *$110.00*

**5897  BRIGANCE Screens: K and 1**

**Curriculum Associates**
**PO Box 2001**
**North Billerica, MA 01862 9914**    978-667-8000
                                      800-225-0248
                                FAX 800-366-1158
                   http://www.curriculumassociates.com
                e-mail: ca@infocurriculumassociates.com
*Albert Brigance, Author*
*Frank Ferguson, President*
*Fred Ferguson, VP Corporate Development/CIO*

The K and 1 Screen is an affordable, easy-to-administer, all-purpose solution. Accurately screen key developmental and early academic skills in just 10-15 mintues per child. School districts nationwide rely on BRIGANCE for screening children before entering kindergarten, grade 1, and grade 2. It meets IDEA requirements and provides consistant results that support early childhood educators observations and judgement.

**5898  Basic School Skills Inventory: Screen and Diagnostic**

**Pro-Ed**
**8700 Shoal Creek Boulevard**
**Austin, TX 78757 6897**             512-451-3246
                                      800-897-3202
                                FAX 800-397-7633
                          http://www.proedinc.com
                      e-mail: info@proedinc.com
*Donald Hammill, Author*
*Don Hamhill, President*

Can be used to locate children who are high risk for school failure, who need more in-depth assessment and who should be referred for additional study.

*Ages 0-4 & 6-11*

**5899  Complete Clinical Dysphagia Evaluation: Test Forms**

**LinguiSystems**
**3100 4th Avenue**
**East Moline, IL 61244**             309-755-2300
                                      800-776-4332
                               FAX 309-755-2377
                            TDY:800-933-8331
                    http://www.linguisystems.com
                 e-mail: service@linguisystems.com
*Linda Bowers, Owner*
*Rosemary Huisingh, Owner*

These test forms are used with The Complete Clinical Dyspagia Evaluation. You'll come away with a complete picture of your patient's behavioral, oral-motor, laryngeal, reespiratory, cognitive, and swallowing abilities and limitations.

**5900  DABERON Screening for School Readiness**

**Pro-Ed**
**8700 Shoal Creek Boulevard**
**Austin, TX  78757 6897**                    **512-451-3246**
**800-897-3202**
**FAX 800-397-7633**
**http://www.proedinc.com**
**e-mail: info@proedinc.com**
*Virginia Danzer, Author*
*Don Hamhill, President*

Provides a standardized assessment of school readiness in children with learning or behavior problems.

*Ages 4-6*

**5901  Developmental Assessment for the Severely Disabled**

**Pro-Ed**
**8700 Shoal Creek Boulevard**
**Austin, TX  78757 6897**                    **512-451-3246**
**800-897-3202**
**FAX 512-451-8542**
**http://www.proedinc.com**
**e-mail: info@proedinc.com**
*Mary Kay Dykes, Author*
*Don Hamhill, President*

Offers diagnostic and programming personnel concise information about individuals who are functioning between birth and 8 years of age developmentally.

*Ages 0-84*

**5902  Educational Developmental Series**

**Scholastic Testing Service**
**480 Meyer Road**
**Bensenville, IL  60106**                    **630-766-7150**
**800-642-6787**
**FAX 630-766-8054**
**http://www.ststesting.com**
**e-mail: sts@mail.ststesting.com**
*John Kauffman, Vice President Marketing*

A standardized battery of ability and achievement tests. Administration time is approximately 2.5 - 5 hours, depending on grade level and subtests. The EDSERIES has the most comprehensive coverage of all the STS tests. It permits teachers, counselors and administrators to evaluate a student from the broadest possible perspective. A school may use the EDSERIES on a lease/score basis or it may purchase testing materials.

**5903  Fundamentals of Autism**

**Slosson Educational Publications**
**538 Buffalo Road**
**East Aurora, NY  14052**                    **716-652-0930**
**800-828-4800**
**FAX 800-655-3840**
**http://www.slosson.com**
**e-mail: slosson@slosson.com**
*Sue Larson, Author*
*Steven Slosson, President*
*John Slosson, Vice President*

Provides a quick, user-friendly, effective, and accurate approach to help in identifying and developing educationally related program objectives for children diagnosed as autistic.

**5904  Goldman-Fristoe Auditory Skills Test Battery**

**Pro-Ed**
**8700 Shoal Creek Boulevard**
**Austin, TX  78757 6897**                    **512-451-3246**
**800-897-3202**
**FAX 800-397-7633**
**http://www.proedinc.com**
**e-mail: info@proedinc.com**
*Ronald Goldman, Author*
*Don Hamhill, President*

An individually administered measure of a broad range of auditory skills. Administer the full battery to receive a total picture of an individual's auditory skills using the Battery Profile. Administer a single test or a cluster of tests as needed.

**5905  Goodenough-Harris Drawing Test**

**Harcourt Assessment**
**19500 Bulverde Road**
**San Antonio, TX  78259**                    **210-339-5000**
**800-211-8378**
**FAX 210-949-4475**
**http://www.harcourtassessment.com**
*Florence Goodenough, Author*
*Jeff Galt, President/CEO*
*Jack Dilworth, Chairman*
*Gail Ribalta, Vice President Marketing*

This test focuses on mental maturity without requiring verbal skills. The fifteen-minute examination provides standard scores for children ages 3-15. *$143.00*

**5906  Kaufman Assessment Battery for Children**

**AGS**
**4201 Woodland Road**
**Circle Pines, MN  55014 1796**             **651-287-7220**
**800-328-2560**
**FAX 800-471-8457**
**http://www.agsnet.com**
**e-mail: agsmail@agsnet.com**
*Alan Kaufman, Nadeen Kaufman, Author*
*Kevin Brueggman, President*

An individually administered measure of intelligence and achievement, using simultaneous and sequential mental processes.

*35-85 min*

**5907  Kaufman Brief Intelligence Test**

**AGS**
**4201 Woodland Road**
**Circle Pines, MN  55014 1796**             **651-287-7220**
**800-328-2560**
**FAX 800-471-8457**
**http://www.agsnet.com**
**e-mail: absmail@absnet.com**
*Alan Kaufman, Nadeen Kaufman, Author*
*Kevin Brueggman, President*

KBIT is a brief, individually administered test of verbal and non-verbal intelligence. Screens two cognitive functions quickly and easily.

*15-30 min*

**5908** **Marshall University: HELP Program**

**Higher Education for Learning Problems**
520 18th Street
Huntington, WV 25703          304-696-6252
                              FAX 304-696-3231
                    http://www.marshall.edu/help
                    e-mail: weston@marshall.edu
*Barbara Guyer, Director HELP Program*
*Lynne Weston, Assistant Director*
*Debbie Painter MA, Coordinator Diagnostics*

The HELP program is committed to providing assistance through individual tutuoring, mentoring and support, as well as fair and legal access to educational opportunities for students diagnosed with learning disabilities and related disorders such as ADD/ADHD.

**5909** **Monitoring Basic Skills Progress**

**Pro-Ed**
8700 Shoal Creek Boulevard
Austin, TX 78757 6897          512-451-3246
                               800-897-3202
                          FAX 800-397-7633
                    http://www.proedinc.com
                    e-mail: info@proedinc.com
*Lynn Fuchs, Author*
*Don Hamhill, President*

A computer-assisted measurement program that tests and monitors progress in three academic areas: basic reading, basic math and basic spelling.

**5910** **National Center of Higher Education for Learning Problems (HELP)**

**Myers Hall**
520 18th Street
Huntington, WV 25703          304-696-6313
                          FAX 304-696-3231
                    http://www.marshall.edu/help
                    e-mail: painter@marshall.edu
*Barbara Guyer, Director HELP Program*
*Lynee Weston, Assistant Director*
*Debbie Painter MA, Coordinator Diagnostics*

The HELP program offers a full battery of comprehensive psychoeducational tests to determine if an individual has learning and/or attention deficits. The team of professionals can identify specific problems for all ages, such as school age children, college students, medical students, and professionals.

**5911** **PPVT-lll: Peabody Test-Picture Vocabulary Test**

**AGS**
4201 Woodland Road
Circle Pines, MN 55014 1796          651-287-7220
                                     800-328-2560
                                FAX 800-471-8457
                          http://www.agsnet.com
                    e-mail: customerservice@agsnet.com
*Lloyd Dunn, Leota Dunn, Author*
*Kevin Brueggman, President*

A measure of hearing vocabulary for Standard American English; administration time: 10-15 minutes.

**5912** **Peabody Individual Achievement Test**

**AGS**
4201 Woodland Road
Circle Pines, MN 55014 1796          651-287-7220
                                     800-328-2560
                                FAX 800-471-8457
                          http://www.agsnet.com
                    e-mail: agsmail@agsnet.com
*Frederick Markwardt Jr, Author*
*Kevin Brueggman, President*

A thorough and updated individual measure of academic achievement; administration time: 60 minutes.

**5913** **Restless Minds, Restless Kids**

**Slosson Educational Publications**
538 Buffalo Road
East Aurora, NY 14052-0280          716-652-0930
                                    800-828-4800
                               FAX 800-655-3840
                         http://www.slosson.com
                    e-mail: slosson@slosson.com
*Rick D'Alli, Author*
*Steven Slosson, President*
*John Slosson, Vice President*

Two leading specialists in the field of childhood behavioral disorders discuss the state-of-the-art approach to diagnosing and testing ADHD. They are joined by four mothers of ADHD children who share their experiences of the effects of this disorder on the family. *$67.00*

**5914** **School Readiness Test**

**Scholastic Testing Service**
480 Meyer Road
Bensenville, IL 60106          630-766-7150
                               800-642-6787
                          FAX 630-766-8054
                    http://www.ststesting.com
                    e-mail: sts@mail.ststesting.com
*John Kauffman, Vice President Marketing*

An effective tool for determining the readiness of each student for first grade. It allows a teacher to learn as much as possible about every entering student's abilities, and about any factors that might interfere with his or her learning.

**5915** **Screening Children for Related Early Educational Needs**

**Pro-Ed**
8700 Shoal Creek Boulevard
Austin, TX 78757 6897          512-451-3246
                               800-897-3202
                          FAX 800-397-7633
                    http://www.proedinc.com
                    e-mail: info@proedinc.com
*Wayne Hresko, Author*
*Don Hamhill, President*

A new academic screening test for young children that provides both global and specific ability scores that can be used to identify individual abilities.

*Ages 3-7*

**5916  Slosson Intelligence Test: Revised**

**Pro-Ed**
**8700 Shoal Creek Boulevard**
**Austin, TX  78757 6897**　　　　**512-451-3246**
　　　　　　　　　　　　　　　　**800-897-3202**
　　　　　　　　　　　　**FAX 800-397-7633**
　　　　　　　　　　**http://www.proedinc.com**
　　　　　　　　　　**e-mail: info@proedinc.com**
*Richard Slosson, Author*
*Don Hamhill, President*

A widely used individual screening test for those who need to evaluate the mental ability of individuals who are learning disabled, mentally retarded, blind, orthopedically disabled, normal, or gifted from ages 4 to adulthood. *$ 111.00*

*Ages 4-Adult*

**5917  Source for Nonverbal Learning Disorders**

**LinguiSystems**
**3100 4th Avenue**
**East Moline, IL  61244**　　　　**309-755-2300**
　　　　　　　　　　　　　　　　**800-776-4332**
　　　　　　　　　　　　**FAX 309-755-2377**
　　　　　　　　　　　　**TDY:800-933-8331**
　　　　　　**http://www.linguisystems.com**
　　　　　　**e-mail: service@linguisystems.com**
*Linda Bowers, Owner*
*Rosemary Huisingh, Owner*

Not sure if you have a student with nonverbal learning disorder? See if this description sounds familiar: ignores nonverbal cues such as facial expressions, is clumsy for no apparent reason, makes inappropriate social remarks, and has difficulty with visual-spatial-organizational tasks. This resource provides you with useful checklists, anecdotes, and methods for dealing with this little understood disorder through the lifespan.

**5918  TOVA**

**Universal Attention Disorders**
**4281 Katella Avenue**
**Los Alamitos, CA  90720**　　　　**714-229-8770**
　　　　　　　　　　　　　　　　**800-729-2886**
　　　　　　　　　　　　**FAX 714-229-8782**
　　　　　　　　　　**http://www.tovatest.com**
　　　　　　　　　　**e-mail: info@tovatest.com**
*Clifford Corman, Medical Director*
*Karen Carlson, Marketing Director*

The TOVA (Tests of Variables of Attention) is a computerized, objective measure of attention and impulsivity, used in the assessment and treatment of ADD/ADHD. It is standardized from 4 to 80 years of age. TOVA's report contains a full analysis and interpetation of data. Variables measured include omissions, commisions, response time and response time variability.

**5919  Test of Memory and Learning (TOMAL)**

**Pro-Ed**
**8700 Shoal Creek Boulevard**
**Austin, TX  78757 6897**　　　　**512-451-3246**
　　　　　　　　　　　　　　　　**800-897-3202**
　　　　　　　　　　　　**FAX 800-397-7633**
　　　　　　　　　　**http://www.proedinc.com**
　　　　　　　　　　**e-mail: info@proedinc.com**
*Cecil Reynolds, Erin Bigler, Author*
*Don Hamhill, President*

TOMAL provides ten subtests that evaluate general and specific memory functions.

*Ages 5-19*

**5920  Test of Nonverbal Intelligence**

**Pro-Ed**
**8700 Shoal Creek Boulevard**
**Austin, TX  78757 6897**　　　　**512-451-3246**
　　　　　　　　　　　　　　　　**800-897-3202**
　　　　　　　　　　　　**FAX 800-397-7633**
　　　　　　　　　　**http://www.proedinc.com**
　　　　　　　　　　**e-mail: info@proedinc.com**
*Linda Brown, Author*
*Don Hamhill, President*

A language-free measure of reasoning and intelligence presents a variety of abstract problem solving tasks.

*Ages 0-89*

**5921  Vision, Perception and Cognition: Manual for Evaluation & Treatment**

**Therapro**
**225 Arlington Street**
**Framingham, MA  01702 8723**　　　**508-872-9494**
　　　　　　　　　　　　　　　　**800-257-5376**
　　　　　　　　　　　　**FAX 508-875-2062**
　　　　　　　**http://www.theraproducts.com**
　　　　　　　**e-mail: info@theraproducts.com**
*Barbara Zoltan, Ellen Siev & Brenda Freishtat, Author*

Details methods for testing perceptual, visual and cognitive deficits, as well as procedure for evaluating test results in relation to cognitive loss. Clearly explains each deficit, provides step by step testing techniques and gives complete treatment guidelines. Also includes information on the use of computers in cognitive training. *$37.00*

*181 pages*

## Math

**5922  3 Steps to Math Success**

**Curriculum Associates**
**PO Box 2001**
**North Billerica, MA  01862 9914**　　**978-667-8000**
　　　　　　　　　　　　　　　　**800-225-0248**
　　　　　　　　　　　　**FAX 800-366-1158**
　　　　　　**http://www.curriculumassociates.com**
　　　　　　**e-mail: ca@infocurriculumassociates.com**
*Curriculum Associates, Author*
*Frank Ferguson, President*
*Fred Ferguson, VP Corporate Development/CIO*

We developed an integrated approach to math that ensures academic success long after the final bell has rung. Together, these series create an easy-to-use system of targeted instruction designed to remedy math weakness and reinforce math strengths.

**5923  AfterMath Series**

Curriculum Associates
PO Box 2001
North Billerica, MA  01862 9914      978-667-8000
                                     800-225-0248
                               FAX 800-366-1158
              http://www.curriculumassociates.com
              e-mail: ca@infocurriculumassociates.com
*Frank Ferguson, President*
*Fred Ferguson, VP Corporate Development/CIO*

Galileo once said that mathematics is the alphabet in which the universe was created. This series helps students master that alphabet. As they puzzle their way through brainteasers and learn math magic, students build critical-thinking skills that are vital to comprehending and succeeding in today's world.

**5924  ENRIGHT Computation Series**

Curriculum Associates
PO Box 2001
North Billerica, MA  01862 9914      978-667-8000
                                     800-225-0248
                               FAX 800-366-1158
              http://www.curriculumassociates.com
              e-mail: ca@infocurriculumassociates.com
*Frank Ferguson, President*
*Fred Ferguson, VP Corporate Development/CIO*

Close the gap between expected and actual computation performance. The ENRIGHT Computation Series provides the practice necessary to master addition, subtraction, multiplication, and division of whole numbers, fractions, and decimals.

**5925  Figure It Out: Thinking Like a Math Problem Solver**

Curriculum Associates
PO Box 2001
North Billerica, MA  01862 9914      978-667-8000
                                     800-225-0248
                               FAX 800-366-1158
              http://www.curriculumassociates.com
              e-mail: ca@infocurriculumassociates.com
*Frank Ferguson, President*
*Fred Ferguson, VP Corporate Development/CIO*

Critical thinking is the key to unlocking the mystery of these nonroutine problems. Your students will eagerly accept the challenge! Students learn to apply eight strategies in each book including: draw a picture; use a pattern; work backwards; make a table; and guess and check.

**5926  Getting Ready for Algebra**

Curriculum Associates
PO Box 2001
North Billerica, MA  01862 9914      978-667-8000
                                     800-225-0248
                               FAX 800-366-1158
              http://www.curriculumassociates.com
              e-mail: ca@infocurriculumassociates.com
*Frank Ferguson, President*
*Fred Ferguson, VP Corporate Development/CIO*

NCTM encourages algebra instruction in the early grades to develop critical-thinking, communication, reasoning, and problem-solving skills. Getting Ready for Algebra exercises these skills in lessons that focus on key algebra concepts: adding and subtracting positive integers; patterns; set theory notation; open sentences; inequality and more.

**5927  Learning Disability Evaluation Scale: Renormed**

Hawthorne Educational Services
800 Gray Oak Drive
Columbia, MO  65201              573-874-1710
                                800-542-1673
                          FAX 800-442-9509
                   http://www.hes-inc.com
            e-mail: edina.laird@hes-inc.com
*Stephen McCarney, Author*
*Edina Laird, Director of External Relations*

The Learning Disability Evaluation Scale (LDES) is an initial screening and assessment instrument in the areas of listening, thinking, speaking, reading, writing, spelling, and mathematical calculations based on the federal definition (IDEA). The Learning Disability Intervention Manual (LDIM) is a companion to the LDES and contains goals, objectives, and intervention/instructional strategies for the learning problems identified by the LDES. *$152.00*

*217 pages*

**5928  QUIC Tests**

Scholastic Testing Service
480 Meyer Road
Bensenville, IL  60106           630-766-7150
                                 800-642-6787
                           FAX 630-766-8054
                    http://www.ststesting.com
             e-mail: sts@mail.ststesting.com
*John Kauffman, Vice President Marketing*

The Quic Tests are used to determine the functional level of student comptetency in mathematics and/ or communicative arts for use in grades 2-12. Administration time is 30 minutes or less.

**5929  Skills Assessments**

Harcourt
6277 Sea Harbor Drive
Orlando, FL  32887               252-480-3200
                                 800-531-5015
                           FAX 512-343-6854
                  http://www.harcourtachieve.com
             e-mail: info@steck-vaughn.com
*Tim McEwen, President/CEO*
*Jeff Johnson, Director Marketing Communication*

This handy, all-in-one resource helps identify students strengths and weaknesses in order to determine appropriate instructional levels in each of five subjects areas: reading; language arts; math; science; and social studies. Assessments are identified by subtopics in each subject.

**5930  Test of Mathematical Abilities**

Pro-Ed
8700 Shoal Creek Boulevard
Austin, TX  78757 6897           512-451-3246
                                 800-897-3202
                           FAX 800-397-7633
                    http://www.proedinc.com
             e-mail: info@proedinc.com
*Virginia Brown, Mary Cronin, Elizabeth McEntire, Author*
*Don Hamhill, President*

Has been developed to provide standardized information about story problems and computation, attitude, vocabulary and general cultural application. *$92.00*

*Ages 3-12*

## Professional Guides

**5931 Assessment Update**

**Jossey-Bass**
**111 River Street**
**Hoboken, NJ 07030**          **201-748-6000**
                              **FAX 201-748-6088**
          **http://www.josseybass.com/wiley**
*William Pesce, President/CEO*
*Trudy Banta, Editor*

Assessment Update is dedicated to covering the latest developments in the rapidly evolving area of higher education assessment. Assessment Update offers all academic leaders up-to-date information and practical advice on conducting assessments in a range of areas, including student learning and outcomes, faculty instruction, academic programs and curricula, student services, and overall institutional functioning.

**5932 Assessment of Students with Handicaps in Vocational Education**

**Association for Career and Technical Education**
**1410 King Street**
**Alexandria, VA 22314**          **703-683-3111**
                              **800-626-9972**
                    **FAX 703-683-7424**
          **http://www.acteonline.org**
          **e-mail: jbray@acteonline.org**
*L Albright, Author*
*Jan Bray, Executive Director*
*Peter Magnuson, Senior Dir Strategic Marketing*

Includes teachers, supervisors, administrators and others interested in the development and improvement of vocational, technical and practical-arts education.

**5933 BRIGANCE Word Analysis: Strategies and Practice**

**Curriculum Associates**
**PO Box 2001**
**North Billerica, MA 01862 9914**     **978-667-8000**
                              **800-225-0248**
                    **FAX 800-366-1158**
          **http://www.curriculumassociates.com**
          **e-mail: ca@infocurriculumassociates.com**
*Albert Brigance, Author*
*Frank Ferguson, President*
*Fred Ferguson, VP Corporate Development/CIO*

Our comprehensive, two-volume resource combines activities, strategies, and reference materials for teaching phonetic and structural word analysis. Two durable binders feature reproducible activity pages. Choose from more than 1,600 activities for corrective instruction or to reinforce your classroom reading program.

**5934 Career Planner's Portfolio: A School-to-work Assessment Tool**

**Curriculum Associates**
**PO Box 2001**
**North Billerica, MA 01862 9914**     **978-667-8000**
                              **800-225-0248**
                    **FAX 800-366-1158**
          **http://www.curriculumassociates.com**
          **e-mail: ca@infocurriculumassociates.com**
*Robert G Forest, Author*
*Frank Ferguson, President*
*Fred Ferguson, VP Corporate Development/CIO*

Students career plans develop and evolve over several school years. Our portfolio will help track of their progess.

**5935 Computer Scoring Systems for PRO-ED Tests**

**Pro-Ed**
**8700 Shoal Creek Boulevard**
**Austin, TX 78757 6897**          **512-451-3246**
                              **800-897-3202**
                    **FAX 800-397-7633**
          **http://www.proedinc.com**
          **e-mail: info@proedinc.com**
*Don Hamhill, President*

Computer scoring systems have been developed to generate reports for many PRO-ED tests and to help examiners interpret test performance.

**5936 Goals and Objectives Writer Software**

**Curriculum Associates**
**PO Box 2001**
**North Billerica, MA 01862 9914**     **978-667-8000**
                              **800-225-0248**
                    **FAX 800-366-1158**
          **http://www.curriculumassociates.com**
          **e-mail: ca@infocurriculumassociates.com**
*Frank Ferguson, President*
*Fred Ferguson, VP Corporate Development/CIO*

Using the Goals and Objectives program, you'll quickly and easily create, edit, and print IEPs. The CD allows you to install the program on your hard drive in order to save students data for future updates. You can easily export IEPs into any word processing program. CD-Rom for Windows and Macintosh.

**5937 Occupational Aptitude Survey and Interest Schedule**

**Pro-Ed**
**8700 Shoal Creek Boulevard**
**Austin, TX 78757 6897**          **512-451-3246**
                              **800-897-3202**
                    **FAX 800-397-7633**
          **http://www.proedinc.com**
          **e-mail: info@proedinc.com**
*Randall Parker, Author*
*Don Hamhill, President*

Consists of two related tests: the OASIS-2 Aptitude Survey and the OASIS-2 Interest Schedule. The tests were normed on the same national sample of 1,505 students from 13 states. The Aptitude Survey measures six broad aptitude factors that are directly related to skills and abilities required in over 20,000 jobs and the Interest Schedule measures 12 interest factors directly related to the occupations listed in Occupational Exploration.

**5938  Portfolio Assessment Teacher's Guide**

Harcourt
6277 Sea Harbor Drive
Orlando, FL  32887                252-480-3200
                                 800-531-5015
                            FAX 800-699-9459
                http://www.harcourtachieve.com
                    e-mail: ecare@harcourt.com
*Roger Farr, Author*
*Tim McEwen, President/CEO*
*Jeff Johnson, Director Marketing Communication*

Start your portfolio systems with tips from the expert.
Roger Farr outlines the basic steps for evaluating a
portfolio, offers ideas for organizing portfolios and
making the most of portfolio conferences, and provides reproducible evaluation forms for primary
through intermediate grades and above. *$21.80*

**5939  Teaching Test Taking Skills**

Brookline Books
300 Bedford Street
Manchester, NH  03101              617-734-6772
                              FAX 603-922-3348
                  http://www.brroklinebooks.com
                  e-mail: brooklinebks@delphi.com
*Margo Mastropieri,Thomas Scruggs, Author*

Test-wise individuals often score higher than others
of equal ability who may not use test-taking skills effectively. This work teaches general concepts about
the test format or other conditions of testing, not specific items on the test. *$21.95*

*ISBN 0-914797-76-X*

**5940  Tests, Measurement and Evaluation**

American Institutes for Research
1000 Thomas Jefferson Street NW
Washington, DC  20007              202-342-5000
                              FAX 202-298-6809
                            http://www.air.org
*Sol Pelavin, President/CEO*
*Nikki Shannon, Administrative Assistant*

Our goal is to provide governments and the private
sector with responsive services of the highest quality
by applying and advancing the knowledge, theories,
methods, and standards of the behavioral and social
services to solve significant societal problems and improve the quality of life of all people.

---

# Reading

**5941  3 Steps to Reading Success**

Curriculum Associates
PO Box 2001
North Billerica, MA  01862 9914    978-667-8000
                                   800-225-0248
                            FAX 800-366-1158
                http://www.curriculumassociates.com
                e-mail: ca@infocurriculumassociates.com
*Frank Ferguson, President*
*Fred Ferguson, VP Corporate Development/CIO*

Equipping your students with the skills and strategies
they need to achieve lifelong success can be a challenge. That's why we developed an integrated approach to learning that ensures academic success long
after the final bell has rung.

**5942  BRIGANCE Readiness: Strategies and Practice**

Curriculum Associates
PO Box 2001
North Billerica, MA  01862 9914    978-667-8000
                                   800-225-0248
                            FAX 800-366-1158
                http://www.curriculumassociates.com
                e-mail: ca@infocurriculumassociates.com
*Albert Brigance, Author*
*Frank Ferguson, President*
*Fred Ferguson, VP Corporate Development/CIO*

Attend to the needs and differences of the children in
your program using Readiness: Strategies and Practice. Skills are introduced, taught, and reinforced using both age-appropriate and individual appropriate
activties. *$174.00*

**5943  CLUES for Better Reading: Grade 1**

Curriculum Associates
PO Box 2001
North Billerica, MA  01862 9914    978-667-8000
                                   800-225-0248
                            FAX 800-366-1158
                http://www.curriculumassociates.com
                e-mail: ca@infocurriculumassociates.com
*Diane Lapp, James Flood, Author*
*Frank Ferguson, President*
*Fred Ferguson, VP Corporate Development/CIO*

Clues for Better Reading Book A develops and
strengthens comprehension through reading activities
in the same skill strands featured in the Kindergarten
level. The 96-page Teacher Guide provides activities
to introduce the unit skill and new vocabulary, followed by guided lessons and extension activities.

**5944  CLUES for Better Reading: Grade 2-5**

Curriculum Associates
PO Box 2001
North Billerica, MA  01862 9914    978-667-8000
                                   800-225-0248
                            FAX 800-366-1158
                http://www.curriculumassociates.com
                e-mail: ca@infocurriculumassociates.com
*Diane Lapp, James Flood, Author*
*Frank Ferguson, President*
*Fred Ferguson, VP Corporate Development/CIO*

Students explore a variety of literacy genres: stories;
poetry; plays, newspaper articles, and others. Related
lanuage activities - writing, word analysis, or study
skills - help students extend reading comprehension to
other areas of language arts.

**5945  CLUES for Better Reading: Kindergaten**

Curriculum Associates
PO Box 2001
North Billerica, MA  01862 9914      978-667-8000
800-225-0248
FAX 800-366-1158
http://www.curriculumassociates.com
e-mail: ca@infocurriculumassociates.com
*Diane Lapp, James Flood, Author*
*Frank Ferguson, President*
*Fred Ferguson, VP Corporate Development/CIO*

Emergent readers explore language with Clues for Better Reading and Writing. Teacher-directed lessons feature minimal text with appealing full-color artwork, and place a strong emphasis on oral literature to develop early reading skills.

**5946  Capitalization and Punctuation**

Curriculum Associates
PO Box 2001
North Billerica, MA  01862 9914      978-667-8000
800-225-0248
FAX 800-366-1158
http://www.curriculumassociates.com
e-mail: ca@infocurriculumassociates.com
*Curriculum Associates, Author*
*Frank Ferguson, President*
*Fred Ferguson, VP Corporate Development/CIO*

Capitalization and Punctuation features structured, easy to understand lessons that are organized sequentially. Students read the rules, study sample exercises, apply the skills in practice lessons, and review the skills in maintenance lessons.

**5947  Effective Reading of Textbooks**

Curriculum Associates
PO Box 2001
North Billerica, MA  01862 9914      978-667-8000
800-225-0248
FAX 800-366-1158
http://www.curriculumassociates.com
e-mail: ca@infocurriculumassociates.com
*Anita Archer, Author*
*Frank Ferguson, President*
*Fred Ferguson, VP Corporate Development/CIO*

Students practice previewing for reading, active reading, indentation note-taking, mapping a visual display of content, and writing a summary paragraph.

**5948  Extensions in Reading**

Curriculum Associates
PO Box 2001
North Billerica, MA  01862 9914      978-667-8000
800-225-0248
FAX 800-366-1158
http://www.curriculumassociates.com
e-mail: ca@infocurriculumassociates.com
*Curriculum Assoociates, Author*
*Frank Ferguson, President*
*Fred Ferguson, VP Corporate Development/CIO*

A unique new program teaching reading strategies and more. Extensions offers rich experiences with nonfiction and fiction. Each lesson extends to include: researching and writing; use of graphic organizers; vocabulary development; and comprehension questions with test-prep format.

**5949  Formal Reading Inventory**

Pro-Ed
8700 Shoal Creek Boulevard
Austin, TX  78757 6897          512-451-3246
800-897-3202
FAX 800-397-7633
http://www.proedinc.com
e-mail: info@proedinc.com
*J Lee Wiederholt, Author*
*Don Hamhill, President*

A national test for assessing silent reading comprehension and diagnosing reading miscues.

**5950  Gray Oral Diagnostic Reading Tests**

Pro-Ed
8700 Shoal Creek Boulevard
Austin, TX  78757 6897          512-451-3246
800-897-3202
FAX 800-397-7633
http://www.proedinc.com
e-mail: info@proedinc.com
*Brian Bryant, J Lee Wiederholt, Author*
*Don Hamhill, President*

Uses two alternate, equivalent forms to assess students who have difficulty reading continuous print and who require an evaluation of specific abilities and weaknesses. *$235.00*

**5951  Gray Oral Reading Tests**

Pro-Ed
8700 Shoal Creek Boulevard
Austin, TX  78757 6897          512-451-3246
800-897-3202
FAX 800-397-7633
http://www.proedinc.com
e-mail: info@proedinc.com
*J Lee Wiederholt, Brian Bryant, Author*
*Don Hamhill, President*

The latest revision provides an objective measure of growth in oral reading and an aid in the diagnosis of oral reading difficulties. *$198.00*

**5952  Reading Assessment System**

Steck-Vaughn Company
PO Box 690789
Orlando, FL  32819              407-345-3800
800-531-5015
FAX 800-269-5232
http://www.steck-vaughn.com
e-mail: info@steck-vaughn.com
*Connie Alden, Vice President of Human Resource*
*Michael Ruecker, Vice President of Human Resource*

The Reading Assessment System provides an ongoing measure of specific student's skills and offers detailed directions for individual instruction and remediation. Up to eight reports are available. This popular program generates individual scores, class scores, school scores, and district reports.

**5953   Scholastic Abilities Test for Adults**

Pro-Ed
8700 Shoal Creek Boulevard
Austin, TX  78757 6897                 512-451-3246
                                       800-897-3202
                                  FAX 800-397-7633
                         http://www.proedinc.com
                         e-mail: info@proedinc.com
*Brian Bryant, James Patton, Caroline Dunn, Author*
*Don Hamhill, President*

Measures scholastic competence, aptitude and academic achievement for persons with learning difficulties. *$164.00*

*Ages 16-70*

**5954   Skills Assessments**

Steck-Vaughn Company
PO Box 690789
Orlando, FL  32819                     407-345-3800
                                       800-531-5015
                                  FAX 800-269-5232
                       http://www.steck-vaughn.com
                       e-mail: info@steck-vaughn.com
*Connie Alden, Vice President of Human Resource*
*Michael Ruecker, Vice President of Human Resource*

This handy, all-in-one resource helps identify students strengths and weaknesses in order to determine appropriate instructional levels in each of five subjects areas: reading; language arts; math; science; and social studies. Assessments are identified by subtopics in each subject.

**5955   Standardized Reading Inventory**

Pro-Ed
8700 Shoal Creek Boulevard
Austin, TX  78757 6897                 512-451-3246
                                       800-897-3202
                                  FAX 800-397-7633
                         http://www.proedinc.com
                         e-mail: info@proedinc.com
*Phyllis Newcomer, Author*
*Don Hamhill, President*

An instrument for evaluating students' reading ability. *$231.00*

**5956   TERA-3: Test of Early Reading Ability 3nd Edition**

AGS
4201 Woodland Road
Circle Pines, MN  55014 1796           651-287-7220
                                       800-328-2560
                                  FAX 800-471-8457
                         http://www.SLPforum.com
                         e-mail: ags@skypoint.com
*Kim Reid, Wayne Hresko and Donald Hammill, Author*
*Kevin Brueggman, President*

Ideal for screening children's early reading abilities. Specifically the revised test measures knowledge of contextual meaning, the alphabet and conventions such as reading from left to right. *$236.00*

**5957   Test of Early Reading Ability**

Pro-Ed
8700 Shoal Creek Boulevard
Austin, TX  78757 6897                 512-451-3246
                                       800-897-3202
                                  FAX 800-397-7633
                         http://www.proedinc.com
                         e-mail: info@proedinc.com
*D Kim Reid, Wayne Hresko, Donald Hammill, Author*
*Don Hamhill, President*

Unique test in that it measures the actual reading ability of young children. Items measure knowledge of contextual meaning, alphabet and conventions. *$236.00*

**5958   Test of Reading Comprehension**

Pro-Ed
8700 Shoal Creek Boulevard
Austin, TX  78757 6897                 512-451-3246
                                       800-897-3202
                                  FAX 800-397-7633
                         http://www.proedinc.com
                         e-mail: info@proedinc.com
*Virginia Brown, Donald Hammill, J Lee Wiederholt, Author*
*Don Hamhill, President*

A multidimensional test of silent reading comprehension for students. The test reflects current psycholinguistic theories that consider reading comprehension to be a constructive process involving both language and cognition. *$ 166.00*

*Ages 7-11*

## Speech & Language Arts

**5959   A Calendar of Home Activities**

Curriculum Associates
PO Box 2001
North Billerica, MA  01862 9914       978-667-8000
                                       800-225-0248
                                  FAX 800-366-1158
                   http://www.curriculumassociates.com
                   e-mail: ca@infocurriculumassociates.com
*Donald Johnson, Elaine Johnson, Author*
*Frank Ferguson, President*
*Fred Ferguson, VP Corporate Development/CIO*

An activity-a-day: 365 activities for parents and children to share at home in just 10-15 minutes each day. Parents support their children's educational experiences in a meaningful and enjoyable way, such as cooking, playing ball, and sculpting clay.

**5960 Activities for Dictionary Practice**

Curriculum Associates
PO Box 2001
North Billerica, MA  01862 9914      978-667-8000
800-225-0248
FAX 800-366-1158
http://www.curriculumassociates.com
e-mail: ca@infocurriculumassociates.com
*Jean Lucken, Author*
*Frank Ferguson, President*
*Fred Ferguson, VP Corporate Development/CIO*

The ideal companion for classroom dictionaries! A wide variety of exercises helps students make efficient use of this important reference tool - the dictionary. Reading, spelling, vocabulary-building, and word-usage skills are reinforced.

**5961 Adolescent Language Screening Test**

Pro-Ed
8700 Shoal Creek Boulevard
Austin, TX  78757 6897          512-451-3246
800-897-3202
FAX 800-397-7633
http://www.proedinc.com
e-mail: info@proedinc.com
*Denise Morgan, Arthur Guilford, Author*
*Don Hamhill, President*

Provides speech/language pathologists and other interested professionals with a rapid thorough method for screening adolescents' speech and language. *$128.00*

*Ages 11-17*

**5962 Adventures in Science: Activities for the School-Home Connection**

Curriculum Associates
PO Box 2001
North Billerica, MA  01862 9914      978-667-8000
800-225-0248
FAX 800-366-1158
http://www.curriculumassociates.com
e-mail: ca@inforcurriculumasociates.com
*Curriculum Associates, Author*
*Frank Ferguson, President*
*Fred Ferguson, VP Corporate Development/CIO*

Process-based and hands-on, these engaging activities get your students investigating and exploring the world outside the classroom. Activities and materials are designed especially for the home, encouraging parents to take an active role in their child's education.

**5963 Aphasia Diagnostic Profiles**

Pro-Ed
8700 Shoal Creek Boulevard
Austin, TX  78757 6897          512-451-3246
800-897-3202
FAX 800-397-7633
http://www.proedinc.com
e-mail: info@proedinc.com
*Nancy Helm-Estrabrooks, Author*
*Don Hamhill, President*

This is a quick, efficient, and systematic assessment of language and communication impairment associated with aphasia that should be administered individually. The test can be administered in 40-45 minutes.

**5964 BRIGANCE Assessment of Basic Skills: Spanish Edition**

Curriculum Associates
PO Box 2001
North Billerica, MA  01862 9914      978-667-8000
800-225-0248
FAX 800-366-1158
http://www.curriculumassociates.com
e-mail: ca@infocurriculumassociates.com
*Albert Brigance, Author*
*Frank Ferguson, President*
*Fred Ferguson, VP Corporate Development/CIO*

Critiqued and field tested by Spanish linguists and educators nationwide, the Assessment of Basic Skills meets nondiscriminatory testing requirements for Limited English Proficient students. *$149.00*

**5965 BRIGANCE Comprehensive Inventory of Basic Skills: Revised**

Curriculum Associates
PO Box 2001
North Billerica, MA  01862 9914      978-667-8000
800-225-0248
FAX 800-366-1158
http://www.curriculumassociates.com
e-mail: ca@infocurriculumassociates.com
*Albert Brigance, Author*
*Frank Ferguson, President*
*Fred Ferguson, VP Corporate Development/CIO*

Designed for use in elementary and middle schools, the CIBS-R is a valuable resource for programs emphasizing individualized instruction. The Inventory is especially helpful in programs serving students with special needs, and continues to be indispensable in IEP development and program planning.

**5966 BRIGANCE Employability Skills Inventory**

Curriculum Associates
PO Box 2001
North Billerica, MA  01862 9914      978-667-8000
800-225-0248
FAX 800-366-1158
http://www.curriculumassociates.com
e-mail: ca@infocurriculumassociates.com
*Albert Brigance, Author*
*Frank Ferguson, President*
*Fred Ferguson, VP Corporate Development/CIO*

Extensive criterion-referenced tool assesses basic skills and employability skills in the context of job-seeking or employment situations: reading grade placement; rating scales; career awareness and self-understanding; reading skills; speaking and listening; job-seeking skills and knowledge; pre-employment writing; math and concepts. *$89.95*

**5967  BRIGANCE Inventory of Essential Skills**

Curriculum Associates
PO Box 2001
North Billerica, MA  01862 9914      978-667-8000
                                    800-225-0248
                            FAX 800-366-1158
        http://www.curriculumassociates.com
        e-mail: ca@infocurriculumassociates.com
*Albert Brigance, Author*
*Frank Ferguson, President*
*Fred Ferguson, VP Corporate Development/CIO*

The Inventory of Essential Skills is widely used to assess secondary level students or adult learners with special needs. *$169.00*

**5968  BRIGANCE Life Skills Inventory**

Curriculum Associates
PO Box 2001
North Billerica, MA  01862 9914      978-667-8000
                                    800-225-0248
                            FAX 800-366-1158
        http://www.curriculumassociates.com
        e-mail: ca@infocurriculumassociates.com
*Albert Brigance, Author*
*Frank Ferguson, President*
*Fred Ferguson, VP Corporate Development/CIO*

Assesses listening, speaking, reading, writing, comprehending, and computing skills in nine life-skill sections: speaking and listening; money and finance; functional writing; food; words on common signs and warning labels; clothing; health; telephone; travel and transportation. *$89.95*

**5969  Bedside Evaluation and Screening Test of Aphasia**

Pro-Ed
8700 Shoal Creek Boulevard
Austin, TX  78757 6897            512-451-3246
                                  800-897-3202
                           FAX 800-397-7633
        http://www.proedinc.com
        e-mail: info@proedinc.com
*Joyce West, Elaine Sands, Deborah Ross-Swain, Author*
*Don Hamhill, President*

Access and quantify language disorders in adults resulting from aphasia. *$143.00*

**5970  Boone Voice Program for Adults**

Pro-Ed
8700 Shoal Creek Boulevard
Austin, TX  78757 6897            512-451-3246
                                  800-897-3202
                           FAX 800-397-7633
        http://www.proedinc.com
        e-mail: info@proedinc.com
*Daniel Boone, Author*
*Don Hamhill, President*

Provides for diagnosis and remediation of adult voice disorders. This program is based on the same philosophy and therapy as The Program for Children but is presented at an adult interest level. *$141.00*

**5971  Boone Voice Program for Children**

Pro-Ed
8700 Shoal Creek Boulevard
Austin, TX  78757                 512-451-3246
                                  800-897-3202
                           FAX 512-451-8542
        http://www.proedinc.com
        e-mail: info@proedinc.com
*Don Hamhill, President*

Provides a cognitive approach to voice therapy and is designed to give useful step-by-step guidelines and materials for diagnosis and remediation of voice disorders in children.

**5972  CLUES for Better Writing: Grade 1**

Curriculum Associates
PO Box 2001
North Billerica, MA  01862 9914      978-667-8000
                                    800-225-0248
                            FAX 800-366-1158
        http://www.curriculumassociates.com
        e-mail: ca@inforcurriculumassociates.com
*Curriculum Associates, Author*
*Frank Ferguson, President*
*Fred Ferguson, VP Corporate Development/CIO*

Clues for Better Writing Book A develops and reinforces skills with creative writing projects, art activities, and vocabulary exercises. The 24-page Teacher Guide scripts each lesson and features spelling exercises, reproducible word lists, and extension activities.

**5973  CLUES for Better Writing: Grades 2-5**

Curriculum Associates
PO Box 2001
North Billerica, MA  01862 9914      978-667-8000
                                    800-225-0248
                            FAX 800-366-1158
        http://www.curriculumassociates.com
        e-mail: ca@infocurriculumassociates.com
*Curriculum Associates, Author*
*Frank Ferguson, President*
*Fred Ferguson, VP Corporate Development/CIO*

Clues for Better Writing Book B-E teach students the five steps to successful writing—brainstorming, planning, writing, editing, and publishing.

**5974  CLUES for Better Writing: Kindergarten**

Curriculum Associates
PO Box 2001
North Billerica, MA  01862 9914      978-667-8000
                                    800-225-0248
                            FAX 800-366-1158
        http://www.curriculumassociates.com
        e-mail: ca@infocurriculumassociates.com
*Curriculum Associates, Author*
*Frank Ferguson, President*
*Fred Ferguson, VP Corporate Development/CIO*

Emergent readers and writers explore lanuage with Clues for Better Reading and Writing. The 64-page student book features teacher-directed lessons with minimal text, appealing full-color artwork, and oral literture to develop early lanuage skills.

**5975 CLUES for Phonemic Awareness**

Curriculum Associates
PO Box 2001
North Billerica, MA  01862 9914     978-667-8000
800-225-0248
FAX 800-366-1158
http://www.curriculumassociates.com
e-mail: ca@infocurriculumassociates.com
*Diane Lapp, James Flood, Linda Lungren, Author*
*Frank Ferguson, President*
*Fred Ferguson, VP Corporate Development/CIO*

Give your preschool, primary, or ESL children a head start on the road to reading and writing by helping them understand that language that they hear and speak is made up of a series of sounds.

**5976 Completing Daily Assignments**

Curriculum Associates
PO Box 2001
North Billerica, MA  01862 9914     978-667-8000
800-225-0248
FAX 800-366-1158
http://www.curriculumassociates.com
e-mail: ca@infocurriculumassociates.com
*Anita Archer, Mary Gleason, Author*
*Frank Ferguson, President*
*Fred Ferguson, VP Corporate Development/CIO*

Focuses on planning assignments, writing answers to factual and opinion questions, and proofreading. Students learn to produce neat, well-organized assignments. *$19.90*

**5977 Connecting Reading and Writing with Vocabulary**

Curriculum Associates
PO Box 2001
North Billerica, MA  01862 9914     978-667-8000
800-225-0248
FAX 800-366-1158
http://www.curriculumassociates.com
e-mail: ca@infocurriculumassociates.com
*Deborah P Adcock, Author*
*Frank Ferguson, President*
*Fred Ferguson, VP Corporate Development/CIO*

This vocabulary enrichment series builds successful writers and speakers by implementing strategic word techniques. Students will add 120 writing words and other word forms to their word banks. Each lesson introduces ten vocabulary words in a variety of contexts: a letter, poem, story, journal entry, classified ad, etc.

**5978 Diamonds in the Rough**

Slosson Educational Publications
538 Buffalo Road
East Aurora, NY  14052     716-652-0930
800-828-4800
FAX 800-655-3840
http://www.slosson.com
e-mail: slosson@slosson.com
*Georgina Moynihan, TTFM*
*Steven Slosson, President*

College referance/rehabilitation guide for people with attention deficit disorder and learning disabilities.

**5979 Easy Talker: A Fluency Workbook for School Age Children**

Pro-Ed
8700 Shoal Creek Boulevard
Austin, TX  78757 6897     512-451-3246
800-897-3202
FAX 800-397-7633
http://www.proedinc.com
e-mail: info@proedinc.com
*Garry Guitar, Julie Reville, Author*
*Don Hamhill, President*

A diagnostic, criterion-referenced instrument to be used with children, to determine which stutterers would benefit from early intervention. *$41.00*

*Ages 5-18*

**5980 Fluharty Preschool Speech & Language Screening Test-2**

Speech Bin
1965 25th Avenue
Vero Beach, FL  32960     772-770-0007
800-477-3324
FAX 772-770-0006
http://www.speechbin.com
e-mail: info@speechbin.com
*Shane Peters, Product Coordinator*
*Jan Binney, Owner*

Carefully normed on 705 children, the Fluharty yields standard scores, percentiles, and age equivalents. The form features space for speech-language pathologists to note phonological processes, voice quality, and fluency; a Teacher Questionnaire is also provided. Item number P882. *$153.00*

**5981 Help for the Learning Disabled Child**

Slosson Educational Publications
538 Buffalo Road
East Aurora, NY  14052     716-652-0930
800-828-4800
FAX 800-655-3840
http://www.slosson.com
e-mail: slosson@slosson.com
*Georgina Moynihan, TTFM*
*Steven Slosson, President*

Symptoms and solutions for learning disabled children. Features issues from a medical, psychological and educational basis and illustrates learning disabilities from emotional and mental impairment.

**5982 Learning Disability Evaluation Scale: Renormed**

Hawthorne Educational Services
800 Gray Oak Drive
Columbia, MO  65201     573-874-1710
800-542-1673
FAX 800-442-9509
*Susan Kurtc, General Manager*
*Edina Laird, Director of External Relations*

The Learning Disability Evaluation Scale (LDES) is an initial screening and assessment instrument in the areas of listening, thinking, speaking, reading, writing, spelling, and mathematical calculations based on the federal definition (IDEA). The Learning Disability Intervention Manual (LDIM) is a companion to the LDES and contains goals, objectives, and intervention/instructional strategies for the learning problems identified by the LDES. *$143.00*

*217 pages*

**5983 Learning from Verbal Presentations and Participating in Discussions**

Curriculum Associates
PO Box 2001
North Billerica, MA  01862 9914     978-667-8000
800-225-0248
FAX 800-366-1158
http://www.curriculumassociates.com
e-mail: ca@infocurriculumassociates.com
*Anita Archer, Mary Gleason, Author*
*Frank Ferguson, President*
*Fred Ferguson, VP Corporate Development/CIO*

Develops oral and written language abilities. Students learn valuable strategies for note-taking, brainstorming, and effectively participating in class dicussions. *$19.90*

**5984 Naglieri: Nonverbal Ability Test-Multilevel Form**

Harcourt
19500 Bulverde Road
San Antonio, TX  78259     800-232-1223
800-211-8378
FAX 800-232-1223
http://www.hbtpc.com
*Jack Naglieri, Author*
*Jack Naglieri*

Provides a group-administered measure of nonverbal reasoning and problem solving that is independent of educational curricula and children's cultural or language background.

**5985 Oral Speech Mechanism Screening Examination**

Pro-Ed
8700 Shoal Creek Boulevard
Austin, TX  78757 6897     512-451-3246
800-897-3202
FAX 800-397-7663
http://www.proedinc.com
e-mail: info@proedinc.com
*Kenneth St Louis, Dennis Ruscello, Author*
*Don Hamhill, President*

Provides an efficient, quick, and reliable method to examine the oral speech mechanism of all types of speech, language, and related disorders where oral structure and function are of concern. *$101.00*

*Ages 5-70+*

**5986 Peabody Picture Vocabulary Test: Third Edition**

AGS Publishing
4201 Woodland Road
Circle Pines, MN  55014 1796     651-287-7220
800-328-2560
FAX 800-471-8457
http://www.agsnet.com
e-mail: agsmail@agsnet.com
*Lloyd Dunn, Leota Dunn, Author*
*Karen Dahlen, Associate Director*
*Matt Keller, Marketing Manager*
*Lisa Dunttam, Development Assistant*

A wide range measure of receptive vocabulary for standard English and screen of verbal ability.

*Ages 2-6*

**5987 Phonological Awareness Test: Computerized Scoring**

LinguiSystems
3100 4th Avenue
East Moline, IL  61244     309-755-2300
800-776-4332
FAX 309-755-2377
TDY:800-933-8331
http://www.linguisystems.com
e-mail: service@linguisystems.com
*Linda Bowers, Owner*
*Rosemary Huisingh, Owner*

What a timesaver! This optional CD-ROM software allows you to accurately, conveniently, and quickly score The Phonological Awareness Test. Just plug in the raw scores and the program does everything else. You'll be able to print out all the scores you need to include in a student's assessment report.

*Ages 5-9*

**5988 Preschool Language Assessment Instrument**

Harcourt
19500 Bulverde Road
San Antonio, TX  78259     800-232-1223
800-211-8378
FAX 800-232-1223
http://www.hbtpc.com
*Marion Blank, Susan Rose, Laura Berlin, Author*
*Marion Blank*
*Susan Rose*

Provides a profile of a child's language skills in order to match teaching with the student's competence. The test is ideal for children ages 3 to 6 and is available in Spanish. *$197.00*

**5989 Preschool Language Scale: Fourth Edition**

Harcourt
19500 Bulverde Road
San Antonio, TX  78259     800-232-1223
800-211-8378
FAX 800-232-1223
http://www.hbtpc.com
*Iria Zimmerman, PhD*
*Violette Steiner, BS*
*Roberta Evatt Pond, MA*

This tool measures a broad range of receptive and expressive language skills. A Spanish version is also available.

*Ages 0-11*

**5990 Preschool Motor Speech Evaluation & Intervention**

Speech Bin
1965 25th Avenue
Vero Beach, FL  32960     772-770-0007
800-477-3324
FAX 772-770-0006
http://www.speechbin.com
e-mail: info@speechbin.com
*Shane Peters, Product Coordinator*
*Jan Binney, Owner*

This comprehensive criterion-based assessment tool differentiates motor-based speech disorders from those of phonology and determines if speech difficulties of children 18 months to six years old are characteristic of: oral nonverbal apraxia; dysarthria; developmental verbal dyspraxia; hypersensitivity; differences in tone and hyposensitivity. Item number J322. *$59.00*

**5991  Receptive One-Word Picture Vocabulary Test (ROWPVT-2000)**

**Speech Bin**
**1965 25th Avenue**
**Vero Beach, FL  32960**          **772-770-0007**
**800-477-3324**
**FAX 888-329-2246**
**http://www.speechbin.com**
**e-mail: info@speechbin.com**
*Rick Brownell, Author*
*Shane Peters, Product Coordinator*
*Jan Binney, Owner*

This administered, untimed measure assessess the vocabulary comprehension of 0-2 through 11-18 years. New full-color test pictures are easy to recognize; many new test items have been added. It is ideal for children unable or reluctant to speak because only a gestural response is required. Item number A305. *$140.00*

**5992  Receptive-Expressive Emergent Language Tests**

**Pro-Ed**
**8700 Shoal Creek Boulevard**
**Austin, TX  78757 6897**          **512-451-3246**
**800-897-3202**
**FAX 800-397-7633**
**http://www.proedinc.com**
**e-mail: info@proedinc.com**
*Kenneth Bzoch, Richard League, Virginia Brown, Author*
*Don Hamhill, President*

Designed to use with at-risk infants and toddlers to provide a multidimensional analysis of emergency language skills.

*Ages 0-3*

**5993  Sequenced Inventory of Communication Development**

**Slosson Educational Publications**
**538 Buffalo Road**
**East Aurora, NY  14052**          **716-652-0930**
**800-828-4800**
**FAX 800-655-3840**
**http://www.slosson.com**
**e-mail: slosson@slosson.com**
*Dona Hedrick, Elizabeth Prather, Annette Tobin, Author*
*Steven Slosson, President*
*John Slosson, Vice President*

A diagnostic test designed to evaluate communications abilities, the SICD was planned for use in remedial programming of the young child with language disorders, mental challenges, and specific language problems. It has been successfully used with children who have sensory impairments, both hearing and visual, and varying degrees of retardation/challenges. *$395.00*

*4mo-4 yrs old*

**5994  Sequenced Inventory of Communication Development (SICD)**

**Speech Bin**
**1965 25th Avenue**
**Vero Beach, FL  32960**          **772-770-0007**
**800-477-3324**
**FAX 772-770-0006**
**http://www.speechbin.com**
**e-mail: info@speechbin.com**
*Shane Peters, Product Coordinator*
*Jan Binney, Owner*

SICD uses appealing toys to assess communication skills of children at all levels of ability, including those with impaired hearing or vision. SICD looks at child and environment, measuring receptive and expressive language. Item number W710. *$395.00*

**5995  Skills Assessments**

**Steck-Vaughn Company**
**PO Box 690789**
**Orlando, FL  32819**          **407-345-3800**
**800-531-5015**
**FAX 800-269-5232**
**http://www.steck-vaughn.com**
**e-mail: info@steck-vaughn.com**
*Connie Alden, Vice President of Human Resource*
*Michael Ruecker, Vice President of Human Resource*

This handy, all-in-one resource helps identify students strengths and weaknesses in order to determine appropriate instructional levels in each of five subjects areas: reading, language arts, math, science, and social stuides. Assessments are identified by subtopics in each subject.

**5996  Slosson Intelligence Test**

**Slosson Educational Publications**
**538 Buffalo Road**
**East Aurora, NY  14052-0280**          **716-652-0930**
**800-828-4800**
**FAX 800-655-3840**
**http://www.slosson.com**
**e-mail: slosson@slosson.com**
*Richard L Slosson, Author*
*Georgina Moynihan, TTFM*
*Steven Slosson, President*

A quick and reliable individual screening test of Crystallized Verbal Intelligence. *$84.00*

**5997  Slosson Intelligence Test: Primary**

**Slosson Educational Publications**
**538 Buffalo Road**
**East Aurora, NY  14052-0280**          **716-652-0930**
**800-828-4800**
**FAX 800-655-3840**
**http://www.slosson.com**
**e-mail: slosson@slosson.com**
*Bradley Erford, Gary Vitali, Steven Slosson, Author*
*Georgina Moynihan, TTFM*
*Steven Slosson, President*

Designed to facilitate the screening identification of children at risk of educational failure. Provides a quick estimate of mental ability to identify children who may be appropriate candidates for deeper testing services. *$116.00*

**5998  Stuttering Severity Instrument for Children and Adults**

**Pro-Ed**
**8700 Shoal Creek Boulevard**
**Austin, TX  78757 6897**          512-451-3246
                                    800-897-3202
                            FAX 800-397-7633
                    http://www.proedinc.com
                    e-mail: info@proedinc.com
*Glyndon Riley, Author*
*Don Hamhill, President*

With these easily administered tools you can determine whether to schedule a child for therapy using the Stuttering Prediction Instrument or to evaluate the effects of treatment using the Stuttering Severity Instrument. *$97.00*

**5999  TELD-2: Test of Early Language Development**

**Pro-Ed**
**8700 Shoal Creek Boulevard**
**Austin, TX  78757 6897**          512-451-3246
                                    800-897-3202
                            FAX 800-397-7633
                    http://www.proedinc.com
                    e-mail: info@proedinc.com
*Wayne Hresko, Kim Reid, Don Hammill, Author*
*Don Hamhill, President*

An individually administered test of spoken language abilities. This test fills the need for a well-constructed, standardized instrument, based on a current theory, that can be used to assess spoken language skills at early ages. Administration Time: 20 minutes. *$272.00*

*Ages 2-11*

**6000  TOAL-3: Test of Adolescent & Adult Language**

**Pro-Ed**
**8700 Shoal Creek Boulevard**
**Austin, TX  78757 6897**          512-451-3246
                                    800-897-3202
                            FAX 800-397-7633
                    http://www.proedinc.com
                    e-mail: info@proedinc.com
*Don Hammill, Virginia Brown, Stephen Larson, Author*
*Don Hamhill, President*

This test is a measure of receptive and expressive language skills. In this revision easier items were added to the subtests, making them more appropriate for testing disabled students. *$177.00*

*Ages 12-24*

**6001  TOLD-3: Test of Language Development, Primary**

**Harcourt**
**19500 Bulverde Road**
**San Antonio, TX  78259**          800-232-1223
                                    800-211-8378
                            FAX 800-232-1223
                    http://www.hbtpc.com
*Phyllis Newcomer, Donald Hammill, Author*
*Phyllis Newcomer*
*Donald Hammill*

An individually administered language battery that assesses the understanding and meaningful use of spoken words, aspects of grammar, word pronunciation and the ability to distinguish between similar sounding words. *$265.00*

**6002  TOWL-3: Test of Written Language, 3rd Edition**

**Pro-Ed**
**8700 Shoal Creek Boulevard**
**Austin, TX  78757 6897**          512-451-3246
                                    800-897-3202
                            FAX 800-397-7633
                    http://www.proedinc.com
                    e-mail: info@proedinc.com
*Donald Hammill, Stephen Larson, Author*
*Don Hamhill, President*

Offers a measure of written language skills to identify students who need help improving their writing skills. Administration Time: 65 minutes. *$193.00*

*Ages 7-17*

**6003  Test for Auditory Comprehension of Language: TACL-3**

**Speech Bin**
**1965 25th Avenue**
**Vero Beach, FL  32960**          772-770-0007
                                    800-477-3324
                            FAX 772-770-0006
                    http://www.speechbin.com
                    e-mail: info@speechbin.com
*Shane Peters, Product Coordinator*
*Jan Binney, Owner*

The newly revised TACL-3 evaluates the 0-3 to 9-11-year old's understanding of spoken language in three subtests: Vocabulary, Grammatical Morphemes and Elaborated Phrases and Sentences. Each test item is a word or sentence read aloud by the examiner; the child responds by pointing to one of three pictures. Item number P792. *$261.00*

**6004  Test of Auditory Reasoning & Processing Skills (TARPS)**

**Speech Bin**
**1965 25th Avenue**
**Vero Beach, FL  32960**          772-770-0007
                                    800-477-3324
                            FAX 888-329-2246
                    http://www.speechbin.com
                    e-mail: info@speechbin.com
*Morrison Gardner, Author*
*Shane Peters, Product Coordinator*
*Jan Binney, Owner*

TARPS assesses how 5-14 year old children understand, interpret, draw conclusions, and make inferences from auditorily presented stimuli. It tests their ability to think, understand, reason, and make sense of what they hear. Item number H787. *$64.00*

**6005**  **Test of Auditory-Perceptual Skills: Upper (TAPS-UL)**

Speech Bin
1965 25th Avenue
Vero Beach, FL  32960

772-770-0007
800-477-3324
FAX 888-329-2246
http://www.speechbin.com
e-mail: info@speechbin.com

*Wayne Hresko, Shelley Herron, Pamela Peak, Author*
*Shane Peters, Product Coordinator*
*Jan Binney, Owner*

This highly respected, well-normed test evaluates a 13-18 year old's ability to perceive auditory stimuli and helps you diagnose auditory disorders in just 15-20 minutes. TAPS: UL measures the auditory perceptual skills of processing, word and sequential memory, interpretation of oral directions, and discrimination. Item number H769. *$95.00*

**6006**  **Test of Early Written Language**

Pro-Ed
8700 Shoal Creek Boulevard
Austin, TX  78757

512-451-3246
800-897-3202
FAX 512-451-8542
http://www.proedinc.com
e-mail: info@proedinc.com

*Wayne Hresko, Author*
*Don Hamhill, President*

Measures the merging written language skills of young children and is especially useful in identifying mildy disabled students.

*Ages 3-11*

**6007**  **Test of Written Spelling**

Pro-Ed
8700 Shoal Creek Boulevard
Austin, TX  78757 6897

512-451-3246
800-897-3202
FAX 800-397-7633
http://www.proedinc.com
e-mail: info@proedinc.com

*Stephen Larsen, Donald Hammill, Louisa Moats, Author*
*Don Hamhill, President*

Assesses students' ability to spell words whose spellings are readily predictable in sound-letter patterns, words whose spellings are less predictable and both types of words considered together. *$82.00*

**6008**  **Testing & Remediating Auditory Processing (TRAP)**

Speech Bin
1965 25th Avenue
Vero Beach, FL  32960

772-770-0007
800-477-3324
FAX 888-329-2246
http://www.speechbin.com
e-mail: info@speechbin.com

*Lynn Baron Berk, Author*
*Shane Peters, Product Coordinator*
*Jan Binney, Owner*

TRAP gives you an easy-to-implement program to assess and treat school-age auditory processing problems. It gives you two major components: Screening Test of Auditoring Processing Skills that identifies children at risk due to auditory processing deficits; and Remediating Auditory Processing Skills that presents interactional stories, sequence pictures, and illustrated activities. Item number 1233. *$38.00*

**6009**  **Voice Assessment Protocol for Children and Adults**

Pro-Ed
8700 Shoal Creek Boulevard
Austin, TX  78757 6897

512-451-3246
800-897-3202
FAX 800-397-7633
http://www.proedinc.com
e-mail: info@proedinc.com

*Rebekah Pindzola, Author*
*Don Hamhill, President*

Easily guides the speech pathologist through a systematic evaluation of vocal pitch, loudness, quality, breath features and rate/rhythm. *$61.00*

## Visual & Motor Skills

**6010**  **BRIGANCE Inventory of Early Development-II**

Curriculum Associates
PO Box 2001
North Billerica, MA  01862 9914

978-667-8000
800-225-0248
FAX 800-366-1158
http://www.curriculumassociates.com
e-mail: ca@infocurriculumassociates.com

*Albert Brigance, Author*
*Frank Ferguson, President*
*Fred Ferguson, VP Corporate Development/CIO*

The Inventory of Early Development simplifies and combines the assessment, diagnostic, recordkeeping, and instructional planning process, and it encourages communication between teachers and parents.

*Ages Birth-7*

**6011**  **Benton Visual Retention Test: Fifth Edition**

Harcourt
19500 Bulverde Road
San Antonio, TX  78259

800-232-1223
800-211-8378
FAX 800-232-1223
http://www.hbtpc.com

*Abigail Benton Sivan, Author*
*Abigail*

Assess visual perception, memory, visoconstructive abilities. Test administration 15-20 minutes. *$189.00*

*Ages 8-Adult*

**6012  Boston Diagnostic Aphasia Exam: Third Edition**

Speech Bin
1965 25th Avenue
Vero Beach, FL  32960          772-770-0007
                              800-477-3324
                         FAX 888-329-2246
                    http://www.speechbin.com
                    e-mail: info@speechbin.com
*Harold Goodglass, Edith Kaplan, Barbara Barresi,
Author*
*Jan Binney, Owner*
*Shane Peters, Product Coordinator*

evised and improved. BDAE-3 now gives you an instructive 90-minute video plus two separate forms of
the test. Item number L235. *$150.00*

**6013  Development Test of Visual Perception**

Pro-Ed
8700 Shoal Creek Boulevard
Austin, TX  78757 9867          512-451-3246
                               800-897-3202
                          FAX 800-397-7633
                     http://www.proedinc.com
                     e-mail: info@proedinc.com
*Don Hammill, Nils Pearson, Judith Voress, Author*
*Don Hamhill, President*

Measures both visual perception and visual-motor integration skills, has eight subtests, is based on updated
theories of visual perceptual development, and can be
administered to individuals in 35 minutes. *$179.00*

*Ages 4-10*

**6014  Developmental Test of Visual Perception
(DTVP-2)**

Pro-Ed
8700 Shoal Creek Boulevard
Austin, TX  78757 6897          512-451-3246
                               800-897-3202
                          FAX 800-397-7633
                     http://www.proedinc.com
                     e-mail: info@proedinc.com
*Don Hammill, Nils Pearson, Judith Voress, Author*
*Don Hamhill, President*

A test that measures both visual perception and visual-motor integration skills, has eight subtests, is
based on updated theories of visual perceptual development, and can be administered to individuals in 35
minutes. *$179.00*

*Ages 4-10*

**6015  Differential Test of Conduct and Emotional
Problems**

Slosson Educational Publications
538 Buffalo Road
East Aurora, NY  14052-0280          716-652-0930
                                    800-828-4800
                               FAX 800-655-3840
                          http://www.slosson.com
                          e-mail: slosson@slosson.com
*Edward Kelly, Author*
*Georgina Moynihan, TTFM*
*Steven Slosson, President*

Designed to address one of the most critical challenges in education and juvenile care. Administration
of test is 15-20 minutes. *$82.00*

**6016  KLPA: Khan-Lewis Phonological Analysis**

Pro-Ed
8700 Shoal Creek Boulevard
Austin, TX  78757 6897          512-451-3246
                               800-897-3202
                          FAX 800-397-7633
                     http://www.proedinc.com
                     e-mail: info@proedinc.com
*Linda Klan, Nancy Lewis, Author*
*Don Hamhill, President*

An in-depth measure of phonological processes for
assessment and remediation planning. Administration Time: 10-30 minutes. *$126.00*

*Ages 2-5*

**6017  Learning Efficiency Test II**

Academic Therapy Publications
20 Commercial Boulevard
Novato, CA  94949          415-883-3314
                          800-422-7249
                     FAX 888-287-9975
                http://www.academictherapy.com
                e-mail: sales@academictherapy.com
*Raymond Webster, Author*
*Anna Arena, President*
*Jim Arena, Vice President*

Provides a quick and accurate measure of a child or
adult's information processing abilities, sequential
and nonsequential, in both visual and auditory modalities. *$92.00*

*Ages 5-75+*
*ISBN 0-878799-40-0*

**6018  Oral Motor Assessment: Ages and Stages**

Therapro
225 Arlington Street
Framingham, MA  01702 8723          508-872-9494
                                   800-257-5376
                              FAX 508-875-2062
                         http://www.theraproducts.com
                         e-mail: info@theraproducts.com
*Diane Chapman Bahr, Author*
*Karen Conrad, Owner*

Provides an overview of available assessments,
checklists, tables, and figures to assist the clinician in
accurately diagnosing muscle function and motor
planning issues. *$55.00*

**6019  Peabody Developmental Motor Scales-2**

Speech Bin
1965 25th Avenue
Vero Beach, FL  32960          772-770-0007
                              800-477-3324
                         FAX 772-770-0006
                    http://www.speechbin.com
                    e-mail: info@speechbin.com
*Shane Peters, Product Coordinator*
*Jan Binney, Owner*

PDMS-2 gives you in-depth standardized assessment
of motor skills in children birth to six years. Subtests
include: fine motor object manipulation; grasping;
gross motor; locomotion; reflexes; visual-motor integration and stationary. Item number P624. *$43.00*

**6020 Perceptual Motor Development Series**

**Therapro**
**225 Arlington Street**
**Framingham, MA 01702 8723**      **508-872-9494**
                                   **800-257-5376**
                             **FAX 508-875-2062**
                  **http://www.theraproducts.com**
              **e-mail: info@theraproducts.com**
*Jack Capon, Author*
*Karen Conrad, Owner*

Use these classroom tested movement education activities to assess motor strengths and weaknesses in preschool and early elementary grades or special education classes. The sequence of easily given tests and tasks requires minimal instruction time and your kids will find the activities to be interesting, challenging, and fun! Each book has 25-54 pages.

**6021 Preschool Motor Speech Evaluation & Intervention**

**Speech Bin**
**1965 25th Avenue**
**Vero Beach, FL 32960**      **772-770-0007**
                              **800-477-3324**
                        **FAX 772-770-0006**
                 **http://www.speechbin.com**
              **e-mail: info@speechbin.com**
*Shane Peters, Product Coordinator*
*Jan Binney, Owner*

This comprehensive criterion-based assessment tool differentiates motor-based speech disorders from those of phonology and determines if speech difficulties of children 18 months to six years old are characteristic of: oral nonverbal apraxia; dysarthria; developmental verbal dyspraxia; hypersensitivity; differences in tone and hyposensitivity. Item number J322. *$59.00*

**6022 Slosson Full Range Intelligence Test Kit**

**Slosson Educational Publications**
**538 Buffalo Road**
**East Aurora, NY 14052**      **716-652-0930**
                               **800-828-4800**
                         **FAX 800-655-3840**
                  **http://www.slosson.com**
              **e-mail: slosson@slosson.com**
*Bob Algozzine, Ronald Eaves, Lester Mann, Author*
*Steven Slosson, President*
*Steven Slosson, President*
*Georgina Moynihan, TTFM*

Intended to supplement the use of more extensive cognitive assessment instruments. Administration of test 25-45 minutes. *$125.00*

*Ages 5-Adult*

**6023 Slosson Visual Motor Performance Test**

**Slosson Educational Publications**
**538 Buffalo Road**
**East Aurora, NY 14052**      **716-652-0930**
                               **800-828-4800**
                         **FAX 800-655-3840**
                  **http://www.slosson.com**
              **e-mail: slosson@slosson.com**
*Richard Slosson, Author*
*Steven Slosson, President*
*Steven Slosson, President*
*Georgina Moynihan, TTFM*

A test of visual motor integration in which individuals are asked to copy geometric figures increasing in complexity without the use of a ruler, compass or other aids.

**6024 Test of Gross Motor Development**

**Pro-Ed**
**8700 Shoal Creek Boulevard**
**Austin, TX 78757 6897**      **512-451-3246**
                               **800-897-3202**
                         **FAX 800-397-7633**
                  **http://www.proedinc.com**
              **e-mail: info@proedinc.com**
*Dale Urlich, Author*
*Don Hamhill, President*

Assists you in identifying children who are significantly behind their peers in gross motor skill development and who should be eligible for special education services in phyiscal education.

*Ages 3-11*

**6025 Visual Skills Appraisal**

**Academic Therapy Publications**
**20 Commercial Boulevard**
**Novato, CA 94949**      **415-883-3314**
                          **800-422-7249**
                    **FAX 415-883-3720**
             **http://www.academictherapy.com**
          **e-mail: sales@academictherapy.com**
*Regina Richards, Gary Oppenheim, Author*
*Anna Arena, President*
*Jim Arena, Vice President*

This test identifies visual problems in children. Can be administered by teachers or other educators who may not have training in assessment. Set includes manual, stimulus cards and test forms. *$85.00*

*Ages 5-9*
*ISBN 0-878794-50-0*

## National Programs

**6026  Alliance for Technology Access**

1304 Southpoint Boulevard
Petaluma, CA  94954              707-778-3011
                                800-455-7970
                            FAX 707-765-2080
                            TDY:707-778-3015
                         http://www.ataccess.org
                    e-mail: atainfo@ataccess.org
*Mary Lester, Executive Director*
*Kelly , Office Assistant*

A national organization dedicated to providing access to technology for people with disabilities through its coalition of 39 community-based resource centers in 28 states and in the Virgin Islands. Each center provides information, awareness, and training for professionals and provides guided problem solving and technical assistance for individuals with disabilities and family members.

**6027  America's Jobline**

National Federation of the Blind
1800 Johnson Street
Baltimore, MD  21230            410-659-9314
                                800-414-5748
                            FAX 410-685-5653
                            http://www.nfb.org
                         e-mail: nfb@nfb.org
*James Gashel, Director Government Affairs*
*M Rorick, Coordinator*

In partnership with the United States Department of Labor the National Federation of the Blind offers a program that assists blind persons in finding competitive employment. The 800 number offers access to 24 hour job announcements in a high quality synthetic speech format instead of printed text. Jobline helps those who do not have or cannot use standard computers, and those who cannot see or read standard video display.

**6028  American College Testing Program**

ACT Universal Testing
500 ACT Drive
Iowa City, IA  52243 0168       319-337-1000
                            FAX 319-339-3021
                            TDY:319-337-1701
                            http://www.act.org
                    e-mail: sandy.schlote@act.org
*Ed Colby, Public Relations*
*Sandy Schlote, Testing Coordinator*

To help individuals and organizations make informed decisions about education and work. We provide information for life's transitions.

**6029  Division on Career Development**

Council for Exceptional Children
1110 N Glebe Road
Arlington, VA  22201            703-620-3660
                                888-232-7733
                            FAX 703-264-9494
                            TDY:703-264-9446
                         http://www.cec.sped.org
                    e-mail: service@ces.sped.org
*Victor Erickson, Exhibits Manager*
*Liz Martinez, Publications Director*

Focuses on the career development of individuals with disabilities and/or who are gifted and their transition from school to adult life. Members include professionals and others interested in career development and transition for individuals with any exception at any age. Members receive a journal twice yearly and newsletter three times per year.

**6030  Independent Living Research Utilization Program**

2323 S Shepherd
Houston, TX  77019              713-520-0232
                            FAX 713-520-5785
                            TDY:713-520-5136
                            http://www.ilru.org
                    e-mail: larry.redd@ilru.org
*Larry Redd, Supervisor*

A national resource center for information, training, research and technical assistance in independent living; produces and disseminates materials, develops and conducts training and publishes a monthly newsletter; provides a listing of Statewide Independent Living Councils (SILCS) in each state.

**6031  Job Accommodation Network (JAN)**

West Virginia University
PO Box 6080
Morgantown, WV  26506-6080     304-293-7186
                                800-232-9675
                            FAX 304-293-5407
                            TDY:800-232-9675
                         http://www.jan.wvu.edu
                    e-mail: jan@jan.wvu.edu
*DJ Hendrix, Director*

Network and consulting resource that provides information about employment issues to employers, rehabilitation professionals, and persons with disabilities. Callers should be prepared to explain their specific problem and job circumstances. Sponsored by the Office of Disability Employment Policy, the Network is operated by West Virginia University's Rehabilitation Research and Training Center. Brochures and printed materials available.

**6032  Minnesota Vocational Rehabilitation Agency: Rehabilitation Services Branch**

Department of Employment & Economic Development
390 N Robert Street
Saint Paul, MN  55101           651-296-5616
                                800-328-9095
                            FAX 651-297-5159
                         http://www.deed.state.mn.us
                    e-mail: paul.bridges@state.mn.us
*Paul Bridges, Director*
*Jan McAllister, Administrative Assistant*

Provides basic vocational rehabilitation services to consumers including vocational counseling, planning, guidance and placement, as well as certain special services based on individual circumstances.

**6033  Office of Vocational & Adult Education**

**US Department of Education**
**330 C Street SW**
**Washington, DC  20202**                  **202-205-5451**
                                  **FAX 202-205-9340**
                                  **http://www.ed.gov**
                                  **e-mail: ovae@ed.gov**
*Susan Sclafani, Assistant Secretary*
*Hans Meeder, Deputy Assistant Secretary*

These agencies can provide job training, counseling, financial assistance, and employment placement to individuals who meet eligibility criteria.

**6034  Transition Research Institute**

**University of Illinois at Urbana-Champaign**
**51 Gerty Drive**
**Champaign, IL  61820**                  **217-333-2325**
                                  **FAX 217-244-0851**
                      **http://www.ed.uiuc.edu/illinoisrcep**
                              **e-mail: jtrach@uiuc.edu**
*John Trach, Director*
*Betty Taylor, Administrative Assistant*

Provides technical assistance on transition-focused projects, policy analysis concerning legislation focused on education and transition services for youths with disabilities, and a wealth of information for teachers, service providers and researchers.

## Publications

**6035  ADD on the Job**

**Taylor Publishing**
**1550 W Mockingbird Lane**
**Dallas, TX  75235**                  **214-637-2800**
                                  **800-677-2800**
                                  **FAX 214-819-8580**
                      **http://www.taylorpublishing.com**
                  **e-mail: brosser@taylorpublishing.com**
*Lynn Weiss PhD, Author*
*Boyd Rosser, Director*
*Charles Kass, Assistant Director*

Practical, sensitive advice for the ADD employee, his boss, and his co-workers. The book suggests advantages that the ADD worker has, how to find the right job, and how to keep it. Employers and co-workers will learn what to expect from fellow workers with ADD and the most effective ways to work with them.

*232 pages  Paperback*
*ISBN 0-878339-17-5*

**6036  Ability Magazine**

**Ability Awareness**
**1001 W 17th Street**
**Costa Mesa, CA  92627**                  **949-854-8700**
                                  **FAX 949-548-5966**
                                  **TDY:949-548-5966**
                      **http://www.abilitymagazine.com**
                  **e-mail: editorial@abilitymagazine.com**
*Chat Cooper, Executive Director*

Brings disabilities into mainstream America. By interviewing high profile personalities such as President Clinton, Elizabeth Taylor, Mary Tyler Moore, Richard Pryor, Jane Seymour and many more, Ability Magazine is able to bring articles to the public's attention that may in the past have gone unnoticed.

*80+ pages  Bimonthly*

**6037  Articulation Models for Vocational Education**

**Center on Education and Training for Employment**
**Ohio State University**
**Columbus, OH  43210**                  **614-292-4353**
                                  **800-848-4815**
                                  **FAX 614-292-1260**
                      **http://www.cete.org/products**
Highlights the vital role of articulations in vocational education today.

**6038  Bottom Line: Basic Skills in the Workplace**

**US Department of Labor**
**200 Constitution Avenue NW**
**Washington, DC  20210**
                                  **866-4-USADOL**
Discusses the issues of meeting basic literacy needs and meeting them within the context of employment.

**6039  Business Currents**

**National Alliance of Business (NAB)**
**1201 New York Avenue NW**
**Washington, DC  20005**                  **202-289-2910**
                                  **FAX 202-289-1303**
Business Currents provides information about legislative and administrative actions affecting employment and training.

*Biweekly*

**6040  Career Inventories for the Learning Disabled**

**Slosson Educational Publications**
**538 Buffalo Road**
**East Aurora, NY  14052**                  **716-652-0930**
                                  **800-828-4800**
                                  **FAX 800-655-3840**
                      **http://www.slossom.com**
                  **e-mail: slosson@slosson.com**
*Steven Slosson, President*
*Mary Buchanan, Author*

These career assessment inventories take personality, ability, and interest into account in pointing LD students toward intelligent and realistic career choices.

**6041  Change Agent**

**Nat'l Center for Research in Vocational Education**
**2150 Shattuck Avenue**
**Berkeley, CA  94704**
                                  **800-762-4093**
                  **e-mail: dcarlson@uclink.berkley.edu**
*David Carlson, Contact*

A quarterly digest of center publications.

**6042 Cognitive Theory-Based Teaching and Learning in Vocational Education**

Center on Education and Training for Employment
Ohio State University
Columbus, OH 43210                 614-292-4353
                                   800-848-4815
                              FAX 614-292-1260
                    http://www.cete.org/products
      e-mail: ericacve@magnus.acs.ohio_state.edu
*Ruth Thomas, Author*
*Ruth Thomas*

This research review explores the relevance to vocational curriculum and instruction of theories of cognition.

**6043 College Students with Learning Disabilities: A Handbook**

Learning Disabilities Association of America
4156 Library Road
Pittsburgh, PA 15234               412-341-1515
                              FAX 412-344-0224
                    http://www.ldaamerica.org
e-mail: ldanatl@usaor.net /info@ldaamerica.org
*Jane Browning, Director*
*Heathe Smith, Clerk*

An overview of related issues, including information on Section 504 as it pertains to students with learning disabilities and college personnel.

**6044 Current Developments in Employment and Training**

National Governors Association
444 N Capitol Street NW
Washington, DC 20001               202-624-5353
                              FAX 202-624-5313
                         http://www.nga.org
                    e-mail: mjensen@nga.org
*Martin Jensen, Editor*

Highlights issues and areas of interest related to employment and training.

*Bimonthly*

**6045 For Employers: A Look at Learning Disabilities**

Learning Disabilities Association of America
4156 Library Road
Pittsburgh, PA 15234               412-341-1515
                              FAX 412-344-0224
                    http://www.ldaamerica.org
e-mail: ldanatl@usaor.net /info@ldaamerica.org
*Jane Browning, Director*
*Heathe Smith, Clerk*

Helps employers understand learning disabilities.

**6046 Fundamentals of Job Placement**

RPM Press
PO Box 31483
Tucson, AZ 85751                   520-886-1990
                                   888-810-1990
                              FAX 520-886-1990
                    http://www.rpmpress.com
                    e-mail: pmccray@theriver.com
*James Costello, Author*
*Jan Stonebraker, Operations Manager*
*Paul , President*

Provides step-by-step guidance for educators, special counselors and vocational rehabilitation personnel on how to develop job placement opportunities for special needs students and adults.

**6047 Fundamentals of Vocational Assessment**

RPM Press
PO Box 31483
Tucson, AZ 85751                   520-886-1990
                                   888-810-1990
                              FAX 520-866-1900
                    http://www.rpmpress.com
                    e-mail: pmccray@theriver.com
*Jan Stonebraker, Operations Manager*
*Paul , President*

Provides step-by-step guidance for educators, counselors and vocational rehabilitation personnel on how to conduct professional vocational assessments of special needs students.

**6048 Handbook for Developing Community Based Employment**

RPM Press
PO Box 31483
Tucson, AZ 85751                   520-886-1990
                                   888-810-1990
                              FAX 520-866-1990
                    http://www.rpmpress.com
                    e-mail: pmccray@theriver.com
*Jan Stonebraker, Operations Manager*
*Paul , President*

Provides step-by-step guidance for educators and vocational rehabilitation personnel on how to develop community-based employment training programs for severely challenged workers.

**6049 JOBS V**

PESCO International
21 Paulding Street
Pleasantville, NY 10570            914-769-4266
                                   800-431-2016
                              FAX 914-769-2970
                         http://www.pesco.org
                    e-mail: pesco@pesco.org
*Joseph Kass, President*
*Charles Kass, Vice President*
*Kathy Griffin, Sales Manager*

A software program matching people with jobs, training, employment and local employers. Provides job outlooks for the next five years.

**6050 Job Access**

Ability Awareness
1001 W 17th Street
Costa Mesa, CA 92627               949-854-8700
                              FAX 949-548-5966
                              TDY:949-548-5966
                    http://www.jobaccess.org
                    e-mail: marketing@jobaccess.org
*Chat Cooper, Executive Director*

Job Access, a program of ability awareness, is an internet driven system dedicated to employ qualified people with disabilities. Employers can list job postings and review our resume bank. People with disabilities seeking employment can also search for jobs.

**6051   Job Accommodation Handbook**

RPM Press
PO Box 31483
Tucson, AZ  85751                    520-886-1990
                                     888-810-1990
                              FAX 520-866-1990
                         http://www.rpmpress.com
                    e-mail: pmccray@theriver.com
*Paul McCray, Author*
*Jan Stonebraker, Operations Manager*
*Paul McCray, President*

Provides how-to-do-it for counselors, job placement specialists, educators and others on how to modify jobs for special needs workers.

**6052   Job Interview Tips for People with Learning Disabilities**

Learning Disabilities Association of America
4156 Library Road
Pittsburgh, PA  15234                412-341-1515
                              FAX 412-344-0224
                       http://www.ldaamerica.org
      e-mail: ldanatl@usaor.net /info@ldaamerica.org
*Jane Browning, Director*
*Heathe Smith, Clerk*

*$18.00*

**6053   Life Centered Career Education: Assessment Batteries**

Council for Exceptional Children
1110 N Glebe Road
Arlington, VA  22201                 703-620-3660
                                     888-232-7733
                              FAX 703-264-9494
                              TDY:703-264-9446
                        http://www.cec.sped.org/
                    e-mail: service@ces.sped.org
*Donn E Brolin, Author*
*Victor Erickson, Exhibits manager*
*Liz Martinez, Publications Director*

The LCCE Batteries are curriculum-based assessment instruments designed to measure the career education knowledge and skills of regular and special education students. There are two alternative forms of a Knowledge Battery and two forms of the Performance Batteries. These assessment tools can be combined with instruction to determine the instructional goals most appropriate for a particular student.

*827 pages*

**6054   National Dissemination Center**

Academy for the Educational Development
PO Box 1492
Washington, DC  20013-149            202-884-8200
                                     800-695-0285
                              FAX 202-884-8841
                              TDY:800-695-0285
                          http://www.nichcy.org
                     e-mail: nichcy@aed.org
*Susan Ripley, Executive Director*

A newsletter offering information on vocational assessment, books and more for the disabled.

**6055   National Forum on Issues in Vocational Assessment**

MCD, Stout Vocational Rehabilitation Institute
University of Wisconsin-Stout
Menomonie, WI  54751                 715-232-2475
                              FAX 715-232-2356
                   e-mail: admissions@uwstout.edu
*RR Fry, Author*
*John Lui MD, Institute Director*
*Marilyn Mars, Director of Purchasing Departmen*

The impact potential of curriculum-based vocational assessment in our schools.

**6056   National Governors Association**

444 N Capitol Street NW
Washington, DC  20001                202-624-5353
                              FAX 202-624-5313
                              http://www.nga.org
                       e-mail: mjensen@nga.org
*Martin Jensen, Editor*

Highlights issues and areas of interest related to employment and training.

*Bimonthly*

**6057   PWI Profile**

Goodwill Industries of America
9200 Rockville Pike
Bethesda, MD  20814                  240-333-5200
                            http://www.goodwill.org/
                     e-mail: contactus@goodwill.org
Newsletter that deals with employment of persons with disabilities.

**6058   Rehabilitation Research and Training Center on Supported Employment**

PO Box 842011
Richmond, VA  23284                  804-828-1851
                              FAX 804-828-2193
                              TDY:804-828-2494
                       http://www.worksupport.com
                   e-mail: vbrooker@mail1.vcu.edu
*Jeanne Roberts, Graphics Designer*
*Valerie Brooker, Associate Director*

Helps disabled persons find and hold a job. Designed to assist persons with significant disabilities to obtain and maintain community integrated competitive employment through high quality research and disseminations.

**6059   School to Adult Life Transition Bibliography**

Special Education Resource Center
25 Industrial Park Road
Middletown, CT  06457                860-632-1485
                              FAX 860-632-8870
                           http://www.ctserc.org
                     e-mail: jlebrrun@ctserc.org
*Jen Lebrun, Director*

A bibliography of references and resources.

**6060    Self Advocacy as a Technique for Transition**

KUAF-University of Kansas
1122 W Campus Road
Lawrence, KS  66045                       785-864-2700
                                        FAX 785-864-4149
                              http://www.soe.ku.edu/sped
                              e-mail: spedrecpt@ku.edu
*Chriss Walther-Thomas, Chairperson*

A joint effort involved in researching the effect of self-advocacy training upon adolescents with learning disabilities.

**6061    Self-Directed Search**

Psychological Corporation
555 Academic Court
San Antonio, TX  78204                    800-232-1223
                                          800-211-8378
                                        FAX 210-949-4475
                              http://www.hbtpc.com
*John Hiolland, Author*
*John Hiolland*

This self-administered, self-scored and self-interpreted test enables the individual to make education and career choices.

**6062    Self-Supervision: A Career Tool for Audiologists, Clinical Series 10**

American Speech-Language-Hearing Association
10801 Rockville Pike
Bethesda, MD  20852                       301-897-5700
                                          800-638-2255
                                        FAX 301-897-7358
                                        TDY:301-897-5700
                              http://www.asha.org
                              e-mail: randerson@asha.org
*Rick Anderson, Marketing Director*
*Eileen Pietrarton, Executive Director*

Describes concepts of supervision, defines and presents strategies for self-supervision, discusses supervisory accountability and covers issues of self-supervision within supervisor format.

**6063    Transition and Students with Learning Disabilities**

Pro-Ed
8700 Shoal Creek Boulevard
Austin, TX  78757                         512-451-3246
                                          800-897-3202
                                        FAX 512-451-8542
                              http://www.proedinc.com
                              e-mail: info@proedinc.com
*Patton Blalock, Author*
*Don Hamhill, President*

Provides important information about academic, social and vocational planning for students with learning disabilities.

**6064    Vocational Entry Skills for Secondary Students**

Learning Disabilities Association of America
4156 Library Road
Pittsburgh, PA  15234                     412-341-1515
                                        FAX 412-344-0224
                              http://www.ldaamerica.org
                    e-mail: ldanatl@usaor.net /info@ldaamerica.org
*Jane Browning, Director*
*Heathe Smith, Clerk*

**6065    Vocational Training and Employment of Autistic Adolescents**

Charles C Thomas Publisher
2600 S 1st Street
Springfield, IL  62704                    217-789-8980
                                          800-258-8980
                                        FAX 217-789-9130
                              http://www.ccthomas.com
                              e-mail: books@ccthomas.com
*Elva Duran, Author*
*Michael Thomas, Director*
*Claire Slagle, Assistant Director*

How professionals and parents are now advocating, demanding and arranging that persons receive vocational training and equal rights for the disabled.

**6066    Work America, Workforce Economics Workforce Trends**

National Alliance of Business (NAB)
1201 New York Avenue NW
Washington, DC  20005                     202-289-2888
                                          800-787-7788
                                        FAX 202-289-1303
                              http://www.nab.com
                              e-mail: jonesr@nab.com

Award winning publications that feature timely articles related to the human resource agenda. Workforce development and education improvement is covered from the business perspective.

**6067    Workforce Investment Quarterly**

National Governor's Association (NGA)
444 N Capitol Street NW
Washington, DC  20001                     202-624-5300
                                        FAX 202-624-7870
                              http://www.nga.org
                              e-mail: info@nga.org
*Rey Scheppach, Director*

Highlights issues and area interests related to employment and training. Contact NGA for more information.

## Alabama

**6068    Department of Human Resources**

Alabama Department of Human Resources
50 N Ripley Street
Montgomery, AL  36130                     334-242-1160
                                        FAX 334-242-0198
                              http://www.dhr.state.al.us
                              e-mail: ogapi@dhr.state.al.us
*Page Walley MD, Commissioner*
*Barry Spear, Audio-Visual Information Officer*

Partners with communities to promote family stability and to provide for the self-sufficiency of vulnerable Alabamians.

**6069  Easter Seals Achievement Center**

510 W Thomason Circle
Opelika, AL  36801                    334-745-3501
                                 FAX 334-745-5808
            http://www.alabama.easter-seals.org
*Cheryl Bynum, Director Rehabilitation Services*
*Barry Cavan, Chief Executive Officer*

Job training and employment services, occupational skills training, job placement/competitive-supported employment, vocational evaluation/situation assessment, work adjustment.

**6070  Easter Seals Adult Services Center**

1180 Fairview Road
Little Rock, AR  72212                501-221-8400
                                     877-221-8400
                                 FAX 501-221-8842
              http://www.ar.easter-seals.org
             e-mail: mail@ar.easter-seals.org
*Priscilla Handley, Administrator*
*Sharon Moone-Jochums, President/CEO*

Adult day programming, personal and social supports, camping and recreation for children, job placement/competitive-supported employment, work services.

**6071  Easter Seals Alabama**

6005-A E Shirley Lane
Montgomery, AL  36617                 334-395-4489
                                     800-388-7325
                                 FAX 334-395-4492
            http://www.alabama.easter-seals.org
              e-mail: alaseal@worldnet.att.net
*Johnny Webster, President/CEO*

Job training and employment services, senior community service employment program.

**6072  Easter Seals Camp ASCCA**

Easter Seals Camp ASCCA
5278 Camp ASCCA Drive
Jackson's Gap, AL  36861              256-825-9226
                                     800-843-2267
                                 FAX 256-825-8332
            http://www.alabama.easter-seals.org
                 e-mail: info@campascca.org
*Matt Rickman, Camp Director*
*John Stephenson, Administrator*

Camp respite for adults and children, camperships, canoeing, day camping for adults, day camping for children, therapeutic horseback riding.

**6073  Easter Seals Capilouto Center for the Deaf**

5950 Monticello Drive
Montgomery, AL  36117                 334-244-8090
                                 FAX 334-244-1183
                                 TDY:334-272-6754
            http://www.alabama.easter-seals.org
                 e-mail: lstokley@jccd.org
*Lynne Stockley, Executive Director*
*Brenda Culpepper, Work Conditioning Specialist*

Job training and employment services, occupational skills training, job placement/competitive-supported employment, vocational evaluation/situation assessment, work adjustment.

**6074  Easter Seals Opportunity Center**

United Way
6300 McClellan Boulevard
Anniston, AL  36206                   256-820-9960
                                 FAX 256-820-9592
            http://www.alabama.easter-seals.org
          e-mail: mikenancyoppcen@aol.com
*Mike Almaroad, Administrator*
*Barry Cavan, Chief Executive Officer*

Job training and employment services, occupational skills training, job placement/competitive-supported employment, vocational evaluation/situation assessment, work adjustment.

**6075  Easter Seals Rehabilitation Center**

2906 Citizens Parkway
Selma, AL  36701-3915                 334-872-8422
                                     800-499-1816
                                 FAX 334-872-3907
            http://www.alabama.easter-seals.org
          e-mail: dwhite@alabama.easter-seals.org
*David White, Program Director*
*Larry Lewis, Chief Executive Officer*

Early education and care for ages zero through five, and preschool educational and developmental services for ages three and five.

**6076  Easter Seals Rehabilitation Center: Northwest Alabama**

1450 E Avalon Avenue
Muscle Shoals, AL  35661             256-381-1110
                                 FAX 256-314-5105
            http://www.alabama.easter-seals.org
               e-mail: easter@hiwaay.net
*Danny Prince, Administrator*
*Shiella Phillips, Director*

Job training and employment services, occupational skills training, job placement/competitive-supported employment, vocational evaluation/situation assessment, work services.

**6077  Easter Seals: Birmingham Area**

200 Beacon Parkway W
Birmingham, AL  35209                 205-942-6277
                                 FAX 205-945-4906
            http://www.alabama.easter-seals.org
              e-mail: esba@eastersealsbham.org
*Johnny Webster, Director*
*Lisa Howard, Office Manager*

Job training and employment services, occupational skills training, job placement/competitive-supported employment, vocational evaluation/situation assessment, work adjustment.

**6078    Easter Seals: West Alabama**

1110 6th Avenue E
Tuscaloosa, AL  35401            205-759-1211
                                 800-726-1216
                            FAX 205-349-1162
        http://www.alabama.easter-seals.org
           e-mail: eswa@eastersealswestal.org
*Lorie Robinson, Administrator*
*Bettye Hughes, Office Manager*

Job training and employment services, occupational skills training, job placement/competitive-supported employment, vocational evaluation/situation assessment, work adjustment.

**6079    Good Will Easter Seals**

2448 Gordon Smith Drive
Mobile, AL  36617                251-471-4303
                                 800-411-0068
                            FAX 251-476-4303
        http://www.alabama.easter-seals.org
*Frank Harkins, Chief Executive Officer*

Job training and employment services, occupational skills training, job placement/competitive-supported employment, vocational evaluation/situation assessment, work adjustment.

**6080    State Vocational Rehabilitation Agency of Alabama**

Division of Rehabilitation Services
2129 E South Boulevard
Montgomery, AL  36116-2455      334-281-8780
                                 800-441-7607
                            FAX 334-281-1973
            http://www.rehab.state.al.us
            e-mail: sshivers@rehab.state.al.us
*Steve Shivers, Commissioner*
*Jim , Assistant Commissioner*

State vocational rehabilitation agencies provide direct services to persons with disabilities, including persons with learning disabilities. The services may include evaluation and diagnosis; counseling, guidance, and referral services; vocational and other training services; transportation to rehabilitation services; and assistive devices.

**6081    Workforce Development Division**

Alabama Dept. of Economic & Community Affairs
401 Adams Avenue
Montgomery, AL  36103-5690      334-242-5100
                            FAX 334-242-5855
            http://www.adeca.state.al.us
            e-mail: stevew@adeca.state.al.us
*Steve Walkley, Division Director*
*Tim Alford, Executive Director*

Customer focused to help Americans access the tools they need to manage their careers through information and high quality services and to help US companies find skilled workers. Alabama's Career Center System is a network of one-stop centers designed to offer these services. These centers are co-located or electronically linked to provide streamlined services.

## Alaska

**6082    Alaska Department of Labor**

1111 W 8th Street
Juneau, AK  99801               907-465-2700
                            FAX 907-465-2784
                http://www.state.ak.us
        e-mail: Commissioner_Labor@labor.state.ak.us
*Greg O'Claray, Commissioner*
*Ed Fisher, Deputy Commissioner*

Responsible for the overall management of the department's programs and resources; serves as a liaison with other state, federal, and local governmental agencies and the legislature.

**6083    State Vocational Rehabilitation Agency of Alaska**

Division of Vocational Rehabilitation Services
1016 W 6th Avenue
Anchorage, AK  99501            907-269-3632
                            FAX 907-269-3632
        http://www.edu.state.ak.us/vocrehab/home.html
State vocational rehabilitation agencies provide direct services to persons with disabilities, including persons with learning disabilities. The services may include evaluation and diagnosis; counseling, guidance, and referral services; vocational and other training services; transportation to rehabilitation services; and assistive devices.

## Arizona

**6084    Division of Employment & Training Rehabilitation Services**

1789 W Jefferson Street
Phoenix, AZ  85007              602-542-4910
                            FAX 602-542-5339
                http://www.de.state.az.us
*David Berns, Director*
*Juanita Hernandez, Executive Assistant*

**6085    Rehabilitation Services Administration**

1789 W Jefferson Street
Phoenix, AZ  85007              602-542-3332
                            FAX 602-542-3778
                            TDY:602-542-6049
            http://www.de.state.az.us/rsa/
                e-mail: azrsa@azdes.gov
*Skip Bingham, Administrator*
*Craig Warren, Deputy Administrator*
*Linda Olson, Planning/Evaluation*

Helping people with disabilities become economically independent and decreasing or eliminating their need for ongoing government supports through integrated, meaningful, sustained work. This is achieved through a rehabilitation process which engages applicants and clients fully in actively exploring their vocational interests, abilities, capabilities and service/process options and in making choices.

## Arkansas

**6086 Arkansas Employment Security Department: Office of Employment & Training Services**

1 Pershing Circle
North Little Rock, AR 72114      501-682-2121
FAX 501-682-2273
http://www.state.ar.us/esd/
e-mail: mel.thrash.aesd@mail.state.ar.us
*Artee Williams, Director*
*Mel Thrash, Deputy Director*
*Ron Snead, Employment Assistance*

Employment related services that contribute to the economic stability of Arkansa and its citizens. These services are provided to employers, the workforce and the general public.

**6087 Arkansas Rehabilitation Services Employment Center: Office for the Deaf & Hearing Impaired**

4601 W Markham
Little Rock, AR 72205      501-686-2800
FAX 501-686-9418
http://www.arsinfo.org
e-mail: jlgatewood@ars.state.ar.us
*John Wyvill, Commissioner*
*Sue Gaskin, Special Programs*

Providing opportunities for individuals with hearing impairment to work and have productive and independent lives.

**6088 Department of Human Services: Division of Developmental Disabilities Services**

Donaghey Plaza N, Slot N503
Little Rock, AR 72203      501-682-8665
FAX 501-682-8380
TDY:501-682-1332
http://www.state.ar.us/ddds/ddsinsti.html
*James Green PhD, Director*
*Kurt Knickrehm, Director Human Services*
*Joe Quinn, Communications*

Offers a wide range of services and supports to Arkansans with developmental disabilities and their families.

**6089 Department of Workforce Education**

Three Capitol Mall
Little Rock, AR 72201      501-682-1500
FAX 501-682-1509
http://www.work-ed.state.ar.us/
e-mail: steve.franks@mail.state.ar.us
*Steve Franks MD, Director*
*Garland Hankins, Adult Education*
*John Davidson, Career/Technical Education*

Provides the leadership and contributes resources to serve the diverse and changing workforce training needs of the youth and adults of Arkansas.

**6090 State Vocational Rehabilitation Agency of Arkansas**

ARS, Vocational & Technical Education Division
1616 Brookwood Drive
Little Rock, AR 72203      501-296-1600
800-330-0632
FAX 501-296-1655
TDY:501-296-1669
http://www.arsinfo.org
e-mail: jlgatewood@ars.state.ar.us
*John Wyvill, Commissioner*
*Barbara Lewis, Field Services*
*Sue Gaskin, Special Programs*

Provides direct services to persons with disabilities, including persons with learning disabilities. The services may include evaluation and diagnosis, counseling, guidance, and referral services, vocational and other training services, transportation to rehabilitation services, and assistive devices. Offering opportunities for individuals with disabilities to lead productive and independent lives.

**6091 Workforce Investment Board**

Arkansas State Employment Board
PO Box 2981
Little Rock, AR 72203      501-371-1020
FAX 501-371-1030
TDY:800-285-1131
http://www.state.ar.us/workforce/
e-mail: arkansasweb@mail.state.ar.us
*Sandra Winston, Executive Director*
*Elroy Willoghpy, Deputy Director*
*Sharon Robinette, Workforce Analysis/Reporting*

Operates workforce centers that offer locally developed and operated services linking employers and jobseekers through a statewide delivery system. Conveinient centers are designed to eliminate the need to visit different locations. The centers integrate multiple workforce development programs into a single system, making the resources much more accessible and user friendly to jobseekers as well as expanding services to employers.

## California

**6092 Adult Education**

California Department of Education
1430 N Street
Sacramento, CA 95814      916-319-0800
FAX 916-319-0100
http://www.cde.ca.gov/adulteducation
e-mail: joconell@cde.ca.gov
*Jack O'Conell, Director*
*Sue Bennett, Educational Options*

Elementary basic skills and tutor/literacy training are offered on or off site using language masters, audiocassettes, videos and computers with internet access. Workplace literacy training will also be provided, with groups of students physically coming into the Center or hooking up to the Center from their workplace by borrowing materials or going online. In the latter case, instructors will meet with students at the work site on a regular schedule for evaluation and consultation.

**6093 California State Deparment of Education GED**

1430 N Street
Sacramento, CA 95814 916-319-0800
800-331-6316
FAX 916-319-0100
http://www.cde.ca.gov/ged/
e-mail: GEDoffic@cde.ca.gov
*Nancy Edmunds, Program Coordinator*

Provides access to a general high school education by
providing many local classes and testing services.

**6094 Department of Rehabilitation**

2000 Evergreen Street
Sacramento, CA 94244 916-263-8981
FAX 916-263-7474
TDY:916-263-7477
http://www.dor.ca.gov
e-mail: publicaffairs@dor.ca.gov
*Catherine PhD, Director*

Assists Californians with disabilities in obtaining and
retain employment and maximizing their ability to
live independently in their communities. Working
with individuals of every type and category of disability, DOR provides vocational rehabilitational services to eligible Californians.

**6095 Easter Seals Central California**

9010 Soquel Drive
Aptos, CA 95003 4002 831-684-2166
FAX 831-685-6055
http://www.centralcal.easter-seals.org
e-mail: donna@es-cc.org
*Donna Alvarez, Vice President Finance*
*Bruce Hinman, Chief Executive Officer*

Recreational services for adults, residential camping
programs.

**6096 Easter Seals Southern California**

11110 Artesia Boulevard
Cerritos, CA 90703 562-860-7270
877-855-2279
FAX 562-860-1680
http://www.essc.org
e-mail: Dee.Prescott@essc.org
*Dee Prescott, Regional Director*
*Sandy Meredith, Program Director*

Adult day programing/personal and social supports.

**6097 Easter Seals Superior California**

3205 Hurley Way
Sacramento, CA 95864-3898 916-485-6711
888-887-3257
FAX 916-485-2653
http://www.easterseals-superiorca.org
e-mail: info@easterseals-superiorca.org
*Gary Kasai, President*

Job training and employment services, occupational
skills training, job placement/competitive-support
employment, vocational evaluation/situational assessment and work adjustment.

**6098 Easter Seals: Redondo Beach**

700 N Pacific Coast Highway
Redondo Beach, CA 90277 310-376-3445
800-404-3445
FAX 310-376-5567
http://www.cssc.org
e-mail: dee.prescott@cssc.org
*Dee Prescott, Regional Director*
*Mark Whitley, President*

Job training and employment services, occupational
skills training, job placement/competitive-support
employment, vocational evaluation/situational assessment and work adjustment.

**6099 Easter Seals: Southern California**

4727 Labrea Avenue 8100 West
Los Angeles, CA 90038 323-257-3006
877-877-8565
FAX 323-954-3775
http://www.essc.org
e-mail: lupe.trevizoreinoso@essc.org
*Lupe Trevizo-Reinoso, Regional Director*
*Mark Whitley, President*

Job training and employment services, occupational
skills training, job placement/competitive-support
employment, vocational evaluation/situational assessment and work adjustment.

**6100 Easter Seals: Van Nuys**

Easter Seals: Van Nuys
16946 Sherman Way
Van Nuys, CA 91406 818-996-9902
800-996-6302
FAX 818-996-1606
http://www.cssc.org
e-mail: paula.pompa-craven@cssc.org
*Paula Pompa-Craven, Regional Director*
*Mark Whitley, President*

Job training and employment services, occupational
skills training, job placement/competitive-support
employment, vocational evaluation/situational assessment and work adjustment.

**6101 Employment Development Department**

State of California
800 Capitol Mall
Sacramento, CA 95814 916-654-7111
FAX 916-653-0597
http://www.edd.ca.gov
e-mail: phenning@edd.ca.gov
*Patrick Henning, Director*
*Sally McKeag, Chief Deputy Director*
*Diego Haro, Job Service Branch*

Vocational training and placement for citizens of California.

## Colorado

**6102 Easter Seals Colorado**

5755 W Alameda Avenue
Lakewood, CO 80226 3500 303-233-1666
FAX 303-233-1028
http://www.eastersealsco.org
*Lynn Robinson, CEO*

Job training and employment services, occupational skills training, job placement/competitive-support employment, vocational evaluation/situational assessment and work adjustment.

**6103 Human Services: Division of Developmental Disabilities**

**Human Services: Division of Developmental Disabil**
**3824 W Princeton Circle**
**Denver, CO 80236**                303-866-7450
                                 FAX 303-866-7470
                                 TDY:303-866-7471
http://www.cdhs.state.co.us/ohr/dds/DDS_center
e-mail: sandi.zagyi@state.co.us
*Fred DeCrescentis, Director*
*Deb Lucero, Administrative Assistant*

Provides leadership for the direction, funding and operation of community based services to people with developmental disabilities within Colorado.

**6104 Human Services: Division of Vocational Rehabilitation**

**1575 Sherman Street**
**Denver, CO 80203**                303-866-4150
                                 FAX 303-866-4905
                                 TDY:303-866-4150
http://www.cdhs.state.co.us/ods/dvr/index.html
e-mail: keri.wells@state.co.us
*Nancy Smith, Director*
*Debbie Powell, Administrative Assistant*

Assists individuals whose disabilities result in barriers to employment to succeed at work and live independently. Building partnerships to improve opportunities for safety, self-sufficiency and dignity for the people of Colorado.

**6105 State Vocational Rehabilitation Agency of Colorado**

**Div. of Rehabilitation/Dept. of Human Services**
**2211 W Evans Ave**
**Denver, CO 80223**                303-866-4150
                         e-mail: diana.huerta@state.co.us
*Diana Huerta, Director*

State vocational rehabilitation agencies provide direct services to persons with disabilities, including persons with learning disabilities. The services may include evaluation and diagnosis; counseling, guidance, and referral services; vocational and other training services; transportation to rehabilitation services; and assistive devices.

## Connecticut

**6106 Bureau of Adult Education & Training**

**25 Industrial Park Road**
**Middletown, CT 06457**                860-807-2110
                                 FAX 860-807-2112
http://www.state.ct.us/sde/deps/adult/index.htm
e-mail: gail.brooks-lemkin@po.state.ct.us
*Maureen Staggenborg, Acting Bureau Chief*
*Gail Brooks-Lemkin, Technical Assistant*

Committed to quality adult education programs which are accessible to all Connecticut adults and lead to mastery of the essential proficiences needed to function as productive citizens in work, family and community environments. Programs are available at local schools throughout the state. Offers basic literacy, elementary education, English language proficiency, secondary school completion and preparation for equivalency examinations.

**6107 Department of Labor**

**200 Folly Brook Boulevard**
**Wethersfield, CT 06109**                860-263-6000
                                 TDY:860-263-6074
http://www.ctdol.state.ct.gov/dol
e-mail: dol.help@po.state.ct.us
*Shaun Cashman, Commissioner*
*Thomas Hutton, Assistant Commissioner*

Assisting workers to become competitive in a global economy, we take a comprehensive approach to meeting the needs of workers, employers and other agencies that serve them.

**6108 Department of Social Services: Vocational Rehabilitation Program**

**25 Sigourney Street**
**Hartford, CT 06106**                860-424-4844
                                 800-537-2549
                                 TDY:860-424-4839
http://www.dss.state.ct.us
e-mail: pgr.dss@po.state.ct.us
*John Galiette, Director*
*Evelyn Knight, Program Assistant*

Provides services to people with most significant physical or mental disabilities to assist them in their effort to enter or maintain employment. The agency also oversees a statewide network of community based, consumer controlled, independent living centers that promote independence for people with disabilities.

**6109 Easter Seals Connecticut**

**174 Williamantic Road**
**Chaplin, CT 06235**                860-455-1331
                                 FAX 860-455-1372
http://www.eastersealsco.org
*Kathy Buck, Director Adult Programs*
*John Quinn, Chief Executive Officer*

Adult day programming/personal, social supports and senior services.

**6110 Easter Seals Employment Industries**

**Easter Seals Rehabilitation Center**
**122 Avenue of Industry**
**Waterbury, CT 06705**                203-236-0188
                                 FAX 203-236-0183
http://www.eswct.com
e-mail: eswct@eswct.com
*Ron Bourque, Director Vocational Rehab Svcs.*
*Francis DeBlasio, Chief Executive Officer*

Job training, employment services, vocational evaluation/situational assessment and work services.

**6111 Easter Seals Fulfillment Enterprises**

226 Upton Road
Colchester, CT 06415      860-537-4595
     FAX 860-537-9673
http://www.ct.easter-seals.org
e-mail: jsalois@easterseals.org
*Jerry Salois, Director Operations*
*John Quinn, Chief Executive Officer*

Job training, employment services, vocational evaluation/situational assessment and work services.

**6112 Easter Seals: Uncasville**

152 Norwich-New London Turnpike
Uncasville, CT 06382      860-456-1727
*Kathy Buck, Director Adult Programs*
*John Quinn, Chief Executive Officer*

Job training, employment services, vocational evaluation/situational assessment and work services.

**6113 Easter Seals: Waterbury**

22 Tompkins Street
Waterbury, CT 06708      203-754-5141
     FAX 203-754-1198
http://www.ct.easter-seals.org
e-mail: fdeblasio@eswct.com
*Francis DeBlasio, President*
*Rupa Gandi, Vice President*

Job training, employment services, vocational evaluation/situational assessment and work services.

## Delaware

**6114 Division of Vocational Rehabilitation**

Delaware Department of Labor
4425 N Market Street
Wilmington, DE 19809      302-761-8275
     FAX 302-761-6611
http://www.delawareworks.com
e-mail: cynthia.fairwell@state.de.us
*Andrea Guest, Director*
*Cynthia Fairwell, Program Specialist*

Mission is to provide information opportunitie, and resources to individuals with disabilities, leading to success in employment and independent living.

**6115 Easter Seals Delaware and Maryland Shore**

61 Corporate Circle
New Castle, DE 19720      302-324-4444
     800-677-3800
     FAX 302-324-4442
     TDY:302-324-4444
http://www.de.easter-seals.org
e-mail: badami@esdel.org
*William Adami, Vice President*
*Sandra Tuttle, President*

Job training, employment services, vocational evaluation/situational assessment and work services.

**6116 Easter Seals Dover Enterprise**

100 Enterprise Place
Dover, DE 19904      302-678-3353
     800-677-3800
     FAX 302-678-3650
http://www.de.easter-seals.org
e-mail: gcassedy@esdel.org
*Gary Cassedy, Chief Executive Officer*
*Sandra Tuttle, President*

Job training, employment services, vocational evaluation/situational assessment and work services.

**6117 Easter Seals Georgetown Professional Center**

600 N DuPont Highway
Georgetown, DE 19947      302-856-7364
     877-204-3276
     FAX 302-856-7296
http://www.de.easter-seals.org
e-mail: cea@gt.esdel.org
*Pam Reuther, Director Sussex County*
*Sandra Tuttle, President*

Job training, employment services, vocational evaluation/situational assessment and work services.

**6118 Workforce Investment: Virtual Career Network**

Department of Labor
4425 N Market Street
Wilmington, DE 19802      302-761-8085
     FAX 302-761-6634
http://www.vcnet.net
e-mail: tsmith@state.de.us
*Barry Butler, Supervisor*
*Anne Farley, Director*

Many area offices for a one-stop employment and training integrated service delivery system. Much of our information is also available online.

## District of Columbia

**6119 Centers for Independent Living Program: Rehabilitation Services Administration**

1400 Florida Avenue NE
Washington, DC 20002      202-388-0033
     FAX 202-398-3018
     TDY:202-388-0277
http://www.dccil.org
e-mail: info@dccil.org
*Richard Simms, Executive Director*
*kandra hall, Coordinator*

Consumer controlled, cross disability, community based, private nonprofit organization that promotes independent life styles for people with significant disabilities in the District of Columbia.

**6120 Department of Employment Services**

Government of the District of Columbia
64 New York Avenue NE
Washington, DC 20002      202-724-7000
     FAX 202-724-5683
     TDY:202-673-6994
*Gregory Irish, Director*

Helps consider career decisions and offer vocational and placement assistance at several area training locations.

**6121 Department of Human Services: Bureau of Training & Employment**

810 1st Street NE
Washington, DC 20002          202-442-8663
                              FAX 202-263-7518
                              TDY:202-442-8598
http://www.rsa@dcgovernment.com
e-mail: answersplease@dhs.washington.dc.us /
                              rsa@dcgo

*Elizabeth Parkers, Administrator*
*Eliza Spermen, Program Support Assistant*

**6122 District of Columbia Department of Education: Vocational & Adult Education**

400 Maryland Avenue SW
Washington, DC 20202          202-205-5451
                              800-872-5327
                              FAX 202-205-8748
http://www.ed.gov/offices/OVAE
e-mail: ovae@ed.gov

To help all people achieve the knowledge and skills to be lifelong learners, to be successful in their chosen careers, and to be effective citizens.

**6123 State Vocational Rehabilitation Agency**

Rehabilitation Services Administration
810 1st Street NE
Washington, DC 20002          202-442-8663
                              FAX 202-442-8742
e-mail: elizabeth.parker@dc.gov

*Elizabeth Parker, Administrator*
*Cheryl Bolden, Administrative Assistant*

Provides direct services to persons with disabilities, including persons with learning disabilities. The services may include evaluation and diagnosis, counseling, guidance, and referral services, vocational and other training services, transportation to rehabilitation services and assistive devices. Our goal is to assist those we serve in becoming independent and self sufficient in the home and in the community and to prepare for, enter and maintain gainful employment.

## Florida

**6124 College Living Experience**

6555 Nova Drive
Davie, FL 33317               954-370-5142
                              800-486-5058
                              FAX 954-370-1895
http://www.cleinc.net
e-mail: secretary@cleinc.net

*Irene PhD, Director*
*Eliza , Assistant Director*

For young adults with learning difficulties who have average intellectual abilities but who would benefit from: intensive academic tutoring, advocacy and guidance, a comprehensive independent living skills program, social skills training, vocational support services and apartment living. One central program with a variety of experiences, including college, vocational school and internships, all within walking distance.

**6125 Division of Vocational Rehabilitation**

Florida Department of Education
2002 Old Saint Augustine Road
Tallahassee, FL 32301         850-245-3399
                              800-451-4327
                              FAX 850-245-3316
                              TDY:800-451-4327
http://www.rehabworks.org

*Linda Parnell, Director*
*Amanda Grines, Office Assistant*

Statewide employment resource for businesses and people with disabilities. Our mission is to enable individuals with disabilities to obtain and keep employment.

**6126 Easter Seals Broward County Florida**

Easter Seals Broward County Florida
6951 W Sunrise Boulevard
Plantation, FL 33313          954-792-8772
                              FAX 954-791-8275
http://www.broward.easterseals.com
e-mail: info@broward.easterseals.com

*Susan Armiger, CEO*

Job training, employment services, vocational evaluation/situational assessment and work services.

**6127 Easter Seals Florida: East Coast Region**

6050 Babcock Street SE
Palm Bay, FL 32909            321-723-4474
                              FAX 321-676-3843
http://www.fl.easter-seals.org
e-mail: gedwards@fl.easter-seals.org

*Gail Edwards, Executive Director*
*Robert Griggs, President*

Job training, employment services, vocational evaluation/situational assessment and work services.

**6128 Easter Seals Miami-Dade**

1475 NW 14th Avenue
Miami, FL 33125               305-325-0470
                              FAX 305-325-0578
http://www.miami.easter-seals.org
e-mail: essdade@aol.com

*Joan Bornstein MD, Director*
*Jorge Alvarez, Information Specialist*

Job training, employment services, vocational evaluation/situational assessment and work services.

**6129 Easter Seals North Florida**

910 Myers Park Drive
Tallahassee, FL 32301         850-222-4465
                              FAX 850-222-5950
http://www.northflorida.easter-seals.org
e-mail: enorthflorida@aol.com

*Christine Hall, CEO/President*

Job training, employment services, vocational evaluation/situational assessment and work services.

**6130 Easter Seals Southwest Florida**

Easter Seals Southwest Florida
350 Braden Avenue
Sarasota, FL 34243-2096    941-355-7637
800-807-7899
FAX 941-351-9711
http://www.swfl.easterseals.com
*Mary Hitchcock, President*

Job training, employment services, vocational evaluation/situational assessment and work services.

**6131 Florida Workforce Investment Act**

Department of Labor & Employment Security
1947 Commonwaelth Lane
Tallahassee, FL 32303    850-921-1119
FAX 850-921-1101
http://www.workforceflorida.com
*Kathleen McLeskey, Acting Director*

Provides job-training services for economically disadvantaged adults and youth, dislocated workers and others who face significant employment barriers.

**6132 TILES Project: Transition/Independent Living/Employment/Support**

Family Network on Disabilities of Florida
2735 Whitney Road
Clearwater, FL 33760    727-523-1130
800-825-5736
FAX 727-523-8687
http://www.fndfl.org
e-mail: fnd@fndfl.org
*Tom Nurse, Program Director*
*Jan , Executive Director*

Provides training information to enable individuals with disabilities and the parents, family members, guardians, advocates, or other authorized representatives to participate more effectively with professionals in meeting the vocational, independent living and rehabilitation needs of people with disabilities in Florida.

## Georgia

**6133 Easter Seals East Georgia**

Easter Seals Georgia
1500 Wrightsboro Road
Augusta, GA 30904-2411    706-667-9695
866-667-9695
FAX 229-435-6278
http://www.eastersealseastgeorgia.org
e-mail: sthomas@esega.org
*Sheila Thomas, Executive Director*

Job training, employment services, vocational evaluation/situational assessment and work services.

**6134 Easter Seals Middle Georgia**

602 Kellam Road
Dublin, GA 31021    478-275-8850
FAX 478-275-8852
http://www.middlegeorgia.easterseals.com
*Wayne Peebles, President/CEO*

Job training, employment services, vocational evaluation/situational assessment and work services.

**6135 Easter Seals Southern Georgia**

Easter Seals Southern Georgia
1906 Palmyra Road
Albany, GA 31701    229-439-7061
800-365-4583
FAX 229-435-6278
http://www.southerngeorgia.easterseals.com
e-mail: benglish@swga-easterseals.org
*Beth English, Executive Director*
*Matt Hatcher, Chief Financial Officer*

Job training, employment services, vocational evaluation/situational assessment and work services.

**6136 Vocational Rehabilitation Services**

Georgia Department of Labor
148 Andrew Young International Blvd
Atlanta, GA 30303    404-232-3910
FAX 404-232-3912
TDY:404-232-3911
http://www.vocrehabga.org
e-mail: rehab@dol.state.ga.us
*Bobby Pack, Commissioner*
*Ken Armstrong, Office Assistant*

Operates 5 integrated and interdependent programs that share a primary goal — to help people with disabilities to become fully productive members of society by achieving independence and meaningful employment.

## Hawaii

**6137 Vocational & Rehabilitation Agency Hawaii: Division of Vocational Rehab & Services for the Blind**

Department of Human Services
PO Box 339
Honolulu, HI 96809    808-692-7719
FAX 808-692-7727
TDY:808-586-5167
http://www.state.hi.us/dhs/vr
e-mail: nshim@dhs.state.hi.us
*Neil Shim, Administrator*
*Lilian Poller, Director*

State vocational rehabilitation agencies provide direct services to persons with disabilities, including persons with learning disabilities. The services may include evaluation and diagnosis, counseling, guidance, and referral services, vocational and other training services, transportation to rehabilitation services, and assistive devices.

## Idaho

**6138 Department of Commerce & Labor**

Department of Commerce & Labor
317 W Main Street
Boise, ID 83735 0001    208-332-3570
FAX 208-334-6430
TDY:800-377-1363
http://www.cl.idaho.gov
e-mail: rvaldez@dds.state.id.us
*Roger Madsen, Director*
*Rogelio Valdez, Disability Determinations*

An equal opportunity employer/program with auxiliary aids and services available upon request to individuals with disabilities.

**6139  Easter Seals-Goodwill Staffing Services**

Easter Seals-Goodwill Staffing Services
1465 S Vinnell Way
Boise, ID  83709                         208-373-1299
                                  FAX 208-378-9965
        http://www.esgw-nrm.easter-seals.org
                  e-mail: marcib@esgw.org
*Marci Bailey, Manager*
*Michelle Belknap, Chief Executive Officer*

Job training, employment services, vocational evaluation/situational assessment and work services.

**6140  Easter Seals-Goodwill Working Solutions**

Easter Seals-Goodwill Staffing Services
1613 N Park Centre Boulevard
Nampa, ID  83651                         208-466-2671
                                  FAX 208-466-2537
        http://www.esgw-nrm.easter-seals.org
                  e-mail: landisr@esgw.org
*Landis Rossi, Coordinator*
*Michelle Belknap, Chief Executive Officer*

Job training, employment services, vocational evaluation/situational assessment and work services.

**6141  Idaho Department of Commerce & Labor**

Idaho Department of Labor
317 Main Street
Boise, ID  83735                         208-332-3570
                                  FAX 208-334-6430
                                  TDY:800-377-1363
                        http://www.cl.idaho.gov
              e-mail: rvaldez@dds.state.id.us
*Roger Madsen, Director*
*Rogelio Valdez, Disability Determinations*

Provides vocational training services for economically disadvantaged adults and youth, dislocated workers and others who face significant employment barriers.

**6142  State Vocational Rehabilitation Agency**

State of Idaho
650 W State
Boise, ID  83720 0096                    208-334-3390
                                  FAX 208-334-5305
                    http://www2.state.id.us/idvr
              e-mail: scook@idvr.state.id.us
*Michael Graham, Administrator*
*Sue Payne, Chief Field Services*
*Sue Cook, Assistant Chief Field Services*

State vocational rehabilitation agencies provide direct services to persons with disabilities, including persons with learning disabilities. The services may include evaluation and diagnosis, counseling, guidance, and referral services, vocational and other training services, transportation to rehabilitation services, and assistive devices.

**6143  Temporary Assistance for Needy Families: Idaho Department of Health and Welfare**

450 W State Street 4th Floor
Boise, ID  83720-0036                    208-334-0606
                                  FAX 208-332-7362
                        http://www.2.state.id.us
              e-mail: BCEH@idhw.state.id.us
*Karl Kurtz, Director of Health and Welfare*
*Dian Prince, Administrative Assistant*

Provides assistance and work opportunities to needy families by granting states the federal funds and wide flexibility to develop and implement their own welfare programs.

# Illinois

**6144  Easter Seals Central Illinois**

2715 N 27th Street
Decatur, IL  62526                       217-429-1052
                                  FAX 217-423-7605
              http://www.easterseals-ci.org
              e-mail: info@easterseals-ci.org
*Janet Kelsheimer, President*
*Margie Malone, Office Manager*

Job training, employment services, vocational evaluation/situational assessment and work services.

**6145  Easter Seals Missouri**

Easter Seals Missouri
602 E 3rd Street
Alton, IL  62002                         618-462-7325
                                  FAX 618-462-8170
              http://www.mo.easterseals.org
        e-mail: lynnstonecipher@mo.easterseals.com
*Lynn Stonecipher, Manager*
*Craig Byrd, Chief Executive Officer*

Job training, employment services, vocational evaluation/situational assessment and work services.

**6146  Easter Seals Youth at Risk**

Easter Seals Illinois
120 W Madison
Oak Park, IL  60302                      708-524-8700
                                  FAX 708-524-4902
              http://www.eastersealschicago.org
              e-mail: wkern@eastersealschicago.org
*Bill Kern, Program Manager*
*F , President*

Job training, employment services, vocational evaluation/situational assessment and work services.

**6147  State Vocational Rehabilitation Agency**

State Vocational Rehabilitation Agency
100 S Grand Avenue
East Springfield, IL  62762              217-524-7551
                                         800-843-6154
                                  FAX 217-558-4270
                                  TDY:217-557-2507
                        http://www.dhs.state.il.us
              e-mail: ors@dhs.state.il.us
*Rob Kilbury, Director*
*Kris Smith, Assistant Director*

We help people with physical or learning disabilities find and keep jobs. Our goal is to help our customers find quality employment that pays a living wage and offers a chance for advancement. Specialized services for the deaf and blind or visually impaired.

**6148  Temporary Assistance for Needy Families**

Department of Human Services
100 E Grand Avenue
Springfield, IL 62762     217-785-0480
FAX 217-557-2134
http://www.dhs.state.il.us
e-mail: carol.adams@dhs.state.il.us
*Marva Arnold, Director*
*Ginger White, Administrative Assistant*

Focus on transitional services. Major points include creating goals, continuation of Work Pays program, cash assistance, subsidized employment, and medical benefits.

## Indiana

**6149  Easter Seals Arc of Northeast Indiana**

Easter Seals Arc of Northeast Indiana
4919 ProjeCourts Drive
Fort Wayne, IN 46825     260-456-4534
FAX 260-745-5200
http://www.eastersealsarcnein.org
e-mail: shinkle@esarc.org
*Stephen Hinkle, CEO*
*Sue Dubai, Administrative Assistant*

Job training, employment services, vocational evaluation/situational assessment and work services.

**6150  Easter Seals Crossroads Industrial Services**

8302 E 33rd Street
Indianapolis, IN 46226     317-897-7320
FAX 317-897-9763
http://www.eastersealscrossroads.org
*Brett Bennett, Division Director*

Job training, employment services, vocational evaluation/situational assessment and work services.

**6151  Easter Seals Crossroads Rehabilitation Center: Indiana**

4740 Kingsway Drive
Indianapolis, IN 46205     317-466-1000
FAX 317-466-2000
TDY:317-479-3232
http://www.eastersealscrossroads.org
e-mail: info@eastersealscrossroads.org
*James Vento, President*
*Judy Otto, Vice President*

Job training, employment services, vocational evaluation/situational assessment and work services.

**6152  Easter Seals: Bridgepointe**

1329 Applegate Lane
Clarksville, IN 47129     812-283-7908
FAX 812-283-6248
e-mail: cmarshall@bridgepoint.org
*Caren Marshall, Executive Director*

Job training, employment services, vocational evaluation/situational assessment and work services.

**6153  Indiana Vocation Rehabilitation Services Goodwill Industries**

Department of Vocational Rehabilitation
1452 Vaxter Avenue
Clarksville, IN 47129     812-288-8261
FAX 812-282-7048
http://www.ivrs.state.in.us
*Delbert Hayden, Supervisor*

Purpose is to assist the community by providing services which allow individuals to maximize their potential and to participate in work, family and the community. To do this we will provide rehabilitation, education and training.

**6154  State Vocational Rehabilitation Agency**

Division of Disability, Aging, & Rehab. Services
402 W Washington Street
Indianapolis, IN 46204     317-232-1319
800-545-7763
FAX 317-232-6478
http://www.in.gov
e-mail: phedden@fssa.state.in.us
*Mike Hedden, Deputy Director*
*Karen Smith, Office Manager*

Provides direct services to persons with disabilities, including persons with learning disabilities. The services may include evaluation and diagnosis; counseling, guidance, and referral services, vocational and other training services, transportation to rehabilitation services, and assistive devices.

## Iowa

**6155  Easter Seals Center**

2920 30th Street
Des Moines, IA 50310     515-274-1529
866-533-9344
FAX 515-274-6434
TDY:515-274-8348
http://www.ia-easter-seals.orgls.org
e-mail: info@eastersealsia.org
*Marcia Tope, Coordinator Intake/QA*
*Donna Elbrecht, Chief Executive Officer*

Job training, employment services, vocational evaluation/situational assessment and work services.

**6156  Easter Seals Iowa**

401 NE 66th Avenue
Des Moines, IA 50313     515-274-1529
866-533-9344
FAX 515-274-6434
TDY:515-274-8348
http://www.ia-easter-seals.orgls.org
e-mail: info@eastersealsia.org
*Marcia Tope, Coordinator Intake/QA*
*Donna Elbrecht, Chief Executive Officer*

Job training, employment services, vocational evaluation/situational assessment and work services.

**6157   Iowa Bureau of Community Colleges**
Department of Education
Grimes State Office Building
Des Moines, IA  50319          515-281-3125
                              FAX 515-281-6544
http://www.state.ia.us/educate/commcoll.html
e-mail: sally.schroeder@iowa.gov
*Sally Schroeder, Director*

**6158   Iowa JOBS Program: Division of Economic Assistance**
Department of Human Services
Hoover State Building
Des Moines, IA  50319          515-281-5011
                              FAX 515-281-7791
http://www.dhs.state.ia.us
*Kevin Cannon, Director*

**6159   Iowa Vocational Rehabilitation Agency**
Department of Education
Grimes State Office Building
Des Moines, IA  50319          515-281-5294
                              FAX 515-281-4703
http://www.state.ia.us/educate/directory.html
*Steve Wooderson, Administrator for Vocational Reh*
*Kathy Petosa, Administrative Assistant*

**6160   State Vocational Rehabilitation Agency**
Iowa Division of Vocational Rehabilitation Service
510 E 12th Street
Des Moines, IA  50319 0240     515-281-4211
                               800-532-1486
                              FAX 515-281-7645
                              TDY:515-281-4211
http://www.dvrs.stste.ia.us
e-mail: swooderson@dvrs.state.ia.us
*Stephen Wooderson, Administrator*
*Teresa Scott, Typist Advanced*

We work for and with individuals with disabilities to achieve their employment, independence and economic goals. Economic independence and more and better jobs are what we are about for Iowans with disabilities.

## Kansas

**6161   Easter Seals Kansas**
3636 N Oliver
Wichita, KS  67220             316-744-1428
                               888-337-6287
                              FAX 316-744-1428
http://www.goodwilleastersealsks.org
*Curtis Tatum, Vice President Programs*
*Marie Mareda, Chief Executive Officer*

Job training, employment services, vocational evaluation/situational assessment and work services.

**6162   Kansas Vocational Rehabilitation Agency**
300 SW Oakley, Biddle Building
Topeka, KS  66606              785-296-3911
                              FAX 785-368-6688
*Joyce Cussimanio, Commissioner*

To assist people with disabilities achieve suitable employment and independence.

**6163   Office of Vocational Rehabilitation**
Department of Vocational Rehabilitation
915 SW Harrison Street
Topeka, KS  66612              785-296-3959
                              FAX 785-296-2173
http://www.srskansas.org
e-mail: cmxa@srskansas.org
*Clarissa Ashdown, Program Support Administrator*
*Laura Letters, Office Assistant*

Partnering to connect Kansans with support and services to improve lives. Vocational and transitional training.

## Kentucky

**6164   Easter Seals Employment Connections-Pennyrile**
755 Industrial Road
Madisonville, KY  42431        270-625-4840
http://www.klucas@eswky.easterseals.com
e-mail: dtinsley@ky-ws.easter-seals.org
*Donna Tinsley, Site Manager*
*Kenneth Lucas, Chief Executive Officer*

Job training, employment services, vocational evaluation/situational assessment and work services.

**6165   Easter Seals: West Kentucky**
Easter Seals
2229 Mildred Street
Paducah, KY  42001             270-444-9687
                               866-673-3565
                              FAX 270-444-0655
http://www.eswky.easter-seals.org
e-mail: info@ky-ws.easter-seals.org
*Kenneth Lucas, President/CEO*
*Lori Devine, Executive Secretary*

Job training, employment services, vocational evaluation/situational assessment and work services.

**6166   State Vocational Rehabilitation Agency**
Department of Vocational Rehabilitation
209 St. Clair Street
Frankfort, KY  40601           502-564-4440
                               800-372-7172
                              FAX 502-564-6745
http://www.kydor.state.ky.us/
e-mail: wfd.vocrehab@mail.state.ky.us
*Bruce Crump, Commissioner*
*Wanda Webber, Director for Finance*

Provides direct services to persons with disabilities, including persons with learning disabilities. The services may include evaluation and diagnosis; counseling, guidance, and referral services, vocational and other training services, transportation to rehabilitation services, and assistive devices.

## Louisianna

**6167   State Vocational Rehabilitation Agency**

Department of Social Services
8225 Florida Boulevard
Baton Rouge, LA  70806          225-925-4131
                                FAX 225-922-1515
                    http://www.dss.state.la.us
              e-mail: jwallace@lrs.dss.state.la.us
*James Wallace, Director*
*Claire Hymel, Assistant Director*
*Ed Barras, Community Rehabilitation*

Responsible for developing and providing social services and improving social conditions for the citizens of Louisiana, and for rehabilitating people with disabilities for employment.

## Maine

**6168   State Vocational Rehabilitation Agency**

Maine Bureau of Rehabilitation Services
2 Anthony Avenue
Augusta, ME  04333 0150          207-624-5950
                                 800-698-4440
                            FAX 207-624-5980
         http://www.state.me.us/rehab/index.htm
                e-mail: penny.plourde@maine.gov
*Laura Fortman, Commissioner*
*Gill Duson, Bureau Chief*
*Penny Plourde, Director*

Works to bring about full access to employment, independence and community integration for people with disabilities. Our three service provision units are Vocational Rehabilitation, Division for the Blind and Visually Impaired and Division of Deafness.

**6169   Temporary Assistance for Needy Families**

Department of Human Services
221 State Street
Augusta, ME  04333               207-287-2736
                            FAX 207-287-3005
                       http://www.maine.gov
*Jack Nicholas, Commissioner*

Focuses on transitional services.

## Maryland

**6170   Maryland Technology Assistance Program**

Department of Disabilities
2301 Argonne Drive
Baltimore, MD  21218              410-554-9230
                                  800-832-4827
                             FAX 410-554-9237
                             TDY:866-881-7488
                        http://www.mdtap.org
                   e-mail: mdtap@mdtap.org
*Jessica Vollmer, Office Manager*

Offers information and referrals, reduced rate loan program for assistive technology, five regional display centers, presentations and training on request.

**6171   State Vocational Rehabilitation Agency**

Div. of Rehab. Services, Dept. of Education
2301 Argonne Drive
Baltimore, MD  21218              410-554-9385
                             FAX 410-554-9412
                     http://www.msde.state.md.us
               e-mail: hdavis@dors.state.md.us
*Robert Burns, Assistant State Superintendent*
*Harvey Davis, Director Field Services*
*Sue Schaffer, Director Workforce/Technology*

Operates more than 20 statewide offices and also operates the Workforce and Technology Center, a comprehensive rehabilitation facility in Baltimore. Rehabilitation representatives also work in many Maryland One-Stop Career Centers.

## Massachusettes

**6172   Easter Seals: Massachusetts**

89 S Street
Boston, MA  02111                 617-226-2640
                             FAX 617-737-9875
                   http://www.eastersealsma.org
             e-mail: maryd@eastersealsma.org
*Mary D'Antonino, Information Specialist*
*Kirk Joslin, President*

Job training, employment services, vocational evaluation/situational assessment and work services.

**6173   Easter Seals: Worcester**

484 Main Street
Worcester, MA  01608              508-757-2756
                             FAX 508-831-9768
                   http://www.eastersealsma.org
             e-mail: maryd@eastersealsma.org
*Mary D'Antonino, Information Specialist*
*Kirk Joslin, President*

Job training, employment services, vocational evaluation/situational assessment and work services.

**6174   JOBS Program: Massachusetts Employment Services Program**

Dept of Transitional Assistance/Office of Health
600 Washington Street
Boston, MA  02111                 617-348-8400
                             FAX 617-348-8575
                http://www.state.ma.us/dta/index.htm
*John Wagner, Commissioner*
*Diana Ward, Assistant*

The Employment Services Program is a joint federal and state funded program whose primary goal is to provide a way to self-sufficiency for TAFDC families. ESP is an employment-oriented program that is based on a work-first approach.

**6175   Massachusetts Job Training Partnership Act: Department of Employment & Training**

Division of Career Services
CF Hurley Building, !st Floor
Boston, MA  02114                 617-626-5680
                             TDY:888-527-1912
                       http://www.detma.org
                  e-mail: ddesousa@detma.org
*David DeSousa, Director*
*Maria Caira, Commissioner Assistant*

Supplies information on the local labor market and assists companies in locating employees.

**6176  State Vocational Rehabilitation Agency**

**Massachusetts Rehabilitation Commission**
**27 Wormwood Street**
**Boston, MA  02210 1616**          617-204-3600
                                   800-245-6543
                                   FAX 617-727-1354
                                   TDY:800-223-3212
           http://www.state.ma.is/mrc.mrc.htm
           e-mail: commissioner@mrc.state.ma.us
*Elmer Bartels, Commissioner*

Provides public vocational rehabilitation, independent living and disability determination services for residents with disabilities in Massachusetts.

## Michigan

**6177  Easter Seal Michigan**

**Easter Seals Michigan**
**1401 N Michigan**
**Saginaw, MI  48602 1516**          989-753-4773
                                     800-757-3257
                                 FAX 989-753-4795
           http://www.mi-ws.easterseals.org
                       e-mail: esofmi@aol.com
*Julie Dorcey, Regional Director*
*John Cocciolone, Chief Executive Officer*

Job training, employment services, vocational evaluation/situational assessment and work services.

**6178  Easter Seals Collaborative Solutions**

**Easter Seals Collaborative Solutions**
**1105 N Telegraph**
**Waterford, MI  48328**              248-975-9769
                                  FAX 248-338-2936
                                  TDY:248-338-1188
                http://www.essmichigan.org
           e-mail: essmichigan@essmichigan.org
*Wendy Standifer, Program Manager*
*John Cocciolone, Chief Executive Officer*

Job training, employment services, vocational evaluation/situational assessment and work services.

**6179  Michigan Commission for the Blind: Deafblind Unit**

**201 N Washington Square, 2nd Floor**
**Lansing, MI  48909**               517-373-2062
                                     800-292-4200
                                 FAX 517-335-5140
                                 TDY:517-373-4025
           http://www.mcb1.org /another website:
                                     www.michi
                e-mail: heibecks@michigan.gov
*Patrick Cannon, State Director*
*Leamon Jones, Director of Consumer Services*

Provides opportunities to the deaf and or blind community to achieve employability and function independently in society.

**6180  Michigan Jobs Commission**

**201 N Washington Square**
**Lansing, MI  48913**               517-373-4871
                                 FAX 517-373-0314
                   e-mail: bolinb@state.mi.us
*Carl Bourdelais, Regional Director*

**6181  Michigan Workforce Investment Act**

**Public Policy Assoc. Inc**
**119 Pere Marquette Drive**
**Lansing, MI  48912**               517-485-4477
                                 FAX 517-485-4488
                http://www.publicpolicy.com
              e-mail: ppa@publicpolicy.com
*Jeffrey Padden, President*
*Nancy Hewat, Executive Officer*

**6182  State Vocational Rehabilitation Agency**

**Michigan Rehabilitation Services**
**PO Box 30010**
**Lansing, MI  48909**               517-373-3390
                                     800-605-6722
                                 FAX 517-373-0565
                                 TDY:888-605-6722
                http://www.michigan.gov/mrs
           e-mail: balthazarj@michigan.gov
*Jaye Balthazar, Director*

State vocational rehabilitation agencies provide direct services to persons with disabilities, including persons with learning disabilities. The services may include evaluation and diagnosis; counseling, guidance, and referral services; vocational and other training services; transportation to rehabilitation services; and assistive devices.

## Minnesota

**6183  Goodwill/Easter Seals Minnesota**

**Goodwill/Easter Seals Minnesota**
**19463 Evans Street NW**
**Elk River, MN  55330**             763-274-1822
                                 FAX 763-274-1825
           http://www.goodwilleasterseals.org
*Tony Cassiday, Coordinator*
*Michael Wirth-Davis, Chief Executive Officer*

Job training, employment services, vocational evaluation/situational assessment and work services.

**6184  Goodwill/Easter Seals: St. Cloud**

**50 S 2nd Street**
**St. Cloud, MN  56387**             320-654-9527
                                 FAX 320-654-9542
           http://www.goodwilleasterseals.org
*Julie Danda, Program Services Manager*
*Michael Wirth-Davis, Chief Executive Officer*

Job training, employment services, vocational evaluation/situational assessment and work services.

**6185 Goodwill/Easter Seals: St. Paul**

Goodwill/Easter Seals: St. Paul
553 Fairview Avenue
St. Paul, MN 55104          651-379-5800
                           800-669-6719
                      FAX 651-379-5804
                      TDY:651-767-3300
           http://www.goodwilleasterseals.org
        e-mail: kjmatter@goodwilleasterseals.org
*Kelly Matter, Program Services Vice President*
*Michael Wirth-Davis, Chief Executive Officer*

Job training, employment services, vocational evaluation/situational assessment and work services.

**6186 Goodwill/Easter Seals: Willmar**

2424 1st Street S
Willmar, MN 56201          320-214-9238
                      FAX 320-214-9140
           http://www.goodwilleasterseals.org
              e-mail: pfwl@wilmar.com
*Melissa Peterson, Program Services Manager*
*Michael Wirth-Davis, Chief Executive Officer*

Job training, employment services, vocational evaluation/situational assessment and work services.

**6187 Minnesota Department of Employment and Economic Development**

Minnesota Workforce Center
332 Minnesota St, Suite E200
St. Paul, MN 55101-1351          651-297-1291
                http://www.mnwfc.org
    e-mail: mdes.customerservice@state.mn.us
*Bonnie Elsey, Director*

The Department of Employment and Economic Development is Minnesota's principal economic development agency, with programs promoting business expansion and retention, workforce development, international trade, community development and tourism.

**6188 School-to-Work Outreach Project**

Institute on Community Integration
111A Pattee Hall
Minneapolis, MN 55455          612-626-7220
                      FAX 612-624-9344
              http://www.ici.umn.edu
             e-mail: walla001@umn.edu
*Terry Wallace, Research Associate*
*David Johnson, Director*

A primary goal of the project is to improve school-to-work opportunities for students with disabilities through the identification and documentation of exemplary school-to-work activities. This is achieved through a nomination/application/review process conducted by the School-to-Work Outreach Project.

**6189 State Vocational Rehabilitation Agency: Minnesota Department of Economics Security**

Rehabilitation Service Branch
390 N Robert Street
St. Paul, MN 55101          651-296-9981
                           800-328-9095
                      FAX 651-297-5159
           http://www.deed.state.mn.us
        e-mail: paul.bridges@state.mn.us
*Paul Bridges, Director*
*Jan McAllister, Administrative Assistant*

State vocational rehabilitation agencies provide direct services to persons with disabilities, including persons with learning disabilities. The services may include evaluation and diagnosis, counseling, guidance, and referral services, vocational and other training services, transportation to rehabilitation services, and assistive devices.

## Mississippi

**6190 Department of Vocational Rehabilitation Services: Mississippi**

PO Box 1698
Jackson, MS 39215          601-853-5100
                           800-443-1000
                      FAX 601-853-5325
                      TDY:601-351-1586
           http://www.mdrs.state.ms.us
*Gary Neely, President*
*Hs McMillan, Executive Director*

**6191 State Vocational Rehabilitation Agency: Vocational Rehabilitation Division**

Mississippi Department of Rehabilitation Services
1281 Highway 51
Jackson, MS 39215          601-853-5230
                           800-443-1000
                      FAX 601-853-5205
                      TDY:601-853-5310
           http://www.mdrs.state.ms.us/
        e-mail: gneely@mdrs.state.ms.us
*Jerry Sawyer, Director*
*Natalie Wagner, Executive Assistant*

State vocational rehabilitation agencies provide direct services to persons with disabilities, including persons with learning disabilities. The services may include evaluation and diagnosis; counseling, guidance, and referral services; vocational and other training services; transportation to rehabilitation services; and assistive devices.

## Missouri

**6192 Rehabilitation Services for the Blind**

Family Support Division
615 E 13th Street
Kansas City, MO 64106
816-889-2677
800-592-6004
FAX 816-889-2504
http://www.dss.mo.gov/dfs/rehab
e-mail: Kimberly.Gerlt@dss.mo.gov
*Kimberly Gerlt, Operations Coordinator*
*Rachel Labrado, Director*

Creating opportunities for eligible blind and visually impaired people in order that they may attain personal and vocational success.

**6193 State Vocational Rehabilitation AgencyDepartment of Elementary & Secondary Education**

3024 Dupont Circle
Jefferson City, MO 65109-0525
573-751-3251
877-222-8963
FAX 573-751-1441
TDY:573-751-0881
http://www.vr.dese.state.mo.us
*Jeanne Loyd, Assistant Commissioner*
*Twyla Yardley, Supervisor*

State vocational rehabilitation agencies provide direct services to persons with disabilities, including persons with learning disabilities. The services may include evaluation and diagnosis, counseling, guidance, and referral services, vocational and other training services, transportation to rehabilitation services, and assistive devices.

## Montana

**6194 Easter Seals-Goodwill Career Designs**

4400 Central Avenue
Great Falls, MT 59405
406-761-3680
FAX 406-761-3680
http://www.esgrw-nrm.easter-seals.org
e-mail: sharonod@esgw.org
*Sharon Odden, Vice President Program Services*
*Michelle Belknap, Chief Executive Officer*

Job training, employment services, vocational evaluation/situational assessment and work services.

**6195 Easter Seals-Goodwill Store**

951 S 29th Street W
Billings, MT 59102
406-656-4020
FAX 406-656-3750
http://www.esgw-nrm.easter-seals.org
e-mail: gwbillings@mcn.net
*Rhonda Haynes, Manager*
*Michelle Belknap, Chief Executive Officer*

Job training, employment services, vocational evaluation/situational assessment and work services.

**6196 Easter Seals-Goodwill Working Partners**

4141 1/2 S Main Street
Conrad, MT 59425
406-278-9121
FAX 406-271-2073
http://www.esgw-nrm.easter-seals.org
e-mail: sandrab@esgw.org
*Sandra Bucher, Case Manager*
*Michelle Belknap, Chief Executive Officer*

Job training, employment services, vocational evaluation/situational assessment and work services.

**6197 Easter Seals-Goodwill Working Partners: Great Falls**

205 9th Avenue S
Great Falls, MT 59405
406-452-2196
FAX 406-453-2160
http://www.esgrw-nrm.easter-seals.org
e-mail: joelc@csgw.org
*Joel Corda, Supervisor*
*Michelle Belknap, Chief Executive Officer*

Job training, employment services, vocational evaluation/situational assessment and work services.

**6198 Easter Seals-Goodwill Working Partners: Hardin**

501 N Center Avenue
Hardin, MT 59034
406-665-3500
FAX 406-665-1395
http://www.esgrw-nrm.easter-seals.org
e-mail: opweasle@state.mt.us
*Oma Weasle, Supervisor*
*Carla Colstad, Office Assistant*

Job training, employment services, vocational evaluation/situational assessment and work services.

**6199 State Vocational Rehabilitation Agency**

Department of Public Health & Human Services
111 N Sanders Street
Helena, MT 59604
406-444-5622
FAX 406-444-1970
http://www.dphhs.state.mt.gov
e-mail: rwynia@mt.gov
*Robert Wynia, Director*

State vocational rehabilitation agencies provide direct services to persons with disabilities, including persons with learning disabilities. The services may include evaluation and diagnosis, counseling, guidance, and referral services, vocational and other training services, transportation to rehabilitation services, and assistive devices.

## Nebraska

**6200 Easter Seals Nebraska**

2727 W 2nd
Hastings, NE 68901
402-462-3031
800-471-6425
FAX 402-462-2040
http://www.ne.easter-seals.org
e-mail: kginder@ne.easter-seals.org
*Karen Ginder, President*

Job training, employment services, vocational evaluation/situational assessment and work services.

**6201 Job Training Program**

**Nebraska Department of Economic Development**
PO Box 94666
Lincoln, NE 68509          402-471-3780
                          800-426-6505
                       FAX 402-471-3365
                  http://www.assist.neded.org
                   e-mail: lshaal@neded.org
*Lori Shaal, Job Training Coordinator*

Provides training assistance on projects that offer an
opportunity for economic development in Nebraska.
Use of the funds is limited to eligible companies and
eligible training projects.

**6202 State Vocational Rehabilitation Agency: Quality
Employment Solutions**

**State Department of Education**
PO Box 94987
Lincoln, NE 68509          402-471-3644
                          877-637-3422
                       FAX 402-471-0788
                http://www.vocrehab.state.ne.us
         e-mail: vr_stateoffice@vocrehab.state.ne.us
*Frank Lloyd, Assistant Commissioner of Ed.*

We help people with disabilities make career plans,
learn job skills, get and keep a job. Our goal is to prepare people for jobs where they can make a living
wage and have access to medical insurance.

## Nevada

**6203 Bureau of Services to the Blind & Visually
Impaired**

**Bureau of Services to Blind and Visually Impaired**
505 E King Street
Carson City, NV 89701          775-684-4244
                          FAX 775-684-4186
                  http://www.detr.state.nv.us
                   e-mail: detbsb@nvdetr.org
*Maureen Cole, Administrator*

Services to the Blind and Visually Impaired (BSBVI)
provides a variety of services to eligible individuals,
whose vision is not correctable by ordinary eye care.
Adaptive training, independence skills, low vision exams and aids, mobility training and vocational rehabilitation are offered.

**6204 Nevada Economic Opportunity Board:
Community Action Partnership**

**Nevada Economic Opportunity Board**
PO Box 270880
Las Vegas, NV 89127-4880          702-647-1510
                          FAX 702-647-6639
                       http://www.eobcc.org
*Marcia Walker, Executive Director*

Located in one of the fastest growing and most diverse
communities in the United States, the Economic Opportunity Board of Clark County is a highly innovative Community Action Agency. Our mission is to
eliminate poverty by providing programs, resources,
services, and advocacy for self-sufficiency and economic empowerment.

**6205 Nevada Governor's Council on Rehabilitation &
Employment of People with Disabilities**

505 E King Street
Carson City, NV 89701          775-684-3200
                          FAX 775-684-4186
                  http://www.detr.state.nv.us
                   e-mail: djsanders@nvdetr.org
*Donna Sanders, Assistant Director*

To help insure vocational rehabilitation programs are
consumer oriented, driven and result in employment
outcomes for Nevadans with disabilities. Funding for
innovation and expansion grants.

**6206 Rehabilitation Division Department of
Employment, Training & Rehabilitation**

**Bureau of Services to Blind and Visually Impaired**
505 E King Street
Carson City, NV 89701 3705          775-684-4244
                          FAX 775-684-4186
                       TDY:775-684-8400
                  http://www.detr.state.nv.us
                   e-mail: detbsb@nvdetr.org
*Maureen Cole, Administrator*

Providing options and choices for Nevadans with disabilities to work and live independently. Our mission
will be accomplished through planning, implementing and coordinating assessment, employment, independent living and training.

## New Hampshire

**6207 Department of Health & Human Services: New
Hampshire**

129 Pleasant Street
Concord, NH 03301          603-271-4688
                          800-852-3345
                       FAX 603-271-4912
                       TDY:800-735-2964
                  http://www.dhhs.nh.gov
*Nicoli Whitley, Public Information Officer*
*John Stephen, Commissioner*

**6208 Easter Seals New Hampshire**

54 Pleasant Street
Claremont, NH 03743          603-543-3795
                  http://www.easterseals.nh.org
               e-mail: cmcmahon@eastersealsnh.org
*Chris McMahon, Chief Operations Officer*
*Larry Gammon, President*

Job training, employment services, vocational evalu-
ation/situational assessment and work services.

**6209 Easter Seals: Keene**

12 Kingsbury Street
Keene, NH 03431          603-355-1067
                          800-307-2737
                       FAX 603-358-3947
                  http://www.easterseals.nh.org
               e-mail: cmcmahon@eastersealsnh.org
*Chris McMahon, Chief Operations Officer*
*Larry Gammon, President*

Job training, employment services, vocational evaluation/situational assessment and work services.

**6210  Easter Seals: Manchester**

555 Auburn Street
Manchester, NH  03103          603-623-8863
                                800-870-8728
                          FAX 603-625-1148
                http://www.easterseals.nh.org
           e-mail: cmcmahon@eastersealsnh.org
*Chris McMahon, Chief Operations Officer*
*Larry Gammon, President*

Job training, employment services, vocational evaluation/situational assessment and work services.

**6211  State Vocational Rehabilitation Agency**

Department of Education
21 South Fruit
Concord, NH  03301          603-271-3471
                            800-299-1647
                      FAX 603-271-7095
                      TDY:603-271-3471
               http://www.ed.state.nh.us/VR
             e-mail: dlebrun@ed.state.nh.us
*Paul Leather, Director*
*Lillian Lee, Program Planner*

Assisting eligible New Hampshire citizens with disabilities secure suitable employment, financial and personal independence by providing rehabilitation services.

## New Jersey

**6212  Division of Family Development: New Jersey Department of Human Services**

PO Box 716
Trenton, NJ  08625          609-588-2163
                      FAX 609-588-3051
               http://www.state.nj.us
*Karen Highsmith, Director*

**6213  Easter Seals: Silverton**

Easter Seals Silverton
1195 Airport Road
Lakewood, NJ  08701          732-257-6662
                      FAX 732-730-0492
               http://www.eastersealsnj.org
*Brian Fitzgerald, President*

Job training, employment services, vocational evaluation/situational assessment and work services.

**6214  Eden Family of Services**

Eden Services
One Eden Way
Princeton, NJ  08540          609-987-0099
                      FAX 609-987-0243
               http://www.edenservices.org
             e-mail: info@edenservices.org
*David Holmes EdD, Executive Director/President*
*Anne Holmes, Director Outreach Support*
*Joani Truch, Administration/Communications*

Provides year round educational services, early intervention, parent training, respite care, outreach services, community based residential services and employment opportunities for individuals with autism.

**6215  New Jersey Council on Developmental Disabilities**

20 W State Street
Trenton, NJ  08625          609-292-3745
                            800-216-1199
                      FAX 609-292-7114
                      TDY:609-777-3238
               http://www.njddc.org
             e-mail: njddc@njddc.org
*Ethan Ellis, Executive Director*
*Jane Dunhamn, Events Coordinator*
*Sue Gottesman, Legislative Coordinator*

Promotes systems change, coordinates advocacy and research for 1.2 million residents with developmental and other disabilities.

**6216  New Jersey Technology Assistive Resource Program**

New Jersey Department of Labor
210 S Broad Street
Trenton, NJ  08608          609-777-0945
                            800-922-7233
                      FAX 609-777-0187
               http://www.njpanda.org
             e-mail: adadvocate@njpanda.org
*G Dickman, Chair*
*Marilyn Goldstein, Vice-Chair*

Assists individuals in overcoming barriers in the system and making assistive technology more accessible to individuals with disabilities throughout the state.

**6217  Programs for Children with Special Health Care Needs**

NJ Department of Health & Senior Services
50 E State Street
Trenton, NJ  08625          609-984-0755
                      FAX 609-292-9288
               http://www.state.nj.us.com
*Gloria Rodriguez, President*
*Cajwar Aamir, Senior Public Health Physician*

**6218  State Department of Education Education for Students with Disabilities**

Office of Vocational-Technical Career & Innovative
PO Box 500
Trenton, NJ  08625          609-633-0665
                      FAX 609-984-5347
               http://www.state.nj.us/education
             e-mail: pharris@doe.state.nj.us
*Patricia Harris, Administrative Assistant*
*Rochelle Hendricks, Director*

Assists the disabled student with changes from the school environment to the working world.

**6219 State Vocational Rehabilitation Agency**

New Jersey Department of Labor
135 E State Street
Trenton, NJ 08625-0398          609-292-5987
                                FAX 609-292-8347
                                TDY:609-292-2919
http://www.nj.gov/labor/dvrs/vrsindex.html
e-mail: dvraadmin@dol.state.nj.us
*Thomas Jennings, Director*
*Janice Pointer, Assistant Director*

Enables individuals with disabilities to achieve employment outcomes consistent with their strengths, priorities, needs, abilities and capabilities. Our division is here to help people with disabilites that are having trouble finding or holding a job because of their disability.

## New Mexico

**6220 Department of Human Services: Project Forward**

PO Box 2348
Santa Fe, NM 87504          505-827-7262
                            FAX 505-827-7203
*Marise McFadden, Contact*

**6221 New Mexico Department of Labor: Job Training Division**

Office Of Workforce Training and Development
1596 Pacheco Street
Santa Fe, NM 87505          505-827-6827
                            FAX 505-827-6812
http://www.dol.state.nm.us
e-mail: reese.fullerton@state.nm.us
*Reese Fullerton, Executive Director*
*Veronica Moya, Office Assistant*

Helps citizens of New Mexico from all walks of life find appropriate vocational trainings, and job placement.

**6222 State Vocational Rehabilitation Agency New Mexico**

Department of Education
435 St. Michaels Drive
Santa Fe, NM 87505          505-954-8511
                            800-224-7005
                            FAX 505-954-8562
http://www.dvrgetsjobs.com
e-mail: cmaple@state.nm.us
*Kathryn Maple-Cross, Director*
*Irene White, Administrative Assistant*

State vocational rehabilitation agencies provide direct services to persons with disabilities, including persons with learning disabilities. The services may include evaluation and diagnosis, counseling, guidance, and referral services, vocational and other training services, transportation to rehabilitation services, and assistive devices.

## New York

**6223 Commission for the Blind & Visually Handicapped**

Department of Social Services
74 State Street
Albany, NY 12207          518-474-1701
http://www.dfa.state.ny.us
e-mail: cbvh@dfa.state.ny.us
*John Johnson, Commissioner Children/Family*

Professionals and paraprofessionals are available to help those with low vision or blindness with vocational rehabilitation services.

**6224 Office of Curriculum & Instructional Support**

State Department of Adult Education
89 Washington Avenue
Albany, NY 12234          518-474-8892
                          FAX 518-474-0319
http://www.emsc.nysed.gov/workforce
e-mail: jstevens@mail.nysed.gov
*Jean Stevens, Assistant Commissioner*
*Richard Mills, Commissioner*

Works with those seeking General Educational Development diplomas and technical training.

**6225 Office of Vocational and Educational Services for Individuals with Disabilities**

New York State Education Department
One Commerce Plaza
Albany, NY 12234          518-474-3852
                          800-222-5627
                          FAX 518-473-9466
http://www.web.nysed.gov
e-mail: nlauria@mail.nysed.gov
*Richard Mills, Commissioner*
*Nancy Lauria, Director*

Promotes educational equality and excellence for students with disabilities while ensuring that they receive the rights and protection to which they are entitled, assure appropriate continuity between the child and adult services systems, and provide the highest quality vocational rehabilitation and independent living services to all eligible people.

## North Carolina

**6226 State Vocational Rehabilitation Agency**

Department of Health & Human Resources
2801 Mail Service Center
Raleigh, NC 27699          919-855-3500
                           FAX 919-733-7968
                           TDY:919-855-3579
http://www.dhhs.state.nc.us
e-mail: george.mccoy@ncmail.net
*Carmen Hooker-Odem, Secretary Health/Human Services*
*George McCoy, Director*

Vocational rehabilitation counselors work with business and community agencies to help them prepare their worksites to accomodate employees who have physical or mental disabilities. The division also provides services that encourage and reinforce independent living for the disabled.

## North Dakota

**6227 Division of Vocational Rehabilitation**

North Dakota Health & Human Services
600 S 2nd Street
Bismarck, ND 58504-5782          701-328-8800
                                 888-862-7342
                           FAX 701-328-8969
                           TDY:701-328-8968
       http://www.state.nd.us.humanservices
*Gene Hysjulien, Director*

Assists individuals with disabilities to achieve competitive employment and increased independence through rehabilitation services.

**6228 North Dakota Department of Career and Technical Education**

Special Needs Project
600 E Boulevard Avenue
Bismarck, ND 58505               701-328-3180
                           FAX 701-328-1255
               http://www.state.nd.us
               e-mail: mwilson@state.nd.us
*Dwight Crabtree, Assistant State Director*
*Gary Freier, Director for Special Needs*

The mission of the Board for Vocational and Technical Education is to work with others to provide all North Dakota citizens with the technical skills, knowledge, and attitudes necessary for successful performance in a globally competitive workplace.

**6229 North Dakota Workforce Development Council**

North Dakota Department of Commerce
1600 E Century Avenue, Suite 2
Bismarck, ND 58502               701-328-7266
                           FAX 701-328-5320
     http://www.growingnd.com/services/workforce
                 e-mail: jhirsch@state.nd.us
*James Hirsch, Director*
*Jill Splonskowski, Secretary*

The role of the North Dakota Workforce Development Council is to advise the Governor and the Public concerning the nature and extent of workforce development in the context of North Dakota's economic development needs, and how to meet these needs effectively while maximizing the efficient use of available resources and avoiding unnecessary duplication of effort.

**6230 Workforce Investment Act**

Governor's Employment & Training Forum
PO Box 5507
Bismarck, ND 58506               701-328-2836
                           FAX 701-328-1612
                           TDY:800-366-6888
               http://www.jobnd.com
               e-mail: mdaley@state.nd.us
*Maren Daley, Executive Director*

Literacy coaching and further vocational training.

## Ohio

**6231 Bureau of Workforce Services**

145 S Front Street
Columbus, OH 43215              614-466-3817
                           FAX 614-728-5938
               http://www.ohioworkforce.org
*Bill Demidovich, Deputy Director*

Oversees the implementation of the job training partnership act and employment and training programs in the state of Ohio.

**6232 State Vocational Rehabilitation Agency**

Ohio Rehabilitation Services Commission
400 E Campus View Boulevard
Columbus, OH 43235 4604          614-438-1200
                                 800-282-4635
                           FAX 614-785-5010
                           TDY:614-438-1726
               http://www.state.oh.us
         e-mail: rsc_rir@vscnet.a1.state.oh.us
*John Connelly, Executive Director*
*Sandra Montgomery, Administration*

State vocational rehabilitation agencies provide direct services to persons with disabilities, including persons with learning disabilities. The services may include evaluation and diagnosis, counseling, guidance, and referral services, vocational and other training services, transportation to rehabilitation services, and assistive devices.

## Oklahoma

**6233 National Clearinghouse of Rehabilitation Training Materials**

Oklahoma State University
206 W 6th Street
Stillwater, OK 74078            405-744-2000
                                 800-223-5219
                           FAX 405-744-2001
                           TDY:405-744-2002
               http://www.nchrtm.okstate.edu
           e-mail: jennifer.ahlert@okstate.edu
*Jennifer Ahlert, Marketing Coordinator*
*Carolyn Cail, Information Coordinator*

Rehabilitation counselor and education materials, disability information and resources.

**6234 State Vocational Rehabilitation Agency: Oklahoma Department of Rehabilitation Services**

3535 NW 58th Street
Oklahoma City, OK 73112          405-951-3400
                                 800-845-8476
                           FAX 405-951-3529
               http://www.okrehab.org
             e-mail: ddcouch@drs.state.ok.us
*David Pittman MD, Commission Chair*
*Susan Randall, Administrative Assistant*

State vocational rehabilitation agencies provide direct services to persons with disabilities, including persons with learning disabilities. The services may include evaluation and diagnosis counseling, guidance, and referral services, vocational and other training services, transportation to rehabilitation services and assistive devices.

**6235 Workforce Investment Act**

**Oklahoma Employment Security Commission**
**2401 N Lincoln Boulevard**
**Oklahoma City, OK  73152**          405-557-7294
                          FAX 405-557-1478
                  http://www.oesc.state.ok.us
            e-mail: denise.burr@oesc.state.ok.us
*John Brock, Executive Director*
*Glen Robards, Assistant Director*

Partnership of local goverments offering resource conservation and development and workforce development.

## Oregon

**6236 Department of Community Colleges & Workforce Development**

**255 Capitol Street NE**
**Salem, OR  97310**                  503-378-8648
                          FAX 503-378-3365
                          TDY:800-735-2900
                  http://www.odccwd.state.or.us
            e-mail: karen.madden@state.or.us
*Karen Madden, Program Manager*
*Jerry Lierow, Coordinator*

Contributes leadership and resources to increase the skills, knowledge and career opportunities for Oregonians.

**6237 Oregon Employment Department**

**875 Union Street NE**
**Salem, OR  97311**                  503-947-1394
                              800-237-3710
                          FAX 503-947-1668
                  http://www.emp.state.or.us
            e-mail: deborah.lincoln@state.or.us
*Deborah Lincoln, Director*
*Greg Hickman, Deputy Director*
*Odie Vogel, Assistant to Director*

Supports economic stability for Oregonians and communities during times of unemployment through the payment of unemployment benefits. Serves businesses by recruiting and referring the best qualified applicants to jobs, and provides resources to diverse job seekers in support of their employment needs.

**6238 Oregon Office of Education and Workforce Policy**

**State Capitol Building**
**Salem, OR  97301 4047**             503-378-4582
                          FAX 503-378-4863
                  http://www.arcweb.sos.state.or.us
            e-mail: annette.talbott@state.or.us
*Annette Talbott, Workforce Policy Coordinator*
*Danny Santos, Education Policy Coordinator*

The Governor's Office of Education and Workforce Policy was established to assist the Governor in examining education and workforce efforts with a view to supporting and strengthening what is working well. The goal is to have Oregonians prepared to meet the education and workforce needs of Oregon businesses rather than having to recruit from outside the state to fill quality jobs.

**6239 Recruitment and Retention Special Education Jobs Clearinghouse**

**Teaching Research**
**345 Monmouth Avenue**
**Monmouth, OR  97361**               503-838-8777
                          FAX 503-838-8150
                  http://www.ode.state.or.us/sped
            e-mail: samplesb@wou.edu
*Bernie Samples, Clearinghouse Coordinator*

A free on-line jobs clearinghouse with access to position openings in Oregon in the area of Special Education and related services. A Job Seeker Listing and resumes also sent via e-mail to districts and agencies looking for qualified individuals.

**6240 State Vocational Rehabilitation Agency**

**Division of Vocational Rehabilitation**
**500 Summer Street NE**
**Salem, OR  97301**                  503-945-5944
                              877-277-0513
                          FAX 503-378-2897
            http://www.dhs.state.or.us/vr/index.html
                  e-mail: info.vr@state.or.us
*Jean Thorne, Director Human Services*
*Stephanie Parrish-Taylor, Program Director*

Uses state and federal funds to assist Oregonians who have disabilities to achieve and maintain employment and independence.

## Pennsylvania

**6241 State Vocational Rehabilitation Agency: Pennsylvania**

**Department of Labor & Industry**
**1521 N 6th Street**
**Harrisburg, PA  17102**             717-787-5244
                              800-442-6351
                          FAX 717-783-5221
                  http://www.dli.state.pa.us
            e-mail: ovr@dli.state.pa.us
*Steven Nasuti, Executive Director*

Provides individualized services to assist people with disabilities to pursue, obtain, and maintain satisfactory employment. Counselors are available for training, planning and placement services.

## Rhode Island

**6242 Rhode Island Department of Employment and Training**

**101 Friendship Street**
**Providence, RI  02914**             401-277-4922
                          FAX 401-861-8030

**6243 Rhode Island Vocational and Rehabilitation Agency**

Rhode Island Department of Human Services
40 Fountain Street
Providence, RI 02903          401-421-7005
                              FAX 401-222-3574
                              TDY:401-421-7016
                              http://www.ors.ri.gov
                              e-mail: rcarroll@ors.ri.gov
*Raymond Carroll, Administrator*
*Valerie Williams, Chief Clerk*

Assists people with disabilities to become employed and to live independently in the community. In order to achieve this goal, we work in partnership with the State Rehabilitation Council, our customers, staff and community.

**6244 State Vocational Rehabilitation Agency: Rhode Island**

Rhode Island Department of Human Services
40 Fountain Street
Providence, RI 02903          401-421-7005
                              FAX 401-222-3574
                              TDY:401-421-7016
                              http://www.ors.ri.gov
                              e-mail: rcarroll@ors.ri.gov
*Raymond Carroll, Administrator*
*Valerie Williams, Chief Clerk*

Assists people with disabilities to become employed and to live independently in the community. In order to achieve this goal, we work in partnership with the State Rehabilitation Council, our customers, staff and community.

## South Carolina

**6245 Americans with Disabilities Act Assistance Line**

Employment Security Commission
1550 Gadsden Street
Columbia, SC 29202          803-737-2593
                            800-436-8190
                            FAX 803-737-0140
                            http://www.sces.org
                            e-mail: rratterree@sces.org
*Regina Ratterree, Program Coordinator*

Provides information, technical assistance and training on the Americans with Disabilities Act.

**6246 South Carolina Vocational Rehabilitation Department**

1410 Boston Avenue
West Columbia, SC 29171          803-896-6500
                                FAX 803-896-6529
                                http://www.scvrd.net
*Jay Rolin, Director*
*Shannon Lindsay, Counselor*

Enabling eligible South Carolinians with disabilities to prepare for, achieve and maintain competitive employment. Training, coaching and job placement services available.

## South Dakota

**6247 Department of Social Services**

700 Governors Drive
Pierre, SD 57501          605-773-3165
                          FAX 605-773-4855
                          http://www.state.sd.us
                          e-mail: dssinfo@state.sd.us
*Maxine Johnston, Administrative Assistant*

**6248 South Dakota Department of Labor**

700 Governors Drive
Pierre, SD 57501-2291          605-773-5017
                               800-952-3216
                               FAX 605-773-4211
                               TDY:605-773-5017
                               http://www.state.sd.us/dol/dol.htm
                               e-mail: miker@dol.pr.state.sd.us
*Michael Ryan, Administrator*

Job training programs provide an important framework for developing public-private sector partnerships. We help prepare South Dakotans of all ages for entry or re-entry into the labor force.

**6249 South Dakota Rehabilitation Center for the Blind**

Department of Human Services
800 W Avenue N
Sioux Falls, SD 57104          605-36752603
                               FAX 605-367-5263
                               http://www.state.sd.us/dhs/
                               e-mail: dawn.backer@state.sd.us
*Dawn Backer, Manager Rehabilitation*
*Nicole Gregor, Administrative Assistant*

Helping people lead a full, productive life — regardless of how much one does or does not see. Upon completion of training, individuals usually return to their community and use these new skills in their home, school or job.

**6250 State Vocational Rehabilitation Agency**

Division of Rehabilitation Services
3800 E Highway 34
Pierre, SD 57501-5070          605-773-5485
                               800-265-9684
                               FAX 605-773-5483
                               TDY:605-773-3195
                               http://www.state.sd.us/dhs/drs/
                               e-mail: steve.stewart@state.sd.us
*Grady Kickul, Director*
*Steve Stewart, Rehabilitation Engineer*

Assists individuals with disabilities to obtain employment, economic self-sufficiency, personal independence and full inclusion into society.

## Tennessee

**6251  State Vocational Rehabilitation Agency**

Tennessee Department of Human Services
400 Deaderick Street
Nashville, TN  37248-0060          615-313-4714
866-311-4288
FAX 615-741-4165
TDY:615-532-8569
http://www.state.tn.us/humanserv/
e-mail: car.w.brown@state.tn.us
*Carl Brown, Assistant Commissioner*
*Terry Smith, Director*

State vocational rehabilitation agencies provide direct services to persons with disabilities, including persons with learning disabilities. The services may include evaluation and diagnosis counseling, guidance, and referral services, vocational and other training services, transportation to rehabilitation services and assistive devices.

**6252  Tennessee Department of Education**

Tennessee Department of Education
710 James Robertson Parkway
Nashville, TN  37243          615-741-2731
800-531-1515
FAX 615-532-4791
http://www.state.tn.us
e-mail: education.comments@state.tn.us
*Phil White, Director of Adult Education*
*Lana Seivers, Commissioner of Education*

Mission is to take Tennessee to the top in education. Guides administration of the state's K-12 public schools.

**6253  Tennessee Department of Labor & Workforce Development: Office of Adult Education**

500 James Robertson Parkway
Nashville, TN  37243          615-741-7054
800-531-1515
FAX 615-532-4899
TDY:800-848-0299
http://www.state.tn.us
e-mail: phil.white@state.tn.us
*Phil White, Director of Adult Education*
*James Neeley, Commissioner*

**6254  Tennessee Services for the Blind**

Division of Rehabilitation
400 Deaderick Street
Nashville, TN  37248 6200          615-313-4914
FAX 615-313-6617
TDY:615-313-6601
http://www.state.tn.us/humanserv/
e-mail: Human-Services.Webmaster@state.tn.us
*Terry Smith, Director*
*Philip Wagster, Director Vocational Rehab.*

Offering training and services to help blind or low-vision citizens of Tennessee become more independent at home, in the community and at work.

## Texas

**6255  Department of Assistive & Rehabilitative Services**

Texas Department of Health & Human Services
4800 N Lamar Boulevard
Austin, TX  78756          512-377-0500
800-252-5204
FAX 512-377-0682
http://www.hhsc.state.tx.us/default.htm
e-mail: terrell.murphy@dars.state.tx.us
*Terrel Murphy, Director*
*Wanda Malveaux, Office Assistant*

Transitional and vocational programs aid independence in the home, community and at work for Texans who are blind, deaf, or have other impairments that would benefit from assistive technology.

**6256  State Vocational Rehabilitation Agency**

Texas State Rehabilitation Commission
4800 N Lamar Boulevard
Austin, TX  78756          512-424-4000
800-628-5115
FAX 512-424-4730
http://www.dars.state.tx.us
e-mail: dars@rehab.state.tx.us
*Terry Murphy, Commissioner*
*San , Office Assistant*
*Mary Wolfe, Field Operations/Communications*

State vocational rehabilitation agencies provide direct services to persons with disabilities, including persons with learning disabilities. The services may include evaluation and diagnosis, counseling, guidance, and referral services, vocational and other training services, transportation to rehabilitation services and assistive devices.

**6257  Texas Education Agency**

1701 N Congress Avenue
Austin, TX  78701          512-463-9734
FAX 512-475-3661
http://www.tea.state.tx.us
*Paul Lindsey, Asst Commissioner/Continuing Ed.*
*Pavlos Roussos, Program Director/Adult Education*

**6258  Texas Workforce Commission**

101 E 15th Street
Austin, TX  78778          512-463-2222
FAX 512-475-2321
http://www.twc.state.tx.us
e-mail: luis.macias@twc.state.tx.us
*Larry Temple, Executive Director*
*Luis Macias, Director Workforce Division*

Provides oversight, coordination, guidance, planning, technical assistance and implementation of employment and training activities with a focus on meeting the needs of employers throughout the state of Texas.

## Utah

**6259  Adult Education Services**

Utah State Office of Education
250 E 500 S
Salt Lake City, UT  84114          801-538-7824
                                   FAX 801-538-7882
http://www.usoe.k12.ut.us/adulted/home.htm
          e-mail: dsteele@usoe.k12.ut.us
*David Steele, Coordinator/Director Education*
*Sandra Grant, Specialist*
*Shauna South, Specialist*

Provides oversight of state and federally funded adult
education programs. Offers adult basic education,
adult high school completion, English as a second language, and general education development programs.

**6260  State Vocational Rehabilitation Agency**

Utah State Office of Rehabilitation
250 E 5th S
Salt Lake City, UT  84111          801-538-7530
                                   800-473-7530
                                   FAX 801-538-7522
                                   TDY:801-538-7530
          http://www.usor.utah.gov
          e-mail: duchida@utah.gov
*Donald Uchida, Director*

Assisting and empowering eligible individuals. Disabled, learning disabled, blind, low vision and deaf
people can prepare for and obtain employment and increase their independence through job training and
assistive technology.

## Vermont

**6261  Adult Education & Literacy State Department of
Education**

Department of Education
120 State Street
Montpelier, VT  05602              802-828-5134
                                   FAX 802-828-3146
          http://www.state.vt.us/educ/
          e-mail: edinfo@doe.state.vt.us
*Amy Brockman, Adult Education*
*John Bradley, Career/Technical Information*

Promotes quality education for area adults as well as
those under age 18.

**6262  REACH-UP Program: Department of Social
Welfare**

Department for Children and Families Economic
Serv
103 S Main Street
Waterbury, VT  05671-1201          802-241-2800
                                   FAX 802-241-2830
          http://www.vt.gov
*Pamela Dalley, Director*
*Barbara Kingsbury, Office Manager*

**6263  Vermont Department of Employment & Training**

5 Green Mountain Drive
Montpelier, VT  05601 0488         802-828-4000
                                   FAX 802-828-4022
          http://www.det.state.vt.us
          e-mail: mcalcagni@det.state.vt.us
*Mike Calcagni, Director Jobs/Training*
*Mike Griffin, Labor Market Information*

Represents Vermont's efforts to provide services, information and support both to individuals to obtain
and keep good jobs, and to employers to recruit and
maintain a productive workforce.

**6264  VocRehab Vermont**

Agency of Human Services
103 S Main Street
Waterbury, VT  05671 2303          802-241-2186
                                   866-879-6757
                                   FAX 802-241-3359
                                   TDY:802-241-1455
          http://www.vocrehabvermont.org
          e-mail: janetr@dad.state.vt.us
*Diane Dalmasse, Director*
*Sandra Hayden, Support for Brain Injury Program*

Works in close partnership with the Vermont Association of Business and Industry Rehabilitation to assist
Vermonters with disabilities to find and maintain
meaningful employment in their communities.

## Virginia

**6265  Department of Rehabilitative Services**

8004 Franklin Farms Drive
Richmond, VA  23229                804-662-7000
                                   800-552-5019
                                   FAX 804-662-9531
                                   TDY:800-464-9950
          http://www.vadrs.org
          e-mail: DRS@DRS.state.va.us
*John Rothrock, Director*
*Barbara Tyson, Administrative Assistant*

Helps people with disabilities get ready for, find and
keep a job. We have a residential training and medical
rehabilitation center known as the Woodrow Wilson
Rehabilitation Center, as well as offices located
across Virginia. The agency also partners with a network of community rehabilitation providers also
known as Employment Service Organizations.

**6266  Office of Adult Education & Literacy**

Virginia Department of Education
PO Box 2120
Richmond, VA  23218-2120           804-225-2075
                                   FAX 804-225-3352
          http://www.doe.virginia.gov
          e-mail: yvonne.thayer@doe.virginia.gov
*Yvonne Thayer, Director*
*Elizabeth Hawa, Associate Director*

Provides leadership and support for adult education
and literacy services, with priority on the development and expansion of quality family literacy and
workforce education programs.

**6267 Virginia Employment Commission**

PO Box 1358
Richmond, VA 23218          804-786-3466
                           FAX 804-371-2814
                  http://www.vec.state.va.us
        e-mail: athornton-crump@vec.state.va.us
*Dolores Esser, Commissioner*
*Alexis Thornton-Crump, Program Manager*

Provides workforce services that promote maximum employment to enhance the economic stability of Virginia.

## Washington

**6268 State Vocational Rehabilitation Agency:
Washington Division of Vocational Rehabilitation**

**Department of Social Services & Health**
PO Box 45340
Olympia, WA 98504          360-438-8000
                           800-637-5627
                      FAX 360-438-8007
                      TDY:360-438-8000
                  http://www.1.dshs.wa.gov
               e-mail: obrien@dshs.wa.gov
*Michael O'Brien, Director*

State vocational rehabilitation agencies provide direct services to persons with disabilities, including persons with learning disabilities. The services may include evaluation and diagnosis, counseling, guidance, and referral services, vocational and other training services, transportation to rehabilitation services, and assistive devices.

**6269 Work First Division: Washington Department of
Social and Health Services**

**6860 Capital Blvd**
Pumwater, WA 98511          877-980-9180
               http://www.onlinecso.dshs.wa.gov

## West Virginia

**6270 West Virginia Division of Rehabilitation Services**

**West Virginia Department of Education & the Arts**
PO Box 50890
Charleston, WV 25305          304-766-4601
                              800-642-3021
                         FAX 304-766-4905
                         TDY:304-766-4965
                     http://www.wvdrs.org
          e-mail: Debbiel@mail.drs.state.wv.us
*Janice Holland, Director*
*Debbie Lovely, Field Services/Programs*

State vocational rehabilitation agencies provide direct services to persons with disabilities, including persons with learning disabilities. The services may include evaluation and diagnosis, counseling, guidance, and referral services, vocational and other training services, transportation to rehabilitation services, and assistive devices.

**6271 Workforce Investment Act**

**West Virginia Bureau of Employment Programs**
112 California Avenue
Charleston, WV 25305          304-558-1138
                              800-252-5627
                         FAX 304-558-1136
                  http://www.state.wv.us/bep/
               e-mail: BGreenle@wvbep.org
*Don Pardue, Commissioner*
*Valerie Comer, Director*

Matching jobseekers with employers in a prompt, efficient manner, to help those in need become job ready, and to analyze and disseminate labor market information. Special placement techniques are also offered which seek to match the physical and mental demands of a job to the capabilities of workers with disabilities. Such services are given by Job Service in cooperation with other community agencies and include counseling and special placement assistance.

## Wisconsin

**6272 State Vocational Rehabilitation Agency:
Wisconsin Division of Vocational Rehabilitation**

**2917 International Lane**
Madison, WI 53702          608-261-0050
                           800-442-3477
                      FAX 608-243-5680
                      TDY:888-877-5939
              http://www.dwd.state.wi.us/dvr/
            e-mail: dwddvr@dwd.state.wi.us
*Charlene Dwyer, Administrator*
*Charlene Dwyer, Administrator*
*Kristin Rolling, Disability Research/Information*

Federal and state program designed to obtain, maintain and improve employment for people with disabilities by working with vocational rehabilitation consumers, employers and other partners.

**6273 W-2 Program: Division of Work Force Solutions**

**Wisconsin Department of Workforce Development**
201 E Washington Avenue
Madison, WI 53702          608-266-0327
                      FAX 608-261-6376
       http://www.dwd.state.wi.us/dws/w2/default.htm
          e-mail: sandy.breitborde@dwd.state.wi.us
*Bill Clingan, Administrator*
*Sandy Breitborde, Workforce Information*

Develops and maintains employment focused programs that enable employers to hire and retain the workforce they need and that provide individuals and families with services that enable them to achieve financial well being as members of Wisconsin's workforce. It delivers services through public-private partnerships and a statewide network of job centers.

**6274 Work Force Information Act**

**Education and Training Policy Division**
PO Box 7903
Madison, WI 53707          608-266-2439
                      FAX 608-267-2392
              e-mail: denisga@dwd.state.WI.us
*Gary Denis, Director*

## Wyoming

**6275 State Vocational Rehabilitation Agency**

**Wyoming Division of Vocational Rehabilitation**
**1100 Herschler Building**
**Cheyenne, WY 82002**          307-777-7389
                              FAX 307-777-5939
                  http://www.wyomingworkforce.org
                     e-mail: jmcint@state.wy.us

*Jim McIntosh, Division Administrator*
*Velta Spear, Office Assistant*

Assists Wyoming citizens with disabilities to prepare for, enter into, and return to suitable employment. Individuals with a disability that prevents them from working may apply for these services as long as a physical or mental impairment which constitutes or results in a substantial impediment to employment exists, and they have the ability to benefit in terms of an employment outcome from vocational services.

A

Boise State University, 4301
Boling Center for Developmental Disabiliti es, 5194
Book Reports Plus, 1064
**Books on Special Children**, 341, 366, 368, 3069, 3095, 3100, 3101, 3107, 3169, 3176, 3180, 3188, 3189, 3208, 3209, 3218, 3222, 3683, 3702, 3733, 3734
Boone Voice Program for Adults, 5970
Boone Voice Program for Children, 5971
Boppie's Great Word Chase, 1718
Boredom Rx, 834
**Boston Centers for Youth & Families**, 470
Boston College, 4550
Boston Diagnostic Aphasia Exam: Third Edition, 6012
**Boston Public Library**, 3932
Boston University, 4551
Bottom Line: Basic Skills in the Workplace, 6038
Bowdoin College, 4503
Bowling Green State University, 4989
**Boy Scout of America**, 502
Boy Scouts of America, 50
Boyce Campus of the Community College of Allegheny County, 5096
Boys and Girls Village, 5505
Bozons' Quest, 1812
Braille 'n Speak Scholar, 1813
Braille' n Speak Classic, 1578, 2089
Brain Injury Association, 51
**BrainTrain**, 1973, 1990
Brainopoly: A Thinking Game, 835, 1327
Bramson Ort Technical Institute, 4824
Brandeis University, 4552
Brandon Hall School, 4263, 5571
Breakthroughs Manual: How to Reach Student s with Autism, 1216
Brehm Preparatory School, 4311, 5588
Brenau University, 4264
Brescia University, 4473
Brevard College, 4928
Brevard Community College, 4215
Brevard Learning Clinic, 5554
Brewton-Parker College, 4265
Briarwood College, 4170
Briarwood School, 5223
Bridgepointe Goodwill & Easter Seals, 203
Bridges Academy, 5800
Bridges to Career Success: A Model for Training Career Counselors, 3661
Bridges to Reading, 3077
Bridges to Reading Comprehension, 1065
Bridgewater State College, 4553
Bridging the Family-Professional Gap: Facilitating Interdisciplinary Services, 3728
Brief Intervention for School Problems: Collaborating for Practical Solutions, 3729
Brigham Young University, 5288
Brigham Young University: Hawaii, 4295
Bright Students Who Learn Differently, 5801
Brightside for Families and Children, 5642
Brislain Learning Center, 5469
Bristol Community College, 4554
Broccoli-Flavored Bubble Gum, 1217
Brookes Publishing, 3351
**Brookes Publishing Company**, 3106, 3152, 3157, 3158, 3160, 3164, 3165, 3438, 3442, 3457, 3515, 3742, 3774, 3789
Brookhaven College, 5195
**Brookline Books**, 364, 839, 3073, 3130, 3191, 3688, 3738, 3787, 3808, 3846, 3866, 3884, 3893, 3905, 5939
Brookline Books/Lumen Editions, 3352
**Brooks/Cole Publishing Company**, 332, 3673, 3681, 3719, 3743, 3749, 3768, 3806, 3837, 3845, 3885
Broome Community College, 4825
**Broschart School**, 5628
Broward Community College, 4216

**Brown Mackie College**, 5037
**Brown University**, 5157, 2870
Brush Ranch School, 4803, 5707
Bryan College: Dayton, 5196
Bryant College, 5158
Bryn Mawr College, 5097
Bubblegum Machine, 1719
Bubbleland Word Discovery, 633
Buddy's Body, 1814
Building Healthy Minds, 3078
Building Mathematical Thinking, 913
Building Perspective, 914, 1884
Building Perspective Deluxe, 915, 1885
Building a Child's Self-Image: A Guide for Parents, 3079
Buncombe County Literacy Council, 2826
Bureau of Adult Education & Training, 6106
**Bureau of Adult Education and Training**, 2221
**Bureau of Adult and Education Training**, 2218
**Bureau of Child & Adolescent Health**, 2442
**Bureau of Correction Education**, 2493
**Bureau of Early Intervention**, 2443
**Bureau of Employment Security**, 2324
**Bureau of Services to Blind and Visually Impaired**, 6203, 6206
Bureau of Services to the Blind & Visually Impaired, 6203
Bureau of Special Education & Pupil Servic es, 2213
Bureau of Workforce Services, 6231
Burlington College, 5300
Business Currents, 6039
**Business Publishers**, 3611, 3640, 3647, 3648
Busy Kids Movement, 1218
Butler County Community College, 4447
Butler University, 4375
Butte College, 4006
Butte County Library Adult Reading Program, 2658

C

**C&C Software**, 1756, 1916
CABE Journal, 3601
**CACLD**, 168
CACLD Spring & Fall Conferences, 1518
**CAP Director, NY Commission on Quality of Care**, 2432
**CASES Executive Office**, 153, 2659
CAST, 1640
CCT Telephone Interface, 1579
**CE Software**, 2004, 1604
CEC Federation Conference: Arkansas, 1519
CEC Federation Conference: Kansas, 1520
CEC Federation Conference: Pennsylvania, 1521
CEC Federation Conference: Virginia, 1522
CEC Today, 3602
**CHADD**, 320, 336
CHADD Educators Manual, 336
CHILD FIND of Connecticut, 2214
CITE Technology Access Center, 1641
CLUES for Better Reading: Grade 1, 5943
CLUES for Better Reading: Grade 2-5, 5944
CLUES for Better Reading: Kindergaten, 5945
CLUES for Better Writing: Grade 1, 5972
CLUES for Better Writing: Grades 2-5, 5973
CLUES for Better Writing: Kindergarten, 5974
CLUES for Phonemic Awareness, 5975
CMECSU Technology Project for Learners with Low Incidence Disabilities, 1642
CONCENTRATE! On Words and Concepts, 1674
COPE Center of Progressive Education, 5506
CREC Summer School, 413
**CREC/ATDW**, 2685
CRISP, 2005
**CT Association for Children and Adults with LD**, 3750, 3783, 3838, 3842, 3941
CUNY Queensborough Community College, 4826
Cabrillo College, 4007

College of Santa Fe, 4805
College of Southern Idaho, 4302
College of St. Catherine: Minneapolis, 4653
College of St. Catherine: St. Paul Campus, 4654
College of St. Joseph, 5302
College of Staten Island of the City University of New York, 4833
College of William and Mary, 5313
College of Wooster, 4999
College of the Canyons, 4030
College of the Desert, 4031
College of the Mainland, 5227
College of the Redwoods: Learning Skills Center, 4032
College of the Sequoias, 4033
College of the Siskiyous, 4034
College: A Viable Option, 3514
Colleges/Universities that Accept Students with Learning Disabilities, 3922
Collin County Community College, 5228
Colorado Adult Education and Family Literacy, 2680
Colorado Assistive Technology Project, 2202
Colorado Christian University, 4142
Colorado Civil Rights Division, 2203
**Colorado Department of Corrections**, 2206
**Colorado Department of Education**, 2680
Colorado Department of Labor and Employment, 2204
Colorado Developmental Disabilities, 2205
Colorado Mountain College, 4143
Colorado Northwestern Community College, 4144
Colorado State University, 4145
Colored Wooden Counting Cubes, 1332
Columbia Basin College, 5355
Columbia College, 4035, 4834
Columbia College Chicago, 4316
Columbia Union College, 4522
Columbia-Greene Community College, 4835
Columbus State Community College: Department of Disability Services, 5000
Columbus State University, 4267
Combining Shapes, 917, 1886
Combining and Breaking Apart Numbers, 918, 1887
Come Play with Me, 1333
**Comforty Mediaconcepts**, 3481
Commerce Library Literacy Program, 2897
Commission for the Blind & Visually Handicapped, 6223
**Commission on Accreditation of Rehabilitation Fac**, 56
Commission on Accreditation of Rehabilitation Facilities (CARF), 56
**Commission on Adult Basic Education (COABE)**, 3304, 3596
Common Ground: Whole Language & Phonics Working Together, 3087
Common Sense About Dyslexia, 3088
**Commonwealth Learning Center**, 5644
Communication Aid Manufacturers Association (CAMA) Workshops, 1526
Communication Aids, 1334
Communication Aids: Manufacturers Association, 57, 1580
Communication Outlook, 3655
Communication Skills for Visually Impaired Learners, 3863
Communication Skills in Children with Down Syndrome, 3089
Community Alliance for Special Education, 5
Community Based Services, 5718
**Community Center**, 2734
Community Child Guidance Clinic School, 5508
Community College of Allegheny County: College Center, North Campus, 5103
Community College of Allegheny County: Allegheny Campus, 5104
Community College of Aurora, 4146
Community College of Baltimore County, 4523
Community College of Denver, 4147
Community College of Philadelphia, 5105
Community College of Rhode Island-Knight Campus, 5159

Community College of Southern Nevada, 4748
Community College of Vermont, 5303
**Community Disabilities Services**, 4785, 4786
Community Education Journal, 3283
Community High School, 4775
**Community Legal Aid/Disabilities Law Program**, 2228
**Community Opportunity Development Agency**, 518
Community School, 4776
Comparing with Ratios, 919, 1888
Comparison Kitchen, 1817
**Compass Learning**, 2008, 1614
Competencies for Teachers of Students with Learning Disabilities, 3739
Complete Clinical Dysphagia Evaluation: Test Forms, 5899
Complete Guide to Running, Walking and Fitness for Kids, 840
Complete IEP Guide: How to Advocate for Your Special Ed Child, 3090
Complete Learning Disabilities Handbook, 3740
Complete Learning Disabilities Resource Library, 3091
Complete Oral-Motor Program for Articulation: Book Only, 636
Complete Oral-Motor Program for Articulation, 637
Complete Oral-Motor Program for Articulation: Refill Kit, 638
Complete Set of State Resource Sheets, 3247
Completing Daily Assignments, 5976
Comprehension Connection, 2040
Comprehensive Advocacy of Idaho, 192
Comprehensive Assessment in Special Education: Approaches, Procedures and Concerns, 3741
**Comprehensive Counseling Center**, 4285
Comprehensive Educational Services (CES), 5745
**Comprehensive Psychiatric Resources**, 359
**Comprehensive Services for the Disabled**, 1646
**Compu-Teach**, 2041, 2101, 2102, 2103, 2104
Computer & Web Resources for People with Disabilities: A Guide to..., 3092
**Computer Access Center**, 1647
Computer Access-Computer Learning, 1628
Computer Accommodation Lab, 1648
Computer Learning Foundation, 58, 1649
Computer Scoring Systems for PRO-ED Tests, 5935
**Computer Technology in Special Education & Rehab.**, 55
Computers in Head Start Classrooms, 1629
Concentration Video, 3466
Conceptual Skills, 1889
Concert Tour Entrepreneur, 920, 1890
Concordia College, 4655
Concordia College: New York, 4836
Concordia University at Austin, 5229
Conducting Individualized Education Program Meetings that Withstand Due Process, 3093
ConnSENSE Conference, 1527
Connect Outloud, 1581
Connect-A-Card, 1069
**Connecticut Assoc. for Children & Adults with LD**, 1518, 1549
**Connecticut Assoc. for Children and Adults with LD**, 2985, 3006, 3043, 3058, 3104, 3133, 3173, 3175, 3179, 3194, 3279, 3406, 3470, 3475, 3486, 3487, 3488, 3509, 3674, 3690
**Connecticut Association Children & Adults with LD**, 3005
Connecticut Association for Children and Adults with LD, 168
Connecticut Association for Children and Adults with Learning Disabilities, 3355
**Connecticut Association for Children and Adults wi**, 361
**Connecticut Association of Boards of Education**, 3601
Connecticut Association of Private Special Education Facilities (CAPSEF), 169
Connecticut Bureau of Rehabilitation Services, 2215
Connecticut Capitol Region Educational Council, 170
Connecticut Center for Augmentative Communication, 5509
Connecticut Center for Children and Families, 5510
Connecticut College, 4173

DHH Outreach, 5198
DLM Math Fluency Program: Addition Facts, 1893
DLM Math Fluency Program: Division Facts, 1894
DLM Math Fluency Program: Multiplication Facts, 1895
DLM Math Fluency Program: Subtraction Facts, 1896
**DMOZ Open Directory Project**, 3548
Daily Starters: Quote of the Day, 642, 1431
Dallas Academy, 5230
Dallas Academy: Coed High School, 5231
Dallas County Community College, 5232
**Dallas Metro Care**, 879
Dance Land, 1224
Daniel Webster College, 4756
Danville Area Community College, 4317
Dartmoor School, 5357
Dartmouth College, 4757
Data Explorer, 922, 1897
**Data Research**, 3045, 3048, 3050
**Dataflo Computer Services**, 1732
Davidson County Community College, 4935
**Davidson Films**, 3491
Davis & Elkins College, 5400
**Davis Dyslexia Association**, 381, 3551
A Day at Play, 1670
A Day in the Life: Assessment and Instruction, 5871
De Anza College: Special Education Divisio, 4040
De Paul School, 5618
DePaul School for Dyslexia, 4219
**DePaul University**, 4350
DeVry Institute of Technology, 4268
Deal Me In: The Use of Playing Cards in Learning and Teaching, 3750
Dean College, 4558
Dearborn Academy, 4559
Deciding What to Teach and How to Teach It Connecting Students through Curriculum and Instruction, 3096
Decimals and Percentages for Job and Personal Use, 923
Decimals: Concepts & Problem-Solving, 924
A Decision Making Model for Occupational Therapy in the Public Schools, 3670
Decoding Games, 1073, 1336
Deep in the Rain Forest, 1179
Defects: Engendering the Modern Body, 3751
Defiance College, 5003
Defiant Children, 3097
Definition Play by Play, 842, 1337
Degrees of Success: Conversations with College Students with LD, 3467
Delaware Assistive Technology Initiative, 2226
Delaware County Community, 5106
Delaware County Literacy Council, 2860
Delaware Department of Education: Adult Community Education, 2688
**Delaware Department of Labor**, 2227, 6114
Delaware Technical and Community College: Terry Campus, 4203
Delaware Valley College of Science and Agriculture, 5107
**Delaware Valley College of Science and Agriculture**, 5107
Delaware Valley Friends School, 5108
**Dell Publishing**, 360
Delta College, 4609
**Delta Corporation**, 3764
Deming Literacy Program, 2807
**Denison University**, 5004
Denver Academy, 4148
**Department for Adult Education & Literacy**, 2312, 2756
**Department for Children and Families Economic Serv**, 6262
**Department for Public Advocacy**, 2311
**Department of Adult Education**, 2250
Department of Assistive & Rehabilitative Services, 6255
**Department of Children, Families & Learning**, 2360, 2785
**Department of Commerce & Labor**, 6138
**Department of Community Colleges**, 2489

Department of Community Colleges & Workforce Development, 6236
**Department of Community Colleges & Workforce**, 2857
Department of Community Colleges and Workforce Development, 2482
**Department of Correction**, 2772
Department of Correction School District, 2180
Department of Correction: Education Coordinator, 2519
Department of Correctional Services, 2433
**Department of Corrections**, 2335, 2225, 2308, 2369, 2476, 2578, 2596
**Department of Corrections & Human Services**, 2377
**Department of Corrections/Division of Institutions**, 2155
**Department of Disabilities**, 5220, 6170
**Department of Disability Services**, 4721, 4941
**Department of Economic Development**, 2289, 2741
**Department of Economic Security**, 2792
**Department of Education**, 2158, 2159, 2213, 2318, 2352, 2355, 2384, 2422, 2428, 2430, 2480, 2517, 2523, 2592, 2736, 2740, 2783, 6157, 6159, 6211, 6222
**Department of Education Pennsylvania**, 1559
**Department of Education,Career & Lifelong Learning**, 2559
**Department of Education: Adult & Community**, 2389
**Department of Education: Office of Adult Education**, 2570, 2574, 2575
**Department of Employment**, 2611
**Department of Employment & Economic Development**, 6032
Department of Employment Services, 6120
**Department of Health & Human Resources**, 6226
Department of Health & Human Services: New Hampshire, 6207
**Department of Human Resources**, 6068, 2449, 2453
**Department of Human Services**, 2323, 2491, 2520, 2738, 2867, 6137, 6148, 6158, 6169, 6249
Department of Human Services: Bureau of Training & Employment, 6121
Department of Human Services: Division of Developmental Disabilities Services, 2527, 2888, 6088
Department of Human Services: Project Forward, 6220
**Department of Industrial Relations**, 2150
**Department of Labor**, 6107, 2152, 2524, 6118
**Department of Labor & Employment Security**, 6131
**Department of Labor & Industry**, 6241
**Department of Personnel & Human Services**, 2579
**Department of Public Health & Human Services**, 6199
**Department of Public Instruction**, 2459, 2229, 2230, 2600, 2688
**Department of Public Safety**, 2247
Department of Rehabilitation, 6094
**Department of Rehabilitation & Correction**, 2465
**Department of Rehabilitative Services**, 6265, 2571
**Department of Social Services**, 6247, 6167, 6223
**Department of Social Services & Health**, 6268
Department of Social Services: Vocational Rehabilitation Program, 6108
**Department of Social Welfare**, 2568, 2927
**Department of Student Support Services**, 5056
**Department of Technical & Adult Education**, 2703
**Department of Technical and Adult Education**, 2245
**Department of Vocational Rehabilitation**, 6190, 6153, 6163, 6166
**Department of Vocational and Adult Education**, 2799
**Department of Workforce Education**, 6089, 2184
**Dept of Transitional Assistance/Office of Health**, 2770, 6174
DesMoines Area Community College, 4411
Designing Clinical Strategies for Language Impaired Children, 3413
Designs for Learning Differences School, 5708
**Deta Corporation**, 3869, 3873
Detroit College of Business, 4610
Detroit College of Business: Warren Campus, 4611
Developing Fine and Gross Motor Skills, 3098
Development Test of Visual Perception, 6013
Developmental Assessment for the Severely Disabled, 5901

**Boldface indicates Publisher**

**Boldface indicates Publisher**

Literacy Volunteers of America: Montana, 2795
Literacy Volunteers of America: Montgomery County, 2910
Literacy Volunteers of America: Nelson County, 2938
Literacy Volunteers of America: New River Valley, 2939
Literacy Volunteers of America: Northern Neck Chapter, 2940
Literacy Volunteers of America: Otero County, 2812
Literacy Volunteers of America: Pitt County, 2829
Literacy Volunteers of America: Port Arthur Literacy Support, 2911
Literacy Volunteers of America: Prince William, 2941
Literacy Volunteers of America: Read West, 2813
Literacy Volunteers of America: Rhode Island, 2869
Literacy Volunteers of America: Sanilac Council, 2778
Literacy Volunteers of America: Santa Cruz County, 2654
Literacy Volunteers of America: Santa Fe, 2814
Literacy Volunteers of America: Shenandoah County, 2942
Literacy Volunteers of America: Socorro County, 2815
Literacy Volunteers of America: Tift County, 2708
Literacy Volunteers of America: Troup County, 2709
Literacy Volunteers of America: Tulsa City County Library, 2846
Literacy Volunteers of America: Wasatch Front, 2917
Literacy Volunteers of America: Washington County, 2841
Literacy Volunteers of America: White County, 2732
Literacy Volunteers of America: Willits Public Library, 2665
Literacy Volunteers of America: Wilmington Library, 2689
Literacy Volunteers of America: Wimberley Area, 2912
Literacy Volunteers of America: Wisconsin, 2965
Literacy Volunteers of Casper, 2970
Literacy Volunteers of Douglas, 2971
Literacy Volunteers of Greater Hartford, 2687
**Literacy Volunteers of Maricopa County**, 2653
Literacy Volunteers of Massachusetts, 2771
**Literacy Volunteers of New York State**, 2823
Literacy Volunteers of Powell North College, 2972
**Literacy Volunteers of Rhode Island**, 2876
Literacy Volunteers of Sheridan/Northern Wyoming, 2973
**Literacy Volunteers of Western County Incorporated**, 2818
Literacy Volunteers of the Lowcountry, 2878
Literacy Volunteers of the National Capital Area, 2694
Literary Cavalcade, 3334
Literary Resources Rhode Island, 2870
**Little Brown & Company**, 3127
Little Keswick School, 5323, 5836
Living Independently Forever (LIFE), 5656
Living Skills, 865
Living with a Learning Disability, 3170
**Lock Haven University**, 2122
Lock Haven University of Pennsylvania, 5124
Long Beach City College Pacific Coast Campus, 4058
Long Island University: CW Post Campus, 4861
Longview Community College: ABLE Program- Academic Bridges to Learning Effectiveness, 4708
Longwood College, 5324
Look At It This Way, 1241
Look! Listen! & Learn Language!: Software, 707, 1758
Lorain County Community College, 5012
Loras College, 4426
Lord Fairfax Community College, 5325
Lorraine D Foster Day School, 5527
Los Angeles City College, 4059
Los Angeles Mission College: Disabled Student Programs and Services, 4060
Los Angeles Pierce College, 4061
Los Angeles School of Gymnastics Day Camp, 408
Los Angeles Valley College, 4062
Los Medanos College, 4063
Lost Dreams & Growth: Parents' Concerns, 3492
Louisburg College, 4945
Louisiana Assistive Technology Access Network, 2317
Louisiana College, 4490
**Louisiana Department of Education**, 2316, 2319

Louisiana State Literacy Resource Center: State Department of Education, 2760
Louisiana State Planning Council on Developmental Disabilities Newsletter, 3324
**Louisiana State University**, 4488
Louisiana State University Agricultural and Mechanical College, 4491
Louisiana State University: Alexandria, 4492
Louisiana State University: Eunice, 4493
**Love Publishing Company**, 3376, 3494, 3710, 3753, 3773
Loyola Marymount University, 4064
Loyola University New Orleans, 4494
Lubbock Christian University, 5245
Lureen B Wallace Community College, 3959
Luther College, 4427
Lutheran Braille Workers: Sight Saving Division, 160
Lycoming College, 5125
Lynn University, 4237

# M

M-SS-NG L-NKS, 708, 1759
MAC Mainstreaming at Camp, 527
MACcessories: Guide to Peripherals, 1630
**MATP Center**, 2332
**MATP Children's Hospital**, 2336
MATRIX: A Parent Network and Resource Center, 87
MAXI, 1465
**MCD, Stout Vocational Rehabilitation Institute**, 6055
MCLA: Measure of Cognitive-Linguistic Abilities, 709
**MNSCU**, 4645
MORE: Integrating the Mouth with Sensory & Postural Functions, 866
**MS Project START**, 2364
Macalester College, 4662
Macon State College, 4279
Madisonville Community College: University of Kentucky, 4480
Madonna University, 4626
Magicatch Set, 1363
Magination Press, 3377
Magnetic Fun, 1364
Mailman Center for Child Development: University of Miami Department of Pediatrics, 185
Maine Bureau of Applied Technical Adult Learning: Adult Career and Technical Education, 2762
**Maine Bureau of Rehabilitation Services**, 6168
**Maine Department of Education**, 2320, 2762
Maine Department of Labor: Bureau of Rehabilitation Services, 2323
Maine Department of Labor: Employment Services, 2324
Maine Human Rights Commission, 2325
Maine Literacy Resource Center, 2763
Maine Literacy Volunteers of America, 2764
Maine Parent Federation, 218
**Mainstream**, 3638, 3617
Mainstreaming Exceptional Students: A Guide for Classroom Teachers, 3807
Make Every Step Count: Birth to 1 Year, 1027
Make It Go, 1760
Make It Today for Pre-K Play, 1028
Make-A-Flash, 1761
Make-a-Map 3D, 1291
Making School Inclusion Work, 3808
Making Sense of Sensory Integration, 3171
**Malden YMCA**, 472
Malone College, 5013
**Manchester City Library**, 2804
Manchester College, 4393
Manchester Community Technical College, 4180
Mandy, 3007
**Manhattan Adult Learning and Resource Center**, 3819
Manhattan Center for Learning, 5731

Merced Adult School, 2667
Merced College, 4068
Mercer University: Atlanta, 4280
Mercy College, 4868
Mercyhurst College, 5129
Meredith College, 4949
Meredith-Dunn School, 5620
**Merit Software**, 1983, 1672, 1692, 1738, 1780, 1821, 1841, 1933, 1989
Merritt College, 4069
Mesa Community College, 3977
Mesabi Range Community & Technical College, 4664
Messiah College, 5130
Metropolitan Adult Education Program, 2668
Metropolitan School, 5678
**Metropolitan Speech and Language Center**, 5702
**Miami Dade Community College**, 4220
Miami University, 5017
Miami University: Middletown Campus, 5018
Michigan Adult Learning & Technology Center, 2779
Michigan Assistive Technology: Michigan Rehabilitation Services, 2348, 2780
Michigan Citizens Alliance to Uphold Special Education (CAUSE), 230
Michigan Commission for the Blind: Deafblind Unit, 6179
Michigan Developmental Disabilities Council, 2349
Michigan Employment Security Commission, 2350
**Michigan Jobs Commission**, 6180, 2345, 2348, 2780, 2784
Michigan Laubach Literacy Action, 2781
Michigan Libraries and Adult Literacy, 2782
Michigan Protection and Advocacy Service, 2351
**Michigan Rehabilitation Services**, 6182
Michigan State Department of Adult Education: Office of Extended Learning Services, 2783
**Michigan State University**, 4627, 1635
Michigan Technological University, 4628
**Michigan University/Artificial Language Laboratory**, 3655
Michigan Workforce Investment Act, 2784, 6181
Micro IntroVoice, 1599
Microcomputer Language Assessment and Development System, 1767
Microsoft Corporation, 2022
Mid City Adult Learning Center, 2669
Mid-Michigan Community College, 4629
Mid-State College, 4507
**Mid-State Technical College**, 5426
Middle School Geometry: Basic Concepts, 965
Middle School Language Arts, 713
Middle School Math, 966
Middle School Math Bundle, 967, 1984
Middle School Writing: Expository Writing, 1468
**Middle Tennessee State University**, 5205
Middlesex Community College, 4576
**Middlesex County College**, 4791
**Middletown Parks and Recreation Department**, 426
Middletown Summer Day Programs, 426
Midland Lutheran College, 4739
Midland School, 5703
Midlands Technical College, 5175
Midwestern State University, 5247
Mighty Math Astro Algebra, 1925
Mighty Math Calculating Crew, 1926
Mighty Math Cosmic Geometry, 1927
Mighty Math Countdown, 1928
Mighty Math Number Heroes, 1929
Mighty Math Zoo Zillions, 1930
Mike Mulligan & His Steam Shovel, 714, 1110, 1768, 2051
Milford Recreation Department Camp Happiness, 427
**Milken Family Foundation**, 3897
Mill Springs Academy, 4281, 5577
Millcreek Schools, 5675
Millersville University of Pennsylvania, 5131
Millie's Math House, 1931

**Milliken Publishing**, 1825, 1838, 2040, 2072
Milliken Science Series: Circulation and Digestion, 2072
Millikin University, 4339
Mills College, 4070
Milwaukee Area Technical College, 5427
Mind Over Matter, 1691
A Mind of Your Own, 3439
MindTwister Math, 968
Mindworks Press, 3379
Minneapolis Community College, 4665
**Minneapolis Public Schools Community Education**, 233
Minnesota Access Services, 233
Minnesota Department of Adult Education: Adult Basic Education, 2785
Minnesota Department of Children, Families & Learning, 2355
Minnesota Department of Employment and Economic Development, 2786, 6187
Minnesota Department of Human Rights, 2356
**Minnesota Disability Law Center**, 234, 2359
Minnesota GED Administration, 2787
Minnesota Governor's Council on Developmental Disabilities, 2357
Minnesota LDA Learning Disabilities Center, 2788
Minnesota LINCS: Literacy Council, 2789
Minnesota Life College, 4666
Minnesota Life Work Center, 2358, 2790
Minnesota Literacy Training Network, 2791
**Minnesota STAR Program**, 2354
**Minnesota State Community & Technical College**, 4667
Minnesota State Community & Technology Col, 4667
Minnesota State University Moorehead, 4668
Minnesota University Affiliated Program on Developmental Disabilities, 4669
Minnesota Vocational Rehabilitation Agency: Rehabilitation Services Branch, 2792, 6032
Minnesota West Community & Technical College, 4670
**Minnesota Workforce Center**, 2786, 6187
**Minot State University**, 4981
Minot State University: Bottineau Campus, 4980
A Miracle to Believe In, 2975, 3055
Miracosta College, 4071
Miriam School, 5679
Mirror Symmetry, 969
**Mississippi Department of Rehabilitation Services**, 6191
Mississippi Employment Security Commission, 2363
Mississippi Project START, 2364
Mississippi State University, 4694
**Mississippi State University/ Student Services**, 3930
Mississippi University Affiliated Program, 4695
Missouri Parents Act (MPACT), 5680
Missouri Protection & Advocacy Services, 2373
Missouri Southern State College, 4710
Missouri Valley College, 4711
Misunderstood Child, 3175
Mitchell College, 4181
**Mobility International USA**, 564, 3946
Modern Consumer Education: You and the Law, 3229
**Modern Learning Press**, 3380, 3087
Modesto Junior College, 4072
Mohawk Valley Community College, 4869
Molloy College, 4870
MonTECH, 2379
Money Skills, 1844
Monitoring Basic Skills Progress, 5909
Monkey Business, 1692
Monroe County Community College, 4630
Monsters & Make-Believe, 1693
**Montana Advocacy Program (MAP) Inc.: Helena**, 236
Montana Advocacy Program (MAP): Helena, 236
Montana Advocacy Program (MAP): Missoula Office, 237
Montana Department of Labor & Industry, 2380
Montana Literacy Resource Center, 2796
**Montana Office of Public Instruction**, 2381, 2382

Northeast State Technical Community College, 5207
Northeast Wisconsin Technical College, 5430
Northeastern Illinois University, 4344
Northeastern Junior College, 4155
Northeastern State University, 5055
Northeastern University, 4581
Northern Arizona University, 3978
Northern Illinois Center for Adaptive Technology, 1658
**Northern Illinois University**, 4345, 3667
Northern Kentucky University, 4482
Northern Maine Community College, 4508
Northern Michigan University, 4632
Northern Montana College, 4730
**Northern Neck Adult Education Program**, 2940
Northern Nevada Literacy Council, 2803
Northern New Mexico Community College, 4812
Northern State University, 5189
Northern Virginia Community College, 5329
**Northland College**, 5431
Northwest College, 5450
Northwest Media, 3384
Northwest Missouri State University, 4713
Northwest Oklahoma Literacy Council, 2847
Northwest Regional Literacy Resource Center, 2951
Northwest School, 5370
Northwest Technical College, 5021
**Northwest Village School**, 5538
Northwest Village School: Wheeler Clinic, 5530
Northwestern College, 4434, 4673
Northwestern Connecticut Community College, 4183
Northwestern Michigan College, 4633
**Northwestern State University**, 4489
Northwestern University, 4346
Northwestern University Communicative Disorders, 4347
Northwood University, 4634
Norwalk Community-Technical College, 4184
Norwalk Public Schools: Special Education Summer Programs, 428
Norwich University, 5307
Note Speller, 1696
Notre Dame College of Ohio, 5022
Now You're Talking: Extend Conversation, 3420
Number Farm, 1932
Number Meanings and Counting, 972
Number Please, 1933
Number Sense & Problem Solving CD-ROM, 973, 1934, 1986
Number Stumper, 1935
Numbers That Add Up to Educational Rights for Children with Disabilities, 3036
Numbers Undercover, 974
**Nursing Department**, 4461

## O

**O'Neill Learning Center**, 4654
**O'Net: Department of Labor's Occ. Information**, 3549
OPTIONS, 5531
OSERS Magazine, 3325
OT Practice, 3643
Oakland Community College: Orchard Ridge Campus, 4635
Oakland University, 4636
**Oakstone Legal and Business Publishing**, 3032
Oakton Community College, 4348
**Oakwood School**, 5839
**Oakwood Solutions**, 1871
Oberlin College, 5023
Occupational Aptitude Survey and Interest Schedule, 5937
Occupational Outlook Quarterly, 3644
Occupations, 1847
Ocean County College, 4789
**Octameron Associates**, 3919
Odyssey School, 5250
**Office Differing Disabilities**, 4758

**Office Disabilities Services**, 4829
**Office For Special Needs**, 5421
**Office Of Workforce Training and Development**, 6221
**Office for Disability Services**, 4119, 5137
**Office for Students with Disabilities**, 4121, 4123, 4225, 4243, 4251, 4403, 4853, 5112
**Office for Students with Learning Disabilities**, 4788
**Office for Students with Special Needs**, 4928
**Office of Academic Disability Support**, 5322
**Office of Access & Learning Accommodation**, 5222
**Office of Accessibility Services**, 4701
Office of Adult Basic and Literacy Education, 2382
Office of Adult Education & Literacy, 6266
**Office of Adult Literacy**, 2704
Office of Advocacy for Persons with Disabilities, 2439
**Office of Civil Rights**, 2208, 2209, 2375, 2445
Office of Civil Rights: US Department of Health and Human Services, 2139
Office of Civil Rights: US Department of Education, 2140
**Office of Community Based Services**, 2391
**Office of Correctional Education**, 3284
Office of Curriculum & Instructional Support, 2440, 6224
**Office of Differing Disabilities**, 4746, 4773
**Office of Disabilities Services**, 4725, 5193, 5319
**Office of Disability Accommodation**, 5280
Office of Disability Employment Policy, 2141
**Office of Disability Services**, 2302, 5251, 4173, 4228, 4270, 4318, 4551, 4596, 4609, 4715, 4720, 4767, 4770, 4908, 4993, 5110, 5252, 5259, 5320
**Office of Disabled Student Services**, 5213
Office of Disabled Students at Manatee Community College, 4238
**Office of Discrimination and Hate Crimes**, 2271
Office of Federal Contract Compliance Programs: US Department of Labor, 2142
Office of Federal Contract Compliance: Boston District Office, 2340
**Office of Handicapped Concerns**, 2475
**Office of Human Resources & EEO**, 2143
**Office of Multi Access Services**, 4227
**Office of P&A for Persons with Disabilities**, 2220
Office of Personnel Management, 2143
Office of Program Operations: US Department of Education, 2144
**Office of Protection & Advocacy**, 2217
**Office of Public Inquiries**, 2146
**Office of School & Community Support**, 2760
Office of Services for Students with Disabilities, 4637
**Office of Special Education & Rehabilitative Svcs.**, 3325
**Office of Special Education Programs**, 2645, 2416, 2418
**Office of Special Education and Rehabilitative Svc**, 54
**Office of Special Needs**, 5146
**Office of Special Services**, 4194
**Office of Special Services for Students with Dis.**, 4131
**Office of Specialized Services**, 4792
**Office of State Libraries**, 2713
**Office of Student Development, Adm. 303**, 4313
**Office of Student Relations**, 4124
**Office of Student Support Services**, 4175
Office of Vocational & Adult Education, 6033
Office of Vocational Rehabilitation, 6163
Office of Vocational and Educational Services for Individuals with Disabilities, 6225
**Office of Vocational-Technical Career & Innovative**, 6218
**Office of the Arizona Attorney General**, 2169
Office of the Governor, 2182, 2456
**Office of the Secretary for Education**, 2660
Oh Say What They See: Language Stimulation, 3495
Ohio Adult Basic and Literacy Education, 2466
Ohio Civil Rights Commission, 2467
Ohio Coalition for the Education of Children with Learning Disabilities, 5758
**Ohio Department of Education**, 2466

**Boldface indicates Publisher**

University of Sydney/School Educational Psychology, 3767
University of Tampa, 4254
University of Tennessee, 5194
University of Tennessee: Knoxville, 5214, 2886
University of Tennessee: Martin, 5215
University of Texas at Austin, 2544
University of Texas: Arlington, 5281
University of Texas: Dallas, 5282
University of Texas: Pan American, 5283
University of Texas: San Antonio, 5284
University of The District of Columbia, 2235
University of Toledo, 5044
University of Topeka, 4469
University of Tulsa, 5070
University of Utah, 5295
University of Vermont, 5309, 5878
University of Virginia, 5342, 5321
University of Washington, 5389
University of Washington: Center on Human Development and Disability, 5390
University of West Florida, 4255
University of Wisconsin Center, 5434
University of Wisconsin Center: Marshfield Wood County, 5434
University of Wisconsin-Madison, 3552
University of Wisconsin: Eau Claire, 5435
University of Wisconsin: La Crosse, 5436
University of Wisconsin: Madison, 5437
University of Wisconsin: Milwaukee, 5438
University of Wisconsin: Oshkosh, 5439
University of Wisconsin: Platteville, 5440
University of Wisconsin: River Falls, 5441
University of Wisconsin: Whitewater, 5442
University of Wyoming, 5452
University of Wyoming: Division of Social Work and Wyoming Institute for Disabilities (WIND), 5453
University of the Arts, 5151
University of the District of Columbia, 4212
University of the Incarnate Word, 5285
University of the Ozarks, 3998, 3993
University of the Pacific, 4131
Unlocking the Mysteries of Sensory Dysfunction, 3223
Untamed World, 1199
Up and Running, 1618
Updown Chair, 1272
Upper Valley Support Group, 247
Upward Bound Camp for Special Needs, 565
Urbana University, 5045
Ursinus College, 5152
Ursuline College, 5046
Utah Department of Special Education, 3698, 3699
Utah Governor's Council for People with Disabilities, 2551
Utah Labor Commission: Utah Anti-discrimination and Labor Division, 2552
Utah Literacy Action Center, 2918
Utah Literacy Resource Center, 2919
Utah Parent Center, 5825
Utah State Office of Education, 6259
Utah State Office of Rehabilitation, 6260
Utah State University, 5296, 1512, 5289, 5822
Utah Valley State College, 5297
Utah Work Force, 2553
Utica College of Syracuse University, 4922

## V

VIP Educational Services, 5820
VISTA, 1619
VISTA Vocational & Life Skills Center, 4198, 5535
VSA Arts, 136
Valdosta State University, 4293
Valencia Community College, 4256
Valencia County Literacy Council, 2817

Valentine Bear, 3018
Vallejo City Unified School District, 3506
Valley Academy, 4539
Valleyhead, 484, 5666
Vanderbilt University, 5216
Vanguard School, 5567, 5788
Vanguard University of Southern California, 4132
Variety School of Hawaii, 5583
Vassar College, 4923
Ventura College, 4133
Verbal Images Press, 2998
Vermont Agency of Human Services, 2560
Vermont Assistive Technology Project: Department of Aging and Disabilities, 2561, 2922
Vermont Department of Corrections, 2923
Vermont Department of Employment & Training, 2562, 6263
Vermont Department of Employment & Training, 2925, 2928
Vermont Department of Welfare, 2563, 2924
Vermont Developmental Disabilities Council, 2564
Vermont Disability Law Project, 2565
Vermont Governor's Office, 2566
Vermont Human Resources Investment Council, 2925
Vermont Legal Aid Client Assistance Program and Disability Law Project, 2567
Vermont Literacy Resource Center: Department of Education, 2926
Vermont Protection and Advocacy, 305
Vermont REACH-UP Program, 2568, 2927
Vermont Special Education, 2569
Vermont Technical College, 5310
Vermont Workforce Reinvestment Act, 2928
Very Special Arts (VSA), 136
Vickery Meadow Learning Center, 5821
Victor Valley College, 4134
Victoria Adult Literacy, 2915
Villa Maria Education Center, 5536
Villanova University, 5153
Vincennes University, 4406
Virginia Adult Education Centers for Professional Development, 2945
Virginia Board for People with Disabilities, 2576
Virginia Commonwealth University, 5343
Virginia Community College System, 5312
Virginia Council of Administrators of Special Education, 2946
Virginia Department of Education, 6266
Virginia Employment Commission, 6267
Virginia Highlands Community College, 5344
Virginia Intermont College, 5345
Virginia Literacy Coalition, 2947
Virginia Polytechnic Institute and State University, 5346
Virginia Wesleyan College, 5347
Virginia Western Community College, 5348
Virtual Labs: Electricity, 1200
Virtual Labs: Light, 1201
Visagraph II Eye-Movement Recording System, 1620
Vision Care Clinic of Santa Clara Valley, 5500
Vision Help Network, 5637
Vision Literacy of California, 2679
Vision and Learning Disabilities, 3858
Vision, Perception and Cognition: Manual for Evaluation & Treatment, 5921
Visual Perception and Attention Workbook, 898
Visual Processes in Reading and Reading Disabilities, 3906
Visual Skills Appraisal, 6025
Visual Voice Tools, 812
Visualizing and Verbalizing for Language Comprehension/Thinking, 3878
Viterbo University, 5443
VocRehab Vermont, 2929, 6264
Vocabulary, 1166
Vocabulary Connections, 813
Vocabulary Play by Play, 814

**Boldface indicates Publisher**

## Alabama

Alabama Aviation and Technical College, 3947
Alabama Commission on Higher Education, 2648
Alabama Department of Industrial Relations, 2148
Alabama Disabilities Advocacy Program, 2149
Alabama Southern Community College, 3948
Auburn University, 3949
Auburn University at Montgomery, 3950
Birmingham-Southern College, 3951
Bishop State Community College, 3952
Camp ASCCA, 392
Chattahoochee Valley State Community College, 3953
Department of Human Resources, 6068
Easter Seals Achievement Center, 6069
Easter Seals Alabama, 6071
Easter Seals Camp ASCCA, 6072
Easter Seals Capilouto Center for the Deaf, 6073
Easter Seals Gulf Coast, 393
Easter Seals Opportunity Center, 6074
Easter Seals Rehabilitation Center, 6075
Easter Seals Rehabilitation Center: Northwest Alabama, 6076
Easter Seals: Birmingham Area, 6077
Easter Seals: West Alabama, 6078
Employment Service Division: Alabama, 2150
George County Wallace State Community College, 3954
Good Will Easter Seals, 5454, 6079
Jacksonville State University, 3956
James H Faulkner State Community College, 3957
John M Patterson State Technical College, 3958
LDA Alabama Newsletter, 355
Learning Disabilities Association of Alabama, 141
Lureen B Wallace Community College, 3959
Marion Military Institute, 3960
National Association for Developmental Dis, 2151
Northeast Alabama Community College, 3961
Special Education Action Committee, 5455
Three Springs, 5456
Troy State University Dothan, 3962
UAB Sparks Center for Developmental and Learning Disorders, 142
University of Alabama, 3963
University of Alabama: Huntsville, 3964
University of Montevallo, 3965
University of North Alabama, 3966
University of South Alabama, 3967
Wireglass Rehabilitation Center, 5457
Workforce Development Division, 6081
Workshops, 5458

## Alaska

Alaska Department of Labor, 6082
Alaska Department of Labor: Employment Security Division, 2152
Alaska Literacy Program, 2649
Alaska Pacific University, 3968
Arkansas Adult Basic Education, 2650
Assistive Technology: Metro Region, 2153
Center for Community, 2154, 5459
Center for Human Development (CHD) University Affiliated Program, 143
Correctional Education Division: Alaska, 2155
Disability Law Center of Alaska, 2156
Juneau Campus: University of Alaska Southeast, 3969
Ketchikan Campus: University of Alaska Southeast, 3970
Learning Disabilities Association of Alaska (LDAALaska), 144
Literacy Council of Alaska, 2651
Sheldon Jackson College, 3995
State GED Administration: GED Testing Program, 2160
State Vocational Rehabilitation Agency of Alaska, 6080, 6083

State of Alaska Community & Regional Affairs Department: Administrative Services, 2161
University of Alaska Anchorage: Disability Support Services, 3971
University of Alaska: Fairbanks, 3972

## Arizona

Academy of Tucson, 5460
Adult & Family Literacy Education, 2162
Adult Education Division of the Arizona Department of Education, 2652
Arizona Center for Disability Law, 145, 2163
Arizona Center for Law in the Public Interest, 2164
Arizona Department of Economic Security, 2165
Arizona Department of Education, 2166
Arizona Governor's Committee on Employment of the Handicapped, 2167
Arizona State University, 3973
Commission on Accreditation of Rehabilitation Facilities (CARF), 56
Devereux Arizona Treatment Network, 5461
Division of Employment & Training Rehabilitation Services, 6084
Easter Seals Arizona, 394
Easter Seals Tucson, 395
Eastern Arizona College, 3974
Fair Employment Practice Agency, 2157, 2169
Fundamentals of Job Placement, 6046
Fundamentals of Vocational Assessment, 6047
GED Testing Services, 2170
Glendale Community College, 3975
Grand Canyon University, 3976
Handbook for Developing Community Based Employment, 6048
Institute for Human Development: Northern Arizona University, 146
Job Accommodation Handbook, 6051
LATCH School, 5462
Life Development Institute (LDI), 5463
Literacy Volunteers of America: Maricopa County, 2653
Mesa Community College, 3977
New Way Learning Academy, 5464
Northern Arizona University, 3978
Parent Information Network, 147
Phoenix College, 3979
Pima Community College, 3980
Raising Special Kids, 5465
Rehabilitation Services Administration, 6085
Scottsdale Community College, 3981
South Mountain Community College, 3982
Spring Ridge Academy, 3983
Turning Point School, 5466
University of Advancing Computer Technology, 3984
University of Arizona, 3985
Yavapai College, 3986

## Arkansas

Arkansas Adult Learning Resource Center, 2655
Arkansas Baptist College, 3987
Arkansas Department of Education, 2172
Arkansas Department of Human Services: Division of Rehabilitation Services, 2173
Arkansas Department of Special Education, 2174
Arkansas Department of Workforce Education, 2175
Arkansas Disability Coalition, 5467
Arkansas Employment Security Department, 2176
Arkansas Employment Security Department: Office of Employment & Training Services, 6086
Arkansas Governor's Developmental Disabilities Council, 2177
Arkansas Literacy Council: Laubach Literacy Action, 2656
Arkansas Northeastern College, 3988

## California

Vincennes University, 4406

## Iowa

American College Testing Program, 29, 6028
Central College: Student Support Services, 4407
Client Assistance Program (CAP): Iowa Division of Persons with Disabilities, 2285
Clinton Community College, 4408
Coe College, 4409
Cornell College, 4410
DesMoines Area Community College, 4411
Dordt College, 4412
Drake University, 4413
Easter Seals Camp Sunnyside, 457
Easter Seals Center, 6155
Easter Seals Iowa, 6156
Ellsworth Community College, 4414
Governor's Council on Developmental Disabilities, 2286
Graceland College, 4415
Grand View College, 4416
Grinnell College, 4417
Hawkeye Community College, 4418
Indian Hills Community College, 4419
International Dyslexia Association: Iowa Branch, 208
Iowa Bureau of Community Colleges, 2736, 6157
Iowa Center for Disabilities and Development, 209
Iowa Central Community College, 4420
Iowa Compass, 5614
Iowa Department of Education: Iowa Literacy Council Programs, 2737
Iowa Employment Service, 2287
Iowa JOBS Program: Division of Economic Assistance, 2738, 6158
Iowa Lakes Community College: Emmetsburg Campus, 4421
Iowa Lakes Community College: Success Centers, 4422
Iowa Literacy Resource Center, 2739
Iowa Program for Assistive Technology, 210
Iowa State University, 4423
Iowa Vocational Rehabilitation Agency, 2740, 6159
Iowa Welfare Programs, 2288
Iowa Wesleyan College, 4424
Iowa Western Community College: Council Bluffs Campus, 4425
Iowa Workforce Investment Act, 2289, 2741
Learning Disabilities Association of Iowa, 211, 2290, 2742, 2742
Library Literacy Programs: State Library of Iowa, 2743
Loras College, 4426
Luther College, 4427
Marshalltown Community College, 4428
Morningside College, 4429
Mount Mercy College, 4430
Mount Saint Clare College, 4431
Muscatine Community College, 4432
North Iowa Area Community College, 4433
Saint Ambrose College, 4435
Scott Community College, 4436
Southeastern Community College: North Campus, 4437
Southwestern Community College, 4438
University of Iowa, 4439
University of Northern Iowa, 4440
Waldorf College, 4441
Wartburg College, 4442

## Kansas

Allen County Community College, 4443
Baker University, 4444
Barton County Community College, 4445
Bethel College, 4446
Butler County Community College, 4447
CEC Federation Conference: Kansas, 1520
Center for Research on Learning, 4448
Client Assistance Program (CAP): Kansas Division of Persons with Disabilities, 2294, 2744
Colby Community College, 4449
Cooperative Thinking Strategies, 1221
Cowley County Community College, 4450
Donnelly College, 4451
Easter Seals Kansas, 6161
Emporia State University, 4452
Families Together, 5615
Fort Scott Community College, 4453
Heartspring School, 5616
Hutchinson Community College, 4454
INSPECT: A Strategy for Finding and Correcting Spelling Errors, 1303
International Dyslexia Society: Kansas Western Missouri Branch, 212
Kansas Adult Education Association, 2295, 2745
Kansas Advocacy & Protective Services, 213
Kansas Advocacy Protective Services, 2296
Kansas Community College: Kansas City, 4455
Kansas Correctional Education, 2746
Kansas Department of Corrections, 2747
Kansas Department of Human Resources, 2297
Kansas Department of Social and Rehabilitation Services, 2298
Kansas Human Rights Commission, 2299
Kansas Laubach Literacy Action, 2748
Kansas Library Literacy Programs: Kansas State Library, 2749
Kansas Literacy Resource Center, 2750
Kansas Literacy Volunteers of America, 2751
Kansas State Department of Adult Education, 2752
Kansas State Department of Education of Education, 2300
Kansas State Literacy Resource Center: Kansas State Department of Education, 2753
Kansas State University, 4456
Kansas University Center for Developmental Disabilities (KUCDD), 4457
Kansas Vocational Rehabilitation Agency, 2754, 6162
Kansas Welfare Programs: Kansas Social and Rehabilitative Services, 2301
Labette Community College, 4458
Learning Disabilities Association of Kansas, 214
Learning Resource Network, 86, 2631
Learning Strategies Curriculum, 1306
Menninger Center for Learning Disabilities, 5617
National Council on Rehabilitation Education, 107
Neosho County Community College, 4459
Newman University, 4460
North Central Kansas Technical College, 4461
Office of Vocational Rehabilitation, 6163
Ottawa University, 4462
Pittsburg State University, 4463
Rural Clearinghouse for Lifelong Education & Development, 129
SLANT: A Starter Strategy for Class Participation, 1308
Saint Mary College, 4464
Self Advocacy as a Technique for Transition, 6060
Seward County Community College, 4465
State GED Administration: Kansas State Department of Education, 2304
Strategic Math Series, 994
Surface Counseling, 1265
Tabor College, 4466
University Affiliated Program, 4467
University of Kansas, 4468
Washburn University of Topeka, 4469
Western Kansas Community Service Consortium, 2305, 2755
Wichita State University, 4470

## Kentucky

American Printing House for the Blind, 34

## Michigan

AVKO Dyslexia Research Foundation, 18
Adrian College, 4599
Adventure Learning Center at Eagle Village, 485
Alma College, 4600
Andrews University, 4601
Aquinas College, 4602
Augmentative Communication Technology, 4603
Bay De Noc Community College, 4604
Calvin College, 4605
Center for Human Development, 5668
Center for the Improvement of Early Readin g Achievement CIERA, 2619
Central Michigan University, 4606
Charles Stewart Mott Community College, 4607
Client Assistance Program (CAP): Michigan Department of Persons with Disabilities, 2346
College of Art and Design: Center for Creative Studies, 4608
Correctional Education: Department of Corrections, 2347
Delta College, 4609
Detroit College of Business, 4610
Detroit College of Business: Warren Campus, 4611
Developmental Disabilities Institute: Wayn e State University, 4612
Easter Seal Michigan, 6177
Easter Seals Collaborative Solutions, 6178
Easter Seals Genesee County, 486
Easter Seals Michigan, 487
Easter Seals Michigan: Saginaw, 488
Eastern Michigan University, 4613
Eton Academy, 4614, 5669
Ferris State University, 4615
Finlandia University, 4616
Fowler Center Summer Camp, 489
Genesee County Literacy Coalition, 2776
Glen Oaks Community College, 4617
Henry Ford Community College, 4618
Hope College, 4619
International Dyslexia Association: Michig an Branch, 228
Jackson Community College, 4620
Kalamazoo College, 4621
Kellogg Community College, 4622
Kendall College of Art and Design, 4623
Lake Michigan Academy, 5670
Lake Michigan College, 4624
Lansing Community College, 4625
Learning Disabilities Association of Michigan (LDA), 229
Let's Write Right: Teacher's Edition, 1462
Literacy Volunteers of America: Lansing Area Literacy Coalition, 2777
Literacy Volunteers of America: Sanilac Council, 2778
Madonna University, 4626
Michigan Adult Learning & Technology Center, 2779
Michigan Assistive Technology: Michigan Rehabilitation Services, 2348, 2780
Michigan Citizens Alliance to Uphold Speci al Education (CAUSE), 230
Michigan Commission for the Blind: Deafbli nd Unit, 6179
Michigan Developmental Disabilities Counci l, 2349
Michigan Employment Security Commission, 2350
Michigan Jobs Commission, 6180
Michigan Laubach Literacy Action, 2781
Michigan Libraries and Adult Literacy, 2782
Michigan Protection and Advocacy Service, 2351
Michigan State Department of Adult Educati on: Office of Extended Learning Services, 2783
Michigan State University, 4627
Michigan Technological University, 4628
Michigan Workforce Investment Act, 2784, 6181
Mid-Michigan Community College, 4629
Minnesota Access Services, 233
Monroe County Community College, 4630

Montcalm Community College, 4631
Northern Michigan University, 4632
Northwestern Michigan College, 4633
Northwood University, 4634
Oakland Community College: Orchard Ridge Campus, 4635
Oakland University, 4636
Office of Services for Students with Disabilities, 4637
Patterns of English Spelling, 1116
Recording for the Blind & Dyslexic Learnin g Through Listening: Michigan Unit, 231
SLD Learning Center, 5671
Saginaw Valley State University, 4638
Sequential Spelling 1-7 with Student Response Book, 764
St. Clair County Community College, 4639
University of Michigan: Dearborn, 4640
University of Michigan: Flint, 4641
Washtenaw Community College, 4642
Western Michigan University, 4643

## Minnesota

Ablenet, 620, 828, 1058, 1058, 1175, 1204, 1312
Alexandria Technical College, 4644
Anoka-Ramsey Community College, 4645
Ants in His Pants: Absurdities and Realiti es of Special Education, 1060
Augsburg College, 4646
Basic Math for Job and Personal Use, 912
Basic Signing Vocabulary Cards, 630
Bemidji State University, 4647
Bethel College: Minnesota, 4648
Calculator Math for Job and Personal Use, 916
Calvin Academy and Special Education Day School, 4649
Camp Buckskin, 490
Camp Chi Rho, 491
Camp Confidence, 492
Camp Friendship, 493
Century College, 4650
Closing the Gap, 55
Closing the Gap Conference, 1524
College of Associated Arts, 4651
College of Saint Scholastica, 4652
College of St. Catherine: Minneapolis, 4653
College of St. Catherine: St. Paul Campus, 4654
Concordia College, 4655
Decimals and Percentages for Job and Personal Use, 923
Families and Advocates Partnership for Edu cation FAPE, 75
Goodwill/Easter Seals Minnesota, 6183
Goodwill/Easter Seals: St. Cloud, 6184
Goodwill/Easter Seals: St. Paul, 6185
Goodwill/Easter Seals: Willmar, 6186
Grammar and Writing for Job and Personal Use, 1448
Groves Academy, 5672
Gustavus Adolphus College, 4656
Hamline College, 4657
Hands-On Activities for Exceptional Studen ts, 852
Hibbing Community College, 4658
Higher Education Consortium for Urban Affairs, 2118
How the Student with Hearing Loss Can Succeed in College, 3933
Inclusion: Strategies for Working with Young Children, 1091
International Adolescent Conference: Programs for Adolescents, 1540
International Dyslexia Association: Upper Midwest Branch, 232
Inver Hills Community College, 4659
Itasca Community College, 4660
LDA Learning Center, 5673
Lake Superior College, 4661
Listening and Speaking for Job and Persona l Use, 703
Macalester College, 4662
Mankato State University, 4663
Mastering Reading Series, 1108

Mesabi Range Community & Technical College, 4664
Minneapolis Community College, 4665
Minnesota Department of Adult Education: Adult Basic Education, 2785
Minnesota Department of Children, Families & Learning, 2355
Minnesota Department of Employment and Economic Development, 2786, 6187
Minnesota Department of Human Rights, 2356
Minnesota Disability Law Center, 234
Minnesota GED Administration, 2787
Minnesota Governor's Council on Developmental Disabilities, 2357
Minnesota LDA Learning Disabilities Center, 2788
Minnesota LINCS: Literacy Council, 2789
Minnesota Life College, 4666
Minnesota Life Work Center, 2358, 2790
Minnesota Literacy Training Network, 2791
Minnesota State Community & Technology Col, 4667
Minnesota State University Moorehead, 4668
Minnesota University Affiliated Program on Developmental Disabilities, 4669
Minnesota Vocational Rehabilitation Agency: Rehabilitation Services Branch, 2792, 6032
Minnesota West Community & Technical College, 4670
Normandale Community College, 4671
North Hennepin Community College, 4672
Northwestern College, 4434, 4673
PACER Center, 120
Peer Pals, 1247, 1307
People at Work, 870
Phonemic Awareness: The Sounds of Reading, 1117
Pillsbury Baptist Bible College, 4674
Punctuation, Capitalization, and Handwriting for Job and Personal Use, 1476
Rainy River Community College, 4675
Reading for Job and Personal Use, 1141
Riverland Community College Student Success Center, 4676
Rochester Community and Technical College, 4677
Saint John's School of Theology & Seminary, 4678
Saint Mary's University of Minnesota, 4679
School-to-Work Outreach Project, 6188
Sign Language Classroom Resource, 765
Southwest Minnesota State University: Learning Resources, 4680
Spelling for Job and Personal Use, 1483
St. Cloud State University, 4681
St. Olaf College, 4682
St. Paul Technical College, 4683
State Vocational Rehabilitation Agency: Minnesota Department of Economics Security, 6189
Taking Part, 1267
That's Life Picture Stories, 889
University of Minnesota Disability Services, 4684
University of Minnesota: Crookston, 4685
University of Minnesota: Duluth, 4686
University of Minnesota: Morris, 4687
University of Minnesota: Twin Cities Campus, 4688
University of St. Thomas, 4689
Winnebago, 494
Working for Myself, 904
Worthington Community College, 4690

## Mississippi

Client Assistance Program (CAP): Mississippi Division of Persons with Disabilities, 2361
Department of Vocational Rehabilitation Services: Mississippi, 6190
Guide to Community Colleges Serving Students with Learning Disabilities, 3930
Heritage School, 5674
Hinds Community College, 4691
Holmes Community College, 4692

International Dyslexia Association: Mississippi, 235
Itawamba Community College, 4693
Millcreek Schools, 5675
Mississippi Employment Security Commission, 2363
Mississippi Project START, 2364
Mississippi State University, 4694
Mississippi University Affiliated Program, 4695
Northeast Mississippi Community College, 4696
State Vocational Rehabilitation Agency: Vocational Rehabilitation Division, 6191
University of Mississippi, 4697
University of Southern Mississippi, 4698
William Carey College, 4699

## Missouri

Central Methodist College, 4700
Central Missouri State University, 4701
Churchill School, 5676
East Central College, 4702
Equal Employment Opportunity Commission, 8, 2132, 2370, 2370
Evangel University, 4703
Fontbonne College, 4704
Gillis Center, 5677
Great Plains Disability and Business Technical Assistance Center (DBTAC), 2371
Jefferson College, 4705
Kansas City Art Institute, 4706
Key Concepts in Personal Development, 857
Learning Disabilities Association of Missouri, 2372
Lindenwood College, 4707
Literacy Investment for Tomorrow: Missouri, 2793
Literacy Kansas City, 2794
Longview Community College: ABLE Program- Academic Bridges to Learning Effectiveness, 4708
Maple Woods Community College, 4709
Metropolitan School, 5678
Miriam School, 5679
Missouri Parents Act (MPACT), 5680
Missouri Protection & Advocacy Services, 2373
Missouri Southern State College, 4710
Missouri Valley College, 4711
North Central Missouri College, 4712
Northwest Missouri State University, 4713
People to People International, 2123
Region VII: US Department of Health and Human Services, 2375
Rehabilitation Services for the Blind, 6192
Saint Louis University, 4714
Sertoma International/Sertoma Foundation, 130
Southwest Missouri State University, 4715
St. Louis Community College at Florissant Valley: Access Office, 4716
St. Louis Community College at Forest Park: Access Office, 4717
St. Louis Community College at Meramec, 4718
State Vocational Rehabilitation Agency Department of Elementary & Secondary Education, 6193
Understanding Me, 1165
University Affiliated Program for Developmental Disabilities, 4719
University of Missouri, 4720
University of Missouri: Kansas City, 4721
University of Missouri: Rolla, 4722
Washington University, 4723
Westminster College, 4724

## Montana

Developmental Disabilities Planning and Advisory Council, 2378
Dull Knife Memorial College, 4725

### Nebraska

### Nevada

### New Hampshire

## New York

## North Carolina

## Rhode Island

## South Carolina

Wiley College, 5287

## Utah

Adult Education Services, 6259
American Council on Rural Special Educatio n Conference, 1512
Assistive Technology Center, 2545
Assistive Technology Program, 2449, 2510, 2546, 2546
Brigham Young University, 5288
Center for Persons with Disabilities, 2547, 5289
College of Eastern Utah, 5290
Disability Law Center, 2548
Easter Seals Utah, 592
Latter-Day Saints Business College, 5291
Literacy Volunteers of America: Wasatch Front, 2917
Mountain Plains Regional Resource Center, 5822
Reid Ranch, 593
Reid School, 5823
SEPS Center for Learning, 5824
Salt Lake Community College: Disability Resource Center, 5292
Snow College, 5293
Southern Utah University, 5294
State Office of Education, 2550
University of Utah, 5295
Utah Governor's Council for People with Disabilities, 2551
Utah Labor Commission: Utah Anti-discrimin ation and Labor Division, 2552
Utah Literacy Action Center, 2918
Utah Literacy Resource Center, 2919
Utah Parent Center, 5825
Utah State University, 5296
Utah Valley State College, 5297
Utah Work Force, 2553
Weber State University, 5298
Westminster College of Salt Lake City, 5299

## Vermont

ABE Career and Lifelong Learning: Vermont Department of Education, 2920
Adult Education & Literacy State Department of Education, 6261
Burlington College, 5300
Champlain College, 5301
College of St. Joseph, 5302
Community College of Vermont, 5303
Easter Seals Vermont, 594
Green Mountain College, 5304
Johnson State College, 5305
Landmark College, 5306
Learning Disabilities Association of Vermont, 304
Learning Disabilities Association of Vermo nt, 2555, 2921
Norwich University, 5307
Pine Ridge School, 5826
REACH-UP Program: Department of Social Welfare, 6262
REACH-UP Program: Department of Social Wel fare, 2557
Silver Towers Camp, 595
Southern Vermont College, 5308
Stern Center for Language and Learning, 5827
University of Vermont, 5309
Vermont Agency of Human Services, 2560
Vermont Assistive Technology Project: Depa rtment of Aging and Disabilities, 2561, 2922
Vermont Department of Corrections, 2923
Vermont Department of Employment & Trainin g, 2562, 6263
Vermont Department of Welfare, 2563, 2924
Vermont Developmental Disabilities Council, 2564
Vermont Disability Law Project, 2565
Vermont Governor's Office, 2566
Vermont Human Resources Investment Council, 2925

Vermont Legal Aid Client Assistance Progra m and Disability Law Project, 2567
Vermont Literacy Resource Center: Departme nt of Education, 2926
Vermont Protection and Advocacy, 305
Vermont REACH-UP Program, 2568, 2927
Vermont Special Education, 2569
Vermont Technical College, 5310
Vermont Workforce Reinvestment Act, 2928
VocRehab Vermont, 2929, 6264

## Virginia

ADA Clearinghouse and Resource Center, 1
Accolink Academy, 5828
Achievment Center, The, 5829
Adult and Employment Training: Virginia Department of Education, 2570
American Counseling Association, 31
American Counseling Association Convention, 1513
American Rehabilitation Counseling Associa tion (ARCA), 38
Assistive Technology System, 2571
Association Book Exhibit: Brain Research, 1517
Averett College, 5311
Blue Ridge Community College, 5312
Brain Injury Association, 51
CEC Federation Conference: Virginia, 1522
Camp Easter Seals East, 590
Campus Opportunities for Students with Learning Differences, 3919
Charlotte County Literacy Program, 2930
Chesapeake Bay Academy, 5830
Children with ADD: A Shared Responsibility, 337
College of William and Mary, 5313
Council for Educational Diagnostic Service s, 2620
Council for Exceptional Children, 59
Council for Exceptional Children (CEC), 60
Council for Learning Disabilities, 61
Council for Learning Disabilities Internat ional Conference, 1529
Creative Mind Workshop: Making Magic with Children and Art, 1532
DCE-LVA Virginia Institutions, 2931
Department of Rehabilitative Services, 6265
Division for Children's Communication Development, 2622
Division for Culturally and Linguistically Diverse Learners, 64, 2623
Division for Early Childhood, 65
Division for Learning Disabilities, 66
Division for Research, 67, 2624
Division on Career Development, 68, 6029
Division on Visual Impairments, 69
Driven to Distraction: Attention Deficit Disorder from Childhood Through Adulthood, 340
Eastern Mennonite University, 5314
Emory & Henry College, 5315
Fairfax County Community and Recreation, 596
Fairfax House, 5831
Ferrum College, 5316
GW Community School, 5317
Grafton School, 5832
Hampden-Sydney College, 5318
Highlands Educational Literacy Program, 2932
Home School Legal Defense Association, 9
How to Teach ADD-ADHD Children, 349
James Madison University, 5319
John Tyler Community College, 5320
Learning Center of Charlottesville, 5833
Learning Disabilities Association of Virginia, 306
Learning Needs & Evaluation Center: Elson Student Health Center, 5321
Learning Resource Center, 5834
Leary School of Virginia, 5835

Wisconsin Indianhead Tech College: Rice La ke Campus, 5448
Wisconsin Literacy Resource Center, 2968
Wisconsin Literacy Services, 2969
Work Force Information Act, 6274

### Wyoming

Adult Basic Education, 2605
Client Assistance Program (CAP): Wyoming D ivision, 2606
Correctional Education: Wyoming Women's Center, 2607
Laramie County Community College: Disabili ty Resource
Center, 5449
Literacy Volunteers of Casper, 2970
Literacy Volunteers of Douglas, 2971
Literacy Volunteers of Powell North Colleg e, 2972
Literacy Volunteers of Sheridan/Northern Wyoming, 2973
Northwest College, 5450
Protection & Advocacy Agency, 2183, 2220, 2228, 2228, 2248,
2257, 2282, 2291, 2311, 2326, 2341, 2359, 2374, 2400, 2412,
2421, 2444
Sheridan College, 5451
State Department of Education, 2159, 2211, 2245, 2245, 2250,
2283, 2293, 2313, 2331, 2366, 2388, 2402, 2472, 2501, 2528,
2558, 2574
State GED Administration, 2184, 2221, 2230, 2230, 2246, 2251,
2259, 2284, 2319, 2353, 2389, 2431, 2447, 2473, 2481, 2502, 2517
State Vocational Rehabilitation Agency, 6123, 6142, 6147, 6147,
6154, 6160, 6166, 6167, 6168, 6171, 6176, 6182, 6199, 6211,
6219, 6226, 6232
University of Wyoming, 5452
University of Wyoming: Division of Social Work and
Wyoming Institute for Disabilities (WIND), 5453
Wyoming Department of Employment and Job Training
Programs, 2611
Wyoming Literacy Resource Center, 2974
Wyoming Parent Information Center, 5852

## ADD/ADHD

## Animation

## Aphasia

## Aptitude

## Articulation

## Arts

## At-Risk

BRIGANCE Screens: Early Preschool, 5895
BRIGANCE Screens: Infants and Toddler, 5896
BRIGANCE Screens: K and 1, 5897
Basic School Skills Inventory: Screen and Diagnostic, 5898
DABERON Screening for School Readiness, 5900
Developmental Assessment for the Severely Disabled, 5901

## Autism

Activity Schedules for Children with Autism: A Guide for Parents and Professionals, 3061
Autism Research Institute, 46
Autism Research Review International, 3600
Autism Screening Instrument for Educational Planning, 5873
Autism Society of America, 47
Autism Treatment Center of America, 48
Behind the Glass Door: Hannah's Story, 3456
Children with Autism, 3082
Community Based Services, 5718
Devereux Center for Autism, 5692
Eden Institute Curriculum: Classroom, 1729
Eden Institute Curriculum: Classroom Orienation, Volume II, 3758
Eden Institute Curriculum: Core, 3759
Eden Institute Curriculum: Speech and Language, Volume IV, 3760
Eden Institute Curriculum: Volume I, 1820
Eden Services, 5695
Effective Teaching Methods for Autistic Children, 3108
Fundamentals of Autism, 2999, 3252, 5884, 5903
General Information about Autism, 3253
Getting Started with Facilitated Communication, 3471
Going to School with Facilitated Communication, 3472
I Want My Little Boy Back, 3476
Ivymount School, 4529
Kaufman Assessment Battery for Children, 5906
Kaufman Brief Intelligence Test, 5907
SEARCH Day Program, 5705
Sensory Motor Issues in Autism, 877
Son Rise: The Miracle Continues, 3203
Son-Rise Program, 131
Son-Rise Program: Autism Treatment Center of America, 5662
Son-Rise: The Miracle Continues, 2987
www.autismtreatment.com, 3540
www.son-rise.org, 3582

## Behavioral Disorders

Behavior Management System, 3674
Calm Down and Play, 1219
Child Behavior Checklist, 5878
Children with Learning and Behavioral Disorders, 3246
Competencies for Teachers of Students with Learning Disabilities, 3739
Defiant Children, 3097
Devereux Deerhaven, 5693
Feelings, 1823
Instructional Methods for Students, 3795
Learning Disabilities and Social Skills: Last One Picked..First One Picked On, 3488
National Institute of Mental Health, 2134
School Behaviors and Organization Skills, 5889
Stop, Relax and Think, 1259
Stop, Relax and Think Ball, 1260
Stop, Relax and Think Card Game, 1261
Stop, Relax and Think Scriptbook, 1262
Stop, Relax and Think Workbook, 1263

## Bilingual Resources

Articulation 3-Vowels: Software, 626
BRIGANCE Assessment of Basic Skills: Spanish Edition, 5964
Bilingualism and Learning Disabilities, 3726

## Camps

American Institute for Foreign Study, 2112
American-Scandinavian Foundation, 2114
Association for International Practical Training, 2115
Camp Arrowhead YMCA YMCA, 558
Camp Easter Seals, 495
Camp Fire USA, 559
Crossroads for Kids, 476
Earthstewards Network, 2116
Easter Seals, 71
Easter Seals ARC of Northeast Indiana, 454
Easter Seals Achievement Center, 6069
Easter Seals Adult Services Center, 396, 6070
Easter Seals Alabama, 6071
Easter Seals Albany, 520
Easter Seals Arc of Northeast Indiana, 6149
Easter Seals Arizona, 394
Easter Seals Bay Area: San Jose, 397
Easter Seals Bay Area: Tri-Valley Campus, 398
Easter Seals Bethlehem, 568
Easter Seals Broadview Heights, 549
Easter Seals Broward County Florida, 6126
Easter Seals Camp, 582
Easter Seals Camp ASCCA, 6072
Easter Seals Camp Carpenter, 500
Easter Seals Camp Hemlocks, 422
Easter Seals Camp KYSOC, 460
Easter Seals Camp Merry Heart, 505
Easter Seals Camp Rocky Mountain Village, 409
Easter Seals Camp Sunnyside, 457
Easter Seals Camp Wawbeek, 607
Easter Seals Camping and Recreation List, 446
Easter Seals Capilouto Center for the Deaf, 6073
Easter Seals Center, 6155
Easter Seals Central California, 399, 6095
Easter Seals Central California: Camp Harmon, 400
Easter Seals Central Illinois, 447, 6144
Easter Seals Central Pennsylvania, 561
Easter Seals Central Texas, 585
Easter Seals Central and Southeast Ohio, 550
Easter Seals Cincinnati, 551
Easter Seals Collaborative Solutions, 6178
Easter Seals Colorado, 410, 6102
Easter Seals Connecticut, 6109
Easter Seals Crossroads Industrial Services, 6150
Easter Seals Crossroads Rehabilitation Center: Indiana, 6151
Easter Seals Delaware and Maryland Shore, 6115
Easter Seals Dover Enterprise, 6116
Easter Seals Downingtown, 569
Easter Seals East Georgia, 6133
Easter Seals East Rochester, 521
Easter Seals Eastern Pennsylvania, 570
Easter Seals Employment Connections-Pennyrile, 6164
Easter Seals Employment Industries, 6110
Easter Seals Eureka, 401
Easter Seals Florida: Central Florida, 437
Easter Seals Florida: East Coast Region, 6127
Easter Seals Franklin, 571
Easter Seals Fulfillment Enterprises, 6111
Easter Seals Genesee County, 486
Easter Seals Georgetown Professional Center, 6117
Easter Seals Greenville, 579
Easter Seals Gulf Coast, 393
Easter Seals Hawaii: Oahu Service Center, 443
Easter Seals Iowa, 6156

Easter Seals Jayne Shover Center, 448
Easter Seals Joliet, 449
Easter Seals Kansas, 6161
Easter Seals Kentucky, 461
Easter Seals Kulpsville, 572
Easter Seals Levittown, 573
Easter Seals Lorain, 552
Easter Seals Louisiana, 463
Easter Seals Madison, 608
Easter Seals Marietta, 553
Easter Seals Massachusetts, 477
Easter Seals Medford, 562
Easter Seals Media, 574
Easter Seals Menomonee Falls, 609
Easter Seals Miami-Dade, 6128
Easter Seals Michigan, 487
Easter Seals Michigan: Saginaw, 488
Easter Seals Middle Georgia, 6134
Easter Seals Missouri, 450, 6145
Easter Seals Monterey, 402
Easter Seals Nebraska, 497, 6200
Easter Seals New Hampshire, 242, 6208
Easter Seals New Hampshire, 501
Easter Seals New Mexico, 509
Easter Seals North Florida, 6129
Easter Seals Northeast Ohio, 554
Easter Seals Northern California, 403
Easter Seals Northern California: Rohnert Park, 404
Easter Seals Oklahoma, 560
Easter Seals Opportunity Center, 6074
Easter Seals Oregon, 563
Easter Seals Pierre, 580
Easter Seals Rehabilitation Center, 6075
Easter Seals Rehabilitation Center: Northwest Alabama, 6076
Easter Seals South Central Pennsylvania, 575
Easter Seals Southeastern Wisconsin, 610
Easter Seals Southern California, 6096
Easter Seals Southern Colorado, 411
Easter Seals Southern Georgia, 441, 6135
Easter Seals Southwest Florida, 6130
Easter Seals Spokane, 602
Easter Seals Superior California, 405, 6097
Easter Seals Superior California: Stockton, 406
Easter Seals Tri-Counties California, 407
Easter Seals Tucson, 395
Easter Seals UCP: Peoria, 451
Easter Seals Utah, 592
Easter Seals Vermont, 594
Easter Seals Volusia and Flagler Counties, 438
Easter Seals Washington, 603
Easter Seals Wayne & Union Counties, 455
Easter Seals West Virginia, 604
Easter Seals Youngstown, 555
Easter Seals Youth at Risk, 6146
Easter Seals of Central Texas, 299
Easter Seals of Greater Dallas, 300
Easter Seals of Northern Kentucky, 462
Easter Seals of Southeast Wisconsin, 310
Easter Seals of Southeastern Pennsylvania, 576
Easter Seals-Goodwill Career Designs, 6194
Easter Seals-Goodwill Staffing Services, 6139
Easter Seals-Goodwill Store, 6195
Easter Seals-Goodwill Working Partners, 6196
Easter Seals-Goodwill Working Partners: Great Falls, 6197
Easter Seals-Goodwill Working Partners: Hardin, 6198
Easter Seals-Goodwill Working Solutions, 6140
Easter Seals: Birmingham Area, 6077
Easter Seals: Bridgepointe, 6152
Easter Seals: Keene, 6209
Easter Seals: Manchester, 6210
Easter Seals: Massachusetts, 6172
Easter Seals: Redondo Beach, 6098
Easter Seals: Silverton, 6213

Easter Seals: Southern California, 6099
Easter Seals: Uncasville, 6112
Easter Seals: Van Nuys, 6100
Easter Seals: Waterbury, 6113
Easter Seals: West Alabama, 6078
Easter Seals: West Kentucky, 6165
Easter Seals: Worcester, 6173
Easter Seals: Youngstown, Ohio, 276
El Paso LDA Vacation Adventure, 586
Good Will Easter Seals, 5454, 6079
No Barriers to Study, 2122
Samuel Field/Bay Terrace YM & YWHA Special Services, 532
Star Ranch: Summer Program, 589
Talisman Summer Camp, 540
Youth for Understanding USA, 2125

### Child Welfare

CHILD FIND of Connecticut, 2214
Caring for Your Baby and Young Child: Birth to Age 5, 3081
Child Care Association of Illinois, 194
Eckerd Family Youth Alternatives, 439
Help Build a Brighter Future: Children at Risk for LD in Child Care Centers, 3126
Iowa Welfare Programs, 2288
Jewish Children's Bureau of Chicago, 198
Sequenced Inventory of Communication Development, 5993
Temporary Assistance for Needy Families, 6148, 6169
Temporary Assistance for Needy Families: Idaho Department of Health and Welfare, 2719, 6143

### Clearinghouses

American Self-Help Clearinghouse of New Jersey, 248
Clearinghouse for Specialized Media, 2192
Clearinghouse on Disability Information, 54

### Cognitive Disorders

Alpine Tram Ride, 1672
Atypical Cognitive Deficits, 3721
Cognitive Approach to Learning Disabilities, 3736
Contemporary Intellectual Assessment: Theories, Tests and Issues, 3094
Hands-On Activities for Exceptional Students, 852
Helping Students Become Strategic Learners, 3688
Implementing Cognitive Strategy Instruction Across the School, 3787
Link N' Learn Activity Book, 1360
MCLA: Measure of Cognitive-Linguistic Abilities, 709
Problem Sensitivity: A Qualitative Difference in the Learning Disabled, 3266
Putting the Pieces Together: Volume 4, 871
Test of Nonverbal Intelligence, 5920
Workbook for Reasoning Skills, 901

### Comic Strips

Teaching Old Logs New Tricks: Absurdities and Realities of Education, 3216

### Communication Disorders

Art of Communication, 3452
Communication Aids, 1334
Communication Skills in Children with Down Syndrome, 3089
If Your Child Stutters: A Guide for Parents, 3257
Learning Problems in Language, 3489
My House: Language Activities of Daily Living, 1845
Now You're Talking: Extend Conversation, 3420
Personal Communicating Device, 1602

## Creative Expression

## Critical Thinking

## Curriculum Guides

## Daily Living

### Databases

### Developmental Disabilities

## Directories

## Discrimination

## Dispute Resolution Dyslexia

## Dyslexia

## Elementary Education

## Equality

## Ethics

## Evaluations

## Eye/Hand Coordination

## Family Involvement

## Family Resources

## Financial Resources

## Fluency

## Gameboards

## Gifted Education

## History

## Hotlines

## Human Services

Administration on Children, Youth and Families: US Department of Education, 2126
Advocacy, 2532
Alabama Disabilities Advocacy Program, 2149
Alaska Department of Labor: Employment Security Division, 2152
American Public Human Services Association (APHSA), 36
Arkansas Department of Human Services: Division of Rehabilitation Services, 2173
Arkansas Governor's Developmental Disabilities Council, 2177
California State Council on Developmental Disabilities, 2190
Center for Human Development (CHD) University Affiliated Program, 143
Client Assistance Program: Governor's Commission on Disability, 2403
Connecticut Department of Social Services, 2216
Delaware Department of Labor, 2227
Department of Health & Human Services: New Hampshire, 6207
Department of Human Resources, 6068
Department of Human Services: Bureau of Training & Employment, 6121
Department of Human Services: Division of Developmental Disabilities Services, 6088
Department of Human Services: Division of Rehabilitation Services, 2527, 2888
Department of Human Services: Project Forward, 6220
Department of Social Services, 6247
Disability Law Center, 2548
Disability Law Center of Alaska, 2156
District of Columbia Office of Human Rights, 2234
Employment Service Division: Alabama, 2150
Employment Standards Administration: US Department of Labor, 2130
Governor's Council on Developmental Disabilities, 2286
Granite State Independent Living Foundation, 2404
Human Development Center, 4488
Human Services: Division of Developmental Disabilities, 6103
Human Services: Division of Vocational Rehabilitation, 6104
Idaho Human Rights Commission, 2256
Illinois Department of Human Rights, 2269
Increasing Capabilities Access Network, 2181
Indiana ATTAIN Project, 2280
Institute for Human Development: Northern Arizona University, 146
Institute on Disability, 2405
Institute on Disability at the University of New Hampshire, 2406
Kansas Advocacy Protective Services, 2296
Kansas Department of Human Resources, 2297
Kansas Department of Social and Rehabilitation Services, 2298
Kansas Human Rights Commission, 2299
Maine Department of Labor: Bureau of Rehabilitation Services, 2323
Maine Human Rights Commission, 2325
Michigan Protection and Advocacy Service, 2351
Minnesota Department of Children, Families & Learning, 2355
Minnesota Department of Human Rights, 2356
Minnesota Governor's Council on Developmental Disabilities, 2357
Nevada Governor's Council on Developmental Disabilities, 2398
New Jersey Programs for Children with Disabilities: Ages 3 - 5, 2418
New Mexico Human Rights Commission Education Bureau, 2426
New York Department of Human Rights, 2434
North Carolina Division of Vocational Rehabilitation, 2453
North Dakota Department of Human Services, 2460
North Dakota Department of Human Services: Welfare & Public Assistance, 2835

Office of Advocacy for Persons with Disabilities, 2439
Oregon Department of Human Resource Adult & Family Services Division, 2487, 2851
Parent Information Center: New Hampshire Coalition for Citizens With Disabilities, 2411
Pennsylvania Human Rights Commission and Fair Employment Practice, 2495
Pennsylvania's Initiative on Assistive Technology, 2497
Programs for Children with Disabilities: Ages 3 - 5, 2441
REACH-UP Program: Department of Social Welfare, 6262
Rhode Island Commission for Human Rights, 2505
Rhode Island Department of Human Services, 2872
Rhode Island Human Resource Investment Council, 2874
ServiceLink, 2413
South Carolina Human Affairs Commission, 2515
South Dakota Department of Labor, 6248
South Dakota Division of Human Rights, 2522
State Council on Developmental Disabilities, 2249
State Department of Adult & Community Education, 2229
State Developmental Disabilities Planning Council, 2446
State of Alaska Community & Regional Affairs Department: Administrative Services, 2161
State of Connecticut: Board of Education for the Visually Impaired, 2223
Texas Commission on Human Rights, 2537
University of Oregon for Excellence in Developmental Disabilities, 285
University of Washington: Center on Human Development and Disability, 5390
Utah Governor's Council for People with Disabilities, 2551
Vermont Agency of Human Services, 2560
Vermont Human Resources Investment Council, 2925
Virginia Board for People with Disabilities, 2576
Washington Human Rights Commission, 2587
Youth Dakota Advocacy Services, 2525

## Inclusion

Andreas: Outcomes of Inclusion, 3449
Backyards & Butterflies: Ways to Include Children with Disabilities, 3073
Center for Community Inclusion (CCI): Maine's University Center for Excellence, 4504
Devereux Mapleton, 5774
Devereux Massachusetts, 5646
Devereux Santa Barbara, 5473
Disabled and Their Parents: A Counseling Challenge, 3680
General Guidelines for Providers of Psychological Services, 3685
Inclusion Series, 3481
Inclusion: An Essential Guide for the Paraprofessional, 3149, 3792
Institute for Community Inclusion (ICI), 4568
Learning Difficulties and Emotional Problems, 3161
Making School Inclusion Work, 3808
Social-Emotional Dimension Scale, 5891
Southern Adventist University, 5211
Take Part Art, 3842

## Infancy

New Jersey Programs for Infants and Toddlers with Disabilities: Early Intervention System, 2419
Programs for Infants and Toddlers with Disabilities, 2443
Tips for Teaching Infants & Toddlers, 896, 1045
www.babycenter.com, 3541

## Information Resources

A Human Development View of Learning Disabilities: From Theory to Practice, 3704
American Heritage Children's Dictionary, 621

BOSC Books on Special Children, 3348
Bethany House Publishers, 3349
Center Work, 3731
Change Agent, 6041
Charles C Thomas Publisher, 3353
Complete Learning Disabilities Handbook, 3740
How to Organize Your Child and Save Your Sanity, 3138
Including Students with Severe and Multiple Disabilities in Typical Classrooms, 3789
Landmark School Resources, 3800
Learning Company, 2021
Learning Disabilities Association of Texas Newsletter, 3321
National Bible Association, 3383
National Dissemination Center for Children with Disabilities, 109
National Resources, 3260
Northwest Media, 3384
Questions to Aid in Selecting an Appropriate College Program for LD, 3941
Reader's Digest Partners for Sight Foundation, 3389
Scholastic, 2028
Sunburst Communications, 2029
Thomas Nelson Publishers, 3396
Thomas T Beeler, Publisher, 3397
Thorndike Press, 3398
Transaction Publishers, 3399
Underachieving Gifted, 3278
www.abcparenting.com, 3534
www.childparenting.about.com, 3544
www.disabilityresources.org, 3546
www.hood.edu/seri/serihome.htm, 3559
www.ldresources.com, 3569
www.wrightlaw.com, 3586

## Integration

Division on Career Development, 68, 6029
Inclusion: 450 Strategies for Success, 3147, 3790
Michigan Developmental Disabilities Council, 2349
Minnesota Access Services, 233
Regular Lives, 3498
South Dakota Council on Developmental Disabilities, 2520

## International Associations

International Reading Association Newspaper: Reading Today, 353
International Reading Association Newspaper: Reading Today, 3316
International Summerstays, 2119
Lisle Fellowship, 2120
People to People International, 2123
World Experience, 2124
www.familyvillage.wisc.edu, 3552

## Intervention

Academic Skills Problems Workbook, 3707
Accessing Programs for Infants, Toddlers and Preschoolers, 3241
Behavior Change in the Classroom: Self-Management Interventions, 3909
Bridges to Reading, 3077
Brief Intervention for School Problems: Collaborating for Practical Solutions, 3729
Child Who is Ignored: Module 6, 3464
Connecticut Center for Children and Families, 5510
Division for Early Childhood, 65
Early Intervention in Natural Environments, 3885
Easy Talker: A Fluency Workbook for School Age Children, 5979
Focus on Exceptional Children, 3773

Guidelines and Recommended Practices for Individualized Family Service Plan, 3123
HELP Activity Guide, 3776
Hammit School: The Baby Fold, 5601
Helping Students Succeed in the Regular Classroom, 3781
Intervention in School and Clinic, 3796
Just Kids: Early Childhood Learning Center, 5727
New Hampshire Easter Seals Early Intervention Program, 245
Practitioner's Guide to Dynamic Assessment, 3692
Reading Writing & Rage: The Terrible Price Paid By Victims of School Failure, 3192
Tomorrow's Children, 3506
When Slow Is Fast Enough: Educating the Delayed Preschool Child, 3887
Yale Child Study Center, 5540

## Job/Vocational Resources

A Student's Guide to Jobs, 3238
Adult Education & Literacy State Department of Education, 6261
Alabama Department of Industrial Relations, 2148
Arizona Governor's Committee on Employment of the Handicapped, 2167
Arkansas Employment Security Department, 2176
BRIGANCE Employability Skills Inventory, 5966
Bottom Line: Basic Skills in the Workplace, 6038
California Department of Fair Employment and Housing, 2185
California Employment Development Department, 2188
Career Inventories for the Learning Disabled, 6040
Career Planner's Portfolio: A School-to-work Assessment Tool, 5934
Colorado Department of Labor and Employment, 2204
Department of Employment Services, 6120
Department of Personnel & Human Services, 2579
Different Way of Learning, 3515
Direct Link, May I Help You?, 3516
District of Columbia Department of Employment Services, 2232
District of Columbia Fair Employment Practice Agencies, 2233
Division of Family Development: New Jersey Department of Human Services, 6212
Easter Seal Michigan, 6177
Employment Initiatives Model: Job Coach Training Manual and Tape, 3517
Fair Employment Practice Agency, 2157, 2169
Florida Department of Labor and Employment Security, 2237
Florida Fair Employment Practice Agency, 2238
Florida Vocational Rehabilitation Agency: Division of Vocational Rehabilitation, 2700
Florida Workforce Investment Act, 6131
For Employers: A Look at Learning Disabilities, 6045
Goodwill/Easter Seals Minnesota, 6183
Goodwill/Easter Seals: St. Cloud, 6184
Goodwill/Easter Seals: St. Paul, 6185
Goodwill/Easter Seals: Willmar, 6186
How Not to Contact Employers, 3519
Idaho Department of Commerce & Labor, 6141
Idaho Fair Employment Practice Agency, 2255
Idaho Workforce Investment Act, 2718
Illinois Department of Employment Security, 2268
Illinois Fair Employment Practice Agency, 2271
Illinois Office of Rehabilitation Services, 2272, 2723
Indiana Employment Services and Job Training Program Liaison, 2281
Iowa Employment Service, 2287
Iowa JOBS Program: Division of Economic Assistance, 2738, 6158
Iowa Workforce Investment Act, 2289, 2741
JOBS Program: Massachusetts Employment Services Program, 2770, 6174
Job Access, 6050
Job Accommodation Handbook, 6051

## Language Skills

## Leadership

## Legal Issues

## Literature

## Sound Recognition

## Special Education

## Speech Skills

## Spelling

## Strategies

## Student Workshops

## Support Groups

## Surveys

## Switches

## Synthesizers

28 Instant Song Games, 1004, 1203

## Transportation

American Red Cross, 37
Division of Vocational Rehabilitation, 2253, 2948, 6114, 6125, 6227
Let's Find Out, 3298
Office of Vocational and Educational Services for Individuals with Disabilities, 6225
Rehabilitation Grants and Contracts Monitor, 3646
Related Services for School-Aged Children with Disabilities, 3272
South Carolina Vocational Rehabilitation Department, 6246
State Vocational Rehabilitation Agency, 6123, 6142, 6147, 6154, 6160, 6166, 6167, 6168, 6171, 6176, 6182, 6199, 6211, 6219, 6226, 6232, 6240, 6250, 6251, 6256, 6260
State Vocational Rehabilitation Agency New Mexico, 6222
State Vocational Rehabilitation Agency Department of Elementary & Secondary Education, 6193
State Vocational Rehabilitation Agency of Alabama, 6080
State Vocational Rehabilitation Agency of Alaska, 6083
State Vocational Rehabilitation Agency of Arkansas, 6090
State Vocational Rehabilitation Agency of Colorado, 6105
State Vocational Rehabilitation Agency: Minnesota Department of Economics Security, 6189
State Vocational Rehabilitation Agency: Oklahoma Department of Rehabilitation Services, 6234
State Vocational Rehabilitation Agency: Washington Division of Vocational Rehabilitation, 6268
State Vocational Rehabilitation Agency: Wisconsin Division of Vocational Rehabilitation, 6272
State Vocational Rehabilitation Agency: Pennsylvania, 6241
State Vocational Rehabilitation Agency: Quality Employment Solutions, 6202
State Vocational Rehabilitation Agency: Rhode Island, 6244
State Vocational Rehabilitation Agency: Vocational Rehabilitation Division, 6191
TILES Project: Transition/Independent Living/Employment/Support, 6132
West Virginia Division of Rehabilitation Services, 6270

## Treatment

ADHD in Adolescents: Diagnosis and Treatment, 3057
AdvoServ, 5541
American Psychological Association, 35, 3346
American Psychologist, 3588
Anger Within Programs 1-4: Walking Through the Storm Life Space Crisis Intervention, 3450
Attentional Deficit Disorder in Children and Adolescents, 3720
BASC Monitor for ADHD, 5874
Behavior Analysis in Education, 3673
Boys and Girls Village, 5505
Camelot Care Center, 5798
Camelot Care Center: Illinois, 5589
Chileda Institute, 5851
Cognitive-Behavioral Therapy for Impulsive Children: 2nd Edition, 3677
Curtis Home, 5513
Devereux Arizona Treatment Network, 5461
Devereux Brandywine, 5772
Devereux Foundation, 5773
Devereux Genesis Learning Centers, 5799
Devereux Glenholme School, 5514
Eastern Associates Speech and Language Services, 5746
Elmcrest Schools, 5516
Emergence: Labeled Autistic, 3110
Full Circle Programs, 5477
Harmony Hill School, 5790
Heartspring School, 5616
Helping Your Hyperactive Child, 3133
Hyperactive Children Grown Up, 3141

Illinois Center for Autism, 5603
International Dyslexia Association Quarterly Newsletter: Perspectives, 3312
International Dyslexia Association: National Headquarters, 82, 2629
Interventions for ADHD: Treatment in Developmental Context, 3153
Journal of Speech, Language, and Hearing Research, 3656
Julia Dyckman Andrus Memorial, 5726
Kennedy Krieger Institute for Handicapped Children, 5634
Klingberg Family Centers, 5523
Lorraine D Foster Day School, 5527
Mental Health Report, 3640
Millcreek Schools, 5675
NAWA Academy, 5482
Natchaug Hospital School Program, 5529
New England Center for Children, 5658
Pines Residential Treatment Center, 5841
Providence Speech and Hearing Center, 5488, 5864
Saint Francis Home for Children: Highland Heights, 5533
Sensory Integration & Vision Therapy Specialists, 5637
Sensory Integration & Vision Therapy Specialists, 5638
Star Ranch, 5818
Stuttering Severity Instrument for Children and Adults, 5998
Treatment of Children's Grammatical Impairments in Naturalistic Context, 3507
Waterford Country Schools, 5537

## Visual Assistive Devices

AppleWorks Manuals: Special Editions, 1624
Benton Visual Retention Test: Fifth Edition, 6011
Braille 'n Speak Scholar, 1813
Braille' n Speak Classic, 1578, 2089
Development Test of Visual Perception, 6013
Developmental Test of Visual Perception (DTVP-2), 6014
Genie Color TV, 1589
Home Row Indicators, 1591
National Association for Visually Handicapped, 3382
Opening Windows: A Talking and Tactile Tutorial for Microsoft Windows, 1631
Self-Adhesive Braille Keytop Labels, 1607
Ulverscroft Large Print Books, 3400
Updown Chair, 1272
VISTA, 1619
Xavier Society for the Blind, 3404
www.allaboutvision.com, 3538

## Visual Discrimination

Associated Services for the Blind, 3347
Bureau of Services to the Blind & Visually Impaired, 6203
Commission for the Blind & Visually Handicapped, 6223
Comparison Kitchen, 1817
Educating Students Who Have Visual Impairments with Other Disabilities, 3106
Gremlin Hunt, 1738
I Can Read, 1089
Illinois Catholic Guild for the Blind, 195
Jewish Braille Institute of America, 3371
Lighthouse Low Vision Products, 1106
Lutheran Braille Workers: Sight Saving Division, 160
Michigan Commission for the Blind: Deafblind Unit, 6179
National Federation of the Blind, 112
Recording for the Blind & Dyslexic Learning Through Listening: Michigan Unit, 231
Recording for the Blind & Dyslexic of Metropolitan Washington, 177
Recording for the Blind & Dyslexic: Berkshire/Lenox/Williamstown, 227
Recording for the Blind & Dyslexic: Chicago Loop Studio & Administrative Offices, 200
Recording for the Blind & Dyslexic: Kentucky Chapter, 216

## Vocabulary

## Voice Output Devices

## Volunteer

## Workshop Training

## Writing

# Glossary

**Accommodations:** Techniques and materials that allow individuals with LD to complete school or work tasks with greater ease and effectiveness. Examples include spellcheckers, tape recorders, and expanded time for completing assignments.

**ADA:** Americans with Disabilities Act.

**Adaptive Physical Education:** A special education program designed to suit a person's limits and disabilities.

**Alternative Assessment:** An alternative to conventional means of assessing achievement; usually means using something other than a paper and pencil test, such as oral testing or work sample review.

**Appeal:** A written request for a change in a decision.

**Aptitude Test:** A test developed to measure a person's ability to learn, and the likelihood of succeeding in academic work or in specific careers.

**Assistive Technology (AT):** Equipment that enhances the ability of students and employees to be more efficient and successful. For individuals with LD, computer grammar checkers, an overhead projector used by a teacher, or the audiovisual information delivered through a CD-ROM would be typical examples.

**Attention Deficit Disorder (ADD):** A disorder of brain function, causing severe difficulty in focusing and maintaining attention, paying attention to details, listening to instructions, and organizing assignments, thoughts and behaviors. Often leads to learning/academic difficulties, and behavior problems at home, school, and work. ADD is not a learning disability.

**Attention Deficit Hyperactivity Disorder (AD/HD):** A disorder of brain function, causing severe difficulty in staying on task, accompanied by hyperactivity. Difficulties can occur in taking turns in games or conversations, controlling temper outbursts, anticipating the consequences of actions, and containing or managing internal restlessness.

**Auditory Discrimination:** The ability to recognize, compare, and differentiate the discrete sounds in words; this ability is crucial for reading skills. Categorized as gross ability (e.g., detecting the differences between the noises made by a cow and a horse) or fine ability (e.g., distinguishing between the "s" sound and the "sh" sound).

**Auditory Figure-Ground Discrimination:** The ability to distinguish significant sounds amid a noisy background, and to focus on the auditory information being presented.

**Auditory Memory:** The ability to remember something heard some time in the past (long-term auditory memory); the ability to recall something heard very recently (short-term auditory memory).

**Auditory Sequencing:** The ability to comprehend and recollect the order of spoken words.

**AYP:** Annual yearly progress.

**Behavior Modification:** A technique intended to alter behavior by positive reinforcement (rewarding desirable actions) and ignoring undesirable actions.

**Binocular Fusion:** The blending of separate images from each eye into a single significant image.

**Brain Imaging Techniques:** Recently developed, noninvasive techniques for studying the activity of living brains. Includes brain electrical activity mapping (BEAM), computerized axial tomography (CAT), and magnetic resonance imaging (MRI).

**Brain Injury:** The physical damage to brain tissue or structure that occurs before, during, or after birth that is verified by EEG, MRI, CAT, or a similar examination, rather than by observation of performance. When caused by an accident, the damage may be called Traumatic Brain Injury (TBI).

**Catastrophic Reaction:** A display of extreme emotion (anger, terror, frustration or grief) without an apparent stimulus, possibly prompted by unexpected events, alteration of set routine, or feelings of over-excitement.

**CEC:** Council for Exceptional Children.

**Central Auditory Processing Disorder (CAPD):** A weakness in how the brain processes auditory information in an individual with functioning hearing ability.

**Central Nervous System (CNS):** The brain and the spinal cord.

**Cerebral Cortex:** The brain's outer layer, which controls thoughts, feelings, and voluntary movements.

**Child Study Committee:** A body of school officers and/or specialists which acts upon referrals of students thought to be disabled, and aids in the students' specialized aptitude assessment.

**Cognition:** The act or process of knowing, as a result of the capacities of various thinking skills and thought processes which are considered cognitive skills.

**Cognitive Ability:** Skills of reasoning and thinking; the ability to perceive intellectually.

**Cognitive Style:** The way a person typically approaches problem solving and learning activities (e.g., methodical analysis or impulsive reactivity).

**Compensation:** The process by which a person is taught to manage his or her learning problems, by manipulating and emphasizing strengths as a way to work around skills and/or abilities which may be limited.

**Conceptual Disorder:** A disturbance in the processes of reasoning, thinking, evaluating, recognizing, generalizing, and/or memorizing.

**Conceptualization:** The process of developing a general idea based on observations, including the ability to recognize similar traits within a group of objects.

**Configuration:** The visual form or shape of words.

**Coordination:** The synchronization and complementary functioning of muscles in the body necessary for completing complex movements.

**Criterion Referenced Test:** A test developed to reflect the specific knowledge or skills possessed by an individual, scored in terms of an individual's knowledge or ability of a relatively small unit of content without reference to other individuals' scores.

**Cross-Categorical:** A term referring to a system in which an instructor addresses more than one handicapping condition within one instructional session.

**Cumulative File:** The general file maintained for any child enrolled in a school. Parents have a right to copy and/or have access to any information in this file.

**Decoding:** The process of acquiring meaning from spoken, written, or printed symbols used in receptive language.

**Developmental Aphasia:** A severe language disorder in the normal acquisition of language.

**Developmental Lag:** A delay in the development of some aspect of a person's mental or physical maturation.

**Direct Instruction (DI):** An instructional approach to academic subjects that emphasizes the use of carefully sequenced steps that include demonstration, modeling, guided practice, and independent application.

**Directionality:** The ability to distinguish direction and orientation, including the difference between right and left, up and down, and forward and backward.

**Discrimination:** The process of differentiating between and/or among separate stimuli.

**Disinhibition:** Lack of restraint in a person's response to a situation, often resulting in impulsive and/or inappropriate reactions.

**Distractibility:** The transferring of attention from the task at hand to stimuli such as sounds and sights that normally occur in a person's surroundings.

**DOE:** Department of Education.

**Due Process:** Application of legal measures to ensure the protection of an individual's rights, e.g., a parent has the right to ask for a full evaluation of any educational program developed for his or her child.

**Dysarthia:** A disorder affecting the muscles necessary for speech, impacting a person's ability to pronounce words.

**Dyscalculia:** A wide range of life-long disabilities involving mathematics and computations, often indicated by severe difficulty in understanding and using symbols or functions needed for success in mathematics.

**Dysgraphia:** A disability affecting writing abilities, characterized by difficulty in spelling, written expression, and producing handwriting that is legible and written at an age-appropriate speed.

**Dyslexia:** A life-long language processing disorder causing the brain to process and interpret information differently, resulting in severe difficulty in understanding or using one or more areas of language, including listening, speaking, reading, writing, and spelling.

**Dysnomia:** A marked difficulty in remembering names or recalling words needed in context for oral or written language.

**Dyspraxia:** A specific disorder in the development of motor skills which inhibits a person's ability to plan and complete intended fine motor activities, marked by severe difficulty in performing drawing, writing, buttoning, and other tasks requiring fine motor skill, or in sequencing the necessary movements.

**Early Intervention Program:** A specially designed program for assisting infants and preschool children who exhibit developmental delay, intended to prevent future cognitive problems.

**EDGAR:** Education Department General Administrative Regulations.

**Educational Evaluation:** An assessment of a child's aptitude, based on multiple tests, analysis of class work, and classroom observation, intended to determine levels of achievement in certain academic areas, as well as the child's learning style and perceptual abilities.

**Electroencephalogram (EEG):** A recording, represented graphically, of electric currents produced in the cerebral cortex during brain functioning; also called a brain wave test.

**ELL:** English language learner.

**Encoding:** The process of expressing language through word selection, ideation, and transferring thoughts to written or spoken form.

**ESEA:** The federal Elementary and Secondary Education Act.

**ESL:** English as a second language.

**Expressive Language:** Communication through speech, writing, and/or gestures.

**FAPE:** Free appropriate public education; a right mandated for every child under federal law.

**Far Point Copying:** Reproducing, in writing, a copy of a model some distance away (e.g., a sentence on a chalkboard).

**FAST:** Functional academic skills test.

**FBA:** Functional behavior assessment.

**FERPA:** Family Educational Rights to Privacy Act (a.k.a. the Buckley Amendment).

**Figure-Ground Discrimination:** The ability to distinguish important information from the surrounding environment, e.g., isolating a particular word within a paragraph, or hearing an instructor's voice amid other noises.

**Fine Motor Skills:** The use of small muscles to complete precise tasks such as writing, drawing, buttoning, opening jars, and doing puzzles.

**General Education (Regular Education):** Any education not considered Special Education.

**Gross Motor Skills:** The use of larger muscles for activities involving strength and balance, such as walking, running and climbing.

**Handicapped:** A person with any physical and/or mental disability which inhibits such actions as seeing, hearing, speaking, learning, walking, or working. According to federal law, a child is handicapped when he or she is mentally retarded, seriously emotionally disturbed, hard of hearing or deaf, visually impaired or blind, speech impaired, orthopedically impaired, other health impaired, or as having specific learning disabilities which require special education services because of these disabilities.

**Haptic Sense:** The combination of kinesthetic and tactile sense.

**Head Start:** Head Start and Early Head Start are federally mandated comprehensive child development programs that serve children from birth to age 5, pregnant women, and their families. They are child-focused programs and have the overall goal of increasing the school readiness of young children in low-income families.

**Hyperactivity (Hyperkinesis):** Behavior characterized by constant and excessive movement, often marked by distractibility and/or catastrophic reactions.

**Hypoactivity:** Underactivity, often characterized by lethargy, dazedness, or sluggishness.

**IDEA:** Individuals with Disabilities Education Act.

**IEP**: Individualized education program.

**IEP Committee**: The group of select individuals who develop a student's Individualized Education Program after the student has been identified as handicapped.

**Impulsivity:** Reacting to a situation without consideration of outcome or consequences.

**Individualized Education Plan (IEP):** The written educational program designed for each handicapped (including learning disabled) individual, incorporating certain information such as educational goals (long-term and short-term), the duration of the program, and provisions for evaluating the program's effectiveness and the student's performance.

**Individualized Family Service Plan (IFSP):** A plan that documents and guides the early intervention process for children with disabilities and their families, as dictated in the Individuals with Disabilities Education Act (IDEA).

**Individualized Transition Plan (ITP):** A plan that must be made by the IEP team for a student, no later than age 16, regarding transition services that student may need to prepare for post-school life. An ITP may include planning for employment, post-secondary education, adult services, independent living, and community participation.

**Information Processing:** The cognitive ability to use and apply the information collected by a person's senses; consists of two important types of processing: auditory processing and visual processing.

**Information Processing Disorder:** A chronic deficiency in a person's ability to use or organize the data that his or her senses have gathered.

**Insertions:** The addition of letters or numbers that do not belong in a word or numeral (involved in spelling, reading and mathematics).

**Inversions:** The confusion of directionality (usually up and down) of letters or numbers, e.g., 9 and 6.

**Itinerant Teacher:** A Special Education Teacher who is shared by multiple schools or school systems.

**Kinesthetic:** Pertaining to the muscles.

**Kinesthetic Method:** A teaching technique that uses muscle control in learning words, e.g., finger-tracing written characters while reciting the letters or sounds which correspond to the characters.

**Laterality:** The preference for, or tendency to use, the hand, foot, eye and ear on a particular side of the body.

**LD:** Learning disabilities; learning disabled.

**LDA:** Learning Disabilities Association of America.

**LEA:** Local education agency.

**Learned Helplessness:** A tendency to be a passive learner who depends on others for decisions and guidance. In individuals with LD, continued struggle and failure can heighten this lack of self-confidence.

**Learning Disability (LD):** A neurological disorder that affects the brain's ability to receive, process, store and respond to information. The term learning disability is used to describe the seeming unexplained difficulty a person of at least average intelligence has in acquiring basic academic skills.

**Learning Modalities:** Approaches to assessment or instruction stressing the auditory, visual, or tactile avenues for learning that are dependent upon the individual.

**Learning Strategy Approaches:** Instructional approaches that focus on efficient ways to learn, rather than on curriculum. Includes specific techniques for organizing, actively interacting with material, memorizing, and monitoring any content or subject.

**Learning Styles:** The ways in which a person best understands and retains learning, e.g., vision, hearing, movement, kinesthetic, or a combination. Learning style-specific approaches to assessment or instruction emphasize the variations in temperament, attitude, and preferred manner of tackling a task. Typically considered are styles along the active/passive, reflective/impulsive, or verbal/spatial dimensions.

**LEP:** Limited English proficiency.

**Licensed Clinical Psychologist:** A specialist who applies the principles and methods of psychological evaluation and psychotherapy to individuals with the intent of counteracting problematic behavior and/or emotional adjustment problems.

**Licensed Clinical Social Worker:** A social worker who is qualified professionally, by education and experience, to provide direct diagnostic, preventative and treatment services in situations where an individual's ability to function is threatened or adversely affected by social and/or psychological stress or damage to his or her health.

**Licensed Professional Counselor:** A person trained in guidance and counseling services, with emphasis on both the individual and group forums of counseling, who helps individuals to achieve more effective personal, social, educational, and career-related development and adjustment.

**Linguistic Approach:** A method for teaching reading which emphasizes the use of word families, e.g., once an individual has learned the word "it," the words "sit," "pit," "bit," and "fit" are introduced.

**Locus of Control:** The tendency to attribute success and difficulties either to internal factors such as effort or to external factors such as chance. Individuals with learning disabilities tend to blame failure on themselves and achievement on luck, leading to frustration and passivity.

**LRE:** Least restrictive environment. According to the Individuals with Disabilities Education Act, keeping a child in general education classrooms with children in his or her grade and age group is a priority. If appropriate, it is preferable for a child to be in a regular class with in-class services and accommodations than in a separate special education class.

**Mainstreaming:** The practice of placing a child who has special education needs into general education classrooms, for at least part of the child's educational program.

**Maturation Lag:** A delay in development in one or more areas of skill or ability.

**MBD:** Minimal brain dysfunction.

**Metacognitive Learning:** Instructional approaches emphasizing awareness of the cognitive processes that facilitate one's own learning and its application to academic and work assignments. Typical metacognitive techniques include systematic rehearsal of steps or conscious selection among strategies for completing a task.

**Milieu Therapy:** A clinical method developed to regulate a child's environment, and to minimize conflicting and/or confusing information.

**Minimal Brain Dysfunction (MBD):** A medical and psychological term originally used to refer to the learning difficulties that seemed to result from identified or presumed damage to the brain. Reflects a medical, rather than educational or vocational orientation.

**MIS:** Management information systems.

**Mixed Laterality (Lateral Confusion):** The tendency to perform some acts with preference for a person's right side and others with a left side preference, or the shifting from right to left (or vice versa) for certain activities.

**Modality:** The sensory channel used to collect information; the most common modalities are visual, auditory, olfactory, gustatory, tactile, and kinesthetic.

**Modified Self-Contained:** Refers to a type of education in which a student is instructed in a self-contained environment for most of the school day, but also receives instruction from a general education teacher for some part of the school day.

**Multi-Categorical:** A classroom model for special education in which students with more than one handicapping condition are assigned to a special education instructor.

**Multi-Disciplinary Team (MDT):** A group of educators and education specialists that evaluates a child's handicap and prepares an Individualized Education Plan (IEP) based on their evaluation.

**Multisensory Learning:** An instructional approach that combines auditory, visual, and tactile elements into a learning task. Tracing sandpaper numbers while saying a number fact aloud would be a multisensory learning activity.

**NCLB (NCLBA):** No Child Left Behind Act.

**NCLD:** National Center for Learning Disabilities.

**NEA:** National Education Association.

**Near Point Copying:** Reproducing, in writing, a copy of a model situated close at hand (e.g., a phrase in a notebook).

**Neurological Examination:** A test of the sensory or motor responses, designed to determine if there is impairment of the nervous system.

**Neuropsychological Examination:** A series of tasks that allow observation of performance that is presumed to be related to the intactness of brain function.

**Norm-Referenced Test:** *See* Standardized Test.

**Norms:** Statistics providing a frame of reference that gives meaning to test scores; these statistics are based upon the performance of students of various ages or grades in the standardization group for the test, and therefore represent average or predictable performance, not standard or desirable achievement levels.

**OCR:** Office of Civil Rights, US Department of Health and Human Services.

**Oral Language:** Verbal communication skills necessary for understanding and using language, such as listening and speaking.

**Organicity:** Brain damage or a disorder of the central nervous system.

**Orton Dyslexia Society:** An organization comprised of learning disabilities professionals, as well as specialists, scientists, and parents.

**Orton-Gillingham Approach:** A technique for teaching individuals with learning disabilities which stresses a multi-sensory, phonetic, sequential, structured approach to learning.

**OSEP:** Office of Special Education Programs, US Department of Education.

**OSERS:** Office of Special Education and Rehabilitative Services, US Department of Education.

**Perceptual Ability:** A function of the brain that supplies an individual with the abilities to process, organize, and interpret information supplied through the senses.

**Perceptual Handicap:** Difficulty in accurately processing, organizing, interpreting, and discriminating among visual, auditory, or tactile information. A person with a perceptual handicap may not be able to distinguish between sounds or words (e.g., "map" and "mop"), or between visual symbols (e.g., the letters "b" and "d") However, eyeglasses or hearing aids do not necessarily indicate a perceptual handicap.

**Perceptual Speed:** The rapidity with which an individual can perceive and complete a given task, e.g., motor speed or visual discrimination.

**Perceptual-Motor:** The muscle activity that results from information obtained through the senses.

**Perseveration:** The repetition of words, movements, or tasks, often characterized by difficulty shifting to a new task; a student may continue working on a certain task long after his or her peers have moved onto a new one.

**Phonics Approach:** A method for teaching spelling and reading that emphasizes the importance of learning the sounds made by individual and various combinations of letters within a word, and then sequentially blending the discrete sounds to form the word.

**Pre-K:** Pre-kindergarten.

**Pre-Referral Process:** A procedure in which special and regular teachers develop trial strategies to help a student showing difficulty in learning remain in the regular classroom.

**Psychiatrist:** A licensed medical doctor who treats emotional and/or behavioral problems, and is qualified to use or prescribe medications for the purposes of treatment.

**Psychological Examination:** The evaluation of an individual's intellectual and behavioral characteristics made by a clinical psychologist or a certified school psychologist.

**Psychomotor:** Relating to the motor effects of psychological procedures. Psychomotor tests are used to assess motor skills that depend upon sensory or perceptual motor coordination.

**Reasoning Ability:** Refers to nonverbal, deductive, inductive, and analytical thinking, depending upon the way in which a given test measures this skill.

**Receptive Language (Decoding):** Language that is written or spoken by others and received by an individual; the skills necessary for receptive language are listening and reading.

**Regular Education (General Education):** All education not considered Special Education.

**REI:** Regular Education Initiative.

**Remediation:** The process by which an individual is given instruction and practice in skills which are lacking or nonexistent, helping to strengthen, develop, and improve these skills.

**Resource Program:** A program model in which a student is in a regular classroom for most of each day, but also receives regularly scheduled individual services in a specialized resource classroom.

**Resource Teacher:** A specialist who works with special education students and who often acts as a consultant for regular teachers. *See also* Transposition.

**Reversals:** A difficulty in reading or reproducing words in sentences, letters within words, or individual letters in their proper spatial position or proper order; also refers to the reversal of mathematical concepts and symbols.

**School Psychologist:** A specialist who works with individuals experiencing problems associated with educational systems and who uses psychological concepts and methods to develop programs in an effort to improve learning conditions for those individuals.

**SEA:** State education agency.

**Section 504:** A part of the Rehabilitation Act of 1973, a civil rights law, making it illegal for any organization receiving federal funds to discriminate against a person solely on the basis of disability.

**Self-Advocacy:** The development of specific skills and understandings that enable children and adults to explain their specific learning disabilities to others and cope positively with the attitudes of peers, parents, teachers, and employers.

**Self-Contained Classroom:** A setting designed specifically for special education students who spend all or most of the school day in this environment.

**Semantics:** Meaning or understanding evinced through oral or written language by virtue of its specific structure and the relationships between its components.

**Sensorimotor (Sensory-Motor):** The relationship between movement and sensation.

**Sensory Acuity:** The ability to react to sensation at appropriate levels of intensity.

**Sequence:** The detail of information in its customary order (e.g., days of the week).

**Sight Word Approach (Whole Word Approach):** A method for teaching reading which is based on an individual's visual memory skills rather than on phonics, emphasizing the ability to memorize and recognize a word based on its visual configuration.

**Slingerland Method:** Developed by Beth Slingerland, a method of teaching which is highly structured and multi-sensory, designed for group instruction of individuals with learning disabilities.

**Soft Neurological Signs:** Abnormalities of the brain which are mild or slight and thus hard to detect, as opposed to gross, or more obvious, neurological irregularities.

**Sound Blending:** The ability to unite the sounds or parts of a word into an uninterrupted whole.

**Spatial Orientation:** A person's awareness of the space around him or her, taking into account distance, form, position and direction.

**Spatial Relationships:** The positioning of objects in space in relation to the person observing them, taking into account physical distance, as well as the relationship of objects and characters described in written or spoken narrative.

**SPD:** Semantic pragmatic disorder.

**Special Education:** A form of instruction developed specifically for handicapped (including learning disabled) students.

**Specific Learning Disability (SLD):** The official term used in federal legislation to refer to difficulty in certain areas of learning. Synonymous with learning disability.

**Standardized Test (Norm-Referenced Test):** A test comparing an individual's performance with the performance of a large group of similar individuals (usually of the same age), e.g., IQ tests and most achievement tests.

**Substitution:** The interchanging of a given letter, number, or word for another in spelling, reading, or mathematics.

**Subtype Research:** A recently developed research method that seeks to identify characteristics that are common to specific groups within the larger population of individuals identified as having learning disabilities.

**Task Analysis:** The careful examination of a specific task in order to recognize its elements and the processes needed to complete it.

**Thematic Maturity:** The ability to write in an organized and logical way so as to effectively and easily express meaning.

**Transition:** Often refers to the change from secondary school to post-secondary programs, work, and independent living typical of young adults. Also used to describe other periods of major change, e.g., from a specialized setting to a mainstreamed setting.

**Transposition:** The confusion or reversal of the order of letters within a word, or numbers within a numeral. *See also* Reversals.

**VAK Approach:** A method of teaching which employs visual, auditory, kinesthetic and tactile abilities, emphasizing a multi-sensory approach to learning skills and/or concepts.

**Verbal Ability:** Generally relates to a person's skill in creating oral or spoken language, depending on the way in which the skill is tested.

**Visual Association:** The ability to relate visually presented concepts and formulate thematic comparisons.

**Visual Closure:** The ability to recognize an object when only parts of it are visible.

**Visual Discrimination:** The ability to use the sense of sight to detect differences and similarities in visually presented items to differentiate one item from another.

**Visual Figure-Ground Discrimination:** The ability to distinguish a shape or printed character from its background.

**Visual Memory:** The ability to remember something seen some time in the past (long-term visual memory); the ability to recall something seen very recently (short-term visual memory).

**Visual Motor Processing:** The ability to use visual observation to coordinate and appropriately apply other motor skills.

**Visual Perception:** The ability to see and interpret material correctly.

**Visual Sequencing:** The ability to see and recognize the order of words, symbols, images or other visual objects.

**WISC-III:** *Weschler Intelligence Scale for Children-Third Edition.* An assessment used to measure a child's intellectual ability.

**WISC-R:** *Weschler Intelligence Scale for Children-Revised.* An assessment used to measure a child's intellectual ability.

**Word Recognition:** The ability to perceive, pronounce, or read a word; usually this term is used to indicate a word which is immediately identifiable by sight and does not require the use of word-attack or analysis skills. (NB: Word Recognition does not necessarily indicate understanding of the word.)

**Word-Attack Skills:** The methods of examining an unfamiliar word by using a phonetic, sight word, or other visual approach in an effort to understand the word.

**Written Language:** All aspects of written expression, including spelling, grammar, punctuation, capitalization, penmanship, and ability to translate thoughts into words.

# The Complete Learning Disabilities Directory

## Available Formats

## Online Database

*The Complete Learning Disabilities Directory* is available in Print and in an Online Database. Subscribers to the **Online Database** can access their subscription via the Internet and do customized searches that instantly locate needed resources of information. It's never been faster or easier to locate just the right resource. Whether you're searching for Testing Materials or Schools or College Programs, the information you need is only a click away with **The Complete Learning Disabilities Directory – Online Database**.

Online Database (annual subscription): $195.00
Online Database & Print Directory combo: $280.00

Visit www.greyhouse.com and explore the subscription site free of charge or call (800) 562-2139 for more information.

---

## Mailing List Information

This directory is available in mailing list form on mailing labels or diskettes. Call (800) 562-2139 to place an order or inquire about counts. There are a number of ways we can segment the database to meet your mailing list requirements.

---

## Licensable Database on Disk

The database of this directory is available on diskette in an ASCII text file, delimited or fixed fielded. Call (800) 562-2139 for more details.

To preview any of our Directories Risk-Free for 30 days, call (800) 562-2139 or fax to (518) 789-0556

# Sedgwick Press - Education Directories

## Educators Resource Directory, 2005/06

*Educators Resource Directory* is a comprehensive resource that provides the educational professional with thousands of resources and statistical data for professional development. This directory saves hours of research time by providing immediate access to Associations & Organizations, Conferences & Trade Shows, Educational Research Centers, Employment Opportunities & Teaching Abroad, School Library Services, Scholarships, Financial Resources, Professional Consultants, Computer Software & Testing Resources and much more. Plus, this comprehensive directory also includes a section on Statistics and Rankings with over 100 tables, including statistics on Average Teacher Salaries, SAT/ACT scores, Revenues & Expenditures and more. These important statistics will allow the user to see how their school rates among others, make relocation decisions and so much more. For quick access to information, this directory contains four indexes: Entry & Publisher Index, Geographic Index, a Subject & Grade Index and Web Sites Index. *Educators Resource Directory* will be a well-used addition to the reference collection of any school district, education department or public library.

*"Recommended for all collections that serve elementary and secondary school professionals." –Choice*

1,000 pages; Softcover ISBN 1-59237-080-2, $145.00 ♦ Online Database $195.00 ♦ Online Database & Directory Combo $280.00

## The Comparative Guide to American Elementary & Secondary Schools, 2004/05

The only guide of its kind, this award winning compilation offers a snapshot profile of every public school district in the United States serving 1,500 or more students – more than 5,900 districts are covered. Organized alphabetically by district within state, each chapter begins with a Statistical Overview of the state. Each district listing includes contact information (name, address, phone number and web site) plus Grades Served, the Numbers of Students and Teachers and the Number of Regular, Special Education, Alternative and Vocational Schools in the district along with statistics on Student/Classroom Teacher Ratios, Drop Out Rates, Ethnicity, the Numbers of Librarians and Guidance Counselors and District Expenditures per student. As an added bonus, *The Comparative Guide to American Elementary and Secondary Schools* provides important ranking tables, both by state and nationally, for each data element. For easy navigation through this wealth of information, this handbook contains a useful City Index that lists all districts that operate schools within a city. These important comparative statistics are necessary for anyone considering relocation or doing comparative research on their own district and would be a perfect acquisition for any public library or school district library.

*"This straightforward guide is an easy way to find general information. Valuable for academic and large public library collections." –ARBA*

2,400 pages; Softcover ISBN 1-59237-047-0, $125.00

# Sedgwick Press - Health Directories

## The Complete Directory for People with Disabilities, 2005

A wealth of information, now in one comprehensive sourcebook. Completely updated for 2005, this edition contains more information than ever before, including thousands of new entries and enhancements to existing entries and thousands of additional web sites and e-mail addresses. This up-to-date directory is the most comprehensive resource available for people with disabilities, detailing Independent Living Centers, Rehabilitation Facilities, State & Federal Agencies, Associations, Support Groups, Periodicals & Books, Assistive Devices, Employment & Education Programs, Camps and Travel Groups. Each year, more libraries, schools, colleges, hospitals, rehabilitation centers and individuals add *The Complete Directory for People with Disabilities* to their collections, making sure that this information is readily available to the families, individuals and professionals who can benefit most from the amazing wealth of resources cataloged here.

*"No other reference tool exists to meet the special needs of the disabled in one convenient resource for information." –Library Journal*

1,200 pages; Softcover ISBN 1-59237-054-3, $165.00 ♦ Online Database $215.00 ♦ Online Database & Directory Combo $300.00

## The Complete Mental Health Directory, 2004

This is the most comprehensive resource covering the field of behavioral health, with critical information for both the layman and the mental health professional. For the layman, this directory offers understandable descriptions of 25 Mental Health Disorders as well as detailed information on Associations, Media, Support Groups and Mental Health Facilities. For the professional, *The Complete Mental Health Directory* offers critical and comprehensive information on Managed Care Organizations, Information Systems, Government Agencies and Provider Organizations. This comprehensive volume of needed information will be widely used in any reference collection.

*"… the strength of this directory is that it consolidates widely dispersed information into a single volume." –Booklist*

800 pages; Softcover ISBN 1-59237-046-2, $165.00 ♦ Online Database $215.00 ♦ Online & Directory Combo $300.00

To preview any of our Directories Risk-Free for 30 days, call (800) 562-2139 or fax to (518) 789-0556

# The Complete Directory for People with Chronic Illness, 2005/06

Thousands of hours of research have gone into this completely updated 2005/06 edition – several new chapters have been added along with thousands of new entries and enhancements to existing entries. Plus, each chronic illness chapter has been reviewed by an medical expert in the field. This widely-hailed directory is structured around the 90 most prevalent chronic illnesses – from Asthma to Cancer to Wilson's Disease – and provides a comprehensive overview of the support services and information resources available for people diagnosed with a chronic illness. Each chronic illness has its own chapter and contains a brief description in layman's language, followed by important resources for National & Local Organizations, State Agencies, Newsletters, Books & Periodicals, Libraries & Research Centers, Support Groups & Hotlines, Web Sites and much more. This directory is an important resource for health care professionals, the collections of hospital and health care libraries, as well as an invaluable tool for people with a chronic illness and their support network.

*"A must purchase for all hospital and health care libraries and is strongly recommended for all public library reference departments." –ARBA*

1,200 pages; Softcover ISBN 1-59237-081-0, $165.00 ◆ Online Database $215.00 ◆ Online Database & Directory Combo $300.00

# Older Americans Information Directory, 2004/05

Completely updated for 2004/05, this Fifth Edition has been completely revised and now contains 1,000 new listings, over 8,000 updates to existing listings and over 3,000 brand new e-mail addresses and web sites. You'll find important resources for Older Americans including National, Regional, State & Local Organizations, Government Agencies, Research Centers, Libraries & Information Centers, Legal Resources, Discount Travel Information, Continuing Education Programs, Disability Aids & Assistive Devices, Health, Print Media and Electronic Media. Three indexes: Entry Index, Subject Index and Geographic Index make it easy to find just the right source of information. This comprehensive guide to resources for Older Americans will be a welcome addition to any reference collection.

*"Highly recommended for academic, public, health science and consumer libraries..." –Choice*

1,200 pages; Softcover ISBN 1-59237-037-3, $165.00 ◆ Online Database $215.00 ◆ Online Database & Directory Combo $300.00

# The Complete Directory for Pediatric Disorders, 2004/05

This important directory provides parents and caregivers with information about Pediatric Conditions, Disorders, Diseases and Disabilities, including Blood Disorders, Bone & Spinal Disorders, Brain Defects & Abnormalities, Chromosomal Disorders, Congenital Heart Defects, Movement Disorders, Neuromuscular Disorders and Pediatric Tumors & Cancers. This carefully written directory offers: understandable Descriptions of 15 major bodily systems; Descriptions of more than 200 Disorders and a Resources Section, detailing National Agencies & Associations, State Associations, Online Services, Libraries & Resource Centers, Research Centers, Support Groups & Hotlines, Camps, Books and Periodicals. This resource will provide immediate access to information crucial to families and caregivers when coping with children's illnesses.

*"Recommended for public and consumer health libraries." –Library Journal*

1,200 pages; Softcover ISBN 1-59237-045-4, $165.00 ◆ Online Database $215.00 ◆ Online Database & Directory Combo $300.00

# The Complete Directory for People with Rare Disorders, 2002/03

This outstanding reference is produced in conjunction with the National Organization for Rare Disorders to provide comprehensive and needed access to important information on over 1,000 rare disorders, including Cancers and Muscular, Genetic and Blood Disorders. An informative Disorder Description is provided for each of the 1,100 disorders (rare Cancers and Muscular, Genetic and Blood Disorders) followed by information on National and State Organizations dealing with a particular disorder, Umbrella Organizations that cover a wide range of disorders, the Publications that can be useful when researching a disorder and the Government Agencies to contact. Detailed and up-to-date listings contain mailing address, phone and fax numbers, web sites and e-mail addresses along with a description. For quick, easy access to information, this directory contains two indexes: Entry Name Index and Acronym/Keyword Index along with an informative Guide for Rare Disorder Advocates. The Complete Directory for People with Rare Disorders will be an invaluable tool for the thousands of families that have been struck with a rare or "orphan" disease, who feel that they have no place to turn and will be a much-used addition to the reference collection of any public or academic library.

*"Quick access to information... public libraries and hospital patient libraries will find this a useful resource in directing users to support groups or agencies dealing with a rare disorder." –Booklist*

726 pages; Softcover ISBN 1-891482-18-1, $165.00

To preview any of our Directories Risk-Free for 30 days, call (800) 562-2139 or fax to (518) 789-0556

# Universal Reference Publications
## Statistical & Demographic Reference Books

## The Value of a Dollar 1860-2004, Third Edition

A guide to practical economy, *The Value of a Dollar* records the actual prices of thousands of items that consumers purchased from the Civil War to the present, along with facts about investment options and income opportunities. This brand new Third Edition boasts a brand new addition to each five-year chapter, a section on Trends. This informative section charts the change in price over time and provides added detail on the reasons prices changed within the time period, including industry developments, changes in consumer attitudes and important historical facts. Plus, a brand new chapter for 2000-2004 has been added. Each 5-year chapter includes a Historical Snapshot, Consumer Expenditures, Investments, Selected Income, Income/Standard Jobs, Food Basket, Standard Prices and Miscellany. This interesting and useful publication will be widely used in any reference collection.

*"Recommended for high school, college and public libraries."* –ARBA

600 pages; Hardcover ISBN 1-59237-074-8, $135.00

## The Value of a Dollar 1600-1859, The Colonial Era to The Civil War

Following the format of the widely acclaimed, T*he Value of a Dollar, 1860-2004, The Value of a Dollar 1600-1859, The Colonial Era to The Civil War* records the actual prices of thousands of items that consumers purchased from the Colonial Era to the Civil War. Our editorial department had been flooded with requests from users of our Value of a Dollar for the same type of information, just from an earlier time period. This new volume is just the answer – with pricing data from 1600 to 1859. Arranged into five-year chapters, each 5-year chapter includes a Historical Snapshot, Consumer Expenditures, Investments, Selected Income, Income/Standard Jobs, Food Basket, Standard Prices and Miscellany. There is also a section on Trends. This informative section charts the change in price over time and provides added detail on the reasons prices changed within the time period, including industry developments, changes in consumer attitudes and important historical facts. This fascinating survey will serve a wide range of research needs and will be useful in allhigh school, public and academic library reference collections.

600 pages; Hardcover ISBN 1-59237-094-2, $135.00

## Working Americans 1880-1999
## Volume I: The Working Class, Volume II: The Middle Class, Volume III: The Upper Class

Each of the volumes in the *Working Americans 1880-1999* series focuses on a particular class of Americans, The Working Class, The Middle Class and The Upper Class over the last 120 years. Chapters in each volume focus on one decade and profile three to five families. Family Profiles include real data on Income & Job Descriptions, Selected Prices of the Times, Annual Income, Annual Budgets, Family Finances, Life at Work, Life at Home, Life in the Community, Working Conditions, Cost of Living, Amusements and much more. Each chapter also contains an Economic Profile with Average Wages of other Professions, a selection of Typical Pricing, Key Events & Inventions, News Profiles, Articles from Local Media and Illustrations. The *Working Americans* series captures the lifestyles of each of the classes from the last twelve decades, covers a vast array of occupations and ethnic backgrounds and travels the entire nation. These interesting and useful compilations of portraits of the American Working, Middle and Upper Classes during the last 120 years will be an important addition to any high school, public or academic library reference collection.

*"These interesting, unique compilations of economic and social facts, figures and graphs will support multiple research needs. They will engage and enlighten patrons in high school, public and academic library collections."* –Booklist

Volume I: The Working Class ♦ 558 pages; Hardcover ISBN 1-891482-81-5, $145.00 ♦ Volume II: The Middle Class ♦ 591 pages; Hardcover ISBN 1-891482-72-6; $145.00 ♦ Volume III: The Upper Class ♦ 567 pages; Hardcover ISBN 1-930956-38-X, $145.00

## Working Americans 1880-1999  Volume IV: Their Children

This Fourth Volume in the highly successful *Working Americans 1880-1999* series focuses on American children, decade by decade from 1880 to 1999. This interesting and useful volume introduces the reader to three children in each decade, one from each of the Working, Middle and Upper classes. Like the first three volumes in the series, the individual profiles are created from interviews, diaries, statistical studies, biographies and news reports. Profiles cover a broad range of ethnic backgrounds, geographic area and lifestyles – everything from an orphan in Memphis in 1882, following the Yellow Fever epidemic of 1878 to an eleven-year-old nephew of a beer baron and owner of the New York Yankees in New York City in 1921. Chapters also contain important supplementary materials including News Features as well as information on everything from Schools to Parks, Infectious Diseases to Childhood Fears along with Entertainment, Family Life and much more to provide an informative overview of the lifestyles of children from each decade. This interesting account of what life was like for Children in the Working, Middle and Upper Classes will be a welcome addition to the reference collection of any high school, public or academic library.

600 pages; Hardcover ISBN 1-930956-35-5, $145.00

**To preview any of our Directories Risk-Free for 30 days, call (800) 562-2139 or fax to (518) 789-0556**

## Working Americans 1880-2003 Volume V: Americans At War

*Working Americans 1880-2003 Volume V: Americans At War* is divided into 11 chapters, each covering a decade from 1880-2003 and examines the lives of Americans during the time of war, including declared conflicts, one-time military actions, protests, and preparations for war. Each decade includes several personal profiles, whether on the battlefield or on the homefront, that tell the stories of civilians, soldiers, and officers during the decade. The profiles examine: Life at Home; Life at Work; and Life in the Community. Each decade also includes an Economic Profile with statistical comparisons, a Historical Snapshot, News Profiles, local News Articles, and Illustrations that provide a solid historical background to the decade being examined. Profiles range widely not only geographically, but also emotionally, from that of a girl whose leg was torn off in a blast during WWI, to the boredom of being stationed in the Dakotas as the Indian Wars were drawing to a close. As in previous volumes of the *Working Americans* series, information is presented in narrative form, but hard facts and real-life situations back up each story. The basis of the profiles come from diaries, private print books, personal interviews, family histories, estate documents and magazine articles. For easy reference, *Working Americans 1880-2003 Volume V: Americans At War* includes an in-depth Subject Index. The *Working Americans* series has become an important reference for public libraries, academic libraries and high school libraries. This fifth volume will be a welcome addition to all of these types of reference collections.

600 pages; Hardcover ISBN 1-59237-024-1; $145.00
Five Volume Set (Volumes I-V), Hardcover ISBN 1-59237-034-9, $675.00

## Working Americans 1880-2005 Volume V: Women at Work

Unlike any other volume in the *Working Americans* series, this Sixth Volume, is the first to focus on a particular gender of Americans. *Volume VI: Women at Work*, traces what life was like for working women from the 1860's to the present time. Beginning with the life of a maid in 1890 and a store clerk in 1900 and ending with the life and times of the modern working women, this text captures the struggle, strengths and changing perception of the American woman at work. Each chapter focuses on one decade and profiles three to five women with real data on Income & Job Descriptions, Selected Prices of the Times, Annual Income, Annual Budgets, Family Finances, Life at Work, Life at Home, Life in the Community, Working Conditions, Cost of Living, Amusements and much more. For even broader access to the events, economics and attitude towards women throughout the past 130 years, each chapter is supplemented with News Profiles, Articles from Local Media, Illustrations, Economic Profiles, Typical Pricing, Key Events, Inventions and more. This important volume illustrates what life was like for working women over time and allows the reader to develop an understanding of the changing role of women at work. These interesting and useful compilations of portraits of women at work will be an important addition to any high school, public or academic library reference collection.

600 pages; Hardcover ISBN 1-59237-063-2; $145.00
Six Volume Set (Volumes I-VI), Hardcover ISBN 1-59237-063-2, $810.00

## The Asian Databook: Statistics for all US Counties & Cities with Over 10,000 Population

This is the first-ever resource that compiles statistics and rankings on the US Asian population. *The Asian Databook* presents over 20 statistical data points for each city and county, arranged alphabetically by state, then alphabetically by place name. Data reported for each place includes Population, Languages Spoken at Home, Foreign-Born, Educational Attainment, Income Figures, Poverty Status, Homeownership, Home Values & Rent, and more. Next, in the Rankings Section, the top 75 places are listed for each data element. These easy-to-access ranking tables allow the user to quickly determine trends and population characteristics. This kind of comparative data can not be found elsewhere, in print or on the web, in a format that's as easy-to-use or more concise. A useful resource for those searching for demographics data, career search and relocation information and also for market research. With data ranging from Ancestry to Education, *The Asian Databook* presents a useful compilation of information that will be a much-needed resource in the reference collection of any public or academic library along with the marketing collection of any company whose primary focus in on the Asian population.

1,000 pages; Softcover ISBN 1-59237-044-6 $150.00

To preview any of our Directories Risk-Free for 30 days, call (800) 562-2139 or fax to (518) 789-0556

# The Hispanic Databook: Statistics for all US Counties & Cities with Over 10,000 Population

Previously published by Toucan Valley Publications, this second edition has been completely updated with figures from the latest census and has been broadly expanded to include dozens of new data elements and a brand new Rankings section. For ease-of-use, *The Hispanic Databook* presents over 20 statistical data points for each city and county, arranged alphabetically by state, then alphabetically by place name. Data reported for each place includes Population, Languages Spoken at Home, Foreign-Born, Educational Attainment, Income Figures, Poverty Status, Homeownership, Home Values & Rent, and more. Next, in the Rankings Section, the top 75 places are listed for each data element. These easy-to-access ranking tables allow the user to quickly determine trends and population characteristics. A useful resource for those searching for demographics data, career search and relocation information and also for market research. With data ranging from Ancestry to Education, *The Hispanic Databook* presents a useful compilation of information that will be a much-needed resource in the reference collection of any public or academic library along with the marketing collection of any company whose primary focus in on the Hispanic population.

*"This accurate, clearly presented volume of selected Hispanic demographics is recommended for large public libraries and research collections."-Library Journa*

1,000 pages; Softcover ISBN 1-59237-008-X, $150.00

# Ancestry in America: A Comparative Guide to Over 200 Ethnic Backgrounds

This brand new reference work pulls together thousands of comparative statistics on the Ethnic Backgrounds of all populated places in the United States with populations over 10,000. Section One, Statistics by Place, is made up of a list of over 200 ancestry and race categories arranged alphabetically by each of the 5,000 different places with populations over 10,000. This informative city-by-city section allows the user to quickly and easily explore the ethnic makeup of all major population bases in the United States. Section Two, Comparative Rankings, contains three tables for each ethnicity and race. In the first table, the top 150 populated places are ranked by population number for that particular ancestry group, regardless of population. In the second table, the top 150 populated places are ranked by the percent of the total population for that ancestry group. In the third table, those top 150 populated places with 10,000 population are ranked by population number for each ancestry group. These easy-to-navigate tables allow users to see ancestry population patterns and make city-by-city comparisons as well. Plus, as an added bonus with the purchase of *Ancestry in America*, a free companion CD-ROM is available that lists statistics and rankings for all of the 35,000 populated places in the United States. This brand new, information-packed resource will serve a wide-range or research requests for demographics, population characteristics, relocation information and much more.

*"This compilation will serve a wide range of research requests for population characteristics … it offers much more detail than other sources." –Booklist*

1,500 pages; Softcover ISBN 1-59237-029-2, $225.00

# Profiles of America: Facts, Figures & Statistics for Every Populated Place in the United States

*Profiles of America* is the only source that pulls together, in one place, statistical, historical and descriptive information about every place in the United States in an easy-to-use format. This award winning reference set, now in its second edition, compiles statistics and data from over 20 different sources – the latest census information has been included along with more than nine brand new statistical topics. This Four-Volume Set details over 40,000 places, from the biggest metropolis to the smallest unincorporated hamlet, and provides statistical details and information on over 50 different topics including Geography, Climate, Population, Vital Statistics, Economy, Income, Taxes, Education, Housing, Health & Environment, Public Safety, Newspapers, Transportation, Presidential Election Results and Information Contacts or Chambers of Commerce. Profiles are arranged, for ease-of-use, by state and then by county. Each county begins with a County-Wide Overview and is followed by information for each Community in that particular county. The Community Profiles within the county are arranged alphabetically. *Profiles of America* is a virtual snapshot of America at your fingertips and a unique compilation of information that will be widely used in any reference collection.

*A Library Journal Best Reference Book* *"An outstanding compilation." –Library Journal*

10,000 pages; Four Volume Set; Softcover ISBN 1-891482-80-7, $595.00

# The Comparative Guide to American Suburbs, 2005

*The Comparative Guide to American Suburbs* is a one-stop source for Statistics on the 2,000+ suburban communities surrounding the 50 largest metropolitan areas – their population characteristics, income levels, economy, school system and important data on how they compare to one another. Organized into 50 Metropolitan Area chapters, each chapter contains an overview of the Metropolitan Area, a detailed Map followed by a comprehensive Statistical Profile of each Suburban Community, including Contact Information, Physical Characteristics, Population Characteristics, Income, Economy, Unemployment Rate, Cost of Living, Education, Chambers of Commerce and more. Next, statistical data is sorted into Ranking Tables that rank the suburbs by twenty different criteria, including Population, Per Capita Income, Unemployment Rate, Crime Rate, Cost of Living and more. *The Comparative Guide to American Suburbs* is the best source for locating data on suburbs. Those looking to relocate, as well as those doing preliminary market research, will find this an invaluable timesaving resource.

*"Public and academic libraries will find this compilation useful…The work draws together figures from many sources and will be especially helpful for job relocation decisions." – Booklist*

1,700 pages; Softcover ISBN 1-59237-004-7, $130.00

To preview any of our Directories Risk-Free for 30 days, call (800) 562-2139 or fax to (518) 789-0556

# America's Top-Rated Cities, 2005

*America's Top-Rated Cities* provides current, comprehensive statistical information and other essential data in one easy-to-use source on the 100 "top" cities that have been cited as the best for business and living in the U.S. This handbook allows readers to see, at a glance, a concise social, business, economic, demographic and environmental profile of each city, including brief evaluative comments. In addition to detailed data on Cost of Living, Finances, Real Estate, Education, Major Employers, Media, Crime and Climate, city reports now include Housing Vacancies, Tax Audits, Bankruptcy, Presidential Election Results and more. This outstanding source of information will be widely used in any reference collection.

*"The only source of its kind that brings together all of this information into one easy-to-use source."* –ARBA

2,500 pages, 4 Volume Set; Softcover ISBN 1-59237-076-4, $195.00

# America's Top-Rated Smaller Cities, 2004

A perfect companion to *America's Top-Rated Cities, America's Top-Rated Smaller Cities* provides current, comprehensive business and living profiles of smaller cities (population 25,000-99,999) that have been cited as the best for business and living in the United States. Sixty cities make up this 2004 edition of *America's Top-Rated Smaller Cities*, all are top-ranked by Population Growth, Median Income, Unemployment Rate and Crime Rate. City reports reflect the most current data available on a wide-range of statistics, including Employment & Earnings, Household Income, Unemployment Rate, Population Characteristics, Taxes, Cost of Living, Education, Health Care, Public Safety, Recreation, Media, Air & Water Quality and much more. *America's Top-Rated Smaller Cities* offers a reliable, one-stop source for statistical data that, before now, could only be found scattered in hundreds of sources. This volume is designed for a wide range of readers: individuals considering relocating a residence or business; professionals considering expanding their business or changing careers; general and market researchers; real estate consultants; human resource personnel; urban planners and investors.

*"Recommended for public and academic libraries and specialized collections."* –Library Journal

1,100 pages; Softcover ISBN 1-59237-043-8, $160.00

# The American Tally, 2003/04   Statistics & Comparative Rankings for U.S. Cities with Populations over 10,000

This important statistical handbook compiles, all in one place, comparative statistics on all U.S. cities and towns with a 10,000+ population. *The American Tally* provides statistical details on over 4,000 cities and towns and profiles how they compare with one another in Population Characteristics, Education, Language & Immigration, Income & Employment and Housing. Each section begins with an alphabetical listing of cities by state, allowing for quick access to both the statistics and relative rankings of any city. Next, the highest and lowest cities are listed in each statistic. These important, informative lists provide quick reference to which cities are at both extremes of the spectrum for each statistic. Unlike any other reference, *The American Tally* provides quick, easy access to comparative statistics – a must-have for any reference collection.

*"A solid library reference."* –Bookwatch

500 pages; Softcover ISBN 1-930956-29-0, $125.00

# The Environmental Resource Handbook, 2004

*The Environmental Resource Handbook*, now in its second edition, is the most up-to-date and comprehensive source for Environmental Resources and Statistics. Section I: Resources provides detailed contact information for thousands of information sources, including Associations & Organizations, Awards & Honors, Conferences, Foundations & Grants, Environmental Health, Government Agencies, National Parks & Wildlife Refuges, Publications, Research Centers, Educational Programs, Green Product Catalogs, Consultants and much more. Section II: Statistics, provides statistics and rankings on hundreds of important topics, including Children's Environmental Index, Municipal Finances, Toxic Chemicals, Recycling, Climate, Air & Water Quality and more. This kind of up-to-date environmental data, all in one place, is not available anywhere else on the market place today. This vast compilation of resources and statistics is a must-have for all public and academic libraries as well as any organization with a primary focus on the environment.

*"…worth consideration by libraries with environmental collections and environmentally concerned users."* –Booklist

1,000 pages; Softcover ISBN 1-59237-030-6, $155.00 ◆ Online Database $300.00

# Weather America, A Thirty-Year Summary of Statistical Weather Data and Rankings

This valuable resource provides extensive climatological data for over 4,000 National and Cooperative Weather Stations throughout the United States. *Weather America* begins with a new Major Storms section that details major storm events of the nation and a National Rankings section that details rankings for several data elements, such as Maximum Temperature and Precipitation. The main body of *Weather America* is organized into 50 state sections. Each section provides a Data Table on each Weather Station, organized alphabetically, that provides statistics on Maximum and Minimum Temperatures, Precipitation, Snowfall, Extreme Temperatures, Foggy Days, Humidity and more. State sections contain two brand new features in this edition – a City Index and a narrative Description of the climatic conditions of the state. Each section also includes a revised Map of the State that includes not only weather stations, but cities and towns.

*"Best Reference Book of the Year."* –Library Journal

2,013 pages; Softcover ISBN 1-891482-29-7, $175.00

To preview any of our Directories Risk-Free for 30 days, call (800) 562-2139 or fax to (518) 789-0556

# Grey House Publishing
## Business Directories

## New York State Directory, 2005/06

*The New York State Directory*, published annually since 1983, is a comprehensive and easy-to-use guide to accessing public officials and private sector organizations and individuals who influence public policy in the state of New York. *The New York State Directory* includes important information on all New York state legislators and congressional representatives, including biographies and key committee assignments. It also includes staff rosters for all branches of New York state government and for federal agencies and departments that impact the state policy process. Following the state government section are 25 chapters covering policy areas from agriculture through veterans' affairs. Each chapter identifies the state, local and federal agencies and officials that formulate or implement policy. In addition, each chapter contains a roster of private sector experts and advocates who influence the policy process. The directory also offers appendices that include statewide party officials; chambers of commerce; lobbying organizations; public and private universities and colleges; television, radio and print media; and local government agencies and officials. A companion volume, Profiles of New York, is also available with detailed demographic and statistical data on the over 2,300 places in New York State. Packed with over 50 pieces of data that make up a complete, user-friendly profile, the directory goes even further by then pulling selected data and providing it in ranking list form for even easier comparisons between the 100 largest towns and cities.

New York State Directory - 800 pages; Softcover ISBN 1-59237-093-4; $129.00
New York State Directory with Profiles of New York – 2 volumes; 1,600 pages; Softcover ISBN 1-59237-095-0; $195

## Nations of the World, 2005  A Political, Economic and Business Handbook

This completely revised edition covers all the nations of the world in an easy-to-use, single volume. Each nation is profiled in a single chapter that includes Key Facts, Political & Economic Issues, a Country Profile and Business Information. In this fast-changing world, it is extremely important to make sure that the most up-to-date information is included in your reference collection. This 2005 edition is just the answer. Each of the 200+ country chapters have been carefully reviewed by a political expert to make sure that the text reflects the most current information on Politics, Travel Advisories, Economics and more. You'll find such vital information as a Country Map, Population Characteristics, Inflation, Agricultural Production, Foreign Debt, Political History, Foreign Policy, Regional Insecurity, Economics, Trade & Tourism, Historical Profile, Political Systems, Ethnicity, Languages, Media, Climate, Hotels, Chambers of Commerce, Banking, Travel Information and more. Five Regional Chapters follow the main text and include a Regional Map, an Introductory Article, Key Indicators and Currencies for the Region. New for 2004, an all-inclusive CD-ROM is available as a companion to the printed text. Noted for its sophisticated, up-to-date and reliable compilation of political, economic and business information, this brand new edition will be an important acquisition to any public, academic or special library reference collection.

*"A useful addition to both general reference collections and business collections."* –RUSQ

1,700 pages; Print Version Only Softcover ISBN 1-59237-051-9, $145.00 ◆ Print Version and CD-ROM $180.00

## The Directory of Business Information Resources, 2005

With 100% verification, over 1,000 new listings and more than 12,000 updates, this 2005 edition of *The Directory of Business Information Resources* is the most up-to-date source for contacts in over 98 business areas – from advertising and agriculture to utilities and wholesalers. This carefully researched volume details: the Associations representing each industry; the Newsletters that keep members current; the Magazines and Journals - with their "Special Issues" - that are important to the trade, the Conventions that are "must attends," Databases, Directories and Industry Web Sites that provide access to must-have marketing resources. Includes contact names, phone & fax numbers, web sites and e-mail addresses. This one-volume resource is a gold mine of information and would be a welcome addition to any reference collection.

*"This is a most useful and easy-to-use addition to any researcher's library."* –The Information Professionals Institute

2,500 pages; Softcover ISBN 1-59237-050-0, $195.00 ◆ Online Database $495.00

To preview any of our Directories Risk-Free for 30 days, call (800) 562-2139 or fax to (518) 789-0556

## The Grey House Performing Arts Directory, 2005

*The Grey House Performing Arts Directory* is the most comprehensive resource covering the Performing Arts. This important directory provides current information on over 8,500 Dance Companies, Instrumental Music Programs, Opera Companies, Choral Groups, Theater Companies, Performing Arts Series and Performing Arts Facilities. Plus, this edition now contains a brand new section on Artist Management Groups. In addition to mailing address, phone & fax numbers, e-mail addresses and web sites, dozens of other fields of available information include mission statement, key contacts, facilities, seating capacity, season, attendance and more. This directory also provides an important Information Resources section that covers hundreds of Performing Arts Associations, Magazines, Newsletters, Trade Shows, Directories, Databases and Industry Web Sites. Five indexes provide immediate access to this wealth of information: Entry Name, Executive Name, Performance Facilities, Geographic and Information Resources. *The Grey House Performing Arts Directory* pulls together thousands of Performing Arts Organizations, Facilities and Information Resources into an easy-to-use source – this kind of comprehensiveness and extensive detail is not available in any resource on the market place today.

*"Immensely useful and user-friendly ... recommended for public, academic and certain special library reference collections."* –*Booklist*

1,500 pages; Softcover ISBN 1-59237-023-3, $185.00 ◆ Online Database $335.00

## The Directory of Venture Capital & Private Equity Firms, 2005

This edition has been extensively updated and broadly expanded to offer direct access to over 2,800 Domestic and International Venture Capital Firms, including address, phone & fax numbers, e-mail addresses and web sites for both primary and branch locations. Entries include details on the firm's Mission Statement, Industry Group Preferences, Geographic Preferences, Average and Minimum Investments and Investment Criteria. You'll also find details that are available nowhere else, including the Firm's Portfolio Companies and extensive information on each of the firm's Managing Partners, such as Education, Professional Background and Directorships held, along with the Partner's E-mail Address. *The Directory of Venture Capital & Private Equity Firms* offers five important indexes: Geographic Index, Executive Name Index, Portfolio Company Index, Industry Preference Index and College & University Index. With its comprehensive coverage and detailed, extensive information on each company, *The Directory of Venture Capital & Private Equity Firms* is an important addition to any finance collection.

*"The sheer number of listings, the descriptive information provided and the outstanding indexing make this directory a better value than its principal competitor, Pratt's Guide to Venture Capital Sources. Recommended for business collections in large public, academic and business libraries."* –*Choice*

1,300 pages; Softcover ISBN 1-59237-062-4, $450.00 ◆ Online Database (includes a free copy of the directory) $889.00

## The Directory of Mail Order Catalogs, 2005

Published since 1981, this 2005 edition features 100% verification of data and is the premier source of information on the mail order catalog industry. Details over 12,000 consumer catalog companies with 44 different product chapters from Animals to Toys & Games. Contains detailed contact information including e-mail addresses and web sites along with important business details such as employee size, years in business, sales volume, catalog size, number of catalogs mailed and more. Four indexes provide quick access to information: Catalog & Company Name Index, Geographic Index, Product Index and Web Sites Index.

*"This is a godsend for those looking for information."* –*Reference Book Review*

1,700 pages; Softcover ISBN 1-59237-066-7 $250.00 ◆ Online Database (includes a free copy of the directory) $495.00

## The Directory of Business to Business Catalogs, 2005

The completely updated 2005 *Directory of Business to Business Catalogs*, provides details on over 6,000 suppliers of everything from computers to laboratory supplies... office products to office design... marketing resources to safety equipment... landscaping to maintenance suppliers... building construction and much more. Detailed entries offer mailing address, phone & fax numbers, e-mail addresses, web sites, key contacts, sales volume, employee size, catalog printing information and more. Jut about every kind of product a business needs in its day-to-day operations is covered in this carefully-researched volume. Three indexes are provided for at-a-glance access to information: Catalog & Company Name Index, Geographic Index and Web Sites Index.

*"An excellent choice for libraries... wishing to supplement their business supplier resources."* –*Booklist*

800 pages; Softcover ISBN 1-59237-064-0, $165.00 ◆ Online Database (includes a free copy of the directory) $325.00

To preview any of our Directories Risk-Free for 30 days, call (800) 562-2139 or fax to (518) 789-0556

# The Grey House Safety & Security Directory, 2005

*The Grey House Safety & Security Directory* is the most comprehensive reference tool and buyer's guide for the safety and security industry. Arranged by safety topic, each chapter begins with OSHA regulations for the topic, followed by Training Articles written by top professionals in the field and Self-Inspection Checklists. Next, each topic contains Buyer's Guide sections that feature related products and services. Topics include Administration, Insurance, Loss Control & Consulting, Protective Equipment & Apparel, Noise & Vibration, Facilities Monitoring & Maintenance, Employee Health Maintenance & Ergonomics, Retail Food Services, Machine Guards, Process Guidelines & Tool Handling, Ordinary Materials Handling, Hazardous Materials Handling, Workplace Preparation & Maintenance, Electrical Lighting & Safety, Fire & Rescue and Security. The Buyer's Guide sections are carefully indexed within each topic area to ensure that you can find the supplies needed to meet OSHA's regulations. Six important indexes make finding information and product manufacturers quick and easy: Geographical Index of Manufacturers and Distributors, Company Profile Index, Brand Name Index, Product Index, Index of Web Sites and Index of Advertisers. This comprehensive, up-to-date reference will provide every tool necessary to make sure a business is in compliance with OSHA regulations and locate the products and services needed to meet those regulations.

*"Presents industrial safety information for engineers, plant managers, risk managers, and construction site supervisors..." –Choice*

1,500 pages, 2 Volume Set; Softcover ISBN 1-59237-067-5, $225.00

# The Grey House Homeland Security Directory, 2005

This updated edition features the latest contact information for government and private organizations involved with Homeland Security along with the latest product information and provides detailed profiles of nearly 1,000 Federal & State Organizations & Agencies and over 3,000 Officials and Key Executives involved with Homeland Security. These listings are incredibly detailed and include Mailing Address, Phone & Fax Numbers, Email Addresses & Web Sites, a complete Description of the Agency and a complete list of the Officials and Key Executives associated with the Agency. Next, *The Grey House Homeland Security Directory* provides the go-to source for Homeland Security Products & Services. This section features over 2,000 Companies that provide Consulting, Products or Services. With this Buyer's Guide at their fingertips, users can locate suppliers of everything from Training Materials to Access Controls, from Perimeter Security to BioTerrorism Countermeasures and everything in between – complete with contact information and product descriptions. A handy Product Locator Index is provided to quickly and easily locate suppliers of a particular product. Lastly, an Information Resources Section provides immediate access to contact information for hundreds of Associations, Newsletters, Magazines, Trade Shows, Databases and Directories that focus on Homeland Security. This comprehensive, information-packed resource will be a welcome tool for any company or agency that is in need of Homeland Security information and will be a necessary acquisition for the reference collection of all public libraries and large school districts.

*"Compiles this information in one place and is discerning in content. A useful purchase for public and academic libraries." –Booklist*

800 pages; Softcover ISBN 1-59237-057-8, $195.00 ◆ Online Database (includes a free copy of the directory) $385.00

# The Grey House Transportation Security Directory & Handbook, 2005

This brand new title is the only reference of its kind that brings together current data on Transportation Security. With information on everything from Regulatory Authorities to Security Equipment, this top-flight database brings together the relevant information necessary for creating and maintaining a security plan for a wide range of transportation facilities. With this current, comprehensive directory at the ready you'll have immediate access to: Regulatory Authorities & Legislation; Information Resources; Sample Security Plans & Checklists; Contact Data for Major Airports, Seaports, Railroads, Trucking Companies and Oil Pipelines; Security Service Providers; Recommended Equipment & Product Information and more. Using the *Grey House Transportation Security Directory & Handbook*, managers will be able to quickly and easily assess their current security plans; develop contacts to create and maintain new security procedures; and source the products and services necessary to adequately maintain a secure environment. This valuable resource is a must for all Security Managers at Airports, Seaports, Railroads, Trucking Companies and Oil Pipelines.

800 pages; Softcover ISBN 1-59237-075-6, $195

# International Business and Trade Directories, 2003/04

Completely updated, the Third Edition of *International Business and Trade Directories* now contains more than 10,000 entries, over 2,000 more than the last edition, making this directory the most comprehensive resource of the worlds business and trade directories. Entries include content descriptions, price, publisher's name and address, web site and e-mail addresses, phone and fax numbers and editorial staff. Organized by industry group, and then by region, this resource puts over 10,000 industry-specific business and trade directories at the reader's fingertips. Three indexes are included for quick access to information: Geographic Index, Publisher Index and Title Index. Public, college and corporate libraries, as well as individuals and corporations seeking critical market information will want to add this directory to their marketing collection.

*"Reasonably priced for a work of this type, this directory should appeal to larger academic, public and corporate libraries with an international focus." –Library Journal*

1,800 pages; Softcover ISBN 1-930956-63-0, $225.00 ◆ Online Database (includes a free copy of the directory) $450.00

**To preview any of our Directories Risk-Free for 30 days, call (800) 562-2139 or fax to (518) 789-0556**

# Thomas Food and Beverage Market Place, 2005

*Thomas Food and Beverage Market Place* is bigger and better than ever with thousands of new companies, thousands of updates to existing companies and two revised and enhanced product category indexes. This comprehensive directory profiles over 18,000 Food & Beverage Manufacturers, 12,000 Equipment & Supply Companies, 2,200 Transportation & Warehouse Companies, 2,000 Brokers & Wholesalers, 8,000 Importers & Exporters, 900 Industry Resources and hundreds of Mail Order Catalogs. Listings include detailed Contact Information, Sales Volumes, Key Contacts, Brand & Product Information, Packaging Details and much more. *Thomas Food and Beverage Market Place* is available as a three-volume printed set, a subscription-based Online Database via the Internet, on CD-ROM, as well as mailing lists and a licensable database.

*"An essential purchase for those in the food industry but will also be useful in public libraries where needed. Much of the information will be difficult and time consuming to locate without this handy three-volume ready-reference source." —ARBA*

8,500 pages, 3 Volume Set; Softcover ISBN 1-59237-058-6, $495.00 ◆ CD-ROM $695.00 ◆
CD-ROM & 3 Volume Set Combo $895.00 ◆ Online Database $695.00 ◆ Online Database & 3 Volume Set Combo, $895.00

# Sports Market Place Directory, 2005

For over 20 years, this comprehensive, up-to-date directory has offered direct access to the Who, What, When & Where of the Sports Industry. With over 20,000 updates and enhancements, the *Sports Market Place Directory* is the most detailed, comprehensive and current sports business reference source available. In 1,800 information-packed pages, *Sports Market Place Directory* profiles contact information and key executives for: Single Sport Organizations, Professional Leagues, Multi-Sport Organizations, Disabled Sports, High School & Youth Sports, Military Sports, Olympic Organizations, Media, Sponsors, Sponsorship & Marketing Event Agencies, Event & Meeting Calendars, Professional Services, College Sports, Manufacturers & Retailers, Facilities and much more. *The Sports Market Place Directory* provides organization's contact information with detailed descriptions including: Key Contacts, physical, mailing, email and web addresses plus phone and fax numbers. Plus, nine important indexes make sure that you can find the information you're looking for quickly and easily: Entry Index, Single Sport Index, Media Index, Sponsor Index, Agency Index, Manufacturers Index, Brand Name Index, Facilities Index and Executive/Geographic Index. For over twenty years, *The Sports Market Place Directory* has assisted thousands of individuals in their pursuit of a career in the sports industry. Why not use "THE SOURCE" that top recruiters, headhunters and career placement centers use to find information on or about sports organizations and key hiring contacts.

1,800 pages; Softcover ISBN 1-59237-077-2, $225.00 ◆ CD-ROM $479.00

# Research Services Directory, 2003/04  Commercial & Corporate Research Centers

This Ninth Edition provides access to well over 8,000 independent Commercial Research Firms, Corporate Research Centers and Laboratories offering contract services for hands-on, basic or applied research. *Research Services Directory* covers the thousands of types of research companies, including Biotechnology & Pharmaceutical Developers, Consumer Product Research, Defense Contractors, Electronics & Software Engineers, Think Tanks, Forensic Investigators, Independent Commercial Laboratories, Information Brokers, Market & Survey Research Companies, Medical Diagnostic Facilities, Product Research & Development Firms and more. Each entry provides the company's name, mailing address, phone & fax numbers, key contacts, web site, e-mail address, as well as a company description and research and technical fields served. Four indexes provide immediate access to this wealth of information: Research Firms Index, Geographic Index, Personnel Name Index and Subject Index.

*"An important source for organizations in need of information about laboratories, individuals and other facilities." —ARBA*

1,400 pages; Softcover ISBN 1-59237-003-9, $395.00 ◆ Online Database (includes a free copy of the directory) $850.00

**To preview any of our Directories Risk-Free for 30 days, call (800) 562-2139 or fax to (518) 789-0556**

# Sedgwick Press
# Hospital & Health Plan Directories

## The Directory of Hospital Personnel, 2005

*The Directory of Hospital Personnel* is the best resource you can have at your fingertips when researching or marketing a product or service to the hospital market. A "Who's Who" of the hospital universe, this directory puts you in touch with over 150,000 key decision-makers. With 100% verification of data you can rest assured that you will reach the right person with just one call. Every hospital in the U.S. is profiled, listed alphabetically by city within state. Plus, three easy-to-use, cross-referenced indexes put the facts at your fingertips faster and more easily than any other directory: Hospital Name Index, Bed Size Index and Personnel Index. *The Directory of Hospital Personnel* is the only complete source for key hospital decision-makers by name. Whether you want to define or restructure sales territories... locate hospitals with the purchasing power to accept your proposals... keep track of important contacts or colleagues... or find information on which insurance plans are accepted, *The Directory of Hospital Personnel* gives you the information you need – easily, efficiently, effectively and accurately.

*"Recommended for college, university and medical libraries." -ARBA*

2,500 pages; Softcover ISBN 1-59237-065-9 $275.00 ◆ Online Database $545.00 ◆ Online Database & Directory Combo, $650.00

## The Directory of Health Care Group Purchasing Organizations, 2004

This comprehensive directory provides the important data you need to get in touch with over 800 Group Purchasing Organizations. By providing in-depth information on this growing market and its members, *The Directory of Health Care Group Purchasing Organizations* fills a major need for the most accurate and comprehensive information on over 800 GPOs – Mailing Address, Phone & Fax Numbers, E-mail Addresses, Key Contacts, Purchasing Agents, Group Descriptions, Membership Categorization, Standard Vendor Proposal Requirements, Membership Fees & Terms, Expanded Services, Total Member Beds & Outpatient Visits represented and more. Five Indexes provide a number of ways to locate the right GPO: Alphabetical Index, Expanded Services Index, Organization Type Index, Geographic Index and Member Institution Index. With its comprehensive and detailed information on each purchasing organization, *The Directory of Health Care Group Purchasing Organizations* is the go-to source for anyone looking to target this market.

*"The information is clearly arranged and easy to access...recommended for those needing this very specialized information." –ARBA*

1,000 pages; Softcover ISBN 1-59237-036-5, $325.00 ◆ Online Database, $650.00 ◆ Online Database & Directory Combo, $750.00

## The HMO/PPO Directory, 2005

*The HMO/PPO Directory* is a comprehensive source that provides detailed information about Health Maintenance Organizations and Preferred Provider Organizations nationwide. This comprehensive directory details more information about more managed health care organizations than ever before. Over 1,100 HMOs, PPOs and affiliated companies are listed, arranged alphabetically by state. Detailed listings include Key Contact Information, Prescription Drug Benefits, Enrollment, Geographical Areas served, Affiliated Physicians & Hospitals, Federal Qualifications, Status, Year Founded, Managed Care Partners, Employer References, Fees & Payment Information and more. Plus, five years of historical information is included related to Revenues, Net Income, Medical Loss Ratios, Membership Enrollment and Number of Patient Complaints. Five easy-to-use, cross-referenced indexes will put this vast array of information at your fingertips immediately: HMO Index, PPO Index, Other Providers Index, Personnel Index and Enrollment Index. *The HMO/PPO Directory* provides the most comprehensive information on the most companies available on the market place today.

*"Helpful to individuals requesting certain HMO/PPO issues such as co-payment costs, subscription costs and patient complaints. Individuals concerned (or those with questions) about their insurance may find this text to be of use to them." -ARBA*

600 pages; Softcover ISBN 1-59237-057-8, $275.00 ◆ Online Database, $495.00 ◆ Online Database & Directory Combo, $600.00

## The Directory of Independent Ambulatory Care Centers, 2002/03

This first edition of *The Directory of Independent Ambulatory Care Centers* provides access to detailed information that, before now, could only be found scattered in hundreds of different sources. This comprehensive and up-to-date directory pulls together a vast array of contact information for over 7,200 Ambulatory Surgery Centers, Ambulatory General and Urgent Care Clinics, and Diagnostic Imaging Centers that are not affiliated with a hospital or major medical center. Detailed listings include Mailing Address, Phone & Fax Numbers, E-mail and Web Site addresses, Contact Name and Phone Numbers of the Medical Director and other Key Executives and Purchasing Agents, Specialties & Services Offered, Year Founded, Numbers of Employees and Surgeons, Number of Operating Rooms, Number of Cases seen per year, Overnight Options, Contracted Services and much more. Listings are arranged by State, by Center Category and then alphabetically by Organization Name. *The Directory of Independent Ambulatory Care Centers* is a must-have resource for anyone marketing a product or service to this important industry and will be an invaluable tool for those searching for a local care center that will meet their specific needs.

*"A handy, well-organized resource that would be useful in medical center libraries and public libraries." –Choice*

986 pages; Softcover ISBN 1-930956-90-8, $185.00 ◆ Online Database, $365.00 ◆ Online Database & Directory Combo, $450.00

**To preview any of our Directories Risk-Free for 30 days, call (800) 562-2139 or fax to (518) 789-0556**